C. Guaid

Ernest John Knapton   Wheaton College   Norton   Massachusetts

CHARLES   SCRIBNER'S   SONS   NEW   YORK

EUROPE

1 4 5 0
1 8 1 5

To DAVID

PREFACE

THIS BOOK deals with the history of Europe over a period of four hundred years, roughly from the middle of the fifteenth century to the opening of the nineteenth century. So complex an age will become intelligible to the reader only if he is made aware of the important inheritance coming to it out of the past, whether from classical antiquity or more immediately from the medieval period with which the beginnings of modern times are so intricately entangled. These matters of inheritance are therefore given brief introductory treatment. It seems essential, too, when one ends an account so precisely in 1815 with the downfall of Napoleon, to inquire what kind of legacy the centuries under consideration have bequeathed to more recent times. The Epilogue attempts a summary of this complicated problem.

The modern European world has its setting in space as well as in time. To the best of my ability I have sketched the pattern of historical events against the essential background of European geography, and have made substantial use of maps in order to clarify various aspects of political development. No historical phenomenon of the last four centuries is more significant than the expansion of European horizons overseas, unless one argues for the reverse phenomenon of the impact made by this wider world upon European life. It would go far beyond the purpose of this book, in which the attention is focused primarily upon the European scene, to deal fully with these matters. There is, I hope, sufficient discussion of overseas developments to make clear their momentous importance.

Historians are aware of the difficulties involved when, in addition to the fundamental themes of politics, war and diplomacy, they undertake to deal with religion, the arts, economic change, technology, speculative thought and various aspects of social evolution. Not the least difficult problem is that of organization, and I cannot hope to have solved it to the complete satisfaction of my readers or, I must admit, even of myself. Politics gives the central thread, for one of the major aspects of modern history, surely, has been the emergence of the strong nation-state. Cultural matters, however, should not be regarded as an appendage or decoration; they help to define the climate of an age and they testify impressively to the rich substance of successive periods in European life.

In writing this book I have tried to keep in mind the abilities and needs of the college students for whom it is primarily intended. The experience of a good many years of teaching here and elsewhere has led me to a few simple conclusions. First, if one cannot catch the interest of students little else matters. To this end one must attempt, for example, to bring to life the vivid personalities of the past and include some of the moments of high drama which may well occupy more space than their intrinsic importance would justify. Secondly, there must be a sure and solid pattern of clearly presented factual material. The gist of this is organized in the comparative chronological tables at the end of the volume. Thirdly, there must be some attempt to give intelligibility and meaning to history, though never in such a dogmatic way as to preclude a student from having opinions and drawing conclusions of his own. A historian may be forgiven, too, if he clings to the hope that some students may be impelled to ask still further questions of the past. The bibliographies are designed to provide this kind of additional material for serious undergraduate readers rather than to be a scientific documentation of the subject. It should be added that the illustrations have been selected with the idea that they may be an integral part of the volume.

Anyone undertaking to write a textbook covering a fairly long period of history will quickly become aware of many old obligations at the same time that he assumes others that are new. Numerous teachers in Canada, England and the United States have put me heavily in their debt, as have many books. It seems to me that Sir Llewellyn Woodward's lectures on European history which I heard thirty years ago in the hall of All Souls College, and which I still remember, offered an unforgettable example of what the analysis and presentation of history might become, even as the ripe work of another distinguished Oxford historian, the late H. A. L. Fisher's *History of Europe,* has set for me a model of urbane lucidity and reflective wisdom that few can hope to approach. I am sure, too, that I can never fully acknowledge my debt to Harvard's Widener Library, the magnificent resources of which are so hospitably made accessible to students.

Among my more immediate obligations I must give sincere thanks to Professor Arthur C. Bining of the University of Pennsylvania, the editor of the Scribner's Historical Series, who in addition to reading my entire manuscript with great care has given me much useful counsel out of his wide experience. I must also thank Professor Preston Slosson of the University of Michigan for his courtesy in offering valuable suggestions at an early stage in planning this work. I desire also to thank Mr. T. J. B. Walsh, College Editor of Charles Scribner's Sons, for his many kindnesses. The skilled editorial counsels and the infectious enthusiasm of Mr. J. G. E. Hopkins of Scribner's have been in evidence at every stage of my work, and Miss Betty Anderson has given expert and meticulous care to all matters connected with the illustrations and maps.

My colleagues at Wheaton College must be well aware of the many demands I have made on their patience and time. Above all, I must thank my good friend, Dr. Geoffrey May, for the painstaking improvements which he has been able to make in the form of my manuscript and for the fertile criticisms and suggestions which I imagine only a non-historian could produce in such generous abundance. The manuscript has also benefited greatly from the special knowledge put at my disposal by a number of my colleagues: Professors Holcombe Austin, Carolyn M. Clewes, Elsie E. Gulley, Mary L. Heuser, Henrietta C. Jennings, J. Arthur Martin, August C. Miller, Jr., Frank W. Ramseyer, Jr., and Jane E. Ruby. None of these, of course, can be responsible for the points of view which I have expressed. I am grateful, too, for the interest which President A. Howard Meneely has shown in the work of a fellow-historian. I should like also to mention two old friends in the historical field, Professor Frederick B. Artz of Oberlin College and Professor Arthur M. Wilson of Dartmouth College from whom, over the years, I have gained more by means of discussion than I am sure either of them realizes.

A book of this kind is long in the making, and I am indebted to all the members of my family both for their forbearance and their help. To my wife, Jocelyn, I am above all grateful for her tireless assistance, her frank criticisms and her never-failing encouragement.

ERNEST JOHN KNAPTON

NORTON, MASSACHUSETTS

ACKNOWLEDGMENTS

GRATEFUL ACKNOWLEDGMENT is made to the following publishers and authors for granting permission to quote at the pages indicated from their copyright works:

THE ABINGDON PRESS: Roland H. Bainton, *Here I Stand: A Life of Martin Luther* (1950), on pp. 188, 190, 192.

APPLETON-CENTURY-CROFTS, INC.: J. R. Strayer, *Western Europe in the Middle Ages* (1955), on p. 23.

PROFESSOR CRANE BRINTON: *The Jacobins* (The Macmillan Company, 1930), on p. 608.

THE CAMBRIDGE UNIVERSITY PRESS: *The Cambridge Modern History* (1934), Vols. I, II, III, VIII, IX, on pp. 71, 193, 198, 259, 580-1, 650; Sir James Jeans, *The Growth of Physical Science* (1951), on p. 472.

COLUMBIA UNIVERSITY PRESS: L. Einstein, *The Italian Renaissance in England* (1913), on p. 160.

HARCOURT, BRACE AND COMPANY, INC.: R. H. Tawney, *Religion and the Rise of Capitalism* (1926), on p. 122; Helen Gardner, *Art Through the Ages* (1948), on p. 516; R. P. Stearns, *Pageant of Europe* (1947), on pp. 187, 670; B. H. Sumner, *A Short History of Russia* (1943), on p. 385.

HARPER AND BROTHERS, PUBLISHERS: H. Heaton, *Economic History of Europe* (1948), on pp. 29, 108, 500; E. P. Cheyney, *The Dawn of a New Era* (1936), on p. 36; F. Nussbaum, *The Triumph of Science and Reason* (1953), on pp. 290, 374; John B. Wolf, *The Emergence of the Great Powers* (1951), on p. 362; W. Dorn, *Competition for Empire* (1940), on pp. 412, 447; Leo Gershoy, *From Despotism to Revolution* (1944), on pp. 522, 551, 703; C. Brinton, *A Decade of Revolution* (1934), on p. 626; G. Bruun, *Europe and the French Imperium* (1938), on pp. 643, 658, 708.

HARVARD UNIVERSITY PRESS: C. H. Haskins, *The Renaissance of the Twelfth Century* (1928), on p. 58.

HENRY HOLT AND COMPANY, INC.: G. L. Mosse, *The Reformation* (1953), on p. 185; L. Packard, *The Commercial Revolution* (1940), on p. 336; Preserved Smith, *A History of Modern Culture* (1930), on p. 706; Preserved Smith, *The Age of the Reformation* (1920), on pp. 217, 222, 245-6.

HOUGHTON MIFFLIN COMPANY: H. A. L. Fisher, *A History of Europe* (1931), on pp. 34, 339, 594.

ALFRED A. KNOPF, INC.: F. B. Artz, *The Mind of the Middle Ages* (1954), on pp. 31-2, 63-4; F. L. Baumer, *Main Currents of Western Thought* (1952), on p. 171; Albert Mathiez, *The French Revolution* (1929), on pp. 561, 584.

LONGMANS, GREEN & CO., INC.: A. R. Hall, *The Scientific Revolution* (1954), on pp. 59, 168, 172, 469, 478; G. M. Trevelyan, *History of England* (1926), on p. 296.

THE MACMILLAN COMPANY: R. Butterfield, *Origins of Modern Science* (1951), on pp. 168-9, 464, 474; H. J. Grimm, *The Reformation Era* (1954), on p. 182; John Hall Stewart, *Documentary Survey of the French Revolution* (1951), on p. 585.

METHUEN AND CO. LTD.: H. Brodetsky, *Sir Isaac Newton* (1929), on pp. 470-1.

W. W. NORTON & COMPANY, INC.: J. W. Thompson and E. N. Johnson, *An Introduction to Medieval Europe* (1937), on pp. 57, 59.

OXFORD UNIVERSITY PRESS, INC.: *The Oxford Book of French Verse* (1926), on p. 151; G. Davies, *The Early Stuarts* (1938), on p. 314; B. Williams, *The Whig Supremacy* (1939), on p. 529; H. A. L. Fisher, *Bonapartism* (1914), on p. 667; Sir Ernest Barker (ed.), *The European Inheritance* (1954), on p. 671.

PENGUIN BOOKS LTD.: Eric Newton, *European Painting and Sculpture* (1951), on pp. 78, 144, 145, 288–9; N. Pevsner, *Outline of European Architecture* (1953), on p. 131; G. Hamilton, *The Art and Architecture of Russia* (1954), on p. 384.

PRENTICE-HALL, INC.: C. Brinton, *Ideas and Men, The Story of Western Thought* (1950), on p. 53.

G. P. PUTNAM'S SONS: J. Boulenger, *The Seventeenth Century* (1920), on pp. 350–1; H. Nickerson, *The Armed Horde* (1940), on p. 426.

THE UNIVERSITY OF CHICAGO PRESS: G. Santillana, *The Crime of Galileo* (1955), on p. 173.

YALE UNIVERSITY PRESS: G. Vernadsky, *History of Russia* (1944), on p. 380.

The illustrations used on the title page are as follows:

SAINT DOMINIC, an anonymous Italian woodcut from the *Meditationes* of Johannes de Turrecremata, printed by Ulrich Hahn, Rome, 1473. This woodcut first appeared in the edition of 1467, the first illustrated book to be printed in Italy. Courtesy of The Metropolitan Museum of Art.

A SOLDIER ON HORSEBACK taken from a steel engraving of the Battle of Mondovi, April 22, 1796. Courtesy of the Picture Collection, New York Public Library.

Contents

List of Illustrations

List of Maps

P A R T   I

BACKGROUNDS

"Wonders are many, and none is more wonderful than man. . . .
Speech, and wind-swift thought,
and all the moods that mould a state hath he taught himself;
and how to flee the arrows of the frost,
when 'tis hard lodging under the clear sky,
and the arrows of the rushing rain;
yea, he hath resource for all. . . .
Only against Death shall he call for aid in vain."

      SOPHOCLES, *Antigone*

Introductory

THE PARTHENON, or temple of Athena, is a supreme example of the Greek genius. Built in the fifth century B.C., and used successively as a Roman temple, a Greek Catholic and a Roman Catholic church, a Turkish mosque and a powder house (shattered by an explosion in 1687), the ruined temple has the tranquil greatness of its first creation. Photograph by Martin Hürlimann, Atlantis Verlag, Zürich.

Chapter 1

■ THE STUDY OF THE PAST

MANY REASONS can be given for the study of history, among them the simple desire to recapture as vividly as possible that which in a literal sense is forever gone from us. The spell of the past has fascinated men in all

3

ages, whether we think of Herodotus marveling at the splendors of Egypt, Gibbon brooding amid the ruins of the Roman Forum, Petrarch vainly holding in his hands a Greek manuscript which he could not read or a museum visitor of today looking at the relics of his forebears. The westerner visits New England; the New Englander visits Europe; the European tourist may stand, like Napoleon, in the shadow of the Egyptian pyramids, summoning up thousands of years of history. By seeking the tangible remains of the past, each in his own way is gaining some sense of its reality. So likewise the written word may serve to kindle the imagination and renew the life of what was once the present.

The study of history suggests patterns of change and development. As we attempt to understand some segments of the past, we discern in it a quality attaching to all life, that of never-ceasing transition. An age seeming outwardly most stable will contain within itself the seeds of change. Considerations of this kind have led some historians to seek a "law" of historical development. They have looked for "principles" underlying historical phenomena and have proposed various and often strange philosophies of history. It would seem wiser to limit our aim to discerning the apparent patterns of change, remembering that these very patterns may not be altogether the product of the events themselves but may owe much to the eye of the beholder. We may note, too, that the speed of change may vary greatly in different periods. The era with which this book first concerns itself—the fifteenth and sixteenth centuries—was one of very rapid change; the close of the eighteenth was another. The historian must see and describe as best he can *what* these changes are; he may try his hand at telling *how* they came about; if he ventures to suggest *why*, he may be sure to encounter different explanations as other historians address themselves to the same problem.

■ ANCIENT, MEDIEVAL AND MODERN

The narrative of man's long development in Western Europe is conventionally broken into the threefold division of ancient, medieval and modern, each a part of a larger, interconnected story. In this scheme the classical world of Greece and Rome stands as one great chapter in human history; and the medieval world, inheriting much and at the same time contributing much, stands as another. A third era is found in the modern world emerging out of its medieval predecessor, a world whose genesis and development, roughly from 1450 to 1815, it is the purpose of this volume to describe. This conventional scheme, in one sense arbitrary and mechanical, corresponds with certain broad historical realities; it is clear that the "climate of civilization" in the first century of our Christian era was not what it was in the thirteenth nor again what it was in the seventeenth.

The closing decades of the fifteenth century in Europe are usually said to mark the beginning of "modern" times. Few historians today would care to defend this thesis literally, for the student will soon note that the beginnings of any historical period are hard to distinguish. If he is to divide his history into periods (and it is extremely helpful to do so), he will recognize the element of artificiality in what he is doing. He will find that these periods are not sharply differentiated like scenes in a play, but are related as autumn is to summer, or manhood to youth. In any age he will find individuals who are ahead of their times. Petrarch, who has been called "the first modern man," died in 1374. The same title has been given to the Emperor Frederick II, "the wonder of the world," who died in 1250; it could with equal justice be applied to the Franciscan friar, Roger Bacon, who died in 1292. The rate of development in one country may be much more rapid than in another; for example, the steady growth of parliamentary institutions in England stands in striking contrast to the greatly retarded political progress of Poland; France achieved political unity far earlier than did Germany or Italy. One country may never pass through stages which are basically important in other countries: Russia felt little if any direct influence from the Renaissance which so powerfully affected Western Europe; Spain was scarcely touched by the Reformation. Broad generalizations about so complex a structure as "Europe" can thus be very dangerous. Orderliness, consistency and simplicity in the historical pattern sometimes appear to be the subjective creation of the historian; they seem to have little place in the whirling confusion of the events themselves. It is hard at times to deny that obscurity, contradiction and even unintelligibility have been part of the historical record.

With all these qualifications, one may take the late fifteenth century as a main point of departure for the beginning of modern times. In doing this one should be careful not to view the medieval world as a "static" era which a new and revolutionary age was quickly to supersede. The twilight zone between the medieval and the modern world was anything but static; it stood rather as a period of many-sided change. It was, inescapably, an age of contradictions, for the old rubbed shoulders with the new. An examination of the process by which the sixteenth century grew out of the centuries which preceded it will show a gradual rather than a revolutionary transformation. It will show the roots of the present lying deep in the past, and it will reveal many survivals from an earlier age embedded, like fossils, in the later strata of history. The old historical clichés must be interpreted with caution; no sudden "Revival of Learning," no dramatic "Rediscovery of Antiquity," could or did put an end to the "Gothic Night" of the Middle Ages. The historian can see in the rich life of the late medieval period the expression of great genius and the anticipation of much that we choose to call modern. It is possible to discover a long pattern of interrelated change leading from the ecclesiastical splendors of the thirteenth century to the secular triumphs of the sixteenth.

The transformation may have been long and unevenly paced, but it was genuine and, in the outcome, definitive. The keenest minds of the sixteenth century were aware of their emancipation from a markedly different past. In their thought certain distinctive qualities appear. The atmosphere is that of a brave new world. The new pattern of life, making all allowances, can now be seen to have some recognizable kinship with our own. This pattern could hardly be found in the thirteenth century. St. Thomas Aquinas, Innocent III and Dante are not of our world in the same sense that Erasmus, Machiavelli and Henry VIII may claim to be.

From 1500 onwards the complex pattern of the world which we know slowly took shape. The fabric of medieval society was slowly replaced by a new system of powerful dynastic states. A revolution in commercial life went along with a vigorous development of overseas trade and settlement. The intellectual ferment of the thirteenth, fourteenth and fifteenth centuries culminated in what is termed the High Renaissance of the sixteenth century. A religious upheaval left permanent divisions within a once united Christian Europe. Dynastic rivalries and power politics found militant expression in a long series of European and overseas wars. From modest colonial settlements grew what may truly be called modern empires. The continuing advances in culture led to the magnificent achievements of the Classical Age and ultimately to the intellectual crusade associated with the Age of the Enlightenment. A revolutionary era, one of the great turning points in modern history, marked the close of the eighteenth century. These years of turmoil, followed by the disciplined order of Napoleon, spelled doom to the old regime under which Europe had lived for so long. They had profound effects upon the economic and social structure of Western Europe and, after the downfall of the Napoleonic regime, they bequeathed to the nineteenth century the main components of the bourgeois, capitalistic, parliamentary society which has come down to our own day.

These topics, with others subordinate to them, are the subjects of this volume. We shall first begin by considering the stage upon which the great drama is to be performed, then the actors who take part and finally the great European traditions to which the modern world fell heir.

■ GEOGRAPHY AND HISTORY

Europe is a peninsula of the great land-mass known as Eurasia.[1] One has but to observe this land-mass upon a globe to see how small Europe is in relation to the whole, for its area of some 3,750,000 square miles is less than one-fifth of the total land surface of which it is a part. A north-south line from the East Prussian coast to southern Greece would be about 1,200 miles long; from Stettin on the Baltic to Trieste at the head of the Adriatic the distance is about half that great. A line drawn from the southern seacoast of Portugal to the northern tip of the Ural Mountains would be about 3,300 miles long; the middle point would lie in what is now Poland. But the active center of European life has always been much further to the west. Comprising about one-fifteenth of the earth's total land surface, Europe today has one-fifth of its population. A guess at the population at about the year 1500 gives us a figure somewhere between 50 and 70 millions. That figure today would be in the neighborhood of 540 millions.

It is not easy to establish a boundary separating Europe from Asia. Conventionally this is often put at the Ural Mountains, though these are low and have at their southern end the great open gap of flat land known as the Caspian Gate. Historically speaking, the eastern limit of Europe has never been clearly marked. It has lain somewhere in the vast wooded plain south of the Baltic constituting over the centuries a kind of zone of uncertainty where political frontiers have moved back and forth. When men ask themselves today, as they may have asked at the time of Peter the Great, whether Russia is a part of Europe, they are putting a question which is as much one of politics as it is of geography.

The oceans which wash the long and intricate seacoast of Europe mark roughly its western and northern limits. The Baltic, Mediterranean and the Black seas give deep access to the interior of the continent and have significantly affected the history of peoples far removed from the Atlantic seaboard. It is important to notice that the Mediterranean is not the true southern boundary of the European world, for throughout history the whole southern and eastern land-fringe of the Mediterranean has been associated with the life on its northern shores. Since sailors have had little difficulty in mastering this inland water, its real function has been that of a link rather than a boundary—a tideless sea over which Egyptian, Cretan, Phoenician, Greek, Roman, Arab, Venetian or Genoese ships have woven their routes of trade. The real southern boundary of this world is a land rather than a water barrier—the great desert belt which begins with the

1. See map, pp. 8–9.

The student should make
careful reference to this map
while reading the section,
"Geography and History," in
Chapter I. Since physical
features are not always shown
on later maps, it will be helpful
to refer back occasionally when
noting the details of territorial
changes.

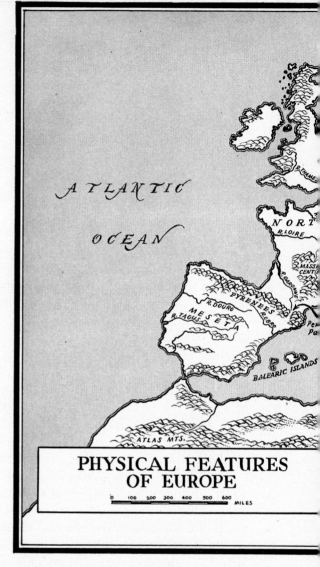

PHYSICAL FEATURES
OF EUROPE

0 100 200 300 400 500 600
MILES

Western Sahara and runs through the Libyan and Arabian Deserts to the
lonely steppes lying to the east of the Caspian and Aral seas.

The surface of Europe is a complex of mountains and plains, so placed
as to create many sharply defined and historically distinct areas, yet such
also that passage from one part to another, whether peaceful or warlike, has
been relatively easy. In simple summary the picture is threefold: a central
mountain backbone running east and west; to the south of it a Mediterranean fringe much broken by lesser mountains and by indentations of the
sea; to the north a great lowland plain leading eastward toward the Urals
and the Asiatic steppe.

The principal mountain backbone consists of the Pyrenees, the Alps,
the Carpathians, the Balkans and the Caucasus Mountains. Subordinate to

8

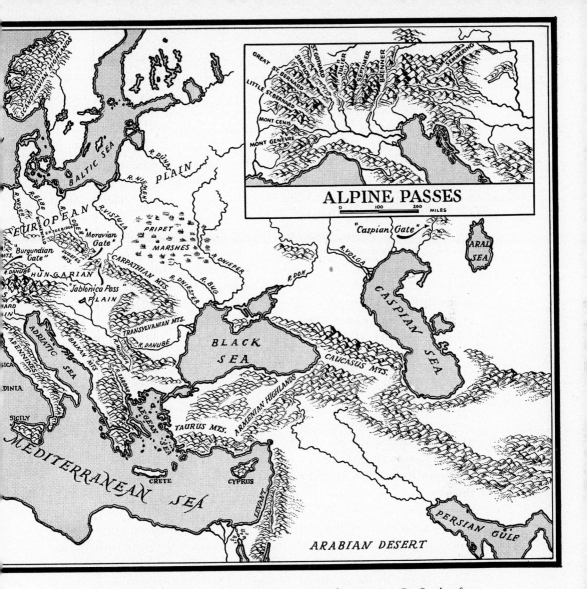

this dominant feature are numerous lesser mountain systems. In Spain, for example, an upland plateau area, the *Meseta,* is broken by the high east-west ridges of the Sierras and drops sharply to the lowland plain of Portugal on the west and to Catalonia on the east. The *Meseta* is relatively isolated from the Mediterranean world and prevents easy transit to the Atlantic shore. The main mountain body of France, the *Massif Central,* has the effect of breaking up France into several regions. Towards the eastern frontier the Vosges and Jura Mountains constitute a kind of defensive, though certainly not an impenetrable, barrier. In central Europe several mountain ranges, the Böhmerwald, the Erzgebirge and the Sudetes, form a protective bastion around three sides of Bohemia. Despite this, German merchants and artisans during the Middle Ages pressed through and settled themselves as a flourish-

9

ing minority in the Bohemian state. From the Bohemian barrier the heavily wooded Carpathians run in a south-easterly direction, eventually meeting with the Transylvanian Alps at a sharp angle so that together they bound the Hungarian Plain. In Italy the Apennines curve southward from the Alps, lying in such a way as to cut off the Lombard Plain (Caesar's Cisalpine Gaul) from the rest of the peninsula. Less immediately important are the Scandinavian Highlands, the mountains of Wales and Scotland, the Atlas barrier south of the coastal plain of North Africa, and the Taurus Mountains and the Armenian Highlands of Asia Minor.

The Mediterranean fringe south of the main European mountain chain includes the peninsular areas of Greece and Italy, the Aegean Islands, Cyprus, Crete, Sicily, Sardinia, Corsica and the Balearic Islands, together with the Levant, the North African coastal fringe and Spain. Much broken up by mountains and inlets, this home of classical civilization preserved those tangible remains which later centuries were to rediscover and admire. Throughout Asia Minor and North Africa the civilization of the Arab-Moslem world established itself and ultimately came into contact with the very different life of Western Europe.

The northern plain may be traced from the foothills of the Pyrenees, stretching northward and then turning eastward across northern France and Germany, steadily widening and becoming sandier and less fertile, dotted with heath and sparse woodlands, cut by numerous gentle rivers and eventually encountering the great conifer forests and steppes of Poland and European Russia. The huge Pripet Marshes, lying in the upper basin of the Dnieper River with a size equal to half that of England, helped to isolate Russia from the west and to establish a kind of boundary area between Russian-speaking and Polish-speaking lands. An extraordinarily complex history has been played out over the great expanses of this northern plain: in the west this history has been marked by the conflict of Latin and Teuton, and in the east by the rivalry of Teuton and Slav. On the northern fringe of Europe lie the peninsular areas of Brittany, Denmark and Scandinavia. Likewise on the fringe, and yet inescapably involved in the affairs of the continent, are the British Isles.

The rivers of Europe have in general been more important as means of communication than as boundaries or obstacles to man's activities. Usually a common life is to be found on both river banks, with the line of demarcation, if any, coming at the watershed.[2] Very commonly European commercial towns have grown up, not at the mouths of rivers, but at an up-river point

2. The Rhine has often served in modern times as the classic example of the dividing line between one people and another. Yet from a geographical point of view Alsace is separated from France by the Vosges Mountains; in its dialect and general pattern of life it has many links with the German territories across the Rhine.

safer from piratical attacks where ocean-borne shipping transfers its cargoes to river craft. Good examples are Bordeaux, Rouen, London and Bremen.

The Rhône has served from ancient times as a highway leading northward from the Mediterranean; its connection with the plateau of Langres makes possible easy transit to the Seine; while its tributary, the Saône, leads toward the Rhineland towns. The map shows clearly how the various rivers of the Paris Basin (the Seine and its tributaries, the Oise, Aisne, and Marne) together with the Loire, Somme and Meuse gave major importance to the city of Paris.

In another area, the Rhine valley grew through the Middle Ages to be one of the great European arteries of commerce; along it or near it like rich jewels lay towns of major importance: Basel, Strasbourg, Mainz, Cologne, and many others. On a smaller scale the river Scheldt showed very much the same pattern as its neighbor, the Rhine. At these river estuaries were the busy urban areas of the Netherlands and Flanders. Hemmed in by the sea and at times half inundated, the low country constituted a sort of natural refuge; partly for this reason the Dutch were able to win their independence from Spain during the sixteenth century.

Eastward from the Rhine and roughly paralleling it in direction lie the Weser, the Elbe, the Oder, the Vistula, the Niemen, and the Düna rivers. Gently flowing and navigable for long distances, these rivers, cutting across the northern plain at regular intervals, are no serious obstacle to east-west movement. Important commercial towns grew up near their mouths: Bremen, Hamburg, Stettin, Danzig, Memel and Riga. Others such as Magdeburg, Breslau, or Warsaw lay at important river crossings or junctions.

The Danube, rising in the Black Forest and flowing for nearly two thousand miles to the Black Sea, though navigable for the greater part of its distance, never assumed the commercial importance of the Rhine. Its lower reaches have served as one of the great invasion routes into central Europe; along it in the early sixteenth century the Turks surged to the very gates of Vienna. A famous route in the Balkans followed the Vardar River northward from the Aegean port of Salonika and continued along the Morava River, meeting the Danube not far from Belgrade. Further to the east, the great river systems of Russia emphasized her isolation from Western Europe, for the magnificent networks making up the Dnieper, the Don, and the Volga basins all flow southward to the Black and Caspian seas. Only the Düna, of relatively minor importance, gave Russia an outlet through the Baltic to the west.

The surface of Europe being so much divided by mountain barriers, the various routes or passes giving access from one area to another have been of great historical significance. Several passes cut through the Pyrenees; one of them, the Perthus, through the eastern Pyrenees, was used by Hannibal. Invaders have had little difficulty in crossing into Italy where, in addition to the coastal route from the south of France, numerous Alpine passes could be employed. The principal passes, the Mont Genèvre, the Mont Cenis, the two St. Bernards, the Simplon, the St. Gothard, the Julier, the Septimer and the Brenner, have echoed for centuries to the voices of soldiers, pilgrims, and merchants. In the western Carpathians the historically famous Jablonica Pass gave access from Galicia to the Hungarian Plain. From Trieste at the head of the Adriatic an important route ran between the Julian and Dinaric Alps, making use of the low-lying Semmering Pass to reach Vienna.

Other features, of significance at certain periods and to certain countries, may be noted. The low-lying Flanders territories on the northeast frontier of France have been of continuous concern to that country, whether as a possible area of expansion, or as a threatening avenue through which an attack might come. The so-called Burgundian Gate, an opening placed between the Rhône-Saône basin and the Rhine basin has presented something of the same problem to the French. Another gap of historical importance is the Moravian Gateway which leads into the quadrilateral of Bohemia. Running roughly from Cracow to Vienna, this passage links the northern plain to the Danubian valley and thus heightens the strategic and economic importance of the Austrian capital.

Such configurations helped to determine the elaborate patterns of European commerce. Some trade routes were inherited from antiquity; many were products of the Middle Ages; a lesser number are products of the modern world. Sea routes cut across the Mediterranean, with Genoa and Venice as the principal points of departure for the Levant (the eastern end of the Mediterranean), and with Constantinople controlling the entrance to the Black Sea. A coastal route which had been known to the Phoenicians led from the Strait of Gibraltar to the English Channel; it was renewed by the Venetian galleys in the fourteenth century; an extension of it led through the Sound into the Baltic; another led to Norway and thus ultimately to the Shetlands, the Faroes and Iceland. From the Strait of Gibraltar ships could turn southward and by the fifteenth century make the occasional adventurous outward voyage to the Canaries or risk the unknown terrors of the African coast. Cities assumed a particular importance through their position at strategic road junctions (Lyons, Milan, Troyes, Nuremberg), on major rivers (Magdeburg, Ulm, Basel, Mainz) or at ports linking major sea and land routes (Hamburg, Marseilles, Venice).

The soil of Europe has been able to support a thriving population. The general fertility of the Mediterranean area in ancient times was due in some degree to the limestone deposits which gave natural fertilization to the soil and made possible widespread small-scale farming. The continued cutting of the hillside forests for wood and charcoal led in time to erosion and soil starvation and had marked effects upon agricultural productivity. The northwest sector of Europe, with its good drainage, its generally mild climate and its abundant rainfall, was well adapted to grain and other crops. Further to the east a steadily poorer, sandy soil is found which could nevertheless be brought to support a substantial population. The subsoil mineral wealth is considerable, the principal items being copper, tin, gold, silver, iron, lead, zinc, salt, coal, glass-sand and building stone of various kinds.

The climate of Europe, which lies almost entirely within the north temperate zone, can be described as generally stimulating and favorable. The Mediterranean climate of mild winters and relatively dry summers contrasts with the more equable climate of the northwest, where winters are cold and where rain falls intermittently throughout the year. East of the Rhine the winters become colder and more snowy. Although hasty generalizations about the determining influence of these climatic and geographic conditions would be unwise, yet it may be stated in simple terms that Europe has afforded a highly favorable physical environment for the development of what we have come to call "Western Civilization."

A few suggestions may be offered as to the way in which the patterns of geography interweave themselves, so to speak, with the patterns of history. In the first place, the Mediterranean area in ancient times to a very considerable degree constituted a world of its own. Greece, Asia Minor, Italy, southern Gaul, Spain, North Africa and Egypt were the true home of classical, Greek and Latin civilizations. In the Levant the Hebrews developed their own important contributions to the western tradition. Lands further afield such as Gaul, Britain and Mesopotamia were subject only in part to these historic influences. It is understandable, therefore, that the legacy of antiquity was preserved and perpetuated in this Mediterranean area, whether on the very soil of Greece and Italy, or less immediately through the Moslem culture which spread across North Africa and into Spain. Geographical circumstance will give at least a partial explanation for Italy becoming the home of what is called the Revival of Learning and experiencing in the fourteenth and fifteenth centuries its phenomenal cutural advance.

It may also be noted that northwestern Europe, principally the land lying between the Pyrenees, the French Alps, the Vosges and the Jura, together with the Low Countries and the British Isles, constitutes in some sense another world. Linked by easy routes with the Mediterranean and once subject to a considerable degree of Romanization, it bore throughout the

Middle Ages the deep imprint of its classical inheritance. But this world was subject also to other powerful influences, notably those of the barbarian invasions, so that its development in modern times was to show significant divergences from that of the Mediterranean lands. Perhaps not so much in its geographical circumstances as in the cultural fusion of the new Germanic elements with the older Latin traditions is to be found the secret of its impressive vitality.

A third world lay north of the Danube and east of the Rhine. For the most part outside the Roman orbit, it was largely Germanic in culture but merged without any clearly defined border into the Slavic world of eastern Europe. In this medieval frontier area various "Marks" or "Marches" were set up on the eastern boundary of Christian, civilized Europe. These ran southward from the Baltic, roughly between the Elbe and Oder rivers. To the east of them lay the great forest hunting lands of Poland and Russia. The Middle Ages witnessed a remarkable advance into these frontier lands, with active colonization, much clearing of forests, drainage of marshes and founding of towns. But the east still remained a "trouble zone" where the absence of clearly defined boundaries led to recurrent war. So also in the west the Rhine basin grew to be another area of conflict. Here, in what had been the "Middle Kingdom" of Lotharingia, set up between the East and West Franks, the Teutonic and Latin worlds met, and here diplomatic maneuver and armed strife became perennial.

It would be unwise to overstress the separateness of the three worlds thus briefly sketched, for during the Middle Ages certain powerful unifying forces were at work by which they were all in some degree influenced. Nevertheless, the differences between the Mediterranean lands with their classical tradition, northwestern Europe with its fusion of cultures, and the more barbarous Europe east of the Rhine continued to be real; and a careful student can detect many ways in which these differences were expressed. The complex patterns of modern history owe much to the interplay of forces between these regions, geographically and culturally distinct yet broadly associated in a common destiny.

Perhaps the most striking geographic consideration which emerges with respect to the course of modern European history is the great northward shift in the centers of political power, accompanied by the tremendous phenomenon of overseas expansion. Ancient civilization had grown around a Mediterranean center. During the Middle Ages a rich culture developed north of the Alps, but this had always been balanced, so to speak, by the prestige and power of the papacy, by the long-drawn-out activity of the crusades and by the vigorous economic life of the Mediterranean world. In the succeeding age the geographic shift is clear. One may speak of the preponderance of the Austrian Hapsburgs, of Spain, of France or of England and one may note the rise of new northern powers such as Russia or Prussia. Never is it possible, however, in the modern era to speak of the preponderance of Rome or of Italy.

■ PEOPLES AND TONGUES

The great variety of peoples and tongues confronting the traveler in present-day Europe gives evidence of the complex human background of modern history. Anthropologists have sought to distinguish three main physical types in Europe and have related them to three distinct zones: the long-headed "Mediterranean" with dark skin, hair and eyes; the round-headed "Alpine" with light brown pigmentation; and the long-headed, tall, fair "Nordic." No such clear-cut distinctions can be made for modern Europe. The swarthy Sicilian may be taken as one extreme, and the blonde Norwegian the other; but, save for isolated groups, the average European people today is a composite representing centuries of intermixture and cross-breeding, so that "race" as a means of distinguishing one population from another has become one of the most abused of all words.

Language divisions in Europe are more clearly marked and have had greater historical significance. Broadly speaking, those which prevail today are those which were found at the opening of the modern era. Most European languages are variants of a common Indo-European parent tongue. Their main divisions can be summarized as follows: (1) The Greek language was found in the southern part of the Balkan peninsula, in the islands of the Aegean Sea and in parts of Asia Minor. (2) The much more widely distributed Latin or Romance group included Italian, Spanish, Portuguese, French, Rumanian and the dialect spoken by the Walloons of southern Flanders. (3) The Germanic group comprised German, Dutch, Flemish, Danish, Norwegian, Swedish and English (the latter in the course of time acquiring a strong Latin and Norman-French admixture). (4) The Slavic group was very complex. The East Slavic languages included what we think of today as Russian, together with the Ukrainian or Little Russian in the south and the White Russian to the west. The West Slavic languages included Polish, Czech and Slovak. In the Southern Slav group were the Serbs, Croats, Slovenes and Bulgars. Along the Baltic coast the Latvian and Lithuanian languages showed some affinity to the Slavic group. (5) In the Celtic group were the relatively unimportant Welsh, Gaelic and Breton tongues.

Apart from the Indo-European languages must be put the Finno-Ugric group, including the Finnish and Estonian tongues on the one hand and on the other the Magyar tongue brought into southeast Europe by the Hungarian invaders of the ninth century. Distantly akin to these were the Turkish invaders who in the fourteenth and fifteenth centuries overran Asia Minor and part of the Balkans, bringing from Asia a language of the Ural-Altaic group. Of much greater cultural and historical significance than these was Arabic, the language of the Moorish-Arabic population of North Africa, which, with the Moorish conquests, was established for a time in Sicily and Spain. To be noted only as primitive survivals and linguistic curiosities were the Basque dialect of the Pyrenees and the Albanian tongue spoken in a remote region of the Balkans.

These linguistic divisions were to be of the utmost importance in the eventual growth of European national states. But the process by which linguistic and national boundaries came roughly to coincide was long and involved with many other factors. Switzerland was the outstanding, though not the only, example of a flourishing state built upon a diversity of speech. It was of unquestioned advantage to countries such as England and France to have a single language as a basis upon which to erect a unified political structure, though even in these relatively advanced countries the persistence of dialects tended to accentuate localism and thereby to create many internal domestic problems. Down to the time of the French Revolution, if not later, a Breton or an Alsatian would feel himself to have little in common with a southerner from Provence. Even in England as late as the close of the eighteenth century, the north-country head of an Oxford college could preach sermons in a Cumberland accent so strong as to be scarcely comprehensible to his southern hearers. It is also to be observed that the common tongue of the German peoples, or of the Italians, was not in itself sufficient to overcome the obstacles which long delayed their unification.

At the close of the Middle Ages Latin still gave to the educated world a common medium of expression; but as the use of this language declined, the bewildering variety of tongues and dialects accentuated the diversities of the European pattern. Greek was essentially the language of the Byzantine world until the Revival of Learning reintroduced it to western scholarship. Broadly speaking, the languages sorted themselves out into groups of Latin, Germanic and Slavic origin; but the peoples of Europe cannot be said to have been consciously influenced by such kinships. Frenchmen and Italians could find almost as many reasons for disagreeing with one another as could, say, the English and the Dutch, or, as time went on, the Russians and the Poles. The deliberate use of linguistic kinship as a means to national unification is a phenomenon mainly of the nineteenth and twentieth centuries.

To some historians the distinctions between peoples based upon physical type, language or geography are less significant than those arising from differences in social levels or classes. It could be shown, of course, that members of the feudal aristocracy in various parts of medieval Europe lived very much the same life, dressed and amused themselves, hunted and fought in very much the same way; that, in brief, they had common interests which were not those of the classes beneath them. So also the priestly class throughout Western Europe, with its single faith, its one vast church organization, its common language and its canon law, constituted in a sense one body. The same could be said for the universities and the European community of learning. Erasmus of Rotterdam was truly a citizen of Europe. Similarly, as trade and banking developed, a certain community of interests and practices grew up between merchants of various lands. Even so, it is not easy to strike a balance between such tendencies: some cut across national lines, accentuating class or occupational interests; while contrary tendencies united the various classes of one country together in support of national aims. If any judgment can be made, it is that only gradually during the seventeenth and eighteenth centuries the sense of national interest and allegiance began to take precedence.

As for the vast, anonymous mass of peasantry who made up the greater part of the European population, it would be true in a very general sense that they were akin to one another in the type of life that they lived and in the burdens that they bore. But they could hardly be aware of this. Although they could be moved to action at times by a keen sense of their own local grievances, hardly any larger incentive united them. Existing in an atmosphere of stupefying parochialism, it was difficult for them even to develop any sense of national obligation, much less to associate their destinies with those of their fellows in other lands.

■ THE LEGACY OF ANTIQUITY

One of the most striking features of European culture is the way in which it has sought periodically to reinvigorate itself by turning to the great traditions of its past. Historical "legacies" are not easy to isolate or define. A student is on tricky ground when he seeks to estimate the basic contributions of one age to another, and glib superficialities may sparkle more brightly than essential truths. Yet it is important to take the longer view, to explore those parts of the European story which most clearly suggest growth and continuity and to consider those achievements upon which it may be shown that later ages have been able to build.

This is particularly true with respect to antiquity. Two major strands are commonly distinguished in the long background of our western world: the classical and the Hebrew-Christian. Separate in one sense and yet in another intermingling, they may be considered the warp and woof of European civilization. Each is so rich, so much the product of complex antecedents, so fertile in its progeny, that nothing more than summary treatment is possible here.

The classical tradition requires us to think of both Greece and Rome. There come to mind at once the magnificent achievements of the individual Greek city states, bathed in the sunshine of Hellas and evolving forms of government startlingly modern in their nature. We think of the brilliance of Greek art, literature and philosophy. On the other hand we recall the widespread sobriety, discipline and order of the Roman Empire which also inherited much that the Greeks had achieved.

We may thank the Greeks for the sophisticated use which they made of the material achievements of the earlier Mesopotamian and Egyptian worlds —for transforming, as it were, the works of the oriental hand with the magic of the Greek mind. We are indebted to their great thinkers for their desire to explore the mysteries of the universe, for insisting upon its intelligibility, for postulating the supremacy of reason, for taking man to be a creature capable of rational development and the universe to be something which he may logically understand. These best Greek minds gave to subsequent ages the fundamental patterns of scientific and philosophical thought; they defined the study of politics and pushed forward its boundaries both in theory and practice; they presented the world with a dazzling series of literary and artistic masterpieces so impressive that the forms in which they were embodied have dominated the West for two thousand years. One may think of the role of Aristotle during the Middle Ages—"The Philosopher," as he was called—or of Plato's subsequent role in idealistic thought. Above all, Greek thinkers enunciated an ideal of life based on balance, restraint and symmetry—"moderation in all things." Thus to summarize the work of the Greeks is to give only a fragmentary sense of their imperishable achievement. This achievement though obscured in some subsequent ages was never lost. Beneath most of the intellectual structures of later Europe are foundations which they first laid.

In comparison with this splendid picture the work of Rome runs the risk of being undervalued. It is all too easy to characterize Roman civilization as a pale shadow of the Greek, a diluted or debased copy of an original whose true greatness Rome was unable to achieve. Thoughtful consideration should dispel such a view. The Roman world, to be sure, preserved much that the Greek world had created, but it added its own considerable genius. Virgil is more than the pallid copy of Homer, and the Roman city state is more than the echo of the Greek *polis*. In two respects—Rome the builder and Rome the lawgiver—the achievement was fundamental and superb. Simply to survey the externals of the Roman Empire with its roads, aqueducts, cities, amphitheaters, temples, villas, frontier defenses and harbors is to receive the impression of a monumental civilization. And to study Roman law not merely as a technical business of paragraphs and codes but as the embodiment of certain living principles of reason, wisely combined with ancient usages and then applied to ever wider circles of human beings, is to be impressed by the humane genius which infused it.

The Hebrew-Christian tradition sprang from the obscure Jewish peoples of Palestine whose sacred books, the Old Testament, embodied teachings with a powerful message for themselves and for later times. The notions of one omnipotent God, of vengeance to be meted out to the sinner and rewards to the good, of a forthcoming Messiah to bring about a reign of justice, were accompanied by a strong sense of being a chosen people who would win salvation through righteousness. This view was developed and modified in the New Testament. The teaching mission of Jesus revealed a way of life which, with many a paradox and many a challenge to complacency, took powerful hold upon the minds of men. Christians were exhorted to seek patience, humility, charity, love and forbearance and to find strength in what formerly they might have considered weakness. They were urged to recognize the fatherhood of God, the brotherhood of all men, the immortality of the soul and the unique mission of Jesus as a Redeemer. No other religion has based itself so unequivocally upon a gospel of love. Ever larger groups throughout the Roman Empire fell under the spell of this message, dramatized for all time in the story of the Crucifixion.

In so complex a world the Christian teachings could not escape the impact of pagan, classical thought. St. Paul, to whom large credit must be given for elaborating and expounding the Christian belief, was a product of the Graeco-Roman world. In his various epistles scholars find significant Greek elements. Suggestions of Platonic ideas can also be seen in the Fourth Gospel. The Christian teaching of human brotherhood echoes, if it does not arise from, a similar teaching of the Stoics. As an organized Christian Church gradually arose it took something of the Roman imperial pattern, with a hierarchy or chain of offices ascending from the deacons through the priests to the bishops and patriarchs. One clear evidence of the classical influence may be seen in the Church's distinctive vocabulary, which was Greek through and through. Tolerated by the Emperor Constantine in the fourth century and declared to be the sole religion by Theodosius in the fifth, Christianity dominated the religious life of the Late Roman Empire and triumphantly survived the decline of the imperial fabric. So complete, indeed, was its triumph that medieval Europe became, as it never since has been, a single society in which the acceptance of Christianity stood as the test of membership.

The classical world continued to exert its influence along with that of the Hebrew-Christian tradition. Actually the two traditions were closely intermingled: it would be almost impossible to disentangle them; and it would prove unrewarding to attempt a precise evaluation of the importance of each to later times. A great church figure such as St. Augustine was heavily indebted to the Stoic teachings of Cicero. In the distorted form of Neoplatonism some of Plato's ideas were later directed upon the Christian belief. The Middle Ages, dominated as they were by the Christian concept, never lost contact with classical antiquity. Not the least important means of maintaining this contact was the Arab-Moslem world of North Africa and Spain which conveyed much Hellenistic learning to Western Europe. When the writings of Aristotle came to be closely studied in the thirteenth century, they had a profound effect; indeed, it became the purpose of St. Thomas Aquinas, one of the greatest of the scholastics, to reconcile Aristotelianism with the Christian revelation. What is often taken as most original, Gothic ecclesiastical architecture, has an ancestry which can be traced back from the soaring cathedral to the Romanesque church, the Roman basilica and ultimately to the buildings of the Hellenistic age.

The debt of the medieval and the later world to classical antiquity was, in short, many-sided and immense. Where the classical, or more precisely the Greek, spirit perhaps found least echo in the Middle Ages was in the view which came to be held of man and the world. Here the Christian teaching depicted man as heavily burdened by original sin, struggling amid the darkness and dangers of this life to attain everlasting blessedness in the next. These burdens of sin and salvation would have rung strange indeed to Greek ears.

Despite large gaps in the medieval knowledge of antiquity, and despite stubborn misinterpretations, the persistent vitality of the classical tradition was apparent all through the Middle Ages. With the Revival of Learning in the fourteenth and fifteenth centuries, the rich treasures of the ancient world became more fully known. Thus they could be reabsorbed into the general stream of European culture and exercise their profoundly stimulating effect upon all later times.

THE ABBEY OF MONT SAINT MICHEL, off the Brittany coast, a famous goal of pilgrims since the ninth century and later the site of a Benedictine monastery. The complex site with its clustering buildings and surrounding walls which can be reached only by a causeway from the shore is crowned by the Gothic abbey church. Photograph by the French Government Tourist Office.

Chapter 2

Medieval Foundations of Modern Times

■ THE MEDIEVAL ERA

A TWELFTH CENTURY MARINER entering the harbor of Boulogne at dusk would be guided by a beacon fire shining from a lighthouse built in the reign of the Roman Emperor Caligula and repaired eight centuries later by order of Charlemagne. Such is one tiny reminder of a rich and complex

21

ancient inheritance. The medieval period in turn left its deep imprint upon the times which followed, so much so that modern history cannot truly be understood independently of it. What is the significance of this middle period lying between the ancient and the modern world?

The term, "Middle Ages," in its somewhat derogatory sense as the scholars of the Renaissance employed it, suggested a kind of long interval or pause between the greatness of classical antiquity and the equal greatness of the modern age. Such a viewpoint is hardly tenable. Nor is it historically correct to propose the thesis that the Middle Ages, although possessed of an authentically rich culture, constituted a civilization so static, so fettered and so essentially unprogressive that it took the sudden explosive force of the so-called Revival of Learning and the Renaissance to break the bonds and to inaugurate a new age. Students are increasingly disposed to see a long period of transition between the "medieval" and the "modern" world, with the corollary that the modern institutions become intelligible only when seen as the outcome of a long process of development.

Conventionally, the medieval period is taken to run from the decline of the Roman world in the fourth and fifth centuries A.D. to the consolidation in the late fifteenth century of a group of strong territorial monarchies in Western Europe. The term, "Dark Ages," if it can be applied to the years roughly from A.D. 400 to 800, suggests something of the confusions and barbarization which succeeded the orderliness of the Roman world.[1] But even this early period was rich in creative possibilities. It began with the great Germanic migrations, shadowy in their historical details but profound in their ultimate effects upon the social and political life of Europe. In some cases, as in Anglo-Saxon England or in Frankish Gaul, the invaders established a pattern of life showing an unbroken continuity with later times. In other cases, as in Visigothic Spain or in Vandal Africa, the results were less dramatic and less permanent. Yet everywhere the Germanic peoples modified the older patterns of Latin culture. They brought new languages and new literary forms, an untutored yet vigorous art, a new type of customary law, of village organization, of landholding, of military allegiance. The old Roman political structure of municipality and province gave way to a simpler pattern based upon the rural village, the tribe and the barbarian kingdom.

1. We owe, perhaps, to Petrarch's expression, *tenebrae*, the concept of a "Dark Age" following the decline of the Roman world. From Leonardo Bruni's *History of the Florentine People* and Flavio Biondo's *History from the Decline of the Roman Empire*, both written about the middle of the fifteenth century, comes the concept of a "Middle Age" of approximately one thousand years lying between the ancient and the modern world. See w. k. ferguson, *The Renaissance in Historical Thought* (1948), pp. 8–14.

By the year 1000 a new Europe was taking shape. Two centuries later a distinctive medieval civilization reached its climax. It was rich, intricate and in many ways profoundly creative. By 1500 this world was being transformed into still another. No attempt to sum up in a few phrases the essentials of the Middle Ages can be wholly successful, but the following passage deserves consideration as a shrewd estimate of some fundamental aspects of medieval life:

> It was a Western European civilization rather than a Mediterranean or an oceanic civilization. Political power was divided among a hierarchy of interdependent governments rather than concentrated in a world empire or a group of sovereign national states. The Church was independent of secular authority, but it was more than a private association with limited functions; it set the standards and defined the goals for all human activities. In economics there was neither state regulation, nor *laissez-faire;* instead local custom controlled farmers, artisans, and merchants in the interest of the whole community. In Gothic art, chivalric poetry, scholastic philosophy, and the university system of education the twelfth century created forms which were neither classical nor modern. These characteristics of twelfth century civilization were not only distinct, they were also interdependent; they fused into an organic whole. . . . The civilization of the twelfth century was remarkably self-sufficient and self-consistent; it had a flavor, a texture, almost a personality, of its own.[2]

To consider briefly how the economic and social framework of the modern age develops out of the medieval period, and to observe similarly the transformation of political institutions and the patterns of religion is the purpose of this chapter.

■ RURAL LIFE

Medieval life was overwhelmingly rural. It carried on the immemorial pattern by which man worked to produce the food and other necessities which his household consumed. Nine out of ten people were to be found within the agrarian framework. But their way of life varied too much for any neat summarization; and the manor, so often taken as the "typical" agrarian unit of the medieval period, was really only one of many rural forms. A full picture, obviously impossible here, would have to include the scattered farmers and crofters, the lonely shepherds, the foresters, the charcoal-burners, hunters, vineyard-keepers and many others.[3]

2. J. R. STRAYER, *Western Europe in the Middle Ages, A Short History* (1955), p. 8.
3. It has been observed that of territory studied in the English midlands only 60 per cent in 1279 could properly be called manorial. H. HEATON, *Economic History of Europe* (rev. ed., 1948), p. 87.

The manor in its various national forms played a profoundly important part in the economy of Western Europe, and its gradual transformation over the centuries was a major factor in social change. It represented a close-knit, interdependent community. The cluster of cottages in the shadow of the manor house suggested the imperative need for protection in a barbarous age. The lord's house with its mill, barns, baking-oven and other outbuildings, together with the nearby church and priest's house, were symbols of authority. The manorial lord might be a great baron or a simple knight or esquire. Of "gentle" birth, he was someone apart from his tenants. His demesne land consisted either of scattered strips or a sort of home farm around the manor house. He or his agent presided over the court of the manor in which he dealt with all kinds of petty disputes. Farming, local administration, family affairs, the sports of the countryside, litigation, and occasional war made up his pattern of life.

The villagers were "base," or "vile," in contrast to the gentility of their lord. Some might be free men, holding their land by payment of a money rent; at the other end of the scale was a steadily declining number of actual slaves. More common was the serf, or villein. He was bound to the soil and subject to the manifold authority of his lord. He could not dispose of his holdings or marry off his children without his lord's consent. He could not appeal from the manorial to the royal courts. He was "rightless before his lord." He gave his lord several days' work each week in addition to further "boon services" at harvest time. He made regular payments either in kind (poultry, eggs and the like) or in money. Yet so long as he rendered these services he and his heirs were protected by the force of custom and could till the acres of which they had the hereditary use.

The communal pattern of life is demonstrated very clearly in methods of medieval agriculture. A farmer must of necessity be something of a conformist; he cannot argue with the seasons; and the medieval peasant, with his wretched minimum of mechanical equipment, was forced to depend very largely upon the help of his fellows. Stretching away from the village center lay the plowlands, meadows, woodland and waste, whither the peasants walked daily to their tasks. No uniform system of cultivation can be assumed, but the division of manorial lands into two or three great open fields cultivated according to an annual rotation existed over large areas.[4] One field was left fallow; one was planted in the autumn to wheat or rye for the peasant's daily bread; one was sown in the spring to oats, peas, beans or

4. Generalizations are dangerous. What follows applies most closely to northern France and large parts of England, less so to Germany, and even less to Spain, Italy and eastern Europe. Local differences were inescapable; upland and mountain areas could hardly follow the lowland pattern.

barley (as the nursery-rhyme still recalls) to provide cattle fodder, porridge and beer. Meadowland was reapportioned periodically to give each villager his share of the hay; the woodland and waste were open for gathering firewood, turf, nuts and berries. After the crops were harvested the common fields, together with the waste land, were used for turning out the livestock.

Under this pattern the peasant holdings were in the form of long, narrow strips, usually one-half to one acre in size and scattered at random throughout the three great fields. Thirty acres was often taken as the "typical" villein holding.[5] The peasant would share in the good and poor soil and would of necessity conform to the common pattern in plowing, sowing and harvesting. Individual enterprise, experiment and innovation would be difficult, if not impossible. Such in brief was the "open-field" system of large parts of Western Europe.

It would seem proper to stress the drab, unfree life of the medieval peasant, periodically assailed by war, famine and pestilence. The hovels where so many people once lived are gone forever; few medieval writers thought them worthy even of description. A common method of construction, lost in immemorial antiquity, made use of a number of long poles placed in a circle, coming together, tepee-like, at the top, and covered with branches, bracken or sod. To give headroom and warmth the ground within might be dug down for two or three feet.[6] In comparison with these huts the timber-framed cottages of a later period with thatched or sod roofs and clay and wattled walls would seem substantial indeed. Yet they fell far below any modern standards of hygiene or decency. Usually lacking windows or fireplace, with an earthen floor and a wretched minimum of furnishings, their two rooms might house cattle, pigs and poultry as well as the human tenants. Only at a still later date do we have the thatched and chimneyed cottages beloved of tourists, their diamond-paned windows wreathed in honeysuckle and roses. Against the drab and anonymous peasant background of medieval life a small upper-class minority acted out its better-known story which we dignify with the name of history.

Hunger, cold, pain and fear were never far from the lives of the peasants. Yet it would be unfair to forget the mitigating circumstances. Feast days and holidays were numerous. The countryside had its rude sports and pastimes. In every hamlet the church brought the vivid pageantry of its

---

5. There were endless variations. Thirty acres might represent what one peasant family could handle with communal assistance. The long, narrow strips can be explained by the use of the heavy northern plow that cut a deep furrow when yoked to a team of oxen and obviated the lighter cross-plowing of the Mediterranean lands.

6. Survivals of this ancient type can be seen in the huts of vagrant English charcoal burners and in the "black houses" of the Outer Hebrides. See the illustrations in H. BRAUN, *The Story of the English House* (1940), pp. 1–5.

service and offered to the promising village lad an occasional chance to rise in a career of learning and piety. In a great many cases villages produced some surplus for sale, and thus the opportunity might come to visit the market of a nearby town and there momentarily to breathe the air of freedom. Slowly, too, some specialization of occupation might grow up in rural areas and craftsmen such as cobblers, carpenters, thatchers and tilers might appear.

Rural life was not absolutely fixed in its patterns. An impressive feature of the later Middle Ages was what may be called the expansion of the frontier. In England the Welsh Marches and the wild north were gradually settled. In the Low Countries much land was rescued from the sea. In France many forests and marshlands were cleared. Above all, in Germany a great eastward colonizing advance recruited peasants from many parts of Europe for settlement across the Elbe and along the Baltic. Like America in the nineteenth century, Europe in the thirteenth and fourteenth centuries saw a movement towards the frontier, a movement which had important social and political effects.

The change which above all others was to transform the life of the medieval peasant was associated with the gradual conversion of the various manorial dues to a money basis. The reasons for this were complex. The main importance of the phenomenon is that the peasant ultimately became in some sense a rent payer and that serfdom in Western Europe declined.[7] Money payments meant the increase of wage labor and the growth of a landless class. It meant social unrest and a growing consciousness of peasant grievances. No overnight transformation occurred, and even with the decline of serfdom oppressive dues and services remained attached to the holding of land. Such services persisted in France until the eighteenth century, and even later in Poland, Austria and Hungary.

Outwardly the pattern of rural life at the opening of the sixteenth century would not seem to have undergone any spectacular transformation. The peasant, though no longer usually a serf, was still very much a tenant and a dependent. He would be respectfully aware of his position in relation to his landlord. The rural outlook was essentially—inescapably—conservative. Roads were still generally atrocious, and it might very well be that an average countryman would hardly travel more than a score of miles from his home or see more than two or three hundred persons during his entire lifetime. His grievances were real, and, with no orderly method of securing a

---

7. In eastern Europe the process was much slower and in some respects operated in reverse. It should be noted that Russian serfdom is not medieval in origin. It was a product of the seventeenth century, when the great nobles, with the aid of the rulers at Moscow, reduced their former rent-paying peasants to complete personal subjection.

remedy, he would, perforce, continue in that tradition of unrest and occasional unpremeditated revolt which had marked the fourteenth and fifteenth centuries.

The main agricultural trends at the close of the Middle Ages may be briefly summarized. Broadly speaking, a "subsistence economy" was giving place to an "exchange economy." With the decline of serfdom in the west, unwritten "customary" tenures were being replaced by specifically defined money tenures which gave the peasant virtually perpetual tenancy so long as he fulfilled certain financial obligations. But peasant ownership of land was not common. There were some improvements in agricultural methods and some tendency to consolidate the scattered open-field peasant holdings. Growth of the class of landless laborers was very marked. The medieval era was responsible for some highly important technological advances such as the use of the horse-collar which after the tenth century greatly increased the working load that could be pulled, the iron horseshoe, the heavy wheeled plow, the wheelbarrow, the spinning-wheel, the windmill for grinding grain and the sawmill operated by water-power. New developments in some areas, such as the conversion of arable land to sheep farming, brought great wealth to the owners and encouraged people with money to invest it in land, thus developing a new *rentier* type. It is customary to speak of the dynamic contribution of the towns to the evolution of the modern world. This is true enough, but their spectacular growth should not altogether obscure the significance of agrarian unrest and rural change at the dawn of a new era.

■ THE URBAN ECONOMY

The network of medieval towns spread across the face of Europe made up a pattern of life in sharp contrast to that of village and manor house. Although for the most part small in size, a few cities had above one hundred thousand inhabitants. Perhaps a score in all counted from six thousand to eighty thousand in population. Many important urban centers fell below even this range.[8]

The medieval town, whether of Roman or Germanic origin, whether growing up in the shelter of monastery or castle, or located at some strategic crossing of trade routes, came to have one distinctive feature: it breathed the air of freedom. To be sure, this freedom was relative, but the list of rights which gradually evolved is an impressive one. Among these were the right

8. Figures vary greatly. One estimate gives the following figures for the thirteenth century: Palermo, 500,000; Paris, 240,000; Florence, Venice, Milan, about 100,000; London, Genoa, Barcelona, Cologne, about 50,000. J. W. THOMPSON and E. N. JOHNSON, *An Introduction to Medieval Europe* (1937), pp. 602–603. Note the estimated figure of 1,000,000 for the medieval population of Constantinople, and 800,000 for Baghdad.

to collect local urban taxes in return for an annual lump payment to the lord on whose ground the town stood; the right to hold court, to elect magistrates, to hold regular markets and fairs, to regulate trade by means of a "gild merchant," to give freedom to the villein who could stay within its walls for a year and a day; and the right to defend itself against outside attack. The town gates, closed at nightfall, and the walls, manned if need be by its burghers, were the concrete embodiment of these freedoms. "Democracy" could hardly be expected to exist, and did not, even in the towns; urban government tended to fall quite generally into the hands of an oligarchy, the wealthy merchant class. But compared with the servile regime of the manor, the town was freedom itself.

One visualizes the medieval town as a compact entity, secure behind its towered walls and sturdy gates. The houses lining its narrow, cobbled streets were often built with projecting upper storeys that almost obscured the sky. Sanitary arrangements were poor, and the danger of fire everpresent. Shops were small and usually attached to the living quarters of the shopkeepers. In the central square where commonly the countryside brought its produce to the weekly market, one would find the town hall, the parish church or cathedral, merchant warehouses and the halls of the various gilds. With increasing prosperity many towns grew in splendor; Florence, for example, came to be dotted with the *palazzi* of its nobles and rich merchants, and some of the German and Flemish towns became famous for their civic architecture. In such crowded quarters squalor and splendor often rubbed shoulders. Yet it was possible for the medieval townsman, as it is not always possible for his urban descendant today, to saunter beyond the town gates to the orchards and meadows of the enfolding countryside.

As agriculture occupied the life of the villager, so the various crafts occupied his urban counterpart. Moreover, just as the peasant had to subordinate himself to the inescapable communal pattern of his environment, so also in a different sense the town artisan had to be a conformist. The craft gilds, with their three stages of apprentice, journeyman, and master, regulated the specific trades or crafts within the town. They determined wages, prices, quality and output and in addition served as social, charitable and religious brotherhoods. They gave dignity and corporate pride to various occupations, tangible expressions of which we may still see in the superb masterpieces of the medieval silversmiths and goldsmiths. The gilds were a good example of the corporate spirit of the Middle Ages; they exemplified the tendency, seen in every aspect of life, to define the individual in terms of his association with a larger group. As times changed and as the gilds tended to become rigid and unimaginative, the virtues of this particular kind of economic organization became less real.

The greatest stimulus to the prosperity of the towns was undoubtedly trade. Never entirely self-sufficient, the medieval towns early began to exchange commodities on a relatively wide basis. Venice, strategically placed at the head of the Adriatic and near the Alpine passes, used her large galleys to bring goods directly from Constantinople and indirectly from the Far East, thus stimulating economic activity in the whole north of Italy. The Flemish towns played a parallel role north of the Alps, having an important trade connection with the Baltic and also a growing cloth manufacture of their own. As the Italian and Flemish towns both extended their sphere of operations, their common meeting place came to be midway on the natural route from Venice to Bruges, in the plain of Champagne, where famous annual fairs grew up.[9]

Regulation of trade within the town came to lie in the hands of the "gild merchant," an association of all its merchants and traders, with power to fix conditions of trade and to determine the rights of foreign merchants. By making reciprocal arrangements with other towns, the gild merchant could contrive to give some sort of economic order to an area wider than that of the town itself. This urban regulation of economic life thus became an important forerunner of what later was called mercantilism—in other words, the regulation of economic life on a national scale by the state itself.

The goods making up the substance of medieval trade were numerous. Salt, wines, wool, dried fish, lumber and grain could be called the great staples. Other commodities were leather and hides, tallow, hemp, honey, wax, pitch and various metals. In another category fell the luxury commodities of the Levant trade: spices, silks, precious stones, ivory, rare woods, drugs, perfumes and, by the fifteenth century, some Chinese porcelains. As the crafts became more specialized, particular towns grew famous for certain products. This gave a market for special types of cloth, for metal wares of various sorts and for such end products as weapons, glassware and leather goods. "A fourteenth century Italian merchant bought his coats of mail in Milan or Nuremberg; his gold handled swords in Florence or Lyons; his blades in Milan, Toledo, Nuremberg or Solingen; his spurs and leather trunks in Paris; and the cords for his crossbows in Hungary." [10]

The fourteenth century saw the establishment of a regular sea route from Venice to England and Flanders traversed by great galleys one hundred and fifty feet in length and carrying crews numbering up to two hundred. The first of such voyages of some two thousand five hundred miles has been described as the longest voyage undertaken by European trading vessels since

9. At one of the most famous of these fairs, Troyes, a system of weights grew up which is still known as Troy weight.
10. HEATON, *Economic History of Europe*, p. 135.

antiquity. Meanwhile, as other Mediterranean cities such as Genoa, Pisa, Florence, Marseilles and Barcelona followed in the path of Venice, there developed in the north around the Baltic that elaborate trade association of towns known as the Hanseatic League. This, with Lübeck as its center, established trading connections at the four key points of Bergen, Bruges, London and Novgorod and exercised such political, economic and military authority in the fourteenth century that it could almost be considered a great power.

Along with the growing number of commodities and the widening of the trading area came significant developments in business techniques. Medieval fairs had their local rules, administered in special courts. The gild merchant, as we have seen, began to regulate inter-municipal trade. With the growth of shipping, codes of maritime law deriving ultimately from the old Roman sea-law of Rhodes were adapted by a number of Italian towns and in one way or another spread to some of the French and Flemish sea-ports. Differences between these codes were gradually ironed out. Similarly the laws governing trade, fairs and markets generally achieved some degree of standardization. By 1250 it could be said that a widely accepted body of maritime and commercial law—in some sense a forerunner of later international law—had come into existence.

Various business practices took something of their modern shape. Banking as a specialized occupation seems to have had its roots in Italy, above all in Florence and Genoa. From the traditional money-changing and money-lending arose such complex developments as the use of bills of exchange, letters of credit and checks, double-entry bookkeeping, insurance and interest-tables. Many of these practices can be traced to antiquity and had had a continuous existence in the eastern Mediterranean; yet the later Middle Ages can be credited with their elaboration and wide dispersal in Italy, Germany, the Low Countries, France and England. In the thirteenth and fourteenth centuries Italian merchants began to substitute the new Arabic notation for the clumsy Roman numerals. In this same period coined money came much more generally into employment. The exclusive use of silver as the metal of currency ended in the thirteenth century; gold florins were struck in 1252 at Florence. Within fifty years other gold coins had been issued in Venice, France and England.[11]

Remarkable technological advances were made during the medieval period. Most of them, though not all, were associated with the urban economy and may, therefore, be most conveniently considered here. Architectural techniques developed impressively. No small amount of skill was required

11. The English "pound" meant originally a pound's weight of silver.

to build a medieval castle; and the construction of a cathedral, with its complicated arches and stone vaulting, its flying buttresses and window traceries, its intricate weights and stresses, raised architectural and engineering problems of the highest degree of refinement. Great technical skill appears in the making of medieval armor and siege engines. The remarkable improvements in navigation and sailing, such as the use of the fore-and-aft instead of the lateen rig, the modern type of rudder, the astrolabe, the quadrant, astronomical tables, elaborate lists of sailing directions and, above all, the compass, constituted in total a veritable revolution. Other devices evolved during the Middle Ages include the use of cast iron, the crank to transmit power from a wheel, the spinning-wheel and fulling-mill, fireplaces and chimneys instead of the brazier centrally located in a room, buttons for clothing, paper, window panes and spectacles for reading. Woodcuts for printing appear as a crude anticipation of movable type. Geared clocks run by weights begin to succeed sundials, hourglasses and water-clocks in the late thirteenth century. With them a precise division of the day was made possible instead of the variable hours earlier associated with the liturgical practices of the Church. Such technological improvements are usually obscure in their first beginnings and undramatic in their development. Nevertheless, by giving man greater control over his environment they constitute as a whole a remarkable advance.

No view of medieval town life and commerce can ignore the tremendous power and activity of the Byzantine Empire. The political significance of this eastern successor to imperial Rome, extending through the Balkans and Asia Minor, will be considered shortly. In an economic sense the life which centered around the great city of Constantinople, or Byzantium, rose to spectacular levels. With its powerful army and navy, its large merchant marine, its coinage of standard weight and purity, its well-established legal procedures and rigorous system of tax-collection, the Eastern Empire was admirably fitted to take advantage of its favorable position at the crossroads of East and West. Although the great mass of the Byzantine population were peasants toiling on the estates of the great landowners, the city of Constantinople grew to a population of one million. Its reputation for splendor spread throughout all Europe:

> Here was the residence of the emperor and of the patriarch; here were palaces, churches—above all *Hagia Sophia*—and monasteries, baths, theaters, orphanages, and parks. When Paris, London, Vienna, and Rome were dirty villages, Constantinople had miles of paved streets, policed at all hours and lighted at night. On the one hand, one found incredible splendor, and on the other, in the dark alleys of the capital, poverty and vice, often a world of dogs, dirt, and thieves. In the harbor were the vessels of Syrians, Egyptians, Russians, Scandi-

navians, Persians, and Venetians, and in the streets and on the quays one found half the nationalities of both Europe and Asia, a motley and cosmopolitan horde.[12]

Byzantium traded on a large scale with the entire East. Many of its commercial techniques, inherited from the Late Roman Empire, were passed on to the western world. In the ninth century it developed a large trade with Russia, especially with the merchants of Kiev who annually banded together and traveled by way of the Dnieper River and the Black Sea. Eventually Byzantine trade was to be weakened by the competition of Venice, Genoa and other Italian towns, but down to the time of the Fourth Crusade and the capture of Byzantium by the Venetians in 1204 this trade provided the economic basis for the splendor of the Eastern Empire.

It must suffice in conclusion to indicate a few consequences of this acceleration of urban life. Clearly, the towns injected an element of dynamism into European society and contributed largely to its transformation. Two new classes were growing in importance: one was the merchant bourgeoisie, the other, the skilled artisans. Still small in number in comparison with the vast rural population, these groups were to play an increasingly important role in the new age. This was to be particularly true of the merchant class, whose alliance with the new monarchies had often served to bring about the decline of feudal authority. As we have seen, the money economy of the late medieval period was beginning to undermine the established pattern of rural life. From the "petty capitalism" of the medieval period the new structure of "commercial capitalism" slowly emerged. Moreover, the new interests and the wider horizons of the wealthy bourgeois made possible a vigorous flourishing of urban culture. This could be seen in the founding of grammar schools, the building of graceful parish churches, substantial gild-halls, homes for the sick and aged and palaces for the new merchant princes. Painters, sculptors, silversmiths and all kinds of craftsmen received encouragement. The towns fostered in their midst a new school of politics. Particularly in Italy they became the eventual home of a cultivated and "urbane" society—the fertile soil for a remarkable growth in almost all fields of culture. The towns were, indeed, in the forefront of progress; they were the harbingers of a new age.

■ THE EXPANSION OF EUROPE

Further to understand the broadening outlook and the secular interests of the urban class, we should glance briefly at the new horizons opened up by trade and exploration during this transitional period. The considerable

12. FREDERICK B. ARTZ, *The Mind of the Middle Ages* (1954), p. 97.

knowledge of the world acquired in classical antiquity survived only in a limited and distorted form during the early medieval period. At this time the Arabs were unquestionably the best informed geographically. But as the Middle Ages progressed, a substantial body of information grew up elsewhere. The Crusades, beginning in 1096, made an important contribution. Thousands of Europeans, either as soldiers or pilgrims, made the long journey by land and sea to the Near East. Those who returned brought back a wider knowledge, some of which was preserved in the medieval chronicles and some in more popular literary forms.

Knowledge developed in other ways. The learned Adam of Bremen, for example, in the eleventh century had no question as to the sphericity of the earth. Adelard of Bath, who died about 1150, traveled fairly widely in the Near East and included among his writings a treatise on the astrolabe. One of the earliest mentions of the compass as an aid to navigation comes in the *De Utensilibus* of the English schoolman, Alexander Neckam, written about 1180, though its common use did not come until at least the fourteenth century. Roger Bacon in the thirteenth century included geography among his many interests. He commented upon the contemporary accounts of religious missions to central Asia such as that of William of Rubruquis, appealed for accurate mapping techniques based on lines of latitude and longitude and, improving upon Ptolemy's calculations, made a very close estimate of the earth's circumference. The *portolani,* or detailed sailing directions giving the distances and lie of the land from one Mediterranean port to another, came to be accompanied by maps of fair accuracy. Perhaps the most important step in the advance of geographical science was the translation of Ptolemy's *Geography* from Greek to Latin in 1410. This invaluable compendium of classical knowledge circulated widely in manuscript form and when printed in 1475 caused Ptolemy to be known as the teacher of the modern world. It led to the use of degree lines on maps and stimulated the search for information concerning new areas which Ptolemy had not covered.

The inroads of the Mongols from Asia into eastern Europe in the thirteenth century brought two utterly alien worlds into contact. The vast Mongol Empire created in central Asia at the close of the twelfth century by Jenghiz Khan soon sent its horsemen through the Caspian Gateway into the plains of southern Russia. By 1240 the Mongols had reached the Dnieper River, overrunning the territories of the ancient Russian state of Kiev. Mongol forces struck beyond, reaching Breslau in Silesia, Cracow in Poland and Budapest in Hungary. Bulgaria, Serbia and Bosnia were ravaged. When this last ferocious onslaught had receded, the general overlordship of the successors of Jenghiz Khan still prevailed in the basins of the

Christian Europe is bounded by the Mongols to the east, the Turks to the southeast and the Moslem states in Africa. The Holy Roman Empire extends into Italy and well beyond the Rhine. England holds Aquitaine. Poland and Lithuania unite in 1386; in 1397 Denmark, Sweden and Norway form the Union of Kalmar. Note the small area of the Byzantine Empire.

THE EUROPEAN STATES
around 1350

Lower Volga, the Don, the Dnieper and the Dniester. Local Russian princes were required to pay tribute to the Khan of the Golden Horde. Although the Greek Orthodox clergy were given a special position and in some ways their growth was actually aided, the Mongol period left permanent marks upon Russian civilization. "It is to this period," a distinguished historian has told us, "that we must trace the final estrangement of Russia from Western Europe." [13] After more than two hundred years one of the princes of Moscow, Ivan III, in 1480 destroyed the long domination of the Golden Horde and opened a new chapter in Russian history.

The Mongols, meanwhile, had aroused the missionary zeal of the Church. In 1245 John of Piano Carpini led an embassy or mission from the pope all

13. H. A. L. FISHER, *A History of Europe* (new rev. ed., 1939), p. 390.

the way on foot across central Asia to Karakorum, in what is now Outer Mongolia, where he was favorably received by the Great Khan. Another monk, William of Rubruquis, reached Karakorum about a decade later. In 1283 a Franciscan named John of Montecorvino went to the Far East where he became Archbishop of Peking, built churches and convents, established other bishoprics and made converts by the thousands. Between 1323 and 1328 Oderic of Pordonone traveled through India, China, Malaya and central Asia. In the course of his travels he reached Lhasa in Tibet—the first European to accomplish this feat. Although vigorous missionary activity was abandoned in the fourteenth century, it had led to a permanent increase in knowledge of the Far East.

Many medieval voyagers left accounts of their travels, among them the

35

aforementioned John of Piano Carpini and William of Rubruquis. The journeys of the Polo family, which fell between the years 1260 and 1295, still captivate the imagination. Nicolo and Marco were merchants who not only covered the laborious Asiatic land routes already traveled, but also saw the wonders of the highly cultured Chinese Empire and heard about Japan before returning along the vast sea route which skirted the whole southern coast of Asia. Marco Polo's *Travels,* dictated by him in French and subsequently translated into Latin, Italian and other languages, achieved a contemporary fame which subsequent ages have not diminished. Columbus, it may be remembered, kept and heavily annotated a copy of Marco Polo's work. While the somewhat later *Travels* attributed to Sir John Mandeville must be put in a different category, yet even this plagiarized account of prodigies and wonders has a substratum of geographic truth; with all its fantasies it suggested the pattern of new and strange worlds. Eighty-five manuscript copies of Marco Polo made before the invention of printing still survive; and two hundred and twenty-five are known of Mandeville. These are doubtless a mere fraction of those once in circulation. Through such writings the educated people of the late Middle Ages could learn about an impressive number of countries and places—"China and India, Thibet and Turkestan, the lands of the Near East, Persia, Mesopotamia, Arabia, the adjacent parts of Asia Minor, the lands south of the Caucasus and around the Black and Caspian Seas, the northern and western parts of Russia, all the shores of the Baltic and even much of Siberia and Mongolia." [14]

In 1291 a Genoese sailor, Ugolino di Vivaldo, set out into the Atlantic with two galleys hoping to reach India by circumnavigating Africa. He was lost in the attempt, but other Genoese sailors may have reached the Canary Islands before 1300. Within the next fifty years Madeira, the Azores and the Cape Verde Islands had been discovered. The Arabian Ibn Batuta, one of the great travelers of the fourteenth century, is reputed to have journeyed down the west African coast as far as the Niger River and the east African coast as far as Mombasa. This would have put him in the neighborhood of the equator, but his narratives were not known to his European contemporaries. French merchants were on the Guinea coast by 1364. Even though these first voyages led to no immediate settlements, it remains true that the fourteenth century saw European sailors and fishermen first beginning to meet the challenge of the Atlantic.

The desire of merchants outside the Mediterranean area to share in the vigorous trading pursuits of the Italian cities is understandable. A new phenomenon of the fifteenth and sixteenth centuries was to be the emergence of various royal dynasties eager to further the desires of the merchant class.

14. E. P. CHEYNEY, *The Dawn of a New Era* (1936), p. 296.

Portugal, Spain, France and England illustrate this tendency, and of these Portugal must be put first in any account of oceanic exploration. Strategically placed for the advance down the African coast, it succeeded with the aid of England in throwing off the yoke of Castile at the close of the fourteenth century. It then turned its attention to overseas expansion and in 1415 captured from the Moors the port of Ceuta, lying across the straits from Gibraltar. The story of Prince Henry "The Navigator," fifth son of John I of Portugal, is one of active encouragement to the theory and practice of exploration. Establishing himself at Sagres, on the southernmost promontory in Portugal, he patronized and helped the study of geography, astronomy, cartography and navigation, and by all this furthered the growth of Portuguese commerce; he took the first steps in colonizing the Azores and sought constantly to fight the infidel and to aid the spread of Christianity. His activities were phenomenally successful; by the time of his death in 1460 his ships were nearing Sierra Leone peninsula on the African coast.

From this point onward the rate of exploration proceeded with dramatic acceleration, and the stage was set for that tremendous surge of overseas activity, both political and economic, which marks the sixteenth century. Perhaps for this reason the great names of this later age of exploration tend to be seen too much in the light of their own times, and the substantial achievements of the medieval period tend to be undervalued. In this respect as in so many others the elements of continuity are real; one should not let the dramatic exploits of the age of Vasco da Gama and Columbus hide the basic importance of the preceding centuries.

■ GOVERNMENT AND POLITICS

The most distinctive political institution of medieval Europe was feudalism. It should be understood less as a romantic business of knights and ladies, troubadours and tournaments, than as a practical method of ensuring order amid the dangers of an unstable world. The barbarian kingdoms which took shape after the decline of Roman authority were unskilled in administration and quite generally weak. Europe experienced a series of shocks as Viking, Arab, Saracen or Magyar invaders spread their terrors. The common desire of the weak and defenceless to place themselves under the protection of the strong can thus be easily understood.

The essential elements of feudalism were two: the concept of *vassalage* and the concept of the *fief*. The vassal was one bound by certain ties to a lord. He paid him homage (that is, became his "man") and solemnly vowed fealty or faith. He owed various services: military service, court service and payments on stated occasions. In return for all this he held a fief. Usually but not necessarily land, a fief may be defined as the right to possession dependent upon the fulfillment of certain well-defined conditions. The lord's fundamental obligation to his vassal, having provided him with a fief, would be to give him protection.

The essence of feudalism appears to be landholding in return for services, with a careful definition of rights and duties on both sides. A powerful ruler, parceling out some of his possessions to a series of vassals, created a kind of political order, and feudalism in this way contributed to the effective government of large parts of Europe in the tenth and eleventh centuries at a time when royal power was generally weak. Eventually, as in England, some royal rulers were able to make use of the feudal bond to strengthen their own authority. The system as it developed came to be marked by notable complexities. By what was known as sub-infeudation a vassal could further parcel out some of his territories to a sub-vassal. The latter could repeat the process. Thus the same person could be overlord and vassal; allegiance could be divided and loyalty uncertain. The Church, moreover, was a great landholder and became deeply involved in feudal conflicts, as we shall see. From another standpoint, it was not always possible to define clearly the local powers of a feudal lord in relation to the overarching authority of his king. In some sense, therefore, feudalism contributed to the disorder as well as to the order of medieval life.

Primarily political, feudalism made other important contributions. Its external symbol was the castle. Originally this was a crude wooden structure on an earthen mound, surrounded by a palisade. The development from this to the elaborate stone structures of the thirteenth century, with their moats, keeps, curtain-walls, halls, and towers, constitutes an important chapter in the history of warfare, of architecture and of society. The code of chivalry, embodying the elaborate rules of "courtesy" or knightly behavior, eventually did something to soften and adorn the harshness of medieval life. From it grew what later ages came to regard as the code of the "gentleman." From feudal society, too, grew the traditional association of the European aristocracy with the occupations and pleasures of the countryside.

Royal power would seem at first glance to be in sharp contrast to feudal power. Feudalism laid stress upon local rights and resented any interference with them, so that centralizing and decentralizing tendencies inevitably came into conflict. Monarchy could claim to be the apex of the feudal pyramid, the point where all allegiances, so to speak, came together. This, however, was much truer at first in theory than in fact, and circumstances varied from country to country. But in the end the general outcome was the decline of feudal authority and the substitution for it of royal power.

In England and Wales the remains of some five hundred "motte and bailey" castles are testimony to an early and widespread feudal pattern.[15] The Norman conquest following 1066 led to the appearance of a very powerful group of feudal nobles, but their localized vigor was quickly countered by the even greater centralizing vigor of the Norman and Plantagenet kings. By various means the local bond was subordinated to the allegiance due the king, and a system of royal administration was slowly worked out. Ultimately local machinery was ingeniously dovetailed into the national framework of government. England, then, had that kind of feudal "pyramid" in which authority centered in the king who stood at its summit.

In France, where the dukedoms of the great nobles were extraordinarily powerful, one sees a more thoroughgoing example of the feudal state. At first royal power prevailed only over a very small territory around Paris, and some of the holdings of the great feudatories were so extensive as to constitute almost kingdoms in themselves. It took several hundred years for the Capetians and their successors to assert their authority and to build up the realm of France as the sixteenth and seventeenth centuries came to know it.

Medieval Germany saw the rise of a particularly militant class of feudal knights whose stubborn local pride was out of all relation to their actual importance. These continued to assert themselves long after feudalism in its true sense had waned. Of greater political significance were the rulers of larger German states, both lay and ecclesiastical, who by the twelfth century had given to Germany the characteristic pattern of a feudal society. In Italy there was no unity of pattern. The Norman Kingdom of Sicily witnessed a strong development of royal authority. Further to the north feudal principalities of the more common type flourished, but here a new element appeared with the growth of the Italian communes. These thriving towns took on some of the attributes of sovereign power; their citizens gradually bought up the lands of the feudal class; and the communes were prepared on occasion to band together and defy even the authority of the Holy Roman Emperor. Spain, Scandinavia, Poland and Hungary each in its own way adapted itself to a feudal regime.

The place of kingship in medieval history requires some brief examination. It was a complex institution. Royal titles were usually hereditary, but the right of blood succession was combined with public ceremonies of acclamation or election, and coronation. Absolutism in its later sense was hardly known. In general the king was held to be "under the law"; custom was very strong; the Church could remind him of his sacred duties; and the barons, or even a vaguely defined "community," could claim some right of

15. The "motte and bailey" is an early form of castle in which there is a fortified mound and a walled enclosure.

protest in the case of tyrannical interference with established ways. Magna
Carta (1215) is the classic example of such a protest. But its importance
should not be overstated. The king was held to be superior to the people
and possessed of inherent independent rights. Roman law could be invoked
to give some support to absolutist tendencies; there were also medieval
writers who ventured the idea that the king was the officer of the people and
that the people had made a compact with him; he could, if unsuitable, be
dismissed by them. But these incipient notions, inclining in the direction
either of divine right or of popular sovereignty, were deviations from the
main current of medieval political thought.[16] Not until the late thirteenth
century, "a turning point in the history of constitutional ideas," was a
machinery created by means of which churchmen, nobles and commoners
could formally share in the royal tasks of government.

The growth of representative political institutions is one of the significant phenomena which link together the medieval and the modern world. A
fundamental right of any feudal overlord was to call upon his vassals for
advice and counsel. Exercising this right, a medieval king could summon
his principal churchmen and lay nobles to meet in a "Great Council" at
more or less regular intervals. When such bodies were enlarged by adding
representatives from the newly developing towns, a "third estate" was added
to the existing two orders, and some form of national assembly could be
said to exist. Its duties were not so much law-making as law-declaring and
advice-giving; it functioned more, perhaps, as a court than as a modern
legislature. In the uncertain realm of royal taxation it took a stand in the
protection of property by claiming the right to give its assent to any proposed new levies of money.

The Cortes in Spain, the Estates General in France and the Parliament in
England all showed a striking parallelism of development. Occasional meetings were summoned in the several Spanish kingdoms of Leon, Castile,
Aragon, Catalonia and Valencia in the twelfth and thirteenth centuries, with
the most impressive developments occurring in Castile. The growth of a
system of estates can be seen in early fourteenth-century France. In England
townsmen and knights of the shire were summoned to the Parliament in
1265 and a generation later to the "Model Parliament" of 1295. In the Holy
Roman Empire the emperors were assisted by diets, in which the representatives of the German cities gradually acquired the right to be present. What
were called provincial estates (*Landtage*) grew up in states such as Pomerania, Württemberg and Bavaria. Not truly parliamentary in the modern
sense, these various bodies are nevertheless a striking illustration of political
evolution. Progress was not always steady; the "premature constitutional-

16. F. KERN, *Kingship and Law in the Middle Ages* (1939), pp. 135–139.

ism," for example, of late medieval England, was followed by the vigorous royal assertiveness of the Tudors. The Cortes of Spain and the Estates General of France failed to live up to the great promise of their beginnings, nor did any national assembly emerge from the local gatherings in Germany or in Italy.

Outwardly the most impressive political institution of the Middle Ages was the Holy Roman Empire. It arose in a sense from the inability or unwillingness of Europe to forget the mighty traditions of imperial Rome. Established by the Frankish king, Charlemagne, in the year 800 so as to include an area corresponding roughly to present-day France, northern Italy and western Germany, and refounded by Otto the Great in 962, this Empire claimed to revive the traditions of the Roman Empire. By the twelfth century it had become largely Germanic, including also what today would be the Netherlands, Belgium, Switzerland, Bohemia, Austria, Italy as far south as Rome, and some part of eastern and southeastern France. Over three hundred states, large and small, were included.

After 1273 the emperorship lay traditionally with the Hapsburg family. By the Golden Bull of 1356 the method of election was fixed, with the choice lying in the hands of the seven electors (the Archbishops of Mainz, Trier and Cologne, and the lay rulers of Bohemia, the Palatinate, Saxony and Brandenburg). The emperor was "assisted" by a diet of three houses, one composed of the seven electors, one of the lesser nobles and one of the free imperial cities. In theory the emperor was the feudal superior of all territorial rulers within the bounds of the Empire; in a vague sense, too, he could claim some political authority over all Christendom. Yet his imperial vassals showed an increasing unwillingness to accept this authority and the emperor had perforce to content himself with the splendid, if hollow, pageantry of his office.

Imperial claims clashed also with those of the papacy, which likewise claimed to be the heir of Rome. As a great landowner the Roman Catholic Church entered deeply into the feudal system. A bishop, drawing revenues from German territory, had certain feudal obligations to his imperial overlord. Did emperor and pope share in the election of a bishop, or did one or the other exercise prime authority? The same problem, it may be noted, arose with other rulers, such as those of England and France. The imperial-papal conflicts rocked the Middle Ages, with victories won or claimed on both sides. Ultimately the question was not so much decided as it was superseded when the political power and assertiveness of the newly arising national states pushed the older dispute into the background. Weak though the Empire was in many ways, it nevertheless gave a certain splendor to the Middle Ages and also a certain sense of unity. Centuries later some persistent memories of it continued to haunt the minds of men.

The imperialism which flourished at Byzantium was far different from that of the Western Empire. This successor to the Late Roman Empire maintained itself during the early medieval period against Slav, Tartar, Persian and Moslem attacks. Byzantium later took the offensive and won back territories so that by 1050 its authority extended from the head of the Adriatic to the eastern tip of the Black Sea and from the Danube as far south as the islands of Crete and Cyprus. This great age of political power continued until the thirteenth century, when it was halted by the Venetian occupation which lasted from 1204 to 1261—the period of the "Latin Empire of Constantinople." The area controlled by Byzantium soon shrank to a fraction of what it had been. Despite a considerable economic and cultural revival in the fourteenth and fifteenth centuries, the Eastern Empire languished until it was finally destroyed by the Turkish conquest of Byzantium in 1453.

The Byzantine Empire continued the autocratic tradition of antiquity. The existing ruler possessed the right to crown his successor during his lifetime, and while the new ruler had to be proclaimed by the senate or the army and acclaimed by the populace, this in fact meant very little. A splendid court and an elaborate ceremonial gave added dignity to the imperial title. The emperors guided the religious life of the state. Government was in the hands of a complicated and highly organized bureaucracy which, with all its defects, made possible an administration uniformly applied over a wide area, a powerful army that shared in the tasks of civil government and a tax system that brought in steady and substantial revenues. In all these respects the Byzantine Empire showed qualities far different from those which characterized the states of Western Europe.

The medieval period revealed some evidences of growing national sentiment in contrast to the vague internationalism of the Holy Roman Empire. At the close of the twelfth century a French writer sought to list the distinctive characteristics of various nations: the French, he said, were proud and womanish; the Germans furious and obscene; the Lombards greedy, malicious, and cowardly; the English were drunkards and had tails. A century later Pierre Dubois wrote: "It is a peculiar merit of the French to have a surer judgment than other nations." On many occasions medieval kings contrived to appeal to the loyalty of their subjects. A long struggle such as the Hundred Years War between England and France (1340–1453) undoubtedly stimulated national self-consciousness and national pride. The growth of vernacular literature in England, France, Germany, Spain and Italy emphasized national differences. In one of his letters Petrarch thanked God that he was born an Italian. Although a distinction must be drawn between the growth of national sentiment and the appearance of a vigorous national state, yet the one seems the necessary precondition of the other. National feeling was much stronger in some areas than in others, but it has been well said that the aspect of thought which most clearly marks the difference between the Europe of 1250 and the Europe of 1450 is precisely the growth of this spirit.[17]

The political contributions of the Middle Ages were, in sum, profound. Feudalism provided the idea of contract, of mutual dependence, of relations which were definable and enforceable. The medieval towns made significant contributions to the art of self-government. The Holy Roman Empire gave some idea of European unity and order in the great tradition of imperial Rome. From the medieval kingdoms came the idea of monarchy that was the mouthpiece of the law and yet itself under the law; these states demonstrated the slow concentration of royal power that could put an end to feudal disorder; they worked out the beginnings of representative government; they revealed an element of national self-assertiveness. As territories were slowly consolidated, the map of Europe was beginning by 1450 to take something of its modern shape.

From the active minds of the medieval period came vigorous contributions to the literature of political controversy. Papal, imperial and royal power each had its champions. Couched in a phraseology unfamiliar to us and dealing with issues that often seem remote, these writings have never achieved the celebrity of the great political classics of the seventeenth and eighteenth centuries. Yet they carried over some basically important concepts from the ancient world, such as the idea of a law of nature by whose universal standards specific human laws might be judged. They developed the study of Roman law and in so doing contributed both to legal theory and to the actual practice of government. From the Germanic peoples came the idea of law as custom and of the need for a ruler to consult his people in order to discover what this custom was. Writers clarified certain concepts such as those dealing with the rights of property, the right of a ruler to tax and the proper functions of the estates of the realm. They put forward ideas which foreshadowed the later doctrine of the social contract. Though much of this medieval political thought soon gathered dust, much of it also was constructive. It was the essential preliminary to the great political writings and some of the actual political developments of the sixteenth century.

■ RELIGION

In theory, at least, medieval Europe was the home of one Christian, Catholic people. The geographic limits to this unity should be noted. An

17. CHEYNEY, *Dawn of a New Era*, p. 337.

uncertain religious frontier existed toward the Slavic East.[18] All Asia Minor and all North Africa were in Moslem hands. A small part of the southern coast of Spain (Granada) remained Moslem until 1492, although the greater part of the country had been freed by the close of the twelfth century from its Moorish conquerors. After 1354 another Moslem people, the Turks, who by then were solidly established in Asia Minor, spread into the Balkans and began to push north towards the Danube.

Nor was Christendom itself united. The Orthodox Eastern, or Greek, Church which had developed in consequence of early disagreements between Rome and Constantinople had definitely become separated from the West in 1054, when a papal envoy arrived in state to lay upon the great altar of the church of Santa Sophia a solemn bull of excommunication. The authority of the Eastern Church extended from Constantinople into the Balkan peninsula and, despite the Turkish advance there, contrived to maintain itself and even to advance. Scattered Jewish communities were found throughout Western Europe, many of them meeting severe persecution at the time of the Crusades. Heresy raised its head from time to time and from country to country. These were the rents in the Christian fabric. Despite such important exceptions, however, the stress should be put upon the general unity of medieval Catholic Christendom.

The Christian Church of the West was the product of long and elaborate growth. The authority of the Bishop of Rome, or pope, as he came to be called, extended over a vast network of officials: cardinals, legates, archbishops, bishops, abbots, monks, nuns and priests. The full development of Roman Catholic organization and faith is the work of the eleventh and twelfth centuries. About the middle of the eleventh century the College of Cardinals emerged as the body charged with the duty of electing the pope from its number and with other important administrative responsibilities. About the same time a great revival of the old monastic orders began to reinvigorate religious life. Around 1150 in the *Sentences* of Peter Lombard (one of the great theological textbooks of the Middle Ages) we find the doctrine of the seven sacraments crystallizing into a definite form.[19] These were declared to be the means of salvation, the visible signs of invisible grace. The Church, through its ordained priesthood, had the responsibility of administering them. Outside the Church, therefore, there was no salva-

18. Hungary did not become Christian until the reign of King Stephen (997–1038). The Grand Duchy of Lithuania remained pagan until 1385 when its ruler, the Grand Prince Jagiello, married a Polish princess, became Catholic and united the thrones of Poland and Lithuania.
19. The seven were: baptism, confirmation, penance, the Eucharist, marriage, ordination and extreme unction. The origin of the sacraments is asserted to be found in scriptural texts, but their actual development covered a long period of time.

tion. The Church declared that in the Eucharist, or Lord's Supper, the body and blood of Christ "are truly contained in the sacrament of the altar under the form of bread and wine, the bread being changed into body, and the wine into blood by divine power." [20] Thus the humble worshiper at the Mass found himself in the presence of a recurring miracle.

The great powers which the Roman Catholic Church claimed for itself were variously expressed: in the stress upon priestly authority, in the system of ecclesiastical courts subject to the final authority of the papal court, in the elaborate machinery of papal taxation developed throughout Christendom, in the employment of excommunication and interdict, in prayers for the dead, in granting indulgences to individuals to reduce the amount of their suffering in purgatory, in preaching crusades against the infidel, in the machinery of the Inquisition used against heresy, in the definition and denunciation of reprehensible business practices such as usury, in the challenge made to the authority of kings and emperors. Such elaborate powers may not have been fully appreciated by the average man; but he knew that the Church through its sacraments stood beside him at every important crisis of his life, and that outside the Church there was no salvation.

Many services that we would not regard as essentially religious were performed by the Church. The cathedral schools and the various monastic establishments were responsible for a large part of such elementary and secondary education as there was, and the medieval universities were in most cases closely associated with the Church. Other services to learning included maintaining libraries, compiling records and chronicles and copying manuscripts. The Church aided government by providing a steady stream of officials who could read and write. Church courts also had jurisdiction over such matters as sacrilege, morals and the annulment of marriages. The monasteries often served as hospitals, inns or poorhouses. With the coming of the mendicant orders—the Franciscans and the Dominicans—in the thirteenth century, an even greater stress was put upon charitable works performed outside the cloister. The name of St. Francis of Assisi (1182–1226) recalls a life dedicated through love to the service of all God's creatures. In another sphere the Church concerned itself actively with practical arts such as agriculture and building. It also spurred many developments in the fine arts. In still another field, that of missionary enterprise, the priest served with the soldier and the merchant to open up the immense vistas of the mysterious, non-European world.

Religion contributed greatly to the vigor of medieval thinking. Only by a great misrepresentation can this thought be regarded as fixed and essen-

20. Quoted from A. C. MC GIFFERT, *A History of Christian Thought,* II (1933), p. 322. The doctrine was officially proclaimed at the Fourth Lateran Council in 1215.

tially unprogressive. There have been, indeed, few more strenuous ages of controversy. The dogmas and teachings of the Church being still in some sense fluid, during this period of elaboration and definition the various Doctors of the Schools (whether described as Angelic, Seraphic, Universal or merely Subtle) went at the task of debate with incomparable vigor. Much of the literature of controversy may seem almost unreadable today because we are not familiar with the issues in the terms in which they were then posed and because we no longer employ the intricate techniques of argument then in vogue. In the person of St. Thomas Aquinas (1225–1274), the greatest of such disputants, we have the superb master of dialectic, or logical reasoning, who worked out in his *Summa Theologica* a powerful demonstration and vindication of God's plan.

The problem of conflict between the Church and the civil power has already been mentioned. The dispute in the late eleventh century between Pope Gregory VII and the Emperor Henry IV over the question of lay investiture (that is, the question of who had the ultimate power of conferring the symbols of temporal and spiritual power upon a new bishop) was settled by a compromise. But the arguments and the struggle went on. At the close of the twelfth century, Pope Innocent III made vast claims on behalf of papal power and was able to assert himself against the rulers of England, France, Scandinavia, Aragon, Castile and Leon, to say nothing of the Holy Roman Emperor himself. At the great jubilee of 1300 Pope Boniface VIII showed himself to pilgrims, seated upon a throne, equipped with sword, crown and scepter, and shouting, "I am Caesar, I am Emperor!" [21]

Such pretensions at such a date had an element of fantasy, for royal power was beginning to assert itself widely. In a dispute with Philip IV of France, Boniface was seized and soon died in prison. The Archbishop of Bordeaux was made pope and the papal capital was transferred to Avignon, a small piece of ecclesiastical land on the border of France. There it remained from 1309 to 1376, a clear symbol of the decline of papal prestige. This decline was not helped by the ensuing Great Schism, when for forty years there was one papal claimant at Avignon and another in Italy. Various Church councils, supposedly representing all Christendom, were summoned to deal with this and other matters—at Pisa, Constance, Pavia, Siena and Basel—but such attempts to settle important religious questions, though interesting as a parallel to the contemporaneous growth of representative political bodies in various countries, failed of their object. In a famous pronouncement the papacy issued the Bull *Execrabilis* (1460), condemning as erroneous and detestable any attempt to appeal from the Roman pontiff to

21. LORD BRYCE, *The Holy Roman Empire* (1922), p. 108.

a Church council. Once again papal claims had been raised very high, but even so the fifteenth century was to find the papacy challenged upon many fronts.

Another challenge to the medieval Church came in the form of heresy. During the later Middle Ages doctrinal disagreements were widespread, and so sharp as to expose certain believers to the charge of heresy. In some cases the new sects seem to have derived from the earlier heresies of the third and fourth centuries. This seems to have been true of the Albigensians in southern France who were a revival of the sect of the Manicheans dating from the time of St. Augustine. They accepted only the New Testament, challenged the authority of the Catholic hierarchy, and looked upon the world as a sort of arena where the forces of darkness and evil battled those of goodness and light. In the early thirteenth century the papacy preached a crusade against them and subjected them to bitter persecution. Another heretical group, the Waldensians, preached "holy poverty" even as St. Francis was to preach; but by attacking the orthodox opinions on the sacraments they exposed themselves to severe attacks. In fourteenth-century England John Wyclif (1320–1384) became an ardent critic of what he regarded as widespread religious abuses, condemning especially the wealth of the Church, its extravagant political claims and its views concerning the sacramental system. His English followers, nicknamed Lollards, eventually experienced a persecution which Wyclif himself contrived to escape. From England his influence spread to Bohemia where John Hus (1369–1415) proclaimed the new ideas at the University of Prague. The Hussites had a powerful impact upon Bohemia and their influence was also felt in Austria, Poland, Hungary and Lithuania. But Hus himself was eventually condemned as a heretic at the Council of Constance and burned at the stake.

Through the machinery of the medieval Inquisition the Church took vigorous action against heretics; it could torture them in order to obtain confession, impose religious penalties, or, in the case of stubbornness, turn them over to the civil authorities to be burned. Yet the heresies continued. Religious uniformity proved impossible to achieve, and the element of dissent remained until, under different circumstances and at a later date, it was to be transferred into open revolt.

To this picture of dissent must be added a few comments about the Eastern Orthodox Church which differed on many points from the Church of Rome. It had no single head with authority like that of the pope, maintaining instead the theory that ultimate decisions were to be made by a general church council. It was administered by the four great patriarchs of Constantinople, Alexandria, Antioch and Jerusalem. It had no formal, official creed; it permitted priests to marry; it admitted painted icons but not "graven images" in its churches; it employed a different calendar; its version of monasticism (which had first developed within the Eastern Empire) retained much of the early notion of a hermitical flight from the world. Services were conducted in Old Greek or Old Slavonic, and sometimes in the other vernaculars, which meant that the humble worshipers in eastern Europe would usually find a language more within their comprehension than was Latin to the worshipers of the western Church.

A significant tendency was for a series of "national" churches to arise in Greece, Bulgaria, Serbia and in what was to be Russia. The Eastern Church tended more and more to be the religion of the Slavic lands; and as it went its way regardless of developments in the West it doubtless added something to the relative isolation in which the Russian people grew up in the later Middle Ages.

The presence of a definitely heathen world upon the fringes of Christendom was a fact of permanent importance in European history. The remarkable spread of Arab-Moslem influence subsequent to the career of Mohammed (d. 632) has already been noted.[22] Following the first great wave of Moslem advance, the Turks, a Mongol people from central Asia, had in their turn pushed westwards. The Seljuk Turks won their first victories against the eastern fringes of the Byzantine Empire as early as 1071 and quickly thereafter set up their rule in parts of Asia Minor and Armenia. By the middle of the thirteenth century another group, the Ottoman Turks, had pushed their dominion through Asia Minor to the banks of the Bosphorus.[23] Bypassing Constantinople, they crossed in 1354 into the Balkans and in 1389 won the historic victory at Kossovo which meant the end of medieval Serbia. Soon reaching the Danube, the Turks became so strongly entrenched throughout the Balkan region that their capture of Constantinople in 1453 was really the epilogue to a tale already told.

The Moslem religion as such made no significant contribution to the spiritual evolution of the West. In a negative sense, however, by helping to provoke the Crusades it contributed to the political and social ferment which they engendered in Europe. The influence of the Turk was much less than that of the Arab and the Moor; and the true contribution of these lay

22. See p. 44. The word, "Moslem," refers to an orthodox follower of the religious teachings of Mohammed embodied in the Koran. "Arabic" refers to the common language which came to be in use all the way from the Middle East through North Africa to Spain. "Saracen" was the current designation among the Crusaders for their Moslem enemies. "Moor," strictly speaking, applies to Morocco and Algeria, but came to be used for the Moslems in Spain. "Islam," meaning submission to the will of God, is the religious teaching of Mohammed.
23. The name "Ottoman," of such long significance in European history, comes from Osman I (d. 1326), the founder of the dynasty.

not in the field of religion but in the realms of art, letters and science, where they were able to pass on to the West their own impressive contributions together with those parts of the classical inheritance of which they had long been the guardians.

The existence of this alien world, of which for two centuries the Mongols were also a part, on the frontiers of Christian Europe had a large significance. To some extent it limited and forced in upon itself a Europe which in a strictly geographic sense could well have expanded more widely. It had at least something to do with the patterns created by fifteenth-century exploration. Its threats and challenges were recurrent, and time and again writers would suggest that the solution to many of Europe's difficulties lay in a joint crusade to exterminate the infidel. Yet the Turks remained, and could not be disregarded as an important element in what came to be known as the European balance of power. In the interests of trade with the Levant and the remoter East it became necessary for Christian states to vie with each other in seeking favorable arrangements with the sultan. Control of the Straits which led into the Black Sea came to be a major aim of diplomacy. The Eastern Question of the nineteenth and twentieth centuries, in which the "Terrible Turk" played the central role, is but the latest manifestation of an ancient problem.

The complex nature of European religious life in the fourteenth and fifteenth centuries makes generalization dangerous. One might safely insist, however, upon the vitality and many-sidedness of medieval Christianity. The claims which the Church made to penetrate all aspects of life and to direct one great Christian Commonwealth (*Respublica Christiana*) were such as to capture the imagination of many, both then and in later generations, even if these claims fell short of actual realization. On the other hand, the Church became subject to powerful criticisms. Some of these involved disagreement in matters of doctrine. Further criticisms dealt not so much with the beliefs as with the behavior of the clergy, in consequence of their growing wealth and worldly interests. Perhaps even more acutely felt were the financial abuses which developed as the Church sought ever larger revenues. Still other criticisms grew out of the political rights which the Church claimed for itself at a time when national self-assertiveness was on the increase. After the effort to subordinate the papacy to the authority of Church councils had subsided, the Church entered into various concordats or agreements with a number of European states. In defining and accepting the respective spheres of ecclesiastical and civil power the Church tacitly acknowledged the political sovereignty of national states and thus reduced the magnificent claims to universal authority which some of its leaders had asserted during the Middle Ages.

Thus, although in the latter half of the fifteenth century Western Europe was still outwardly one united Christendom, it had become subject to heavy stresses and strains. In a strictly chronological sense the great religious upheaval which was to put an end to this Christian unity belongs to the sixteenth century. But the predisposing conditions, the ferment and indeed not a little of the actual strife can be found in the age which preceded.

THE EMERGENCE
OF THE MODERN ERA
1 4 5 0 – 1 6 5 0

"Now is it that the minds of men are qualified
with all manner of discipline,
and the old sciences revived, which for ages were extinct.
Now it is that the learned languages
are to their pristine purity restored. . . .
Printing likewise is now in use,
so elegant and so correct that better cannot be imagined. . . .
All the world is full of knowing men,
of most learned schoolmasters, and vast libraries;
and it appears to me as a truth that neither in Plato's time,
nor Cicero's, nor Papinian's,
there was ever such conveniency for studying
as we see at this day there is."

      RABELAIS, *Gargantua and Pantagruel*

VIRGIN AND CHILD, from the "Portal of the Virgin" on the west front of Amiens Cathedral, early thirteenth century. This is the first great cathedral doorway that is wholly Gothic in character, and the Virgin and child fit into their rather austere setting with elegance and dignity. Photograph by the French Government Tourist Office.

Chapter 3

The Cultural Transition

■ MEDIEVAL SCHOLARSHIP

A STUDY of the transition from the cultural life of the Middle Ages to that
of the succeeding period reveals problems of unusual complexity. The word
"culture" is not easy to pin down. In one sense it may be taken to mean an
entire pattern of life, as when we speak of the culture of the Eskimo. In
another sense it may be taken to mean a particular refinement of tastes,
interests and conduct, as when we speak of the culture of a gentleman.
To some degree the historian is concerned with both usages. He can hardly
disregard the ideas and outlook, the "culture," of the common man. But
he will probably be much more concerned with the outlook and ideas of
what we may call the creative minority, those who write the books, paint
the pictures, design the buildings and invent the machines. It may well be
that the task of the intellectual historian is to try "to find the relations
between the ideas of the philosophers, the intellectuals, the thinkers, and the
actual way of living of the millions who carry the tasks of civilization." [1]
In undertaking this task, we would be seeking the connection between
what have been described as the high and the low intellectual traditions.
By necessity this search must give its principal attention to the achievements
of the creative minority.

The medieval peasant, we may be sure, even more than his urban
brother, was generally deficient in his knowledge, crude in his manners
and gross in his appetites. He knew little of the vast world which enclosed
his immediate horizon. Beyond the tiny circle of his daily experiences lurked

1. CRANE BRINTON, *Ideas and Men* (1950), p. 7.

a terrifying army of demons and evil spirits. Such beliefs long antedated Christianity. Children's fairy-tales still carry some savor of these ancient fears of the forest, the storm and the night. Medieval folk-lore was full of prodigies, monstrosities and marvels. In church frescoes or carvings the medieval worshiper could see depicted the terrors of Hell and the ever-present devils waiting to snatch up the unwary. The common man lived under a cloud of ignorance and fear, subject to the kind of occasional mass hysteria that could set thousands of French and German children off on foot on a Crusade to the Holy Land. The dark shades of such a picture may be relieved in part when we recall that these attitudes were not unique to the Middle Ages, that parts of popular mythology were innocent and charming, that the great period of the witchcraft persecutions came later, from the fifteenth to the seventeenth century, and that men today cannot claim to have shaken themselves free from superstition and mass hysteria.

We must likewise be cautious in judgments about the educated minority. The medieval veneer of learning and culture was often very thin. Noblemen were usually content to leave a knowledge of letters to church dignitaries and learned clerks. Despite the external graces of chivalry, manners among the upper classes would seem startlingly uncouth today. So elegant a lady as Chaucer's Prioress was graceful in that she did not dip her fingers "deepe" in the sauce. The total mass of unalleviated human suffering, the omnipresent beggars and cripples, the general acceptance of physical discomfort even by the well-to-do, would seem intolerable to us. Of superstition, too, in the upper classes there was no doubt plenty. As late as the seventeenth century court astrologers still cast horoscopes for their royal masters.

Yet all this must be kept in proportion, and here, as in so many other respects, it would be unwise to draw a sharp contrast between the medieval scene and that which was to follow. Limited though the horizon of the common toiler might be, he showed in many ways his skill, adaptability and craftsmanship. At his best he did work of a very high order. Men like St. Francis did not accept suffering and poverty with indifference; and they had their ardent followers. Considering the small libraries (often a mere shelf or cupboard) of medieval scholars, and considering, too, disparities in manuscripts, the difficulties of communication and the absence of the printed word, the wonder is that learning achieved as much as it did. If any concept of a "Dark Age" is to be retained, it should be limited, certainly, to those early centuries when a new order was slowly emerging from the ruins of the Roman world.

One of the main phenomena often taken to distinguish the beginnings of modern times is, by a kind of paradox, the "Rediscovery of Antiquity," for it is held that the humane influence of the Greek and Latin classics had a powerful effect in releasing medieval thought from its supposed fetters. We may begin, therefore, by considering how much knowledge of classical antiquity the Middle Ages actually possessed. Had classical learning ever really been lost?

There were in existence during the Middle Ages many widely used compendiums based upon classical sources. One such was the vast hodge-podge of learning and lore, the seventh century *Etymologies* of Isidore of Seville. Another famous work was Priscian's *Grammar,* with its ten thousand lines of quotations from Greek and Roman texts. Through these and many others a large, if uncritical, body of classical allusion and mythology was preserved. Substantial portions of Latin literature were never lost. Virgil led the list as the supreme poet of the Middle Ages, with Ovid a close, and perhaps a surprising, second. Horace, Juvenal, Lucan, Martial, Persius and Statius were also read. The dramas of Seneca and Terence and a good portion of the prose of Cicero, Seneca and the elder Pliny were known. But of the great Roman historians the Middle Ages knew surprisingly little, at least at first hand. The medieval sense of history was highly deficient, and the Latin writers, as scholars have remarked, were not seen in their individual settings of time and place but were accepted *en bloc* without critical discrimination.

Toward the end of the twelfth century came the great flood of translations of Greek works, many of them from the Moslem scholars of Spain and Sicily, and with them a much enlarged area of knowledge; for the "thin stream of Platonism" present during the earlier period had not sprung from a direct acquaintance with the master. Owing much to the Arabs, these translations from Greek into Latin gave to the scholars of the later Middle Ages the main body of Aristotle's writings. They also made known the major works of the Greek scientists and mathematicians: Ptolemy, Hippocrates, Galen and Euclid. One must note the absence of the great Greek poets and dramatists, and the fact that knowledge of Plato was limited to three dialogues (the *Meno,* the *Phaedo* and the *Timaeus*). This may be ascribed to the preponderantly scientific interests of the Arab scholars whose own scientific writings added substantially to the sum of medieval knowledge. The names of Averroes of Cordova, the translator of Aristotle, and Avicenna, the medical scholar and learned student of Plato and Aristotle, indicate the high position which Moslem scholarship had achieved. One should remember, however, that a Latin translation of an Arabic translation of a Syriac translation of a lost Greek original could hardly retain the fine flavor of its source. A few men in the twelfth and thirteenth centuries such as Albertus Magnus, Robert Grosseteste and Roger

Bacon were competent in Greek, but broadly speaking the classical tradition of the Middle Ages was overwhelmingly Latin. The enlarged classical interests failed to awaken any large body of students to the "humane" values of ancient culture. It may well be that an unusual individual such as John of Salisbury had something of this broader interest, but in general the emphasis was directed towards the scholastic fields of logic and theology.

The undergraduate studies of the medieval universities were derived from the famous Seven Liberal Arts which had been elaborated in the schools of the earlier medieval period. These subjects had been divided into the *Trivium* (grammar, logic and rhetoric) and the *Quadrivium* (geometry, astronomy, arithmetic and music). This plan was linked indirectly with the schools of the Late Roman Empire and thus continued something of the classical tradition. In the twelfth century the renewed study of "grammar" (really much more than that) led to a short-lived revival of the Latin classics, until the new logic of Aristotle, the new astronomy and the new mathematics swung the emphasis away from letters and toward logic, or to the practical studies of law and rhetoric. The growing concern with Roman law led certain Italian students of the thirteenth and fourteenth centuries to interest themselves in the classical setting amid which Roman law had developed and thus to obtain a truer perspective of the ancient world.

For advanced studies, the medical texts in common use were those of Galen and Hippocrates; other standard scientific works were Pliny, Ptolemy and Euclid. Civil law was studied in the *Digest* of Justinian and canon law in Gratian's *Decretum,* a twelfth-century compilation. In theology the text of the Bible was customarily supplemented by the famous *Sentences* of Peter Lombard, a collection, condensation and classification of the utterances of the Christian fathers on matters of belief which became the great theological manual of the Middle Ages. Aristotelian teachings took firm hold in the thirteenth century; in 1255 the whole of the new Aristotle was prescribed at Paris for the degree of Master of Arts.

There developed, then, a substantial corpus of classical knowledge, much of it relevant to the purposes of medieval life. The universities cannot fairly be condemned as homes of dead learning. With the rise of Paris, Oxford and Montpellier came the concept of the *Studium Generale*—the idea of a corporation of masters and scholars, admitting students from all parts, training them professionally and granting them the famous *Jus ubique docendi,* the right to teach everywhere. The common criticism of medieval instruction as being simply dry exposition and dogmatic commentary upon texts loses much of its point when one recalls the absence of printed books and the scarcity, even, of manuscripts. The combination of formal and informal lectures, the rote memorizing and above all the public disputations in which a student was required to debate publicly with his teachers and fellows suggest a stimulating variety of pedagogical methods. Graduate training for professional careers in theology, law or medicine, while obviously different in many respects from training today, was in its own way disciplined and thorough. It took about eighteen years of audition, lecturing and discussion to produce a Doctor of Theology. The bitter criticisms of university teaching uttered by Rabelais and Erasmus in the sixteenth century refer to a time when the genius of the medieval university had waned. No one acquainted with teachers such as Abelard or John of Salisbury would be disposed to doubt their acuteness and vigor.

The fine flower of the medieval intellect was revealed in scholasticism, "the organization of all knowledge into one coherent system subordinate to theology." [2] As a fully developed system it reached its height in the thirteenth century. Its main problem was that of harmonizing Christian and Greek ideas, or, as we may put it, of showing the compatibility of revelation (that is, biblical truth) and reason (pagan truth). Grave questions dealing with such matters as the nature of the Trinity, the number and validity of the sacraments, the doctrine of the atonement or the problem of sin and punishment called for precise definition. Could the rational teachings of Aristotle support the Christian revelation? St. Anselm (d. 1109) had sought harmony in his famous *credo ut intellegam* ("I believe in order that I may understand.") In the twelfth century Abelard had mercilessly exposed the inconsistencies in matters of doctrine which he found in the views of his colleagues and forerunners. Albertus Magnus (d. 1280) made wide use of Aristotle in his writings; he accepted revealed truth but sought also to test it rationally in the light of experience.

Incomparably the greatest of the schoolmen was St. Thomas Aquinas (d. 1274), the Angelic Doctor. In his monumental *Summa Theologica* he attempted one of those vast and typically medieval summations in which the existence and nature of God, the creation, the Trinity, the Incarnation of Jesus Christ, the sacraments, the end and moral obligations of man and other fundamental problems of theology were analyzed. He recognized two sources of knowledge: the Christian faith and the truths revealed by human reason, particularly as Aristotle had set them forth. He was also deeply concerned with questions of ethics. His conclusion was that man, endowed with freedom of will, could in a sense make the choice between good and evil, yet in so doing he must seek the support of heavenly grace which God has supplied through the sacraments. In recent times the papacy has directed that this monumental systematization of religious and philo-

2. THOMPSON and JOHNSON, *Introduction to Medieval Europe*, p. 706.

sophical thought should be taken as a cornerstone of Roman Catholic theology.

The decline of scholastic thought towards the close of the Middle Ages should not blind us to its great importance. Through it the philosophic heritage of Greece and Rome made its first great impact upon Western European culture. The theology emerging out of this period combined a study of the Christian tradition with a considerable attention to the philosophical teachings of classical antiquity. By opening wide areas of thought to vigorous debate scholasticism had played a significant part in the development of the modern mind. "Within the limits of the doctrines of the Church," one of the profoundest students of this period has written, "men were free to speculate as they would, and these limits were not felt as a restriction to the degree that we might imagine. Teachers of law and medicine, of grammar and logic, of mathematics and astronomy, did not find themselves held down by the prescribed rules. . . . Philosophy, then, was free, save where it trespassed upon theology." [3]

This freedom we may also observe in some aspects of medieval science. It was, inevitably, "bookish" to a large degree, and many writings could be quoted to impress us with their naiveté. But the twelfth-century revival of Greek and Arabic texts gave currency to the great scientific works of antiquity. The famous thirteenth-century *Speculum* of Vincent of Beauvais, which fills three large folio volumes in the edition of 1624, used Greek and Arab writers in its discussions of natural science, philosophy and history. From the Arabs who were brilliant mathematicians in their own right came much knowledge from Greek and some ultimately from Hindu sources. This led to our use of arabic numerals, to the enormously valuable and hitherto unused concept of zero and to the beginnings of algebra and trigonometry. Arab knowledge also enlarged the medical lore coming from the Greek manuscripts.

Even though this bookish knowledge involved the highly unscientific pursuits of alchemy and astrology, we should not let the attempts to turn base metals into gold and to cast horoscopes obscure the presence of what would be recognized today as genuinely scientific interests. In the late Middle Ages, for example, doubts persisted concerning the truth of the Ptolemaic system of the cosmos in which the earth was its fixed center, and some fragments survived of the Greek literature which placed the sun in the central position. Alchemy, whatever its defects, has been described as chemistry in the making. The claims of observation and experiment were pushed by various writers. "What is authority but a halter?" asked Adelard of Bath. Albertus Magnus wrote treatises on optics, geography,

3. C. H. HASKINS, *The Renaissance of the Twelfth Century* (1928), pp. 360–362.

botany, zoology and astronomy and criticized the ancients for their neglect of experience.

Two great Oxford Franciscans, Robert Grosseteste (1175–1253) and Roger Bacon (1214–1292), occupy an important place in any account of medieval science. Grosseteste knew Greek and wrote upon mathematics, astronomy, optics, perspective, heat, sound and color. His pupil, Roger Bacon, combined striking credulity with a versatile interest in natural phenomena. Dramatizing Bacon's work is dangerous, in that it may suggest uniqueness; Bacon did not stand alone in attacking what he called "frail and unworthy authority, long-established custom." Other thirteenth-century scholars possessed, along with their understandable limitations, something of his interest in the natural world. Bacon devoted one section of his *Opus Maius* to "experimental science" (*scientia experimentalis*), writing of "one more perfect than all, which all serve and which in a wonderful way certifies them all: this is called the experimental science." [4] He discussed optics, systematic geography and mechanics. He understood the use of lenses and may have devised a crude microscope or telescope. He knew how to make gunpowder. He seems to have had odd gifts of prophecy, speculating upon ships without rowers, chariots without animals to pull them and machines which flew through the air. He also found time to compile a Greek and a Hebrew grammar.

The significance of these scientific interests during the Middle Ages is thus characterized by a modern scholar:

> Medieval science . . . as a system of ideas, with all the imperfections of its methods and information, was true science. It offered a system of explanation, closely related to the facts of experience and satisfactory to those who used it, giving them a degree of control over their natural resources and allowing them to make certain predictions about the course of future events. . . . All that can rightly be said, when we have understood that medieval men had prejudices, purposes and hopes totally different from our own, is that they were less inquisitive and self-critical than they might have been. They were less interested in natural philosophy, for to them it was but a step forward to higher things. Science was a means, not an end.[5]

■ LITERATURE AND THE ARTS IN THE MIDDLE AGES

The cultural vigor of the medieval period may also be observed in the field of literature. The greater part of medieval writing was, of course, in Latin. Naturally enough, the elegance of classical Latin tended to disappear at an early date and the scholastic devotion to logic hardly encouraged the graces of style. Yet medieval Latin at its best was both fluent and

4. THOMPSON and JOHNSON, *Introduction to Medieval Europe*, p. 716.
5. A. R. HALL, *The Scientific Revolution, 1500–1800* (1954), p. 33.

forceful. It was used for theological and devotional works, schoolbooks of all kinds, legal compendiums, scientific treatises, histories, chronicles, biographies, political tracts and many other works. Its total volume was enormous. An impressive body of medieval Latin poetry also accumulated. Some of this was religious and included great hymns of the Church such as the *Dies Irae*. The so-called Goliardic poetry—the secular Latin lyrics of the wandering scholars which celebrated the lusty joys of this life—constituted a new form of poetic art.

More indicative of vitality and growth were the various types of vernacular literature which emerged in the late Middle Ages. Men increasingly employed the language of everyday life as a means of literary expression. The exquisite lyrics of the troubadours, with their curious amalgam of stylization and deep personal feeling, displayed the ideal of courtly love. The great medieval epics such as the *Song of Roland,* the *Cid* and the *Nibelungenlied* corresponded in their own way to the epic tradition of antiquity. The elaborate literature of the Arthurian cycle blossomed in the last half of the twelfth century; and the *fabliaux,* or versified folk-tales, "often gross, sometimes satirical, and usually intended to be hilarious," became the favorite poetry of the medieval townsmen. The popular ballads further illustrate the variety of literary expression. Beginnings of the drama are found in the miracle, mystery and morality plays in which biblical or allegorical subjects were presented. The transition from performances within the churches to those given by local gilds in public places suggests another aspect of the process of secularization.

Above all, one should call attention to three of the best-known vernacular works of the Middle Ages. Chaucer's *Canterbury Tales* breathe the very life of late fourteenth-century England. The French *Romance of the Rose,* written by Guillaume Lorris and Jean de Meun, has been described as the most widely read poem of the thirteenth century. In part a romantic allegory of courtly love and in part a satire on this same subject, it seems to have far surpassed Chaucer in contemporary popularity. Dante's *Divine Comedy,* the supreme poem of the Middle Ages, is the mirror of an entire world. It helped to make the Tuscan dialect the language of Italy.

The full development of Gothic architecture can be taken as one of the most distinctive illustrations of the creative abilities of the medieval period. In one sense a matter of engineering—involving the problem of devising better methods of lighting and roof support than were obtained by the heavy columns, rounded arches, thick walls and small windows of the Romanesque style—Gothic architecture developed a system of pointed arches, groin vaulting, narrower columns, flying buttresses and ever larger window areas. Such a style invoked many subsidiary arts such as stone and wood carving, stained glass, tapestries, metal-working, enamels, frescoes and altar painting, but in every case the architectural pattern was dominant. This architecture had its first beginnings and highest development in France, especially in the Seine basin, but it soon came to dominate northern Europe and spread into the Mediterranean lands. Stained glass caught what there was of the northern sunlight, and in some of the later examples, such as the superb Sainte Chapelle at Paris, the window area was so large as to give the visitor the impression of standing within a cage of colored light. The style proved highly adaptable to a variety of purposes so that collegiate buildings, the halls of the gilds, the homes of the merchants, in fact almost every architectural type yielded to its sway.

The Gothic style has come to be so symbolic of the Middle Ages and the "revolt" against it so much the mark of the new age that one may tend to underestimate its continued influence. In Italy, it is true, where Gothic architecture never seemed altogether at home, the employment of architectural models from classical antiquity was sweeping in its effects. But in France the chateau architecture of the sixteenth century continued to show, together with the new classical-Italian elements, recognizable marks of its medieval provenance. The same may be said of the new architecture of Tudor England where there was important Gothic building well into the seventeenth century, and of much of the civic architecture of the new German states. In Spain and in Portugal, too, the tradition of Gothic architecture continued to show its vitality. João de Castilho, the distinguished Portuguese architect of the late fifteenth century, contrived to "modernize" his Gothic designs by mingling with them motifs which reflect the influence of the oriental world which the explorers were discovering.

In its early stages medieval painting showed the powerful influence of the frescoes and mosaics of Byzantium. In the Gothic church, however, with the expansion of window areas and the steady diminution of wall-space, little scope existed for the full development of the fresco form. Altar-pieces, frequently executed on wood, usually had a gold or blue background and were stiff and one-dimensional in effect. Toward the end of the thirteenth century the Florentine Cimabue (c. 1240–1302) broke away from the Byzantine tradition with his free and flexible frescoes. These were the inspiration of his greatest pupil, Giotto (c. 1267–1337). This epoch-marking figure, an anti-traditionalist who sought something of the direct inspiration of nature, contrived a three-dimensional quality, a sense of color, light and shade and above all a feeling for humanity and for nature that have captivated observers ever since.

In northern Europe we may take as the first significant development the work of the miniaturists who, as in the example of the wonderfully vivid *Book of Hours* made for the Duke of Berry, reproduced the world of nature with an inspired fidelity. In the tradition of these brilliant miniaturists appeared the oil painting of Hubert and Jan van Eyck who, along with such artists as Roger van der Weyden and Hans Memling, created the great fifteenth-century Flemish school which so profoundly affected all European painting. It developed with extraordinary virtuosity the technique of painting in oils and thus was able to produce an unrivaled brilliance of color. The Flemish artists lovingly reproduced the smallest details of the scenes and figures which they selected; but they were also able to convey the effect of a deep spirituality. In this way they opened a window upon the entire world of the late Middle Ages. Taken by some historians as important contributors to the new artistic tradition of the Renaissance, they have been regarded by others as carrying into the fifteenth century a lingering and extraordinarily brilliant medievalism.

The important developments in music during the Middle Ages were both religious and secular. The type of chanting which came to accompany the liturgical services of the Church, whether its development be attributed to St. Ambrose in the fourth century or to the encouragement of Pope Gregory the Great in the sixth, was that in which the voices sang either in unison or at octave intervals. This "plain-song" or "Gregorian chant" was the great basis of medieval church music. The gradual elaboration of this music from the tenth century onward into different "voices" did not mean the production of harmony in the modern sense. It meant rather the emergence of "polyphonic" music in which several voices participated, each carrying its own melody and rhythm, separate but blending musically together. Through this interweaving of voices the art of "counterpoint," or contrapuntal music, developed. Vocal compositions in polyphonic style intended for use in church services and using Biblical or similar prose texts were known as motets. In all this development it will be seen that the modern concept of a harmonic accompaniment for voices singing a single melody was entirely absent.

Secular music took various forms. The poems of the minstrels—the French troubadours and the German minnesingers—were often sung to the accompaniment of instruments such as the harp, the viol, the lute or the oboe, but there is no clear evidence that these accompaniments were harmonized. Some secular music was composed for instruments alone, and in the late Middle Ages large numbers of instrumentalists were often assembled to play. Four hundred and fifty performers, for example, are said to have entertained the Diet of the Holy Roman Empire at Frankfort in 1397. The best-known surviving example of fourteenth-century secular music is the round, "Sumer is icumen in," where four voices carrying the same air enter one after the other, while two other voices carry a simple and independent bass. The medieval period had also the great importance of developing a method of musical notation which in a modified form is still in use.

In the fifteenth century an Englishman, John Dunstable, and a Netherlander, Guillaume Dufay, brought polyphonic, contrapuntal music to a splendid level of development. This growth was particularly noteworthy in Flanders and Burgundy, constituting an interesting parallel to the great contemporary Flemish school of painting. By the close of the Middle Ages, then, musical techniques had developed in such a way as to bring into existence a large body of music: the motets and masses associated with the services of the Church; the madrigals which originally could be either religious or secular; and such explicitly secular forms as the chanson, the catch and the round. In all these forms the versatile genius of the medieval period found an eloquent means of expression.

Any estimate of the cultural achievements of Western Europe in the Middle Ages must take into account the powerful impact of the Moslem and Byzantine worlds. The great contributions of the Arabs in the field of learning have already been briefly noted. Their high skill in the arts and crafts taught many lessons to the Christian world. In architecture, among their numerous contributions were the pointed arch, ribbed vaulting, the use of columns bound together in clusters, stone tracery in window openings and the art of stained glass.

Byzantine architectural techniques were most spectacularly exemplified in the Emperor Justinian's great church, the Hagia Sophia at Constantinople. The influence of this Byzantine style was felt in Italy, notably in churches at Venice, Ravenna and in Sicily, as well as in the Romanesque churches of France and the Rhineland. Byzantine architects commonly undertook to erect churches in the square form of a Greek cross, without the long nave so typical of the West. They developed great skill in the use of the dome, superimposed upon a square supporting structure by means of ingenious connecting devices ("pendentives" and "squinches"). Lesser domes were usually clustered around the corners of the central structure. Within, elaborate use was made of colored marble, of carvings and, above all, of huge, colored mosaics set against a golden background. The influence of the great Byzantine mosaics and of the fresco and tempera painting of the churches is evident in early Italian painters such as Cimabue, Duccio and Giotto. Byzantine ivory carvings, reliquaries, textiles, metalwork and embroideries found their way into the West.

> Scandinavian rulers were crowned and buried in Byzantine silks, with lions, elephants, eagles, and griffins woven in them; they kept their Byzantine jewels and enamels on gold in Byzantine-carved ivory chests. The same was true of

the Russian princes of Kiev, the doges of Venice, the abbots of Monte Cassino, the Norman kings of Sicily, and the wealthy merchants of Amalfi.[6]

The Byzantine Empire possessed numerous schools and higher centers of education. These, for the most part, were devoted to the traditional learning. The Byzantine scholars catalogued and copied, made anthologies and abridgments of the Greek classics but in general showed no talent for creative activity. Yet they preserved many of the great works of antiquity and eventually were able to make these available to the much more vigorous scholars of the Italian Revival of Learning.

These Byzantine influences, so fertile in Western Europe, were even more prevalent in the development of Russian civilization. Late in the ninth century missionaries of the Greek Church had converted the ruler of Kiev to their faith. Two famous missionary figures, St. Cyril and St. Methodius, about the same time adapted the Greek alphabet to the Slavic tongue and undertook a translation of the Bible into one of the Slavic dialects. Through the steadily developing channels of commerce and through other contacts the rich stream of Byzantine culture moved into the Slavic lands, profoundly influencing their architecture, their art, their religion and their literature.

Such were some aspects of the medieval culture which, in ways both tangible and intangible, seemed by the fourteenth century to have passed its zenith. The flowering of this civilization had been to a very considerable extent a northern phenomenon; Paris and Chartres had been the great centers of learning, art, literature and music to which people were attracted from all parts of Europe. At the height of this medieval period, as it has been well said, all Latin Christendom seemed to be made up culturally of a series of provinces of northern France. The restlessness and confusion of the fourteenth century were in one sense the marks of a world in decline; they suggest the waning of an extraordinarily rich and many-sided culture. In another sense this restlessness could be taken as the first stirring of a new era. What seems indisputable is the shifting of the center of cultural interest from north to south of the Alps. The many signs of a new age are most clearly evident in the busy life of the Italian towns where almost every aspect of human activity came to be pursued with a new and spectacular enthusiasm.

■ THE ITALIAN SETTING OF THE REVIVAL OF LEARNING

The remarkable ferment of Italian life in the fourteenth and fifteenth centuries must be seen against this complex background made up of both conservatism and change. Those who first used the terms Revival of Learn-

6. ARTZ, *The Mind of the Middle Ages,* p. 128.

ing and Renaissance meant to suggest a "rebirth" of the thought and art of classical antiquity after the long "night" of the Middle Ages. So simple an explanation does less than justice to a most complex phenomenon; the night was not so dark, nor was the new day immediately so bright as the contrast implies. Yet long usage hallows such terms and makes them difficult to discard.

Nor are scholars nowadays content to focus their attention solely upon Italy. They can find in other lands the vigorous stirrings of new life, and they therefore will explain the rich cultural advances eventually made in England, France, the Netherlands or Germany partly, to be sure, as a result of Italian influences but partly also as the result of a native evolution. It remains true, however, that the spirit of the new age was first dramatically evident south of the Alps and that there, especially in the arts, the achievements were more brilliant. The Revival of Learning and the great developments in architecture, sculpture and painting can best be understood, then, if the Italian achievement is considered first.

Italy in the fourteenth and fifteenth centuries exhibited in a particularly intense form many of the social, economic and political changes that were taking place over a wider area. An unusually vigorous development of town life brought about important changes in the old feudal-agrarian pattern. Neither the Church nor the Empire could permanently maintain the vast claims that had been put forward during the High Middle Ages. Instead there emerged a new, prosperous, urban, "bourgeois-aristocratic" society, the product and expression of the growing secular interests and the wider horizons of the new age. The Italian towns were, at least for a time, the fortunate beneficiaries of the change whereby the "petty capitalism" of the medieval period began to give place to a more vigorous and more complex economic organization.

Such changes were due in part to the highly favorable location of the Italian peninsula between Western Europe and the Near East. Italy was, moreover, the land where classical culture once had flourished and where its tangible remains were still visible. It lay within the shadow of Byzantine civilization. It had the great traditions and prestige which came from its being the home and center of papal power. But the reasons for the flourishing of genius almost always defy full explanation. One may stress the ancient heritage, the wealth, the leisure, the political vigor of the new urban aristocracy and still be unable to say precisely why the fires of the New Learning were to burn in Italy as brightly as they did.

In the earlier medieval period Italy had been made up of a network of feudal territories, many of them under the suzerainty of the Holy Roman emperors. But by the twelfth century a vigorous growth of the towns or communes of northern Italy had led to a successful defiance of the imperial power which reached across the Alps. This same growth spelled the end of territorial feudalism in north and central Italy. The wealthy merchant families tended to form a patrician ruling class which bought up large country areas and brought this rural territory within the political orbit of the towns. In this way some of the leading cities took on the aspect of territorial states. Florence came to control all Tuscany. Venice extended her mainland authority within a few miles of Milan and controlled a sea empire reaching along the Adriatic coast to the Ionian Islands, Crete and Cyprus. Milan came to dominate a vitally important economic area in northern Italy. The papacy began to extend its authority over the very considerable territory which came to be known as the States of the Church. Naples was the center of a kingdom which included the whole of southern Italy and, at least in theory, the island of Sicily. Less brilliant, but each in its way important were Genoa, Ferrara, Mantua, Siena and Urbino.

How much the economic factor contributed to the importance of these cities may be illustrated in the case of Florence. By the early fourteenth century over thirty thousand people were employed in making or finishing cloth in or near the city. Florentine merchants were the leading buyers of wool in Spain and the British Isles. Florentine textiles were sold in the markets of North Africa, Spain, the Black Sea and western Asia, as well as throughout Europe. Other trades such as the manufacture of silk and leather goods brought still more wealth. The prosperity thus gained led Florence to an outstanding position as a money market and a banking city. In 1252 it had begun the issue of its famous gold florins, of which by 1300 there were an estimated two million in circulation. Meanwhile the Florentine bankers had come to handle most of the work involved in collecting, guarding, transshipping and investing the papal income. Among the Florentine families which prospered by these various pursuits, one, the Medici, rose to play a dominant part also in the political and cultural life of the city. Giovanni, who died in 1429, may be regarded as the founder of the family's financial greatness. His son, Cosimo, acquired political control of the city in 1434 and became a princely patron of the arts. Cosimo's grandson, Lorenzo the Magnificent (1449–1492), shone even more brilliantly. Two Medici became popes, two became queens of France. Later the family acquired the titles of dukes of Florence and grand dukes of Tuscany. The greatness of the Medici family was thus inseparably connected with the greatness of the city.

The older wealthy merchant families in the major towns tended to form a patrician ruling class, the *grandi*. In time they were challenged by a sort of new rich who commonly had the backing of the ordinary citizens, the *popolo.* In the natural political turmoil which ensued, a frequent phenomenon was the appearance of a single powerful figure, the despot, who usurped the role of the older families, appealed in various ways for popular support and at the same time contrived to gather effective political power into his own hands. Vigorous and ruthless in their seizure of authority, and relying upon mercenary soldiers under adventurous leaders known as *condottieri*, these despots commonly became patrons of culture, for culture was one of the marks of a city's greatness.

Powerful families became closely associated with the political domination of certain towns: the Visconti and then the Sforza in Milan; the Medici in Florence; the house of Gonzaga in Mantua; the house of Este in Ferrara; the Montefeltro family in Urbino. Rome, of course, was under the political control of the popes. Naples was under the royal house of Anjou and, later, of Aragon. Venice never yielded to the rule of a single despot but was governed through the long period of its greatness and decline by a no less powerful oligarchy of merchant families. Under the rule of these aggressive, individualistic despots who often acquired noble titles and lived in princely state, the arts flourished as never before and Italy made the astonishing cultural advances of the fourteenth and fifteenth centuries.

■ THE ACCOMPLISHMENT OF THE REVIVAL OF LEARNING

The city of Florence harbored some of the greatest figures of this new era. It had been the home of Dante, the supreme spokesman of the Middle Ages. A Florentine, too, was Francesco Petrarch (1305–1374). An instinctive artist and nature lover, an eager traveler and correspondent, a minor diplomat, a man of affairs who refused both a papal secretaryship and the greater honor of becoming rector of the newly-founded University of Florence, Petrarch was versatile in his abilities. He is remembered as a master of the Italian lyric, the composer of sonnets to his beloved Laura so perfect as later to enchant one of the greatest lyric poets, Shelley. Equally significant was his devotion to Virgil and, above all, to the stylistic elegance of Cicero. In 1341 he was crowned with laurel on the Capitol in Rome, the foremost man of letters in Europe. Petrarch is called the first of the humanists—in Symonds' sweeping phrase, "the Columbus of a new spiritual hemisphere." In order to gain contact with the antiquity which so absorbed him he collected ancient manuscripts, coins and inscriptions. A friend in Constantinople sent him Greek manuscripts containing the text of Homer's works and sixteen of Plato's dialogues. These he could treasure but never read, albeit his friend, Boccaccio, was able to send him a Latin translation, if a wretched one, of the *Iliad* and the *Odyssey*. Petrarch's devotion to the classics had a twofold significance: it stressed the need for excellence in matters of literary form and it sought in the classics a more rational and at the same time a more joyous approach to life. It is from this *humane* interpretation of the documents of antiquity that the term, humanist, is derived.

Of Petrarch's devoted friend, Giovanni Boccaccio (1313–1375), there is a story, true in spirit if not in word, which tells how as a young man preparing for his father's profession of banking he visited the tomb of Virgil and, brooding there, resolved to devote his life to poetry. Boccaccio was a prolific versifier, but he is better remembered as a prose master of the Tuscan tongue who in the ever fascinating tales of the *Decameron* set forth a vivid and somewhat scandalous world of sensuous enjoyment, heedless of the threats of ecclesiastical authority. Though his enthusiasms always outran his scholarly achievements, Boccaccio was led by Petrarch to a delight in learned studies. In 1360 he sought Greek lessons from one Leontius Pilatus, of Constantinople, whom he aided to become "professor" of Greek at Florence; but this uncouth Byzantine master knew so little of the true classical tongue that Boccaccio's knowledge of it never became more than superficial. With his aid, nevertheless, Boccaccio made rough translations of Homer into Latin and prepared dictionaries of mythology and geographic names which had considerable use as textbooks. In this sense Boccaccio earned his title as the first Grecian of the modern world; but classical scholarship still awaited its truly great exponents.

Both Petrarch and Boccaccio must be regarded as transitional figures. The verses in Petrarch's *Canzoniere* show their indebtedness to the earlier poetry of the Provençal troubadours, just as the urbane and sophisticated stories of the *Decameron* owe something to the cruder medieval *fabliaux* which had preceded them. One of the most curiously revealing of Petrarch's writings is his *Secret,* an imaginary Latin dialogue between himself and St. Augustine. The saint urges him not to confuse earthly love with the love of God: he questions the value of pagan and scholarly studies; and he urges Petrarch, above all, "to enter upon the meditation of your last end, which comes on, step by step, without your being aware." Petrarch's and Boccaccio's mastery of the vernacular did not at once establish a cult, for the immediate sequel to their age was an attempt to turn from the vernacular in order to revive the classic purity of the Ciceronian style and to unlock the hidden store of Latin and Greek texts. Not until a century later did the vernacular really come into its own.

The fifteenth century in Italy was marked by a vigorous devotion to classical scholarship. Petrarch and Boccaccio had set a new "humane" value upon the Latin authors already known in a greater or less degree to the

Middle Ages and had encouraged the search for further texts, both Greek and Latin. Few stories are more dramatic than this richly rewarded quest. Petrarch made many journeys in Italy searching for lost manuscripts of Cicero and other Latin authors. Boccaccio, visiting the monastery of Monte Cassino, was shocked at the neglected condition of the manuscripts he found there, among them the *Histories* and part of the *Annals* of Tacitus. Another collector of Latin manuscripts and an ardent cultivator of the pure, Ciceronian style was Coluccio Salutati, a correspondent and friend of Petrarch and Latin secretary to the government of Florence.

Easily the most spectacular and successful of these searchers was Poggio Bracciolini, a papal secretary and an ardent scholar. He has been likened, with justice, to a bloodhound. While attending the Council of Constance in 1415 he made use of the opportunity to ransack nearby monasteries in Switzerland and South Germany. Among his finds was a complete text of Quintilian's *Institutes of Oratory,* a work until then imperfectly known and one that was to influence profoundly the educational thought of the times. The manuscript was discovered, Poggio says, "safe as yet, and sound, though covered with dust and filthy with neglect and age. The books . . . were lying in a most foul and obscure dungeon at the very bottom of a tower, a place into which condemned criminals would hardly have been thrust." Poggio also discovered works of Lucretius, Plautus, the Younger Pliny, Ammianus Marcellinus, Vitrivius and Columella, and some of the Ciceronian *Orations.*

The labors of scholars were aided by noblemen and wealthy merchants who provided subsidies and themselves built up collections of manuscripts. Vespasiano da Bisticci's *Lives of Illustrious Men* has a revealing passage concerning Nicolao Nicoli, a Florentine merchant who became an ardent student of the new learning:

> He collected a fine library, not regarding the cost and was always searching for rare books. He bought all these with the wealth which his father had left, putting aside only what was necessary for his maintenance. . . . If he heard of students going to Greece or to France or elsewhere he would give them the names of the books which they lacked in Florence, and procure for them the help of Cosimo de' Medici who would do anything for him. . . . There was no copy of Pliny in Italy; but, news having been brought to Nicolao that there was a fine and perfect one at Lübeck in Germany, he worked so effectively through Cosimo de' Medici that he, by the agency of a kinsman of his living there bargained with the friars who owned it, giving them a hundred Rhenish ducats in exchange for the book.

Many Greek manuscripts were brought directly from Constantinople. In 1413 Giovanni Aurispa brought some of the texts of Sophocles, Euripides and Thucydides to Italy. In 1423 he is said to have brought 238 separate manuscripts. His contemporary, Guarino of Verona, is credited with 54 and Francesco Filelfo with 40. The fall of Constantinople to the Turks in 1453 was in no sense the beginning of a flow of scholarly riches; indeed, it may well be that most of the important Greek manuscripts which had survived the great fire of 1204 had been brought to Italy in advance of the capture of the eastern capital.

It is difficult to evaluate the exact significance of this new interest in the Greek tongue, but the emphasis which some of the earlier historians of the Revival of Learning gave to it would perhaps seem to be exaggerated. In 1393 Manuel Chrysoloras, a Greek scholar, came on a diplomatic mission from Byzantium to Italy, and in 1397 he was invited by the magistrates of Florence to teach Greek there. He stayed in Florence for three years and also taught at Milan, Pavia, Venice and Rome. Chrysoloras translated Homer and *The Republic* of Plato and compiled the first Greek grammar to be used in the West. He had both scholarship and eloquence, lecturing to crowded audiences which had among them men such as Poggio Bracciolini and Leonardo Bruni, destined to eminent places in the ranks of the humanists.

We can still catch something of the ardor of these first academic disciples. "I delivered myself over to Chrysoloras," wrote Bruni, "with such passion that what I received from him by day in hours of waking, occupied my mind at night in hours of sleep." Bruni first gave currency to the word, *humanitas,* in relation to the literary culture of antiquity, and his translations of Aristotle and Plato have been called milestones in the history of classical philology. Nicolao Nicoli collected so ardently that on his death in 1437 he was able to leave eight hundred manuscripts to the city of Florence, among them the famous eleventh-century codex containing works of Aeschylus and Sophocles. Interest of a somewhat different sort was shown by Nicholas V, the first of the great humanist popes (1447–1455), who sponsored and encouraged an impressive project for translating the major works of Greek literature into Latin.

From the Byzantine scholar, Gemistos Plethon, who was at Florence at the time of the Church council of 1438–1439 came a stimulus to Platonic studies. Plethon, to be sure, hardly taught the pure doctrines of Plato, but steeped himself in the obscure verbiage of Neoplatonism which distorted Plato's idealism into a kind of Christian mysticism. Greek studies were aided in another way and on another level by the famous school which Vittorino da Feltre established at Mantua in 1425 under the patronage of the Gonzaga family. Vittorino combined Christian devotion with a passionate enthusiasm for the best in the classics. He encouraged a pure Ciceronianism in style and urged his pupils to avoid the use of the vernacular in writing. Gradually they were introduced to the Greek classics and encouraged to attempt Greek composition. Some time was also given to mathematics, astronomy, natural history and music, as well as to healthy outdoors training and to good manners. "The idea which dominated his whole system was the classical, primarily Greek, idea of an education in which mind and body should be harmoniously developed.... It was humanistic, in a deeper sense, because it was at once intellectual, moral, and physical." [7]

In 1462 Cosimo de' Medici founded the famous Florentine Academy, an informal association of some of the leading Florentines meeting at a villa outside the city to discuss Plato's works. The Academy was placed under the direction of the distinguished young humanist, Marsilio Ficino, and had considerable influence both in Italy and on German scholars further afield such as Melanchthon and Reuchlin. All Plato's dialogues were translated and various commentaries were composed. The cult of Plato involved holding a banquet on his birthday, and crowning his bust with flowers and burning lamps before it on the anniversary of his death.

The outstanding figure associated with the Academy after Marsilio was the precocious Pico della Mirandola, a prince of one of the lesser states, the master of twenty-two languages who eventually burned his love poems, became a follower of Savonarola, and proposed to walk barefoot through the world, preaching the Gospel. There were academies, too, in Venice, Rome and Naples for the pursuit of Greek studies, and Greek lecturers in many cities. By the middle of the fifteenth century, then, the cult of classical learning was in full swing.

Another aspect of scholarship was to be found in Hebrew studies. The language itself gave direct access to the original text of the Old Testament. Moreover it was held by some scholars that the medieval system of Jewish theosophy known as the *Cabala* would aid in reconciling classical philosophy with Christian doctrine, for similarities with Neoplatonism could be found in cabalistic literature. Thus Greek and Hebrew learning might be combined in the approach to the ultimate truths of the Christian faith. Pico della Mirandola stands out as one of the most brilliant of such students, and he was responsible for training the great German Hebraist, Reuchlin. Hebrew manuscripts were steadily accumulated in the Vatican library, that at Urbino and in those of individual scholars.

The development of scholarship also found expression in historical writing. Leonardo Bruni's *History of the Florentine People*, at which he worked until his death in 1444, reflects the new attitude in that Bruni saw the history of Florence in relation to the broad background of classical

7. *The Cambridge Modern History,* I, p. 558

antiquity and to the rising importance of the Italian towns during the medieval period. Flavio Biondo's *History from the Decline of the Roman Empire,* completed in 1453, is even more important in that it set up as a complete period in itself the thousand years from the fall of Rome (which Biondo wrongly gives as A.D. 412) to the year 1412, the beginning of "modern" times. Thus he suggested the schematic division of history into the now familiar classification of ancient, medieval and modern. Such works, as well as Poggio's *History of the People of Florence,* were written in Latin. The great vernacular histories of Guicciardini and Machiavelli, epoch-marking in their significance, belong to the sixteenth century.

Another type of historical work is that of Lorenzo Valla, who after an education at Rome and Florence taught oratory at the University of Pavia and then entered the service of Alfonso, King of Aragon and Sicily. In 1440 Valla wrote his famous criticism of the so-called Donation of Constantine— a document, now believed to have been forged in the eighth century, giving an account of the Emperor Constantine's "donation" of the western half of the Roman Empire to the papacy. Valla not only criticized the Donation by employing the known evidence of history but also subjected the text itself to a powerful attack, making brilliant use of philology, numismatics and even psychology to prove his points. This famous exposé has often been taken as a triumph of the new humanistic scholarship, and indeed it was. It is salutary to remember, however, that almost simultaneously with Valla an English scholar, Reginald Pecock, demolished the Donation even more thoroughly and entirely without benefit of the New Learning.

The founding of libraries is a further illustration of the growth of scholarly interests. Nicolao Nicoli's famous bequest of his eight hundred volumes to Cosimo de' Medici and other Florentine trustees has already been mentioned. Cosimo, a noble patron of the New Learning, had previously founded the library of San Giorgio Maggiore in Venice. In this same city Cardinal Bessarion had bequeathed his famous collection to the library of St. Mark's. Using half of Nicolao's bequest, Cosimo also established a library in the Convent of San Marco in Florence. His own collection, together with the rest of Nicolao's volumes, served as the nucleus for the great Laurentian Library. He founded still another library at nearby Fiesole. In Rome, Pope Nicholas V (d. 1455) transformed the modest Vatican collection by adding a large number of manuscripts so that at his death it held more than 800 Latin and about 350 Greek manuscripts, largely theological in nature. Sixtus IV (d. 1484) was responsible for enlarging the collection even further, establishing a permanent building and preparing a catalogue of its treasures which then amounted to about 3,600 manuscripts. At Urbino, Duke Frederick had an unrivaled private library in which a permanent staff of copyists was kept at work. The texts were copied on the finest vellum and decorated with exquisite miniatures. Each volume was bound in crimson velvet held with silver clasps. In this treasured collection no printed work was permitted to intrude.

Much has been made of the introduction of printing as a phenomenon of the new age. It was of inestimable value in the spread of knowledge, but it came too late to be regarded as a "cause" of the Renaissance and it was not always cordially received at first by the scholarly world. Like most inventions, its origin was complex. Paper had been made in Europe since the thirteenth century.[8] The so-called "block-books," in which an entire page of lettering was carved out of one wooden block from which multiple impressions could be taken, came into use in the first half of the fifteenth century, if not earlier. The great step beyond this was to devise some form of movable type, to develop the techniques necessary in order to have a good casting metal, good type faces, molds, matrices and inks, and to combine all these elements in a workable printing establishment. Such seems to have been the achievement of Johann Gutenberg of Mainz, around the year 1450.[9] Why, with Italy so clearly in the lead in the New Learning, this epoch-marking advance came in another area may be left to speculation. It can be noted, however, that the Rhineland towns were a part of the vigorous economic and social life of this transitional period and had a high tradition of craftsmanship. In Italy, nevertheless, printing soon made some of its greatest contributions. The Aldine Press established by Aldus Manutius at Venice in 1490 was dedicated principally to printing the Greek and Latin classics. Much more than mere printing was involved, for Aldus Manutius gathered in his household a veritable academy of scholars and editors. The first Greek texts were printed by him in 1493 and by the time of his death in 1515 he had printed twenty-eight first editions of the principal writings of antiquity. No major Greek author remained unpublished. These small, carefully edited, beautifully printed and inexpensive volumes constituted a veritable revolution in the printer's art.

8. The invention of the spinning wheel around 1300 greatly reduced the price of cloth and expanded its use. Hence the supply of linen rags used in making paper was much increased. Without this large and cheaper supply of paper it is doubtful whether the printing of books on a large scale would have been economically feasible.

9. Several fragments and scraps of books now lost have been assigned by the experts to the period between 1444 and 1448. Most scholars now accept the Constance Missal, of which three copies exist, as the earliest surviving printed book. Typographical evidence indicates that it antedates the Gutenberg Bible which was completed before August, 1456. The first *dated* book is the Mainz Psalter of 1457. Printing spread with astonishing rapidity. In Italy the first press was at Subiaco (1465), followed by Rome (1467), Venice (1469), Milan (1469) and Florence (1471). A press was set up at Basel in 1467. For other countries the dates may be summarized: Bohemia (1468), France (1470), the Low Countries (1473), Spain (1473), Hungary (1473), Poland (1475), England (1477), Austria (1482), Denmark (1482), Sweden (1483), Portugal (1489), Montenegro (1494), Turkey (1494).

Laborious modern research has made it possible to analyze the content of the books which appeared during the first fifty years of printing. These *incunabula,* as they are called, were for the most part the standard works of the Middle Ages. Almost half of them dealt with religious subjects. The most frequently printed book was the Bible, of which the Latin text (the Vulgate) appeared in one hundred and thirty-three editions. There were fifteen different editions in German, thirteen in Italian, eleven in French, two in Bohemian and one each in Spanish and Dutch. No complete English Bible was printed before 1535. The Church Fathers and the various scholastic writers were published, together with a great output of religious manuals, books of devotion, compilations, sermons and liturgical works. There were many works of civil and canon law. The great medieval encyclopedias, the scientific treatises, the books on geography, astronomy, mathematics and medicine known to the Middle Ages were now given wider circulation in printed form. Toward the close of the century more and more of the great works of classical literature began to see the light. There were also books in the vernacular, such as Dante, Boccaccio, Petrarch, Villon and Chaucer in addition to a large number of miscellaneous textbooks of all kinds.

The impression gained in looking over a listing of early printed books is that of a gradual rather than of a revolutionary shifting of interest from the works which had occupied the attention of the Middle Ages to those exemplifying the New Learning.[10] A striking illustration, however, of the way in which printing could spread new ideas comes in the famous *Letter* by which Columbus announced his discovery of the New World. This two-leaf folder of folio size was first printed at Barcelona in 1493. Within a year there were twelve editions, at places as far distant as Rome, Paris, Antwerp, Basel and Florence. Within five years at least seventeen editions had appeared, in four languages and six different countries.

The New Learning differed in many significant ways from medieval scholasticism. Much humanistic activity, to be sure, was still concerned with theological subjects and much of it was devoted to splitting the fine hairs of pedantic controversy. Nevertheless, if we take the definition of humanism as being an enthusiasm for the literature of Greece and Rome, both for its style and its ideas, it may be possible to bring out some important points. Whereas scholastic thought had been centered upon the Christian tradition, humanistic thought swung at least some of the emphasis in the direction of the classics. The new knowledge of antiquity made the

---

10. A rough summary and estimate of the subject matter up to 1500 has been offered as follows: religion, 45 per cent; literature, 30 per cent; law, 10 per cent; science, 10 per cent; miscellaneous, 5 per cent. DOUGLAS C. MCMURTRIE, *The Book* (1943), p. 320.

ancient world appear to be a living civilization from which men could draw their present inspiration. In another sense, by making use of the printed word the humanists were able to break away from the confined world of the university and the cloister and make their appeal to a wider audience. They were supremely conscious, moreover, in a way that save for rare intervals the medieval world never had been, of the importance of style. This cultivation of classical Roman models, this "Ciceronianism," led often to artificiality and a mere aping of antiquity; nevertheless, it had its own merits and established some link between the activities of the scholars and the elegant graces of Renaissance society.

In thus summarizing and cataloguing the first great achievements of Italian humanism the danger is that one may give too much attention to the letter and obscure the full significance of the spirit. Amid much that was pedantic and bookish a new confidence in man's limitless capacities was being asserted. No more eloquent testimonial to this faith has ever been penned than that proclaimed in Pico della Mirandola's famous *Oration on the Dignity of Man,* probably written in 1486. He has God address man thus:

> The nature of all other things is limited and constrained within the bounds of law prescribed by me; thou, coerced by no necessity, shalt ordain for thyself the limits of thy nature in accordance with thine own free will, in whose hand I have placed thee. . . . I have made thee neither of heaven nor of earth, neither mortal nor immortal, so that thou mayest with greater freedom of choice and with more honor, as though the maker and moulder of thyself, fashion thyself in whatever shape thou shalt prefer.

This action of God is hailed by Pico as representing the highest wisdom:

> O supreme generosity of God the Father, O highest and most marvellous felicity of Man! to whom it is granted to have that which he chooses, to be that which he wills. . . . On Man when he came into life the Father conferred the seeds of all good and the germs of every form of life. Whatever seeds each man cultivates, those seeds will grow to maturity and bear in him their own fruit. If they be vegetative, he will be like a plant. If sensual, he will become brutish. If rational, he will issue as a heavenly being. If intellectual, he will be an angel, and the son of God. And if, happy in the lot of no created thing, he withdraws into the center of his own unity, his spirit, made one with God, in the solitary darkness of God who is set above all things, shall surpass them all.

Thus Pico expresses his confidence in the boundless capacity of man—"this our chameleon"—to make himself over in whatever pattern man himself may choose. Such inner restlessness, such belief in the human capacity to achieve good or evil by one's own powers, is, surely, the mark of the new age.

■ THE TRANSFORMATION OF THE ARTS IN ITALY

A further aspect of the great cultural changes coming over Italy and one that has principally commanded the world's admiration is to be seen in the arts. Here only a few highlights of this rich and intricate field can be suggested. Italy had not been immersed in the flood of Gothic art to the same extent as had the countries to the north. It had never altogether departed from the artistic traditions of classical antiquity, and it saw the noble ruins of this earlier civilization on every hand.[11] In addition to the legacy of antiquity the powerful influence of Byzantine art made itself felt, especially in Venice, Ravenna and southern Italy. Save in Venice, where a local architecture of great vitality developed, Italian Gothic tended to be something of an importation, decorative rather than truly functional and never completely at home under the skies of the peninsula.

In 1403 a young Florentine metal-worker, Filippo Brunelleschi (1377–1446), went to Rome, determined to study the imposing remains to be found there. He was accompanied by a sixteen-year-old youth, Donatello (1386–1466). These two, destined to be the leading figures of the new movement in the arts, remained for several years, measuring and observing. On his return to Florence, Brunelleschi began his career as an architect. In 1419 he won approval for his plan to erect a superb octagonal dome upon the unfinished medieval cathedral of Santa Maria del Fiore—a proposal combining in its details classical inspiration with great originality. His plan, as much a triumph of engineering as it was of art, was brilliantly realized. In the Pazzi Chapel which he built in 1429, the first complete ecclesiastical building of the Renaissance, Brunelleschi skilfully made use of such Roman elements as Corinthian pilasters and circular wall medallions in combination with a floor plan that was still essentially medieval.

Interest in the new architectural style rapidly developed. The manuscript of the great Roman treatise, Vitruvius' *De Architectura,* had been recovered by the ever-searching Poggio from a Swiss monastery and came to have a profound effect upon Renaissance design. One has only to compare the old, fortress-like structures such as the Palazzo Vecchio in Florence with the new buildings of the fifteenth century—the Riccardi, the Rucellai and the Strozzi palaces, and even more the elegant country villas of the nobility—to see the change at work. From Florence the fashion spread. In the Church of Sant' Andrea at Mantua another brilliant architect, Leon Battista Alberti (1404–1472), employed the Roman triumphal arch to provide the motif for the façade. The many elements of the new style, notably the use of the dome, barrel vault, Roman columns joined by semicircular arches, pilasters, medal-

11. Not a little of the noble ruin was deliberately created, for the ancient marble could be, and was, easily burned into lime.

lions and elaborate cornices and the emphasis upon symmetrical patterns, all gradually combined to produce the masterpieces of the new age.

In the closely related field of sculpture one may go back to Nicola Pisano (c. 1206–1278) and the pulpit which he made in 1260 for the Baptistery at Pisa. While Gothic in some respects, its carvings clearly show the influence of surviving Roman sarcophagi. Pisano must, however, be regarded as a gifted forerunner, and it is the work of Donatello, the friend of Brunelleschi, which really marks the arrival of the new age in sculpture. Inspired like the latter by his Roman sojourn, Donatello showed himself to be no slavish copier of antiquity; his St. George brilliantly combined the elements of the old and the new. His David was the first nude statue of the Renaissance, free-standing and independent of any architectural setting. Donatello was equally at home in carving an altar piece as he was in making the great equestrian statue of the *condottiere* Gattamelata—a powerful figure of the modern world in the costume of a Roman general. Lorenzo Ghiberti (1378–1455), his contemporary, occupies an equally important place. In 1401 as a young man he submitted a prizewinning design for the north doors of the Baptistery in Florence to be carved in bronze with biblical scenes. These were completed in 1424 and their fame led to a further commission for the east doors. The work was ended in 1452, more than fifty years after Ghiberti made his first venture. The scriptural themes were expressed in a masterly pattern which combined an exquisite feeling for nature with a classical elegance of form, so that what might have been merely skilled craftsmanship rose through a lifetime of inspired labor to the heights of great art. The work of Luca della Robbia (1399–1482), Verrocchio (1435–1488) and Pollaiuolo (1429–1498) further expressed the greatness of the Florentine school of sculpture.

It must be clear that one significant aspect of this age was the growing importance of the artist as an individual. The Middle Ages had been to large degree the age of the craftsman, working with his fellows to adorn a cathedral or illuminate a breviary. Much of the best work, therefore, was anonymous and the distinction between artisan and artist not always clear. But with the rise of the great merchant princes, the growing rivalry and civic pride of the Italian cities, the flourishing of the despots and the secular splendor of the papacy, patronage of the arts contributed to a new trend. The man of affairs gave importance to the artist whom he sponsored and befriended, and it is touching to recall that the sculptor, Donatello, and his close friend, Cosimo de' Medici, were buried in the same tomb. With the increased importance of the patron there developed inevitably a larger role for the artist existing as a distinct and important type within the framework of Renaissance society.

The field of painting saw important developments in technique. The method of *fresco* painting required the artist to cover a wall, on which he had sketched his design, with a coat of fresh plaster, then apply his paints at once to it and let both paint and plaster dry together. The *tempera* method required the artist to cover a wooden panel with glue and plaster of Paris (*gesso*), and then to "temper" his paints by mixing them with egg-white before applying them. The method of oil painting, whether on wood or canvas, involved the use of linseed oil to mix the colors. It was developed in Flanders by the Van Eycks and made possible a remarkable brilliance of technique. It seems to have been acquired from some of their disciples and taken to Italy about the middle of the fifteenth century where it became widespread, but never, of course, to the exclusion of the older techniques.

The point of departure for Renaissance painting must be the Florentine, Giotto, who by the time of his death in 1337 may be said to have started a school marked by naturalism, exquisiteness of perception, religious devoutness and deep human sympathies.[12] Not all responded immediately to the influence of this "great humanizer of painting." Fra Angelico (1387–1455) has been called the last of the medievalists. The golden backgrounds and the glowing colors with which he portrayed his hosts of exquisite angels suggest the work of the illuminators of manuscripts; these paintings, together with the superb frescoes with which he decorated the Convent of San Marco, make him something of an anomaly. Symonds compares him to a secluded lakelet lying quietly apart from the ever-broadening stream of the great Renaissance painters.

The truly significant advances came from other quarters. Great technical advances were made by painters such as Masaccio (1402–1429) and Uccello (1396–1475). The former employed light, shadow, foreshortening and a technically skilful depiction of the human form, as in his "Expulsion from Paradise," where the vividly human figures of Adam and Eve are shown wracked with emotion. Uccello's concern with perspective, light and pattern was almost mathematical, and yet he produced paintings of great interest and power. The culmination of this early period of Florentine painting may be put in the work of Sandro Botticelli (c. 1444–1510), marked by an elegant technique of line and form and equally by an elusive charm. His religious paintings have a genuine tenderness; but in addition to these are the many works of direct classical inspiration. His "Primavera" was suggested by a

12. "The Byzantines . . . had created an aloof world in which the human body, so devotedly worshipped by the Greeks, had no place. Giotto gave his figures a physique and brought them back to earth; he took them out of the vague indeterminate space in which they had existed for so long and set them in definite places on the earth's surface, set them among rocks or in meadows or houses. They have structure, they breathe." ERIC NEWTON, *European Painting and Sculpture* (Penguin Books, 1951), pp. 53–54.

passage from Lucretius; his "Birth of Venus" may embody a neo-Platonic allegory of the school of Ficino. With his naturalism, color and grace, his happy combination of religious and pagan elements, Botticelli seems almost as much a poet as a painter and sums up much of his age. Other schools of painting developed, such as the Umbrian and the Venetian, but in the fifteenth century Florence reigned supreme.

By the close of the fifteenth century in Italy, then, the powerful ferment of new ideas and new practices was making itself felt. The long process of transition frequently meant the confusion of the old and the new, but in the end among the brilliant élite of the Italian cities a new outlook had been born. It came to be marked by a reaction against "medievalism" and a passion for "antiquity." In literary matters it showed great concern for elegance and purity of style. It had a highly developed esthetic sense and it savored to the full the joys of this world. To call this outlook pagan is to do less than justice to the strength of the religious tradition. But the age was, at some times and in some respects, subject to powerful non-Christian influences. It was avid of success and enchanted by worldly brilliance. Its ideal was the elegant, urbane, self-reliant man, possessed of what the Italians called *Virtù,* a word meaning a combination of force and intellect best translated, perhaps, as virtuosity. Molded in part by ancient tradition, in part by bold ventures into new fields, Italian culture clearly demonstrated the arrival of a new age.

These magnificent achievements had come about largely before 1500. In the ensuing decades Italy was to reach an even higher peak of achievement, and other lands in their own way were to vie with her. Before considering the various manifestations of this High Renaissance culture we must turn to the contemporaneous trends in the political and social life both north and south of the Alps. Such a study is important, because this new and more complex society provided the necessary stimulus and setting for the further elaboration of literature and the arts.

CHARLES V AS COUNT OF FLANDERS. This colored bust by Konrad Meit, now in the Bruges Museum, is a fine example of the transition from Medieval to Renaissance sculpture. Made in 1517, two years before the imperial coronation, it shows Charles wearing the famous Order of the Golden Fleece. His sensitive face is that of a youth seemingly aware of the heavy responsibilities lying ahead of him. Photograph by the Belgian Government Information Center.

Chapter **4**

The New World
of Politics

■ THE EUROPEAN STATES SYSTEM: SPAIN, ENGLAND AND FRANCE

AN OUTSTANDING DEVELOPMENT in the complex pattern of sixteenth-century Europe was the growth of a number of vigorous monarchical states, each seeking an efficient machinery of centralized administration, proud of its independence and eager to further its dynastic interests. These states, to be sure, were not new, nor was the pattern uniform. Earlier, however, the medieval monarchies had been in some degree counterbalanced by the power of the feudal nobility and in a general sense they had also to compete with the splendid externals and the lofty theoretical claims of the Holy Roman Empire. By the sixteenth century the new monarchies were beginning to free themselves from such encumbrances.

At the risk of over-simplification some listing of the typical marks of these new monarchies may be attempted. They were seated in a definite territory; and their subjects tended to have a common language, a common outlook, a common pride and common ideals. At least in embryo there existed what we have come to call nationalism. The rulers leaned, as we shall see, toward authoritarianism and therefore faced a possible challenge in the various representative bodies or estates of which the medieval period had so many examples. For various reasons kings were in need of larger revenues, the customary sources of which—income from the royal domains, customs, tolls, occasional special levies and the like—proved in most cases to be no longer adequate. A tendency arose, therefore, for royal power to assert itself in the financial realm against what the medieval world had looked upon as the property rights of the subjects. Nor was it uncommon for monarchy to find itself in conflict with the claims of the Roman Catholic Church. Roman law was studied with renewed vigor; its "reception" in various continental countries had important effects, for in its paragraphs could be found many precepts suitable to bolster royal authority. A modern theory of "divine right," strange in many ways to the Middle Ages, was in the making.

With all this came an increased royal regulation of economic life upon a nation-wide scale. The slow standardization of the coinage, the more efficient and uniform collection of taxes, the granting of charters for exploration, trade and settlement, the regulation of imports and of domestic manufacture and sale—in short, the conscious direction of economic life in the interests of the state—were diverse aspects and beginnings of what later came to be known as mercantilism. This vigorous assertion of national economic interests was one of the forces helping to create more ambitious and more militant foreign policies.

No single explanation can suffice for such complex phenomena. In one simple sense the decline or disintegration of an older pattern of political life made possible the new monarchies. Feudal power in Western Europe had become much weaker, partly as a consequence of the long-drawn-out Hundred Years' War (1338–1453) between England and France and the Wars of the Roses (1455–1485) in England. In each case monarchy benefited by the weakening of the noble class. One must likewise note the failure of the Holy Roman Empire to exercise over its members the powers to which it

The eastern frontier of France is still far from the Rhine, the Hapsburg lands are widely scattered and Venice has a "sea empire." The Ottoman Turks have pushed into the Balkans and across the Danube. Aragon's island possessions draw Spain, now united, into the orbit of Mediterranean politics. In 1492 Granada is cleared of the Moslems.

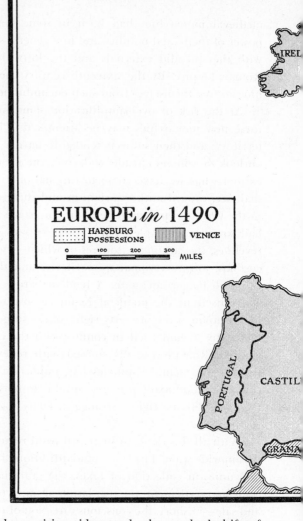

EUROPE *in* 1490

HAPSBURG POSSESSIONS   VENICE

0   100   200   300
MILES

IREL

PORTUGAL   CASTIL

GRANA

made theoretical claim. On the positive side stands the gradual shift of economic activity from the Mediterranean to the Atlantic seaboard with the consequent advantage to those countries—Portugal, Spain, France and England—first able to profit by the new state of affairs. Here an increase in general wealth came about, with the possibility of larger royal revenues and stronger royal authority. As a new mercantile class arose, various ambitious dynasties were able to profit by its prosperity and to make political arrangements that were to the advantage of both king and subject. Under such conditions the power of the old feudal class was even further weakened. Particular developments, such as the use of gunpowder and shot against medieval armor or the artillery train against the baronial castle, contributed to the same end. The new monarchies often benefited by the religious

ferment and unrest which served to rally opinion against papal pretensions. Famous maxims drawn from the Roman legal tradition, such as "what pleases the prince has the power of the law," certainly strengthened, if they did not themselves create, the authority which lay in royal hands. In a broader sense, too, the ruthlessly competitive nature of the times may be taken as a partial explanation of these governmental changes.

In the opening decades of the sixteenth century nothing is more striking than the way in which a splendid cast of royal figures dominated the European stage. Not only were their aims and methods very similar, but each also seemed to embody in his person something of the state over which he ruled. Even a relatively hasty survey would reveal to the enquirer common elements in the public careers of a remarkable series of monarchs, the brilliant light of whose rule illuminated the entire century.[1] The outstanding examples were found in Spain, England and France.

In the Iberian Peninsula the union of the various kingdoms into which it had been divided came about in 1479 when Ferdinand, ruler of Aragon, Catalonia and Valencia, and his wife, Isabella of Castile and Leon, undertook their joint rule. The conquest of Granada, completed in 1492, saw the destruction of the last Moslem power in the peninsula, and in the same year the Jews also were expelled. In 1512 Ferdinand acquired that part of the Kingdom of Navarre which lay on the southern slope of the Pyrenees. By a process of coalescence, rather than of annexation, Spain had now in a geographical sense become one.

The major domestic problem confronting the Spanish rulers was to establish an efficient machinery of administration for their complex territories. This purpose was achieved by taking advantage of the weakness of the Cortes or estates to be found in the various provinces, and by vesting greater powers in a royal council. It was not possible to impose a new and mechanical unity upon the old variety of regional institutions, but by a relentless extension of royal authority a kind of "decentralized despotism" was set up. Both Ferdinand and Isabella contrived to appeal to the interests of the towns against those of the old feudal class. Lawyers and other members of the new bourgeoisie were introduced into the higher levels of royal administration. Royal power worked very closely with ecclesiastical power, one example being the revival of the Inquisition in 1478, the control of which was transferred from papal to royal hands. By a Concordat in 1482 the crown acquired the right to nominate all bishops and other high church officials. It also supervised all church property, determined whether papal bulls were to have force in Spain and assumed the headship of the three ancient Spanish crusading orders.

The great wealth which flowed in from the New World was directed in substantial part to the royal coffers. This made possible the creation of a large standing army and enhanced Spain's position in relation to other European countries. The upland territory of Castile had lain somewhat apart from the larger currents of European affairs, but Aragon, situated in the valley of the Ebro and having the important seaport of Barcelona, was essentially a Mediterranean power. Its dynasty, as we shall see, had a connection with the Kingdom of Naples and was thereby drawn into Italian

1. The list is a long one. In the first half of the century note: Henry VIII (1509–1547) of England; Francis I (1515–1547) of France; Charles V (1519–1556), Hapsburg Emperor and King of Spain; Emmanuel the Fortunate (1495–1521) of Portugal; Gustavus I (1523–1560) of Sweden; Christian II (1513–1523) of Denmark; Ivan IV (1533–1584) of Russia; Joachim II (1535–1571) of Brandenburg; Sigismund II (1548–1572) of Poland; and Suleiman II (1520–1566) of the Ottoman Empire.

affairs and from there into the wider turmoil of European politics. Spain's magnificent overseas conquests, too, rapidly widened her interests and her influence. An astute series of dynastic marriages created political ties with England, Portugal and Austria. Queen Isabella died in 1504 and Ferdinand in 1516. Their grandson, Charles of Hapsburg, who succeeded them on the Spanish throne was thus able to assume a position in European affairs of hitherto unequaled brilliance.[2]

The growth of royal power in England was no less real. The Wars of the Roses, in which the feudal nobility rallied in support either of the white rose of York or the red rose of Lancaster, spelled the end of the political preponderance which this class had exercised. Monarchy remained the victor after the nobility exhausted itself in armed strife. Following the Battle of Bosworth in 1485 when Richard III, the last of the Yorkist kings, lost his life, the throne went to the Welsh Henry Tudor, a royal claimant who by blood and marriage was linked with both the Yorkist and Lancastrian lines. England's greatness under this Tudor dynasty (1485–1603) surely owes as much to the shrewd, niggling, unspectacular Henry VII, the only child to survive infancy of the twenty-two his mother had borne, as it does to his brilliant son, Henry VIII, or to the equally brilliant granddaughter, Elizabeth.

Henry VII made no violent political revolution. He contrived to work with Parliament, though he saw no necessity to summon it regularly. There were ten sessions in the first twelve years of his reign, but only one in the second. Much local administration he wisely left in the hands of those generally competent amateurs, the six or seven hundred justices of the peace. Henry did not hesitate to set apart a special branch of the royal council which came to be known as the Court of Star Chamber and which had arbitrary power to curb what Bacon later called the "overmighty subjects." He not only limited the political power of the nobility but also enriched his treasury by ingenious devices such as "benevolences" and "forced loans." Seeking economic prosperity and, above all, a full treasury, he encouraged legislation to benefit the merchant class which was now profiting as never before from the growth of the wool trade. Henry made shrewd diplomatic marriages—his daughter Margaret to James IV of Scotland (then a separate kingdom), and his son Arthur, and on Arthur's death a younger

2. The marriage arrangements of Ferdinand and Isabella must surely stand as a classic of matrimonial politics. They married their only son, John, to Margaret, daughter of the Hapsburg Emperor Maximilian. Their daughter, Joanna the Mad, was married to Maximilian's son, Philip. Her sister, Catherine, was first married to Arthur, son of Henry VII of England, and then on Arthur's death to his brother, the future Henry VIII. Another daughter, Isabella, was married to Alfonso of Portugal, and on his death to his brother, King Emmanuel. On Isabella's death a last sister, Maria, then married Emmanuel.

son Henry, to Catherine of Aragon, daughter of Ferdinand and Isabella and
the aunt of the future Emperor Charles V. There was little of the spectacular but much of the admirable in this king who, while keeping England out
of major war, built up her domestic strength and engaged skilfully in
diplomatic maneuvers abroad. Francis Bacon, his first biographer, truthfully speaks of him as " a wonder for wise men."

With the accession of Henry VIII in 1509 the Tudor monarchy entered
a more dramatic and assertive era. England became much more deeply involved in foreign affairs. The great conflict with Rome led to the creation
of the Church of England with Henry as its supreme head. All the while
Parliament was subservient but never destroyed, and a new nobility, rising
from the middle class, moved steadily into public office.[3] Exhibiting in
his youth much of the attractive versatility of the traditional Renaissance
king, Henry in his later years was often tyrannical, cruel and gross. Yet his
reign made possible the greatness of Elizabeth's. The queen whom Edmund
Spenser immortalized as Gloriana followed the unhappy interlude of the
boy Edward VI and the grimly fanatical Mary Tudor. Elizabeth's reign,
which opened under the shadow of a very great foreign danger and which
was also threatened with domestic treason, ended in a blaze of glory. Secure
at home, prosperous in its commerce, rich in literature and the arts, Elizabethan England watched its sailors make those voyages beyond the seas
which brought an entirely new perspective to its history.

Something of this new pattern of kingship can clearly be seen in France.
In 1438, by the so-called Pragmatic Sanction of Bourges, elections to French
bishoprics and abbacies had been taken from papal control and placed,
subject to royal recommendations, in the hands of the French clergy. The
financial and judicial authority of the papal court with respect to France
had also been greatly reduced. In 1439 the Estates General (more or less the
equivalent of the English Parliament) had given up their claim to vote
approval of the celebrated taille, a general tax levied upon the value of
land. With this power of taxation now under his own control, the king had
the means to maintain a permanent armed force as a guarantee of his own
authority. In 1453 the English gave up their century-long struggle and withdrew from all of France save Calais.

The way was clear for Louis XI (1461–1483) to develop and demonstrate
a new concept of royal power which came into striking conflict with a now
outmoded range of ideas. This crafty, penurious and unattractive ruler,
watched over by a strange crew of astrologers and physicians, fought the
power of the feudal nobility and put into operation a new system of courts

3. Henry VIII nominated in his will sixteen regents to act during the minority of his son,
Edward VI. Not one of these noblemen had a title of more than twelve years' standing.

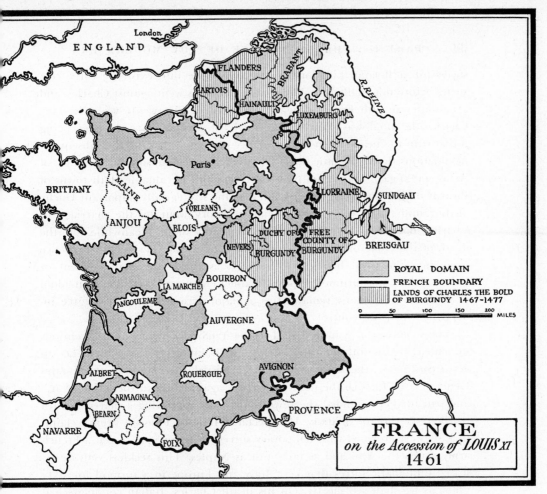

London
ENGLAND

FLANDERS
ARTOIS
HAINAULT
BRABANT
LUXEMBURG
R. RHINE

BRITTANY
MAINE
ANJOU
ORLEANS
BLOIS
NEVERS
Paris
LORRAINE
SUNDGAU
DUCHY OF BURGUNDY
FREE COUNTY OF BURGUNDY
BREISGAU

BOURBON
LA MARCHE
ANGOULEME
AUVERGNE

ALBRET
ROUERGUE
AVIGNON
ARMAGNAC
BEARN
NAVARRE
FOIX
PROVENCE

ROYAL DOMAIN
FRENCH BOUNDARY
LANDS OF CHARLES THE BOLD
OF BURGUNDY 1467-1477

0   50   100   150   200
MILES

FRANCE
on the Accession of LOUIS XI
1461

The basic internal and external problems confronting the French kings can be seen. The principal domestic concern is to extend the royal domain by reducing the power of the great feudal nobles. On the northeast frontier lie the Burgundian lands of Charles the Bold, an echo of the much earlier "Middle Kingdom" of Lotharingia and a challenge to Louis XI and his successors as they consolidated their power.

of law. He relentlessly collected money, consciously and deliberately playing off the wealthy bourgeoisie against his rebellious nobles. It is said that he planted bribes as if they were investments in the courts of his enemies. He summoned the Estates General only once, and then to inform them that he could raise his revenues without consulting them. The army he was able to strengthen with the aid of Swiss mercenaries.

The problem of territorial consolidation raised questions of both domestic and foreign policy. Abroad there arose the dangerous challenge of Charles the Bold of Burgundy, the ruler of a "Middle Kingdom" made up of scattered territories running along France's eastern border southward from the Low Countries to Switzerland. Had this duke, whose court at Brussels displayed the last flamboyant splendors of the Middle Ages, been successful, a Belgian kingdom might have come into existence three centuries before it actually did. The chance of events went against Charles, and a tedious war with France dragged along for nearly twenty years. In 1477 Charles the Bold was slain at the Battle of Nancy, his body later being found with the head frozen fast in the ice of a pond. During the subsequent negotiations the diplomatic skill of Louis XI prevailed, so that the Peace of Arras (1482) gave France not only the economically valuable cloth towns of Picardy on her northeast frontier but also the strategically important Duchy of Burgundy.[4] All other Burgundian territory went by the marriage of Charles' daughter, Mary, into Hapsburg possession. Meanwhile, on the death of the Duke of Anjou, the great fiefs of Anjou, Maine and Provence came into the royal hands. In this way, as the historic enlargement of the royal domain continued, Louis was able to bequeath to his son a kingdom in which only Brittany remained as a major area still to some degree independent of royal control.

Louis' successor, Charles VIII (1483–1498), "a young and licentious hunchback of doubtful sanity," sought with infinitely less competence to act according to the same pattern. He resisted the claims of the Estates General, tried to curb the nobles who rose against him in the "Mad War," and still further extended the royal domain by contriving a marriage with the heiress, Anne of Brittany. His spectacular efforts to assert French claims in Italy were crowned with temporary success when in 1494 he led a French army across the Alps and as far south as Naples. This reckless venture released diplomatic forces that kept Italy and Europe in a turmoil for sixty years, as we shall see shortly. On his death Charles' Italian conquests had to be abandoned; but his successors kept up the will-o'-the-wisp adventure. Among them Francis I (1515–1547) was a distinguished embodiment of the Renaissance ideal of monarchy. He pursued the old Italian claims not merely on the battlefields of the peninsula but also in the critical areas of the Low Countries and the Rhineland so that his wars became a major adventure to secure diplomatic leadership in Europe. Although opposition from the French nobles had somewhat subsided, this gnawing domestic problem was by no means solved; it remained for Cardinal Richelieu in a later generation to take the decisive steps which placed nobles and commoners alike in undoubted subservience to the monarchy.

One may sum up this period in French history by a brief sketch of the system of government which was developing. Despite the high claims occasionally made by some of the members, the Estates General clearly had been

4. The Duchy of Burgundy, of which Dijon was the ancient capital, must be distinguished from the adjoining Free County of Burgundy (Franche Comté), with Besançon as its capital. This latter lay nearer the Rhine and was still a part of the Holy Roman Empire. Franche Comté was later secured for France by Louis XIV.

thrust into the background. Financial power had gone from them; legislative authority they had never truly possessed. Although the Wars of Religion were to show that the nobles could still raise substantial opposition to the crown, their power in general was on the decline. Many of the new bourgeoisie were being won over by titles and by appointment to public office of which (for a price) they were guaranteed the hereditary tenure. The French church was tamed. The Concordat of Bologna (1516), replacing the outmoded Pragmatic Sanction of Bourges, put all nominations to the ten archbishoprics, the eighty-three bishoprics and the five hundred and twenty-seven abbacies of France in royal hands. The royal council, made up of royal appointees and now gradually being divided into sections for various purposes such as foreign affairs, finances and judicial matters, exercised a kind of legislative power through its right to issue ordinances. These, it is true, had to be entered upon the registers of the *Parlement* of Paris, a semi-hereditary body of lawyers and functionaries with the right of "remonstrance" or temporary veto. But such a veto could in the last instance be overridden by the royal will. The estates or assemblies found in some of the provinces were privileged bodies, not genuinely representative, and in any case they had administrative rather than legislative duties. Nor were the various provincial *parlements,* of which by 1553 there were seven, in any position seriously to impede royal power. The king counted on the assistance of various officers of the royal household such as the chancellor and the constable who in the course of time were gradually becoming officers of state; but they, like the royal governors of the provinces, were usually subordinate to the king's wishes. Thus the administrative pattern was set: while it could as yet hardly be called despotism, the powerful French monarchy of the sixteenth century, defined and in some sense limited by the ancient traditions of the realm, adorned by the graces of a Francis I and tempered by the wit and good sense of a Henry IV, was on its way to the ponderous, semi-oriental despotism of a Louis XIV.

■ THE MONARCHICAL PATTERN IN THE LESSER STATES

The pattern of monarchy thus surveyed in Spain, England and France had its parallels in other countries. Portugal, for example, had been pushed by the dramatic successes of its early explorers into a position of unanticipated prominence and wealth, so much so that in 1500 King Emmanuel took the resounding title, "Lord of the Conquest, Navigation, and Commerce of India, Ethiopia, Arabia and Persia," and had it confirmed by the pope. Such magnificent claims were somewhat unreal, and Portugal proved herself in the end no more capable than was Spain of making wise use of the riches coming from overseas. When the direct line to the throne died out in 1580, Portugal was united for sixty years with Spain.

The little Electorate of Brandenburg which originated in the sandy and infertile lands lying between the Elbe and the Oder rivers slowly acquired scattered territories and in 1417 received a famous dynasty, the Hohenzollerns, destined to rule for five centuries. Joachim I (1499–1535) had a very high idea of his power as margrave, or ruler. He was responsible for furthering the use of Roman law, disciplining unruly nobles and bringing the towns more closely under his authority. Joachim II (1535–1571) undertook an elaborate reform program. He accepted certain of the new Protestant ideas and declared himself to be *Summus Episcopus,* or head of the church in Brandenburg. The whole system of administration was reorganized, the old feudal council being divided into various commissions to supervise finances, justice, religion, foreign affairs and domestic policy. While Joachim was compelled to concede various rights to the local estates in the different parts of his domains, he was careful to see that they did not secure positive powers of legislation. Brandenburg was not yet strong enough to count as a major power, nor had it as yet acquired those Prussian territories to the east that so influenced its destiny. In this period, nevertheless, the first steps toward the efficient centralization of authority had been taken.

In the Scandinavian lands royal authority was also strengthened. Between 1397 and 1448 Norway, Denmark and Sweden had been united in the Union of Kalmar, with a single king, but in the fifteenth century this union fell apart. In 1450 Denmark and Norway concluded a permanent union under the rule of the House of Oldenburg which sought likewise to renew the link with Sweden. In the end a peasant uprising drove the Danes from Sweden; and in 1523 a Swedish nobleman, Gustavus Eriksson, took the title of king. He was the founder of the great House of Vasa and, like the Tudors in England, was responsible for vigorously asserting royal authority, restoring order and developing the royal revenues. The old royal council (*Riksrad*) became a subservient body and the strength of the nobles was broken. Great prosperity came to Sweden from her northern mines, her manufactures and her trade. At the time of his death in 1560 Gustavus I had come to exercise more authority than had any earlier king of Sweden. Royal power also flourished in Denmark.

In its own way the distant territory of Muscovy experienced a consolidation of royal authority. Ivan III ("The Great") ruled as Grand Duke of Moscow from 1462 to 1505. In 1480 he successfully challenged the long Mongol domination of the Golden Horde and doubled his territories by acquiring the areas of Novgorod and Pskov. By marrying the niece of the last emperor at Constantinople he could make some claim to be regarded as the heir of Byzantium. Greek and Latin architects and engineers were invited to his court where a Bolognese architect supervised the rebuilding of the Kremlin. The greatest of his immediate successors, Ivan IV ("The Terrible"), took in 1547 the grandiose title, Tsar of All the Russias. Ruthless and bloodthirsty in stamping out opposition, he surrounded himself with able administrators; but he was still largely out of contact with the West. His main fame, perhaps, comes from his conquest of Kazan and Astrakhan, territories which first gave to Muscovy the great basin of the Volga and made this mighty stream a Russian river. Such conquests were, significantly, toward the east, so that Ivan's possessions remained largely a stranger to European civilization. British seamen, nevertheless, contrived to reach Moscow by the northerly route through the White Sea, and negotiations for trade were undertaken though with no great results. Ivan broke with the old Russian nobility, the *Boyars,* and in 1550 actually summoned representatives from all Russian towns and provinces to meet with him at Moscow. From this, too, little resulted. Ivan has been described as a man of genius, one who anticipated the aims of Peter the Great; but somehow his genius never matured; his reign was marred by an almost incredible bloodthirstiness and ferocity and he failed in major respects to reach the ambitious goals which he set for himself.

The Hapsburg rulers of the sixteenth century held territories so widespread and so variously administered as to make the nature of their government unique. The imperial authority as such was not great, but the huge extent of the family lands automatically made the Hapsburgs a dynasty of major importance. Although the emperorship was elective and theoretically open to all, since 1273 one Hapsburg had tended to follow another, and from 1438 this family succession had been continuous. Inheritance and fortunate marriages brought a close relationship with Spain, Italy and the Netherlands. But at the close of the fifteenth century the cumbersome machinery of imperial administration led the Emperor Maximilian (1493–1519) to accept the demands of a reform party and undertake various changes. One of these was the creation of an Imperial Court of Justice to deal with disputes among the princes and to unify the application of Roman law throughout the Empire. Another was the proclamation of a Public Peace in an attempt to curb the marauding tendencies of the imperial knights. A third was the creation of a Privy Council dependent upon the emperor and having administrative and judicial powers. Still another was the levying of the Common Penny, a general property tax to defray military and other expenses. For administrative purposes the imperial territories were divided into ten Circles. With his better organized revenues Maximilian set about creating an imperial army. Such legislation was more striking in its aims than in its actual accomplishments; it proved unable to counteract the dead weight of localism and ancient prejudice, so that imperial and local authority remained in an uneasy opposition.

Maximilian had been able to further the dynastic fortunes of the Hapsburgs (as distinct from their imperial authority) by means of his elaborate marriage negotiations.[5] He himself married Mary of Burgundy, the daughter of Charles the Bold, and thus secured a claim to the Netherlands, Luxemburg and Franche Comté. His son, Philip, married Joanna the Mad, daughter of Ferdinand and Isabella of Spain. When Maximilian died in 1519 the seven electors chose as his successor to the imperial title his grandson Charles, the son of Philip and Joanna. As a Hapsburg heir Charles inherited his grandfather's vast possessions, and as son of Philip and Joanna he likewise became the heir of Castile and Aragon. With the imperial dignity added to the rule of his family lands, Charles assumed a station the like of which had hardly been seen since the days of Charlemagne.[6] It has been estimated that his territories were three times as large as those of the Roman Emperor, Trajan. In this sense, therefore, he could well be called the colossus of the sixteenth century. But he was immediately confronted with bitter strife at home and was also involved in the endless complications of the Italian wars. Thus Charles was not destined to be the architect of any new political unity and his long reign ended in 1556 in abdication, bitterness and defeat. The policy of dynastic marriages for the purpose of territorial gain made European conflict almost inevitable. In the wedding procession of Maximilian and Mary of Burgundy, once wrote the great French historian, Lavisse, walked the shadows of numberless soldiers—symbols of all those who were to die in the wars that this marriage engendered.

Italy produced no strong national state to compare with those of England, France or Scandinavia. Some aspects of the evolution of the Italian city states have already been suggested, and it has been pointed out how Venice, Milan and Florence in the north had become masters of substantial territories. One notable development of the late fifteenth century was the reappearance of the papacy as a political force. Since the period of the

5. This tradition is expressed in the famous Austrian motto: *Alii bella gerant, tu, Austria felix, nube!* (Others shall wage war; thou, O happy Austria, shall marry!)
6. The origin and extent of the Hapsburg family lands can be listed thus:
    From Maximilian: Austria, Carinthia, Styria, the Tyrol.
    From Mary of Burgundy: The Netherlands, Luxemburg, Franche Comté.
    From Isabella of Spain: Castile and the Spanish Indies.
    From Ferdinand of Spain: Aragon, Navarre, the Balearic Islands, Sardinia, Naples, Sicily.
    Charles' brother, Ferdinand, took the title of King of Bohemia after the Turkish victory
        at Mohàcs in 1526. In 1527 Ferdinand was also elected King of Hungary, but actually
        ruled only the small portion not under Turkish control.
    The Hapsburgs acquired the Duchy of Milan in 1535.

Avignonese captivity in the fourteenth century the papacy had gone into something of a decline; territories once under its control had broken away. The Borgia Pope Alexander VI (1492–1503) sought by every means to aid the ambitions of his natural son, Caesar Borgia, who wished to carve out a kingdom for himself in the territory known as the Romagna. These ambitions ended with the death of Alexander VI. His successor, Julius II (1503–1513), who moved directly to re-establish the territorial authority of the papacy, was spectacularly successful. Perugia, Bologna and most of the Romagna were secured and the Papal States assumed the general form which they were to hold until the middle of the nineteenth century. In attaining this goal the papacy had become the center of opposition to French interference; but the price which had to be paid to get rid of the French was to see the power of Spain firmly established at Naples. This kingdom fell to King Ferdinand of Aragon in 1504 and remained under his dynasty until 1713.

Venice, Milan and Florence each flourished in the hands of a relatively small governing group. Their rivalries and territorial ambitions contributed to the complex pattern of alliances and war which marked the close of the fifteenth century and the opening decades of the sixteenth. Given such an atmosphere, the possibility of political unification which Dante had dreamed of in his *De Monarchia* was practically non-existent. In the last chapter of his famous book, *The Prince,* Machiavelli appealed to the Medici to take the lead in expelling the foreigner and restoring Italy's unique greatness. But the appeal, however eloquent, remained unheard. Politically, Italy exhibited a miserable pattern of diplomatic intrigue and recurrent war at a time when European cultural life was profoundly enriched by its artistic and intellectual genius.

In some other countries monarchical power labored under heavy difficulties. Poland, which in the fourteenth century had reached from the Baltic to the Black Sea and was still one of the largest states in Europe, saw the triumph of neither a strong monarchy nor of the popular forces. Burdened with an elective kingship, a highly privileged nobility and a wretched peasantry, and failing at the same time to develop a thriving middle class or a healthy commercial economy, the country slowly sank into confusion, to become in the end the victim of its more powerful neighbors.

The medieval kings of Bohemia had had a proud history, winning the rank of elector in the Holy Roman Empire. But the throne was elective, and in 1526 it was arranged that Ferdinand of Hapsburg, the younger brother of the Emperor Charles V, should rule. Thus Bohemia lost its independence as a nation and became little more than a Hapsburg province in which the proud traditions of Bohemian politics and culture were steadily suppressed. A similar fate attended the ancient Hungarian monarchy where Ferdinand of Hapsburg had likewise won the crown in 1526. A hopeless struggle against the Turks ended in 1547 with the acceptance of the fact of partition. Most of Hungary fell into the hands of the sultan and remained there for a century and a half. Ferdinand maintained the title of king over what was left; but the vitality, such as it was, of Hungarian political life had come to an end.

If the Ottoman Empire is to be included in the list of powerful sixteenth-century political societies, it must be remembered that it was an empire rather than a national state and remained in many significant respects foreign to the traditions of Western Europe. From its first beginnings in Asia Minor it had grown dramatically, pushing forward under the able Mohammed II (1451–1481), the captor of Constantinople, into the Balkan and Black Sea areas. Under Selim I (1512–1520) Syria, Egypt, Tripoli, Tunis and Algeria were gained. By seizing Baghdad he acquired the caliphate, or lordship over the orthodox Moslems. Europe became most familiar, however, with Suleiman II, "The Magnificent" (1520–1566), whose policies made him an active participant in the European balance of power. By winning the island of Rhodes from the ancient crusading order of the Knights Hospitallers he gained control of the Aegean Sea. In 1521 he captured Belgrade and from this fortress was able to pour his armies into the great plain of Hungary. At Mohàcs in 1526 he defeated the Hungarians and secured for himself seven-tenths of the kingdom. Three years later the Turkish hosts with their silken tents and oriental war-trumpets were at the gates of Vienna. Defeat of the Turks saved Austria; but they won Budapest in 1541 and for one hundred and fifty years held the greater part of Hungary. Europe found no way to unite permanently in the face of the Turkish peril; on the contrary, more than one Christian power, thinking in terms of immediate advantage, bid ardently for the sultan's support.

This Ottoman Empire was one in which a powerful minority ruled over a vastly greater non-Turkish population. Only Moslems could be regarded as citizens. The government was autocratic, the sultan having the power to appoint a grand vizier responsible to him alone. The legal system was based upon the teachings of the Koran. Revenues were secured by a general land tax, customs duties in Turkish ports and a head tax on all non-Moslems. A standing army was at the sultan's command; its compulsory levies included the *spahis,* or cavalry, and also the unique force of *janissaries,* a small, highly trained, professional body of troops made up of boys taken from tributary Christian peoples and brought up in the Mohammedan faith.

The government encouraged trade with Christian Europe; and the merchants of Venice, Ragusa, Genoa or Marseilles had no reason to be dissatisfied with the profits. Special concessions, or "capitulations," were eventually obtained by the French who in 1536 were granted freedom of trade and navigation, subject to a five per cent duty, in Turkish ports. No foreign vessel was to enter save under the French flag, and Frenchmen were to have extraterritorial rights, religious freedom and the custody of the so-called "Holy Places" in Palestine. The Turks seem to have been unusually indulgent to their Christian subjects; these could worship as they chose, and the Greek Church was permitted to have its patriarch at Constantinople, though he was appointed by the sultan. In such matters the Ottoman Empire, whatever its larger defects, embodied a greater degree of religious toleration than would be found contemporaneously in the Christian states of Western Europe.

Monarchy, then, usually strong but occasionally weak, dominated the political life of the sixteenth century. Some of its domestic problems will be considered in due course. Meanwhile, as a sequel to the general picture just sketched, one may consider the complicated international problems which arose at the end of the fifteenth century in consequence of French intervention in the turbulent life of the Italian states.

■ THE ITALIAN WARS

Between 1494, when Charles VIII led a French army through the Alps in quest of an Italian inheritance, and 1559, when peace of a sort temporarily descended, Europe witnessed an extraordinary series of alliances and wars, originating in Italy but gradually extending further afield until they became more generally European in scope. These times still arrest the imagination; for the splendors of a dying feudalism are evoked by the meeting of Henry VIII and Francis I on the Field of Cloth of Gold, by the knightly exploits of the Chevalier Bayard, "without fear and without reproach," or by the soldierly renown of "the Great Captain," the Spaniard Gonsalvo di Cordova. In another sense the wars seem but a tedious embodiment of dynastic ambitions—an illustration of the ruthless politics of power.

Considered as a mere catalogue of politics and diplomacy, then, the story would hardly be worth telling. Yet it rises above tedium because in it one may observe the emergence of major European problems. The chief of these was to be the long rivalry between the royal houses of France and Austria—a rivalry which in oversimplified terms might be described as one between the Latin world to the west of the Rhine and the German world to the east of it. This rivalry found its first expression in French dynastic claims to Naples and Milan; the claims aroused the suspicion and then the active hostility of the Hapsburgs; in time the struggle shifted from Italy to an even more critical area of conflict—the long corridor running from the

North Sea to Switzerland where Louis XI had fought Charles the Bold and where, seven hundred years before, the "Middle Kingdom" of Lotharingia had arisen out of the broken empire of Charlemagne.

It may be doubted whether a consistent French policy was yet at work. But the outward pressure, so to speak, of the French monarchy, profiting by small gains and slowly pushing into areas where the flimsy authority of the Hapsburgs still prevailed, was of far deeper consequence than any French territorial ambitions in Italy itself. And thus the peace of 1559, which marked the terminus of the French candidacy in Naples and Milan, was no more than a truce in an age-long struggle for the control of the historic Middle Kingdom.

Certain predisposing circumstances seemed to favor the French claims in Italy. Royal authority was in process of asserting itself in France, where the reign of Louis XI in some sense marked the transition from the medieval to the modern world. The French nobility were restive and eager for adventure. In Italy, on the other hand, disunity was the rule. Although a kind of political equilibrium between the various states had been reached by the middle of the fifteenth century, it was uneasy. Italy was menaced, too, by countries other than France. A later generation was responsible for the saying that Italy is an artichoke to be eaten leaf by leaf; but even in this earlier age the aphorism had much truth.

Charles VIII of France had some legal claim to inherit the Kingdom of Naples but his position was certainly not unassailable, and the Spanish House of Aragon had in fact succeeded to the Neapolitan throne. Charles VIII could also make claim to the Duchy of Milan through his cousin, Charles of Orleans, a descendant of the former ruling house, the Visconti. The actual ruler of Milan, Ludovico Sforza, was highly unpopular in Naples and Florence, and now feared that these two states might form a coalition against him. He therefore encouraged the eager Charles VIII to assert his claims to Naples in the hope of diverting a threat to his own territory. Charles had dreams of glory; he held a reasonably secure kingdom; funds could be secured, ironically enough, from Italian bankers; and his army, medieval in some respects, had the invaluable advantage of a powerful artillery train.

The new statesmanship of this age is seen in the careful steps which Charles took to prepare his ground. England, which had attacked Boulogne in 1492, was bought off with a money ransom. Aragon and Castile were momentarily placated by the return of Cerdagne and Roussillon, territories on the northern slope of the Pyrenees won for France by Louis XI. Maximilian of Hapsburg was reassured as to his possession of the territories gained by his marriage to Mary of Burgundy. These concessions were the

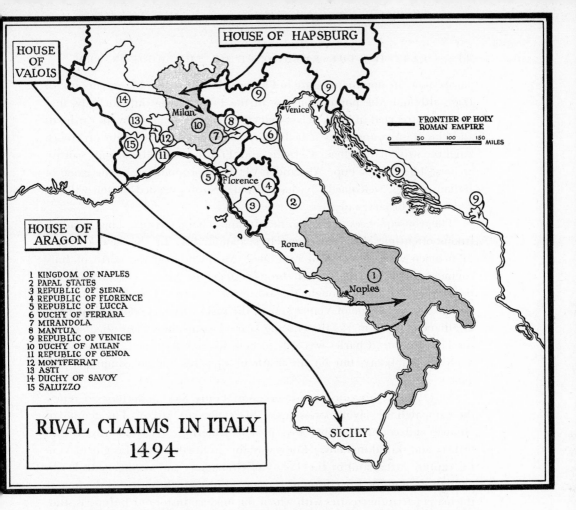

RIVAL CLAIMS IN ITALY
1494

At the close of the Middle Ages Italy is disunited. Access through the Alpine passes (page 9) is easy for its northern neighbors, while Spain had long used the sea route. Constant rivalries among the Italian states, intensified by repeated outside interventions, provide a seedbed for the growth of modern "power politics" and the techniques of the "balance of power." Italy becomes a European battleground.

crude payments to be tossed on the table in the gamble for what Charles conceived to be the all-important Italian prize. But in view of the fact that Ferdinand I, the ruler of Naples, was of the House of Aragon, it could be foretold that trouble with Spain would almost inevitably ensue. Moreover the frontier of the Holy Roman Empire still ran so far to the south as to encompass a good part of northern Italy, including the Duchy of Milan. It was improbable, therefore, that the Emperor Maximilian would long remain silent.

The French army of thirty thousand troops which issued from the Mont Genèvre Pass into the North Italian plain in 1494 at first met easy success. Ludovico Sforza welcomed Charles at Milan. The Dominican friar, Savonarola, now the dominant figure in Florence, hailed him as the regenerator of Italy, although the population saw in the French king only an ugly, misshapen figure, clad in black velvet and cloth of gold, escorted by his cardinals and closely surrounded by a bodyguard of bowmen and a train of French knights, Swiss halberdiers, German and French footsoldiers and Scottish archers. The Borgia Pope Alexander VI, deeply committed to the game of Italian politics, welcomed Charles at Rome. Naples yielded to him without a blow in February, 1495.

The consequences were significant and characteristic. The invading troops oftentimes behaved themselves abominably. In the new kingdom Frenchmen were quickly put into office. Meanwhile, in the north of Italy common dislike of the French brought together Venice, Milan and the papacy. These likewise sought the aid of the Empire, of Spain and later of Florence. The League of Venice (1495), the first of the kaleidoscopic pattern of alliances which marks the ensuing years, cast an immediate shadow over the French plans. Charles was able to fight his way back to France carrying a substantial booty, but on his death in 1498 his Italian conquests were gone.[7]

Nevertheless, his cousin and successor, Louis XII, undertook to renew the campaign by laying stress upon his claims to Milan. The tempo of alliance and counter-alliance rose in a bewildering crescendo.[8] By shrewd bribery and skilful maneuver Louis was able to break up the League of Venice, capture Milan and by the Treaty of Granada (1500) arrange with Ferdinand of Aragon for a partition of Naples. This is worth noting as the first of the many partition treaties with which the modern history of Europe is stud-

7. The often repeated view that the French took back with them across the Alps the new cultural interests of the Italian Renaissance hardly fits in with what we know of Charles VIII or of the general behavior of armies. It was at this time that syphilis, possibly brought from the New World by the first explorers, spread to northern Europe where it rapidly reached epidemic proportions.

8. The complex diplomatic maneuvers of these years almost defy description. The following is a rough summary of the sequence of alliances:

	LEAGUE OF VENICE, 1495	LEAGUE OF CAMBRAI, 1508	HOLY LEAGUE, 1511	HOLY LEAGUE, 1521	LEAGUE OF COGNAC, 1526
Principal Members	Papacy Empire Spain Venice Milan Florence	Papacy Empire Spain England France	Papacy Empire Spain Venice England	Papacy Empire Spain England	Papacy Venice Milan Florence England France
Directed Against	France	Venice Milan	France	France	Empire Spain

ded. But the agreement did not last, and by 1504 Louis had lost his share. By vigorous diplomacy France was then able to create a new alliance, the League of Cambrai (1508). Skilful counter-diplomacy in the end shattered this League and raised the old anti-French cry. In 1511 the Holy League was formed by the papacy which still maintained its purpose of driving the French from Italy. It included Venice, Spain, England and later the Empire. Such a grouping in opposition to France is a clear indication that the major problem of power was regarded as broadly European rather than narrowly Italian. Louis was obliged to abandon Italy and devote his efforts to coping with an English invasion of northern France. He likewise had to meet an imperial attack upon Dijon, the capital of the Burgundian territory won by France a generation earlier.

Death made little difference to French ambitions, for Francis I, who succeeded Louis in 1515, immediately proceeded to renew the claim to Milan. By now the major conflict lay clearly between France and the Empire, as the long list of disputed frontier areas—Flanders, Artois, Burgundy and Navarre—shows. The young king made a brilliant beginning, invading Italy, winning the battle of Marignano and forcing Charles, the grandson of Maximilian, to recognize the French seizure of Milan. In 1516 Francis was able to make the Concordat of Bologna with the papacy, securing for himself a powerful hold upon the French church.[9] It was not unnatural, therefore, that Francis should entertain dreams of being elected emperor and should intrigue (albeit in vain) to that end. By 1516, with the Treaty of Noyon, there was even talk of a general European peace to be consolidated by that supposedly infallible prescription, a united crusade against the Turk now pressing northward through the Balkans.

In 1519, when the imperial election fell to the Hapsburgs, the new Emperor Charles V vigorously asserted his power. War with France was renewed, and at Pavia in 1525 Francis was defeated and captured. He secured his release by agreeing to the Treaty of Madrid (1526) in which France gave up all its territorial claims. Immediately on his release, in the true spirit of Machiavelli, Francis resumed his claims and renewed the war. Profiting by the general mistrust of the wide powers of the new emperor, Francis was able to counteract the old hostilities and by the League of Cognac (1526) find allies in Milan, Venice, Florence and the Papal States. Charles replied by seizing Milan. His imperial troops, mutinous and out of hand, captured Rome, made the pope a prisoner in the Castle of St. Angelo and subjected the city to the worst ravaging in its long history.

Exhaustion on both sides led to the Peace of Cambrai (1529). France was to keep Burgundy but was to renounce her claims to Milan, Naples, Artois

9. See p. 89.

and Flanders. In this way Spain, now directly in control of Naples and Milan, moved into that position of prominence in Italy which she was to hold for nearly two hundred years. But even yet peace had not been definitely secured; in 1535 war was renewed. The miserable pattern of war, truce, diplomatic maneuver and further war continued even after the death of Francis I in 1547. His son and successor, Henry II, a good Catholic who was married to Catherine de' Medici, a relative of the pope, intrigued with the German Protestant princes and secured their alliance in the Treaty of Friedwald (1552), obtaining from them also the promise of the three Lorraine bishoprics of Metz, Toul and Verdun. The importance of these territories was certainly not ecclesiastical; it was strategic, for they lay directly across a critical route of advance between Germany and France.

The Treaty of Cateau-Cambrésis (1559) between France and Spain ended the long struggle. Three separate problems demanded solution: that of Calais, that of the northeastern frontier and that of Italy. In a separate treaty England agreed to yield Calais to the French, thus abandoning her last foothold upon the continent. In Italy, France abandoned all claims to Naples and Milan. She did retain, however, several important fortress points lying in Savoy upon the Italian slope of the Alps—Chieri, Pinerolo, Chivasso and Villanova. Although these held out to France no prospect of a political establishment, they gave her an important military advantage, making it possible for France to maintain that strategic interest in Italy which can be observed all the way from Richelieu to Napoleon. Most important for France was the situation on the northeast frontier. Here she retained several small fortified points; but her major acquisitions were Metz, Toul and Verdun. These first stepping stones toward the Rhine, the marks of the new orientation of French foreign policy, had an ultimate importance in European history that it would be hard to exaggerate.

◼ THE EUROPEAN BALANCE OF POWER

As much as any year, then, 1559 may be said to be a landmark in the history of the sixteenth century. Spain's hand now fell with deadening effect throughout Italy, for this Hapsburg influence was not limited to the territories of Naples, Sicily and Milan which Spain actually held. French foreign policy had assumed an orientation toward the Low Countries and the Rhineland, and in that same general direction French statesmen had discovered the rich possibilities for intrigue which existed amid the confused politics of the German states. England, under the skilled direction of Cardinal Wolsey and his successors, concerned itself more actively, too, with European affairs. In the narrow military sense, the new Spanish tactics and the enlarged use of mercenary armies paid for out of royal treasuries were making war a professional business of cold calculation and ruthless exploitation. The related field of diplomacy was slowly moving from an amateur to a professional status. The age, as we have seen, was one in which alliances were made and broken with startling rapidity. The enlargement of territory seemed almost a necessity for any ambitious ruler, and war served as a normal means to gain his ends.

In these tedious and often frustrating struggles a new pattern of international conduct was slowly emerging. The phrase which has come to be used in description of the new diplomatic technique is that of the principle of the balance of power. In an age when intensely realistic statesmen were quick to employ almost any means to further their own ends, the expression, "principle," is perhaps not quite convincing. It would seem proper, however, to speak of a diplomatic policy governed by the growing realization that states must band together for their own advantage whenever one— whether France, Spain or the Empire—seemed overambitious and over-powerful. In this sense the sixteenth century saw the development of a pattern of diplomatic behavior that has continued down to our own day.

This ruthless skill in the conduct of international affairs did not escape the notice of contemporary observers. The Florentine, Niccolò Machiavelli, and the Englishman, Thomas More, both were holders of important political office and active participants in great events. From their observations came books written within two or three years of one another—*The Prince* and the *Utopia*—which have a permanent place in the political literature of modern times.

Sir Thomas More (1478–1535) was one of the most distinguished figures of the early Tudor period. A scholar who was removed by his father from Oxford on account of his passion for the new Greek learning, a lawyer who rose in a brilliant career to be knighted, to serve as Speaker of the House of Commons and to be an intimate of Henry VIII, More reached the pinnacle of his career when he became Lord Chancellor of England. He had gone on various embassies to the Low Countries and had been posted for a time at Calais as agent for the diplomacy of his royal master. Thus More, like Machiavelli, had some first-hand knowledge of continental politics. Unlike the Florentine, however, he was devoutly Catholic, and at the same time he shared with his devoted friend, Erasmus, a broadly humane view of mankind. Expediency could never take the place of principle with him; in the end he chose the headsman's axe rather than repudiate papal supremacy and recognize Henry VIII as supreme head of the Church of England.

More's *Utopia,* which he published in Latin in 1516, is one of the great classics in the literature of ideal commonwealths. It can be related to the sixteenth-century political world by virtue of the devastating criticisms which it contains of social conditions in England and also of those European diplomatic practices which Machiavelli so complacently accepted. These criticisms, rather than the magnificent vision of a Utopia beyond the seas, make it an interesting parallel and contrast to the work of the Florentine. More draws upon his diplomatic experience by imagining that on a trip to the Low Countries he came upon a sailor, Raphael Hythloday, a much traveled man and a shrewd observer. It is to be remembered that More wrote at a time when France was making a vigorous bid for the domination of Italy and in this effort had provoked a bewildering series of alliances and counter-alliances, all inspired by the motive of political power. The words of Raphael, supposedly addressed to More, are full of significance.

> Suppose [Raphael says] that I were with the French king, and there sitting in his council, whiles that in that most secret consultation, the king himself there being present in his own person, they beat their brains and search the very bottoms of their wits to discuss by what craft and means the king may still keep Milan, and draw to him again fugitive Naples, and then how to conquer the Venetians, and how to bring under his jurisdiction all Italy, then how to win the domination of Flanders, Brabant, and of all Burgundy: with divers other lands, whose kingdom he hath long ago in mind and purpose invaded. . . .

These words, it will be noted, give an almost precise picture of the diplomatic aims that French policy had pursued. Raphael then continues with a startlingly unorthodox hypothesis:

> If I, silly man, should rise up and will them to turn over the leaf, and learn a new lesson, saying that my counsel is not to meddle with Italy, but to tarry still at home, and that the kingdom of France alone is almost greater, than that it may well be governed by one man . . . and that therefore it were best for him to content himself with his own kingdom of France, as his forefathers and predecessors did before him; to make much of it, to enrich it, and to make it as flourishing as he could, to endeavour himself to love his subjects, and again to be beloved of them, willingly to live with them, peaceably to govern them, and with other kingdoms not to meddle. . . .

The advice is unexceptionable, but neither Raphael nor More has any illusions as to its reception. Raphael puts the question to the author: "This mine advice, Master More, how think you it would be heard and taken?" More's answer is simple: "So God help me, not very thankfully."

This powerful intellect, then, saw war as one of the great curses of his time. It is not surprising that an equally shrewd observer, More's dear friend, Erasmus, should think similarly. His *Antipolemus* was written in eloquent denunciation of war, and in his *Education of a Christian Prince* he spoke sadly of the Christian failure to meet its challenge:

Plato calls it sedition, not war, when Greeks war with Greeks; and if this should happen, he bids them fight with every restraint. What term should we apply, then, when Christians engage in battle with Christians, since they are united by so many bonds to each other? . . . Among such great and changing vicissitudes of human events, among so many treaties and agreements which are now entered into, now rescinded, who can lack a pretext—if there is any real excuse —for going to war? But the pontifical laws do not disapprove all war. Augustine approved of it in some instances, and St. Bernard praises some soldiers. But Christ himself and Peter and Paul everywhere teach the opposite.

Between More and his Italian contemporary, Machiavelli (1469–1527) it would be difficult to find a greater contrast. Machiavelli was a Florentine who grew up in the great days of Lorenzo de' Medici. After the expulsion of the Medici in 1494 he served as a secretary to the republican government of Florence, which sent him on diplomatic missions in Italy and to France. On the return of the Medici in 1512 he was imprisoned for a short time and then went into exile. He began the writing of his *Discourses on Livy,* and interrupted this in 1513 to write his study of the problems of ruling which he entitled *The Prince* and which he dedicated to Lorenzo di Piero de' Medici, Duke of Urbino. The book remained in manuscript until 1532, after Machiavelli's death.

Machiavelli's best-known work has quite generally been regarded as a collection of callous maxims about the art of government, completely devoid of any concern for morality. It has been taken as the supreme expression of those public policies in which the end justifies the means. It can also be seen as a manifesto addressed to a particular person in the light of a particular problem, namely, what to do about the disunion of Italy and about the constant threats from abroad. Machiavelli must likewise be regarded as an objective student of politics, interested in the natural workings of human society and greatly concerned to discover and explain the forces animating both rulers and subjects.

Whatever the general purpose of Machiavelli's writing, it is clear that he made shrewd comments upon his own times. He had observed the ruthlessness with which Pope Alexander VI sought material advantage for himself and territories for his son, Caesar Borgia. He had seen the great success of Julius II in refounding the Papal States. He pointed out that Louis XII of France blundered badly in helping the papacy to occupy the Romagna and thus enlarge the temporal power of the Church, and that Louis blundered again by agreeing to divide Naples with Ferdinand of Aragon, for the result was to bring Spain into the peninsula. Machiavelli saw as one of the outstanding facts of his age the great prestige and power of the French and Spanish monarchies, and he made it clear that the fortunes of these countries depended upon the skill and determination of their rulers.

Machiavelli's discussion of politics concentrates upon the role of the prince, or ruler. Any prince must take account of what Machiavelli calls *Fortuna,* which is certainly more than mere luck or chance. It may more nearly resemble those enveloping forces of nature and environment which man cannot escape but which with skill he may be able to moderate. Fundamentally, the prince should be possessed of what Machiavelli calls *Virtù,* the ability to think and then to do, or, as Machiavelli would say, the sum of those qualities which make a man great, powerful and famous. A ruler is not bound, as the thought of the Middle Ages held, either by Divine Law or by Natural Law; his business is simply to maintain the state. To do this, to be sure, he should command the devotion of his subjects, and to this end he must "seem" to be possessed of wide virtues. A proper care for religion, Machiavelli says, is a valuable means of strengthening a state. But all this falls in the category of means, not of ends. "Thus it is well," Machiavelli says, "to seem merciful, faithful, humane, religious and upright, and also to be so; but the mind should remain so balanced that were it needful not to be so, you should be able and know how to change to the contrary."

The self-interest of the ruler must come first. "He who is the cause of another's greatness is himself undone." The ruler must accept the realities of his age and meet force with force.

> A prince, therefore, should have no care or thought but for war, and for the regulations and training it requires, and should apply himself exclusively to this as his peculiar province; for war is the sole art looked for in one who rules, and is of such efficacy that it not merely maintains those who are born Princes, but often enables men to rise to that eminence from a private station.

The ruler must impose his authority upon his own state:

> Since love and fear can hardly exist together, if we must choose between them it is far safer to be feared than loved. For men it may generally be affirmed that they are thankless, fickle, false, studious to avoid danger, greedy of gain, devoted to you while you are able to confer benefits upon them, and ready, as I said before, while danger is distant, to shed their blood, and sacrifice their property, their lives, and their children for you; but in the hour of need they turn against you.

In his relations with other states the ruler must be completely ruthless: "A prudent Prince neither can nor ought to keep his word when to keep it is hurtful to him and the causes which led him to pledge it are removed. . . . He ought not to quit good courses if he can help it, but should know how to follow evil courses if he must." The ruler must play the game of balance and maneuver, with no other thought than that of his own advantage: "And here let it be noted that a Prince should be careful never to join with one stronger than himself in attacking others, unless, as already said, he be driven to it by necessity. For if he whom you join prevails, you are at his mercy." Perhaps the simplest and clearest of all Machiavelli's statements about politics is contained in a passage from his *Discourses on Livy:*

> For where the very safety of the country depends upon the resolution to be taken, no considerations of justice or injustice, humanity or cruelty, nor of glory or of shame, should be allowed to prevail. But putting all other considerations aside, the only question should be, "What course will save the life and liberty of the country?"

These counsels have established Machiavelli as the great immoralist of politics. It is not perhaps sufficiently realized that as a man of his times he was giving realistic advice in a tough and dangerous world, or that he was shrewd enough to see that the ruler should seek to command the trust and affection of his people. Nor should it be forgotten that Machiavelli was looking for some kind of inspired leadership that would end the divisions of Italy. In a magnificent peroration he called upon the illustrious house of Medici to take the lead in uniting Italy against the foreigner—"the barbarian tyranny"—from which Italy had suffered so much.

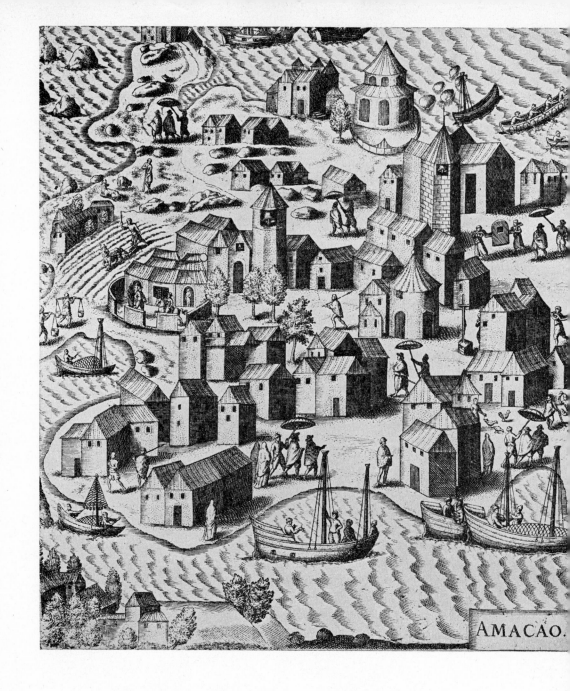

The New World
of Exploration and Commerce

PORTUGUESE SETTLEMENT OF MACAO IN CHINA. Here the Portuguese dried cargo in the early sixteenth century, and in 1557 were permitted to settle. This engraving comes from the finely illustrated VOYAGES of Theodore de Bry (first German edition, Frankfort-on-the-Main, 1606). De Bry's illustrations, although not always accurate, gave a vivid picture of the new lands beyond the seas. Courtesy of the Rare Book Room, New York Public Library.

Chapter 5

■ THE GREAT VOYAGES

IN MARKED CONTRAST to the tedious intricacies of the European struggle for power stand the vast sweep and panorama of overseas expansion. During the medieval period Europe herself had been subject to a variety of Asiatic onslaughts: Tartars, Finns, Arabs, Magyars, Bulgars and Turks had all moved in upon her from the east with lasting effects upon the population.

The crusading movement of the twelfth and thirteenth centuries sent men in the other direction and brought the west, if only transiently, into touch with the fringe of the oriental world. The great overland voyages of the thirteenth century had reached as far as central Asia; nevertheless, the various Christian missions established in the cities of China had all died out during the fourteenth century. These contacts, then, lacked permanence; their importance for the west was that they helped to build up a certain literary tradition exemplified in such books as those of Marco Polo, Mandeville and John of Pontecorvo. This tradition exercised some of Europe's acutest minds and helped to keep alive the spark of geographic interest.

During the fifteenth century the urge to discovery and trade, of which the beginnings have already been sketched, gathered steady momentum.[1] Adjacent to Europe proper lay those parts of Africa and Asia which had been linked with the European world since the time of classical antiquity. Through them flowed the luxury goods, like spices and silks, which Europe's upper classes valued so highly.[2] Beyond this known world there existed another, vaguely described in the Greek and Roman geographers and fitfully illuminated by the tales of medieval travelers. This was primarily the vast continental expanse of Africa and Asia. The medieval tradition also included an even more shadowy region—the elusive islands of the Atlantic. Substance was given to at least part of this tradition when Madeira, the Cape Verde Islands, the Azores and the Canaries became known. Beyond them lay the truly fabulous realms: Atlantis; Antillia, or the Island of the Seven Cities; the Island of Brasil, long sought by Bristol merchants; and the Island of St. Brandan whose bells, ringing through the mists, Irish sailors were said to hear but never find.

In the fifteenth century geographical knowledge began to be systematized. It was based on the writings of the classical geographers, modified and enlarged by the comments of medieval authors such as Roger Bacon. The Greek Ptolemy had made no question of the earth's roundness and he called attention to the huge size of the Asiatic land mass. A Latin translation of Ptolemy's *Geography* was made around 1410 and first printed in 1470. Around 1410, too, Pierre d'Ailly, a French cardinal, wrote his *Imago Mundi,* in which he accepted with other men of learning the sphericity of the earth, but unlike Ptolemy greatly exaggerated the size of Asia. This meant that, in the absence of any knowledge of the western hemisphere, it would seem to require no very great westward voyage to reach Cathay. The

1. See pp. 32–37.
2. Spices were not so general an article of consumption as is often believed. They were too expensive. The average consumer "relied upon such local herbs as mint or sage to give taste to the flesh of elderly cattle, muscular hogs and sinewy sheep." HEATON, *Economic History of Europe,* p. 151

Imago Mundi was first printed between 1480 and 1483. Another important geographical work, the *Historia Rerum* of Aeneas Sylvius (later Pope Pius II), published in 1477 also embodied a great deal of Ptolemy's geographic knowledge. In addition, then, to the practical knowledge and experience which the sailors of Prince Henry of Portugal had gained as they edged slowly down the African coast, there developed this learned view of the world in which, save for the staggering omission of North and South America, the parts were being brought into a crudely correct relationship. Such was the knowledge available to Columbus; it was knowledge of which the components were partly classical and partly medieval.

Geographical knowledge alone does not command men to action. One must note the ambition, the vigor and the competitive rivalries of the rulers of the various maritime kingdoms, especially those of Portugal and Spain. One must also include the role of the merchant. The advantages which shipmen could draw from the African trade of which the foundations had been laid by Prince Henry were enormous. The little Portuguese caravels went out with their supply of glass beads, red caps and hawks' bells, often adding a deckload of horses for the African chiefs with whom they dealt. They returned with pepper, elephant tusks, slaves and chests of gold dust. Profits, even taking into account the heavy risks, were spectacular.

Techniques of navigation and sailing were steadily improving. The compass was in general employment in the fifteenth century so that the *portolani,* or sailing charts, could carry reasonably accurate directions for known coastal points. The quadrant, cross-staff and astrolabe were coming into use for measuring the altitude of sun or stars and thus roughly determining the latitude. But the techniques were still very crude. Vasco da Gama was in the habit of going ashore and hanging his astrolabe from a tree or tripod to measure the sun's angle. When Columbus used his quadrant in 1492 in Cuba in order to determine his latitude, instead of the correct twenty-one degrees his figure was forty-two, which would have put him in the neighborhood of Cape Cod. Mariners could make use of several almanacks, notably the *Ephemerides* giving astronomical data for the years 1474–1506 which Johann Müller of Königsberg printed in 1474. Longitude was a constant puzzle and remained so until the perfection of the chronometer in the eighteenth century. To calculate an east-west position it was necessary to rely mainly upon dead reckoning at which many shipmasters, including Columbus, developed phenomenal skill.

Sailing vessels became much more seaworthy in the fifteenth century. The Venetian galleys, used for the coastal trade from the Mediterranean to the Baltic, were useless for deep navigation, but the Portuguese sailors steadily improved their caravels. These were sturdy seagoing vessels with a

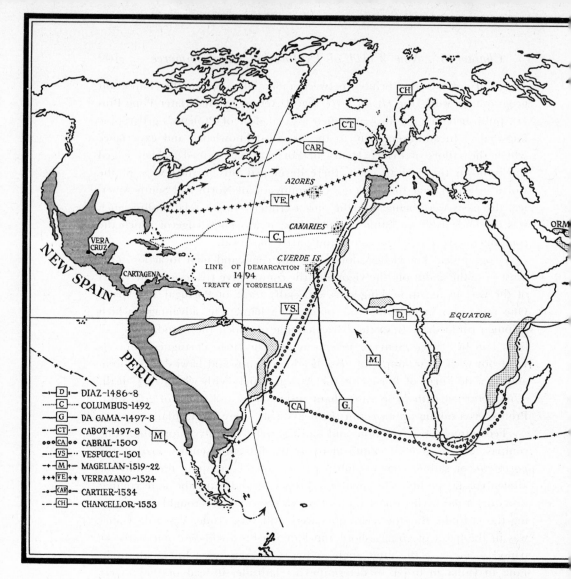

CH

CT

CAR

AZORES

VE.

CANARIES

C.

C. VERDE IS.

VS.

D.

EQUATOR

M.

CA

G.

ORM

VERA CRUZ

NEW SPAIN

CARTAGENA

PERU

LINE OF DEMARCATION
1494
TREATY OF TORDESILLAS

-·-[D]·- — DIAZ~1486~8
······[C]····· — COLUMBUS~1492
——[G]— — DA GAMA~1497-8
-··[CT]··· — CABOT~1497-8
°°°[CA]°°° — CABRAL~1500
-··-[VS]-·· — VESPUCCI~1501
-·+[M]+·- — MAGELLAN~1519~22
+++[VE]++ — VERRAZANO~1524
-·°-[CAR]°- — CARTIER~1534
-·-[CH]-·- — CHANCELLOR~1553

M

high forecastle and poop-deck, and were rigged with three masts. Originally
fishing vessels, they had either lateen or fore-and-aft sails which were later
replaced by a square rig. The caravels averaged perhaps fifty or sixty tons,
with a keel of fifty feet, and drew about six feet of water. The *Niña,* a
caravel that sailed with Columbus, had a crew of twenty-four; the *Pinta*
carried a slightly larger number. His flagship, the *Santa María,* was a true
Nao or "ship," derived from the Mediterranean carrack; it may have been
about a hundred tons burthen and carried a crew of forty. Such vessels
were tiny indeed in comparison with modern ocean-going vessels, but they
were reliable craft, capable of great deeds. At the close of the fifteenth
century came changes in sailing methods. Chaucer's shipman of the fourteenth century is described as knowing "every creek in Brittany and in
110

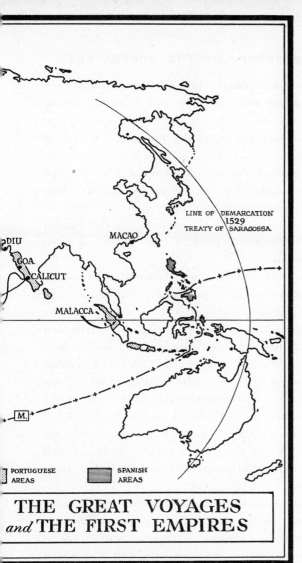

LINE OF DEMARCATION
1529
TREATY OF SARAGOSSA

MACAO

DIU
GOA
CALICUT

MALACCA

M.

PORTUGUESE
AREAS

SPANISH
AREAS

THE GREAT VOYAGES
and THE FIRST EMPIRES

Note how the well-traveled route from Europe to the Canaries provides the start for the great voyages. The areas of Portuguese and Spanish trade stand out clearly, as do the limited areas of French and English explorations. A globe will better show the spatial relationships and the great distances involved.

Spain"—a valid description of the sailor who is never far from shore. In this tradition the navigators of Prince Henry of Portugal had usually hugged the coast of Africa in their southward advance. But the men of the new age were of another type. Columbus was out of sight of land for thirty-three days, navigating westward into the unknown. Vasco da Gama on his epochal voyage to India left the Canaries and did not sight land again for ninety days—an odyssey unsurpassed until Magellan sailed the Pacific for nearly four months without replenishing his provisions. Skill, courage and almost unbelievable endurance were the marks of men such as these.

The sea route to India was established by Portuguese sailors, following in the traditions of the servants of Prince Henry. It is hardly correct to say that the Turkish capture of Constantinople in 1453 meant "cutting" the old trade routes to the Far East. No important spice route ran through Constantinople, and the Turks did not seize the most widely used points of transshipment until as late as 1516 and 1517. An alternative to the Levant route was economically desirable whether or not the Turks were in control of Constantinople. To reach India by sea would mean a reduction in the very heavy costs long associated with the complex land and sea passage, where tolls en route sometimes quadrupled the original price of merchandise. Cheap trading goods, impractical to carry by land, could easily be shipped by sea to the Orient and used there to purchase valuable cargoes for the return voyage. The inducements, therefore, to find an unbroken sea route to the Indies were enormous.

In 1487–1488 Bartholomew Diaz, who had been ordered to follow the African coast until he reached Abyssinia, the supposed home of the Christian potentate, Prester John, finally rounded the Cape of Good Hope. Actually only about eight hundred miles of the coast of East Africa now remained unknown, for Arab sailors had pushed far down southward from the Red Sea. At this same time King John II of Portugal sent Pedro de Covilham overland on an eastern mission to find the elusive, and as it turned out mythical, Prester John. Covilham traveled through Egypt to Aden at the mouth of the Red Sea and then went by Arab ship across the Indian Ocean to Calicut on the Malabar Coast of India. On his return he sent letters from Egypt urging John to seek the completion of the voyage around Africa, past the Island of the Moon (Madagascar) and so on to India, saying that the trip would be an easy one.

Then followed the four voyages of Columbus, beginning in 1492 with the great Atlantic crossing which Europe accepted, not as the finding of a new world, but rather as establishing a shorter and less hazardous route to the Far East. Columbus died in this belief, always hoping that his caravels sailing the Caribbean would come someday upon the fabled cities of Cathay. Those who are pleased to detect the element of chance in history will note that Columbus had long sought to make his voyages under the flag of Portugal; that failing this he was ready with overtures to the courts of France and England; and that he was able to secure the patronage and support of Spain at the very last moment by something approaching the mere whim of Queen Isabella. One may justifiably speculate as to what different fortunes the New World might have seen had Columbus sailed under another flag.

Emmanuel the Fortunate succeeded John II in Portugal in 1495 and commissioned Vasco da Gama to follow in the path of Diaz and complete the sea route to India. Da Gama left the Cape Verde Islands with four ships and a complement of 118 men on August 3, 1497. Unlike his predecessors he headed boldly southward in mid-Atlantic and was out of sight of land until November 4, when he touched the African coast about one hundred miles north of the Cape of Good Hope. This voyage covering over five thousand miles was one of the greatest feats in the history of maritime exploration. Da Gama then worked around the tip of Africa and up to Mozambique, whence an Arab pilot took him on the relatively uneventful voyage to Calicut. Here he found himself at the great Indian trading center of the eastern world, where Arab merchants dominated the great flood of oriental commerce. Da Gama returned to Portugal, his two surviving ships laden with pepper, ginger, cinnamon, cloves, nutmeg, rubies and other precious stones. He had sailed 24,000 nautical miles and half his crew were dead. But the profits of the voyage were sixty times its cost. It remained for Portugal to break the Arab trading monopoly in the east and seek to replace it with her own.

By the turn of the century the Great Voyages, as they have come to be known, had opened the sea routes to the East and West Indies. Other voyages added to this knowledge, notably those of Cabral and Vespucci along the coast of South America, of Cabot to Labrador and Newfoundland and the great adventure of Magellan which led to the circumnavigation of the globe. Only at a later date did English and French activity become permanently important. Before this happened, Portuguese and Spanish empires, rich almost beyond belief, had come into existence.

■ PORTUGAL AND SPAIN AS IMPERIAL POWERS

The progress of the Portuguese Empire, imposed at the sword's point, must be briefly sketched. The battles in Asia, it should be noted, were fought not so much against the native populations as against the Mohammedan traders and their allies who had already established themselves throughout the Orient. In 1501 Pedro Alvarez Cabral compelled the native ruler at Calicut to accept a Portuguese trading post. After a fierce war a line of forts and trading establishments was set up all along the Malabar Coast. A wider area of maritime control, however, was needed, and beginning in 1505 the Viceroy, Francisco Almeida, undertook the task of securing a network of bases on both sides of the Arabian Sea. He was succeeded in 1509 by Alfonso da Albuquerque. A naval victory (1509) off Diu on the northwest coast of India destroyed the Moorish fleet and led to the Portuguese seizure of Goa in 1510. Other conquests soon followed. Ormuz on the Persian Gulf, Sokotra at the mouth of the Red Sea and Malacca near the tip of the Malay Peninsula formed a vast strategic triangle within which Goa became the administrative center. Portuguese ships, touching at Ceylon, Sumatra, Java, Borneo and Celebes, quickly went beyond this triangle to the Moluccas, the fabulous spice islands of incomparable wealth. The true architect of this rapidly-won empire was Albuquerque, "the last and greatest Portuguese empire-builder," who died in 1515 leaving unachieved his fantastic dreams of ruining Egyptian commerce by diverting the Nile to the Red Sea or of stealing Mohammed's body from its shrine at Medina.

Portuguese ships first reached Canton in 1516, though Macao later replaced it as the principal center for the China trade. In 1542 Japan also was reached. The long, narrow line of forts and trading posts constituting the Portuguese Empire stretched from the African coasts through India, Ceylon and Siam to the farthest Indies, and flourished for half a century. It was an empire of wealth and exploitation, of trade not settlement, controlled by ruthless force yet rendered less harsh by the great mission of the Jesuit, St. Francis Xavier, who between 1542 and 1552 carried the Christian message from Goa through the Indies as far as Japan.

This empire was highly centralized and subject to the same spirit of autocracy that had developed in Portugal itself. At home the *Casa da Mina* (Guinea House) and the *Casa da India* (India House) directed the African and Indian trade. The viceroy of India at Goa had vast but vague authority. It would seem that the population of Portugal, numbering less than one and a half millions, was clearly not adequate to any program of settlement, had such been desired. Trade thrived at first under royal monopoly, but wealth which poured into the homeland went to selfish rather than to productive uses, and in the end it was foreign rather than Portuguese merchants who benefited. A slowly demoralized Portugal enjoyed for one or two generations an empire which it was unable permanently to maintain at its first spectacular level.

As Portuguese explorers pushed their empire further and further to the east, Spain's destiny became associated with the New World to the west. Columbus' first voyage in 1492 had revealed the islands of the Caribbean. In the three subsequent voyages (1494, 1498, 1502) he rounded out the knowledge of this area and traced the mainland coast from Honduras to Venezuela, still never doubting that he had reached the Indies. After Columbus' first voyage the possibility of conflict between Spain and Portugal became real, with the result that in 1493 the pope issued a bull assigning to Spain all newly found lands beyond a north-south line one hundred leagues west of the Azores. This was unsatisfactory to the Portuguese, who by direct negotiation with Spain secured in 1494 the famous Treaty of Tordesillas which moved the line two hundred and seventy leagues further west. As a line of demarcation was later applied also to the Pacific, there came about the rough division of the entire overseas world into Portuguese and Spanish areas of exploitation.[3]

3. But in 1500 the Portuguese, Cabral, planning to follow the South Atlantic route of Da Gama to India, came in sight of the coast of Brazil. This land, as it turned out, lay

Of the numerous voyages which followed those of Columbus, two are most worthy of notice. Amerigo Vespucci in 1499 and 1501 skirted the greater part of the Atlantic coast of South America, and, thanks to the aid of a German geographer and map-maker, Martin Waldseemüller, gave the New World its name. Another explorer, Balboa, led an expedition in 1513 from a Spanish settlement at Darien across the Isthmus of Panama and saw for the first time the Pacific Ocean, whereupon the geographic pattern of the New World took definite shape.

Settlement followed very closely on the heels of exploration, for the backing which Ferdinand and Isabella had given to Columbus was inspired by the hopes of the great wealth to be derived from permanently established centers of trade. On his second voyage Columbus brought 1,500 laborers, soldiers and priests for the colonies of Isabela and Santo Domingo which he planted on the Island of Hispaniola (now Haiti). Santo Domingo so became the first permanent site of European settlement in the New World. No great wealth was secured from the Spanish posts scattered through the Caribbean, so that Columbus died with his original hopes bitterly disappointed.

The great change in Spanish fortunes came with an expedition sent in 1519 from Cuba, under the direction of Hernando Cortes, for the conquest of Mexico. This tiny expedition of six hundred infantrymen and sixteen cavalrymen, armed with a few cannon and aided by native auxiliaries, revealed an Aztec kingdom of fabulous wealth and with a level of civilization far above that of the naked savages of Cuba and Hispaniola. By 1521 Montezuma's golden kingdom had fallen to the Spanish *conquistadores,* and in 1522 the first large shipment of treasure reached Spain. A new age had begun.

A decade later (1532) Francisco Pizarro launched even smaller Spanish forces against the great Inca empire of Peru, marched to the capital city of Cuzco in the Andes, and brought this equally rich and fabulous land under the Spanish heel. A new capital was established in 1535 at Lima, and gradually Spanish control spread from Peru into what are now Ecuador, Bolivia, Northern Chile, Paraguay and the northwestern parts of Argentina. The last of the Andean territories, Colombia, came under Spanish rule in 1538. It may be noted that this Spanish conquest was aided significantly by South-German capitalists. The Fugger family of Augsburg supplied funds and founded settlements in Peru. Another German banking family, the Welsers, established a colony at Coro in Venezuela and started copper mines in Santo Domingo. German capital was sent in substantial amounts to Spain itself. Thus, although Germany was in no position to become an overseas power

---

east of the line set up by the Treaty of Tordesillas and thus gave Portugal her one great colony in the western hemisphere.

like Portugal or Spain, it played some part in the opening of the New World.

As Spanish authority thus radiated from the original Caribbean bases into both North and South America, a new move was made by a Portuguese sea-captain in the employ of Spain who sailed from Seville in 1519, hoping to reach the Indies by rounding what was now clearly defined as South America. Ferdinand Magellan discovered and passed through the dangerous straits named after him, and sailed for ninety-eight days with appalling suffering across the Pacific. The crew ate the ox-hides that covered the top of the mainyard and sold rats for half a ducat apiece. In the Philippines, which he claimed for Spain, he was killed in a skirmish with the natives, but his crews went on to the Spice Islands, finding them already in Portuguese possession. Only one ship, the *Victoria,* eventually returned home in 1522 carrying eighteen European and four Asiatic survivors of an epic voyage which, within a generation of Columbus' great venture into the west, finally corrected the geographical misconceptions for which he was in some measure responsible.

The Spanish empire in the New World lay under the control of the Council of the Indies, one of the several bodies through which the Spanish kings exercized their authority. Royal officials were sent from Spain to govern what were eventually the two great viceroyalties: New Spain (including Mexico, the West Indies, Central America and what is now Venezuela) and Peru (covering all Spain's remaining possessions in South America). The viceroy was checked by the *Audiencia,* a combined governor's council and supreme court that made reports to the home government. There was also in Spain the *Casa de Contratación,* a kind of board of trade, court and clearing house which regulated the economic life of the colonies. The commercial importance of this new colonial world must be left for later discussion. But its general development went far beyond that of the Portuguese. It has been estimated that by 1575 there were about two hundred Spanish towns and some 175,000 Spanish settlers in America. The University at Lima was founded in 1551 and the University of Mexico City two years later. The first printing press in the New World was set up at Mexico City in 1539.

England and France played a much less impressive part in the first stages of this exploring activity. Something of the same royal interest, to be sure, existed, carrying with it an understandable desire to profit by the anticipated wealth of the new lands. But action was all on a much smaller scale. Francis I of France sent out Verrazano in 1524 to seek, if possible, a northwest passage to the Indies. In 1534 Jacques Cartier reached the mouth of the St. Lawrence and in the following year sailed up it as far as the present

Quebec and Montreal. The Lachine ("China") Rapids, near Montreal, still testify to Cartier's hope that he was nearing the Orient. No permanent French settlements were made, however, until Port Royal in Acadia was founded in 1604 and Quebec in 1608.

England likewise lagged behind. Bristol merchants had a long but unsuccessful interest in finding the islands of the Atlantic. Bartholomew Columbus is said to have approached Henry VII shortly before his brother succeeded in winning the support of Spain for the great westward voyages. The first positive English step was taken in 1497 when the Italian John Cabot sailed from Bristol with a commission to seek out unknown lands. He evidently skirted the Labrador-Newfoundland area, which he revisited in 1498. The main result of his voyages seems to have been the encouragement which it gave to the European fishing fleets to make their annual trips to the banks off Newfoundland. The interest in a northwest passage persisted, and in the sixteenth and seventeenth centuries sailors such as Frobisher, Davis, Hudson and Baffin boldly steered into the perilous waters still marked by their names. Nevertheless, the passage itself remained unachieved.

Other efforts were made to find the elusive passage to the Orient by sailing to the northeast, around the tip of Norway. An expedition headed by Willoughby and Chancellor left England for this purpose in 1553. Willoughby and his crew were lost, but Chancellor succeeded in reaching the White Sea whence he went overland to Moscow. From this journey a trade connection between England and Muscovy eventually developed. Other voyages were made, the most notable being that of an official of the Muscovy Company, Anthony Jenkinson, who sailed to the White Sea in 1557 and then went overland to Moscow and down the Volga to the Caspian. Jenkinson traveled with a caravan of a thousand camels into central Asia, reached the famous trading center of Bokhara and brought back to Ivan the Terrible in Moscow the gift of a yak's tail. These and other exploits of high adventure produced no quick results remotely comparable to the splendid empires that had been set up by Spain and Portugal. It would have been hard for the two powers which had so complacently divided the overseas world between themselves by the Treaty of Tordesillas to foresee that in the end they would be far outshadowed by their belated rivals.

Enormous consequences flowed from this first age of exploration and discovery. The oceans had been mastered by intrepid seamen to whom, nevertheless, hardships were ever present. Not until the eighteenth century, for example, was a defense found against the terrible ravages of scurvy. But as geographical knowledge widened, the nameless dread of the unknown gradually disappeared. If one takes the famous Behaim globe of 1492, with its highly inaccurate calculation of distances and its omission of the western hemisphere, and compares it with the Waldseemüller map of 1507 which gives at least some indication of the Atlantic coasts of North and South America, one may see the beginning of an accurate geographic perspective. Schoner's globe of 1523 was sufficiently informed to show Magellan's route around the world.

Modern scientific geography began to take shape in the work of men such as Sebastian Münster and Gerhard Mercator. The former's *Cosmographia* (1544), a geographical compilation dealing with human and political geography on a regional basis, devoted one of its five parts to the new discoveries. It remained standard for nearly a century, during which time it went through forty-six editions and appeared in six languages. Mercator was a Flemish scholar who developed a method first used by Spanish geographers for projecting segments of the curved surface of the globe upon maps. He applied this "Mercator's projection" to a world map which he originally produced in 1538 and greatly improved in later editions. Despite its great distortion of polar areas the method was correct for short distances and gave true directions, so it has continued to have value down to our own day. By the close of the sixteenth century, then, a fair knowledge of the main patterns of global geography, with the exception of Australia, the Antarctic regions, and the northern land rim of the Pacific Ocean, had been obtained. Scholars began to collect the original narratives made by the explorers; one of the most famous of these collections being the *English Voyages* of Richard Hakluyt which he published in three volumes between 1588 and 1600. There were many others.

In addition to these advances in knowledge one can only note the profound changes beginning to affect the general tenor of European life. In a political sense the European states were becoming the masters of new and distant realms; they were enlarging the sphere of their rivalries and finding new occasions for war. At the same time certain European states such as Spain and later England were gaining wealth from overseas which enabled them to bring greater economic and military strength into the pursuit of their European ambitions. The intellectual, social and general economic consequences were likewise enormous. The next problem, therefore, is to see in what ways the age of exploration and overseas settlement was associated with important changes in the economic patterns of European life.

■ THE IMPACT OF THE OVERSEAS WORLD UPON EUROPE

The revolution of outlook brought about by the Great Voyages was so vast and the ultimate consequences so profound that there is some danger of overstressing the causal connection between the process of overseas expansion and the economic changes actually occurring in sixteenth-century Europe. These economic changes were real and substantial, so much so that the phrase, "Commercial Revolution," has been applied to them; and they were related, of course, to developments overseas. It is also true, however, that a process of economic evolution was at work in Europe itself, independent of the explorations and anterior to them. In the economic field, as in so many others, medieval antecedents may be discovered for some of the most significant trends of the new age.

In its own way, as we have seen, medieval economic life had possessed unmistakable vigor. Manufacture, to be sure, was limited in scope and was intended basically for a local market. Trade was conducted largely on an inter-urban basis. Goods moved along certain well-defined land routes, the geographical significance of which has been previously suggested.[4] Water transport followed the rivers, hugged the seacoast or ventured as far only as the confines of the Mediterranean, the Black, the Baltic and the North seas. Throughout the area thus covered there was a substantial exchange of basic commodities such as wool, textiles, grain, wines, fish, lumber, furs and hides. By a process of frequent transshipment various luxury goods came into Europe over the long routes from Asia.

Medieval capitalism, even if we choose to describe it as "petty," certainly existed. Fortunes were made, money was "risked" in commercial ventures, banking techniques were developed and, despite considerable disapproval from the Church, lending at interest was widely practiced. Certain medieval industries such as the production of textiles in Italy and Flanders, or of wool in England, and the highly organized shipbuilding industry at Venice reflected a fairly elaborate type of capitalistic enterprise. On the whole, however, it would be proper to stress the intra-European rather than the extra-European character of business life and to recognize the local rather than the national character of the regulation that was imposed upon it.

The first significance of the Great Voyages was to open the sea routes to the Indies, East and West. Direct oceanic contact was now made with the traditional wealth of the Orient, and a hitherto unknown Western Hemisphere of apparently limitless economic possibilities was revealed. The immediate advantage fell, of course, to those countries most favorably situated with respect to the new sea routes—in the first instance Portugal and Spain, and later France, England and the Netherlands. The disadvantage fell to such trading centers as Venice and Genoa which were tied most closely to the medieval trade routes. Oceanic commerce meant a spectacular reduction in the costs of transport. It has been calculated that oriental goods coming to medieval Europe overland had their price multiplied at least fourfold

4. See pp. 10–12.

en route. Much of this cost, as we have previously seen, could now be avoided.

The Italian cities were not the only ones to feel the adverse effects of the new direction of trade. South German towns such as Augsburg, which lay in a key position for the distribution of goods sent to them from Italy, found themselves in a changing world. The growing centers of trade were along the Atlantic fringe—at first Lisbon and Cadiz, later such ports as La Rochelle, Nantes, Bristol, London, Amsterdam and, above all, Antwerp, situated at the mouth of the Scheldt and the gateway to a very rich hinter-land. In 1532 the famous Flanders galleys of Venice made their last voyage to the Channel. The new patterns of commerce had rendered them obsolete.

An obvious result of the growing trade with the Indies was the larger number of commodities available to a considerable segment of the European population. Ultimately such products as tea and coffee, unknown to the medieval world, came to be staples of diet. Sugar-cane from Africa was taken to the West Indies and thus sugar, hitherto little used outside the Moslem world, became one of the great exports to Europe. Of the five great native products of the Western Hemisphere—tobacco, potatoes, chocolate, cotton, and Indian corn—the first three were quickly added to the list of Europe's basic requirements. African slaves, of little direct economic importance in Europe, came to be widely used in the plantations of the New World, and traffic in them served as another rapid means to wealth. The Orient fur-nished Europe with spices, drugs, cottons, silks, gold, ivory, rare woods, jewels, tea, coffee, new breeds of horses, new poultry and plants. Such items as luxurious fabrics and oriental rugs became part of what has been de-scribed as a new and magnificent "consumers' civilization."

The immediate gains from this commerce were at first confined to rela-tively limited circles, and it may be doubted whether a substantial part of the population benefited immediately in any significant way. But for those who were favorably situated the profits were enormous. The number of Portuguese ships engaged in the India trade between 1497 and 1612 has been given as 806. Of these 96 were lost. But from a two-year voyage which might cost (including the value of the ship) some $20,000 in modern money a return of $750,000 was not impossible. The reward went to the merchants who "adventured" on such enterprises and to the monarchs who gave authorization to them. The king of Portugal, for example, levied taxes of from 30 to 60 per cent upon the spices that were sold upon the European market. By a decree of 1504 the *quinto,* or royal fifth, was to be taken by the Spanish crown on all treasure found or mined in the Indies. With some occasional modifications this remained the law until the eighteenth century. It can readily be seen, therefore, that at least some part of the explanation for Spain's vigorously aggressive European policies lies in the new wealth which made such ventures possible.

Capitalism itself underwent a process of change and evolution. The term "petty capitalism" does not do full justice to the elaborate developments of the medieval period, but it is certainly true that by the sixteenth century capitalism broadened its scope as the greater availability of money, the flood of new commodities and the new spirit of enterprise led to the creation of large new areas for capitalistic investment. Not all of this new financial activity necessarily received its stimulus from overseas. The vigorous mining activities in Bohemia, the Tyrol, Transylvania and Hungary owed much to the steady development of European mining and engineering techniques, and resulted in the production of substantial quantities of gold, silver and copper.[5] The great fortunes acquired by the famous Fugger family of Augsburg came in part from textiles, but in substantial part also from an investment in the silver mines of the Tyrol and the copper mines of Hungary.

New industries, sometimes with royal sponsorship and assistance, made impressive headway. Such was the silk industry of France. Book publishing was another development requiring substantial amounts of capital and elaborate technical organization. This industry soon assumed very large proportions and distributed its products very widely in Europe. Still another was the casting of cannon and the manufacture of firearms. The prosperous manufacturer, not yet so important as the great merchant, is nevertheless a new and interesting type. An example is John Winchcombe—"Jack of Newbury"—a clothier who is said to have entertained Henry VIII and his court, to have marched to the battle of Flodden Field at the head of a hundred of his own men and to have maintained under one roof two hundred handlooms for the weaving of cloth. Associated with this business growth one may note the development of new bookkeeping methods. In 1494 an Italian, Luca Pacioli, published a general treatise on mathematics, *Summa de Arithmetica,* including a section on double-entry bookkeeping which is the starting point of modern accounting methods.

The profession of banking likewise developed. Italy had seen the rise of the great banking families—the Medici at Florence, the Chigi at Rome, the Strozzi, the Bardi and many others. North of the Alps equally famous banking families arose, notably the Fuggers, the Welsers, the Hochstetters and the Imhoffs. Usually making their start in some venture such as textiles, mining or the spice trade, these concerns gradually assumed duties that we would regard as more specifically financial. As Antwerp developed into the

---

5. George Agricola's *De Re Metallica* (1556) is a classic work on the subject of mining and smelting. It could be compared in its own way with the treatise of Copernicus on astronomy or of Vesalius on anatomy.

great European money market with its stock exchange, or *bourse,* the banking houses flourished. Over the entrance of the Antwerp *bourse* was the inscription, "For the use of the merchants of all nations and tongues." To exploit the spice trade large supplies of credit were needed. European bankers provided funds for overseas ventures, handled credit transactions and foreign exchange, developed techniques of insurance, made possible various kinds of speculation and provided large loans to public figures for political purposes. The Fuggers, for example, lent huge sums to the Emperor Maximilian in order to further some of his marriage plans; they furnished money to Albert of Hohenzollern when he maneuvered to become Archbishop of Mainz; and they heavily subsidized the future Charles V when he bribed his way to the Holy Roman emperorship. Jacob Fugger, it has been recounted, "died in the odor of sanctity, a good Catholic and a Count of the Empire, having seen his firm pay 54 per cent for the preceding sixteen years."[6]

Some degree of agricultural specialization was called forth by the greater specialization of town life. Business men were acquiring a money surplus some of which could be invested in land. One of the most important examples of such investment was the conversion of former arable land to pasture for the very profitable raising of sheep. The extent of this should not be exaggerated; even in England, where the "enclosure" of the old commons so as to create a pattern of hedged-in, private fields and to deprive the villagers of their former pasturage, has often been singled out as a revolutionary phenomenon, it can be shown that only a very small proportion, perhaps three per cent of the arable land, was affected. In Spain the ancient association of wealthy sheep raisers known as the *Mesta* was able to secure important privileges from the crown which gave the association widespread pasturing rights and turned large areas of crown and church lands from cultivation to grazing. This was to the immediate advantage of the sheep raisers, but in the long run worked great damage to the Spanish economy as a whole. Various parts of Europe saw some drift of rural population to the growing urban centers; in England, for example, the disturbance in farming areas caused considerable unrest. The sharp rise in prices, too, was responsible for genuine hardship, so that peasant risings came to play their part in both the political and the religious developments of the sixteenth century.

One of the most significant phenomena of the times was a rapid price rise in Western Europe. This was due in part, but not altogether, to the large inflow of bullion from the New World. It would seem that Europe's supply of precious metals had actually diminished down to 1450, in consequence,

6. R. H. TAWNEY, *Religion and the Rise of Capitalism* (1938), p. 84.

perhaps, of the failure of new production to keep up with the outgo of gold and silver used in purchasing luxury goods from the East. Thenceforth, however, new supplies of precious metal came in, partly from the African trade and partly from the scientifically exploited mines of central Europe. The first important quantities of American gold arrived in 1503; Mexican treasure was first seized by Cortes in 1519, and that of Peru in 1534. An enormously rich silver deposit was discovered in Mexico in 1545, and about the same time the wealth of the fabulous silver mines of Potosi, in Peru, was first exploited. Throughout the sixteenth century, then, this flow of treasure continued, with the result that the European gold and silver supply has been estimated to have increased fivefold between 1500 and 1600. Most of the bullion shipped from the New World to Spain quickly left its original destination and found its way into the strong boxes of bankers and merchants in Italy and northern Europe. Studies show that the general price level in Spain around 1600 was more than three times what it had been in 1500; in France the corresponding figure came to roughly twice, and in England, two and one-half times. As wages did not go up as fast as prices, the immediate consequences to large groups of the population were very unfortunate. It has been calculated that the average real income in Western Europe, that is to say, income calculated in terms of what money would buy, fell rather than rose between 1450 and 1650.

The growing interference of government in economic matters was an outstanding phenomenon of the times. In a sense this was nothing new, for medieval economic life had been subject to elaborate regulation. But regulation had been largely upon a local basis, whereas the new aspect of the sixteenth century was the growth of regulation and control on a *national* scale. Many illustrations can be given. Royal governments sponsored and subsidized the Great Voyages and authorized the planting of their flags in new lands and over alien peoples. Royal agencies such as the Portuguese *Casa da India* were devised to control the new commerce and to ensure royal participation in the profits. Governments granted trade licenses, chartered companies and regulated colonization. The Muscovy Company, established by English merchants in 1555 for trade with Russia, represents the first of many such companies. Royal governments sought, with great difficulty and often unavailingly, to establish a truly national coinage that would supersede the medley of local currencies and avoid the dangers of debasement. Governments issued innumerable regulations to cope with the problem of rising prices and fluctuations in standards and quality. The sixteenth century is studded with royal edicts concerning these matters. Queen Elizabeth's great Statute of Artificers (1563) substituted for local control an elaborate machinery intended to deal with wages and conditions of employment for the country as a whole. Other regulations sought to protect native industries against competition from outside sources: an Elizabethan statute, for instance, forbade the importation of knives, daggers, and swords that would compete with articles of home manufacture. This policy of *mercantilism,* or the fostering of the commercial interest of a country through direct governmental intervention, began to take shape in the sixteenth century and, with increasing complexity, became a standard pattern in the seventeenth.

The rapid rise of these national economic interests raised many problems. It led inevitably to armed conflicts. The running fights which English adventurers carried on across the Spanish Main with the merchant vessels and treasure ships of the Hapsburgs were little removed from piracy. Smuggling became a highly organized and highly profitable occupation. Later on, as commercial wars of a new type and scale were fought—usually for enormous stakes—it became necessary to create sea-power and build up armies of a new type, for the old feudal contingents were totally inadequate to the new demands. The ancient devices of borrowing funds, of imposing arbitrary levies or of crudely debasing the coinage failed to provide monarchs with the sums they needed. New sources of revenue were required, and it became the business of governments to find them. In this search important questions were raised: Who should be taxed? By whose authority? On what basis? What accounting must a king give of his expenditures? What are the property rights of subjects against him? It can be seen, then, that some of the most important constitutional questions of the sixteenth and seventeenth centuries are implicit in these new economic developments.

▪ PATTERNS OF SOCIAL CHANGE

The complex structure of European society gave evidence in the sixteenth century of significant changes. Some countries were more deeply affected than others; some were slow to feel the effect of forces actively at work elsewhere. A simple summary is bound, therefore, to be inexact; it may, nevertheless, shed some light on the changing times and illustrate the interrelationships between economics, politics and culture.

Basically, it may be ventured, one can speak of a new dynamism in European life. The old, orderly pattern of the medieval world in which everyone was presumed to have an appointed task—the serf in his field, the craftsman at his bench, the merchant in his counting-house, the monk in his cloister— was giving place to a new Europe where life was lived on a broader and freer scale. With larger horizons and new wealth it is understandable that men should have developed the habit of turning their hands to new enterprises and of venturing into new paths.

Such changes do not come about overnight. The medieval gild, as one illustration, had been a unit of production and also a unit of society well suited to a small-scale urban economy. It gave in its way impressive strength to the economic life of the Middle Ages. But as economic and political conditions changed, the gild system showed signs of being outdated. Like many institutions, however, it had a survival value which permitted it to continue long after its original usefulness had declined. This "cultural lag" affords a good example of the dangers of sweeping generalization. New business forms took away from the gilds a great deal of their old importance, yet in France, for example, the gilds contrived to cling to many of their ancient privileges to the close of the eighteenth century.

One would not expect, and one does not find, a dramatic transformation of the agrarian class. The increasing vigor and dynamism of the urban economy was paralleled by some changes in the agricultural pattern, though these were not spectacular in nature. Serfdom in Western Europe was clearly going; the steady commutation of personal services into money payments meant that the peasant was no longer bound hand and foot to his landlord. But he was still a tenant rather than a free proprietor, and many objectionable obligations and forms of payment remained. East of the Elbe River, indeed, the great landlords were able to maintain and even to increase the extent of agrarian servitude.

The European population was still overwhelmingly rural, but some signs could be detected in Western Europe of a shift to the towns. The slow beginnings of a process were at work which by the twentieth century was to result in the preponderance of urban over rural population in important parts of the continent. The new age meant a certain diminution in the power and prestige of the old landed aristocracy. The decline, of course, was relative and it remained true, for example, that the "country gentry" contrived to dominate English political life well into the nineteenth century. East of the Elbe River, as we have noted, the landholding class actually grew in power, so that a great Polish, Hungarian, or Russian nobleman of the eighteenth century actually exercised control over his tenantry and lived in a state that few medieval landlords could have approached. Yet the main generalization holds: a new class was on the way to winning economic and ultimately political power. In Western Europe the impoverished nobleman well endowed with marriageable daughters became a stock figure of literature and the stage as he was, no doubt, in real life.

The New Monarchies clearly owe much to changing economic conditions. In many cases rulers were able to end or transform the old feudal relationships, to enlarge their wealth and to make profitable bargains with towns or even with individual representatives of the new commercial class. It became the responsibility, if not the privilege, of the monarchy to regulate the national economy and defend it by force of arms. The tendency towards "strong" government in the sixteenth century must be explained by a variety of reasons; one of them, clearly, was this need for a firm hand when states were in increasingly bitter conflict.

A corollary to the decline of the old landed class would be the growth of a new merchant aristocracy whose members often rose from modest beginnings. Their first fortunes usually came from some specific occupation such as weaving or mining. From this, as in the case of the Medici or the Fuggers, it was an easy transition to commercial transactions and to banking. The Atlantic seaports and the new inland commercial centers became the homes of substantial merchant capitalists. The owners of new fortunes might arrange marriages with ancient families, or they might secure noble titles of their own: the Fuggers were Counts of the Empire; the Medici became Grand Dukes of Tuscany. Under Henry VIII and Queen Elizabeth in England a new Tudor nobility developed, luxuriantly endowed with confiscated monastic lands and, naturally enough, the loyal servants of the monarchy. A new type of civil servant drawn from this aristocracy came into prominence. Such were the Cecils, the Walsinghams and the Burghleys. Perhaps, as it has been argued, great bankers like the Fuggers did not exercise so much behind-the-scenes power as they might have done; but influential they undoubtedly were. In various ways the rulers recognized this; even so exalted a monarch as Louis XIV of France later found it expedient to make use of advisers and subordinates drawn from the prosperous bourgeoisie. Such men exercised a wide influence in many ways. They were patrons of the arts, building splendid estates for themselves, founding grammar schools for their children and endowing colleges where their sons could be trained as gentlemen. The merchant aristocracy of the City of London, holding splendid banquets, electing their Lord Mayors and diverting parts of their substantial fortunes to works of charity and civic beneficence, are typical of the new age.

As a part of this new middle class appears the figure later to be called the entrepreneur—the venturesome individual who is out to make a profit by engaging in trade or money transactions or who is quick to attempt some new organization of manufacture. Such a man, for example, would buy up a supply of wool and then "put out" this wool to be carded and spun; or he might distribute yarn to a number of hand-loom weavers and later collect and market the cloth which they made. A business man of this type pays cash for the manual labor which he requires; he takes risks; he finds a market for his goods; and he makes, or hopes to make, a profit. Although this "putting-out system" was certainly not unknown in the Middle Ages, it became widespread only at a later period; it flourished in Western Europe until largely superseded by the new and more complex factory pattern of the nineteenth century. As a social phenomenon the putting-out system is important in that it substituted for the older personal relationships of the gild era something which can be called the "cash nexus"; in other words, the link between this new figure and the laborer is entirely monetary, expressed in terms of the wage paid for the piece-work which has been done. It is a stage in the creation of what came to be known as the industrial proletariat.

The changing economic pattern meant the development of new skills and the rise of new occupations. To stress these is certainly not to undervalue the abilities of the medieval craftsmen whose work, both technically and artistically, was often of a high order. The advancing times, however, saw new occupations: watchmaking, lens grinding, making of nautical and scientific instruments, map making, improved pottery, cannon founding, paper making, printing, engraving, bookbinding, type casting and scores of others. New machines, such as the lathe for wood and metal working, were developed. As some medieval occupations, such as those of the illuminators and copyists, declined, others took their places.

The lower classes were subject to stresses and strains inevitable at a time of complex social change. The decline of serfdom and the growth of a money economy did not always and everywhere mean an immediate advantage to the peasantry. There was considerable human dislocation, misery and unrest. The "sturdy beggars" of Tudor England were usually dispossessed village tenants who roamed the countryside and created constant problems for the authorities. The "cash nexus" could mean ruthless exploitation by the new masters. The severe rise in prices hit the lower classes hard; consequently there were sporadic risings in various parts of Europe by peasants who could hardly be aware of the full significance of the changes that were at work. In eastern Europe the decline in the status of the peasant class was genuine and severe. In the cities there was also unrest, and with it the growth of what can properly be called an unskilled proletariat. The rise of the prosperous middle class meant in some cases that the simple town artisan lost political rights which he had held at an earlier period. Against such considerations must be put the improvements in housing, furniture, clothing and more generally in the comforts and refinements of urban "civilization." Still intolerably crude by our standards, the life of the working classes in the sixteenth century would, on balance, seem to show substantial advances over what it had been in the Middle Ages.

Some historians have made considerable point of the fresh outlook which came to be associated with these economic and social changes. It has been pointed out, for example, that the medieval Church had given only a cautious and limited approval to the business practices of its times. It had denounced usury, supported the principle of the "just price" in contrast to the methods of unscrupulous business competition and generally minimized the importance of worldly success. It has been argued that the Protestant leaders, Calvin in particular, were much more ready than were Catholics to extol the virtues of a business, capitalistic society. Every man should take pride in his vocation, or "calling." By urging his followers to "thrift, industry and sobriety" Calvin is said to have formulated what has been called the "Protestant ethic." It may well be, as we shall see later, that there were certain aspects of Protestant thought that were more readily adaptable to the new commercial age than were some of the traditional Catholic teachings, but it is dangerous to push the generalization too far. The Roman Catholic Church, too, proved able to maintain itself and its doctrines in a world where secular and business interests grew apace.

The wider horizons of the new age of exploration and commerce unquestionably affected what may be called the horizons of European thought. Gradually the peoples of the old world became aware of the strange civilizations across the seas, whether exemplified by the naked savages of Hispaniola or by the ancient and rich cultures of the Orient. Not only in the books of travels, but also in writers such as Montaigne, Rabelais, Shakespeare, Francis Bacon, the Portugese Camoëns or the Spanish Las Casas it is possible to see the impact of the discoveries and the development of new perspectives.

One illustration of this new outlook may be given. Michel de Montaigne, a gentle skeptic and detached observer of life, published in 1580 a volume of *Essays* giving his varied reflections upon the complex world of men. In the essay which he entitles "Of Cannibals," Montaigne shows a deep interest in stories told him by a sailor "who had lived ten or twelve years in that other world which has been discovered in our time." Montaigne saw no reason to consider this other world as "barbarous," for he was shrewd enough to see that "everyone calls barbarism that which is not his own usage." The picture of a life unspoiled by civilization enchanted him.

> These nations, then, seem to me to be so far barbarous as they have received very little fashioning from human wit, and are still very near to their original simplicity. The laws of Nature govern them still, very little debased with any mixture of ours; but they are in such a state of purity that I am sometimes vexed that the knowledge of them did not come earlier, at a time when there were men better able to judge of them than we are. I am sorry that Lycurgus and Plato did not know them; for it seems to me that what we now actually

see in those nations does not only surpass all the pictures with which the poets have adorned the golden age and all their inventions in feigning a happy state of man, but even the conceptions and the very desire of philosophy. They could not imagine so pure and simple an innocence as we by experience see to be in them, nor could they have believed that human society could be maintained with so little artifice and human cementing. This is a nation, I should say to Plato, wherein there is no manner of traffic, no knowledge of letters, no science of numbers, no name of magistrate or political superiority, no use of service, no riches or poverty, no contracts, no successions, no partitions of property, no employments but those of leisure, no respect of kinship save the common ties, no clothing, no agriculture, no metal, no use of corn or wine. The very words that signify lying, treachery, dissimulation, avarice, envy, detraction, pardon, never heard of.

The lyric contrast between the noble savage in the state of nature and the unhappy member of civilized society was later to become one of the commonplaces of European literature; in the sixteenth century it had at least something of the novelty of the discoveries themselves. Nor was the question, as in the case of Montaigne, always one for idle speculation. With the first small beginnings of migration and settlement the possibility arose that people might create for themselves a new life overseas if the old life should prove unendurable. Such matters are not capable of precise demonstration, but it might be suggested that here we have the beginnings of a historical process which could be called one of the great liberating forces of modern times.

   Montaigne's cordial interest in "that other world" beyond the seas was that of a comfortable recluse to whom the problems and worries of public life meant little. Even so, his interest and sympathy suggest something of the ferment at work in a changing society. It has been a commonplace to single out the Rediscovery of Antiquity as one of the chief intellectual contributions to the transition from medieval to modern times. The evidence of this chapter would suggest that the transition was likewise influenced by the dramatic discovery of the vast world in which men actually lived. In the case of men such as Montaigne and Sir Thomas More it would seem that the fascination of the antique world and the spell of the new maritime discoveries were about equally combined. The pages of More's *Utopia* were inspired in part by Plato's ancient vision of an ideal republic, in part also, we may believe, by the rumor, stimulated by the voyages of discovery, of some mysterious island paradise safely lying at the stormy confines of the Western Ocean.

Chapter 6

The Culmination
of the Renaissance (1)

■ ART AND LETTERS IN ITALY

AMID THE POLITICAL and economic changes of the sixteenth century, Renaissance culture became richer and more complex. A notable shift occurred in the great centers of activity. Florence, so long the focus of Italy's artistic life but now torn by civil strife, began to surrender its primacy to Rome, where popes such as Julius II, Leo X and Clement VII aspired to the dominant positions as patrons once held by the Medici dukes. Venice began to rival Rome as a magnificent home of the arts. North of the Alps, too, an intellectual and artistic ferment was at work. This "High Renaissance" represented a fully matured culture, endowed in some of its manifestations with regal splendor.

Rome saw a heightened appreciation of the great works of antiquity. Not only were there imposing ruins on every side, but sculptures such as the Belvedere Apollo were actually unearthed from the soil where for so long they had lain. The achievements of this climactic age were on the grand scale: one thinks of the stupendous plans for rebuilding St. Peter's, of the monumental frescoes of Michelangelo, of the vast panoramic canvases of Veronese. One remembers Titian painting until his hundredth year or, in contrast, Giorgione whose meteoric brilliance ended at the age of thirty-two. The period saw a rich cross-fertilization of culture between Italy and the northern lands. Yet the creative power of the age could hardly be maintained; men of a lesser breed followed Michelangelo and Titian. These later figures, still under the spell of their predecessors, showed something of the earlier brilliance. They tended however, to decline later in the century into an elaborate formalism and an extravagance of style to which the term "Mannerism" has been applied.

Architecture showed no revolutionary developments. The main trend was towards a certain monumental quality. Julius II planned to surround the huge tomb which he intended for himself with a new edifice; to this end the ancient basilica of St. Peter's which in part went back to the age of Constantine the Great was ruthlessly destroyed. Bramante drew up the first plans for a church which was to be in the form of a Greek cross surmounted by an enormous dome, but he lived to see only the preliminary work undertaken. Other architects, including Raphael, continued the planning and supervision until in 1546 the seventy-two-year-old Michelangelo was called in. The dome, redesigned under the inspiration of his unique genius, would have produced a magnificent effect had not the view later been obscured by lengthening the nave and adding a mediocre façade. The huge colonnade in St. Peter's square, designed by Bernini in the seventeenth century, added still further complexity to the original plan.[1]

Outside Rome the work of Andrea Palladio (1518–1580) at Vicenza had a wide influence. His various public buildings were stamped with the classical perfection of the "Palladian" style, having a type of window opening that much later became a common feature of the Georgian architecture of England and America. Palladio, deeply influenced by the work of Vitruvius and Alberti, published in 1570 his *Four Books on Architecture* with woodcuts attempting to reproduce the lost illustrations from Vitruvius. This book in its turn had a profound influence upon subsequent architectural developments. One should also notice the work of Jacopo Sansovino (1477–1570) at Venice. Among his many buildings the great library of St. Mark's may be taken as a superb example of the way in which elements of classical tradition could be newly adapted to the ornate pattern of Venetian life.

The danger that architectural style would degenerate altogether into an academic formalism was averted later in the century by what has been called an "escape into the new and dangerous freedom of the Baroque." This style, with its flowing lines, its sumptuousness of detail and its suggestion of deep emotionalism, owes much to the rich genius and powerful influence of Michelangelo. At times tending to be florid, over-ornate and

1. "So the eternal city is crowned not by a symbol of Renaissance worldliness, as Julius II had visualized it, but by an overwhelming synthesis of Mannerism and Baroque, and at the same time of Antiquity and Christianity." N. PEVSNER, *An Outline of European Architecture* (1951), p. 159.

bombastic, the Baroque style had an element of swagger and a spirit of self-dramatization which conveyed a feeling of genuine vitality. First employed in churches and palaces, the style was applied to colonnades, fountains, formal gardens and carefully designed vistas, reaching its full development in the seventeenth century.

In the sculpture of the Italian High Renaissance the name of Michelangelo (1475–1564) far outdistances all others. His art was partly the product of classical inspiration (he was present when the Laocoön group was dug up in a Roman vineyard), partly a reflection of his close study of nature and partly the outcome of his own profoundly creative genius. Michelangelo lived long and suffered much; his early statue of David is alive with youthful vigor, his exquisite Pietà full of profound delicacy and mournful sensitivity. Michelangelo was commissioned to create in St. Peter's a magnificent tomb for Julius II, but his plans met with frustration and disappointment. We have only his preliminary drawings, his powerful seated statue of Moses and his Bound Slaves, figures which seem to be struggling to free themselves not merely from their bonds, but from the very rock out of which they are carved.

Michelangelo was also commissioned to design the famous Medici tombs in the sacristy of the Church of San Lorenzo in Florence. In this setting the artist completed only two of the four projected parts: the vigorous representation of Giuliano, cousin of Clement VII, as the man of action and the shadowy, brooding figure of Lorenzo of Urbino, nephew of Giuliano, as the man of thought. Even more powerful are the figures of Night and Day on one sarcophagus and of Morning and Evening on the other. In their forms Michelangelo depicted the tragic contrast between superb bodily strength and evident emotional exhaustion—"a withering commentary upon the futility of all human endeavor before the forces of ignorance and evil." [2]

Of an entirely different inspiration is the sculpture of Benvenuto Cellini (1500–1571). This incorrigible rascal, a virtuoso who could rise to any degree of technical skill, had no such depths of emotion as inspired Michelangelo. Yet his Perseus holding the head of Medusa is a statue of great technical brilliance. Cellini, a craftsman and goldsmith as much as a sculptor, could also produce superb minor masterpieces such as the Rospigliosi Cup now in the Metropolitan Museum in New York or the ornate gold and enamel salt-cellar which he designed for Francis I of France.

The painting of the High Renaissance, like its sister arts, was the climax of a long process of development. While Michelangelo can be truly said to have dominated the field of sculpture, he had in such painters as Leonardo da Vinci (1452–1519) and Raphael Sanzio colleagues of genius equal to his

2. DAVID M. ROBB and J. J. GARRISON, *Art in the Western World* (1942), p. 531.

own. Leonardo's Mona Lisa, his Madonna of the Rocks and his Last Supper are among the best known of all paintings, and with reason, for they have that rare quality of being immediately appealing to the novice and at the same time full of profound significance to the connoisseur and specialist. Leonardo shows himself the technical master in all that he does—a master of perspective, of design, of color, of the knowledge of the human body and of nature—but along with his technical mastery he likewise conveys his psychological subtlety, his feeling for the unfathomed mysteries of existence, such as is revealed in the famous "enigmatic" smile on the face of the Mona Lisa or on the face of St. Anne. No one can study the paintings of Leonardo and not feel himself to be in the presence of a unique artist and great man whose interests and capacities were as wide as humanity.

Raphael (1483–1520) has been called "the Mozart of painting"; he has been compared to Phidias in the sure and confident ease of his work and it has been said that he could create nothing but beauty. Technically incomparable, whether in his magnificent portraits, his exquisite Madonnas or in the great frescoes with which he adorned the papal apartments (the *Stanze*) of Julius II, Raphael suggests a golden age of genius from which the mysteries and struggles which possessed a Leonardo or a Michelangelo are absent. The four famous frescoes in the *Camera della Signatura* representing the fields of Christian theology, pagan philosophy, jurisprudence and letters express better, perhaps, than almost any other work of the time the effort to synthesize the two great traditions of the Christian and the classical world. The student may draw from these frescoes endless lessons in color, design, perspective and spatial relationships, but it remains true that Raphael holds his great place in the history of art largely by virtue of the human tenderness which breathes through the classic perfection of his Madonnas. He died at thirty-seven, mourned by the papal court that had stood ready, so it is said, to make him a cardinal.

Versatility seems a totally inadequate word to characterize Michelangelo's work as a painter. Although few of his oil paintings have survived, his great frescoes in the Sistine Chapel suffice to put him among the greatest artists. The decoration of this lofty ceiling, undertaken almost single-handed and completed in about four years, is a feat to be remembered for all time. The work involved making a series of panels, among them the Drunkenness of Noah, the Deluge, the Creation of Adam, and God the Father: these can be taken as an allegorical portrayal of the progress of man from the lowest materialism to the divine, and thus may echo the Platonic concepts of Ficino and Pico della Mirandola. The whole work is enriched with a profuse elaboration of human forms, Sybils, Prophets and nude athletes displaying Michelangelo's powerful plastic and sculptural technique and his almost unbelievable virtuosity in foreshortening. Later Michelangelo finished the decoration of the chapel by painting on the east wall above the altar his huge fresco of the Last Judgment. This magnificent chapel, then, epitomizes the complex nature of Michelangelo's life. If we may call Raphael the Mozart of painting, we may with equal appropriateness compare Michelangelo to Beethoven.

The powerful influence of these men committed their immediate successors to the established patterns and techniques of painting. Inevitably therefore, convention replaced originality, so that the succeeding school which has come to be known as the Mannerists showed little creative ability. To find any continuance of the vitality of the earlier masters we must turn to Venice where in the luxurious atmosphere of the Adriatic city the art of painting reached new brilliance. Here, according to tradition, the use of oils was first borrowed from the Netherlands. Here the two Bellinis, Gentile (1427–1507) and Giovanni (1428–1516), ushered in a new generation of the artists that were to bring even greater fame to the city. Here, too, Giorgione (1477–1511) may be said to have founded that school for which Venice became famous—the tradition of brilliant color, of altar pieces rich in classical allusion, of ornate landscapes, of fleshly beauty and superb portraiture. Of this Venetian school Titian, who died in 1576 in his hundredth year, was the supreme master. He painted a series of incomparable portraits, a number of enchanting landscapes, biblical scenes and superb depictions of pagan myths. Veronese (1528–1588) and Tintoretto (1518–1594) continued this tradition, elaborating their imagery and increasing the size of their canvases until at times they would seem to be creating not simply a picture but a pageant.

Renaissance music in Italy inherited the great medieval tradition of polyphonic composition. This seems to have been particularly reinforced by the migration of a number of Flemish musicians and composers in the fifteenth century. At Venice, especially in the choir attached to St. Mark's, a rich school of contrapuntal music developed under the great master, Andrea Gabrieli. At Rome the musical growth was even more impressive. Here Giovanni Palestrina (1526–1594), a papal organist and choirmaster, raised the older school of pure counterpoint to new heights. He composed masses, motets and some superb religious madrigals. A legend says that he wrote his great Mass of Pope Marcellus in order to convince the authorities at the Council of Trent that polyphonic music could still be devout.

Music, whether religious or secular, was an aspect of the many-sided virtuosity of Italy in this golden age. Instrumental music became more elaborate and more popular. It became one of the marks of the Renaissance gentleman to perform skilfully and gracefully on some instrument such as the lute or viol. The instruments themselves were in process of evolution, so that eventually the violin was to develop out of the earlier viols and the harpsichord out of the virginals. In the year 1600 a Florentine composer, Jacopo Peri, was commissioned to write a musical drama on the occasion of the marriage of Henry IV of France to Marie de' Medici. The result was the performance of "Eurydice," a landmark in the history of the opera, for in this revival of a Greek tragic theme the soloists were permitted to declaim their parts and the musical accompaniment was made subordinate to the sense of the words. A new musical form was in the making.

The literature of the High Renaissance carried on many of the interests associated with the earlier period of humanistic culture. Scholarship, for example, was highly prized. The development of printing and the growth of humanism north of the Alps caused ideas to interchange with a new vigor. One of the best examples is found in the work of Pietro Bembo (1470–1547), a papal secretary at the court of Leo X. He was a famous Latinist, the master of a pure Ciceronian style and yet at the same time a lover of the vernacular as Petrarch had written it, and himself the author of a work, *Della Volgar Lingua,* extolling the use of the Tuscan dialect. Bembo moved in many courtly circles, corresponded gracefully and widely and left behind an elegant library.

Other writers turned their attention to history. Machiavelli (1469–1527) wrote a *History of Florence* in the vernacular which began with the decline of Rome and carried the story in increasing political detail down to 1492. His *Discourses on the First Ten Books of Livy,* roaming freely over the history of the Roman Republic, drew many supposed lessons for his own times. Guicciardini (1483–1540) wrote a *History of Florence,* dealing mainly with the fifteenth century, and also a most elaborate *History of Italy* covering the years 1492 to 1534, a prolix narrative which nevertheless has been described as the first clear exposition of the emerging European political system. Such writings were overwhelmingly political because in their age politics seemed the clue to all else. In this general category of histories but very different in content was Vasari's famous *Lives of the Most Eminent Painters, Sculptors and Architects* published in 1550, a vast store of information about eminent artists from Cimabue to Michelangelo.

The age likewise witnessed an active interest in poetic expression, an inheritance from the great tradition of Dante and Petrarch. In Tuscany there was a considerable revival of earlier lyric forms. At the court of Ferrara the poet Ariosto (1474–1533) pictured in his *Orlando Furioso* the heroic world of chivalry with Orlando as its near-mad hero. This elaborate narrative poem "Of loves and ladies, knights and arms, . . . of courteisies, and many a daring feat" described an outworn age and set a romantic pattern which European writers eagerly accepted and imitated—Spenser, for example, in Ariosto's own age, Byron and Scott in an age to come. The *Jerusalem Delivered* of Tasso (1544–1594), which Voltaire considered superior to Homer, carried into a later generation something of this same spirit of medieval romance.

The world would be the poorer without the flamboyant literary genius of Benvenuto Cellini. This versatile artist became an intimate of Pope Clement VII, quarreled with his successor, stayed for a time at the court of Francis I and then returned in his last years to Medicean Florence. His *Autobiography* gives a fascinating picture of the political and artistic life of his times. It shows him as the prince of extroverts, a talented, conscienceless adventurer willing to seduce and even to murder, a lover of all the arts and himself a sculptor of high ability. He was, too, a magnificent liar. A faint halo, he tells us, could be observed around his head in the early morning and in the evening.

In the same tradition but of far less attractiveness, must be put Pietro Aretino (1492–1556), "the scourge of princes" and the prince of liars. This lampooner and scurrilous blackmailer brought a not uncharacteristic Renaissance activity to its highest—or lowest—level. Princes were afraid of his foul pen; yet he had the favor of the sultan, of the emperor, of Francis I and Henry VIII. The pope, it was rumored, considered making him a cardinal; his portrait was painted by Titian. According to tradition he met his death laughing uncontrollably at an indecent joke.

Italian writing of the High Renaissance also produced many examples of the literature of "courtesy," dealing with the education and nature of the Renaissance gentleman. Of this, Baldassare Castiglione's *Book of the Courtier,* first printed in 1528 and endlessly republished and translated, is the supreme example. In one sense the book is a manual of manners. The ideal courtier should be, preferably, of good birth; this, however, is not essential; "study and toil" can "amend natural defects." He must first be trained in arms, but he must also acquire all the courtly graces, be well read in the humanities, both Latin and Greek, and be modest and restrained in his bearing. He must be able to "lead his prince along the thorny path of virtue, decking it as with shady leafage and strewing it with lovely flowers to relieve the tedium of the weary journey." For, says Castiglione in a striking metaphor, the prince must himself be good so as to make others good, "like that square used by architects which not only is straight and true itself, but also makes straight all things to which it is applied."

The *Courtier,* however, is much more than a manual of courtesy. Like so much of Renaissance thought it is marked by a strong current of Platonism. "I believe," Castiglione has one of his characters say, "that there exists in everything its own perfection, although concealed; and that this can be determined through rational discussion by any having the knowledge of the thing in hand." Or again, like Plato, he conceives of a Great Chain of Being by which all aspects of reality, large and small, are linked together:

> Look at the state of this great fabric of the world, which was made by God for the health and preservation of every created thing. The round firmament . . . and the earth; . . . the sun . . . and the moon . . . and the five other stars which separately travel the same course. . . . Think now of the shape of man, which may be called a little world; wherein we see every part of the body precisely composed with skill, and not by chance. . . . And we may say that the good and the beautiful are in a way one and the same thing, and especially in the human body; of whose beauty I think the most immediate cause is beauty of the soul. . . .

Castiglione's book has another fame, in that it reveals with exquisite art the intellectual interests of his age and the grace with which they were pursued. In the little mountain dukedom of Urbino, where the palace windows today still look down upon the valley of the Metaurus, an elegant company was wont to discourse freely and happily upon every sort of human problem. Few passages in literature have more enchantment than Castiglione's account of how one of these night-long sessions came to an end:

> Then every man arose upon his feet with much wonder . . . and not one of them felt any heaviness of sleep. . . . When the windows were opened then upon the side of the Palace that has the prospect towards the high top of Mount Catri, they saw already risen in the east a fair morning like unto the color of roses, and all stars gone save only Venus, from which seemed to blow a sweet blast that, filling the air with a biting cold, began to quicken the tunable notes of the pretty birds among the hushing woods of the hills nearby. Then they all, taking their leave with reverence of the Duchess, departed toward their lodging without torch, the light of the day sufficing.

■ HUMANISM AND THE ARTS IN GERMANY AND THE NETHERLANDS

Renaissance culture in Germany and the Netherlands was to differ significantly from that of Italy. During the Middle Ages the connections between these two areas had been considerable. Commerce, flowing back and forth over the Alpine trade routes, provided one link. The political activities of the medieval emperors provided another. A third arose from the complex activities of the medieval Church. In the intellectual realm, however, medieval Germany could offer little to compare with the extraordinary vigor of thirteenth-century France or with the great initial ferment of the Italian Revival of Learning. The first German universities, for example, were not founded until the late fourteenth century—Erfurt in 1379 and Heidelberg in 1385.[3] These did little at first to revive the tradition of classical learning. Moreover, royal or imperial patronage of the arts, save in the case of an occasional ruler such as Maximilian I, remained weak, so that no parallel existed in Germany to the brilliant culture of the courts of the Italian despots. The artistic tradition of late medieval Flanders, however, was, as we have seen, profoundly creative. With it went a high level of craftsmanship in various fields which continued on into the fifteenth and sixteenth centuries.

Such intellectual ferment as there was had a strong religious element. To this the Rhineland mystics of the fourteenth century, notably Tauler, Suso and Meister Eckhart, made important contributions. They were followed in the next century by Thomas à Kempis (1380–1471) whose *Imitation of Christ* became one of the best known works of Christian piety. The mystics stressed the individual's search for God, the immediacy of religious experience and a general devoutness of life. In this same tradition and more directly important for the growth of northern humanism was Gerard Groote (1340–1384), a Netherlands ascetic who founded a teaching order known as the Brethren of the Common Life. Many schools were founded under the auspices of this order which, though its primary purpose was that of piety, later through careful teaching became famous as a nursery of humanistic scholarship. Altogether some twenty-two Netherlands schools have been listed in which improved textbooks, a strict grammatical discipline and the reading of both the Bible and the Latin classics became standard. The greatest of these, the school at Deventer, was said to have had as many as two thousand pupils.

The religious and scholarly contacts between Germany and Italy during the fifteenth century gave an impetus to the northern tradition of learning which the schools of the Brethren of the Common Life represented. Here the name of Nicholas of Cusa (1401–1464) first deserves attention. A native of Cues, on the Moselle River, he left Heidelberg to study canon law for six years at Padua. He wrote on political theory and philosophy and later rose to be a cardinal. Cusanus, as he was called, became familiar with the humanist circle in Rome, achieved fame by the discovery of the manuscript of twelve plays of Plautus and went on a mission to Constantinople during which he acquired some ancient Greek manuscripts. At his home in the Rhineland he built up a private library which included translations of many Greek authors. He was also keenly interested in science, made the first modern map of central Europe, anticipated Copernicus' views on the solar system, was a friend of the geographer Toscanelli, wrote on mathematics, professed to have squared the circle, developed a philosophy of

3. The University of Prague dates from 1347 and Cracow from 1364, so that these central European foundations antedate the German. The founding dates of other universities may be listed as follows: Vienna, 1364; Leipzig, 1409; Rostock, 1419; Freiburg, 1455.

pantheism and was, understandably, much admired by a kindred spirit, Leonardo da Vinci. All in all, this many-sided genius can well be described as the greatest name in the northern Renaissance before Erasmus.

In the second half of the fifteenth century the number of German humanists rapidly increased. Their lives show something of a common pattern: education in a monastic school or at one of the foundations of the Brethren of the Common Life, study at a northern university, and then the inevitable Italian sojourn bringing an acquaintance with the new world of scholarship and a devotion to the new learning. While the German humanists, much more than the Italian, have won principal fame for their concentration upon biblical studies, some of the earlier Germans displayed an engaging versatility. Most nearly resembling the Italians, perhaps, in this respect was Rudolf Agricola (1443–1485), "the father of German humanism," a Netherlander who studied first in Germany and then in Italy, where he became proficient in Greek. Agricola's talents suggest something of what the Italians described as the *uomo universale;* he was a musician, an artist and an athlete as well as a scholar. His three brief years at Heidelberg, where he lectured on classical literature, helped to make that university a center of humanistic studies. John Wessel (1420–1489), known as "The Light of the World," studied at Deventer in Holland, and in Paris and Rome, moved in a circle which included Erasmus and lectured on philosophy at Heidelberg. Another pioneer was Alexander Hegius (1433–1498), a pupil of Thomas à Kempis who settled at Deventer and enlarged the fame of its already distinguished school. Among his many pupils was the young Erasmus. Influential in still another way was Conrad Celtes (1459–1508), one of the "wandering humanists." He was no great scholar but rather a versifier, an enthusiast for learning and an organizer of the new classical studies at Nuremberg, Cracow and Vienna.

Humanistic studies were also forwarded by individual scholars in some of the thriving German towns; Augsburg, for example, claimed Conrad Peutinger (1465–1547) as one of its ornaments, with his varied interests in the classics, in archaeology, in geography and in the chronicles of the medieval period. At Nuremberg, Wilibald Pirckheimer (1470–1528), a fluent writer and a friend of the Emperor Maximilian I, was similarly distinguished. At Strasbourg Jakob Wimpheling (1450–1528) won renown for his efforts to develop new methods of teaching the ancient languages.

A brilliant example of the humanist was Johann Reuchlin (1455–1522), who at the age of twenty published a Latin dictionary and went on to develop a profound interest in Hebrew studies. For a time he was a distinguished figure at Heidelberg University. His *De Rudimentis Hebraicis* (1506), a Hebrew grammar and dictionary, has been described as epoch-making. Reuchlin's interest in Hebrew cabalistic literature led to a great controversy, for there were those in Germany who thought that Hebrew studies were incompatible with Christianity and should be banned. One outcome of the controversy which raged between Reuchlin's defenders and attackers was the famous satire, *Letters of Obscure Men* (1514). This was a defense of Reuchlin by means of biting attacks upon the scholastic follies of his opponents. The work, authored in part by the Franconian knight, Ulrich von Hutten, aided notably in marshalling the forces of German humanism on the side of religious reform. The greatest example of the combination of classical and biblical studies was to be found in a scholar of a later generation, Philip Melanchthon (1497–1560), the friend of Luther and one of the pillars of the new Lutheran movement.

Rather than continue this catalogue of humanists one may consider at some length a northern scholar, a giant in an age of greatness, a figure of European fame in his own times and one whose personality shines almost as vividly today. Desiderius Erasmus—"of Rotterdam," as he usually subscribed himself—was born about 1466 and educated at the famous school in Deventer conducted by the Brethren of the Common Life. He then entered the Augustinian order and took priestly vows. Erasmus does not seem to have had any great vocation for the monastic life from which much later, in 1517, he managed to secure papal absolution. In Paris, where he studied for a time without enthusiasm, he found the new learning rubbing shoulders with the old. Then, in 1499, he went to England. Here he made the acquaintance of an extraordinarily attractive circle: Colet, Grocyn, Linacre and, above all, Sir Thomas More. Without exception they were devotees of Greek studies. "When I hear my Colet," Erasmus wrote in one of his inimitable letters, "I seem to be listening to Plato himself. In Grocyn, who does not marvel at such a perfect world of learning? . . . What has nature created more gentle, sweet or happy than the genius of Thomas More?" For Erasmus England was indeed a world of almost infinite attraction.

Another challenging world presented itself in Italy, which Erasmus first visited in 1506. At Bologna he saw with misgiving the warrior pope, Julius II, enter the conquered city through a breach in its walls, riding in military state behind the Holy Sacrament. At Florence, we are told, his interest was wholly in the new scholarship; he seemed totally unaware that his neighbors were Leonardo, Raphael, Michelangelo and Andrea del Sarto, or that the secretary of the Florentine Republic was Niccolò Machiavelli. His subsequent visits to Rome, Venice and Padua brought him into close contact with the brilliant world of learning and enhanced his growing fame.

By this time Erasmus had found his vocation; his career now led him from one important center to another, editing, writing, lecturing on Greek at

Cambridge, supervising the publishing of his works at Basel, enjoying travel by barge down the Rhine to the Netherlands. On one famous occasion he was enchanted to discover that a humble customs officer on the river was an ardent admirer of his works. And always Erasmus kept up his enormous correspondence. Although a friend of Luther, he parted company in matters of religious doctrine, contriving to keep aloof from the profound turmoils of the Lutheran era. He died, honored as were few of his contemporaries, in 1536.

The impressively diversified writings of Erasmus are one of the great monuments of the Northern Renaissance.[4] The *Adages,* first published in 1500 and frequently republished and enlarged, took the form of extracts from classical authors together with Erasmus' own comments upon them. At first simply a kind of classical anthology, the *Adages* grew to be a celebrated work of Erasmian wit and learning, one of the most widely quoted books of the age. The *Praise of Folly,* hastily composed in 1509 and published in 1511, is one of the most inclusive of satires, for there is hardly a corner of human society, civil or religious, where the goddess of Folly cannot discover her devotees. The satire is on the whole good-natured; some of the comment is scathing enough, but in a few pages at the end Erasmus creates a new mood and holds up the lives of innocent little children and the meditative pursuits of saintly people as models which are worth more than the life of reason itself. The *Colloquies* were originally published in 1522 as dialogues intended to teach grammar and perhaps also conduct, but as the process of enlargement and revision went on they, like the *Adages,* became a storehouse of wisdom and satire. Their content is so varied that no summary can do justice to the riches found in them.

In still another type of writing Erasmus concerned himself with technical problems of education, such as grammar, style and methods of teaching. He was also concerned with public issues. He wrote, for example, a treatise *On the Education of a Christian Prince* (1516) for his royal patron, the future Emperor Charles V. The work is strongly Platonic in flavor. A prince, Erasmus says, should seek "the highest power, the greatest wisdom, the greatest goodness," and he quotes approvingly Plato's famous remark that no state will be blessed until philosophers are at the helm. The chief hope for a good prince lies in his education. This should be both biblical and classical. In addition to the Scriptures he should read Plutarch, Seneca, Aristotle, Cicero and, above all, Plato. If he is truly wise he will keep faith with his brother monarchs and "work for the ending of that madness for war which has persisted so long and so disgracefully among Christians." The *Complaint of Peace* (1517) is a further attack upon the evil of war.

4. The great folio edition of Erasmus published at Leyden between 1703 and 1706 fills eleven volumes.

The *Handbook of a Christian Knight* (*Enchiridion Militis Christiani,* 1503) outlines the Christian life as a war of the soul in which the chief weapons are knowledge and prayer. Erasmus pleads feelingly that the letter be not mistaken for the spirit, as is often the case in the cult of relics: "Honorest thou the bones of Paul hid in the shrine, and honorest thou a piece of his carcass shining through glass," he asks, "and regardest thou not the whole mind of Paul shining through his letters?" Erasmus was in search of a life of true piety, unfettered by formalism and dogma. The *Paraclesis,* or introduction to Erasmus' translation of the New Testament, contains his moving appeal that all men read the Gospels:

> I would desire that all women should read the gospel and Paul's epistles, and I would to God they were translated into the tongues of all men. So that they might not only be read and known of the Scots and Irishmen, but also of the Turks and Saracens. . . . I would to God the plowman would sing a text of the scripture at his plowing, and that the weaver at his loom with this would drive away the tediousness of time. I would the wayfaring man with this pastime would assuage the weariness of his journey.

It remains to consider Erasmus in his great role as editor, translator and scholar. His passion for classical learning equaled his love of the Bible, and it is very revealing that in 1506 he should have undertaken to translate two plays of Euripides from the Greek in preparation, so he explained, for the greater task of translating the Scriptures. Erasmus edited and published many classical texts—Cicero, Seneca, Aristotle and Ptolemy among them—and likewise translated such diverse authors as Euripides, Galen and Xenophon. He delighted in the prospect of wedding the reason of antiquity to the faith of Christianity: "I have brought it about," he wrote, "that philosophy has begun to celebrate Christ."

Erasmus' greatest fame has come from his edition of the Greek text of the New Testament which appeared in 1516 and of which he made a Latin translation in 1519. Scholars have not been slow to point out that this Greek version was derived from inadequate manuscript sources and thus constituted no great monument of biblical scholarship. There is the famous story of how, lacking a few concluding verses of the original Greek text of Revelations, he manufactured an "original" by translating back into Greek the current Latin text of the Vulgate. Erasmus, as Mark Pattison said, was a man of letters and not a dry-as-dust scholar. With all its defects, the Erasmian text was epoch-making in that it was widely diffused, frequently re-edited and provided the basis upon which a definitive scholarly text could later be established. Erasmus wrote commentaries on the Psalms and a very popular paraphrase of the New Testament. He also edited with enormous labor the writings of many of the Christian Fathers, among them Jerome, Cyprian, Ambrose, Augustine. Chrysostom, Basil and Origen. This scholarly work was carried on with the aid of a correspondence which reached out to all corners of the learned world.

Erasmus seems a bundle of contradictions—strong in mind and sickly in body, devout and yet skeptical, learned yet popular, a meticulous grammarian and a recklessly witty phrase-maker, an outspoken critic of social abuses and yet so prim in manner as to lead one eminent historian of the Reformation to describe him as seeming to be descended from a long line of maiden aunts. Holbein's famous portraits have caught something of this complexity of character. Yet the overall impression is one of commanding influence. A whole age of scholarship gave itself to him in veneration and affection. Such, then, was this richly endowed, versatile and lovable figure, a Christian humanist in the truest sense of the word, a giant in his own times and a man the fragrance of whose character has persisted from that day to our own.

In the field of the arts Germany was slow to follow in the path of the great Italians of the fifteenth century. German architecture, for example, carried on the Gothic tradition well into the sixteenth century. The old-style brick and timbered houses as well as the traditional gildhalls and warehouses with their steep roofs and picturesque gables continued to be erected in the thriving merchant cities. To these buildings, however, were added certain touches of the new Italian style: scrolls, broken pediments, pilasters, carvings of human figures and so forth. Germany was much more the home of skilled anonymous craftsmen than it was of artistic *virtuosi*. The lands north of the Alps did not hesitate to import talent from the south. Italian workmen were employed on buildings at Prague in the 1530's, and Italian motifs are clearly visible in the façade of the castle at Heidelberg or in the courtyard of the palace at Dresden, both begun about the middle of the sixteenth century. Gothic influences nevertheless persisted and not until the arrival of the Baroque style in Austria, South Germany and the Rhineland toward the close of the sixteenth century was the full influence of Italy demonstrated.

In sculpture, similarly, the skilled traditions of the medieval carvers continued to be displayed in the altarpieces, tombs, statuary and crucifixes of a later time, but again with nothing comparable to the classically inspired masterpieces of the Italian fifteenth century. The transition from the spirit of the Middle Ages to that of the Renaissance can perhaps best be observed in the workshop of the two Peter Vischers, father and son, at Nuremberg in the early 1500's. These and others of their family were master-craftsmen in bronze; a work such as their shrine of St. Sebald, completed in 1519, is overwhelmingly Gothic in general form, but the details are clearly Italianate. The eighteen magnificent bronze statues of medieval rulers which ornament the tomb of the Emperor Maximilian at Innsbruck likewise evoke in one sense the spirit of the Middle Ages, yet at the same time they suggest the spirit of a new era.

Trends in painting in Germany and the Low Countries are more complex. The late medieval period produced, as has been seen, a distinguished school of Flemish painters: the Van Eycks, Hans Memling, Roger van der Weyden, Van der Goes and many others. This Flemish school, which had had an important influence upon the evolution of Italian painting, carried on its domestic tradition in such men as Hieronymus Bosch (1460–1516) and Quentin Matsys (1466–1530). No such school existed in Germany proper, and yet here too a late Gothic tradition in painting had its influence. In the course of time the northern painters began to modify their native style by acceptance of the new elements which they found in Italy. Artists such as Grünewald, Cranach, Holbein and Dürer illustrate the way in which men with their roots deep in the German past begin to develop in new directions.

Matthias Grünewald (d. 1531) was a painter of extraordinary visionary power. His masterpiece, the celebrated Altarpiece of Isenheim, is a complex work which combines superb coloring with deep religious feeling. It has been described as untouched by any classical or Italian influences, and yet it rises above the obvious medievalism of its subject-matter to the level of universality. "There is nothing at all like it in the whole history of art. Tortured almost to the point of hysteria, grotesque yet sublime, it has the curious effect of looking back to the Gothic artists and forward to the Baroque masters at the same time."[5] Lucas Cranach (1472–1553) became court painter to the Elector of Saxony. His religious works have something of the naïveté of their medieval predecessors, but Cranach added to this a large interest in nature. He was also a skilled portraitist, so closely connected with the leaders of the German Reformation that he might be called their official artist. Hans Holbein the Younger (1497–1543) is the German artist who would perhaps seem to approach most closely the sophistication and brilliance of the great Italian portraitists. Holbein, however, left Basel for Tudor England where he depicted its leading figures so superbly as to identify him more with his adopted land than with his own Germany.

The artistic achievement of this new age would seem best exemplified in the work of Albrecht Dürer (1471–1528). Significantly, his father, who first trained him as a goldsmith at Nuremberg, had had his own training in the Netherlands and had worshiped at the shrine of the Van Eycks and Roger van der Weyden. Dürer's first visit to Italy in 1494 has been called the beginning of the artistic renaissance in the north, for it opened a new world to the German artist. Dürer observed at first hand, took up related studies such

5. ERIC NEWTON, *European Painting and Sculpture* (Penguin Books, 1951), p. 138.

as mathematics and philosophy, and began to read Leonardo's great *Treatise on Painting*. On a later trip he wrote that he was going to Bologna to be instructed in "the secret art of perspective." Dürer worked in oils but was even more famous for his drawings, etchings and engravings. He also published three books: one on fortifications, one on geometry or measurement and one on human proportions.

Few engravings of this period are better known than the famous *St. Jerome in His Study,* or the equally famous *Melancolia I.* They were usually paired by Dürer himself and may perhaps be taken to represent his two conflicting interpretations of life. The *St. Jerome* breathes serenity and tranquility. The geometrical orderliness of the whole design, the harmonious proportions, the neatness of the setting and the calm confidence of the central figure suggest a mind at peace with itself. In the *Melancolia* all is strain and disorder. The pattern of lines is criss-crossed and irregular. There is no simple harmony to the design. A brooding figure sits surrounded by the tools and devices with which man might be expected to dominate nature—but the tools are cast aside and the figure remains impotent. Are these two engravings simply an exercise of artistic virtuosity, or do they represent Dürer's own sense of frustration as a new world of knowledge flung down its disturbing challenge to the complacency of the old? [6]

Flemish painters of the sixteenth century continued in many respects to build upon and enlarge their own brilliant medieval tradition. Quentin Matsys (1466–1530), the founder of what is known as the Antwerp School, was the first of these to drink deeply at the new Italian fount of inspiration. He was surpassed in accomplishment, however, by Pieter Bruegel the Elder (1525–1569). Like his medieval predecessors Bruegel was a lover of color and detail. He was also a superb landscapist who saw how man and nature were inseparably joined. Bruegel was a satirist and genre painter whose vivid depictions of peasant life have an almost photographic quality. At the same time they have such earthy and tumultuous vitality as to suggest comparison with Rabelais. An utterly different world radiated from the lavish canvases of Peter Paul Rubens (1577–1640), "the greatest colorist known to painting." Rubens' world is anything but a peasant's world. His opulent works suggest those of Venetians such as Tintoretto and Veronese, and yet they reflect an environment and breathe a life which is that of the north. "Rubens was afraid of nothing, had no limitations except the serious one of having both feet firmly planted on earth." [7] In Rubens we leave the artistic world of the High Renaissance for that of the Baroque.

In summary, the intellectual and artistic movements of this age in Ger-

6. See the comments in M. P. GILMORE, *The World of Humanism* (1952), pp. 269–270.
7. NEWTON, *European Painting and Sculpture,* p. 140.

many and the Netherlands form a complex pattern significantly different from what can be observed in Italy. In a social sense Germany could not equal the elegant sophistication and literary brilliance of the Italian courts. The German princes were won more easily by the pleasures of the tankard and the tournament than by the attractions of the New Learning and the new art. Germany produced no artist to equal the many-sided genius of Michelangelo and Leonardo, though in his own way Albrecht Dürer caught much of their spirit. Yet Germany made its own profound contributions. The printing press, it should be recalled, was cradled upon German soil. The foundation of new universities (Tübingen, Basel, Wittenberg, Frankfort-on-Oder, Marburg, Königsberg, Jena) was an expression of active enthusiasm for the New Learning. Christian humanism was in large degree a German creation. Added to the new achievements in the arts was the rich harvest of scholarship, which may perhaps be taken as the greatest contribution of Germany and the Netherlands. The Hebrew scholarship of a Reuchlin, the Greek learning of a Melanchthon, the versatile talents of an Erasmus are monuments to the greatness of an age. Nor can one ignore the work of Martin Luther, especially in his vernacular writings. One should recall, too, that the great art of a Dürer or a Bruegel was paralleled by the no less significant art of many an anonymous craftsman and artisan. In the totality of these achievements Germany and the Netherlands contributed in generous measure to the culture of the Renaissance.

■ THE FRENCH RENAISSANCE

Although France had played an outstanding role in medieval cultural life, during the fourteenth and fifteenth centuries she had yielded precedence in this respect to Italy. After the long confusions of the Hundred Years' War (1340–1453), France now at long last began to show the evidences of a new vigor, not the least of these signs being the success of shrewd policies of Louis XI. Whatever his political skill, it must be recognized, however, that he was hardly a devotee of the art and learning of Italy.

To explain the rich culture of Renaissance France one must do more than call it an inheritance or borrowing from Italy. Three main forces can be seen at work. One such force was found in the richness of France's own late medieval tradition. Another came from the east and northeast, from the court life and urban culture of Flanders and the other possessions of the Dukes of Burgundy. A third stream of influence crossed the Alps from Italy. These complex forces cannot wholly be disentangled.

The native French tradition is best seen in the ornate patterns of the late Gothic architectural style (known from its exuberance as the Flamboyant) which persisted through the fifteenth century. This style was exemplified in church architecture, in domestic buildings such as the elaborate town house which Jacques Coeur, the merchant prince of Bourges, built for himself in 1443 and in such famous chateaux of the Loire valley as Amboise and Blois. This same suggestion of late Gothic ornateness is found in the paintings of Jean Fouquet (1415–1482), in the glowing pages of the chronicler Jean Froissart (1337–1410) or in those of the historian Philippe de Commines (1445–1509). The late Gothic world breathes, too, in the haunting verses of François Villon (1431–1463), the poet of the thieves' kitchen, the gutter and the gallows. These examples we may call authentically French.

The influences coming from France's eastern and northeastern borders were largely those of the great Flemish school of painting. They may also be observed in the fashions of French court circles where the extravagance in dress and manners of the last Burgundian dukes was faithfully reflected. They may be found, too, in the link between the Christian humanism of the Dutch Brethren of the Common Life and a similar type of Christian humanism which grew up in France. These, then, were forces working independently of those coming from Italy.

The Italian influences which without question were important and profound were not really new. As in the case of Germany, the Roman Catholic Church had long provided one powerful link with the south. Medieval merchants and bankers provided another. Political connections arose from the claims long made by certain French families (notably the houses of Orleans and Anjou) to Italian inheritances. The importance of these varied connections in relation to French culture is not easily assessed, though some specific points of detail can be listed. After the invasion of Italy by Charles VIII, he sent back Italian workmen to his chateau at Amboise; he also brought back with him the Greek scholar Lascaris. Francis I when in Florence became the patron of Leonardo, Andrea del Sarto and Benvenuto Cellini. George, Cardinal of Amboise, emulated many of his Italian confreres in becoming an ardent devotee of the new art. These examples all suggest the beginnings of a new age, yet the student has only to turn the pages of any work illustrating French Renaissance architecture or to catch the flavor of a poet such as Ronsard and prose writers such as Rabelais or Montaigne to see how much of an older France still mingled with the new.

French humanistic scholarship followed belatedly in the path marked out by Italians. Although some scattered teaching of Greek began at Paris in the middle of the fifteenth century, it was hardly important. A printing press was set up at Paris by three Germans in 1470; it soon issued a few antique Latin texts, but the first Greek book was not issued until 1507. Interest in both the Greek and Latin classics grew rapidly: when, for example, the Italian humanist Aleander lectured at Paris in 1511 on Ausonius he delivered his opening address to an audience of two thousand persons.

In French scholarship the outstanding name was that of Guillaume Budé (1468–1540). Having turned from the conventional study of law to that of the classics, he rapidly became an ardent devotee of Greek studies, stimulated by Lascaris, the scholar whom Charles VIII had brought back to France. Budé, an intimate of Francis I and of Francis' sister, Marguerite of Angoulême, went to Italy on several diplomatic missions. His scholarly fame comes from several works, notably his learned annotations on the ancient Roman legal texts, the *Pandects,* his treatise on Roman coinage and his brilliant *Commentaries on the Greek Language.* Budé was a scholar of legendary devotion; tradition tells of him seeking relief from the cruel headaches which impeded his studies by having a red hot iron applied to the crown of his head; there is also the story of how on his wedding day he reluctantly limited his time at his books to three hours. By his contemporaries he was ranked as a scholar equal to Erasmus. Not the least of his services to learning was that of arousing an enthusiasm in Francis I, which led to the royal sponsorship and subsidizing of Greek studies in France.

A somewhat different type of scholarship is exemplified in the Estienne family, founders of a publishing house worthy to be compared with that of the Aldines in Venice. Robert was responsible for a Latin New Testament (1523), a Greek New Testament (1546) and altogether eleven editions of the entire Bible. He also published an enormous Concordance to the Bible and a Latin Dictionary (1532) that long remained standard. His son Henri published the texts of fifty-eight Latin and seventy-four Greek authors. Of these eighteen were first editions.

Perhaps as important as the actual work of scholars was the assistance and patronage given them by Francis I. In 1530 he authorized the creation of the "Corporation of Royal Readers" to further the study of Greek and Hebrew, to which the Sorbonne was still hostile. Out of these and other studies in mathematics, Latin, medicine and philosophy developed the famous humanistic center which came to be known as the Collège de France. Francis also (1539) subsidized the casting of a special Greek type made by Claude Garamond, a creation of such elegance that it can properly be included among the artistic triumphs of the period. Among the great patrons one should also mention the king's sister, Marguerite of Angoulême, who kept a brilliant literary court in the south of France, encouraged new writers and herself wrote the *Heptameron,* a collection of stories in imitation of those of Boccaccio.

Some of the interests in the new learning quickly moved over into the field of religion. Marguerite of Angoulême was sympathetic toward the reformed doctrines. At Meaux a small group of scholars gathered around

Bishop Briçonnet and began to re-examine the doctrines and teachings of the Church. Of these scholars the most noted was Lefèvre d'Etaples (1455–1536) whose *Commentaries on the Pauline Epistles* (1512) antedated the views of Martin Luther on the question of salvation by faith. These trends have an important place in the growth of Protestant thought and are, therefore, better reserved for treatment with the general subject of the Reformation.

Humanistic scholarship in the second half of the sixteenth century was inevitably impeded by the confusions of the French Wars of Religion. One should note that, while Paris naturally remained the chief center of learned studies, other French cities such as Bordeaux, Lyons, Orleans, Nîmes, Bourges, Angers, Poitiers and Toulouse all made distinguished names for themselves. One should also call attention to two scholars of this later generation, Joseph Scaliger (1540–1609) and Isaac Casaubon (1559–1614). Casaubon had a superb mastery of the Greek language. Scaliger, the greatest name in the history of French classical scholarship, was a brilliant editor of classical texts. He placed all subsequent historians in his debt by his epoch-marking *De Emendatione Temporum* (1583), a monumental systematization of classical chronology.

In the arts, a combination of native traditions and external influences helped to create the rich culture of the French Renaissance. The transformation began slowly at the end of the fifteenth century; its effects were marked during the reign of Francis I; its climax came during the succeeding reign of his son, Henry II; after Henry's death in 1559 it was not long before a slackening of the artistic impulse became evident.

The innovations coming out of Italy are first and most clearly seen in French architecture, especially in the chateaux of the Loire Valley. Here the kings of France had made their residence during the last stages of the Hundred Years' War and here, as a more elegant and peaceful mode of life took shape, the new taste found exquisite architectural expression. The grim, fortified castle could now be transformed into the elegant country home with large window areas and graceful galleries. Charles VIII sent Italian workmen to remodel his royal castle at Amboise. One may see at Blois a wing added by Louis XII (*circa* 1500) which is still Flamboyant in character, with the typical late medieval pointed arches and exuberant foliation. The wing added by Francis I (*circa* 1515–1519) with its famous outdoor staircase shows, however, the late Gothic tradition only as a faint survival amid the ordered elegance and grace of the new classicism. At Chambord, built a generation later, the new architectural style clearly took precedence over the old. With its multiplicity of windows and its patterns of classical ornamentation superimposed upon a structural pattern harking back to the Middle Ages, Chambord seems a parody of a medieval castle.

The royal chateau of Fontainebleau near Paris has been called "the second Rome," for here Francis I summoned droves of Italian craftsmen and artists to give full expression to the new elegance. Elaborate frescoes, carved stucco work, tapestries, gilded ceilings, ceramics and enamel work were carefully planned by Italian experts such as Il Rosso and Primaticcio. These products of the so-called "School of Fontainebleau" were pagan in spirit, graceful, cosmopolitan and highly decorative. They have been charged with representing little more than elegant vacuities, and yet they constituted a landmark in a cultural transformation.

By the middle of the century interest was directly centered in classical antiquity, the artistic standards of which were now closely observed. In 1547 the great architectural work of the Roman Vitruvius was translated into French. French architects traveled widely in Italy; the Italian, Primaticcio, brought back from there a celebrated collection of casts of antique sculpture. In 1546 Pierre Lescot (1510–1578), one of the greatest names of this new period, undertook to rebuild the Louvre, parts of which dated from the Middle Ages. The great court which he designed shows an ordered and scholarly classicism now divorced from the native Gothic tradition and yet clearly French rather than Italian. The spirit of Lescot's art, which was original rather than merely imitative, was carried on by others such as Bullant and Delorme. So also in sculpture, Jean Goujon (1510–1566), who worked on the façade of the Louvre and whose gracefully sculptured Water Nymphs recall the purity of the ancient Greek masterpieces, has an elegance which is typically French.

French Renaissance painting produced no school comparable to that of the great Italians or of the Netherlands. Yet there was some distinguished portraiture in which the continuing influence of the Flemish tradition may be observed. François Clouet (d. 1572) painted many of the celebrated figures of his time. His work includes a brilliant portrait of Anne of Austria and a charming drawing of the youthful Marguerite of Valois. But the tradition did not continue, and Clouet's death has been taken to mark the end of an era.

For the arts in general it would seem true that the last part of the century showed a considerable slackening in creative vigor. To be sure, the court of Catherine de' Medici was marked by an outward brilliance to which court dances, masques, ballets and music all contributed. The bitterness and cruelty of the Wars of Religion, however, as well as the decadence of the last Valois rulers, created an atmosphere in which the artist could not truly thrive.

In the field of letters sixteenth-century France made notable contributions. From the translations of Petrarch and Boccaccio, which had long been

current, there developed a close interest in the general life and culture of
Italy. The first great patroness of letters, as we have seen, was the royal
Marguerite of Angoulême, herself an author and poet. One of her consuming
interests was the Platonic tradition of Medicean Florence which, through
translations of the Neoplatonic writings of Marsilio Ficino, began to make
itself felt in France.

In 1549, the year of Marguerite's death, a young French poet named
Joachim du Bellay (1522–1560) wrote his famous *Deffense et Illustration de
la Langue Françoise.* This epoch-marking "defense" and "rendering illustrious" of the French language was a manifesto inspired in part by Du
Bellay's association with another young poet, Pierre de Ronsard (1524–1585).
Both were ardent lovers of classical literature. Du Bellay urged his brother
poets to abandon the old French forms and to seek "models of nobility" in
the poetry of Greece and Rome. They should not, however, become slavish
imitators of antiquity, he declared; on the contrary, they should enliven and
enrich their own French language with terms drawn from Greek, Latin, Old
French and from the special vocabularies of hunting, hawking and falconry.
Above all, they must derive from the classics a supreme sense of the importance of form. The name, *La Pléiade,* was taken by this talented group of
seven poets who dedicated themselves to such ideals. Although some of these
writers, not unexpectedly, wrote poetry by rule, one of them at least has
achieved a sure immortality. As the Greek lyricists once had done, so Ronsard
caught a vision of "the exquisite sense of beauty of youth and the spring,
and the pathos of winter in the fields and winter in the heart." [8]

Although Latin was still the language of scholarship, more and more
translations were being made into French. Lefèvre published a French
version of the New Testament in 1523. Calvin's *Institutes,* originally written
in Latin, were translated into French in 1541. Of the various vernacular
renderings of the classics, the greatest was undoubtedly Jacques Amyot's
translation of Plutarch's *Lives,* which began to appear in 1559. This spirited
and idiomatic translation which brought to life the great names of antiquity
passed over into Elizabethan England through Thomas North's English
version.

François Rabelais (1490–1553) is a giant figure in the literary history of
this age. He was a Benedictine monk by training and a wanderer by instinct,
a doctor of medicine who edited ancient Greek medical texts such as those
of Galen and Hippocrates. Among his many eccentric claims to distinction
is the fact that he was the first Frenchman of modern times to dissect a corpse.

8. ST. JOHN LUCAS (ed.), *The Oxford Book of French Verse* (Oxford, 1926), p. xv. The flavor
of Ronsard's sonnet beginning "Quand vous serez bien vieille, au soir, à la chandelle," has
been perfectly caught by William Butler Yeats in his famous rendering, "When you are
old and gray and full of sleep."

His enduring fame, however, has come from other sources. In 1533 he began to publish the account of the fantastic adventures of the giant Gargantua and his son Pantagruel, continuing to add further portions until his death in 1553. An enthusiast for the New Learning, a close follower of the discoveries overseas, an advocate of the Renaissance code of gentlemanly behavior and a hater of all sham and pretense, Rabelais was highly characteristic of his age and yet at the same time a figure of unique proportions.

So huge and chaotic a work as the *Gargantua and Pantagruel*—a vast quarry or storehouse from which every type of mind can draw pretty much what it wills—defies neat summary. Its main characteristic, perhaps, is an enormous zest for life in all its forms. A strong suggestion of the medieval *Fabliaux* appears in the evident love for a good story, as it does also in Rabelais' inveterate coarseness and bawdry. He had an enormous contempt for the sniveling teachers of an outworn scholasticism. He disliked idle and selfish monks, greedy lawyers and worldly popes. Underneath all these vigorous criticisms, however, underneath the fantasies, prodigies and earthy crudities are constructive ideas of extraordinary power and attractiveness.

One great concern of Rabelais was education. He wrote scathingly of the medieval follies to which Gargantua was subjected and sketched with enthusiasm the new education which Gargantua contemplated for his son Pantagruel:

> Now all the Sciences [Gargantua writes] are restored; the languages are established: Greek, without which a man may be ashamed to count himself a scholar, Hebrew, Chaldean, Latin; and printed books are now in use, so elegant and correct, an invention of my age by divine inspiration as artillery is a counter-invention though the invention of the devil. All the world is full of learned men, of most skilled preceptors, of vast libraries.

Gargantua urges Pantagruel to study Greek, Latin, Hebrew, history, geography, geometry, arithmetic, music, astronomy and civil law. He is to apply himself to a study of the works of nature, to medical books and to "frequent anatomies." He is to read the New Testament in Greek and the Old Testament in Hebrew. And with all this he is to live virtuously. Pantagruel is advised "to love and fear God, and in Him place all thy thoughts and all thy hope."

Rabelais also proposed the founding of a new order at the Abbey of Thélème, where men and women can live together happily in the pursuit of goodness and truth. In contrast to those who follow the monastic vows of poverty, chastity and obedience, they are to seek riches, marriage and freedom. The abbey itself seems an imaginative reconstruction of one of the great new chateaux of the Loire, inhabited by richly clad, elegantly housed ladies and gentlemen who recall the splendid figures of a sixteenth-century tapestry. They must learn to become masters of every art: to sing, dance, play upon musical instruments and excel at sports.

> Their life was spent not in laws, statutes or rules, but at their own free will and pleasure. They rose from bed when they thought good, drank, ate, worked, slept when the desire came to them. None did waken them, none constrained them either to drink or eat, nor to do any other thing; for so had Gargantua established it. The rule of their order had but one clause: *Do What Thou Wilt.* Because persons that are free, well born, well educated and accustomed to good company, have by nature an instinct and spur which prompts them to virtuous acts and withdraws them from vice. This they call honor.

This is a far cry from the Rabelais of gross appetites and earthy humor, and yet it is as much a part of him as the side which has been accepted in popular reputation. One may see Rabelais as a writer powerfully impressed by the new ideas of his age and brilliantly endowed to express them—a man who wore the face of a buffoon in order to preach the wisdom of truth and love.

It would be hard to find a greater contrast than between Rabelais and the great prose writer of the later part of the century, Michel de Montaigne (1533–1592). For even as Rabelais delighted in the surging life of his day, so Montaigne seemed to draw himself apart and retire into the quiet of his tower study where with his beloved classics he could reflect upon the world of men. The antithesis, however, is not total; Montaigne had been a man of affairs; he had held various public offices in his youth and served as mayor of Bordeaux even as late as 1580 when the first book of *Essays* was written. As one looks over the extraordinary list of subjects which Montaigne chose for his essays (and he may be credited with inventing the essay as we know it), one is struck by the variety of his interests. His titles, which include *Of Cannibals, Of Liars, Of Sleep, Of Smells and Odors, Of the Education of Children,* suggest that Montaigne in his own delicate and aloof way found an absorbing interest in the manifold aspects of the same human spectacle that attracted Rabelais.

Montaigne was a gentle skeptic. He lived through the cruelties of the French Wars of Religion and he had no real answer to their problem save in a kind of intellectual detachment which would enable him to comprehend and endure what he could not change. In his long essay on the education of children he proposed, like Rabelais and like many another Renaissance educator, the development of both body and mind. Mere scholarliness and bookishness should give place to the creation of the well-rounded man. "Greek and Latin are fine accomplishments," he wrote, "but we pay too high a price for them." In sum, although he could toy brilliantly with many ideas, Montaigne had little dedication to any outside purposes. "The greatest thing in the world," he wrote, "is to know how to belong to oneself."

HATFIELD HOUSE, built by Robert Cecil between 1607 and
1612. The H-shaped plan, the large windows, clusters of
chimneys and Italianate arches are all marks of the Renaissance age. Photograph, copyright by A. F. Kersting, London.

Chapter 7

The Culmination
of the Renaissance (2)

■ THE RENAISSANCE IN ENGLAND

ENGLAND'S RELATIVELY SLOW DEVELOPMENT in the great age of the Renaissance
was due in part to its geographical position on the sea frontier of Europe, in
part to the domestic political confusions of the fourteenth and fifteenth centuries and in part to England's late commitment to the tangled game of
continental politics. Isolation did not mean the absence of culture, for
English talents had found vigorous expression in such fields as architecture,

vernacular letters and the learning of the medieval universities. England's receptivity to the new life of Italy may have been belated, but it ultimately bore a rich harvest. This harvest was varied: in painting and sculpture England could not produce the equals of the great Italians, but English scholars were distinguished; in music England reached the level of greatness; and the poetry and the drama of the Elizabethan age were incomparable.

Italian influences were first impressed upon England in the field of scholarship. In 1425, for example, Humphrey, Duke of Gloucester, brother of Henry V, began to visit the Italian courts and patronize the Italian humanists, some of whom he commissioned as translators. Duke Humphrey assembled a famous library of the New Learning from which he made generous gifts to Oxford University. His example, however, was not at first widely followed, and Poggio Bracciolini, searching the English monastic libraries for classical manuscripts, concluded that they were "full of foolishness." Although by 1450 a few Oxford scholars had made the Italian pilgrimage, progress was still slow. The earliest English teacher of Greek seems to have been a William Sellyng who between 1470 and 1472 gave instruction, not at the universities, but at Canterbury.

Four Englishmen and one Dutchman are entitled to be called the founders of English humanism. Thomas Linacre (1460–1524), a youthful pupil of Sellyng, studied medicine, law and the classics at Bologna and elsewhere in Italy between 1487 and 1499. On his return to England he became an ardent advocate and teacher of Greek. His interests were numerous: he was one of the founders of the Royal College of Physicians, he translated various works of Greek science and he corresponded widely. William Grocyn (1446–1519) likewise studied in Italy where he helped the Aldine Press to bring out the first great edition of Aristotle's works. He returned to Oxford and for a time lectured there daily in Greek. To say that Linacre and Grocyn were the teachers and inspirers of Colet, More and Erasmus is to underline one important aspect of their greatness. The range of their influence was, of course, limited, and official support not at first generous. We are told, for example, that the University library in Cambridge at the end of the fifteenth century consisted of between five and six hundred volumes, largely on medieval scholastic philosophy, and contained not one Greek or classical Roman author. The founding of Corpus Christi College at Oxford in 1516 as a home of humanistic studies and the establishment of a Greek lectureship at Cambridge in 1519 marked the secure establishment of Greek in academic circles.

Succeeding these first teachers were others whose main sphere lay outside the universities. John Colet (1467–1519), for example, had read Plato as an undergraduate and had lectured on the Pauline Epistles at Oxford. These lectures have been described as a landmark in English humanism in that they abandoned the scholastic method of his predecessors and employed instead the new "grammatical" and philological approach. Later Colet became Dean of St. Paul's and founder of St. Paul's School in London. This famous foundation he placed under lay control and appointed as its High Master William Lily, who had learned Greek in Italy and had been Grocyn's pupil at Oxford. In addition to the usual Latin the pupils were to be taught both Christian doctrine and the Greek language—the latter, so it was stipulated, "without the usual amount of flogging." Other grammar schools on the model of St. Paul's were soon founded.

Thomas More (1478–1535) combined an active political career and a devout Catholic faith with a passionate interest in the new studies. More's singularly happy domestic circle, into which Erasmus was warmly received, suggests something of the affection and enthusiasm of the first generation of English humanists. "Did you but know the blessings of Britain," Erasmus wrote, "you would clap wings to your feet and run hither." After his first visit in 1499 Erasmus declared that classical learning could better be acquired in England than in Italy itself. This new scholarship had varied interests: it was concerned with the literature of antiquity, with technical problems of language and grammar, with Neoplatonism, with theology and biblical scholarship, with science and the scientific texts of antiquity. Occasionally, as in the *Utopia* of Sir Thomas More, it could launch itself into brilliant flights of fancy.

One looks in vain for any great English Renaissance school of painting or sculpture. Nor were there architects of the same prestige as those at work in Florence, Rome or Venice. The "surveyor," as the English builder was known, had hardly yet attained the dignity of professional status. Yet architectural progress was very real, for with the order and prosperity of the Tudor era the bleak medieval castle and the somewhat crude manor house began to give way to the stately homes of an essentially peaceful age. The main domestic feature of the medieval English castle or manor house had been the great hall, where most of the life centered; it had a dais at one end, the kitchen and buttery opening off the other, and behind the dais certain retiring rooms for the head of the house ("solar," "parlor," and "chamber"). Although the great hall, ever more elaborately constructed, continued as a distinctive feature of the Tudor manor house, around it grew up a very unmedieval complex of staircases, chambers and paneled galleries. Windows grew larger and more numerous. Kenilworth, the home of the Earl of Leicester, was described by a contemporary as "so glittering of glass anights by continual brightness of candle-fire and torchlight, transparent through the lightsome winds [windows], as if it were the Egyptian

Pharos [lighthouse] relucent unto all the Alexandrian coast." Oak became the favorite wood of Tudor and Jacobean times, as walnut was to be that of Queen Anne and mahogany that of the Georgians.

Tudor architecture had many distinctive features: the greater use of brick in place of stone; the introduction of long, mullioned windows, high pitched gables and clusters of chimneys; the Tudor arch; the employment of classical pillars and pilasters on the façade; the new note of privacy within; the elaborate carved plaster ceilings; the paneled woodwork; the huge fireplaces and overmantels. Staircases, formerly crude and utilitarian, now assumed an imposing quality. Formal Italian gardens with clipped shrubs and hedges began to provide the setting for the new buildings. Much of the detail and ornamentation was Italianate, and for its execution it became increasingly common to import skilled Italian workmen. Another stream of influence came from the Dutch workmen who in the late sixteenth century escaped in large numbers from the Spanish persecution in the Low Countries. The typically "Dutch" gables and the brick construction of many country houses in East Anglia illustrate their contribution.

Continental influences, however, did not destroy England's native traditions. Such monuments as Cardinal Wolsey's vast palace at Hampton Court may echo the opulent culture of the Italian Renaissance, but the great entrance gates, the simulated battlements and the hall have an unmistakably English flavor. Of church building there was very little, and of cathedral building none. The Henry VII chapel in Westminster Abbey, Magdalen College tower in Oxford and King's College chapel in Cambridge, all early sixteenth-century construction and three gems of the Tudor age, really belong to "the sunset splendor of English Gothic." One has to wait for Inigo Jones (1573–1652), the great English disciple of Palladio, or for the even later appearance of Sir Christopher Wren (1632–1723) to see on a truly grand scale English acceptance and mastery of the architectural traditions of the Italian High Renaissance.

The greatest glories of this period unquestionably were in the field of literature. Even so, one cannot fail to notice how slowly these developments came. The one great original prose work of the first half-century which is still read is More's *Utopia;* this was first composed in Latin and translated only after More's death. The Great Bible, based on the translations of Tyndale and Coverdale, which Thomas Cranmer brought to publication in 1539, and Cranmer's English Prayer Book of 1552, are in a special category; their superb English renderings influenced much more than the literary taste of their users.

In the second half-century English prose became a workmanlike vehicle for various fields of endeavor, though some writing, such as John Lyly's

Euphues (1578), were intolerably affected. Sir Philip Sidney's *Defence of Poesie* (1580), on the other hand, is simply and clearly wrought. This was an age of antiquarians; Raphael Holinshed published his famous *Chronicles* in 1578 and William Camden his *Britannia* in 1586. In other fields Hakluyt's *English Voyages* began to appear in 1588 and Hooker's *Laws of Ecclesiastical Polity* in 1594. The increasing interest in continental literature may be seen in the work of the translators, much of which rose almost to the level of genius. Among these one may note Sir Thomas North, the translator of Plutarch. John Florio made a widely-read translation of Montaigne; George Chapman did the same for Homer and Thomas Hoby for Castiglione's *Courtier.*

In the field of poetry the Italian influence was powerful, both in matters of form and in matters of content and spirit. Such influence, together with that of the French group known as the *Pléiade,* merged with the rich native traditions of English poetry. Edmund Spenser (1552–1599), for example, in his *Faerie Queene* used the form of the Italian romantic epic for which he was indebted to Ariosto and Tasso, but at the same time he consciously employed the idiom of an earlier age of English speech. Sidney's *Defence of Poesie,* which has been said to epitomize the literary criticisms of the Italian Renaissance, admits the appeal of the old English border ballads. "I never heard the old song of Percy and Douglas," he wrote, "that I found not my heart moved more than with a trumpet." The two poets, Wyatt and Surrey, who were to English poetry what Grocyn and Linacre were to scholarship, consciously developed their verse forms on the model of the Italians; they were indebted to Petrarch as was "the age's paragon," Sidney, for the sonnet form. Lyrics, odes, madrigals and ballads added to the richness of the poetic harvest.

Great as were these achievements, it was the English drama that gave this period its principal glory. The drama was to some degree a native development, springing from the miracle and mystery plays, the moralities and the interludes of earlier times. The growing interest in antiquity now brought to these older English traditions the classical conventions as to subject matter and form. The Roman Seneca rather than the Greek dramatists became the model. Moreover, the contemporary Italian ideal of the heroic figure, the man of *virtù,* found concrete embodiment in the tragic heroes of the Elizabethan stage.

Again it is important to point out the relative lateness of such dramatic development. It was little in evidence before 1590, when Marlowe, Shakespeare, Kyd, Greene and Lyly all appeared. One can only note in passing the incredible richness and power of the Elizabethan stage. Playwriting was no elegant distraction to occupy an idle hour; it was undertaken to meet the interests of a lusty audience—a goodly cross-section of English life. The plays of William Shakespeare (1564–1616) are a perfect reflection of this atmosphere and this manifold vitality in their color, their range, their naturalness, their patriotism, their humor, their sympathy, their matchless poetry and their unbounded humanity. But the very universality of Shakespeare's genius may keep us from realizing how closely he was wedded to his times; we may better in consequence capture the strengths and weaknesses of the age in thinking of the dramatic pageant which we find in lesser lights such as Dekker, Kyd, Beaumont, Fletcher and Ben Johnson. Perhaps in the tumultuous and boldly overreaching genius of Christopher Marlowe (1564–1593), the "cut branch" that "might have grown full straight," dying at twenty-nine in a tavern brawl, we may find the most typical, if not the greatest, manifestation of the turbulent power of this Elizabethan age.

The particular genius of Tudor England found one of its most exquisite expressions in music. Visitors were constantly impressed by the widespread popularity of music on all social levels and by the high degree of excellence which it attained. This may have been due to the rich legacy of religious music, rounds, catches and part-songs coming out of the late Middle Ages and in part to the direct interest and patronage of the Tudors. The versatile Henry VIII tried his hand at musical composition, and Elizabeth was quick to grant a place in her Chapel Royal to talented musical figures. Music, too, had a close association with the development of Elizabethan poetry and drama, as one may observe in the extraordinary effectiveness of a song such as "O Mistress Mine" in Shakespeare's *Twelfth Night*. The English madrigal, a part-song without musical accompaniment usually for five or six voices, reached a degree of perfection never attained elsewhere.

The long list of English musicians must include Thomas Tallis (1515–1585), "the father of English cathedral music" and one of the greatest masters of the English contrapuntal school. One of his most extraordinary, though by no means his greatest, accomplishments was to compose a motet for eight five-part choirs so that the music had to include forty separate parts. Orlando Gibbons (1585–1625), organist of the Chapel Royal and of Westminster Abbey, was also famous for his madrigals, motets and anthems. The appropriately named John Bull (1562–1628), in addition to being a skilled organist and performer upon the virginals, has been credited with composing the air of the British national anthem, "God Save the Queen." Rising above his fellows, William Byrd (1540–1623), equally skilled in the writing of church motets and exquisite secular madrigals, has rightly come to be regarded as one of the greatest of all English composers.

Important changes were under way in the general pattern of upper-class life. Henry VII, the first of the Tudors and himself no particular devotee of the New Learning, had introduced a number of Italians to his court; his magnificent tomb in Westminster Abbey was the work of an Italian artist, Pietro Torrigiano. Under Henry VIII the tour of Italy became fashionable, with the result that a good many handbooks on travel were written. To the considerable disgust of some sturdy Englishmen, etiquette, manners and dress began to reflect the elegance of the Italian courts. An English physician, Andrew Borde, protesting against the ever more elaborate and effeminate Italian fashions, was prompted to publish a small work in which he drew a picture of himself naked and put under it the following lines:

> I am an Englishman and naked I stand here,
> Musing in my mind what raiment I shall wear;
> For now I will wear this, and now I will wear that;
> Now I will wear I cannot tell what.[1]

Italian books on "courtesy," notably Castiglione's *Courtier,* were translated into English. There was much grave discussion of the question whether one had to be born a gentleman or could be made such by training. Some books concerned themselves with the duties of princes; Sir Thomas Elyot's *Boke of the Governour* (1531), leaning heavily upon Plutarch, Plato and Aristotle, proposed a pattern of conduct inspired by reason and moderation. A boy, he said, should go in for all moderate types of harmonious exercise but should avoid the "beastly fury" of football. Roger Ascham, the greatest educationist of his time, declared in *The Scholemaster* (1570) that Castiglione's *Courtier,* "advisedly read, and diligently followed but one year at home in England, would do a young gentleman more good, I wis, than three years travel spent abroad in Italy." From Italy came instruction in riding, in fencing and even in the Englishman's native pastime, the chase. Masques, modeled upon those of Italy, were offered at court. As these new influences developed, whether at the universities, at court or through the wider distribution of books, they led to a new coloration of aristocratic life and manners. To speak and read Italian, or at least to pepper one's speech with Italian phrases, became the mark of fashion. A new luxury in dress, a new profligacy in behavior, and in some quarters the parading of "Italian vices" challenged the standards of the older generation with the very different standards of the new. These trends in the arts, in literature and in manners gave evidence of a vigorous, restless and militantly self-conscious age.

■ SPANISH CULTURE IN THE SIXTEENTH CENTURY

The foreigners who accompanied Charles of Hapsburg to Madrid in 1517 were said to have been struck by the prevailing barbarousness and by the widespread contempt for letters. Although such impressions may have

1. Quoted in LEWIS EINSTEIN, *The Italian Renaissance in England* (1913), p. 79.

been exaggerated, they were not altogether without truth, for even if the sea connection with Italy was fairly close, the land barrier of the Pyrenees effectively curbed Spain's outside contacts. A general economic backwardness hung over the peninsula. During the Middle Ages a rich culture combining both Christian and Moorish elements had developed in Spain. The scholars of Toledo and Cordova had been able to preserve and translate many of the Greek, Hebrew and Arabic texts coming from the ancient world and thus to enlarge the medieval European horizons of knowledge. This cultural vigor had not been maintained. The initiative in the great Revival of Learning of the fourteenth and fifteenth centuries came, as we have seen, not from Spain but from Italy.

Spanish scholars in some numbers were found in Italy about the middle of the fifteenth century. One of the most famous, Antonio de Lebrija, returned in 1473 to teach at Seville, Alcalá and Salamanca and to establish a reputation as the leading Spanish humanist. The Portuguese Arias Barbosa, who had studied under Poliziano, lectured on Greek at Salamanca. A Sicilian, Lucio Marineo, migrated to Spain and undertook the task of developing a purer Latinity than that which he found. Another Italian, Peter Martyr, coming to Spain in 1489, was much favored by the intellectually inclined Queen Isabella. He opened a school at the court, with the royal Prince John as one of his pupils. Another figure of importance was Juan Luis Vives, a Spaniard who spent most of his life in the Low Countries. Vives was famous for several treatises on education, proposing schools somewhat like that of Vittorino da Feltre at Mantua in which ancient and modern languages would be taught in the new atmosphere of humanistic scholarship.

Among Spanish scholars the most distinguished figure was that of Cardinal Ximenes (1436–1517). After serving during his youth in Rome, he later became confessor to Queen Isabella, then Archbishop of Toledo, Cardinal, Primate of Spain and Grand Inquisitor. He undertook a reform of the Spanish church, employing the University of Alcalá as a center where a better education for the clergy could be provided. Here they could study theology, law, Latin, Greek and Hebrew. Ximenes is most famous for his undertaking to publish the Bible in its original languages. This famous "Complutensian Polyglot," as it is known, had the Old Testament in parallel columns of Hebrew, Latin and Greek, and the New Testament in Greek and Latin. Work on the New Testament was completed in 1514, but the entire Bible was not issued until 1522. Although the Polyglot is a landmark in the history of biblical scholarship and one of the great glories of Spain, its purpose was more to reinforce than to correct the authority of the traditional Latin version, the Vulgate. In this sense the appearance of Erasmus' Greek New Testament of 1516 was fundamentally more important.

Following the introduction of printing to Spain in 1473 came an impressive output of printed books. Several new universities were added to the ancient foundations of Salamanca, Valladolid and Lerida: Valencia in 1501, Seville in 1505, Alcalá in 1508, Santiago in 1526 and Granada in 1531. The first university in the New World, it may be noted, was that of San Marcos in Lima, Peru, established by charter of the Emperor Charles V in 1551. Erasmus for a time had a considerable influence in Spain; his *Enchiridion* was translated into Spanish and there were numerous editions of his *Colloquies.* Royal patronage was uneven. Ferdinand of Aragon was almost illiterate, but Isabella was an ardent patron of learning and Philip II established an impressive royal library at the Escorial with a famous collection of Greek manuscripts.

These accomplishments were real, yet Spanish humanism did not live up to its first promise. The decline which set in by the middle of the sixteenth century has been attributed to various causes. The pressure of the Inquisition in Spain gradually subdued any interest in new ideas. In 1530 Charles V made the Compact of Bologna with Pope Clement VII, promising a repressive Spanish intervention in Italy; the fulfilment of this promise had bad effects on intellectual life, both in Italy and in Spain. The Jesuit Order proved itself hostile to new ideas. Moreover, the long, grim reign of Philip II (1556–1598), in which royal absolutism found full expression and religious intolerance prevailed, was anything but favorable to the free growth of learning.

Spanish architecture continued in the old Gothic tradition (with its own unique Moorish flavor) well into the sixteenth century. As the new architectural models of Italy came to be known, they began to have an influence, even if this was first expressed in ornamentation and external adornment rather than in basic design. The *Plateresque,* or silversmith's, style gave Spanish architects an opportunity to exhibit an attractive delicacy of technique and modeling, much of it influenced by the Moorish workmanship of an earlier period. Extremely rich ornament, combining Gothic, Mohammedan and Italian Renaissance ingredients, was applied to structurally simple forms. Later in the century Spanish builders undertook a more conscious imitation of Roman monumental architecture, notably in the case of the Escorial, that enormous combination of monastery, royal residence, church and tomb which Philip II built in the wild and barren countryside near Madrid. Its church is one of the great monuments of the Spanish Renaissance. Toward the end of the century architectural design moved in the direction of the Baroque, a style which was carried to the Spanish possessions in the New World and in Asia.

Spanish medieval painting had shown the various influences of the Sienese school in Italy, the French miniaturists and the Flemish painters. Little immediate and direct influence seems to have been exerted by the brilliant artistic developments of the Italian Renaissance. Scholars would probably put as the great landmark in the history of Spanish painting the decade of the 1570's when Domenico Theotocopuli (1548–1614), better known as El Greco ("The Greek"), came to Spain after studying in Venice. This extraordinary figure, whose genius long failed of recognition, showed a marvelous capacity to employ color and rhythm for the expression of emotion, and displayed, as it has been well said, the combination of realism and mysticism which are the two poles of Spanish art. El Greco was a master of the Baroque style; he was a mystic and seer, " a mixture of ice and flame" whose distorted figures often express greater truth than the most perfectly contrived representations of lesser artists. Velasquez, a superb portraitist, landscapist, and close observer of common life, was born in 1599. This great court painter, "the most perfect artist produced by Spain," carries the story into the later period of the Baroque and can therefore only be mentioned here.

The last years of Philip II and the succeeding reign of Philip III have been characterized as a time of social and moral decline. This period of social decadence strangely enough coincides with the rise of the golden age of Spanish literature, a period of literary revival which provided the world with masterpieces of imagination, verbal felicity and satire. In 1605 Miguel Cervantes (1547–1616) published his *Don Quixote,* the story of an eccentric knight who, accompanied by his squire, Sancho Panza, went forth in search of romantic adventure. Just as the word "machiavellian," has become an adjective of almost universal use, so the word "quixotic" has entered many other languages than Spanish. *Don Quixote* was a pitiless exposure of an outworn ideal, a satire upon the kind of chivalry which still lingered in Spain. The fantastic adventures of Don Quixote, "The Knight of the Rueful Countenance," laughed this outworn ideal out of existence. Yet one must not forget that it was the attendant, Sancho Panza, the "practical man," who was the follower and the eccentric visionary, Don Quixote himself, who led.

Other literary forms developed in Spain. The European popularity of the Spanish rogues' tale was enormous; one must note that these "picaresque" expressions of rascality had a widespread influence upon later European literature. Spain also produced many works on exploration, navigation and the arts of war—all reflecting her own manifold activities. The most striking developments were in the field of the drama, where the output reached an almost unbelievable total. The greatest dramatist, Lope de Vega (1562–1635), claimed to have written fifteen hundred full-length comedies and four hundred shorter pieces. Lope had gone on an expedition to the Azores and in 1588 sailed with the Armada. His plays, and those of his fellows, were of the "romantic," "point of honor," "cloak and sword" type. This extraordinary literary ebullience was carried on into the next century by the dramatist Calderon.

Portugal, meanwhile, followed much of the same pattern, with a vigorous literary output of plays, romances, lyric poems and works on history, travel and exploration. In the person of Luis de Camoëns (1524–1580) it produced its greatest literary figure. His *Lusiads,* an epic poem which dealt with the heroic exploits of Vasco da Gama, sought to display the drama of Portugal's great conquests in the Far East. Camoëns had taken part in these adventures and according to tradition had been shipwrecked and washed ashore on the coast of Cambodia holding the manuscript of the *Lusiads* above his head. Only Milton's *Paradise Lost,* it has been said, can provide a modern equal to Camoëns' great work.

■ POLITICAL THOUGHT IN THE SIXTEENTH CENTURY

The sixteenth century saw the appearance of a considerable literature which concerned itself with such matters as the nature of the state, the extent of its authority and the justification of political obedience. This literature may be taken as a mark of growing political maturity. The Middle Ages, to be sure, had witnessed a large and active discussion of political matters, but in a very different context. In theory at least the "universal community" of medieval times had been dominated by the concept of Natural Law—the old Roman doctrine of an eternal order which sets standards for what is right and fitting. Under this theory the laws of particular states could be regarded as "just" to the extent that they conformed to the basic tenets of this Law of Nature. Moreover, on account of the long rivalry between the empire and the papacy, it is understandable that great controversy should have raged as to the theoretical bases and extent of imperial and papal authority and as to the relations between the two. Questions were raised, too, as to the nature of royal power and the duties of kings towards their subjects. But in the nature of things the political problems of the medieval state differed from the new and sharply etched issues which were to arise in the sixteenth century.

The medieval era bequeathed certain ideas to later times. The state, for example, should exist to support justice. Politics must be something more than mere expediency. The state should maintain the Christian religion. The property rights of subjects should be free from arbitrary interference on the part of rulers. This last notion was to be of profound importance in that it affected the concrete problem of the position and powers of the various estates or representative bodies which, as we have seen, had developed during the medieval period.[2] At the opening of the sixteenth century an unresolved conflict existed between the claims of royal power and the claims of the various estates or assemblages which spoke for "the people" in matters of taxation.

In the emergence of modern political thought two fifteenth-century figures, the German, Nicolas of Cusa, and the Englishman, Sir John Fortescue, play an important transitional role. Cusa's *De Concordantia Catholica* (1433), a product of the so-called conciliar movement, claimed that the pope should be subject to a general council made up of the representatives of all Christendom. The emperor, in turn, should collaborate with a properly elected federal diet or assembly. Cusa's whole emphasis was upon reasonableness or "concord." Fortescue's *Monarchia, or Governance of England* (1470) and his other works consider the peculiar qualities of English kingship. Some countries may be subject to the rule of a powerful law-making monarch, but England is under the rule of law. The king rules with the aid of laws to which his subjects have assented. There must, therefore, be both a strong monarch and also a system of estates to consent to grants of money required for extraordinary expenditures.

To these ideas the new currents of thought in the sixteenth century offer some telling contrasts. Erasmus, in his *Education of a Christian Prince* (1516), stressed the importance of moral training in producing a genuinely able and good monarch. Nevertheless, the decline of the universal outlook and the harshly realistic politics of the Italian Wars brought into sharp relief the powers claimed by the political ruler. Niccolò Machiavelli, the Florentine who was an active participant in Italian political life in its most ruthless stage, best illustrates the growth of these new forces. The essential idea in his classic work, *The Prince* (1513), is that the ruler must create public order by the effective exercise of his power. Men are a poor lot and the times are difficult. Unless the state can survive, what else matters? Machiavelli made the great severance from the preceding period by denying the existence either of Divine Law or Natural Law. Instead he asserted his belief in the omnipotent lawgiver. Machiavelli says that the ruler must seek by every means, free from all moral scruples, to maintain his power. *Virtù*, as we have seen, means the ability to combine intellect and force, but ethics as such has no part in it.[3] To be sure, the maintenance of religion, the provision of some type of assembly and the participation of the people in a

2. See pp. 40–41.
3. See pp. 103–105.

"republican" constitution may all serve to improve the morale and fiber of a state. If the people, however, share in the government of a state, they act not because of any right but because it is expedient for the ruler to have them do so.

Although Martin Luther does not occupy a large place in the history of political thought, there are significant aspects of his views which deserve consideration. Luther was strongly impressed with the need for obedience to the temporal ruler. "I would rather," he said, "suffer a prince doing wrong than a people doing right." One may speculate as to how much this arose from Luther's own reliance upon the favor and protection of his temporal lord, Frederick the Wise of Saxony. "Disobedience is a greater sin than murder, unchastity, theft and dishonesty," Luther wrote. In general it was Luther's argument, as it was Calvin's, that a subject must accept the ruler whom God gives him, and that the ruler, though under an obligation to rule justly, is subject to the authority of God rather than of man if he fails to do so.

John Calvin devoted one section of his *Institutes of the Christian Religion* (1536) to political matters. According to Calvin the remedy which the people have against a tyrant is very slight. All government is a reflection of divine authority. In Paul's words, "There is no power but of God; the powers that be are ordained of God." In general even a bad king ought to be obeyed. "The most iniquitous kings," Calvin wrote, "are placed on their thrones by the same decree by which the authority of all kings is established." There can be a kind of passive resistance or flight if a ruler seeks to defy the law of God "to whose will the desires of all kings ought to be subject." The remedy against tyranny cannot be actual revolt, however; it is that of "tears and prayers," for "we truly perform the obedience which God requires of us when we suffer any thing rather than deviate from piety." Of the three forms which civil governments may take, monarchy, aristocracy and democracy, each may be good in its own way but each may be subject to perversion. "I shall by no means deny," Calvin wrote, "that either aristocracy, or a mixture of aristocracy and democracy, far excels all others. . . . The vice or imperfection of men therefore renders it safer and more tolerable for the government to be in the hands of the many. . . . But if those to whom the will of God has assigned another form of government, transfer this to themselves so as to be tempted to desire a revolution, the very thought will be not only foolish and useless, but altogether criminal."

The break from Calvin, in which active resistance is justified, comes in later Protestant writing in both Scotland and France. "It is blasphemy," the sturdy John Knox declared, "to say that God hath commanded kings to be obeyed when they command impiety." In France a number of important writers, animated by the bitter struggles of the Wars of Religion, sought to discover restraints on the power of rulers. Francis Hotman's *Franco-Gallia* (1573) tried to make the appeal to history, saying that the French monarchy had once been elective and that its powers were limited by the Estates General.

Another approach was that of "reason" or "philosophy." Of this litera- ture the most important work was the celebrated *Vindiciae Contra Tyrannos,* or *Vindication Against Tyrants* (1579). This anonymous work declared that society is bound together by a contract or covenant. If the ruler departs from God's laws or neglects the duties of his office, he may be resisted by the lawfully constituted authorities. On account of the contract, declares the *Vindiciae,* the true lord and sovereign is the people, but this term really means the various magistrates and public officials who guard the compact on which political society is based. Very important consequences may be seen to flow from such an argument. The *Vindiciae,* indeed, has been described as "the first work in modern history that constructs a political philosophy on the basis of certain inalienable rights of man." [4] As such it could be regarded as the fountain head of a literature of enormous later importance both in Europe and America. One must also note that such ideas, first employed by Protestant writers against Catholic rulers, were later employed by Catholics when the situation was reversed. Such, for example, was the case with the Spanish Jesuit writer, Mariana, whose *De Rege* was published in 1599.

The theory of a limited power attaching to kingship could be, and was, opposed. What came to be known as the divine right of kings was really a variant of the Christian view of God's supreme authority, finding expression on earth through established rulers. No very systematic argument was brought forward in support of this authority, nor indeed was it required, for divine right could always be asserted as a kind of mystery. "The state of monarchy," wrote the future King James I of England in his *Trew Law of Free Monarchies* (1598) "is the supremest thing upon earth." The theory was to cause profound trouble in England, where it clearly found itself on alien soil; it found a more sympathetic reception in France where to many the only answer to the disorders of the civil wars seemed to be an elaboration of centralized, monarchical power. Divine right, then, can be regarded as a theory, or perhaps better an elaborate rationalization, associated with a certain stage in the development of some European states.

The sixteenth-century writer whose works most intelligently dealt with the problem of the state was the Frenchman, Jean Bodin. His *Republic,* first published in 1576, dealt with many topics, not the least interesting being his recognition of the importance of geography, climate and general

4. G. P. GOOCH, *English Democratic Ideas in the Seventeenth Century* (1927), p. 14.

environment in determining the nature of a particular state. Although Bodin has often been taken as an advocate of absolutism, this would seem to be a superficial and incorrect interpretation of his views. Bodin did recognize the important place which monarchy held in the sixteenth century, and he placed its powers on a very high plane. His definition of sovereignty would apply, of course, to other governments as well as monarchies. "Sovereignty," he says, "is supreme power over citizens and subjects, unrestrained by law." A prince or people possessed of sovereignty is not required to render an account to any save God. This does, indeed, seem like a high interpretation of sovereign power. But Bodin also says that there are three checks or bridles upon it. One of these is the law of God and Nature, or what we might think of as a moral law. Another check consists of the fundamental laws and constitutional usages found in a state. Such would be the Salic Law of France excluding women from the throne, which no French monarch could alter. A third limitation arises from the property rights of subjects which do not fall within the sphere of the sovereign and which cannot be subject to his taxation without the consent of the Estates. It can be seen, therefore, that Bodin presented an analysis of the state which, in accordance with the realities of the sixteenth century, gives a very high place to sovereign power but which likewise recognizes that the king is not a tyrant and does not rule by divine right. Under Bodin's theory an important role remains for the lawfully constituted estates of the realm.

In summary, then, the political thought of the sixteenth century can be seen as reflecting its own times. It was influenced by some important traditions coming out of the past, and yet, as in the case of Machiavelli, it made a sharp breach with that past. Theory in the sixteenth century, responding very quickly and sensitively to the actual state of affairs, was not just the rationalization of a particular set of circumstances. The age produced a number of ideas and writings which, if they were not the equal of the great political classics of the seventeenth and eighteenth centuries, were nevertheless essential as a foundation for them.

■ THE BEGINNINGS OF THE SCIENTIFIC REVOLUTION

"Rational science . . . by whose methods alone the phenomena of nature may be rightly understood, and by whose application alone they may be controlled, is the creation of the seventeenth and eighteenth centuries." [5] This statement requires the important qualification that developments in the sixteenth century made the later scientific revolution possible. The cumulative effect of such a transformation can hardly be overstated. "Since that

5. HALL, *The Scientific Revolution, 1500–1800*, p. xii.

revolution overturned the authority in science not only of the middle ages but of the ancient world—since it ended not only in the eclipse of scholastic philosophy but in the destruction of Aristotelian physics—it outshines everything since the rise of Christianity and reduces the Renaissance and Reformation to mere episodes, mere internal displacements within the system of medieval Christendom." [6]

It is clear that medieval scholars were not so ignorant or so indifferent in scientific matters as was once thought. They possessed some part of the scientific knowledge acquired in antiquity, to which they could add the further knowledge coming from Moslem sources. In the field of technology they had given evidence of a surprising amount of inventiveness and mechanical adaptation. It is also true that men like Roger Bacon or Robert Grosseteste were not isolated and eccentric figures; there was a more active medieval interest in the world of nature and in the process of experimentation than many have supposed. Nevertheless, the medieval scientific outlook labored under disadvantages that should not be minimized.

Medieval thought, as we have seen, had been profoundly influenced by Aristotle, interpreted by St. Thomas Aquinas in the light of the Christian tradition. To explain the world of nature, the *end* for which a thing existed was stressed more than any other aspect. Aristotle, to be sure, was closely interested in observing nature itself, and it may well be that in their tremendous emphasis upon ends some of the later Aristotelians could be accused of "forgetting their founder." The method could be most fruitful in some fields; it had enabled Aristotle himself to analyze the state by considering the *purpose* for which it existed, and declare it to be an institution intended to further the true end of man as a rational being. For science, however, as science is generally understood in modern times, we may see that to concentrate on the question "Why?" at the expense of the question "What?" could lead to distorted theorizing.

The leaders of sixteenth-century humanism do not seem to have been greatly interested in science as a discipline. They were essentially "bookish," though not in the same way as their medieval predecessors had been. The humanists gave their age a better knowledge of such great scientific writers of antiquity as Ptolemy, Archimedes, Galen and Pliny. The first important scientific work to be printed was Pliny's *Natural History* which appeared at Venice in 1469. The humanists developed a new interest in Plato and, through him, in Pythagoras, thereby emphasizing the idea of mathematical harmonies which underlie all life. As printing developed, the accumulated scientific knowledge of Greek and Roman antiquity became available to inquiring minds.

6. H. BUTTERFIELD, *The Origins of Modern Science* (1951), p. viii.

Astronomy can be given pride of place in this development. Since ancient times it had been associated with man's major interests—with religion and prophecy, with chronology, with agricultural pursuits, with travel and geography and, of course, with mathematics. The ancient world had left a particularly rich legacy, and the medieval world had listed astronomy as one of the Seven Liberal Arts. The skies, it has been observed, had been plotted far more accurately than any European coastline. It is hardly surprising, therefore, that the steady accumulation of astronomical data led men to consider the reasons for the behavior of the heavenly bodies and to re-examine their theories as to the nature of the cosmos.

Inherited from the past was a view of the cosmos in which the world stood as the fixed, immutable center. Globular in shape, the world was believed to have dry land only in its northern hemisphere, surrounding which lay the vast mass of the oceans. About the earth revolved a series of eleven concentric, crystalline spheres in perfect circular orbits. The first sphere contained the Moon; the second, the planet Mercury; the third, Venus; the fourth, the Sun; then followed Mars, Jupiter and Saturn. The eight sphere, the Firmament, contained the fixed stars. The ninth was the Crystalline Heaven. The tenth, or Primum Mobile, rotated once in twenty-four hours, giving regular, diurnal motion to the whole. Lastly came the eleventh, the outermost sphere, the Empyraean Heaven where God and all the elect dwelt. Most eloquently in the pages of Dante this inheritance from Aristotle and Ptolemy had been assimilated to the Christian view of the universe.[7]

Departing briefly from the subject of astronomy, we may note that material substance was taken to be made up of Aristotle's four "elements" (earth, air, fire and water) mixed in various proportions. By invoking a theory of primary "qualities" (heat, cold, dryness and moistness) it was possible to account for a transmutation from one element to another; heat applied to water, for example, produced "air." Thought had been given to the problems of motion (which on earth was held to proceed in straight lines), to the problem of "inertia" and to "impetus" as an explanation of motion.

The physical nature of man was studied in close dependence upon the writings of antiquity. During the Middle Ages the great master of anatomy and physiology was the Greek Galen. The authority of his texts was unchallenged, and while some practice of dissection went on in such medical schools as Salerno and Montpellier, in general the purpose of the demonstrations was to illustrate the sacred words of Galen.[8] It is hardly surprising,

7. One may note that this accepted view of the crystalline heavens did not affect the practical skill of Columbus and his fellows as navigators.
8. At such medieval dissections the professor would read and comment upon the text of Galen from his lofty chair while below him an *ostensor* directed the work of a lowly *demonstrator* whose business it was actually to wield a knife.

therefore, that fundamental misconceptions about the working of the body existed.

Nicolas Copernicus (1473–1543), the son of a Polish merchant, is a giant figure on the horizon of modern science. He combined a career of scholarship with the office of canon in the Cathedral of Frauenburg. Here, near the mouth of the Vistula River, far removed from the great intellectual centers of the new age, he undertook those studies which have immortalized his name. Copernicus had received his first training in mathematics and astronomy at the ancient Polish University of Cracow. He had then further pursued his studies in Italy where he had as a teacher one Domenico di Novara, a Platonist and disciple of Pythagoras who was in the habit of criticizing Ptolemy's astronomical theory because of its lack of mathematical simplicity. Later on, at his simple observatory near the Baltic, Copernicus made various observations of the heavenly bodies and compiled some astronomical tables which long remained in use.

Copernicus seems to have been as much influenced by his studies of the ancient writers as by the evidence of the heavens. He knew that the natural philosophy of Aristotle and the astronomy of Ptolemy, accepted by the universities and the Church, taught that the earth was a fixed center around which the heavenly orbs revolved. He also knew of the opposing theory of Pythagoras and Aristarchus, suggesting that the planets, revolving on their own axes, also traveled around the sun. To Copernicus this latter theory had the great virtue of making rational sense and of requiring relatively simple mathematical formulas, in contrast to the intolerably complex mathematics to which Ptolemy's disciples were driven.

> The planetary theories of Ptolemy and most other astronomers [Copernicus wrote] although consistent with the numerical data, seemed likewise to present no small difficulty. . . . Having become aware of these defects, I often considered whether there could perhaps be found a more reasonable arrangement of circles, from which every apparent inequality would be derived and in which everything would move uniformly around its proper center, as the rule of absolute motion requires. After I had addressed myself to this very difficult and almost insoluble problem, *the suggestion at length came to me how it could be solved with fewer and much simpler constructions than were formerly used, if some assumptions (which are called axioms) were granted me.*[9]

The most important axiom listed by Copernicus declared: "All the spheres revolve around the sun as their mid-point, and therefore the sun is the center of the universe." With this and other correlative assumptions he was able to offer a relatively simple mathematical explanation of celestial phe-

9. From the *Commentariolus*, a brief sketch of Copernicus' views issued a few years before his great work. See F. L. BAUMER, *Main Currents of European Thought* (1952), pp. 272–273. Italics not in the original.

nomena. His conclusions were embodied in the famous work, *De Revolutionibus Orbium Celestium (On the Revolutions of the Celestial Orbs)*. It was published in Nuremberg in 1543 and dedicated to Pope Paul III. According to the traditional story, a completed copy of the work, fresh from the press, was put into the hands of Copernicus only a few hours before his death.

The radical implications of the theory of Copernicus were not at first realized. Accepted initially by the Catholics, it was denounced by Protestant leaders such as Luther and Melanchthon. Students gave the hypothesis a mixed reception; Francis Bacon remained unconvinced, as did William Harvey, the discoverer of the circulation of the blood. The great astronomer, Tycho Brahe, declared that Copernicus' theory was opposed to the principles of physics and contrary to the authority of Scripture. In 1616 the Roman Catholic Church at last placed the *De Revolutionibus* on the *Index of Prohibited Books* where it remained until 1835.

It is well to recognize the large conservative element in Copernicus' thought. He was as much concerned to have a theory that would validate the known tables of the astronomers as to account for actual observations made of the heavens. Having no concept of elliptical orbits for the planets, he insisted upon the inviolable perfection of circular motion. In his new scheme crystalline sphere still revolved within crystalline sphere. "Apart from his one great innovation," a modern scholar has written, "all Copernicus' astronomical thought is thoroughly medieval. Truly he reformed the medieval universe, because he brought its pattern into a new order, but he introduced no new doctrine concerning its composition or the deeper logic of its various appearances." [10]

To follow astronomical developments along the path which Copernicus had plotted would lead well into the seventeenth century, and it must suffice here to indicate the general trend. Tycho Brahe (1546–1601), although rejecting the heliocentric theory, constructed an elaborate observatory near Elsinore in Denmark where, despite the fact that the telescope was still unknown, he was able to assemble a remarkable quantity of astronomical data.[11] This "undigested mass of observations of unparalleled accuracy" in turn made it possible for Tycho Brahe's assistant, Johann Kepler (1571–1630) to make further important advances. Never for a moment abandoning his delight in "mathematical harmonies" and astrological pursuits, Kepler applied to his vast astronomical knowledge a genius for mathematics. "Where matter is," he declared, "there is geometry also." The difficulties he en-

10. HALL, *The Scientific Revolution, 1500–1800*, p. 63.
11. These materials, enlarged by Kepler, were later published under the patronage of the Emperor Rudolph II. The so-called "Rudolphine Tables" (1627) are a landmark in astronomical history.

countered in dealing with the assumed circular orbits of the planets led Kepler to make new assumptions which in the end were conclusively borne out by the evidence. His great discovery, a tremendous advance upon Copernicus, was that planets move in elliptical rather than circular orbits. Kepler therefore formulated his first law of planetary motion, declaring that each planet moves in an elliptical course with the sun as one focus. His second and third laws of planetary motion related the speed at which the planets moved to their distance from the sun. Kepler saw a common principle of design running through the universe. Mathematics had been harmonized with observed data so as to make possible universal generalizations.

Galileo Galilei (1564–1642), a contemporary of Kepler, made astronomical contributions of equal importance but of a very different nature. Learning in 1609 of a Dutch optical device, he constructed a telescope with the aid of which he was able to describe in his *Sidereal Messenger* (1610) the four satellites of Jupiter, the phases of Venus, the surface of the moon, the star clusters in the Milky Way and the spots on the sun's surface. Galileo was soon in conflict with the "Aristotelians" at the University of Padua, for his views tended to be those of Copernicus whose *De Revolutionibus* the Inquisition had condemned in 1616. Whereas Kepler's works were so technical as to be read only by scholars, Galileo reached a wider audience. In 1632 he published his *Dialogues on the Great World Systems,* a discussion between supporters of the Ptolemaic and Copernican theories. The *Dialogues* were readable, clever and obviously dedicated to the new astronomy—the Aristotelian champion, for example, is named "Simplicio"—and there is little question as to who gets the better of the argument. The work has been described as "the story of the mind of Galileo . . . the mind of a man who knew very well where he was going . . . a charge of dynamite planted by an expert engineer." [12] The Inquisition quickly moved upon the elderly Galileo with the result that in 1633 he was forced, in the words of his recantation, "to abandon the false opinion that the sun is the center of the world and immovable, and that the earth is not the center of the world and that it moves." The remaining nine years of his life Galileo spent under perpetual house arrest, pursuing his scientific studies under the shadow of oncoming blindness.

The sixteenth century was likewise a most important age for the development of mathematics. An invaluable device for rapid calculation, the use of Arabic numbers, had come in during the Middle Ages. Another, the use of decimals, was advocated and explained by Simon Stevinus of Bruges in a work published in 1585. A third great means of simplifying calculations, the use of logarithms, was published to the world by John Napier, a Scot, in

12. G. DE SANTILLANA, *The Crime of Galileo* (1955), pp. 174, 176.

1614, though he may have communicated his method to Tycho Brahe twenty years earlier. The sixteenth century, too, saw the use of the common mathematical symbols (plus, minus and so forth) which quickly became standard. With the publication of the *Ars Magna* of Girolamo Cardan in 1545, algebra may be said to have come into its own, to be further developed by great mathematicians such as Vieta and Tartaglia. Geometry, which in the form of Euclid's *Elements,* had been one of the great staples of the medieval period, was elaborated and enlarged. All this mathematical growth went hand in hand with the great advances in the natural sciences.

Few students of the physical world have shown more absorbed curiosity than Leonardo da Vinci (1452–1519). Scholars have with reason denied him the title of true scientist, for the endless observations and reflections upon nature which fill his secret notebooks were never reduced to an orderly system. It has been said, too, that there is nothing in his assumptions that could not be found in the scientific writing of the later Middle Ages. Yet Leonardo lived in the exciting atmosphere of an inquiring age and was fascinated by the revelations which he found in the world of nature. He was a gifted technician who devised portable bridges, siege-engines, water-pumps, mortars, mining and metal-casting equipment. His notebooks have sketches of flying machines with action based on a study of the wings of birds. Leonardo was also an ardent student of nature, concerning himself with anatomy and dissection, botany, geography, geology, mineralogy, astronomy and with the phenomena of light, color, optics and perspective. Much of this, to be sure, he related to his art: "Perspective," he wrote, "is the bridle and rudder of painting." The fascination of this versatile genius is undeniable, but it was a genius that lacked focus, that showed no capacity to classify, to arrange and to generalize.

The contrast is all the more marked when one turns to the great work of Galileo in the fields of physics and dynamics. Galileo was powerful in those very respects where Leonardo was weak, namely in the capacity to draft hypotheses concerning observed natural phenomena, to observe further and experiment in the light of these hypotheses and, finally, to arrive at generalizations. Most historians now question the literal truth of the stories told by one of Galileo's disciples in which the master timed with his pulse the swinging lamps in the cathedral at Pisa and used the leaning tower in an attempt to study the speed of falling bodies. Galileo did in fact test experimentally his hypothesis about the acceleration of falling bodies. He built an inclined plane twelve yards long with an inch-wide trough down the center. A polished brass ball was rolled down the trough which had first been lined with parchment to reduce friction. An ingenious water-clock measured the time taken to cover a given distance. The experiment was repeated with the plane at different angles and the results collated so as to show that a body falling perpendicularly could be regarded as a special case of the general experiment. Galileo was able to demonstrate that the distance covered by a rolling or falling body was proportional to the square of the time consumed.

Ultimately Galileo formulated certain generalizations of enormous importance: the laws of the pendulum; the law of falling bodies, or acceleration; the plotting of the parabolic curve of a projectile fired by a cannon. These phenomena could be expressed in mathematical terms. "True philosophy," Galileo wrote, "expounds nature to us; but she can be understood only by him who has learned the speech and symbols in which she speaks to us. This speech is mathematics." His conviction that the laws derived from the particular experiments which he performed were applicable to all bodies laid the basis for an entire cosmology.

Advances in physics were made under experimental conditions of great difficulty. In 1600 men were without means accurately to measure temperature, air pressure or small intervals of time. Although the compass had, of course, long been in use, it was not until 1600 that William Gilbert wrote his famous book, *On the Magnet,* describing the properties and behavior of the lodestone and supposing the earth itself to be a magnet. The Flemish scholar, Stevinus, made the very important formulation known as the parallelogram of forces and also showed that the pressure of liquid at the bottom of a vessel depends upon the height of the liquid and not upon the shape of the vessel. Such work laid foundations for the great advances of the seventeenth century.

Other fields must be given briefer treatment. In medicine the problem seemed in one sense to be that of breaking away from slavish dependence upon the ancient medical texts, notably those of Galen. There is evidence that as early as 1528 students and doctors at Paris participated in the actual process of dissection. About this time a number of treatises on anatomy were written. A young Flemish student, Andreas Vesalius (1514–1564), the holder of the chair of anatomy and surgery at the University of Padua, transformed the study of anatomy by publishing in 1543 his great folio of drawings, *De Humani Corporis Fabrica (On the Structure of the Human Body).* Appearing in the same year as the *De Revolutionibus* of Copernicus, it deserves to be ranked with the astronomical treatise as a landmark in the history of science. The superb woodcuts of the volume, artistic as well as scientific masterpieces, were prepared under the immediate direction of Vesalius and were based upon a close observation and painstaking study of the human body in all its minute details unaided by microscopic techniques. The book, completed before Vesalius had reached his thirtieth birthday, is one of the supreme expressions of the "virtuosity" of the Renaissance. Yet even this work could not altogether break away from the traditional dependence upon Galen, whom Vesalius accepted as a master, whose errors he occasionally repeated and from whose physiological teachings he departed only when compelled by his own direct observations.[13]

The sequel was a rapid development of knowledge of the human body and its more careful study. The French surgeon, Ambroise Paré, published his *Method of Treating Gunshot Wounds* in 1545, a practical treatise which revolutionized surgical techniques. Paré, for example, proposed that wounds be treated with ointments instead of with boiling oil, and that bleeding be stopped by using ligatures instead of red-hot irons. A permanent theater designed so that medical students could conveniently observe dissections was built at the University of Padua in 1594. A successor of Vesalius at Padua, Hieronymus Fabricius, discovered and wrote a treatise upon the valves of the veins. Such work led up to the monumental achievement of the English doctor, William Harvey, who in 1628 published his famous treatise, *On the Motion of the Heart and the Blood,* which, by describing the process of circulation through the arteries and the veins, made one of the greatest of all contributions to the knowledge of human physiology. In the sense of establishing a new hypothesis which gave consistent meaning to a mass of hitherto discordant data, Harvey's scientific work was more epochal than that of Vesalius.

Some account has already been given of developments in geography during the sixteenth century.[14] It must suffice, therefore, to refer to these as part of the picture of steady scientific advance. Other studies, such as botany and zoology, had their devotees. The Swiss, Conrad von Gessner, gave himself to the work of classifying flora and fauna and published a *Catalog of Plants* and a *History of Animals,* the latter having been called the basis of modern zoology. The basically important *De Re Metallica* (1556) of Georgius Agricola covered all phases of mining and metallurgy. Bernard Palissy, the Huguenot potter, published his *Admirable Discourses* in 1589, a remarkable pioneer treatise on physics, chemistry, mineralogy and geology. "My only book," he wrote, "is the sky and the earth." The century also saw important manuals and writings on the general subject of engineering, a field which was stimulated both by the remarkable activity in building and by the ever-recurrent military campaigns.

13. Our own age has not dealt kindly with Vesalius. A special copy of his *Epitome,* printed upon vellum for presentation to the Emperor Charles V, was one of the treasures of the University of Louvain. It was lost when the Germans burned the university library during the First World War. The original blocks from which the woodcuts of the *De Fabrica* were made, among the prize possessions of the University of Munich, were destroyed by Allied bombing during the Second World War.
14. See p. 118.

The question may be asked: How far did all this scientific development effect a transformation in the outlook of the sixteenth century? The age clearly is one of transition as old attitudes were giving place to new, and much confusion of interpretation inevitably arises. Some people were astonishingly "modern" in their chosen fields, stubbornly "ancient" in other respects. Leonardo, as it has been noted, assembled an impressive mass of interesting data and speculations, but brought all this to no important synthesis. Indeed, efforts to reach some such synthesis might spell disaster. The Italian philosopher Giordano Bruno (1548–1600) was so impressed by the evidences of orderliness and law pervading the physical universe that he declared God could not exist beyond and apart from the things of the world. This philosophy of pantheism caused him in 1600 to be burned at the stake in Rome. For the magnificent scientific synthesis of a Newton one had to wait for a later age.

The name of Bacon is frequently put forward as best symbolizing the new attitude being developed by men of science. Francis Bacon, Lord Verulam (1561–1626), was a lawyer, Lord Chancellor of England, and a superb master of English prose. This controversial figure, whose writings, one might note, carry us well into the seventeenth century, seems to have been captivated by the possibilities that he saw in the new field of science. He wrote much, including a utopian fantasy, *The New Atlantis* (1627), in which he pictures a world where the methods of science are employed to bring about a better life. His "House of Solomon" with its oddly named types of researchers: Merchants of Light, Pioneers, Compilers, Mystery Men, Lamps, Inoculators and Interpreters of Nature, suggests nothing so much as one of our great modern research foundations. Bacon had in mind that these men should perform various tasks, some digging out secrets from books, some conducting experiments, some planning new lines of research, some compiling the results and some spreading the new findings abroad. "The end of our foundation," he wrote, "is the knowledge of causes, and secret motions of things, and the enlarging of the bounds of human empire to the effecting of all things possible." The *New Atlantis* is a magnificent dream, but it marks Bacon as a poet and a prophet rather than a scientist.

Bacon proposed to write an *Instauratio Magna,* or *Great Undertaking,* which was to formulate the aims and methods of the new science. Though he drew up plans for the whole, only a part was actually completed. The *Novum Organum* (1620), as one segment of it was entitled, offered a new method, so-called, for achieving truth. This "Method," or "Organon," involved three parts: (1) the search for principles themselves; (2) the rejection of the old, deductive, syllogistic method as "letting nature slip out of its hands"; and (3) the use of induction, leading to what Bacon called "inevitable conclusions." By the method of induction one would proceed to assemble individual bits of evidence from the world of nature until, out of their multiplicity, some acceptable generalization or "truth" would emerge. "Those, therefore," he wrote, "who determine not to conjecture and guess, but to find out and know . . . must consult only things themselves."

Bacon's critics have insisted that he had really produced nothing new and, moreover, that his proposal to replace the deductive by the inductive method was far too sweeping a move and actually not in harmony with the procedures which scientists commonly employed. They have also pointed out with much truth that Bacon was not himself a man of science. It is easy to criticize him nowadays as being too confident concerning the "Great Undertaking" and what could be gained from it. Nevertheless, Bacon is marked by a certain heroic quality in that he had caught a vision of what men of a succeeding age were to attempt—namely, to seek for certainty of knowledge amid the immediate confusions of the world of sense.

In long retrospect it can be seen that the pioneering scientific efforts of the sixteenth century were but scattered anticipations of what were to be the superb achievements of the seventeenth. In the earlier period the hand of superstition still lay heavy upon Europe; science in the modern sense was in its infancy; the number of its devotees was not large; and as yet little in the way of bold synthesis had been attempted. Work of lasting importance had none-the-less been done, with the result that by the close of the century men stood upon the threshold of an age whose supreme glory was to be found in its scientific achievement.

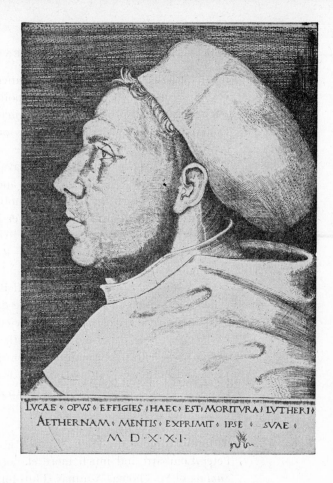

MARTIN LUTHER, an etching by Lucas Cranach the elder, of Wittenberg, who after 1504 held a position at the court of the Elector of Saxony. This second earliest known likeness of Luther was made in 1521 by one of his greatest admirers. The idealized profile has strength, devoutness and more than a suggestion of peasant solidity. Beneath the Latin inscription is Cranach's signature of a winged snake. Courtesy of the Print Room, New York Public Library.

LVCAE ✦ OPVS ✦ EFFIGIES ✦ HAEC ✦ EST ✦ MORITVRA ✦ LVTHERI ✦
AETHERNAM ✦ MENTIS ✦ EXPRIMIT ✦ IPSE ✦ SVAE ✦
M D · X · X I ·

Chapter 8

The Age of the Reformation
1517–1598 (1)

■ BACKGROUNDS

THE TREMENDOUS INTELLECTUAL, artistic and social changes of the sixteenth century were paralleled by equally tremendous changes in the sphere of religion. The unified world of western Christendom which had been one of the principal creations of the Middle Ages was subjected to a great upheaval, the immediate outcome of which was a division of Western Europe

179

into "Catholic" and "Protestant." Other no less important effects soon revealed themselves in the spheres of politics, economic life and culture. To refer to this great process as a "Reformation" is a matter of viewpoint. The Protestant will regard this period as one which brought about, albeit at great cost, an urgently needed restatement of religious belief. The Roman Catholic will see a period of upheaval in which the religious unity of medieval life was tragically shattered and in which the only true "Reformation" was that which the Roman Catholic Church itself was able to effect in its own internal discipline. Whichever the point of view, it remains true that this great movement touched the lives of the average European far more directly and poignantly than did the Renaissance and that in addition to its religious significance the political and social consequences were profound.

As a starting point one may recall the large pattern of Christian unity which had existed in Western Europe during the Middle Ages. This unity may be regarded from two points of view. It had found external expression in the growth of "papal monarchy"—that vast organization of Latin Christendom most effectively maintained by popes such as Innocent III (1198–1216) and Boniface VIII (1294–1303). The elaborate nature of this organization has already been described.[1] Catholic unity was also expressed in the sphere of ritual and belief. The medieval definition of belief, which in a sense had been in the making ever since the founding of Christianity, reached its formulation in the High Middle Ages in works such as the *Sentences* of Peter Lombard and much more elaborately and definitively in the great *Summa* of St. Thomas Aquinas. Thus fortified, the Church had been able in no small measure to dominate the life of the Middle Ages.

The unity of medieval Christendom had nevertheless experienced many challenges.[2] The papal monarchy with its vast claims came into conflict with the political interests of the medieval Empire and with those of the newly rising national monarchies, particularly of England and France. As early as the fourteenth century the English Parliament had passed the Statutes of Provisors and Praemunire, limiting papal authority with respect to church appointments and legal cases in church courts. France eventually contrived to place the power of appointing French bishops in royal hands. The fifteenth century also saw great efforts to subordinate the authority of popes to that of general church councils. One must recall, too, the continued disagreement of the various heretical groups over the questions of Christian doctrine. All this implies an atmosphere of ferment long antedating the revolts which came to a head in the sixteenth century.

1. See pp. 44–46.
2. See pp. 46–48.

Why did a major religious crisis eventually develop? It must be obvious that for so complex a phenomenon no single explanation will suffice. To some degree the new critical thought which is associated with humanism had its effects in the sphere of religion. This was certainly true of the Christian humanists such as Erasmus or Colet but one can hardly ignore the enormous distance between the semi-paganism of many of the Italian humanists and the religious devoutness of their German counterparts. Moreover, much of the impetus for religious reform came from groups that were in no sense devotees of the New Learning. In this respect one should recall the importance of the so-called Rhineland mystics—that considerable group of late medieval writers and teachers who attached first importance to inner devoutness and much less to externals. It is surely inadequate to see the Reformation, as some historians have done, as "merely" the religious side of the Renaissance. The Reformation was part of a long continuing ferment. In one sense it may seem to be "a revolt against medievalism"; in another sense it can be called "the last great flowering of the piety of the Middle Ages." Rather than view it as a sudden explosion of new forces, one may better interpret the Reformation as a culminating stage in a process of attack or disintegration with which the Church had been threatened ever since the thirteenth century.

The mounting criticisms of the Church were of various sorts. First, under the heading of moral criticism, we may include the numerous condemnations of ecclesiastical misconduct. The growth in clerical wealth, seen in its most ostentatious form in the Renaissance papacy, had long been a target for attack. Many church offices were held by unworthy and often by ignorant men. The ideal of celibacy was widely ignored. Pluralism, or the holding of several offices at once, nepotism, or the favoring of relatives, and simony, or the sale of church office to the highest bidder, were widespread abuses. Under this heading of moral criticism, then, it was not so much the question of what the Church *taught* as of how the Church *behaved* that was at issue.

Secondly, we may consider economic matters. The Church was a huge landowner, in some countries possessing as much as one-fifth or even one-third of the total land. It drew all the regular revenues of any landlord. In addition, the regular payment of tithe to the local parish church was required and, beyond this, large payments (annates and "Peter's pence") to Rome. Add the host of other contributions that could be exacted, and add further the various exemptions which the Church claimed from lay taxation, and it can be seen how much of an issue finances could become.

Thirdly, political matters had become of large importance. It is clear that the medieval Church had assumed many of the characteristic marks of a political society. In so doing it ran counter to the claims of the medieval Empire and also to the growing national assertiveness of states such as England and France. A particular situation developed in Germany where the local interests (the "particularism," as it came to be called) of the various German princes opposed the claims of the emperors. When Charles V became the outspoken champion of the Catholic cause it was only natural that some German rulers should throw their support to Protestantism, less perhaps for religious than for political reasons. One must not fail to remark also that a large body of political literature developing during the Middle Ages was designed to rebuff the political claims of the papacy; this writing strengthened the hands of the opposition when the religious breach came.

A fourth and fundamentally important cause of conflict lay in the field of doctrine or belief. The tendency of some modern historians is to emphasize the moral, the economic and the political sides of the religious conflict. Important, however, as these matters were they should not obscure what to the sixteenth century was the fundamental question: How shall a man achieve his salvation? [3] The Roman Catholic Church had elaborated its system of theology which, while insisting upon the sinful nature of man, endowed him with a freedom of will enabling him to choose between good and evil. In this choice, however, man needed the assistance of God's grace communicated to him through the sacraments. By the performance of good works ordered by the Church man could contribute to his own salvation; nevertheless the tremendous—the inescapable—role of the Church remained. Without it there could be no salvation. This central doctrine had come to be associated with a centuries-old pattern of worship and belief: appeals for the intercession of the Virgin, veneration of the saints, the cult of relics and pilgrimages, the belief in purgatory, prayers for the dead, confession and penance, fasting, the insistence upon clerical celibacy, the acceptance of papal supremacy and the recognition of the supernatural authority of the priest.

It is to be remembered that the elaborate pattern of the Roman Catholic faith had not come suddenly into existence. The writings of the Church Fathers quite naturally showed a tremendous wrestling with questions of belief. In some passages St. Augustine had drawn the picture of an omnipotent God looking down upon sinful man unable to achieve his own salvation. Man could not be saved through his own efforts but only by a faith in God who had predestined and elected some to salvation through grace. At the time of the Reformation this doctrine, if logically pursued, seemed for some

3. "The Reformation had its inception in the search for the answer to a typically medieval question, How can I be saved?" HAROLD J. GRIMM, *The Reformation Era, 1500–1650* (1954), p. 1.

individuals to raise serious questions concerning the necessity of the vast mediating machinery of the Church, and would clearly constitute a revolution in belief (as later Calvin relentlessly sought to demonstrate). In addition, therefore, to the moral, political and economic grounds for disagreement which existed in the late fifteenth century, it was also possible for acute minds to question sincerely whether certain of the Church's teachings, especially on the basic problem of the method of salvation, were necessarily true.

Finally, we must see why these matters came to a head in Germany rather than elsewhere. In Italy, save for the short-lived outburst of Savonarola at Florence, there was much more concern with art and learning than with religious reform. France had forfeited the intellectual leadership which she had held during the Middle Ages. This leadership was not regained even by the appearance of an important group of religious reformers around the cathedral at Meaux, one of whom, Lefèvre d'Etaples, published a *Commentary on the Epistles of St. Paul* (1512) which anticipated some of the religious ideas of Martin Luther. In England, too, the religious situation was hardly explosive. In Germany, however, religious ferment seems to have been very great. There had grown up a strong tradition of religious devotion and mystical piety of which, as we have seen, the so-called Rhineland mystics and the schools of the Brethren of the Common Life were the best expression.[4] The development of printing in Germany resulted in an enormous output of works of popular devotion. One such work entitled *A German Theology,* originally widely circulated in manuscript, claimed that man could find God not through learning and study, but only by complete surrender to Him. Luther published the *German Theology* in 1516, with a prefatory statement to the effect that he had learned more from it than from any works save the Bible and St. Augustine.

In Germany, too, the stirrings of national sentiment seemed to render particularly objectionable the abuses prevalent in ecclesiastical life. While some of the German humanists had drunk deep at the fountains of Italian culture, on the whole there remained a tradition of sturdy northern independence. Papal interference in German affairs, particularly when it took the form of financial demands causing money to wing its way over the Alps to Rome, could easily create bitter resistance. A certain tradition of social unrest, too, springing from the wretched condition of large parts of the peasant class, had not infrequently found expression in actual revolt. This peasant unrest had its own causes not directly connected with the religious revolution of the sixteenth century but one may well see how an attitude of dissatisfaction and unrest in one sphere might have its effects in another. In a word, then, the situation in Germany was explosive.

4. See p. 138.

■ LUTHERANISM IN GERMANY AND SCANDINAVIA

At times the history of an age seems to be almost identical with the biography of a man. Seldom has this been truer than in the Germany of Martin Luther. We can see him in the portrait painted by Lucas Cranach, a heavy-set, bull-necked, peasant type, clearly someone of solidity and determination. His admirers have seen him as the rock upon which the German Reformation was built and as the sturdy champion of a newly born German nationalism. His critics have found in him intolerance, wilfulness, coarseness of fiber, neuroticism, over-great concern with the problem of his own salvation, an indifference to the new culture of the Renaissance and, in many important matters, a persistent medievalism of outlook. Whatever the viewpoint, admirers and critics alike have found him a figure of impressive stature.

Martin Luther (1483–1546) was the son of a Thuringian miner sufficiently well off to send his boy from the village school to the grammar school at Eisenach and thence to the University at Erfurt, at that time the most famous in Germany. Luther was intended for a career in law, but whether because of the theological studies which were included as part of his program, or because of the general atmosphere of piety in which he had grown up, or, as tradition has it, because of a terrifying thunderstorm which overtook him on a hot July day in 1505, he made the sudden decision to enter a monastery of the Augustinian Order. Here Luther developed a strong sense of God's absolute power and of man's helplessness; this affected him so deeply that, according to another famous tradition, Luther on his first celebration of the Mass was barely able to proceed with the ceremony.

In the monastery Luther sought complete dedication. "If ever a monk had got to Heaven by monkery," he wrote later, "I should have been he. For all that a monk could do, I did." His abilities were so apparent that in 1508 he was sent to the recently founded University of Wittenberg in Saxony to teach theology. Here between 1513 and 1516 he gave his famous lectures on Psalms and Romans, important for the gradual definition of his ideas. Meanwhile in 1510 he had made a journey to Rome, another landmark in his spiritual evolution, for the worldliness and corruption which he saw made it hard for him to believe that this was the Church which through its sacraments could provide man with the sure means of salvation. Some historians have seen the problem as an intensely personal one; Luther was less concerned with reforming the Church than with ending his own agonizing doubts and confusions. The doctrine of justification by works which was implicit in the sacramental system of the Roman Catholic Church Luther found increasingly shaky; it failed to give him that sense of forgiveness which he ardently craved. Luther was deeply convinced of his own unworthiness and powerlessness; in the writings of St. Paul he began to find evidence of a struggle very like his own; the answer to his doubts he ultimately found in the seventeenth verse of the first chapter of Paul's Epistle to the Romans, "The just shall live by faith."

> Night and day [Luther recalled] I pondered until I saw the connection between the justice of God and the statement, "The righteous shall live by his faith." Then I grasped that the justice of God is that righteousness by which through grace and sheer mercy God justifies us through faith. Thereupon I felt myself to be reborn and to have gone through open doors into Paradise.[5]

Luther was not the first to develop such ideas, for justification by faith had already been asserted by various more or less obscure German writers and also by the French scholar, Lefèvre. Luther did not consider himself an innovator. He found support for his views in the writings of St. Augustine and also in those of the medieval German mystics such as Eckhart and Tauler. Whether or not Luther's recently acquired convictions would have remained a matter of local concern can hardly be answered; for at this particular turning point in his spiritual evolution a dramatic crisis came about in consequence of the sale of indulgences in nearby territory. This crisis, in one sense a mere episode, raised the curtain upon a drama of monumental proportions.

To appreciate the crisis it is first necessary to understand something of the nature of an indulgence. In the Catholic view, when an individual commits a mortal sin he becomes burdened with guilt and is liable to eternal punishment in hell. The danger of eternal punishment can be removed through the sacrament of penance if a sinner is truly contrite; but the temporal penalty, according to God's immutable justice, still remains to be paid. An indulgence makes possible the remission of this temporal punishment, seeing that the pope through the exercise of the power of the keys can draw upon the merits stored up in heaven because of the sufferings of Christ and the saints and apply these merits to help a contrite sinner. This theory of the "Treasury of Merits" had been taken by many to mean that an individual could, after showing himself truly contrite, buy an indulgence and avoid the necessity of performing any good work. Indulgences, originally granted to those fighting the heathen, had proved to be a plentiful source of church revenue and thus were employed for many charitable purposes during the Middle Ages. They could be, and were, used in other ways. The outward sign of contriteness might be nothing more than a declared willingness to pay; the virtues attaching to an indulgence might be extended from an actual contributor so as to apply to the souls of relatives suffering in purgatory; the nature of indulgences might be enlarged improperly by claiming for them an efficacy in absolving a sinner from guilt. The pro-

5. Quoted in GEORGE L. MOSSE, *The Reformation* (1953), p. 15.

ceeds, moreover, might be used for something less than a truly worthy purpose.

All these dubious aspects became evident in the indulgence crisis of 1517. Albert of Hohenzollern, Bishop of Magdeburg and Halberstadt, had ambitions in 1514 to become Archbishop of Mainz and thereby the leading church dignitary in Germany. The Medici Pope Leo X was willing to install him if Albert would contribute, in addition to the usual fees, the sum of ten thousand ducats toward the rebuilding of St. Peter's—a project close to the pope's heart. As this sum was difficult for Albert to raise, the pope suggested the proclamation of an indulgence for eight years in Albert's territories, one-half of the proceeds to go to the archbishop and one-half to the rebuilding of St. Peter's. With his share of the proceeds Albert could undertake to repay the loan which the Augsburg banking family, the Fuggers, had made to him. The actual issuing of the indulgences was put into the hands of a ruthless Dominican monk, John Tetzel, who undertook his task with all the enthusiasm of a modern super-salesman and with manifest contempt for the spiritual safeguards that should have accompanied the proceedings. Indulgences were issued with lightning speed. A contemporary cartoon showing Tetzel preaching beside an open money-chest carried the doggerel rhyme:

> As soon as the coin in the coffer rings,
> The soul from purgatory springs.

Although Tetzel was not permitted to enter the territories of the Elector of Saxony, he approached close enough to these borders to create a sensation and to encourage many of the Elector's subjects to cross the frontier in order to visit him. To Luther, who had already questioned the earlier sale of indulgences in Saxony, Tetzel's conduct was intolerable. On October 31, 1517, Luther posted on the door of the Castle Church at Wittenberg a list in Latin of ninety-five theses dealing with the subject of indulgences—theses which, according to academic custom, Luther was prepared to maintain in debate against all comers. The ninety-five theses, although certainly not meant by Luther as such, played a significant part in precipitating the religious upheaval in Germany. Soon translated into German and printed in pamphlet form, they were widely distributed and avidly read, thus serving to rally an opposition that hitherto had been formless and undisciplined.[6]

Luther sent a copy of his *Theses* to the Archbishop Albert. "I grieve," he wrote, "at the very false ideas which the people conceive from them [the indulgences] and which are spread abroad by common talk on every side—namely, that unhappy souls believe that, if they buy letters of indulgences,

6. By the beginning of 1518 they were being sold in Switzerland, France, the Netherlands, England, Spain and even outside the Vatican in Rome.

they are sure of their salvation. . . . By no function of a bishop's office can a man become sure of his salvation, since he does not even become sure through the grace of God infused into him. . . . Indulgences confer absolutely no good on souls as regard salvation or holiness, but only take away the outward penalty which was wont of old to be canonically imposed." [7]

A few of the *Theses* will serve to indicate Luther's general pattern of thought:

(1) Our Lord and Master Jesus Christ, in saying 'Repent ye,' etc., intended that the whole life of believers should be penitence.

(5) The pope does not wish, nor is he able, to remit any penalty except what he or the Canon Law has imposed.

(6) The pope has no power to remit any guilt, except by declaring and warranting it to have been remitted by God. . . .

(21) Thus those preachers of indulgences are in error who say that, by indulgences of the pope, a man is loosed and saved from all punishment.

(28) It is certain that, when the money rattles in the chest, avarice and gain may be increased, but the suffrage of the church depends on the will of God alone.

(37) Every true Christian, whether living or dead, has a share in all the benefits of Christ and of the church given him by God, even without letters of pardon.

(50) Christians should be taught that, if the pope were acquainted with the exactions of the preachers of pardons, he would prefer that the Basilica of St. Peter should be burnt to ashes, than that it should be built up with the skin, flesh and bones of his sheep.

(86) Why does not the pope, whose riches are at this day more ample than those of the wealthiest of the wealthy, build the one Basilica of St. Peter's with his own money, rather than with that of poor believers?

With the publishing of the ninety-five theses the fortunes of Luther, whether he willed it or not, became associated with the public affairs of Germany. The papacy was soon bound to take notice. Luther's first summons to appear in Rome was changed to a request that he appear before the papal legate, Cajetan, at Augsburg in October, 1518. Here, although he was treated with much consideration, he stoutly maintained his position. The papal attitude seems at first to have been almost conciliatory; in November, 1518, a bull was issued in which some of the current abuses of indulgences were conceded and denounced. The political situation in the Holy Roman Empire, the threat from the Turks, the death of the Emperor Maximilian in January, 1519, and the possibilities of a bitterly contested election all help to explain papal reluctance to move too sternly. Gradually the political situation in Germany became clearer. In June, 1519, Maximilian's grandson

7. Quoted in RAYMOND P. STEARNS, *Pageant of Europe* (1947), p. 103.

was elected Charles V of the Holy Roman Empire. He was nineteen years old, and comparatively unknown, although already king of Spain. Unable to speak German, so that he had to be addressed in Flemish or French, Charles was a devout Catholic, but too concerned at first with Spanish affairs to devote much attention to the mounting religious problem in Germany.

In 1519 Luther agreed to debate the religious issues at the University of Leipzig. His opponent was to be a redoubtable theologian from the University of Ingolstadt, John Eck. Luther proceeded from Wittenberg accompanied by some of his fellow theologians who rode with him in a farm cart; he was escorted by two hundred students equipped with halberds and steel helmets. At the inns in Leipzig where Luther's party was quartered, armed soldiers were stationed to keep order. In this dramatic atmosphere Luther and a few of his companions engaged in an eighteen-day debate with Eck. A contemporary account gives the setting:

> Martin is of middle height, emaciated from care and study, so that you can almost count his bones through his skin. He is in the vigor of manhood and has a clear, penetrating voice. He is learned and has the Scripture at his fingers' ends. He knows Greek and Hebrew sufficiently to judge of the interpretations. A perfect forest of words and ideas stands at his command. He is affable and friendly, in no sense dour or arrogant. He is equal to anything. . . . Eck is a heavy, square-set fellow with a full German voice supported by a hefty chest. He would make a tragedian or a town crier, but his voice is rather rough than clear. His eyes and mouth and whole face remind one more of a butcher than a theologian.[8]

There was no decision or verdict as such in the debate itself. The real significance of the Leipzig meetings was that Luther committed himself to a more extreme position. He was led, for example, to endorse some of the ideas of the heretic, John Hus, and so directly opposed the papacy.

By June, 1520, Leo X was sufficiently sure of his stand to issue the bull, *Exsurge Domine,* in which Luther's views were declared to be heretical and in which he was given sixty days to recant or else be excommunicated. This document, formally conveyed to Germany, Luther burned dramatically in public session before his students at Wittenberg. To present his ideas to the German people Luther issued in the autumn of 1520 three pamphlets which, like the ninety-five theses of 1517, quickly became weapons of major importance in the great battle of beliefs which began to rage in Germany.

The *Address to the Christian Nobility of the German Nation* was political in tone. It appealed to the German ruling class from the emperor down to assume its responsibilities in the ordering and the reform of the Church. Luther argued in favor of the independence of the civil power. The spiritual

8. Quoted in ROLAND H. BAINTON, *Here I Stand: A Life of Martin Luther* (1950), p. 113.

power is not superior to the temporal, for all Christians are of one body. It is wrong to maintain that only the pope can interpret Scripture or summon a church council. Magistrates have God's command to punish evil-doers; they should take over the civil powers and the temporal wealth of the Church. "Every town," Luther wrote, "should elect a pious and learned citizen from the congregation and charge him with the office of minister; the congregation should support him and he should be left at liberty to marry or not."

The second pamphlet, *The Babylonian Captivity of the Church,* was a sweeping attack upon the sacramental system of the Catholic Church. Only baptism and the Lord's Supper were to be retained as true sacraments, and these in sharply modified form. Luther denied that the bread and the wine were transubstantiated into the actual body and blood of Christ, though Christ, in some real sense, was present. His proposals, pushed to their logical conclusion, would so completely have destroyed the claims of the Catholic Church that Erasmus on reading them is said to have exclaimed, "The breach is irreparable!"

The Freedom of the Christian Man is unusual in that despite the "irreparable breach" which Erasmus had prophesied Luther now prefaced this work with a conciliatory letter to Leo X. "I bring with me this little treatise," he wrote, "published under your name, as a good omen of the establishment of peace and of good hope. By this you may perceive in what pursuits I should prefer and be able to occupy myself to more profit, if I were allowed, or had been hitherto allowed, by your impious flatterers." Luther's argument was that a man is free for the reason that his salvation is not dependent upon the carrying out of rules imposed from without. Inward liberty arises from having a sure and certain faith in God's mercy; "One thing and one alone is necessary for life, justification and Christian liberty; and that is the most holy Word of God." Although a Christian man will naturally be impelled to do good works, these are not the means of his salvation, but the expression of his faith in God's grace. The challenge was explicit.

Charles V, who had been crowned Holy Roman Emperor in October, 1520, had made up his mind to take firm steps to preserve religious orthodoxy in his realms. Luther was, therefore, ordered to appear under an imperial safe-conduct before the Diet of the Empire which was to meet at Worms. Here, in April, 1521, the simple Augustinian monk met the assembled splendor of the Imperial Court. An indication of the remarkable literary output of Luther was the presence on a table near him of twenty-five books and pamphlets that he had written. He was asked whether he would retract their contents. Luther requested a delay of twenty-four hours. His historic reply, as accurately as it can be reproduced, was then made as follows: "Since then Your Majesty and your lordships desire a simple reply, I will answer without horns and without teeth. Unless I am convicted by Scripture and plain reason—I do not accept the authority of popes and councils, for they have contradicted each other—my conscience is captive to the Word of God. I cannot and I will not recant anything, for to go against conscience is neither right nor safe. God help me. Amen!" [9]

Charles V, genuinely concerned, appealed to his nobles to support him in defending "the Catholic faith and the honor of God." On May 26 he signed the Edict of Worms, prepared by the papal representative, in which Luther, officially to be regarded as a convicted heretic, was placed under the ban of empire. Luther quickly left Worms, intending to return to Wittenberg, but with the connivance of his friend, the Elector of Saxony, he was "seized" by a band of armed men and went into hiding in the castle of the Wartburg. Here, in seclusion for ten months, he undertook his translation of the Bible into German, a work which, completed in 1534, was one of his greatest achievements and has left a permanent mark both upon German religious life and the German tongue. Eighteen translations of the Vulgate into German are known to have existed before Luther's. He, however, sought to get away from the mistakes of the Vulgate and the earlier translations by incorporating the results of Greek and Hebrew scholarship into his work. Moreover, by using the "High German" of Saxony he helped to make this dialect the national tongue.

Bit by bit Luther had developed a system of belief of which the main points could be given as follows: (1) Man is "justified" and saved, not by his own works, but by faith in Jesus Christ. His status in relation to God is determined by this faith and nothing else. Consequently the vast hierarchy of the Roman Church is not necessary as a means to salvation. (2) The Word of God, found in the Bible and interpreted by right reason, is the authority for Christian doctrine and practice. (3) All men are priests in the sense that every believer can and should mediate between God and man. Monks and nuns may leave the cloister; they, as well as priests, may marry and the Church should no longer claim authority over the lay state. Services should be conducted in German; all should have direct access to the Bible; all should participate more actively in the church services through hymn singing and prayers. (4) There are only two sacraments, baptism and the Lord's Supper. No miracle can make possible the transubstantiation of the bread and wine at the Mass into the body and blood of Christ. But Christ is present "as fire is in a red hot iron."

At this point the account of Luther's activities may properly give place to some notice of the wider pattern of events in Germany. On all sides the

9. *Ibid.*, p. 185. There is no contemporary record of the famous phrase, "Here I stand, I cannot do otherwise." Bainton seems to think its use not improbable.

old unrests seem to have been stimulated by the religious crisis. One problem was that of the German knights—that large body of medieval landholders who were clearly out of date and were yet stubbornly clinging to their ancient privileges. The German knights regarded the great princes of the Empire, both lay and ecclesiastical, as their worst enemies, and only a little less so the governments of the towns. The outstanding leader of the knights was an eccentric figure, Franz von Sickingen, a friend and ardent supporter of Luther. In 1522 Sickingen organized a League of Knights on the Upper Rhine and attacked the lands of the Archbishop of Trier. The attack failed, and Sickingen was killed in the defense of his own home. Cannon were used to destroy his castle, and these marks of a new age may be taken as symbolic of the victory not only over Sickingen but also over the forces which he represented. Luther had wisely refused to commit himself to this movement, for such a selfish effort to reform the Empire could hardly have succeeded.

Luther was increasingly harassed by reformers who went beyond what he was willing to seek. His old colleague at Wittenberg, Andreas Carlstadt, was one of these. Carlstadt wrote vehemently against celibacy, the veneration of images and the Catholic order of the Mass and persuaded the town council of Wittenberg to issue ordinances in this spirit. His actions attracted even more extreme persons such as the so-called "Zwickau Prophets" from a neighboring town who claimed to have such direct inspiration from the Holy Spirit that not even the Bible was needed in order to convey the truth to them. In various parts of Germany groups arose that rejected infant baptism, on the grounds that baptism without faith was meaningless; from them grew up the later sect of the Anabaptists. They represented an extreme interpretation of the appeal to Scripture as the rule of life. One should also notice the views of Thomas Muenzer, the pastor at Zwickau, who foretold a bloody purification of the Church which would begin with the immediate slaughter of all those who opposed him and end with the community of all goods. Such fanaticism was abhorrent to Luther; hearing of it he left his refuge in the Wartburg and returned to Wittenberg where he preached eloquently and successfully against the extremists.

The Peasants' Revolt of 1524–1525 was also associated with the Lutheran protest. Agrarian unrest, which had a long history in Germany, was easily aroused in the atmosphere of ferment which Luther had helped to create. Moreover, extremists such as Carlstadt and Muenzer preached in such a way as to give active encouragement to peasant demands. Revolts which in 1524 became widespread in South Germany had swept still further afield by 1525. The general demands of the peasants are best seen in their Twelve Articles of 1525. These articles, making an appeal to Scripture, claimed the right of the peasants to elect their own ministers and to pay them a fair tithe. They asked for freedom from serfdom "unless it should be shown us from the Gospel that we are serfs." They sought liberty of the chase, fishing and woodcutting, freedom from excessive services, judgments according to written law and the restoration of meadows and fields to the community. The articles, it can be seen, were preponderantly economic in nature: nevertheless the various claims were given a religious sanction and Luther was hailed as a peasant champion.

In actual fact Luther's economic and social views were emphatically conservative. Despite the revolutionary aspect of his religious beliefs, he had a profound sense of the legitimacy of civil power. "No one has the right to overthrow authority," he wrote in his *Exhortation to Peace,* "for Paul says, 'let every soul be subject unto the higher powers.'" Luther spoke out vehemently and savagely against the peasant threats to the social order. His pamphlet of 1525, *Against the Murderous and Thieving Hordes of Peasants,* shows the depth of his indignation:

> If the peasant is in open rebellion, then he is outside the law of God, for rebellion is not simply murder, but it is like a great fire which attacks and lays waste a whole land. . . . Therefore, let everyone who can, smite, slay and stab, secretly or openly, remembering that nothing can be more poisonous, hurtful, or devilish than a rebel.[10]

After much bloodshed the revolts were put down, the principle of authority vindicated and the grievances of the peasants left unalleviated. The effect on Luther was, perhaps, to intensify in him the fear of chaos and to make him intolerant of those religious leaders who spoke also the language of radical social reform.

As it became clearer that the religious ideas which Luther had championed were taking a firm hold upon large sections of the German people, the major problem for public authorities became to decide what compromise if any they would have to make. Charles V had declared himself at the Diet of Worms to be an ardent champion of orthodoxy in religion; this could not prevent him from being bedeviled by a variety of problems. In 1526 the Turks won Mohàcs and overran Hungary. In 1529 they were actually besieging Vienna. Charles found himself carrying a series of coalition wars in Italy and elsewhere against Francis I of France, his rival in 1519 for the imperial throne. Charles was also committed to conflicts with the Moslem pirates at Tunis and Algiers. He discovered a spirit of unrest among the princes of Germany, some of whom, for example Frederick of Saxony and Philip of Hesse, were on the side of the religious reformers.

The religious question was considered at the Diet of Nuremberg in November, 1522, where, although majority sentiment was still on the side

10. BAINTON, *Here I Stand,* p. 280.

of orthodoxy, papal abuses in Germany were frankly conceded. At the Diet of Speyer in 1526 it was agreed that, until a church council should meet, each state should "so live, rule and conduct itself as it shall be ready to answer to God and his Imperial Majesty." This was meant to be purely provisional, but following it the Elector of Saxony and Philip of Hesse proceeded to confiscate monastic property and to set up "reformed" churches. The breach had been made and the territorial principle asserted. At the second Diet of Speyer in 1529 Charles revoked the decree of 1526, thus leading the dissenting princes to draw up the protest from which the historic term, Protestant, takes its origin.[11] The Protestants, however, were divided. Three different statements of belief were presented by them to the Diet of Augsburg in 1530. One of these, drawn up by Luther's colleague at Wittenberg, Philip Melanchthon, has become celebrated as the Augsburg Confession. Although Melanchthon intended it to be a means of securing some measure of agreement between Lutherans and Catholics, the Augsburg Confession in the end proved to be one of the great documents of the Lutheran Church. Justification by faith, adherence to the letter of the Scripture, taking of the sacrament in both kinds, marriage of the clergy, and a clear distinction between the spiritual and temporal power of the bishops, he said, should not be reasons for conflict. Yet conflicts continued, some of them among the Protestants themselves.

About the same time that doctrinal differences were being defined, political factions began to crystallize. A group of Protestant princes meeting at the little town of Schmalkald formed a league to protect themselves against the attempted enforcement of Catholicism by the emperor. Luther, who extolled obedience to authority and at the most would have counseled passive resistance, now witnessed the spectacle of organized opposition. Brandenburg officially adopted Lutheranism in 1539. A considerable lull followed so that not until 1546, the year of Luther's death, did resistance to the emperor actually result in bloody strife. The Schmalkaldic War then saw Charles win the victory of Mühlberg in 1547, with the consequence that in the "Interim" of 1548 he tried to put what the Protestants called a straitjacket upon them. His attempts led to revived opposition and to foreign assistance (notably from France) for the Protestant cause. In deep discouragement Charles decided late in 1554 to abdicate. No alternative to compromise seemed possible. His brother Ferdinand summoned the imperial Diet to meet at Augsburg where, in September, 1555, the historic Peace of Augsburg was signed.

11. The protest of 1529 was signed by the rulers of Saxony, Brandenburg, Brunswick, Hesse and Anhalt, and by fourteen imperial cities. "Of such slender dimensions was the original Protestant Church." (*Cambridge Modern History*, II, p. 205.)

The peace reached at Augsburg was an agreement to differ. The main terms were as follows: (1) For the future each secular prince in the Empire could choose between the Catholic and Lutheran faith, and his subjects were to conform or depart. This was the famous *cujus regio, ejus religio* clause. No alternatives to Catholicism or Lutheranism were to be accepted, although Charles' successor, Ferdinand, gave the Lutherans secret verbal assurance that they would be tolerated in the Catholic ecclesiastical states. (2) If any ecclesiastical prince abandoned Catholicism, he was to relinquish the revenues and patronage of his office to the Catholic Church. This was later interpreted as the famous "ecclesiastical reservation clause" by which the Protestants subsequently declared that they did not consider themselves bound and from which much trouble was to spring. (3) Ecclesiastical property which had been secularized before 1552 was to remain in the hands of its Protestant possessors; hereafter no further "secularizations" were to be allowed.

Such were the main terms of the religious settlement which was to give Germany peace of a sort for sixty-three years. One must note the fundamental importance of what had taken place. Most significantly, the medieval attempt to regard Western Europe as a single Christian community had failed. It had been affirmed and widely accepted that man could reach salvation by a route other than that which the Roman Catholic Church provided. The territorial principle, *cujus regio, ejus religio,* gave tremendous impetus to princely power not only in the sense of making these rulers independent of the emperor but also in the sense of giving them in large measure control of a state church.

Luther was thus in a way responsible for a pattern of churches organized on the territorial basis. The prince, or lay ruler, was at the head. In Brandenburg, for example, the Elector took the title of *Summus Episcopus;* the affairs of the church were directed by a consistory. There was also a general synod or meeting of church representatives and in addition officers known as superintendents who took the place of bishops. Beneath these were the lower clergy. Clerical salaries were paid by the state. Lutheranism, then, which had attacked the hierarchical principle of the Catholic Church, produced its own though admittedly very different hierarchical pattern. Power in large measure still came from above.

The degree of religious toleration achieved in Germany can be seen to be relatively small; the dissenting individual, it has been remarked, now had instead of the remote prospect of being burned the more imminent prospect of being banished.[12] This "lame and halting conclusion of nearly forty

12. The Ecclesiastical Ordinance issued in 1540 by Joachim II of Brandenburg provided: "If any one should be so obstinate as to refuse to conform to this very Christian regulation, we shall permit him, by our generosity, to go and reside in some other land."

years of strife" was only the first step toward true religious liberty. Luther nevertheless had made some tremendously important contributions to the religious life of Germany. He had raised the question of conscience and of individual judgment. He had been accepted as a great champion of the German people. He had led the common man directly to the Bible, and had made it available to him in his epoch-marking translation. He had emphasized the importance of the sermon, the tract, the catechism, the communal hymn and the prayer. The first collection of Luther's hymns appeared in 1524. His best-known composition, "A Mighty Fortress Is Our God," has been described by the poet Heine as the Marseillaise or battle-hymn of the Reformation. And, above all, Luther had directed a tendency into channels where it was to flow for centuries to come.

The spread of Lutheran teachings to the Scandinavian countries was made possible largely by the effective power and determination of their rulers. In Denmark the change came about between 1527, when Frederick I granted toleration to the growing body of Lutheran believers, and 1536 when his successor, Christian III, fully established a Lutheran state church with himself as its head. A state church was likewise imposed upon Norway where Catholicism contrived to exist only in secret. In Sweden, where the House of Vasa had led the revolt from Denmark and the Union of Kalmar in 1523, Gustavus Vasa proclaimed the reformed religion in 1527 and proceeded to organize a Swedish Lutheran Church. The *Riksdag,* or assembly of estates, transferred church revenues to the crown and fixed the appointment of bishops. Changes in doctrine were accepted somewhat later. By the middle of the century churches organized on the basis of Lutheran teachings and the Confession of Augsburg dominated Scandinavia and spread southward so as to cover perhaps two-thirds of the German states. South Germany, the Rhineland and of course the Austrian family lands remained preponderantly Catholic.

■ THE PROTESTANT REFORMATION IN SWITZERLAND

It is perhaps not surprising that Switzerland, of relatively minor importance in the system of European politics, should have become the scene of significant religious changes. It could hardly escape the effects of the great religious storms undergone by the German neighbor to the north. Despite the relative isolation of the thirteen cantons of the Confederation behind their mountain barriers, they were repeatedly involved in the affairs of a larger world. From Italy trade routes of first importance led across Switzerland to the northern lands. The Swiss had long provided France with mercenary troops. Although after their great defeat at Marignano (1515) the cantons joined the Holy League against France, some of them were soon won back to the French alliance. On the other hand, cultural and economic connections with South Germany were extremely close. Basel, a town which Erasmus held in deep affection, was the home of one of the most famous printing houses in Europe; its university grew to have a European reputation and made the city a center of the new scholarship. Although the Confederation was nominally subject to the authority of the Holy Roman Empire, a sturdy tradition of local independence contrived to flourish.

The first distinguished name in the history of the Swiss Reformation is that of Ulrich Zwingli (1484–1531). Growing up under the influence of humanism and collecting a fine private library, he looked with greatest admiration upon Erasmus. Zwingli became a priest in 1506; in 1519, just when the Lutheran storm was blowing up in Germany, he began to preach at Zurich. His ideas show the influence both of the humanists and of Luther's tracts. In his sermons he began to present one challenge after another. He was notably aided by an enthusiastic local printer who eagerly put Zwingli's ideas into book and pamphlet form. Zwingli condemned the collection of tithes, the use of images, fasting and indulgences. He declared the Mass to be simply a service of commemoration. Finding no biblical authority for clerical celibacy, Zwingli in 1522 took himself a wife. In 1523 the Great Council, or governing body, of Zurich sponsored a public disputation in which Zwingli vigorously pressed his views. These were later given reasoned expression in his work, *On the True and False Religion* (1525). Man, he wrote, is justified by faith through which he can become wholly virtuous and free to perform God's will.

Like Luther, Zwingli challenged the sacramental system, transubstantiation, the veneration of saints and relics and the institution of monasticism. Differences over the question of the nature of the Eucharist, however, went deep: Zwingli regarded communion as a simple service of commemoration in which Christ was present only symbolically. Moreover, while Luther was disposed to accept all those conventional beliefs which the Bible did not explicitly forbid, Zwingli would accept only those which the Bible explicitly authorized. This, indeed, may be taken as one of the fundamental differences between the Lutheran and the Swiss Reformations. Luther believed that the word of God was to be found in the Bible but was not necessarily to be identified with the text of Scripture. Zwingli (and later Calvin) made this identification and took the sacred text as a definitive rule of life. These differences were such that when Luther and Zwingli came together at the Marburg Conference in 1529 in the hope of finding agreement they failed to do so. Referring to the Eucharist, Luther chalked the words, "This is my Body," on the table in front of him and refused to take Zwingli's outstretched hand. The breach was decisive.

The establishment of what came to be called the Reformed service, as distinct from the Lutheran, can be dated from 1525 when the Zwinglian form of worship was accepted at Zurich. Sympathizers grew in other parts of Switzerland. The prosperous city of Bern accepted the new views in 1528; Basel did so in 1529. Since the thirteen cantons had always enjoyed a large measure of autonomy the sharp religious cleavage now led to the forming of rival leagues within Switzerland and the outbreak of religious war. The Catholic cause was championed by the three ancient "Forest Cantons" of Uri, Schwyz and Unterwalden, along with the newer cantons of Luzern, Zug, Solothurn and Freiburg. Protestantism had its champions in the thriving "City Cantons" of Zurich, Bern and Basel, as well as in Glarus, Schaffhausen and Appenzell. In some sense, therefore, an economic division characterized the conflict. In the battle of Kappel (1531) Zwingli, who served both as a military chaplain and soldier, was found lying wounded under a pear tree and slain. The Peace of Kappel in the same year provided a compromise by which each canton was free to determine its own religious affairs; thus a roughly equal division was reached in Switzerland between Protestant and Catholic cantons which has persisted down to our own day. This territorial settlement, therefore, resembled in general and antedated that which was reached in Germany by the Peace of Augsburg.

The church, according to Zwingli, "is nothing but the total of all Christian believers, assembled in the Spirit and the will of God." More than Luther, Zwingli worked in the direction of the close association of the congregation and the civil power. He set up a board of discipline in Zurich with both ministers and magistrates upon it, so that civil and ecclesiastical authorities joined in regulating conduct by means of a militant attack upon unchastity, theft, avarice, usury and fraud. Zwingli seems to have been more hopeful than was Luther of setting up the kingdom of God upon earth; it has been observed that while the statue at Worms shows Luther holding only a Bible, that of Zwingli at Zurich shows him with the Word of God in one hand and a sword in the other.

The name of Martin Bucer of Strassburg deserves mention, in that he strove by various means to harmonize the views of different Protestant reformers. His doctrines resembled those of Luther, save that he approached Zwingli's position on the question of the Eucharist. Bucer tried unsuccessfully in 1529 to reconcile Luther and Zwingli. Later on he tried the same tactics of harmony with the Catholics, but again without success. Appointed professor of divinity at Cambridge in 1549, he acquainted English religious leaders with the views of the continental reformers.

The greatest name in the history of the Swiss Reformation, inseparably connected with Geneva, is that of a Frenchman, John Calvin. One may find in the geographical location and political circumstances of Geneva some explanation for the all-important role which it was to play in the religious struggle of the sixteenth century. This vigorous city, once under the rule of a local bishop and of the counts of Savoy, had succeeded in throwing off the authority of both. Though Geneva itself had not joined the Confederation, it had secured an alliance with the powerful Swiss Canton of Bern. Thus it could hardly escape the reform ideas that were in the air, ideas to which it became notably subject after 1533 when it heard the sermons of William Farel, "a fiery, red-bearded Elijah bellowing at the priests of Baal." It was perhaps Farel's greatest contribution to persuade a transient student of theology, John Calvin, to stay in the city and there undertake the work of the Lord.

John Calvin (1509–1564) was born at Noyon, in Picardy. He belongs, therefore, to the generation which followed that of Luther. Intended at first for the church, he turned to the study of law at Orleans and Bourges. All his writing shows the influence of a rigorous training which combined biblical and classical studies with a deep knowledge of the early Church Fathers, especially of St. Augustine.[13] He was well read, a brilliant stylist, intellectually acute and unhesitatingly self-confident. Calvin grew up in the 1520's when Luther's ideas were being felt in France. His native land moreover had its own sources of discontent independent of those visible across the Rhine. It could be shown, for example, that the moral, doctrinal, economic and political grievances which have been discussed in relation to Germany all had their counterparts in France, though perhaps in not such an acute form. These grievances, however, were sufficient to influence a significant minority and to produce occasional disturbances. The year 1534, for example, when John Calvin, under suspicion of heresy, found it advisable to leave France was the "Year of the Placards," when from time to time in the various French cities mysterious posters appeared denouncing the Mass in coarse and offensive terms. One such placard, describing the pope, cardinals, bishops, priests and monks as "vermin," was found on the very door of the royal bedchamber at Amboise. In response to such attacks the burning of heretics began.

Calvin took refuge in Switzerland, where at Basel he wrote and in 1536 published in Latin his *Institutes of the Christian Religion*.[14] He hopefully but vainly dedicated his work to Francis I with a plea that the monarch would take the lead in freeing the Church from its errors. In its directness,

13. "Without Augustine we never should have had Calvinism." *Cambridge Modern History*, II, p. 364.
14. The work was translated into excellent French in 1541. Calvin steadily revised and enlarged it, so that in the final version of 1559 it had grown from 6 to 81 chapters and was five times its original size. There were 25 editions during his lifetime.

its skill in presentation and its ruthless logicality the book has been described as a lawyer's brief designed to meet the marshaled logic of Catholic dogma. This, one of the most significant and influential of all Protestant writings, must be given analysis.

Central to Calvin's argument is the tremendous fact of the overpowering majesty of God. Everything else derives from this idea, which runs like a mighty theme through all that Calvin wrote. "For the will of God," Calvin declared, "is the highest rule of justice; so that what he wills must be considered just, for this very reason because he wills it. When it is inquired, therefore, why the Lord did so, the answer must be: Because he would."

Calvin's beliefs were based squarely upon the Scriptures. "No one," he wrote, "can receive even the smallest taste of right and sound doctrine unless he has become a disciple of the Scriptures." Like St. Thomas Aquinas, Calvin sought to establish a rational explanation for his religious beliefs. The picture of Calvin's all-powerful God is derived much more from the pages of the Old Testament than from those of the New. God has created the world by his power and governs every part of it by his providence. Since the fall of Adam man has been steeped in sin and depravity. He cannot contribute to his own salvation. He is "despoiled of freedom of will and subjected to a miserable slavery." Or, in the words of the later New England Primer, "In Adam's fall we sinned all." Christ is the mediator making possible salvation for fallen man. Salvation, Calvin says with rigorous logic, must be the work of God, not of man; for God is all-powerful.

God has from all time determined or predestined man's fate. "Predestination we call the eternal decree of God, by which he has determined in himself, what he would have to become of every individual of mankind." By predestination and election some are called to salvation; these are the elect—the "saints." All others are doomed to eternal damnation, for God "gives to some what he refuses to others." Such a doctrine, says Calvin, is "productive of the most delightful benefit," yet man cannot fully understand it. "It is unreasonable," he explains, "that man should scrutinize with impunity those things which the Lord has determined to be hidden in himself." This terrible doctrine might seem certain to drive man to a condition of hopeless and despairing passivity. In actual fact it does not seem to have had any such effect. Although sinful man could not save himself by his own efforts and although he could never truly know whether he was of the elect, the Calvinist proceeded to act as if he were. The Calvinist honored God, lived soberly and wrestled against the temptations of the devil. And he never ceased to exhort and denounce the unregenerate.

Of great importance for the historian is the view which Calvin takes of the true church and man's relation to it. This he discusses in the fourth and final book of the *Institutes,* along with some concluding considerations as to the nature of civil government. Calvin regarded the church from two points of view. There is an Invisible Church, "into which none are admitted but those who by the gift of adoption are sons of God." The church in this sense includes not only "the saints who dwell on earth" but also "all the elect who have existed from the beginning of the world." In another sense the Visible Church, or Church Universal, is made up of all those men, scattered through the world, "who profess to worship one God and Christ." In this church, unhappily, there will be "a very large mixture of hypocrites," for only God can truly know who are the elect and who are the reprobate. Admission must therefore depend on a certain standard of outward conduct. Membership in the church should be open to all "who by confession of faith, regularity of conduct and participation in the sacraments, unite with us in acknowledging the same God and Christ." The church administers two sacraments, baptism and the Lord's Supper. These are external signs of an individual's faith and are in no way a means of salvation.

These passages are important, for in them one may see what became highly characteristic of Calvinism: the combination of a rigid external standard of conduct with an equally rigid code of belief. The true Christian is one who professes his faith, lives an upright life and participates in the two sacraments of his church, baptism and the Lord's Supper. As Christian faith came to mean unwavering assent to a system of doctrine derived from Scripture, so Christian life came to mean unwavering obedience to a set of Scriptural rules governing conduct. There developed what has come to be known as Puritanism—in one sense austere, forbidding and perhaps unattractive, yet in another sense singularly dignified and compelling. It must be the business of the church to proclaim and maintain the standards by which the Puritan lived.

If one wishes to recapture the atmosphere of early Calvinism one may think of a gathering in the New England meeting house—a service simple and austere, without ornamentation or elaborate ceremonial. Here, with a communion table taking the place of the altar, the minister in his black "Geneva gown" looked down from his pulpit upon the congregation, sitting upon their hard benches for the two or three hour service. Listening to the long, emotionally charged sermons and prayers, and joining ardently in singing the hymns and psalms, the worshipers found a Protestant alternative for the drama of the Catholic Mass.

At Geneva we may see how this new type of church organization became closely associated with the political and social life of the city. Geneva was not a democracy, for out of some 13,000 inhabitants only 1,500 of the wealthier class could vote. In 1537 Calvin drafted a series of proposals for Christian belief and church government. The Lord's Supper should be celebrated at least monthly; the church should have the power to excommunicate or expel unruly members; there should be a system of elders to watch over individual life and conduct; and the young should be carefully trained in religious truth. The civil power should profess its belief in the true doctrine and aid the church in maintaining religious discipline. Such views must at first have seemed too extreme, for Calvin and Farel were banished in 1538 and were not able to return until 1541. Calvin then was able to draft the celebrated Ecclesiastical Ordinances of 1541 in which his system is most clearly expressed.

The central organ of church government was to be the Consistory, a body composed of six ministers and of twelve elders coopted annually by the clergy. The Consistory had the general supervision of religious life and public morals. The city was divided into districts within which the elders were to make periodic visits and inspections. They could sit as a court and visit condemnation upon those who erred, turning them over to the civil power for punishment. In this way a severe censorship and control was exercised over public morals, a control which led to such terrible results as burning Calvin's old friend Servetus at the stake for questioning the doctrine of the Trinity. The clergy of Geneva were organized into what was known as the Congregation, or Venerable Company of Pastors. This body approved the appointment of teachers and preachers and generally exercised an oversight over the work of the ministry and the schools. The Ordinances likewise stressed the importance of teachers who were to educate the children, and of a body of deacons to care for the homeless and the sick. All in all, Calvin created a machinery whereby the godly life as he conceived it was to be rigorously followed. Religion in Geneva had really taken precedence over politics, so that although the town council was nominally supreme, in actuality the ministers were the real masters of the city.

Calvin's political views were not elaborated until the last edition (1559) of the *Institutes*. They have already been summarized in the section dealing with political thought in the sixteenth century. Here one may simply compare his teachings with those of Luther. Both had a very high view of civil authority. "It is the will of God, that while we are aspiring towards our true country, we be pilgrims on the earth," Calvin wrote, in a phrase that Governor William Bradford was later to immortalize in his *History of Plimouth Plantation*. In general it should be the purpose of civil government to support religion and "establish general peace and tranquility." Magistrates are "commissioned of God." The estates of the realm or any duly constituted magistracy may, indeed, take a stand against tyranny, but for the individual, passive resistance to a ruler who disobeys the laws of God is as much as

Calvin will allow. What has been called "the break from Calvin," in other words the right of the individual actively to resist oppression, came later.

Calvinism, whether in its religious or in its political sense, would at first glance seem to have little in common with the democratic tradition of a later period. Certain germs of democracy may nevertheless be observed, notably in the idea of the priesthood of all believers, in the organization of the Calvinistic churches with their elders and deacons, in the regional meetings ("colloquies") of the neighboring churches and in the eventual national "synods" which bound the local churches of France together. In Scotland the general assembly of the Scottish church was actually more representative of the nation than parliament, which was feudal in its make-up. One has only to recall, however, the nature of the early New England town to realize that such democracy was far from complete; in some sense the principle was not so much democratic as it was theocratic; if one cannot speak precisely of the government of God, one may certainly stress the concept of government by the godly.

It is Calvin's great importance that he established these ideas and practices in the little city state of Geneva. In so doing, he made Geneva the "Protestant Rome"—the center to which devotees came from all over Europe; here he preached, wrote his treatises and conducted his voluminous correspondence. Above all, Calvin sought to bring his followers directly to the Bible. He encouraged one of his associates to make a French version to which in 1535 he wrote the preface. "He wished," so it was said, "nothing more than to be obedient to what was the voice of God directly made audible in the words of the Bible." From Geneva a stream of influence went forth which profoundly affected France, Germany, the Low Countries, Scotland, England, America, and, to a lesser degree, Poland, Austria and Hungary.

■ THE FRENCH REFORMATION

The reform movement in France was the outcome both of domestic forces and of influences coming into the country from Germany and Switzerland. Luther's works, which had a large vogue in France, were condemned and burned by the Sorbonne. Francis I, who had secured administrative control of the Church in France by the Concordat of 1516, with the papacy, was content to remain a champion of orthodoxy at home. Political considerations, however, led him to adopt seemingly contradictory policies. On the one hand Francis decreed instant burning for any man convicted by three witnesses of being a Lutheran. On the other, in 1534 he allied secretly with the Protestant princes of Germany against the Emperor Charles V. Francis' sister Marguerite, who married Henry of Navarre and whose grandson was to be the future Henry IV of France, gave her sympathies to the side of religious reform. She encouraged the translation of the New Testament which appeared in 1523; she wrote a book of piety, *The Mirror of the Sinful Soul;* and she corresponded ardently with the humanist scholar, Briçonnet.

Despite the beginnings of religious persecution, which were evident in France before 1530, Calvin's followers, nicknamed Huguenots, soon became a significant group.[15] Calvin had been rebuffed in his appeal to Francis I. Many of the nobles, however, turned to Calvin, as did goodly numbers of the middle class. The French edition of the *Institutes* was burned by order of the Sorbonne in 1544. In 1545 the king authorized an attack on the Protestant Waldensians in Provence. This armed assault resulted in the destruction of three towns and twenty-two villages and the ruthless massacre of three thousand men, women and children.

Under Francis' son, Henry II (1547–1559), the crisis became more acute. It was now as much political as religious, for certain great families were playing for political advantage and perhaps even for the crown itself. The Guise and Montmorency families were dominated by ardent Catholics, while other names—Bourbon, Condé, Châtillon, Coligny—began to appear on the side of Protestantism. In this situation Henry's wife, the Florentine Catherine de' Medici, played an important role. Lacking strong religious convictions and schooled in the political traditions of Machiavelli, she sought, by compromise if need be, to preserve order and to maintain royal authority. Above all she was determined to secure the succession for her weakling sons. A special court, nicknamed the *Chambre Ardente* ("Burning Chamber") which was set up in 1547 to deal with cases of heresy, made persecution official. Although some Protestants were sentenced, nevertheless their cause continued to grow, so that by 1559 the number of Huguenot churches was large enough and the atmosphere sufficiently relaxed to permit the meeting of a national synod in Paris. In the same year the Protestants accepted a profession of faith, strongly Calvinist in character. Calvin boasted that there were now 300,000 Huguenots in France.

The crisis really came to a head in 1559 with the death of Henry II. His three sons (the future Francis II, Charles IX and Henry III) were either immature, sickly or depraved. Despite the efforts of the Queen Mother, Catherine de' Medici, to maintain royal authority, the great families of the Guises and Bourbons came into open rivalry. Seeing that Protestantism had now been openly accepted by many of the nobility, in 1562 Catherine sum-

---

15. Like the later Puritans, Methodists and Quakers, the Huguenots derived their name from a slang expression, perhaps in this case a corruption of the German word *Eidgenossen,* or Confederates.

moned both sides to the Colloquy of Poissy, seeking a religious compromise. But when this failed, and when the Duke of Guise permitted his retainers to slaughter a group of Protestant worshipers (the Massacre of Vassy), a long and vicious era of civil war was precipitated.

These Wars of Religion, which might almost equally well be called Wars of the Succession, ran their tedious length from 1562 to 1598; they thus fall into the period following the Peace of Augsburg when religious compromise had brought a halt to the strife in Germany. In this confused period historians have been able to distinguish eight separate wars, punctuated by repeated attempts at compromise and reconciliation. The recurrent efforts at compromise and their repeated failure are of more significance than the tedious details of the wars themselves. Although Catherine would doubtless have been willing to accept limited toleration, factional jealousies ran very deep; moreover, the final decrees of the Council of Trent (1564) seemed to render any Roman Catholic compromise with Protestantism impossible. After the Chancellor, L'Hôpital, was dismissed for urging toleration, the wretched wars dragged on. Violence steadily increased. In 1572 the Guises contrived the murder of Admiral Coligny, a leading Protestant and advocate of moderation. In the bloody massacre of St. Bartholomew (August, 1572), for which Catherine and her son Charles must accept responsibility, some three thousand Huguenots met their deaths in Paris alone, where the red waters of the Seine were choked with their bodies. The St. Bartholomew massacre, for which the papacy struck a medal and at which Philip II of Spain rejoiced, rang a warning to the Protestant cause everywhere in Europe.

During the last stage of these increasingly savage wars, Spanish intervention gave further powerful aid to the extreme Catholic faction. Consequently, a group of moderate Catholics known as the *Politiques* now began to put the goal of order and peace, rather than religious uniformity, in first place. Their efforts, however, were unavailing and the so-called "War of the Three Henries" ensued. Henry III, the last and certainly the most corrupt of the Valois, supported the Catholic cause while at the same time working to enlarge his own royal power. A second leader, Henry of Guise, represented the forces of the Catholic "League" organized to resist any concessions to Protestantism. He likewise sought to advance the fortunes of his own house and even to seize the person of the king. A third figure, Henry of Navarre, the Protestant grandson of Marguerite of Navarre, had the support of the *Politiques* along with whom he championed a policy of moderation.

Only violence, however, could bring a solution. Henry III contrived the murder of Henry of Guise in the royal ante-chamber at Blois; the Guise family in return contrived the murder of Henry III. Henry of Navarre, the next in line to the throne, took the crown in 1589 and found himself facing the combined opposition of the Catholic League and of Spain. In the course of this struggle he made the shrewd decision in 1593 to return to the Catholic faith, this being the only condition upon which royal leadership of his war-torn country could be effective. Soon becoming the master of France, Henry then obtained the Peace of Vervins with Spain in 1598, at long last ridding his country of the hated foreigners. This outcome then made it possible in the same year for him to issue the Edict of Nantes.

The Edict of Nantes, a historic landmark in the growth of religious toleration, can be summarized as follows:

(1) The "Catholic Apostolic and Roman religion" was to be restored and re-established in France wherever its exercise had been interrupted.

(2) No member of "the so-called reformed religion" (i. e., the Huguenots) was to be molested because of his faith.

(3) Private worship could be practiced by the Huguenots within their homes or castles anywhere in France.

(4) Public Protestant worship was to be allowed in a long list of designated places (but not within five leagues of Paris).

(5) Calvinists had all the legal rights of Catholics, could be admitted to schools, hospitals and universities, and could hold any public office.

(6) Calvinists were permitted to hold religious synods, and about two hundred fortified towns such as La Rochelle, Montpellier and Nîmes were to be in their hands.

The religious outcome in France, then, was markedly different from what it had been in Germany. In the latter case the individual had to accept the public religion of his state or emigrate to another. In France one could be a Calvinist in private anywhere. Although Catholicism remained the official religion of the state, Calvinism was guaranteed an assured, albeit a minority, status. The Protestants, therefore, did not secure the full degree of liberty granted to the Catholics. It has been suggested that Henry IV himself regarded the Edict as provisional rather than as permanent. Certain it is that at his coronation he had promised to drive all heretics from France. Toleration, then, may have been to Henry an expedient. For his subjects in general, to whom liberty of conscience was still unfamiliar, this toleration has been described as a hateful concession made under hard necessity. Only with difficulty was the Edict accepted by the various provincial bodies in France. In any event, the provision which gave the Huguenots fortified towns was to be nullified by Cardinal Richelieu; and in 1685 the guarantees of religious toleration in France were ended by the Grand Monarch, Louis XIV. At the time of its issuance, however, the Edict must be regarded as a notable achievement in the struggle for religious liberty.

THOMAS CRANMER, ARCHBISHOP OF CANTERBURY, painted by Gerlach Flicke in 1546 when Cranmer was at the height of his influence and ten years before he was burned at the stake in Oxford. Scholar, politician, churchman and martyr, Cranmer has left his great memorial in the Anglican Litany and Prayer Book. Photograph, copyright by the National Portrait Gallery, London.

Chapter 9

The Age
of the Reformation
1517–1598 (2)

■ THE ENGLISH REFORMATION

THE IMPETUS to religious change in England was to be found partly in influences coming from abroad and perhaps even more in certain native trends. Opposition to papal interference was of long standing, for as early as the fourteenth century Parliament had enacted legislation to limit papal control of church appointments and of ecclesiastic courts. Although these statutes were not rigidly enforced and although a technique of "live and let live" had been worked out between civil and ecclesiastical authority, the tradition of opposition nevertheless existed. Criticism of Catholic dogma, which likewise had a long history going back at least to Wyclif and the Lollards, continued to have its further exponents. Without doubt, too, there was a large discontent with the worldliness of the clergy, the reported corruption of the religious houses and the widespread neglect of clerical duties.

In another sense the new nationalism of which the Tudor Henry VII and his successors were the spokesmen contributed to the religious crisis. A growing antagonism to Spain, as sixteenth-century England became involved in the tangle of European politics, led to a strong suspicion of that Catholic religion of which Spain had become the outstanding champion. The papacy, moreover, because of its political and territorial ambitions was regarded as a temporal power of some importance. Thus there were many reasons why England should oppose papal demands, whether these demands involved matters of doctrine or dealt with the equally pertinent questions of church appointments, church courts and church finances.

New ideas were coming in at the opening of the sixteenth century. England had its biblical humanists—men such as John Colet who were happy in the company of Erasmus and who, like Erasmus, were capable of stimulating their fellows to new courses of thought and action. In addition to the well-known Oxford Reformers there was also a small university group at Cambridge accustomed to meet at the White Horse Tavern (known as "Little Germany") and discuss the new ideas of Dr. Martin Luther. These "Germans," as they came to be called, included some famous names; among them were Tyndale, Coverdale, Latimer and Cranmer.

It is perhaps unfortunate that the beginning of religious reform in England has been so closely associated in common understanding with what was really an episode—a marital problem in the life of Henry VIII. His divorce, or, more properly, the desired annulment of his marriage with Catherine of Aragon, was not the cause of the English Reformation, though it was certainly the precipitating event. When Henry VIII had succeeded his father, Henry VII, in 1509 he seemed, in the brilliant and complicated world of European politics, to be the epitome of Renaissance kingship. For political reasons his father had arranged that he should marry Catherine of Aragon, the daughter of Ferdinand and Isabella. Catherine had previously been married to Henry's brother, Arthur, who had died before the marriage had been consummated; a dispensation therefore had been obtained from the pope so that Henry could marry the widow of his deceased brother. Although Catherine had borne Henry a daughter, the future Mary Tudor, none of her remaining six children had survived infancy.

Three reasons could be given for Henry now wishing an annulment of his marriage. In the first place, it was clear by 1524 that Catherine would not bear him a son. England had never had a queen regnant, and considering the ruthless politics of the age it was very questionable whether the destinies of the kingdom could safely be left in the hands of a young princess. A second reason could be found in that curious phenomenon, the conscience of Henry VIII. Had the pope been justified in issuing a dispensation, and if he had not was Henry legally married to Catherine? A third consideration was Henry's new infatuation for a lady of the court, Anne Boleyn; but, while this infatuation was real enough, it is only fair to Henry to point out that he had contemplated ending his marriage with Catherine long before he fell in love with Anne.

By 1527 Henry had instructed his principal minister, Cardinal Wolsey, to undertake the necessary proceedings at Rome to have his marriage annulled. Wolsey, the son of an Ipswich butcher and one of the most spectacular figures of a spectacular age, was Henry's principal minister from 1515 to 1529. Rising rapidly to be Archbishop of York, Lord Chancellor, Cardinal and papal legate, he also held the bishopric of Bath and Wells, then Durham and then Winchester; and he seriously aspired to become pope. "He is," wrote a contemporary, "the proudest prelate that ever breathed." His income was enormous. "This cardinal," wrote the Venetian ambassador with some exaggeration, "rules both the king and the entire kingdom." [1] It has been truly observed that he understood little of what we call the Reformation, and he made no real contribution to solving political questions; yet he dramatized for Henry VIII the nature of political power and showed his royal master how it could be used.

For the pope the prospective annulment raised huge problems. The papacy was threatened by Charles V whose troops in 1527 had seized and sacked Rome. Charles was the nephew of Catherine. Could the papacy risk provoking the imperial anger? It was a serious business, moreover, for one pontiff to reverse the decision of a predecessor. It seemed, therefore, that the best policy for Clement VII was to temporize. Accordingly, he first authorized Wolsey and an Italian cardinal to hear the case in England and then, after many calculated delays, revoked it to Rome. Wolsey, who had been steadily growing in Henry's disfavor, now came under violent royal attack. In thus agreeing to let an ecclesiastical case be appealed to Rome, he was accused of a breach of the ancient statute of *Praemunire* and compelled to surrender his office as chancellor. He died in November, 1530, while on his way, under arrest, to the Tower of London. In this long drawn out crisis, rendered sordid by Henry's consuming desire to make Anne Boleyn his bride, the religious conflict came to a head.

In 1529 Henry summoned the so-called Reformation Parliament which sat until 1536 and which joined with him in effecting the breach with Rome. One need not speak of royal dictatorship or tyranny, for the majority of Parliament was disposed to do those things which Henry required. The new figure to assume the mantle of Wolsey was Thomas Cromwell, risen like his predecessor from humble origins. The clergy were required to pay a collective fine of one hundred thousand pounds for their error in recognizing Wolsey's legatine authority and were required to accept Henry as supreme head of the church "so far as the law of Christ allows." This headship was conceived of in political and not religious terms. No future church laws were to be proclaimed without royal approval. The payment of annates to Rome was abolished and the power of church courts limited. Royal influence in the election of bishops became decisive. Papal jurisdiction in Eng-

---

1. A. F. POLLARD, *Wolsey* (1929), pp. 102–103.

land was declared at an end, and thus the Houses of Convocation (the official assembly of the Church in England) annulled Henry's marriage with Catherine (1533). Whereupon the pope excommunicated Henry, and Henry in reprisal ended all money payments to Rome. The climax came in 1534 with the Act of Supremacy. By this the clergy were required to recognize Henry as "only supreme head on earth of the Church of England" and to renounce the "usurped jurisdiction of the bishop of Rome." For refusal to take this oath Fisher, Bishop of Rochester, and the chancellor, Sir Thomas More, were sent to the scaffold. Despite some unrest in the north, England as a whole accepted the changes which Henry was making. The first great breach had been effected.

Another important issue was that of the monasteries. Not as numerous as in some continental countries (one estimate gives 7,000 monks, 2,000 nuns and 35,000 lay members), they nevertheless were highly important as landowners.[2] Many accusations had been made of monastic indifference, idleness and corruption. The commissioners whom Thomas Cromwell sent around compiled a shocking series of reports, designed, it may be suspected, as much to please the royal master as to give an accurate reflection of what they found. Yet the evidence could not be ignored. In 1536 Parliament voted the suppression of the lesser monasteries (those with an annual income of less than two hundred pounds); in 1539 it was the turn of the greater establishments. The inmates were not treated too harshly, provided that they would conform; some were given benefices; abbots and priors were given pensions; some were permitted to renounce their vows completely. Six new bishoprics were created. A portion of the old monastic revenues was applied to these new ecclesiastic foundations; relatively small amounts were turned over as gifts to courtiers and officials. By far the greater part of monastic property was sold, much of it to the gentry and the rising middle class whose members were now tied by a strong bond of personal interest to the monarchy.

Still further developments were to come. In 1533 Thomas Cranmer (1489–1556) had been made Archbishop of Canterbury. Cranmer had had some contact with the Lutherans of Germany (whom Henry denounced in a little book for which the pope had awarded him the title, Defender of the Faith), but on the whole he was regarded as a moderate. The so-called "Great Bible" of 1539, a translation which was really the work of Tyndale and Coverdale but which had an introduction written by Cranmer, was ordered (1541) to be read every Sunday from every pulpit in the land.

2. J. D. MACKIE, *The Earlier Tudors* (1952), pp. 372–373. The author quotes estimates of from one-third to one-sixth of all the land of England as being in monastic hands.

Meanwhile in 1536 Henry had forced Convocation to accept a document quaintly entitled, "Articles devised by the King's Highness to establish Christian quietness." These Ten Articles, the first restatement of belief in England, deserve notice. Although they generally reaffirmed the Roman Catholic faith, they included some significant changes. The Articles reduced the sacraments to three, referred to salvation by faith and questioned the doctrine of purgatory. Above all, they set up the Bible, the three historic Creeds and the first four church councils as the bases of the Christian faith. Henry made these changes because they seemed best to embody the temper of the times. However, in 1539, warned by the northern Catholic rising known as the Pilgrimage of Grace, he reversed his direction. Parliament in that year was induced to draft the Six Articles—the "Whip with Six Strings," defining religious belief and penalizing disbelief. These articles maintained Catholic doctrine essentially unchanged, including the belief in transubstantiation, the use of the confessional and the custom of clerical celibacy. Denial of transubstantiation was punishable by death. The provision concerning clerical celibacy caused much embarrassment to Archbishop Cranmer, who had married and was compelled on at least one occasion when traveling to carry his wife hidden in a chest. Efforts were made to enforce the articles. In London, for example, a man was hanged for eating flesh on Friday and a Dr. Barnes, who "leaned to Anabaptism," was burned at the stake. Such punishments were not new, and yet they were significant in their time as marking an embitterment of the current controversy. On the whole, however, by the time of Henry's death in 1547 England had accepted the great administrative changes consequent upon the first royal actions.

The permanent doctrinal changes were yet to come. Henry, it has been well said, was no Protestant, yet he had successfully challenged the authority of the pope, and had seen the Bible, the Creed, the Lord's Prayer and the Ten Commandments authoritatively published in English.[3] Major state offices were now generally in lay rather than in clerical hands. Most significant of all, the English church was being nationalized. Henry had demonstrated the power not so much of absolutism as of a strong king working through Parliament. Thus, at a time when royal authoritarianism seemed to be growing elsewhere in Europe, Henry associated himself with popular forces in order to deal with the great problem of religion.

The six-year reign of the boy king, Edward VI (1547–1553), was responsible for a doctrinal reformation, as distinct from the essentially political reformation undertaken by his father. The two Protectors of the realm, first Somerset and then Northumberland, were both Protestants and pushed

3. *Ibid.*, p. 433.

the cause of reform. An Act of Uniformity was passed in 1549 making compulsory the use of Cranmer's Book of Common Prayer. This, the first to be written in English, leaned in the direction of Lutheran doctrine. It was intended to replace the older Latin Mass-books, but in matters of belief was so unclear as to be described as an exercise in ambiguity. This Prayer Book, it must be noted, was adopted by Parliament rather than by the official assembly of the clergy and therefore was definitely state-imposed. Yet inquisitorial methods were not used. Provided that Englishmen conformed outwardly, they could still differ as to the precise meaning of their beliefs.

In these years, too, the views of Calvin and Zwingli as distinct from those of Luther began to make themselves felt. Cranmer himself showed Calvinist influence. "They teach," he wrote of his opponents, "that Christ is in the bread and wine, but we say, according to the truth, that he is in them that worthily eat and drink the bread and the wine." Repeated demands were made for the simplification of the church service and for a higher standard of clerical ability. There was need for such a raising of standards. In a visitation of the diocese of Gloucester in 1551, for example, it was found that out of 311 clergy questioned 170 were unable to repeat the Ten Commandments and 10 could not even recite the Lord's Prayer.

In 1552 a second Act of Uniformity was passed requiring all to attend church and authorizing a Second Prayer Book. Written in the stately English of Thomas Cranmer this book went much further than its predecessor in the direction of Zwinglian ideas. Communion was regarded as an act of remembrance; the phrase, communion table, was used instead of altar; vestments were simplified; and a general confession was substituted for private confession. The Forty-Two Articles of belief, which retained only baptism and communion as sacraments and explicitly repudiated transubstantiation, were now drawn up. They asserted the doctrine of justification by faith and emphasized the sole authority of the Bible. All papal authority was rejected, and a most powerful emphasis was placed upon the rights of the monarchy. "The Civil Magistrate," it was asserted, "is ordained and allowed of God; wherefore we must obey him not only for fear of punishment, but also for conscience' sake." With little change the Forty-Two Articles were later taken over by Elizabeth.

On Edward's death his half-sister Mary, the daughter of Catherine of Aragon, succeeded him. This tragic interlude (1553–1558), in which Mary sought to restore the Catholic faith in which she so profoundly believed, was destined to fail. Her marriage in 1554 to the future Philip II of Spain was unpopular. Under the spur of her principal advisor, Reginald, Cardinal Pole, Parliament meekly repealed the ecclesiastical legislation of her predecessors. It was impossible, however, to restore the confiscated monastic lands and it proved impossible, too, to destroy the Protestant allegiance of the majority of Englishmen.

Mary's persecutions were notable, not for their number, but for the rank of those who were attacked. Latimer, Bishop of Worcester, Ridley of London, Hooper of Gloucester, Taylor of Lincoln and Ferrar of St. Davids were burned, some of them outside their cathedrals. The aged Cranmer, Archbishop of Canterbury, after seven recantations found courage finally to profess his Protestant faith and was burned publicly in Oxford, steadfastly holding to the flames the hand with which his recantations had been signed. Altogether more than three hundred went to the stake in four years. The *Actes and Monuments* of John Foxe (1563), better known as the *Book of Martyrs,* gave Englishmen the record of these and earlier persecutions. For the next two hundred years it was often placed beside the Bible in parish churches and there read. In this reign many Englishmen sought safety on the continent; these eight hundred or so "Marian exiles" came into contact with the leaders of continental Protestantism, especially in the Rhineland and Switzerland, in consequence of which when they did eventually return they were disposed to carry the religious reformation in England even further.

The reign of Elizabeth (1558–1603), one of the most fateful in English history, gave to English Protestantism its permanent definition. The daughter of Anne Boleyn, Elizabeth was only twenty-five at her accession. She had been proclaimed illegitimate by the papacy.[4] Enormous dangers hung over the kingdom, making it essential for her to move carefully. Elizabeth herself was not unlike the French *Politiques;* wishing to establish a secure order in the state on the basis of compromise or toleration, she displayed nothing of her half-sister's religious fanaticism. As she moved through the uncertainties and dangers of her first years—dangers which actually could not be said to have been vanquished until the defeat of the Armada in 1588—Elizabeth showed an unshakable determination to assert royal power within the general framework of the parliamentary system. Her attitude toward religious questions must, therefore, be considered in this light.

Elizabeth would not, like her father, assume the title of Supreme Head of the Church. The Act of Supremacy of 1559 declared simply that "the Queen's Highness is the only supreme governor of this realm . . . as well in all spiritual or ecclesiastical things or causes as temporal." As Marian legislation was swept away, an Act of Uniformity (1559) restored with some slight modifications the Prayer Book of 1552. All clergy, public officials and candidates for university degrees were to take the oath of supremacy, and

4. In 1536, after Henry VIII had caused Anne Boleyn to be beheaded on the charge of adultery, Parliament had declared her daughter Elizabeth to be illegitimate.

death could be imposed upon anyone who challenged the queen's authority. Of nine thousand clergy only about two hundred refused the oath. Attendance at church was made compulsory.[5] A certain moderation and compromise could be found in the rewording of the Prayer Book, notably in dealing with the communion. A similar desire for caution might also be seen in the fact that the Thirty-Nine Articles of faith, drawn up by Convocation in 1563, were not given legal sanction by Parliament until 1571. This was the year after the pope had issued his bull of excommunication against Elizabeth, who did not press Parliament to take such action until reconciliation with Catholics appeared out of the question.

The Thirty-Nine Articles declared that the Scriptures contained all that was necessary to salvation. They included a statement on the Lord's Supper that could be accepted both by Lutherans and Calvinists. Men were to be saved only by faith, from which good works would naturally follow. Only baptism and the Lord's Supper were recognized as sacraments, and belief in purgatory was condemned. The queen was authorized to "restrain with the civil sword the stubborn and evil-doers," and papal authority in England was explicitly condemned.

It seems clear that Elizabeth's policies met the desires of the majority of Englishmen, for by 1585 the number of practicing Catholics had shrunk to a small minority of the total population.[6] Her *Via Media,* or Middle Way, found its classic defense in Richard Hooker's *Laws of Ecclesiastical Polity,* written towards the close of the reign. Reason as well as Scripture, Hooker argued, will justify the form of religious settlement which England has secured. The Anglican Church has been established by a Parliament which is surely possessed of that reason in which all men participate. "With us," he wrote, "one society is both the Church and commonwealth."

Despite Elizabeth's moderation she was not able to avoid some forcible measures. On the one side was the Roman Catholic interest, principally embodied abroad in the policies of the hated Philip II of Spain, and at home in those groups who had never at heart accepted the new order and were now reinforced by outside encouragement, notably from the Jesuits. Elizabeth was confronted with various Catholic plots, most of which seemed to lead to Mary, Queen of Scots, the nearest successor to the English throne and a devout Catholic. Expelled in 1568 from her kingdom by Knox and

---

5. The fine of one shilling for non-attendance in the statute of 1559 was often exacted, but the savage twenty-pound fine of 1581 remained largely a dead letter.

6. J. B. BLACK, *The Reign of Elizabeth* (1936), p. 374, n. 1, states that it is impossible to determine the number of Roman Catholics in Elizabethan England. He cites, without accepting it, a possible figure of 120,000 which would be some 4% or 5% of the total population. There were doubtless far more Catholics than would declare themselves openly.

his followers, Mary had flung herself upon the mercy of Elizabeth and had been held in semi-captivity. She was unquestionably involved in Catholic intrigue, though how much she was the instigator is still debated. In 1587 Elizabeth sent Mary to the block, yet this harsh act was hardly typical. Toward English Catholics Elizabeth was generally less ruthless. Her concern was less with heresy than it was with treason; but against the Jesuits and others who sought to win proselytes the penalties became very severe. Jesuits, for example, were ordered to leave the kingdom within forty days under penalty of death. Even so, under the penal laws of Elizabeth only some 250 victims perished over a twenty-year period.

Elizabeth's policies were also subject to attack from other quarters. In England those who came to be known as Puritans were eager to push the religious reformation even further. Under the influence of Calvin's teachings they were opposed to the institution of bishops and to the degree of ceremonial which the Prayer Book envisaged. They laid much stress upon lay preaching and "prophesying." In the form of Presbyterianism similar ideas took powerful hold in what was then the separate Scottish kingdom. One of the more radical English leaders, Robert Browne, insisted upon the importance of each little religious group, thus leading in the direction of "congregationalism." This was hardly as yet an explicit creed, but was clearly opposed to the episcopal organization of the English church. These radical ideas spread from the arena of religion into that of politics. Luther and Calvin had both insisted on the high position of the civil power and the duty of obedience. The generation subsequent to Calvin, however, was exposed to the bitterness of the French wars of religion and the Dutch struggle for independence. It therefore developed the more active doctrine of resistance to an oppressor, finding Biblical justification for armed resistance and even for assassinating a tyrant. In this atmosphere it is understandable that Elizabeth and her ministers, with their strong sense of order, should have looked upon the newly arisen sects with profound misgivings.

In summary, the religious settlement in England was one which sought to include as many as possible in a single church without too much insistence upon dogmatic niceties. It was well suited to a people who kept the question of political unity uppermost. England produced no giants such as Luther or Calvin; on the other hand she was spared the cruelty of religious war and large-scale persecution. Elizabeth worked for a solution that would satisfy the vast majority of her subjects and at the same time not bear down too heavily upon those who disagreed. It may be some indication of the value of the settlement which she achieved that, despite the religious conflicts of the seventeenth century, its main outlines have persisted down to our own day.

■ THE REFORMATION IN SCOTLAND

Although the reform movement in Scotland followed a path somewhat different from that in England, yet the two were closely related. The most important political outcome—the eventual union of the two thrones—would hardly have been possible had not religious reform prepared the way.

The turbulent history of Scotland had favored the growth of some heretical movements, and the evident corruption of the Catholic Church had led to active criticisms which resembled those arising contemporaneously in other countries. This domestic situation was complicated by the problem of the Scottish monarchy and its foreign relations, especially with France and England. In 1542 the week-old infant, Mary Stuart, great-granddaughter of Henry VII of England, succeeded to the throne of Scotland under the regency of her mother, Mary of Guise. The close connection with Catholic France was deeply resented by a group of Scottish nobles who became sympathetically disposed to religious reform. Leader of the Catholic group in Scotland was Cardinal Beaton, Archbishop of St. Andrews, who sought by rigorous measures to stamp out the growing Protestant ideas. The opposition to Beaton was such that in 1546 he was murdered.

The man around whom the Scottish Reformation took shape was John Knox, a priest of humble birth who had turned to the teachings of Calvin, preached with tremendous eloquence and, amid many other adventures, spent some time in Geneva at the feet of Calvin himself. In 1557 a group of Scottish noblemen and gentlemen, the "Lords of Congregation," signed a solemn oath or Covenant in which they promised to set forth "the most blessed Word of God and His Congregation" in accordance with the reform ideas. They invited Knox to come from Geneva to be their spokesman. Knox had just written his *First Blast of the Trumpet Against the Monstrous Regiment of Women* (1557), a militant denunciation of feminine influence in high places, notably in the cases of Mary of Guise, Mary Stuart and Mary Tudor of England, all ardent Catholics. Coming as it did on the very eve of the accession of Elizabeth of England to whom the Scottish reformers were soon to look for help, the book must be regarded as spectacularly ill-timed. Elizabeth never forgave Knox for it. The "Reformed Kirk" of Scotland was proclaimed in 1558 and in the following year Knox returned as its champion.

The bitter conflict which ensued was as much political as religious. Mary, who had been married in 1558 to the dauphin of France, and had been queen during Francis II's brief reign of one year returned to Scotland in 1561, a widow of eighteen. Meanwhile English aid to the Lords of Congregation had helped to drive out the French. With these political moves came also religious changes. The Scottish Parliament had declared in 1560 that the "Bishop of Rome" had no authority in the land. The ministers of the Reformed Kirk drew up a Confession of Faith (Calvinistic in tone) and a Book of Discipline which outlined a pattern of church organization abolishing the bishops and setting up a framework of local churches or kirks, periodical synods and a general assembly presided over by an elected moderator. Government of the church was not so much to be by the people as by the elders and the ordained ministers. In place of the old prayer book was substituted a Book of Common Order.

In this atmosphere the young queen vainly sought to restore the Roman Catholic faith and to assert her own absolute power. Her long discussions with Knox, preserved in the quaint pages of his *History of the Reformation,* are still moving. "Ye have taught the people to receive another religion than their princes can allow," she declared, "and how can that doctrine be of God, seeing that God commands subjects to obey their princes?" Knox's reply, "if their princes exceed their bounds, Madam, they may be resisted and even deposed," shows the great gulf, not only between the stern old reformer and the young queen, but between the new doctrine of open resistance and the old teaching of passive obedience which both Luther and Calvin had earlier espoused. The armed conflict in Scotland lasted until 1568 when the Parliament forced Mary to abdicate in favor of her son, James VI, born of her marriage with Lord Darnley. Mary gave up the struggle, fled to England, and placed herself at the mercy of her Protestant cousin, Elizabeth. Presbyterianism, after some further struggle, became the established religion in Scotland, as Anglicanism was in England. That the northern country moved further away from Rome than did England may be attributed in some measure to the later period at which religious changes came about in Scotland. "England cast loose from Rome at a time when the conservative influence of Luther was predominant; Scotland was swept into the current of revolution under the fiercer star of Calvin." [7] Such differences as came about have shown an impressive permanence.

■ THE SPREAD OF CALVINISM: THE RADICAL SECTS

Calvinism, like Lutheranism, spread to other lands. The Netherlands, long the home of considerable religious diversity, were very susceptible to reform ideas. Here, where groups such as the Brethren of the Common Life had set a high standard of religious devotion, the Bible had been translated into the vernacular and printed as early as 1477. Luther's writings quickly found a welcome, so much so that as early as 1522 Charles V ordered them publicly burned. Calvin's ideas likewise spread, as did the teachings of some of the extremist groups such as the Anabaptists. The first Calvinist

7. PRESERVED SMITH, *The Age of the Reformation* (1920), p. 353.

church was organized in 1561. When in 1565 Philip II, the successor to Charles V, insisted upon publishing the decrees of the Council of Trent, this was taken by the provinces of Holland and Brabant as an infringement upon their constitutional liberties. Thus, although the revolt against Spain which followed was in considerable degree political, the religious issue also loomed large. This revolt will be described later; meanwhile we may note simply that provisional freedom from Spain was secured in 1609 after a long struggle and confirmed in 1648 at the Peace of Westphalia.

Calvinist teachings gained some unofficial and fugitive hold in various parts of Germany, notably in the Rhineland, in Württemberg and in Brandenburg. Other Calvinist groups appeared in Austria, Poland and Hungary; there was, indeed, for a time a most impressive acceptance of Calvinism in Polish and Hungarian noble circles which a later generation of Catholics finally succeeded in counteracting. It can be noted, too, that the Turkish overrunning of Transylvania did not destroy the Calvinist groups which had taken root there, for the Turk showed at times a degree of tolerance which far exceeded that of his Christian contemporaries.

In Spain and Italy the reform ideas hardly went beyond certain restricted intellectual circles. The new discipline given by Cardinal Ximenes to the Spanish Church by the opening of the sixteenth century placed it fundamentally in opposition to reform. Yet at the University of Alcalá there was an Erasmian circle which sympathized with the ideas of the great Dutch humanist, and there were similar groups at Seville and Valladolid. The Church, however, moved severely against the innovators; the Inquisition was invoked and one of the leaders of reform, the Archbishop of Toledo, was sentenced to seventeen years imprisonment. In this way the new teachings, which had taken a relatively slight hold, were quickly stamped out.

In Italy, similarly, there were small groups at Naples, Siena, Lucca, Ferrara and elsewhere toying with the new religious ideas. Calvin spent some time at Ferrara where the duchess welcomed him to her court. But when the Roman Inquisition was reorganized in 1542 and when the growing influence of Spain in the peninsula reinforced the local authority of the papacy the movement sympathizing with Protestantism faded away.

So far this chapter has concerned itself with the larger movements of "protest" which developed in the sixteenth century—Lutheran, Calvinistic, Anglican or Presbyterian—and only brief notice has been given to lesser and more extreme groups such as the Anabaptists. It remains to inspect these aspects of radical Protestantism somewhat more closely, remembering that during the sixteenth century they were always minority groups, often subject to severe persecution and seldom effective or influential in any large way.

The Anabaptists, as we have seen, were groups arising first in Germany and the Netherlands who were opposed to infant baptism, declaring that this rite should be reserved for adults. The essence of the Anabaptist viewpoint seems to be an insistence upon the autonomy of each religious group, to which admission should be voluntary and only upon condition of living a moral life. With this as a starting point the Anabaptists naturally had little regard for the machinery of the state as an instrument of religious reform. Some of them took a very hostile view of conventional society, going so far as to renounce worldly wealth and, on occasion, to set up a kind of primitive communism. They were led often to refuse military service, or to go to law or swear an oath. Some became polygamists. The group led by John of Leyden which sought for a year to put such ideas into effect at the Germany city of Münster was in the end obliterated with the greatest cruelty. Other groups, such as that led by Menno Simons in the Netherlands, sought to live a Christian life of the utmost simplicity with only a rudimentary form of church organization; from these has developed the modern sect of the Mennonites, "a people," as Simons himself wrote, "separated from the world." In the sixteenth century such groups endured much persecution.

Of another type were the English followers of Robert Browne known as the Brownists. They could be regarded as the initiators of the modern congregational type of church, for Browne, the author of *Reformation Without Tarrying for Anie,* put forward the argument that any small group of devout Christians itself constituted a church and should be self-governing. Similar groups, known sometimes as Independents or Separatists, grew up. They could be regarded as the end product of the movement which had first impelled men to make their separation from the Church of Rome. The common ground of the Independent groups would be their doctrine of a "Covenant" as the basis of church membership and their opposition to what was known as episcopacy, in other words, to the elaborate church organization of which the system of bishops was an integral part.

Still another radical development was Unitarianism, which went beyond the attack on the sacraments launched by Luther and Calvin to question the very doctrine of the Trinity itself. The Spaniard, Miguel Serveto, was one of the first to profess such belief. At Geneva he tried to convert Calvin to his anti-trinitarian views; for this attempt he was burnt at the stake. Lelio and Fausto Sozzini (from whose name comes the label Socinian) also preached Unitarian doctrines, the former in Switzerland and Germany, the latter, with lasting effects, in Poland and Hungary. Still another designation known to the sixteenth century was that of Arminian, a word applied to the Dutch followers of Jacob Hermansen (Arminius) who argued against predestination and declared that man could exercise his free will with the assistance of God's grace. Such names—Separatist, Socinian or Arminian—occur frequently in the controversial religious literature of the sixteenth century, usually applied as a term of reproach to those individuals who went beyond the degree of religious reformation that the majority in a given area had been disposed to accept. These radical sects, never very large in numbers, bore witness to what the sympathizers with the Protestant revolt would probably call its dynamism and vitality, and what its opponents would probably call its hopelessly divisive tendencies.

■ THE REFORMATION IN THE ROMAN CATHOLIC CHURCH

It would be a mistaken view of the period of the Reformation to see it as concerned solely with the emergence and definition of the various Protestant churches. The Roman Catholic Church itself was gravely concerned with the problem of reform, whether in the more or less external matters of conduct or in the fundamental questions of dogma and belief. Ideas of reform within the Church were by no means new, for the medieval period—an age of vigorous religious controversy—had actively concerned itself with the discussion and formulation of belief. In a different sense, too, the work of the great church councils in the fourteenth and fifteenth centuries had been directed to matters of "reformation." It is also to be remembered that the first Protestant reformers of the sixteenth century regarded themselves as men seeking to bring about purification and change *within* the existing Catholic Church, and only at a later stage did they take a stand which led to their expulsion from it.

The papacy of the late fifteenth century was subject, as we have seen, to the powerful and complex influences of the Renaissance, one immediate consequence of which was a definite lowering of spiritual standards and a strong emphasis upon worldly splendor. The new atmosphere could be seen at its best in the brilliant artistic patronage of Julius II or Leo X, and certainly at its worst in the scandalous corruption of the Borgia pope, Alexander VI. His death in 1503 ended a flagrant period of papal licentiousness. Julius II (1503–1513), deeply involved in the political problems of the Italian Wars, was not unaware of the gathering religious clouds. In 1512 he summoned the Fifth Lateran Council, supposedly a council of all Christendom but actually overwhelmingly Italian, to consider the need of reform. For five years it sat, pointing its finger at a good many abuses and making some sensible proposals for reform; these proposals, however, never were put into effect and the council closed in the spring of 1517 just as the Lutheran storm in Germany was about to break.

Meanwhile Leo X (1513–1521), a Medici, had succeeded Julius II. He was less concerned with religion than with complicated political matters and with the patronage of the arts. The Concordat which he made with France in 1516 was what we today would call a "deal": Francis I gained the right to nominate French bishops in return for the resumption of the flow of papal revenues from France to Italy and for a kind of political guarantee of the House of Medici in Tuscany. Leo, who is reputed to have expressed his determination to enjoy the papacy which God had given him, failed to perceive the extent of the religious dangers in Germany. His approval of the issuing of indulgences there has been called a stupendous miscalculation, as indeed it was; for although he did eventually issue the famous bull excommunicating Luther he was in no wise able to stem the rise of German Protestantism. Under his immediate successors this movement gathered ever-increasing strength.

It remained for a later pontiff, Paul III (1534–1549), sometimes called the last Renaissance pope, to make some effort to reconcile existing religious differences. The new ideas had not been without their effect upon the Catholic Church; heretical opinions had taken hold in some exalted circles; and at least a few Italian churchmen were, as one historian puts it, "steering for Wittenberg." There had been, too, a certain revival of piety exemplified in the founding of the Oratory of Divine Love, an association of distinguished prelates and laymen who dedicated themselves to work and pray for the purification of the Church. Several new religious orders—the Theatines, the Capuchins and the Ursulines—likewise sought to inspire a greater devotion and piety. In 1537 Paul III established a Commission of Nine to survey ecclesiastical conditions. Its report condemned such prevalent abuses as the general unfitness of the clergy, the scandals in religious houses, the misuse of church funds, the sale of indulgences and the weakness of the cardinalate. But the report brought only modest results.

In 1541 Paul III went so far as to seek reconciliation with the German Protestants by sending a delegation to confer with their leaders at the Diet of Ratisbon. In consequence of the remarkable spirit of compromise which seemed at first evident, preliminary agreements were reached on certain vexed points. Man, it was agreed, is saved by faith (according to Luther's doctrine), but this faith must be living and active (according to the Catholic doctrine of good works). It was tentatively agreed that clerical marriage could be permitted though not encouraged. The papacy, however, subsequently rejected some of the accepted statements on the grounds of their ambiguity, and when, added to this, Luther denounced the statement on transubstantiation, what might have been a promising reconciliation fell through. This was indeed the last chance, the parting of the ways. By 1541 schism was an accomplished fact. Henceforth the reforms undertaken in the Roman Catholic Church were not designed to effect a reconciliation with Protestantism. They were intended, on the contrary, to strengthen the ramparts against further onslaughts and to win back ground that had already been lost. In this great battle the Catholic Church had considerable success.

One of the most dramatic moves in the Catholic struggle against disbelief came in the founding of the Society of Jesus. An obscure Spanish nobleman, Inigo Lopes de Recalde (1491–1556), lamed in battle in 1521, experienced during his convalescence a religious conversion which led him to a new life. After years of pilgrimage, study and devotion [8] the future St. Ignatius of Loyola succeeded in 1540 in obtaining papal approval for a new religious order, the Society of Jesus. Its purposes are best given in St. Ignatius' own words:

> Whoever wishes to fight for God under the standard of the Cross and to serve the Lord alone and his vicar on earth the Roman pontiff shall, after a solemn vow of perpetual chastity, consider that he is part of a society instituted chiefly for these ends, for the profit of souls in life and Christian doctrine, for the propagation of the faith through public preaching, the ministry of God's word, spiritual exercises and works of charity, and especially for the education of children and ignorant persons in Christianity, for the hearing of confession and for the giving of spiritual consolation.[9]

With the usual vows of poverty, obedience and chastity, a vow of allegiance to the pope was required of full-fledged members of the order—the so-called "professed of the four vows." The long and arduous training included a novitiate of two years, then five years given to the study of the liberal arts, then four or five to theology. The members wore no distinctive monastic garb. *The Constitutions* which Ignatius drafted in 1550 for his order covered every detail of life with elaborate care. All members were subject to an iron discipline and were to obey unquestioningly the authority of their head, the General of the Society. "Consummate prudence," it was declared, "allied with moderate saintliness is better than greater saintliness and mere prudence." "To attain the truth in all things," Ignatius wrote in his *Spiritual Exercises*, "we ought always to hold that we believe what seems to us white to be black, if the Hierarchical Church so defines it." These *Exercises*, a classic in the field of religious literature, offered a carefully worked out plan of meditation and self-discipline and were designed to give the novice spiritual training for the arduous work of his order.

8. It may be ranked among the extraordinary coincidences of history that Calvin and Ignatius were contemporaries at the Collège Montaigu in Paris.
9. Quoted in SMITH, *Age of the Reformation*, pp. 402–403.

At first small in numbers, the Jesuits soon began to exert an important influence in the religious conflict that was raging. Militancy was a mark of the order. "No storm is so dangerous as a calm," declared Ignatius, "no enemy is so dangerous as having none." Such militancy provoked reprisals. Against English Jesuits, trained on the continent, Queen Elizabeth directed her severest penalties, requiring those who were caught to be punished with death. The Jesuits played a leading role in winning back Poland to the faith. Missionary enterprise soon carried others far afield. Seminaries were established in Portugal, Italy, Spain, South Germany, France, Poland and the Spanish Netherlands. When St. Ignatius died in 1556 members of his order were to be found literally at the ends of the earth: in China and Japan, in India, Tibet, the Congo, Abyssinia and Brazil.[10]

The Church of the Gesù in Rome not only became the spiritual center, so to speak, of the Jesuit Order, but also with its ornate Baroque architecture constituted a model which was imitated in Jesuit church architecture both in Europe and overseas. In the field of teaching the Jesuits soon became active, founding schools that were famous for the care and thoroughness of their methods. "The chief crime of the Jesuits," wrote an eighteenth-century critic, Helvétius, "was the excellence of their teaching." Jesuit teaching laid great stress upon careful organization, drill, examination and review. It seems to have devised the system of marks or grades to regulate the work of the classroom. As preachers, too, the Jesuits made their name, though in time they became subject to criticism for a kind of ruthlessness, a determination to achieve their ends by an over-cleverness of argument and an intellectual agility to which the adjective "jesuitical" has come to be applied. The Jesuits likewise became noted for their pre-eminence in the work of the confessional. To say that they became confessors to the rulers of Catholic Europe is hardly an exaggeration, and it serves as a striking illustration of their power.

The most dramatic example of the Catholic effort to stem the tide of revolt may be seen in the work of the Council of Trent. This, the last of the great Church councils before the nineteenth century, was first summoned by Paul III in 1542; it sat intermittently until 1563.[11] Representation was largely Italian and Spanish, with some members also from France and Germany. On one occasion, in 1552, there was a brief and unavailing appearance of Protestant spokesmen. The Council, sitting at a time of political conflict between France and Spain and between the Emperor and the German Protestants, was marked by bitterness, denunciation and even beard-pulling. Much work, nevertheless, was eventually done.

10. For the work of the Jesuit St. Francis Xavier, the "Apostle of the Indies," see p. 114.
11. Trent was chosen as a meeting place because of its location in the Italian Tyrol on the frontiers of the Italian and German worlds. The Council convened officially in 1545.

The two great subjects of the Council were those of dogma and discipline. In respect to the first, the traditional positions of the Roman Catholic Church were in the end unhesitatingly reaffirmed—a result achieved in no small measure by the determination of Jesuit representatives. The seven sacraments, the authority of the text of the Vulgate, the veneration of the saints, the cult of the Virgin, the use of images and relics, the undertaking of pilgrimages, the use of indulgences and the belief in purgatory were all approved. Doctrinally, then, there was to be no yielding.

In the field of discipline and morals, however, the great need for improvement was frankly recognized, with the consequence that elaborate reform measures were taken. Bishops were to reorder their dioceses in every one of which there should be a seminary to train priests. Nepotism, pluralism and simony were condemned. The discipline of the monastic orders was to be tightened. A catechism, new service books and a new edition of the Vulgate were to be prepared. Celibacy was to be strictly enforced. Services were to be conducted in Latin, though it was also provided that preaching could be carried on in the vernacular. Unquestionably these measures brought about a remarkable improvement in the general standards of the Church.

The Council also concerned itself with regulating the flood of books coming from the printing presses, a matter which had long been the concern of the papacy and also of various civil governments. In 1559 Paul IV issued an *Index* of prohibited books, grouping them in three categories: those that were definitely heretical, those tending to heresy and those anonymous works unwholesome in doctrine. The list included the complete works of Erasmus. A later *Index,* the so-called *Tridentine Index* (including the writings of Machiavelli and Boccaccio), was published in 1564, and in 1571 a special Congregation, or commission, on the *Index* was established in Rome. The lists then established have been periodically revised to our own day. In Spain an *Index Expurgatorius* was set up in 1571 which concerned itself not with the condemnation of whole works but with the more delicate task of finding offensive passages deserving to be deleted.

Still another aspect of this work was the revival of the Roman Inquisition. This medieval technique for rooting out heresy by examination, exhortation and, if need be, torture had been officially authorized and revived in Spain as early as 1478 and had brought heavy suffering principally to Moors and Jews. The burning of heretics in an *auto da fé* ("act of faith") often became a great public spectacle. After formal ceremonies the victims were wrapped in yellow garments painted with devils and red flames. They were given tall, conical caps to wear. Those who repented at the last moment were treated with clemency—they were strangled. The unrepentant were burned.[12] The Spanish Inquisition was extended later to the Netherlands. In 1542 by papal decree a Roman Inquisition was created, to be directed by a body of six cardinals named the Holy Office. The work of this body was extended from Rome to other Italian cities, and though it never achieved the ferocity of its Spanish counterpart it had its bloody side. It contrived to root out small bands of heretics and dissenters which had quietly appeared in various parts of the peninsula. Among many others, the philosopher, Giordano Bruno, was condemned to death by the Inquisition in 1600; Galileo was compelled to recant before it in the seventeenth century; and Casanova, perhaps not unreasonably, was imprisoned by its order in the eighteenth.

Up to the middle of the sixteenth century, then, it would seem that the Protestant cause was in the ascendant. Thereafter the Catholics managed to hold their ground, and in time to win back much that had been lost. The outcome, first recognized in the *cujus regio, ejus religio* provision of the Peace of Augsburg, was a permanent religious division in Western Europe. The savage strife of the Thirty Years' War was soon to make clear, however, that this outcome fell far short of ending the conflict.

■ THE CONSEQUENCES OF THE RELIGIOUS CONFLICT

The religious pattern of Western Europe at the close of the sixteenth century was complex. The countries remaining invincibly Catholic were Spain, Portugal, Italy, most of South Germany, Austria, Bohemia, Ireland, Lithuania and those parts of the Low Countries later known as Belgium. A substantial Protestant minority persisted among the Hungarian nobility. Poland, originally subjected to strong Protestant influences, eventually reverted to a devout Catholicism. Firmly on the Protestant side were North Germany, Scandinavia, Finland, Estonia, Latvia, the United Netherlands, England and Scotland.

Such toleration as was found arose from the looseness with which dogma was defined and from the unwillingness of some authorities to use undue severity against Catholics or dissenters. In Germany, where the will of the prince made the decision for Catholicism or Lutheranism, dissenting minorities had little right save that of emigration. Yet in practice they often were permitted to remain. Similarly, while the Anglican settlement in England placed great political disabilities upon dissenters, they were not actively

12. When Philip II made his first public appearance on returning to Spain in 1559 from the Netherlands he celebrated the occasion by presiding over a "splendid" *auto da fé* at Valladolid where fourteen distinguished victims perished before his eyes. History has recorded Philip's terrible answer to a Spanish nobleman who, crippled by torture, reproached the king as he limped towards the stake: "If my son were as perverse as you, I myself would carry fuel to burn him."

Religious divisions can be shown only approximately. Although state churches were the rule, few countries could enforce complete religious uniformity. Minorities were found in almost every country and sometimes could worship with few restrictions. The broad distinction between a Protestant north and a Roman Catholic south is apparent.

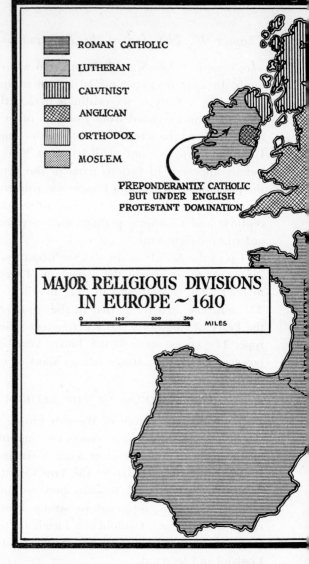

ROMAN CATHOLIC

LUTHERAN

CALVINIST

ANGLICAN

ORTHODOX

MOSLEM

PREPONDERANTLY CATHOLIC
BUT UNDER ENGLISH
PROTESTANT DOMINATION

MAJOR RELIGIOUS DIVISIONS
IN EUROPE ~ 1610

0   100   200   300   MILES

persecuted. In Switzerland toleration existed in the sense that it was agreed to differ; some cantons followed the path of Catholicism, some the path of Calvinism. Although France remained officially Catholic or "Gallican," the Edict of Nantes (1598), as we have seen, extended a remarkable degree of toleration to the Calvinistic or Huguenot minority—more, indeed, than was granted officially to a minority in any other country. Yet it has been said of Henry IV of France that toleration was to him really no more than a political expedient. In Bohemia, Transylvania and Hungary, Protestant minorities contrived to exist amid alien surroundings.

In so complex a movement as the Reformation it is not always easy to know what is cause and what is effect. The sixteenth century was so much an era of spectacular change that one must be careful not to attribute reli-

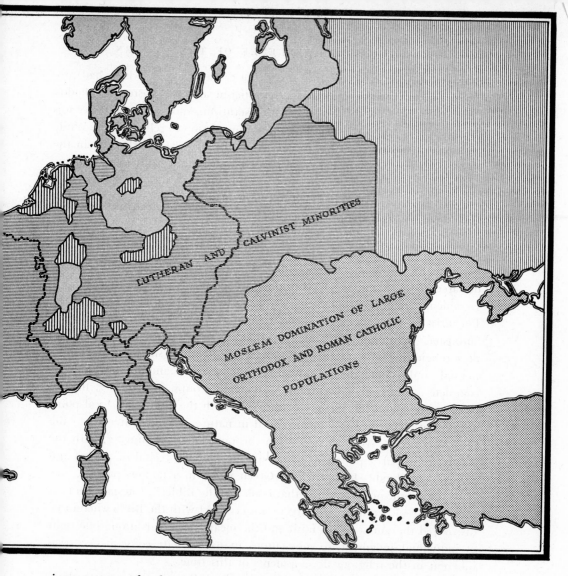

LUTHERAN AND CALVINIST MINORITIES

MOSLEM DOMINATION OF LARGE ORTHODOX AND ROMAN CATHOLIC POPULATIONS

gious causes to developments which might equally well be due to political or economic forces. Whatever its full explanation, the increasing *secularization* of society stands out as one of the major phenomena of this period. The altered relations between church and state meant that the state took over many of the duties which the church had formerly performed, as for example in the fields of charity and education. The state felt justified in confiscating large segments of ecclesiastical wealth. It undertook to define and regulate the type of church that should function within its borders. It undertook bit by bit to issue commands and set standards for its subjects in large areas where formerly the church had considered itself supreme.

Several specific results of the religious conflict may be listed. In the broadest sense, Europe had to accept the fact of religious divisions far deeper

227

than ever before; now, in addition to the earlier cleavage which had produced the two worlds of Roman Catholicism and the Eastern Orthodox
Church, emerged the third world of Protestantism. Another consequence was
the heightened importance of nationalism in relation to religious life. While
nationalism was not new, its increased significance was clearly seen in the
close relationship existing between church and state in Lutheran Germany,
in Scandinavia, in Scotland and in England. We may also observe the slow
beginnings of toleration, founded less on principle than on expediency, but
none the less powerful in its ultimate effects.

Protestantism had repudiated the Roman claim to be the Church Universal and had successfully challenged papal authority. It had denied the
necessity for the elaborate sacramental system which the Catholic belief
declared to be essential to salvation. It had reduced the number of the
sacraments, retaining baptism as a rule but refusing to admit in the
Eucharist its miraculous character. It had converted the "priest" into the
"minister," maintaining in some cases that any sincere layman could officiate
at a religious service. It had reduced the degree and significance of ceremonial—only moderately in the Lutheran services, and to the point of
complete austerity in the extreme Calvinistic groups. The service, instead
of centering about the mystery of the Mass with the altar as its focal point
and the priest as the officiator, changed in nature so as to center about the
preaching of the Word of God from the pulpit by the minister, with the
congregation participating in hymn singing and the recital of psalms and
prayers. "England," John Richard Green wrote in a famous passage, "became the people of a book, and that book was the Bible." Protestantism thus
brought the individual more directly into contact with the Bible wherein he
discovered the source of his faith and the means of his salvation. The right
of individual judgment, so momentous in its ultimate consequences, was
inherent in the religious developments of this time.

It has also been argued that the growth of Protestantism, particularly
in its Calvinistic form, helped the growth of the commercial, business
civilization which marked the new age. Such an argument rests partly upon
a consideration of the supposedly hostile view which the medieval Catholic
Church had officially taken of usury, lending at interest and worldly practices in general. In its extreme form this interpretation of the Roman
Catholic viewpoint can hardly stand, for the Church had found many
ways to modify the rigor of its economic prohibitions. The argument is
also based on those aspects of Calvin's teachings in which he stressed man's
earthly "vocation" or "calling" and insisted upon the virtues of thrift, industry and sobriety. These are the virtues of a middle-class civilization,
supposedly best exemplified in the Swiss or the Dutch. It is clear enough

that the rapid growth of the modern world of commerce and industry was contemporaneous with the beginnings of the Protestant revolt, and it is also true that many business interests in many countries were glad to be free of the various money payments which the Roman Catholic Church had exacted. They were ready, too, to lay their hands upon the landed wealth of the Church, as they did in England. It is usually agreed now, however, that it would be difficult to demonstrate a consistently close relationship of cause and effect between the appearance of Protestantism and the rise of a modern capitalistic economy. Other forces were at work, and too many examples could be found where the given "cause" did not produce the anticipated "result."

The religious upheaval produced some outcomes that were inconsistent with others. Certain Protestant communities seemed to contribute to the growth of the democratic spirit; others, as in the case of Prussia, were on the side of monarchical absolutism. In some cases religious change led quickly to toleration, in others, to savage intolerance. Men were exiled or burned for their faith by Catholic and Protestant alike. Witch hunting grew throughout the sixteenth century until it actually reached its hysterical climax in the seventeenth. Its victims must be numbered in the thousands. Protestantism may have contributed to the liberation of the spirit of man; but in attacking the ceremonials and "superstitions" of Catholicism it in many cases destroyed artistic works of inestimable value. In these matters a simple verdict is not easy to give; the England of Edward VI, for instance, which witnessed the ruthless destruction of medieval sculptures, wall-paintings and stained glass, was also the England that first heard the superb cadences of Cranmer's Prayer Book. Opinions will differ as to the ultimate significance of this fateful age. No Catholic can contemplate without regret the tremendous breach in the structure of his church; no Protestant can look without deep feeling at the founding years of his faith.

PORTRAIT OF PHILIP II OF SPAIN by Titian, painted in 1553, before Philip assumed his heavy burdens as king. The portrait brilliantly suggests Philip's invariably regal bearing, and hints at the elements of strength and weakness in his character. From the Galleria Pitti in Florence. Photograph, Alinari.

Chapter 10

The Age of Philip II
1555 – 1598

❧ THE BURDEN OF INHERITANCE

THE HISTORICAL USAGE which tends to see an epoch in terms of its leaders designates the second half of the sixteenth century the age of Philip II. All such designations are of course relative. Englishmen may be disposed to see the sixteenth century first in terms of Henry VIII and later in terms of the great Elizabeth. Frenchmen may recall the recklessly ambitious role of Francis I at the opening of the century, the wise toleration of Henry IV at its close. Dutchmen revere the memory of William the Silent. In a religious sense the powerful figures of Luther and Calvin cast their long shadows across the entire century. But it remains true that in respect of the actual realities of power imperial Spain reached a position in the middle sixteenth century for which neither its past nor its future history holds any parallel. To direct the fortunes of his country in this fateful period was the heavy responsibility of Philip II.

When the Emperor Charles abdicated in 1555 he left a divided inheritance. To his brother Ferdinand went the Austrian crown, the Hapsburg family lands associated with it, and, eventually, the imperial dignity. To his son Philip went what actually turned out to be an even more impressive legacy: first of all, Spain; then the lands comprising the Burgundian inheritance (the Low Countries, Luxemburg and the Free County of Burgundy); then the Italian possessions (Naples, Sicily and Milan); and, added to all this, the vast colonial possessions beyond the seas. One does not know whether to be more impressed by the brilliance of the inheritance which

231

now fell to the sombrely dedicated young king or by the grave problems which his lands presented. Philip was first and foremost King of Spain, determined in that capacity to govern justly and devoutly according to his lights. But he was led inescapably into an endless series of European embroilments: into the everlasting confusions of Italian politics, into the politico-religious conflicts in Germany and France, into conflict with the Turks in the Mediterranean, into naval war with the English on the high seas, into the bloody revolt of the Netherlands and into the vast problems of the New World.

Bitter diplomatic and military encounters marked the international scene in the first half of the sixteenth century, even as religious upheavals characterized the domestic scene. European rivalries which, as we have seen, had first found their battleground in Italy had then spread to the wider areas of the Rhineland and Flanders. The basic rivalry of Hapsburg and Valois became complicated by a constantly shifting pattern of alliances, created originally by the small Italian states at the center of the conflict and later extended to include England and various states within the Holy Roman Empire.

England represented something of a new element in this struggle. Under the tutelage of Cardinal Wolsey, it had seemed more favorably disposed to the imperial cause than to France, though it flung its weight back and forth, seeking to maintain what came to be known as the European balance. England was allied briefly with France at the time of the "Field of Cloth of Gold" (1520), then in return for substantial payments joined Charles V, then, after the imperial sack of Rome in 1527, swung back to the French side. Much later, with the marriage in 1554 of Charles' son Philip to Mary Tudor, England found itself once more in alliance with the Empire and in conflict with France. At the time of Charles' abdication in 1555 he left Philip faced with an uncertainty as to what England's future action would be.

The legacy of Charles V was complicated in other ways. The Turks had by 1541 advanced from their victory at Mohàcs to the nearly total overrunning of Hungary. As the northern, land arm of this Turkish pincers reached up the Danube another arm advanced by sea along the southern fringe of the Mediterranean and by 1535 had reached Tunis. The Turk quickly made the discovery than His Most Christian Majesty, the King of France, was not averse to an alliance with the infidel in order to further French diplomatic ambitions against the Empire. Heavy burdens consequently were thrust upon the Hapsburgs.

In addition to this conflict on the frontiers of Europe Charles was also embroiled in the heart of Germany with the Protestant princes who had

HAPSBURG DOMINIONS *on the*
ABDICATION *of* CHARLES V 1556

IMPERIAL FRONTIER

AUSTRIAN HAPSBURGS   SPANISH HAPSBURGS

0   100   200   300   MILES

NETHERLANDS

SILESIA

LUXEMBURG

BOHEMIA

FRANCE

AUSTRIA

HUNGARY

FRANCHE
COMTE'

TYROL

STYRIA
CARINTHIA
CARNIOLA

OTTOMAN

MILAN

EMPIRE

SPAIN

NAPLES

BALEARIC ISLANDS

SARDINIA

MELILLA   ORAN

BONA   BIZERTA

TUNIS

SICILY

While the Austrian Hapsburgs consolidated their central position in Europe, the widely
scattered lands of the Spanish Hapsburgs drew them into a variety of conflicts.

formed the Schmalkaldic League to defend their local rights. By 1544 he
had contrived to make a peace with France by which this country renounced
most of its rights in Italy as well as in Flanders. The peace, however, turned
out to be little more than a breathing spell. The French secretly undertook
negotiations with the Turks and also with various German Protestant
princes, notably Maurice of Saxony, who had deserted the imperial cause.
By the Treaty of Friedwald (1552) France, in return for giving military aid

to the German princes, was promised the three so-called "Lorraine Bishop-rics"—Metz, Toul and Verdun. These critical frontier points, controlling one of the great strategic passages from France to Germany, opened up the possibility of momentous developments not only in the immediate years ahead but also in the long distant future.

In 1555 the long and wearisome conflict was still in progress, with France in actual possession of the three Bishoprics. The war had lost almost com-pletely its Italian character and was now being waged in the old territories of Charles the Bold running from the shores of the North Sea southward along the Rhine. Although peace had come to Germany by the settlement of Augsburg, this great internal struggle now had as its sequel an external conflict of even larger proportions. The Protestant issue, provisionally set-tled in Germany, was still unresolved elsewhere. Savage religious war was soon to break out in France and the Netherlands, while religion was to provide the English with a rallying cry in support of their young Queen Elizabeth. The prospect seemed to be one of international conflict on a growing scale.

In this situation Philip's stand was unhesitating. Although his strong sense of personal power frequently put him at odds with Rome, he conceived himself to be the sword-arm of the Counter Reformation and Spain to be the true bulwark of the Roman Catholic faith. The Inquisition had flour-ished most luxuriantly on Spanish soil; the disciplinary work of the Council of Trent had Philip's ardent support. Soon he was to bend all his energies to the fight against Protestantism—most directly in the Netherlands, but also in France and eventually also against England. Of first importance, however, was the problem of establishing his authority in Spain itself.

INTERNAL AFFAIRS IN SPAIN

Philip II had undergone long training for his task as king. Born and educated in Spain, he was "as Spanish as a Castilian grandee." In 1543 Charles V had made him regent of the Spanish kingdom. Later he obtained the title of Duke of Milan and King of Naples. In a moving ceremony at Brussels in October, 1555, Philip accepted the sovereignty of the Nether-lands from his weary and disillusioned father. In the following January, likewise at Brussels, he accepted the crown of Spain. Philip did not actually return to his Spanish kingdom until 1559 when he made it clear that his purpose was to maintain the structure of royal absolutism which his father had developed.

Charles had built up a pattern of government based on foundations laid earlier by Ferdinand and Isabella. These two had united the crowns of

Castile and Aragon but had not really combined the various realms of Spain into one administrative structure. Charles, it is true, held title to all the Iberian states save Portugal, but rather than proceed in the direction of a genuine unification he had embarked on the policy of what has been called "decentralized despotism." The decline of the historic Spanish parliamentary bodies, the Cortes, especially that of Castile, was due less to the desire of Charles, who had made some effort to invigorate them, than to their own seemingly incurable weaknesses. In default of these bodies the king directed the work of the state through an elaborate series of royal councils appointed by him and composed largely of trained lawyers and professional administrators.

Such was the general pattern which Philip II inherited and continued to employ. The Cortes were not abolished but sank further into insignificance. The municipalities, which once had had some independent vigor and which had served as a kind of feeding ground for the Cortes, lost all remnants of their earlier independence. The royal councils were increased in number. Of these the Council of Castile was the chief agency for judicial matters and internal administration. The Council of State, composed largely of nobles, dealt perfunctorily with foreign affairs, the real conduct of which remained in the king's hands. The great Council of the Indies directed the affairs of the New World, while a body called the *Suprema* was in charge of the work of the Inquisition. A newly created Privy Council helped to govern the Netherlands. In addition there functioned a Council of Aragon, a Council of Italy and, after its annexation in 1580, a Council of Portugal. Like the later Frederick the Great of Prussia, Philip tried to keep all the threads of administration in his own hands; he worked long hours, read and endorsed countless papers and permitted his ministers to be little more than diligent clerks.[1]

Several significant domestic aspects of Philip's long reign may be noted. In 1580, on the failure of the direct royal line in Portugal, Philip was able to have his claim to the throne recognized by part of the Portuguese nobility and to repress such opposition as there was. Portugal, known as the garden of Europe, was united to Spain until 1640, bringing with her the vast wealth of her overseas possessions. This move on the part of Philip could be regarded as part of what might be called a new "western" or Atlantic emphasis in contrast to the Mediterranean or Aragonese interests of his predecessors. The same trend can be noted in Philip's codification of Spanish law, the

---

1. Philip's passion for annotating documents amounted to a mania. Once when his ambassador in London sought to interest the king by including in a despatch a detailed account of tiny insects that he had observed crawling on his window panes, Philip solemnly noted in the margin, "probably fleas."

Nueva Recopilación, which emphasized Roman law and Castilian procedures rather than those of Aragon.

Philip was, above all, fanatical in matters of religion. The Inquisition received his ardent support. Spanish representatives at the Council of Trent were required to take a militant stand in maintaining orthodoxy in dogma. Throughout his reign Philip often found himself in disagreement and indeed at times in open conflict with the papacy, for his concept of royal power was so high and his determination to control the Spanish church so great that amicable relations with Rome were hardly possible.

An important religious issue was presented by the Moriscoes in Granada. These were the Moorish population who after their conquest by Ferdinand and Isabella had renounced their Moslem faith for Christianity. Philip suspected with some reason that these thrifty and industrious people still maintained secretly many of their Moslem practices and despite earlier promises of toleration he turned the power of the Inquisition upon them. Old laws were revived forbidding the Moriscoes to wear Moorish costume or to veil their women. Ancient folk dances were forbidden, as were Moorish names, and it was decreed that in a few years Arabic was to be replaced by the Spanish tongue. Such edicts provoked a ferocious revolt which began in 1568 and lasted for three years. Men, women and children were slaughtered by the thousands and the fertile countryside of Granada was devastated. In the end the Moriscoes were defeated and scattered throughout Castile, with the result that Spain's economic life to which they had contributed much was dealt a severe blow.

Nothing more clearly demonstrates the strange quality of Philip's religious devotion than the Escorial, that extraordinary combination of palace, monastery and sepulcher which he caused to be built in the bleak countryside a day's journey from Madrid. Designed to commemorate the martyr, St. Lawrence, on whose day Spanish troops had won the Battle of St. Quentin, the vast structure was built in the form of a huge grill, representing the object on which the saint, according to tradition, had met his fiery death. The architect Juan Bautista de Toledo, a pupil of Michelangelo, was responsible for the first stage of the work. The enormous group of buildings, 740 feet in length and 580 feet broad, had 16 courtyards and 86 staircases. Bronzes were brought from Saragossa, marble from Andalusia, tapestries from the Netherlands, lamps from Toledo, woolen blankets from the Andes, gold and silver from Peru and red and green featherwork from Mexico. The visitor could admire paintings by the great masters—Raphael, Titian, El Greco, Roger van der Weyden or Hieronymus Bosch. A splendid library held four thousand rare volumes and priceless Greek, Persian and Arabic manuscripts. This, incidentally, seems to have been the first library where books were kept on shelves rather than in cupboards or in chests. Above all else sounded the note of religious dedication. The royal apartments were so designed that from his bedroom Philip could gaze down through a window upon the high altar of the monastery church. Several hundred cases holding bones and relics of saints and martyrs were moved in. Philip became accustomed to spend more and more of each year at the Escorial. Here he toiled night and day at the tasks of government and here, at the end, surrounded by the coffins of his father, his brother, his three wives and his children, in circumstances of hideous suffering he was to die.

Economic problems in Spain under Philip II cannot be understood apart from his colonial policy. His predecessors had developed an empire of almost unbelievable wealth; now after the first fury of conquest the problem facing the Spaniards was to organize this empire for effective exploitation.[2] Whether politically, through the Council of the Indies, or economically, through the *Casa de Contratación,* elaborate efforts were made in Spain to regulate the life of the colonies, as efforts were also made overseas in the great viceroyalties of New Spain and Peru. Trade with the New World was channeled through the port of Cadiz under close government regulation and with the provision that the monarchy was entitled to a fifth of the value of all bullion mined. The wealth of the Spanish Empire was further developed under Philip with the reoccupation of the Philippines and the founding in 1571 of Manila. Still further treasure was in prospect when Portugal and her possessions came under Spanish rule in 1580.

To this overseas wealth were added the resources that Spain had at home. Much of the soil of the peninsula was not well suited for agriculture, nor were the river systems favorable for water transport. The merino wool, however, which Spain produced in huge quantities, was reputed to be the best in the world. The Mediterranean areas produced grain, olives, oranges, silk and vines. Spanish craftsmen were still famous for certain products, for example, the sword blades made at Toledo. All this would seem to furnish a substantial basis for a thriving economy.

In point of actual fact the economy of Spain in the sixteenth century was subject to many severe handicaps. The Church held enormous areas of land which were exempt from taxation and thus deprived the government of a large revenue. Castilian nobles also were exempt from regular taxation, while the Cortes of Aragon voted its financial contributions only with the greatest reluctance. The landowning nobility, whose concern was with sheep raising rather than with agriculture, were banded together in a privileged association known as the *Mesta* which perpetuated a system of sheep pasturage and a generally wasteful use of land that made healthy agricultural

2. See p. 116.

development almost impossible. Urban life which had earlier shown some signs of development received little if any deliberate stimulation. The wealth of the Americas was not used to encourage Spanish industry but for the most part was shipped to other European countries to buy luxuries and thus to enrich the manufacturers and merchants of foreign lands. Much of the treasure sent from the colonies never indeed saw Spain. English free-booters intercepted some of it and other large quantities were pledged in advance to German or Genoese bankers. Thus the failure of Spain to develop substantial industries of her own meant that the colonies, despite formal prohibitions, were themselves compelled in some cases to attempt manu-facture or more commonly to purchase elsewhere badly needed goods which Spain ought to have supplied.

Philip II was able to do very little about these complicated problems. Royal revenues were a constant problem to him. The basic home source of funds was the *Alcabala* or sales tax of ten per cent on all purchases. This fantastic tax was supposedly applied whenever goods changed hands, no matter how many times. The end result was to discourage trade on anything but a strictly local basis. An elaborate network of taxation was imposed upon the colonies. At home money was secured from import and export duties, from an excise tax on the main foodstuffs, from the proceeds from the sale of offices and the sale of indulgences (which never were denounced in Spain as they had been in Germany), from the profits of the state salt monopoly and from the income produced by the king's private lands.

All these sources of revenue failed to provide Philip with the funds he needed. Much wealth was lost on the Spanish Main through piracy. At the close of the century the output of the colonial mines began to decline. The great administrative machine over which Philip presided so anxiously did not work well. Taxes were wastefully collected, finances were corruptly administered and money was unwisely spent. Italy produced very little revenue while the Netherlands in armed revolt proved to be a terrible drain on the royal treasury.

In essence, therefore, it could be said that Spain, in the period of her political and military greatness, undertook policies which were beyond the economic capacity of the country to maintain. The influx of bullion during the sixteenth century meant a threefold rise in Spanish prices, with no equivalent increase in wages. Hardship for the average man, therefore, was very real. At the close of Philip's reign the economic picture, as most his-torians will agree, was deplorable. The population of the principal towns dwindled; large areas of the countryside were depopulated; in order to cope with famine the prohibition of imports had to be suspended and wheat brought from abroad. Contrary to the general European trend, the population of Spain between 1500 and 1700 is estimated to have dropped from seven to six millions. An idle and cynical nobility flaunted its wealth in the face of widespread beggary and misery. Such grim conditions Philip can hardly said to have created, yet it proved beyond his capacity to find a remedy for them. Baffling to himself, they remained an equally baffling legacy for his successors.

■ THE REVOLT OF THE NETHERLANDS

No part of the policies of Philip II shows more clearly his failure to adapt himself to the temper of the times than his treatment of Flanders and the Dutch Netherlands. These ancient territories of Charles the Bold had come by marriage into Hapsburg hands in 1477 and had been the favorite resort of the Flemish-speaking Charles V. Each of the seventeen component provinces, though banded into a loose confederation, was nominally independent. The southern parts had prospered enormously during the Middle Ages; they lay in a most favorable geographic position across the busy estuaries of the Rhine, the Meuse and the Scheldt and had built up a thriving cloth manufacture. In typical medieval fashion these various towns—Ghent, Bruges, Ypres, Brussels and Antwerp among them—had secured charters, privileges and liberties which they jealously treasured. Farther north, new centers such as Amsterdam, Rotterdam, Delft, Leyden and The Hague gradually grew in importance. Here, in addition to the wealth which came from linens, woolens, lace, carpets and tapestries, a thriving fishing industry also developed. The northern provinces, many parts of which were reclaimed from the sea by means of dykes and irrigation, were the home of a prosperous agriculture. From all these substantial lands it was estimated that Charles V had derived nearly half his revenues.

Philip II, who spoke no Flemish and was a thoroughgoing Spaniard both in heart and manners, regarded these provinces otherwise than had his father. No hint of toleration showed itself in a ruler who was determined at all costs to root out heresy and to maintain the Roman Catholic faith. The principle of royal absolutism was sacred to the one who seemed to take particular pleasure in signing royal documents with the ancient and proud Spanish formula, *Yo el Rey* ("I the King"). Added to Philip's authoritarian convictions, however, was a certain dilatoriness and inertia which served only to aggravate a situation in the Netherlands which was already difficult.

Among the numerous grounds for unrest in these provinces was the problem of finances. The huge sums which Charles V had raised with no great trouble were now denied to Philip. Delegates from the various provinces, meeting together in what was known as the States General, refused to grant him the money necessary to meet the debts incurred by his predecessor so that in the end Philip was obliged to settle for a much smaller amount than he had proposed.

A second ground was that of religion. Lutheran, Calvinist and Anabaptist teachings had gradually crept into the Low Countries, despite the efforts of Charles V to repel them. When Philip in 1560 issued an edict against heresy and announced that he intended to put into effect the machinery of the Inquisition, although he was really only carrying out measures introduced earlier by his father, he encountered strong opposition. Against the advice of his Council he admitted the Society of Jesus. His further announcement that he intended to transform drastically the existing four bishoprics so that there would be three archbishoprics and fifteen bishoprics, was denounced by both Catholics and Protestants.

Other grounds for resentment were political in nature. After 1559 Philip never again saw the Netherlands. He appointed his half-sister, Margaret of Parma (the natural daughter of Charles V by a Flemish mistress), as regent. Although Margaret was no fanatic, she was closely advised and guided by a small group of royal agents, whose chief, Cardinal Granvelle, was nicknamed *le diable rouge;* these men loyally served the will of the Spanish king. Opposition to Philip was hardly democratic in nature as some of the romantic historians of the Netherlands have implied. It could be more truly described as oligarchic in that it arose from the nobles and prosperous townsmen whose interests were being injured. The opposition to some extent could also be called nationalistic, for the presence of large numbers of German and Spanish soldiers was bitterly resented.

In this atmosphere a steadily growing and remarkably stubborn opposition to Spanish policy emerged. It was inspired fundamentally by the program of centralization applied to a people with a long medieval tradition of self-government. It was not exclusively religious, it was found as much in Flanders and Brabant as in the northern provinces and it did not at first aim at complete independence. It expressed, rather, the local resentment against certain of Philip's moves such as his announcement in 1564 that all the decrees of the Council of Trent were to be promulgated as law, and his attempts to impose heavy financial contributions. In 1566 riots broke out in which churches were desecrated and images smashed. Margaret of Parma, finding it impossible to control the situation, reported starkly to Philip, "There is neither law, faith nor king."

Leadership of the revolt was assumed by a number of Dutch noblemen, notably Counts Egmont and Hoorn and, above all, by William of Nassau, Prince of Orange. These were not at first open revolutionaries. Egmont and

THE NETHERLANDS 1609

UNITED NETHERLANDS

SPANISH NETHERLANDS

BISHOPRIC OF LIÈGE

0   25   50   75 MILES

LINGUISTIC BOUNDARY

GRONINGEN

FRIESLAND

DRENTHE

OVERYSSEL

Deventer

Amsterdam

HOLLAND

UTRECHT

GELDERLAND

The Hague

Rotterdam

ZEELAND

"COMMON LANDS"

E. GELDERS

Antwerp

BRABANT

Bruges

Ghent

MECHLIN

LIÈGE

LIMBURG

Brussels

FLANDERS

FLEMINGS

WALLOONS

NAMUR

ARTOIS

HAINAULT

BISHOPRIC OF LIÈGE

CAMBRESIS

LUXEMBURG

Luxemburg

Note that the frontier between the Spanish and the United Netherlands was fixed more by defense needs, which involved the use of the rivers, than it was by language or religion.

Hoorn had served Charles V with distinction in the campaigns against France. William was of a family which had extensive holdings in the Rhineland and in Brabant. By marriage into the French house of Orange-Châlons the head of the family had acquired a relatively insignificant new territory in the south of France, a new title and the status of sovereign prince. Henceforth the name of Orange was to be inseparable from the history of the Netherlands. William had been educated as a Catholic. He had been a favorite page of Charles V and had risen steadily in dignity and imperial approval. Although Philip II did not like him, he recognized William's importance and confirmed him in his office of Stadholder or principal minister in the Provinces of Holland, Zeeland and Utrecht. William was, then, a figure of some stature who had played a part in urging the States General to maintain their traditional rights against Spanish encroachments. Egmont and Hoorn were likewise widely known and widely respected. Growing numbers of noblemen, gentry and merchants supported these leaders.

By 1567 the minor disturbances had grown to the stage of open revolt. To meet this, Philip at once sent to the Netherlands as Captain-General an outstanding servant, the Duke of Alva. This experienced soldier assembled an army of some ten thousand men at Genoa, then proceeded northward under the suspicious eyes of the French and Swiss, crossing the Mont Cenis Pass and directing his Spanish, Italian and German troops through Burgundy, Lorraine and Luxemburg safely to their destination in the Netherlands. Marching with this army, disciplined and organized into battalions and platoons, were two thousand Italian courtesans.

Alva quickly took over control in the Netherlands from the mildly disposed Margaret of Parma, setting up to assist him an emergency council which has come down in history under the name of the Council of Blood. This tribunal, whose members were preponderantly Spanish, had no formal legal status. It met twice daily and was presided over by Alva himself, who retained the right of final decision. The Council relied heavily upon informers and sent out sub-committees to all parts of the Netherlands. Its work was to punish treason and to compel obedience, to which end it was responsible for the wholesale burning or beheading of thousands of victims. From the confiscated estates of those who were sentenced a stream of gold flowed into the royal treasury. Counts Egmont and Hoorn were seized and brought before this Council. Although as Knights of the Order of the Golden Fleece they were entitled to trial by their Order, this right was denied them and in 1568 they were executed publicly at Brussels—historic martyrs in a historic cause. William of Orange, who was declared an outlaw and whose estates were confiscated, by this time was clearly the leader of the Protestant side.

The name of "Beggars" (*Gueux*) was contemptuously applied by the Spaniards to the organized resistance. The Dutch quickly took up this title, some of them even adopting the beggar's wallet and wooden bowl as insignia of the revolt. With the assistance of their naval forces—the "Sea Beggars"— they were able to harry the Spanish. Towns such as Flushing, Brill, Rotterdam, Schiedam and Gouda expelled their garrisons and became centers of resistance so that little by little the northern provinces were made free of

Spanish control. In the south, where resentment against Philip's rule was also bitter, Alva was able to maintain a firmer hand.

As one follows the course of this dramatic struggle one is shocked, even today, by the appalling fury and savagery with which it was waged. Alva's regime has been called a classic example of military despotism, enforced by troops who were in large part mercenary and from whom all humanity seemed to have departed. Towns which endured terrible hardships during siege were, after capture, exposed to wild excesses in which men, women and children perished. Alva, a hardened soldier of long experience, told Philip it was the bloodiest war he had known. Some dramatic touches mitigated the horror, as for example when Leyden was relieved in 1574 by Dutch ships coming full sail across the flooded countryside, or when Spanish war vessels on another occasion were captured by Dutch infantry gliding silently on skates across the ice. Antwerp was seized in 1576 and sacked with such unheard-of violence as to make this "Spanish Fury" and the name of Philip anathema to the Protestant cause throughout Europe.

So great was the general resentment throughout the Netherlands that in 1576 representatives of the seventeen provinces signed the Pacification of Ghent, agreeing to band together until all foreign troops should have gone and a new assembly of the provinces could meet to consider the religious problem and find some means of maintaining their ancient rights. This agreement marked the zenith of the revolt. Alva had been recalled in 1573, to be succeeded by Don Juan of Austria, fresh from his victory over the Turks at Lepanto. In 1579 Philip sent one of his ablest generals, Alexander Farnese, Duke of Parma and son of the former regent, Margaret of Parma. With him came twenty thousand additional troops. Parma skilfully subdued the southern, Catholic provinces which had been concerned at the growth of Calvinism in the north and at William of Orange's open espousal of Protestantism. These southern provinces formed the Union of Arras while at the same time the northern group formed the Union of Utrecht. The cleavage was followed in 1581 by the decisive landmark, the Act of Abjuration, in which the northern provinces solemnly deprived Philip II of his sovereignty over them and thus asserted their independence.[3]

The division turned out to be permanent. The determination of a final boundary between the northern and southern provinces was influenced more by strategic considerations than by anything else. A defensive line roughly corresponding to the course of the Rhine and the Scheldt made possible the freedom of the United Netherlands. Other differences, such as

3. The seven northern provinces, as ultimately organized, were: Holland, Zeeland, Utrecht, Gelderland, Overyssel, Friesland and Groningen. The ten southern provinces were: Brabant, Limburg, Luxemburg, Flanders, Artois, Hainault, Namur, Mechlin, East Gelderland and Antwerp.

language, religion and occupations contributed, yet the settlement left substantial numbers of Catholics in the northern provinces and substantial numbers of Flemish-speaking peoples in the southern provinces.

No deliberate plan to create a Dutch republic seems to have been intended. William of Orange had already accepted, albeit with some reluctance, sovereignty over the maritime provinces of Holland and Zeeland. It remained uncertain, however, who should be at the head of the new union. By the Treaty of Plessis-les-Tours signed by Dutch representatives in 1580 with the Duke of Anjou it was proposed that this brother of Henry III of France assume the sovereignty of the entire Netherlands; he was, however, in many respects a most unpromising candidate against whom there was a strong Dutch resentment so that the treaty never became effective. Although republicanism in the end triumphed, it would seem that the Dutch Republic, as its great historian, Motley, remarked, came into existence without deliberate intention on the part of its people or its leaders.

In the year 1581 Philip II, in a stern attempt to deprive the revolt of its leader, issued his celebrated ban against the head of the House of Orange:

> We expose the said William Nassau as an enemy of the human race, giving his property to all who may seize it. And if any one of our subjects or any stranger should be found sufficiently generous of heart to rid us of this pest, delivering him to us, alive or dead, or taking his life, we will cause to be furnished to him immediately after the deed shall have been done, the sum of twenty-five thousand crowns in gold. If he have committed any crime, however heinous, we promise to pardon him; and if he be not already noble, we will ennoble him for his valor.

Three years later this William of Orange, known to his devoted countrymen as The Silent, fell at the hand of an assassin.

Political independence is seldom easily achieved, and for twenty-five years following the death of William the struggle continued. Leadership was assumed by William's son, Maurice of Nassau, only seventeen at the time of his father's death. Help sent by Queen Elizabeth in 1585 was not effective, but in 1596, when a formal alliance was concluded with the French and the English, the Dutch had come substantially into control of their own territories and were fighting a defensive war along the frontiers of their state. In 1609 a truce was signed between Spain and the States General which was to last for twenty years. The conflict was renewed during the Thirty Years' War so that it was not until the Peace of Westphalia (1648) that the independence for which the Netherlands had carried on so bloody and lengthy a struggle gained formal European recognition.

Philip II did not live to see the effects of the disastrous policies which he had tried to impose upon his ancient Burgundian inheritance. He had wished to maintain the Catholic faith unchallenged, to impose his absolute authority and to exploit for his own purposes the wealth of these thriving lands. In all respects he had failed. The United Netherlands became in the seventeenth century one of the major powers of Europe and a cornerstone of the Protestant cause. The state took the form of a confederation in which each part was theoretically held to be sovereign. An assembly of delegates known as the States General met at The Hague. There was also a Council of State made up of twelve members. The office of stadholder, or governor-general, ultimately became hereditary in the House of Orange which by 1625 had also gained the hereditary stadholdership in six of the seven component provinces.

For the United Netherlands in general the seventeenth century proved to be a time of unparalleled advance—a veritable golden age. The province of Holland, within which lay the important cities of Amsterdam, Haarlem, Rotterdam, Delft, Leyden and The Hague, far outshone any other, so much so that its name has often been taken as synonymous with that of the confederacy as a whole. Amsterdam replaced Antwerp as a European financial center. Even in the midst of the epic struggle for freedom great overseas developments were undertaken. Dutch ships, for example, reached the East Indies in 1594. The Dutch East India Company was founded in 1602, the Dutch West India Company in 1621, and actual trade with Japan began in 1634. By 1650 the United Netherlands could rightly be regarded as the chief shipping, trading, manufacturing and financial nation in Europe. This great economic prosperity was accompanied by a no less impressive development in the arts and sciences.

The contrast between the provinces which had secured their freedom and those which remained under the hand of Spain was striking. In the south, what once had been the thriving areas of Brabant and Flanders were now suffering heavily from the effects of the long war. Wolves roamed the streets of desolated towns, while ancient centers such as Ghent and Bruges never recovered their former preeminence. These Spanish Netherlands, later to come under the control of Austria, lagged behind the brilliant advance of their northern neighbor. It should be observed that the division into a Protestant north and a Catholic south came about really after the rebellion and was in the truest sense a result rather than a cause of the revolt. A distinguished student of this period has shrewdly set down his view of the basic reasons for this disparity, and particularly for the persistence of Catholicism in the south:

> If we look closely into the causes why the North should become predominantly Protestant while the South gradually reverted to an entirely Catholic faith, we must see that the reasons were in part racial, in part geographical and in part

social. Geographically and linguistically the Northern provinces looked for their culture to Germany, and the Southern provinces to France. Moreover the easy defensibility of Holland and Zeeland, behind their moats, made them a natural refuge of a hunted sect and, this tendency once having asserted itself, the polarization of the Netherlands naturally followed, Protestants being drawn and driven to their friends in the North and Catholics similarly finding it necessary or advisable to settle in the South. Moreover in the Southern provinces the two privileged classes, clergy and nobility, were relatively stronger than in the almost entirely bourgeois and commercial North.[4]

These divisions, in process of realization during the sixteenth century and fully achieved during the seventeenth, are the basis for the overwhelmingly Catholic allegiance of present-day Belgium and for the rise of the official Calvinistic Reformed Church of the United Netherlands. The contrast cannot be ignored, moreover, between the policy of toleration of the northern provinces where a substantial Catholic minority has persisted to this day and the continuing intolerance of the Spanish provinces where Protestantism was forced out of existence and has never in any substantial degree reappeared.

■ THE TURKISH MENACE IN THE MEDITERRANEAN

Not the least of the complex problems facing Philip II was the Turkish threat in the Mediterranean. Geography had made Spain a Mediterranean power, and despite the rapid growth of Spanish interests in the New World during the sixteenth century her Mediterranean obligations remained. The historic interests of the House of Aragon extended from ports such as Barcelona through the Balearic Islands and Sardinia to Naples and Sicily. These maritime interests could not fail to be threatened by the Ottoman Turks whose great land advance up the Danube was paralleled, as we have seen, by a naval advance along the North African coast. Moslem raiders, putting out from North African ports, became a constant menace to Mediterranean shipping and a challenge to the Christian powers of the West.

In 1535 the Emperor Charles V, standing upon the deck of a great galley with a crucifix lashed to its masthead, had directed the operations of a fleet which won back Tunis from the infidel—a victory which he always regarded as one of his greatest. But the fortunes of war soon turned. Gradually regaining their lost ground, the Turks harried the entire Mediterranean with their pirate raids. Spain was able to hold only a few outposts (Mers-el-Kebir, Oran, Melilla and Goletta) on the African coast. The greatest of Spain's Moslem opponents, Khaireddin, nicknamed "Barbarossa," became the terror of the Mediterranean, attacking Nice on the French coast and even threaten-

4. SMITH, *Age of the Reformation*, p. 271.

ing Rome. One of his most spectacular exploits was to transport seventy thousand Moors from Spain to Algiers, saving them from the threats of the Inquisition and strengthening his own territories in the process. Death removed Barbarossa in 1547 but the menace continued.

This ominous situation was inherited by Philip II, who promptly accepted the obligation to carry on a conflict which in his eyes was nothing less than a crusade. The Spanish met heavy disaster at Tripoli in 1560, but five years later their fleet was able to relieve the siege of Malta, stubbornly defended against the Moslems by the ancient crusading order of the Knights of St. John. In 1570 the Turks succeeded in capturing Cyprus, flaying the commander of the garrison and sending his stuffed skin as a trophy to Constantinople. In the following year the papacy, gravely concerned at the growing menace which seemed to threaten all Christendom, organized a league with Genoa, Venice and Spain as its principal members to take common action against the Turk.

A fleet of some two hundred galleys, together with large numbers of supporting craft, was organized and the command given to Don Juan of Austria, Philip's half-brother, who had already made a great name for himself in the campaign against the Moriscoes. His huge Armada, with fifty thousand sailors to man the craft and thirty-one thousand soldiers to fight them, assembled at Messina, each departing vessel being blessed in turn by the papal nuncio.

At this time the galley was still the queen of the Mediterranean. Long and low, with from one to three banks of heavy oars and a single mast carrying a huge lateen sail, it was well suited to an inland sea, as its long history reaching back to Carthaginian and Greek times would indicate. The huge oars or sweeps were manned by as many as seven men apiece and were fitted into a framework standing out from the hull and running parallel to it. These galleys, brought to a high pitch of perfection by the Venetians and Genoese, were not maneuverable as a true ship would be; they were designed either to ram and sink their opponents or to come alongside for a bloody hand-to-hand encounter. A recent Mediterranean development, the galleass, was shorter, wider and higher than the galley; it had three masts, each with a lateen sail, and could also be rowed with oars. It carried heavy cannon which could be fired forward. Six of these, marking a transitional stage in naval architecture, took part in the battle of Lepanto (1571).

The great battle, fought near the entrance to the Gulf of Corinth, has the historic significance of being the last sea encounter in which the galley played a decisive role. The crushing defeat of the Turks spread Don Juan's renown throughout Europe. Was this victory, however, which has been compared to that of the ancient Greeks over the Persians at Salamis, truly decisive? Although in the first flush of victory Don Juan wished to go on and assault Constantinople, counsels of caution prevailed. In 1573 he recaptured Tunis and its neighbor, Goletta, but these were soon lost so that at the end of Philip's reign only a few of the African ports, or "presidios," remained in his hands. Failure of the maritime powers to continue united as allies meant that in some sense Lepanto was a hollow victory. It has been argued, indeed, that Don Juan did Philip and his advisers a disservice in that he led them to believe that the tactics of a galley battle ("a clash of armed rowboats") could be equally effective in the Atlantic where naval construction was vastly different and seamanship everything.

Nevertheless, Lepanto had a profound psychological significance, for a Turkish fleet had never before thus been beaten at sea. The Turkish maritime advance was at an end, and while piracy remained a problem until the nineteenth century the naval situation in the Mediterranean, where Spain was clearly the leading power, took on a new aspect. Actually, the failure of the Turks to make any further advances was due only in part to their crushing defeat and as much to the internal decay which now beset the Ottoman Empire. When the great Suleiman the Magnificent died in 1566 he was succeeded by one of whom it is sufficient to record that he is known to history as Selim the Sot. Selim's successor, Murad III, began his reign by strangling his five brothers and is notable chiefly for fathering more than a hundred children. The decline in political leadership made it clear that any large-scale Turkish naval threat in the Mediterranean was a thing of the past.

ENGLAND AND THE BALANCE OF POWER

In the reign of Philip II English foreign policy in the hands of Elizabeth and her able ministers Cecil and Walsingham made significant advances. During the first half of the century England had begun to commit herself to an active role in European politics, being concerned increasingly to see that neither the Hapsburgs nor France should dominate the European balance of power. Formerly an obscure country which lay on the very fringes of Europe and counted for little, she was in process of becoming a powerful nation with whom all her contemporaries had to reckon. Such in a broad sense was the evolution of England to which Spain contributed not a little.

Wolsey and his royal master Henry VIII may take much credit for having directed their country into this new path. To Wolsey France had seemed the principal foe, and the Low Countries, long a market for English wool and cloth, the principal friend. The game, however, was one in which no alliance was really sacred and in which one might have to shift partners overnight in the interest of diplomatic advantage. Under Edward VI England was definitely committed to the Protestant cause. The ensuing brief reign of Mary Tudor had seemed to reverse this trend, for she was married to Philip of Spain. Yet Philip's marriage did not enable him to secure a firm alliance with England or to dominate English policy. He drew England, it is true, briefly into a war with France, the outcome of which was that England lost Calais. To Mary's subjects he was always unpopular, and now in retrospect her tragic reign seems little more than a deeply unhappy episode, running counter to the major trends of her country's history.

When Elizabeth succeeded her half-sister in 1558 England's prospects both in foreign and domestic affairs were uncertain. The Peace of Cateau-Cambrésis (1559) temporarily closed the long duel between the Hapsburgs and Valois which had begun in 1494. Philip reaped the harvest which had really been Spain's since the defeat and capture of Francis I at Pavia in 1525. He was now King of Naples and Sicily and Duke of Milan, from which possessions Spain derived an authority in Italy that was to last more or less undiminished until 1713. In some way Elizabeth had to steer between the dangers arising from the menacing ambitions of France and Spain.

At home Elizabeth felt bound to move slowly in religious matters; yet she contrived to establish a *Via Media,* or middle path, and in the end clearly aligned her country on the Protestant side. Even though Philip's hints of a possible marriage with Elizabeth had been rebuffed, Spain did not seem at first to present any immediate danger. The real danger seemed to come from France which, deeply interested in the fortunes of Mary Queen of Scots, had sent troops to Scotland to support her and the Catholic cause. Mary, now the widow of Francis II of France, had included the arms of England with those of France and Scotland on her escutcheon. Elizabeth's decision, therefore, to send troops to Scotland and thus to force the French to withdraw (1560) led to a diplomatic victory of the first importance, for it was to be followed in the not too distant future by the triumph of the Protestant cause in Scotland.

If Wolsey may be regarded as the principal architect and agent of Henry VIII's foreign policy, then Sir William Cecil (later Lord Burghley) may equally be regarded as playing the same role for Elizabeth. He served her faithfully for forty years, seeking patiently to employ the methods of maneuver and intrigue rather than those of open war. A master of negotiation, he directed a vast espionage service of remarkable efficiency. Elizabeth called him her "spirit" and her "oracle"; to the court he was known as "the old fox." In the end he was able to pass on to his son, Robert Cecil, the powers which he exercised so masterfully.

Elizabeth's first great aim seems to have been to seek a peace that would genuinely favor English interests. This was hardly a true policy of alliance but rather one of assisting and linking together the various Protestant communities against the dangerous threat of Catholic aggression. The dangers were various. For his third marriage Philip II had taken a French wife and might be able to effect a diplomatic alliance between the courts of France and Spain. In France, Catholic and Huguenot rivalries had brought the country to the brink of civil war. In Germany, the ambitions of the Protestant princes had by no means been satisfied by the recent Peace of Augsburg. In the Low Countries armed revolt against Spain was imminent.

The French situation seemed to the English the most delicate of these matters, for Elizabeth did not wish to see the powerful Guise family, ambitious for the throne and ardently Catholic, win out, seeing that such a victory would in all probability mean a close alliance of Guise and Hapsburg. In order to give encouragement to the opponents of the Guises, Elizabeth's advisers for a time contemplated her marrying either the Duke of Anjou or later his brother, the Duke of Alençon. Elizabeth joined in a scheme which it is difficult now to see as anything other than a fantastic and preposterous comedy. Alençon was twenty years junior to Elizabeth, very puny, with a face pitted with smallpox and an enormous nose. Elizabeth danced with him and kissed him in front of the court. She called him her "frog" and the envoy who represented him her "monkey." On one occasion this envoy wrote to her: "Be assured on the faith of a monkey that your frog lives in hope." Alençon had encouraged both the French Huguenots and the Netherlands Protestants and so in responding to his overtures Elizabeth was really supporting the Protestant cause against both France and Spain. Decisions in these matters were long deferred, with the result that in 1584 Alençon died, unwed. Elizabeth was content to see France prevented by its domestic difficulties from playing a leading role in European affairs. The natural sequel, however, was that Spain under Philip II soon rose to the position of England's principal rival.

The antagonism between England and Spain took some little time to develop. Philip at first conceived that it might be better to have Elizabeth on the throne than to see it go to Mary Stuart, linked by marriage to the French crown and thus potentially able to bring about the Anglo-French alliance which Philip feared above all. On the other side, however, various forces were at work making the rivalry between England and Spain increasingly bitter.

One such force was English sympathy for the Dutch revolt against Spain. This did not at first mean armed resistance, but it did lead to the offer of hospitable asylum for thousands of Netherlands refugees, many of them skilled artisans. Another cause of Anglo-Spanish antagonism was trade on the high seas. English seamen, restive at the Spanish claims to a commercial monopoly in the Caribbean and elsewhere, did not intend to let such claims pass unchallenged. In 1562 an English sailor, John Hawkins, laid the foundation for the subsequent slave trade by carrying a cargo of Negroes in his ship, the *Jesus,* from West Africa to Hispaniola (Santo Domingo). A second trip, favored with royal and noble patronage, followed and then a third, in which Francis Drake captained a ship in Hawkins' squadron. The English were moving into an area where Spain claimed a monopoly, so that illegal trade, slaving, plunder and armed conflict soon went hand in hand.

Nearer home something in the nature of a trade war also developed. In the Netherlands, the English had long enjoyed a lucrative market for their cloth which Spain now sought to curb. She imposed severe restrictions upon English trade, and England retaliated in kind. Such retaliation thrived in an atmosphere where international law on the high seas was practically unknown. English ships engaged in what was really piracy by preying upon the great ships running between Spain and the rich port of Antwerp. English ships of war demanded a salute from all vessels, regardless of nationality, that passed through what were called the "narrow seas," while the Strait of Dover was complacently known to the English as "Her Majestie's Streame." In 1568 when Spanish treasure ships carrying huge funds to the Low Countries put in at Plymouth and Southampton to escape pirates, Elizabeth "borrowed" the treasure, saying that as it was really only on loan from Italian bankers to Philip she would be glad to assume his indebtedness to them. This type of action was usually disapproved by Cecil but encouraged by Elizabeth's other principal adviser, Walsingham, an ardent Protestant and a man impatient at Cecil's caution. In a practical sense the aggressive policy seemed certainly to be the better choice. When Drake's *Golden Hind* reached England in 1580 after his famous expedition around the world, it carried a cargo (the product of his various raids) estimated to be worth between a quarter and a half of the whole annual product of the Spanish mines in the New World, or a whole year's revenue of the English crown.

The picture, then, is one of Anglo-Spanish conflict which became more and more open. When the Dutch "Sea Beggars" took up their activity in the Channel they were allowed to use English ports. In 1585, a year after the assassination of William of Orange, Elizabeth finally agreed to give open aid to the Dutch. Spain retaliated by seizing the British ships in her ports, and the English replied in turn by sending Drake on a spectacular raiding mission. Beginning with an attack on Vigo, in Spain, he proceeded to the Canaries, then across the Atlantic to Santo Domingo and Cartagena, returning home with an enormous booty to receive the plaudits of his admiring queen. In December, 1585, the Earl of Leicester was sent to the Netherlands with 6,000 men. Although his campaign was not a success, the die had been cast. By this time, too, there seemed little doubt that Philip was encouraging conspiracies in England to overthrow Elizabeth and replace her with Mary Stuart. In 1587, after the discovery of Babington's plot to murder Elizabeth, the queen reluctantly took the advice of her ministers; Mary, nearly twenty years a prisoner, was beheaded in the great hall of Fotheringay Castle.[5]

Philip's plans to send a great force against England seem to have begun as early as 1585. In the following year he received papal backing for them. A great, threefold operation was envisaged: a huge naval force would be sent from Spain to destroy English seapower; Parma's troops in the Netherlands would supply an invasion force to cross the Channel; and simultaneously a rising in England would be undertaken by disaffected English Catholics. In 1587 Drake boldly raided Cadiz, creating great destruction and thereby setting back Spanish plans until the following year. Nevertheless, Philip pushed ahead; a great fleet was prepared, the command of which was given to the Duke of Medina Sidonia, a soldier uniquely unfitted for his task.

The Spanish plan of attack could have little hope of success. Tactically, the great mistake was to assume that the huge Spanish galleons could maneuver and fight as the galleys of the Mediterranean traditionally had done by coming alongside, grappling with the enemy and then sending infantry over the bulwarks for hand-to-hand encounter. The English, with much smaller ships, had learned the technique of refusing to grapple and instead maneuvered into position to fire broadsides in salvos against their much heavier opponents.[6]

When Lord Howard of Effingham with Drake and his other commanders met the Spanish fleet in the Channel in July, 1588, he was able to employ these new tactics with brilliant success. As the fleets drew near, the English could observe Spanish soldiers standing in rows on the decks of their ships, musketeers in front and pikemen behind, waiting for the moment of hand-to-hand combat. The English met them with broadsides. The Spanish

5. Elizabeth signed the death warrant herself, but would not agree to its release. Cecil summoned the Privy Council and arranged to have the warrant issued without Elizabeth's knowledge.
6. The Spanish galleons were huge ships, reaching perhaps a thousand tons and thus being ten times the burthen of Columbus' *Santa Maria*. Henry VIII had commissioned naval architects to redesign English ships of war. They were very maneuverable, having a length roughly three times the beam, as compared to the medieval "round" ships with a length twice the beam. Gunners were trained to fire their rows of iron or brass cannon simultaneously. Drake insisted upon a high level of discipline and skill from all his crews. "I must have the gentlemen," he declared on one occasion, "to hale and draw with the mariners."

fleet, badly mauled, put in to Calais, but was driven out by fire-ships and then made its way northward through the dangerous shoals along the Flemish coast where it suffered further losses. Rather than risk a return, the decision was at last made to beat back to Spain around the north of Scotland and Ireland. Of an original Spanish fleet of more than 130 vessels, some 63 were destroyed—as much by the fury of the storms as by actual combat. The Spaniards inflicted no loss at all upon the English. "They did not in all their sailing round about England," wrote a contemporary, "so much as sink or take one ship, bark, pinnace, or cockboat of ours, or even burn so much as one sheepcote in this land." Equally as impressive as the triumph at sea was the consideration that Parma's superb Spanish infantry remained helpless in the Netherlands, unable without effective naval support to pass over "Her Majestie's Streame." Such was Elizabeth's great victory.

Glorious as was the outcome, England did not press the triumph over the Armada to a really decisive conclusion. She maintained military vigilance at home against the prospect of further Spanish attacks. Raiding expeditions on the Spanish coast and across the Atlantic continued to bring back substantial booty, though the evidence does not suggest that England could truly have grown rich from these adventures. English troops were sent again to the Netherlands where they contrived to win some victories and secure valuable training in the art of war. After 1589 England openly supported Henry of Navarre who on the death of Henry III succeeded to the title of king. Elizabeth sent five expeditions totaling in all some twenty thousand men to France between 1589 and 1595 and expended heavy sums upon them. In this way she gave aid to the "common cause" against the House of Guise and against its ally, Philip II. When Henry IV made his peace with Spain at Vervins in 1598 he was able at long last to dismiss the hated foreigner from his soil. But not until 1604, the year after Elizabeth's death, could England bring the long conflict with Spain to an end.

This whole period, then, clearly marks the decline of Spain and the corresponding rise of England to a new European importance and to new destinies overseas. In 1583 Sir Humphrey Gilbert had gone down with his little ship, the *Squirrel,* returning from the ill-fated attempt to set up a colony in Newfoundland. Two years later Raleigh made his equally ill-fated settlement at Roanoke on the Carolina coast. Failures in a literal sense, they were nevertheless the harbingers of greatness, for the settlements of Jamestown and Plymouth were soon to follow. In the year 1600 the great East India Company was chartered. The sharp contrast between the fortunes of England and Spain was thus dramatic. When Philip died in 1598 amid the gloomy splendors of the Escorial he left his realms to a son who showed little enthusiasm for the vast imperial schemes of his father. Meanwhile England, bathed in the golden sunshine of the last years of the Elizabethan age, looked forward to the prospect of an even more brilliant future.

■ FRANCE AND THE BALANCE OF POWER

If Philip's reign saw England rise to a new importance, it saw France endure the long confusions of the Wars of Religion and suffer the dangers of intervention from abroad, until at the end of the century the firm hand of Henry IV brought the ship of state to a steady course. In the background lay the long period of the Italian wars and the Hapsburg-Bourbon rivalry which had been personified in the conflicts between Francis I and the Emperor Charles V. In the background, too, lay religious cleavage, slowly developing in France as the influence of Luther, Zwingli and Calvin made itself felt. France's role in the second half of the critical sixteenth century seems to have been much more passive than active; it was the scene of a bitter religious conflict in which outside powers, notably Spain and England, tried to play a part. Yet France was sufficiently important for its help to be sought by England against Philip II. French assistance was also invoked by the Netherlands against this same Spanish danger.

Down to the time of his death in 1547 the ambitions of Francis I set the direction of French policy. None of his successors could play quite the same role as he had done; indeed, the unhappy picture in the ensuing decades is that of progressive decay in the Valois line until in the person of Henry III the family reached the utmost miserable depths of incompetence and degeneracy. The reign of Francis' son, Henry II (1547–1559), closely paralleled that of Edward VI and of Mary Tudor in England. As in their case, the principal domestic matter in France was that of religion, but whereas events in England were tending in the direction of a settlement by compromise, in France religious differences were becoming more acute and were to lead to bitter civil war.

Henry II was violently anti-Protestant and subject to the strong influence of the Guise family. Yet "reasons of state" loomed large, and in renewing the war with Charles V in 1551 Henry was willing to ally, by means of the Treaty of Friedwald, with the German Protestant princes and later, after the abdication of Charles, to carry on the war against Philip II of Spain. The gains which France made in 1559 by the Peace of Cateau-Cambrésis— Metz, Toul and Verdun on the Rhineland frontier, Chieri, Pinerolo, Chivasso and Villanova towards Savoy, and Calais on the Channel—show that in the European game of diplomacy she had won some shrewd strategic advances. By a tragic irony, however, Henry II was killed in the tournament which celebrated the return of peace and the three sons who successively followed him on the throne proved unable to maintain the advantageous position which he had won.

The reigns of the three sons of Henry II cover precisely three decades (1559–1589). The first, Francis II, ruled for only a year, dying at the age of seventeen; his successor Charles IX was only ten on his accession. Heavy responsibilities, therefore, fell upon the shoulders of the queen mother and regent, Catherine de' Medici. Her name, which is always associated with the Massacre of St. Bartholomew, has come to have a sinister connotation; yet in many respects her aims and policies were not unworthy. Desiring, understandably enough, to maintain the authority of her dynasty, she sought to harmonize differences within France. She would therefore have been willing to accept some degree of compromise and toleration in religious matters. A Catholic herself, she showed considerable favor toward Protestantism, only to be swept by the course of events into extreme measures which of her own volition she probably never would have undertaken.

The savage wars of religion that filled the reigns of Charles IX and his brother, Henry III, have already been sketched.[7] Not until near the end of this long period did foreign affairs assume a major importance, yet the time was without question conducive to active intrigue from abroad. The great landmark was the Massacre of St. Bartholomew in 1572, for this tragic attack upon the Huguenots had a profound impact in Europe, helping to intensify Protestant sympathy for the Huguenots and at the same time bringing Philip II more closely into the support of the Guises. Philip II is reported to have rejoiced on hearing the news which to him seemed to indicate the coming triumph of the Catholic cause in Europe. Thus in the ensuing years foreign intervention in the French civil wars became more active. England sent money to the Huguenots and German troops were mustered in the Rhineland to fight under the Duke of Condé, a leader of the French Protestant cause. Philip II of Spain now began to take a more vigorous part since he bitterly resented the willingness of the Duke of Anjou, brother of Henry III, to accept the sovereignty of the United Netherlands. After 1580, when Philip took over the crown of Portugal, he had further grounds for resentment in the help which France had given to the Portuguese opposition. With the death of the Duke of Anjou in 1584 Henry of Navarre, the leader of the Protestant cause, was the next in the direct line for the French crown. This prospect, too, Philip was determined to oppose.[8]

England meanwhile had come out more clearly on the Protestant side.

One of Henry of Navarre's entourage wrote to Walsingham in England as follows: "France is the stage on which is being played a strange tragedy in which all Christendom has a share. Many persons will come on, if not in the earlier acts, at any rate in the later." The outcome, as we have seen, was that by 1589 Henry of Navarre as king of France found himself fighting the organized might of the Catholic League, which meant in practical terms that he encountered mainly the open opposition of Philip II and his Spanish forces.

A Catholic victory in the French religious wars would without question have meant Spanish domination over France and might even have meant Philip's recovery of the Netherlands. But Philip's day was nearly over. In a series of victories Henry began to make his military position in France secure. He then made himself doubly sure of public backing by returning to the faith of the great majority of Frenchmen and becoming Catholic. "Paris," as he said, "was worth a Mass." The capital, long the stronghold of the League, fell to Henry in 1594; a contemporary cartoon shows him smiling shrewdly down upon the Spanish troops passing outward and homeward through its gateways. To end the opposition, which now came much more from Spain than from the League, a further military effort was needed. The ensuing campaign was fought principally in Burgundy and on the northeast frontier, an area by now well established as the classic battleground for the two great European rivals. In 1598, four months before Philip II died, peace between France and Spain was signed at Vervins.

The Peace of Vervins has been described as a truce, for the military conflict between France and Spain had not been truly ended; within a generation under the direction of Cardinal Richelieu, it was to be renewed. The general principle at Vervins was that of a mutual restoration of conquests; in addition, concern over the future of the Netherlands loomed large. The Dutch and English interest was to see that Philip of Spain surrender all sovereignty over both the Dutch and Flemish provinces; the Dutch in particular, now reasonably sure of their own freedom, wished to see the southern area also separated from the Spanish crown. In the end a compromise was attempted; it was agreed that sovereignty over Flanders (henceforth known as the Spanish Netherlands) should go to Philip's daughter, the Infanta Isabella, who was to marry the Archduke Albert of Austria, son of the Emperor Maximilian II.[9] In default of offspring from this marriage, however, the Spanish Netherlands later reverted to the Spanish crown. The Treaty of Vervins, then, contained no terms of profound significance in

9. The fact that Albert was Cardinal and Archbishop of Toledo proved no insuperable obstacle. He renounced his ecclesiastical dignities, married, and assumed his new title.

the immediate diplomatic history of the period. But in the longer perspective it assumes importance as a kind of historical marking point on one side of which lay the period of Spanish ascendance, while on the other lay a coming age of even more striking French achievement.

■ THE CONTRIBUTION OF IMPERIAL SPAIN

The increasing evidences of decline should not be taken to obscure the tremendous impact which Spain made upon the sixteenth century. Nor should one ignore or underestimate the importance of Spain's legacy to later times. Master of enormous wealth, powerful at home and overseas, in the forefront in diplomacy and war, an ardent champion of Roman Catholicism, Spain seemed long destined to carry on in the brilliant role which Charles V had assumed. Not until the close of the century were the signs of her weakness fully apparent.

The fields of Spain's contributions were various. In this chapter the emphasis has so far been upon politics and diplomacy, yet there was much more. An important field of Spanish influence concerned naval and colonial affairs. With her great empire and her traditions of seamanship and exploration Spain early took the lead on the high seas, a position emphasized all the more by her annexation of Portugal in 1580. Not even the success of England against the Armada in 1588 could destroy Spain's colonial supremacy, and it is understandable that Spanish books on exploration, navigation and seamanship became standard and were translated into various foreign languages.[10] It should be remembered, moreover, that despite Spain's ruthless treatment of the natives in her colonial possessions it was a Spanish priest, Bartolomeo Las Casas, the "Apostle of the Indies," whose writings first denounced these iniquities and championed a humane treatment of Spain's new subjects.

In military affairs Spain's role during the sixteenth century was unquestionably brilliant. The long line of commanders, from Gonsalvo di Cordova to the Duke of Alva and Alexander of Parma, laid the foundations of modern military methods of organization, strategy and tactics. The Spanish in the sixteenth century were the first to maintain a true standing army. In the Italian wars the long bow and the crossbow disappeared, to be replaced by the arquebus and the pike. The clumsy arquebus, supported on a portable fork, developed later into the musket, a powerful weapon capable of

---

10. The Spanish school of seamanship at Seville was responsible, among much else, for the publication of Marten Cortes' *Art of Navigation* (1551) which the Muscovy Company later considered sufficiently important to have translated into English.

disabling a horse at five hundred paces. The pike in its way was equally formidable—it grew to be eighteen feet in length and was so heavy that the expression, "trailing a pike," became a literal description of the pike-man's only practical method of marching. The pike held its place in warfare until it was superseded by the development of the bayonet in the last quarter of the seventeenth century. The Spanish commanders combined pikemen and musketeers into elaborately organized and highly trained battalions capable of maneuvering from square formations into battle line and performing their tasks with a very high morale. The Spaniards developed a school of fencing which competed with the Italian and helped to displace the old-fashioned combat with sword and buckler. Spanish infantry, gaining experience first in Italy and later in the Netherlands, became the model for all European troops, so much so that the Thirty Years' War may be said to have been fought largely with Spanish tactics. The military innovations of the great Swedish commander, Gustavus Adolphus, were really based upon Spanish foundations.

The Netherlands became a great testing ground for new developments in the art of war—for example, the use of the military telescope, the time-fuse and the hand-grenade. Troops were trained while in winter quarters, and there were important advances in the design of entrenchments and fortifications. Maurice of Nassau, who carried on the struggle for independence after the death of William of Orange and doubtless learned much from the Spanish, is said to have been the first general in history to climb a church tower and watch an enemy through a glass.

The tremendous social prestige of Spain was likewise unmistakable. The elaborate marriage pattern which brought the royal house of Spain into close connections with other dynasties cannot be described in detail; it will suffice to recall that the four marriages of Philip II linked him with the ruling families of Portugal, England, France and Austria. His children's marriages continued the old Austrian connection and created a new one with the Dukes of Savoy. Philip II's granddaughter, Anne, married Louis XIII of France and his great granddaughter, Maria Theresa, married Louis XIV. In this way Spain remained in the diplomatic foreground and perhaps because of this the dress, manners, deportment and etiquette of the Spanish court became a European possession. It has often been observed that the fantastically elaborate ceremonial of the court of Versailles under Louis XIV bore much more of the marks of Spain than of France itself.

The brilliance of Spanish literature in the last half of the sixteenth and the opening decades of the seventeenth century has already been mentioned.[11] Spanish influence can be traced in the literature of other coun-

11. See pp. 163–164.

tries, notably in the evolution of the drama and in the beginnings of the modern "picaresque" novel. These influences were effectively at work long after the day of Spain's true greatness had passed, and never more impressively than at the court of Anne of Austria, wife of Louis XIII of France.

> Anne of Austria throughout her life kept a Spanish court; and for forty years Spanish actors and authors flocked into France. Spanish dress, demeanour, and manners were the rage. Scores of Spanish words were accepted into French. The games, dances, the favorite dishes, even the terms of endearment, of Spaniards were naturalized; and Spanish was the modish language. Spanish plays and novels were translated into French, and thence into English or other tongues; or, at least, their ingenious plots and intrigues were appropriated. . . . Where France led, England followed; and the dramatists of the late seventeenth and early eighteenth centuries perpetuated on the English stage, and at this time in English form, the romantic story of intrigue which had its origins in Spain.[12]

What was thus true of Spain's influence in France was also true to a lesser degree elsewhere. Yet the widespread influence of Spanish culture was asserted, paradoxically enough, at a time when the reign of Philip III began to exhibit a shocking deterioration in Spanish society. An ostentatious and corrupt court, a spendthrift nobility, a hypocritical clergy and a miserable peasantry were the components in a domestic picture of what truthfully has been called complete social decadence. Europe could hardly realize the extent to which internal decay had weakened the structure of Imperial Spain, or how transient was to be the period of its greatness.

12. *The Cambridge Modern History,* III, pp. 547–548.

The Age of the
Thirty Years' War
1598–1648

THE PASSAGE OF THE LECH, 1632, engraving by Matthew Merian from THEATRUM EUROPAEUM, Frankfurt am Main, 1637. Swedish troops of King Gustavus Adolphus defeat Tilly's imperial forces by crossing the Lech aided by a smoke-screen and a prefabricated bridge. Note the formal pattern of war in the seventeenth century. Courtesy of the New York Public Library.

Chapter 11

■ HENRY IV, SULLY AND THE RECOVERY OF FRANCE

THE DEVELOPMENT of strong, centralized monarchical power in certain European countries, notably in France and Prussia, stands out as one of the major aspects of the seventeenth century. This process contrasts sharply with the continued difficulties of Hapsburg rule in Germany and with the waning of Spanish prestige. In consequence of these changes a political and cultural pattern began to emerge by the middle of the century which had

261

its best expression in the brilliant achievements of the French monarchy. The first stages of these new developments must now be considered.

When Henry IV became king of France in 1589 he could be described as ruler in little more than name. The country was torn by civil war, bitterly divided by religious conflict, economically exhausted and still threatened by the power of Spain. Kingship involved making urgent decisions and assuming staggering responsibilities. Henry's return, in 1593, to the Catholic Church made it possible for him to be crowned in the following year at Chartres. Partly by military force and partly by substantial bribes he proceeded to win over the hostile forces of the Catholic League, until by 1598 the last large center of resistance, Brittany, was secured. Meanwhile Spain, against which he had come to open war in 1595, was likewise defeated. With the return of peace in 1598 Henry was able to issue the Edict of Nantes and thereby secure the general allegiance of Frenchmen, both Catholic and Protestant.

The work of Henry IV was inseparable from that of his great minister, Maximilian de Béthune, Baron Rosny, better known to history by his later title of Duke of Sully. Brought up as a Protestant, Sully had joined the court of Navarre in 1571, proving himself to be a loyal and able servant. In 1598 he entered Henry's royal council as superintendent of finances; to this office other duties and other titles were soon to be added, so that without any question Sully soon became the principal pillar of the reign. Under a governmental system which still lacked any formally organized body of ministers, the powers of such a man were enormous.

An immediate problem was that of the machinery of government. During the confusions of the Wars of Religion royal authority had been unavoidably weakened and the local powers of the great nobles correspondingly increased. One of Henry's principal tasks, therefore, was to curb the power of disaffected nobles and to reassert his own. In this effort he was remarkably successful. He put down conspiracies with a ruthless hand. Though Henry never chose to summon the Estates General, he recognized the place of the various provincial assemblies in the government of France and consulted them on more than one occasion. In 1596, for example, he summoned a meeting at Rouen of the "Notables" (a gathering of some eighty representatives of the Church, the nobility and the various administrative bodies), urging them most tactfully to join in seeking new sources of taxation and a better organization of the government. The system of the *Paulette*, introduced in 1604, by which office-holders were required to make an annual contribution to the state of one-sixtieth of their income was doubtless the regularization of a haphazard practice which had long been accepted. It had grave defects, yet it was later defended by so shrewd a statesman as Richelieu on the grounds that it prevented even greater abuses.

Finances were a constant challenge to the government. Making all allowances for the unreliability of sixteenth-century statistics, one may consider a few broad indications. The public debt in 1560 has been estimated at 43½ million *livres;* in 1576 it was 101 millions; in 1598 it rose to 350 millions; and in 1610 it had dropped to 224 millions.[1] The work of tax-collecting was let out or "farmed" as a kind of business venture to individuals or corporations who turned over only a fraction of their takings to the state, keeping the rest as their profit. The technique of tax-farming was wasteful in the extreme; it has been estimated that only about one-quarter of what the public paid in taxes ever reached the royal treasury. A parallel abuse was that by which whole classes of persons, notably the clergy and the nobles, were exempt from certain taxes, leaving the burden to be carried by the middle and lower classes. Other inequities arose from the varying incidence of taxation in different provinces in France.

It would be too much to expect that Henry and Sully could end such complex abuses, yet they strove hard. Certain economies in administration, together with an insistence upon greater efficiency, resulted in a substantial reduction of the public debt between 1598 and 1610. Though the pernicious system of tax-farming defied full-scale assault, an end was put to the practice of sub-farming the taxes. Better methods of bookkeeping were employed and efforts made to cut down the size of the *taille* (a sort of income tax) and to impose its burden upon a wider number of people. Attempts were also made to secure a lower rate of interest upon public loans. The annual payments made to the government by office-holders were put upon a more systematic basis. No one of these measures could in itself be described as wholly successful, yet the overall effect was unquestionably beneficial. With a clear balance of 18 million *livres* on hand by the end of his reign Henry could claim to have substantially increased the annual income of the government and to have left a full treasury.

Direct efforts were also made to stimulate and encourage economic life. Henry had read and evidently been much impressed by a sixteenth-century farming treatise, the famous *Théâtre d'agriculture* (1600) of Olivier de Serres. Some of its practical advice, for example on the better utilization of land, was put into effect. Dutch workers were brought in to drain marshy areas, forests were improved and patrolled, roads and canals were built so that farmers could more readily get their produce to market. New crops such as maize and mulberries were encouraged, the latter making possible

1. The *livre* was the old French equivalent of the later franc.

an important growth of the silk industry. Efforts were made to remove inter-provincial tariffs which hindered the free sale of grain, and also to further the sale of grain abroad by removing the restrictions upon its export. Peace and order were stressed as the basic foundations of a healthy economy.

The policies which thus improved agriculture were paralleled by others in the field of industry. Official encouragement, usually in the form of boun-ties, loans or tax-exemptions, was given to the manufacture of silk, tapestries, linen, carpets, glassware, pottery and iron wares. With royal encouragement specialized groups of workers such as jewellers, clock and instrument-makers, painters and sculptors were set up at the Louvre. The obvious corollary to such efforts came in various measures to stimulate trade. A Commission of Commerce was set up in 1601 under the hard working Barthélemy de Laf-fémas. Within France improvements in roads, bridges and canals, together with a new network of post-houses, helped in the freer movement of goods. Fiscal exemptions were granted to certain towns. Commercial treaties with the Hansa League (1602), with England (1604) and with Spain (1607) were designed to stimulate the flow of commodities. Encouragement was also given to overseas trade and settlement; Port-Royal, in Acadia, was founded in 1605 and Quebec in 1608.

A further sign of the king's intentions may be observed in his efforts to improve and beautify the city of Paris; this involved completing the Tuil-eries, building the great gallery of the Louvre, improving public sanitation, paving some streets and erecting the famous Pont Neuf over the River Seine. All in all, then, one is justified in seeing in the work of Henry and Sully a conscious effort to increase through royal leadership the economic and social well-being of the state. To this policy the name mercantilism may legiti-mately be applied. Few French kings, it may be ventured, have concerned themselves so actively with their country's economic good.

The foreign policy of Henry IV seems to have been based upon a real-istic appraisal of the problems of his age. The enormous growth of Haps-burg power had led to various counter moves on the part of France, Eng-land and the Netherlands. As the century closed, Henry was determined that the Hapsburgs, now divided into the Spanish and Austrian branches, must not dominate the continent; some evidence, indeed, indicates that Henry would not have been averse to taking over the major role which the Hapsburgs formerly had played. He wished, nevertheless, to move cautiously, to avoid unleashing a general war, and to acquire further ter-ritory only as an incidental outcome of his other purposes and not as in itself a major goal.

The map of Europe in 1600 shows clearly enough the situation. On all France's land frontiers lay the shadow of Hapsburg power. To the south, where the Pyrenees met the Mediterranean, was the small territory of Roussillon—a Spanish possession on the French slope of the mountains. On the northeastern border were the rich territories of Flanders, now directly under Spanish control. Due east, in imperial hands, lay Franche Comté, the "Free County" of Burgundy. To the southeast, beyond the rampart of the French Alps, were the territories of the Dukes of Savoy within which stood strategic fortresses such as Saluzzo and Pinerolo guarding critical routes into Italy. Control of these border points would have made it possible for French armies to issue forth from the Alps and to menace Turin and the whole north Italian plain. Such were the main strategic considerations which Henry IV had to consider.

The French moves were varied and cautious. Henry IV seems to have toyed for a time with the notion of becoming a candidate for the emperorship of the Holy Roman Empire. In another move he went briefly to war with Savoy, gaining in 1601 two important small areas, Bresse and Bugey, which brought the French frontier to the western tip of Lake Geneva. He sought friendship with the Swiss Cantons and with Sweden. In Italy he sought to counter Spanish influences by friendly gestures towards the various Italian duchies. In southeast Europe he encouraged the Turks to renew their old hostility against Austria and Spain. He showed great sympathy towards the United Netherlands, granted them subsidies and had some share in securing for them the favorable truce terms of 1609. Most significant of all, and echoing an earlier French policy, he encouraged the various German Protestant princes to league together for their own advantage in the Evangelical Union of 1608—a classic example of French efforts to stimulate political opposition to the emperor.

Historians have been long attracted by what would appear to be one of the most dramatic undertakings of this decade, the so-called Great Design, attributed to Henry IV and Sully. The account which can be distilled from Sully's *Memoirs* suggests a plan to reorganize the existing states system of Europe, setting up in its place a federal structure somewhat like that of the later United States of America with a senate, various lesser councils, a common meeting place, a common army and a common treasury. Intended to remove the danger of war, the plan was broached, according to some accounts, to the English and the Dutch and but for Henry's tragic murder might have been pushed even further. Fascinating as the plan appears, there are serious historical doubts as to whether it ever approached the point of concreteness.[2] The Great Design may well have been little more than a

2. The chapter in Sully's much-doctored *Memoirs* purporting to deal with the Great Design is really made up of a series of scattered passages assembled by an editor in 1745 and thus conveying a far greater suggestion of coherence than the plan probably ever had.

dream in the mind of Sully, and this dream may have concerned itself much more with astute power politics than with international utopias.

The Great Design envisaged a new organization of states, all roughly equal in strength: six hereditary monarchies (France, Spain, England, Denmark, Sweden and Savoy); five elective monarchies (Austria, Poland, Bohemia, Hungary and Rome); and four sovereign republics (Venice, the Netherlands, Switzerland and a new grouping in northern Italy). This much at least seems clear, that before any such proposal could ever be put into effect Hapsburg power would have to be broken into fragments and one of the great aims of French diplomacy automatically realized. Realistic considerations such as these seem to give a better explanation of Sully's plan than those which see its inspiration in the lofty vision of a united Europe.[3]

In the last years of his reign, when a crisis arose over the fate of the two Rhineland duchies of Jülich and Cleves, Henry IV acted vigorously. When the Catholic rulers of these lands died in 1609, among the several claimants to the succession was the Elector of Brandenburg, a leader of the Protestant cause in Germany. The emperor at once indicated his interest. If the Hapsburgs were to control these disputed territories they would have an admirable jumping-off point for an attack upon the United Netherlands. The dispute thus grew to wider proportions than a mere matter of succession, with the result that in 1609 a Catholic League was organized in Germany to oppose the support which the Evangelical Union of certain German Protestant princes gave to the Elector of Brandenburg. Henry IV of France, despite his Catholicism, formally allied himself in 1610 with the German Protestants. Mustering the resources of the French state, Henry planned to put an army of 30,000 men in the field, a force of major proportions intended to challenge Hapsburg authority in a critical area.[4] The issue, however, was never joined, for in 1610, on his way to take command of his armies, Henry was assassinated.

Death, as it has been put, may have saved Henry from his greatest blunder.[5] However this may be, martyrdom left Henry's reputation secure in the hearts of his countrymen. Few French kings have made so great an impression of sincerity, moderation and devotion to the public weal. The boudoir scandals of Henry's private life, never more notable than in his last months, had little adverse effect upon his popularity. His great achievements in establishing order at home and raising French prestige abroad

3. See the sensible discussion in D. OGG, *Europe in the Seventeenth Century* (1931), pp. 77–81.
4. See map, pp. 368–369.
5. The Cleves-Jülich question was not settled until 1614 when by the Treaty of Xanten it was agreed to divide the territories, Jülich going to a Catholic claimant and Cleves to the Protestant House of Brandenburg. In 1815 Brandenburg acquired the entire territory.

laid the firm foundations upon which his brilliant successors could build.
If Henry's rule had the flavor of absolutism, it was an absolutism devoted
to the public good. Such, in general terms, would seem to be the nature of
Henry's work as we can now see it at a distance of three centuries. To his
contemporaries, however, the immediate sequel was to be a decade of confusion and threatening danger.

■ FRANCE UNDER RICHELIEU AND MAZARIN

As Frenchmen look to Henry IV as one of their greatest kings, so they
regard Richelieu as one of their greatest public servants. Such, indeed, is
the fame of Armand Jean Duplessis, Cardinal de Richelieu (1585–1642),
that it has tended to becloud the achievement of his royal master and to
deny Louis XIII the substantial share of a credit which is rightly his. Not
the least achievement of this unspectacular yet able king was to give Richelieu a relatively free hand and a firm backing in the conduct of public affairs.

The two decades of Richelieu's great achievements were prefaced by
ten years of uncertainty. Since Louis XIII was only nine years old on the
death of his father in 1610, a regency was established by the Queen Mother,
Marie de' Medici.[6] This regency meant the arrival of certain royal favorites,
notably the Italian Concini and his wife, in positions of power and the
squandering of the treasure that Sully had built up. It also meant a definite
reversal in foreign policy. The queen steered her country away from the
Rhineland war that Henry IV had contemplated and instead moved deliberately towards an alliance with Spain and Austria. To this end the young
king was betrothed to Princess Anne of Austria, daughter of Philip III of
Spain; his sister was married to the future Philip IV.

Concini was murdered in 1617 by nobles jealous of his position; the
same uprising forced Marie de' Medici and her entourage (which included
the young Richelieu) into exile at Blois. Louis XIII, now growing in years
and self-confidence, sought to govern with the aid of his own favorite, the
Duke of Luynes. A confused period followed in which a kind of reconciliation was effected between the king and his mother, with the consequence
that Richelieu quietly moved into the center of the stage.

As a younger son of a noble family Richelieu had early entered the
Church, becoming bishop of Luçon, in a fashion not uncommon at the time,
at the age of twenty-one. In 1622, when he was only thirty-seven, he became
a cardinal. Richelieu, who had proved himself a shrewd adviser to the
Queen Mother, was no less useful to Louis XIII. His ambition was realized

6. She is described by ALDOUS HUXLEY in his *Grey Eminence* as "a large, fleshly, gloriously
bedizened barmaid."

in 1624, when the king made him a member of the royal council; here his rank of cardinal, rather than any clearly defined office, entitled him to the appellation of "first minister." However little this title may have meant at first, the course of events soon showed that Richelieu stood incomparably above his fellows. Despite various attempts to overthrow him, his position remained secure until his death in 1642.

Richelieu's name is one of the greatest in the entire history of French foreign policy. His profound importance lies in the clear aims which he set, and the skill and determination with which he pursued them. Richelieu sought to exalt the authority of the state—an authority of which he willingly took the king to be the living embodiment—by every possible means. All domestic obstacles to royal authority must be removed so that France could proceed to establish a commanding position in Europe free from the menace of any rival power. To these twin aims Richelieu devoted his life. Endowed with an uncanny skill, he contrived in a remarkable degree to achieve them. The criticism has been made of him that as a cardinal of the Church he might have had a larger concept of the European Christian community and have worked for something more noble than simply the security and prestige of France. To make this criticism is to ignore the climate of the seventeenth century. Richelieu was a man of his times.

At home the main problem seemed to be that created by the Huguenots. The religious toleration which was provided by the Edict of Nantes had given the Protestants a remarkable degree of political autonomy. The real danger was that of creating a state within a state. Could, for example, the Huguenots be permitted to retain the two hundred fortified towns which the Edict had conceded them? Even before Richelieu came to power the matter had led to open conflict, following which arrangements had been made in 1622 continuing the Huguenot liberty of worship but reducing the number of their fortified towns to three. Dissatisfied with this, some Protestants had organized active resistance centering at the west coast port of La Rochelle and had sought help from Protestant England.

Finally deciding that the Huguenot danger was a political threat which would have to be ended by military means, Richelieu prepared to besiege La Rochelle. The great cardinal himself accompanied and directed the siege operation, striding about among his troops in military cloak and riding-boots while a huge mole or breakwater was constructed in an effort to block the harbor. In October, 1628, after English attempts to relieve the city by sea had failed, La Rochelle capitulated; this led to the acceptance by both sides in the following year of the Peace of Alais. The Protestants were to continue to have unimpaired freedom of worship; they had, however, to turn over their remaining fortified places to the government, with the consequence that their organization was seriously weakened. The year 1629, then, may be taken as the final termination of the religious wars in France; it marks the time when the Huguenots lost any claim to political autonomy. Henceforth the Protestant community could concern itself less with defending its religious liberties and more with improving its economic condition. It may also be noted that the Roman Catholic Church began a vigorous and not unsuccessful drive to reconvert the Huguenots to their old faith.

Richelieu's policies likewise involved an attack upon the continuing privileges of the great nobles who more often than not were jealous of his powers. From time to time (in 1626, 1630, 1632 and 1642) he was compelled to take ruthless action against conspiracies, most of which seem to have been inspired by that eccentric character, Gaston of Orleans, the royal brother who in the words of one historian flitted through Richelieu's life like some vicious insect. A royal edict of 1626 provided for the destruction of all fortresses not situated on the frontiers of France. Another forbade duelling under pain of death. A noble practice so long established could hardly be abolished by decree, hence it is understandable that the duelling edict was hailed with derision by the young bloods. Yet one of them who ostentatiously fought a duel under Richelieu's own windows was arrested and, to the general astonishment, sent to the scaffold.

Various administrative changes were devised to strengthen the authority of the central government. Lest centers of opposition should develop, Richelieu arranged that nobles who held provincial governorships should periodically be reshuffled. Royal agents known as intendants were usually drawn from the middle class and were set up beside the governors to supervise the administration of justice and police and to collect taxes. Rebels and traitors were tried before specially appointed judges. In 1630 a severe press censorship was established, and a year later the *Gazette,* soon to be the official mouthpiece of the government, began to appear. The Estates General were never summoned, while the *Parlement* of Paris, a kind of supreme law court, was told in 1641 that it must not busy itself with affairs of state. A small advisory body of noblemen, the Notables, was summoned in 1626 and again in 1627, but it was made up entirely of royal nominees. Thus, while the French nobility remained secure in its economic and social privileges, it was in no position to challenge the political authority of the king and his great minister.

Closely allied with the specific problem of the nobles was the more general problem of governmental administration. Here one may observe the growth of a disciplined, centralized machinery of control. The old royal council was on the way to becoming the recognized agent of the royal will.

In 1630 it was reorganized so as to have three subordinate branches to discuss details. The *Parlements* which, on the model of the *Parlement* of Paris, existed in some of the provinces, found their legal and administrative authority challenged by the new royal intendants. In six provinces there also existed what were known as provincial estates, local administrative bodies privileged to vote their own exceptional subsidies and thus not subject to the general assessment which had been recognized by the Estates General. In three of these cases (Burgundy, Dauphiné and Provence) Richelieu was able to remove their privileges. The other three he left alone.

Despite the constructive work of Henry IV and Sully, finances remained a continuing problem in France. That Richelieu seems to have proceeded by means of expedients is suggested by his admission to Claude Bullion, the appropriately named minister of finance, that he was ignorant of financial matters. In 1640 a standard gold coin, the *louis d'or,* was issued at Paris. (The minister of finance celebrated the occasion by a dinner at which each happy guest was served with a plateful of the new coins.) There was, however, no substantial reorganization of finances. Old taxes such as the *taille* and *gabelle* were continued; indirect taxes were farmed; there was no efficient audit; nearly one-half of the famous salt-tax was absorbed in the costs of collection; borrowing went on at very high rates of interest; and it was estimated that one-fourth of the population still remained exempt from all direct taxation. Since deficits continued, Richelieu must be charged with having made no lasting contribution to a financial problem that was increasingly to harass France until the time of the Revolution.

In the related fields of industry and commerce Richelieu's achievements were less than spectacular. He made some improvements in roads, bridges and canals and organized an efficient post service for travelers and goods. France was divided into twenty postal districts with connections to seven foreign countries. Although Richelieu cannot properly be termed a full-fledged mercantilist, yet he sought by various means to direct the economic life of France. Special favors were granted to some industries, notably to those manufacturing silks, rugs and tapestries. Some efforts were made to ease the circulation of manufactures within France and to restrict the import of foreign goods. Edicts were issued to curb purchases abroad and to require all exports to be carried in French vessels. These edicts, however, were only partly effective.

The charters which Richelieu issued to French trading companies were not followed by impressive results. Various grants were made of exclusive trading or colonizing rights in Canada, the West Indies, Africa, Russia, Madagascar and the East Indies. Despite these moves, the French accomplishments were small in comparison with the active work of the English and the Dutch. The Company of One Hundred Associates, for example, which had been organized in 1627 with the plan to send four thousand colonists to North America in fifteen years could show by 1642 only two hundred settlers. The conclusion seems to be that in this field Richelieu was not in firm enough contact with practical realities; the charters were so drawn as to make the companies dependent upon close governmental control, but in actual fact Richelieu's interests and his energies were focused elsewhere.

In religious matters the age was one of considerable Catholic revival, as the founding of several new orders such as the Lazarites and the Sisters of Charity will indicate. In this age, too, the abbey of Port Royal became the center of an ardent religious activity later to become famous under the name of Jansenism. Although Richelieu's own interests were strongly political he sought for a better standard of appointments in the Church, seeking to steer a middle path between the "Gallicans" who insisted upon the rights of the French clergy and those whose first allegiance was to Rome. In foreign affairs Richelieu had no hesitation in taking the Protestant side, nor did he hesitate to ask large sums from the clergy in support of his wars abroad. If Richelieu had a theory on the subject of church and state relations it would seem to be that he was disposed to recognize the rights of king and pope, each in his own sphere. In a crisis, nevertheless, if affairs of state made such a decision necessary, Richelieu would not hesitate to act firmly against the Church.

The successor to Richelieu and inheritor of his policies was Cardinal Mazarin (1602–1661), an Italian who had entered the service of France, become naturalized and risen spectacularly in rank and fame. In foreign affairs Mazarin, as will appear, reaped where Richelieu had sown. At home he was able to outmaneuver the Council of Regency which had been set up to conduct affairs during the minority of Louis XIV. Mazarin won the favor and the affection of the Queen Mother, Anne of Austria, to whom it is even possible that he may have secretly been married.

By 1648 Mazarin ran into a domestic opposition, the *Fronde,* which reached the proportions of a minor civil war.[7] The conflict had two stages. In the first, the *Parlement* of Paris resisted Mazarin's efforts to extend taxes and drew up a series of fifteen demands centering upon their right to share in the levying of taxes and including a demand that all French subjects be tried according to the law of the land. While this corresponded in some ways to the contemporary parliamentary struggles in England, the "Parliamentary *Fronde*" was in essence an effort of a privileged group of office-

7. The name, *Fronde,* is a slang expression for the sling with which Paris urchins threw mud at passers-by.

holders to defend its selfish interests. By 1649 Mazarin and the Queen Mother had been compelled to accept the *Parlement's* demands.

A second disturbance, the "Princes' *Fronde*," was inspired by the desire of a group of high nobles (and their wives) led by the ambitious Prince of Condé to take over power from Mazarin, of whom they were intensely jealous. They were powerful enough for a time to force Mazarin to leave France. Condé, however, was unable to maintain his alliance with the *Parlement* of Paris, so that when the conspirators fell out, Mazarin returned in 1653 and regained his authority which he exercised until his death in 1661.

Three points can be made about Mazarin's struggle with the *Frondeurs*. In the first place, the crisis showed the selfish motives which inspired a large segment of the French nobility. In the second place, the effort to base the struggle on an appeal to the ancient constitutional traditions of France was a failure. In the third place, the obvious cynicism and incompetence of many of the leaders of the *Fronde* seem to have reconciled large numbers of Frenchmen to accepting royal absolutism as an alternative to recurrent disorder.

■ RICHELIEU AND FOREIGN AFFAIRS:
THE FIRST PHASE, 1624–1631

Richelieu's handling of foreign affairs could not wait upon the establishment of order at home. From the beginning to the end of his administration he found the larger questions of European policy pressing in upon him. Sometimes, indeed, the appearance of a crisis at home, as in the case of the revolt of the Huguenots at La Rochelle, made it impossible for him to act as decisively abroad as he would have wished. As far as possible, therefore, he sought a united kingdom as the necessary prerequisite to his diplomatic maneuvers.

Like Henry IV, Richelieu took seriously into account the threat to French interests which came from Hapsburg power both in Spain and Austria. Military strength was a prime necessity to meet this threat. Although Richelieu clearly saw the need for an efficient, centrally organized army to replace the mixed feudal levies of the past, he can hardly be said to have brought any such modern army into existence. The great names of the French military tradition—the Condés, the Turennes and the Vaubans—belong to a later generation. Nevertheless a considerable amount was done to improve discipline and to develop organization and tactics.

Richelieu's best work was done in maritime affairs. As early as 1626 he assumed the title of General Superintendent of Navigation and Commerce. Hitherto the navy had had very little central organization, its admirals really being provincial officials who were responsible for the defense only of their immediate coasts. In a sweeping change Richelieu abolished the old office of admiral, and by his famous Marine Ordinance (1627) brought the entire French coast under the central control of the state. He acquired a series of ports which were to be used as naval bases, requiring each of them to build naval vessels for the government. A naval council (*Conseil de la Marine*) was created and placed under the direction of a controller and an efficient staff. Through these means Richelieu secured by 1636 an Atlantic fleet of thirty-eight ships organized in three squadrons, and a Mediterranean fleet of twelve galleys and thirteen auxiliaries. A curious detail of this reorganization was that in his search for a commander of the Atlantic fleet Richelieu finally hit upon the unlikely figure of the Archbishop of Bordeaux.

Richelieu's *Political Testament,* a lengthy document in which he embodied many of his ideas for posterity, stressed the need to find friends abroad and to maintain bridgeheads to them. In this search he was aided by some devoted servants, notably the Capuchin monk, Father Joseph, the "Grey Eminence" of legend.[8] To certain frontier areas such as Artois, Flanders, Franche Comté, Lorraine and Milan, France could put forward historic claims. Richelieu's policies were in no sense crudely annexationist; the very term, "natural frontiers," for example, seems to have been the creation of a later generation. He was concerned rather with the questions of French security and the European balance. If to obtain these ends it was necessary to gain certain strong points, of which Strasbourg and Versoix to the east and Casale and Pinerolo in Italy may be taken as examples, then well and good. Territorial expansion in itself was not, however, his primary aim.

Another matter was that of alliances. Although the fires of religious conflict which had died down in France still burned abroad, religion was not the key to Richelieu's foreign policy. In order to weaken the Hapsburg emperor he turned to the German Protestant princes, offered subsidies to Protestant powers such as Denmark, the Netherlands and Sweden, and arranged for a marriage between the future Charles I of England and Henrietta Maria of France. It was also necessary to keep a close eye upon strategic areas where the Hapsburgs might gain a dangerous military advantage. For this reason the questions of the Valtelline and the Duchy of Mantua, in one sense minor, took on an urgent significance.

8. Joseph was unquestionably a practising mystic who lived a life of great austerity and devoutness. Only reluctantly would he accept a dispensation permitting him to use a coach while traveling on business of state. Nevertheless he furthered and defended to the full his master's realistic and ruthless policies.

The Valtelline is a long Swiss valley which runs northeasterly from Lake Como in Italy towards the valley of the Inn River.[9] It thus provided a strategic corridor extending from the Spanish-controlled Duchy of Milan to the Austrian Tyrol and, less directly, to the head waters of the Rhine. In a military crisis, then, Spanish or Italian troops could be shuttled via Genoa and Milan to the support of the Hapsburg cause in Germany or the Netherlands. The Catholic Valtelline had long been under the control of its Protestant Swiss neighbors, the so-called Grisons League, but by 1622 it had with Spanish help thrown off this control and granted the right of passage to the Spaniards. Papal troops, it was agreed, should hold the forts controlling the valley.

This was the situation that Richelieu sought to overthrow. Allying with Venice and Savoy, he succeeded in 1625 in driving out the occupying garrisons. The Huguenot revolt at home, however, forced him to withdraw his troops and modify his plans. The Treaty of Monzon (1626) with Spain was an arrangement by which the Grisons resumed their control and the Spanish fortresses in the valley were dismantled. In point of actual fact, Richelieu was unable to prevent the Spaniards at a later date from using the valley. In 1634, for example, the Spaniards were able to send twelve thousand troops through it and help to win the important battle of Nordlingen over the Swedes. The real importance of the episode lies in Richelieu's instantaneous recognition of the high strategic importance of this area and his prompt support of the Protestant Grisons in order to further French policy against the Hapsburgs.

The problem of the Mantuan succession likewise illuminates Richelieu's aims. Mantua was a small Italian duchy lying in the Lombard plain at the junction of the Po and Mincio rivers. In 1627 it fell to a French claimant, the Duke of Nevers, whose rights were immediately challenged by the Hapsburgs. Here again strategic considerations proved to be more important than any inherent value attaching to the duchy itself. Richelieu strongly backed Nevers' claims and in 1629 king and cardinal led a French army across the Alps. The outcome of two years of war and negotiation was the Treaty of Cherasco (1631). The Duke of Nevers was recognized as the ruler of Mantua and its western appendage, the territory of Montferrat. Within this lay the important fortress of Casale. The French were permitted to keep Casale and also Pinerolo, which they had captured during the campaign. These two strong points, lying on the Italian slope of the Alps, gave the French an excellent military base for operations in northern Italy. In a strategic sense, therefore, Richelieu's shrewd diplomacy had been well rewarded.

9. See map, p. 283.

By 1631 the essential pattern of Richelieu's foreign policy had clearly emerged. He was secure at home and he had moved vigorously abroad in defense of French interests. He was increasingly concerned over the great political and religious conflict that raged in central Europe. To understand this conflict it is necessary to retrace our steps and examine more closely the nature of Hapsburg power in Germany and observe the various issues which were at stake in the Thirty Years' War.

■ THE HAPSBURGS AND THE PROBLEM OF GERMANY

The settlement made at Augsburg in 1555 created as many problems as it solved. Hapsburg power had been weakened to some extent, seeing that the princes won certain rights in religion which the emperor had long sought to deny them. The first beginnings of religious toleration had appeared, and with it the hope that further concessions could be achieved. Nevertheless, large problems remained so that within fifty years political and religious differences flared up again. In the end large parts of Europe became embroiled in what was originally a civil war within Germany.

Political and geographical circumstances made it very hard for either the Spanish or the Austrian Hapsburgs to mind their own business. Spain's control extended over the Duchy of Milan, Franche Comté, Luxemburg and the Spanish Netherlands. These all lay within the territorial limits of the Holy Roman Empire and therefore were theoretically subject in some degree to its authority. The Austrian Hapsburgs at Vienna exercised a control over Germany which was more apparent than real. Their interests, if not their power, nevertheless were widespread. A common Catholicism dominated the outlook of the two branches. A common concern for the affairs of Italy was traditional. A common antagonism was felt towards France, towards England and towards the newly powerful Protestant states of Sweden and the United Netherlands. It must therefore be clear that large possibilities for trouble existed, and that in the event of major disturbances in Germany Spain would almost automatically be involved.

The immediate imperial successors to Charles V were his brother Ferdinand I (1556–1564), then Ferdinand's son Maximilian II (1564–1576), and then Maximilian's son Rudolf II (1576–1612). All were beset by difficulties arising from those questions of religion, internal politics and foreign relations which by 1600 were reaching a critical stage. In a religious sense it had become clear that with the growth of Calvinism the Augsburg settlement of 1555 which recognized only the Lutheran or the Roman Catholic faith was no longer adequate. In addition to Calvinism other sects had arisen; in Bohemia, for example, there were groups such as the Utraquists (believing that the layman could receive the communion in either form) and the Bohemian Brethren. At this time, too, the Roman Catholic Church, strengthened by the work of the Counter Reformation, was making vigorous attempts to win back those who had left the fold. Its success was considerable.

A special problem arose from one particular aspect of the Peace of Augsburg, the so-called "ecclesiastical reservation" clause. This was really an imperial ruling to the effect that if an ecclesiastical prince went over to the Protestant faith he could not, so to speak, take his lands and revenues along with him, but would have to turn them over, or "reserve" them, to the Catholic authorities who would thus keep the lands under their administration. In a number of cases this principle had been violated. On the other hand, instances appeared where the imperial authorities by favoring the Catholics had outraged the established rights of Protestant communities. In Bohemia a special problem arose from the Letter of Majesty which the Emperor Rudolf had granted to his Protestant subjects in 1609. This ostensible charter of rights gave no protection to the Calvinists or Bohemian Brethren, and what rights it did grant to the Lutherans came to be ignored. In consequence of all this, religious unrest mounted steadily to a climax.

The major political issue in Germany was the old problem of "particularism." Local rulers were traditionally jealous of their rights and were enormously suspicious of imperial authority. The machinery of administration which Maximilian I a century before had sought to regularize and improve still functioned badly. The three houses of the imperial Diet, the complex system of imperial courts and the administrative subdivisions known as the imperial circles all operated with fantastic clumsiness. For a time, too, it looked as if imperial authority would be fatally weakened by the tendency of the emperors to apportion various parts of the Empire (Austria, Bohemia and Hungary) to different members of the Hapsburg family. The Emperor Matthias (1612–1629), however, being childless undertook to reverse this tendency. He indicated that he wished his cousin, Ferdinand of Styria, to succeed him and he further arranged to have Ferdinand elected King of Bohemia in 1617 and of Hungary in 1618. This example of imperial consolidation was all the more ominous to the Protestants since Ferdinand's Catholicism was of the most ardent kind. Selfish interests on the part of the princes were clearly involved, for many Protestant rulers could see golden vistas opening before them if only they could lay their hands upon the great wealth coming from confiscated church lands. An Evangelical Union of German Protestant rulers had been formed in 1608 and an opposing Catholic League in 1609.[10] Inspired more by politics than by religion, these associations made an already explosive situation even more precarious.

10. See pp. 265–266.

The complex interests of foreign powers added to the troubles of Germany. Ever since the Italian Wars at the close of the fifteenth century the ruthless game of alliance and counter-alliance had grown in intensity. Protestant states such as Sweden, Denmark and the United Netherlands were understandably concerned at the fate of their fellow-Protestants in Germany. At the same time they were interested in the prospect of territorial gains for themselves. The ruler of Denmark, for instance, some of whose scattered lands lay within the frontiers of the Empire, had his eye upon the neighboring bishoprics of Osnabrück and Halberstadt. The king of Sweden had imperial dreams to ring the Baltic with new Swedish provinces. James I of England had wed his daughter Elizabeth to the Calvinistic ruler of the Palatinate. France, as always, was willing to fish in troubled waters.

Broadly speaking, then, the situation was that of a growing challenge to the old imperial power. In the years between 1555 and 1618 various princes found occasion to consolidate their position and take the first steps to modernize their administrative machinery. As the powers of these princes thus expanded, they stood ready to challenge such imperial pretensions as still remained. No effective means existed to curb these new military, dynastic, political and religious interests. In such circumstances a spark would be sufficient to set off a conflagration. Such a spark was to be found in 1618 in the ancient Kingdom of Bohemia.

■ THE THIRTY YEARS' WAR

The chronicle of the Thirty Years' War is a record of diplomatic intrigue, military campaigns and savage destruction. Its interest to the historian lies less in these matters than in its demonstration of the disruptive forces at work in German national life and in its evidence of the vigorous participation of outside powers in imperial affairs. The foreign interest is brought out especially in the various "periods"—Bohemian, Danish, Swedish and French —into which the war is conventionally divided. Even more important than the war itself was the settlement which ended it, for the Peace of Westphalia was to constitute a landmark in the political, diplomatic and religious history of Europe.

The war opened with a revolt in Bohemia where a bitter resentment grew up against what was regarded as unjustifiable interference by the Hapsburgs in the internal affairs of the ancient kingdom. The Emperor Matthias, who held also the title of King of Bohemia, had arranged for his cousin Ferdinand to succeed him in 1617 as king. Protestant and national opinion reacted sharply against this with the result that two imperial emissaries, appearing in 1618 before a gathering of Bohemian nobles in Prague, were unceremoniously thrown from a high window of the Hradschin Palace. By this historic "defenestration of Prague" war upon the emperor was unofficially declared.

Matthias died in the following year. When Ferdinand then succeeded him as emperor, the Bohemian Estates proceeded at once to renounce Hapsburg rule and to invite a Rhineland prince, Frederick, the Elector of the Palatinate, to be their king. Frederick, an ardent Calvinist and the son-in-law of James I of England, was hopefully regarded as the leader of the Protestant cause. He went to Prague and was crowned. Here he became something of a curiosity, driving about in a bright red cloak with a large yellow feather stuck in his hat, or bathing stark naked in the River Moldau before the queen and her ladies, to the horror of the good burghers of the capital.

Imperial forces were soon mustered against Frederick. At the Battle of White Hill (1620) outside Prague he was defeated by the Austrian commander, Count Tilly. The defeat meant ultimately not only the loss of his Bohemian crown but also the loss of Frederick's ancestral territory, the Palatinate, which went to Maximilian of Bavaria, an ardent supporter of the imperial cause.[11] An extraordinarily severe repression was imposed upon Bohemia. Leaders of the revolt were executed, their lands were confiscated and redistributed, education was largely given over to the Jesuits, and many scholars including the great Bohemian educator Comenius were driven into exile. Roman Catholicism was firmly reestablished. The old political rights guaranteed by the Letter of Majesty were abrogated and it was eventually provided that the Bohemian crown was to be hereditary in the House of Hapsburg. The Bohemian revolt, then, had turned out to be a catastrophe for the Protestant and Bohemian cause.

On the larger scene complications soon developed. Most of the German Protestant princes for various reasons had chosen to stand aside rather than come to the aid of Bohemia. Catholic Spain soon took the opportunity to renew its old war with the Dutch who, despite aid from England and France, were compelled by 1625 to surrender the fortress town of Breda. In this situation a new challenger to the progress of the Catholic cause appeared in the person of Christian IV, King of Denmark. Some of his lands lay within the frontiers of the Empire. Ambitious to acquire more, and concerned at the fate of his Protestant brethren, he decided to intervene.

The "Danish period" of the Thirty Years' War opened in 1625 when Christian IV led his troops southward into Germany. Here he met not only

---

11. Maximilian also obtained the rank of imperial elector formerly held by the ruler of the Palatinate.

the already famous imperial general, Tilly, but a dramatic new figure, Count Wallenstein. This Bohemian adventurer, who had deserted Protestantism for Catholicism, had made a fortune by selling grain to the imperial armies. He seemed to be of the view that the emperor could strengthen his position by paying less attention to his scattered dynastic interests and by seeking instead to build up a strong German-Austrian block in the center of Europe. Obsessed by notions of his own destiny, Wallenstein had risen high in imperial favor and had gathered around him a polyglot army which he commanded with brilliant ability. In 1626 Wallenstein overwhelmingly defeated Christian IV at the Battle of Lutter, with the consequence that the Protestant cause once again seemed dashed to the ground. By 1629, thoroughly defeated, Christian withdrew from the war.

A significant indication of the trend of events was the Edict of Restitution which the Catholic League persuaded the emperor to issue in 1629. By its terms all ecclesiastical property seized by the Protestants since 1552 was to be restored to the Catholic Church. It was also stated that under no circumstances could any form of Protestant belief other than Lutheranism be tolerated. The imperial commissioners who were appointed to enforce the Edict were so thorough that by 1631 five bishoprics in north Germany, about a hundred monasteries and much other land had been regained. This clearly was a matter of ominous significance to the whole Protestant cause.

The conflict steadily took on larger dimensions. Richelieu, as we have seen, had shrewdly perceived the interest of France in Spanish and imperial matters and had acted quickly both in the Valtelline question in 1626 and the Mantuan succession in 1628. These had been maneuvers of relatively minor importance. Now, as the entire field of German affairs began to open before him, he was not yet ready to commit France openly but still was prepared to give secret support where it would be most effective. His opportunity came in Sweden.

Gustavus Adolphus, King of Sweden, was an extraordinary figure. Coming to the throne in 1611, he had been spectacularly successful in reorganizing the machinery of his government, winning the support of the townsmen and the nobles and securing the backing of the *Riksdag,* the Swedish assembly of the estates of the realm. He had some knowledge of ten languages. A huge man, with tawny hair and beard, he was known as the Lion of the North. His remarkable gifts as a soldier had been developed in his wars with Denmark, Russia and Poland. Under Gustavus Adolphus the Swedish army had become a superb military machine led by a king who was prepared if need be to spend fifteen hours a day in the saddle.

The reasons for Swedish intervention in German affairs were numerous. Gustavus was a good Lutheran. In his earlier campaigns he had won Ingria,

Karelia and Livonia which, added to Finland and Estonia, made Sweden a powerful Baltic state. He aspired to secure further territories across the Baltic and to play an active part in imperial affairs. He was concerned over the power of the Hapsburgs and also over the possible threat to the Swedish dynasty from his Catholic cousin who sat on the throne of Poland. He was, moreover, under strong pressure from France to intervene.

In July, 1630, Gustavus brought his Swedish troops across the Baltic and landed upon the coast of Pomerania. Unable at first to secure a close alliance with the leading German Protestant princes, he was urged on secretly by Richelieu who made the subsidy Treaty of Bärewalde with him in 1631, promising him large sums of money in return for keeping his Swedish army in the field. Gustavus made a spectacular march southward across Germany, winning the battle of Breitenfeld against Tilly, occupying Munich and then marching down the valley of the Main towards the Rhine. Meanwhile the ferocious sack of the old Hansa town of Magdeburg by the imperial forces brought several Protestant states, notably Brandenburg and Saxony, to the side of Sweden. Now that Gustavus had cut a path from the Baltic almost to the western frontier of the Empire, it seemed that all Germany was in his hand.

At this juncture the emperor decided to recall Wallenstein, whom some of the Catholic princes had persuaded him earlier to dismiss. The two great generals met at the battle of Lützen (1632) where the Swedes won a meaningless victory, seeing that in the course of the fighting Gustavus Adolphus was killed. Even though the Swedish chancellor, Oxenstjerna, conducted affairs of state with considerable ability under the rule of Gustavus' daughter, Queen Christina, the period of Sweden's military greatness was now over. The Protestant command passed into the hands of a much less distinguished figure, Bernhard of Weimar. Corresponding changes occurred on the opposing side. Wallenstein, embittered at the loss of the battle of Lützen, opened secret negotiations with the Swedes. Ferdinand II, aware of this, announced Wallenstein's dismissal and soon after gratefully rewarded a small group of adventurers who contrived to assassinate the emperor's most brilliant commander.

The growing challenge to the French interest became evident in 1634 when the imperialists won a great victory over the Swedes at Nordlingen, following which they were able to impose the Peace of Prague (1635) on a number of the Protestant states. If enforced, the peace would have meant the mutual restoration of territories, the end of all princely leagues in Germany and the subordination of all armed forces to the emperor. Here Richelieu's grasp of the situation clearly showed itself. France could no longer afford to stand apart. Nine days before the terms of the Peace of

Prague were published Richelieu invoked the ancient formalities of war. A French herald accompanied by a trumpeter was sent posthaste to Brussels where in the presence of a curious throng he proclaimed the intentions of the King of France, threw to the crowd a formal declaration of war upon Spain and then galloped off. After long years of hesitation France was committed to war upon a European scale.

The "French period" of the Thirty Years' War was to drag on for thirteen years. France made alliances with Sweden, the United Netherlands and Savoy, directing her principal efforts against the power of Spain. She fought campaigns in Flanders, in the Free County of Burgundy, in northern Italy and in the Pyrenees—in other words, in all those border areas where French interests were at stake. The first advantage seemed to lie with Spain who, however, found herself weakened by revolts in Catalonia and Naples and by a vigorous resurgence of Dutch opposition. In 1635 the French staved off an actual threat to Paris. Later, at the battle of Rocroi which was won by the French in 1643, the names of Condé and Turenne, destined to shine so brilliantly in French military annals, first became known. Despite this victory, something approaching a stalemate of exhaustion had appeared. Although it was to take five years to complete them, in that same year formal negotiations for peace were begun.

■ THE PEACE OF WESTPHALIA

Tentative negotiations to end the long drawn-out war had begun as early as 1641, the year before Richelieu's death. Not until 1643, however, did the delegates formally begin to assemble. Difficulties over precedence were so great (should the papal representative, for example, have a canopy over his chair?) and Catholic-Protestant rivalries so real that French negotiations with the imperialists had to be carried on at Münster and Swedish negotiations at Osnabrück in Westphalia. When in 1645 all the German princes and imperial cities won the right to have their spokesmen, the Catholic representatives were obliged to attend at the former city and the Protestant at the latter. Endlessly tedious and preposterous as many of the ambassadorial conflicts were, they had some value in raising questions of "protocol" and diplomatic rights, and in causing some rules eventually to be accepted which have become the staples of modern diplomatic procedure.

The general terms finally gathered together in the cumbersome Latin text of the Treaty of Westphalia (October, 1648) were of various sorts. The main territorial provisions can be summarized as follows:

(1) France was confirmed in possession of Metz, Toul and Verdun (towns first secured in 1552), of a number of towns in Alsace and of some fortresses along

Important gains are here made by France in the Rhineland, by Sweden in Pomerania and by Brandenburg both to the east and west. The power of the Hapsburgs is consequently weakened. In the insert note the strategic importance of the Valtelline and the Duchy of Mantua in relation to the old battlegrounds of Italy.

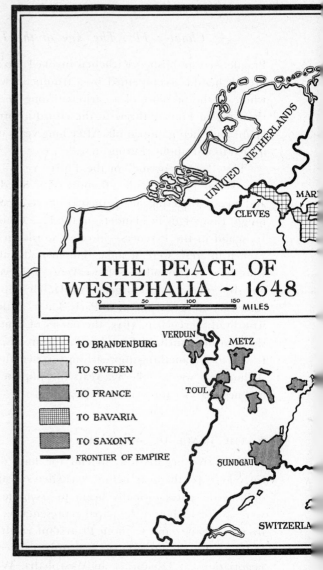

THE PEACE OF
WESTPHALIA ~ 1648

0   50   100   150
MILES

▦ TO BRANDENBURG
▧ TO SWEDEN
▨ TO FRANCE
▦ TO BAVARIA
▨ TO SAXONY
━ FRONTIER OF EMPIRE

UNITED NETHERLANDS
CLEVES
MAR
VERDUN   METZ
TOUL
SUNDGAU
SWITZERLA

the upper Rhine. France's precise legal title to these Alsatian lands, which were separated by imperial soil from France proper, was not clear and later became the subject of long dispute. France also obtained the fortress of Pinerolo on the Italian slope of the French Alps.

(2) Sweden obtained Western Pomerania on the southern shore of the Baltic, thereby gaining control of the mouth of the Oder River. She likewise secured the former bishoprics of Bremen and Verden to the west of the Danish peninsula, giving her control of the mouths of the Elbe and the Weser rivers. As a member of the Holy Roman Empire Sweden could now have three votes in the Diet of princes.

(3) Brandenburg obtained Eastern Pomerania, several secularized bishoprics lying between the Elbe and the Rhine, the right of succession to Magdeburg, and confirmation of her earlier acquisition of Cleves and Mark. She had acquired a seacoast and steppingstones to the Rhine.

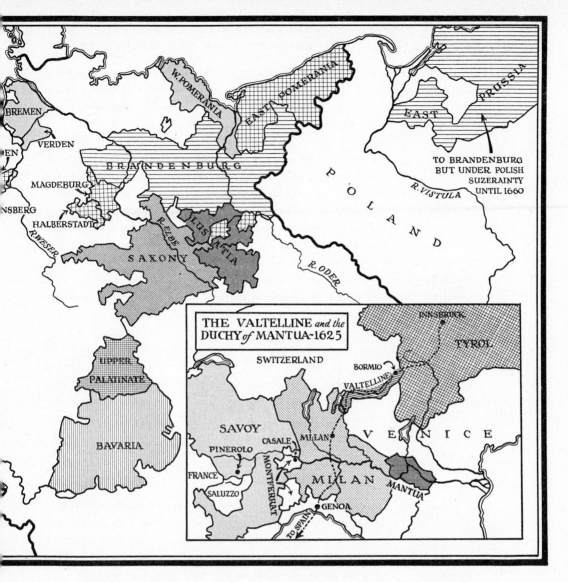

THE VALTELLINE *and the*
DUCHY *of* MANTUA-1625

(4) Bavaria acquired some territory and now had an electoral vote, while the son of the old Elector Palatine was restored to the Rhenish Palatinate with the rank of elector. This meant that henceforth there were eight votes instead of seven in the imperial electoral college.

(5) Saxony acquired the substantial territory of Lusatia on her eastern border.

With respect to the general structure of the Empire, it was weakened by declaring the United Netherlands and Switzerland free of all imperial control. In Bohemia the crown was declared to be hereditary in the Hapsburg line. All the states of the Empire were now regarded as sovereign, having the right to make alliances with each other and with foreign powers, provided that these alliances were not directed against the Empire. Another severe blow had thus been struck against the ancient imperial structure, justifying the description of it by the jurist, Samuel Pufendorf, as a monstrosity. An inventory of the component states of the Holy Roman Empire in 1648 would show 158 under secular rulers, 123 under ecclesiastics and 62 free cities—a grand total of 343 "sovereign" states.

In the religious sphere, the rights formerly enjoyed by Lutherans throughout the Empire were now extended to the Calvinists. This concession was still far from constituting true religious toleration, for the power of determination lay with the princes, who had the *jus reformandi,* or right to enforce conformity by threat of expulsion. That they did not exercise this right on any large scale was due more than anything else to economic reasons; they could hardly afford to suffer the losses that large-scale expulsions would produce. All church property was to remain in the hands of those holding it in January, 1624. The treaty also provided that when the imperial Diet had to discuss matters of religion it was to divide into sections representing the Protestants and the Catholics. Such a provision only added to the confusions of the imperial body.

A significant aspect of the Peace of Westphalia was that it underscored the rough division of Germany into a Protestant north and a Roman Catholic south which henceforth remained more or less permanent. It also indicated a decline in papal prestige, for its terms were totally unacceptable to the pope who issued the bull, *Zelo Domini Deus,* declaring the treaty in resounding phrases to be "null, void, invalid, iniquitious, unjust, damnable, reprobate, inane, empty of meaning and effect for all time." We may take it as a mark of the new age that the protest passed almost completely unnoticed.

More than any preceding treaty, the Peace of Westphalia began to give definition to the essential features of the map of modern Europe. Its provisions with respect to particular states are a significant clue to the pattern of history for the ensuing century. Sweden, for example, stood on the threshold of an era of great, if transitory, power. Brandenburg was committed to a program of territorial expansion which ultimately would permit her to dominate German affairs. An independent and extraordinarily prosperous Netherlands was to make the seventeenth century the greatest in its history. France, making strategic gains on her frontiers and building up at home an effective machinery of centralized administration, was about to enter a brilliant age under the most resplendent of her kings.

In contrast to these harbingers of greatness it is customary to stress the economic and social havoc wrought by the wars in Germany. The older historians have been wont to paint a picture in the very darkest colors, a picture which emphasizes the incredible ferocity of the invading armies, the destruction of towns, villages and crops, the massacres of civilians, the widespread famines, the evidence, even, of cannibalism. It has been said that the cultural evolution of Germany was set back for a hundred years and the war has been taken to explain why Germany until the much later age of Goethe and Schiller was unable to produce intellectual talents equal to those so profusely displayed in France, Holland and England.

One may well question whether any so sweeping a verdict should be passed. A heavy loss of population there undoubtedly was, but whatever cultural decline occurred in Germany could be shown to have antedated rather than be the result of the Thirty Years' War. On the other hand, it could be argued that German cultural achievements in the decades following the war were by no means lacking. Moreover, although the contemporary statistical evidence is extremely unreliable, it would seem that the German national income, productive power and standard of living were higher about 1650 than they had been in 1600. The cultural pattern of German life, it may safely be concluded, was disrupted rather than destroyed.[12]

Discussion of the extent of depopulation and economic decline should not obscure one significant trend. It is evident that certain moves in the direction of German unity, observable at the outset of the Protestant Reformation, had received a severe setback. The divisive tendencies in Germany —the centrifugal rather than the centripetal forces—were now in the ascendant. If progress were to be made in Germany, it would have to be within the narrow limits of the numerous territorial states, and it was to take the form of bureaucratic rule and dynastic centralization. The Empire as a political power henceforth counted for very little.

■ THE AGE OF THE BAROQUE

In the first half of the seventeenth century, while Europe north of the Alps was torn by the confusions of the Thirty Years' War, cultural changes of high significance were under way. These changes were the outcome of a long process of development going back to the age of Michelangelo and the splendors of the High Renaissance, a development resulting in what has come to be called the Age of the Baroque.[13] The term Baroque, applied

12. This is the conclusion of Miss C. V. Wedgwood, whose *Thirty Years' War* (1939) is the most recent careful study of this problem. She confesses herself suspicious of all contemporary statistics of population, though she concedes that the German Empire, excluding Bohemia, may have dropped in population from twenty-one millions in 1618 to thirteen and a half in 1648. It is interesting also to note the small size of the armies involved: the Catholic League could put only about 15,000 men in the field; Gustavus Adolphus invaded Germany with about the same number; Wallenstein commanded about 20,000 men; the French gave Bernard of Weimar subsidies for 18,000; and Condé's army in 1645 numbered only 12,000.

13. The word baroque is of uncertain origin. It may come from the Spanish *barrueco*, meaning a large, irregularly shaped pearl. Another suggested derivation is from *barocco*, a scholastic term applied to a complex figure in formal logic.

originally to architecture and sculpture, suggests greater freedom, elaboration and extravagance than were found in the ordered, classical traditions of the Renaissance. The term has widened in scope so that today some students are disposed to go beyond the usual references to the arts and speak even of a "Baroque" way of life. Although the ornateness and emotionalism of some Baroque creations may give rise to the charge of theatricality, it is also true that the masterful splendor of the best work has aroused very high and justifiable praise. Not many, however, would probably go so far as the scholar who has proclaimed Baroque to be "the high water mark of European creative effort." [14]

In its essence the Baroque style, owing much to the brilliant legacy of Michelangelo, expresses a deep sense of man's restless energies. In form it is strongly decorative, yet the elaborate rhythms are such that the plastic details, say, in an architectural work, do not serve merely as adornment but rather provide an essential means of linking together all the components. This overall unity can be seen in the disposition of figures in a painting or sculptured group; it is best illustrated, perhaps, in the symmetrical design of a Baroque villa, where the building cannot properly be considered apart from the ordered pattern of its setting—terraces, walks, gardens, vistas, sculptures, fountains and pools all making a subtly harmonious whole.

The Baroque arts reached their climax in Italy and Spain by mid-seventeenth century. In Austria and South Germany their development came somewhat later. The style had many brilliant manifestations as far afield as Poland and the Ukraine and perhaps a lesser influence in North Germany and Scandinavia. From Spain and Portugal the patterns of Baroque church architecture spread overseas to the colonies, so that manifestations of this style can be found to the farthest limits of the Americas and the Indies. Strong Baroque elements can be observed in the classical culture of seventeenth-century France and, in some aspects at least, in England.

In Baroque architecture the starting point is often taken to be the erection of the famous Jesuit church, the Gesù, built in Rome between 1568 and 1584 from the designs of Giacomo Vignola. Few churches have had wider architectural influence. Among its many typically Baroque characteristics may be listed the imposing classical façade, the huge tunnel-vault over the nave, the dome erected over the crossing of nave and transept, the rich marble decor and the elaborate pattern of ornamentation imposed upon the formal arrangement of classical arches and columns. A characteristic device is the artful use of light which shines down upon the chancel with most theatrical effect from windows concealed in the dome. Another famous landmark of the early Baroque is the Church of San Carlo of the Four

14. C. J. FRIEDRICH, *The Age of the Baroque* (1952), p. 91.

Fountains in Rome, designed by Francesco Borromini and begun in 1633. Here the curving lines of the exterior façade and the complicated pattern of ovals which form the ground plan of the interior demonstrate the artistic subtlety and unity of a characteristic design.

The outstanding name in the architecture of this period is that of Lorenzo Bernini (1598–1680). He is best known for his great work in connection with St. Peter's in Rome: his contributions include the elaborate canopy or *baldacchino* over the high altar, the dramatically contrived royal staircase or *Scala Regia* leading to the papal apartments and, above all, the design of the great square in front of St. Peter's with its central obelisk and the huge colonnade curving away on either side of the façade. Here one might recall the earlier name of Carlo Maderna who modified the original plans for St. Peter's by lengthening the nave and imposing upon the exterior the mediocre façade which obscures Michelangelo's superb dome.

In Spain the spirit of Baroque architecture was carried to extremes which often bordered on the fantastic. To conventional taste, the ornamentation of the sacristy of the Charterhouse at Granada and of many other Spanish examples would seem wildly overdone, so that the structural pattern of a building seems to disappear beneath a riotous profusion of detail. From the work of the Spanish architect, José de Churriguera (1650–1725), comes the name "churrigueresque" to identify this luxuriant extreme in Baroque style.

Many of the truly exquisite examples of Baroque architecture were created north of the Alps, at a period somewhat later than in Italy. In Germany the ornateness of the late Gothic style flowed easily into the new patterns imported from Italy. Churches in Austria, Saxony and Bavaria gave enchanting expression to the art, and we may say the artifice, of the Baroque. Yet the great designers of these regions—Fischer von Erlach, Asam, Neumann and Poppelmann—really belong to the eighteenth century. The elaborate staircase in the electoral palace at Bruchsal designed by Neumann in 1730 has been described as the high water mark and end of the Baroque style.

One may also demonstrate the Baroque element in French and English architecture. The wing built by François Mansart (1598–1666) in 1635 to the royal chateau of Blois contrasts significantly with the Renaissance work of the time of Francis I. In the huge, quarter-mile east front of the Louvre, begun in 1665 by Claude Perrault (1613–1688), we may see a certain Baroque pomposity. In England, the work of Inigo Jones (1573–1652) shows that he had learned much from the Italian Palladio, and he continued to exercise a "classical" restraint very unlike the style of his contemporaries across the Channel. St. Paul's Cathedral, the masterpiece of Sir Christopher Wren

(1632–1723), was begun in 1675. Its interior has a rich magnificence which has caused it to be described as a Baroque version of Classicism, as we may also describe Vanbrugh's work at Blenheim Palace. In England, however, as in France, one must note the absence of the exuberance which is so characteristic of Italian, Spanish and central European Baroque.

The patterns of Baroque sculpture have much the same quality that can be found in architecture. Individual figures were very commonly a part of a larger unity and were not intended, like much of the work of the Renaissance, to stand alone. Bernini, famous as an architect, was equally famous as a sculptor, so much so that one may select his altar of St. Theresa (1646) in the Church of Santa Maria della Vittoria in Rome as an illustration. In this celebrated composition the saint is shown transfixed in ecstasy while a youthful angel, holding an arrow, smiles down upon her. The whole work is a mass of billowing shapes and lines. Behind the figures are gilt metal shafts suggesting rays of light; the marble surrounding the scene is gold, amber and pink; a window high above bathes the figures in a mellow radiance. To the right and left of the altar are niches from which sculptured representations of members of the Cornaro family, seated behind balustrades, seem to be watching the miraculous scene. The effect is theatrical to a degree, reminding one that Bernini was a Neapolitan to whom, perhaps, a high sense of drama came almost instinctively.

It is well to remember the anonymous character of much Baroque sculpture. "It is almost always a part of a whole, a detail in a larger conception, and it therefore loses its meaning when it is detached from its context." The tritons and sea-nymphs adorning fountains in public squares, the statues artfully placed at the end of avenues of cypress trees, or the elaborate sculptures on the façades or interiors of Baroque churches all served this larger purpose and are to be understood in this sense.

The influences contributing to the Baroque spirit in painting are to be found in some of the great works of the sixteenth century—the Sistine frescoes of Michelangelo, the deeply moving paintings of El Greco and the opulent products of Venetian artists such as Titian, Tintoretto and Veronese. It was a discovery of seventeenth-century painting that the mind could grasp the whole complex texture of a scene in one moment, and therefore that it was the work of the artist to convey this sense of unity and not simply to combine a number of completely separate objects.[15] Painting of this type led to an increased subtlety in the handling of light and color, the production of a three dimensional quality, an elaboration of rhythm and the merging of shadow and substance into new and unexpected patterns.

15. NEWTON, *European Painting and Sculpture*, p. 60.

No one showed more superbly the ability to produce these effects than the Dutch painter, Rembrandt van Rijn (1606–1669). "Rembrandt was no longer conscious of painting a set of definable and therefore separable objects. His eye could pass from a figure to the floor under its feet and the wall behind it and the cloud seen through the window in the wall without being conscious of passing from one *thing* to another. The whole texture of his picture is one." [16] The figures in his Night Watch are not simply a collection of portraits; they are combined in a masterly grouping to give a vivid impression of color, life and motion. Sometimes shadow seems dominant in his portraits. In his Man With a Gold Helmet a ray of light catches one part of the ornamentation leaving all else in obscurity. In his Christ at Emmaus a dim light, reflected from the table around which the four figures gather, illuminates them as they emerge from the surrounding shadows. The same mysteriously pervasive quality of light and shadow can be seen in his deeply moving Simeon in the Temple, or in his Christ in the Storm on the Lake of Galilee where the fishing boat is revealed as if by a flash of lightning amid the tempest. This, surely, is a world different from what has been described as the cool morning light of Botticelli or the splendid noon of Raphael and Leonardo.

In their own very different way the superbly lighted landscapes and interiors of Jan Vermeer of Delft (1632–1675) have an equal sense of space and rhythm, as do the dignified portraits of Anthony van Dyck (1599–1641) and the vigorously cheerful compositions of Franz Hals (1580–1666). The consummate master of the Baroque style in painting, both in its strength and its weaknesses, may be taken to be the Flemish painter Peter Paul Rubens (1577–1640). He could turn his hand to any subject, from a Crucifixion to a Venus. Rubens was above all a master of fleshly beauty. His crowded canvases shine forth with golden sunshine, rich fabrics, blue skies and exuberant vitality. In the workshop where Rubens first sketched the outlines of his paintings with a masterly hand, skilled craftsmen worked with him to complete the details of more than two thousand canvases. Rubens, a critic remarks, had every equipment for scaling the heavens except a pair of wings.

Spanish Baroque painting had its chief exponent in Diego Velasquez (1599–1660), the court painter to Philip IV. His great series of royal portraits as well as his landscapes and his varied depictions of Spanish life have a quality of timelessness which sets them apart from the more conventional representations of his age. One of his most admired successors was the sentimentally religious Murillo (1617–1682). Among the French one would include Philippe Champaigne (1602–1674), perhaps best remembered

16. *Idem.*

for his extraordinarily revealing portraits of Richelieu. Two others, Claude Gelée, better known as Lorrain (1600–1682), and Nicholas Poussin (1594–1665), are really more "Roman" than French; they are of the Baroque school, but lack the fire of the great masters.

No summary, however brief, of Baroque painting could properly ignore the vogue of elaborately painted walls and ceilings. The European visitor today finds the evidence on every hand in churches, palaces and public buildings. He may exhaust himself in contemplation of the saints and angels, the gods and goddesses, the dizzily flying cupids, the billowing clouds and flowing draperies, the miracles of perspective and foreshortening, the exquisite symphonies of color that this artistic technique displayed.

Developments in music suggest many parallels to the growth of the visual arts. The sixteenth century had been one of the great ages in the history of music, evolving in turn out of the techniques of the late medieval period. Contrapuntal music, a style in which several voices were set one against another, each having its own melodic line and together forming an elaborate "polyphony" or harmony of sound, had held the main interest. The music of the Baroque era leads into a new world. A fundamental change, the "monodic revolution," is the development of harmonic music in which solo voices or instruments carry the main air and the accompaniment is harmonized but definitely subordinate. "The combination of solo voices with richly developed accompaniment made it possible to express depths of passion, of devotion, of agony and delight of which the old polyphony could only speak objectively." [17]

New musical forms, of which the most important was the opera, developed in the seventeenth century. Claudio Monteverdi (1567–1643) used classical subjects such as Orpheus, Ulysses and Ariadne for a whole series of operatic works. These spectacles, combining drama and music in a stage setting to which painting, sculpture and architecture all contributed, can thus be taken as a many-sided expression of the Baroque spirit. The vogue developed very rapidly. The first opera house was opened in 1637 at Venice; before 1700 more than seven hundred operas had been produced in Italy alone. The composition of the first French opera in 1659 soon set a fashionable pattern north of the Alps. The court musician, Jean-Baptiste Lully (1639–1687), composed at least one opera a year from 1672 until his death. The Italian fashion soon spread so that in the late seventeenth century Dresden, Vienna and Hamburg became important centers of the new musical form. Other compositions such as the oratorio, the passion and the cantata showed the continuing power of religion. The oratorio was an extended musical work, usually based on a religious theme, for solo voices,

17. F. L. NUSSBAUM, *The Triumph of Science and Reason* (1953), p. 38.

chorus and orchestra. The passion and cantata were less elaborate but similar types. The prolific composer, Heinrich Schütz (1585–1672), for over sixty years director of the Saxon court chapel, brought the Italian monodic style into German church music. Jan Sweelink (1562–1621) carried the new organ style to the Netherlands whence it spread to Germany.

Such developments led to the use of a wider variety of musical instruments. The organ grew from a crude, portable instrument sometimes played by striking it with the fist to the elaborate construction which we know today. Frescobaldi, at St. Peter's, has been called the greatest organist of the seventeenth century. The violin as we know it is associated with the work of certain families of Italian craftsmen, notably the Amati, the Guarneri and the Stradivari. Other instruments such as the clavichord and harpsichord were perfected and music written for them. Strings and woodwinds were assembled in groups so that their effects could be made more definite and so that *concerti grossi* could be written with their distinctive tonal qualities in mind. The larger emphasis upon solo parts, whether for instruments or voices, led to the growth of a professional class of *virtuosi*. The year 1685, distinguished by the birth of two giant figures in musical history, Johann Sebastian Bach and George Frederick Handel, may be taken as a landmark. They carried the Baroque musical style well into the eighteenth century.

In literature one may well run considerable risk in attempting to unite wide varieties of individual expression within the limits of a defined "Baroque" style. There are, clearly enough, Baroque elements in the many-sided genius of Shakespeare, as there are also in Cervantes and in the Spanish playwrights of the Golden Age. In the Spanish poet, Luis de Góngora (1561–1627) were displayed an affected elegance and a preciosity in style to which the name "gongorism" has been given. One may have been led to think too much, perhaps, of the ordered dignity and reasonableness of French classical literature to recognize Corneille and Racine as dramatists of truly Baroque character. Yet the ornate style of their plays, the formalized conflicts, the burdens which fate imposes upon the heroes and the heroines are all in the Baroque tradition. Nor is it possible to ignore in this connection the extraordinary richness and humanity of Molière's comedies. One must list, too, the German author, Grimmelshausen, whose *Simplicissimus* (1669) pictures the adventures and confusions of a guileless hero during the Thirty Years' War.

If one were to select a single author whose work best exemplifies the spirit of the Baroque, the choice might well be John Milton (1608–1674). His great epics show the titanic struggles of the powers of darkness against those of light. His Satan could be called as striking a portrait of Baroque man as the age created. The grandeur of Milton's conceptions is equaled only by the splendid sonority of the language in *Paradise Lost* and *Paradise Regained,* while the lyrical quality of the shorter works—*L'Allegro, Il Penseroso* or the masque, *Comus*—like the ornamental element in Baroque architecture is of an incomparable enchantment.

The student who is interested in seeking a common pattern of culture in various aspects of an age may relate many of these developments of the arts to some broader aspects of human behavior. He will note a certain theatrical quality attaching to many expressions of seventeenth-century life. He will note the degree of artifice used by architects in planning the interiors of the great homes of the age; the long sequence of rooms, often lined with mirrors, opening vista-like into one another; the elaborate crystal chandeliers producing a dazzling display of light; the monumental staircases which gave a theatrical background for the grand exits and entrances of kings and princes. He will observe a high sense of drama in the stylized manners and the courtly etiquette which owed so much to imperial Spain. He will recall the fantastic elaboration of late seventeenth-century costume, the huge wigs now beginning to be worn by gentlemen, the imperial Roman costumes in which monarchs such as Louis XIV were pleased to be sculptured. He will see great soldiers and great noblemen assuming the dignity of kings: the mighty Prince Eugene, victor of Belgrade, welcomed like a Roman general; Wallenstein building for himself the huge Baroque palaces of Sagan, Gitschin and Prague; or the great Duke of Marlborough moving grandly amid the splendors of Blenheim Palace.

Above all, the student of this age will be conscious of powerful tensions and strains. An ardent sense of religious devotion could be turned all too easily into fanaticism or hysteria. Dedication to one's own purposes could lead to savage intolerance of others. An exquisite artistic perception might be the close neighbor to the grossest sensuality. Extravagant display and enormous wealth took little account of the direst poverty. Such we may take to be some of the components of the complex "Baroque" structure of seventeenth-century life.

THE STABILIZATION

OF THOUGHT

AND INSTITUTIONS

1650–1750

"There is nothing so far removed from us as to be beyond our reach,
or so hidden that we cannot discover it,
provided only we abstain from accepting the false for the true,
and always preserve in our thoughts the order necessary
for the deduction of one truth from another."

DESCARTES, *Discourse on Method*

The title page of Thomas Hobbes' *Leviathan*, 1651. The *Leviathan* has been called one of the great books of the world. The crowned figure is made up of a mass of tiny people who have "contracted" to form a sovereign power.

Chapter 12

The Struggle for Parliamentary Government in England

■ THE LEGACY OF THE TUDORS

IN MARCH, 1603, Queen Elizabeth of England lay speechless and dying at Richmond. The anxious members of the Council sought access to her bedside in order to discover some indication of her will as to the succession. For the Tudors had always regarded the crown as their property, and with their dying breath Henry VIII, Edward VI and Mary had all named their

294

successors. Henry VIII had stipulated that on the death of his three children the crown should go to the heirs of his younger sister, Mary, rather than to the heirs of his elder sister, Margaret. On this basis Edward Seymour, Lord Beauchamp, would take precedence over James VI of Scotland. The Council put various names to the dying queen, asking her to indicate her will by a motion of her finger. At the mention of the King of France she was unmoved. At the mention of James of Scotland she still made no response. The name of Lord Beauchamp suddenly roused her from silence: "I will have no rascal's son in my seat, but one worthy to be a king!" These were Elizabeth's last and only words. Taking what meaning they could from them, the Council proclaimed James VI of Scotland as the new monarch and Parliament loyally recognized his title.

James VI of Scotland was the son of Mary Stuart and the great-great-grandson of Henry VII, the founder of the Tudor dynasty. On his accession to the English throne he was, in contemporary parlance, "James Sixt and First," the ruler by separate titles of both England and Scotland. Save for a brief interlude under Oliver Cromwell, the two kingdoms were to retain their separate Parliaments and identities until joined by the Act of Union in 1707.

The seventeenth century was to see profoundly important parliamentary developments in England. These were the outcome of a dramatic period of rebellion and civil war during which "Cavaliers" with their laces and curls rode into battle against somber "Roundheads" who sang psalms as they advanced to smite the enemies of the Lord. An anointed king was publicly beheaded in Whitehall and the age-hallowed monarchy gave way for a time to the strange experiment of a republic having a simple country gentleman—a squire of Huntingdonshire—at its head. After a restored monarchy had seemed curiously unable to learn its lessons, a second, bloodless revolution forced another king to flee ignominiously into the night and at length gave England the means to safeguard those parliamentary institutions which she still treasures.

These advances, so contrary to the absolutist trends in contemporary France, were not easily won, for at the outset the new Stuart line made claims not unlike those of the Bourbons. More than three-quarters of a century were needed to bring the parliamentary cause to success. During this period circumstances uniquely favorable helped the island kingdom to work out its destinies behind the defensive moat of the Channel in a fashion to which continental developments offered no parallel.

England had reason to be grateful for the legacy of the Tudors. She was free from the foreign dangers which for so long had threatened her. Order prevailed at home. A religious settlement had been made which the majority seemed well pleased to accept. Although finances were none too secure and although Elizabeth left a large public debt, a substantial measure of prosperity had arisen. Of this prosperity the splendid manor houses and estates of the Tudor nobility, as well as the solidly built seaports and market towns were ample evidence. Despite the hardships of the enclosure movement the English villages, too, had some share in the general wealth; the wooden-floored, thatched cottages with their brick chimneys, diamond-paned windows, huge fireplaces and oak furniture suggested an entirely different standard of life from that found in the hovels of their medieval predecessors.

The Tudor age had left a brilliant tradition in literature, architecture and music. The proud nationalism of a superbly confident age was perfectly expressed in Shakespeare's *Richard II* (1597):

> This royal throne of kings, this scepter'd isle,
> This earth of majesty, this seat of Mars,
> This other Eden, demi-paradise . . .
> This happy breed of men, this little world,
> This precious stone set in the silver sea
> Which serves it in the office of a wall . . .
> This blessed plot, this earth, this realm, this England.

In the light of such confidence one tends to forget England's modest rank, stated in terms of population and resources, among the European powers. The estimate of 4½ million people for England and Wales (with an additional million apiece for Ireland and Scotland) falls far behind the estimated 20 millions for the Holy Roman Empire, 16 millions for France, 11 millions for Poland or 7 millions for Spain.

Parliament, despite the frequently high-handed actions of the Tudors, had contrived to assert its basic rights to vote taxes and share in legislation; and at the same time it had given its support to the monarchy. The House of Commons in particular had developed a tradition of frank speech. "In face of Spain and the Pope it was more Elizabethan than the Queen herself. Members were in a perpetual fever of loyalty, urging her to more vigorous measures in self-defense—to get married, to name her heir, to execute the Queen of Scots, to persecute the Catholics more and the Puritans less—everything in short except raise higher taxes. . . ." [1] The position of monarchy seemed secure, as Elizabeth was proud to assert in one of her last messages to Parliament:

> Though God hath raised me high, yet this I count the glory of my crown, that I have reigned with your loves. This makes me that I do not so much rejoice that God hath made me to be a Queen, as to be a Queen over so thankful a people.

1. G. M. TREVELYAN, *History of England* (1926), p. 373.

These eloquent words could not altogether obscure the fact that in the relations of crown and Parliament elements of danger were lurking. Elizabeth had often acted as a despot. If her rule was a despotism, it was, however, sincerely intended for her country's good, and exercised so as to win a large measure of popular assent. No one could say in 1603 what claims the new monarchy would make, or how these would be received. In the interests of order and authority the Tudors had set up a number of "privileged" or "prerogative" courts: the Court of the Star Chamber, the Court of High Commission, the Council of the North, the Council of Wales; these had vigorously asserted royal authority against the over-powerful nobles. Such courts, "accepted organs of law and order under the Tudors, engines of despotism under their successors," ventured upon dangerous ground. Men had some hope that the common law of England—that age-old pattern of tradition, usages and unwritten precepts—would protect their persons and their property against the arbitrary exactions of a royal innovator. It was by no means certain, however, that the Stuarts would display the tact and skill of their predecessors, or that if they sought to act tyrannically the means existed to keep their power in check.

■ THE REIGN OF JAMES I

James I had been King of Scotland since 1567 when at the age of one he succeeded his ill-fated mother.[2] He had grown up amid a stormy period in which, even though Presbyterianism had been established as the official faith, bitter rivalry between Protestant and Catholic leaders continued. Although James, unlike his mother, accepted Protestantism he conceived in the process a powerful dislike for the dour Covenanters of Scottish politics. His extraordinary precociousness (Henry IV of France called him "the wisest fool in Christendom") soon displayed itself. This king who fell sick at the sight of cold steel, whose tongue was too large for his mouth and whose

2. The following genealogy shows the problem of descent:

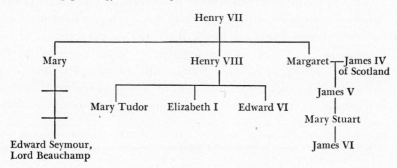

knees knocked together as he walked, delighted in the pleasures of author-ship. Some of James' political ideas were soon to embroil him with his Eng-lish subjects.[3]

The theory of the divine right of kings had had little popularity upon English soil, yet long before its arguments were propounded by Louis XIV's court preacher, Bishop Bossuet, James asserted it vigorously. "The state of monarchy," he wrote, "is the supremest thing upon earth; for kings are not only God's lieutenants upon earth, and sit upon God's throne, but even by God himself they are called gods." In a speech to the Star Chamber he insisted: "It is atheism and blasphemy to dispute what God can do, . . . so it is presumption and high contempt in a subject to dispute what a king can do, or say that a king cannot do this or that. . . ." In his most famous work, *The Trew Lawe of Free Monarchies,* James had stated: "And as ye see it manifest that the king is overlord of the whole land, so is he master over every person . . . having power of life and death of every one of them; for although a just prince will not take the life of any subjects without a clear law, yet the same laws whereby he taketh them are made by himself or his predecessors; and so the power always floweth from himself."

A crisis soon developed over the problem of royal prerogative. From medieval times onward the monarch had, without any question, been pos-sessed of certain powers or "prerogatives" which he exercised and which no one else could exercise. He gave assent to laws; he granted pardons; he was responsible for the coining of money; he appointed ministers; he vetoed bills; he called out the army. The real question at issue was not whether royal prerogative existed but rather who was to decide the point beyond which royal authority could not go. If James was able to fix the limits of his own authority, then he would be truly absolute; if, on the other hand, the king was to be "under the law" then it was important to discover who made, amended or "declared" the law.

Put in this way, the problem seemed essentially political and constitu-tional. It involved, however, fundamental economic questions. Since the price-revolution of the sixteenth century had raised the costs of government along with the costs of everything else, there was a constant tendency for the executive to seek new sources of funds. If the traditional revenues were no longer adequate, would the royal prerogative go so far as to let the king impose new taxes (that is to say, interfere with the property rights of his subjects) without the assent of the estates of the realm? A venerable medieval maxim had asserted that "what touches all must be approved by all." How

---

3. James, among his other undertakings, wrote a *Demonologie,* a learned treatise on witch-craft. In view of the common acceptance of witchcraft this, however, would hardly mark him as an eccentric.

was this to be taken? In other words, could James challenge Parliament's claim to control of the purse-strings? Queen Elizabeth had on the whole been a good manager; James' extravagance was notorious. Financial difficulties, then, soon raised major problems for him and for his subjects.

Religion made other difficulties. The apparently acceptable Elizabethan Settlement steered a middle course, and it is often the weakness of a middle course to leave both extremes dissatisfied. On one wing were the Catholics, or "papists." "Popery" to the average Englishman meant Mary Tudor's burning of Latimer, Ridley and Cranmer; it meant the Armada; it meant the long series of plots against the life of Good Queen Bess. In 1603 there may have been 150,000 Catholics in England who contrived to exist more or less unmolested and to worship in private. James I had a Catholic mother and although he himself was a determined Protestant he eventually sought a Catholic marriage for his son and heir. His attitude to the Catholics, then, had an ambiguity which went beyond that found in the policies of Elizabeth.

At the other extreme were those Protestants to whom the established church was less than acceptable. The Puritan wing within the church was willing to accept a state church provided that ritual could be simplified and the powers of the bishops reduced to a minimum. But as the Puritans developed their belief that the Holy Spirit manifests itself directly to the hearts of men, they progressively minimized the state's function in religious life. Outside the established church were the Presbyterians, committed to a simpler formulation of belief and utterly hostile to "episcopacy." Of growing importance, too, were those to whom the name, "Independent," came to be given. These opposed the idea of a state church altogether, attaching basic importance to the local group or congregation, hence the name "Separatist" or "Congregationalist." This same divisive tendency produced even more radical groups of which some such as the "Diggers" and "Levellers" sought to establish a pattern of primitive Christianity in which all distinctions of rank, wealth and ownership would be abolished.

Out of this seething mass of conflict—in part political, in part economic and in part religious—was slowly to develop an explosive situation. James' own viewpoint was strongly episcopalian and "Erastian." [4] Criticism and eventually open resistance came from a wide variety of sources. Some was offered by members of Parliament who saw their powers under attack. Some came from the law students and jurists who championed the venerable traditions of the common law. Some came from the historians and antiquarians who in the spirit of Renaissance scholarship had busied themselves

---

4. "Erastian" refers to the policy of subordinating the church very emphatically to the authority of the state.

with tracing and interpreting the history of past struggles between king and people. Some came from the prosperous merchants and landed proprietors. Criticism was raised by the spokesmen of the various groups of religious dissenters, among them country squires like Oliver Cromwell whose normal allegiance would unhesitatingly have been to the king, but who were now disturbed at heart by the new trends. "Religion," said Cromwell simply, "was not the thing at first contended for, but God brought it to that issue at last."

Well received at the outset, James soon plunged into a variety of controversial matters. At the Hampton Court Conference, for example, summoned in 1604 to hear the grievances of the Puritan leaders, he spoke very sharply in defense of the episcopacy and in opposition to the Dissenters. "I will have one doctrine," he declared, "one discipline, one religion in substance and one ceremony." He denounced the Presbyterians, saying that a Scottish presbytery "agreeth with monarchy as well as God with the devil." As for the Dissenters in general, James served blunt warning: "I will make them conform, or I will harry them out of the land, or else worse." Nor was James speaking idly. Three hundred clergy who refused to comply with the Prayer Book and the new codification of discipline were deprived of their livings.[5]

Tension of another sort was engendered by the discovery in 1605 of the Gunpowder Plot. One Guy Fawkes, a Catholic who resented the strictness of the anti-Catholic laws, was found hidden in the vaults under the Houses of Parliament, surrounded by thirty-six barrels of gunpowder and ready to blow up himself, king, Lords and Commons. When Fawkes was tortured and executed, evidence was uncovered to implicate a group of noblemen and some Jesuits. The result was a strong wave of anti-Catholic feeling.[6]

In addition to these religious matters, the extravagant James had major troubles with finances. He found himself in sharp conflict with Parliament over such seemingly trivial matters as his right to impose an extra tax of five shillings per hundredweight on imported currants. When in the celebrated Bate's case a merchant refused to pay the tax, the Court of Exchequer upheld James, "who guideth all under God by his wisdom." James, too, was not averse to raising money by ingenious techniques of improvisation. He frankly sold noble titles for substantial sums and actually created the new title of "baronet" (an hereditary knighthood) for a stipulated price of a thousand pounds.

James' high-handed actions brought him also into conflict with the

5. For another outcome of the Hampton Court Conference—the King James Bible—see p. 519.
6. The date, November 5, still survives in England as "Guy Fawkes' Day." From the dummies which have ever since annually been burned in commemoration of the occasion comes the use of the word "guy" as a term of disrespect.

judiciary. Here Sir Edward Coke, Chief Justice of the Court of Common Pleas, emerged as a militant champion of the common law which, he urged, set definite legal limits upon royal prerogative. These limits James was constantly outstepping. Coke rose in protest and particularly attacked the conduct of the Court of High Commission. When James transferred Coke from Common Pleas to King's Bench, he still spoke out, denying the king's right to alter any law or create new offences by royal proclamation. In 1616 Coke, "Oracle of the Common Law," was dismissed from office, but soon after was returned as a member of Parliament in which capacity he became a leader of the popular cause.

In Parliament, where the troubles with James were recurrent, the issue of royal prerogative was hotly debated. In December, 1621, after James had tried to limit the matters which the Commons could discuss, they adopted a protestation: "That the liberties, franchises, privileges and jurisdictions of Parliament are the ancient and undoubted birthright and inheritance of the subjects of England." James dissolved Parliament, sent for the journals of the Commons and in a fit of rage tore out the offending page from the record.

Other quarrels stemmed from James' ineffective conduct of foreign affairs. In 1604 he made an unpopular peace with Spain. Even though his daughter Elizabeth was married to Frederick, the Elector Palatine and "Winter King" of Bohemia, James showed great reluctance in 1618 to come to the aid of the Protestant cause in the Thirty Years' War. Later James shocked English opinion by sending his son Charles and the unpopular favorite, the Duke of Buckingham, on a matrimonial mission to Spain seeking the hand of the Infanta for Charles. James evidently thought that he might best help the cause of his outcast son-in-law, the Elector Palatine, by ingratiating himself with Catholic Spain. The effort was a disastrous failure; nor was the ultimate solution, the betrothal of Charles to Henrietta Maria, sister of Louis XIII of France, one that England could welcome with enthusiasm. Thus James' death in 1625 meant that unsolved problems of major proportions were bequeathed to the new reign.

■ CHARLES I AND THE COMING OF CONFLICT

Charles I had large abilities and considerable personal charm. He carried himself with dignity and proved to be an intelligent patron of learning and the arts. Lacking his father's extraordinary fluency of pen and tongue, he likewise lacked James' combativeness of manner. Often, however, he showed himself an unwise judge of men and policies, as in his favors for the Duke of Buckingham or in his marriage to the Catholic Henrietta Maria of

France. Moreover, in his stubborn way he was as wedded to authoritarian principles as his father had been, so that between 1625 and 1642 conflicts between crown and Parliament grew in intensity until the outcome was civil war.

As Charles embarked upon courses which aroused the antagonism of Parliament he found himself opposed by an unusual group of Englishmen, among them John Hampden, John Pym, Oliver Cromwell and Sir John Eliot. They and their fellows were sober men of substance, country squires for the most part, university bred and generally having some training in the law. Seldom have leaders of a great revolution looked less like revolutionaries; and seldom were men who ultimately won great military victories less inherently warlike.

Charles began by blundering in his foreign policy. Leaning heavily upon the advice of his favorite, the Duke of Buckingham, he carried on a brief war with Spain, mismanaged it badly and withdrew from it in 1630 with considerable discredit. He also sought to give assistance to the French Protestants at La Rochelle who were defending themselves against the assaults of Richelieu. Charles' hope, probably, was that in this way he would encourage Protestant support at home; he did not see that since Richelieu was committed to an anti-Hapsburg policy abroad, England's interests would have been better served by taking the Cardinal's side. Wise or unwise, Charles' policy failed in its immediate purpose of aiding the Protestants, and his reputation suffered in consequence. Parliament in its indignation had sought to impeach Buckingham. Although Charles headed off this move, he soon witnessed the public jubilation which arose when Buckingham was assassinated by a Puritan fanatic. All in all, Charles' ill-advised foreign moves contrasted sharply with the diplomatic skill and caution earlier shown by the Tudors.

Charles' main troubles, however, arose in connection with domestic matters. Parliament grew intensely suspicious of the means he used to secure funds. At the opening of the reign it had granted the king tunnage and poundage for one year only instead of the customary grant for life.[7] As Charles nevertheless continued to raise money by what Parliament considered illegal devices including, for example, the imposition of "forced loans" upon his wealthier subjects, resistance soon developed and was met with savage penalties. The average Englishman had been accustomed to depend upon the common law for his protection. He now found that the prerogative courts were making use of the Roman civil law as studied by Renaissance scholars. Such law favored the king's servants and in general took a

---

7. "Tunnage" refers to customs duties imposed upon incoming "tuns," or casks, of wine. "Poundage" means a tax levied on merchandise according to weight.

very exalted view of royal authority. In 1628 the Court of Star Chamber fined one Richard Chambers the staggering sum of £2,000 for saying that "the merchants are in no part of the world so skrewed and wrung as in England."

In 1628 Parliament drew up the famous Petition of Right, a document which assumes a major place in the great tradition of English freedom descending from Magna Carta. The Petition listed and denounced four great abuses: (1) Levying taxes and forced loans without consent of Parliament; (2) imprisoning individuals without cause shown; (3) billeting soldiers upon householders; (4) imposing martial law. Reluctantly Charles was compelled to give his assent to the Petition, using the ancient phrase, "Soit droit fait!" ("Let right be done!").

Charles continued nevertheless to resent and oppose those members who were most outspoken against him. On one occasion, when Charles ordered the Speaker of the Commons to terminate the discussion and he seemed disposed to obey, members forcibly held their presiding officer in the chair until their resolutions of protest could be passed. After a violent quarrel with the Commons in 1629 Charles contrived the arrest of three members and flung them arbitrarily into the Tower of London. Sir John Eliot, steadfastly refusing to sign a submission, died in 1632 in his cell, a martyr to the cause of parliamentary freedom. His two companions did not regain their liberty for eleven years. Meanwhile, in March, 1629, Charles exercised his royal prerogative and dissolved Parliament, speaking bitterly of "the undutiful and seditious carriage in the lower house." It was not to meet again for eleven years.[8]

In the following decade Charles was compelled to govern by what devices he could. He raised money by reviving antiquated statutes, by fining nobles who had encroached upon the ancient and forgotten limits of the royal forests, by continuing to levy tunnage and poundage, by selling various monopolies and privileges and by imposing heavy fines in the Court of Star Chamber. A new device was "ship money." By ancient tradition coastal towns were required to raise money for naval defense; the innovation consisted in now requiring inland areas also to contribute. A Buckinghamshire squire, John Hampden, who protested lost his case in court (one of the judges declaring bluntly, *"Rex is lex"*); nevertheless Hampden had stood for a principle and immortalized himself, even in defeat, as the champion of a good cause.

In the mounting conflict two names became outstanding in their support

8. It may be noted that the Spanish equivalent of Parliament—the Cortes—had lost practically all power; that the Estates General of France were sent home in 1614 and not resummoned until 1789; and that the Diet of the Holy Roman Empire had become a mere shadow.

of Charles. Thomas Wentworth, later Earl of Strafford, had risen to be Lord Deputy in Ireland, where he efficiently and ruthlessly imposed the rule which his royal master desired. Returning to England, he was quickly suspected of being ready to employ no less ruthless means in order to smash opposition at home. The other figure was William Laud, a stiff-necked churchman whom Charles made Archbishop of Canterbury. Laud was "High Church"; he enraged the Puritan wing by insisting on full ceremonial in • the service; he moved, for example, the communion table back to the east end of the church where it was separated by the altar-rail from the congregation. Through efficient visitations he enforced discipline on his subordinates, making use of the Star Chamber and Court of High Commission when severe measures were needed. In 1637 three Englishmen, Prynne (a lawyer), Burton (a clergyman) and Bastwick (a doctor) were fined, pilloried, had their ears cut off and were imprisoned for life for publishing Puritan attacks upon the bishops.

Questions of religion ultimately set off armed conflict. Laud rashly insisted upon issuing new orders in Scotland making Charles officially head of the church and proposing to institute there a system of bishops. The pattern of the Reformation in Scotland, it will be remembered, had given laymen a larger share in church government than was the case in England; for this reason Laud's innovations were all the more objectionable. In 1637 Laud ordered the Anglican Prayer Book to be read in all Scottish churches. A tablet in St. Giles Church in Edinburgh still commemorates the historic occasion when one Jennie Geddes, her ears offended by what she took to be the popish service, rose wrathfully and hurled her stool at the minister, crying "Will ye say the Mass in my lug?"

The outcome was war. The so-called "Bishops' Wars" of 1639 and 1640 were in themselves indecisive. To carry on the struggle, however, Charles was compelled at long last to summon Parliament to vote funds. The "Short Parliament" of 1640, the first in eleven years, stipulated that "redress of grievances must precede supply" and was in consequence dissolved by the indignant Charles I. He was nevertheless obliged soon after to summon another, famous in English history as the Long Parliament. In one form or another some remnants of this historic body survived as late as 1660.

Those Englishmen who had earlier made some name for themselves by opposing the actions of Charles—Pym, Hampden, Strode and Cromwell— dominated the House of Commons, though it is also true that other parliamentarians such as Hyde and Falkland gave Charles able and honorable support. Parliament, as a result of its varied activities in Tudor and early Stuart times, had come to be an efficiently operating machine. Especially through its committees, the House of Commons was able to dispose of business in most workmanlike fashion. It had, moreover, the inestimable advantage of being able to count upon the support of the wealthy and vigorous city of London.

Parliament moved fast, enacting in 1641 a fundamentally important body of legislation. It declared ship money illegal and asserted that no subsidy, custom or tax could be levied without consent of Parliament. It abolished the Court of Star Chamber, the Court of High Commission, the Council of Wales and the Council of the North. It declared that the interval between two Parliaments could not be more than three years, and, ignoring precedents, it forced Charles to agree that this present Parliament could not be dissolved without its own consent.

Conflict with the king was expressed most forcibly in parliamentary actions against Strafford and Laud. The Commons voted a bill of attainder accusing Strafford of subverting the laws, of introducing arbitrary government and slandering the Commons. In May, 1641, after agonized hesitation, Charles signed the bill which sent his most ardent servant to the scaffold. He may have thought that by this sacrifice he could save the rest. Pym, however, saw more clearly. "Hath he given us Strafford?" Pym exclaimed, "Then can he deny us nothing." Archbishop Laud was likewise sent to the Tower where, fainting with emotion, he gave a last blessing from his cell window to Strafford as the earl walked by on his way to the executioner's block. Four years later at the height of the Civil War Laud, too, was beheaded on Tower Hill. Between 1645 and 1660 there was no Archbishop of Canterbury.

Questions of religion, meanwhile, surged to the fore. A "Root and Branch" petition introduced in the Commons by the Puritans urged the abolition of the whole system of bishops. Although Parliament was not yet ready for such drastic action, it went so far as to reverse some of Laud's policies, ordering, for example, that the communion table be put back in the middle of the church, that images be removed and ritual simplified. In November, 1641, it passed by the narrow margin of eleven votes the Grand Remonstrance asking that Charles select advisers whom Parliament trusted and that further church reform be undertaken. For Cromwell this was decisive. He told Falkland, a moderate royalist, that if the vote had gone otherwise he would have given up and emigrated with the Puritans to Massachusetts. "Thus near," wrote the royalist Lord Clarendon in his *History of the Rebellion,* "was the Kingdom to its deliverance."

These measures infuriated Charles to such an extent that in January, 1642, he took the unprecedented step of coming with soldiers to the floor of the Commons, seeking to arrest Pym, Hampden and three other members. As they were conveniently absent, Charles retired in discomfiture, followed by cries of "Privilege! Privilege!" Henceforth it was clear that peaceful compromise could hardly be secured. Charles left London for the north where his support was stronger. In the next few months both sides jockeyed for position until at long last, in August, 1642, the king raised his standard at Nottingham, urging all loyal subjects to rally to him. England's fate now turned upon the decision of the sword.

■ CIVIL WAR

The English Civil War has been well described as a war of ideas in church and state. Much of the support given Charles came from those nobles and landed gentry for whom allegiance to the crown was traditional and instinctive. "I do not like the quarrel," wrote Sir Edmund Verney, "and do heartily wish that the king would yield and consent to what they [Parliament] desire. . . . I have eaten his bread and served him over thirty years, and will not do so base a thing as to forsake him." [9] Other support came from those Englishmen, well satisfied with the established church, who were afraid of what Presbyterians and Independents might do to it. Others, doubtless, were fearful of the social and economic changes that would come about if merchants and shopkeepers got the upper hand in Parliament or if, even worse, the radical ideas of the Levellers should prevail. The Catholic minority naturally enough was on the side of the king.

On the side of Parliament stood the opponents and critics of the established church, whether loosely named Puritans, or more precisely identified as Presbyterians, Independents and members of the various sects. The parliamentary cause included preeminently the merchant class, most especially those in London, Bristol and other seaports. It included many students and practitioners of the common law, champions of the parliamentary tradition. It included people with grievances of all types, among them the devotees of new sects such as "Diggers," "Levellers" or "Fifth-Monarchy men" who like some of the continental Anabaptists aspired to radical changes in the social order. The term "Roundhead" came to be applied to the close-cropped, hymn-singing, prayerful champions of Parliament, as the term "Cavalier" was contrastingly given to the long-haired, dashingly attired champions of the king.

The war itself, though hard-fought and decisive in its outcome, worked no such havoc upon England as did the contemporary Thirty Years' War upon Germany. Many Englishmen were little affected. Both sides secured troops as best they could, raising money in order to train and maintain

9. Verney carried the king's standard at Edgehill, the first battle of the Civil War, and was slain holding it.

the raw levies that somehow had to be whipped into shape. Parliament had two inestimable advantages: first, control of the navy, and second, control of much larger financial resources than ever were available to the king. Through Pym's initiative it eventually got valuable help from the Scots, some of whose leaders had served as adventurers or mercenaries abroad in the Thirty Years' War and were able to put to use their knowledge of the new tactics which the Swedes had so successfully employed. Drawing his support from the country gentry, Charles was strong in cavalry; this meant that a leader like Prince Rupert of the Rhine initially could score some dashing victories. In the long pull, however, Parliament discovered able generals, built its armies and forged ahead. Charles never truly overcame the handicap of weak finances, even though the country gentry gave what they could, and the colleges at Oxford, where he first made his headquarters, loyally melted down their ancient silver to contribute to his cause.

The war first seemed to favor Charles. Since 1641 Ireland had been in a state of savage rebellion. By generous promises Charles made a truce with the Irish and thus released troops to be put in the field at home. To gain strength Parliament sought active assistance from Scotland. By the Solemn League and Covenant (1643) it was agreed to preserve the Presby-terian Church of Scotland and to work for the reform of religion in England and Ireland so as to bring the churches of all three to as much uniformity as possible, most especially by ending "popery" and "prelacy." The West-minster Assembly, a meeting of English and Scottish clergy, drew up a creed designed to bind the churches of the two realms. In effect, therefore, Parliament had agreed to establish Presbyterianism in order to win Scottish support. The bargain seemed justified, for at the Battle of Marston Moor (July, 1644), the largest of the war, a combined Scottish and English army destroyed the Royalist forces of Rupert of the Rhine.

Meanwhile increasingly severe measures were taken against the estab-lished church. The use of the Book of Common Prayer was forbidden and local authorities were instructed to proceed against "idle, disaffected and scandalous clergy." In one way or another perhaps three thousand Anglican clergy—about one third of their total number—were ejected. Although some succeeded in defying the law with impunity, for the most part Anglicans were subject to the severest restrictions and only those remained who would accept the new practices. Baptism, marriage and burial became in effect civil ceremonies.

As the war progressed, the name of Oliver Cromwell won steadily larger importance on the parliamentary side. This Cambridge-educated Hunting-donshire squire had been elected to the Parliament of 1628, to the Short Parliament of 1640 and to the Long Parliament which succeeded it. He was deeply attached to the popular cause and as deeply concerned about the religious issue. Undertaking his duties as a soldier Cromwell grew rapidly in reputation, for the well-disciplined, psalm-singing cavalry which he led—the "Ironsides," as Prince Rupert nicknamed them—soon proved themselves the equal of any on the royalist side.

In 1645 Parliament, having met unexpected losses, agreed to raise a "New Model Army" consisting of 14,000 foot soldiers and 7,000 cavalry. Sir Thomas Fairfax was put in command, with Cromwell as his deputy. At Naseby, in 1645, the New Model broke the royalist cause, and in the following year Charles surrendered to the Scots.

The New Model was now invaded by a strange variety of "Sects," as the Reverend Richard Baxter observed when he visited it after Naseby. An essential feature of the Independent churches was that, unlike the Presbyterians, they abandoned altogether the broad territorial system of organization and took the isolated congregation as the autonomous unit. They thus went a long way toward tolerating varieties of worship. They disliked the Presbyterians almost as much as they disliked the Anglicans or papists. Thus the way was preparing for a breach between the army, dominated by Cromwell's Independents, and Parliament where the Presbyterian element prevailed.

The best example of the growing radicalism is seen in the action of a Leveller group headed by John Lilburne which sought to give England a written constitution. In 1647 these "Jacobins of the Puritan Revolution" drew up a scheme, the Agreement of the People, proposing a popularly elected Parliament based upon an agreement or contract of the whole people, who were possessed of certain natural rights. The proposals of the Levellers were debated by the victorious Army Council in 1647 at the parish church in Putney. Some striking questions were raised: whether, for example, the vote was the birthright of all Englishmen, as the Levellers insisted, or whether it was a right conditional upon the ownership of real property, as the more cautious army spokesmen maintained.

In 1647 the Scots turned Charles I over to Parliament. The next struggle took place between the victors. Although the episcopal system in England had come to an end, Presbyterians and Independents found it hard to agree. During these confusions Charles contrived to escape. He maneuvered for Scottish aid, offering to support Presbyterianism and to suppress the Independents. A second civil war followed, in which Charles actually received some Scottish aid. Nevertheless, Parliament's forces were so strong that the army, led by Cromwell, emerged as victor. To complete the triumph, the army attacked the Presbyterian-dominated Parliament. A Colonel Pride and a file of soldiers stationed themselves at the door of the Commons in December, 1648, to prevent all the Presbyterian members from entering. By this "Pride's Purge" about 100 members were expelled, leaving only a remnant of about 90 Independents. Cromwell had not been consulted but expressed his pleasure. The so-called "Rump" remained to carry out the will of the army. As Charles was again a prisoner the immediate problem was to determine his fate and that of the monarchy.

Brushing aside the House of Lords, the Rump appointed a court of 135 commissioners to try Charles Stuart—"that man of blood," as a contemporary pamphlet described him. Students are agreed that it would be difficult to find a legal basis or precedent for this action and for the methods by which the trial was conducted. Charles was accused of seeking to erect a tyrannical and unlawful power instead of governing according to the laws of the land. His principal defense was simply to refuse to acknowledge the jurisdiction of the court and to insist upon his royal authority. "Where the word of a king is," he said, "there is power." After three days Charles was found guilty; sentence was pronounced upon him that he should be put to death by beheading "as a tyrant, traitor, murderer and public enemy of the good people of the land." Only a fraction of the 135 commissioners had attended the trial and in the end only 59 could be induced to sign the death warrant.

On January 30, 1649, Charles, dressed in black velvet, was publicly beheaded in Whitehall, meeting his end with dignity. From the scaffold he spoke somewhat as follows:

> For the people, truly I desire their liberty and freedom as much as anybody whatsoever, but I must tell you their liberty and freedom consists in having government, those laws by which their lives and goods may be most their own. It is not their having a share in the government. . . . A subject and a sovereign are clear different things.

The execution of Charles, "the Lord's anointed," stands, as Professor Trevelyan writes, like a gigantic interrogation point across the page of English history. Charles' persistent misgovernment had been evident; his violation of the rights of Parliament was outrageous; yet the nature of his trial and the pathos of his end had the ironical result of bringing the majority in a deeply divided England to sympathy with him. The republic which now automatically came into existence was not popular; it could be maintained only by the armed force of a ruthlessly determined minority.[10]

10. John Milton justified the execution in a pamphlet of 1649 of which the full title conveys his argument: *The Tenure of Kings and Magistrates, Proving That It Is Lawful, and Hath Been Held So Through All Ages, for Any, Who Have the Power, to Call to Account a Tyrant or Wicked King, and after Due Conviction to Depose and Put Him to Death.* This tract was far outshadowed by another seeking to win sympathy for Charles. The famous *Eikon Basilike, the Pourtraicture of His Sacred Majestie in His Solitudes and Sufferings,* first published on the day of Charles' funeral, went through some fifty editions in one year.

◼ COMMONWEALTH AND PROTECTORATE

The years from 1649 to 1660 are a strange interlude in the constitutional history of England. From a narrowly legal point of view, they might never have been. Having quarreled with the king and beheaded him, the leaders of one parliamentary group tried the experiment of republicanism, only to have England decide in the end that republicanism was not for her. The "Restoration" of 1660, therefore, sought to link itself directly to the year 1641, ignoring all that had happened in between. History, however, does not stand still, much less run backwards, and it is now possible to see that during the years of the Commonwealth some developments occurred which were to have no small importance for the future.

With the execution of Charles I, England found itself a republic. On the day of his death the Rump ordered to be printed the following statement:

> That the people are, under God, the original of all just power: . . . that the Commons of England, in Parliament assembled, being chosen by, and representing, the people, have the supreme power in this nation.

Parliament, or what was left of it, then proceeded formally to abolish the monarchy and the House of Lords. Government was to be in the hands of the Rump Parliament and of a Council of State numbering 41 which the Rump nominated.

Cromwell, now fifty years old, had come to be the dominant figure of the time. As a soldier his reputation was secure, while as a statesman he likewise spoke with a voice that commanded the respect of his fellows. He was faced by large domestic difficulties, for the army profoundly distrusted the Rump, and the Sects were clamoring for a large measure of social reform. Scotland and Ireland for different reasons were both in open revolt. To Cromwell Parliament entrusted the responsibility of restoring order.

Ireland received Cromwell's first attention. In August, 1649, he landed at Dublin with a Puritan army of 12,000 men. The Irish garrisons in the small towns of Drogheda and Wexford were particularly defiant, rejecting all Cromwell's warnings that by not surrendering they would subject themselves to the severest penalties of war. When the garrison of 3,000 at Drogheda continued to resist, Cromwell himself led the final assault, the outcome of which he described as follows:

> Being thus entered we refused them quarter; having, the day before, summoned the town. I believe we put to the sword the whole number of the defendants, I do not think thirty of the whole number escaped with their lives. Those that did, are in safe custody for Barbadoes.

Wexford suffered a similar terrible fate. When Cromwell left Ireland in 1650 his son-in-law, Henry Ireton, carried on the work of subjugation, causing thousands of Irish to be driven into the western counties from their homes. Order was eventually restored but in such a manner that the evil memories of the Cromwellian occupation have continued from that day to this.

Scotland, where Presbyterian sentiment had unwisely calculated its chances to be better under Charles I or his son than under the Independents, was subdued in 1650 and 1651. Cromwell won the victory of Dunbar in 1650, then marched north to conquer Perth. Meanwhile a Scottish army invaded England. Cromwell defeated this army in 1651 at Worcester in a battle which he described as his "crowning mercy." From this battle the future Charles II was lucky enough to escape with his life, leaving the parliamentarians in unchallengeable control.

The great questions now were political. How should England be governed? Cromwell and the army discovered that the Rump, the incompetence of which was clear for all to see, was most reluctant to destroy itself. In April, 1653, Cromwell appeared before it with a file of musketeers. After listening briefly to the debate he rose, praised the members for their earlier good work, condemned them for their present behavior and then bluntly ordered his soldiers to clear the house. In the light of Charles I's earlier attempt to arrest the five members no action could have been more bitterly ironical. Pointing to the mace, the historical symbol of the Speaker's authority, Cromwell exclaimed: "Take away that bauble!" In this way the army and the Independent leaders prevailed over what was, after all, the last vestige of constitutional authority.

Nothing but expedients in goverment now remained. Cromwell first arranged for the ministers of the Independent churches to nominate a list of candidates from which the army picked 140. This Nominated Parliament (remembered as "Barebones Parliament" from the strange name of one of its Puritan members, Praise-God Barebones), having proposed the abolition of Oxford and Cambridge Universities, accomplished little more than to agree to its own dissolution, resigning its powers to Cromwell.

Meanwhile some army leaders prepared a more elaborate and more revolutionary scheme, embodied in a document known as the Instrument of Government, and persuaded Cromwell, now very much the ruler in fact, to accept it (December, 1653). This, the only written constitution in English history, provided that supreme legislative authority for England, Ireland and Scotland should reside in a Lord Protector and in "the people assembled in Parliament." Executive power was to be wielded by the Lord Protector and a Council of twenty-two. Cromwell was named as Lord Protector and fifteen of the Council members were likewise indicated. England was to have 400 members in Parliament, Scotland and Ireland were to have thirty apiece. Seats were to be redistributed and a general property qualification of

£200 was to be a prerequisite for voting in the counties. Parliament was to meet intermittently; when it was not in session the Lord Protector and the Council were supreme. Toleration was extended to all professing Christians save "papists" (Catholics) and "prelatists" (Episcopalians).

The Instrument of Government which established the "Protectorate" as a variant of the "Commonwealth" which preceded it was significant in giving partial recognition to the popular basis of political rule and in attempting for the first time to combine England, Scotland and Ireland under one authority. Nevertheless, when accepted by Cromwell it worked so badly that after five months he exercised his right as Protector to dissolve the first Protectorate Parliament. He now (1655) arranged to divide England and Wales into twelve districts, each administered by a Cromwellian major-general—clearly a move in the direction of greater authoritarianism.

The last years of the Protectorate are an object lesson in the difficulties of dictatorial rule. The second Protectorate Parliament offered Cromwell in 1657 the "Humble Petition and Advice," urging him to assume the title of king. This Cromwell refused although he agreed to nominate his successor and to establish an upper chamber the members of which he would nominate and the lower chamber approve. Many historians have suggested that Cromwell might ultimately have been tempted to put on the crown, for he seems to have been acutely aware of the ancient traditions of England which so closely interwove parliamentary and royal authority. Amid the confusions arising from such changes as were made, Cromwell died in September, 1658. Even the most skilful of dictators find it hard to provide for their successor. Oliver's son Richard had been indicated to succeed him, yet seldom was a candidate more reluctant and less capable. Failing a leader, the republican cause rapidly disintegrated.

Before attempting any final estimate of Cromwell's work, we must glance at his foreign policies. Domestic affairs kept him from intervening too closely in the tangled game of continental politics where the skill of Cardinal Mazarin was being displayed to the full. The execution of Charles shocked Europe but provoked no direct reaction. Mazarin, for his part, was content to leave well enough alone in England if the distractions of the Civil War and its aftermath kept that country from impeding France's continental ambitions. Ultimately, indeed, Mazarin proved eager to have Cromwell's support in his war against Spain.

Cromwell was keenly aware of some of the larger issues abroad. Having brought England, Scotland and Ireland, if only temporarily, under one rule he desired to see his country act as a major power, especially on the high seas. He has been called the first ruler of England who was consciously an imperialist. The Navigation Act of 1651 which forbade the importing of goods save in English ships or ships of the producing nations was clearly directed against the Dutch carrying trade. The war with Holland (1652–1654) was the immediate consequence, showing Cromwell's concern with the techniques of mercantilism.

His vigorous anti-Spanish policy led to an alliance with France, the seizure and eventual colonization of Jamaica and the capture of Dunkirk in the Spanish Netherlands. English military prestige on the continent grew greatly. "I have seen the English," Marshal Turenne wrote to Mazarin in 1657; "they are the finest troops possible." At the same time the navy, brilliantly commanded by Admiral Blake, gave England control of the sea. Between 1649 and 1660 no less than 207 ships were added to the Royal Navy. Cromwell and Blake together, therefore, carried forward to new heights the work which Elizabeth and Drake had begun nearly a century before.

Whether Cromwell could have anticipated all the results that were to flow from this period may be doubted. They were, nevertheless, substantial. In the first place, the cause of absolute, divine right monarchy had lost any chance of permanently asserting itself. Conversely, the power of the House of Commons, despite all the curious distortions of the Cromwellian period, was moving into the ascendant. England's general rejection of Roman Catholicism was assured. The dangers of a standing army and of military extremism had been brought home. Royal independence of Parliament in financial matters was gone, as was the danger of the prerogative courts. Englishmen seemed convinced that republicanism was not for them. In the field of religion the Dissenters, to whom the appellation of Nonconformists soon came to be more generally applied, became a permanent and powerful force in English life.

Puritan "intolerance" has been much decried. The efforts to impose a godly and austere pattern of life upon England by closing the theaters, by requiring church attendance, by attacking drunkenness, swearing and gambling, by abolishing the festivals of Christmas, Easter and Whitsuntide, imposing the Puritan Sabbath and requiring sober clothing and demeanor were sincerely intended, yet they were often niggling and preposterous. There was, however, another side. An ordinance of 1650 repealed the penalties against those not attending their parish church provided that they were present at some religious exercise, and Cromwell seems to have been disposed not to take harsh measures against any religious group that would conduct itself quietly.

John Milton in England and Roger Williams in America have won themselves an immortal place in the literature devoted to the cause of freedom of conscience. "Let her and falsehood grapple," wrote Milton in 1644 in his *Areopagitica.* "Who ever knew truth put to the worse in a free and open encounter?" Cromwell sympathized, too, with the long-persecuted Jews, making arrangements which permitted them to enter England, to trade and to open synagogues. Under the Protectorate the Quaker movement also came into being. After George Fox began to "publish the Truth" in 1647 the Quakers' extreme views caused many to be imprisoned. Yet Cromwell seems to have realized and respected the value of their faith.

No historian can ignore the permanent influence of Puritanism upon the English character, whether in such specific ways as in daily Bible readings, in family prayers, in the Puritan Sabbath, or in more subtle respects. It is true that the new age of the Restoration was to be marked by a sharp reversal of public and private behavior and would suggest, superficially, that the lessons had not been learned. Nevertheless, powerful new forces had been generated. In the political sphere, above all, the policies of the later Stuarts were soon to be brought to a sharp halt. The speed with which the "Bloodless Revolution" of 1688 was to be accomplished and the very wide measure of acceptance which Englishmen gave it are clear indications that the sober leaders of the Puritan epoch in their own way had done work of lasting value.

Oliver Cromwell's problem was the problem of a sincere and godly man brought in times of profound disagreement to a position of demanding eminence. Many of his actions look like those of a tyrant, yet in our own age the House of Commons has chosen to erect his statue outside its entrance. He had found himself in the presence of a very great danger—that of arbitrary royal power—and had not hesitated to exercise an arbitrary power of his own to combat this danger. He had fought fire with fire.

> During his last hours [writes one of the most learned historians of this period] Cromwell was heard to murmur that the Lord had made him, though most unworthy, a mean instrument to do His people some good. To serve the minority of the nation that seemed to him to be the people of God had been the guiding principle of his life. To try and secure for them their civil liberties as men, and their spiritual liberties as Christians, he had fought to destroy the old monarchy and the ecclesiastical system associated with the name of Archbishop Laud. For their sake he had fought the Scottish presbyterians when they had tried to force upon Englishmen a yoke too grievous to be borne. For their sake, too, he had not hesitated to disregard civil rights when they seemed to conflict with freedom of conscience. For forms of church government or for sectarian creeds he cared as little as for constitutional forms. To him the essence of puritanism was the good life.[11]

11. G. DAVIES, *The Early Stuarts, 1603–1660* (1938), p. 186.

■ THE AGE OF THE RESTORATION

In a narrow and precise sense the Restoration of 1660 was a transition from Puritan, republican, revolutionary rule to the rule of the Stuarts, brought about after the obvious failure of Oliver Cromwell's son Richard in the role of Lord Protector. Having neither the talents, the character nor the desire to succeed at his post, Richard soon gave his resignation to what was left of the old Long Parliament of 1640, summoned by the army leaders after Richard had dissolved the second Protectorate Parliament. The dominant figure in England was General Monck, a parliamentary leader whose power lay in his military command. Monck, however, seemed to have no political ambitions for himself. Marching southward with his troops, he first restored the surviving Presbyterian members and then ordered the fragmentary Long Parliament to summon a Convention Parliament in order to determine the future government of England.

The results of this election showed a strong current of royalist sympathy. Meanwhile negotiations were undertaken with the exiled Charles II at Breda, in Holland. This shrewd figure played his cards well. He issued the Declaration of Breda, dating it "in the twelfth year of our reign," promising to govern with the aid of a free Parliament, to issue generous pardons, to give guarantees to the legitimate purchasers of forfeited estates, to grant "liberty to tender consciences" in matters of religion and to secure the army its arrears of pay. The Convention Parliament likewise played its cards well. It accepted the Declaration of Breda with the statement "that, according to the ancient and fundamental laws of this kingdom, the Government is and ought to be, King, Lords and Commons." With this understanding Charles was enthusiastically welcomed at London in May, 1660, and the restoration of the Stuarts was effected.

In a broader sense the Restoration was a repudiation of the ideals of the Puritan Commonwealth. It has been described as a provisional compromise between kingly and parliamentary power. The critical question was whether there would be a conservative revolution leading England back to the principles and policies of the first two Stuarts. It is clear now that the ultimate aims of the restored monarchs involved at least two points: regaining authority for themselves and reestablishing the Roman Catholic faith. In these respects Charles II did not make his real purposes clear. Consequently he was able to remain upon the throne for twenty-five years, as he never could have done had his deepest beliefs been plainly displayed. Only on his deathbed did he declare himself a Catholic. His brother James, on the other hand, who made public profession of Catholicism as early as 1673, reigned only from 1685 to 1688, during which brief period there could be little doubt of his purposes or of the dangers to which English institutions were thereby being exposed.

Charles II, who, according to the diarist, Samuel Pepys, "discovered a most delicious method of walking called sauntering," was considerably more than the pleasure-loving, self-indulgent, Merry Monarch that tradition has seen sauntering across the stage of English history. His immediate aim in 1660 was to bring back to his country some kind of order and harmony. An Act of Indemnity and Oblivion, though it was sharply criticized by returning royalists as failing in its purpose, was supposed to cover all offences committed during the Civil War and Commonwealth. The standing army received its arrears in pay and was disbanded.[12] Lands that had been confiscated during the revolution were restored wherever possible to their rightful owners, though not without much dissatisfaction. The established church recovered its authority, a certain number of non-Episcopalians, however, being allowed to retain their pulpits. Charles renounced some ancient feudal sources of income and was granted instead an annual revenue of over a million pounds.

In other respects action was less moderate. The Convention Parliament ordered twenty-eight surviving regicides (those who had voted for the death of Charles I) to stand trial; thirteen of these were executed. The once-honored bodies of Pym, Blake and Cromwell were torn from their graves in Westminster Abbey; that of Cromwell was dragged through the streets and given shameful burial at a public crossroads. These were the emotional reactions of a sort unhappily to be expected at the close of an age of revolution and upheaval.

The elections of 1661 resulted in the election of the "Cavalier Parliament," a body dominated by the landed aristocracy. As his principal adviser Charles leaned upon a faithful royalist, Edward Hyde, now Earl of Clarendon and Lord Chancellor. Parliament, more perhaps than Clarendon, was responsible between 1661 and 1665 for a series of measures known as the Clarendon Code which imposed very harsh disabilities upon Dissenters. The Corporation Act (1661) required all members of city or borough governments to be members of the Church of England. The Act of Uniformity (1662) required all clergymen and teachers to accept the Anglican Prayer Book. The Conventicle Act (1664) forbade meetings of more than five persons for worship except in accordance with this Prayer Book. The Five Mile Act (1665) forbade all dissenting clergy to come within five miles of a town or to teach. In 1663, when Charles sought to mitigate the force of some of these measures by asserting his royal power to "dispense" with the laws, Parlia-

12. Save for a few units, the Coldstreams, Grenadiers and Horse Guards, that now boast some of the proudest traditions of the British army.

ment sharply rebuffed him. Widely unpopular, Clarendon was impeached for high treason, deserted by his royal master and ultimately died in exile.

The years immediately following Clarendon's fall (1667–1673) were marked by the interplay of domestic and foreign affairs, both of which were strongly colored by the Catholic issue. Charles now governed with the aid of the "Cabal," a group of five political adventurers led by Anthony Ashley Cooper who embarked upon a reckless foreign policy. England had in the past fought one trade war under Cromwell against the Dutch and a second between 1665 and 1667 from which she acquired "New Amsterdam," or New York. As the danger now seemed to come chiefly from France, in 1668 England joined the Netherlands and Sweden to form the Triple Alliance against Louis XIV.[13] When the war ended Charles II moved selfishly to reverse this wise national policy. In 1670 he concluded the secret Treaty of Dover with Louis XIV whereby France and England agreed to attack and partition Holland. Charles was to restore Catholicism in England and in return get £200,000 a year secretly from Louis XIV. The first provision was known to the entire Cabal, the others only to its two Catholic members. In 1672 England launched her third war against the Dutch, this time in company with France. Almost simultaneously Charles favored the English Catholics (and with them the Dissenters) by issuing a Declaration of Indulgence suspending all penal laws in matters of religion.

The result was a sharp revulsion of opinion. The Cavalier Parliament forced Charles to withdraw the Declaration of Indulgence and then passed the Test Act (1673) requiring all persons holding civil or military office to take the sacrament according to the rites of the Church of England. When Charles' brother and heir, James, resigned his office of Lord High Admiral rather than do this, he openly admitted himself to be a Roman Catholic. Public opinion likewise forced Charles to withdraw from the Dutch war and broke up the Cabal.

A development of cardinal importance in these years was the first emergence of a party system in English politics. Men had taken sides, to be sure, during the Civil War, but hardly in the modern party sense. Now on the twin issues of religion and royal power feelings became violently embittered. Following the downfall of the Cabal, Charles took as his principal adviser the Earl of Danby, the leader of a High Anglican, strongly monarchist group known as the "Court Party" and later, through a slang term, as the Tories. Danby was a skilful manipulator, able to find jobs or bribes for those whose support he needed.

Opposition to the Tories centered in a disgruntled member of the old Cabal—Anthony Ashley Cooper, now Earl of Shaftesbury. Indignant at the

13. See p. 343.

king's Catholic intrigues, Shaftesbury became leader of the "Country Party," seeking toleration for Dissenters, subordination of the king to his ministers and the exclusion of Charles' brother James from the succession. To this group another slang term, "Whigs," was eventually applied. All feelings were inflamed in 1678 when Titus Oates, an adventurer, professed to have knowledge of a Catholic plot to murder the king and have his brother James succeed him. By his outrageously false testimony Oates sent a number of "Tory" Englishmen to the scaffold. Shaftesbury took advantage of this "Popish Plot" excitement to seek Danby's impeachment, a move that Charles II averted only by using his power to dissolve the seventeen-year-old Cavalier Parliament.

Three new Parliaments followed in quick succession (1679, 1680, 1681), each to be dissolved by Charles as he saw his authority threatened. Under the first, the all-important Habeas Corpus Act was passed providing strict punishment for officials who failed to respond to a writ of Habeas Corpus either by justifying the detention of a prisoner or by producing him in court for trial.[14] Religion, however, provided the major issue. The Country Party had pledged its members to introduce an Exclusion Bill specifically designed to keep James from the throne. Charles saved the day by dissolving the Parliament of 1679, as he did again in the case of the Parliament of 1680. When a third Parliament met at Oxford in 1681 this, too, was dissolved by royal command, so that during his last four years Charles was able to rule with power in his own hands—more nearly absolute than any other Stuart had been. On his deathbed in 1685 he received the last rites of the Roman Catholic Church.

■ THE GLORIOUS REVOLUTION

The four-year reign of James II brought the Stuart cause to disaster. At the outset, even when Mass was celebrated openly at court, public opinion was not too much aroused. James had two Protestant daughters by his first wife: Mary, married to William of Orange, the leader of continental Protestantism, and Anne, married to George of Denmark. Time might therefore put the succession in safe hands. Yet even this prospect was clouded, for James had married again, this time to the Catholic Mary of Modena.

The wild effort of the Duke of Monmouth, an illegitimate son of Charles II, to organize a Protestant rising in the southwest of England and seize the throne met with failure as did a smaller rising in Scotland. Nevertheless, the savagery with which Judge Jeffreys punished the English peasantry who

---

14. BISHOP BURNET's *History of My Own Times* is authority for the famous story that the act would not have passed the House of Lords had not one of the tellers, in a jocose mood, counted one very fat lord as twelve men.

had risen in support of Monmouth shocked public opinion. James then outraged his subjects by keeping a standing army of 20,000 men on the outskirts of London. He sought to have Habeas Corpus and the Test Act repealed, proroguing Parliament when it refused. The church was dominated and bullied by reestablishing the old Court of High Commission. A Declaration of Indulgence, issued in 1687, sought by the exercise of royal prerogative to exempt Dissenters and Catholics from the penalties of the existing laws. At Oxford and Cambridge, strongholds of Anglicanism, James expelled some who were vocal in their opposition to him and introduced Catholics who were amenable.

Two events brought matters to a head. In 1688 James issued a second Declaration of Indulgence which the clergy were required to read from the pulpit. Seven bishops, including the Archbishop of Canterbury, who submitted a petition in protest were committed to prison for trial amid intense public emotion. As they walked into the Tower of London the watching people and the very guards knelt to ask their blessing. Crowds gathered around Westminster Hall where the trial was held and rejoiced wildly on the eventual news of the bishops' acquittal. The second event directly concerned the succession. Shortly before the trial, Mary of Modena had borne James a son who automatically took precedence over his Protestant half-sisters. Hence England now had the prospect of one Catholic ruler succeeding another.

On the very day of the acquittal of the bishops, a group of seven prominent Whig and Tory leaders joined in a secret letter to William of Orange, offering their support if he would come over and help them. He was not promised the crown. "We, who subscribe this," they wrote simply, "will not fail to attend your Highness upon your landing." Unlike the situation in 1642 the Tories were now against the king. The choice of William of Orange was shrewd: through his mother, Mary, he was the grandson of Charles I; through his wife he was the son-in-law of James II; he could be counted upon, too, to have the continental backing of those, including even Catholic Spain and Austria and the papacy itself, who feared the encroachments of Louis XIV. Moreover, it must be remembered that in October, 1685, Louis had revoked the Edict of Nantes, sending a stream of French Huguenots into exile and adding a strong religious opposition to the already widespread distrust of his political and military aims.

An admiral disguised as a bluejacket carried the ciphered message of invitation across the Channel. William's decision and preparations were known to Louis XIV who made no attempt to interfere, thinking that William's arrival would throw England into a long turmoil of civil war. It was perhaps the greatest of all Louis' miscalculations. William sailed from the Netherlands in November, 1688, with a flotilla of 600 ships, large and small, carrying some 15,000 troops. Crowds on the English and French coasts saw the imposing force pass through the Strait of Dover, the winds having prevented a landing on the Yorkshire coast as first planned. William came ashore at Torbay in Devon, whence, with an array of English footsoldiers, Dutch guards, Brandenburgers, Swiss mercenaries and Swedish horsemen he advanced through the English rain along the muddy roads toward London. William's banners carried the words, *Pro Religione Protestante, Pro Libero Parlemento* and the proud motto of the House of Orange, *Je Maintiendrai*.

No armed conflict was needed. James, having sent his wife and infant ahead, left London in December, burning the writs which he had prepared for the summoning of a new Parliament and throwing the great seal of England spitefully into the Thames as he was rowed across at the dead of night. Seized later by fishermen off the Kentish coast and brought back, James was wisely allowed by William to depart a second time. He celebrated Christmas at the court of Louis XIV. The great seal, without which the operation of government was greatly impeded, was eventually dredged up from the Thames.

England was now technically without a king. No Parliament being in existence, William summoned an unofficial gathering of peers and "all such persons as have served as Knights, Citizens and Burgesses in any of the Parliaments that were held during the reign of the late King Charles the Second," together with representatives of the City of London. On their advice he then summoned a Convention Parliament to meet in January, 1689. This body, when elected, declared that James, by attempting to break the original contract between king and people, had abdicated and that the throne was thereby vacant.[15] It was also stated to be "inconsistent with the safety and welfare of this Protestant Kingdom to be governed by a Popish prince." It was then decided to offer the crown jointly to William and Mary. Before the offer of the crown was made a Declaration of Rights was drawn up, listing James' misdeeds and enumerating the basic rights of Englishmen. In February, 1689, William and Mary accepted this essentially conservative document in the banqueting hall of Whitehall Palace from which Charles I had walked to his execution forty years before. They were then declared to be the rightful rulers of the realm and the "Bloodless Revolution" was accomplished.

In Scotland, where James II had sought to crush the Presbyterians, a Convention Parliament declared the crown forfeit and offered it to William

---

15. The concept of "abdication," whether true or not, was most welcome to the Tories, many of whom had espoused the theory of divine hereditary right and did not wish to be accused of expelling a legitimate monarch by force.

and Mary on condition that they reestablish Presbyterianism. Opposition from the Western Highlanders led by Graham of Claverhouse ("Bonnie Dundee") was soon put down.

In Ireland the problem was more difficult, for James, with the active backing of Louis XIV, could look for the support of the Catholic majority. Escorted by a French fleet, James landed in Ireland in March, 1689, where soon he had the greater part of the country with him. The Protestant North offered resistance, but only when William himself came over in 1690 could a decision be reached. The victory of the Protestant "Orangemen" at the Battle of the Boyne on July 1 ruined the last hopes of James II. With his escape to France Ireland fell once more under the English heel. Although Catholics were promised the same degree of freedom that they had had under Charles II, actually they were not permitted to sit in or vote for the Irish Parliament, to enter the learned professions, carry arms, purchase land, marry Protestants or buy a horse worth more than five pounds. A new era of oppression had begun.

■ THE REVOLUTIONARY SETTLEMENT

A series of parliamentary enactments, most of them completed in 1689, were needed to give full definition to the new status of the English monarchy. Constitutional changes are seldom in themselves dramatic, and yet the changes wrought in these years have profoundly affected the fortunes of all England's subsequent political life. This legislation—the "Revolutionary Settlement"—was mainly the work of the Convention Parliament summoned after the departure of James by William of Orange at a time when he was not yet king. Hence one may properly emphasize its extra-legal and revolutionary nature. The legislation was, nevertheless, permanent and fundamental.

The Bill of Rights, completed in October, 1689, gave formal parliamentary definition to the Declaration of Rights which William and Mary had previously accepted. It lacked fine phrasing or lofty theorizing. Severely practical in nature, the Bill of Rights first listed and condemned a series of illegal acts of which the Stuarts had been guilty. The sovereign cannot suspend the laws, use his dispensing power to get around them, levy money without consent of Parliament, create special courts or maintain a standing army in peace time. The Bill then asserted the basic rights of all subjects: to petition the king, to bear arms, to have free elections and frequent Parliaments, to enjoy freedom of speech and to be secure from excessive fines, excessive bail and cruel or unusual punishments.

Included with this Bill was an Act of Succession stipulating that no one who was a papist or married to a papist could be king, and that the succession was to go to the heirs of Queen Mary, then to her sister Anne and Anne's heirs, then to the heirs of William by another wife.

In the same year Parliament passed a Toleration Act (though the word toleration does not appear in it) granting freedom of worship to all who would take an oath of allegiance and subscribe to a declaration against popery. Although this was broad enough to cover Congregationalists, Quakers and Baptists, it did not apply to disbelievers in the Trinity, so that the total effect was to exclude Unitarians as well as Catholics from its provisions. The Act, moreover, did nothing to remove the civil disabilities of Catholics and Dissenters who still could not hold crown or municipal office or attend the Universities. "Toleration" did not mean religious equality.

A Mutiny Act (1689), in addition to fixing death as the penalty for mutiny, sedition or desertion, declared that keeping a standing army in times of peace without consent of Parliament was illegal. The Act was strictly limited in duration, with the consequence that by its periodic renewals Parliament could remind the crown of the limitations imposed upon royal authority.

The Triennial Act of 1694 limited the duration of any Parliament to three years and the interval between Parliaments likewise to three years. Still another step came with the failure to renew the Licensing Act in 1695. Previously all publishing had been subject to government license; failure to renew this act meant the establishment of liberty of the press, subject now only to the important safeguard of the law of libel. William on his own initiative made the tenure of judges permanent, commissioning them *quam diu se bene gesserint*—so long as they behave properly. This provision was put on a statutory basis in 1701. Placing the judges in this way above politics constituted a tremendous step forward and made English justice unique. Another statute required that a person accused of treason be given a copy of the indictment and be defended by counsel. An overt act of treason had to be substantiated by two witnesses. Still other arrangements fixed the annual peacetime revenues of the Crown at £1,200,000 and by providing for commissioners to audit accounts made certain that appropriations would be spent only for purposes authorized by the House of Commons.

The remaining great measure, the Act of Settlement (1701), was designed to make more precise the conditions of succession to the throne. Queen Mary had died childless in 1694. Her sister, Queen Anne, lost her only child, the ten-year-old Duke of Gloucester, in 1700.[16] Seeing that the question of succession to the Spanish throne was casting Europe into a turmoil, Parliament had good reason to wish to clarify the dynastic problem at home. It was specifically provided that, on failure of the earlier provisions, the succession should go to the Electress Sophia of Hanover, granddaughter of

16. Anne had endured fifteen other unsuccessful pregnancies.

James I, and to her heirs on condition of their being Protestant. It was precisely stipulated that "whosoever shall hereafter come to the possession of this Crown shall join in communion with the Church of England as by law established." In this way the crown passed to George I of Hanover in 1714 on the death of Anne and the privileged position of the Anglican Church was maintained.

Although not strictly a part of the Revolution Settlement, the Act of Union with Scotland (1707) must be recorded as closing an embittered chapter in the relations of the two countries. Not the least of the difficulties arose from the Presbyterianism of the Scottish majority and also from the strong "Jacobite" element in Scotland that supported the cause of the exiled James II and his son, James Edward, the "Old Pretender." After laborious negotiations an agreement was reached whereby a United Kingdom was to be created with one Parliament in which Scotland would be represented by forty-five members in the Commons and by sixteen peers in the Lords.[17] The Presbyterian Church was to remain unaltered and the Scottish courts were to operate, as they still do, under their own historic laws and procedures. Various trade regulations, guarantees and commercial privileges were also involved. All in all, an agreement was reached that has stood without major embarrassment from that day to the present.

In the opening years of the eighteenth century England could contemplate a great political achievement at home. Major problems and difficulties, to be sure, still remained. The Jacobites—those whose allegiance was given to the exiled James II or to his son (the "Old Pretender") or later to his grandson (the "Young Pretender")—drank the famous Jacobite toast to "the king over the water" and were still capable of making trouble, as they showed in the risings of 1715 and 1745. Parliament still was elected by only a very small number of Englishmen. Great restrictions had been placed upon royal power, yet precisely what powers remained, as for example in vetoing legislation or dismissing ministers, still was not clear. Moreover, no real scheme of cabinet government had as yet been worked out, and no well defined system of prime-ministership had been created in order to harmonize the workings of the legislative and executive branches. These were problems for the eighteenth century to tackle. Yet, it must be repeated, a magnificent work had been achieved. The eminent historian, Lord Acton, has called the Revolution of 1688 and its aftermath the greatest thing done by the English nation. Authority, he says, was limited, regulated and controlled. England, having ordered her own affairs, stood as a shining example from which later generations upon the continent were to draw an increasing measure of hope and inspiration.

17. The sixteen were to be elected by the Scottish peers from their total number.

Vüe et Perspective du Château   de Ve
                        Dédiée   Au Roy
              Par son tres humble tres obeissant   et tres fidele Serviteu

...inc et Gravé d'après le Baurel par P. Menant.

The Age of Louis XIV

de la Cour .

Se vend a Paris chez Demortain pont R Dame CPR.

Chapter 13

■ THE MONARCHY OF THE KING'S PLEASURE

ON ALMOST ANY MORNING in the life of Louis XIV a stately and in many
respects fantastic ritual was enacted in the closely shuttered royal bedchamber of the great palace of Versailles. Lit by the flickering gleam of a night
lamp stood a huge four-poster bed, surmounted by an elaborate canopy hav-

325

ing a white plume at each corner. Its gold-embroidered, red velvet hangings were drawn close. A small camp-bed on which a *valet de chambre* had slept occupied one corner of the room. On a table nearby were the remains of the night collation: bread, water, wine, plates, napkins, the royal cup and a trial cup for the attendant.

The *valet de chambre,* having left the room to dress, returned, accompanied by menials who renewed the fires in the two fireplaces, opened the shutters, removed the camp-bed, the night lamp and the collation and then retired. As the clocks struck eight the *valet de chambre* approached the royal bed, drew back the curtains and announced respectfully to the sleeping occupant, "Sire, it is the hour." The valet then went to the great gold and white doors, preparing to open them for the first *entrée* of the morning.

Meanwhile, in the sumptuous antechamber had assembled the princes of the blood, the chief nobles of France, the great officers of the crown, the officers of the chamber, the officers of the wardrobe and distinguished visitors. Even at this early hour they would be elaborately dressed, periwigged and bejeweled, conversing among themselves in hushed tones.

The first entrance (which was sought by scratching lightly on the panels of the door and never by knocking) was the *entrée familière.* This was the prerogative of the immediate male members of the royal family who were uniquely privileged in having both sides of the double doors opened for them and in being permitted to speak to the king while he was still in bed.

Next came the *grande entrée* for an imposing list of court officials: the grand chamberlain, the first gentleman of the chamber, the grand master of the wardrobe, others who carried the king's clothes, the first doctor, the first surgeon and the nurse. The doctor and the surgeon rubbed the king and changed his shirt; wine was poured upon the royal hands; he was presented with a vase of holy water and with a missal from which he recited a few prayers. Most of the gathering then withdrew to permit a short religious service, following which the great nobles returned and the ceremony of dressing began. The king selected a wig for the day from those offered by the royal barber; his slippers were presented by the first *valet de chambre* (a duke); his dressing gown was offered by the grand chamberlain (a prince). The king then walked to his armchair where he prepared to complete his toilet as further groups of visitors were admitted.

The *petit lever* then admitted all those who by right of office were entitled to present themselves. During their comings and goings the royal nightcap was removed, the king shaved himself (on alternate days) and the chosen wig was donned.

The *grand lever,* which now followed, was the time when such distinguished persons as cardinals, archbishops, ambassadors, dukes, governors of provinces, presidents of the *Parlements* and marshals of France were admitted. For each of these the door must be ceremoniously opened and shut. The royal officers meanwhile were assisting with the king's dressing. He was solemnly presented with underclothes, breeches, silk stockings and diamond buckled shoes. Breakfast was offered on a service of porcelain and gold. His dressing gown was held discreetly in front of him while the royal shirt, previously warmed at the fireside, was passed from the valet of the wardrobe to the grand chamberlain who passed it either to the Dauphin or to one of the princes of the blood, from whom the king at length received it. He was next handed his sword, vest, ribbons, jeweled decorations and coat. A basket of cravats and a silver tray of lace handkerchiefs were presented for his choice. His dressing complete, the king knelt for the final prayers; he again took holy water; then, having received his plumed hat, gloves and tall cane, he passed from his bedchamber to his cabinet.

Such was the fantastic ritual with which Louis XIV of France, seldom in the presence of less than two hundred people, began his day. A corresponding ceremony attended his nightly retirement. Ceremonial, indeed, in one form or another dominated Louis' entire life. While thus setting his stamp of magnificence upon France he at the same time aspired to dominate Europe. His era, then, merits careful analysis, for the pattern of the French monarchy gives significant clues to the spirit of an entire age.

An element of prodigy marked Louis throughout his life. He succeeded his father as king in 1643 at the age of five. His first childhood memories are said to have been of sitting on a throne with his mother standing beside him, and of watching his ministers kneel at his feet. During his minority the effective conduct of affairs lay in the hands of Cardinal Mazarin, Richelieu's worthy successor. Following Mazarin's death in 1661 Louis, at the age of twenty-three, took into his own hands power which he subsequently never relinquished. When he died in September, 1715, he had completed over seventy-two years on the throne—the longest recorded reign in European history. By far the greater number of Frenchmen had lived and died knowing no other king.

His long reign must be seen in relation to what preceded it. Feudal France—a confusion of warring duchies and principalities—had given way to the France of Henry IV, Richelieu and Mazarin. Although these men had imposed some degree of royal discipline and centralization upon a badly disrupted country, their work was, nevertheless, incomplete. What one historian describes as "the multiplied tyranny of anachronistic localisms" we may explain by saying that in many parts of France there were individuals and local bodies still ready to challenge, or at all events to bypass, the authority of the central government. Sully, Henry IV and, above all, Richelieu had gone far toward ending the era of feudal anarchy. Inheriting their work, Louis XIV was able to produce and direct a machinery of government, still cumbersome and wasteful to be sure, yet generally workable and in its own way monumentally impressive.

The successes of Louis XIV derived more from certain aspects of his character than from his abilities. Although not of brilliant intelligence, he was deeply devoted to what he called *le métier du roi*—"the business of being a king." Few men have worked harder at the task, have attended so meticulously to its every detail, have surrounded themselves so completely with its pageantry and ceremonial or enjoyed their position so keenly. Even billiards, it is said, Louis played with a regal air. His grandeur of bearing has been contrasted unfavorably to the cheerful *bonhomie* of Henry of Navarre; the elaborate ritual of the court of Versailles has been said to owe more to the stiff ceremonial of imperial Spain (Louis had a Hapsburg wife and a Hapsburg mother) than to the native traditions of France. Yet Louis gave his name to an age and later was to command the admiration of so shrewd and intelligent an observer as Voltaire.

What kind of government did Louis give to France? The word "despotism," so often used to describe it, must be interpreted with caution. Since the close of the Wars of Religion the tendency in France certainly had been in the direction of a vigorous royal power. Louis regarded himself not so much as the steward of an estate as the inheritor of a patrimony which was his in full ownership to care for and make prosper. At the very beginning of his reign Louis asserted that he intended to take upon his shoulders the whole responsibility of government. What he did was to seek a guarantee of order where very easily there might have been chaos. In this light his distrust of the old nobility and his reliance upon men of moderate station are understandable. "It was not to my interest," Louis wrote in his *Memoirs*, "to take men of eminence for my ministers. I wanted before all things to let the public know, by the rank from which I chose them, that I had no intention of sharing power with them."

The complex mechanism of the French government included some survivals from feudal times. The great officers of the court, for example, still held their titles, but in actuality were little more than elegant ornaments. The Estates General, a feudal body which, like the English Parliament, might have risen to great power, was never summoned. Legislation and administration issued from the Royal Council. This, originally a body of feudal office-holders summoned to advise the king, had by the seventeenth century split into four main parts. The Council of State (*Conseil d'Etat*) concerned itself with great problems of state and with foreign affairs. The Council of Despatches (*Conseil des Dépêches*) dealt with internal affairs, sending out written instructions to royal officers in the provinces. The Council of Finances (*Conseil des Finances*) dealt with taxation and revenues. The Privy Council (*Conseil Privé*) was primarily a judicial committee acting in a vaguely defined way as a supreme court. Other lesser councils dealt with religion and commerce.

No one could claim that these councils worked efficiently. Since the king was theoretically if not actually present at their meetings, the decrees issuing from the councils began with the ancient formula, *De Par le Roy,* "By Order of the King." The Council of State usually met on Sundays and Mondays; on Tuesdays the Council of Finances sat. The Council of Despatches met only fortnightly, and the Privy Council, with a full membership of over one hundred, had to be subdivided into various committees in order to do its work. Louis never permitted his ministers to sit in any fixed order lest the suggestion of a "prime minister" should emerge. The privy councillors, usually presided over by the chancellor, wore flowing robes and sat on folding seats covered with black morocco. The royal armchair upholstered in red velvet was always present but usually empty. Symbolizing the king, it faced a long table which was covered with a cloth of purple velvet ornamented with golden lilies.

The princes of the blood could claim the right to be present at sessions of the Royal Council. Actually, the conduct of affairs fell more and more into the hands of the new type of official drawn from the middle class. These men, if holding titles at all, were members of the administrative nobility— the "nobility of the robe," as it was called in contrast to the older "nobility of blood" or to the "nobility of the sword." There were originally four secretaries of state, at first charged with the duty of overseeing different parts of France but later assuming in addition the duties of a particular department such as war, marine or foreign affairs. As the ministries developed more clearly the secretaries of state assumed the nature of experts answerable directly to the king. Of the various public officers, the Superintendent of Finances grew most noticeably in importance.[1]

In the provinces the intendants continued their efficient work and almost superseded the work of the more ancient officers, the provincial governors. Towns, whose liberties were supposedly guaranteed them by medieval charters, felt the royal hand. An ordinance of 1683 required mayors to submit all their accounts to the intendants who in future were to draft municipal budgets and to exercise close supervision over them. In various other ways local powers were reduced. Governors of frontier provinces were

1. The secretaries of state emerged only slowly from the status of minor officials. At Fontainebleau they were entitled to a daily ration of two loaves, a quart of wine, some game and some bacon. On fast days they received six carp from the royal fishponds and three pounds of butter.

limited in their right of raising troops. Assemblies of the clergy found their powers reduced, as did the local *Parlements* and the local Estates. These latter bodies, found in outlying parts of France such as Brittany, Artois and Provence, finally numbered fifteen. They were not elected legislatures but rather privileged bodies whose members often transmitted their rights to their heirs. They assisted in the work of administration, carried out royal orders and supervised taxes but were in no real sense a genuine check upon royal power.

Justice was a chaos of privilege and of overlapping jurisdictions. The king was "the fount of law." He could increase or mitigate penalties and in some cases grant pardons. Through his *lettres de cachet* he had the power of arbitrary imprisonment. The *Parlement* of Paris, a body of feudal origin with a full membership of about two hundred, had some of the duties of a supreme court, hearing cases on appeal. Members held office for life, and their seats were to all intents hereditary. The *Parlement* of Paris also had the duty of enregistering royal edicts upon its rolls. If these edicts seemed in conflict with historic precedents, the *Parlement* could employ the right of remonstrance and refuse to enregister them. Should it continue to defy specific orders from the king he could appear before the *Parlement* in a solemn ceremony known as a "Bed of Justice" (*Lit de Justice*). Seated in semi-oriental state upon a couch or divan, the king commanded that his orders be obeyed. To this there was no reply. The duties of the provincial *Parlements* corresponded on a lower level to those of the great court in Paris.[2]

Such was the royal monarchy of Louis XIV. That it was dominated by him to a remarkable degree is unquestionable, for his prestige was enormous and his powers to reward favorites and to remove those he disliked were ever-present. To justify Louis' position, the celebrated court preacher, Bossuet, Bishop of Meaux (1627–1704), enunciated a full-blown theory of divine right. Royal authority, he said in his *Politics Drawn From the Holy Scriptures,* is sacred; it is absolute; it is paternal; and it is in accordance with reason. "The royal throne is not the throne of a man, but the throne of God himself." Or, again: "The prince need render account of his acts to no one." Or, again: "As in God are united all perfection and every virtue, so all the power of all the individuals in a community is united in the person of the king."

While Louis did not hesitate to bask in the warm sunlight of Bossuet's adulation, it remained true that such a theory of royal power ran counter

2. Nine *Parlements* had come into existence between 1443 and 1633: Languedoc, Dauphiné, Guienne, Burgundy, Provence, Normandy, Brittany, Béarn and the Three Bishoprics (Metz, Toul and Verdun). Two were added under Louis XIV: Flanders and Franche-Comté. Lorraine was added in 1769.

to some of the ancient traditions of the French monarchy. Even in the absence of any written stipulations, certain historic limitations seem to have been operative. For one thing, the king could not abdicate. For another, he could not alter the succession, fixed by the Salic Law in the male line. He could not give away or sell any of the royal domain. He could not in theory initiate new taxes or interfere arbitrarily with the property rights of his subjects without the consent of the Estates. He could not change the customary private law regulating manorial rights and privileges. He could not, in a broad sense, alter the general framework of government through which he exercised his power.

On the other hand, from 1600 to 1789 a *tendency* towards absolutism developed. Louis' power of appointment and dismissal was unquestioned. At Versailles he surrounded himself with a horde of royal courtiers, idle, useless, often dissolute, all enjoying his favor and obsequious to his will. Theory and fact, we may say, diverged so that Louis XIV and his successors were more nearly absolute than tradition supposedly would allow. This conceded, it may still be well to employ caution in attaching the uncritical label of absolutism even to so powerfully inspired a government as that of Louis XIV.

Scores of lesser monarchs throughout Europe aped the pageantry of the Grand Monarch at Versailles. The French pattern of royalty thus contributed to the growth of a similar pattern at Berlin, Vienna, St. Petersburg, Madrid and in the tiny courts of obscure German princelings. In this way Louis may be said to have set his stamp not merely upon France but upon Europe.

■ COLBERT AND FRENCH MERCANTILISM

The economic life of seventeenth-century France well illustrated the workings of the authoritarian state. What has come to be called mercantilism implied that political power should be used in order to organize, control and develop all major aspects of economic life and that conversely the increase in national wealth should strengthen political power. Such careful organization, it is clear, would strengthen France for what the age regarded as the inevitable conflicts which had to be waged abroad. Mercantilism in this sense, then, was more than a domestic policy; it could be an invaluable contribution towards realizing the military and territorial ambitions of the dynasty. In essence it became an all-important element in the great struggle over the balance of power.

The name inescapably associated with the growth of French mercantilism is that of Jean-Baptiste Colbert (1619–1683). Of bourgeois origin, he began as a minor official during the early years of Louis XIV, rising soon by virtue of thrift and hard work. He came into prominence, quite typically, by pressing the trial and securing the imprisonment of Fouquet, the Superintendent of Finances who for years had misappropriated public funds. In 1667 a grateful Louis gave Colbert the new title of Controller-General of Finances. Other offices were soon added so that Colbert ultimately carried what would seem to be a crushing burden.[3]

Until his death in 1683 Colbert attempted the twofold task of pleasing Louis and at the same time putting French economic life into healthy working order. To please Louis, Colbert had to indulge the royal passion for splendor, to strengthen Louis' personal power and to find somehow the huge sums necessary for the king's foreign adventures. The history of the reign will show how far these exorbitant demands interfered with the economic program which Colbert envisaged.

Colbert was more of a practical man, aiming at results, than he was a theorist. His economic policies have been described as a sort of "offer" to France. Let Frenchmen cultivate the virtues of thrift and hard work; let the government provide France with a strong navy and merchant marine; let the country strive for self-sufficiency and give up any dependence on foreign manufactures; let the government rid France of obstructive internal tariffs; let it provide uniform currency, good roads and canals; let it establish new industries and if need be subsidize old enterprises. If all this or even a substantial part could be realized, then the government would rejoice in a full treasury, the whole economy would prosper and France would be prepared to compete successfully in what Colbert liked to call the *guerre d'argent* —the war of money. For Colbert shared the view held by most of his contemporaries that all nations were competing for a relatively fixed amount of wealth and that one nation could genuinely prosper only at the expense of another. At times the war of money might unhappily have to turn into a war of bullets; yet Colbert held that the victories won by peaceful means were infinitely preferable to those won by outright war.

In the realm of finances Colbert sought first to systematize governmental operations. Despite all that Sully and Richelieu had done, financial disorder was widespread. Securing regular statements of accounts from government creditors, he reduced the amount of overcharges and was able to lower the rate of interest which the government was committed to pay. Along with all this he worked for a regular system which would account for all receipts and expenditures.

3. His various responsibilities included the direction of the following: Finances, Commerce, Industry, Colonies, Navy, Public Works, Public Instruction, Fine Arts, Postal Service, Agriculture and Foreign Affairs (in part). It would be simpler to say that Colbert had authority over practically all departments save War.

A closely related problem was that of governmental income. The revenues which the crown drew from the royal domains were raised phenomenally; according to one account they grew from 80,000 *livres* in 1661 to 5,500,000 *livres* in 1682. The various traditional sources of taxation, however, were much harder to stimulate. With the *taille* (a direct property tax) he could do little, for the clergy and nobility who were generally exempt from it clung closely to their privileges. Perhaps only a third of the population, and that the poorest, contributed to the *taille*. The *gabelle,* or salt tax, varied greatly in the different provinces; although Colbert could not equalize its burden, he contrived to increase the total amounts taken in. The *aides,* or excise taxes on wine and tobacco, were in a confusion that defied remedy.

Customs duties at the frontier known as *traites,* were likewise very complex, for France was divided into various areas where different rules applied. Indirect taxes (customs, excises, salt tax) had this virtue, that they were paid by the privileged classes of society as well as the unprivileged. They were the source of a substantial revenue. Yet such taxes had to be paid at various frontiers within France and often at different rates. Colbert contrived to establish the "Five Great Farms," a large "free trade" area in the center of France where goods were at least free from internal tolls.[4] A second area of more recently acquired territory including Brittany, Provence, Franche Comté, Flanders and Artois, had no such internal free trade arrangements. The most recent acquisitions (Metz, Toul and Verdun, for example) in some cases still retained free trade privileges with foreign countries. Although Colbert attempted to bring order out of these complexities, he could hardly succeed. Certain new taxes, such as a stamp tax on legal documents or payments for being granted a noble title brought discontent and, on occasion, rioting.

Another realm of interest was that of agriculture. While Colbert always put this second to industry and trade, yet he sought to do what he could. Marshes were drained and some roads built. Horse-breeding was encouraged. Colbert, who always disliked to see so large an amount of land given over to vineyards (he was a teetotaller), encouraged the growth of flax, hemp and mulberries (this last as a basis for the silk industry). An Ordinance of the Forest (1669) sought to improve the stands of timber. On occasions decrees were issued forbidding the export of grain.

The heart of Colbert's program lay in the twin fields of industry and commerce. We find him encouraging a larger population by offering tax-relief to large families and by forbidding emigration. Industrial life he tried

4. The name Five Great Farms comes from the five great tax-farming concessions which handled the customs collections on the outer borders of this entire region.

to stimulate by various means. Sometimes, as in the case of the Gobelins tapestries, a royal workshop was actually set up. In other cases the government attempted to furnish subsidies, guarantee a domestic monopoly or prevent foreign competition. Strict rules were imposed on manufacture in order to maintain standards and prices. Thirty-two elaborate sets of regulations and over a hundred and fifty edicts were issued. The edict of 1671 for the cloth industry, for example, provided that if cloth of inferior quality was produced, samples should be labeled and fastened to a public post for all to see; if the offence was repeated, then the manufacturer himself should be temporarily fastened to the same post. By one means or another impressive advances were made in such industries as linens, tapestries, lace-making, glass-manufacture, woolens, sugar refineries, iron works, armaments, copper and lead mining.

Colbert's trade policies followed as a natural corollary to those concerning industry. The government, he believed, should use every device to stimulate exports and to reduce imports—hence his aim was to reduce internal tolls and to erect a high tariff wall around France. By building canals, most notably that linking the Seine and Loire (completed in 1692, after his death) and that linking the Atlantic and the Mediterranean (the *Canal des Deux Mers* of 1681), he hoped to make transport more efficient. The canal from Toulouse on the Garonne to the Mediterranean was 190 miles long and cut transportation charges by three-fourths. The moderate tariff of 1664 was stiffened in 1667 so as to exclude foreign goods almost completely.

Trade required shipping, and here France was far behind. Colbert's often-quoted statement that there were some 20,000 ships in the world's commerce, of which the Dutch had 16,000 and the French only 600, although exaggerated, nevertheless revealed a painful truth—that France was far behind her competitors. Efforts to remedy this could be seen at the time of the war of 1672 with the Dutch (one of the few wars of which Colbert approved). The navy grew from 20 ships in 1661 to 196 in 1671, and to 270 in 1677; it was eventually manned by some 50,000 sailors. Along with this growth were developed arsenals, dockyards and all the incidentals of a vigorous maritime life.

The list of Colbert's trading companies is impressive: the East and West India Companies of 1664, the Company of the North (for the Baltic trade) in 1669, the Company of the Levant in 1670 and the African Company in 1673. Although these were given monopolies or subsidies, unfortunately they were often hampered by over-elaborate regulations. Compared to their English and Dutch counterparts they scarcely prospered. Colonies were the logical sequel to trading activities, and here again, although Canada showed a modest growth and although Martinique and Guadeloupe had been purchased and settlements made in Santo Domingo and Louisiana, the results were far from spectacular. Colbert inherited from the age of Richelieu a colonial policy more impressive in theory than in practice. During the period which saw French Canada increase from 2,500 to 10,000 inhabitants the English colonies in North America grew from 10,000 to 100,000. Some of Colbert's most imposing colonial dreams never materialized. He thought in terms of a French occupancy of Egypt, of a canal at Suez and of French outposts dotting the Red Sea and the Indian Ocean. These were gains which France was unable to make but which nineteenth-century Britain subsequently exploited with brilliant success. Only in the West Indies, where a lucrative sugar industry was supplemented by the production of tobacco, indigo, cotton, fruits, coffee and chocolate, was there a really profitable commerce.

Some incidentals deserve notice. To regulate this elaborate pattern of economic life a simplification and standardization of legal codes was almost essential. Colbert sought to improve civil and criminal procedures; a code of commerce was set up in 1673, a marine code in 1681. Good in general intent, these codes helped to perpetuate a number of pernicious practices; it could be said, too, that Colbert showed more readiness to safeguard the rights of his royal master than to protect those of the average Frenchman.

France gave the world the word *bourgeoisie*. While Louis made available profitable careers for large numbers of the middle class in the ranks of officialdom, Colbert also made it possible for members of this same class to thrive in other ways. They could benefit from the profits of the endless loans and advances which the government sought. They could invest in new industries and import new luxury goods from overseas. This growth in economic activity made possible a golden age for the financier, the contractor and the speculator. The reign of Louis XIV thus presents something of a paradox in that during a period when royal power was most ostentatious, the bourgeois class, still denied any semblance of political rights, was able to make substantial economic advances.

In 1682, the year before Colbert died, Louis XIV installed his court in the magnificent but still far from completed palace of Versailles. Colbert had long been in rivalry with Louvois, the Minister of War, who encouraged Louis in his extravagant ventures at home and abroad. When death brought an end to the restraining influence of Colbert in 1683, Louis' foreign policy took on an even more reckless aspect so that the heavy burden of war played havoc with French finances. It may well be true that the great public servant had never correlated his ends with the means available, that his economic policies were more effective within France than abroad and that he could never genuinely convert his royal master to his views.

Colbert's "offer to France," though failing of complete acceptance, put new vigor into the country. He had been faced with evils, especially in the fiscal system, too deeply entrenched for him to remove. Yet his energies did much for France. "Without this vigor she could have never survived for three-quarters of a century the wars and extravagance of Louis XIV." [5]

■ CHURCH AND STATE UNDER LOUIS XIV

"God establishes kings as his ministers and reigns by them over his people." Thus wrote Bishop Bossuet for the instruction of Louis XIV's son, the Dauphin of France. Seeing that the Church likewise considered itself divinely ordained to carry out God's will upon earth, it becomes important to consider the relations between the two powers.

Over the years the government of France had reached a tolerably satisfactory working arrangement with the papacy. By the Concordat of Bologna the king had the right of "nomination" to French archbishoprics, bishoprics and abbacies, the pope had the right of "institution." To a very considerable degree this "Gallican" church managed its own affairs. Protestantism, meanwhile, had won a tolerated minority status which certainly brought no threat to the great Catholic majority. As the seventeenth century progressed, the founding of several new religious orders demonstrated the continued vitality of religious life. Figures such as St. Francis de Sales, the author of distinguished devotional works, and St. Vincent de Paul, whose lifelong concern was with the most wretched of mankind, bore witness to this new vigor.

Louis XIV never doubted his own authority in church matters. How strongly he was prepared to act was soon shown in a dispute over the *régale,* or the right of the monarch to enjoy the episcopal revenues of a bishopric while it stood vacant and to dispose at pleasure of all the benefices, or clerical posts, depending on it. In 1673 Louis asserted that this royal right, heretofore limited to the older bishoprics, would be applied throughout France. Despite papal protest and denunciation Louis nevertheless went his way, stoutly backed by Bishop Bossuet, and by the majority of the clergy.

In 1682 an assembly of the French church summoned by the king to meet at Meaux issued a famous Statement of Gallican Liberties embodying four points: (1) Sovereigns are not subject to the papacy in things temporal. (2) A general council is superior to the pope. (3) The pope cannot decide anything contrary to the rules and customs of the church in France (the "Gallican liberties"). (4) Papal judgments are not absolutely final until they have received the consent of the Church. These resolutions, passed by the clergy,

5. L. PACKARD, *The Commercial Revolution* (1945), p. 70.

were registered by the *Parlements* and accepted by the Sorbonne, the theological faculty of the University of Paris.

The pope immediately condemned the decrees, threatening Louis with "the vengeance of Heaven" and refusing to sanction the consecration of new French bishops who accepted them. In a number of years thirty bishoprics in France thus became vacant. Ultimately, when Louis was involved in war in 1693 and a new pope sat in Rome, a compromise of sorts was reached. The French bishops repudiated the four articles of 1682 and the pope agreed henceforth to sanction all royal nominations. In point of fact the actual practice of the French monarchy changed very little. "Gallicanism remained officially condemned in Rome, officially enforced in Paris. . . . And the two parties, contending with mellifluous acrimony, were officially on the best of terms." [6]

The Protestants, who at the opening of Louis XIV's reign numbered more than a million, created a much more troublesome problem. Richelieu's Edict of Alais (1629) had taken from them the very large degree of political independence which they had been granted by the Edict of Nantes. In a religious sense, however, they were still remarkably free. Among these Huguenots could be reckoned, moreover, outstanding industrialists and financiers as well as many of the most highly skilled and most prosperous craftsmen in France. The official attitude towards the Huguenots was one of steadily increasing hostility. For this there were two main explanations: one lay in the personal feelings of the monarch, himself a devout Catholic who assumed that in matters of religion he spoke with the same authority as he did in matters of politics; the other lay in the insistent pressure of the Roman Catholic Church. Louis' own attitude was doubtless influenced by personal considerations. He had come strongly under the influence of Madame de Maintenon, formerly governess to some of his illegitimate daughters, whom he secretly married in 1684 following the death of the queen. In 1679 Madame de Maintenon, an ardent Catholic had written as follows: "The king acknowledges his weakness and recognizes his faults. He is thinking seriously of the conversion of the heretics, and soon earnest efforts will be made to achieve it."

The general policy of the reign towards the Protestants was that of a "strict construction" of the Edict of Nantes: it was held that the Edict did not apply to lands (such as the Pays de Gex) acquired by France after 1598. Here the Protestants, even though in a majority, were denied the rights granted their co-religionists elsewhere in France. Severe pressure was steadily increased in various ways, for example a decree of 1681 ordered that Prot-

6. A. GUÉRARD, *The Life and Death of an Ideal* (1928), p. 189.

estant children at the age of seven be permitted to "decide" for themselves whether or not they wished to become Catholics. Other decrees undertook to debar Huguenots from the professions. Few Huguenots were appointed to public office. By various legal devices Protestant churches were closed, so that by 1684 some 570 out of an estimated 815 congregations were unable to assemble. The most ruthless of all devices was the employment of the *dragonnades,* a term given to the practice of quartering French dragoons and other soldiers in Protestant communities with the understanding that the troops, no matter how badly they behaved, would go unpunished. As a result emigrants began to cross the frontiers, and "conversions," whether real or feigned, took place in large numbers.

In these circumstances, and under the influence of his Jesuit confessor and of counsellors such as Louvois and Le Tellier, Louis proceeded to the ultimate step: in October, 1685, the Edict of Nantes was officially repealed. Protestant worship was entirely forbidden and the "temples" of the reformed faith were to be demolished; Protestant schools were closed; ministers were to quit the realm within fifteen days, leaving behind any of their children over seven; no other members of the reformed religion were to leave France under penalty of being sent to the galleys if caught.

The consequences of revoking the Edict were disastrous. Despite the ban on emigration and the promise that no Protestant would be molested if he remained quiet, a large movement of surreptitious emigration took place. One estimate puts the number of departures at 250,000; these were in large part skilled workmen whose talents henceforth were put to the service of England, the Netherlands, Switzerland, Brandenburg and even the Dutch colony at the Cape of Good Hope. France suffered, too, in a military sense, for there were substantial desertions from the army and navy. Internal disorders left a tragic stain on the last years of Louis XIV. A Protestant revolt in the mountainous Cevennes area in the center of France was put down (1702–1705) with great cruelty. The desperate struggle of these Camisards (so called because in default of other identifying uniform they fought with their shirts, *chemises,* hanging out) has become legendary. Louis' policy of religious intolerance no doubt contributed to the attitude of skepticism and criticism which grew vigorously among intellectuals in the last years of his reign. In few of the Great King's actions, it may be ventured, can so much harm and so little good be seen as in the revocation of Henry IV's generous Edict.

Another aspect of Louis XIV's religious policies involved what was known as Jansenism. This name was applied in France to an attitude or body of belief adopted by certain Catholic groups which was derived from the writings of Cornelius Jansen, Bishop of Ypres in the Spanish Netherlands.

In his three folio volumes, the *Augustinus* (1640), Jansen proclaimed certain doctrines which he professed to find originally in St. Augustine. Men could be saved only by the grace of God, which was given to some and denied others. Jansen, therefore, proposed a doctrine of election and predestination reminiscent of Calvin. Every devout Christian must experience a kind of inner conversion and should lead a life of holiness. Such Catholics, often called "the Puritans of the Roman Church," displayed an austere morality and an intimate personal piety.

Jansenism was associated with a famous foundation, the Abbey of Port Royal, outside Paris. Here a convent of nuns had been organized by Angelica Arnauld, a member of a distinguished French family. At the original headquarters of the nunnery, soon forsaken for a new location nearer Paris, a body of earnest men, some clerical and some lay, began to pursue a life of meditation and study. These were the famous "solitaries" or hermits of Port Royal; among them were Antoine Arnauld, brother of Angelica, who published a book arguing that frequent communion could not atone for an evil life, and Blaise Pascal (1623–1662), one of the most brilliant minds in France.

The Jansenists were soon in sharp conflict with the Jesuits who had come to occupy an important place at the court and in French religious life. The Jesuits were above all anxious to make converts and therefore not infrequently exposed themselves to the charge of leniency in the confessional. "The Jansenist thought the Jesuit too lax; the Jesuit thought the Jansenist too narrow. The one held that mankind would never be led up to the throne of God by a fierce and inhospitable virtue, the other that God would never accept a politic compact with vice. The one strove to make the way to heaven easy and accessible to the many; the other maintained that it must always be difficult and confined to the few." [7] As confessors and directors of conscience the Jesuits seemed often disposed to use extreme interpretations of a general rule so as to exonerate a sinner from almost any sin. "Casuistry" and "probabilism" were the names for these procedures of the confessional.

The controversy was sharpened by papal action. In 1653 the pope officially condemned five propositions contained in the *Augustinus;* the Jansenists neatly sidestepped the issue by questioning whether the propositions condemned could actually be found in the *Augustinus.* Their most eloquent defense, however, came from Pascal who mercilessly attacked the Jesuits in his *Provincial Letters* (1656) for their worldly attitude, their opportunism, their "casuistry" and their loose interpretation of ethical standards.

Louis XIV was hardly the one to be deeply influenced by elaborate theological arguments, but he had Jesuit confessors and he was concerned

7. FISHER, *A History of Europe,* p. 705.

over the maintenance of order and authority. Pascal's *Provincial Letters* were ordered burned by the common hangman. In 1656 the "solitaries" of Port Royal were dispersed; from 1664 to 1669 the nuns were put under interdict; and even though they returned for a time the interdict was later renewed. In 1710 the buildings of Port Royal were razed to the ground. Not even the dead were spared; their very tombstones were destroyed.

It would seem, then, that the French Jesuits had won a great victory, all the more so since in 1713 the papacy issued the famous bull, *Unigenitus,* denouncing one hundred and one Jansenist propositions as heretical. Nevertheless, the victory was far from complete. Jansenist allied with Gallican in protest against active papal interference in French affairs. The Jesuits, still powerful under Louis XIV, grew increasingly unpopular. Much later, in 1764, the Order was expelled from France. Jansenism, though officially condemned, had a powerful influence on important groups: upon literary figures such as Racine; upon some portions of the clergy; upon officials of the *Parlements;* and upon segments of the economically powerful middle class. It helped to mobilize certain forces which in the eighteenth century heard the appeal of conscience and began to educate a political opposition to the absolute monarchy.

Still another counter-current in the religious life of this age was Quietism. Stressing inner devotion and a life of contemplation, Quietism owed much to Miguel de Molinos (1640–1697), a Spanish priest living in Rome. The Catholic authorities officially looked askance at a doctrine which emphasized man's mystical union with God and minimized the importance of the external church. At the royal court Madame Guyon ardently advocated Quietist views, as did Fénelon, Archbishop of Cambrai and tutor to Louis' grandson. Encountering the opposition and criticisms of Louis XIV and Bossuet, Madame Guyon was ordered to a nunnery and Fénelon to reside quietly in his diocese.

In summary, the religious history of the reign shows the king's authoritarian tendencies in conflict with the industrious Huguenots, the devout Jansenists and the mystically inspired Quietists. In an external sense Louis was able to impose his will and maintain the order which he desired. Yet the Jansenists retained their hold over a devout segment of the French people and the forces of criticism which Louis had been unable to quell gathered strength and grew steadily throughout the eighteenth century.

■ FRANCE AND EUROPE

Two important treaty settlements had marked France's foreign successes during the minority of Louis XIV: the Peace of Westphalia with the Empire in 1648 and the Peace of the Pyrenees with Spain in 1659. By the former

France had secured the strategic advantages coming from the possession of Metz, Toul, Verdun, parts of Alsace and the Italian fortress of Pinerolo. By the latter France gained Artois, a few Flemish towns on the northeast border and the territory of Roussillon in the eastern Pyrenees. Maria Teresa, daughter of Philip IV of Spain, was to marry Louis XIV, renouncing with her marriage all claims to the Spanish inheritance and bringing with her instead a dowry of 500,000 crowns.

As Louis embarked upon his personal rule in 1661 he could congratulate himself upon a much strengthened frontier position and upon an at least temporary atmosphere of good relations with the Hapsburgs. In many respects it appeared that the work of Richelieu and Mazarin had brilliantly succeeded and that something approaching diplomatic stability had been achieved.[8] If so, it was not to last long. Colbert, who wished above all else to develop the economic life of France, was greatly averse to military adventures abroad. Thinking in terms of finances and trade, he urged his royal master to strengthen the state, carrying on, if necessary, the *guerre d'argent* against France's economic rivals abroad. Other advisers went much further in urging the employment of military means. In these matters, however, Louis was prepared to make his own decisions.

Louvois, who was Minister of War from 1666 to 1691, carried on the work of military reorganization begun by his father, Michel le Tellier. Great improvements were made in the system of recruiting, in the methods of training, in equipment and in provisioning while in the field. Weapons were modernized in various ways: the cumbersome pike was replaced by the bayonet fixed to the musket; the old musket fired by a match was replaced by the newer flintlock. Manuals of drill were rewritten. Hospitals were built for veterans. Officers, drawn from the noble class, found that they were no longer as privileged as before. The name of Louvois' inspector-general, Jean Martinet, has become synonymous with severe military discipline. Louvois raised the number of available troops to more than two hundred thousand—an enormous figure when compared to the armies of twenty or thirty thousand which his predecessors had put in the field.[9]

Under Vauban, an engineer of genius, French fortifications were transformed. In place of heavy stone structures, some of them medieval survivals, Vauban designed complicated earthworks and entrenchments some of which have lasted almost to our own day. Moreover, he worked out elaborate and

8. In 1660 Mazarin had helped to negotiate the Peace of Oliva, ending the war between Poland and Sweden and, among other provisions, ensuring to Brandenburg full sovereignty over East Prussia. In this way Brandenburg was strengthened as a counterweight to the Hapsburgs.
9. In the eighteenth century Montesquieu gave a rough estimate that a nation could support an army of one per cent of its population, as did Adam Smith.

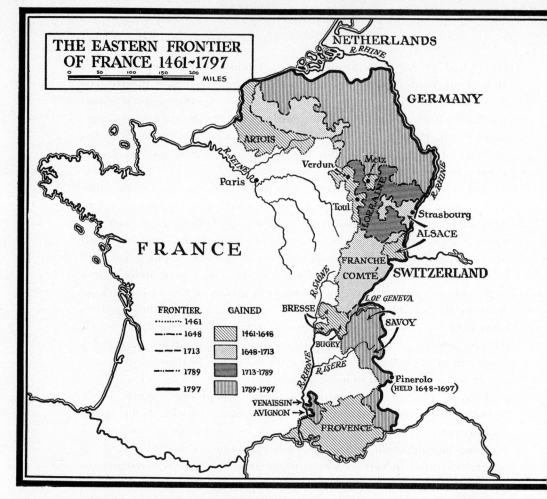

THE EASTERN FRONTIER
OF FRANCE 1461~1797

0   50   100   150   200
MILES

NETHERLANDS

R.RHINE

GERMANY

ARTOIS

Verdun   Metz

Paris

Toul   Strasbourg

ALSACE

FRANCE

FRANCHE
COMTÉ   SWITZERLAND

L. OF GENEVA

FRONTIER   GAINED   BRESSE   SAVOY
.... 1461
—·—·— 1648   ▨ 1461-1648
——— 1713   ▨ 1648-1713   BUGEY
—··—··— 1789   ▨ 1713-1789   R. ISERE
——— 1797   ▨ 1789-1797   Pinerolo
(HELD 1648~1697)

VENAISSIN→
AVIGNON→

PROVENCE

The map demonstrates what is often stressed as "continuity" in French foreign policy:
the advance toward the Rhine. Note that Revolutionary gains exceed those of Louis XIV.

almost mathematically precise engineering techniques for the reduction
and assault of enemy fortifications. Along the French frontier, town after
town was encircled by the new web of defences. Colbert, meanwhile, devoted
similar energies to the strengthening and transformation of the French
navy.[10] All this work of preparation so competently undertaken at home was
soon to be supplemented by the work of brilliant commanders in the field
such as Condé and Turenne.

In 1667 Louis suddenly launched a war against Spain for the seizure of
the Spanish Netherlands. His ostensible reason was that his father-in-law
had died in 1665 leaving Maria Teresa's dowry unpaid. Louis claimed that
the Netherlands "devolved" upon his wife, seeing that she was a daughter
by her father's first marriage and thus (by an old Brabant law dealing with

10. Colbert regarded these moves as a means to safeguard French commerce rather than
as a preliminary to aggressive war.

private property) had priority over the rights of a half-brother born of a second marriage. No discussion need be given to Louis' monstrous legal claim which in reality counted much less than other very practical considerations. French ministers had constantly warned of the dangerous nearness of the northeastern frontier to Paris and of the risk of invasion, as in the last stages of the Thirty Years' War. Hapsburg-Bourbon rivalry was still a fact and the tide of Louis' ambition in full flood.

The War of Devolution, as it was called, displayed the French military machine in brilliant operation. In three weeks Turenne had seized Charleroi, Tournai, Douai, Courtrai, Oudenarde and Lille. Then, with his ambitions mounting, Louis directed his troops southeastwards into Franche Comté, the old Burgundian area which denied him direct access to the Alsatian gains won at Westphalia. This successful move brought into existence a coalition of Protestant powers against France. England, the United Netherlands and Sweden were concerned at the threat to the European balance; consequently in 1668 they formed an alliance. Louis quickly decided to negotiate and in the same year signed the Treaty of Aix-la-Chapelle. Giving up Franche Comté, he was permitted to keep a chain of fortress towns along the northeastern frontier, among them Lille, Douai, Tournai, Armentières and Charleroi. Although the gains were not in themselves large, they were economically valuable and in addition they constituted a possible jumping-off point for further military adventures.

After a brief interval of four years Louis again plunged into war, this time against the United Netherlands. The Dutch were pillars of Protestantism; they were vigorous rivals in the *guerre d'argent;* they were republicans; and they had allied against Louis in 1668. This time Louis prepared the ground more thoroughly. Charles II of England was won over by substantial bribes, in return for which he promised by the secret Treaty of Dover to give Louis naval assistance in the projected war and, at a suitable moment, to introduce Roman Catholicism in England. Subsidies were also promised to Sweden where a change of government had taken place. The Elector of Cologne, who was also Bishop of Liège, was bribed by the French in order to let them advance along his territories in the Meuse Valley and thus attack the Dutch without actually crossing the soil of the Spanish Netherlands.

In 1672, accompanied by a galaxy of generals—Turenne, Vauban, Condé, Luxemburg and Louvois—Louis launched his triumphal advance northward. He commanded armies of some 172,000 men. Maestricht fell; the Rhine was crossed; Utrecht, Nimwegen, Zutphen and other famous Dutch towns were seized; Amsterdam itself was threatened. In July, 1672, the States General of the Netherlands recalled William of Orange (great-grandson of

William the Silent) and appointed him supreme commander.[11] Only by the desperate measure of flooding large stretches of land was Amsterdam kept from the French.

The outrageous terms which Louis announced as his basis for peace helped in the formation of another coalition against him. The alliance this time comprised Brandenburg, Lorraine, Denmark, Spain, the Palatinate and eventually the Holy Roman Empire. These powers were united in the fear of what Louis might do across the Rhine. "The scent of the lilies," it was written, "is growing too strong in Germany." The war broadened in scope so that the French were maintaining armies in Flanders, the Palatinate and Franche Comté. As the costs of war pressed more heavily upon France and as public opinion in England forced Charles II away from Louis and into alliance with Holland, France finally agreed to negotiate.

The Treaty of Nimwegen (1678) marked a further step in the French advance toward the Rhine. Louis' most important gain was Franche Comté. He also acquired a number of towns along the Flanders border, notably Ypres, Cambrai and Valenciennes. In point of territory, war had repaid Louis well; in other respects, notably in the costs involved and in the antagonism of a large part of Europe, he had paid dearly.

For the next decade Louis embarked upon a new policy recommended to him by his advisers. The Westphalian peace treaty had been notably vague in certain respects. France, for example, had been ceded some areas in Alsace "with their dependencies," but these had never been defined. Would it not now be possible to examine such doubtful areas to see if some could be "reunited" to France? Louis set up special courts known as "Chambers of Reunion" which sought confirmation of his claims by taking evidence and exploring musty records going back in some cases to the Middle Ages. As these special chambers were invariably French-dominated, it is not surprising that large areas were now adjudged to belong to France, among them some of the principal towns of the Saar Basin and the whole of Alsace including the great city of Strasbourg.

The countries which had allied against France either in 1668 or 1672 because of its military aggressiveness must have felt that it had now found a highly profitable alternative to war. Moreover, Louis' revocation of the Edict of Nantes in 1685 had caused a wave of indignation and alarm throughout Europe. After initial failures an alliance, The League of Augsburg (1686), was formed which included Spain, the Empire, the Netherlands, England, Sweden, Denmark, Bavaria, Brandenburg and Savoy.

---

11. In 1651 a republican party had wrested the hereditary headship of the state from the House of Orange and accepted the leadership of John De Witt. In 1672 De Witt was murdered.

The War of the League of Augsburg followed the pattern of its predecessors. Louis' generals won some brilliant victories; the Palatinate was ruthlessly devasted by the French in such fashion as to leave bitter memories even to the present day; nevertheless, France was forced eventually to the defensive.[12] This war, it may be noted, was the first European conflict which was to be fought as vigorously in the New World and in Asia as it was at home. France's real weakness lay in finances, for since the death of Colbert in 1683 there had been no actual successor to him. Dwindling resources, together with a succession of bad harvests, sharpened the demand for peace.

For the third time in twenty years negotiations were undertaken, with the Peace of Ryswick (1697) as the outcome. France kept Strasbourg and other Alsatian areas, otherwise she gained little; she was, indeed, required to return earlier conquests such as Charleroi, Courtrai, Pinerolo and Casale. Louis agreed to recognize William and Mary as legitimate rulers in England and to withdraw his support from the exiled James II. He was to make a favorable treaty of commerce with the Dutch who were to be permitted to garrison a chain of "barrier fortresses" in the Spanish Netherlands as a protection against the French. Louis thus was obliged to abandon some of his boldest designs, for he had encountered powers that together seemed capable of denying him the hegemony of Europe.

One spectacular way remained for Louis to recoup his fortunes. As the century drew near its close Charles II, the diseased and imbecilic King of Spain, was dying miserably without offspring. The vast Spanish inheritance would soon be in dispute, for several claimants were in the field.[13]

12. The ravaging of the Palatinate took place with appalling thoroughness. Town after town was razed, peasants were forbidden to plant crops within five leagues of the banks of the Moselle and the great castle at Heidelberg was blown up. "All the buildings at Mannheim," Louvois wrote, "are to be destroyed. Not one is to be left standing."
13. The following chart indicates the problem of the succession:

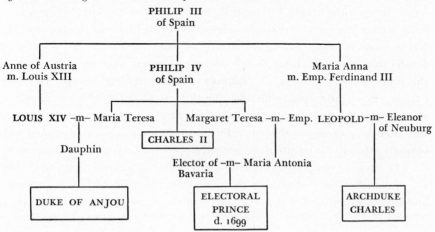

Charles II had two half-sisters, one of whom, Maria Teresa, had married Louis XIV of France; the other, Margaret Teresa, had married the Emperor Leopold (himself a grandson of Philip III of Spain). Maria Teresa's renunciation of the Spanish inheritance had been conditional on the payment of a dowry which in point of fact had never materialized, so that Louis could still conjure up some legal claim to the succession. The Emperor Leopold could assert his interest either on behalf of a son, the Archduke Charles, or a grandson, the Electoral Prince of Bavaria. It was a matter of national pride in Spain that the inheritance should be undivided, though there was no unanimity as to who the next ruler should be.

The whole problem was further complicated by the active interest taken by the major European powers. From their point of view it would clearly be better to insist upon partition than to see such widespread territories in the hands of one ruler, whether French or Austrian. The rivals of France feared, moreover, that if she were to add the great Spanish colonial areas to her own she could win a tremendous commercial advantage by excluding other powers from this trade monopoly. The issue, then, was of vital concern to countries such as England and the Netherlands from whose viewpoint partition was the only solution.

As early as 1668 Louis, foreseeing the problem, had agreed in general terms with the emperor as to the need for an eventual partition. As the years went by, however, this first arrangement no longer seemed to him realistic. In 1698 Louis signed a Partition Treaty with England and the Netherlands agreeing that on the death of Charles II the Dauphin of France should get Naples and Sicily, while the remainder of the inheritance should be divided between the two Austrian claimants. The solution was unacceptable to Spanish opinion and to the Emperor Leopold. It might, however, have been made to work with the backing of the powers, had not fate taken a hand: in 1699 the young Electoral Prince of Bavaria died of smallpox.

A second Partition Treaty was signed between England, France and the Netherlands in 1699, adding the Duchy of Milan to the earlier promise of Naples and Sicily for Louis XIV's grandson. Seeing that the remainder of the inheritance, including the Spanish crown, would go to the Archduke Charles, this would greatly increase the prestige of Austria. Spain, however, was regarded as a very weak state and France's position in Italy now would be very strong, so that most European opinion (save for Leopold who obtusely refused all compromise) seemed disposed to accept the arrangement.

The decisive step, ironically enough, was taken in Spain. A group led by the Archbishop of Toledo felt that the inheritance should be kept intact and that it would be better safeguarded in the hands of a Bourbon than in the hands of a Hapsburg prince. In a melodramatic scene the dying king was persuaded by some of his Spanish advisers to sign a will leaving all his possessions to the grandson of Louis XIV, on condition that the crowns of France and Spain should never be united.

It would seem that Louis now had it in his power to decide whether or not Europe would be plunged into war. To accept the inheritance would almost certainly mean sooner or later the creation of still another coalition. Nevertheless, there was at stake a glittering prize and he could count, as he had not been able to count before, on having Spain on his side. The decisive step was soon taken. Louis appeared in the great hall of mirrors at Versailles, his hand on the shoulder of his seventeen-year-old grandson. Here he made his historic announcement: "Messieurs, you behold the King of Spain."

Europe's first reactions were so slow that Louis seemed to have scored an easy victory. By certain rash acts, however, he aroused widespread opposition. Contrary to the terms of the will, he made it known that he did not consider his grandson, now Philip V of Spain, necessarily debarred from the French throne; he sent troops to expel the Dutch from their garrisons in the Spanish Netherlands; and, worst of all, on the death of the exiled James II of England he recognized his son, the Old Pretender, as the rightful king. Such acts did not remain unchallenged. Negotiations were undertaken at The Hague which resulted (September, 1701) in the Grand Alliance. England, the Netherlands, the Empire, Brandenburg, Hanover and later Portugal pledged themselves to oppose by force the vast ambitions of Louis XIV and to guarantee a partition of the Spanish possessions. France had the support of Spain, Bavaria and (for a time) Savoy.

The general conflict which followed holds a large place in the history of European warfare. It was not uncommon for generals to command armies of 100,000 men; during the war France alone had about 400,000 troops under arms. The costs, as it may well be imagined, were staggering. Warfare became more specialized, with better weapons, more mobile artillery and with "fusiliers," "bombardiers," "grenadiers" and "engineers" all undertaking their particular tasks. Campaigns were fought in the traditional areas of Flanders and northern Italy. Another area of conflict touched Bavaria, where at Blenheim, on the Danube, the Duke of Marlborough won one of his greatest victories, saving Vienna and forcing the French to the defensive. Efforts were made by the allies to invade Spain and France. Naval battles were fought in the Mediterranean, off the coasts of North and South America and in the West Indies. In 1704 the British seized Gibraltar, a strongpoint of incalculable value which they have never since relinquished.

Despite the brilliant campaigns of the Duke of Marlborough in the Low Countries, signalized by the victories of Ramillies, Oudenarde and Malplaquet, and the campaigns of the imperial commander, Prince Eugene, in Italy, no decisive military conclusion could be reached. Moreover, when the Archduke Charles unexpectedly won the imperial crown in 1711, there seemed little point in pushing his claims to the Spanish throne. Even before this, some preliminary negotiations for peace had been undertaken. These were carried on until 1713 when the Peace of Utrecht was finally concluded.[14]

The principal terms of the Treaties of Utrecht and Rastadt can be grouped together as follows:

(1) Philip of Anjou, grandson of Louis XIV, was recognized as Philip V of Spain and the Indies (a title actually held since 1701) on condition that the crowns of Spain and France should never be united.

(2) The Austrian Hapsburgs were to be compensated by obtaining the Spanish Netherlands, Luxemburg, Milan, Naples and the Island of Sardinia.

(3) England won Newfoundland, Nova Scotia and the Hudson's Bay Territory from France and Gibraltar and Minorca from Spain. She also was granted the *Asiento,* or favorable trading privileges with the Spanish Indies.

(4) France was recognized in possession of Strasbourg and Alsace. She had to renounce possession of territory on the right bank of the Rhine and some Flemish towns. She was to recognize Queen Anne of England, expel the "Old Pretender" and destroy the fortifications at Dunkirk which England regarded as a threat.

(5) The Dutch were allowed to maintain their barrier fortresses against France in the Austrian Netherlands.

(6) The Elector of Brandenburg was recognized as King of Prussia.

(7) The Duke of Savoy likewise was recognized as king. He obtained Sicily (which in 1720 he exchanged with Austria for Sardinia).

This great settlement attempted to give definition to Europe's frontiers on a scale even larger than that achieved at Westphalia in 1648. In essence it maintained the principle of partition that had been declared acceptable before Louis XIV moved to secure the entire Spanish inheritance for his grandson. In very simple terms it could be said that every major power made some gains though there were, to be sure, counteracting losses.

In the case of France, although Louis' efforts to dominate Europe had been thwarted, yet if one surveys his entire reign he can be seen to have won much.[15] The Bourbon dynasty on the Spanish throne was to maintain a close "family" connection with France throughout the eighteenth century. The French frontier had been notably advanced in Flanders, Alsace,

14. It was really a bundle of separate treaties, supplemented in 1714 by the Treaty of Rastadt between France and the Empire.
15. See map, p. 342.

Franche Comté and Roussillon. Yet Louis had lost important overseas territories, he had made the name of France suspect abroad and had imposed crushing burdens on a country already suffering from his domestic extravagances. His "policy of excess" had permanently tarnished the glory of the Grand Monarch.

Austria's acquisition of the Spanish Netherlands brought new diplomatic complexities to that troubled area. Her Italian gains threw the unwelcome shadow of Hapsburg power over the peninsula for well over a century. England's new overseas territories along with Gibraltar and Minorca in the Mediterranean underlined her steadily growing leadership in the maritime and colonial sphere. The rise of Brandenburg-Prussia to the dignity of a kingdom marked a further challenge to the Hapsburgs. Essentially, then, a new balance of power, quite unlike anything Louis XIV had intended, marked the close of his long reign.

■ THE GREAT AGE

Writing in the eighteenth century, Voltaire distinguished four great ages in the world's history: the age of Periclean Athens, the Roman age of Caesar and Augustus, Renaissance Italy and the age of Louis XIV. "Of these," happily declared Voltaire, "the last is perhaps the age which most nearly approached perfection."

While Louis XIV was engaged in the War of the League of Augsburg, a Frenchman, Charles Perrault, published a poem with the title, *Parallel of the Ancients and the Moderns.* In it he argued for the doctrine of progress. Seeing that his own times had benefited by the knowledge of all that had gone before, they would obviously outstrip the past. "Our age," Perrault wrote, "has in some sort arrived at the summit of perfection. And since for some years the rate of progress is much slower and appears almost insensible . . . it is pleasant to think that probably there are not many things for which we need to envy future generations." This fantastic complacency, which set off a long debate, may serve to introduce a discussion of the "Great Age" of Louis XIV.

Although not himself endowed with talent in the arts, Louis was pleased to be their patron and sponsor. Eminent critics have called the seventeenth century the greatest of France's literary centuries, and with some reason, for seldom has so splendid a galaxy of talent presented itself in a limited and well-defined period. Even as one can attach a conventional meaning to the phrase, "Renaissance painting" or "Baroque sculpture," so the term, "Classical Age," is appropriately applied to the pattern of French culture in this second half of the seventeenth century.

The prevailing spirit in the arts could be defined as an acceptance of certain principles of order, discipline, balance and good taste. These had found their first great expression in ancient Greece and Rome; consequently it was upon the creations of this world that modern standards of excellence should be based. The critic, Nicolas Boileau (1636–1711), enunciated in his famous *Poetic Art* (1674) general rules for the language of poetry, following them with specific discussion of the pastoral, the elegy, the ode, the epigram, the satire, tragic poetry and the epic. He urged the study of nature, to be sure, but it was to be a nature which excluded the imagination and which should be approached with logic and a sense of discipline on the model of ancients such as Horace. Such was the creed of this "draftsman of the poetical statutes of the seventeenth century."

Certain externals of this age can easily be grasped. Royal patronage for the arts was generously provided. Colbert, doubtless with the attitude of the practical man, saw the advantage of mobilizing artistic talent for such enterprises as the state manufacture of porcelains and tapestries. Doubtless, too, advantage would come from encouraging less practical aspects of the arts and sciences. At all events he gave blessing and encouragement to a surprising number of royal academies: the Academy of Inscriptions and Belles Lettres (1663); the Academy of Science (1666); the Academy of Painting and Sculpture (1664); the French Academy in Rome (1666); the Academy of Architecture (1671); the Academy of Music (1672). Another practical type of encouragement came from the endless commissions issued by Louis and his court to painters, sculptors, architects, playwrights and musicians.

Of all the illustrations that could be given, perhaps the building of Versailles will best exemplify the merits and defects of Louis' association with the arts. First begun in 1662 on the swampy site of a hunting lodge that had caught the royal fancy, the project was sufficiently advanced by 1682 that Louis could move in with his court. Nevertheless, 36,000 men were still at work and the chapel, the last major undertaking, was not completed until 1710. To J. H. Mansart, who followed Louis Levau as architect, Versailles owes its main features. The grandiose plan (the garden façade measures a quarter of a mile), a culmination of the Baroque style, gave perfect expression to the elaborate etiquette, ceremonial and formality of the court of Louis XIV.

André Le Nôtre, the great master of landscape design, laid out the twenty thousand acres of gardens, avenues, woods, lakes and fountains. The clipped hedges, the formal walks, the mathematically proportioned canals and pools suggested that nature itself submitted to the will of the great king: "Everything harmoniously arranged; white statuary and dark groups of trees, marble vases and flower-beds, green bronzes and yellow porphyry, the slender jets of fountains and the calm surface of pools, the regular or *baroque* figures of the ornamental waters; in general, a complete subordination of the parts to the whole."[16] What Le Nôtre did for the exterior, Charles Le Brun did within, outlining heroic paintings, sketching designs for the walls and determining details of fittings for the various chambers.

At times the line is impossible to draw between art and ostentation. The flooring of the main rooms was originally of marble, and the furniture in the state apartments—tables, chairs, cabinets and balustrades—of solid silver. On gala occasions orange trees bloomed in carved silver tubs. Four thousand wax candles lit the Hall of Mirrors in which hung sixteen silver and twelve crystal chandeliers. The windows were hung with white damask embroidered in gold. The upholsteries changed with the seasons: green and flame-colored velvets for the winter; gold, silver and flowered brocades for the summer.

One should not forget the other side of the picture. In 1678 an epidemic made it necessary for cartloads of dead to be carried away nightly from the sheds where the workmen were housed. Most of the attendant nobles lived in cramped and chilly apartments where one could hardly stand upright. Plumbing was unknown. Eventually the marble floors had to be replaced with hardwood when water seeping through caused the supporting beams to rot. In the harsh winter of 1695 wine froze in the glasses on the king's table. Costs finally proved to be so far beyond the royal purse that in 1690 Louis had to send nearly two thousand pieces of his silver furniture to the mint to be melted down.

Painting and sculpture, like architecture, reflected the spirit of the Classical Age. Along with Poussin, Lorrain and Champaigne, already mentioned as exponents of the Baroque style, Henri Rigaud is remembered for his characteristically pompous portraits of Louis XIV. Charles Le Brun achieved distinction less for his own work than for his planning and supervision at Versailles where the elaborately ornamented walls and ceilings and the grandiose battle-paintings look down upon the beholder. As for sculpture, it was not considered incongruous to represent Louis in the dress and armor of a Roman emperor, the whole crowned with an exceedingly French periwig.

Music likewise gave adornment to the age. To the court ballets and masquerades which were so popular under Louis XIII, Mazarin had added opera in the Italian style. Lully, a Florentine, was made superintendent of the king's music. A versatile composer, he created thirteen "lyrical tragedies" in addition to cantatas, dances, ballets and some incidental music for the plays of his friend, Molière.

16. J. BOULENGER, *The Seventeenth Century* (n.d.), p. 366.

The literature of this Classical Age can be described as its greatest glory. Deriving in considerable part from sources which owed little to royal patronage, it was essentially a continuation of the great literary tradition of an earlier France. Under Louis XIV it developed a new character, rose to new heights and expressed itself in an extraordinary variety of forms.

The drama in particular was unsurpassed. The *Cid* of Pierre Corneille (1606–1684), appearing in 1637, created a sensation with its dazzling portrayal of the great Spanish hero. It could be taken as an illustration of the influence of the Spanish tradition in French literature. Later Corneille turned to classical subjects such as *Cinna* or *Horace,* adapting himself to the formal conventions of the classical drama and continuing to portray in heroic terms man's struggle against the blows of fate.

The great master of the French classical drama was Jean Racine (1639–1699). Adopting the unities of time, place and action, Racine produced a brilliant series of plays of which the classically inspired *Andromaque* and *Iphigénie* and the biblically inspired *Athalie* and *Esther* may be given as examples. Racine's faultless diction and carefully polished style make him unique. In his analysis of motives he sought to embody in each character one ruling passion such as honor, love or jealousy. Described as "generalized art from which the local, the temporal, the particular are almost excluded," his work was admirably suited to its age.

In Molière (1622–1673), a bourgeois who knew well the types whom he satirized so skilfully, France found one of its very greatest artists. Molière wrote a long series of comedies which portrayed devastatingly but not unkindly the miser, the would-be gentleman, the hypocritical priest, the ignorant doctor, the arrogant courtier, the bluestocking and scores of other types. Underneath his satire and humor Molière was always the moralist, seriously concerned to teach. His greatness lay in his capacity to conceal the art with which his utterly human characters were depicted.

Other great names reflect the versatile interests of the age. The *Letters* of Madame de Sévigné (1626–1696) are a classic example of the cultivated epistolary style of a great lady. The brilliant *Memoirs* of the Duke of St. Simon (1675–1755), bitterly critical of the court of Louis XIV, are a monument of another type. One should mention, too, the shrewdly critical *Maxims* of La Rochefoucauld (1613–1680) and the skilfully interpreted *Characters* of the essayist La Bruyère (1645–1696). The two sentences in which this latter etches a portrait of the French peasant remain as one of the most poignant of all descriptions of man's inhumanity to man:

> One sees certain sullen animals, male and female, scattered about the country, dark, livid, scorched by the sun, attached to the earth they dig up and turn over with invincible persistence; they have a kind of articulate speech, and

when they rise to their feet, they show a human face, and, indeed, they are man. At night they retire to dens, where they live on black bread, water, and roots; they save others the toil of sowing, ploughing, and garnering in order to live, and thus deserve not to lack the bread they have sown.

The eminent critic, Emile Faguet, has described the *Fables* of Jean de la Fontaine (1621–1695) as perhaps the masterpiece of all French literature. These deceptively simple poetic tales of animals in the tradition of Aesop are in reality exquisitely wrought works of art, each one using some well-known plot to comment upon the weakness and foibles of man. Their unfailing charm consists perhaps in the perfect adaptation of form to the purpose which the author has in mind.

The Classical Age saw the French language take its modern shape. Richelieu's foundation, the French Academy, had undertaken to sponsor a dictionary of the French language with the intention of establishing acceptable standards of usage and good taste. Begun in 1639, this work was completed in 1694. More than academies, however, writers may claim to establish tradition and a literary style, so that one may well attach more importance to the great authors of this age than to the rulings of the academicians in making the French language what it is.

This rich culture was essentially aristocratic, the prerogative of the court and the drawing-rooms of the nobly born. Early in the century the Marquise de Rambouillet (1588–1665) had established her famous *salon* in Paris, an elegant and witty place of meeting where the world of fashion could exchange ideas with the world of art and letters. It gave a particular importance to the intellectual role of women whose foibles Molière so shrewdly satirized. Later in the century the overwhelming prestige of the court at Versailles made it hard for the tradition of the *salon* to flourish. It was, however, never wholly lost, and this characteristically French combination of fashion and intellect continued into the eighteenth century where it was to have profound effects.

One further aspect of this age must be noted, the somewhat unexpected growth of a vigorous and independent spirit of criticism inspired, one may feel sure, by some of the policies of Louis and his court. Huguenot refugees such as Pierre Jurieu not unnaturally carried on a relentless war of words against the king who had expelled them. La Bruyère, as we have seen, embodied in his *Characters* a powerful message of social criticism. Fénelon (1651–1715), tutor to the royal family, as well as being a pioneer of the eighteenth-century cult of sentiment was a bitter critic of Louis' wars. His *Examination of Conscience on the Duties of Royalty* (1692) was so censorious of Louis that the authenticity of the work was at first doubted. The versatile Abbé de St. Pierre, eager like Fénelon to end the European curse of war, wrote his *Project of Perpetual Peace* in 1712, although it was not published until 1717. The *Project,* much more carefully worked out than the Great Design of Sully, proposed the setting up of an international machinery which in many respects was a striking anticipation of that provided by the Covenant of the League of Nations.

Challenging ideas appeared in other fields. Pierre Bayle (1647–1706) published his *Critical Dictionary* in 1696–1697. He was willing to take little on authority, least of all the ideas of conventional religion. The *Critical History of the Old Testament* (1678) of Richard Simon (1638–1712) insisted that the Bible be subjected to the same critical investigation that one would give to any other book. Bernard Fontenelle (1657–1757) attacked oracles and mysteries in his *History of Oracles* (1686); in his *Conversations on the Plurality of Worlds* (1686) he described with great charm and for popular consumption a celestial system in which the various moons spun around their planets and the planets revolved in regular orbits around the sun. Other elements of criticism, such as Pascal's famous attack on the Jesuits, will come to mind. By the close of the century, moreover, the new political and philosophical ideas of the Englishman, John Locke, were likewise beginning to find acceptance in France. These complex developments suggest a considerable ferment beneath the relatively calm surface of the Great Age.

Classicism, in the eloquent metaphor of Paul Hazard, created for a brief while in France the illusion that man could at last halt in his forward march and observe around him a European landscape so perfectly proportioned and so magnificently wrought that it would be impossible for it ever to be surpassed. As the eighteenth century, the heir of the seventeenth, was to show, the illusion was only momentary.

THE "TOBACCO PARLIAMENT" OF FREDERICK WILLIAM I OF PRUSSIA.
An unknown artist depicts King Frederick William, father of
Frederick the Great, with his cronies. The king sits at the head
of the table, his companions occupy benches, and the crown
prince remains reluctantly at his father's side. The Hohenzollern
Museum, Berlin. Steinkopf Photo.

Chapter 14

Monarchy in Central Europe

■ THE SETTING AND THE PROBLEM

THE COMPLEX WORLD of central Europe presented problems very different
from those of the west. In France, Louis XIV built up the structure of his
despotism within the limits of a country already possessing a substantial
degree of political and cultural unity. He could profit, too, from the work

355

of his able predecessors. In England, as we have seen, the great parliamentary advances were made in a uniquely favorable setting.

Europe east of the Rhine, on the other hand, was a land of confusions and contrasts. In a geographic sense it comprised several worlds rather than one. The House of Hohenzollern pursued its destinies very largely in the northern plain, in territories which lacked natural defenses or boundaries and which were broken by a series of rivers. The interests of the ruling house extended all the way from the Rhine to the Vistula. The House of Hapsburg, similarly, held sway in the mountain-girt quadrilateral of Bohemia, in the uplands of Austria, in part of the great Hungarian plain, and in the mountains stretching southwards to the Adriatic. These diverse lands lacked any sense of political unity, any common language, any common tradition, any consistent level of culture. Large parts had fallen under the alien sway of the Turk.

Despite all obstacles, the House of Hapsburg and the House of Hohenzollern brought order to these lands. Their work not infrequently receives less than full justice because of the attention given to the better known and perhaps more spectacular developments of the west. Yet the Hapsburgs freed large parts of Europe from Turkish control and set up an effective rule that lasted for more than two hundred years. The Hohenzollerns by some strange alchemy were able to transform their scattered, unpromising domains into one of the most efficiently administered and militarily most powerful states in Europe. One will look in vain, to be sure, for the intellectual brilliance and artistic triumphs of the Great Age of Louis XIV. One will not find the winds of political freedom beginning to blow as they were in England. Yet in these lands, where the art of public administration was slowly being turned into the science of "cameralism," where Prussian military efficiency rose to new heights and where, late in the eighteenth century, an Austrian emperor was to seek the establishment of uniform justice, equitable taxation and elementary education for all, developments can be found which deserve to be set beside the more familiar achievements of the west.

■ THE TERRITORIAL EXPANSION OF THE HAPSBURG MONARCHY

A survey of the fortunes of the Austrian Hapsburgs in the seventeenth and early eighteenth centuries will reinforce the point that the truly significant developments in Europe's history were not to be found exclusively in its western areas. The problems of the ruling house were complicated because much more than politics was involved. Austria's fortunes over widely different areas were bound up with questions of economics, of religion and of conflicting cultures. One may reduce the confusion somewhat by recalling that the House of Hapsburg ruled in two capacities. In one the Hapsburgs were emperors of the Holy Roman Empire; in the other they held the headship of the Hapsburg family lands, acquired over the centuries by marriage, inheritance and conquest. Most, but not all of the Hapsburg family lands lay within the frontiers of the Holy Roman Empire. Some brought Austria into close rivalry with its historic rival, France. It is important, consequently, to look at the Hapsburg situation both from the imperial viewpoint and from that of the family lands.

The Austrian monarchy enjoyed the mixed blessings of advancing age. First elected to the emperorship in 1273, the Hapsburgs had contrived ever since 1438 to make that title almost automatically theirs. By the seventeenth century, and more especially by the close of the Thirty Years' War, the imperial crown remained a dignity but hardly a power. The imperial boundary line, enclosing the Spanish Netherlands, touched the frontiers of France well west of the Rhine, skirted the northern border of Switzerland (which had received its final independence in 1648), dipped down to the Adriatic near Trieste, then turned northeast to follow the western border of Poland to the Baltic. The area thus delimited corresponded roughly to what we would think of as Germany, Belgium and Austria. Some three hundred states, large and small, lay within this sprawling central-European area, but of effective political power the emperors had practically none. Since 1648 all members had been guaranteed "sovereign" rights. Since 1663 the Diet of the Empire sat in permanence, instead of periodically, at Ratisbon—a somnolent, utterly ineffective gathering of princely and urban ambassadors. Cases in the imperial courts dragged on interminably, on occasion for more than a hundred years. Still able at times to conjure up something of the glamor associated with its ancient traditions (Goethe as a boy in the imperial city of Frankfort was awed by the evidences of past Hapsburg splendor), the Empire existed until 1806 when Napoleon, mistrustful of history and intolerant of all inefficiency, rudely destroyed it.

The continuing prestige of the Hapsburgs in the seventeenth century came both from the extent of their family lands and from their widespread dynastic connections. In the sixteenth century Charles V, it will be recalled, had ruled both the Empire and Spain. On his abdication his huge territories had been divided between his brother and his son. They had never been reunited. Yet the Hapsburgs at Vienna were always conscious of the link with Madrid, and never more so than when Louis XIV through his grandson sought to intrude himself into the Spanish succession.

In the seventeenth century the main parts of the Hapsburg family lands lay clustered along the huge basin of the Danube River, extending from the mountains of South Germany to the great plain of Hungary. The map will

The importance of the Danube and of the mountain barriers around the Hungarian plain is clear. Note the small part of Hungary in Hapsburg hands in the 16th century. Trieste gives Austria a useful port on the Adriatic. The successive dates of reconquest indicate the steady Hapsburg advance down the Danube.

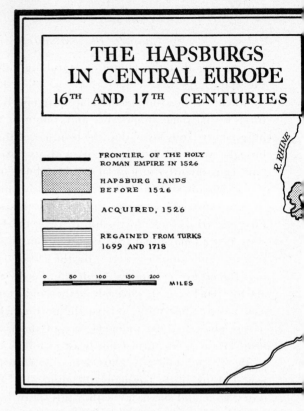

THE HAPSBURGS IN CENTRAL EUROPE
16TH AND 17TH CENTURIES

FRONTIER OF THE HOLY ROMAN EMPIRE IN 1526

HAPSBURG LANDS BEFORE 1526

ACQUIRED, 1526

REGAINED FROM TURKS 1699 AND 1718

R. RHINE

0   50   100   150   200
MILES

show a series of mountain ranges which roughly delimited this whole area: at the northwestern extremity were the various ranges enfolding Bohemia, then the various eastern ranges of the Alps, the complex Balkan massif to the south and finally the Carpathian and the Transylvanian Alps on the farther side of the Hungarian plain.[1] To this whole area, more than half of which lay outside the imperial frontier, the name "Danubia" can appropriately be given. The Hapsburg interest in "Danubia" to some extent offset their declining power, so evident after 1648, within the Empire itself.

A vast complex of peoples and tongues lay under Hapsburg rule. A first administrative area was that of the "Old Dominions" centering around Vienna and Austria proper. These, which included the Tyrol, Styria, Carinthia and Carniola, were preponderantly German. A second division comprised the "Lands of the Bohemian Crown," which in 1627 had been declared hereditary in the Hapsburg line. Of these, Bohemia and Moravia were peopled by "Western Slavs"; another dependency, the fertile valley of Silesia, was largely German. Since 1627 a ruthless policy of repression had created a Teutonic preponderance in Bohemia, replacing Protestantism by Catholicism as the official faith and going far towards suppressing the Czech language. Much later Bismarck was to remark that the control of this Bohemian bastion meant the domination of Europe. A third division com-

1. See map above.
358

prised the ancient kingdom of Hungary, where the elective crown had fallen
to the Hapsburgs at the time of the first Ottoman conquest of 1526. Only a
fragment of the original Hungarian kingdom remained free of Turkish
control. Its southern parts had a substantial Croatian minority, its northern
a substantial Slovak minority. The principality of Transylvania, a Ru-
manian-speaking area once part of the Hungarian kingdom, now lay almost
completely under the rule of the Turks.

In an international sense, the Hapsburgs were menaced on two sides.
In the early sixteenth century the Danubian area had been subject to the
tremendous Ottoman advance from the southeast which had enabled the
Turks to occupy Transylvania and the greater part of Hungary. At the
same time a rivalry in the west between the French and Austrian houses,
originating far back in the Italian Wars, had proved to be fundamental and
persistent. This rivalry was evident in the policies of Henry IV, Richelieu
and Mazarin. It was displayed in an acute form under Louis XIV who,
whether pressing into the Spanish Netherlands, the Palatinate, Franche
Comté, northern Italy or Spain itself, demonstrated an unswerving hostility
to the Hapsburgs. The challenges directed against them from east and west
were not necessarily uncoordinated, for, if the occasion required it, Louis
was perfectly willing to stir up revolt amongst the Hungarians or even to
ally himself with the Turks.

359

In mid-seventeenth century such a situation presented a threefold problem to the Hapsburgs. First, could they cope with a new wave of Turkish aggression and in so doing regain the territories lost during the sixteenth century? Secondly, could they do their share in curbing the grandiose ambitions of Louis XIV in the west? Thirdly, could they at the same time make sorely needed improvements in the government of their scattered and widely different realms? Success, of course, is relative, yet in all three respects the Hapsburgs scored impressive victories.

Leopold I, whose reign from 1658 to 1705 paralleled very closely that of Louis XIV, left no such great impression either on his own or succeeding times as did the Sun King. Yet he had his own not inconsiderable claims to greatness, while his military commander, the renowned Prince Eugene of Savoy, won for himself a dazzling European fame.[2] Leopold was quick to realize that with the declining prestige of the Holy Roman Empire he must base his policies upon the regaining of lost territory and the wise administration of the family lands.

The Turkish question pressed in upon Leopold from the beginning of his reign. The lethargic Ottoman Empire, in general decline ever since the Battle of Lepanto (1571), took on a new vitality when about mid-seventeenth century the energetic Albanian family of Kuprili succeeded in winning the office of grand vizier. Taking advantage of local unrest in Hungary and Transylvania, Mohammed Kuprili sent in Turkish armies which seemed invincible until aid from Western Europe was mobilized against them. Then the Turkish advance was halted and in 1664 the Peace of Vasvar established the Twenty Years' Truce between Hapsburg and Ottoman.

Leopold now undertook a mild policy towards that long narrow strip of Hungarian territory, the poor remnant of the proud kingdom of which his house had assumed the crown in 1526. His task was not easy, for Protestantism, which had taken considerable hold upon the Hungarian nobility, had survived the efforts of the Counter-Reformation to suppress it. Leopold now agreed to rule with the aid of a Hungarian council and to guarantee religious freedom. Unrest nevertheless continued, for it was an undeniable fact that in many respects the Moslems had proven themselves more tolerant overlords in their part of Hungary than the Christians in theirs. Some dissident nobles, consequently, were willing to seek Turkish aid. Far in the west,

2. Prince Eugene offers the supreme example of the extraordinary military career possible to a nobleman of the age. Born at Paris, the fifth son of a Prince of Savoy, he was refused a commission in the French army by Louis XIV. Hence he entered the service of the Emperor Leopold and fought for him for over fifty years. He campaigned in Italy, Bavaria and Flanders but his greatest victories and his greatest fame were won against the Turks, most notably at the siege of Belgrade (1717) where he was wounded for the thirteenth time. To have served under the great Prince Eugene, "whose only passion was glory," was the boast of soldiers all over Europe.

meanwhile, Louis XIV was alternately probing and hammering at the imperial frontiers.

In 1683 the Turks renewed the war with 250,000 men. One of the greatest armies that Europe had ever witnessed overran what was left of Hungary and then surged up the Danube to the very walls of Vienna.[3] The city, desperately resisting the assault, was saved only by the timely intervention of the Polish king, John Sobieski, who, ignoring the blandishments of the French, led his troops triumphantly against the Turks. The papacy then gave its blessing to the formation of a new anti-Turk Holy League comprising the Empire, Poland, Venice and Muscovy. Out of this alliance came success, for by the end of the century the Turks were expelled from the remaining lands which they had long held. The Hapsburgs won back Hungary and Transylvania; Venice gained lands along the Adriatic and in Greece; and Poland gained the area of Podolia and part of the Ukraine. Russia, by winning the port of Azov, came within striking distance of the Black Sea.[4]

The Peace of Carlowitz (1699), which confirmed these gains for Austria, can properly be regarded, therefore, as a great landmark in the political evolution of eastern Europe. By surrendering Hungary and Transylvania which it had held for a hundred and fifty years Turkey was pushed back to the line from which its great advance began. This line, running east and west along the lower Danube and its tributary, the Save, and leaving the great fortress of Belgrade as a Turkish outpost, was to mark the southern boundary of the Hapsburg state until our own day.[5] The brilliantly successful campaigns of Prince Eugene furnish proof of the important role of the soldier in history. In subsequent campaigns the Hapsburg armies led by Prince Eugene made still further territorial gains, and for a time held the fortress of Belgrade, but ultimately the Peace of Belgrade in 1739 confirmed the earlier line of the Save and the Danube. Austria had thus succeeded in assembling those lands which it was to administer for nearly two centuries.

War in the southeast was paralleled by war in the west. Coincident with their great work in driving the Turks down the Danube, the Hapsburgs allied with other powers to meet the threat of Louis XIV. Austria, as we have seen, joined the coalitions against France which arose from the Dutch War (1672–1678), the War of the League of Augsburg (1687–1697) and the

---

3. Collaboration with France was close. The siege of Vienna began on July 16. Louis XIV invaded the Spanish Netherlands in December.
4. Venice won back the southern part of Greece known as the Morea from Turkey. During the fighting in 1689 the Parthenon at Athens, on which the Turks had erected a minaret and which they used as an ammunition store, was blown up.
5. The old Hungarian province, the Banat of Temesvar, lying north of the Danube was still in Turkish hands. It was won in further fighting and granted to Austria by the Peace of Passarowitz in 1718 along with further gains. See map, pp. 406–407.

War of the Spanish Succession (1701–1713).[6] The flashing genius of Prince Eugene, victor over the Turks, was displayed again in Italy, Bavaria and Flanders. Unable, however, in this last conflict to place their candidate upon the throne at Madrid, the Hapsburgs acquired as compensation the Spanish Netherlands, Luxemburg, Milan, Naples and (eventually) Sicily. Such gains clearly were to affect the political fortunes of the dynasty during the eighteenth century.

■ THE ORGANIZATION OF THE HAPSBURG STATE

The fantastically complex problems of the Hapsburg state might well have been the despair of statesmen living in an age dedicated to the principles of authority and order. How were these various lands to be administered? To duplicate the system of Louis XIV was out of the question; to attempt a parliamentary solution à l'anglaise would have been totally incredible. Yet the emperors had to deal somehow with the problems of government and simultaneously to chart a safe course amid the rocks and shoals of European politics. Surprisingly enough they had a large measure of success. "Out of a heterogeneous collection of provinces and kingdoms with different languages and cultures, and out of their shadowy pretensions to imperial dignity the Hapsburgs created the state that defended central Europe successively against Turkish, Swedish, French, German and Russian aggression, and was overwhelmed only by the avalanche of 1914–1918." [7]

Leopold was able to benefit by the preliminary work of administration undertaken by Ferdinand I, the successor of Charles V, in mid-sixteenth century. Ferdinand had sought to reorganize his Imperial Council (the Aulic Council) by setting up divisions to deal with legal, financial, military and political affairs. This, however, was only a beginning and was hampered by the strong tendency of the Hapsburgs to look upon their various lands "patrimonially," that is, as family possessions to be parceled out at will to whatever relatives seemed most in need of substantial endowment. No systematic effort was made to tackle the problem of administration scientifically or as a whole.

Bohemia, after its revolt in the first stages of the Thirty Years' War, had been reduced by the Emperor Ferdinand II to complete subjection. Protestantism was condemned; a new nobility, largely German and Catholic, replaced the old; all essential administrative decisions were made henceforth by a special "Bohemian chancellery" at Vienna. German became both the official language and the language of culture, while the Bohemian crown now became hereditary in the Hapsburg family. Meanwhile, a special chan-

---

6. See pp. 343 ff.
7. JOHN B. WOLF, *The Emergence of the Great Powers, 1685–1715* (1951), p. 128.

cellery was set up in 1620 to administer the affairs of Austria proper. The local nobles were disciplined by being required to share in the court life and the administrative system, while simultaneously many administrators were brought from other parts of the Hapsburg lands to serve at Vienna.

Administrative problems in Hungary proved to be very difficult. When Leopold I came to the throne in 1658 he ruled, as we have seen, over only a small part of the ancient Hungarian kingdom. One of his first acts had been to renew an earlier promise of religious liberty, yet this was inadequate to curb the high-handed actions of some of the Catholic nobles. Various powerful families, notably that of Rákóczy, resented control coming from Vienna; consequently they engineered revolts and were prepared even to seek the aid of Louis XIV. After 1679, therefore, Leopold tried milder tactics, agreeing (1681) to concede some further local autonomy to the Hungarian nobles.

By 1699, when all Hungary and Transylvania had been won back from the Turks, it was possible to consolidate the work of reorganization. In 1687 the Hungarian Diet had formally surrendered its right to elect a king, recognizing the crown as hereditary in the Hapsburg family.[8] In the following year a high commission for the organization of Hungary was set up without a single Hungarian member. It left the great families in possession of the land, allowing them to act as government agents on the local level, but stipulating that the most important Hungarian matters were to be decided in the Hungarian chancellery at Vienna. From Vienna likewise a large reorganization was undertaken in taxation, judicial matters and general administration. Transylvania lost its old connection with Hungary and received its special chancellery at Vienna. These various measures drawing Hungary within the orbit of a new administrative system were only partially effective, for the Rákóczy revolt of 1702–1705, although unsuccessful, showed that a large element of Hungarian resentment was still present. Yet on the whole the plan worked.

Leopold was also responsible for some efforts to undertake a division of labor and a systematic reorganization in the central government at Vienna. A kind of Privy Council (*Geheime Konferenz*) dealt with matters of highest importance. A Court Chancellery (*Hofkanzlei*) took control of general foreign and domestic policies. A Court Chamber (*Hofkammer*) administered revenues and finances, while a War Council (*Hofkriegsrath*) directed the army. These were changes which corresponded in general terms to those occurring in other countries; in Austria it must be said that they were more impressive upon paper than in actual operation.

8. Leopold did not assume the crown himself, but permitted his eldest son Joseph to be crowned Apostolic King of Hungary.

Throughout the widely diversified realm which extended ultimately from Flanders to Transylvania the systematization attempted at Vienna could hardly be undertaken. Ancient patterns of administration were allowed to remain, while the local estates or assemblies were often permitted to assess and collect taxes, regulate the enlistment of troops and administer the police. Much power lay in the hands of the local nobles, but at the same time a large number of non-nobles were admitted into various ranks of the civil service. In general, one must recognize the great administrative work attempted under Leopold I and at the same time concede its serious weaknesses. Little real unity was achieved. The head of the "Danubian Monarchy" included among his titles those of Archduke of Austria, King of Bohemia and Apostolic King of Hungary. Differences of language, religion, laws and local customs were still enormous. In 1713 Leopold's son and successor, Charles VI, aware of the dangers that might arise on his death, sought by issuing his Pragmatic Sanction to guarantee that the diverse lands of the Hapsburgs would remain an indivisible inheritance, to go to his own heir, male or female. Although this principle was accepted at home and even, for a time, by the great powers abroad, events were to show that in a real crisis the Pragmatic Sanction was not strong enough to stand unchallenged.

As the eighteenth century began, the Hapsburg monarchy had reached its most brilliant level. The rulers of this polyglot empire moved in a setting of Baroque magnificence. The old imperial palace at Vienna, the Hofburg, was remodeled and enlarged by Fischer von Erlach, one of the finest of Baroque architects. Schönbrunn, the exquisite summer palace of the Hapsburgs, with its gardens and its formal yew hedges thirty feet high, was completed. Prince Eugene commissioned another great architect, Johann Lucas von Hildebrandt, to design a summer palace, the Belvedere, one of the most perfect monuments of its kind. The great abbey of Melk, rebuilt between 1707 and 1737, raised its splendid Baroque towers above the Danube. Churches, public buildings and the new palaces of the nobility reflected the opulence of the governing class.

The imperial court, blazing with color, dominated the cultural life of the Empire. It became a great center of the Italian opera. Its elaborate Spanish court ceremonial was all the more impressive because of the exotic element contributed by the dashing uniforms of the Hungarian, Croatian and Transylvanian nobility. The emperor's German Guards wore red uniforms faced with black velvet and gold lace. The Hungarian Life Guards wore a scarlet hussar uniform decorated with silver lace, a tiger-skin cape, high yellow boots and a tall fur shako surmounted by a heron's plume. Their horses had green harness and silver bridles. Always one was aware of the nearness of the exotic east. The Turkish ambassador entered Vienna in 1719 with a suite of 763 men, 645 horses, 100 mules and 180 camels. His brilliantly colored coach was escorted by a cupbearer and sharpshooter in scarlet robes, white felt bonnets and tiger-skin cloaks; their silver-handled sabers were in red velvet scabbards. Oriental music was provided by a military band of clarinets, cymbals, trumpets and tambourines. As a symbol of Hapsburg pride the dynasty proclaimed the strange motto, "AEIOU," which long before the Emperor Frederick III, father of Maximilian I, had caused to be inscribed on his buildings and his belongings: *"Austriae Est Imperare Orbi Universo"*; in German, *"Alles Erdreich ist Oesterreich Untertan"*; and in translation, "To Austria Is Given Rule of All the Earth."

■ THE BEGINNINGS OF BRANDENBURG-PRUSSIA

The history of Brandenburg-Prussia involved a geographical setting and a way of life far different from that of the House of Hapsburg. In the early Middle Ages a frontier region of the northern plain lying between the Elbe and the Oder rivers had constituted one of the "Marches" or "Marks" of Christian Europe where a Germanic outpost stood guard against the heathen world of the Slavs. The term "North Mark" was first used to describe it. This land of sand, swamp, heath and pine forest, lacking any seacoast and woefully deficient in natural resources, had little economic or cultural riches. The towns of the North Mark were small, their commerce inconsequential. The area slowly assumed the military characteristics that one would associate with a frontier position, and its ruler—the "Mark Graf" or "Margrave" —came to be a figure of note, ultimately recognized in the Golden Bull of 1356 as one of the Seven Electors who chose the Holy Roman Emperor. As the territories between the Elbe and the Oder were consolidated, the name Brandenburg, actually applying to the principal town, came into use to describe the Elector's total possessions.

Having been ruled by several different families, Brandenburg passed in 1417 by inheritance to the House of Hohenzollern, a minor noble family originating in South Germany where, amid the mountains of the Black Forest, its ancestral castle still stands. For almost five hundred years the fortunes of the Hohenzollerns were to be identified with those of Brandenburg and later of Imperial Germany, enduring until the German collapse in 1918 at the close of the First World War. Growth was slow but persistent. To the original nucleus, the Old Mark, there had been added by 1455 the Middle Mark and the New Mark, so that the Hohenzollerns then held lands some ten thousand square miles in extent running from a point fifty miles west of the Elbe to a point perhaps a hundred miles east of the Oder. By a famous document, the *Dispositio Achillea* (1473), the governing family stipulated that these lands must always pass undivided to the eldest son.

The Hohenzollerns gave a vigorous administration to Brandenburg; bit by bit they gained scattered land eastward toward the Vistula and westward toward the Rhine. Such gains, one must note, almost automatically generate a pressure to fill in the remaining gaps. In the course of the sixteenth century the Electorate became Protestant. Under the rule of Joachim II (1535–1571) it took on many of the characteristics of the "strong monarchies" of the sixteenth century. The church was brought under Joachim's control, the monasteries dissolved, legal procedures revised, taxes reorganized and a tentative beginning made at subdividing, in the interest of efficiency, the old feudal council so that experts could handle the particular kinds of business for which they were best equipped. In the century that ensued, Joachim II's immediate successors did little to enlarge what he had achieved.

The subsequent history of Brandenburg-Prussia during the seventeenth and eighteenth centuries could be written as a series of biographies of four rulers: Frederick William, the Great Elector (1640–1688), the true founder of his country's modern greatness; Frederick I (1688–1713), his son, who by being crowned at Königsberg in 1701 transformed the Electorate into a kingdom; Frederick William I (1713–1740), grandson of the Great Elector, "The Drillmaster of Prussia"; and Frederick II (1740–1786), his great-grandson, a versatile genius and one of the principal figures of the eighteenth century, which did not hesitate to entitle him, "The Great." For the purpose of grasping the general development of a state and not simply recording the chronology of its rulers it may be well to consider those three main fields where Brandenburg-Prussia made remarkable progress. These were, first, the enlargement of its territories, secondly, the creation of an army and, thirdly, the development of a centralized machinery of government. Even in summarizing the dry essentials of these administrative matters it is not possible, however, to avoid the personal element. Above all others the grim, hard-working figure of the Great Elector stands like a giant. Because he pioneered so shrewdly and wrought so well, his successors were able to reap a bountiful harvest where he had sown.

■ THE TERRITORIAL GROWTH OF BRANDENBURG-PRUSSIA

The electors of Brandenburg seldom failed in what they considered to be their sacred duty to enlarge their possessions. Even so, at the opening of the seventeenth century the Electorate was still small in population and poor in resources. In 1609 a dispute over the succession to certain Rhineland duchies led Brandenburg to assert a claim of its own, with the result that after a brief conflict its elector was granted provisional possession of the

Duchies of Cleves and Jülich.[9] Unimportant in extent, these duchies had a profound importance in bringing the Electorate of Brandenburg into a new area of political interest, for their acquisition may be said to mark the beginning of Prussia's "Watch on the Rhine."

This westward thrust was paralleled by an equally significant thrust to the east. Beyond the Vistula lay Prussia, the storied home of the Teutonic Knights. The Prussians were originally a savage Baltic people, certainly not Germanic, whose name ("Borussi") suggests an affinity with the Slavs. In the thirteenth century the rulers of Poland, finding it difficult to subdue these pagan tribes who cut them off from the sea, had commissioned a German crusading order, the Teutonic Knights, to undertake the task of conquest. This they did with such efficiency and such unchristian savagery that few of the natives survived. The Teutonic Knights, assuming the role of land-lords and masters, brought in settlers from Germany and the Low Countries, establishing themselves meanwhile in their grim castles as a governing class throughout the land. At their head was the elective Grand Master of the Order. In the course of time a number of towns such as Riga and Königs-berg developed, and with them a vigorous Baltic trade.

Through a complicated chain of events East Prussia came into the pos-session of the House of Brandenburg. Eventually the Teutonic Knights, that strange combination of monk, warrior and manorial lord, fell upon evil days. Part of their territory, the New Mark, they sold in 1455 to Branden-burg. After a bitter war with Poland they were compelled in 1466 to cede the lower valley of the Vistula (West Prussia), thus interposing an area of Polish control between themselves and the Electorate of Brandenburg. They likewise became vassals of Poland for their remaining possessions. In 1511 they elected a member of the Hohenzollern family as their Grand Master. Falling under the influence of Luther, this Albert of Hohenzollern first adopted Protestantism and then in 1525 secularized the Order, ending its religious nature and turning its lands into a hereditary duchy for himself and his descendants, subject to the traditional Polish overlordship. In 1618, through the death of a cousin, the ruler of Brandenburg acquired the Duke-dom of East Prussia; in 1660 his successor, Frederick William, the Great Elector, was able to shake off Polish overlordship and acquire the land in full sovereignty. By such a circuitous process, then, Brandenburg came into possession of this most valuable eastern territory. Just as the Rhineland acquisitions brought the Electorate into closer contact with the west, so the gaining of East Prussia meant a closer involvement in the politics of eastern

9. This was the same controversy which impelled Henry IV of France to take up arms against the claim of the Hapsburg Emperor. See p. 266.

Neither the rivers nor the contours of the northern plain obstructed the growth of the Mark of Brandenburg. By 1648 its scattered territories touched the Rhine, the Niemen and the Baltic. For further details of gains and losses see the maps on pages 406–407, 417, 657, and 691.

THE GROWTH OF
BRANDENBURG~PRUSSIA
TO 1795

MINDEN

LINGEN

CLEVES

RAVE

GELDERS

MARK

MORS

R. RHINE

R. EMS

R. W

0   50   100   150   MILES

Europe. Equally significant, it brought the rulers of Brandenburg into contact with a land where a military, feudal tradition was deeply rooted in the social life of a conservative, landholding class.

Other territorial gains resulted from Brandenburg's part in the Thirty Years' War. No great purpose would be served by analyzing in detail the complex moves of this essentially selfish struggle—first neutrality, then a Swedish alliance, then an Austrian alliance, then neutrality again. When Frederick William began his rule in 1640 he found his lands overrun with hostile Swedish troops, so that he was concerned first to make an armistice with them and then maneuver so as to gain as much as possible for himself. At the Peace of Westphalia (1648) Brandenburg was confirmed in possession of the scattered western territories of Cleves, Mark and Ravensberg. In addition it acquired the secularized bishoprics of Minden and Halberstadt together with the "expectancy" to the bishopric of Magdeburg. These lands constituted a series of stepping-stones, as it were, in the direction of the Rhine. Along the Baltic coast the territory of Eastern Pomerania was secured, giving Brandenburg for the first time a sea outlet, albeit a poor one, and lessening the gap in the direction of East Prussia. The Elector of Brandenburg now was the ruler of territories larger in size than those of any German prince save the Hapsburgs.

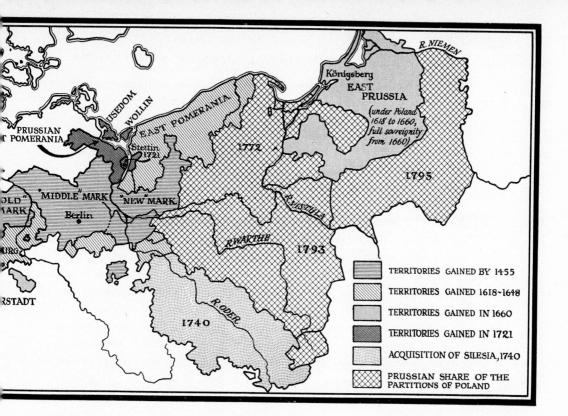

To complete the picture it must be noted that in 1660 the Great Elector (in return for swinging over to the Polish side in the Polish-Swedish War) obtained East Prussia in full sovereignty. Still later, under Frederick I, the successor to the Great Elector, Brandenburg joined the coalition against Louis XIV in the War of the Spanish Succession, gaining at the Peace of Utrecht a few minor areas in the vicinity of Cleves and Ravensberg. More important, perhaps, the signatories now recognized Frederick I as King—a title which he had assumed by putting the crown on his own head in 1701 at Königsberg, in the presence of the Estates of East Prussia. Strictly speaking his title was that of "King in Prussia," but little by little the usage shifted until Europe spoke of the "King of Prussia," and, by an odd transference, applied the name Prussia loosely to the entire Hohenzollern possessions. This kingship also received approval from the emperor.

Still further gains were made by the next ruler, Frederick William I, who in 1713 joined Russia in the Northern War against Sweden. By the Treaty of Stockholm (1720) he enlarged his Pomeranian holdings by obtaining the estuary of the River Oder, a strip of Swedish Pomerania and, most valuable of all, the prosperous city of Stettin. This control of the lower reaches of the Oder River and of the traffic which flowed along it was important in the future, for Frederick II, as we shall see, was consumed with a desire to control the river along its entire length—in political terms, to wrest the fertile and strategically important province of Silesia from its Austrian owners.

If, then, one takes inventory of the lands of Brandenburg-Prussia in 1740, the year of the accession of Frederick II, one will note their distribution across the northern plain (with significant gaps) all the way from the Rhine to the Niemen. Although it now owned the valuable port of Stettin on the Baltic, Prussia could not be counted as a maritime power. Save that they were German-speaking, its territories had no strong common tradition, no common religious faith, no common pattern of life. In this diversity they bore some resemblance to the lands of the Hapsburgs, though of course the provincial differences throughout the Prussian realm were not as profound as was the case in the Austrian lands. It proved to be impossible for the Hapsburgs ever to weld their huge empire effectively together, so that their administration never could avoid a suggestion of patchwork and compromise. In Prussia, on the other hand, the rulers were able to establish an extraordinarily efficient machinery of centralization and to create out of their scattered possessions one of the great states of the eighteenth century.

THE MAKING OF THE PRUSSIAN ARMY

"War," wrote the French statesman, Mirabeau, on the eve of the French Revolution, "is the national industry of Prussia." The growth of a superbly efficient military machine deserves to be singled out as a major force in Prussian history. The chief architect of this development, as of so many others, was the Great Elector. On his accession in 1640 he found the troops at his command poorly trained, badly organized and woefully few in number. They represented either a system of antiquated feudal levies or a monstrously inefficient militia. Regiments were raised by "colonels," in reality little more than contractors agreeing to provide a certain number of men. The harsh discipline which prevailed was maintained by punishments such as flogging, running the gauntlet or slicing off a culprit's nose and ears. The officer corps was composed in considerable part of Scottish, Irish or Polish adventurers. During the last stages of the Thirty Years' War the Great Elector probably never had at one time more than 8,000 effective troops under his command.

The work of Frederick William was to transform this uncouth rabble into an efficient soldiery. By 1648 he had weeded out the worst and was building up a small army, uniformed, disciplined, well-paid and well-officered. During the first Northern War (1655–1660) he came into possession of a professional standing army which at its close numbered about 27,000 men. With it he won his great victory at Warsaw, and later on defeated the Swedes at Fehrbellin. The army was recruited from all parts of the realm. Foreigners were frequently used; for example, when after Louis XIV's revocation of the Edict of Nantes the great French immigration reached Prussia, some of the arrivals were permitted to organize themselves in separate regiments of cavalry, infantry and engineers. In order that he might cope with the threat of Louis XIV's ambitious foreign policy, the Great Elector succeeded in raising the number of his troops to 40,000—a very large number for so small a state. A unified command was first set up in 1655 and a general staff in 1668.

A permanent army of this type entailed very heavy costs in pay, food, clothing, weapons and munitions. The pressure of military necessity, then, forced the state to devise an efficient system of military revenues and financial administration. In 1655 a board called the General Commissariat was set up, having beneath it a widespread network of commissioners and agents. It first supervised the new land tax which was intended to provide military revenues. Later it sought new sources of military revenues in excise taxes, poll taxes, stamp taxes, and a levy upon the first year's income of public officials. The General Commissariat also handled recruiting, provisioning, hospital services and the like. It worked well, so that administrative efficiency, then, first came to Brandenburg under the shadow of military necessity.

No great change in the military picture was made by Frederick I. His successor, Frederick William I (1713–1740), however, has been called the real father of the army of modern Prussia.[10] Inheriting an army of 40,000 men and a bankrupt administration, he contrived to leave a full treasury and an army grown to 83,000 men—the best military force in Europe. This he did by economies in administration and by seeking new sources of revenue. The army received Frederick William I's constant attention, and he is said to have been the first Prussian ruler habitually to wear uniform. The Prussian landed aristocracy provided most of his officers, while the men were recruited through a cantonal system in which each local area was required to produce a stipulated number of recruits for long-term service. Weapons and drill were improved, uniforms prescribed down to the tiniest detail and discipline rigorously enforced. Large garrisons were established in the principal cities; Berlin, for example, with a population now nearing 100,000, had 20,000 troops permanently in barracks.

One of the eccentric aspects of this period was Frederick William I's creation of two regiments of "Potsdam Giants"—those famous "long fellows" all over six feet tall that the king so dearly loved and that he collected

10. R. ERGANG, *The Potsdam Fuehrer, Frederick William I* (1941), p. 6.

by fair means or foul from all corners of Europe. They made an extraordinary appearance on parade, yet, save as military curiosities illustrating the fanatically military enthusiasm of their master, they added little to his fame. Frederick William I should be remembered, however, less for his military eccentricities than for the dedicated labor which he gave to the service of his state.

Frederick II inherited this powerful military machine. Originally far more of a dilettante than a soldier, and interested in flute playing and French poetry rather than in war, he was bullied and driven by his father to accept the traditional militaristic discipline of his house. The powerful fighting force which he inherited he contrived ultimately to enlarge to the total of 200,000 men. What this meant in terms of the Prussian economy can be seen from the following table:

DATE	1648	1740	1786
Population of Prussia	750,000	2,500,000	5,000,000
Size of the standing army	8,000	83,000	200,000

Frederick II, then, came to be in command of armies which could equal those of France, Austria or Russia, even though the population and resources of these states were many times those of the poorly endowed Prussian kingdom. A professional force with some of the traits of a national army had come into existence and was ready to contribute powerfully to the making of modern Prussia.

■ THE PRUSSIAN ADMINISTRATIVE MACHINE

The development of governmental machinery in Prussia kept pace with the enlargement of territory and the growth of military power. In a general sense the process resembled that in other countries where changing conditions resulted in the emergence of specialized agencies of government out of the crude, unspecialized machinery of the medieval state. In characteristic fashion the early rulers of Brandenburg had been assisted by a *Rath*, or a council of noblemen, and in addition had been surrounded by "household officers" with traditional duties to perform. As the territories grew larger the electors also had the assistance of the local estates (*Stände*) of the various provinces; these were in a limited sense representative bodies and always the jealous guardians of local privilege.

During the early sixteenth century, at the time of Joachim II, the old feudal *Rath,* or council, had begun to divide itself into special branches for special purposes: a Treasury (*Kammer*) to handle finances, a Consistory (*Konsistorium*) for church matters and a High Court (*Kammergericht*) for legal affairs. By 1604 one finds that a particularly trustworthy group of councillors, the Privy Council (*Geheime Rath*), concerned itself with weighty matters of state, especially in the field of foreign affairs.

These various developments were all in the direction of making the central power more efficient. At the same time the problem of income led Joachim II to seek the approval of his local estates for new taxes on beer and on landed property. To obtain these he was obliged to grant the estates the right to set up their own machinery for supervising and controlling money grants, and thus his own powers were to some extent weakened.

The necessities of war, as we have seen, pushed the Great Elector into further centralizing measures. The first problem to consider is that of the estates or local assemblies in the old Electorate of Brandenburg and also in the new territories of Cleves, East Prussia and Pomerania. These estates were old and privileged bodies, jealous of their rights. In Brandenburg itself Frederick William summoned the estates in 1653 to agree to new taxes which were to be collected over a six year period. In 1659 Frederick William failed to resummon the estates and simply went on collecting taxes without them. New appointees known as War Commissars were sent out to supervise the collecting of taxes, direct the movement of troops and exercise some police powers. Out of this system grew later the Rural Magistrate (*Landrath*) an invaluable agent and servant of the monarchy. Other agents controlled the new taxes on consumption goods.

In a similar way the estates were tackled in Cleves and Mark, though here the privileges of the "native-born" were such that Frederick William had to move with considerable caution and eventually to compromise. The estates retained their right to meet and to grant taxes, but in the end accepted most of the machinery of centralization which the Great Elector imposed upon them.

In East Prussia a bitter fight with the estates had to be waged. Some of the leaders, who in point of fact were much more the selfish champions of local privilege than spokesmen of a popular cause, were ruthlessly executed. In the end the Elector prevailed; he was able to impose the taxes he desired; and after 1705 the estates, save on rare ceremonial occasions, ceased to meet. So likewise in Eastern Pomerania the estates were quickly brought into subjection.

The Great Elector gave particular attention to the military problem. The General Commissariat of 1655 has already been noted as an agency intended to seek out and exploit new sources of revenue for the army.[11] Money was quickly found, although the somewhat confusing result was that machinery for administering military revenues now existed alongside that concerned with civil revenues. An obvious problem was to harmonize the new centralized machinery with the elaborate network of local officials that had long existed. This the Great Elector did with marked success, so that in each province there grew up a body of regularly paid local officials responsible to Berlin alone.

> Brandenburg-Prussia had become a state. The process had been peculiarly abstract-mechanical, and of uniform simplicity throughout. An active administrative organization had gradually overlaid the local organizations. When resistance was provoked, it was obliterated by the use of force, by an army without local attachments.[12]

The authoritarian pattern of the Prussian state was notably advanced during the reign of Frederick William I, that boorish, bad-tempered, uncultivated drill-sergeant who liked nothing better than to sit of an evening with his male cronies in his informal "Tobacco Parliament" to talk, smoke, swill and perhaps plan some new business of state. Yet Frederick William in his own way worked hard and sternly impressed upon the bureaucracy the need to carry out his orders with precision and punctuality. At the beginning of his reign he declared that faithful officials were so rare that one had to seek them with a light during the day. This condition he strove to correct. "Everyone," he wrote, "must do his duty without arguing and must render complete obedience to the printed and written regulations and orders."

The most striking innovation of this reign was the creation in 1723 of the General Directory—a new board intended to resolve the conflict between the two parallel organizations responsible for the civil and military revenues. Its complexity almost defies clear explanation, for the members operated in two different ways: the four sections into which the General Directory was organized were responsible for the general oversight of the four main *geographical* divisions of the realm while at the same time they were *functional* divisions each charged with a separate work such as agriculture, military affairs, posts or coinage. The General Directory was not a true cabinet; there was no prime minister; and more often than not the king failed to attend. Nevertheless it had importance in providing a kind of apex to the pyramidical structure into which the officialdom of Prussia had been built.

The term "cabinet," especially under Frederick William I and his son Frederick II, is better applied to the private room where the King of Prussia

11. See p. 371.
12. NUSSBAUM, *The Triumph of Science and Reason*, p. 121.

sat at his desk directing the machinery of state, than to any body of officials. Royal responsibility was enormous. To serve the ruler a professional civil service was being trained in the art of "cameralism," that is, in the technical procedures necessary to procure adequate revenues, efficient administration and a healthy economic life. (The expression "cameralism" comes from the German *Kammer,* referring to a "Chamber" or administrative board, as in our "Chamber of Commerce.") A formidable mass of paper-work was indispensable, with the consequence that an interminable stream of reports flowed in from all quarters, each one demanding royal attention and a royal answer.[13] "I am the first servant of the state," Frederick II once wrote. He could almost as truly have called himself its slave.

In economic matters the picture which emerged in Prussia was one of diluted Colbertism. The devastation of the Thirty Years' War had resulted in a severe loss of population and property. The Great Elector was keenly aware of the need to act positively, especially to raise the level of industrial and commercial activity. To this end he encouraged the immigration of skilled Dutch artisans and welcomed large numbers of French Huguenots fleeing from the tyranny of Louis XIV. Swiss Protestants came in from the Canton of Bern, Lutherans from the Palatinate, Calvinists from Saxony and Jews from Poland. All were granted religious toleration—a policy in respect of which the Great Elector stood head and shoulders above his contemporaries. Between 1670 and 1770 some 600,000 immigrants comprising perhaps one-sixth of the total population are said to have arrived.

Agriculture was encouraged by bonuses to those who would take up abandoned homesteads and by the free distribution of seed and livestock. Protection was offered to new industries and strict regulation applied to those already in existence. The beer industry was enlarged. Iron, textiles, paper, tapestries and silks were all produced in larger quantities. Roads and rivers were improved and a great canal built (in part with the labor of the standing army) so as to connect the Elbe and the Oder rivers. The Baltic ports were modernized. A governmental postal system was set up, so efficient for that period that letters could go from Berlin to Cleves in six days and from Berlin to Königsberg in five. Expeditions were sent to the Gold Coast of Africa where for a time a trading post, Grossfriedrichsburg, was in operation. All this direction of economic life suggests the conventional pattern of the paternalistic mercantile state.

Vigorous economic activity is not infrequently accompanied by manifestations of cultural growth. Yet Brandenburg's backwardness in this latter

---

13. The interested student may note that this widespread phenomenon, described in English as "red tape," has as its French equivalent, *paperasserie,* and as its German, *Vielschreiberei.*

respect was notorious; and by no stretch of the imagination could the Great Elector be regarded as a dangerous competitor of Louis XIV in patronage of the arts. Berlin, with a population during the Thirty Years' War of perhaps 6,000, grew rapidly, yet this city, where pigs roamed the streets in medieval fashion looking for garbage, lacked any cultural distinction. The Great Elector made some efforts at beautification with pleasure gardens, new suburbs, drainage, street lights, an enlargement of the old palace and a fine new avenue, *Unter den Linden.* A number of new secondary schools, or *Gymnasia,* were founded. The old universities of Königsberg and Frankfort-on-the-Oder were subsidized and a new university, Duisburg, set up in the Rhineland. The Elector patronized a few scientists and scholars, among them the great jurist, Samuel Pufendorf; he established a botanical garden and built up a State Library at Berlin which in time was to become one of the great libraries of the world. Frederick William's modest achievements must be viewed in the light of the fact that he was building upon very shallow foundations. His capital, Berlin, was almost a new creation and the Electorate as a whole had no great intellectual tradition comparable to that of Italy, France, or even of the Rhineland and South Germany.

The Great Elector's successor, Frederick I, showed a more active interest in the world of culture, perhaps because of his wife, Sophie-Charlotte of Hanover, a bluestocking of formidable energy. Much building in the Baroque manner was undertaken at Berlin where the work of the architect and sculptor Andreas Schluter won considerable fame. Painters, musicians, engineers and architects were brought in from France and Holland. Sophie-Charlotte made the philosopher Leibniz an ornament of the Prussian court and with his encouragement founded the Berlin Academy of Sciences and the Academy of Art. A fourth Prussian university, Halle, was established in 1694. These were notable achievements and yet in some sense they were externals which did not deeply affect the pattern of an essentially autocratic, bureaucratic and militarized state. Nor were they encouraged by the next ruler, of whom Frederick the Great later wrote a bitter indictment. "Under Frederick I," he said, "Berlin was the Athens of the North; under Frederick William I, she became the Sparta."

One important social development east of the Elbe River deserves emphasis. The old knightly class, no longer able to engage in its traditional pursuits, became more and more a class of large-scale agrarian landowners. These succeeded in depressing large numbers of tenant farmers and peasant owners into a kind of agricultural proletariat, truly to be described as serfs. Deprived of many of their old customary rights and subject to a crushing burden of obligatory service, the Prussian serfs did not get their freedom until the Emancipating Edict of 1807. Meanwhile the landlord class—the

"Junkers"—became, next to the monarchy, the dominant influence in the Prussian state, holding commissions in the army, monopolizing the key places in the bureaucracy and controlling the largest part of Prussia's economic life. One is compelled to note the contrast between this Prussian aristocracy, a "service nobility" devoted in its own way to the monarchy, and the aristocracy of France which was deliberately kept by Louis XIV from major posts in the administration and which increasingly surrendered its powers in order to maintain its social privileges. The Junkers of Prussia, on the contrary, followed a course which was doubtless profitable to them but which was also directed by a stern and dedicated sense of duty.

Thus Prussia stood in 1740, a state unique in European history. The parallels and contrasts to be observed in the evolution of Austria and Prussia are enlightening, but cannot be rehearsed here. It may suffice in conclusion to observe that for each state the late seventeenth century was a critical period in which new institutions took shape, new European commitments were accepted and a historical course charted which would affect its destinies for centuries to come.

THE CHURCH OF ST. PETER AND ST. PAUL, in the new capital of St. Petersburg, erected by the Italian architect, Tressini, between 1714 and 1725. Note the Baroque and Classical influences brought by Peter I from the outside world. Lithograph by A. Durand, in Demidov's *Album du Voyage Pittoresque et Archaeologique en Russie, 1839.* Courtesy, New York Public Library.

Chapter 15

Monarchy in Eastern Europe

■ THE RISE OF RUSSIA

THE DRAMA of Russian history was enacted upon a huge plain stretching southward from the Arctic Ocean to the Black and Caspian seas. Along the northern fringe lay the barren tundra region; south of this came the dense conifer forests, gradually changing into the cultivable zone of mixed forest made up of spruce, fir, larch, birch, oak and elm; this was "the core of Muscovy." Then came the vast steppes or prairies of southern Russia. The climate in general was more severe than that of Western Europe; the River Neva, for example, at Peter the Great's northern capital of St. Petersburg was frozen for six months of the year.

Separated from the west by long distances and wretched communications, Russia developed in its own unique way.[1] Its ill-defined western borders merged gradually into what has been called the "trouble zone" where Poles, Lithuanians, Swedes and Germans engaged in endless conflicts. Commercial access to Russia could be had, but only indirectly and with difficulty through a number of Baltic ports which in the Middle Ages carried on a fairly extensive trade in such commodities as furs, timber, grain, beeswax, hemp and tar. To Western Europe, however, Russia itself seemed almost as distant as Tibet.

The first important Russian civilization had arisen well to the south, around the city of Kiev on the lower Dnieper River. By the tenth century Kiev had accepted the protection of Viking or Varangarian warbands that

1. For general backgrounds see pp. 90–91.

had moved southward from their earlier center at Novgorod. These Varangarians, in time merging with the Slavs of the Dnieper, brought with them the name, "Russ," eventually applied to the whole area. Kiev also had strong links with Byzantium. Examples of the Byzantine connection could be seen in the arrival of Christianity during the tenth century, in the establishment of the Eastern Orthodox Church, the forming of a Russian alphabet on a Greek model, the development of "Church Slavonic" as the literary language and the strong Byzantine contributions to music, architecture and religious painting. Another influence was that of the Mongol or Tartar invasions of the thirteenth and fourteenth centuries which led ultimately to the fall of the Kievan state. From these Asiatic overlords (the "Golden Horde") came some influences in art and architecture, some slight mingling of blood, a certain strain of barbarousness and an emphasis upon the autocratic power of the ruler.[2] They were responsible in large part for swinging Kievan Russia away from the orbit of western culture. By the middle of the fifteenth century, however, the Mongol overlordship had been thrown off. Meanwhile Russia's European neighbors had begun to exercise a pressure of their own: "It was Europe," wrote Lavisse, "which first advanced toward Russia." The Swedes in Finland, the German crusading orders in Prussia and Livonia, the Poles thrusting eastward across the Pripet Marshes, the English in the White Sea, or the Turks extending their rule north of the Black Sea—these afforded illustration of the external pressure from Russia's western and southern neighbors.

In the sixteenth century, as already noted, English sailors far to the north won a commercial entry through the White Sea to Archangel. Trade did not bring Russia closely into contact with the west, for such connections as developed were more like those which Europe was making with the overseas world. In a cultural sense, save for a few imported Italian architects and artists, Russia was untouched by the Renaissance, or later by the Reformation. Certainly Poland in the sixteenth century held much greater prominence as a Slavic state than her little-known eastern neighbor.

Following the decline of the Mongol power, the rulers of the small principality of Muscovy began to win a leading position for their lands. Founded in the twelfth century amid a forest clearing, Moscow had grown to be a huge, ramshackle, wooden city of 200,000 when in 1571 it was attacked by the Tartar Khan of the Crimea, captured, burned and all but 30,000 of its inhabitants slain or expelled. Such a catastrophe only temporarily inter-

2. "The Mongolian state was built upon the principle of unquestioning submission of the individual to the group. . . . The power of the Khan was one of merciless strength. It was autocratic; submission to it was unqualified. This view of the authority of the prince was transferred to the Grand Duke of Moscow when the rule of the Khans was weakened." G. VERNADSKY, *A History of Russia* (1944), p. 56.

rupted the rise of Muscovy. The work of Ivan III, "The Great" (1462–1505), who has been compared in importance to his western contemporary, Louis XI of France, as well as the work of Ivan IV, "The Terrible" (1547–1584), have already been sketched.[3] It is sufficient to record here that in 1472 Ivan III had married Sophia, niece of the last emperor at Constantinople. She had encouraged Ivan to develop an elaborate Byzantine court ceremonial and to regard himself as the successor of the imperial Caesars. Just as Byzantium, so it was argued, had long ago fallen heir to the dignities of ancient Rome, so now, when in 1453 Byzantium was seized by the Turks, Moscow had become the "Third Rome," unique in its nature and possessed of a far more splendid destiny than any rival could claim.

Ivan III and Ivan IV extended the control of Muscovy north to the Arctic and south to the Caspian, meanwhile imposing the yoke of autocracy upon their subjects. Ivan IV, moreover, actually sought to break through to the Baltic, where he managed to win the port of Narva from the Swedes and to hold it between 1558 and 1581. He also sought, though with limited success, to bring skilled artisans and technicians from the west into his lands.

Still barred from direct contact with the west, sixteenth-century Russia began a spectacular eastward advance. The march through Siberia to the Pacific was the work of fur-traders and adventurers. It constituted a kind of "internal colonization" deserving to be set beside the great overseas advances made contemporaneously by the maritime powers of the west. The Ural Mountains were no serious barrier. Tobolsk, lying to the east of them, was founded in 1587; Tomsk, in Central Siberia, was established in 1604; Yeneseisk, still further east, was founded in 1618; the waters of the Pacific were first touched at Okhotsk in 1639. The magnet which drew men on was the fur trade—the golden opportunity for wealth coming from the superb Russian sables which Siberia produced. At the time of this great Russian advance no white man had penetrated even halfway across what is now Canada or the United States. It is indeed worthy of notice that the Russians were able to march eastward all the way across Siberia to the Pacific more than eighty years before Peter the Great could take the short step to the shores of the Baltic and nearly a century and a half before Catherine II could gain the coast of the Black Sea.

The close of the sixteenth century in Russia was marked by the "troublous times" during which it seemed that internal dissensions and foreign invasion might undo what had been achieved. In 1613 a great assembly at Moscow including representatives of the nobles, clergy, merchants, the various professions, the palace guards and the Cossacks elected as ruler or "tsar" Michael Romanov, nearest of kin to the ancient dynasty and the

3. See pp. 90–91.

founder of a line that, like the Hapsburgs and Hohenzollerns, was to rule unbroken until the great revolution of 1917.

The first fifty years of Romanov rule saw the beginnings of a new territorial expansion, this time in the direction of Western Europe. Conflict with Poland and Sweden led to the winning of Smolensk and Kiev in 1654 and together with these valuable cities a frontier line along the Dnieper River about a hundred miles west of the old boundary.[4] At the same time Sweden, by extending her Baltic possessions southward to include Livonia, made all the more difficult Russia's advance to the sea.

The same period saw some development of a central bureaucracy. Tsar Alexis (d. 1676), son of Michael Romanov, asserted his authority over the towns, some of which were in revolt, formulated a new legal code, set up a secret police and attempted to turn the noble class into a group holding their possessions in return for service to the state. To the south, in the basins of the Dnieper, the Don and the Volga, particular problems were created by the Cossack tribes. These were frontier settlers, organized in semi-independent republics, who could be brought into submission only by the use of force. Their most famous rebellion was that led by the Cossack Stenka Razin; it lasted from 1667 to 1671 and was ended only when Razin was seized, taken to Moscow and dismembered joint by joint. Some rights of self-government were stubbornly maintained by the Cossacks almost to the end of the eighteenth century.

Another important development came in the sphere of religion. In 1653 the Patriarch Nikon undertook to make changes in the various service books of the Russian Church which had become corrupted through the centuries and needed to be revised in accordance with the older and more accurate Greek texts. The reformers immediately found themselves opposed by the conservative defenders of the "old Russia": peasants, merchants, monks and a large part of the lower clergy who were content with the practices which they knew. These, known as the "Zealots," found a leader in the priest Avvakum, an extraordinary figure whose autobiography, one of the few seventeenth-century Russian works written in the vernacular, is a significant document in the evolution of Russian literature. The extent of Avvakum's fanaticism for the old faith is illustrated in his statement that it were better for a man never to have been born than to cross himself with three fingers instead of two.

In the end, though Nikon himself fell foul of the tsar's authority, his changes in the service books were maintained. Avvakum was burned at the stake in 1681 and his followers severely punished. One consequence was the growth, despite persecution, of a large number of "Old Believers," and the

4. See map, opposite.

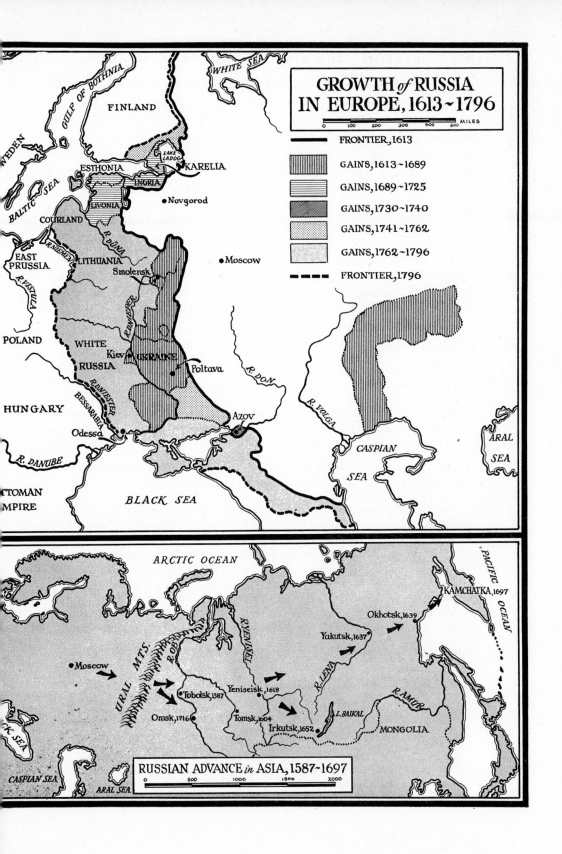

GROWTH *of* RUSSIA
IN EUROPE, 1613~1796

MILES
0   100   200   300   400   500

———— FRONTIER, 1613

GAINS, 1613~1689

GAINS, 1689~1725

GAINS, 1730~1740

GAINS, 1741~1762

GAINS, 1762~1796

– – – FRONTIER, 1796

WHITE SEA

GULF OF BOTHNIA

FINLAND

SWEDEN

BALTIC SEA

LAKE LADOGA

KARELIA

ESTHONIA

INGRIA

•Novgorod

LIVONIA

COURLAND

R. DÜNA

EAST PRUSSIA

R. NIEMEN

LITHUANIA

Smolensk

•Moscow

R. VISTULA

POLAND

WHITE

RUSSIA

R. DNIEPER

Kiev

UKRAINE

•Poltava

R. DON

R. DNIESTER

HUNGARY

BESSARABIA

Odessa•

Azov

R. VOLGA

CASPIAN

SEA

ARAL

SEA

OTTOMAN
EMPIRE

R. DANUBE

BLACK SEA

ARCTIC OCEAN

PACIFIC OCEAN

KAMCHATKA, 1697

Okhotsk, 1639

Yakutsk, 1637

R. YENISEI

R. OB

URAL MTS.

•Moscow

•Tobolsk, 1587

Yeniseisk, 1618

R. LENA

Omsk, 1716

Tomsk, 1604

Irkutsk, 1652

L. BAIKAL

R. AMUR

MONGOLIA

BLACK SEA

CASPIAN SEA

ARAL SEA

RUSSIAN ADVANCE *in* ASIA, 1587~1697

0   500   1000   1500   2000

penetration of Russian religious life by numerous fanatical sects, the *Raskolniki*. Subject to official attack, many of the dissenters fled to the dense forests and the boundless steppes where they aided in the new work of colonization. In one sense they represented a protest against change in general and a devotion to "Mother Russia" which on more than one occasion led them to mobilize opinion against reforming influences coming from abroad. Conversely, the Nikonian reforms can be regarded as a breach in the structure of Russia's conservatism and an anticipation of the work of Peter the Great. Finally, the official church, which had been aided by the state to win its victory, came to be more than ever dependent upon the civil power.[5]

During the first seventy-five years of Romanov rule Russia presented a strange picture to those few westerners able to visit it. Russian cities and towns were still largely of wood, using a method of log construction which seems to have been widely employed in northern Europe and which was later brought by the Swedes to America around 1650. These cities had been described by an English traveler, Giles Fletcher, in 1588:

> The streets of their cities and townes instead of paving are planked with fir trees, planed and layed even close the one to the other. Their houses are of wood without any lime or stone, built very close and warm with firre trees plained and piled one upon another. They are fastened together with dents or notches at every corner, and so clasped fast together. Betwixt the tree or timber they thrust in mosse (whereof they gather plenty in their woods) to keep out the aire.

A later visitor, Archdeacon Coxe, described a striking system of mass production and prefabrication which was used for these buildings:

> Among the curiosities of Moscow I must not omit the market for the sale of houses. It is held in a large open space, in one of the suburbs, and exhibits *ready-made houses,* strewed on the ground. The purchaser who wants a dwelling, repairs to this spot, mentions the number of rooms he requires, examines the different timbers, which are regularly numbered, and bargains for what suits his purpose. The house is sometimes paid for on the spot, and removed by the purchaser; or the vendor contracts to transport it and erect it upon the place where it is designed to stand. It may seem incredible, that a dwelling may be thus bought, removed, raised and inhabited, within the space of a week. . . .[6]

Moscow, like other Russian cities, was still subject to the recurrent hazard of devastating fires and remained so until, as a result of the great conflagration of 1812, a city ordinance made masonry construction obligatory.

A small but steadily increasing number of foreigners—merchants, doctors, craftsmen and specialists of various kinds—established themselves at Moscow in what came to be known as the "German Quarter." A regular

5. It has been estimated that by the time of the Revolution of 1917 the Old Believers may have numbered from twenty to twenty-five millions.
6. Quoted in GEORGE H. HAMILTON, *The Art and Architecture of Russia* (1954), pp. 106, 107

postal service was established between Moscow and the west. The ancient city of Kiev, long famous for its trade, was won back from Poland in 1654. Under Polish rule it had become a kind of cultural outpost where education, music, art and architecture reflected western influences. Kiev had cordially welcomed, for example, the Baroque style in architecture. Its seizure by the rulers of Muscovy meant a flow of clergy trained in the liberal, latinized academies at Kiev who brought with them to Moscow some western ideas. An architectural style known as "Moscow Baroque" came into existence. Ballet seems to have been introduced from the west by the German colony in Moscow in the 1670's, making use of some of the music of Heinrich Schütz. Thus in various ways it was possible for Russia dimly to feel something of the new life of Western Europe.

Despite these developments, the stubborn pride and conservatism of the Russians offered almost insuperable obstacles to genuine progress. Some of the early tsars, it is said, carefully washed themselves after having been in the presence of westerners. The few accounts written by foreign visitors emphasize the native ignorance, the barbaric manners, the widespread drunkenness and gluttony, the hostility to new ideas found on every hand. Anything beyond elementary arithmetic was incomprehensible; nothing was known of western methods of shipbuilding or metal working or of the modern art of war. Though much had been accomplished, a major work remained to be done. Such was the state of affairs at the time of the accession of Peter I.

■ PETER THE GREAT AND EUROPE

"The impact of Peter the Great upon Muscovy," it has been said, "was like that of a peasant hitting his horse with his fist." [7] Grandson of the first Romanov, Peter began his personal rule in 1689. Previous to this he had lived through a period of bloody civil strife during which he shared the throne with an imbecile half-brother under the regency of his half-sister, Sophia. Peter was a contemporary of Louis XIV, though in all save the exercise of power these two had little in common. As a young man Peter had fallen into the company of a reckless Swiss soldier of fortune, François Lefort, who, having taught him every art of dissipation, then encouraged Peter to learn from travel abroad what impressive advances European civilization had made. Scandalously reared, a figure of demonic energy, gross in his appetites, unbelievably brutal in behavior, subject to fits of epilepsy, Peter was a barbarian dedicated to the cause of progress. Undertaking tasks which to lesser men would have seemed impossible, by the time of his death in 1725 he had largely succeeded in what he set out to do.

7. B. H. SUMNER, *A Short History of Russia* (1943), p. 94.

It was Peter's aim to have Russia count among the great powers of Europe. For twenty-eight consecutive years, from 1695 to 1723, he was at war. Military affairs, therefore, occupied so much of his thoughts that it could be argued his ambitious program of domestic reform was intended to make possible his achievements abroad. In essence, Peter's foreign policies were policies of expansion to the south against the Turk, to the west against Sweden and to the east against whatever unknown obstacles delayed the Russian advance into Asia.

Peter did not hesitate to take up the old conflict with the Turk. Nowhere did his southern possessions touch the waters of the Black Sea. The nearest point of access would be the fortress of Azov, controlling the mouth of the River Don. Although Peter's first impulsive expedition of 1695 failed, it had the valuable consequence of leading him to plan more carefully, to learn how to construct suitable shipping and, when his forces were properly mobilized in 1696, to capture the fortress.

The famous European voyage which Peter and a select group of Russians undertook in 1697 and 1698 may well have been inspired by his desire to win further victories against the Turks. His obvious interests were in technology, especially in the methods of shipbuilding which he observed so closely in the Netherlands and in England. He also sought, unsuccessfully as it happened, to form a western alliance against the Turk. In addition Peter saw at first hand a good deal of the workings of European politics and heard much about a possible coalition against Sweden. Moreover, he was able to arrange for craftsmen and experts of various kinds to go to Russia and impart what they knew. In this sense the "European embassy" was epochal both for Peter and for Russia.

Peter's return home was speeded by a revolt of the *streltsi,* or palace guard, which he put down with brutal efficiency, beheading many of the leaders with his own hand. His main problem was not domestic, however, but foreign. Charles XII, "The Swedish Meteor," had become King of Sweden in 1697 at the age of fifteen. This spectacular figure was determined to defend his extensive possessions around the Baltic. He was threatened by an alliance of Saxony, Poland, Denmark and Russia, inspired by a Livonian nobleman, Johann Patkul, who sought independence from Sweden. A man of military genius, Charles nevertheless was so lacking in balance that his wild adventures brought him to disaster in the end. His opponents were his Baltic neighbors, for the western powers, as we have seen, were deeply involved in the complex problems of the Spanish Succession.

The first stage of this Northern War, which ran from 1699 to 1721, meant disaster for the allies. In one year Charles XII defeated the Danes at Copenhagen, the Polish-Saxon troops at Riga and the Russians at Narva, on the Gulf of Finland, where Peter had sought amid a blinding snowstorm to capture the fortress. Some 8,000 Swedes had routed 40,000 Russians—a bad omen, as it seemed, for Peter's military future. Charles XII became overnight the phenomenon of Europe. Although he might well have decided to defend his gains he chose instead to plunge into a six-year struggle for the elective Polish throne upon which he succeeded in imposing his own candidate. Meanwhile Peter with a reorganized army had overrun the Baltic provinces, captured at long last the key fortress of Narva (1704) and undertaken to build himself a new strong point, later named St. Petersburg, at the head of the Gulf of Finland.

Charles XII, having made his peace with Poland and Saxony, next undertook a move which history again and again has shown to be fatal. Like Napoleon and Hitler after him, he determined to destroy Russian opposition upon Russian soil, plunging his armies into the vast depths of the country in disregard of its distances and its merciless winter climate. Marching first towards Moscow, he wheeled south to the Ukraine hoping in vain to be aided by a secret ally, the Cossack leader Mazeppa. Instead, he had to endure the terrible winter of 1708–1709, the worst in a century, when birds, it is said, fell frozen out of the sky. Eventually, after horrible suffering, Charles XII met a huge Russian army at Poltava, in the Ukraine (July, 1709). The result was disaster for the Swedes. Charles escaped almost alone to Turkey where he stayed until 1714, persuading his hosts to renew the war against Russia and thus regain their old fortress of Azov.

The last period of the Northern War brought large gains to Russia. In 1714 Charles XII, wearing a wig and disguised as "Captain Peter Fiske," made a dramatic dash back to Sweden where he found political groups willing to reverse the older policies and to concede Peter the lands he desired along the Baltic. Carrying on the war which the Danes had renewed, Charles died in 1718, leading an assault, bareheaded, against an obscure Norwegian fortress. Three years later the Northern War ended in the Peace of Nystad (1721), a settlement which marked the secure establishment of Russia in the west. Peter won diplomatic recognition as ruler of the Baltic lands which he had long occupied: Ingria, Karelia, Estonia and Livonia. With a window to the Baltic now assured, Russia's diplomatic and military position among the great powers was drastically transformed.

In his few remaining years Peter sought to strengthen his position in Asia. He tried unsuccessfully to establish a Russian embassy at Pekin. In 1719 he sent an expedition to explore the Kurile Islands, north of Japan. A few weeks before his death he sent one of his naval captains, Vitus Bering, on the long journey across Siberia with instructions to build ships and explore the northwest coast of America. Bering's historic explorations, which lasted until 1741, were thus the fruit of an inspiration coming from Peter I. In still another move Peter undertook in 1722 and 1723 a war with Persia from which he acquired Baku on the Caspian and temporary possession of the southern shore of this great inland sea, an area which Peter said was "indispensable" to Russia. Despite these gains, it remains true that Peter's major victories had been won in the west, where Russia's chief interests now clearly lay. These western gains, more than any other, justified Peter in accepting at the close of the Northern War a new title, "Father of the Fatherland, Peter the Great, Emperor of all Russia."

■ "THE BARBARIAN OF GENIUS"

Peter's great domestic work in "westernizing" his country represented a continuous and militant intensification of changes already hesitantly under way before his time. The earlier beginnings, to be sure, were so fragmentary and Peter's own work so dramatic that the latter stands out by contrast in heroic proportions. Much of what he did was inspired by the need to make Russia strong, primarily, no doubt, in the military sense. Peter's reforms, spread over a long period of years, were not systematic; they were piecemeal, chaotic, seldom without a flavor of improvisation. Even so, they touched almost every aspect of Russian life. Though one may group them in categories for convenience of discussion, one should not forget that they made no such orderly pattern in the tumultuous life of Peter's own Russia.

Reforms in government take a large place in any account of Peter's work. His ferocious repression of the *streltsi* revolt in 1698 showed that he was determined to rule with a strong hand. One of the worst obstacles to efficient government was created by the *boyars,* the ignorant, filthy, selfish, hopelessly reactionary nobility of ancient Russia. Their assembly, or *duma,* while in no sense a genuine governing body, had some administrative powers. These Peter effectively terminated by 1700, so that the *boyars* as a class could no longer interfere with the work of government.

The actual conduct of public affairs in the Muscovite state had, through the passage of time, come under the control of an incredibly complicated network of thirty-six "departments," arranged partly on the basis of geography, partly on the basis of the kind of work which they handled. About eighty "secretaries" served as the principal administrative officials. By 1715 Peter had replaced the overlapping "departments" by a system of ten "colleges," or boards, each a kind of commission on the Swedish model charged with one particular class of work such as military affairs or finances. Foreigners with expert knowledge were often brought in to serve in these colleges.

In 1711 Peter set up a small senate of nine members which he later enlarged. Originally entrusted with full governing powers during his absences, it eventually became a kind of "ministry of ministries" with one of its representatives on each of the collegiate boards. Answerable only to Peter, the senate has been called his other self.

To give still further regularity to the administration, Russia was divided into twelve "governments" (*gubernii*), ultimately subdivided into forty-three provinces. Royal appointees were set up as governors, with a subordinate in each of the provinces. In order to carry on the work of the state, they had the assistance of provincial councils drawn from the local landowning aristocracy. Other decrees provided for burgomasters (*burmistri*) in the large towns and for elected town councils. Their duties were mainly to ensure the collection of taxes and to carry out Peter's will. Order was further sought by a revision of the law codes in 1718 on the Swedish model and the creation in 1720 of a new pattern of local courts of justice. The work of justice was aided by a reinvigorated secret police, one branch of which was designed to watch over the conduct of public officials. Peter also sought to establish regular embassies abroad, though his representatives did not always fit easily into the elegant pattern of Europe's governing class.[8]

Another very important approach to the problems of government lay in Peter's treatment of the nobility. A century earlier, Ivan IV, like the Tudors in England, had weakened the old *boyar* aristocracy by creating a new "service" nobility closely dependent upon the ruler. Ivan's work, however, was limited in its effect. Peter now strove to convert all types of Russian aristocracy into this "service nobility" (*dvoriantsvo*), that is to say, he wished to establish a system under which rank and income would be proportional to services rendered to the state. A "Table of Ranks" was drawn up in 1722, by which a kind of ladder of state service was devised having fourteen naval and military rungs and fourteen corresponding civilian rungs. Appropriate titles and landed wealth went with each rung. Peter did not hesitate to admit people of moderate or humble birth to the nobility if they could serve his cause, so that he was soon surrounded by thousands of loyal servants closely dependent upon himself.

All these administrative reforms would have been meaningless had they not been accompanied by a drastic transformation of the army. Peter was bitterly humiliated by his early defeats in the field. He sought, therefore, to enlarge the size of his forces, give them uniforms and modern equipment, train them and arrange for a regular system of recruitment. An elaborate

---

8. Lord MACAULAY, in a notable passage in his *History of England,* describes the sumptuously dressed Russian ambassadors turning up at court balls "dropping pearls and vermin."

network of boards was set up to deal with every aspect of military life and provided with generous funds. Each region was held responsible for a constant quota of men, so that gaps occurring during campaigns would be filled immediately. By the end of his reign Peter had an army of over 200,000 and a Baltic fleet of 50 large and 800 small vessels with crews totaling some 28,000 men.

In economic affairs Peter was inevitably a mercantilist. The real question was how fast and how far so backward a country as Russia could enable its ruler to proceed. Peter's wars gave him windows on the Baltic. He made commercial treaties with countries such as England and Holland and sought to encourage the manufacture of carpets, leather goods, silks and other cloths. Shipbuilding, which had fascinated Peter since childhood, saw a large growth. In agriculture he tried to develop the cultivation of grapevines, the mulberry and the tobacco plant. Experts were brought in to supervise the mining of iron, silver and copper. Some attempts were made to set up government monopolies and to establish state factories, often with the use of state labor. These and other measures show Peter striving mightily to galvanize the economy of his lethargic realm.

The financial problem was always acute, for Peter's actions involved enormous expenditures. Expedient after expedient was tried; Peter, it has been said, "declared war on the taxpayer"; he undertook "financial brigandage." Wherever it seemed possible that income could be secured, there a tax was levied: on salt, tobacco and stamped documents, on graves and coffins, on cabmen and caviar, on baths, births, beards, brandy and bees. The budgets which Peter required the various departments to submit showed that in spite of everything the expenses steadily mounted. Obvious tricks, such as reducing the metallic weight of coins, were attempted; state farms were set up; fishing and inn-keeping were declared government monopolies; a census of all households was imposed; and still the difficulties remained. The problem of "modernizing" the economy of Muscovy in truth remained unsolved.

The Russian Church easily fell under governmental control. From 1589 onward the patriarchate, or directing body, had separated itself from Constantinople and had come closely under the influence of the civil power. When, therefore, the Patriarch Adrian died in 1700 Peter neglected to appoint a successor. He ordered an inquisition into the affairs of the very numerous Russian monasteries, the outcome of which was a decree depriving them of their landed estates and making the monks salaried state officials. Decrees of 1716 and 1718 required everyone to confess at least once yearly and to attend church every Sunday. Finally, a decree of 1721 set up the so-called Spiritual Department, later known as the Holy Synod. This was a board appointed by Peter to spread knowledge of God's law and to extirpate superstition. Among other duties it recommended all candidates for high church office. It had one lay member, later known as the procurator, who in time came to govern its policies. Eventually, therefore, religious affairs came closely under the control of the state.

A whole series of reforms, large and small, were designed to lift Russia out of its medieval, semi-oriental pattern of life. On his return from the west Peter had ordered his subjects to discard their long gowns and to wear the short coats and hose of western fashion. Models of the new clothing were to be hung at town gates so that all could see and copy. All men were required to shave their beards and the popular western use of tobacco was encouraged. Women were to be brought out of seclusion and given some legal share in their marriage arrangements. The Russian calendar was revised, over conservative objections, so as to have the year begin on January 1 and to calculate dates from the birth of Christ rather than from the supposed creation of the world.[9]

Peter seems to have had faith in education. He encouraged Russians to go abroad to learn, especially to pursue the practical arts. A school of mathematics and navigation was set up at Moscow, and another where, in addition to geography, ethics, politics, philosophy and dancing, instruction was given in French and German. An Academy of Sciences was opened in 1725 after correspondence with Leibniz and with the Royal Society in London. It was Peter's hope that this Academy would develop into a university—a hope which was long delayed. Nevertheless a beginning had been made and nobles were told that if they expected to rise in the Table of Ranks they would need to have some educational training.

Peter also gave attention to the printed word. To obtain cheap books in the Russian tongue he was obliged to have many of them printed abroad, in Holland. Certain popular manuals were issued; one rather significantly was entitled *The Art of War*. Another, *An Honorable Mirror of Youth, or a Guide to Deportment* (1717), had much interesting advice. Young nobles should not get drunk in the daytime, dance in heavy boots, spit in the middle of a group of people or eat like pigs. They should cultivate foreign languages and never speak Russian before peasants or servants. In 1703 the first Russian gazette appeared: *News of Military and Other Events Worthy of Knowledge and Remembrance*. Still another significant change was the introduction in 1707 of what was known as the "civil script"—a reduction of the old Cyrillic alphabet which consisted of forty-eight letters. Peter removed eight letters, simplified the rest and had a new type cast in

9. The full Gregorian calendar was not accepted in Russia until 1918, when fourteen lost days were made up.

Holland. With this new script he established a printing press and with his own hand corrected the proofs of some of the earlier books which it issued.

One cannot fail to be impressed by the tireless surge of energy which Peter invariably displayed. He seemed a man possessed by a demon. Building a new capital, St. Petersburg, was his most splendid gesture. On a swampy site at sixty degrees north latitude where winter lasted from November till April and where wooden piles had to be driven into the ground before building could be undertaken, Peter set 150,000 men to work. The city was almost literally built upon their bones, for they died by the thousands. It is significant that Peter's first two projects were a fortress and a shipyard. Nobles were required to build homes at their own expense and in harmony with the general plan. Labor, materials, tools and even prospective inhabitants were requisitioned from other parts of Russia. To obtain building materials, masonry construction for a time was forbidden elsewhere. An elaborate system of canals made St. Petersburg akin to Venice, Amsterdam and Stockholm. The two empresses, Elizabeth and Catherine, continued what Peter had begun, so that in the end there arose a splendid northern capital on the grey banks of the Neva, echoing the contemporary architectural vogue of Western Europe and reflecting little of Russia save the powerful autocracy which had inspired its creation.

Peter died in 1725 without making clear who was to succeed him. For the good-for-nothing Alexis, Peter's son by his first wife, he had nothing but contempt and eventually accused him of plotting against the tsar and fleeing abroad. Alexis died in the fortress of St. Peter and Paul in St. Petersburg in 1718 a few days after having twice been tortured on his father's orders. In 1724 Peter proclaimed his second wife, Catherine, empress with the consequence that upon his death she succeeded him—one of the four women to rule Russia during the eighteenth century.

Peter's work "cleft the soul of Muscovy." Russia was brought into contact with the west and some of its upper classes were powerfully influenced by the new currents which this contact brought. Henceforth Russia could not be ignored in any manipulations of the diplomatic balance. Yet the vast inertia of the Russian people created a problem that could hardly be overcome; in many fundamental respects the transformation of Muscovy remained something of a veneer, beneath which still existed much of an older Russia—powerful, unrepentant, suspicious and unpredictable.

■ SCANDINAVIA

While Austria, Prussia and Russia loomed largest in the life of central and eastern Europe, other areas, among them Scandinavia, played roles of considerable importance. The pattern of internal development in these northern countries reflects certain major trends of the time and helps to make such trends clearer. Their foreign policy was largely concerned with the long struggle for the control of the Baltic.

Scandinavia in the seventeenth century meant two political units: a Danish-Norwegian kingdom extending north from the Jutland Peninsula to the Arctic Ocean, and a Swedish kingdom on the shores of the Baltic that for a time took on some of the characteristics of an empire. Denmark's old control of the Scandinavian Union of Kalmar had ended with Gustavus Vasa's success in winning the Swedish throne in 1523. In addition to Norway proper, Denmark also controlled the maritime provinces of Bohus, Halland and Scania in what today would be southern Sweden; by the possession of these coastal lands it effectively controlled the sea passage, the Sound, from the North Sea into the Baltic. During the Reformation period a powerful Lutheran state church had been established in Denmark. The kingdom had intervened actively, as we have seen, on the Protestant side in the Thirty Years' War, though with no profit to itself. Following the war, Denmark's principal rival turned out to be not the Catholic powers but rather its closest neighbor, Sweden. Between 1643 and 1660 these two engaged in desultory and intermittent war, the outcome of which was Denmark's loss to Sweden of the Baltic Islands of Osel and Gottland, as well as a substantial inland area on the Swedish-Norwegian border and the provinces of Scania, Halland and Bohus on the eastern shores of the Sound.[10] Denmark's losses, therefore, contributed significantly to the growth of the Swedish state.

Simultaneously an important constitutional revolution took place in Denmark. This came as a reaction against the attitude of a powerful group of nobles who, claiming various privileges such as exemption from taxes, sought to overshadow the monarchy itself. By 1665 representatives of the church and the towns, in opposition to the nobles, had succeeded in declaring the monarchy hereditary and in getting Frederick III to issue the famous *Kongelov,* or "King's Law." This declared the monarchy to be absolute, hereditary and subject only to the twin obligations of maintaining the Lutheran Church and preserving the territorial unity of the kingdom. By weakening the selfish power of the nobles the old distinctions of rank were lessened so that all Danish citizens were regarded as equal under the absolute rule of the king. Gradually an efficient bureaucracy developed, with "colleges" or administrative boards in charge of different departments and with a new "service nobility" to carry out the royal wishes. One may perhaps detect in these developments an echo not so much of the absolutism of Louis XIV as of the "popular despotism" of Tudor England.

10. See map, p. 395.

While Denmark thus established its own variant of absolute rule, Sweden in this same period built upon the strong foundations that the brilliant House of Vasa had provided. Despite the eccentricities of Queen Christina, the country had scored impressive gains at the Peace of Westphalia, winning Western Pomerania and the Bishoprics of Bremen and Verden. These, added to the possession of Finland and the earlier acquisitions of Ingria, Karelia, Estonia and Livonia, gave Sweden a commanding Baltic position. At this time, moreover, a member of the House of Vasa sat on the Polish throne. Charles X, who succeeded Christina in Sweden in 1654, acquired, as we have seen, substantial territories from Denmark, and also, at the conclusion in 1660 of the war with Poland, legal confirmation of the earlier acquisition of Livonia. Something in the nature of a Swedish empire had emerged. All the Baltic islands, save those closely dependent on the Jutland Peninsula, were in Swedish hands; the estuaries of important German rivers such as the Weser, the Elbe and the Oder were likewise Swedish, as were most of the coastal cities. A substantial portion of north European sea commerce passed through the Swedish-held ports of Riga, Stettin, Stralsund and Bremen. Swedish rule extended over a polyglot area which included Finns, Estonians, Lithuanians, Poles and Germans, an area of unassimilated peoples having, to be sure, a certain economic and geographic unity, yet held together largely by the force of arms.

During the seventeenth century Sweden experienced a vigorous economic development. The New Sweden Company, organized in 1637, established a settlement, New Sweden, on the banks of the Delaware River which lasted until it was seized by the Dutch in 1655. At home, the Swedish forests were a valuable source of timber needed for masts and spars. An important iron industry also emerged. Around 1700, Christopher Polhem, a Swedish industrialist of genius, developed an important manufactory at Stiernsund which turned out a remarkable variety of products including iron bars, sheet iron, nails, tools, plowshares, cogwheels and parts for clocks. Polhem was a pioneer in producing standardized interchangeable parts. His use of specialized machinery, water power, the division of labor and carefully organized production methods marks him as one of the great forerunners of modern industrial techniques.

With Charles XI, who came to the throne in 1660 as a boy of four, it seemed that the era of aggressive foreign policy had come to an end. Under the regency Sweden joined the Triple Alliance of 1668 against France, only to be bribed a few years later to swing over to the French side.[11] By the Peace of Lund in 1679 Denmark and Sweden established an intimate commercial and military alliance that was to last twenty years. Charles XI's great work

11. See p. 343.

SWEDISH TERRITORY
IN 1523

GAINED IN 1645,
1648, 1658

GAINED, LATER LOST
(1721)

THE RISE *and* DECLINE
of SWEDISH POWER
1523 ~ 1721

0   100   200   300
MILES

was done at home. Faced by a selfish noble opposition resembling that in Denmark, he moved firmly against it. Much crown land had fallen into the hands of the aristocracy; by examining every title-deed in the kingdom Charles was able to "reduce" the possessions, and therefore the degree of independence, of his nobles. The "Reduction" of 1681 thus whipped the nobles into line by depriving them of much of their landed power. The Swedish Assembly (*Riksdag*) then declared that the king was no longer dependent upon his Council of Nobles (*Riksrad*) for advice. Sweden, like Denmark, had become an absolute monarchy with the difference that the Swedish people through their Assembly still had some right to be consulted.

Administratively, Charles XI did for Sweden what his contemporary, the Great Elector, did for Brandenburg. He gave the Swedish crown an independent economic position, he created a new, dependent nobility, built up a corps of civil servants, reduced the national debt by three-fourths, established a regular budget, reorganized the army and navy and created a "collegial" type of departmental administration which Peter the Great later imitated. With some reason, therefore, he can be regarded, after Gustavus Vasa and Gustavus Adolphus, as one of the greatest of Swedish kings, bringing about a general pattern of administration which, though now no longer despotic, has existed down to the present.

The brilliant military adventures which for a time made his successor, Charles XII (1697–1718), the wonder of Europe disguised the weakness of his position in Sweden.[12] The country, failing to develop its domestic resources, seemed to have made war its national industry; during the century which extends from 1611 to 1721 Sweden fought five wars with the Danes and three with the Poles. Coming to the throne at the age of fifteen, Charles XII staked his career, as we have seen, on a military conflict with Russia. The high point of the Swedish king's fortune came in 1701 when, after defeating the Russians at Narva in the preceding year and going on to dominate Poland, Charles seemed to have the control of the European balance of power in his hands. By 1704 he had forced his candidate upon the Polish throne and by 1706 he had invaded Saxony and compelled its elector to renounce the royal title in Poland which he formerly had held. Charles then made the fateful decision not to join hands with Louis XIV in Western Europe but rather to seek a reckoning with Peter I on Russian soil.

For Sweden everything changed after its catastrophic defeat at Poltava in 1709. Charles XII was a fugitive in Turkey, playing chess and reading Racine while Poland and Denmark returned to the attack on his homeland. Russian armies meanwhile overran the Baltic provinces and a Russian fleet harried the Swedish coast. Augustus II of Saxony resumed the Polish throne. Charles' dramatic return in 1714 could not redress the balance of power. His desperate attempts to mobilize all Sweden's resources bled the country white, while his death on the battlefield in 1718 only made Sweden's imperial downfall doubly certain. The Treaties of Stockholm and Fredericksborg in 1719 and 1720 gave Bremen and Verden to Hanover; half of Swedish Pomerania, including Stettin, went to Prussia. By the Treaty of Nystad in 1721 Russia was confirmed in possession of Karelia, Ingria, Estonia and Livonia. Thus there remained to Sweden only Finland and that small part of Western Pomerania which included the port of Stralsund.[13] Sweden's de-

---

12. See pp. 386–387.
13. Finland was lost in 1809 to Russia and the Stralsund area in 1815 to Prussia.

cline came at a time when other powers, too, were finding that their ambitions to expand met European opposition. Just as the Turkish threat on the Danube had been ended at Carlowitz (1699) and Passarowitz (1718), and just as the great bid of Louis XIV in the west had been foiled at Utrecht (1713), so now the treaties ending the Great Northern War put an end to Swedish ambitions and readjusted the northern balance in favor of Russia and Prussia.

■ POLAND

Poland, a country of the northern plain, had the misfortune to be lacking in natural defensive features and clearly defined geographic boundaries. Surrounded by ambitious, aggressive and unscrupulous states, Poland has been described as having neighbors rather than a history.

At its greatest extent the Polish state reached from the Baltic to the Black Sea and had a population of perhaps eleven millions—nearly ten times that of Sweden. The old Principality of Lithuania had been linked with Poland to make a sort of dual realm under one king until, by the Union of Lublin in 1569 the two parts were merged under the rule of Sigismund II and the capital shifted from Cracow to Warsaw. This "last great act of the Jagellon dynasty" seemed to hold out some hope that Poles, Lithuanians, White Russians, Ukranians, Germans and Jews might somehow be welded together in a powerful state. Such was not to be Poland's destiny.

Poland was a country of startling contradictions and paradoxes. Its peasant class, by far the largest portion of the population, followed the general social trend east of the Elbe River and declined steadily in well-being. Living in hovels and sod huts which perpetuated the wretched conditions of the Middle Ages, the peasants were bound by servile ties to their land. No vigorous native merchant bourgeois class had emerged to take the economic life of the Polish towns away from German and Jewish hands. Culturally Poland was tied to the west; its universities dated from the late Middle Ages; its architecture showed the influence of the Renaissance; in the realm of scholarship it was capable of producing brilliant figures such as Copernicus. The nobility constituted nearly ten per cent of the population. Of these by far the greater number were the gentry, or *szlachta,* proud in possession of their ancient privileges yet often ignorant and poverty-stricken. The great nobles, or *pans,* had close contact with the culture of Western Europe; they maintained a princely dignity on their huge estates, in this respect being equaled only by the great Hungarian magnates.

The workings of Poland's fantastic constitution could be described without too much exaggeration as a kind of organized paralysis. With the end of the native Jagellon dynasty in 1572 kingship had become elective; usually members of foreign dynasties—French, Swedish or Saxon—were chosen. Actually, only in two cases after 1572 were native Poles elected. In theory, at least, severe restrictions were placed upon royal power. The Articles of 1573 really made Poland a republic, with a chief magistrate elected for life by the Diet. The king was to have no voice in choosing his wife or his successor, he was to be neutral in religious matters and he could not lead his troops across the border without the consent of the nobles and then only for three months. In the various parts of the Polish state existed provincial diets, made up of the local gentry and actively concerned to maintain their own privileges. The provincial diets sent delegations to a national diet, or *Sejm,* meeting every two years. Any delegate could by his individual act veto legislation, having only to say *Nie pozwalam* ("I disapprove"). He could likewise, by individual action, dissolve or "explode" the *Sejm.* This *liberum veto,* as it was called, made anarchy in the country's internal affairs almost inevitable. It demonstrated how far an antiquated feudal tradition could go in maintaining local rights that ran contrary to the interests of the state as a whole.[14]

In the seventeenth century Poland suffered heavily at the hands of its neighbors. As early as 1629 it had lost Livonia to Sweden. In 1660 at the Peace of Oliva this loss was confirmed and Prussia's full sovereignty over East Prussia also recognized. A few years later at the Peace of Andrusovo (1667) Poland lost Smolensk, Kiev and large areas of White Russia and the Eastern Ukraine to Russia, an event of cardinal importance in this country's western advance. The aggrandizement of neighbors at Poland's expense had thus become a phenomenon of Polish political life long before the great partitions of the eighteenth century.

The one glorious page in Poland's seventeenth-century history was the reign of its native king, John Sobieski (1674–1696). His defeat of the Turks at the siege of Vienna in 1683, where he led a cavalry charge in person, made him a European hero. Shortly after his death Poland was able at the Peace of Carlowitz (1699) to regain the province of Podolia on the Turkish border —the one example of territorial gain in the general course of national disintegration.

The reign of Sobieski could be taken as the late seventeenth-century climax of Polish brilliance. The Baroque style found its expression in churches such as that of the Holy Cross in Warsaw, and in the royal palace, an echo of Versailles, built between 1682 and 1696. A large element of romantic bravura always characterized the Polish nobility. In the museums

14. A contemporary Polish writer declared: "With a single word God created the world; with a single word, *veto,* we destroy Poland."

of Warsaw and Cracow have been preserved examples, dating from this age, of the extraordinary equipment of the Winged Hussars of Poland. These wore complete suits of armor having a pair of wings some five feet long made of gray eagle's plumes and fastened to the shoulder and down the back so that they opened and fluttered menacingly during a cavalry charge. In a sense they could be taken as the ultimate expression of fantasy and unreality which haunted the Polish nobility in a hard and ruthless age.

As the elective monarchy dragged Poland into foreign entanglements, so also it dragged alien powers into Poland's domestic conflicts. When the throne became vacant in 1697 no less than eighteen candidates presented themselves. The victor, Augustus the Strong of Saxony, is reputed to have won because he arrived late, amply furnished with bribe-money at a time when his rivals in the election had spent all theirs. Poland suffered tragically through the ambitions of Charles XII of Sweden who ravaged the country and overthrew Augustus II for a time, only later to see him return. When Augustus, the reputed father of 365 illegitimate children, died in 1733 all Europe was concerned with the problem of the "Polish Succession." The miserable dynastic war which ensued had the effect of switching thrones and inheritances in half a dozen countries.[15] For Poland it was a still further example of the country's incompetence to handle its own problems amid the seething rivalries and ambitions of a hostile Europe.

■ THE POLITICAL PATTERN OF THE LATE
SEVENTEENTH CENTURY

In following the general patterns of development in the European states during the half-century or so which followed the Peace of Westphalia as they have been summarized in this and the preceding chapters one will observe many conflicting features. The type of constitutional growth, for example, to be seen in England diverged widely from the patterns of political evolution in the continental despotisms. As some states increased their military or economic strength others went into a relative or even an absolute decline. Despite these contrasts, however, it would seem that enough common features existed to make possible some kind of general evaluation.

In the first place, it may be ventured that by the time of the Peace of Utrecht in 1713 and even more clearly by the time of the Peace of Nystad in 1721 the political map of Europe had assumed the general form that it was to maintain well into the nineteenth century. France was firmly established along the upper Rhine in Alsace, Russia along the Baltic coast and Austria along the lower Danube and in Italy. The Ottoman Empire had

15. See pp. 408–409.

been pushed back to the Balkans with a frontier along the Save-Danube line; Sweden had lost most of its trans-Baltic possessions; while Prussia, benefiting by important gains of territory, was well on the way to dominate its German neighbors.

In the second place, the flagrantly acquisitive instincts of the newly developing states were strongly in evidence. Wars were generally carried on for the avowed purpose of territorial gain. So inevitable, indeed, did these warlike policies seem that students of the as yet unnamed subject of international law sought not so much to abolish war as to find the rules that would permit military conflict to be conducted in an orderly fashion understood and accepted by all.

Thirdly, although the force of what we call nationalism certainly found expression in various ways, it ran a poor second to what might be termed dynasticism. Rulers with few exceptions regarded themselves as the possessors or owners of their states. The state was a "patrimony" to be passed on to one's heirs. A good ruler, to be sure, "served" his people even as Frederick the Great was later to declare himself to be the first servant of the Prussian state. Yet the element of possessiveness and personal glorification on the part of the reigning dynasties was seldom absent, as the veritable mania for building palaces, summer retreats, private theaters, art galleries, memorial statues, royal parks and gardens will testify.

Fourthly, and of major importance, must be listed the widespread growth of centralized administrative machinery. While few states could provide an equal to the efficient bureaucratic edifice built in Prussia upon the foundations laid by the Great Elector, most of them produced some at least roughly comparable equivalents. Evidence of this is found in the widespread growth of ministries and the increasing specialization of governmental work under the direction of "boards," "councils" or "colleges." It is also seen in the beginnings of trained, professional bureaucracies, in the spread of the techniques of mercantilism and cameralism, and in the growing professionalism of armies and navies.

Fifthly, it seems clear that the attempts to create some kind of international order were woefully weak. Although writers on what was called "The Law of Nations" sought for universally recognized principles of justice and attempted to tabulate the accepted usages of states in their relations with one another, they made slow progress. Nations were guided by crude considerations of self-interest. The thunders which the papacy directed against the terms of the Treaty of Westphalia were as little heeded as would have been any corresponding pronouncements coming from the Holy Roman Emperor. The only ordering principle of any effectiveness in Europe as a whole was that of the balance of power. If one state became too strong, or showed dangerous signs of over-ambition, then other states more often than not would form a coalition against it in order to redress the balance. This procedure was evident in the case of the various coalitions which opposed Louis XIV. Ultimately, however, the balance of power technique was one that worked erratically and with uncertain effectiveness.

Lastly, one must briefly note certain developments in political thought which help to illuminate the process of political history. The numerous seventeenth-century works on international law, beginning with Hugo Grotius' great monograph, *On the Law of War and Peace* (1625), and including Samuel Pufendorf's *Law of Nature and of Peoples* (1672), indicate the effort being made to bring "sovereign states" somehow under the regulation of certain natural principles of justice, and to codify the various international usages that civilized states were in the habit of employing.

The concept of the state as the embodiment of power was most brilliantly expressed by the Englishman, Thomas Hobbes, who published his *Leviathan* in 1651 at a time when England had been rocked by the conflict between king and parliament. Hobbes, a ruthless materialist, "discovered society," as it has been well put. He saw men living in social groups, at first in a state of nature where, with the lack of any authority "to keep them all in awe," their lives were "solitary, poor, nasty, brutish, and short." Hence men willingly contracted to turn over their uncertain power to one man or group of men—the Sovereign—who has the power, as Hobbes says, to reduce all their wills to one will. "Nor is there any power on earth that can be compared to it," is the terrifying phrase on the title page of the *Leviathan*. Thus is created "that *Mortall God,* to which we owe under the *Immortall God,* our peace and defence." The essence of sovereignty to Hobbes was power, and the sovereign (whether one, few or many) remained sovereign only as long as his power lasted.[16]

Later in the century Hobbes' views were to be modified and transformed by a different version of the social contract coming from the profoundly intelligent pen of John Locke. Such views, however, lead into the eighteenth century and into an atmosphere of natural rights and of revolutionary political philosophy far different from that which Hobbes enunciated. Locke wrote what he considered a justification of the English Revolution of 1688. In this sense he was a man of his times, yet Hobbes was far more characteristically the man of the seventeenth century, reflecting the contemporary concepts of the state in which power, responsibility and all effective initiative were usually combined in the person of the ruler. These, it may be ventured, constituted the basic political ideas by which the greater part of continental Europe lived.

16. For a fuller discussion of Hobbes as a political theorist, see pp. 494–495.

Chapter 16

War and Diplomacy
in Europe, 1713–1789

■ INTRODUCTION

FROM THE TIME of the Peace of Utrecht to the outbreak of the French
Revolution the various European states, more perhaps than ever before,
were busily engaged in maneuvering for diplomatic advantage and in un-

dertaking a series of wars for territorial gain. The eighteenth century could be taken indeed as a classical era of dynastic self-interest, when rulers joined alliances and launched campaigns in dizzying succession in order to strengthen, as each thought, his realm. The century likewise was one in which overseas conflict assumed an intensity previously unknown. The general fact of these colonial rivalries, which had a powerful influence upon the more narrowly European policies of the various states, must always be kept in mind even if, for purposes of discussion, their specific nature must be reserved for treatment in the next chapter.

The signatories of the great treaty settlements associated with the Peace of Utrecht seemed disposed at first to maintain them. Military costs had been so huge that no one could seriously think of unleashing a new war of major proportions. Peace was needed, too, in order to bolster up certain regimes the future of which was not altogether sure. In England, for example, the first of the Hanoverians, George I, succeeded Queen Anne in 1714 only to be challenged almost immediately by the Jacobite rising of 1715. For this reason and others of an economic nature Robert Walpole, who by 1721 came to be the king's principal minister, deplored any venturesome or militantly aggressive foreign policy.

In France the throne passed in 1715 to Louis XV, a frail boy of five who was, barring Philip V of Spain, the only direct surviving male descendant of Louis XIV. The regency was held by his dissipated and scandalous relative, Philip, Duke of Orleans, who had become sole regent by the arbitrary step of ignoring the stipulations in the will of Louis XIV. Meanwhile the lawyers of Philip V of Spain, grandson of Louis XIV, were making it clear that they did not consider Philip's renunciation of the French throne to be necessarily and legally binding. It was a French interest, therefore, as it was an English, to have a period of quiet. Hence, despite the fact that England and France had been bitter rivals during the War of the Spanish Succession, their policies now tended to converge, and their two principal spokesmen in foreign affairs, Earl Stanhope and the Abbé Dubois, exhibited a common concern to maintain the European peace. In general it might be said that the majority of European states subscribed to this interest.

Two powers, however, found little satisfaction in things as they were. These were Austria and Spain. In 1711 the Emperor Charles VI had succeeded his brother Joseph on the imperial throne. This Charles, who as Archduke had been a candidate for the Spanish inheritance, had never ceased regretting his failure to win so rich a prize. He regarded Austria's gains in Italy and the Netherlands as poor compensation, for he had not obtained Sicily, and the value of the Spanish Netherlands was weakened by the establishment within them of the Dutch barrier fortresses. His dissatisfaction might well have led him to take steps that would throw all Europe into confusion.

The other danger to the peace came from Spain where, as we have seen, Philip V aroused European apprehensions by his interest in the French crown. To revive this claim would be to raise the ghost of Louis XIV.[1] An even greater source of trouble lay in his queen, whom Thomas Carlyle named the Termagant of Spain. In 1714 Philip V had taken as his second wife Elizabeth Farnese, daughter of the Duke of Parma. Elizabeth's domination of her husband was a phenomenon of the age. Spain, it is said, was ruled from the low four-poster where, side by side in their bed-jackets the king and queen received their ministers, Philip meekly reading his despatches while Elizabeth dictated and decided. She bore him two sons whose prospects of succeeding to the Spanish throne were dimmed by the existence of two older step-brothers. Hence Elizabeth sought to find lands for her own sons in Italy, preferably Tuscany and Parma. By her intricate, frenzied and ceaseless maneuvers to this end she kept Europe's foreign ministries in a turmoil for a generation.[2]

In the first two decades following the Peace of Utrecht there could be observed a rudimentary form of the "Concert of Europe," that is to say, an association of powers seeking to maintain the existing order. The powers thus wishing the status quo (mainly England, France and the Netherlands) found Spain and Austria intermittently ranged against them. It is this period, running from 1713 to 1740 and studded with minor wars, which

1. The position of Philip V with respect to the French dynasty, and the relationship between Louis XV and the Regent Orleans are shown most simply in the following chart:

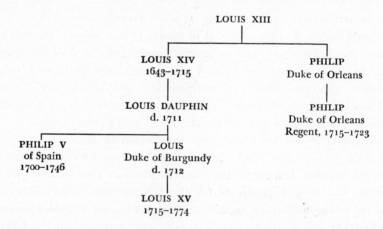

2. Elizabeth's behavior illustrates the value of persistence; her elder son, Don Carlos, was successively Duke of Parma (1731), King of Naples (1735) and of Spain (1759); in 1748 the younger, Don Philip, became Duke of Parma.

commands first attention, less for the tedious detail of its diplomacy than for the underlying aims which can be discovered. Following this we may distinguish a second period extending from 1740 to 1763 when the restless energies of Frederick II of Prussia brought him to the center of the stage, produced a new series of wars and effected an important change in the balance of power. The last three decades of the Old Régime constitute a third period where the main interest seemed to shift eastward, centering upon the portentous questions of the future of Poland and of the Ottoman Empire.

■ THE TERMAGANT OF SPAIN

Spain provided the major impetus for the series of European conflicts which first disturbed the calm of the post-Utrecht period. This calm, it must be recalled, was only relative, for the Northern War, fought for the control of the Baltic, did not end until the Treaty of Nystad in 1721; while Austria carried on intermittent war with the Turks until the Peace of Belgrade in 1739. In Spain Philip V had taken as his principal adviser an Italian priest, Alberoni, who by helping to arrange the king's marriage to Elizabeth Farnese had become a power at court. Alberoni had achieved the rank of cardinal, and in the tradition of Richelieu and Mazarin devoted himself to diplomatic adventure on a grand scale. His policy was to build the economy until Spain became a first-rate power and then undo the Utrecht settlement by seeking to gain, or regain, substantial possessions in Italy. Naturally enough, in view of her ambitions for her sons, the queen ardently supported Alberoni's ideas.

In the light of these and other dangers to the peace, England and France came together. In January, 1717, along with the United Netherlands they formed the Triple Alliance to guarantee the terms of the Peace of Utrecht. Almost immediately Spain reacted by attacking the Austrian possessions in Italy. A Spanish fleet seized Sardinia and Spanish troops were sent to invade Naples. To make matters worse, Alberoni tried to organize a Jacobite rising in England and also plotted to overthrow and kidnap the Duke of Orleans in France. In the face of such threats the Triple Alliance responded with war. Austria, by joining the western powers, made their association a Quadruple Alliance. A British fleet destroyed the entire Spanish fleet off Cape Passaro in the Mediterranean, so completely that Spain received no news of the disaster for a month. The odds now being heavily against Spain, Philip V dismissed Alberoni and agreed to the terms of the Treaty of The Hague (1720). Austria was allowed to take Sicily in exchange for Sardinia which it had received at Utrecht, and Elizabeth

The Treaty of Utrecht (1713) dealt largely with the west, Nystad (1721), with the Baltic area. Austria replaces Spain in the Netherlands and Italy (where Spain, however, later returns). Note the enlarged Hungary, the Hapsburg advance on the lower Danube and the growth of Prussian power. For Russia and Sweden see maps on pages 383 and 395.

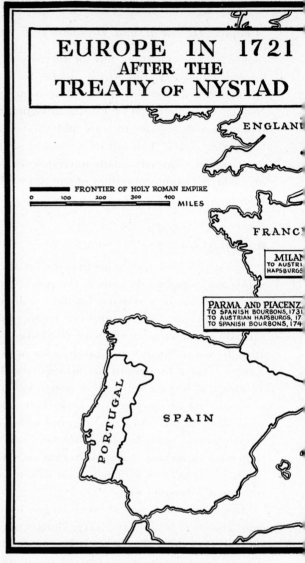

EUROPE IN 1721
AFTER THE
TREATY OF NYSTAD

▬▬▬ FRONTIER OF HOLY ROMAN EMPIRE

0   100   200   300   400
▬▬▬▬▬▬▬▬▬▬ MILES

ENGLAND

FRANCE

MILAN
TO AUSTRI
HAPSBURGS

PARMA AND PIACENZ.
TO SPANISH BOURBONS,1731
TO AUSTRIAN HAPSBURGS, 17
TO SPANISH BOURBONS, 174

PORTUGAL

SPAIN

Farnese was promised that her son, Don Carlos, could look forward eventually to ruling the Italian duchies of Parma and Piacenza. Thus ended in a kind of compromise the first Spanish effort to overthrow the Utrecht settlement. In view of the insistent maternal ambitions of Elizabeth Farnese the compromise was not likely to last.

Spain, as before, took the initiative. The royal adviser succeeding Alberoni was a Dutchman, Ripperda. Inasmuch as Austria had now developed certain resentments against the Triple Alliance, Ripperda's policy was to win that country over to an alliance with Spain.[3] Consequently, in a

3. Austria was resentful that the members of the Triple Alliance would not support the Pragmatic Sanction (see above, p. 364), or agree to Austria forming the Ostend Company to trade with India.

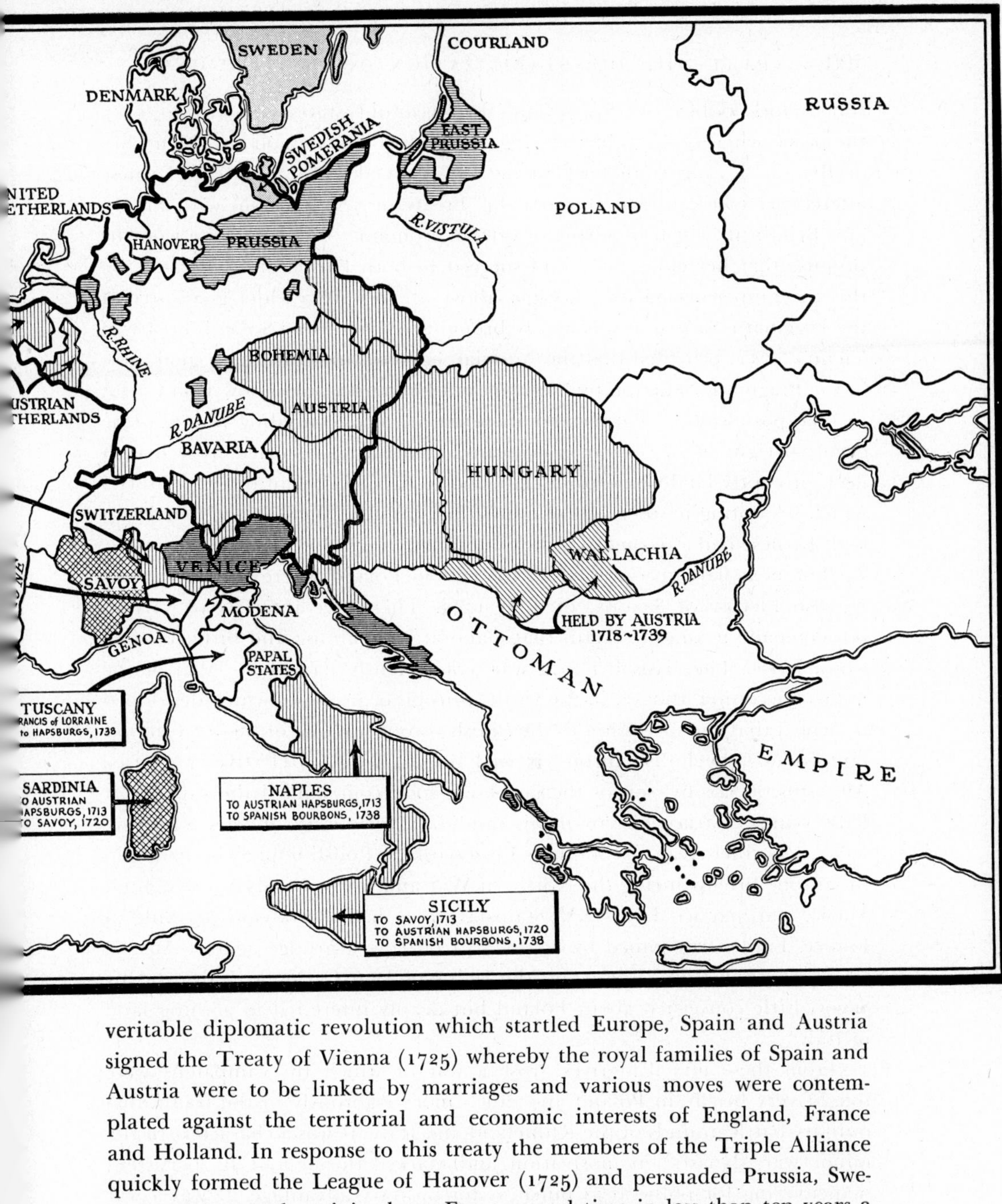

SWEDEN
COURLAND
DENMARK
RUSSIA
SWEDISH POMERANIA
EAST PRUSSIA
NITED
ETHERLANDS
POLAND
R. VISTULA
HANOVER
PRUSSIA
R. RHINE
BOHEMIA
USTRIAN
THERLANDS
R. DANUBE
AUSTRIA
BAVARIA
HUNGARY
SWITZERLAND
WALLACHIA
R. DANUBE
VENICE
SAVOY
MODENA
OTTOMAN
HELD BY AUSTRIA
1718~1739
GENOA
PAPAL STATES
TUSCANY
RANCIS of LORRAINE
to HAPSBURGS, 1738
EMPIRE
SARDINIA
O AUSTRIAN
APSBURGS, 1713
O SAVOY, 1720
NAPLES
TO AUSTRIAN HAPSBURGS, 1713
TO SPANISH BOURBONS, 1738
SICILY
TO SAVOY, 1713
TO AUSTRIAN HAPSBURGS, 1720
TO SPANISH BOURBONS, 1738

veritable diplomatic revolution which startled Europe, Spain and Austria signed the Treaty of Vienna (1725) whereby the royal families of Spain and Austria were to be linked by marriages and various moves were contemplated against the territorial and economic interests of England, France and Holland. In response to this treaty the members of the Triple Alliance quickly formed the League of Hanover (1725) and persuaded Prussia, Sweden and Denmark to join them. For a second time in less than ten years a European "concert" had come into existence to cope with a Spanish threat.

The effect of the League of Hanover was to cause the downfall of Ripperda and steer the indefatigable Elizabeth Farnese into new paths as she undertook her perpetual quest to find Italian thrones for her heirs. In France, Cardinal Fleury had come into full power in 1726. The patient and conciliatory policy of this seventy-three-year-old statesman was to keep the peace wherever possible, relying in the first place upon the friendship of Britain. Losing confidence in her Austrian alliance, Elizabeth Farnese altered her course and negotiated the Treaty of Seville (1729) with France and Britain in which by virtue of certain economic concessions she won the promise that her elder son could succeed to both Parma and Tuscany. To this the Emperor Charles VI, eager above all to have a wider guarantee of the Pragmatic Sanction, was finally brought to agree. The Second Treaty of Vienna (1731) provided that the Austrian emperor in return for a guarantee of the Pragmatic Sanction by England and Holland would allow Don Carlos to take possession of Parma and Piacenza at once, conceding him also the eventual right of succession in Tuscany. Don Carlos, escorted by a British fleet, promptly landed troops in Italy and took possession of those territories which his doting mother had sought so persistently. Were it not that Elizabeth Farnese had a second son, the atmosphere might have continued quiet.

The next flare-up came far to the east in Poland where King Augustus II, also Elector of Saxony, died in 1733. The active interests of various powers made it almost certain that elaborate bargaining and bitter conflict would arise. The crisis led to a war, conveniently named the War of the Polish Succession, though in the vast confusion of purposes which developed it seemed that the succession to the Polish throne was one of the least important issues. The Polish throne, it will be recalled, was elective. Frederick Augustus of Saxony, son of the late king, soon commanded the support of Russia and Austria who saw in his candidacy various advantages for themselves. His chief rival was Stanislas Leszczynski, a Polish noble who had held the throne briefly during the Northern War and whose handsome daughter, Maria, had married Louis XV. Stanislas, then, had the obvious backing of France. France was joined by Spain, still bearing a grudge against Austria for her hesitancy in recognizing the rights of Don Carlos in Italy, and by Savoy, little concerned about Poland but deeply interested in gaining land in Italy.

From these mixed motives arose a war of which the campaigns were fought very briefly in Poland and much more vigorously in the traditional military battlegrounds of the Rhineland and Italy. It was a characteristically minor war, dynastic in motivation and marked throughout by persistent maneuvering for political as much as for military advantage. It was a war which the peace-loving Robert Walpole contrived to avoid. "Madam," he told Queen Caroline in 1734, "there are fifty thousand men slain this year in Europe, and not one Englishman." It was also a war in which Russian troops, sent to assist the Austrian emperor, were seen in the Rhineland for

the first time in European history. It ended in 1738 when the various contestants were able to contrive a settlement with something in it for everyone.

By the Third Treaty of Vienna (1738) Stanislas, defeated in his bid for
the Polish throne, was to be given the Duchy of Lorraine for life, the duchy
on his death to go to France. The gain here was clearly as much that of
France as it was of Stanislas. The dispossessed Francis, Duke of Lorraine,
was to be shifted to Tuscany on the death of its ruler, and to marry the
emperor's daughter, Maria Theresa. The emperor, in turn, was to retain
Milan and receive Parma and Piacenza from Don Carlos, the son of Elizabeth Farnese. Austria agreed that this same Don Carlos, losing Parma and
Piacenza, was to become King of Naples and Sicily. Russia was pleased to
see its candidate on the Polish throne. France, finally, was to recognize the
Pragmatic Sanction. Truly, this was a treaty with something for everyone—
except possibly Savoy, which obtained only a negligible "rectification" of its
eastern frontier. The outstanding features of the settlement were, first, that
it provided for France's advance towards its "natural frontiers." Secondly,
it made even stronger the Austrian hold in North Italy. Thirdly, it placed
the Spanish Bourbons in Naples and Sicily where they were to remain until
1860, thus crowning the ambitions of Elizabeth Farnese. In contrast to these
portentous developments the seating of the trivial Augustus III on the
Polish throne was a mere incident.

■ THE WAR OF THE AUSTRIAN SUCCESSION

The petty conflicts which ended in the peace settlement of 1738 were
soon followed by a war of major proportions. Its prologue took the form of a
maritime and colonial conflict between Britain and Spain (the "War of
Jenkins' Ear"). The opening episode in Europe was Prussia's dramatic
seizure of the Austrian province of Silesia. From these events the contest
developed so as to involve other geographical areas and to raise other political issues. The war ended in a decisive victory for the ruler who started it—
Frederick II of Prussia.

At least three large questions were involved. One was that of the Hapsburg inheritance and the imperial crown. The Emperor Charles VI had
hoped to transmit his Hapsburg lands intact to his daughter, Maria Theresa.
To this end he had undertaken in 1713 to secure the famous Pragmatic
Sanction, first accepted by the spokesmen for his own scattered domains and
subsequently by the powers of Europe.[4] All save Bavaria (a keen rival for
the imperial dignity) had agreed—France last of all in 1738 as one of the
terms of the treaty ending the War of the Polish Succession.

4. See p. 364.

The second large issue concerned Prussia. Here, in the spring of 1740, a young king of great talent and consuming ambition succeeded his father, Frederick William I. This Frederick II saw in Silesia a fertile and strategically valuable province, the seizure of which would be the first logical move in an eastward advance that could someday link the old Electorate of Brandenburg with the territory of East Prussia. Both in a military and in an economic sense Silesia would be a powerful addition to the Prussian state and one that would tip the balance away from Austria.

The third large issue was more broadly European. It arose from the general desire of many powers to fish in troubled waters: the Elector of Bavaria, for example, sought the imperial crown; the Elector of Saxony, who was also King of Poland, wished some part of Silesia; Savoy, frustrated by the peace of 1738, was eager to push eastward into the Hapsburg Duchy of Milan; Spain, as always, sought to rearrange Italy still further in the interest of the sons of Elizabeth Farnese; and France stood ready to march once more into the Austrian Netherlands. Granted such ambitions, a Prussian attack on Silesia would be followed almost inevitably by the formation of an anti-Austrian coalition, for Austria, more than any other power, seemed the guardian of the status quo.

The Prussian ruler whose impulsive actions set off this large train of events was now twenty-eight. As a youth he had been the opposite of everything his drill-master of a father wished: a dilettante, a poet, a flute-player, a devotee of French literature. The crown prince had, indeed, once sought to run away; he had been seized, imprisoned, compelled to watch the beheading of his closest friend and to keep a long public vigil over the body. Whatever inner scars this experience may have left, Frederick thereupon had accepted the harsh discipline his father imposed. He had even agreed to wed Elizabeth Christine, the unhappy, unattractive princess whose married life was fifty-three years of loneliness and sorrow. In the years before becoming king, Frederick, now on much better terms with his father, contrived to maintain his cultural interests while at the same time concerning himself with political and military affairs.

A coincidence of events precipitated the crisis of 1740. Frederick II succeeded his father on May 31; the Emperor Charles died on October 20, trusting that, in virtue of general acceptance of the Pragmatic Sanction, his lands would pass unimpaired to his daughter. Less than two months later, on December 16, and against the advice of his foreign minister and his generals, Frederick led his Prussian troops across the Silesian border. He, like the others, had guaranteed the Pragmatic Sanction; by his own admission he now acted solely for reasons of ambition and selfish aggrandizement. Rather than undertaking a carefully prepared plan, he was in reality improvising rapidly in order to take advantage of what looked like a fortunate situation.

Although inexperienced and at first nervous in battle, Frederick had little difficulty in winning Silesia from the weak grasp of Maria Theresa. His lawyers were not slow to provide him with pseudo-legal claims, yet essentially the victory was one for ruthless force. Paralleling his actions, other countries quickly moved against the Hapsburgs. Bavaria and Saxony launched attacks on Bohemia, while Spain moved to regain lands in Italy such as Parma and Piacenza which had been lost in 1738. France was at first hesitant, for the eighty-seven-year-old Cardinal Fleury saw little point in military adventures. However, a war party whipped up the traditional anti-Hapsburg sentiment so that in 1741 France, too, sent one army to attack the Austrian Netherlands and a second to aid Bavaria on the Danube.

In the face of this greedy hostility Maria Theresa could find few allies. Within her own lands she made an eloquent appeal to the Hungarian nobles who rallied loyally to their queen. Savoy, which had at first chosen the opposing side, was lured to support Austria by the promise of gains in Lombardy. The Dutch gave their sympathy, but little more. England, at war with Spain since 1739 over the colonial issue, was concerned at the Prussian threat to Hanover, at the French in the Netherlands and more generally at the changing European balance. Hence it gave military support to Maria Theresa, and provided the interesting spectacle at Dettingen (1743) of English and allied troops moving into a victorious battle led by King George II himself—the last such royal occasion in English history.

Frederick's whole conduct of the war was marked by complete cynicism. On two occasions he withdrew when he felt his gains secure, only to return when they seemed threatened. Meanwhile Charles Albert of Bavaria had realized his great ambition by winning the imperial election of 1742.[5] When he died in 1745, however, Maria Theresa had the satisfaction of seeing the imperial title revert to her husband, Francis of Lorraine, and later to her son, Joseph II. In this sense, then, despite her adversities, Maria Theresa was able to aid the fortunes of her house.

In 1744 the Second Silesian War welled up as the two sides again strove for mastery. The French Marshal de Saxe avenged the defeat at Dettingen by winning the victory of Fontenoy (1745) in the Netherlands, while in the same year Frederick won his great victory of Hohenfriedberg over the Austrians. Following this and again acting on his own he made the Peace of Dresden (1745) with Maria Theresa, compelling her to recognize once more

---

5. This is the only example of a non-Hapsburg on the throne of the Holy Roman Empire between 1438 and 1806. His successor, Francis I of Lorraine, although not a Hapsburg, was married to Maria Theresa.

his conquest of Silesia. Henceforth the struggle became largely colonial in nature.

At long last the "Maritime Powers" (Britain and Holland) undertook negotiations with France at Aix-la-Chapelle. Their decisions, reached in 1748, were later accepted by Austria. The general basis of peace was the restoration of conquests, with certain significant exceptions. Frederick, of course, kept Silesia. Savoy won a few "leaves from the Italian artichoke" by gaining certain western portions of the Hapsburg Duchy of Milan. And Elizabeth Farnese had the rare satisfaction of seeing her second son, Don Philip, installed as Duke of Parma and Piacenza. Of these changes the Prussian gain of Silesia was unquestionably the most important:

> In truth, Frederick's acquisition of Silesia was the greatest permanent conquest of territory hitherto made by any power in the history of modern western Europe. It became not merely the largest, but, with its rich linen industry and undeveloped iron ores, the wealthiest province of the Prussian monarchy. Without it Prussia could never have become a great power. Its transfer to the Hohenzollern, therefore, marks one of the incisive changes in the history of central Europe.[6]

■ THE DIPLOMATIC REVOLUTION AND THE SEVEN YEARS' WAR

The peace which followed the Treaty of Aix-la-Chapelle was in reality no peace at all, but rather a breathing spell during which diplomatic maneuvering went on at full speed while England and France, nominally at peace in Europe, began a further colonial war in the New World.[7] This Anglo-French antagonism, representing basic rivalries on the world stage, was fundamental. The rivalry between Austria and Prussia likewise was fundamental, for Prussia's capture of Silesia and its seeming determination to dominate German affairs left Austria wholly unreconciled. Was it, however, essential that Austria should consider France its enemy and England its friend? This was the problem which presented itself to Prince Kaunitz, the brilliant statesman who became chancellor and foreign minister of Austria in 1753.

As early as 1749 Kaunitz had begun to insist that the Hapsburgs' real enemy was Prussia rather than France, and that in order to aid in the destruction of Prussia France might even be turned into a friend. Sent to Versailles as Austrian ambassador in 1750, Kaunitz made his first tentative overtures, seeking to win the attention of Louis XV through the royal mis-

6. W. DORN, *Competition for Empire, 1740–1763* (1940), pp. 174–175.
7. French expansion into the Ohio Valley in North America had been followed by the failure of Washington's expedition across the Alleghenies in 1754 and by General Braddock's defeat in 1755.

tress, the Marquise de Pompadour. Meanwhile, with the assistance of Count Haugwitz, another able servant, Maria Theresa had undertaken a far-reaching reorganization of her whole administrative system in the interest of greater efficiency.[8] The provincial agencies of government were subordinated much more effectively than ever before to the centrally organized bureaucracy at Vienna. Austria was thus hopeful, despite the heavy loss of Silesia, of being able to launch military action on a European scale.

The desire of Kaunitz for a reversal of alliances ultimately became a reality as the result of moves coming not from Austria but from Great Britain. This latter country was nervous, as always, at the prospect of a French attack upon the Low Countries; and now, with the Hanoverian dynasty upon the throne, it was concerned, too, about the safety of the Electorate of Hanover. Having found out by inquiry that Austria was less than willing to guarantee help, England looked in other directions. In 1755 it secured a treaty with Russia by which, in return for subsidies, Russia agreed to maintain 50,000 men on the frontiers of East Prussia. Next, in January, 1756, England signed the Convention of Westminster with Prussia, agreeing to oppose the entrance into Germany of any foreign troops. While this had the ultimate effect of counteracting the Anglo-Russian agreement, its immediate effect was to produce action in France. Louis XV now ordered his ministers to accept the overtures from Austria. The outcome was the Treaty of Versailles (May, 1756) in which France and Austria agreed to defend each other's possessions in Europe. Almost simultaneously the Empress Elizabeth of Russia offered Maria Theresa her assistance against Frederick II of Prussia.

Thus, by what looked like a complete reversal of policy the "Diplomatic Revolution" of 1756 had been accomplished. Despite the long tradition of Hapsburg-Bourbon rivalry, France and Austria were now allied, standing with Russia against the Protestant powers of Great Britain and Prussia. Thus when Frederick suddenly invaded his German neighbor, Saxony, in August, 1756, he set off a train of events which led to another European conflict—the Seven Years' War—more violent and wider in extent than that of 1740–1748. Only after Frederick had thus started it did Austria and France sign a Second Treaty of Versailles (May, 1757) by which the signatories pledged themselves in sweeping language to the total destruction of Prussia.[9] It is a striking commentary on Kaunitz's skill that he had won the unwitting support of France in his effort to reestablish Hapsburg leadership in Germany. However necessary this might seem in the light of the new danger from Prussia, it remains true that what France now was doing under the

8. For details see pp. 541–543.
9. The French text of the treaty read: *la destruction totale de la Prusse.*

guidance of Louis XV and Madame de Pompadour ran contrary to the policy of every French statesman since Richelieu. The war which developed had, moreover, a greater significance on the colonial than on the European scene. It was, indeed, permanently to alter the overseas balance of power to the great disadvantage of France and to the great advantage of Great Britain.

In Europe Frederick II could count on very little direct help from his English ally. Having invaded Saxony and then Bohemia he won some early victories, notably at Prague, only to experience a shattering defeat at Kolin. He found Prussia ringed by the hostile coalition of Austria, France, Russia and Sweden. In a series of brilliant battles—Rossbach, Leuthen and Zorndorf—he displayed his magical skill as a commander and his incomparable determination. In wretched health, Frederick forced himself to the limits of physical endurance. He never bathed and seldom washed, and with his unkempt hair and filthy, snuff-strewn uniform must have presented an extraordinary spectacle. "If you saw me now," he wrote at the age of forty-seven to Voltaire, "you would hardly recognize me. I am old, broken, gray-haired, wrinkled. I am losing my teeth and my gaiety." Danger pressed in upon him from all sides. He could not prevent a Russian army from reaching and ravaging the suburbs of Berlin, and he met near-disaster in the defeat of Kunersdorf in 1759 where 19,000 of his 43,000 Prussians were killed or wounded. English help (confined to some campaigning in Hanover) availed him little. In 1759 England was faced, as it had been at the time of the Armada and as it was to be at the time of Napoleon and again at the time of Hitler, with the prospect of invasion, for the French assembled troops and flat-bottomed transports for this purpose. But the British navy blockaded every French port from Dunkirk to Toulon, and when in November Admiral Hawke smashed the French fleet in the resounding victory of Quiberon Bay, the danger was averted.

Frederick, indeed, seemed more than once on the point of defeat. To say that he was saved by the chance happening of the death in 1762 of his bitter opponent, the Empress Elizabeth of Russia, and the accession of his ardent admirer, Peter III, is to attach too much importance to a single event. A combination of factors will better explain Frederick's ultimate victory. One such factor was the general weakness and uncoordinated strategy of the coalition formed against him. Another was the disciplined strength of the Prussian army. Another was the efficient machinery of the Prussian bureaucracy which worked well, maintained order and somehow provided Frederick with the sinews of war. Another lay in the tactical brilliance of Frederick on the field of battle. Still another (the factor singled out later by Napoleon) was the indomitable will power of "Old Fritz"—a moral leadership with which he was able to inspire his country at moments when the future seemed utterly dark.

By 1763 France had been beaten to her knees in the colonial struggle; Catherine II, the successor of her husband, Peter III of Russia, was well disposed towards Frederick; and Austria was exhausted. The Peace of Paris confirmed Britain's colonial victory over France.[10] The Treaty of Hubertusberg in the same year reestablished peace in Europe on the basis of the status quo. This meant, essentially, that Frederick II kept Silesia and that the original Austrian hopes of dismembering Prussia had evaporated. Prussia and Austria pledged mutual friendship and Frederick II promised his future electoral vote to Maria Theresa's son, Joseph, when he became a candidate for the imperial crown. Clearly enough, Frederick II had contrived to assert his position as the leading power in Germany where he had effectively challenged the primacy of the Hapsburgs. Amid great peril and at a heavy cost he had staved off the threat of a coalition designed to effect the destruction of his country. As Peter the Great had acquired new dignities at the victorious close of the Northern War, so now in 1763 Frederick's admiring subjects began to call him "The Great."

■ THE PARTITIONS OF POLAND

The lull following the "settlement" of 1763 was soon succeeded by the long drawn out and tragic spectacle of Poland's disappearance from the map of Europe. To understand the ruthless destruction of this ancient kingdom once reaching from the Baltic to the Black Sea one must focus the historical spotlight upon a relatively narrow segment of the European scene. In another sense, however, the problem was of widespread concern, to be understood not as an internal Polish problem but rather in terms of the conflicting interests of the European powers.

Despite the Peace of Paris, many general problems remained and many European aspirations stood unfulfilled. To Frederick II of Prussia the urgent need was peace, for his country had suffered terribly during two decades of war. Yet he had not lost interest in territorial expansion, any more than had Catherine II of Russia who conceived of her country's future in terms of an advance of frontiers to the west and south. Austria, with no great expansionist aims of its own, deeply resented the loss of Silesia and had no desire to see its powerful neighbors make still further gains. Prussia, it will be recalled, had won reconciliation with its former enemy, Russia, in the last stages of the Seven Years' War when first Peter III and then his wife, Catherine II, succeeded to the throne formerly held by Frederick's bitter opponent, the Tsarina Elizabeth. To Frederick it was a matter of prime impor-

10. For details see pp. 452–453.

tance to maintain this friendly link with Russia. Placed so as to be the neighbor of these three powers was the Kingdom of Poland. Here, then, was the setting for a political drama of major proportions and of long consequences.

In the decade following 1763 the problem of Poland's future revealed itself as a matter of acute concern for its powerful neighbors. The staggering weaknesses in Poland's social and political structure have already been described.[11] The tragedy of Poland was that these weaknesses made themselves glaringly apparent precisely at a time when Russia, Prussia and Austria were at the height of their struggle for territory and power. Prussia in Silesia, Austria on the lower Danube and Russia along the Baltic all had their memories of recent and impressive gains. Their continuing ambitions and rivalries led them consequently to an ingenious solution whereby, at least for a time, they liquidated their other disagreements in a joint plan to take land from their weak neighbor. Such, in essence, is the explanation of that cold-blooded exercise in power politics known as the First Partition of Poland.

In October, 1763, Augustus III, the Saxon Elector who was also ruler of Poland, had died. In opposition to the new Saxon candidate appeared a native Polish nobleman, Stanislas Poniatowski, a discarded lover of Catherine II somewhat blemished in reputation. The Russian empress saw in his election the prospect of exercising, as she desired, control over Polish affairs. Frederick, whose correspondence with Catherine reveals a marked congeniality of temperament, was willing to give his approval and support because with Silesia now in his hands he felt the need of some ally against a recurrence of trouble with Austria. It is equally clear that he looked forward himself to acquiring Polish territory. East Prussia still was separated from the rest of the kingdom by that Polish area (once in the hands of the Teutonic Knights) known as West Prussia. As early as 1752 Frederick had composed a Political Testament in which he indicated West Prussia along with Saxony and Swedish Pomerania as lands someday to be won. Doubtless with the idea of seeking selfish advantage within the Polish state, Prussia and Russia signed an agreement in 1764 pledging themselves to support the candidacy of Stanislas and to oppose any changes in Poland's antiquated constitution. The election took place with Russian troops stationed in Poland and Prussian troops massed along the borders. Under such circumstances it was not hard for Stanislas to win the election, thereby becoming the last native-born king of Poland.

Trouble soon developed in Poland where a native "patriotic" party, led by the great family of Czartoryski, resented Catherine's active inter-

11. See pp. 397–398.

In the map:

BALTIC SEA

RUSSIA

Konigsberg
Danzig

EAST PRUSSIA

Vilna

Smolensk

PRUSSIA

Berlin

1772

Thorn

1795

1795

R. NIEMEN

R. DWINA 1772

R. ODER

Warsaw

1793

R. BUG

1795

R. PRIPET

1793

Kiev

R. DNIEPER

AUSTRIA

R. VISTULA

Cracow

1772

R. DNIESTER

TO RUSSIA
1792

ZIPS
1770

BOUNDARY OF
POLAND ~ 1772

BUKOVINA

1776

R. PRUTH

TO RUSSIA
1783

TO RUSSIA
1792

Vienna

R. DANUBE

Budapest

HUNGARY

R. DRAVE

R. SAVE

OTTOMAN

Bucharest

R. DANUBE

BLACK
SEA

EMPIRE

Legend:

1772
1793
1795
TO RUSSIA

1772
1793
1795
TO PRUSSIA

1772
1795
TO AUSTRIA

THE PARTITIONS of POLAND
1772 ~ 1793 ~ 1795

0   100   200   300   400   500
MILES

In 23 years one of Europe's largest states completely disappeared. Russia's gains were largest in area; Prussia gained the most strategically; Austria won the least.

ference in Poland's affairs. King Stanislas was persuaded to recommend to the Diet the abolition, at least in financial affairs, of the notorious *liberum veto*. Such moves, challenging the vested interests of the nobles, if successful might have put Poland on the path of strength. Further trouble came from the demands of Polish religious minorities, both Protestant and Greek Orthodox Catholic, for full religious toleration. These looked, not unnaturally, either to Protestant Prussia or Orthodox Russia for help. The disagreements reached the point of civil war in 1767 when two rival Polish "confederations," or gatherings of nobles, fell into conflict over the religious issue. Catherine actually sent in troops to help the religious dissidents; some of the Russian soldiers, pursuing their opponents across the southern border of Poland, provoked an incident with the Turks.

The ensuing Russo-Turkish War (1768–1774) was clearly due to much more than this border incident, for rivalry between Moscow and Constantinople was fundamental. Catherine's military advance against the Turks proved to be highly successful. Azov, won by Peter the Great and subsequently lost, was regained; Bessarabia was overrun and Russian troops advanced into the Principalities of Moldavia and Wallachia, seizing Bucharest and threatening to cross the lower Danube.[12] The prospect of Russia pushing beyond the Danube into the heart of the Balkans was disturbing, for it would have seriously endangered the European balance and been of grave concern to Austria. Even Frederick II, the friend and admirer of Catherine, could not approve of the possible annihilation of the Ottoman Empire.

In 1769 Frederick informally suggested a partition of Poland to his Russian ally. In 1770, reviving a fifteenth-century legal claim, Austria sent troops into the Polish border area known as Zips. Frederick held two interviews with Maria Theresa's son, Joseph II, and sent his brother Henry to talk with Catherine II at St. Petersburg. Catherine made it clear (December, 1771) that she would be willing to withdraw from most of her Turkish conquests if she could find compensation in Poland, for she saw a possible war with Austria if she continued hostilities with the Turks. Maria Theresa seemed the most reluctant to join in a partition. Yet she, too, could not be so unrealistic as to forego her portion of Poland if the others took theirs. In the sardonic words of Frederick II, "She is always in tears, yet she is always ready to take her share." A preliminary agreement having been reached by Russia and Prussia in February, the decisive agreement of the three powers was signed in August, 1772, after the final crushing of Polish resistance. Poland's official acceptance was not obtained until September, 1773.

By the terms of the partition Russia obtained lands which brought her frontier to the Düna and the upper Dnieper and gave her some 1,800,000 new subjects. These were mainly White Russians, Eastern Orthodox in religion and therefore easily assimilable in the Russian state. The commercial value of these lands, especially in view of the control of the Düna waterway, was considerable. Frederick acquired West Prussia with its 400,000

12. The Russians even sent a small fleet from the Baltic to the Mediterranean, picking up a British admiral en route to take charge, seeing that the distinguished Russian commander, Count Orlov, had never been to sea before. With expert British advice a Turkish fleet was neatly destroyed at Tchesmé, off the coast of Asia Minor (1770).

population of mixed Polish and German tongues. The territorial link with East Prussia was thus established, even though the valuable port of Danzig at the mouth of the Vistula River remained in Polish hands. The Hapsburgs won some 2,700,000 subjects, chiefly in Galicia. This Polish territory, lying on the northern slope of the Carpathians, had neither linguistic, geographic nor economic affinity with Austria's other possessions, yet in point of numbers and size it was the largest gain made by any of the three participants. Poland's territory was reduced by nearly one-third and her population by even more. Finally, it must be recorded that the European states as a whole looked upon the partition with toleration, cynicism or indifference.

Poland's ultimate destruction was accomplished during the stormy days of the French Revolution, when Frederick II and Maria Theresa had both passed from the scene. In briefest summary the story can be told as follows. Continued Russian interference after the first partition led to a surge of national feeling and a strong demand on the part of Polish liberals for genuine reform. The outcome was the constitution of 1791, a truly enlightened document which, by setting up a limited hereditary monarchy and a parliamentary regime and by proposing large social reforms, seemed to echo the contemporary changes occurring in France.

Catherine II took this constitution of 1791 as an act of defiance. In the following year Russian troops occupied the country, defeated the Polish patriots and won the backing of Prussia, though not of Austria. In the ensuing partition of 1793 Prussia took the rich province of Posen, gaining the valuable cities of Danzig and Thorn which it had failed to secure in 1772. Altogether this meant an increased Prussian population of about 1,500,000 souls. Catherine took an area four times as large with about 3,000,000 inhabitants, so that only a rump of the great Polish state which once extended "from sea to sea" was left. When a last great patriotic Polish uprising led by Thaddeus Kosciusko proved unavailing, the three original participants were able in October, 1795, to divide what was left of the Polish state. Warsaw became a Prussian provincial city, Cracow fell to Austria and Vilna to Russia. Poland did not emerge again as a truly independent state for over a century. Thus was concluded "as callous a diplomatic transaction as a century not without some distinction in *Realpolitik* was to witness." [13]

■ THE LAST RIVALRIES OF FREDERICK II AND JOSEPH II

The closing years of the Old Régime were marked by renewed rivalry between Prussia and Austria over the question of German leadership. Joseph II, who had been elected Holy Roman Emperor in 1765, serving at the same time with his mother as co-regent of the Hapsburg lands, became

13. LEO GERSHOY, *From Despotism to Revolution* (1944), p. 174.

sole ruler in 1780 on the death of Maria Theresa. He had acquired the Bukowina from Turkey in 1775, a useful adjunct to the land just taken from Poland, and soon afterwards won the port of Fiume, on the Adriatic. The ambitions of the young emperor, eager for even further gains, soon brought him into conflict with Frederick II.

The source of trouble lay in Joseph's effort to secure part of the valuable Electorate of Bavaria, the ruler of which died in 1777. There being no direct heir, various claimants were in the running. Joseph, who had some doubtful claims of his own, sought to strengthen them by buying up the claims of the Elector Palatine to at least part of Bavaria. Such moves immediately aroused Frederick II who did not wish to see the position of his country menaced by any growth of his Austrian rival. Ingeniously, however, Frederick professed to speak in the name of the German princes as a whole and in defense of the terms of the Treaty of Westphalia. He further disguised his essentially selfish policy by professing to back the claims of another candidate, the Duke of Zweibrücken. Consequently, when Joseph actually began to occupy Bavaria in 1778, Frederick sent two columns of troops into Bohemia, one led by himself, one by his brother, Henry.

This War of the Bavarian Succession, unlike its predecessors, turned out to be something of a farce. A huge Austrian army installed itself in a vast entrenched position which Frederick approached and carefully surveyed for two months, only to decide at long last that it was impregnable. Consequently he withdrew ingloriously. The troops, foraging for sustenance, had spent so much time digging up frozen potatoes that the name "The Potato War," was given to the campaign. Russia and France assisted in negotiating the Peace of Teschen in May, 1779, by which Austria agreed to withdraw its claims, keeping, however, a useful frontier strip of Bavarian territory along the River Inn, the so-called "Innviertel." Frederick was promised that the small territories of Ansbach and Baireuth, then in the hands of distant relatives, could revert ultimately to Prussia. Thus, despite his unheroic military role, he had in the end achieved his purpose of minimizing the ambitions of Joseph II, meanwhile making a little profit on the transaction.

The Austrian ruler, however, was still ambitious, even more so when death removed the restraining hand of his mother. He contrived to maneuver himself into the favor of Catherine II, forming a defensive alliance with Russia in 1781 which left Frederick II out in the cold. In 1784 Joseph attempted a move of spectacular proportions. He offered the elector of Bavaria an exchange, the elector to take the Austrian Netherlands (a political hornets' nest for which Joseph had a low regard) and Joseph to take Bavaria. In this way Joseph could rid himself of a troublesome distant province and at the same time greatly strengthen Austria's position in central Europe. The implications for the balance of power within Germany were obvious.

Frederick II, old and ill, once more assumed the pose of "protector of German liberties." He first invited the electors of Saxony, Hanover and Mainz to join him in maintaining the status quo (1785), and later enlarged this League of Princes (*Fürstenbund*) to the number of fourteen. The plan was purely selfish and cannot properly be regarded, as some German historians have seen it, as a move on the part of Prussia to reconstruct the dying Empire along the lines of a truly unified Germany. The princes were mobilized simply to repel the ambitions of Joseph II, to minimize the prestige of Austria and to maintain the status quo. In this they succeeded, so that the moribund Holy Roman Empire remained unchanged, dragging itself along for precisely two more decades until Napoleon consigned it to oblivion.

The death of Frederick II in August, 1786, may well be taken as a terminal point in this age of dynastic conflict. He did not live to see the vast political and social changes born of the French Revolution. It had been his work to enlarge the territory of the Prussian state, to invigorate its domestic life, to raise it to the ranks of the great powers and to create within Germany an effective rival to the traditional authority of the Hapsburgs. In all this he had succeeded.

■ THE EUROPEAN POWERS AND THE OTTOMAN EMPIRE

The Ottoman Empire, so powerful in the sixteenth and seventeenth centuries, so apparently weak in the eighteenth, provided Europe with one of its most distracting problems. In the face of the aspirations and rivalries of its powerful neighbors, what was to be the fate of this decaying empire? The "Eastern Question," as the problem came to be known, remained as one of the most controversial legacies from the eighteenth century to its successor, the nineteenth.

The conflict of Moslem and Christian went back at least to the time of the Crusades. In the late fourteenth century, as we have seen, the Turks had established themselves in the Balkans. In 1453 they took Constantinople. In the sixteenth century they surged up the Danube to the very gates of Vienna, managing to bring the greater part of Hungary under their control and to keep it for a century and a half. Still another forward advance startled Europe in 1683 when the Turks once again besieged Vienna, only to be repulsed and eventually driven out of all Hungary and Transylvania. The boundary of 1699 established at the Peace of Carlowitz became the permanent line of division between the Hapsburg and Ottoman Empires.[14] While the Hapsburgs were thus advancing to the line of the Save and Lower Danube rivers, the Poles regained their old province of Podolia and Peter the Great won temporary possession of the port of Azov.

In these conflicts, which provide the setting for the developments of the eighteenth century, certain basic attitudes on the part of the great powers were becoming clear. Austria, naturally enough, had a long and almost inflexible tradition of hostility to the Turks. Russia, which was not a major power before the time of Peter I, was, like Austria, anti-Turkish. The facts of geography clearly contributed to Russia's attitudes, for a series of great rivers, the Don, the Dnieper, the Bug and the Dniester, all flowed into the Black Sea which by virtue of the Ottoman power along its shores was in essence a Turkish lake. Russian opposition to the Turks did not necessarily mean an alignment on the side of Austria, for the desire of one power to benefit at the expense of the Turks might well lead to intense suspicion of another power with similar aspirations.

The other great powers were not as closely involved in Turkish affairs as were Austria and Russia. France's traditional attitude towards the Ottoman Empire was as generally friendly as Austria's was hostile. The advantageous commercial rights which France had obtained in the Levant as early as 1535 had been periodically renewed. More than once France had allied (either openly or secretly) with the Turks against the Hapsburgs. In the eighteenth century this general attitude still continued. Neither Britain nor Prussia was committed closely to a consistently pro-Turkish or anti-Turkish policy, but tended either to minimize the problems of this area or to act in any given case on the basis of expediency.

During the first two decades of the eighteenth century Peter the Great of Russia had been too much concerned with the Baltic question to concentrate decisively upon the Black Sea area. His early conquest of Azov (which he subsequently lost) showed, however, a keen realization of the need for a southern maritime outlet. During the War of the Polish Succession (1733–1738) Russia again picked a quarrel with the Turks, and by the Peace of Belgrade (1739) rewon Azov. In this period the Russian frontier, though still not touching the Black Sea, was pushed westward from the Dnieper River to the Bug.[15] In this same general area further minor additions of territory were made between 1740 and 1762. As the map will show, the actual coast of the Black Sea, despite these gains, was still denied to Russia.

14. See p. 361.
15. See map, p. 425.

The accession of Catherine II in 1762 meant a new vigor in Russia's foreign policies. The empress, urged by some of her advisers to champion the cause of the Greeks and Slavs under Turkish rule, was later to dream of establishing a "Greek Empire" at Constantinople to be ruled by her grandson, appropriately christened Constantine. In 1768, when Russia and Prussia were deeply involved in the affairs of their joint neighbor, Poland, Catherine also became involved in a war with Turkey. After a slow beginning her troops startled Austria by marching through Bessarabia, Moldavia and Wallachia, occupying Bucharest and winning sea control of the Aegean. The complete overrunning of Turkey now seemed a possibility. The first partition of Poland (1772) was therefore in one sense intended as a means of heading off Russia from these large Turkish conquests, for Catherine proved willing to evacuate much Turkish territory in anticipation of substantial gains to be made in Poland.

Two years after the first partition of Poland the Russo-Turkish war was ended by the Treaty of Kuchuk-Kainardji (1774), an agreement of profound importance for the whole future of Russo-Turkish relations. Russia's territorial gains were modest—a confirmation of its title to the port of Azov, some land extending westward along the Black Sea coast to the mouth of the River Bug, and some small areas guarding the outlet from the Sea of Azov to the Black Sea. The Crimea was declared independent of Turkey under its Tartar rulers. The non-territorial terms were really of greater significance. Russia was to maintain a permanent embassy at Constantinople and to have commercial rights in Turkey equal to those of any other power (meaning France). Russia was permitted to maintain Greek Orthodox churches in Constantinople, to have the right of pilgrimage to the Holy Places in Palestine and in general to exercise rights of supervision over Christian worship. These terms, more than any other, were Russia's justification in later years for claiming as it did a privileged position within the Ottoman Empire.

Following the peace of 1774, Austria rather than Russia seemed for a time to take the initiative in Ottoman affairs. Joseph II persuaded the Turks that in return for his share in negotiating the peace he was entitled to the Bukowina, a useful border area which he neatly took in 1775. Catherine II was soon able to win him to an informal agreement for joint action against Turkey, holding out vast prospects for its eventual partition and for the realization of her favorite "Greek Empire" scheme. In 1783 she announced the formal annexation of the Crimea to Russia, a step to which Joseph gave his silent blessing and which the Turks soon accepted. A few years later she made her famous state voyage down the Dnieper, accom-

Russia, Austria and, for a time, Poland were concerned with the Ottoman territories adjoining them. Russian rulers from Peter I to Catherine II were active in seizing land and in making Russia a Black Sea power. Note, however, the continuance of Turkish rule in the Balkans.

panied by Joseph II. At Kherson she passed under a triumphal arch with the inscription "The Way to Byzantium." Tradition tells of her favorite, Potemkin, erecting sham villages on the river banks to impress the visitors. Catherine watched the launching of three warships on the waters of the Black Sea and inspected a new naval arsenal at Sebastopol. Her ambitions could hardly have been more clearly indicated.

Not surprisingly in this same year, 1787, war again broke out between Russia and Turkey, a war in which Austria obligingly soon joined her ally. True to her general intentions Catherine sent an army to seize the port of Otchakov, at the mouth of the Bug River—a step in the direction of the ultimate goal, Byzantium. Austria overran Moldavia and Wallachia. The situation soon changed, however, through the deaths of the Turkish sultan and Joseph II in 1790. Moreover, the dramatic pressure of events in revolutionary France and a growing concern on the part of other powers over Russia's advance had their influence. In 1790 Prussia made an agreement with Austria persuading it to pull out of the Turkish war. In 1792 Catherine herself, once more actively involved in Polish affairs, decided upon peace. By the Treaty of Jassy (1792) the old terms of 1774 were renewed, Turkey promising in addition to recognize Russia's annexation of Otchakov and of the entire Crimea.

The map shows clearly the general pattern of Russia's eighteenth-century advance at the expense of the Ottoman Empire. By 1792 Russia was

POLAND

R. BUG

RUSSIA

R. DON

R. VOLGA

1792
Otchakov

1783

Azov

Kherson

1784

1792

Sevastopol

BLACK   SEA

CASPIAN

1784

SEA

stantinople

EMPIRE

THE OTTOMAN EMPIRE *and its* NEIGHBORS
IN THE EIGHTEENTH CENTURY
0   100   200   300
MILES

HELD FROM
1723 TO 1732

firmly established on the shores of the Black Sea, upon which it could maintain naval armaments and send forth its merchant vessels at will. The map will also show that any further advance of Russia across the Dniester boundary in the direction of Constantinople would bring it, so to speak, upon the southern flank of the Hapsburg Empire. Here was a source of potential conflict destined to last down to our own day. As the eighteenth century closed, however, it seemed principally that a new and vigorous Russia was moving forward at the expense of an old and worn-out Turkish Empire. The German-born Catherine II was not unmindful of what she had achieved. Thinking both of the Polish partitions and of her Turkish conquests, she said, "I came to Russia a poor girl; Russia has dowered me richly, but I have paid her back with Azov, the Crimea and the Ukraine." She spoke no more than the truth.

■ THE AGE OF DYNASTIC CONFLICT

A few generalizations will help to sum up the significance of this century of dynastic politics. First could be listed the widespread devotion to the policy of *Raison d'Etat*—"Reason of State." Governments maneuvered consistently and cold-bloodedly for political or military advantage and with a remarkable disregard of scruple. This, doubtless, they had done long before the eighteenth century began and would continue to do far into the future; it was, perhaps, the distinction of the age in question to pursue "Reason of State" more ruthlessly than ever before through a more or less standardized sequence of alliances, wars, treaties, counter-alliances, further wars, further treaties and so on in dizzying succession.

One will observe certain changes from the general climate of the seventeenth century. The spirit of religious fanaticism had declined, so that wars of religion, in the explicit sense, were a phenomenon of the past. Wars were fought for a variety of reasons, but religion, as such, could hardly be considered one of them. Even the continuing conflicts with the Turk no longer possessed any genuinely crusading spirit but were carried on for the purpose of territorial, economic or political advantage.

In another respect the whole conduct of international relations revealed a larger element of professionalism. French had become the accepted language of diplomacy. Diplomats and ministers were better trained for their tasks; the processes of diplomatic intercourse were becoming regularized; congresses and conferences came to have their established rules of procedure; manuals of diplomacy, collections of treaties and textbooks on the "Law of Nations" grew more numerous and more elaborate.

War, too, was becoming a specialized occupation in the hands of highly trained experts who planned their campaigns and went about their business largely by means of mercenary or professional troops. The famous Swiss writer on international law, Emerich de Vattel, recognized this fact in his *Law of Nations* (1758):

> At the present day war is carried on by regular armies; the people, the peasantry, the towns-folk, take no part in it, and as a rule have nothing to fear from the sword of the enemy. Provided the inhabitants submit to him who is master of the country, and pay the contributions demanded, and refrain from acts of hostility, they live in safety as if they were on friendly terms with the enemy; their property rights are even held sacred; the peasants go freely into the enemy camp to sell their provisions and they are protected as far as possible from the calamities of war.[16]

Although the eighteenth century was studded with wars, these did not, like the earlier Thirty Years' War or the vast upheavals of our own age, wreak havoc wherever they were fought. A campaign could often be won simply by keeping an army in the field. The great French military expert, Vauban, in his work, *On the Assault and Defence of Fortresses,* repeatedly stressed the need for economy of manpower. Frederick II warned his generals not to fight near woods and villages where mercenary troops might desert. He wrote in his *Political Testament* that ideally when his armies were in

16. Quoted in H. NICKERSON, *The Armed Horde* (1940), p. 38.

the field the civilian population should not know that a state of war existed. The Marshal de Saxe maintained that a field army should never be larger than 46,000 men: "a greater army is only an embarrassment." Armies, to be sure, were steadily increasing in size; yet the modern concept of a nation in arms had not appeared. Louis XIV may have increased the size of the French army from 125,000 in 1660 to 400,000 at the time of the War of the Spanish Succession, but this latter figure was phenomenal; on the eve of the French Revolution the regular French army numbered about 170,000 men—somewhat less, it may be recalled, than the army of Prussia which had only one-fifth the population of France. None of these figures, however, can compare with the "total mobilizations" of our own day. Campaigns were conducted in the summers, armies went into winter quarters when the weather was bad and troops were severely restricted in their movements by what we would call logistical considerations. To initiate a campaign huge supplies of stores would be collected near the frontier, and it was estimated that no army could advance more than five days beyond its base of supplies. For the French the Low Countries and Catalonia were therefore ideal campaigning grounds. In the realm of strategy, the movements of armies had to be planned, like those of a chess game, in relation to the fixed points provided by the elaborate fortifications of the age.

Tactics reflected the long hours of drill and maneuver on the parade ground. Brightly uniformed troops wheeled into action and advanced slowly in line formation. They were trained to hold their fire if possible until the other side had fired first, to stand steady and then reply. At Blenheim, for example, the French held their fire until the English line was only thirty paces away. One "perfect volley" (like that of Wolfe's troops at Quebec) could decide a battle, as could the skill of perfectly trained regiments marching in formation from one set position to another. Yet with all the elements of parade and panoply losses could on occasion be very heavy; at Zorndorf, in the Seven Years' War, the Russians in one day lost 21,000 men of the 42,000 engaged. The aftermath of battle, with antisepsis unknown and medical treatment and first aid at a minimum, often presented a picture beyond the power of a pen to describe.

Whether employing the newly developing techniques of diplomacy or trusting to the well-established routines of the art of war, all states were out to make material gains for themselves. Yet the time was beginning to pass when a small country, endowed with military vigor or brilliant leadership could successfully vanquish a larger neighbor. God, in the Napoleonic phrase, was coming to be on the side of the big battalions. The victories of the eighteenth century went to the states that could most effectively combine their military and domestic resources. Smaller countries such as Sweden, and large states like Poland and the Ottoman Empire which were clearly in decline, paid the bills.

The gains of the great powers were impressive. European Russia, for example, with an estimated population of perhaps fourteen millions at the opening of the century could count twice that number at its close. It had made solid territorial gains along the Baltic, in Poland and on the Black Sea coast. Prussia, though small in comparison, likewise had doubled its population, rising from two and a half to five millions. It contrived, moreover, to exploit the resources of Silesia and the Polish provinces to the profound advantage of its general economy. It is also true that the Hapsburg monarchy by its reconquest of Hungary and Transylvania and the later additions of Galicia, the Bukowina, Fiume and the Innviertel made gains both in territory and population far outweighing the loss of Silesia or the transfer of Naples and Sicily to the Spanish Bourbons.

Although France's European gains in the eighteenth century could not compare in size with those just listed, yet the confirmation of its possession of Alsace in 1713 and the reversion of Lorraine in 1766 were of major significance. France's colonial conflicts with Great Britain were in a sense disastrous, and the overseas losses by 1763 very heavy. Even so, its remaining colonial possessions were the source of rich revenues. That France's population should rise as it did from eighteen million in 1715 to twenty-five million on the eve of the French Revolution indicates a domestic economy that was fundamentally healthy. Great Britain had no concern with European territorial expansion save that its new dynasty held the Electorate of Hanover and that it had won the great strategic prize of Gibraltar. Its real gains and its real strategic interests were overseas where, despite the loss of the American colonies, the value of the empire steadily increased.

The eighteenth century witnessed a striking proliferation of treatises urging the need to abolish war and to provide some machinery that would organize the states of Europe so that they could handle their joint problems by peaceful means. Following the Abbé de St. Pierre's *Project of Perpetual Peace* published in 1717, writers such as Montesquieu, Voltaire, Diderot, Rousseau, Alberoni, Bentham and many others pointed out the evils of war and made their alternative proposals. Kant's essay, *On Perpetual Peace,* which appeared in 1795 may be taken as the climactic point in this eighteenth-century literature. He proposed to abolish standing armies, to forbid external borrowing for military purposes and to base all governments on popular will. Only then would it be possible, he felt, for a federation of free states to submit jointly to a law of nations based on enlightened reason. The first comment which must be made on all such writing is that it reflected credit upon the intelligent men who saw the evils of a society burdened by recurrent war. Yet it must also be added that such writings served rather to illuminate the problem than to offer practical measures for its solution. At the close of the eighteenth century the practice of nations continued to be what it had been at the opening—the pursuit of dynastic self-interest by means of the cultivation of power. Thus the strident nationalism of the French Revolution was in this sense to be a new variation upon a familiar theme.

Overseas Expansion
and Imperial Conflicts
1600–1789

THE BOURSE AT AMSTERDAM, 1670, a contemporary painting by J. Berckheyde. This picture, which shows the equivalent of a modern stock exchange, gives a fine expression of dignity and substance, as the prosperously clad merchants transact their business. Copyright, Rijksmuseum, Amsterdam.

Chapter 17

■ BACKGROUNDS: DECLINE OF PORTUGAL AND SPAIN

The great expansion of Europe overseas during the seventeenth and eighteenth centuries, the continuance of an earlier process of which the beginnings have already been described, is a major force in the history of the modern world.[1] Small in scale as were the first daring expeditions of the

1. See ch. v.

Portuguese and Spanish sailors, they had nevertheless achieved splendid results, establishing the main geographic lines along which further developments were to take place. With the knowledge gained from the first great voyages, merchant adventurers setting out from European ports now had challenging alternatives to the old coastal and Mediterranean trade routes. They could either pursue the course of the Portuguese navigators leading down the African coast, around the Cape of Good Hope and so on to India and the Spice Islands, or alternatively they could head westward in the path of Columbus to the Caribbean and South America. As a modification of this western route they could head towards the coast of North America, hoping perhaps by some lucky chance to find the elusive northwest passage to Cathay.

Some of the larger results of the early explorations may be reviewed here. In the first place, two vast empires, the Portuguese and the Spanish, had come into existence, separated by the famous line of demarcation first proposed by Pope Alexander VI in 1493. In the second place, it was soon clear that England, France and the Netherlands, developing somewhat later as maritime powers, did not propose to remain excluded from these two vast imperial preserves. Though they established no permanent colonies during the sixteenth century, they became active upon the high seas, England in particular engaging in freebooting on the Spanish Main and in pushing the search for a northeast or northwest passage to China. French explorers such as Verrazano and Cartier, encouraged perhaps by the familiarity of Breton fishermen with the waters off Newfoundland, headed in this general direction. The men of the Netherlands tended to look elsewhere, for many Dutch sailors and navigators, long accustomed to European coastal waters, took service in Portuguese vessels trading to the Indies, acquiring knowledge and skill that later they were able to put to their own advantage.

From the European point of view one significant result of the maritime advances of the sixteenth century was the phenomenon of the Commercial Revolution. This economic manifestation of the changing times meant new commodities, new wealth, new commercial practices and a newly powerful bourgeois class which gave its support to the European "strong monarchies." Maritime and commercial advance meant the growth of chartered companies of a new type. The older "regulated" companies (of which the English Merchant Adventurers was an example) were made up of individuals who accepted certain common rules of trade and certain obligations for mutual defense, but financed their own share of the business and made their own profits, often limited to a single voyage. The new joint-stock company was one in which individuals bought shares or stock in a chartered organization and benefited regularly according to the number of shares they held. The Muscovy Company of 1555, formed originally to seek a northeast passage to China, constituted the first recorded joint-stock enterprise in English history. The rise of this type of organization, both in England and elsewhere, meant the participation of a steadily growing number of people in overseas affairs.

A further significant development of this period was to be a change in the European balance of power. The Commercial Revolution generated new forces and stimulated new countries to growth. Spain and Portugal, which had taken the lead with so little seeming effort, found themselves challenged from more than one quarter. In addition to Spain's conflict with England another arose with the United Netherlands, a tiny country inspired by a maritime tradition which led it to undertake great ventures at sea even before its independence had been fully won. The meteoric rise of the Netherlands Empire in the Indies is one of the great romances of the seventeenth century. Dutch successes were paralleled but not at first equaled by the colonial activities of England and France. These countries in time, however, won colonial possessions in both hemispheres and developed a military and economic power which outdistanced that of the Dutch. In process of so doing, England and France became committed to a mighty overseas duel, first undertaken at the time of Louis XIV and carried on intermittently until the overthrow of Napoleon in 1815. This "Second Hundred Years' War" which, despite the loss of its American colonies, ended with the advantage very much on England's side is the climactic point of the first great age of imperialism.

■ THE DUTCH COLONIAL EMPIRE

The remarkable success of the Dutch in embarking on a career of overseas expansion at a time when they had scarcely won freedom from the yoke of Spain is to be explained by the circumstances both of their environment and of their past. Few areas were more favorably located than the Netherlands to take advantage of the general movements of European commerce. They had, moreover, a vigorous tradition of cloth and other manufactures going back to the Middle Ages. On land which in part was reclaimed from the sea (the *polders*), the Dutch had built a flourishing and diversified agriculture. The people were extraordinarily sea-minded; Dutch sailors played a very large part in the medieval herring fisheries; they held a dominant place in the coastal trade, for which they eventually devised the famous "fly-ship" (*fluit-schip*)—a tub-like craft, "almost as warlike as a coal-scuttle," but able to carry from 100 to 900 tons of cargo along the

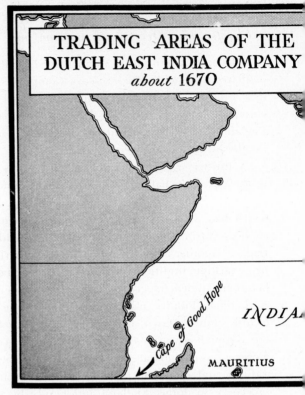

Profits from the trade in these areas compensated for the great distances and risks involved. Note the key posts in India, Ceylon, Formosa and the Netherlands Indies and the trade connection with Japan. From western Sumatra to New Guinea is farther than from San Francisco to New York.

TRADING AREAS OF THE DUTCH EAST INDIA COMPANY *about* 1670

Atlantic coast or into the Baltic. These ships the Dutch had learned to build by assembly-line techniques at the rate of one a day, and with them they prospered. In 1503, out of 1,222 ships passing into the Baltic, 718 were Dutch. The shipyards of Holland were soon constructing vessels for France, England, Scandinavia and even for the great enemy, Spain.

Although Dutch seamen had often voyaged on Portuguese ships going to the East Indies, and had ventured on exploring voyages into the northern latitudes (thereby discovering Spitzbergen and the Barents Sea), not until nearly the close of the sixteenth century did Netherlands merchants undertake distant commercial voyages of their own. They seemed at first to have been well satisfied to profit indirectly from the eastern trade by sending their ships into the Mediterranean or by transshipping to northern ports the oriental wares brought by the Portuguese to Lisbon and Cadiz. After Spain overran Portugal in 1580, however, and closed Lisbon to the transshipment trade (1591), the Dutch soon began to undertake voyages to the Far East on their own. This was no sudden and impulsive act, certainly, but rather the logical consequence of a steady maritime growth. The process was doubtless aided by a number of Dutch books which had begun to tell about the wonders of the Far East, the most notable being the *Navigatio ac Itinerarium* (1595) of Jan van Linschoten, a vivid work deserving to be ranked with that of Hakluyt. Linschoten had visited the Portuguese settlement of Goa in 1589 and gone on Dutch exploratory voyages to the Arctic.

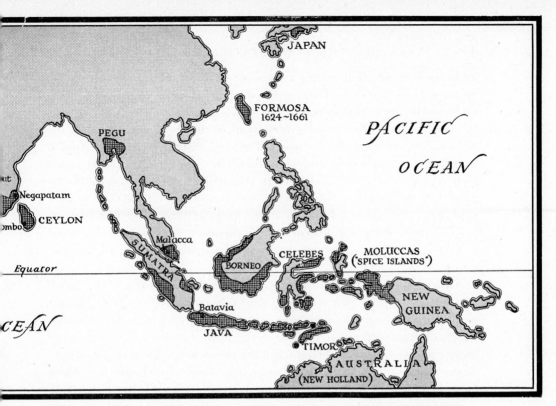

"My heart is longing night and day," he once wrote to a friend, "for voyages to far-away lands." His *Itinerary* became a work of extraordinary popularity and was quickly translated into English, German, Latin and French. Public interest was likewise aroused by Theodore de Bry who began to publish in 1590 his superbly illustrated collection of voyages to the East and West Indies.

The first great name in the history of Dutch voyages to the East Indies is that of Cornelius van Boutman, a skipper formerly in Portuguese service who left Holland in 1595 with four ships. He rounded the Cape of Good Hope, visited India, pushed on to Sumatra, Java and Bali, made a treaty with a native ruler and returned home with great tales and a cargo of spices. Some 145 men out of a total of 249 had died on the outward voyage and the first actual profits were not high, yet hopes for the future were undimmed. The year 1598 saw 22 Dutch ships sail for the Indies; in the following year there were 36.[2]

With the rapid growth of the East Indies trade, the Dutch East India Company was organized in 1602. It was a joint-stock concern, an amalgam of earlier organizations, having a capital of about £540,000 (as compared with the British East India Company's original capital of £30,000). It held

2. Of the 22 Dutch ships sailing in 1598 for the Indies, 13 undertook the route by the Cape of Good Hope. Of these 12 made the trip safely; the other capsized off Dover. The remaining 9 went by the Strait of Magellan; only one returned. The "normal" crew loss on these Dutch voyages has been estimated at 25 per cent.

435

exclusive trading privileges for twenty-one years in the vast area from the Strait of Magellan to the Cape of Good Hope. It could occupy territories, build and fortify trading posts, arm its vessels and declare war in the regions specified in the charter. All the inhabitants of the Dutch Republic had the right to buy shares in the Company. The sixty directors were to be chosen from all the Dutch provinces and cities. An "inner circle" of seventeen men remained actively in charge. In Amsterdam the company built the great East India House with offices, warehouses, an arsenal and a ship-yard. Bales of fragrant spices were stored in the cellars; armor and weapons from all parts of the world decorated the corridors. For nearly two hundred years the Company paid annual dividends ranging from ten to fifty per cent.[3]

Other important business developments paralleled the rise of the Dutch East India Company. Antwerp, long the leading financial center of Europe, went into a decline in consequence of the great conflict between Spain and the Netherlands. It suffered badly in the great crash of 1557, was sacked in 1576 and saw its trade shrivel when the Dutch won control of the mouths of the Rhine and Scheldt. In its place, the Amsterdam Bourse soon won fame as the chief European money market and stock exchange. The Bank of Amsterdam, founded in 1609, became a leading financial center, issuing gold coins that were recognized as an international standard of currency. Commerce was only one source of Dutch wealth. In addition to the manu-facture of cloth the Dutch developed other industries such as book publish-ing (in which they led Europe), sugar refining, brewing, distilling, pottery-making, diamond-cutting, lens-grinding and the manufacture of clocks, microscopes and telescopes.

The beginnings of a Dutch empire in the Far East meant conflict with Portugal and also, seeing that from 1580 to 1640 the Portuguese crown was in Spanish possession, conflict with Spain. In 1606 the Dutch won an important advantage by defeating a Spanish-Portuguese fleet in the Strait of Malacca. Dutch prestige later soared with the appointment in 1618 of Jan Pieterszoon Coen, "the Dutch Albuquerque," as governor-general. He built trading posts throughout the East Indies, founded the capital city of Batavia on the island of Java, drove the Portuguese from practically all their ports except Goa and Macao and laid the foundations of a great commercial empire. England's intervention in this area was quickly rebuffed. The torture and execution of nine English prisoners in 1623 (the "Massacre of Amboyna") was followed by England's withdrawal from the Moluccas. Gradually Dutch influence extended through Java, Sumatra, Celebes and

3. The Dutch East India Company ceased to pay dividends in 1783 and was dissolved in 1794.

the Moluccas. Dutch traders had reached Japan as early as 1609, obtaining rights of trade which they contrived to hold after 1640 when other Europeans were denied them. In 1624 the Dutch reached Formosa, planting a colony which lasted until 1661.

Coen died in 1629 but the great work of expansion went on. In 1641 the Dutch seized Malacca from the Portuguese. In 1642 a Dutch captain, Abel Tasman, sent by the governor-general, Van Diemen, sailed south of Australia, discovered the island of Tasmania, skirted the shores of New Zealand and returned north of New Guinea to Batavia. This greatest of Dutch navigators had completed a voyage which has been called the most important contribution to maritime exploration since Magellan. Other areas were likewise mastered. The Dutch rounded and named Cape Horn in 1615, boldly venturing into those stormy waters at the tip of South America where the "Flying Dutchman" is still reputed to sail. A Dutch crew, shipwrecked at the Cape of Good Hope in 1648, laid the foundations for an African colony formally established there three years later. In 1658 the Dutch completed the ejection of the Portuguese from Ceylon.

By mid-seventeenth century, then, the Dutch had achieved an amazing empire in the Far East. The pepper, nutmeg, cloves and mace of Indonesia yielded a much greater financial return than did the silks, calico and indigo obtained by their rivals at the Indian trading stations. The Dutch capital city of Batavia on the island of Java, with its canals, its brick buildings with brown tiled roofs and diamond-paned, shuttered windows, its European fortifications and its green, exotic setting offered a curious combination of east and west. The Dutch capital soon replaced the Portuguese city of Goa as the center of far eastern commerce. The empire included Java, Sumatra, Borneo, Celebes, the Moluccas (or Spice Islands), part of New Guinea, the Malay Peninsula, Formosa for a time, a few Indian ports, Ceylon and Cape Colony.

These territories were organized into eight governorships subordinate to the semi-despotic governor-general at Batavia. Unlike their practice in the Western Hemisphere, the Dutch sought to mitigate the degree of native slavery which they found on their arrival. In addition to the trade in commodities between the East Indies and Europe they likewise organized an extensive trade between various parts of the oriental world, in this way finding substantial amounts of capital to counter somewhat the steady drain of gold and silver from Europe. The leadership of the Dutch, based essentially on their eastern trade, continued until the eighteenth century when, for a variety of reasons, the Dutch "withdrew from the pursuit of power and devoted themselves to dividends." [4]

4. w. c. ABBOTT, *The Expansion of Europe* (revised ed., 1929), II, p. 84.

Important possessions were also won in the New World. A Dutch expedition captained by an Englishman, Henry Hudson, explored as early as 1609 the great river that bears his name. In 1626 Peter Minuit bought Manhattan Island—where a settlement had been made in 1615—from the Indians and founded New Amsterdam. Flourishing Dutch estates spread up the Hudson as far as Albany while further south land was obtained from the Swedish settlements along the Delaware. Extensive Dutch claims were made, therefore, to the large area known as New Netherland. Following the establishment of a West Indies Company in 1621, the islands of Tobago and Curaçao were seized from Spain between 1632 and 1634. In South America the Portuguese colony of Brazil was invaded in 1624 and Dutch posts were founded and held for almost thirty years. In the end the Dutch colony of Guiana (Surinam) was the sole remainder of this South American venture. When Dutch shipping joined with that of other countries in carrying African slaves to the New World, forts were built on the African coast as bases of operations.

The spectacular successes of the Netherlands in the colonial field and the resultant domestic prosperity were not to last indefinitely. To see this Dutch decline as a consequence of the trade wars with England between 1652 and 1674 is to offer too narrow an explanation for a complex process. Nor can it be explained altogether on the basis of confusions and weakness in Dutch political life. The fundamental reason for the change that can be observed in the eighteenth century, when the Netherlands "ceased to be *the* fisherman, shipbuilder, distributor, finisher and financier of Europe, and became *one* of them," seems to be that they were not equipped in population, area or resources to match the enormous growth and vigor of states such as Great Britain or France in that new age of economic and political conflict where, as it has well been said, coal and iron were more important than spices and herrings.[5] The Dutch decline, moreover, was relative. Although the East India Company was dissolved in 1794 and the Bank of Amsterdam about the same time, and although Ceylon and Cape Colony were seized by England during the Napoleonic wars, the structure of the East Indian empire remained almost intact. The industrious Dutch were able to repair their damaged fortunes and to enjoy an imperial prosperity which has lasted down to our own day.

■ THE RISE OF THE BRITISH EMPIRE

England's imperial developments, destined to surpass those of all her rivals, had their roots in the sixteenth century. Under Queen Elizabeth adventurers and freebooters occasionally rubbed shoulders with other men

5. HEATON, *Economic History of Europe*, p. 287.

such as Sir Humphrey Gilbert and Sir Walter Raleigh, who sought, the one in Newfoundland (1583) and the other on Roanoke Island on the Caro-lina Coast (1585, 1587), to found colonies in the New World. Both were unsuccessful, yet by the opening of the seventeenth century sailors such as Gosnold, Pring and Weymouth were skirting, charting and making favor-able reports about the coast of North America.

The new device of the chartered companies made possible organized plans for settlement on a substantial scale, with provisions for economic development, political organization and established religious worship. The charter, for example, granted to the Virginia Company of London in 1606 led to the first permanent English settlement in the New World—the little group of 105 who landed on the James River in Virginia in 1607 and founded Jamestown. In 1620 came the historic settlement of the *Mayflower's* company, the "Pilgrims," as Governor Bradford called them, at Plymouth. This small group, inspired at least in part by the idea of religious freedom, set up the Plymouth Colony which grew slowly in numbers and prosperity until in 1691 it was absorbed in the much larger neighboring settlement, the Bay Colony, first established by the Massachusetts Bay Company in 1629–1630. Offshoots, likewise inspired by a desire for greater religious and politi-cal liberty, were set up in Connecticut and Rhode Island (1636) and New Hampshire (1679).

Another type of English settlement took the form of the "proprietary grant" in which one person or a group of persons ("Proprietors") usually by charter undertook in return for extensive privileges the prime responsibility of settlement. Maryland was founded as the result of a grant to Lord Balti-more in 1632. Carolina went as a proprietary grant to a group of eight nobles in 1663; New York was transferred from the Dutch to the Duke of York in 1664. Two of the Carolina proprietors were granted New Jersey in 1664. William Penn received the proprietary charter of Pennsylvania in 1681 and of Delaware in 1682. The territory known as Georgia was estab-lished in 1732 by a charter granted to General Oglethorpe, the Earl of Eg-mont and others as trustees of the colony for 21 years.

The important generalization to be made about these several ventures is that they quickly became areas of settlement rather than simply areas of commercial exploitation. In other words, they were truly colonies and not simply "posts," "forts," or "factories." It is notable, too, that while the original charters had generally envisaged a group of directors or managers sitting in London, the prevalent tendency was for the charters to migrate to the colonies where the general direction of affairs was soon established. In this way charters tended to form the bases of constitutions. Although a royal governor might still speak in the name of the king and be assisted by a governor's council, nevertheless, the institutions of self-government began to develop overseas. Early charters often stipulated that settlers should have "the rights of Englishmen." Thus, when the governor of Virginia, on instructions from the General Court in England, summoned representatives of the colony to meet in 1619, his action reflected the desire of the colonists to regulate their own affairs. In the words of a contemporary, a House of Burgesses "broke out in Virginia." Burgesses and Council met together for several years. A General Court, out of which grew an assembly, was authorized in the Massachusetts charter of 1629, and a similar body in Rhode Island in 1644. The development of the New England system of town government with its elected officers and regular town meetings marked the same tendency on a lower level.

By the close of the seventeenth century, with an estimated population of 200,000, the North American colonies were thriving. Primarily agricultural, they were largely self-supporting and increasingly able to send some of the products of the land—rice, tobacco, lumber and furs—across the ocean. The small-scale industries in the New World served chiefly, however, to supply the basic needs of the colonists. The population of Boston in 1689 had reached perhaps 7,000; New York had about 4,000 inhabitants; Philadelphia had less. By the time of the Revolution Philadelphia had a population of 30,000, New York had 25,000 and Boston, 20,000.

An important group of British colonies also grew up in the West Indies. Bermuda, where Englishmen had first landed in 1609, has the distinction of providing the setting ("the vex'd Bermoothes") for Shakespeare's *Tempest* and of having a parliamentary assembly which, dating from 1620, ranks second only to Virginia's House of Burgesses in colonial antiquity. The West Indies were soon settled: St. Christopher in 1623, Barbados in 1625, Nevis in 1628, Montserrat and Antigua in 1632, St. Lucia in 1638. Jamaica was seized by Cromwell from Spain in 1655. Several points are to be noted about the West Indian settlements. The profitable raising of tobacco was soon followed by the even more profitable introduction from Brazil of the sugar-cane. This led to the growth of larger estates, the increased investment of capital and the importing of large numbers of African slaves. It led, too, to a rapid increase in population. Barbados alone had 18,000 white inhabitants by 1643, while by 1650 there were perhaps 40,000 people in what were coming to be known as the Sugar Islands.

As early as 1562 John Hawkins had sold to the Spaniards in Hispaniola a shipload of three hundred slaves which he had seized on the African coast. The first Negroes to arrive in North America proper were brought by the English to Jamestown in a captured Dutch vessel in 1619 and used as indentured servants. From then on, both in the West Indies and in the North American colonies the profitable slave trade steadily developed. In 1672 the Royal African Company was allowed a slave monopoly which was soon broken, however, by English and New England merchants. Black-hulled slave-ships designed to carry as many as seven hundred were built with tiers of decks so close together that the manacled Negroes crowded between them were unable to stand upright. Of every hundred slaves shipped, an average of seventeen died during or shortly after the voyage and perhaps only fifty lived to be effective laborers. Profits from this sinister trade were increased when by the Peace of Utrecht England obtained the *Asiento,* or contract to supply the Spanish colonies with slaves. The total number of Negroes carried to the British colonies in America and the West Indies between 1680 and 1786 has been estimated at over two millions—an annual average of about twenty thousand. French, Dutch, Danes and Portuguese joined in the trade, of which in 1790 over half was still in British hands.

Newfoundland, long the haunt of European fishing fleets, was settled in 1610. In still another area Charles II granted a charter (1670) to Prince Rupert and his associates to form the "Governor and Company of Adventurers Trading into Hudson's Bay." The area roughly defined was so large as to cover one-third of the continent of North America, the Company having the right to trade for furs, minerals and other commodities, to hold land by legal title, to administer the law and "to make war or peace with any prince or people that are not Christian." This implied, obviously, a huge grant of power. By 1671 the governors had begun to send three ships annually into Hudson's Bay; soon they were building trading posts on its coast and sending agents into the western wilderness. The magnetism of the fur trade was irresistible; in time the agents and factors of the Hudson's Bay Company were to push their way across the plains, traverse the mountain wilderness and establish outposts on the shores of the Pacific.

Paralleling these advances in the Western Hemisphere were others in the Far East. The English, whose historic alliance with Portugal can be traced back to 1386, knew of the early Portuguese voyages down the African coast. Englishmen made voyages of their own at an early date to the Guinea Coast and were active, as we have seen, in seeking the northeast passage to China. A Jesuit, Father Thomas Stevens, who visited the Portuguese establishment at Goa in 1579, is the first recorded Englishman to visit India. Another, Ralph Fitch, having reached India traveling through the Levant from one Portuguese post to another, spent the years 1585–1591 at the court of the Mogul Emperor Akbar at Agra. His importance is that he was summoned home to advise the founders of the East India Company. Another adventurer, James Lancaster, cruised the Indian Ocean between 1591 and 1593, preying on Portuguese ships and bringing home seductive tales of the wealth of the Indies.

On December 31, 1600, Queen Elizabeth issued a charter to "The Governor and Company of Merchants of London Trading to the East Indies," giving them the right to trade in the whole area "beyond the Cape of Good Hope to the Strait of Magellan, not yet occupied by any friendly power." The governor and directors were to be elected annually, were authorized to establish trading posts, or "factories" and were empowered to make and enforce laws "not contrary to the laws of this our realm." Many of the directors, we may note, had seats in Parliament. Thus was established, by 101 subscribers with a joint stock of some £30,000, the great East India Company destined to play so momentous a part in British imperial history.[6] In time the shares of the company brought a steady annual profit of 20 or 25 per cent, while appreciating regularly in value.

The first three voyages of the Company (1601–1603) were to Java, Sumatra and the Moluccas, but soon it was decided to establish trade on the Indian mainland. The Company at once set its face against any policy of colonization or settlement. "Let this be received as a rule," wrote the first governor, "that if you will profit seek, seek it at sea and in quiet trade." Consequently, in 1609 William Hawkins went on a mission to Agra where Jahangir, the dissipated successor to Akbar the Great, ruled over the Mogul Empire. This empire, established in the sixteenth century by the Moslem conquerors coming down from the northwest, had imposed a loose unity over the complex network of warring states, preponderantly Hindu in religion, that made up India.

In essence, the seventeenth century saw England withdraw from any great conflict with Holland in the Netherlands Indies and concentrate instead upon establishing cordial and at the same time highly profitable relations with the Mogul emperors.[7] A trading post was set up in 1612 at Surat, on the west coast, north of Bombay. The first Indian cargo of indigo and cotton aboard a ship appropriately named the *Hope* reached England in 1614. In 1633 establishments were begun at the mouth of the Ganges in the great area of Bengal; these led to the founding of Calcutta in 1686. Meanwhile, Madras, to the southeast on the Coromandel Coast, had been occupied and fortified in 1639. Bombay came to Charles II as a dowry in 1661

6. By the revised Charter of 1661 the directors were empowered to coin money, appoint governors of fortresses, enlist soldiers, arm ships, enforce martial law, hold Courts of Admiralty, levy war and negotiate treaties with non-Christians.

7. One of the puzzling problems of English diplomacy was to find gifts acceptable to the fabulously wealthy Mogul rulers. The English finally had luck with a cornet which the emperor Jahangir delighted to blow for an hour at a time; they were successful, too, with hunting mastiffs and cases of French wine.

when he married the Portuguese Catherine of Braganza and was soon turned over by him to the Company. A glance at the map will show, therefore, that in the years between 1612 and 1686 England had established her three principal trading posts at corners of a great strategic triangle which might well lead to the domination of all India. In 1687 Bombay, "the gateway to India," became the Company's chief trading post.

Like the Dutch in the East Indies, the British had difficulty in finding goods that could be sold in India to pay for the indigo, saltpeter, sugar, pepper, calicoes and silks that they shipped to Europe. Most Indian purchases, therefore, were paid for in silver bullion, with the resultant draining of a very substantial amount of treasure from Europe into the coffers of the Indian nabobs. A side result was that English merchants, also like the Dutch, sought to obtain further funds by trading ventures in other areas such as Persia and China; in this way they introduced coffee and tea to English consumers. "That excellent Drink . . . called by the Chineans Tcha, by other nations Tay, alias Tee" was advertised for sale in England as early as 1658.

English overseas policy had been marked during the seventeenth century by a twofold development. In the Western Hemisphere there were substantial settlements numbering about 200,000 souls, as well as a valuable trade in fish, furs, sugar and other commodities. At the other side of the world the British East India Company was reaping a golden harvest. Such was the setting for a mighty duel with the French who likewise were embarked upon the course of empire.

■ FRANCE IN AMERICA AND THE INDIES

French exploration of the New World began under the patronage of the versatile Renaissance king, Francis I. It had been preceded, doubtless, by numberless unrecorded voyages of Norman and Breton sailors to the fishing grounds off Labrador and Newfoundland.[8] In 1524 the Florentine, Verrazano, sailing for France, seems to have skirted the Atlantic coast from Hatteras to Newfoundland. The three great voyages of Jacques Cartier (1534, 1535–1536, 1541–1542) which took him up the St. Lawrence as far as the present Montreal and Quebec, around Prince Edward Island and along the shores of the Gaspé Peninsula, made him the real discoverer of Canada, even though actual settlement had to wait nearly a hundred years.

In 1604 Samuel de Champlain, under authorization from Henry IV of France, succeeded in planting the little settlement of Port Royal on what is now the Bay of Fundy in Nova Scotia. This was the beginning of the

8. It has been estimated that by 1600 there were some 600 French craft engaged in the North American fisheries in addition to those of England, Portugal and Spain.

French colony of Acadia which, constantly in dispute, had a stormy history until permanently ceded to England in 1713 by the Treaty of Utrecht. In 1608 another settlement was made on the St. Lawrence at Quebec; from this, the first permanent French colony in Canada, Champlain launched a series of explorations which took him well into the interior and set the pattern for further French expansion. The Company of New France chartered by Cardinal Richelieu in 1627 was but a faint echo, to be sure, of the great English and Dutch establishments. Intended both to develop the fur trade (of which it had a permanent monopoly) and to plant 4,000 settlers in fifteen years, it won only insignificant success, for French settlements in the New World, despite governmental backing, grew far more slowly than those of their English rivals.

In 1664 the situation was transformed. Louis XIV canceled the old charter and created a new Company of the West, thereby bringing all French overseas activities directly under royal control. Colbert had become Louis' principal economic adviser, pressing the general policies of mercantilism upon his master. Henceforth Canada resembled a French province, having its royal governor, its intendant, its official clergy and its appointed public officials. Rather than trace the narrative of New France's slow expansion, one may more profitably single out those features which made the development of Canada so different from that of its southern neighbors.

One characteristic was, as we have seen, the retention of governmental power in the hands of the authorities in France. Another was the devoted work of the Jesuits in undertaking missions to the Indians at the cost of hardships and even martyrdom. Another was the growth of the fur trade to the exclusion of any such concentration upon agriculture, commerce and settlement as marked the English colonies. With the fur trade developed that extraordinary type of adventurer, the *coureur de bois,* half-French and half-Indian, who gave so much color to this period. Another feature was the steady process of exploration which opened up the Great Lakes and the Ohio Valley and in 1682 brought La Salle down the full length of the Mississippi to its mouth. Also to be emphasized was the relatively slow growth in population which meant that at the end of the seventeenth century, while the English colonists numbered about 200,000, those in French Canada hardly totaled 15,000.

A unique type of "seigneurial" regime was established along the St. Lawrence River. Land was granted to nobles or men of substantial bourgeois status—the *seigneurs*—who in turn settled tenants—the *habitants*—upon it. These tenants were really peasants, bound to their landlords by a series of personal obligations and by payments in money and kind not unlike those of a medieval serf. Everywhere the hand of the Roman Catholic

Church made itself evident. Such a social system, so strikingly different from that of the New England colonies, unquestionably hampered the free growth of New France. Whatever its strengths and weaknesses, it has left its powerful imprint upon French Canadian life down to our own day.

France likewise made settlements in the West Indies where the French corsairs had long preyed on Spanish commerce. A Company of the Islands of America was organized in 1635 with the result that Martinique and Guadeloupe were settled. Other islands were soon obtained, so that by 1665 the French held fourteen, with a white population of more than 15,000. Slave labor was imported to work on the profitable sugar plantations. At the death of Colbert in 1683 the white population of the French West Indies was put at 19,000, the Negro slave population at 27,000 and the remainder at 1,500. This total of some 47,500, while much less than that of the British colonies, was triple the population of French Canada. The French treatment of slaves in the West Indies was regulated by the famous *Code Noir,* or Black Code, drawn up in 1685, which guaranteed them at least a minimum of civilized treatment. A French West India Company, organized in 1664 by Colbert, was intended to build up ocean-borne trade. Although in ten years the company was hopelessly bankrupt, largely through blunders in administration, the economic life of the French islands continued to prosper. These colonies, like Canada, were administered as provinces of France.

France likewise obtained a foothold in the 1630's at Senegal, on the west coast of Africa. At first engaging in the usual trade in tropical produce, the French merchants gradually turned to supplying slaves for America. By 1789 France took a substantial, if minor, part in the trade which carried from twenty to thirty thousand Negroes annually across the Atlantic.

A few French ships made the voyage to the Indian Ocean in the sixteenth century but not until 1615 was a "Molucca Company" chartered for trade with the Spice Islands. It did little. Under Richelieu a number of missionaries, principally Capuchins, were sent overland to the Orient. Active trade really began when Colbert organized his French East India Company in 1664. Ports were established on the Indian coast at Surat (1668), Masulipatam (1669), Pondichéry (1674) and Chandernagor (1690). Trade was also undertaken with the East Indies, Siam and the China Coast. The Ile de France (now Mauritius) and Ile de Bourbon (now Réunion) became important French way-stations in the Indian Ocean. By the close of the seventeenth century France had established an important trading connection with India where it was in a position of rivalry with Britain as it also was in North America and the West Indies. With the Dutch no longer politically or militarily ambitious, this Anglo-French colonial rivalry became the distinctive feature of Europe's overseas conflicts.

■ THE IMPERIAL DUEL BETWEEN ENGLAND AND FRANCE

Before 1660 there had been no serious conflict between the French and English in America. Between 1689 and 1815 the two countries engaged in a series of seven wars. The reasons for this long-continued antagonism lay partly in the general European rivalry over the balance of power (in none of these seven wars, it will be noted, were England and France the sole participants), partly in the general economic antagonisms inherent in the system of mercantilism and partly in direct colonial conflicts.

At a time when the Dutch were slackening the pace of their colonial endeavors, England and France showed an extraordinary vigor. During the reign of Charles II (1660–1685), for example, England acquired Bombay and New York, founded Philadelphia and Charleston, built powerful African forts on the Gold Coast and the Gambia, chartered the Hudson's Bay Company and the Royal African Company, saw the beginnings of the Board of Trade and Plantations and undertook the systematization of its various Acts of Trade. In France, concurrently, Colbert, by founding new trading companies and mobilizing the economic resources of the state, strove to increase the number and prosperity of the French settlements in Canada and the West Indies and to win a larger share of the trade with Africa and India.

At this time, it will be recalled, the European scene was dominated by Louis XIV whose ambitions were made clear in the War of Devolution (1667–1668) and its sequel, the Dutch War (1672–1678).[9] These in turn led to the greater conflicts of the League of Augsburg (1689–1697), the War of the Spanish Succession (1701–1713) and the armed strife of the 1740's and 1750's provoked by the aggressive designs of Frederick II of Prussia. In every case a European war had its colonial counterpart. Yet these colonial wars were not merely incidents or appendages of a struggle being waged in Europe, despite the often quoted passage in Macaulay's *History of England.* "In order," Macaulay wrote, "that [Frederick] might rob a neighbor whom he had promised to defend, black men fought on the Coast of Coromandel and red men scalped each other by the Great Lakes of North America." In truth, the vast conflict which in time spread to North America, the West Indies, Africa and India was inspired by causes far more complex than simply the European ambitions of any statesmen or rulers.

In a broad sense the great overseas conflict illustrates the working of what has come to be known as the old colonial system. Both England and France looked upon their colonies as integral and exceedingly valuable parts of the whole national economy. In the eighteenth century, for example, France was steadily pushing toward the point where trade in colonial

9. For these and the subsequent wars see pp. 340–349.

products made up one-third of its entire foreign commerce—a point actually reached by England in 1774. The wealth of the aristocratic and mercantile classes in eighteenth-century England, with their imposing country estates and lavish expenditures, was based to a substantial degree upon profits from overseas. In the French seaports a highly prosperous merchant class likewise developed, even though in this respect as well as in the growth of an adequate system of commercial banking France could not keep pace with England.

The most important difference between the British and French overseas empires lay in the techniques of settlement and administration. England, as we have seen, permitted local self-government, leaving the colonists very much to themselves under a policy often described as "salutary neglect." France, on the other hand, transferred the domestic pattern of its centralized, autocratic administration to the colonies. These, under the control of the Ministry of Marine, "were governed as if they were war vessels permanently at anchor." [10] The French colonies existed, not to receive large scale emigration, but to produce a commercial profit. Hence France's pride in the sugar-producing West Indies and its relative neglect of French Canada. Hence, too, the French dismissal of the great Indian proconsul Dupleix in 1753, when instead of confining himself to seeking commercial profits he attempted a policy of territorial conquest.

In other respects the British and French systems showed similarities. Both made use of slave labor. Both undertook regulation of the economic life of the colonies (the French through what was known as the *Exclusif* and the English through the Acts of Trade and Navigation). Under this system the colonies would trade mainly with the mother country, providing it with its "colonial wares" and raw materials, and receiving in return manufactured goods. All imports and exports were to be carried in a national merchant marine. The fallacy of the system, of course, was to assume that the economic life of parent and child could be kept in perfect balance. Since there was no such balance, either the home government had to make many exceptions (as it did), or the colonists made smuggling into a major occupation. The English navigation laws also protected colonial commerce and shipbuilding. Colonial ships, theoretically, could sail to all parts of the Empire, receiving protection from the British navy.

Powerful economic rivalries were apparent in the New World. French and English fishermen competed off the Grand Banks of Newfoundland and in the waters of Nova Scotia. The fur trade, with the French headquarters at Montreal and the English at Albany, led the traders and trappers ever further into the wilderness. Each side sought Indian support—the French

10. DORN, *Competition for Empire*, p. 258.

cultivating friendship with the Algonquin tribes, the English urging on the great opponents of the Algonquins, the Iroquois confederacy. Armed raids in America had long preceded the European crisis of 1689, so that while they were not the real cause of conflict, they were indubitably a contributing factor to the coming of war.

The conflict in North America corresponding to the War of the League of Augsburg (1689–1697) was known as King William's War. The governor of New France, Count Frontenac, encouraged Indian attacks on frontier settlements in Maine, Massachusetts and New York. The English countered with the capture of Port Royal, in Acadia, and made unsuccessful thrusts against Montreal and Quebec. On the other side of the Atlantic the English fleet regained command of the Channel by the victory of La Hogue in 1692. The Peace of Ryswick (1697), although it stipulated a mutual restoration of conquests, could not halt the march of events. Though neither side made any territorial gains, England was now committed to a continuing colonial war against France.

The War of the Spanish Succession (1701–1713) had its American counterpart in Queen Anne's War. The French encouraged Indian raids on Berwick in Maine and Deerfield and Haverhill in Massachusetts. The Spaniards, now allied with the French, launched a raid on Carolina. The English again captured Port Royal, naming it Annapolis in honor of their queen, and sent unsuccessful expeditions against Montreal and Quebec.

When the war ended, the Peace of Utrecht (1713) brought about momentous changes in the maritime and colonial scene. France recognized the English title to Acadia (now renamed Nova Scotia), Newfoundland and the vast Hudson's Bay territories. The French, however, kept Cape Breton Island and maintained their rights to the Newfoundland fisheries. In the West Indies, England was granted by Spain the *Asiento,* that is, a thirty-year monopoly in supplying slaves to the Spanish colonies. This grant, which was given to the South Sea Company, meant that the Company could supply a minimum of at least 4,800 slaves annually. In thirty years about 144,000 Negroes were thus sent across the Atlantic.[11] England was also permitted to send one 500-ton ship a year to trade at the Isthmus of Panama and to cut logwood in the Bay of Honduras. The significance of these terms was that England had broken into the exclusive trade monopoly which Spain had tried to maintain in the West Indies. With a foot in the door, England could soon be expected to seek still further advantages—legally or otherwise. Finally, England retained Gibraltar which it had captured from Spain in

11. The South Sea Company held the slaving monopoly until 1751 when the Spanish government bought it back for 100,000 pounds and threw the trade open to all comers.

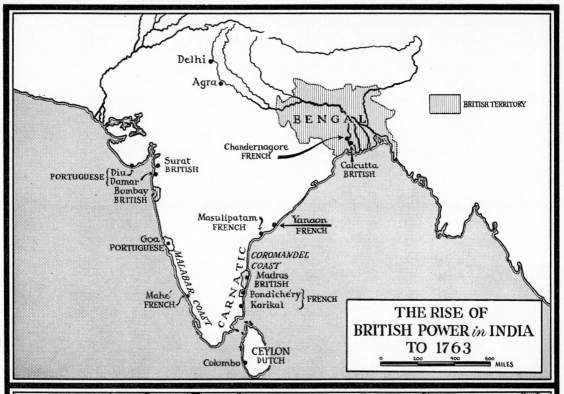

Delhi

Agra

BENGAL

BRITISH TERRITORY

Chandernagore
FRENCH

Surat
BRITISH

Calcutta
BRITISH

PORTUGUESE { Diu
Damar
Bombay
BRITISH

Masulipatam
FRENCH

Yanaon
FRENCH

Goa
PORTUGUESE

MALABAR COAST

CARNATIC

COROMANDEL
COAST

Madras
BRITISH

Mahé
FRENCH

Pondichéry
Karikal

FRENCH

CEYLON
DUTCH

Colombo

THE RISE OF
BRITISH POWER *in* INDIA
TO 1763

0   200   400   600
MILES

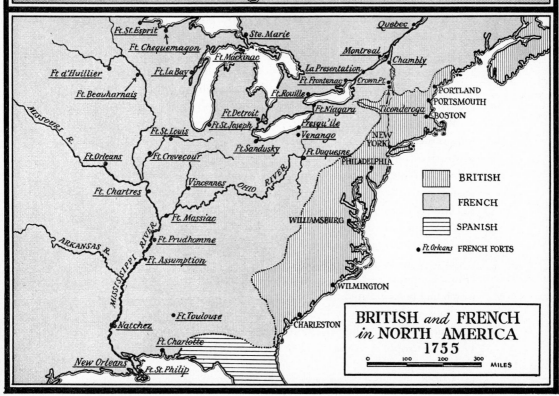

Ft.St.Esprit

Ste.Marie

Quebec

Ft.Chequemagon

Ft.Mackinac

Montreal

Chambly

Ft.d'Huillier

Ft.La Bay

La Presentation

Ft.Frontenac

Crown Pt.

PORTLAND
PORTSMOUTH

Ft.Beauharnais

Ft.Rouille

Ft.Niagara

Ticonderoga

BOSTON

Ft.Detroit

Presqu'ile

NEW
YORK

MISSOURI R.

Ft.St.Louis

Ft.St.Joseph

Venango

Ft.Orleans

Ft.Crevecour

Ft.Sandusky

Ft.Duquesne

PHILADELPHIA

Ft.Chartres

Vincennes

OHIO   RIVER

ARKANSAS R.

Ft.Massiac

WILLIAMSBURG

MISSISSIPPI RIVER

Ft.Prudhomme

Ft.Assumption

WILMINGTON

Ft.Toulouse

Natchez

CHARLESTON

Ft.Charlotte

New Orleans

Ft.St.Philip

BRITISH

FRENCH

SPANISH

Ft.Orleans FRENCH FORTS

BRITISH *and* FRENCH
in NORTH AMERICA
1755

0   100   200   300
MILES

1704, along with the Mediterranean island of Minorca. Britain, it was clear, had assumed a commanding position on the seas.

The two decades following the Peace of Utrecht were marked by a lull in the colonial conflict. Considerable colonial activity nevertheless manifested itself. Having lost Acadia but not Cape Breton Island, France quickly began in 1720 to build the huge fortress of Louisburg on the island so as to command the Gulf of St. Lawrence. Simultaneously France extended its fortified posts throughout the distant interior lands: Frontenac, Rouillé, Niagara, Detroit, Duquesne—the latter on the headwaters of the Ohio. The French flag likewise flew over outposts extending all the way to New Orleans and Fort St. Philip at the mouth of the Mississippi.[12] Nevertheless, under the administration of Cardinal Fleury, France, like England, sought peaceful colonial development rather than war.

A quarrel with Spain rather than France led to the renewal of conflict. Despite peaceful intentions, England found itself at war with Spain in 1739, after the fantastic episode of "Jenkins' Ear." British trade with Spanish America undoubtedly had been pushed far beyond the limits permitted by the Peace of Utrecht, with consequent Spanish resentment and reprisals. When the British Captain Jenkins appeared before the House of Commons with tales of Spanish cruelty and what purported to be his severed ear packed in a box to prove it, the upsurge of feeling led to war.[13] In 1740, in consequence of the problems of the Austrian Succession, England was also at war with France. In the colonial struggle ("King George's War") the New England settlers captured Louisburg, only to see it restored to the French in 1748 who in turn gave up Madras which they had taken.

By this time colonial problems were beginning to assume as large an importance as those of Europe. For this reason a kind of undeclared war was carried on in America during the supposed years of peace. English and French forcibly disputed the precise boundaries of Nova Scotia. The French pushed into the Ohio Valley where a formal expedition was sent in 1749 to claim it in the name of Louis XV. Meanwhile the British colonists were making much of their old claims to this land west of the Alleghenies. In the same year, 1749, that the French made their move and began building a chain of forts, prominent British and Virginia merchants organized the Ohio Company to develop half a million acres of land near the upper Ohio which had been granted them by the crown.

The ensuing conflict in North America, the French and Indian War, was under way long before the formal outbreak in 1756 of the Seven Years' War in Europe. A young Virginian officer, George Washington, had gone

12. See map p. 449.
13. Actually, the episode seems to have been staged by Walpole's political opponents who objected to his long-continued policy of peace.

over the Alleghenies in 1753 hoping to establish a title to the Ohio Valley; he was, however, unable to prevent the French from building Fort Duquesne at the point where the Monongahela and Allegheny rivers come together. In 1754 Washington's small force had to surrender to the French. General Braddock's famous expedition of 1755 to the Ohio met with disaster. In the same year, seeking to destroy a possible trouble center, the English removed the remaining French in Nova Scotia (the "Acadians") to scattered homes in the American colonies.

When war was formally declared in Europe in 1756, the already bitter American conflict soon grew to major proportions. As has more than once happened in the opening stages of a great war, England did not at once find leaders equal to the occasion. The Newcastle administration wallowed in incompetence until William Pitt entered the cabinet. Rapidly rising to a dominant position, Pitt mobilized large forces for a colonial war of which he alone seemed to realize the true importance. With 20,000 regulars and an additional 22,000 colonial volunteers, as well as substantial naval forces, he prepared England for large-scale operations having for their goal the destruction of France as a maritime power.

Pitt, with whom Winston Churchill has often been compared as a war leader, knew how to mobilize the support of the people of England to great ends. His well-planned strategy was, first, to blockade the French coast with superior naval forces. In America he would seize those key military points which the French had systematically built up. Louisburg was captured in 1758; Ticonderoga, at the head of Lake Champlain, fell in 1759. British expeditions seized Fort Frontenac at the lower end of Lake Ontario, Fort Niagara, Fort Duquesne and other important points. The climax came in 1759 when General Wolfe, one of Pitt's "young men," risking all on a daring gamble, sent his Highlanders up from the St. Lawrence to the Plains of Abraham and won Quebec. Although Wolfe and his chivalrous opponent, the Marquis of Montcalm, both died on the battlefield, the great decision had been reached. With the capture of Montreal in 1760 the curtain fell upon one of the most romantic periods in French colonial history.

British naval forces quickly seized the French West Indies, as well as Senegal and Gorée on the African coast. Spain being in the war as an ally of France, British ships eventually seized the port of Havana in Cuba and, at the far end of the world, Manila. When the French fleet at Brest put to sea in 1759 for a raid on the English coast, it was destroyed at Quiberon Bay. These victories added to the brilliant roster of achievement which British seapower could claim.

The other major theater of operations was India. Here existed a confused world strangely different from that of North America. With the death of

Aurangzeb in 1707 the great Mogul Empire went into a decline, as various native states flung off the yoke and asserted their own rule. In the west a strong Hindu power, the Mahratta Confederacy, had arisen. A new Moslem invader from the north, the Persian Nadir Shah, came down through the Khyber Pass in 1739, plundering the Mogul court at Delhi of its state jewels and throwing India into still further turmoil. Both the English and French sought to take advantage of these confusions.

As the names of Wolfe and Montcalm gave heroic interest to the last days of the struggle for French Canada, so the names of Robert Clive and Joseph Dupleix added luster to the conflict in India. Clive was a servant of the British East India Company, an industrious pen-pusher who unexpectedly displayed extraordinary genius as a leader and general. Dupleix likewise rose brilliantly above the routine performance of his duties as French governor of Pondichéry. He was determined to make French influence supreme. Having been granted the title of Nawab by the Mogul Emperor at Delhi, Dupleix lived in oriental splendor, winning the favor of a local ruler, the Nawab of the Carnatic, and building up a native sepoy army of infantry and artillery by means of which he succeeded in imposing the authority of the French upon the states of southern India. In 1746, at the height of the War of the Austrian Succession, French forces seized Madras from the English, only to return it, however, on the news of the Peace of Aix-la-Chapelle.

At this point the twenty-six-year-old Robert Clive persuaded his superiors to give him a military command and to let him plunge into the melée of native affairs. He captured Arcot, near Madras, in 1751 with only 500 troops against native enemy forces numbering 10,000. This enormously enhanced British prestige, all the more so when the French government foolishly recalled Dupleix in 1754. The ruler of Bengal having seized the British post at Calcutta, Clive successfully recaptured the city in 1757.[14] He followed this by capturing the French post of Chandernagor and by defeating the Nawab of Bengal at Plassey (1757). With 3,000 troops, of which only 900 were European, Clive had routed an army of over 50,000. By 1761, when the British captured Pondichéry, the French cause reached the point of disaster. England's great victories in India must be attributed in part to Pitt's inspired leadership at home, in part to Clive's remarkable genius as a leader in the field, and in part to the British success in retaining control of the sea.

The Peace of Paris (1763) brought about an impressive rearrangement in overseas affairs, for the British Empire now stood without an equal. In India the French were given back their few trading posts provided that these

14. The occasion is remembered for the tragic death of 120 British captives imprisoned for the night in a stifling prison—the "Black Hole of Calcutta."

remained unfortified. Some years later the French East India Company was dissolved, and the six French outposts still held on the Indian coast were henceforth administered as colonies. As France recognized England's claims over Bengal, the way was now prepared for the steady advance of British power in India.

France's most sweeping losses were in the New World, where she gave up her entire Canadian possessions save only the two tiny fishing islands of St. Pierre and Miquelon in the Gulf of St. Lawrence. All French territory east of the Mississippi save New Orleans became British. Spain obtained the Louisiana territory west of the great river, and ceded the Floridas to Britain in return for getting back Manila and Havana.

In the West Indies France recovered Martinique and Guadeloupe, obtaining also St. Lucia. Great Britain added St. Vincent, Dominica and Tobago to what she already possessed. It is an interesting commentary on the contemporary value of these Sugar Islands that a pamphlet war raged for a time in England as to whether it would be better to take Canada or Guadeloupe from the French. In 1761, indeed, the Board of Trade had declared that Newfoundland "as a means of wealth and power" was worth more than Canada and Louisiana put together. On the African coast France got back the island of Gorée, while England won some land at the mouth of the Senegal which she held until 1783. In the Mediterranean England recovered Minorca and retained her control of Gibraltar. The peace settlement, therefore, made after Pitt had fallen from office was not in all respects an overwhelming victory for England, and was bitterly denounced by some of the commercial interests of "the City." Yet it left her in a position of undoubted maritime and commercial supremacy—at the pinnacle of what is often called "the First British Empire."

■ THE AMERICAN REVOLUTION

The revolt of Britain's American colonies, so momentous in its ultimate consequences, must be seen in relation to the large trends of eighteenth-century imperial and colonial developments. Basically, the revolt was the outcome of a tradition of sturdy self-reliance which, growing up in the American settlements, had doubtless received additional stimulus from the parliamentary achievements of the English revolutions of the seventeenth century. The American revolt was precipitated by sharp disagreements over financial questions and its outcome was certainly influenced by the assistance which other powers, rivals of England, gave to the colonists. Finally, we may note that the theoretical arguments which were brought up in support of the revolution grew directly out of some of the main currents of eight-

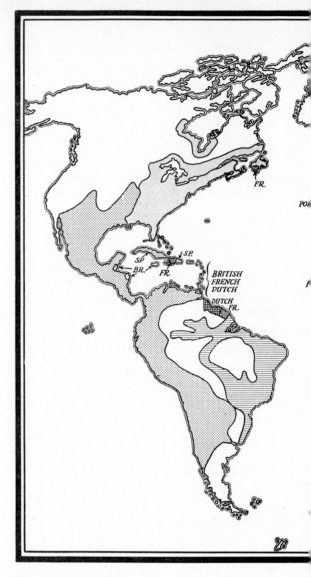

Compare this map with the one on pages 110–111 showing the first colonial empires. Now Portugal and Spain have receded in importance, the Netherlands have prospered greatly, and Britain, through its victories over France, is in a leading position. France and Britain are to continue their rivalries during the American Revolution and the Napoleonic wars.

eenth-century thought—a product of the enlightened tradition of Locke and Montesquieu.

The thirteen American colonies, having by 1763 a total population of two millions, possessed the essential institutions of local self-government, qualified by the powers of various royal officials acting under instructions from the government in England. So numerous, however, were the various directing boards and committees in London, and so uncertain or indifferent as to their duties, that a considerable degree of colonial freedom had in practice developed. The colonies were theoretically subject to the elaborate pattern of mercantile regulation stemming from the old Navigation Acts of 1651 and 1660. Trade to and from the colonies was to be limited to English or colonial-built ships, manned by English crews. The colonists were depend-

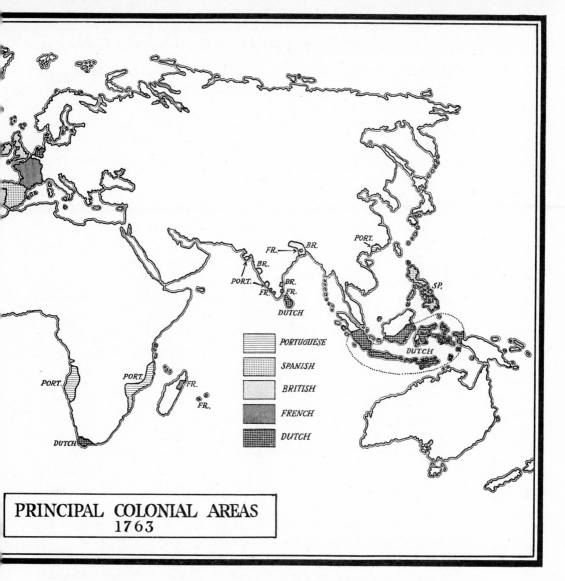

FR. → BR.

BR.

PORT.

PORT.

FR. BR.

FR.

DUTCH

PORT.

SP.

	PORTUGUESE
	SPANISH
	BRITISH
	FRENCH
	DUTCH

DUTCH

PORT.

PORT.

FR.

FR.

DUTCH

PRINCIPAL COLONIAL AREAS
1763

ent in large degree upon English manufactures. Such European goods as
were destined for America had to be shipped through English ports. A long
list of "enumerated articles" grown or made in the colonies could be shipped
only to England. Carelessness and indifference on the part of the English
government, however, meant that methods, legal or otherwise, could usually
be found by the colonists to avoid the most irksome restrictions imposed
upon them. The controls, nevertheless, in theory were there.

After the great victories of 1763 came changes of British policy in respect
to three major issues, military, political and economic. The first concerned
imperial defense. Heavy military expenses had been incurred in the recent
wars which were fought, so the English argued, as much for the good of the
colonists as for that of the mother country. The colonies should therefore be

455

asked to carry a larger share of current military cost, involving the maintenance of a permanent military establishment of some 10,000 troops in the New World.

George III, who acceded in 1760, was determined to restore the powers of the crown. In time, as he was able to find ministers agreeable to his will, the government seemed to act with a firmer hand. A royal proclamation of 1763 closed all new lands west of the Alleghenies to settlement, "for the present." This action caused an uproar in those colonies whose earlier charters gave them vast, if ill-defined and overlapping, claims to these western lands. The Grenville ministry (1763–1765) undertook a general tightening of colonial controls, notably by the Sugar Act of 1764 which sought new revenues by means of an import duty on sugar and molasses.[15] Even more objectionable was the Stamp Act of 1765 requiring a special stamp or tax on legal and business documents, newspapers and pamphlets. These measures led to a storm of protest in the colonies, one of the main arguments being that the new taxes were imposed by a legislature in which the colonists were not represented. The distinguished English jurist, Lord Mansfield, tried to defend the government by invoking the argument of "virtual representation," claiming that the American colonists were "represented" in the House of Commons in the same way as were the nine-tenths of the English people who had no vote. It was hardly a welcome argument. At a Colonial Congress held in 1765 to protest, Christopher Gadsden of South Carolina linked the immediate issue to the new outlook of the eighteenth century: "We should stand," he declared, "on the broad common ground of natural rights." Others, such as Patrick Henry, likewise spoke out.

The crisis was accentuated by the muddled policies of Grenville's successors. Although the Stamp Act was quickly repealed in 1766 by the Rockingham ministry, a Declaratory Act reasserted the full power of Parliament to legislate for the colonies. In 1767 Lord Townshend, the new chancellor of the exchequer, contrived to get Parliament to impose duties on paint, lead, paper, glass and tea going into the colonies, and to take steps to enforce the Navigation Acts and other laws producing revenue. Again there was an uproar. In 1770, after Lord North became prime minister, these were repealed except the tax on tea. A new Tea Act (1773), however, gave the East India Company a monopoly of the export trade to America, with the rapid consequence of protests in various cities and Boston's celebrated "Tea Party" in December, 1773. Lord North's next move was to obtain the so-called "Coercive" or "Intolerable" Acts of 1774 which closed Boston

---

15. The rates actually were lower than some already in existence. But these latter had frequently been ignored, whereas the new rates were to be strictly enforced.

harbor to trade, suspended the charter of Massachusetts, removed power from some of its courts of justice and required local authorities to furnish quarters for British troops on request. In this same year the American colonies were likewise aroused by the Quebec Act which granted the free practice of their religion and the use of French civil law to the Catholic French Canadians and declared the borders of Canada to include all territory north of the Ohio River. The British government seemed to be extending particular favors to the Catholic Canadians while at the same time repudiating the old American colonial claims to the western lands. The Quebec Act brought Canada directly under control of the Crown, thereby alarming the American colonists.

It is clear, then, that the rapidly mounting crisis was both economic and political in nature. The First Continental Congress which met at Philadelphia in 1774 represented all the colonies save Georgia. It issued a Declaration of American Rights and Grievances, considered measures for closer union of the colonies, took steps to maintain an embargo on British goods and submitted a petition to the king. By creating an "Association" to direct the workings of the embargo and take further needful measures, its radical members were clearly moving in the direction of organized rebellion.

The dispute was rapidly causing men on both sides of the Atlantic to take sides. Some parliamentary spokesmen in England such as Pitt and Burke were almost as critical of the actions of their government as were the colonial leaders. When the Second Continental Congress convened in May, 1775, armed conflict had already begun. British regulars had been met by the fire of colonial minute-men at Lexington Green and Concord Bridge in April. Bunker Hill was fought in June. Ethan Allen meanwhile took Fort Ticonderoga; and General Washington assumed command at Cambridge in July of the "Continental Army" which had been authorized by the Congress in Philadelphia. By seizing Dorchester Heights, overlooking Boston, he forced the British to evacuate the city in March, 1776. What can be properly called a civil war, then, was under way in America at least a year before independence was declared. Yet as late as January, 1776, General Washington, who had stated that he "abhorred the idea of independence," was still presiding over an officers' mess where the health of George III was drunk nightly.

Many American "Loyalists," to be found especially among the conservative merchants, landowners, officials and Anglican clergy, did not want independence. Equally as many were indifferent. Perhaps one-third—the "Patriots"—were zealous for the cause of political freedom. The idea of independence was aided, doubtless, by the appearance of a revolutionary pamphlet, *Common Sense*, in January, 1776. This little work by an English immigrant, Tom Paine, the son of a Quaker artisan, greatly influenced opinion; according to Washington, Tom Paine's appeal for an independent popular republic "worked a powerful change in the minds of many men." Other factors responsible were the British use of Hessian troops and the realization that if the rebellion was put down the leaders might be captured and tried for treason. The real voting of independence came on July 2 when the Continental Congress unanimously accepted the resolution of Richard Henry Lee of Virginia, submitted earlier on June 7, "that these United Colonies are, and of Right ought to be, Free and Independent States . . ."

The formal Declaration of Independence, the work of a committee of five headed by Thomas Jefferson and including John Adams and Benjamin Franklin, was in reality the justification of an action already taken. It eloquently mobilized the arguments, derived essentially from John Locke, in favor of the contract theory of government and issued a ringing call for public support of independence:

> We hold these truths to be self-evident, that all men are created equal, that they are endowed by their Creator with certain unalienable Rights, that among these are Life, Liberty, and the pursuit of Happiness. That to secure these rights, Governments are instituted among Men, deriving their just powers from the consent of the governed. That whenever any Form of Government becomes destructive of these ends, it is the Right of the People to alter or to abolish it, and to institute a new Government, laying its foundation on such principles and organizing its powers in such form, as to them shall seem most likely to effect their Safety and Happiness.

In such a passage the historian of ideas cannot fail to observe how deeply men such as Jefferson had been influenced by the new movements of European thought.

The narrative of the American War of Independence must be passed over very briefly. The conflict proceeded with uneven fortunes, the English being hampered by their lengthy communications and their unpopular cause, the Americans by inexperience and the difficulty of holding their scattered supporters together in pursuit of a common goal. The English withdrawal from Boston to New York soon gave confidence to the colonials, yet Washington's subsequent plans to win control of the Hudson Valley went badly astray. Washington soon won decisive victories at Trenton and Princeton, and the surrender of General Burgoyne at Saratoga in 1777, after marching down from Canada, aroused the hope of still further victories. The surrender likewise impelled the French, stinging from the defeat of 1763 and now subjected to expert pressure from the shrewd Benjamin Franklin, to join the war in 1778. Spain followed in 1779 and the Netherlands in 1780. Other

European powers formed the League of Armed Neutrality to oppose Britain's highly unpopular policy of searching neutral ships.

Washington's calm determination in the face of all obstacles, equally as much as his generalship, held together the American cause. A French fleet turned the balance of naval power against England. Thus the surrender of Lord Cornwallis at Yorktown in 1781 with his army of 7,000 troops marked the beginning of the end. From the first shots on Lexington Green the war had spread steadily so that before it was over the British were capturing French outposts in India, losing Senegal, winning under Admiral Rodney the great West Indian naval victory at the Battle of the Saints, and conducting a stubborn, three-year defense of Gibraltar against the Spaniards.

Lord North, deeply shocked by the news of Yorktown, resigned in March, 1782, and his successor, Lord Rockingham, leader of the Old Whigs, soon opened preliminary negotiations with Franklin in Paris. The definitive Peace of Paris was signed by the Shelburne government in 1783. By its terms the thirteen colonies received their independence as the United States of America, within limits extending from the Atlantic to the Mississippi and from the Great Lakes to the Floridas. Spain held East and West Florida, and the Louisiana Territory. France recovered St. Lucia and Tobago in the West Indies, Senegal on the African coast and its Indian establishments. Britain, having lost Minorca to Spain, kept its hold on Gibraltar.

The subsequent process by which the thirteen colonies, coming together under the Articles of Confederation, completed the drafting of a Constitution in 1787 and embarked on a new career in 1789 as the United States of America with Washington as the first president, leads into the field of American history. It seems impossible, however, to exaggerate the importance of the American Revolution as a turning point in modern history. It was the first large-scale experiment in republicanism. It produced a federal structure far larger and more impressive than either the Swiss or the Dutch. It went beyond any European achievement in emphasizing popular sovereignty as the basis of political organization. It effected a complete separation of church and state. These achievements of people who in the eyes of Europe were rude farmers, merchants, artisans or fisher-folk living on the very edge of civilization, profoundly affected European opinion. A rising curiosity greeted the ever-increasing body of literature depicting the life of the New World. *The Letters from an American Farmer*, for example, by a French immigrant and traveler, Michel-Guillaume de Crèvecoeur, who farmed near Chester, New York, were published in England in 1782 and soon translated into French. The huge popularity of these letters with their picture of "a new race of men" suggests something of the widespread European interest in the republican experiment across the seas.

■ THE IMPERIAL BALANCE SHEET
AT THE CLOSE OF THE OLD RÉGIME

The loss of the American colonies, clearly a severe blow to Britain, has been taken to mark the end of that "First British Empire" which had grown up under the protecting wing of the old colonial system. England had without question experienced many humiliations; the surrenders of Burgoyne and Cornwallis came within twenty years of the brilliant victories of Wolfe and Clive; the navy had lost prestige; England had been obliged to recruit mercenaries from Germany in order to fight the colonists; it had for a time lost control of the Channel; Gibraltar had been besieged and nearly lost; a large part of the merchant fleet had been sunk. And in the end the thirteen colonies won their independence. "You must be happy now," wrote Horace Walpole, "not to have a son who would live to grovel in the dregs of England." Following the loss of the colonies a considerable body of opinion, which included the shrewd Jeremy Bentham, believed with Turgot that colonies were destined someday to fall like ripe fruit from the parent tree.

Such a mood, however, was not permanent. Despite all reverses, England's overseas commerce continued to prosper through the eighteenth century, the volume of trade in the 1780's being estimated to have reached two and one-half times what it was in the 1720's. The Indian settlements grew steadily. The Regulating Act of 1773 required officials of the East India Company to have royal confirmation, and established a governor-general at Calcutta with authority over the three presidencies of Bengal, Madras and Bombay. Warren Hastings, the first governor-general (1774–1785), furthered the brilliant work of Robert Clive. Some powers were taken from the East India Company when in 1785 a governmental Board of Control was created. Henceforth the authority of the governor-general, under the crown, was practically despotic. Two later governors, Lord Cornwallis and Lord Wellesley, established order and spread British authority from Bengal into other areas—Oudh, Orissa, the Carnatic, Travancore, Mysore and Malabar. They likewise made subsidiary treaties with some of the native states.

British power grew in other respects. In the very years when troubles were coming to a head in America a Yorkshire farm lad rose to become one of the most distinguished of all England's naval officers. Captain James Cook undertook those three great Pacific voyages of exploration (1768–1779) which removed the mysteries from that vast ocean, paved the way for the settlement of Australia and New Zealand, began to chart the northwest coast of America, caught glimpses of the two polar regions and by scientific regulation and diet successfully mastered the hitherto dread menace of scurvy.[16] Cook's charts were so admirably constructed that they are still in

16. Although James Lind published his *Treatise on Scurvy* in 1754, advocating the use of

use. "I had ambition," Cook wrote simply, "not only to go further than any man had ever gone before, but to go as far as it was possible for a man to go."

The close of the eighteenth century saw steps for the further development of British North America. The Canada Act of 1791, made necessary by the large influx of "loyalists" from the American colonies, set up the two provinces of Upper Canada (Ontario) and Lower Canada (Quebec), granting to each its own assembly, laws, language and church, and some beginnings of representative government. A similar process of loyalist migration led to the separate establishment of New Brunswick, Cape Breton Island and Nova Scotia as colonies. The first settlements were made in Australia in 1788. In still another area the Straits Settlements, Penang and Malacca were established in 1795.

Thus, despite the losses of 1783, a new British Empire was slowly coming into being. The overseas wealth which had enriched the English aristocracy and merchant class of the early eighteenth century—the "nabobs," the West Indian planters, the noble investors, the bankers and the company promoters —continued to flow. With the wider use and the cheapening prices of tea, sugar, tobacco, coffee, India prints and the like, some of this prosperity spread downward to the middle and lower classes. In a more general sense the commercial wealth coming from Britain's overseas possessions associated itself with the new phenomena of the slowly developing industrial revolution.

In France, likewise, despite the great colonial loss of 1763, a substantial wealth remained. The sugar plantations in the West Indian Islands of San Domingo, Martinique, Guadeloupe, St. Lucia and Tobago produced an enormous wealth. The values of French imports and exports in 1700 are given as 93 million francs and 122 million francs respectively. In 1789 the figures were 634 millions and 438 millions, which, even allowing for a substantial rise in the price level, is impressive. Despite the confusions of governmental finance and the crying inequalities of the social system, the growing prosperity of French merchants, importers and investors in the eighteenth century was an undeniable fact. France actually maintained a larger trade with continental Europe and the Levant than did Britain. Only in India, where its five coastal trading posts were the weak survivals of what might have become a substantial empire, did France fail to develop an important commerce. The French East India Company was finally dissolved in 1769. On the whole the prospects for further expansion of trade on the eve of the French Revolution were promising. A commercial treaty

---

green food, fresh fruit and lime-juice, it took until 1795 for the Admiralty to require lime-juice to be served on British ships at sea. Captain Cook kept his crews healthy by the use of malt and sauerkraut and by insisting on cleanliness, proper ventilation, daily exercise, variety in diet, good morale and dancing on the foc'sle.

was made with England in 1786, and one with Russia in 1787, while still further markets were anticipated in the newly founded United States of America.

The Dutch, although no longer an aggressive colonial power, were in a position to enjoy the wealth coming from what they already possessed. The French revolutionary era, it is true, was to see them lose the Cape of Good Hope and Ceylon to the British. Spain and Portugal were so clearly in a decline as colonial powers that one does not always realize the vast extent of their continuing possessions. In addition to Brazil and some of the Atlantic islands (the Azores, Madeira and the Cape Verdes) Portugal held the slender chain of African posts that linked it with Goa, Diu and Daman in India, and even further outposts in New Guinea and at Macao on the China coast. Spain held the greater part of South and Central America, Mexico, the great southwest areas beyond the Mississippi, the larger portion of the West Indies, the Canary Islands off Africa and the Philippines in the Far East. In short, imperialism whether waxing or waning was still clearly to be a profound force in European history. As communications improved, the overseas world presented new problems and new challenges of even larger dimensions to its European conquerors.

Chapter 18

The Intellectual Revolution:
The World of Nature

■ BACKGROUNDS

THE GREAT STRUCTURE of modern science has grown out of the fundamental
work done during the seventeenth century. Earlier ages had made their
contributions, to be sure, for men have never ceased to ask questions and to
propound theories about the mysterious universe surrounding them. The

ancient Greeks, aided by the extraordinary collection of fact and lore coming to them from Egypt and Mesopotamia, had been tireless in their inquiries. The Hellenistic scholars of Alexandria added substantially to the knowledge of their predecessors. Medieval thinkers inherited at least part of this knowledge, and some of them sought to ask questions directly of the world of nature. All this lay in the background of the modern age.

The sixteenth century produced many students who sought to enlarge their knowledge of the physical universe. Yet the Renaissance, which to a very large degree turned man's gaze from the crabbed manuscripts of the schoolmen to the fresh face of the living world, was not truly a great age of science. It lacked the technical equipment, the massive accumulation of data, the mathematical discipline which would make it possible for men to generalize and create unified systems of thought.

By the seventeenth century the old conceptual framework by which men explained their universe was breaking down. New questions were being asked about the world in which man lived, the varieties of its phenomena, the nature of its laws, the means whereby it could be understood. Francis Bacon had appealed for experiment and inductive thinking, but he never truly understood the nature of mathematical reasoning. More important for later developments was the effort to make scientific studies amenable to a mathematical mode of treatment, to "geometrize" the problems and to stress shape, size, quantity and motion. Galileo declared that the book of the universe was written in mathematical language, its alphabet consisting of triangles, circles and geometric figures. In his studies of physical phenomena he used the technique of "abstraction," that is, he abstracted or removed everything but the universal element in a particular phenomenon and thus sought to reach the essential generalizations. Newton, in turn, put forward his mathematically formulated laws of motion as laws of nature whose conclusions could be confirmed by direct observation. "Without the achievements of the mathematicians," says a modern scholar, "the scientific revolution, as we know it, would have been impossible." [1]

This great transformation of outlook affected other fields than those of science. Old questions about man, his place in history and in society, his obligations to his fellows, his esthetic delights and his ultimate purposes were subjected to a new analysis. Often these questions—not in themselves "scientific"—were answered in a way which echoed the methods used by the scientists in their studies of natural phenomena. The phrase, "Intellectual Revolution," refers in the broadest sense to the change from the concept of a mysterious world directed by the inscrutable will of God to one in which the complex phenomena of life could be regarded as orderly processes, sub-

1. H. BUTTERFIELD, *The Origins of Modern Science,* p. 66.

ject to laws which the mind of man was competent to discover. So likewise the phrase, "The Age of Reason," widely applied to the eighteenth century, reflects the conviction of this age that man could, by the exercise of his power of reason, pluck the mystery out of the universe and lead his fellows into a future of ever-increasing happiness. Still another term came into use late in the eighteenth century to characterize man's victory in this mighty struggle. Whether one takes the German word *Aufklärung,* the French *Eclaircissement* or the English "Enlightenment," the connotation is always that of a victory brought by the forces of light over those of darkness. "The Enlightenment," the German philosopher Immanuel Kant wrote in 1784, "is the liberation of man from his self-imposed minority."

It will be important, then, to see how the incredibly complex phenomena of the physical world were brought within the scope of man's rational understanding. Such is the purpose of the present chapter. It will be equally important to observe how the behavior of man, too, was brought under rational scrutiny and to note the manner in which history, politics, economics and the like were held to be obedient to the reign of "law." These matters will be the subject of the chapter which follows. To pursue them is to recognize that the historian must be as much concerned with the structure of ideas as with the structure, say, of the Holy Roman Empire, and that the battles of the mind are as much a part of the human pageant as are the campaigns of Frederick the Great.

To understand the background and genesis of modern science, it must be recalled that the humanists of the Renaissance had devoted much of their time to resurrecting and editing the great writings of classical antiquity, among which were many scientific texts. They did so, however, under the growing pressure of new forces: the tendency to reject authority, the emphasis upon man as an individual, the growing confidence in his creative powers. It could be pointed out that even the literary and grammatical interests of the humanists involved techniques which were in some sense "scientific." To compare, say, the different manuscript versions of a classical author in order to establish a "true" reading, or to assemble evidence from which one could formulate the "laws" of Greek grammar was to employ methods which the modern scientist would understand. Even the development of a naturalistic approach in painting can be suggested as a contribution to the more careful study of the world of nature. All these, however, were little more than tendencies and beginnings.

The span of a century running from the appearance of Copernicus' *De Revolutionibus* in 1543 to the death of Galileo in 1642 marks out a critical era in the history of science. Towards its close Francis Bacon expressed confidence that his *Novum Organum*—"The New Method"—would lead to "the knowledge of the causes and secret motions of things." The attention of thinking men—the educated minority—began to turn more closely to the physical world with its evidences of regularity and law. Some parts of this evidence Galileo and Kepler were able to formulate in mathematical statements such as the former's law of acceleration and the latter's three laws of planetary motion. Still to be attained was a generalized mathematical statement concerning the behavior of matter. This was to be the momentous achievement of the age of Newton. If, then, the century running from 1543 to 1642 may be taken as a period of important scientific beginnings, the succeeding half-century is marked by spectacular achievement. In 1637 a brilliant French mathematician, René Descartes, published his *Discourse on the Method of Rightly Conducting the Reason and Seeking the Truth in the Sciences*. Precisely fifty years later, in 1687, an Englishman, Isaac Newton, completed the printing of his *Mathematical Principles of Natural Philosophy*. In its own way each book enunciated principles on the basis of which men were convinced that they could master the secrets of the physical universe. Seldom have two books so profoundly affected the outlook of an age. An attempt to understand the spirit which inspired the authors of these epochal works may well precede a survey of the achievements in the various fields of natural science.

■ DESCARTES AND CARTESIANISM

The life of René Descartes extends from 1596 to 1650. A boy of good French family, he received a characteristically thorough training at the Jesuit school of La Flèche, following this with legal studies at the university. In what may have been a revulsion against this discipline Descartes then determined to study what he described as "the book of the world." He traveled in Holland, Germany, Denmark and Italy, was a soldier for a time in the Netherlands and may have been with the imperial forces in the first stage of the Thirty Years' War. During the winter of 1619 which he spent isolated at a small inn in a Bavarian village, he seems to have passed through a kind of intellectual and emotional crisis.[2] After further years of wandering during which Descartes describes himself as "trying to be a spectator rather than an actor in all the comedies which the world displays," he settled in the Netherlands, devoting himself to a profound study of mathematics.

In his hospitable Dutch environment Descartes made himself a brilliant mathematician. He was anxious to find a mathematical technique to describe the forms dealt with in geometry; as he put it, he sought "a universal

2. Descartes tells of three dreams during this period of emotional unrest, in one of which he was lame and took refuge in a church during a thunderstorm; in a second he heard thunder and was surrounded by fiery sparks; in a third he opened the Latin author Ausonius and read: "What manner of life shall I lead?"

mathematics that would explain all." In developing the numerical or algebraical formulas that could be applied to geometric figures and solids, he
thus became the founder of analytical geometry. It is noteworthy that such
studies likewise directed Descartes to the question of how one could win a
certainty, comparable to that of mathematics, in *all* fields of knowledge—a
certainty that would reassure one as to the nature of man, the reality of the
physical world and the existence of God. In 1637 Descartes published his
Philosophical Essays, including the epoch-making *Discourse on Method.*
The *Discourse* was intended as a preface to three further treatises appearing
almost simultaneously: the *Dioptric,* the *Meteors* and the *Geometry.* Planned
to give concrete illustration of Descartes' method, they profoundly impressed
his contemporaries and won him an important position in the world of
science. The *Dioptric,* for example, was a fundamental treatise on light, first
stating the law of refraction; the *Geometry,* which has been called Descartes'
most valuable contribution to the scientific revolution, laid the foundations
of algebraical, or analytical, geometry. Newton read these treatises as a
Cambridge undergraduate. Later, in his *Principles of Philosophy* (1644),
Descartes clearly stated the law of inertia.

The *Discourse on Method* gives a deeply moving account of Descartes'
efforts to find certainty of knowledge. His early training, he tells us, had
been scholastic; it had depended upon the authority of books; the syllogisms
of his teachers, Descartes wrote rather bitterly, never increased the sum
total of his knowledge but were good only for communicating what one already knew. Echoing the skepticism of Montaigne, he declared that there
was no opinion, however absurd, that some philosopher had not been
willing to maintain.

"I thought," wrote Descartes, "that the sciences contained in books . . .
are farther removed from truth than the simple inferences which a man of
good sense using his natural and unprejudiced judgment draws respecting
the matters of his experience." Hence Descartes decided, "like one walking
alone and in the dark," to set for himself four guiding precepts. These
were, first, never to accept for true what he did not clearly know to be so
without any ground of doubt; second, to divide all his difficulties into as
many parts as possible; third, to order his thoughts so as to proceed always
by the simplest and easiest steps, "that I might ascend little by little"; and,
fourth, to make constant enumerations and reviews so as to be sure of omit-
ting nothing. These were essentially the procedures of a practical man seeking
a mathematical technique of measurement in order to solve a concrete problem. The method, it will be noted, is that of geometry.

Armed with these precepts, Descartes made his famous formulation of
the method that he believed would lead to absolute truth:

I thought . . . that I ought to reject as absolutely false all opinions in regard to which I could suppose the least ground for doubt, in order to ascertain whether after that there remained aught in my belief that was wholly indubitable. Accordingly, seeing that our senses sometimes deceive us, I was willing to suppose that there existed nothing really such as they presented to us. . . . But immediately upon this I observed that, whilst I thus wished to think that all was false, it was absolutely necessary that I, who thus thought, should truly exist . . . and as I observed that this truth, *I think, hence I am,* was so certain and of such evidence, that no ground of doubt, however extravagant, could be alleged by the Sceptics capable of shaking it, I concluded that I might, without scruple, accept it as the first principle of the Philosophy of which I was in search.

Descartes would thus cast out from his mind any belief—for example, the existence of the external world or of God—concerning which possible doubt could be raised. One could not doubt, however, the existence of the doubter. "I think," said Descartes, "therefore I am." From this premise, as sure as any axiom in geometry, he could now advance, step by step, erecting a coherent, supposedly incontrovertible system that would explain man, God and the physical world.

How Descartes was able to do this in detail is the concern of the philosopher rather than of the historian. Given the fact of his own existence he deduced to his own satisfaction the existence of an omnipotent God and a material universe. The two attributes of matter according to Descartes are, first, that it has dimensions which cause it to occupy space and, secondly, it is not wholly passive. "Give me extension and motion," declared Descartes, "and I will construct the universe." [3] To explain the complex structure and motions of the physical universe Descartes had recourse to a theory of "vortices," that is to say, matter continually spins about in a series of whirlpools, infinitely small and infinitely great, thereby accounting for the regular pattern of physical phenomena. All substances, including the bodies of animals and men, are part of a mechanistic universe, self-operating in consequence of the initial impulse given by God. By thus insisting upon the separate existence of mind and matter, Descartes in philosophic parlance created a system of dualism: mind is that which thinks, and matter is that which has extension and motion.

What had Descartes achieved? He had made basic contributions in mathematics and physics. He had asserted that man must shed the entire burden of knowledge accepted on authority, and should exercise his unrestricted right to doubt. Descartes would begin with those simple truths which he knew *intuitively* to be true (as one knows that the whole is equal to the sum of its parts) and using his power to reason he would advance by

3. By having "extension" is meant that matter occupies some definite, measurable portion of space.

the method of *deduction* from these simple truths to others more complex. The vast world of nature (which Descartes had persuaded himself really existed) would be compelled to yield its mysteries, for Descartes was convinced of its order and regularity. Every science of natural phenomena would be reduced to a branch of mechanics. "Thus the science of Descartes is a centrifugal system, working outwards from the certainty of the existence of mind and God to embrace the universal truths or laws of nature detected by reason, and then . . . revealing the mechanisms involved in particular phenomena. . . . The influence of Descartes . . . was so great because he produced a mechanistic world system of infinite scope." [4]

Ours, then, is an orderly, intelligible world. The completeness of Descartes' conviction is revealed in the following famous passage from the *Discourse* of 1637:

> The long chains of simple and easy reasonings by means of which geometers are accustomed to reach the conclusions of their most difficult demonstrations had led me to imagine that all things, to the knowledge of which man is competent, are mutually connected in the same way, and that there is nothing so far removed from us as to be beyond our reach, or so hidden that we cannot discover it, provided only we abstain from accepting the false for the true, and always preserve in our thoughts the order necessary for the deduction of one truth from another.

The "geometrical spirit" of Cartesianism dominated the ensuing age. It did not, however, pass unchallenged, and one may be helped to appreciate the strength and weakness of Cartesianism by considering an alternative view. Another Frenchman, Blaise Pascal (1623–1662), like Descartes a brilliant mathematician and a devout Catholic, raised troubling questions. Pascal had experienced a religious crisis which took him into the company of the ardently religious and scholarly little group of Catholics known as the Port Royalists and left him dissatisfied with the claims of pure reason. The very majesty and immensity of the universe made it impossible for Pascal to believe that his puny intelligence would ever be able to encompass it. In his *Thoughts,* an eloquent and deeply moving collection of fragments, Pascal poured out his questions.

The great world of nature bombards us with its endless torrent of phenomena which are beyond our power to explain but which we are bound to accept. "The perceptions of our senses," wrote Pascal, "are always true." In another passage he wrote: "Nature is an infinite sphere of which the center is everywhere and the circumference nowhere." In another he compared man to a reed bending helplessly before the wind, but he is "a reed that thinks." Looking at the starry heavens, Pascal confessed his profound

4. HALL, *The Scientific Revolution,* pp. 179, 184.

emotion: "The eternal silence of these infinite spaces," he wrote, "frightens me." This, then, is man's fate, to sail "within a vast sphere, ever drifting in uncertainty." Man hungers after God; he is miserable without him; yet he will not find God by reason, but only by faith, for "the heart has its reasons that reason does not understand." Eloquent though it was, the troubled voice of Pascal, raised in protest against those who expected an adequate, all-embracing philosophy to arise from the *esprit géometrique,* did not prevail in the face of the growing assurance of seventeenth-century thought.

■ NEWTON AND THE NEWTONIAN SYNTHESIS

The great figure of Sir Isaac Newton has come to be regarded as a giant in the modern world of science. Born in 1642, the year when Galileo died, he followed Descartes by a generation. This son of a yeoman farmer, who showed little distinction as a Cambridge undergraduate, developed a mathematical and scientific bent that soon led to a brilliant career. Holding a professorship at the age of twenty-seven, Newton became a mathematician, a physicist whose first interests were in the phenomena of light, an astronomer, a Fellow of Trinity College, President of the Royal Society, Warden and Master of the Mint. He was knighted by Queen Anne. The story is told that in 1696 the Swiss scholar Bernoulli circulated two complex problems among the mathematicians of Europe, defying them to find a solution within six months. Newton submitted his answers, which he wrote out in one day, anonymously. The distinction of his work caused him, however, to be recognized at once by Bernoulli—*tanquam ex ungue leonem,* "as a lion is recognized by his claws."

Newton's close friends idealized their master. He was "very meek, sedate, and humble," one wrote, "never seemingly angry, of profound thought, his countenance mild, pleasant and comely." He lived quietly. "His breakfast was orange peel boiled in water, which he drank as tea, sweetened with sugar, and with bread and butter." At Cambridge he lectured rapidly to very small audiences, returning quietly to his rooms if no one appeared. He had no recreations. According to Sir James Jeans there is only one recorded instance of Newton ever laughing, and that at a friend who saw no use in learning Euclid. He seems to have had no interest in art, music, literature or poetry.

He ate very sparingly [wrote a friend], nay, oftentimes he forgot to eat at all, so that, going into his chambers, I have found his mess untouched. . . . He very rarely went to bed till two or three of the clock, sometimes not till five or six, lying about four or five hours, especially at spring and fall of the leaf, at which times he used to employ about six weeks in his elaboratory, the fire scarce going out either night or day, he sitting up one night and I another, till he had finished his chemical experiments. . . . I cannot say that I ever saw him drink wine, ale, or beer, excepting at meals, and then but very sparingly. He very rarely went to dine in the hall, except on some public days, and then if he had not been minded, would go very carelessly, with shoes down of heels and his head scarcely combed. . . . He kept neither dog nor cat in his chamber. . . . As for his private prayers, I can say nothing of them; I am apt to believe his intense studies deprived him of the better part.[5]

This picture, doubtless correct in itself, does not bring out what have been called the "other, darker qualities of Newton's mind and character." He quarreled with many of his fellow scientists, notably with Robert Hooke, whom he particularly disliked. He had no interest in biology. He preferred alchemy to chemistry, laboriously copying millions of words from obscure alchemical texts. He was likewise devoted to biblical chronology, and tried to calculate the number of generations that had elapsed from the creation of the world. Fascinated by the prophetic books of the Bible, Newton wrote a treatise on Daniel and Revelations. The social, religious and philosophic implications of the scientific revolution of which he was a part concerned him hardly at all.

Newton could make use of the learning of extraordinarily distinguished forerunners; he said that he stood upon the shoulders of giants, among whom one would number men such as Kepler, Borelli, Boyle and Descartes. He seems, oddly, to have owed little directly to the writings of Galileo. Almost simultaneously with Leibniz he developed the infinitesimal calculus as a means of solving complex mathematical problems by formulas which involved relationships between changing quantities. His great mathematical learning served, indeed, as an indispensable basis for his later scientific contributions.

The central problem in solving which Newton won his fame arose from the changing views of the cosmos. If one abandoned the Aristotelian scheme of concentric crystalline orbs holding aloft the planets and stars and moving them regularly in their courses, then on what new theory could one account for the complex movements of the heavenly bodies? By what power were they held in their paths? Copernicus had been aware of the problem; Gilbert had suggested the idea of magnetic attraction; Kepler had written of mutual attraction between bodies in space such as the earth and the moon. In 1643 Descartes had stated the law of inertia, that motion continues in a straight line until it is interrupted by something. In addition to the concept of a "gravitational pull" was the further concept of centrifugal force, that is, of bodies flying away from a rotating earth to which otherwise they would have been drawn. The three ideas, then, of inertia, gravitational pull and

5. Quoted in s. BRODETSKY, *Sir Isaac Newton* (1929), pp. 70, 99–100.

centrifugal force, were well known by mid-seventeenth century. In 1665 an Italian scientist, Alphonso Borelli, stated that gravity would cause the planets to fall into the sun were it not for a counteracting tendency which caused them to fly away. In the same year an Englishman, Robert Hooke (with whom Newton frequently quarreled), stated that the moon might have a "gravitational principle" like the earth; and later he not only enlarged his view to include all parts of the solar system, but was able to state the proposition that the attraction between two bodies is inversely proportional to the square of the distance between them (1680). Newton afterwards re-called that in 1666 he "began to think of Gravity extending to the orb of the Moon and . . . deduced that the forces which keep the Planets in their Orbs must [be] reciprocally as the squares of their distances from the centers about which they revolve." [6] He was so dissatisfied, however, with his mathe-matical calculations in support of this hypothesis that he laid the problem aside.

Newton's great "discovery" of 1687 was in reality the completion and full mathematical demonstration of concepts slowly developing and widely held.[7] In 1684, encouraged by his friend, Edmund Halley, and using more precise astronomical data he worked out proofs and submitted them to the Royal Society in London. Then, in 1687, he published in Latin his *Mathe-matical Principles of Natural Philosophy (Philosophiae Naturalis Principia Mathematica)*—"the greatest scientific work ever produced by the human intellect." [8]

"We offer this work," Newton wrote in his preface, "as the mathematical principles of philosophy; for all the difficulty of philosophy seems to consist of this—from the phenomena of motions to investigate the forces of nature, and then from these forces to demonstrate other phenomena. . . ." What Newton did, in a way far too technical for any summary, was to develop a theory of physical nature within which the motions of the heavens could be accounted for. Turning the pages of the *Principia,* one seems to be looking at an elaborate treatise on geometry with postulates, definitions, theorems and proofs. In it Newton formulated his three laws of motion, to which he added his postulate on gravitation, that every particle of matter attracts every other with a force proportional to the product of their masses and inversely proportional to the square of the distance between them. The formula was soon shown to apply to astronomical observations two centuries

6. HALL, *The Scientific Revolution,* p. 248.
7. The story about Newton and the apple seems to be true, in that he told contempo-raries the idea of attraction between two bodies being proportional to their mass first suggested itself to him when he saw an apple fall to the ground in the family orchard at Woolsthorpe.
8. The phrase is that of one of the most distinguished of modern scientists, Sir JAMES JEANS, in his *Growth of Physical Science* (1951), p. 190.

old. Edmund Halley used it to calculate the path of "Halley's Comet," which had appeared in 1682, and to predict (correctly) that it would reappear about 1759.[9] This was the first time that any such scientific prediction concerning comets had been made.

For the historian of thought the general nature of Newton's achievement is profoundly significant. "He defined mass and the laws of motion. He gave to science formal concepts of space and time which needed no revision for two centuries. He expounded—and exemplified—a 'method of philosophizing' that is still regarded as a valid model. He virtually created theoretical physics as a mathematical science in the form which it preserved to the end of the last century." [10] Newton's four "Rules of Reasoning" are contained in the third book of the *Principia:*

(1) We are to admit no more causes of natural things than such as are both true and sufficient to explain their appearances.

(2) To the same natural effects we must, as far as possible, assign the same causes.

(3) The qualities of bodies . . . which are found to belong to all bodies within the reach of our experiments, are to be esteemed the universal qualities of all bodies whatsoever.

(4) In experimental philosophy we are to look upon propositions collected by general induction from phenomena as accurately or very nearly true, notwithstanding any contrary hypothesis that may be imagined, till such time as other phenomena occur, by which they may either be made more accurate, or liable to exceptions.

One will note the contrasts between what may be called Cartesianism and Newtonianism. Both were profoundly influenced by mathematics; both used man's reason to demonstrate the patterns of an orderly universe. Descartes, however, would have man employ his reason in elaborating upon those self-evident truths which he came upon intuitively by the process of self-examination. Newton's empiricism required him to begin with the world of nature. His method has been summarized as follows: (1) Examine the known facts and frame a hypothesis to reduce them to order. This is *induction.* (2) Draw the logical consequences from the hypothesis by mathematics or otherwise. This is *deduction.* (3) Compare these consequences with observation or experiment. (4) If they agree, call the hypothesis a theory.

English scholars tended to accept Newton's views; Frenchmen tended to adhere to Descartes and his theory of vortices as an explanation of the behavior of matter. In the end, however, Newton's concepts were victorious

9. This was the comet shown on the famous Bayeux Tapestry commemorating William of Normandy's crossing of the English Channel in 1066.
10. HALL, *The Scientific Revolution,* pp. 269–270

over those of Descartes. "The clean and comparatively empty Newtonian skies ultimately carried the day against a Cartesian universe packed with matter and agitated with whirlpools for the existence of which scientific observation provided no evidence." [11] Thus the victory of Newton meant a victory of geometry, allied with the experimental method, over the deductive system of Descartes.

Posterity hailed Newton for his work and in some sense conceived him to be greater than he actually was. Voltaire, whose admiration for Newton was profound, did much to establish his continental reputation. Voltaire was present in 1727 at Newton's funeral in Westminster Abbey, and was deeply impressed by the honors done him. The English buried Newton, he wrote, as they would a king and benefactor of his people.

■ THE TOOLS OF SCIENCE

The broad formulations of Descartes and Newton were made in a world alive with an astonishing variety of scientific activities. As a preliminary to examining the spectacular victories that were being won in almost every field of endeavor it is important to notice the new tools which became available to the scientist—those instruments of precision and those mathematical and other devices which scholars now take for granted. Today one finds it hard to realize how clumsy some of the early techniques of measurement had been; the first clocks of the fourteenth century, for example, were known on occasion to err as much as three hours in twenty-four. Even in the sixteenth century the error was as much as fifteen minutes a day. Copernicus and Brahe watched the heavens without benefit of the telescope, while Vesalius had produced his incredibly detailed anatomical drawings simply by using the human eye. In the period between 1600 and 1650 a remarkable number of technical improvements saw the light—an indication, surely, of the way in which invention is associated with the intellectual climate and the needs of an age and is not simply the product of isolated genius.

In the Netherlands, where lens-grinding and glass-blowing were highly skilled arts, a patent for making a telescope was issued to a Dutchman, Hans Lippershey, in 1608; a year later, hearing of the device, Galileo seems to have made one for himself. He rigged a telescope on a church-tower in Venice, making it possible for astonished merchants to see the details on approaching ships hours before these details were visible to the naked eye. With his telescope Galileo explored the heavens; he saw the satellites of Jupiter, Saturn's rings, the craters of the moon and the sunspots by which he could confirm the rotation of the sun and estimate its speed at fifteen degrees in an hour.

11. BUTTERFIELD. The Origins of Modern Science, p. 121.

Other instruments soon followed. The microscope, which in its simple form seems to have been devised by another Dutchman, Zacharias Jansen, between 1590 and 1610, developed into an instrument of considerable power. An Italian, Evangelista Torricelli, first stated the principle of the mercury barometer in 1643; the instrument itself was further developed by Pascal and Robert Boyle. Around 1650 a German, Otto von Guericke, devised the air pump for creating a near-vacuum. This he was able to display in the form of his celebrated "Nuremberg Spheres"—two hollow brass hemispheres which, when fitted together and exhausted of their air, defied the efforts of sixteen horses to pull them apart. The technique of collecting gases over water was developed early in the eighteenth century.

Clocks and watches driven by coiled springs had been devised in the early sixteenth century, but were very erratic. In 1641, after he had become blind, Galileo dictated to his son instructions for building a pendulum clock that would keep accurate time. About 1650 a Dutchman, Christian Huygens, devised a workable weight and pendulum clock having a degree of error amounting to only ten seconds a day, a quantity later reduced to one-tenth of a second. What this meant for delicate astronomical calculations is obvious. Huygens and the Englishman, Robert Hooke, separately devised also a balance spring that could be used in watches.[12] Delicately contrived scales and balances, accurate to a tenth of a gram, likewise contributed to exact measurement. Crude forms of the thermometer were available in the seventeenth century, and sufficed until a German, Gabriel Fahrenheit, produced a thermometer in 1724 graded with the scale that has become standard. In 1631 Paul Vernier first described the ingenious measuring scale which bears his name and which made possible measurements of the highest refinement. The tangent screw also came into use for making fine adjustments in precision instruments, the outcome of improved techniques in lathe-turning and screw-cutting. At the University of Leyden in 1746 were devised the "Leyden jars" which were the prototypes of later electrical condensers. In 1752 the ever-curious Benjamin Franklin was able to charge a Leyden jar with electricity from a kite during a thunderstorm.

Tools of another sort should also be listed. Algebraical and decimal notation had come into use during the sixteenth century. The conventional

12. The need for accurately recording time at sea was early recognized as a prerequisite to determining a ship's position east or west of a "prime meridian," eventually set at Greenwich. As early as 1598 Spain offered a reward of 1,000 crowns for an accurate means of determining longitude, and much greater prizes were later offered by the Netherlands, Venice, France and England. Seeing that the earth rotates once in 24 hours and its equator is divided into 360 degrees, a rotation of 15 degrees will be effected in one hour. If one observes a ship's clock which keeps Greenwich time at the moment when the sun is precisely overhead and finds that it registers one o'clock, then the vessel is 15 degrees west of Greenwich. Pendulum clocks were highly impractical at sea, but the alternative, an accurate chronometer, was not developed until John Harrison perfected his in 1762.

symbols for multiplication, division and so forth were standardized. Only a mathematician can appreciate the enormous forward steps made possible by Napier's invention of logarithms in 1614. Anticipating the computing machines of today, logarithms reduced what would have been infinitely tedious calculations to the work of a few minutes. The slide-rule, based on logarithmic techniques, was devised by a German, Gunther, in 1624. One must also list Descartes' combination of algebra and geometry into his new analytical geometry, Pascal's studies of mathematical probability and the work of Newton and Leibniz in developing the calculus. The mathematical tools were at hand for those who were eager to use them.

■ THE PHYSICAL WORLD

The study of the physical world went on apace. As it had throughout history, astronomy continued to absorb the attention of men of science. A brilliant sequence of names led, as we have seen, from Copernicus through Brahe, Kepler and Galileo to Newton. The great generalizations of Newton once established, the further advances were largely those of tabulation, computation and more precise measurement. The sun's distance from the earth, for example, was calculated with fair accuracy. Voyages to the southern hemisphere made possible large additions to the catalogue of stars. Such an increase in the available data eventually resulted in the studies of celestial mechanics made by the French astronomer, Pierre Laplace (1749–1827), whose *Mécanique céleste* (1799 ff.) "extended in time the laws that Newton had traced in space" and who defined the new concepts of physics in elegant and precise mathematical equations.

The variety of advances made under the general heading of physics defies any simple summary, so that it must suffice to indicate the principal fields and the type of work done. In 1600 William Gilbert in his *De Magnete* had discussed the strange properties of the lodestone, proceeding then to describe the magnetic field of the earth itself and using for the first time the word "electricity." Other distinguished figures of the seventeenth century such as Guericke and Newton were interested in the phenomenon of magnetism but did little to advance its study until Benjamin Franklin in the eighteenth undertook his simple experiments.

A long list of great names is found in the field of optics. Kepler had described what is known as the *camera obscura*.[13] Galileo, of course, understood the workings of the telescope and Descartes described the refraction of light, a phenomenon which also interested an Italian Jesuit, Grimaldi. Newton split a ray of light by means of a prism, made a study of the spectrum

13. If a ray of light is let into a darkened room through a small aperture so as to shine on the opposite wall, it will project the inverted images of figures moving outside.

of colors and found that if the seven colors were projected one on top of the other, white light would be the result. The great Dutch physicist Huygens rejected Newton's "corpuscular" theory of light in favor of a wave theory which he presented to the French Academy of Science in 1678 and later published in his classic *Treatise on Light* (1690).

Great developments also occurred in dynamics, statics and mechanics. Galileo elaborated and described various applications of the lever, the wedge, the inclined plane and the pulley. He was also able to propose laws of velocity and of the pendulum which explained the motions of falling bodies. Torricelli, whom we have noted as the inventor of the barometer, was more generally concerned with the phenomena of air pressure upon the surface of liquids, as were his contemporaries Boyle, Descartes and Pascal. Robert Boyle, the fourteenth son of the Earl of Cork, among his other wide interests formulated "Boyle's Law" describing the behavior of gases under pressure.

Meanwhile Huygens had published in 1673 an elaborate study of the pendulum. Further advances were made, too, in the study of sound. Guericke, for example, was able to use his vacuum chamber to show that the sound of a striking clock will grow faint as the air is exhausted, thus suggesting a wave theory of sound. Other advances were made in the direction of applied science. Suction pumps were greatly improved because of the advanced knowledge of atmospheric pressure. A rudimentary steam engine was designed by a Frenchman, Denis Papin, around 1706 for the purpose of pumping water in the royal gardens at Versailles. Almost simultaneously two Englishmen, Thomas Savery and Thomas Newcomen, designed crude steam pumps for getting water out of coal mines.

Chemistry made important, though not such elaborate, advances. Its background was largely that of medieval alchemy. Some sixteenth-century students such as Paracelsus had been much concerned with the medical properties of drugs. In seeking to refine them they were naturally concerned with the question of "pure" substance and how to reduce matter to simpler forms. Such investigations could be said to mark a kind of beginning in the search for "elements" and thus led to the problem of the nature of matter. Students could not rest content with the old division of substances into "fire, air, earth and water." Observations of the phenomena of heat led a Belgian scientist, Jean van Helmont (1577–1644), to consider the nature of gases. Helmont, who took the word "gas" from the Greek *chaos,* produced a definition of it which is worth recording: "A spirit or wild exhalation which can neither be confined nor coagulated, belched forth from fomenting things as though it were an enemy to them, and often fatal to incautious by-standers."

These were the beginnings. The great name in seventeenth-century chemistry is that of the versatile Robert Boyle whose book, *The Skeptical Chymist* (1661), is a classic. It attacked the old theory of the four elements and conjectured that matter might ultimately consist of varieties of tiny particles or "corpuscles" combining in various ways to form chemical substances. Boyle likewise studied the phenomena of combustion which he shrewdly related to the process of chemical change, as did his compatriot Robert Hooke. But they were unable to forestall the growth of a theory (fully developed later by a German, G. E. Stahl) that combustion was due to a mysterious "fiery substance" called *phlogiston*. This erroneous but "useful provisional scheme for the explanation of many experiments" dominated chemical thought for a century. It remained for the Frenchman, Antoine Lavoisier, with the help of discoveries made by Joseph Priestley and Henry Cavendish, to demolish the *phlogiston* theory late in the eighteenth century by isolating hydrogen, oxygen and other gases and to evolve a theory of matter as composed of various chemical "elements." In 1789 Lavoisier drew up a list of 33 elements of which 25 are still held to be such. The road which led from Boyle to Lavoisier had thus made possible the creation of the modern science of chemistry.

The details of these various advances in the physical sciences should not obscure the larger significance of the scientific revolution. The method by which problems had been attacked, most especially in astronomy and physics, led to a view of the cosmos in which the earth and the heavens could be reduced to one fundamental system of law to be described in mathematical terms. Many scientists, including Newton, stipulated God as the First Cause. "This most beautiful system of the sun, planets, and comets," Newton wrote in the concluding section of his *Principia*, "could only proceed from the counsel and dominion of an intelligent and powerful Being. . . . He endures forever, and is everywhere present." The operations of nature, however, were increasingly regarded as manifestations of a mechanistic design:

> The only sort of explanation science could give must be in terms of descriptions and of processes, mechanisms, interconnections of parts. Greek animism was dead. Appetites, natural tendencies, sympathies, attractions, were moribund concepts in science, too. The universe of classical physics, in which the only realities were matter and motion, could begin to take shape.[14]

■ THE BIOLOGICAL SCIENCES

The seventeenth century also pushed forward those various studies associated with the living world of nature. In the preceding century a number of encyclopedias and summaries of natural phenomena, more or less in

14. HALL, *The Scientific Revolution*, p. xvii.

the tradition of Pliny's *Natural History* and Aristotle's scientific writings, had been produced. Travel and exploration had something to do, no doubt, with turning man's attention to the endless complexity of the natural world. It was the work of the new age to delimit the various fields more precisely, to accumulate vast stores of information, to observe, to classify and in some measure to explain and generalize about what was known.

In the field of biology and physiology much depended upon the develop-ment of the microscope. In 1661 Marcello Malpighi, professor of medicine at the University of Bologna, was able to observe microscopically the actual flow of blood in the lung of a frog from the arteries through the capillaries into the veins. The same phenomenon in the case of a tadpole was described in 1680 by the Dutch scholar, Antonius van Leeuwenhoek: "I saw," he wrote, "not only that in many places the blood was conveyed through ex-ceedingly minute vessels from the middle of the tail towards the edges, but I saw that each of the vessels had a curve or turning that carried the blood back toward the middle of the tail, in order to be conveyed again to the heart." The microscope enabled Leeuwenhoek to observe the red blood corpuscles and to study protozoa, bacteria and spermatozoa. Robert Hooke, another brilliant microscopist, carried his knowledge in new directions. He was able to show (1667) that a dog could be kept alive in the absence of all movements of the chest or lungs by artificial respiration. This soon led to the study of the functions of venous and arterial blood. The Danish scientist, Nicolaus Stensen, lectured at Paris in 1669 on the physiology of the brain, pointing out that its fibers were arranged "on some definite pattern, on which doubtless depends the diversity of sensations and movements." An Englishman, Stephen Hales (1677–1761), by attaching a long tube to the carotid artery of a horse, was able to demonstrate the phenomenon of arterial blood pressure—a discovery said to be second in importance only to Harvey's discovery of the circulation of the blood.[15]

Botany and zoology grew to be important scientific disciplines. Hooke described the cellular structure of plants, coining the word "cell" as the basic element in plant physiology. Malpighi demonstrated the sexuality of plants and the process of cross-fertilization. A remarkable Englishman, John Ray (1627–1705), undertook with his friend, Francis Willughby, to work out a systematic description of the whole organic world. Ray's *New System of Plants* (1682) attempted to classify plants on the basis of their fruits and leaves. His *Synopsis of Quadrupeds and Serpents* (1693) was the first truly systematic arrangement of animals, making use of fingers, toes and teeth of

15. Hales was versatile. He wrote a treatise, *Vegetable Staticks*, which has earned him the title of father of vegetable physiology, devised a ventilator to convey air to ships' holds, proposed new methods to distil fresh water from salt and wrote a stern *Admonition to Drinkers of Gin, Brandy, Etc.*

the animals concerned as a basis of classification. Another brilliant Dutch microscopist, Jan Swammerdam, assembled much knowledge in his *General History of Insects* (1685). His *Bible of Nature,* which has been called the finest collection of microscopical observations ever published, appeared posthumously in 1737 and is still in use by naturalists.

The steady march of knowledge concerning the structure and variety of living things continually emphasized the need for systematic classification. In this respect the various strands came together in mid-eighteenth century in the hands of the great Swedish botanist, Karl von Linné, or Linnaeus (1707–1778). This "greatest of the systematists" undertook a classification of all life in his *System of Nature* (first drafted in 1735). Linnaeus was a biological dictator whose passion for classification caused him to put every known plant and animal in a defined place. We owe to Linnaeus the familiar "mineral, vegetable and animal" classification, as we owe his separation of the three kingdoms of nature into the subdivisions of class, order, genus and species. He also devised the "binomial" system by which every animal and plant was given a two-word designation, the first denoting the genus and the second the species. In this arrangement, for example, man becomes *Homo sapiens.* Linnaeus' great French contemporary, Count Buffon (1707–1788), who disagreed with him in many respects, undertook in the forty-four volumes of his *Natural History* (begun in 1749) to assemble and classify the whole body of knowledge concerning animal life, suggesting, though not actually accepting, the theory that "not only the ass and horse but even man himself, the apes, the quadrupeds, and all animals might be regarded as forming members of one and the same family." Buffon, moreover, insisted on the importance of rigorous method in science. In the introduction to his first volume he declared that we must increase and sharpen our observations, generalize from facts and combine facts so that we can see by analogy how particulars are connected with the whole.

The study of life inevitably involved the question of the physical environment. Descartes had ascribed the origin of the earth and the planets to the cooling of an originally incandescent mass like the sun. These ideas were later elaborated by Leibniz. The versatile Danish scholar, Nicolaus Stensen, was responsible for a little tract (1669) in which he suggested that fossils embedded in various layers of the earth were the remnants of plants and animals and should be associated with geological changes covering a long period of time. An Englishman, John Woodward, published a *Natural History of the Earth* in 1695 containing a great deal of information about the various strata and the fossilized remains of plants and animals contained in them. These remains, however, he was content to explain as the product of the Deluge. Buffon's great work already mentioned included one volume, the *Epochs of Nature* (1779), which sought to draw up a chronology of the earth divided into six periods based upon the supposed rate of its cooling from a first molten stage. Not until 1795, however, did an amateur Scottish scientist, James Hutton, publish his *Theory of the Earth* proposing the view that the various geological formations are the long distant products of forces which are still in operation and are still to be observed.

The general growth of biology and kindred studies did not lead to such revolutionary outcomes as in the case of the physical sciences. Fundamental work, to be sure, had been done. Descriptive biology and the general process of classification made impressive advances. There were some hints of radical developments to come. Yet the tremendous concepts associated with the nineteenth-century names of Darwin and Mendel lay far in the future.

■ THE RISE OF A POPULAR INTEREST IN SCIENCE

A striking feature of the growth of science in the seventeenth century, far more than in the sixteenth, was a vigorous dissemination of its findings among steadily widening groups of people. What this meant for the outlook of the cultivated classes must be emphasized. In the professional sense it meant that the world of scholarship became more closely knit and therefore able to pool its knowledge, so to speak, in the interest of still further progress. More generally, it meant that something of the attitude and even of the specific findings of scientists could be conveyed to the educated public.

Among the several means for aiding the wider spread of scientific knowledge were the various academies and learned societies which grew in impressive numbers during the seventeenth and eighteenth centuries. In Renaissance Italy a number of associations for the discussion of new ideas had been organized, the most famous being the Academy at Florence founded by Cosimo de' Medici in 1462 to discuss Platonism.[16] Such associations, however, were concerned usually with literature, philosophy and the arts and only rarely with science. A new tendency can first be observed about the middle of the sixteenth century. An Academy of the Secrets of Nature was organized at Naples about 1560 and flourished briefly until suppressed by Philip II of Spain. A major landmark was the founding at Rome in 1603 of the Academy of the Lynx-Eyed (*Accademia dei Lincei*), for the study of natural sciences. Its members, among whom Galileo was included, had to declare themselves opposed to the methods of Aristotelianism; they published reports on subjects of scientific interest. A similar group, the Academy of Experiment (*Accademia del Cimento*), was founded at Florence in 1657 under Medici patronage. It carried out important researches on the nature

16. See page 71.

of heat, on the vacuum and on barometric phenomena. It, too, undertook to publish accounts of its proceedings. These academies, of which the names suggest a first-hand approach to the phenomena of nature, may be taken as examples of the many which grew up in various parts of the peninsula.

England and France were each responsible for a distinguished addition to the ranks of learned societies. The Royal Society for the Improving of Natural Knowledge, established in London in 1660 and granted a royal charter in 1662, grew out of an earlier informal association of scientists going back to the 1640's. Charles II, an amateur of science who enjoyed watching dissections, gave his blessing to it, although according to Pepys "he mightily laughed at [the Society] for spending time only in weighing of ayre and doing nothing else since they sat." He likewise seems to have failed to provide it with funds. The members were to discuss "experimental philosophy," were granted certain curious rights such as that of dissecting the bodies of criminals and could publish their findings in the celebrated *Transactions* which still appear. Their statutes indicate the general purpose of the Society:

> . . . to examine all systems, theories, principles, hypotheses, elements, histories, and experiments of things natural, mathematical, and mechanical, invented, recorded or practised by any considerable author, ancient or modern. . . . In the meantime the Society will not own any hypothesis, system or doctrine of the principles of natural philosophy, proposed or mentioned by any philosopher ancient or modern . . . but will question and canvass all opinions, adopting nor adhering to none till by mature debate and clear arguments, chiefly such as are deduced from legitimate experiments, the truth of such experiments be demonstrated invincibly.

Still another virtue was pointed out by Thomas Sprat in his *History of the Royal Society*. At a time when the English tongue suffered from what Sprat called "this vicious Abundance of Phrase, this Trick of Metaphors, this Volubility of Tongue," the Society insisted upon a simple, workmanlike method of expression: "They have exacted from all their Members," wrote Sprat, "a close, naked, natural way of Speaking; positive Expressions, clear Senses; a native Easiness; bringing all Things as near the mathematical Plainness as they can; and preferring the Language of Artizans, Countrymen, and Merchants, before that of Wits, or Scholars." To set this as a goal, if not to achieve it, was no small distinction.

In Paris, the Academy of Science (*Académie des Sciences*) was established on the advice of Colbert in 1666, mainly because Richelieu's earlier foundation, the *Académie Française,* concerned itself largely with literary and philological matters. Louis gave the Academy of Science his generous support. Pensions were provided for the members, rooms and laboratories were set apart in the Louvre and a magnificent observatory was built by the architect Perrault. In addition to the large telescope and other astronomical equipment, the observatory had rooms for physics and chemistry, a botanical garden, a well for experiments with pendulums and falling bodies and specially built cellars or caves for other experimental purposes. Colbert characteristically instructed the Academicians to seek the means whereby their discoveries could be made to further the progress of French industry.

An academy was established at Vienna in 1687. In Prussia, the Elector Frederick III undertook in 1700 to establish the Berlin Academy of Sciences which under the sympathetic guidance of Frederick the Great later acquired European distinction. In Russia, Peter the Great founded the Imperial Academy of Sciences at St. Petersburg in 1724 upon a plan devised by Leibniz. For nearly a century this Academy was practically the only organized center of higher learning in Russia. Other academies were founded at Dublin (1684), Upsala (1710), Stockholm (1739) and Copenhagen (1743). In France it has been calculated that by 1760 there were thirty-seven local societies concerned with the advancement of learning. Benjamin Franklin's American Philosophical Society founded at Philadelphia in 1743 and reorganized in 1766 was part of the same movement. It kept closely in touch with the European societies and included Buffon and Linnaeus among its foreign members.

The societies encouraged the publication of research by their members. The *Transactions* of the Royal Society in London began in 1665, as did the *Journal des Savants* in Paris. A famous German publication, the *Acta Eruditorum,* was begun at Leipzig in 1682. These periodicals, the ancestors of scholarly journals of today, made possible the exchange of information on a wide scale; the *Transactions* of the American Philosophical Society, for example, were sent to similar organizations in Sweden, Germany, Russia, England, Scotland, Ireland, France and Italy, to all the great universities and to outstanding scientists. Such new channels of communication were an obvious stimulus to scholarship. Newton's computations which led to his *Principia* were previously formulated as a paper submitted to the Royal Society in 1684. John Ray was given money by the Society to publish his *History of Plants.* In the eighteenth century Rousseau's first treatise, the *Discourse on the Arts and Sciences,* was submitted in a prize contest organized in 1750 by the Academy of Dijon.

Still other means of arousing interest in natural phenomena were found in the establishment of botanical gardens, zoos, museums, observatories and galleries. Gardens of herbs were often maintained by the early medical schools; from them developed the larger botanical gardens at Padua, Pisa,

Bologna and Leyden. The most famous of these came to be the Jardin du Roi at Paris which gradually evolved under the direction of Buffon into a splendid botanical and zoological establishment.

Collections of minerals, jewels, medals, coins, cameos and "natural curiosities" had been a favorite interest of the princes of the Renaissance. Some of these royal collections and others made by emulators of royalty provided the basis for later museums and galleries. In Oxford, for example, the Ashmolean Museum, the first in modern times, grew from Dr. Elias Ashmole's collection of "natural curiosities." The British Museum was founded in 1753 out of the great natural history and scientific collections assembled by Sir Hans Sloane. Its manuscript treasures were based on those collected by Sir Robert Cotton and Sir Robert Harley. George II granted it the right to a copy of every book entered at Stationers' Hall. The Paris Observatory, built in 1667, and that at Greenwich, built in 1675, might also be listed as examples of new centers which, in addition to arousing popular interest and developing scientific theory, made invaluable contributions for the practical benefit of navigators. The new knowledge was dramatized in various ways. By the late seventeenth century France took the lead in scientific map-making. A revolutionary new outline map of the world was laid down by Giovanni Cassini on the floor of the Paris Observatory in 1682, making large corrections in the work of earlier cartographers. These changes so startlingly reduced the old dimensions of France that Louis XIV is said to have told Cassini that all the king's military conquests could not compensate for the losses which the successes of the Academy had imposed upon France.

Towards the close of the seventeenth century a considerable literature devoted to the popularization of science began to appear. Among the numerous books which sought to bring the complicated world of the scientists within the comprehension of laymen, the Abbé Fontenelle's *Conversations on the Plurality of Worlds,* first published in 1686, was outstanding. The six "conversations" into which the gracefully written work is divided correspond to the six evenings which a beautiful marquise spends with the clerical author in a starlit garden. Here they behold the wonders of the heavens and consider the workings of the planetary system. That the first conversation should begin by likening the day to a blonde and the night to a brunette, and then proceed to some general considerations about blondes and brunettes adds to the charm of this widely read work of popularization.

Fontenelle's use of a marquise as the principal figure of his little book suggests the fashionable cult of science—a cult which may have had only slight seriousness of purpose. Joseph Addison poked fun in one of his essays at the lady who kept a copy of Newton on her boudoir table and who marked her place in Locke's writings with a paper of beauty-patches. Charles II of England dabbled in chemistry, as did the Duke of Orleans, regent of France during the minority of Louis XV. The eccentric Queen Christina of Sweden was not content to correspond with European scientists; she invited the unfortunate Descartes to her northern court and, it would seem, brought about his death by requiring him to instruct her in philosophy at five o'clock on freezing winter mornings. When, in mid-eighteenth century, Diderot undertook the publication of his great *Encyclopedia,* no less than eleven volumes of magnificent plates were required to illustrate for the general reader the remarkable advances being made in science and technology.

The wider interest in science served doubtless to lessen the cult of superstition. Pierre Bayle's treatise, *On the Comet* (1682), illustrates the effort to explain unusual phenomena on a natural basis. He argued that the appearance of a comet, which had widely been taken as an evil omen, was a purely natural phenomenon which could have no significant effect upon the happiness or misery of mankind. In 1691 a Dutch pastor, Balthasar Bekker, wrote *The World Turned Upside Down* attacking witchcraft, magic and superstition partly on the basis of natural reason but even more on the basis of a religious faith that had no need for such supports. Within four years Bekker's work was translated into French, German and English. These are examples of the growing impact of what one might call the scientific viewpoint upon a wider audience, which in time was gradually to transform the outlook of the educated world.

To say that reason had driven out superstition would be to say far too much. As late as 1727 a woman in Scotland was found guilty of sorcery by a court and sentenced to death.[17] The English and Scottish laws against witchcraft were repealed in 1736, yet Blackstone's famous *Commentaries on the Laws of England* (1765) declared flatly that the existence of witchcraft and sorcery "is a truth to which every nation in the world hath in its turn borne testimony." John Wesley agreed with him, expressing regret that men of learning "have given up all accounts of witches and apparitions as mere old wives fables." Nevertheless, as the eighteenth century progressed the champions of enlightenment and science drew to themselves a steadily increasing body of disciples.

17. The scholar, Preserved Smith, finds that the last recorded burnings for witchcraft took place in Poland in 1793.

THE MOZART FAMILY, by Johann Nepomuk della Croce, done at Salzburg in 1780 when Mozart was 24. This charming picture shows Mozart and his sister at the piano, his father holds a violin and there is a portrait of his late mother. Courtesy, Austrian Information Service, New York.

Chapter 19

The Intellectual Revolution: The World of Man

■ INTRODUCTION

"THE PROPER STUDY of Mankind is Man." Pope's famous line provides the keynote for a survey of further aspects of the Intellectual Revolution. The careful investigation of the world of nature had meant the systematic accumulation of data followed by analysis and interpretation. The outcome of this close scrutiny was a view of the physical world as a vast, smoothly operating mechanism subject to natural law—in brief, a cosmos sometimes described as the Newtonian World Machine. With such a view coming into general acceptance it would be inconceivable that the behavior of man himself, the inhabitant of this orderly cosmos, could undergo any less searching a scrutiny.

Something of the new spirit of the physical scientist, it would seem, took possession of the age-old studies of history, law and politics. New disciplines such as statistics, economics, pedagogy and psychology were developed. With the challenging theories of Descartes as a point of departure, the elaborate structure of modern philosophic thought began to arise, and venerable systems of religious belief were subjected to criticisms so searching that on occasion men appeared whose intention seemed not so much to modify religious faith as to destroy it. Important changes made themselves evident, too, in those various forms of esthetic expression—literature, music, painting, sculpture and architecture—which in any age convey so much of the spirit of man.

A study of these varied activities will not, to be sure, reveal an entirely coherent or harmonious pattern of human behavior, for no age is in all its aspects entirely consistent with itself. Yet one may discover certain major uniformities. One may observe how this Intellectual Revolution generated the modern view of man, whether as an individual or as a member of society. For this new being Pope again may provide the text:

> Created half to rise, and half to fall;
> Great lord of all things, yet a prey to all;
> Sole judge of truth, in endless error hurl'd;
> The glory, jest and riddle of the world!

Finally, it will be possible to see how these new insights into the nature of man and society eventually built up a critical attitude toward existing social institutions and, in the particular case of France, by 1789 contributed to the coming of revolution.

■ THE STUDY OF SOCIETY: HISTORY

As long ago, certainly, as the time of Herodotus men found interest in the story of their past. The age of the Renaissance had produced narrative historians such as Machiavelli and Guicciardini. It had seen in the work of men such as the Italian Lorenzo Valla and the German Ulrich von Hutten the first modern beginnings of what is called "textual criticism," that is, the subjection of historical documents to a rigorous scientific analysis in order to determine their authenticity. It had witnessed many works devoted to antiquarian lore and, in another field, it had read with fascination the numerous accounts of the overseas voyages together with some accompanying crude efforts to describe alien cultures. Yet it was not so much the intellectual enthusiasms of the Renaissance as it was to be the bitter conflicts of the Reformation era that gave impetus to the development of modern historical writing.

A few examples will illustrate the type of history arising in this age of religious controversy. The *Magdeburg Centuries,* a long work put together between 1559 and 1574 at Magdeburg, represented a Protestant attempt to assemble a large, documentary history that would attack the traditions of the medieval Church. It was answered in the twelve volumes of the *Ecclesiastical Annals* of Cardinal Baronius appearing between 1588 and 1607. Other examples that could be given of history generated in the fires of religious controversy are the *History of His Own Time* (1604–1608) composed by the Catholic, Jacques de Thou, dealing with the French Wars of Religion, and Paolo Sarpi's *History of the Council of Trent* (1619), a Catholic and at the same time anti-papal account of this momentous council.

With the consolidation of national states the interest in political history grew apace. Juan de Mariana's *History of Spain* (1592–1595) may be taken as an example of this trend, while John Camden's *Britannia* (1586) is a celebrated work of antiquarianism and at the same time of national patriotism. Lord Clarendon's *History of the Rebellion and Civil Wars in England* written between 1646 and 1671 is noteworthy as a full length account of a momentous period written by one who had been an active participant in it.

The transition from the historical writing of the sixteenth century to that of the seventeenth was marked by a growing concern with technique and method. In this respect one may detect some parallel to the contemporaneous progress of the natural sciences. As early as 1566 the French scholar, Jean Bodin, in his *Method for Easily Understanding History* had divided the history of the world into three great periods culminating in the history of the peoples of northern Europe. Joseph Scaliger's *On the Restoration of Chronology* (1583) had boldly attempted to harmonize the ancient chronologies of the Greek, Hebrew, Chaldean, Egyptian, Persian, Ethiopian, Armenian and Christian peoples. His calculation of the date of man's creation at B.C. 3939 was later amended by an Irish bishop, James Usher, in his *Annals of the Old and New Testament* (1650) to read October 28, B.C. 4004, a date subsequently inserted into the margins of the King James Bible. Periodization was made more precise by a German, Christian Cellarius, who, adopting a method already employed in church history, divided his *Tripartite History* (1685–1696) of the world into three volumes dealing with the "ancient," the "medieval" and the "new" ages.

Another contribution to the scientific study of history was the systematic collection and publication of a wide range of source materials. To do this, it was necessary to devise techniques for authenticating ancient documents. Hence there developed the so-called "auxiliary sciences" such as paleography (the study of handwriting), epigraphy (the study of inscriptions), diplomatic (the identification of different types of documents) and numismatics (the study of coins). A group of Jesuit priests in Belgium, inspired by one of their number, Jean Bolland, undertook to make a monumental collection of the biographies and legends of the saints. The Bollandists published the first volume of their famous *Acta Sanctorum* in 1643, inaugurating a vast work that still continues in our own day. Another group, the Maurists, or members of the Congregation of St. Maur in Paris, likewise undertook scientific studies of source materials. The greatest of their number was Jean Mabillon, whose *De Re Diplomatica* (1681) still remains a standard work on "diplomatic," or the evaluation of historical documents.

One can only sample the names of this growing army of historical scholars. In France André Duchesne (1584–1640), "the father of modern French history," left behind over a hundred manuscript folios of medieval documents that he had copied. Charles Du Cange published in 1678 a famous three-volume "glossary" of medieval Latin (*Glossarium mediae et infimae latinitatis*). In England Thomas Rymer published the fifteen folios of his *Foedera* (1704–1735), a vast collection of medieval charters, treaties and other documents. In Germany the versatile Leibniz began in 1703 to collect the materials later published as the *Annals of the House of Brunswick*. In Italy one of the greatest of all such compilers, Ludovico Muratori, wrote a year-by-year account in seventeen volumes of Italian history and in addition published twenty-five large folios of Italian source materials, the *Rerum Italicarum Scriptores* (1723–1751). Muratori's output has been described as perhaps the greatest of any isolated worker in the whole history of historiography.

We may gain further insight into the general trend of historical studies by considering briefly a few of the major works which were produced. Bishop Bossuet's *Discourse on Universal History* (1681), written for the benefit of the Dauphin of France, tried to show how during ten epochs, arbitrarily taken to run from the creation of man in B.C. 4004, to Bossuet's own age, the hand of God had constantly been present to guide and direct human affairs. This was, in effect, Bossuet's view of the meaning of history. Having little, if any, sympathy for the new age of rationalism, he was deeply shocked and embittered at the efforts of one of his contemporaries, Richard Simon, to apply scientific standards of historical criticism to the books of the Old and New Testament.

Bossuet's historical writing marks the end of an epoch. In 1697 another Frenchman, Pierre Bayle, published his *Historical and Critical Dictionary*, purportedly a general book of reference on Biblical and theological topics, but actually a destructive masterpiece of a high order. Bayle cast doubts on the conduct of the great Biblical heroes and employed his very substantial learning to ridicule the controversies between the sects. Bayle can thus be regarded as the herald of a new age of skeptical thought.

The versatile talents of Voltaire were likewise turned to historical studies. In 1751 he published his *Age of Louis XIV,* a brilliant work in which he examined the Great Age from all angles—its institutions, politics, commerce, wars, art, music, letters and society. "It is not only the life of Louis XIV that I propose to write," explained Voltaire, "but a much greater thing. I shall try to paint for posterity not the actions of one man, but the spirit of the men of the most enlightened age of all time." In his later *Essay on the Manners and Spirit of the Nations* (1754) Voltaire set himself the even more ambitious task of surveying the general evolution of culture from Charlemagne to Louis XIII. Before presenting the main narrative, fourteen introductory chapters attempted a grand survey of history from primitive times, touching upon the civilizations of China, Persia, Arabia and the classical world. No careful student would put this work, with its confident generalizations and its violently anti-religious prejudices, in the same category with the scholarly works of Voltaire's learned and laborious contemporaries. Yet his brilliance, if occasionally superficial, made the past live again, so that Voltaire may share with Herodotus the distinction of being one of the great masters of "social history."

Many students would rank the six majestic volumes of Edward Gibbon's *Decline and Fall of the Roman Empire* (1776–1787) as one of the greatest monuments of the Age of Reason. The vast project, first contemplated in 1764 as Gibbon "sat musing amidst the ruins of the Capitol, while the barefooted friars were singing vespers in the Temple of Jupiter," took him twenty-three years to complete. It included not merely an account of the decline of the Roman Empire in the West but also a history of Byzantium to its capture by the Turks in 1453. Two qualities of Gibbon's work deserve emphasis. One is the amazing industry with which he ransacked the huge mass of published materials which the historical scholarship of his time had made available and built from them a stately work of art. The other is the powerful stamp of Gibbon's personality. Everywhere is the evidence of his deep admiration for classical antiquity, his eighteenth-century sense of form, his fondness for the rolling phrase, his superb irony, his elegant distaste for the dedicated ardors of the early Christians.

To pursue the long list of historical writers whose works crowd this era would be an endless task. The Age of Reason was an age of books. Old libraries were enlarged, new foundations established. In the splendid new homes of the aristocracy, libraries were as essential as dining-rooms or drawing-rooms. On their shelves stood the array of calf-bound folios and quartos among which historical works assumed a prominent place.[1] A few tentative generalizations about these works may help to establish their general importance.

By mid-eighteenth century historical studies had assumed impressive stature. Scholars had made great progress in developing the technical or "scientific" aspects of historical research. They showed, too, a decided fondness for undertaking works of large scope. Gibbon, for example, undertook to survey the entire sweep of the Roman Empire; Voltaire wrote a general history of culture; the philosopher, David Hume, composed a five-volume history of England.

A further trend of the eighteenth century was a renewed interest in antiquity, especially in that supposed home of all virtue, republican Rome, and in Athens, the incomparable center of great art. This historical interest can be seen to parallel the developments in architecture, sculpture and painting known as the Classical Revival. Montesquieu wrote his *Considerations on the Grandeur and Decadence of the Romans* in 1734 more as an analysis of political forces and a treatment of the philosophy of history than as a narrative of historical events. Two Englishmen, James Stuart and Nicholas Revett, published in 1762 the first volume of their *Antiquities of Athens*. The German scholar, Johann Winckelmann, who issued his famous *History of Ancient Art* in 1764, was not concerned simply to compile biographies of artists and to catalog their works but rather to demonstrate the true nature and principles of Greek art on the basis of what he called "its noble simplicity and tranquil greatness."

Much historical writing of the eighteenth century fell far short of scientific objectivity. The Abbé Raynal's ponderously entitled *Philosophical and Political History of the Establishments and the Commerce of Europeans in the Two Indies* (1770)—a work to which a number of his brother *philosophes* contributed—had more fine phrases about natural rights and liberty than it had history. Its popularity led to numerous subsequent editions; in 1779 it was banned in France and ordered burned by the public executioner. Many other historical works, like that of Raynal, fell within the category of propaganda.

Most characteristic of this age's self-confidence was the repeated assertion of the idea of progress. In 1688 Fontenelle, the brilliant popularizer of science, had published a brief *Digression on the Ancients and the Moderns* in which he insisted on the steady progress visible in modern times. The

1. Sir Hans Sloane, whose private library became the foundation of the British Museum, owned some 50,000 volumes. Robert Harley, first Earl of Oxford, developed an even more notable collection of books and manuscripts.

Abbé St. Pierre's *Observations on the Continual Progress of Universal Reason* (1737) and A. R. J. Turgot's *Discourses on Universal History* (1750) are two further illustrations of a large literature devoted to the thesis that human intelligence, building upon the achievements of the past, was steadily creating a better world. The German writer, Gotthold Lessing, wrote a brief sketch, *On the Education of the Human Race* (1777), in which he considered the complex spiritual evolution of mankind, concluding that history reveals a definite law of progress, even if occasional retrogressions hamper the march of mankind towards its lofty goal. This concept, an almost necessary ingredient of the Age of Reason, was most eloquently expressed by the versatile Marquis de Condorcet whose *Sketch of a Historical Picture of the Progress of the Human Mind,* written during the French Revolution while in hiding from his enemies, was published in 1795 soon after he had died in prison. According to Condorcet, mankind after having passed through nine historical epochs was on the verge of a tenth that would witness the destruction of all inequalities and make possible genuine perfection. Soon, Condorcet concluded, man would be able to live "in an elysium which his intelligence has created and which his love for humanity has adorned with the purest forms of enjoyment."

■ THE STUDY OF SOCIETY: POLITICAL THOUGHT

Second only in interest possibly to matters of religion has been man's perennial concern with politics and its accompanying theories. As modern states slowly evolved from the "strong monarchies" of the sixteenth century they not uncommonly rode rough-shod over ancient privileges and made steadily increasing demands upon their subjects. Protests and even occasional revolutions resulted. Out of these great politico-religious controversies of the sixteenth and seventeenth centuries developed a large literature dealing with the basic problems of political obligation. Whom should a man obey? How far does his obedience go? Whence does a ruler derive his powers? Are these in any way limited? How does a state come into existence? How far can the civil government interfere in religious matters? What is the best form of government? Who may overthrow a wicked ruler? Such questions had already provoked important discussions. During the seventeenth and eighteenth centuries the answers given by thoughtful men produced some of the great documents of political theory.

Luther and Calvin had insisted that subjects should obey their rulers, good or bad, or at the most resist passively, leaving to God the duty of punishment. Yet from the doctrine of "passive resistance" a new concept of active resistance to tyranny gradually emerged. The Religious Wars in

France and the Civil Wars in England hastened the progress of political theory. French writers formulated a doctrine of tyrannicide, that is, a justification of the actual slaying of a wicked ruler.

John Milton's various political tracts composed between 1641 and 1659 contained an eloquent advocacy of republicanism based on the agreement of the people who have the right to determine their own government. To extol monarchy, Milton wrote, "is treason against the dignity of mankind." A similar republicanism appeared in James Harrington's *Oceana* (1656) with the novelty that Harrington recognized the influence of economic forces on society. Since land (i.e., wealth) was passing into the hands of the middle class, then, said Harrington, this class should exercise political power and set up a republic. Even more radical ideas of complete equality were aired by the extreme sects of the Levellers and Diggers. Whatever their eccentricities, these groups developed certain views about the equality of all men, about "indefeasible liberties" (what we would call natural rights) and about the "compact" or social contract as the basis of government that were to be highly important in subsequent political thought.

In an age where the claims of reason were rising in importance a theory of "natural law" developed according to which political relationships could be regarded as natural phenomena to be studied analytically as a scientist would study the phenomena of nature. The German writer, Johannes Althusius, argued in his *Politica Methodica Digesta* (1603) that people have a natural propensity to come together and create, by means of an unspoken agreement or contract, the institutions of civil society. On this basis he justified the contemporary efforts of the estates or assemblies in some German territories to assert their authority. The celebrated Dutch writer, Hugo Grotius, tried in his *Law of War and Peace* (1625) to discover the fundamental "law of nature" lying behind the civil laws of various states. One could find the underlying principles upon which specific laws were built, Grotius felt, partly by exercising one's rational faculties and partly by examining the customary practices of states in which reason would, as it were, be found embedded. Grotius, to be sure, was more concerned with the rules governing the relations between states than he was with their internal problems; in this sense he has come to be regarded as "the father of international law."

The conviction steadily grew that man's reason could lead him to see the underlying principles governing the organization of states. Human societies had grown up, so it was felt, in obedience to principles as clear, as "rational," as those of geometry. "Laws in their most general signification," declared Montesquieu's *Spirit of the Laws* (1748), "are the necessary relations arising from the nature of things." Or, again, "Law in general is human reason."

Almost a century before Montesquieu wrote, Thomas Hobbes (1588–1679) composed those works which make him one of the greatest names in the history of modern political theory. In his general view of the world he was a materialist, arguing that one's mental life is built up solely on the basis of sense impressions. It is also significant that Hobbes lived and wrote during one of England's greatest periods of political turmoil. In his *Leviathan* (1651) Hobbes, who had left England during the height of the Civil War, expounded a theory of the state which he sought to base scientifically upon his materialistic view of the individual. The state, Hobbes argued, arises from the nature of men who are roughly equal in their endowments and who seek above all else their own preservation. Without organized society they would be in a "state of nature":

> In such a condition there is no place for industry, because the fruit thereof is uncertain, and consequently no culture of the earth; no navigation, nor use of the commodities that may be imported by sea; no commodious building; no instruments of moving and removing such things as require much force; no knowledge of the face of the earth; no account of time; no arts; no letters; no society; and, which is worst of all, continuall feare, and danger of violent death; and the life of man, solitary, poore, nasty, brutish and short.

In this assumed state of nature Hobbes believed that man is aware of certain "natural laws" or general rules. He should, for one thing, seek peace and follow it. For another, he should be content with as much liberty for himself as he will allow to other men. However, though he may be aware of these "laws," it is all too evident that in a state of nature no means exists to enforce them. Hobbes therefore assumes the operation of a "social contract." Men institute restraint upon themselves for their own good. By agreement they set up a commonwealth, conferring all their power and strength upon one man or assembly of men henceforth known as the sovereign. The ultimate test of sovereignty is *power*—the ability to provide that orderly rule which men through their separate efforts cannot provide. The sovereign may be one man (a monarch), the few (an aristocracy) or the many (a democracy); in every case the sovereign must be regarded as absolute and will remain sovereign only so long as it can exercise power. Hobbes made no defense of any particular regime. He was certainly no theorist of divine right, for any ruler that could maintain his authority must be regarded as legitimate.

Hobbes dealt a heavy blow at the medieval tradition of customary rights and privileges growing up over a long period of time and embodied in venerable charters and other documents. To Hobbes all this would be so much lumber. He found the explanation of political society not in ancient guarantees of rights or privileges but in certain "laws of nature" which are automatically at work. Such a theory as this powerfully reinforced the actual practices of the centralized monarchies of the late seventeenth century. "This," wrote Hobbes in summarizing his account of the creation of a commonwealth, "is the Generation [i.e., the method of creation] of that Great Leviathan, or rather (to speak more reverently) of that Mortall God, to which we owe under the Immortall God, our peace and defence." Hobbes became the spokesman of an age.

As Hobbes' ideas developed during the critical period of the Cromwellian Revolution, so those of John Locke (1632–1704) took shape during the Stuart Restoration and were published almost simultaneously with the Glorious Revolution of 1688. Seldom has the life of a powerful thinker reflected more closely the currents of his age than in the case of Locke. Trained for the church and then turning to the study of medicine, Locke soon moved into the political circle of the Earl of Shaftesbury, one of the founders of what came to be the Whig party. Locke read Descartes with enthusiasm, experimented in chemistry and meteorology and during his three-year political exile in France met some of its leading men of science. Later, in Holland, he likewise came into contact with a distinguished circle of intellectuals. It is significant, too, that Locke returned to England in 1689 on the ship that carried Princess Mary, wife of William of Orange.

In the second of his *Two Treatises of Government* (1690) Locke gave the problems of the state a brilliant analysis. Like Hobbes he assumed that men had once existed in a state of nature from which they had emerged by the device of a contract. Unlike Hobbes, however, Locke was concerned to show that the individual has rights, existing prior to the contract, which he brings into political society with him. With some suggestion of those narratives picturing happy, far-off lands peopled by noble savages, Locke portrayed the state of nature as one of "peace, good will, mutual assistance and preservation." The right to property (property being anything with which an individual "hath mix'd his labor") exists in the state of nature, as do the rights to health, life and liberty. Unhappily, however, there is no guaranty that these "natural rights" will be observed. Hence, argues Locke, "the great and chief end . . . of men uniting into commonwealths and putting themselves under government is the preservation of their property. . . ."

Locke assumes a kind of first contract made by men in order to form a *society* "for their comfortable, safe, and peaceable living one amongst another, in a secure enjoyment of their properties and a greater security against any that are not of it." He then assumes a kind of second contract between people of the newly-created community and the *government* which they set up. As long as this government is faithful to its duties it is supreme. If it violates its trust, then the people, invoking the sacred right of revolution, may rebel.

The ideas of Locke influenced the theory and practice of the eighteenth century on both sides of the Atlantic. As further parts of the world were known, they seemed to confirm his theories of a state of nature, while the history of the recently founded English colonies provided a long list of "charters" and "compacts" by means of which organized societies had come into being.[2] Locke's ideas of "inalienable rights," of the sanctity of property, the responsibility of governments and the right of rebellion became commonplaces of later liberal thought. As Newton was hailed by continental thinkers as the incomparable master in the realm of physical law, so likewise Locke, who said, "Freedom of men under Government is to have a standing Rule to live by, common to every one of that Society and made by the Legislative Power erected in it," gave political inspiration to the whole age.

Charles Louis, Baron de Montesquieu (1689–1755) carried the development of political thought forward into the eighteenth century. This member of the French administrative nobility was not as original a genius as Hobbes or Locke, yet his political treatise, *The Spirit of the Laws* (1748), shapeless and diffuse as it seems today, had a powerful influence. The particular laws of any state, Montesquieu argued, while embodying in general the principle of human reason, should be related to such environmental factors as climate, soil, situation, the temperament of the people, their occupations, manners and traditions. Montesquieu's famous threefold classification of states into despotisms, of which the principle is fear, monarchies, of which the principle is honor, and republics, of which the principle is virtue, can be criticized as an obvious oversimplification, yet it is an interesting expression of the desire to discover some kind of ordering principle in political systems.

Perhaps Montesquieu's greatest service was to dramatize the virtues as he saw them of the British system of government. While he misinterpreted the British "separation of powers" and the system of "checks and balances" which he professed to find in the separate functioning of the legislative, executive and judicial branches, nevertheless Montesquieu was an eloquent champion of British liberties. Whatever the logical defects of his theories, they served as a powerful indictment of the tendency towards despotism which he saw at work in France.

Many distinguished names, among them Voltaire, Diderot and the group in France generally known as the Encyclopedists worked hard to popularize the theories of Locke and Montesquieu. Strong admirers of the English constitution, they were no revolutionaries but tended rather to look for a

2. The most famous of these agreements antedated Locke by two generations. The Mayflower Compact, drawn up in the cabin of the *Mayflower* as it lay at anchor off Cape Cod in November, 1620, contained the signatures of those who "doe by these presents solemnly and mutually in the presence of God and one of another, covenant and combine ourselves together into a civill body politick, for our better ordering and preservation. . . ."

benevolent monarch who would transform society in accordance with the ideals of the Enlightenment. As the century progressed, these men of the *salons* were overshadowed by a writer of a type altogether different, the obscure, shiftless son of a Genevan watchmaker and as powerful a force in subsequent thought as the eighteenth century was to produce.

Jean-Jacques Rousseau (1712–1778) was a man of the people, an "original" with little formal education, a social misfit who drifted through life living with an illiterate servant girl whose five children he turned over to an orphanage, a brilliant writer who was never at home in a society that attempted to lionize him and never at home with himself. The first great spokesman of the democratic cause, Rousseau was heard because of his extraordinary power to think, to feel and to write.

The Bohemianism of Rousseau's private life, his early essays attacking "civilization" and his intensely egocentric work, the *Confessions,* have produced the interpretation of Rousseau as the uninhibited advocate of a return to nature. In his *Discourse on the Origins of Inequality* (1754) Rousseau had declared that the first man to fence in a piece of common land and make it his own was the creator of private property and the originator of the evils of civil society. Despite this view, Rousseau was not the enemy of all organized society; he was the enemy of that kind of society which, he believed, kept men from realizing their true selves.

Rousseau's greatest work, *The Social Contract* (1762), was intended to show how the state, rightly conceived and ordered, will permit men to live well. "Man is born free," Rousseau wrote, meaning presumably that man is born for freedom, "and everywhere he is in chains." The chains are the bonds put upon him by civil society. Rousseau's purpose was to show that the "chains" of civil society can be considered "legitimate" if we understand the way in which a state comes into being, and if we undertake to organize its institutions properly. Rousseau began like Hobbes and Locke with the idea of a state of nature, following which he assumed a contract which differs, however, from those of his predecessors in that it involves no surrender. "Each," wrote Rousseau, "while uniting himself with all, may still obey only himself alone and remain as free as before." Individuals do not surrender themselves to the one with power (as Hobbes said) nor do they contract on certain terms to accept the rule of a defined government (as Locke said). The contract is a "social" contract binding the members only to one another. They put themselves "under the supreme direction of the general will" which is their own. The people, therefore, always are (or always should be) sovereign.

Many complex and subtle problems of theory are raised by Rousseau's arguments. It suffices for the historian to recognize that despite all conflicts

of interpretation Rousseau stands out as the supreme theorist and spokesman of the democratic cause. He did not become so at once, for in point of
fact his political writings were far outdistanced in contemporary popularity
by his *Confessions,* by his novel, *The New Héloïse,* and his educational
treatise, *Emile. The Social Contract* was much better known to subsequent
generations than to Rousseau's own. The cautious and moderate leaders of
the American Revolution gave less welcome to Rousseau than they did to
Locke and Montesquieu, nor did he come into his own during the French
Revolution until the earlier, moderate phase was succeeded by the era of
Robespierre. The men of this age then hailed him as their greatest prophet.

The general patterns of political thought so far sketched were those
which contributed most notably to the evolution of ideas during the Age of
Reason. Another viewpoint, that of utilitarianism, rejected the view that
men had certain natural rights which society should guarantee. Men, it was
argued, simply pursue pleasure and avoid pain, consequently they organize
themselves in society the better to accomplish these ends. An Italian nobleman, the Marquis of Beccaria (1738–1794), concerned with the problems
of the Milanese prison system, published his book, *On Crimes and Punishment,* in 1764. He argued that the purpose of punishment should not be
vengeance or the imposition of an abstract idea of justice, but the preven-
tion of further crime. The guiding principle of social regulation should be
"the greatest happiness of the greatest number" (a phrase which he may have
borrowed from the French *philosophe,* Helvétius). These views were further
stated by that most versatile Englishman, Jeremy Bentham (1748–1832). His
concept of "enlightened self-interest" in contrast to the theory of natural
rights was first put forth in his *Fragment on Government* (1776) and elaborated in the *Principles of Morals and Legislation* (1789). The powerful
influence of Bentham, who lived long and wrote much, was not fully evident until the great reforming movement of the early nineteenth century.

A minor and emphatically different component of eighteenth-century
thought appeared in certain writings that could be called socialistic. The
early Rousseau, for example, in his *Discourse on the Origins of Inequality*
(1754) declared that the creation of private property was the great source
of evil since it led to the inequality of mankind and to the age-long rivalry
between different classes. It is hard to believe that Rousseau seriously desired men to return to a condition antedating civil society, so that the comment of Voltaire that he was too old to recommence walking on all-fours
was doubtless beside the point. In his *Social Contract* (1762) Rousseau, moreover, gave a closely reasoned justification of that civil society which the
earlier *Discourse* found so distasteful and within which the institution of
private property was imbedded. In one sense, nevertheless, it remains true
that Rousseau stands at the beginning of modern socialist thought.

A few other writers likewise attacked the institutions of private property. The various works of the Abbé Gabriel de Mably (1709–1785) proclaimed the equality of all men, denounced private property as the root of all misfortunes and claimed that men could be brought to live and work as the result of other motives than those of private gain. Mably, however, seems to have been possessed of a remarkable pessimism as to whether the better world toward which he aspired would ever actually come into being. Even more obscure than Mably was Morelly, whose *Code of Nature* (1755) likewise attacked property and pictured a kind of communal society.[3] Man, who is fundamentally good, has been corrupted by society. He can be redeemed only by turning to that kind of society where there will be no private property, where all citizens will be maintained at public expense and where everyone will contribute to the public good according to his strength, his talents and his years. In such writers, it must be insisted, no powerful influence upon contemporary thought is to be discovered. Their significance is that they represent an extreme form of the social criticism which developed during the eighteenth century and that they are the shadowy precursors of the much more important socialist writers of the nineteenth century.

In the whole history of political thought few periods are richer than that which extends from the publication of the *Leviathan* in 1651 to the *Social Contract* of 1762. Out of this discussion emerged the modern theories of the social contract, of natural rights, of constitutional checks and balances, of the supremacy of the general will and of popular sovereignty. These were seminal ideas which can be seen to have played a part in dissolving the structure of an old and outworn society, even as they entered into the life and outlook of a new age.

■ THE STUDY OF SOCIETY: ECONOMICS

The development of the study of economics during the seventeenth and eighteenth centuries was made possible by the growth of a new kind of political society, the nation-state, within which economic life assumed new dimensions. Just as men had come to ask a variety of questions about the nature of their political relationships, so also they began to probe the complex problems of agriculture, trade and manufacture in order to understand them, seek their "laws" and establish public policies for dealing with them.

Much controversial writing on subjects such as usury, taxation, money, banking, trade, manufacture and husbandry long antedated the eighteenth century. In general, statesmen had come to adopt the policies known as

3. Scholarly research has failed to provide Morelly with a first name or even with initials. Save for his books, nothing is known of him. He is not to be confused with another eighteenth-century writer, the Abbé Morellet.

mercantilism, although this term was not precise, and the best methods of applying mercantilist policies were long subject to debate.[4] A "bullionist" controversy, for example, developed in England as to whether the "favorable balance" (obtained by exporting more goods than were imported and thus receiving a net balance in gold or silver) should be sought with *each* country, or whether it was enough to have a favorable *general* balance. Thomas Mun's *Discourse of Trade from England into the East Indies* (1621) took the latter viewpoint; the author defended England's export of precious metals to the East Indies because of the eventual wealth which England secured by selling eastern goods in European markets. In his *England's Treasure by Forraigne Trade,* a work composed about 1630 but not published until 1664, he wrote: "The ordinary means to increase our wealth and treasure is by foreign trade, wherein we must ever observe this rule—to sell more to strangers yearly than we consume of theirs in value." To this end the elaborate governmental machinery of the mercantilist state should be employed.

Two seventeenth-century Englishmen, Sir William Petty and Gregory King, are notable for making the attempt to apply mathematical techniques to the study of economics and social problems. Petty, a fellow of the Royal Society, employed statistical material in his *Political Arithmetic* (1691). "I have taken the course . . . ," he wrote in phraseology reminiscent of the physical scientists, "to express myself in terms of number, weight or measure; to use only arguments of sense, and to consider only such causes as have visible foundations in nature." Gregory King, a writer and most industrious compiler, offered a number of tables dealing with the population, social classes and economic resources of England and Wales. His *Natural and Political Observations and Conclusions Upon the State and Condition of England* (1696) is still a valuable source of information upon such matters.[5]

In France a new economic literature developed that was highly critical of the complex machinery of the mercantilist state. A provincial magistrate, Pierre de Boisguillebert, began in 1695 to publish his *Détail de la France,* a powerful attack upon French economic policies. The state, he declared, should meddle as little as possible with agriculture and commerce. The financial exemptions enjoyed by the noble class he held to be outrageous. There should be a general tax from which none should be exempted, grain should be sold freely without export duties, and import duties should be

---

4. "Historically, the mercantilist pattern or frame has been, except for brief periods in a few places, the popular one. The state has always tended to favor policies that promised to add to its financial and fighting strength." HEATON, *Economic History of Europe* (1936 ed.), p. 396.

5. King made out the population of England and Wales in 1696 to be 5,500,000. He also included, from unknown statistical sources, the figure of one million rabbits and 24,000 hares and leverets.

lessened. This greater freedom, when achieved, would encourage industry. Boisguillebert insisted that the production of commodities such as grain, wine, salt and cloth rather than the accumulation of gold constitutes real wealth.

Another eloquent writer was Marshal Vauban. In 1707, amid the desperate economic conditions brought about by the follies of the War of the Spanish Succession, the old soldier composed his *Dîme Royal,* a scathing attack upon current financial confusions. He had the temerity to present it to Louis XIV who instantly suppressed it. The true sources of revenue, Vauban wrote, are men themselves, and it is the working class that unjustly bears the major burden of taxation. Class privileges are ruinous to the state. Labor is the origin of all wealth and agricultural enterprise is the most important form of labor. Vauban's chief proposal was a proportionate tax upon all income, something like the clerical tithe. Because of its frontal attack upon deep-rooted abuses Vauban's little book has been described as the most important work on public economy before Adam Smith's *Wealth of Nations.*

In mid-eighteenth century a group of French writers later called the Physiocrats came into prominence.[6] The Physiocrats were important not so much because they gave the right answers as that they asked the right questions. How are the wealth and welfare of a community to be increased? Certainly not by the mechanical manipulation of a balance of trade or by simply hoarding gold. In the end the welfare of a state will be measured by the excess of the annual product over its cost. A great flaw in the French economy was its outrageously unjust system of taxation which by its one-sidedness violated the true rights of property. The cumbersome network of local tariff barriers within France should be swept away. Agriculture, above all, must be given the fullest freedom and encouragement, for from the soil ultimately a nation's wealth will come.

The peerless leader of the public officials, businessmen and gentlemen-theorists who made up the Physiocratic group was a court physician, François Quesnay (1694–1774), known to his admiring followers as "the Confucius of the West." Quesnay's main contribution was his *Tableau économique* (1758) written in the belief that the rules of economics were as demonstrable as those of algebra or geometry. The "wise legislator" will see to it that the farmer is free to increase his wealth and thereby contribute to the general well-being of society. Manufacture and trade are "useful," to be sure, but "sterile"—they do not add fundamentally to the world's wealth. "It is agriculture," Quesnay wrote, "which furnishes the material of industry and

6. They called themselves "the economists." One of their number, P. S. Dupont de Nemours, later devised the term "Physiocrat" from the Greek words meaning "ruler of nature."

commerce and pays for both." He argued that the surplus created by agriculture—what he called the "net product"—flowed through the economy in such a way as to enrich its every aspect. To meet the needs of the state a single, direct tax falling upon the land should be imposed. In this way the domestic restrictions on the circulation of goods within France created by the chaos of taxes, tolls, imposts, feudal dues and excises would be swept away under the general principle of *laissez-faire*—leave things alone. "The most useful work any legislative body can do," said Quesnay, "is to abolish useless laws."

Another distinguished Physiocrat, Anne Robert Jacques Turgot (1727–1781), served for a time as intendant of the province of Limoges and also for two years as controller-general of finances. In 1766 Turgot wrote for the benefit of two Chinese students his *Reflections on the Creation and Distribution of Wealth* containing the standard Physiocratic argument that land is the only true source of wealth and that only the "net product" of the land should be taxed. Commerce and industry should be left alone, so that under the principle of *laissez-faire* the buyer will be entirely free to buy and the seller to sell.

These ideas of a natural order were impressively formulated across the Channel in a work, *An Inquiry Into the Nature and Causes of the Wealth of Nations* (1776), which remains one of the greatest classics in the history of economic thought. Its author, Adam Smith (1723–1790), was a Scot who had traveled widely in France and met the Physiocratic leaders. For a time Smith was professor of moral philosophy at the University of Glasgow. With the Physiocrats, he believed in the existence of a beneficent "natural order" in economic matters. Undertaking to demonstrate the true source of the wealth of nations, Smith delivered one of the most powerful of all attacks against the mercantile system.

Money, Smith argued, is not wealth; it is an instrument, a "wheel of trade." Labor is the true source of wealth which can be increased only by making labor more effective and by husbanding its products. Production will be more efficient if men concentrate upon the particular tasks which they do well. In one of those vivid passages which make the *Wealth of Nations* so effective Smith describes the division of labor involved in the manufacture of a pin: "One man draws out the wire, another straights it, a third cuts it, a fourth points it, a fifth grinds it at the top for receiving the head; to make the head requires two or three distinct operations; to put it on is a peculiar business, to whiten the pins is another; it is even a trade by itself to put them into the paper. . . ." By extending the area within which goods are sold the division of labor can be carried still farther. In other words, the process of the division of labor is limited by the extent of the market.

The complicated restrictions of the mercantile system, according to Smith, will stifle a healthy economic life. Wealth does not consist in money, but in what money purchases. The purpose of foreign trade is not to secure gold, it is to export surplus products for which there is no demand and to bring back goods for which there is a true demand. "It is the maxim of every prudent master of a family, never to attempt to make at home what it will cost him more to make than to buy. . . . What is prudence in the conduct of every private family can scarce be folly in that of a great kingdom." Smith therefore argued in favor of free trade:

> All systems either of preference or restraint, therefore, being thus completely taken away, the obvious and simple system of natural liberty establishes itself of its own accord. Every man, so long as he does not violate the laws of justice, is left perfectly free to pursue his own interests his own way, and to bring both his industry and his capital into competition with those of any other man, or order of men.

There may be times, to be sure, when the general principle of *laissez-faire* may not apply, but these will be very exceptional cases and do not disprove the general rule. The wealth of nations is the outcome not of control but of freedom.

Smith's economic analysis is a typical product of the Age of Reason in that he saw beneath the external complexities and contradictions of economic life the evidences of order and law. He had faith in this natural order which need no longer be impeded by the short-sighted selfishness of ignorant men. On the contrary, the free play of competing individual interests holds out the prospect of a future of unbounded prosperity. Economic literature before Adam Smith consisted of tracts, monographs and pamphlets on special subjects. His great achievement was to arrange and to synthesize, so that with him the science of economics in the true sense begins.

■ EDUCATION

Changes in educational theory and practice are an important aspect of cultural evolution. The Renaissance ideal of education which combined the traditions of the classics with the standards of the Christian life had found varied expression, for example, in the school of Vittorino da Feltre at Mantua, in the Brethren of the Christian Life, in the Christian humanists of Germany and England and above all in the work of Erasmus. A new aspect of Renaissance culture stressing the education of the gentleman was exemplified by such writers as Rabelais, Castiglione, Montaigne and Thomas Elyot. It later appeared in modified form in John Milton's *Tractate on Education* (1644). "I call therefore a compleat and generous Education," he wrote, "that which fits a man to perform justly, skilfully and magnanimously all the offices both private and publick of Peace and War." One should read the classical authors, study science, be acquainted with modern disciplines and, above all, be in touch with the world of actualities—what Milton called "solid things."

The immediate effects of the Reformation on the progress of learning were little short of disastrous, for the religious reformers tended to denounce the universities as the strongholds of scholastic theology, while the era of religious wars had obviously damaging consequences. In Germany, nevertheless, Melanchthon stood out as an intellectual champion eager to encourage the founding or refounding of schools and universities. In England, too, some substantial progress was made. The age of Elizabeth witnessed the founding of nearly two hundred new grammar schools. The United Netherlands, eager to have a university in each province, saw several appear during the bitter struggle with Spain: Leyden in 1575, Franeker in 1585, Groningen in 1614 and Utrecht in 1634. In the course of Sweden's Baltic expansion were founded the University of Dorpat (1632) in Estonia, Åbo (1640) in Finland, and Lund (1666) in the new Swedish province of Scania. The Catholic foundations of Bamberg (1648), Innsbruck (1672) and Breslau (1702) appeared in central Europe. The Jesuits were energetic in founding their various seminaries and colleges. By 1623 their school in Vienna boasted a thousand pupils. In France these Jesuit establishments completely overshadowed the work of the older universities, the great college of Clermont having by 1675 nearly three thousand pupils. Several Jesuit foundations were established in Germany, while in Poland the order dominated the country's entire educational life.

The seventeenth century was a confused age in the field of education. With the decline of Latin as a practical language, the conventional classical curriculum easily fell under attack. In France many of the nobility were educated in courtly academies soon to be imitated in the knightly schools (*Ritterakademien*) of Germany. A more significant development, due largely to the initiative of Richelieu and Colbert, was the founding of various technical schools giving expert training in engineering, military science, marine architecture and navigation. The impact of science was felt in other ways. New foundations such as the French Academy or the British Royal Society sponsored various types of important scholarly research.

Two German universities, Halle and Göttingen, made notable contributions which significantly reveal the trends of the times. The great teacher, Christian Thomasius (1655–1728), turned Halle into "the very citadel of the rational, the useful and the practical." Thomasius defied tradition by lecturing in German instead of Latin and by encouraging the study of modern languages, mathematics, science, law and geography. At Göttingen, in the

Electorate of Hanover, a group of brilliant scholars gave new luster to the classical tradition by their critical studies of Greek and Roman literature, jurisprudence, mathematics and medicine. Halle and Göttingen, indeed, stood in shining contrast to the more general eighteenth-century decline of university life. At Oxford, Gibbon wrote scornfully of the "Protestant monks," celibates with no vocation for celibacy, who neglected to teach him, while Bentham declared he learned only "mendacity and insincerity."

The Age of Reason was an age of contrasts. At a time when Lord Chester-field poured forth worldly advice in his *Letters to His Son,* offering "a veneer of superficial culture and artificial politeness covering, but not hiding, the most cold-blooded selfishness," the German, August Herman Francke (1663–1727), was encouraging the founding of orphan schools supported by public charity. In France, the Brothers of the Christian Schools undertook similar dedicated work, as did the Society for the Promotion of Christian Knowledge in England. Noteworthy, too, is the name of Robert Raikes, an English printer who in 1780 organized the first Sunday school.

The late seventeenth and the eighteenth century contributed several important documents to the history of educational theory, some of which directly influenced the educational policies of those enlightened despots whose work will be considered in the following chapter. A Czech, Johann Amos Comenius, or Komenski (1592–1670), can rightly be regarded as the great pioneer in the formulation of modern techniques of teaching. Comenius, a bishop of the Moravian Brethren, was driven by the Thirty Years' War to travel widely abroad. His interest in education led him to compose several books on the teaching of languages, notably the *Orbis Pictus,* or *Illustrated World* (1658), in which he associated the Latin vocabularies with pictures for convenience in remembering. This has been said to be the first illustrated school text ever printed. Comenius' chief work was his *Great Didactic,* first published in Czech in 1632 and widely translated. This is an elaborately organized treatise on education, discussing its aims and principles together with a detailed presentation of a course of study and a statement of the methods to be used in teaching the sciences, the arts, languages, morals and "piety." As a psychologist, Comenius held that the child should be trained concurrently to think, to say and to do. The *Great Didactic* concludes with a comprehensive plan of school organization from the "mother school" through the elementary and Latin school to the university. Comenius, it will be observed, first published his *Great Didactic* in the Czech vernacular. Whatever the defects of this cumbersome work, it placed Comenius at the beginning of the list of outstanding educational theorists of the modern age. In the succeeding centuries, much more than in his own time, its value was recognized and its principles applied.

The versatile John Locke, whose *Thoughts on Education* (1693) offered advice on the proper means to educate a youth of good station through a wisely chosen tutor, clearly had set himself a much less ambitious goal than that of Comenius. A few years before, in his *Essay on the Human Understanding* (1690), Locke had compared the mind to a blank page (*tabula rasa*) upon which the hand of experience writes. In the *Thoughts* he speaks of the gentleman's son, "whom, being then very little, I considered only as white paper or wax, to be moulded and fashioned as one pleases." Locke puts great stress on habit formation under the guidance of a kindly hand. He complains that conventional education "fits us rather for the University than for the World." The actual subjects of study, however, are a means to an end and not an end in themselves. They are "as it were the Exercise of his Faculties and the Employment of his Time. . . . But of good Breeding, knowledge of the World, Virtue, Industry and a love of Reputation he cannot have too much."

The most original educational work of the eighteenth century was Rousseau's *Emile* (1762), supposedly written for a sensitive mother in order to show how Emile should be reared from infancy to manhood. With all his literary art, although in generalities, Rousseau depicted a child who had been brought up in perfect naturalness to grow, to unfold from within, to feel and to be. Emile is subject only to the discipline which his experiences and disappointments give him. He should remain, Rousseau says, as long as possible in touch with the world of nature and be kept away from the artificial world of books at least until the age of twelve. The simple truths of natural religion will be a late study. Emile will discover the problems of society only as he grows to take his place in it. This extraordinary work, clearly no part of the conventional pattern of the Age of Reason, has been ardently hailed as the Charter of Childhood and has been equally strongly condemned. Rousseau was perhaps at his best in insisting that virtue cannot be hammered into the mind, and in pointing out to a century that tended to make puppets and dolls out of its children that a child is something other than a small adult. In this sense the *Emile* came as a refreshing and curative breeze into the stifling *salons* of the eighteenth century.

A German, Johann Bernard Basedow (1723–1790), and a Swiss, Johann Heinrich Pestalozzi (1746–1827), contrived to do what Rousseau had never been able to do, that is, put some of his ideas into practice. Basedow opened his school, the Philanthropinum, at Dessau in north Germany in 1774. His *Elementary Book* published in the same year was an illustrated text for children which sought constantly to keep them in touch with the actual world of things. At Yverdun in Switzerland, Pestalozzi likewise maintained a school where instruction from books was kept to a minimum and the child was surrounded by those plants, animals and other objects which he sought to understand. Never too successful in a narrowly practical sense, Pestalozzi was so inspired by a spirit of love for the children whom he taught and by a dedication to the living world of nature that he acquired European fame, in time attracting visitors from all parts of the continent and as far away as America.

■ TRANSITION TO MODERN PHILOSOPHY

Through philosophy men have sought answers to the basic problems of existence: the nature of man, of God, of the external world, of the mind, of knowledge, of truth, of morality. In the new age where the leading spirits were increasingly influenced by the attitude of the scientists it is understandable that for these answers they should tend to reject the guiding hand of "revealed" religion. Man could not accept uncritically the authority of the sacred texts. If the mysteries of the universe were to be solved, they must be solved by other means. Above all, there must be a free play of ideas. In 1700 a friend of Boileau wrote to him from Lyons to say that he was a member of a new society formed to discuss science and belles lettres and that the first two meetings had been devoted to considering Descartes' proofs of the existence of God.

The record of this change, the opening chapter in the history of modern philosophy, is an important aspect of the Intellectual Revolution. A strong current of skepticism, as in the case of Montaigne, had marked the age of the Renaissance. While the Reformation contributed little directly to the development of modern philosophy, it may have stimulated in various circles a tendency to speculative thought. In general, philosophy tended to sever the ties which bound it to religion and to associate itself with the viewpoint of mathematics and physics. Francis Bacon had declared theology to be the principal enemy of science. The Italian, Giordano Bruno, who was burned at the stake at Rome in 1600 for his views, rejected all supernatural explanations. God, he wrote, was a living force to be discovered in *all* aspects of the natural world. He enthusiastically welcomed the Copernican hypothesis. "By the stars," he wrote, "we are moved to discover the infinite effect of an infinite cause . . . and to contemplate the Deity not as outside of, apart from and distant from us, but as in ourselves and more within us than we are in ourselves." The true founder or father of modern philosophy, however, was the mathematician, René Descartes.

Descartes, as a mathematician and as an inquirer probing the nature of reality, was confident that his "method"—starting with the self-evident maxim of his own existence and proceeding from it by pure deduction—would give scientist and philosopher alike the means of reaching ultimate truth. Descartes' two great contributions were to insist that human reason could adequately demonstrate the existence of God, thinking man and matter and that in addition to the world of thought there existed a material world having simply the two qualities of extension and motion.[7]

This dualism of mind and matter raised problems for all subsequent philosophy. Hobbes, a contemporary of Descartes, tried to turn philosophy in the direction of a thoroughgoing materialism. Matter and motion alone make up the universe. Mind is simply a motion in the brain and man is governed by no higher forces than his appetites and his aversions.

A much subtler and more attractive figure than Hobbes was the Jewish lens-grinder of Amsterdam, Baruch Spinoza (1632–1677)—expelled from the synagogue at the age of twenty-four because of his ideas. Reversing Hobbes, Spinoza argued that what we choose to call matter is but one aspect of a fundamental substance which is God. God is not a creator apart from his creation. "There is only one reality in the universe," he wrote, "one substance which may be called God and which is known under two of its attributes, extension and consciousness." Spinoza thus accepted the mechanism and rationalism of Descartes but not his dualism. The severely logical nature of Spinoza's demonstrations may be illustrated by the following passage from his *Ethics:*

> PROP. XIV.—Except God no substance can be granted or conceived.
>
> *Proof.*—As God is a being absolutely infinite, to whom no attribute expressing the essence of substance can be denied (Definition VI), and as he necessarily exists (Proposition XI), if any other substance than God be given, it must be explained by means of some attribute of God, and thus two substances would exist possessing the same attribute, which (Proposition V) is absurd; and so no other substance than God can be granted, and consequently not even be conceived.

For "blessed Spinoza" the highest form of happiness was to realize God's all-pervading role in the universe. "The greatest good," he wrote, "is the knowledge of the union which the mind has with the whole of nature."

Still another speculative thinker who deserves notice on account of the widespread acceptance of his ideas was the versatile Gottfried Wilhelm Leibniz (1646–1716), a mathematical prodigy sharing with Newton the honor of inventing the infinitesimal calculus, a historian, lawyer, theologian and philosopher. He was without doubt the leading intellectual of seventeenth-century Germany. To explain the universe Leibniz devised his theory of monads, saying that all creation was made up of a myriad tiny centers of force, each capable of perceiving, some only dimly and others more acutely. The mind itself was a grouping of a particular type of monads.

---

[7] Although Descartes continued to regard himself as a good Catholic, his works were placed on the *Index* in 1663.

God, "the monad of monads," is the creator of all. Unity is given to the universe by a "preestablished harmony" (the work of God) which brings the monads together in a purposeful order. The monads do not influence each other but operate as if they were a series of clocks that God has wound up and regulated so that, although entirely independent, they will keep time together. We must believe that this is the best of all possible worlds in which what we call evil is a necessary and not clearly understood incident. The views of Leibniz, although brilliantly satirized in Voltaire's clever novel, *Candide,* were in perfect accord with the temper of the eighteenth century and were never better expressed than by Alexander Pope:

> All nature is but art, unknown to thee;
> All chance, direction, which thou canst not see;
> All discord, harmony not understood;
> All partial evil, universal good.
> And, spite of pride, in erring reason's spite,
> One truth is clear, 'Whatever is, is right.'

Such rationalist systems were opposed by the views of the empiricists, those who take their point of departure not from any innate ideas or lofty abstractions but from the evidence of the senses.[8] "Laws" to the empiricist are merely statements of experience gathered together by association. Cause and effect are nothing more than sequences of events. John Locke as a psychologist refused to accept Descartes' theory of innate ideas, arguing instead that man's mind is originally a blank page owing everything to the hand of experience which writes upon it. The simple ideas coming from sense perception are combined by the power of human reason or reflection into complex ideas. The existence of God may be demonstrated by arguing the need for a First Cause from which all else must spring. An external, physical world likewise exists, for our senses bring us emphatic testimony about it. "Nobody," declared Locke, "can, in earnest, be so skeptical as to be uncertain of the existence of those things which he sees and feels." Locke's *Essay Concerning the Human Understanding* (1690) is thus a powerful attack on Descartes' theory of innate ideas.

The eighteenth century ardently pursued the philosophical question of how we may acquire certainty of knowledge. The celebrated George Berkeley (1685–1753), later Bishop of Cloyne, in Ireland, wrote his *Treatise on the Principles of Human Knowledge* at the age of twenty-five.[9] The champion

8. The Bishop of Worcester inquired of Locke how, if there is no innate idea of God, one can refute an atheist? Locke answered neatly that if the idea of God were really innate, no one would be an atheist.

9. Berkeley exhibits some of the versatile interests of the eighteenth century. He secured a grant of £20,000 from Parliament to found a university in the New World from which it was hoped would grow a higher civilization than any at home. He spent three years in Rhode Island waiting in vain for the plans to materialize. Later he devoted much energy to the promotion of tar water as a cure for all physical ills.

of an extreme idealism, Berkeley questioned whether the human mind could ever come into contact with a world of matter, reaching the conclusion that we had no way of proving the existence of a material world and that therefore we could assume no reality save that of the mind. The *cause* of our ideas "is an incorporeal, active substance, or spirit," namely, God.

French thinkers such as Etienne de Condillac, Julian de la Mettrie and Baron Holbach in opposition to the idealistic viewpoint took refuge in a complete materialism. Condillac, for example, argued in his *Treatise on Sensations* (1754) that if we could take a statue and endow it with the sense of sight we would have a statue that could see; endow it with hearing, and we would have a statue that could see and hear; endow it with all five senses and we would have a man. La Mettrie's *Man a Machine* (1748) used the evidence of physiology to argue that man, like all animals, is a pure mechanism.

A shrewd Scot, David Hume (1711–1776), recognizing the power of Berkeley's attack on Locke, turned it to his own purposes. If Berkeley's arguments could be used to destroy physical certainty, Hume would use them also to destroy metaphysical certainty.[10] The mind is simply a bundle of impressions. In his *Treatise of Human Nature* (1739) he denied the absolute certainty of mathematical knowledge and he insisted that what we call cause and effect are really no more than observed sequences of events with which we have become familiar but the outcome of which we could not possibly tell in advance. We see one billiard ball strike another; we see the second leap forward; we see the experiment repeated many times; actually we have not observed "cause and effect" but only a customary sequence. " 'Tis not, therefore, reason which is the guide of life," declared Hume, "but custom." This skepticism so challenged the assumptions of the Enlightenment that an entirely new approach was needed. It was to be provided by the German philosopher, Immanuel Kant, when he "awoke from his dogmatic slumbers."

■ RELIGION

The religious attitudes of the Age of Reason were a sequel to those born of the Reformation. The various consequences of the great religious upheaval had been numerous: a permanent division of the Western Christian world, a proliferation of Protestant creeds, a vigorous reassertion of the Roman Catholic faith and an oppressive period of theological controversy, persecution and actual, bloody war. The literature of these religious controversies was enormous and, to modern judgment, largely sterile. The guess could be ventured that in European libraries which preserve their seventeenth-century collections the greater part is devoted to these debates.

10. Hume also attacked supernatural explanations. In his *Essay on Miracles* (1747) he stated that it is always easier to believe that the individual reporting a miracle is deceiving or being deceived than that the miracle occurred.

It is not perhaps surprising that by the late seventeenth century Western Europe saw a considerable decline in religious ardor.[11] This might be explained in part as the natural swing of the pendulum. In England, for example, the cynical age of the Restoration had succeeded the austere age of Puritans. In France the reign of Louis XIV, despite the monarch's personal piety, lost much of the devoutness seen in the early seventeenth century. In Germany it was a common complaint that the public worship became increasingly routine. The interests of a ruler such as Frederick II were strongly on the side of the freethinkers of France.

The lack of "enthusiasm," notable in many quarters, may likewise be attributed in some degree to a sincere wish for further religious toleration. "Latitudinarianism" within the Church of England, an attempt to agree on religious essentials while minimizing the importance of religious differences, was inspired by this spirit. Many Englishmen were less concerned with a "High Church" (inclining toward Rome) or with a "Low Church" (turning militantly against Rome) than they were with a less dogmatic position that would look tolerantly even upon Dissenters. They thought that theology should always have a rational basis and aim at an enlightened moderation. The externals were not too important. "The form of church government," wrote Edward Stillingfleet in 1662, "is a mere matter of prudence, regulated by the word of God." The most famous of the works which tried to show that no essential disagreement existed between the teachings of the Bible and those of reason and common sense was the *Analogy of Religion, Natural and Revealed* (1736) of Bishop Butler.

A harmonization of divergent views was not always possible. As men sought simple rules to explain the mechanism of the physical universe they were often concerned at what they conceived to be the tyranny of "revealed" religion. The deists, as they came to be known, sought the simple bases of a "natural religion" that would be as clear-cut as the physical laws of Newton. They believed in the existence of God (whom they were apt to describe rather vaguely as "The Great Architect," "The First Cause," or "The Clockmaker"); they believed in "natural laws" operating without God's miraculous intervention; and they believed in man as a moral and intelligent being endowed with freedom of will, and in a life after death. They were inspired by a general optimism which suggests the philosophy of Leibniz. Deism was never an organized faith but rather an attitude of mind common to a select group of enlightened spirits, chiefly in England.

Lord Herbert of Cherbury (1583–1648), a contemporary of Descartes, laid the foundations of English deism. Other great names were those of

---

11. Montesquieu ventured the opinion in his *Notes on England* (1734) that not more than four or five members of the House of Commons regularly attended church.

Bolingbroke and Shaftesbury. From England it spread to France in the circle of Voltaire and his school. The limits which deism imposed upon Christian belief are not easy to define. Some men were able to reconcile deism with their more or less conventional beliefs. Edward Gibbon, on the other hand, displayed such animosity that the celebrated chapters XV and XVI of his *Decline and Fall* must be taken as a full scale attack upon organized Christianity. The great German representative of deism, Lessing, felt that his faith in Christianity must be justified on rational grounds, for no religious system could have a monopoly of truth. His play, *Nathan the Wise* (1779), has as its principal character a Jew who is bold enough to tell the Mohammedan ruler, Saladin, that it is impossible to claim an absolute superiority for either Judaism, Islam or Christianity. All religions, to Lessing, were an expression of man's age-long search to attain a knowledge of God.

Other writers pushed on further in the direction of skepticism; some reached the goal of an unabashed atheism. Pierre Bayle's *Historical and Critical Dictionary* (1697) has already been mentioned as a fertile inspiration for much highly critical thought. The witty tongue of Voltaire served a similar purpose.[12] David Hume's famous *Essay on Miracles* (1747) skilfully put the rationalist case and no doubt contributed to the skeptical trend. About the middle of the eighteenth century in France a substantial group of writers risked the penalties of the censorship (admittedly lax and ineffective) to voice a frankly atheistic doctrine. D'Alembert's *Treatise on Dynamics* (1743) declared that the laws of nature could be understood without any reference to a Supreme Being. La Mettrie's *Man a Machine* described man as a biological product to be regarded indifferently as an animal, a plant or a machine in which all mental processes are the result of physical factors. Diderot's *Interpretation of Nature* (1754) frankly arrived at a materialistic philosophy. Baron Holbach wrote in his *System of Nature* (1770) that the idea of God arises only "in ignorance, fear and calamity." "If we go back to the beginning, we shall always find that ignorance and fear have created the gods; fancy, enthusiasm or deceit has adorned or disfigured them; weakness worships them; credulity keeps them alive. . . ."

In contrast to these ideas, generally the possession of a clever and cynical minority, were others which gave to religion a new vitality and to some of the organized churches a new importance. This counter-current appeared in Germany under the name of pietism. It was not a formal creed but rather an attitude observable in many congregations as a kind of reaction against

12. Voltaire defined a miracle as "a breach of mathematical, divine, immutable, eternal laws. This definition makes a miracle a contradiction in terms. A law cannot be both immutable and broken."

the dry conventionality of much religious life. It insisted that religion must be *felt,* and that the true Christian must combine an inward life of devoutness and even ecstasy with an outward life dedicated to piety and good works. In 1675 Philip Spener (1635–1705), a Lutheran pastor, published a widely-read book, *Pia Desideria, or Heartfelt Longings for a Reform of the True Evangelical Church,* urging these ideals. Akin to Spener was August Hermann Francke (1663–1727) who made the University of Halle a center for the training of theologians inspired by pietistic ideals. A Silesian nobleman, Count Zinzendorf, in 1722 welcomed a group of Bohemian Protestant refugees to his estate at Herrnhut; from these grew the Moravian Brethren, a group of religious devotees living communally and sending forth bands of missionaries as far afield as India, South America, Greenland and South Africa. Pietism, with its hymn-singing, its public prayer meetings and its popular devotional literature was a considerable force in eighteenth-century Germany, a counter to the trend of rationalism and with its "sentimental" approach contributing not a little to the birth of German Romanticism.

England, too, experienced a kind of religious awakening. The Quaker movement, or more correctly the Society of Friends, had been organized by George Fox (1624–1691), who began his public ministry in 1647.[13] The Quakers believed that true religion had nothing to do with external forms but was rather a deeply personal experience of the "inner light." Never large in numbers, austere in dress and demeanor, refusing to establish a formal ministry, to bear arms or to swear an oath, the Quakers soon became a respected minority commanding the admiration even of Voltaire.

The most important religious movement in eighteenth-century England was that associated with the names of John Wesley (1703–1791), his brother Charles (1707–1788) and their friend, George Whitefield (1714–1770). The fifteenth child of a country parson, John was gravely concerned while at Oxford about the prevailing religious indifference. With Charles and a few associates he organized the Holy Club to engage in regular private worship and charitable works. They were nicknamed "Methodists" because of their orderly religious life. In 1735 John and Charles accepted the invitation of General Oglethorpe to visit the new colony of Georgia. Here they met members of the Moravian Brethren and on their return visited the Brethren's headquarters in Silesia.

Some of the links binding together various aspects of Protestantism are revealed in the story of Wesley's conversion. On his return from Georgia he had flung himself into a feverish round of religious activities in London until on a May evening in 1738 he attended the Wednesday prayer meeting

13. It was not until 1668 that a complete system of organization was established by introducing Fox's rules for the management of meetings.

of a small society in Aldersgate Street. Someone read Luther's preface to his commentary on Paul's Epistle to the Romans. "About a quarter before nine," Wesley records, "while he was describing the change which God works in the heart through faith in Christ, I felt my heart strangely warmed, I felt I did trust in Christ, Christ alone, for salvation, and an assurance was given me that he had taken away *my* sins, even mine, and saved me from the law of sin and death."

The two Wesleys and Whitefield do not seem to have sought to break with the Church of England. They were prepared to speak from any pulpit that would welcome them. As little welcome was offered, John Wesley took steps of the utmost importance. One was to create Methodist "societies" and to build "chapels," designed at first to supplement rather than replace the work of the existing churches. Another was to institute "field preaching," a technique by which Wesley and Whitefield came to address outdoor gatherings of five, ten and even twenty thousand. They were aided by a steadily growing number of lay preachers.

John Wesley, who in his own creed was a high churchman, adopted the methods that have come to be called "evangelistic." Having borrowed from the Moravians the doctrine that salvation is the result of a sudden personal conversion, he undertook to preach in that spirit. He appealed directly to the hearts of his hearers, often rousing them to a frenzy of religious emotion. At times he encountered grave bodily risks from unsympathetic crowds, yet he accepted these risks as he did the constant toil of travel.

As John Wesley was the great preacher and organizer, so his brother Charles was the great hymn-writer, having composed, it is estimated, over 6,500 hymns, among them some of the best-known in the language: "Jesu, Lover of My Soul," "Hark the Herald Angels Sing," and "Love Divine, All Loves Excelling." Whitefield was the incomparable popular orator, seldom preaching less than ten times a week and having produced an estimated eighteen thousand sermons. John Wesley was equally tireless; he is said to have traveled 250,000 miles, largely on foot or on horseback, in the fifty years of his devoted ministry.

Wesley established religious "societies" but did not intend to found a new denomination. Nevertheless, the organization of a formal Conference in 1784 gave the Methodist body a legal constitution. The Methodists brought back an element of emotion and personal piety to religious life. They reached the coal miners, the factory workers of England's new industrial areas and in general those whose lives the Church of England hardly touched. Thus the man who wrote in his last year, "I live and die a member of the Church of England," was responsible for the growth of England's largest body of nonconformists.

A certain "evangelical" spirit likewise took possession of some parts of the Church of England. Although William Wilberforce, Lord Shaftesbury and other devout laymen were not prepared to join the Dissenters, they sought to encourage a more devout religious life. These "Evangelicals" hoped to arouse in their "high and dry" fellow churchmen something of the spirit animating the Methodists. While they can be charged with having more concern over slavery in the colonies than over "slavery in Yorkshire," they came in time to consider the immediate social evils of their surroundings. While Methodism was largely a phenomenon of the middle and lower classes, Evangelicalism made its influence felt more especially in the higher and politically more influential levels of society.

Still further contrast to the general spirit of the Enlightenment can be seen in certain relatively minor groups. Freemasonic lodges were widely established on the Continent following the establishment of the Grand Lodge at London in 1717. While most of these were fraternal, charitable and colored in general with a tincture of deism, some of the continental lodges lent themselves to strange tendencies in the direction of occultism, astrology and prophecy. Other groups—Illuminists, Theosophists and Rosicrucians—likewise turned to the exploration of "the invisible world." A number of distinguished figures, most notably the great Swedish scholar and scientist, Emmanuel Swedenborg, persuaded themselves that they could raise ghostly spirits, commune with the dead and extract from the prophetic books of the Bible literal foreknowledge of future events. Although many sincere people doubtless turned to these creeds, the way was opened also for such eccentric figures as that prince of charlatans, Joseph Balsamo, Count of Cagliostro who professed (literally) to have raised the devil in the Colosseum at Rome, or the incredible Count of St. Germain who claimed to be able to turn base metals into gold, to have lived for two thousand years and to have attended the Crucifixion. In these fantastic figures the wheel had turned full circle from the advocates of those doctrines which are conventionally associated with the Age of Reason.

■ THE ARTS AND LETTERS IN THE AGE OF CLASSICISM

The term Classicism, for all its suggestion of discipline and symmetry, is not wholly precise. It is obviously applicable to the Great Age of Louis XIV when all aspects of culture seemed to fit together in a monumental structure of antique inspiration. In the form of Neo-Classicism (a renewed interest in antiquity more Greek than Roman) it had a particular revival in the late eighteenth century. About mid-century, by contrast, the first stirrings of the Romantic Revival were evident. Nevertheless, the Neo-Classical spirit continued to manifest itself during the turmoil of the French Revolution,

for example in the massive paintings of David, and later and somewhat differently in the splendors of the Napoleonic Empire.

The arts of the eighteenth century at first showed no great breach with
the seventeenth. A new term, Rococo, which was applied particularly to
architecture and interior *décor,* superseded Baroque.[14] This most characteristically French form caught the pleasure-loving spirit of the age of Louis
XV even as the Baroque was appropriate to the splendors of the court of
Louis XIV. "Slender proportions and never-ending movement in easy curves
with a definite avoidance of straight lines and angles; light color with much
gilding; the use of many mirrors to add vivacity with their reflections—these,
in general constituted the rococo style, the light, sparkling, thoroughly
French version of baroque." [15]

The Rococo style reflected the taste of an aristocracy of the boudoir and
the salon, and also to some extent the taste of a wealthy, ambitious middle
class. It gave evidence, too, of certain technological advances in such fields
as woodcarving, enameling, porcelain manufacture, weaving, lacemaking
and the production of bric-à-brac. In architecture it produced some buildings
of very great charm, notably the Petit Trianon Palace of Marie Antoinette or
Frederick II's exquisite little palace of Sans Souci at Potsdam. In furniture
it produced that gracefully ornate style known as "Louis XV."

As far-off lands became better known, eighteenth-century taste showed a
growing cult of the exotic. Along with tea drinking came Chinese porcelains
and lacquer works, silks, oriental furniture and wallpapers. It became fashionable to erect Chinese pagodas, as in Kew Gardens, near London, or the
little summer residence of the Elector of Saxony, at Pillnitz, which was built
in pagoda style. Although to a lesser degree, Persian, Turkish, Arabian and
Moorish influences could also be detected.

In the eighteenth century, English architecture, never surrendering itself
to the vagaries of the Rococo, developed that "Georgian" style of straight
lines and subtle proportions in the classical tradition with which Americans
are familiar. The best English architecture of the eighteenth century appeared in those superb country houses which broke away from the older
native traditions and produced masterpieces such as Chatsworth, the seat of
the Duke of Devonshire, with its harmonious proportions, balustraded terraces and classical statuary. The Neo-Classical style likewise produced elegant
town houses with fine doorways and Palladian windows.

The excavations of Herculaneum after 1738 and Pompeii a decade later
aroused a fashionable interest in the Antique Roman style. A particularly

14. The term may derive from the French *rocaille* meaning the rockwork or shellwork so
often found in Rococo ornament. It may also be a pun on the French *roc* intended to
parody the older term, *barocco.*
15. HELEN GARDNER, *Art Through the Ages* (1948), p. 602.

fine manifestation appeared in the work of Robert Adam (1718–1792), a decorator as well as an architect, who, strongly influenced by Pompeii and by the Etruscans, designed interiors of exquisitely proportioned grace and delicacy. A still further development was the designing of large groups of town houses to form one unit. Some of the best examples are the squares and crescents laid out by John Wood at Bath—a fine example of eighteenth-century city planning.

The field of painting likewise presents the evidence of an elegant, sophisticated and privileged age. The French artist, Antoine Watteau (1684–1721), a Fleming trained in the tradition of Rubens, painted sentimental scenes and pastorals, a world of Arcadian shepherds perfectly suited to his time, but also, in the case of his minstrels and pierrots, a world which offered a poignant suggestion of unhappiness and frustration. Jean Fragonard (1732–1806) captured the elegant artificiality of the French aristocracy, while François Boucher (1703–1770) in his frankly amorous paintings of shepherdesses, nymphs and Venuses proved himself a boudoir decorator without peer. The village scenes of Jean-Baptiste Greuze (1725–1805) suggest the influence of the Dutch painters. Jean Chardin (1699–1779), a much greater figure, painted still-life scenes and representations of humble peasants that depict a rustic world far removed from the fashionable society of the court.

The glory of English painting lay in its portraitists and in the slowly developing schools of landscapists and water-colorists. Sir Joshua Reynolds (1723–1792), Thomas Gainsborough (1727–1788), George Romney (1734–1802) and Sir Henry Raeburn (1756–1823) were professional portraitists in the most precise sense of the term, unsurpassed in the grand style which they employed to depict the features of the governing class. The powerful figure of William Hogarth (1697–1764) moves in another world. He was an accomplished portraitist and a master of all the technicalities of his profession. Yet he was even more a satirist of eighteenth-century society. His bitter series of paintings and engravings—"The Rake's Progress," "The Harlot's Progress," "Marriage à la Mode"—as well as the gruesome "Gin Lane" and the less repulsive "Beer Street" are unsurpassed as social documents. In the background of many eighteenth-century portraits appear the suggestions of landscapes which later were to develop into the school of Richard Wilson (1714–1782) and John Crome (1768–1821).

The lonely genius of Francisco Goya (1746–1828) is almost the sole survival of the great age of Spanish art. Goya was for a time a royal painter who, however, so relentlessly exposed the depraved characteristics of a decadent court that it is a puzzle how he retained his post. Goya's technical expertness was accompanied by a deep human feeling and a powerful sense of satire and social criticism. His series of etchings, *The Disasters of War,* spared nothing in realistic horror; while attacking the specific evils of the Napoleonic period they seem at the same time universal in their condemnation.

A distinctive mark of French literature in the eighteenth century was its perpetuation of those graces of language and form which had developed so brilliantly during the seventeenth century. Voltaire and Rousseau, for example, were literary artists of the highest order, making use of the French language as an admirable vehicle for the precise expression of ideas. It has been said that this evolution owes much to the demands of science which must, above all else, have clear and exact language at its command. It may be due in part to the disciplining work of the various French academies. The change has likewise been attributed to the growing number of readers and the consequent need for a simple, immediately effective manner of presentation. "Almost all rules of style," wrote Helvétius, "reduce themselves to the production of clarity."

A further aspect of French literature in the eighteenth century is that many of its exponents were engaged in a great crusade, whether to expose flagrant abuses, to confront readers with new theories about man and the state or in general to persuade them of the value of free inquiry. Montesquieu's *Persian Letters* (1721), Voltaire's *Letters on the English* (1733), his novel, *Candide* (1759), and Beaumarchais' play, *The Marriage of Figaro* (1784) are but a few examples of a literature employing the highest artistic skill for the purpose of indicating and condemning abuses in contemporary life. Rousseau's novel of sentiment, *The New Héloïse* (1760), while impressing the average reader today as intolerably diffuse, spoke "the language of the heart" and offered a powerful message of social morality. It is remarkable that an age which produced so great a literature of social criticism should also have been responsible for a mass of third-rate poetry and mediocre romances which with few exceptions are now almost unreadable.

The early eighteenth century in England was preeminently an age of prose. The language, once so subject to the tortured "conceits" of the Elizabethans and the overelaborate eloquence of the Stuart divines, had won dignity, simplicity and power through the work of the translators of the King James Bible (1611) and the simple prose of John Bunyan's *Pilgrim's Progress* (1678). One may well ask whether the English tongue has ever spoken more greatly than when Bunyan, the tinker of Bedford jail, tells of the death of Mr. Valiant: "When the day that he must go hence was come, many accompanied him to the River-side, into which as he went he said, *Death, where is thy Sting?* And as he went down deeper he said, *Grave, where is thy Victory?* So he passed over, and all the Trumpets sounded for him on the other side."

The age of Queen Anne saw a brilliant procession of prose stylists such as the urbane essayist, Joseph Addison (1672–1719), or Daniel Defoe (1660–1731), equally effective as a pamphleteer, a journalist and, in his *Robinson Crusoe,* as a superb story teller. Jonathan Swift (1667–1745) is England's greatest master of satire whose *Gulliver's Travels* tells its story so successfully that its hidden contemporary satire is usually ignored. As the century advanced, England had the distinction of first developing the form of the modern novel in the sequence which takes us from Samuel Richardson's *Pamela* (1740) and *Clarissa* (1748) to Tobias Smollett's *Roderick Random* (1748), Henry Fielding's *Tom Jones* (1749) and Laurence Sterne's *Tristram Shandy* (1764). The most notable figure of literary England was the great lexicographer, Dr. Samuel Johnson (1709–1784), whose works now are seldom read save by specialists but whose personality has been immortalized by his disciple and biographer, James Boswell. Johnson's pomposity of style was in striking contrast to the literary charm and grace of his friend, Oliver Goldsmith, a poet, novelist and playwright of rare versatility.

Among the many eighteenth-century poets who sought to wear the mantle of their great predecessor, John Dryden (1631–1700), the writer most characteristic of the Classical Age was Alexander Pope (1688–1744). Both in his strengths and his weaknesses he admirably summed up his period: he was a polished, witty and urbane stylist, a master of the epigram ("A little learning is a dangerous thing"; "Fools rush in where angels fear to tread"; "What oft was thought but ne'er so well expressed"; "Hope springs eternal in the human breast") and a thinker of invincible conventionality. Pope's *Essay on Man* is a perfect summing up of the rationalism and optimism of the eighteenth century without a single suggestion of originality or independent critical power.

What gives profound importance to the literary and intellectual evolution of the eighteenth century is the gradual replacement of the conventional creeds of Classicism by the new outlook of Romanticism.[16] Here one can only touch upon a few essential points. Classicism came to exercise a declining hold upon the arts while interest grew in the world of nature, in exotic lands overseas and in the glamor of the Middle Ages. In England, to take one illustration, the great country homes of the eighteenth century were usually set, not in formal Italianate gardens like those of Versailles, but in the newly fashionable "English garden" with rolling lawns, informal clumps of trees, winding paths, romantic vistas, lakes and not infrequently a classical "ruin" artfully contrived for the occasion. These were planned (with much artifice) by landscape gardeners of whom the great master was Lancelot, or "Capabil-

16. French scholars, seeking accurate distinction, use the term, *préromantisme* (preromanticism), for this age leaving the more familiar term for the developments of the early nineteenth century.

ity," Brown (1715–1783). The cult of things oriental, especially Chinese, has already been indicated. About mid-eighteenth century, as taste inclined towards various aspects of medieval life, the "Gothic Revival" began to develop. In 1750 the very fashionable Horace Walpole (a son of the great Sir Robert) began to remodel his estate, Strawberry Hill, at Twickenham with a very strange overlay of Gothic turrets, gateways, windows and fire-places. Books were written on the elements of medieval architecture. In 1772 the young Goethe, standing before the great medieval cathedral at Strasbourg, was struck by the beauties which the modern world seemed long to have ignored. "It rises," he wrote, "like a most sublime, wide-arching Tree of God. . . . Stop, brother, and discern the deepest sense of truth . . . quickening out of strong, rough, German soil."

Certain English poets took the lead in this new interest in nature's simplicity and beauty. James Thomson's *Seasons* (1726), William Collins' *Ode to Evening* (1746) and Thomas Gray's *Elegy in a Country Churchyard* (1750) all have the note of emotion and feeling for the natural world as do the deeply human poems of the great Scottish poet of a later generation, Robert Burns (1759–1796). The cult of a romantic past could lead in unusual directions. One of the strangest episodes in English literary history was the enthusiastic welcome given in 1760 to James Macpherson's publication of the epic poems of a supposed ancient Gaelic poet, "Ossian, Son of Fingal." These were actually the most flagrant forgeries. Poor artistically and yet important also as a part of the new trend were the "Gothic romances," fantastic tales of mystery and terror.

The literary change appeared in France with those writers of sentiment or "sensibility" among whom Rousseau was supreme. The *Confessions,* the *Emile* and especially the *New Héloïse* rejected the rational doctrines of the Enlightenment in order to preach the gospel of nature and proclaim the simple virtues of the human heart. These works stimulated a whole school of disciples and imitators.

The literature of Germany in the first half of the eighteenth century had been marked, as Frederick II noted in his essay, *On German Literature,* by an unfortunate imitativeness of French models. When Johann Gottfried Herder (1744–1803), a product of Germany's eastern borderlands, undertook to study and collect the folk-songs and customary lore of the German and Baltic peoples he stimulated an interest in that which was "natural" and "simple," thereby becoming a pioneer of German Romanticism and German nationalism. The plays of Friedrich Schiller (1759–1805), notably *The Robbers, William Tell* and *The Maid of Orleans,* likewise struck a romantic note.

The significant movement in German literature known as "Storm and Stress" (*Sturm und Drang*) is associated inseparably with the youthful Johann Wolfgang von Goethe (1749–1832). He published *The Sorrows of Young Werther* in 1774, a novel which showed obvious indebtedness to Rousseau's *New Héloïse*. Werther, a lovesick youth, becomes the victim of an unmasterable passion for Charlotte, the fiancée of his closest friend, Albert. His efforts to free himself from Charlotte's innocent spell are unavailing, so that in the end Werther, with the moon's rays streaming in upon him through his casement window, shoots himself with Albert's pistol. On the appearance of this little book a Werther craze, marked by the sale of Werther engravings, Werther cups, Werther medallions and Werther embroidery, swept Germany. A generation of youth dressed itself in the celebrated "Werther costume"—white breeches, yellow waistcoat, blue coat and a black, three-cornered hat—sighing over Werther's sorrows but, save in rare occasions, happily avoiding the extreme of suicide. "Storm and Stress" was a passing phase in German literature, as it was also in the literary career of Goethe, yet it was important in leading to the great developments in Romanticism of a later generation.

The general growth of European music during the Baroque age has already been discussed.[17] Musically, the eighteenth century was an age of giants—of Bach, Handel, Haydn and Mozart. Johann Sebastian Bach (1685–1750), coming of a family of musicians and one of the greatest names in all musical history, made his career as an organist, choirmaster and composer at Weimar and Leipzig. His virtuosity as a composer of polyphonic counterpoint music, in which several melodies were blended and which was best exemplified in his many fugues, has never been equaled. Bach was a master both of the organ and the clavichord and made important contributions to the technique of playing, for example by using the thumb on the keyboard. His magnificent fugues, cantatas, suites, concertos, sonatas and masses have led him to be called the musician's musician, for he composed in a mathematical idiom and displayed a degree of technical perfection almost impossible for an amateur fully to appreciate. Yet his music has profoundly stirred millions and his great *Mass in B Minor* has been compared in importance to Milton's *Paradise Lost*.

Bach contributed greatly to stabilizing and defining the rules of harmony and musical composition. In 1722 a French scholar, Jean Philippe Rameau, published his *Treatise on Harmony*, an important work on the nature of the major and minor scales, chords and tonality. In the same year Bach

17. For a brief summary of the "monodic revolution," the development of opera, oratorio and cantata and the elaboration of orchestral instruments, see pp. 290–291.

began the publication of his *Well Tempered Clavichord,* a series of twenty-four preludes and fugues intended to show that the use of a new system of tuning (that is, the "tempered scale" having a single note to represent both F sharp and G flat) would facilitate composition. On this orthodox structure of harmony the great works of Handel, Mozart and Beethoven were built.

George Frederick Handel (1685–1759) was a German-born composer who came from the Electorate of Hanover to England, having through youthful visits to Italy familiarized himself with Italian opera. In England he made his great reputation by his operas, oratorios, cantatas and anthems. His famous *Water Music* was composed for a river-fête organized for George I in 1717. It was George II, the friend and admirer of Handel, who rose in tribute at the singing of the great "Hallelujah Chorus" of *The Messiah* and thus initiated a custom that has lasted to our own day. On Handel's tomb in Westminster Abbey are carved the words and music of the famous passage from the same work, "I Know that My Redeemer Liveth."

Joseph Haydn (1732–1809) rose from the background of a humble Croatian peasant family to become *Kapellmeister,* or musical director, to the great Hungarian family of Esterhazy. With expert musicians at his command he was able to experiment with orchestral forms and to elaborate this type of music. Haydn was the first great master of the string quartet and has been called the father of the symphony; of this latter form he composed more than a hundred. Mozart said that Haydn taught him to write quartets, and for about a year "papa Haydn" gave musical instruction to Beethoven. Drawing upon his Croatian background, Haydn, with a suggestion of the new era of Romanticism, introduced many themes from popular folk music into his works. One of the most attractive figures in musical history, he composed, so he said, that "the weary and the worn, or the man burdened with affairs, may enjoy a few moments of solace and refreshment."

The last name in the great roster is that of Wolfgang Amadeus Mozart (1756–1791), a musical prodigy composing at the age of five and giving recitals at the age of six. During his pathetically short life he contributed notably to the opera which Gluck had revived. The *Magic Flute, Don Giovanni* and the *Marriage of Figaro* are his chief operatic works. His symphonies and other compositions give Mozart the claim to be a master of melody and elegant form. "The truth of the matter is that Mozart was thoroughly eighteenth century in his style, the balanced, measured and beautifully proportioned style that typified the ideal and rarely the reality of true sophisticates and aristocrats." [18] With Mozart, as with Bach, Handel and Haydn, the music of the Classical Age received its superb definition and expression.

18. GERSHOY, *From Despotism to Revolution,* p. 257.

THE AGE

OF REVOLUTION

1 7 5 0 – 1 8 1 5

"The legislator commands the future;

to be feeble will avail him nothing;

it is for him to will what is good and to perpetuate it;

to make man what he desires him to be.

For the laws, working upon the social body,

which is inert in itself,

can produce either virtue or crime,

civilized customs or savagery."

SAINT-JUST *to the Convention, Paris, April, 1793.*

Europe on the Eve
of Revolution

Chapter 20

■ INTRODUCTION

THE ORDERLY, self-confident world of the eighteenth century, so attractive to those having wealth, position and political power, came to an end in 1789. In the ensuing years France alone experienced a violent, nation-wide revolution powerful enough to make profound changes in its economic and social, as well as its political, structure. All other European countries were influenced to some degree by the revolutionary spirit. Armies swept

525

Compare with the maps on pages 406–407 and 691. By gaining Silesia and part of Poland Prussia is much stronger. Russia continues to move its frontier westward. France has a strong position on the upper Rhine. Austria holds Milan and the Austrian Netherlands, but has lost southern Italy to the Spanish Bourbon dynasty.

EUROPE IN 1789

more than once through Italy's northern provinces. Its political structure was completely reorganized. The Low Countries and large parts of Germany, likewise feeling the hand of war, underwent sweeping political changes. The impact of the Revolution manifested itself as far afield as Spain, Scandinavia, Turkey and Russia. England, although spared revolution, twice faced the menace of actual invasion and stood at war with revolutionary France longer than did any other power.

The necessary preliminary to the study of such developments is an examination of the structure and internal workings of the major European states on the eve of the revolutionary era. Some countries, it is clear, helped to create a revolutionary situation, others were its more or less innocent victims.

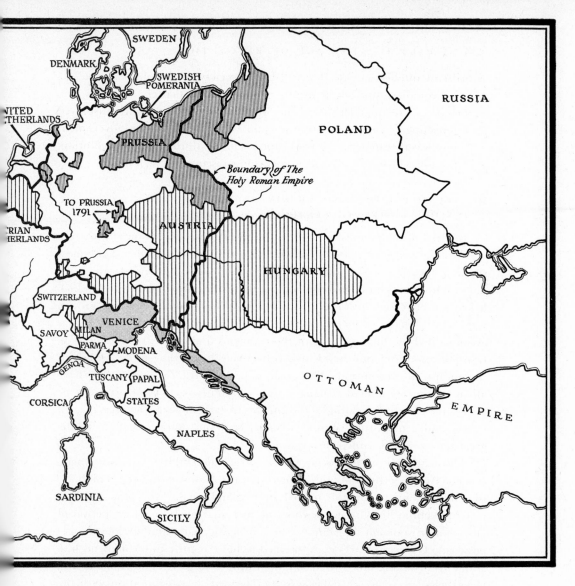

All in one way or another participated in bringing the new age into existence.

The structure of late eighteenth-century European life was far from uniform. England was able to build with reasonable steadiness upon the political and economic foundations which had been laid earlier. Austria, Prussia, Russia, Spain, Portugal and Tuscany exhibited in varying degrees the phenomenon of "Enlightened Despotism." Scandinavian life lacked much of the vigor it had earlier displayed. Poland was a dying state. The Ottoman Empire met defeat after defeat at the hands of its neighbors.

France, more than any other country, seemed the home of paradox. Despotism of a sort there was, but it was neither efficient nor enlightened.

527

A brilliant intellectual life flourished in a society marred by flagrant economic inequalities and social injustices. In domestic matters ministers who were heirs to a distinguished tradition of public service frequently displayed an astonishing incompetence. While commerce prospered, the government of France was threatened with bankruptcy. Out of all this came a revolutionary situation which first affected France and subsequently all Europe.

■ ENGLISH POLITICS AND SOCIETY IN THE EIGHTEENTH CENTURY

Internal developments in eighteenth-century England followed a pattern very different from that found generally on the continent. One of the most significant aspects of England's growth was undoubtedly political—the gradual evolution of cabinet government and the party system, phenomena which led to the increased authority of the House of Commons. Economic growth was almost equally momentous, for a revolution in English agriculture was accompanied by the beginning of those various developments in commerce, transportation and industry which collectively have come to be known as the Industrial Revolution. The great imperial advances of this age have already been considered. Changes in social outlook likewise were to be important. These, revealing a certain dissatisfaction with the structure of society and a mounting volume of social criticism, were a prelude to the great reforms of the nineteenth century.

The death in 1714 of Queen Anne, who left no children, put into operation the Act of Settlement and inaugurated the Hanoverian age.[1] The boorish and uncouth George I arrived in England unable to speak English. Leaving behind his wife, with whom he had quarreled, to a long period of virtual imprisonment in Hanover and bringing with him various unprepossessing German mistresses, he seemed to have as little to recommend him as did his dissolute, slow-witted son, the future George II. The Hanoverians, nevertheless, were accepted because they seemed, in collaboration with the Whigs whom they backed, able to avert the danger of a Stuart restoration and the possible destruction of the liberties won in 1689.

In 1715 the "Old Pretender," James Stuart, son of the exiled James II, raised a revolt in Scotland. This, the "Fifteen," was easily put down. It indicated, nevertheless, the presence of the Jacobite danger and the existence of substantial Tory groups favoring the old dynasty. In 1745 a second Stuart uprising, this time in support of the "Young Pretender" (Charles Stuart, grandson of James II), seemed a much more serious threat. The "Forty-Five"

---

1. George I (1714–1727) was followed by his son, George II (1727–1760). George III, grandson of George II, reigned from 1760 to 1820, his son becoming regent in 1811 on account of the father's insanity.

caused widespread disturbances in Scotland, a Scottish invasion of England which reached Derby, and a final pitched battle in Scotland (Culloden) after which the Young Pretender was forced into inglorious exile. No further serious challenges ensued. "Between 1714 and 1760 the English people, wearied with struggles and sated with glory, was content to stabilize the results of the revolution under a dynasty for which it had no love and accept an oligarchic system of government which for the time being seemed exactly suited to its needs." [2]

Recent scholarship has successfully challenged the view of the older "Whig historians" that early eighteenth-century England saw the secure establishment of cabinet government, responsible to Parliament and free in large measure from royal control. Important beginnings undoubtedly there were, yet the whole process was much longer and much less deliberate than the traditional interpretation has suggested. The great settlement of 1688-1689 had averted the danger of royal tyranny but in no sense had created a parliamentary democracy. England was in reality governed by a tight little oligarchy. The two members chosen from each county (eighty in all) were elected by a very small number of voters. In the towns it has been calculated that the total electorate for England's 204 boroughs numbered not more than 85,000 in all. Some old boroughs with the right to be represented in Parliament had shrunk so as to have a mere handful of voters. The extreme case was an East Anglian coastal town that had been washed away by the sea but still returned its members. Voting was public and thus subject to influence and bribery. Many seats were uncontested; many were looked upon as the possession of a great local family and were sold at a substantial price to someone who would pay. At mid-century some 51 noblemen and 55 country gentlemen actually had under their control over 190 seats in the House of Commons. The surprising fact is that under such circumstances Parliament, which clearly reflected the interests of the nobility, the landed gentry and the mercantile class, showed as much concern for the general welfare as it did.[3]

In this "unreformed House of Commons" some of the modern techniques of government were slowly evolving. Political parties ("Whigs" and "Tories") had first emerged in the latter years of the reign of Charles II, though the monarch had felt no compulsion to select his ministers exclusively from one party or another.[4] Both Whigs and Tories in Parliament represented privileged, landowning groups. The former, however, tended to be the spokes-

---

2. BASIL WILLIAMS, *The Whig Supremacy, 1714–1760* (1939), p. 1.
3. Membership of the Commons in 1754 comprised 63 army and navy officers, 36 merchants, 10 planters, 36 lawyers and 314 landed gentry.
4. See pp. 317–318. The first exclusively one-party ministry was chosen by William III in 1696, but it did not constitute a precedent.

men of the mercantile interests whereas the latter were more strongly agricultural, "High Church" and in some degree Jacobite. The old Privy Council, a group of distinguished officers from whom the monarch traditionally received advice, became after 1713 little more than a formal body with certain routine duties. A smaller group of these councillors, the "Cabinet Council," gradually became more important and regularly included certain key officials: the First Lord of the Treasury, the two Principal Secretaries of State and the Lord Chancellor. As the eighteenth century progressed, political parties slowly took on a clearer definition and the cabinet likewise underwent development.

The period down to 1763 constituted the great age of the Whigs. From 1721 to 1742 Walpole was their unquestioned leader, so that to understand him is to understand a great deal of this age. He was a bluff, coarse-grained country squire, devoted to his landed estates. As leader of the House of Commons it is said that he would sit in the chamber, first reading the daily reports from his gamekeeper before attending to business of state. Walpole was determined to keep England at peace, to foster its mercantile interests and to avoid sensational issues that might split the country in two. He frankly accepted the political morality of his day, making use of large-scale bribery and political patronage to achieve his ends. "All these men have their price," was his comment on a particular group in the Commons that he sought to influence.

Walpole was on excellent terms with George I and subsequently, through the influence of Queen Caroline, with George II. George I rarely attended cabinet meetings, not so much because of his inability to speak English as because of his easy-going disposition to leave the conduct of affairs to his ministers. Yet neither George I nor George II lost control of the government. They were influential in selecting ministers and in causing dismissals. They insisted upon a large share in military affairs. They were in control of substantial funds with which to influence policy and reward their favorites. They did not feel obliged to accept the advice of their ministers. Under such circumstances it was all the more necessary to have someone serving as an intermediary between the monarch and the House of Commons. Walpole performed this duty so well that while it is wrong to describe him as "prime minister" in the modern sense (the office did not exist), nevertheless, as First Lord of the Treasury, he certainly led the other ministers.

No description of the government of eighteenth-century England would be complete without some reference to local administration, and particularly to that uniquely English institution, the justices of the peace. These members of the squirearchy or landed aristocracy were appointed by the crown on recommendation of the lord-lieutenant of each county, and held office for life. In addition to administering local justice (in which capacity they could have their decisions appealed to the quarter-sessions or assizes) the justices of the peace had many administrative duties. They supervised the poor law, saw that highways were kept in repair, issued licenses to tavern-keepers and tradesmen, supervised jails and in some cases set wage-rates. The rule of these "local despots" was on the whole benevolent. The central government managed to keep watch over them, but in a manner far different from that of the centralized despotisms of the continent. On the whole, the justices of the peace (immortalized in Addison's Sir Roger de Coverley) could be regarded as part of the system under which most Englishmen accepted rule by their "betters."

The immediate Whig successors to Walpole were undistinguished. The most notable, the Duke of Newcastle, surpassed even Walpole in the art of parliamentary manipulation. He took active part in every election for forty-six years. It is said that he knew to a penny what it would cost to buy the votes of every member of the House of Commons. Newcastle's incompetent leadership at the opening of the Seven Years' War (1756) was such that he was compelled to resign in favor of a man of outstanding talent, William Pitt.

As Walpole had given England internal order and economic stability a generation earlier, so the elder Pitt now directed the affairs of England during four epic years (1757–1761) of overseas victories.[5] His position changed, however, on the accession of George III in 1760. The new king, who had no intention of submitting to parliamentary rule, preferred the Tories to the Whigs. Pitt, moreover, had antagonized many of his followers by his excessive self-confidence, his theatrical manners and his pompous bearing. "I know that I can save this country," he declared on one occasion, "and I know no other man can." Pitt resigned in 1761 when the cabinet refused to declare war on Spain. His subsequent promotion to the House of Lords as the Earl of Chatham (1766) and his recurrent illness prevented him from ever again equaling his first great accomplishments.

George III meanwhile set out to become the "Patriot King" that his mother and his mentor, Lord Bolingbroke, had once urged him to be. Living an exemplary life, "rejoicing in the name of Britain," he commanded for a time much public sympathy. Yet he was stubborn and tricky. George III did not bring about a new "constitutional crisis" in 1760 by exaggerated claims to royal power; the gist of his position was that, while accepting the Revolutionary Settlement, he would not surrender those constitutional rights which he considered still to be his. Gradually, by the distribution of bribes

5. Pitt held the office of Secretary of State, letting Newcastle, the political manager, hold the prime ministership.

and favors, he brought the long rule of the Whigs to an end. He carefully watched the voting in the House of Commons, rewarding his friends and seeking to penalize his opponents. As the power of the "King's Friends" grew, the old authority of the Whigs declined. When, finally, in 1770 George III appointed his friend, Lord North, to office, he had a docile servant leading the cabinet and an obsequious majority in the House of Commons.

The attempt to assert strong royal power lasted through the period of the American Revolution. Ultimately, as British fortunes declined in this war, so likewise did royal prestige at home. In 1780 the Commons passed by a vote of 232 to 215 the famous resolution of George Dunning: "That the influence of the crown has increased, is increasing, and ought to be diminished." North's resignation in 1782 meant a new era, for now the Whigs returned briefly to power, to be followed in 1783 by the "New Tories." These, under the leadership of the younger William Pitt, son of the Earl of Chatham, announced their intention to undertake parliamentary reform. Prime minister at the age of twenty-three, Pitt was the phenomenon of his times. His reform plans were made ineffective by the tremendous revolutionary developments in France, yet the truly significant fact was that George III's attempts at political control had failed. With Pitt in office, the greater part of royal authority was quietly but firmly transferred to the Cabinet, where it has remained.[6] Incipient madness had first been suspected in the unhappy sovereign as early as 1765. In 1788 a violent seizure overcame him, to be followed by recurrent attacks in subsequent years. These, together with total blindness, removed the old king from the scene of public affairs and left him, a tragic figure at Windsor, from 1811 until his death in 1820.

In summary, cabinet government in the modern sense, with ministers directly and collectively responsible to the House of Commons, had not been achieved in eighteenth-century England. Four important trends, however, were manifest: (1) The crown was gradually losing control of public policy. (2) By the time of the younger Pitt's ministry the idea of a prime minister (though not the legally defined office) was becoming clear. (3) The cabinet had come to be composed of members each in charge of one particular function of government. (4) Cabinet members were aware of their responsibility to the House of Commons, though this was not as yet truly a collective responsibility. In these various respects, therefore, English political developments, far in advance of those on the continent, were of the utmost consequence for the future.

6. See the very able essay of E. T. Williams, "The Cabinet in the Eighteenth Century," in R. L. Schuyler and H. Ausubel, *The Making of English History* (1952).

■ ECONOMIC AND SOCIAL CHANGE
  IN EIGHTEENTH-CENTURY ENGLAND

The life of eighteenth-century England cannot be understood solely in terms of its politics. This was an age of extraordinary prosperity for the "governing classes" whether the old aristocratic families or the newer mercantile elements that steadily intermarried with them. It was an age of splendid country houses in the Palladian style, of Georgian town houses, furniture by Chippendale and Hepplewhite, portraits by Reynolds, Romney and Gainsborough, interior decoration in the neo-classical fashion by the brothers Adam. It was an age that admired the elegant poetry of Alexander Pope, that heard the first romantic poetical notes of Gray, Thomson and Collins, that thrilled to the *Messiah* of Frederick Handel, and witnessed the arrival of the Italian opera. It read the histories of Gibbon, the novels of Sterne, Smollett and Fielding. An aristocracy so sure of itself as was England's could not wish to see any drastic change in the pattern of its life. Yet major change was in the air.

A veritable revolution in English agriculture made itself evident during the eighteenth century as enlightened landowners such as Coke of Holkham, Jethro Tull, Lord Townshend and Arthur Young experimented with new methods of planting, cultivating, soil fertilization and stock breeding. Lord Townshend won the nickname of "Turnip Townshend" through his new four-crop rotation which included turnips and clover along with arable farming. Robert Bakewell developed breeds of cattle producing far more meat than formerly. Arthur Young, though not himself a successful farmer, organized agricultural societies, traveled much and wrote so voluminously as to be one of the greatest agricultural publicists of all time. The "Farmer King," George III, undertook model agriculture at Windsor.

A second wave of enclosures by parliamentary enactment, much greater than the enclosures of the Tudor age, steadily destroyed what was left of the village common lands and open fields. The modern system of hedged fields, farmed by the owner or let out to tenants, ended the age-old system of communal village agriculture. This transformation meant a decline in the sturdy old class of yeoman farmers who found it hard to compete with the great landowners. It also meant hardships to the villagers, some of whom now became day-laborers. Many others drifted towards the cities to seek their fortunes amid the strange conditions that a new industrial age was beginning to create.

Eighteenth-century England stood on the eve of an industrial revolution.[7]

7. There seems a tendency on the part of economic historians to play down the "revolutionary" aspects of this development and stress its long-time, evolutionary nature. Certainly it was no sharp change occurring in mid-eighteenth century, as Arnold Toynbee's classic *Lectures on the Industrial Revolution* (1884) assumed.

Hitherto its great wealth, apart from that created by agriculture, had been largely the product of the sailor, the merchant and the financier who together had brought the products of English artisans into the channels of foreign trade. The new makers of wealth were to be the manufacturers, aided and spurred on by the inventors and the scientists who vastly enlarged England's productive capacities. While the full development of the Industrial Revolution was a phenomenon of the nineteenth and twentieth centuries, its earlier growth merits at least some brief consideration.

The signs of an economic transformation were first evident in England's thriving cloth industry. Here the trickle of technical improvements which had been made during the sixteenth and seventeenth centuries came during the eighteenth century to assume the proportions of a flood. A *Society for the Encouragement of Arts, Manufactures and Commerce,* organized in 1754, offered money, medals and rewards for specific improvements, established a museum and issued various publications.[8] The principal problem was to find techniques for spinning yarn and weaving cloth that would improve upon the spinning-wheel and the hand loom. In 1733 John Kay devised his "flying-shuttle"—a cigar-shaped instrument with small wheels which was struck back and forth by hammers, thus expediting the process of weaving. Richard Arkwright's "water-frame," patented in 1769, made possible the production of stronger yarn in larger quantities by a machine operated by water power. The "spinning-jenny" which James Hargreaves devised in 1764 was really a multiple spinning-wheel worked by hand and capable of manufacturing eight, then sixteen and finally over a hundred threads at one time. Samuel Crompton devised his "spinning-mule" in 1779 (a "hybrid" product of the water-frame and spinning-jenny) which made it possible to use water power to spin four hundred threads at once. The final development was for Edmund Cartwright, a clergyman, to devise a power-loom in 1785 which first made use of horses and later of steam power. The whole process by which one invention led to, and in a sense called forth, another is extremely instructive.

The development of steam power was likewise momentous. Thomas Newcomen devised a steam pump as early as 1706 and subsequently improved it. By mid-century such pumps, known as "the miners' friend" were widely used in the coal industry. In 1769 James Watt devised "a new method of lessening the Consumption of Steam and Fuel in Fire Engines." This was a great improvement upon Newcomen's engine. Later, in partnership with Matthew Boulton, Watt produced engines equipped with crank and flywheel which could be used for general industrial purposes. By 1800 about

8. The Society did not limit itself to industry. It offered many agricultural prizes, for example, a premium of £20 and a gold medal for "The best account of a Method of Rearing and Fattening Hogs, verified by Experiments."

320 "Watt engines" were in use, averaging, however, only about 16 horse power each.

English iron production grew from 20,000 tons in 1740 to 156,000 tons in 1800. Abraham Darby devised a method for using coke instead of charcoal for smelting iron in the first part of the eighteenth century, thereby leading to an increased production of cast iron.[9] Not until 1783, however, was the economical production of wrought iron made possible. Henry Cort then developed methods of "puddling" the molten metal to remove impurities and of using rollers to turn out bar iron.

An example of individual initiative revolutionizing a particular industry is seen in the case of Josiah Wedgwood (1730–1795), a Staffordshire potter of remarkable abilities. Wedgwood aimed with equal success at two markets, the "useful" and the "ornamental." His famous works at Burslem and Etruria were the scene of persistent technological experiments concerning clays, glazes, firing and coloring. Wedgwood was an artist and also a skilled salesman with a keen sense of the market. He sold a dinner service to Catherine II of Russia composed of 952 pieces, each with a different English scene upon it. Wedgwood, in short, has been well described as "a scientific potter, an enterprising business man and a man of taste and artistic talent."

The elaborate growth of England's industrial life, illustrated in the increased coal output from $2\frac{1}{2}$ million tons in 1700 to 10 million tons a century later, defies simple summary. Urban population was on the increase. Inland transportation was vastly improved, partly as a result of the "Turnpike Trusts" which maintained stretches of road in return for collecting tolls, partly because of a series of parliamentary acts after 1760 for improving roads, partly because of the development of a network of canals with horse-drawn barges. The new industrialism brought added wealth and with it added problems of which public opinion was not immediately aware. Adam Smith's *Wealth of Nations,* advocating the doctrines of *laissez-faire,* appeared in 1776. He wrote, it is true, before the evils of unregulated industrial life, of long hours and low wages, of child labor and noisome slums had made themselves evident. The dark shadows of the new industrialism did not fully develop until a later generation.

In a century of which the last decade was to be dominated by the French Revolution, it is instructive to observe a current of social criticism which developed in England. The complacent acceptance of "things as they are" and the view of a world in which all was "for the best" did not pass unchallenged. To some extent the currents of criticism were religious in inspiration; they may have been the product of what is sometimes called "the

9. A cast iron bridge was built across the River Severn in 1779.

Nonconformist conscience"; they were at all events marked by a strong degree of humanitarian sentiment.

In 1728 William Law, an Anglican clergyman, published his *Serious Call to a Devout and Holy Life,* a treatise on practical Christianity appealing for the kind of evangelical Christianity which the Wesleys soon were to undertake. Despite the official apathy of the Anglican Church, the age saw societies formed to promote Christian knowledge, to distribute the Bible and to relieve the poor. Women such as Selina, Countess of Huntingdon, and Lady Elizabeth Hastings constituted "the first heralds of the army of modern spinsters who have made England a stronghold of philanthropy." The Evangelical group led by Wilberforce and Thomas Clarkson worked for the abolition of slavery. The Society for the Abolition of the Slave Trade was founded in 1787. Other reformers were concerned with the abuses of the poor law. John Howard undertook in 1773 his dedicated work for prison reform, while a decade later Hannah More began that long series of "improving" novels and tracts which, while urging the poor to rely upon the virtues of piety, industry and resignation to their lot, still showed a humanitarian awareness of the problem of suffering. Meanwhile the first stirrings of modern English radicalism became evident in scattered demands for parliamentary changes. In 1780 a Society for Promoting Constitutional Information was founded, and in 1785 Pitt actually introduced, but did not succeed in passing, a mild scheme of parliamentary reform. When revolutionary changes came about in the France of 1789, a considerable number of Englishmen through "Corresponding Societies" and other devices showed a warm sympathy with the aims of the French reformers.

Such were some elements in the complex picture of an England that grew and changed greatly during the eighteenth century. On the fringe of continental affairs, England was able to weather the storms of the new revolutionary age far better than most of its European contemporaries.

■ ENLIGHTENED DESPOTISM IN PRUSSIA

Prussia under Frederick II offered a striking contrast to Hanoverian England, for it embodied the spirit, not of parliamentary government, but of enlightened despotism. The rule of Frederick II (1740–1786) was built squarely upon the achievements of his predecessors. Despite their important work in disciplining and strengthening the Prussian state, neither the Great Elector (1640–1688), nor Frederick I (1688–1713), nor Frederick William I (1713–1740) could be called "enlightened" in the eighteenth-century sense of the term. According to this view, reason must rule the world, operating through the agency of an enlightened autocrat who has the welfare of his state at heart. He will seek, therefore, to give it uniform legislation and an equitable tax system. He will grant as much religious toleration as is consistent with national security. He will end privileges for special groups and seek justice for all. He will subordinate the church to the state. He will concede a considerable degree of intellectual liberty and he will be concerned to provide some elementary, useful education for his subjects. He will nurse and foster the economic life of his realm. Never will it occur to him that his subjects need participate actively and responsibly in this work of government. They are to be the recipients of the order and prosperity which the ruler provides.

Frederick II was one of the greatest of enlightened despots. His sympathies were with those French writers who proclaimed the gospel of reason. He and Voltaire were, at least for a time, bosom friends and ardent admirers, maintaining a correspondence which, despite personal quarrels, ran for forty years. Frederick himself was a versatile author who composed a history of Brandenburg, a history of his own times, an essay on Machiavelli, another on the art of war and still another on German literature. He drafted at least two shrewd political testaments for the benefit of his successors. Frederick loved books, music and good food. He played the flute excellently, composed creditable music and wrote bad French verse. Delighting in the company of witty men, he was noted for the cynical power of his own judgments.

Frederick's views on enlightened despotism are most clearly stated in his *Essay on the Forms of Government and on the Duties of Sovereigns:*

> The prince stands in relation to the society over which he rules as the head stands to the body; he must see, think and act for the community in order to procure for it all the advantages which it is capable of enjoying. . . . He is merely the first servant of the State, obliged to act with probity, wisdom and complete disinterestedness, as though at any moment he might be called upon to give an account of his administration to his fellow citizens.

In assuming such a leading role Frederick saw no need to make drastic administrative changes. He kept the General Directory of 1723, but in a minor capacity, choosing rather to exercise his own discretion than to depend too much on the advice of any group of ministers. The most striking feature of his administration was the phenomenal energy with which he worked. All authority centered in Frederick. Day in and day out he sat at his desk, receiving reports from all parts of the kingdom, making his annotations and sending out his written instructions. A detailed calendar informed him of the business to be transacted on every day and almost at every hour of the year. This stupefying routine was interrupted only by periodic inspection trips throughout the kingdom. Otherwise, Frederick's ceaseless devotion to his paper-work lasted until his death.

Frederick stood at the pinnacle of an administrative pyramid. He undertook to create certain specialized ministries or departments (Commerce and Industry in 1741, War Supplies in 1746, Excise and Tolls in 1766, Mines in 1768 and Forestry in 1770), but these were not directed by chiefs comparable in authority to those found in England or France. Instead, Frederick made great point of holding all the guiding strings in his own hands. He kept closely in touch, too, with the fifteen provincial Chambers (*Kammern*), one of which was found in each province. These were administrative boards, largely concerned with finances, designed to see that the king's will was done. They were "the classic workshops of the Prussian mercantilist state." Frederick likewise supervised closely those local officials—the *Landrat* in each rural area and the *Steuerrat* in each urban community—who had authority to deal with local matters.

When it is realized that the Prussian civil service was a career for which individuals were first carefully selected, then in many cases given training in "cameralism" at the universities as well as having practical field experience before taking qualifying examinations, it may be seen what an effective machinery Frederick had at his disposal. Making no radical changes in the Prussian administrative structure, his work was rather to impose his own personality and to dominate every aspect of the government with his phenomenal energies.

Under the direction of a distinguished jurist, Samuel von Cocceji, legal reforms were undertaken. The quality of judges and lawyers was improved, salaries raised, legal procedure simplified and a uniform civil code, the *Corpus Juris Fredericiani,* actually a strange patchwork of Roman, feudal and ecclesiastical procedures, was drafted.[10]

Frederick likewise concerned himself with education, building on the work done by his father. A decree of 1717 had required all parents in localities where schools existed to send their children to them daily. Yet in 1732 a government commission reported that only one-tenth of Prussian children received any education at all. Frederick II's celebrated School Code of 1763 required all children to be taught between the ages of five and thirteen, stipulating that parents too poor to pay fees be assisted by the local authorities. Between 1771 and 1788 Frederick's plan was encouraged by the vigorous efforts of his Minister of Public Instruction, K. A. von Zedlitz. Actually, one is justified in questioning the effectiveness of his ambitious scheme. Many village schools were little more than snug berths for Frederick's old soldiers. The king's purpose, moreover, seems to have been to train children to accept the station into which they were born. "Instruction in the country," he wrote,

---

10. This did not actually come into effect until 1794 when it had been expertly revised. It remained in force until 1900.

"must be planned so that they only receive that which is most essential for them but which is designed to keep them in the villages and not influence them to leave." Rather than stimulate brilliance and originality, he sought conformity and obedience.

Frederick, whose own views were similar to those of the deists, encouraged religious toleration. In general he had no lofty inspiration for his policies, being indifferent in matters of dogma and expecting simply obedience and loyalty from the clergy whom he was pleased to call his "spiritual drill-sergeants."

Economic policy was based on the techniques of mercantilism. Frederick regarded serfdom as a great evil, yet because of noble opposition he was compelled to limit himself to improving the condition of serfs on the royal estates. These were in some cases granted the hereditary possession of their lands. The general condition of the Prussian peasantry can hardly be said to have improved. Actually, most Junker landlords were in process of enlarging their possessions, so that the tendency east of the River Elbe was for landed estates to grow still larger and for the peasants to continue either as serfs or as landless laborers.

The kind of agricultural improvements that Frederick was able to make were technological in nature; he drained swamps, built roads, joined the Oder and Vistula by the Bromberg Canal and distributed free grain, fodder and building-materials as a means of recovery from the damage of war. Experts were sent to England to learn about the agricultural improvements being made there. Turnips and potatoes became for the first time a common food crop. The systematic planting and care of pine and fir forests—a science in which Germany took the lead—was first undertaken by Frederick's experts. Agriculture was also stimulated by colonization. During Frederick's reign an estimated 300,000 settlers were brought in from other parts of Germany and settled for the most part in newly acquired or newly reclaimed lands. Some fifty new villages, for example, were built in the West Prussian lands acquired in the first partition of Poland.

Mercantilist techniques were likewise applied to industry and commerce. Frederick believed in a high tariff and a system of monopolies in order to build up a thriving, self-sufficient national economy. He used large sums of public money in "pump-priming" operations and stood ready either to grant monopolies to new enterprises or even to undertake governmental monopolies on his own. A Prussian state bank was set up in 1765 on the advice of an Italian expert, Calzabigi, to provide credit for new business enterprises. Silesia, acquired by military conquest, Frederick regarded as a source of vast wealth (his "Peru," as it was termed). Silesia had a flourishing textile industry, was rich in iron, lead and coal and was strategically located so that its products could be shipped by river and canal to Danzig, Stettin or Hamburg for export. The general results of Frederick's economic policies seemed most impressive. By 1783 Prussian exports so much exceeded imports as to produce a favorable trade balance of three million thalers. Industrial development had been phenomenal. On Frederick's accession in 1740 Prussia's main exports were wool, linen and timber. By 1786 the list of manufactures included cotton, silks, glass, copper, paper, leather, porcelains and embroideries. Tobacco raising and sugar refining were well-established. One-third of Prussia's manufactures were exported and a promising shipbuilding industry grew up at Stettin.

Efforts to reorganize taxes so as to reduce the burden which fell so heavily on the peasants were less successful. The military land-tax (except in East Prussia and Silesia) continued to be imposed almost exclusively upon peasant holdings. In an attempt at efficiency and fairness Frederick reorganized the various customs and excise duties, setting up a special administration with De Launay, a French expert, at its head. Nevertheless, the burdens here, too, fell most heavily upon the common people who paid substantial taxes on their meat, salt, tobacco, coffee and beer.

A very cautious verdict must be passed upon the enlightened despotism of Frederick II. By his military conquests and his various domestic policies he had caused his country to grow in population from 2½ millions to 6 millions and the standing army from 80,000 to 200,000 men. Frederick ended his reign with cash reserves of 52 million thalers—a sum equal to three full years' revenues. Yet it may be questioned whether a policy of "freezing" such large cash reserves for military emergencies really worked to the country's good.

Frederick so disciplined and dragooned his country that it showed not the least disposition to follow in the path of reform and revolution along which France was to adventure in 1789. He was tireless in his labors, yet trained no subordinates to carry on in his tradition. There was no court, no ceremonial, no stage-setting except the parade-ground before which Frederick could dramatize his position as Louis XIV had done at Versailles. Happy in the company of men of intellect, Frederick did little in any true sense to stimulate the intellectual life of his country. No parallel could be found in Prussia to the group of *philosophes* who gave such distinction to French society. When the French scholar, Thiebault, professor of literature at the Prussian Academy, confessed to Frederick his ignorance of German, the king's reply was: "You are fortunate in your ignorance. Give me your word of honor that you will not learn our language." Frederick built up one of the most powerful states in Europe, yet under his nephew and successor, Frederick William II, it was to undergo a startling deterioration.

Frederick seems to have approached his tasks with an astonishing cynicism. "Mankind," he wrote in his *Testament* of 1768, "move if you urge them on, and stop so soon as you leave off driving them." Concerning his hard-working local officials he expressed the opinion that one could safely hang ninety-nine out of a hundred, since the chance was so small of there being an honest man in the lot. When a school-inspector once assured Frederick that the inborn inclination of men is to good rather than to evil, the king's celebrated reply was, "Ah, my dear Sulzer, you don't know this damned race!" He seemed to have no faith in true progress. "We pass half our life," he wrote, "in shedding the errors of our ancestors, but at the same time we leave truth resting at the bottom of the well from which posterity will not extract it despite all our efforts."

Frederick has been called a reforming reactionary, more concerned to reinforce outworn institutions than to build new. He died miserably in 1786 in the arms of his valet, alone and without family, leaving instructions that he should be buried near his favorite greyhounds, the closest companions of his last years.

■ ENLIGHTENED DESPOTISM IN THE HAPSBURG REALM

The various lands governed by the Hapsburgs at the opening of the eighteenth century had so far acquired the essentials of a workable administration that the Emperor Leopold I and his two sons, Joseph I and Charles VI, were able to rule with reasonable stability. Nevertheless, when Maria Theresa, daughter of Charles VI, inherited the Hapsburg lands in 1740 it was obvious that political unity and genuine administrative efficiency were sorely lacking.[11] Little could be done at once, for Frederick II's sudden onslaught in 1740 upon the province of Silesia obviously thrust questions of reform into the background. From 1740 to 1765 Maria Theresa ruled her Hapsburg lands alone. When her son, Joseph II, then succeeded to the imperial title she invited him to serve with her as co-ruler—an arrangement which lasted until her death in 1780.

Maria Theresa was sober, industrious and devout. Conscientious to a degree, the mother of sixteen children, and constantly aware of the governmental problems which pressed in upon her, she was not "enlightened" in the sense of belonging to that group of ardent spirits which worshiped at the shrine of reason. A ruler who, like Maria Theresa, could forbid the teaching of English in the Austrian universities "because of the dangerous

11. Maria Theresa ruled by many titles, but was never empress in her own right. She was Archduchess of Austria, Queen of Bohemia and Queen of Hungary. In 1745 her husband, Francis of Lorraine, became Holy Roman Emperor. He died in 1765 and the imperial title passed to their son, Joseph II.

character of this language in respect of its corrupting religious and ethical principles," could hardly be claimed by the *philosophes* as one of them. The great reforms which eventually were achieved came about in large degree because of the intelligent efforts of Maria Theresa's principal advisers, Count Haugwitz and Prince Kaunitz. The latter in particular she trusted implicitly. This fantastic product of the Austrian aristocratic tradition who boasted twenty-four generations of distinguished forebears, who spent from two to three hours regularly at his toilet and changed his clothes twenty to thirty times a day, who detested fresh air and never appeared outdoors without a scented handkerchief pressed to his nostrils, served the monarchy as its chancellor and principal adviser from 1750 to 1792—a longer term even than that of Metternich. Kaunitz's competence extended to all fields. Count Haugwitz, on the other hand, was concerned above all with problems of domestic administration. An admirer of the efficiency of the Prussian civil service, he hoped to introduce its main patterns into Austria.

The stresses and strains of public policy clearly called for a high level of administrative efficiency. From 1740 to 1763 Maria Theresa was never free from the actuality or the shadow of war. With her approval a new Council of State (*Staatsrath*) was set up in 1760. This was a large, advisory council of experts to discuss internal and external problems, to examine all projects of reform and to make its recommendations. These recommendations were to be considered as binding on the administrative authorities. The plan of reorganization, chiefly the work of Haugwitz, also involved the definite establishment of a number of ministries: Foreign Office (*Staatskanzlei*); War Council (*Hofkriegsrath*); Ministry of Commerce (*Kommerzdirektorium*); Ministry of the Interior (*Direktorium*), created by combining the chanceries of Austria and Bohemia; and a Supreme Court for the entire monarchy.

The real question was how far this central machinery could be imposed upon a variegated and in many respects medieval pattern of provincial and local administration. How much power, for example, should be left in the hands of the provincial assemblies or estates? Maria Theresa had considerable success in taking power from these estates and in creating for the German-Bohemian lands a new arrangement of ten provincial units each with a directing body of officials appointed from Vienna. A large number of district officers or civil servants, likewise responsible to Vienna, were also appointed. By grouping her German-Bohemian lands in one structure and her Hungarian-Transylvanian in another, Maria Theresa really created the "dualism" of Austria-Hungary which lasted through the nineteenth century.

These administrative reforms were not applied to the Austrian Netherlands or to northern Italy. They met strong opposition in the old Kingdom of Hungary, where a powerful Magyar nobility had firmly entrenched itself in power by means of its Diet and its vast landed wealth. Maria Theresa made no frontal attack on the Hungarian nobility, treating them rather with what has been called *douce violence*—"the gloved hand." In return for position at court, new titles, new honors, advantageous marriages and larger estates, the members of the Hungarian nobility safeguarded their privileges by assuming the new role of an office-holding aristocracy basking in the favor of the monarchy.

Much-needed economic and fiscal reforms were also undertaken. In 1758 Maria Theresa had been obliged to pawn her jewels in order to help meet the costs of the war. To obtain revenue the nobility and the clergy were required to pay property and income taxes. An attempt also was made to convert some of the personal services of the peasantry into cash payments. Steps were taken to reduce the number of internal tariff barriers impeding the flow of commerce and to revise the customs system. It has been estimated that during Maria Theresa's reign the annual revenues were tripled.

In other fields a beginning was made at codifying the criminal and civil laws. The main result of this was the criminal code, the *Nemesis Teresiana* of 1770, which abolished some of the most cruel punishments and declared that sorcery was no longer a crime. The harshness with which landlords imposed their authority upon their peasants was modified by requiring manorial services to be entered in official registers. Haugwitz also undertook military reforms. By securing a ten years' grant of funds from the various estates it was possible to build up through a kind of conscription an army of 108,000 troops, well-uniformed, well-officered and drilled on the Prussian model.

Maria Theresa's reforms were fundamental. An inexperienced young woman of twenty-three when she ascended the throne, she ultimately contrived to take those important steps which imposed a centralized, workable, bureaucratic rule upon her variegated possessions. As her son Joseph moved into a position of authority he was able to push the great administrative revolution still further.

In the public career of Joseph II enlightened despotism may be said to have reached its climax. This extraordinary figure, who died on the eve of his forty-ninth birthday protesting that his life's work had been a failure, somehow mingled the confident philosophy of the Age of Reason with the deeply distrustful outlook of a curiously tortured personality. Maria Theresa had given elaborate attention to her son's upbringing, surrounding him with scholars, priests, soldiers and men of affairs. Yet he seemed fated to unhappiness. The death of his twenty-one-year-old wife of smallpox after three idyllic years left him heartbroken. When he received the ancient title of King of the Romans at Frankfort in the following year he complained to his mother of "the trash and idiocies" to which he had been compelled to listen all day. Even in his most vigorous and seemingly most successful period Joseph could not avoid the sense of frustration. "Everything is in arrears," he wrote to his brother Leopold in 1773, "nothing is done, people kill themselves for nothing and affairs go from bad to worse."

On the death of the Emperor Francis I in 1765 Joseph was elected to the imperial throne, at the same time being invited by his mother to serve with her as co-regent of the Hapsburg lands. Though unable to give absolutely free rein to his own ideas, he could now participate actively in the reform program which she had launched and which appealed to his every instinct. Only in the ten years between 1780 and 1790 when, following the death of his mother, Joseph ruled in his own right could he undertake those full, sweeping and perhaps reckless measures from which he hoped so much.

Joseph's general purpose was to bring order, progress and efficiency to his widespread possessions by means of a rationally planned program of reform. These reforms should be uniformly applied under the firm guidance of the central authority. Had Joseph been more willing to compromise, to accept differences and to be grateful for small mercies, he would have run into much less trouble. He seemed, however, committed to a complete program and would settle for nothing less.

The reform work was intended to touch every aspect of public life. After 1780 Joseph tended to dispense with the Imperial Council, relying more upon the advice of individual statesmen. In a political sense he wished to complete his mother's work of centralization. The provincial diets, once centers of local opposition, were helpless, for they could meet only on the royal summons. Bohemia had been fully co-ordinated and cowed. The Italian provinces in Lombardy made little difficulty. The occasion, therefore, seemed ripe for further moves.

In Hungary Joseph abandoned Maria Theresa's *douce violence* for a vigorous attack upon the privileges of the Magyar nobility. The Hungarian Diet was weakened and ignored. Austrian governors were appointed for Hungary and Transylvania, a large corps of civil servants was sent in, German became the official language, conscription was introduced and as a final blow to Magyar pride the famous iron crown of St. Stephen was transferred from Budapest to Vienna. Somewhat similar policies of assimilation were attempted in the Austrian Netherlands. In both cases the outcome was to be protest and revolt.

In the judicial sphere Joseph employed the Supreme Court which his mother had established as a means of supervising and regulating the provincial and local courts of justice. Better training was provided for law officers. Some courts were abolished and others transformed. A Civil Code dealing with persons and property was promulgated in 1786, a Penal Code in 1787. Marriage was declared a civil contract. In keeping with the humane trends of the time the death penalty was abolished for most crimes, a system of appeals set up and class distinctions before the law terminated. All this work was of permanent value.

Important moves were made in economic matters. Here Joseph considered the great blight to be serfdom. A decree of September, 1781, gave the peasant for the first time legal right of appeal against his landlord's actions. In November, 1781, serfdom as a legal status was ended in the lands of the Austrian and Bohemian crowns, so that the peasants could hold land and marry freely without their lord's consent. In subsequent years this abolition was declared to apply to Hungary and Transylvania. The peasants, though now legally freed, were still burdened by heavy traditional dues to landlord, state and church. Joseph therefore ordered a great survey to be made of all his lands with the intention of replacing the complex burdens of the peasantry by a single land-tax. A decree, the so-called Urbarial Patent, was finally issued to this effect in 1789.[12] It was almost immediately repealed, however, by his brother and successor, Leopold, in 1790. In 1798 the bonds of serfdom in Austria were fully reestablished, to remain until the great revolution of 1848.

Joseph sought further means of economic improvement. He enjoyed the friendship of the famous Viennese professor and teacher of cameralism, Josef von Sonnenfels. He likewise regarded himself as a Physiocrat, maintaining a correspondence with the distinguished French writer and public servant, Turgot. In this tradition he sought to end the selfish privileges of the old gilds and to lift many of the restrictive controls which his mother had put upon industry. To some extent this was done, trade and manufacture becoming considerably freer. A tariff, nevertheless, was retained about the Hapsburg lands as a whole. The emperor built a highway, the Via Josephina, across the Carniolan Alps to the Adriatic. He gave titles to wealthy bourgeois. Some immediate prosperity seemed to arise from his reforms, revenues increasing substantially until the climactic year, 1787. Costs of administration, notably for the army, rose likewise so that Joseph's last years saw an acute

---

12. Under the servile system the peasant's disposition of his income has been summarized as follows:

    Payments to the Church .... 10 per cent
    Payments to the landlord .... 29 per cent
    Payments to the state .... 34 per cent
    Retained by the peasant .... 27 per cent

Under the Urbarial Patent the proposal was roughly as follows :

    Payment to the landlord .... 15 per cent
    Land tax to the state .... 15 per cent
    Retained by the peasant .... 70 per cent

economic depression.[13] Nevertheless, Joseph had taken important steps, not the least significant being to establish the beginnings of a free trade area or "customs union" in the great Danubian basin. He still lacked, however, the steadying support of an interested and substantial middle class.

Joseph also took action in the field of religion. In 1773 he had joined with his mother in banning the Jesuit Order, which had become widely unpopular throughout Europe. As a child of the Enlightenment Joseph had little patience with religious traditionalism, elaborate ceremonial and special privilege. His famous Patent of Toleration (1781) granted a wide degree of freedom in worship and belief, excluding only professed deists and atheists from its provisions. Toleration and freedom of worship were extended even to the Jews who, long subject to many disabilities, were now no longer required to wear a distinctive costume. The severe censorship of books and periodicals was also very much lightened.

Joseph's attempts to favor freedom of inquiry were sometimes blundering. When some students at the University of Innsbruck protested that one of their professors had taught that the creation of the world must be dated much earlier than B.C. 4004, Joseph ordered the complaining students to be sent home "because heads as poor as theirs cannot profit from education." It must also be recorded that three months before his death Joseph, alarmed by what he saw in France, terminated the freedom of the press and restored the censorship.

The Church had been calculated to hold three-eighths of the land in Austria. Joseph attacked the monasteries in a decree of 1781 which abolished the contemplative orders, with the result that some 700 out of more than 2,000 monasteries and convents were closed. About 38,000 monks and nuns out of a total of 65,000 were turned out of their houses. The wealth of the confiscated establishments was put into a special Religious Fund of which the income was to be used for charitable, educational and similar purposes. Joseph used some of the money to establish a General Hospital, a Lying-In Hospital, a Foundling Asylum, a Medical-Surgical Academy and an Institute for the Deaf and the Blind—steps which notably contributed to the rise of Vienna as a distinguished medical center. Joseph also sought to reduce church ceremonial, to limit its elaborate public processions and to reduce the public celebration of Saints' Days.

In general Joseph wished to bring the Church into dependence upon the state. The nomination of bishops lay in his hands. No papal bulls were to be issued without royal authorization. The clergy were to take an oath to the emperor and were forbidden to take cases being tried in church courts

13. This was the economic crisis which led Prince Kaunitz to limit the dinners served at his table to eight courses.

on appeal to Rome. This policy, known as "Josephism" or "Febronianism," caused such papal consternation that in 1782 Pius VII paid an urgent visit to Vienna, vainly seeking to persuade Joseph to reverse his policies.[14] Joseph continued on his path, setting up training schools for the clergy and seeking in general to make the Church a useful servant of the state.

Enlightened despotism involved, necessarily, the problem of education. Advised by the forward-looking Abbot Felbiger, Maria Theresa had issued the famous School Ordinance of 1774 providing that throughout her realms there should be an integrated scheme of elementary, technical and "Latin" schools (*Gymnasia*) as well as normal schools and universities. Funds for elementary schools were to be provided from local sources with the aid of state subsidies when these proved inadequate. Higher education should become more practical, with German as the universal language of instruction, and emphasis given to training for medicine, law and the civil service. Although Joseph's plans, which made primary education compulsory, were more impressive on paper than in fact, they remain as one of the most ambitious ventures of the Old Régime.

The pattern of a Hapsburg empire which emerged under Joseph's rule was that of a benign absolutism operating supposedly under uniform laws and procedures. Local privileges and liberties no longer were to be tolerated. The old provincial estates were mere shadows. The empire was divided symmetrically into thirteen states or provinces and these in turn into "circles" (*Kreise*). A bureaucratic system of boards and commissions conveyed the desires of the central authorities down to the local level.

In Joseph's last years the opposition to his reforms reached the stage of revolt. The introduction of German as an official language in non-German lands, the conscription, the suppression of local privileges all led to trouble. Disturbances arose in the two extreme limits of the realm, Hungary and the Austrian Netherlands. Unrest in Hungary caused Joseph as one of his last acts to revoke most of his reform measures. Trouble in the Netherlands arose from a series of edicts which, beginning with the Patent of Toleration of 1781, threatened the vested interests of the local authorities. The final crisis was produced by imperial decrees of 1787 which converted the historic states of the Austrian Netherlands into a single province divided into nine "circles" and subsidiary districts. The situation therefore differed from that which had provoked revolution in seventeenth-century England and in eighteenth-century America. In the case of Joseph II it was the monarch who took the side of reform and the revolutionary party which tried to defend the conservative interests. After various preliminary disturbances, an assembly at

14. The term, Febronianism, comes from "Febronius," the pen-name of Johan Nikolaus von Hontheim, a Rhineland bishop, who published his *De Statu Ecclesiae* in 1763 denouncing papal interference in civil matters.

Brussels in December, 1789, proclaimed the deposition of Joseph II and the foundation of the Republic of the United States of Belgium.

Amid these confusions, all the more frustrating because of a war with the Turks and news of revolutionary disturbances in France where his sister reigned as queen, Joseph II died in February, 1790. Six days before his death the desperately ill monarch had decreed that everything, save for the abolition of serfdom, should be restored to the condition at the time of the death of Maria Theresa. The epitaph which he composed for himself read: "Here lies Joseph II who was unfortunate in all his enterprises." It did the great reformer less than justice.

■ ENLIGHTENED DESPOTISM IN RUSSIA

The two great names of Peter I and Catherine II so dominate the stage of Russian history in the eighteenth century that all else tends to be obscured. Peter's immediate successors were, to be sure, so weak or corrupt as to deserve little attention, save in the case of his daughter Elizabeth who finally contrived to win the imperial throne in 1741, sixteen years after her father's death.

The reign of Elizabeth (1741–1762), though less famous than that of Peter I or Catherine II, nevertheless influenced the course of Russian history. She won the throne by a military *coup,* boldly riding in armor at the head of a regiment of guards. She relied heavily upon a succession of favorites. She permitted the Russian nobility, which Peter tried to make into a "service nobility," to regain their traditional local powers. The nobility became a "patrimonial" class with absolute authority on their estates. In consequence the serfs were reduced to an even more rigorous subjection. This period saw considerable economic growth. With state subsidies the manufacture of textiles, glass, porcelain and munitions developed substantially. The iron industry of the Urals was actually larger than that of any other country in Europe.[15]

Elizabeth was a staunch admirer of France and French culture. In her reign a notable current of French influence made itself felt in contrast to the "northern" and German influences which had prevailed under her predecessors. An Academy of Fine Arts was founded, visitors from abroad were encouraged, French books were circulated and French became the language of fashion. The University of Moscow was founded in 1755. Artistically, Elizabeth's tastes were essentially those of the age of Rococo. Through her patronage an Italian, Bartolommeo Rastrelli, became Russia's chief architect. Among his works were the building or rebuilding of the new Summer Palace, the Winter Palace at St. Petersburg and the Great Palace at Tsarskoe Selo. Something, therefore, of the spirit of enlightened despotism can be said to have entered Russia during the reign of this predecessor of Catherine II.

Elizabeth's immediate successor in 1762 was her nephew, Peter III, whom she had groomed for the emperorship. She likewise had arranged the marriage of this dissolute and subnormal nephew to the sixteen-year-old daughter of an obscure German princeling—a bride subsequently known to history as Catherine the Great. Catherine seems to have accepted the husband, whom she despised, as a means to power. Peter III met his death six months after his accession during a palace revolt in which Catherine openly participated. Such was the bloody beginning of her reign.

This empress of German parentage and French culture contrived, nevertheless, to identify herself with Russia, accepting its religion, learning its language and ardently championing its causes. Like Peter the Great, she launched upon a militant foreign policy which won her rich returns and a distinguished European reputation. At home she undertook to bring about many changes, making frequent references to the "philosophic" writers of the eighteenth century with whose works she was familiar. She knew and corresponded with such leading figures as Voltaire, Diderot, Grimm and d'Holbach. These men obviously welcomed and made much of their imperial friendship. Diderot professed to find in Catherine "the soul of Brutus and the charms of Cleopatra." In her various reforms, therefore, Catherine had what we would call a good press—a consideration to be kept in mind in attempting an evaluation of her work.

Catherine's intentions with respect to the government of Russia were displayed in the history of the celebrated Legislative Commission which she summoned in 1767. This impressive body of 564 members was the first attempt to represent the whole nation since the meetings of the venerable assembly, the *Zemsky Sobor,* in the sixteenth and seventeenth centuries.[16] Its purpose was to redraft into one code the vast body of imperial and local legislation so as to provide Russia with the basis for an orderly and rational government. Catherine issued a famous *Instruction* (1767) for the guidance of her servants—a document full of fine phrases from Montesquieu and Beccaria ("The people do not exist for the ruler, but the ruler for the people"), and yet hardly disguising her autocratic purpose ("The ruler is the source of all civil and political power"). After holding more than two hundred meetings, the members in 1768 turned over their work to subcommittees. These met intermittently until 1775, by which time Catherine seems to have forgotten all about them.

16. The membership of the Legislative Commission was as follows: nobility, 161; townsmen, 208; peasants, 79; Cossacks, 54; "foreign peoples" from the Asian steppes, 34; government representatives, 28.

In a more concrete and practical sense, Catherine's chief reform was the Administrative Decree of 1775. This undertook a large-scale reorganization of the twenty provinces (*Gubernia*) into which Peter I had divided Russia. There were now to be fifty such units, each with from 300,000 to 400,000 inhabitants and each with a governor appointed by the empress. The governor would be aided by nominated boards which dealt with administration, finances and justice. The courts were divided into civil and criminal branches. The provinces in turn were divided into districts, each with 20,000 to 30,000 inhabitants and a set of local officials. The fundamental principle remained that of centralization in the hands of the sovereign; hardly any element of genuine self-government was conceded.

Catherine made little use of the Senate which Peter I had created, and she actually abolished some of his "collegiate" administrative boards. Her first reliance was upon herself, her second was upon those favorites with whom she successively dallied and her third was upon the nobility as a class. To favor them she issued a Letter of Grace in 1785 defining their prerogatives. They were to be exempted in general from military service, from personal taxation and from corporal punishment. They had absolute powers over their peasants. They had various economic rights, such as being able to buy and sell land freely, set up factories, sink mines and engage in trade if they desired. The essence was contained in one striking phrase. Catherine declared that henceforth the nobles were to be "an estate . . . separated by its rights and privileges from the rest of the people."

For the townsmen, a very small minority of the total population, Catherine likewise issued a Charter in 1785, recognizing that those with the necessary property qualifications formed a separate estate. Such people were exempt from military service, obtained tax favors and were granted supposed rights of local self-government which turned out to be largely illusory.

Catherine's reign was marked by tremendous peasant unrest, due in part to the repressive policies of her predecessor. In 1773 the great Pugachev revolt flared up in south Russia, led by Pugachev, an illiterate Don Cossack. The peasants rose against their lords and seized a number of cities in an orgy of violence. Regular troops drove Pugachev down the Volga and finally captured him. He was brought to Moscow in a specially built iron cage, then hanged, drawn and quartered. Henceforth Catherine renounced any plans to ameliorate the lot of the serfs, so that her reign was in this respect a capitulation to the landed class. She gave large parts of the royal domain to her favorite nobles, and transferred 800,000 crown peasants to private ownership as serfs. Peasant allotments grew smaller and their services heavier. Catherine's view of serfdom is tersely summarized in one sentence of a letter to Diderot: "Landowners do whatever seems good to them on their estates except inflict capital punishment; that is forbidden." The verdict of a recent student that for the Russian peasant the "enlightened" Catherine was a blight and a calamity does not seem unjustified.

Catherine's religious policies reflect her own nature. She abandoned her native Lutheranism for the Russian Orthodox faith as a part of the attempt to identify herself with her new realm. She gave shelter to the Jesuits when their order was dissolved by Clement XIV in 1773. Some wealthy Jews were granted the right of holding municipal office. Administratively, her concern was to maintain close control over the Russian Church. Hence she carried out Peter III's intention of taking control of all church lands. These were put under the direction of a special commission which employed the revenues to maintain the clergy and to support some ecclesiastical schools, hospitals and asylums. About two million "church peasants" became government serfs.

Catherine's economic policies resembled in general those of the Physiocrats. Her purpose was to make trade as free as possible within Russian borders, to end the old state monopolies and encourage private enterprise. Her greatest successes were in the export trade where a series of commercial treaties with foreign countries made possible a sharp rise in a large variety of Russian exports. This trade, which was conducted largely through the Baltic, was supplemented by a growing commerce on the Black Sea and with Asia. Between 1762 and 1796 Russia's foreign trade grew fourfold. Manufactures made some progress, for the Russian noblemen, unlike those in France, were encouraged to undertake industrial ventures many of which depended upon manorial factories operated by servile labor. Nevertheless, by 1794 only four per cent of European Russia's population could be classified as urban.

Catherine also made some name for herself as a patron of the arts, as a sponsor of French culture and, somewhat paradoxically, as a sponsor of Russian nationalism. She took some interest in education, though how important her achievements were may be questioned. The empress founded a few schools and in 1786 accepted the recommendations of a school commission that a national system of elementary education be set up. These recommendations never became effective. On Catherine's death in 1796, "Russia's entire educational apparatus comprised the University of Moscow and the provincial academies; the Smolny Institute for the daughters of poor but deserving noblemen; some technical schools and gymnasia for the well-to-do; a large number of miserable village schools kept by the clergy; and private schools established by benevolent landlords for their own serfs. Of free public elementary schools there were in the entire vastness of Russia only slightly more than 300, staffed by only 600 or so teachers." [17]

17. GERSHOY, *From Despotism to Revolution*, p. 280.

Catherine II's claims to be regarded truly as an enlightened despot would seem to be much less than those of Frederick II or Joseph II. Her interests were too closely identified with those of the landed aristocracy whose prestige and economic power she enormously strengthened. It may be true that her reign first witnessed the scattered appearance of those free-thinking types, the "conscience-stricken nobility." Yet when the most notable of them, Alexander Radishchev, wrote his outspoken *Journey from St. Petersburg to Moscow* (1790) describing the evils of serfdom he was first sentenced to death and then banished to Siberia. The enormous difficulties in a country like Russia may serve as a partial extenuation of Catherine's failure. The question, however, can be asked whether she ever really intended to set her country on the path of reform as Joseph II hopefully sought to do in his realms. She widened the cleavage between the ruling class and the people. In large part her reforms were a façade behind which the ruthless power of an autocratic state still prevailed.

■ ENLIGHTENED DESPOTISM IN THE LESSER STATES

Many of the lesser European states exhibited during the eighteenth century the characteristics of enlightened despotism. That they should have done so is hardly surprising, seeing that the problems confronting governments were widely similar in their general nature while the rulers, often related by blood, tended to resemble each other closely in their training and outlook. The persuasive spirit of the Enlightenment spread so widely that few statesmen or rulers were entirely alien to it.

Italy was by no means as generally decadent as is often assumed. Old commercial centers such as Genoa and Venice were, to be sure, in decline. The Papal States displayed little vitality. In other areas, nevertheless, a considerable vigor was evident. Piedmont, for example, under the rule of Charles Emmanuel III (1730–1773) exhibited surprising strength. The little kingdom of three million people played an important part in European affairs, acquired some Lombard territory and, above all, developed a well-organized administration with uniform laws and an equitable tax system. The power of the Church was restricted and serfdom ended. The generally progressive tendencies of the Piedmontese state were unfortunately curbed, however, by the spirit of reaction which set in during the reign of Charles Emmanuel's immediate successor.

In Tuscany an impressive reform program was undertaken by Leopold, brother of Joseph II of Austria, who ruled from 1765 until 1790. Less spectacular than Joseph, Leopold nevertheless undertook to reorganize taxes and finances, to build roads, drain marshes, encourage scientific farming and remove those internal tariffs which hampered trade. Serfdom was gradually ended. A uniform penal code which forbade the use of torture and capital punishment was introduced. The Inquisition was banned, some monasteries were suppressed and papal interference rebuffed. Native Tuscans were put into government office. When Leopold left in 1790 to succeed Joseph as Holy Roman Emperor he had performed an impressive work of enlightened reform. His work found some echo in the Kingdom of Naples, where Don Carlos, son of Elizabeth Farnese of Spain, ruled from 1735 to 1759. Here administrative improvements, largely inspired by the king's gifted adviser, the Marquis of Tanucci, were made.

The Iberian Peninsula experienced some of the same reforming tendencies. Charles, King of Naples, became Charles III of Spain in 1759, bringing with him to that decaying land an ardent interest in reform. At Madrid he faced a situation of complete political, economic and cultural stagnation. In coping with this Charles was notably aided by several talented Spanish noblemen, Count Aranda, Count Campomanes and, later, Count Floridablanca, all well-read in the works of the *philosophes*. Having repressed the violent Madrid riots of 1766 which broke out in opposition to some aspects of his reforms, Charles soon ordered the expulsion of the Jesuits whom he suspected of inspiring much of the opposition. He also reduced the powers of the Inquisition. His political reforms sought a more efficient centralization, chiefly by setting up a Council of State (1783) which combined in one body the authority formerly exercised by various boards or "colleges." In economic matters the king tried to break down the privileges of the aristocratic sheep farmers who, along with the Church, controlled huge expanses of the Spanish countryside. Success was not easy, nor was it possible to do much to provide land for a new class of small, independent farmers. Charles' various aids to manufacture and commerce constituted a kind of Neo-Colbertism. He built roads and canals, established a new postal system, a new coinage and new weights and measures. He lowered and in some cases abolished the internal customs duties, and tried to destroy the powers of the various gilds. With the encouragement given to the manufacture of silks, woolens and cotton cloth, Spain's foreign trade increased five-fold during the reign. The methodical and well-intentioned Charles died in 1788, on the very eve of the French Revolution. No king since Philip II had so strongly impressed himself upon his country. None in an equal time had done so much. Yet the tragedy of Charles III's work was that he could not perpetuate it.

Enlightened despotism in Portugal is associated more closely with a royal minister, Sebastian Joseph Carvalho, Marquis of Pombal, than it is with the Portuguese monarchy. From 1750 to 1777 Pombal was principal minister to Joseph I of Portugal and for most of the time virtual dictator. He made his first great reputation by his vigorous handling of the great Lisbon earthquake disaster of 1755 when 30,000 persons died. Pombal's reforms were introduced in a backward country where an arrogant, privileged nobility exploited a wretched peasantry. Pombal ruthlessly employed royal power to balance the finances, to simplify legal machinery, reorganize the army, build schools, stimulate commerce and subsidize manufactures. He tried, with fair success, to revive trade with the Portuguese colonies. Never scrupling to use violence and espionage for his ends, Pombal did not adopt remedies adequate to meet his country's grave political and economic weaknesses. Utterly unable to arrest Portugal's steady decline, he fell from power in 1777 on the death of his royal master.

In some of the lesser German states, a modest pattern of enlightened leadership was in evidence. Karl Friedrich of Baden, whose long reign stretched from 1748 to 1816, initiated reforms that reflected almost every action of the great Joseph II. He freed the serfs on the grand-ducal estates, encouraged manufactures and scientific agriculture, welcomed immigrants, proclaimed religious toleration, reformed the tax structure and built schools. Karl August, Duke of Saxe-Weimar from 1775 to 1828, made his duodecimo principality a center of German artistic and intellectual life. Among many others, the great names of Goethe, Schiller and Herder were inseparably connected with this "German Athens."

The Scandinavian kingdoms also contributed their share. In the Danish-Norwegian realm, the royal absolutism of the late seventeenth century was followed by long periods of decadence and political intrigue. In Sweden the *Riksdag,* or assembly of estates, had managed to regain so much power that the country appeared almost to be a republic with a monarchical façade. In 1756, for example, the *Riksdag* boldly informed King Frederick that kings in general are the natural enemies of their subjects and can exist only on sufferance. Gustavus III, who came to the throne in 1771, was steeped in contemporary French literature and culture. By a *coup* in 1772 he assured his own power, revised the constitution and governed for twenty years as an enlightened despot. For a time he worked with the *Riksdag,* eventually, however, choosing to act alone. His program was so similar in pattern to the work of the rulers already described that it need not be itemized. By 1792 his reign had become a true despotism in which the nobility now were his principal opponents. Gustavus died during a midnight masquerade at the Stockholm Opera, shot in the back by a leader of the aristocratic conspiracy against him.

The fantastic ministry of Count Struensee in Denmark is a minor yet intriguing aspect of the history of enlightened despotism. Christian VII, who became king in 1766, was dissolute and without question mad. A young German, Johann Friedrich Struensee, who became court physician and thus indispensable to the monarch, contrived also to win the queen as his paramour. Then, in 1770, Struensee maneuvered so as to get control of the government. A veritable torrent of reform legislation followed. In ten months Struensee issued 1069 ordinances, or an average of three a day. The old council of state, the *Rigsraad,* was abolished. A new machinery of administration, directly responsible to the crown, was set up. Vested interests and ancient privileges of all kinds were attacked. Struensee decreed freedom of trade, religious toleration, new educational opportunities, judicial reforms and equality of all before the law. Such sweeping measures provoked an inevitable reaction. In January, 1772, a group of noble conspirators won the ear of the mad king and persuaded Christian to order Struensee's arrest. The minister was charged with breaking the fundamental law (*Kongelov*) through issuing decrees without the royal signature. He was executed by being publicly hewn to pieces. Although the reactionaries then annulled Struensee's legislation, something of value remained. This fanatical propagandist of the ideas of the Enlightenment had at least indicated the great areas where reforms were needed, leaving it for others to undertake them at a later date and by less impetuous means.

Poland's political decline and final disappearance from the map would seem to set it apart from the course of enlightened reform as seen in other countries. Nevertheless, even here an element of this spirit of progress marked the last days of Polish independence. After the first partition of 1772 King Stanislas led a movement of national regeneration. Influenced in part by the ideals of the *philosophes,* this movement was also stimulated by a distinguished group of Polish intellectuals and political leaders. The general suppression of the Jesuit Order in 1773 gave the Polish government substantial revenues, some of which were used for educational purposes. An Educational Commission sought to reorganize methods of teaching and to revive the decayed universities at Vilna and Cracow. A considerable economic revival occurred with some building of factories and growth in trade. A decree of 1788 ended the life-and-death power of nobles over their serfs. In some cases serfs actually were freed. Efforts were made to reorganize and liberalize the system of town government. The final great step came with the Constitution of 1791 which turned Poland from an elective to a hereditary monarchy, with ministerial responsibility and a parliament elected for two-year terms. In effect Poland obtained a constitution very similar to that which France established in the same year. Unhappily, these enlightened measures taken within Poland only precipitated the determination of its neighbors to proceed with a second and then a third partition so that by 1795 Polish independence was extinguished for more than a century. The Polish reformers sought the right measures at a tragically wrong time.

VOLTAIRE

ROUSSEAU

Chapter 21

The Crisis
of the French Monarchy

■ PROBLEMS OF GOVERNMENT IN THE EIGHTEENTH CENTURY

FRANCE HELD a unique place in the history of the eighteenth century. To its European neighbors the great achievements of the age of Louis XIV were not easily forgotten. With a population of some 16 millions in 1715, rising to perhaps 25 millions in 1789, France could be regarded as the most powerful state in Europe. Its overseas empire, even though greatly weakened in 1763, was still large, its commercial prosperity unquestioned. In Paris a *salon* life of rare charm and sophistication developed—the perfect setting for a

556

MONTESQUIEU

DIDEROT

CRITICS OF THE REGIME
The statue of Voltaire by Houdon is in
the Théatre Français; the bust of Montesquieu by Lemoyne, in the Museum of Bordeaux; and the busts of Diderot by Pigalle
and Rousseau by Houdon, in the Louvre.
Courtesy, Caisse Nationale des Monuments
Historiques, Paris.

gifted circle of writers. Frenchmen, however, were denied the active political
life of their English contemporaries. They could intrigue for court sinecures
and they could serve the state as agents of the royal will, but they had no
way to express themselves in any elected or genuinely parliamentary capacity.

Monarchy gave no leadership to eighteenth-century France, for neither
Louis XV nor his grandson, Louis XVI, had the qualities of an enlightened
despot. Their ministers, generally skilful in the conduct of foreign affairs,
were markedly ineffective in domestic matters. Enlightened despotism may
have had this influence upon France, that it won writers such as Voltaire and
Diderot to be its ardent admirers and advocates. In sum, France offered the
paradox of a country where a growing commercial prosperity and a thriving
intellectual life existed in the company of governmental incompetence and
under the mounting shadow of public bankruptcy.

The political narrative of French history in the eighteenth century runs
in oversimplified summary as follows. From 1715 to 1723 France was under
the corrupt rule of the Orléans regency, at the close of which Louis XV, then
thirteen, technically came of age. A brief period (1724–1726) dominated by
the Duke of Bourbon followed. Louis then entrusted the control of affairs

557

to Cardinal Fleury whose long ministry (1726–1743) paralleling that of Robert Walpole in England resembled it in many respects. Fleury gave France a sober, able and markedly successful administration. The ensuing period (1743–1774) was the age of Louis XV's personal government—an age of complete political cynicism and moral deterioration, of royal mistresses and petticoat government and of an inescapable decline in monarchical popularity. When finally the well-intentioned but utterly weak Louis XVI became king in 1774 neither he nor his queen proved equal to the situation. A rapid succession of ministers grappled vainly with the related problems of administration and finances. Some were distinguished, some appeared charlatans, all were unsuccessful. By 1788 a financial crisis of the first order was at hand.

The government of France retained in general the structure which it had at the time of Louis XIV.[1] A hereditary monarch claiming divine authority governed with the help of royal appointees who made up the various branches of the Royal Council. He was also served by the heads of the several ministries whom he likewise appointed. In some provinces *Parlements* existed (thirteen in all), acting as courts to register royal edicts and to perform local administrative duties. Some provinces also claimed the right to have provincial estates; these were not legislatures but rather privileged bodies of office-holders assisting in the work of administration. The most effective agents of the central government were the intendants, of whom there were about thirty, each exerting large powers in an area known as a *généralité*, usually corresponding to an old province.[2]

France was stamped everywhere with the marks of privilege and inequality. The southern half of France, very roughly, was administered under the "written law" derived from Rome (*pays du droit écrit*); the northern half was administered under the unwritten, "customary law" derived from the usages of the early Frankish tribes (*pays du droit coutumier*). Justice, if such it can be called, was enforced through a chaotic series of royal, manorial and ecclesiastical courts so confused as to defy any clear understanding. Arbitrary arrest under a royal order (*lettre de cachet*) was always possible. The bribery of judges was notorious, while special privileges were available for the nobility and clergy. In general, centralization was supposedly operative, but it was scandalously inefficient. "A strict rule," wrote De Tocqueville, "a loose enforcement."

The practice of Louis XIV had been to rely largely upon public officials drawn from the middle class rather than from the aristocracy. These officials usually acquired titles, so that the category of "nobility of the robe," in

1. For details see pp. 328–331.
2. In 1789 there were 40 provinces, or *gouvernements,* and 34 intendancies, or *généralités.*

FRANCE *in* 1789

0   100   200   MILES

R. RHINE

Arras   Douai

Rouen

Metz

Paris

Nancy

Rennes

Colmar

Dijon   Besançon

Grenoble

Bordeaux

Aix

Toulouse

Pau

Perpignan

PAYS D'ÉTAT

■ PROVINCIAL PARLEMENTS

— PROVINCIAL BOUNDARIES

BOUNDARY BETWEEN
DROIT COUTUMIER *and* DROIT ÉCRIT

Note the extension of frontiers since 1461 (page 87). Variations in size of provinces and
differences in law and government suggest the confusions of the Old Régime.

contrast to the "nobility of the sword," won public prominence. The purchase of office and its transmission in many cases from father to son served
as a major impediment to efficiency. One of the characteristics of the eighteenth century had been the growth in various countries of trained, professional bureaucracies acting under the direction of a strong, central power.
This was not true of France. Men of ability and training there undoubtedly

were, yet they could make little headway against the paralyzing tendencies of the system as a whole.

■ SOCIAL AND ECONOMIC CONDITIONS

Social and economic conditions in France may be considered together, for economic privilege was closely tied to social status. The king administered a realm of three estates. First came the clergy, or spiritual lords, then the nobility, or temporal lords, and finally the "Third Estate," or the commoners. The privileges and disabilities of these three classes go far to explain the critical situation that slowly evolved in France.

The First Estate, the clergy, numbered some 130,000 of whom about 60,000 were "regulars," that is, members of monastic orders, and about 70,000 were "seculars," that is, engaged in the usual priestly and parochial duties. A more important distinction was that between the upper and the lower clergy. Nomination to bishoprics and abbacies was in the hands of the king, which meant that members of noble families could obtain high church rank with little regard to their spiritual qualifications. Talleyrand, Count of Périgord, surely one of the worst of all French bishops, entered the church because his nurse dropped him as an infant, permanently injuring his foot and making impossible a career in the army. In 1785 a French cardinal became involved in the "diamond necklace affair," spending a million and a half francs for a necklace which he thought would win him the favors of Marie Antoinette, and holding moonlight assignations in the Tuileries gardens with an adventuress impersonating the queen. In 1789 every French bishop was of noble birth.

In contrast to the worldliness and scandal which characterized the behavior of a large part of the upper clergy the lives of the parish priests were marked by a general dedication to their calling. Seeing that many of them were of humble origin, it is understandable that in the early days of the Revolution, before the attacks on religion began, they should have tended to side with the reformers rather than with the defenders of privilege.

The Roman Catholic Church held great landed wealth, estimated at somewhere between six and ten per cent of the total soil of France. From this it drew a valuable income. In addition it had the income from the tithe, an annual collection of about one-thirteenth of the value of all farm and dairy produce in France. Although the clergy were exempt from regular taxation, at periodical intervals their general assembly voted "free gifts" to the king. Their position, in summary, was emphatically one of privilege.

The nobility, who may have numbered some 400,000, were marked by great variations in dignity, wealth and outlook. In addition to the ancient nobility "of blood" and "of the sword" was the newer, administrative nobility "of the robe." Many others, hardly distinguishable from the peasantry, lived boorishly and meagerly on their farms, claiming the various privileges due them because of their noble lineage. Some nobles, the court group, spent their time at Versailles fawning upon the monarch. To win his sometimes substantial favors they endured almost intolerable inconveniences and endless boredom. Some enlightened nobles gave themselves to the stimulating life of the Paris *salons,* toying with ideas which often must have seemed dangerously at variance with the selfish interests of their class. Some followed the conventional noble career of military service in the French army, where a commission could be granted only to one of noble birth. In marked contrast to English practice, few of the French nobility concerned themselves seriously with pursuing the new developments in scientific agriculture and improving their estates. "Whenever you stumble on a Grand Seigneur," the English traveler Arthur Young noted in 1787, "even one that was worth millions, you are sure to find his property desert. . . . Go to their residence, wherever it may be, and you would probably find them in the midst of a forest, very well peopled with deer, wild boars and wolves. Oh! if I were the legislator of France for a day, I would make such great lords skip again."

Among the Third Estate the bourgeois groups have been estimated to number about two millions.[3] Their upper segment showed notable prosperity. This group included the merchants engaged in overseas trade, the West Indian sugar planters, the silk manufacturers of Lyons and the makers of porcelains, cloths and various luxury goods. Between 1715 and 1789 French annual exports grew fourfold. A commercial treaty with England in 1786 seemed to promise a steadily increasing and mutually advantageous exchange of goods. The growth of French industrial life, second only to that of England, deserves emphasis. Large-scale enterprises were still exceptional and "manufacture" was for the most part literally by hand. Nevertheless, France took quick advantage of the new inventions—flying shuttles, spinning jennys and water frames—which England had devised. It likewise made solid advances of its own in mining and metallurgy. "The Revolution," Mathiez has written, "was not to break out in an exhausted country, but, on the contrary, in a flourishing land on a rising tide of progress." [4]

The prosperity won by some parts of the French bourgeoisie stood in marked contrast to their conditions in other respects. Socially, they were snubbed on all sides by the aristocracy. When Voltaire satirized a nobleman, his response was to send lackeys to horsewhip the injudicious author, who

3. The population of Paris in 1789 was about 650,000. Lyons had 135,000, Marseilles, 90,000, Bordeaux, 76,000 and Rouen, 72,000.
4. A. MATHIEZ, *The French Revolution* (1929), p. 12.

subsequently could find no recourse at law. Madame Roland, a respectable member of the provincial bourgeoisie, recalled in her memoirs how she and her mother when visiting an aristocratic neighbor were invited to stay for lunch, only to find that they were required to take their meal with the servants. Barnave, a leader of the revolutionary era, was powerless to prevent his wife from being rudely expelled from a theater box by an arrogant nobleman. On a more substantial level, the bourgeoisie had to assume the burden of tax payments from which the nobility and clergy were largely exempt. Under such circumstances it is not surprising that many bourgeois were avid readers of the new literature of social criticism, that they joined the literary and debating societies (the *sociétés de pensée*) where such works were read and discussed and that they were in the forefront of the reforming activities of 1789.

The peasantry numbered about 22 millions out of a total population of 25 millions. It should be noted parenthetically that the French word, *paysan,* literally means a country-dweller and includes a wide variety of types, from the serf at the bottom of the scale to the comfortably-off farmer at the top. A million or so Frenchmen were serfs, largely in the newly-acquired lands on the eastern borders. Five million could be classed as landless day-laborers (*roturiers*). By far the largest number were *métayers,* a term usually trans- lated as "share-croppers," farming a piece of land and turning over about half the crop to the landlord. The number of fifteen million would include these *métayers* and other peasants perhaps owning small portions of land and farming other land by dependent tenures. Those peasants who truly owned their land free of major encumbrances (*francs-alleux* or *laboureurs*) may have numbered about a million.

The picture of the French peasantry as an utterly miserable, half-human class, ground down by their lords, does not tally with the evidence. Arthur Young's vivid *Travels in France,* telling of conditions in 1787, 1788 and 1789, conveys a mixed impression of prosperous countryside alternating with other areas of acute poverty. The trend to peasant ownership in the eighteenth century was definite. Moreover, the French peasant without any doubt was far better off than his counterpart in central and eastern Europe.

What must be stressed about the French rural classes is the burden of taxation and services, at times almost intolerable, they were forced to carry. The nobility and clergy being practically free from taxes, the load fell all the more heavily upon the peasantry who constituted almost nine-tenths of the population. They were subject to manorial, ecclesiastical and royal exactions.[5] The tithe which they paid the church may have averaged one-

5. The famous French historian, Taine, is responsible for the often-quoted but clearly unverifiable statement that the peasant on the average gave 14 francs out of every hundred

fifteenth of their income. The heavy taxes to the state included the *taille* (originally a payment instead of military service), the *capitation* (a poll-tax) and the *vingtième* (an income tax amounting to about 11 per cent). The indirect taxes included the famous *gabelle* (on salt), the *aides* (excise taxes) and the *traites* or *douanes* (customs dues). The peasant also paid another royal tax, the *corvée*. This required all country dwellers living within five or ten miles of royal highways to contribute the labor necessary for their maintenance. The peasant suffered under the further grievances that the collection of these taxes was "farmed," that is, let out to contractors who profited hugely from them; that the privileged groups were largely exempt; that the taxes varied greatly from one part of France to another and that the proceeds were spent with obvious extravagance.

The manorial dues, though less in amount than the royal taxes, were even more keenly felt. It must be emphasized that although actual serfdom was of minor consequence, most of the soil of France was burdened with services, both personal and monetary, surviving from medieval times. Even those peasants who had bought land found that the landlords often retained the title-deeds and continued to demand various services. Some of these were the old manorial payments in money or produce; others, more deeply resented, required labor services. Most exasperating of all were the *capitaineries,* or hunting rights, which prevented the farmer from driving off the game which ate his crops and permitted the lord of the manor to hunt freely over newly-planted fields. After 1750 there seems to have been a growing tendency for the landlords to reexamine their title-deeds and discover neglected sources of revenue to which they were legally entitled. They then proceeded to collect these additional sums. This "feudal reaction," coming at a time of sharp growth in population and rising food prices, added greatly to the general resentment. The period was punctuated by recurrent crises and near-famines. Poor housing and clothing, frequent epidemics, vagrancy, begging, coarse and inadequate food all took their toll. Two days before the fall of the Bastille, Arthur Young made the following entry in his journal:

> Walking up a long hill to ease my mare, I was joined by a poor woman who complained of the times and that it was a sad country. . . . It was said, at present, that something was to be done by some great folks for such poor ones, but she did not know who nor how, but God send us better, for the *taille* and the manorial rights are crushing us. This woman, at no great distance, might have been taken for 60 or 70, her figure was so bent and her face so furrowed and hardened by labor; but she said she was only 28.

Although the mass of the peasantry were hardly vocal, this peasant problem was one of the important constituents of the mounting crisis.

---

he earned to the church, 14 more to his seigneur and 53 to the king, keeping only 19 for himself.

■ THE CRITICISMS OF THE PHILOSOPHES

Amid these stresses and strains of French life a remarkable body of liberal and critical thought developed. Those writers known as the *philosophes* were rarely philosophers in the technical sense. They were speculative thinkers, articulate social critics and skilled publicists, seeking to mold public opinion. Their intellectual equipment was an inheritance from Newton and Locke, tinctured by the skepticism of Bayle and Fontenelle. In general their purpose was to champion the claims of human intelligence, using the weapons of reason to attack all outworn systems of thought based upon tradition and authority. They hated intolerance, mobilizing their forces very strongly against organized religion which to them seemed to breathe the spirit of reaction. "Now is the time," Holbach wrote in his *System of Nature* (1771), "for reason, guided by experience, to attack at their source the prejudices of which mankind has so long been the victim."

Montesquieu and Voltaire were responsible more than any others, perhaps, for beginning the popularization of Newton and Locke on the continent. They both made skilful use of satire and criticism. Montesquieu's *Persian Letters* (1721) used the device of letters written by an imaginary Persian visitor to satirize French society. Voltaire's *Letters on the English* (1733) were the product of a visit abroad; they condemned, under cover of his praises of English life, the many abuses which he saw in France. He showed the same propagandist zeal in his novel, *Candide* (1759), and in his *Philosophical Dictionary* (1764). Describing France in *Candide,* Voltaire wrote as follows: "Imagine all the contradictions, all the possible incompatibilities, you will find them in the government, in the law courts, in the churches and in the theaters of this oddity amongst nations."

By mid-century a younger generation of writers mobilized an even more devastating attack. A strong current of philosophic materialism and of contempt for supernatural values was shown by men such as La Mettrie, Diderot, Condillac, Helvétius and Holbach. From another side, Rousseau, whose unique character kept him from ever being fully identified with the *philosophes,* launched important criticisms in his political treatise, the *Discourse on the Origins of Inequality* (1754); the *Social Contract* followed in 1762.

Diderot's great work was to publish the *Encyclopedia,* the seventeen volumes of which appeared between 1751 and 1765, soon followed by eleven volumes of plates and several supplementary volumes. Originally hired as a kind of literary hack to bring out a French revision of Chambers' English *Cyclopaedia,* Diderot determined to make a new synthesis of human knowledge that would embody the spirit of the Age of Reason. To that end he sought the assistance of his most distinguished contemporaries. The mathematician, D'Alembert, wrote the famous preliminary essay invoking the

Newtonian scientific method and Locke's empirical philosophy as a means of unifying all fields of knowledge. Buffon, Voltaire, Montesquieu, Holbach and Rousseau contributed articles. While much material was routine and much was adapted from earlier compilations, the *Encyclopedia* also exemplified the new spirit of criticism. Superstition and intolerance were attacked. Strong emphasis was given to the role of science, to new viewpoints in politics and to the creeds of humanitarianism and progress. The eleven fine volumes of plates devoted very largely to technology are an impressive display of eighteenth-century advances in industry and the arts. The *Encyclopedia* was twice suppressed—for a time in 1752 after the publication of the first two volumes and again in 1759 after five more volumes had appeared —a testimony in itself to the concern which the government felt over its influence. This influence can hardly be doubted. There were 4,300 subscribers to the original edition, following which six further editions were issued before the end of the century.

The propaganda of the *philosophes* was spread in various ways. Royal censorship was completely ineffective in curbing the publication of books, pamphlets, journals and newspapers. The *salons* carried on the tradition of urbane, sophisticated, critical talk that had first grown up in an earlier age. New ideas were spread in the theater. Clubs, local academies, debating societies, Masonic lodges, lending libraries and similar groups were remarkably active. In the circle of the *sociétés de pensée* it was possible for many intelligent and ambitious members of the bourgeois class to formulate and clarify their ideas. Here many of the subsequent leaders of the Revolution received their training.

How much these currents of critical thought contributed to the revolutionary crisis of 1789 has long been debated by historians. Some have gone even so far as to develop a theory of "conspiracy," arguing that a relatively small group of men deliberately inoculated France with the poison of dangerous ideas. Others have chosen instead to emphasize the insistent pressure of intolerable economic and social conditions. Taking a middle ground, one may recognize the contributing influence of the "critical spirit" at a time when the government seemed constantly to demonstrate its incompetence to deal with flagrant abuses.

None of the great *philosophes*, with the exception of Condorcet, lived to see the actual coming of revolution. Montesquieu died in 1755. Helvétius, Quesnay, Voltaire and Rousseau died in the decade of the 1770's, Condillac, D'Alembert, Diderot and Buffon in the 1780's. In 1767 Voltaire had prophesied to a correspondent that revolution would come in ten years' time. "A man of my age," he wrote, "will not see it, but we will die in the hope that men may become more enlightened and more gentle. . . . I shall not see

those beautiful days, but I shall see their dawning." In 1774 he wrote to
Turgot: "You are bringing to birth a beautiful century of which I shall see
only the earliest dawn. I foresee great changes, and France stands in need
of every one of them."

■ THE TWILIGHT OF THE MONARCHY, 1774–1789

The new king, Louis XVI, was a striking contrast to his grandfather
whom he succeeded in 1774. Virtuous, honest, pious and well-meaning, he
gave long hours to duties in which he took little real interest. His conduct
was marked by hesitancy and lack of initiative. He knew little of public
affairs. Easily influenced by his advisers, he found it almost impossible to
impose his will upon them. Louis XVI had no liking for the splendors of
monarchy. He spent hours at the table. His great passion was hunting; his
hobby, repairing locks. In 1770 he had married Marie Antoinette, fifteen-
year-old daughter of Maria Theresa of Austria. His queen was charming,
witty and frivolous. While innocent of the vicious charges that her enemies
made against her, she undoubtedly tended to engage in political intrigue
which injured the true interests of both France and the monarchy.

Louis attempted to meet the growing administrative and financial crises
by summoning one minister after another to deal with them. His first choice
was Turgot, the physiocratic minister and writer who had made a great
name for himself as intendant of the province of Limoges. Unfortunately,
Louis accompanied this action by resummoning the old *Parlements* which
immediately took up their earlier opposition to reform.[6] Turgot launched
a number of physiocratic reforms: economies in administration, free-trade
in grain throughout France, the suppression of the hated *corvée,* or compulsory work on the roads, and the abolition of the urban gilds on the
ground that they were interfering with freedom of enterprise.[7] He also established a Discount Bank to aid the government with loans in time of crisis.
These measures and others which contemplated large revisions of the tax
system would, if successful, have truly set France upon the path of enlightened despotism. In 1776, as a result of selfish intrigues in which Marie
Antoinette joined, Louis dismissed Turgot. This fateful decision can be regarded as one of the worst that Louis ever made, for it ended the prospect
of genuine monarchical reform.

6. In 1771 Louis XV, after a long quarrel with the *Parlement* of Paris, had dissolved it and
the provincial *Parlements.* He had then set up a body of 75 royal nominees called, after
Louis' chief adviser, the *"Parlement* Maupeou." By this means he had hoped to circum-
vent the growing opposition of the privileged classes.
7. The preamble to the decree of January, 1776, abolishing the gilds has the striking
sentence: "The right to work is the property of every man, the most sacred and inviolable
of all."

Turgot's successor, Necker, was a Genevan banker and Protestant whose financial expertness enabled him to grope through the maze of French finances for five years without disaster. He sought economies, naturally enough, and to this end issued in 1781 his famous Financial Statement (*Compte rendu*)—the first serious attempt to analyze in detail the financial status of the government. Opposition of the *Parlements,* the queen and the privileged classes in general forced Necker's resignation in May, 1781.

Henceforth government seemed to be a matter of expedients. Calonne (1783–1787) spent freely and floated enormous loans in the hope of reviving public confidence. Although for a time he had outward success he was compelled in 1786 to recommend the same type of economies that had been proposed by Turgot and Necker. Since these would almost certainly arouse the old opposition of the *Parlements,* Louis and Calonne decided to submit recommendations to an advisory body of 144 eminent figures known as the Assembly of Notables. This met in February, 1787, heard Calonne's proposals for economy and rejected them. Calonne was replaced by Loménie de Brienne, Archbishop of Toulouse.

The essence of the government's problem was finances. With about half of the government's expenditures devoted to debt services, and with tax-rates already heavy, the obvious solution was to ask the clergy and nobles to assume their fair share of the burden. The Notables agreed to some part of Brienne's schemes but rejected the key proposal for a general land-tax which all should pay. The young Marquis of Lafayette, fresh from his American adventures, made the striking proposal to summon the ancient Estates General. In May, 1787, Louis dismissed the Notables and submitted Brienne's measures to the *Parlements.* These, the inveterate champions of privilege, opposed the imposition of new taxes, saying that only the nation, meeting in the Estates General, could give assent to new taxes. When the *Parlement* of Paris objected to a royal *lit de justice* the king exiled the body from Paris (August, 1787). A month later, with typical lack of clear purpose, he restored it.

These conflicts between king, Notables and *Parlements* were accompanied during the spring of 1788 by disturbances in various parts of France. Some were occasioned by food scarcity and high prices, some were deliberately fomented by the king's noble opponents. Finally, Louis made the great decision. Promising to summon the Estates General which had last met in 1614, he issued a decree on July 5, 1788, requesting information from provincial and municipal officers concerning the method of convoking this ancient body. In August Brienne, having announced national bankruptcy, was dismissed and Necker for the second time assumed the position of principal royal adviser.

The immediate preliminaries to the summoning of the Estates General showed how tense the situation in France had become. The Notables, re-summoned in November to give advice, were clearly on the side of con-servatism. The close of 1788 witnessed a surprising torrent of pamphlet liter-ature, much of it championing that great majority of the French people, the Third Estate, whose rights seemed to have been flouted by the two privileged orders. The most famous of these pamphlets, *What is the Third Estate?* written by the Abbé Sieyès, appeared in January, 1789. It was a bold appeal to the French people to recognize that the Third Estate, rather than being one of three orders, was in reality a complete nation:

> I pray that they will keep in mind the enormous difference between the as-sembly of the third estate and that of the other two orders. The first represents 25,000,000 men, and deliberates concerning the interests of the nation. The two others, were they to unite, have the powers of only about 200,000 individ-uals, and think only of their privileges. The third estate alone, they say, cannot constitute the *Estates General.* Well! So much the better! It will form a *National Assembly.*

Louis XVI made only a partial concession to this viewpoint. A decree of December 27, 1788 ("A New Year's Gift for France"), announced that the Third Estate would have double representation—600 deputies as against 300 for each of the other orders. No promise was made, however, that these orders would all meet and vote as one body, in fact the traditional practice had been that they should meet separately.

Rules for the elections provided that the nobility and clergy would each choose their deputies in their own assemblies. For the Third Estate it was stipulated that every male who had reached the age of twenty-five and was registered on the tax-rolls could vote for electors who in turn would choose deputies. To determine how many were thus able to vote would now seem impossible. Nevertheless it is clear that the Third Estate was to be elected by a phenomenally broad franchise.

All local electoral groups, in accordance with an old tradition of the Es-tates General, were asked to submit formal statements of grievances (*cahiers de doléances*). Those of the nobility and clergy were usually drafted in their local assemblies. Those of the Third Estate were compiled in the secondary electoral assemblies from the more numerous first drafts composed in the local parishes. Although many of the *cahiers* show the influence of some model, they were a genuine expression of grievances and thus remain an invaluable source of information about the general state of public opinion in France. On the whole, this opinion was marked by its moderation.

A few generalizations about the opinions expressed in the *cahiers* may be listed. The three orders agreed in their opposition to despotic rule,

though expressing their personal loyalty to the king. They wished a hereditary monarchy, limited in power and having an elected, representative assembly to carry on the main work of government. They wished a general
guarantee of civil rights and a major revision of the tax system. The *cahiers*
of the peasants, not unnaturally, made bitter protests against manorial
dues and the unfair burden of taxes. Some of the bourgeois groups spoke
in scathing terms of the many privileges of the noble class. Members of
the lower clergy spoke out similarly against the privileges of the bishops
and the monastic orders. In sum, the *cahiers* gave evidence of widespread
demand for social, economic and political reform, while at the same time
offering no signs of violent, revolutionary intent. This in general was the
atmosphere which could be said to have marked France on the eve of the
meeting of the Estates General.

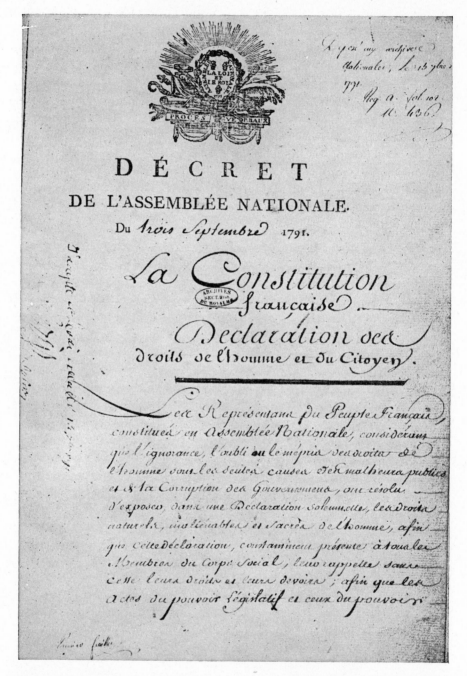

DECREE OF SEPTEMBER 3, 1791, PROCLAIMING THE NEW FRENCH CONSTITUTION. This first written constitution in the history of France, and one of the first in Europe, begins with the celebrated Declaration of the Rights of Man. Note Louis XVI's signature at the left side: "J'accepte." Courtesy, French Press and Information Division.

Chapter 22

The Revolution of Moderation
1789–1791

■ FROM ESTATES GENERAL TO CONSTITUENT ASSEMBLY

THE TREMENDOUS CHANGES taking place in France between 1789 and 1815 make up one of the great revolutionary epochs of modern times. On the one side of this decade lay the ordered, privileged society of the Old Régime. On the other was to emerge the very different bourgeois society of the nineteenth century. Because of the profound impact of these years the period has long commanded the detailed attention of many historians. Only in our own day, however, has a pattern of even more profound revolutions brought home the fact that the French Revolution was not a unique phenomenon but was rather a part of the endless flux of human affairs.

When the Estates General met in May, 1789, few could realize the full significance of the event. The French upper classes had so successfully opposed the efforts of Louis XVI's ministers to reform taxes and finances that their actions have been called a "privileged revolution"—a "feudal reaction" in relation to which the summoning of the Estates General stood as a "second revolution." It now became the turn of the royal ministers to mobilize the spokesmen of the French people in order to see what could be done to remedy the continuing financial crisis.

In one sense it is quite true to say that the summoning of the Estates General was not revolutionary in intent. Yet the pamphlets of 1788, the *cahiers* of grievances, and, even more, the attitude of the leading figures of the Assembly all show how widespread was the desire to end the era of privilege and to create a truly constitutional structure. Many members were ready to make sweeping changes, to equalize the burden of Frenchmen, to define and limit the powers of the monarchy, and to alter drastically the position and powers of the Roman Catholic Church. Though one may well doubt whether the deputies came to Versailles with the details of any such program clearly in mind, one cannot but be impressed by the speed with which the majority of them turned in the end to the great tasks of reform.

· The Estates General, meeting for the first time in 175 years, were an unwieldy body. The clergy, the First Estate, had 308 representatives; the nobility, or Second Estate, had 285 representatives; the Third Estate, representing the commoners, numbered 621.[1] The kind of leadership which the Estates General produced was on the whole impressive. Sieyès, Gobel and Grégoire may be taken as examples of churchmen who had been deeply influenced by the critical spirit of the eighteenth century and who stood ready to support a major pattern of reform. Soon to be the most famous of all the clerical representatives, Charles Maurice Talleyrand, Bishop of Autun, was marked less by intellectual brilliance or high purpose than by an extraordinary capacity to set his sails to the prevailing winds of doctrine and to advance his own fortunes. A nobleman like the Marquis of Lafayette, who had made a distinguished reputation in America and who in the assembly of the Notables had demanded the summoning of the Estates, commanded for a time a tremendous popularity and seemed destined to a spectacular career. Outwardly less promising was Count Mirabeau, elected as the representative of the Third Estate from the town of Aix-en-Provence. His life, which under the Old Régime had been one of dissipation and versatile scandal, had led for a time to imprisonment under a royal *lettre de cachet*. Yet he was well read in the critical literature of the philosophers; he had served in the French embassy at Berlin and written a shrewd analysis of the Prussian monarchy; he was an effective debater, a vigorous orator and, as it turned out, a man of great courage. Seeking as he did to reconcile the cause of monarchy with that of the people, he might have held the Revolution to the path of moderation. He died, however, in the spring of 1791, precisely at the wrong time, a victim of his own excesses.

The representation of the Third Estate included some of the ablest men in France. Malouet, an experienced civil servant, had been intendant of Toulon. Mounier, a magistrate from Grenoble, was a student of Montesquieu

1. The student may profitably analyze the following rough summary of membership: First Estate—46 bishops, 55 abbots, 9 monks, 198 parish priests; Second Estate—265 nobility of the sword (i. e., hereditary), 20 nobility of the robe (i. e., administrative); Third Estate—210 lawyers, 150 judicial officers, 130 merchants, bankers and so forth, 40 farmers and peasants, 25 municipal officers, 20 royal officers, 15 doctors, 15 noblemen, 4 ecclesiasts, 12 miscellaneous. See *Cambridge Modern History*, VIII, p. 133.

and an ardent admirer of the English constitution. Barère, a young lawyer from Toulouse and like many other deputies a Freemason, was likewise steeped in the ideas of the Enlightenment. Bailly, a distinguished astronomer and scientist, had been elected among the deputies from the city of Paris. One might also have noted, although he was by no means distinguished, a prim and somewhat old-fashioned-looking lawyer from Arras. Few would have prophesied that within four years Maximilien Robespierre would be the master of France. The Muse of History might also have marked out an obscure Doctor Guillotin from the south of France. Contributing little to the political work of the Assembly, he was, for "humanitarian" reasons, to recommend the use of that efficient instrument of decapitation which has given his name a gruesome immortality.

At the crowded, uncomfortable opening session of the Estates General held in one of the great halls at Versailles on May 5 the king delivered an awkward address. Necker followed with a staggeringly dull, three-hour report on the subject of finances. It was then intended that the three Estates should organize themselves as separate groups. They adjourned for this purpose, but in the ensuing days it soon became evident that the Third Estate obeyed its instructions with the greatest reluctance, doing little more than name Bailly as its president. "The spectators in the galleries," wrote the English traveler, Arthur Young, "are allowed to interfere in the debates by clapping their hands, and other noisy expressions of approbation; this is grossly indecent; it is also dangerous. . . . Another circumstance is the want of order among themselves; more than once there were an hundred members on their legs at a time, and M. Bailly absolutely without power to keep order."

The real problem facing the Estates General was that of "vote by order" or "vote by head." If the three Estates voted separately and as units, then clearly the commoners would be outnumbered. Hence, on June 17 the Third Estate with the backing of a few of the clergy took a historic step. It declared itself by vote to be a National Assembly and urged the deputies of the other orders to join it forthwith. This decision was followed by even more dramatic action. On June 20, finding their regular meeting place locked (ostensibly because of the need for repairs), the deputies of the Third Estate proceeded to the nearest convenient spot, an indoor tennis court. Here, on the proposal of Mounier and amid intense excitement, they adopted the famous "Tennis Court Oath," agreeing "not to separate until the constitution of the kingdom is established and consolidated upon firm foundations." This pledge, one of the most important decisions of the Revolution, clearly showed the intention of the Third Estate to undertake the fundamental work of making a constitution. It also implied that the Third Estate regarded its authority as coming not from the king but from the people of France. On June 22 about 150 clergy and a few noblemen agreed to join.[2]

In a royal session on June 23 the king, having promised certain reforms, ended by ordering the three Estates to resume their separate meetings. On his withdrawal the clergy and nobles obeyed him, but the Third Estate remained stubbornly in session. Replying to the command of a royal official, Mirabeau thundered his famous answer: "Go and tell those who sent you that we are here by the will of the people, and will leave our places only if compelled by armed force." In the face of this defiance and to avoid a crisis Louis acted characteristically: he capitulated. When on June 27 he ordered the clergy and nobles to meet with the Third Estate, another decisive landmark in the history of the Revolution had been reached, for now a united body existed that could claim to speak not simply for the privileged orders but for France as a whole. Meanwhile Louis had secretly given orders for twenty thousand trustworthy troops to be assembled at Versailles.

■ BLOODSHED AND REFORM

Closely pressing upon these developments came the first manifestations of violence. At Paris the atmosphere of crisis may in part be explained by the growing concern over food shortages and high prices. Criticisms also were directed against the reactionary advisers who were supposed to be dominating the king. News came, too, of the arrival of further troops, largely Swiss and German mercenaries, at Versailles. That a few individuals were deliberately fomenting unrest is a hypothesis for which some evidence seems to exist. On July 12 Necker, the royal minister who had come to symbolize the hopes of the reformers, was dismissed by the king and ordered out of the kingdom. In the tense situation which now arose mobs began to roam the streets of Paris looking for arms in gunsmiths' shops; some of the crowds clashed with the troops. Bourgeois groups thereupon undertook to organize an impromptu civic militia (the genesis of the later National Guard) and to set up an emergency municipal organization based upon the sixty new electoral divisions of the capital. Finally, after listening to some inflammatory speeches in the gardens of the Palais Royal—notably one by a militant young journalist named Camille Desmoulins—the mobs began to converge on the old fortress-prison known as the Bastille.

The Bastille, guarded by little more than a hundred men, had, as it turned out, only seven inmates. The grim pile had long seemed the vivid expression of tyranny; here without trial had been imprisoned many French-

2. David's famous painting of the Tennis Court Oath shows a monk, a priest and a Protestant minister in fraternal embrace before an enthusiastic crowd of deputies. Actually only a few clergy and no nobles were present.

men against whom the famous symbols of royal displeasure, the *lettres de cachet,* had been issued. The immediate explanation of the attack, nevertheless, seems to have been only the continuing search for arms. The Bastille was clumsily defended; its commandant rashly undertook to parley with the assailants; and after some confused fighting the mob broke in. At the cost of some Parisian lives the prison was captured, whereupon the head of the slain commandant was paraded on a pike through the streets. Bloodshed had made its appearance. A monument of tyranny was destroyed, for the Bastille was soon dismantled, stone by stone. The July 14 assault on the Bastille, in itself an episode of mob violence, thus became overnight and has ever since remained for republican France a great symbol of revolutionary triumph.

The political consequences followed fast. Louis XVI, weak and irresolute as usual, accepted the situation. Dismissing the conservative ministry, he recalled Necker and went to Paris where the local authorities presented him with the red-white-and-blue cockade, a symbol of the new age.[3] Meanwhile his younger brother, Count of Artois, and many of the nobility began to flee abroad—the first wave of what was to be a mounting tide of emigration.

Shortly after the events of July 14 the National Assembly sent two of its most respected members, Lafayette and Bailly, to confer with the provisional municipal leaders in Paris. Bailly was thereupon chosen mayor of Paris and Lafayette commander of the National Guard, or militia. In this way something of an official sanction or blessing was given to those popular forces in Paris which seemed ready to undertake further changes, and a closer link was established between Paris and the National Assembly.

In the country districts, meanwhile, further manifestations of violence appeared. Various circumstances such as the deplorable conditions of peasant life in certain areas, the heavy tax burdens, the outmoded manorial services, the recurrent food shortages and unemployment doubtless contributed to these provincial outbreaks. One must also take into account the "mob psychology" of this tense summer of 1789. Moreover, there is some evidence of the deliberate spreading of rumors; alarming stories were circulated, for example, that "the brigands" were coming and that the peasants should take arms against them. Whatever the reasons, large parts of rural France underwent disturbances in which ancient manorial records were destroyed, hayricks and manor-houses were burned, and occasionally the landlords or their local agents were put to death. By autumn the "Great Fear," as it was called, had died down. Its effects upon the National Assembly were clear. Some deputies, hitherto lukewarm on the subject of

3. This historic revolutionary tricolor was made by adding the red and blue colors of the city of Paris to the ancient white banner of the Bourbons.

reform, now found good reason to become its advocates. Throughout the provinces, moreover, local communities began to create their own militia and to reorganize their governments in rough imitation of what had been done in Paris.

At Versailles a committee of the National Assembly was set up late in July to consider remedies for the provincial disturbances. Alarmed because rebels were attacking that most sacred of all rights, property, the committee recommended that no concessions be made to them. At the same time the concern of the aristocracy was mounting. On the night of August 4 a noble-man, the Viscount of Noailles (himself landless), acquired a certain immortal-ity by dramatically proposing three measures: (1) taxes should be paid by all in proportion to their incomes; (2) seigneurial obligations involving serfdom and similar personal servitudes should be abolished without compensation; (3) all other feudal dues should be redeemable by the peasantry for a money payment. After a series of highly emotional speeches a formal motion em-bodying the second and third of these proposals was carried amid frenzied enthusiasm.

The results, although less sweeping than had at first seemed likely, were fundamental. By abolishing such outworn survivals as personal servitude, manorial rights of justice over the peasants, hunting and fishing rights, ecclesiastical tithes and the purchase of office, the Assembly made clear its hostility to the privileges of the Old Régime. Nevertheless, when the pro-posals were put into definite shape a week later the peasant found that he could obtain relief from *real* or land dues only by a process of payment not yet determined. Consequently the opening phrase of the final decree of August 11 which read, "The National Assembly abolishes the feudal regime entirely," is clearly inaccurate as a precise statement of fact and yet remains a profoundly significant declaration of intentions.

On August 10 the Assembly announced that it would help to establish civil order by authorizing a system of National Guards throughout France. These citizen groups, already springing up in imitation of the National Guards of Paris, were to be subject to local authority and to take an oath to the nation, the king and the law. Significantly, the officers were to swear never to use such troops against the citizenry except upon the orders of civil-ian officials.

The most impressive of all the documents of this period was the cele-brated Declaration of the Rights of Man, a manifesto worthy to be placed beside earlier charters such as the English Bill of Rights of 1689 or the American Declaration of Independence of 1776. Several drafts were sub-mitted, of which the one produced by Mounier, Sieyès and Lafayette seems to have been the most important. After much debate and amendment the various drafts were hammered together into the Declaration which was voted on August 27, 1789.

The rights which were proclaimed were those of "man and citizen," not, it will be noted, merely those of "Frenchmen." Issued "under the auspices of the Supreme Being" they included the following statements:

(1) Men are born and remain free and equal in rights; social distinctions may be based only upon general usefulness.

(2) The aim of every political association is the preservation of the natural and inalienable rights of man; these rights are liberty, property, security and resistance to oppression.

(3) The source of all sovereignty resides essentially in the nation; no group, no individual, may exercise authority not emanating expressly therefrom.

(4) Liberty consists of the power to do whatever is not injurious to others; thus the enjoyment of the natural rights of every man has for its limits only those that assure other members of society the enjoyment of those same rights; such limits may be determined only by law.

(6) Law is the expression of the general will; all citizens have the right to concur personally, or through their representatives, in its formulation. . . .

(7) No man may be accused, arrested or detained except in cases determined by law and according to the forms prescribed thereby. . . .

(10) No one is to be disquieted because of his opinions, even religious, provided their manifestation does not disturb the public order established by law.

(11) Free communication of ideas and opinions is one of the most precious of the rights of man. Consequently, every citizen may speak, write and think freely, subject to responsibility for the abuse of such liberty in the cases determined by law.

(17) Since property is a sacred and inviolable right, no one may be deprived thereof unless a legally established public necessity obviously requires it, and upon condition of a just and previous indemnity.

Historians have read various meanings into this Declaration of Rights. Its main significance, surely, is that the framers felt that an explicit gospel of human rights needed to be proclaimed. These rights centered upon the questions of liberty and equality. The Declaration has been said to be republican in spirit in that it makes no allusion to monarchy or to royal power. It has been called essentially bourgeois because of its inadequate treatment of the rights of labor and its concluding stress upon the rights of property. The Declaration has also been said to proclaim political ideals for all citizens which the restrictive provisions of the Constitution of 1791 actually brushed aside. Whatever its emphasis and whatever its inconsistencies, the document dramatized for Frenchmen the new era upon which they were embarking. It is quite understandable, therefore, that they should have inscribed the Declaration, like the Tables of the Law, upon the walls of their National Assembly.

From May until October the legislators of the new France sat at Versailles. Here they were under the shadow of the royal court and relatively free from the turbulent passions of Paris. Had Louis sought to follow the advice of the moderate leaders of the Assembly, events might have taken a different course. As it happened, he made several unfortunate moves. He refused his assent to some of the constitutional articles that were being drafted. He initiated no actions against food shortages or unemployment. He summoned the Flanders Regiment to Versailles and permitted its officers at a banquet to make extravagant professions of loyalty to the royal family and of hostility to the course of the Revolution.

Early in October exaggerated reports of these proceedings reached Paris where, under the further stimulus of food shortages and high prices, a mob of men and women (or men dressed as women) undertook a march to Versailles. On arriving, the crowd first created some disturbance in the Assembly and then surged beneath the windows of the royal apartments. Louis received a delegation with the usual polite assurance of his good intentions. Later, during the night of October 5, unruly groups burst through the line of guards that Lafayette had posted and stormed along the corridors seeking "the Austrian woman"—the unpopular Marie Antoinette. Desperately seeking refuge in her husband's apartment, the queen avoided death only by an instant. Next day, when Lafayette and the National Guard had reestablished order, the royal family appeared on a balcony before the people. Louis now made another of his fateful decisions: he announced that he would sign the decrees which were in question and at once establish his court at Paris.

A strange procession left Versailles for Paris at noon on October 6. The royal family, escorted by National Guards, traveled in lumbering coaches. Accompanying them was a nondescript mob crudely armed and carrying on pikes the heads of two murdered palace guards. Hasty preparations were made at the Tuileries to receive the king and to convert the royal riding school into a suitable meeting-place for the Assembly which, of necessity, followed Louis. By October 12, when the members resumed their duties, it was evident that another turning-point had been reached. Henceforth the debates were likely to be influenced by the various pressure groups and the incipient political parties that were growing up in Paris, and even, as happened on occasion, by the actual intrusion of an armed mob. This transfer of the Assembly to Paris, in the opinion of Albert Mathiez, one of the greatest historians of the Revolution, was even more fateful in its consequences than the fall of the Bastille.

■ THE ATMOSPHERE OF A CHANGING WORLD

Now that the legislators had moved to Paris, the reform program under-taken at Versailles gathered greater speed. It was stimulated by the gradual emergence of political groups, hardly as yet to be described as parties in the true sense but tending in that direction. From the first days of the Estates General groups of deputies had formed the habit of occasional meetings, whether for convenience in dining, for sociability, or for intellectual interests of the sort which had been manifested in the *salons* of the Old Régime. After the migration of the Assembly to Paris these informal groups began to assume greater definiteness.

In certain Parisian *salons* groups of noblemen were still ardently devoted to the royalist cause and the traditions of the past. Their importance, how-ever, was not great. Less reactionary in tone were middle-of-the-road groups such as the club entitled "The Friends of the Monarchical Constitution" or the group, sponsored by Lafayette, known as "The Club of 1789." This latter met in sumptuous apartments in the Palais Royal and included as members Sieyès, Condorcet, Mirabeau, Brissot and Talleyrand. These were among the most distinguished leaders in the Assembly. Ultimately of much greater importance was a group originating in an informal gathering of Breton deputies at Versailles. Moving to Paris, they organized themselves under the name, "Society of the Friends of the Constitution," enlarged their member-ship and looked around for a home. This they found in the abandoned library of an order of Jacobin monks—a branch of the Dominicans. Soon the name "Jacobin" came to be applied to this political group, which rapidly forged ahead, established branches in the provinces and at the height of its power in 1793 had perhaps half a million members. Much of the history of the Revolution can be written around its proceedings. Another club, like-wise named from the former monastery in which it was installed, was the Cordeliers; its official but little used title was "The Society of the Friends of the Rights of Man." With its lower membership dues it attracted persons of relatively modest station and soon became notable for the violence of its pronouncements. The Cordelier symbol was the open eye, suggesting the role of watchdog of public affairs. Men such as Danton, Hébert, and Marat were among its most active members. Militant as it was, the club never acquired the eminence or power of the Jacobins.

Students may well reflect upon the relation between these clubs and the processes of democracy. Sociologists and political scientists have made familiar the term, "pressure group." To some extent these clubs of the left served to channel the interests and desires of the people of Paris, and in so doing they doubtless furthered the cause of what might be termed direct democracy. In another sense they served as a platform where powerful figures such as

Danton or Robespierre could demonstrate their leadership and mobilize support. It is significant, for example, that Robespierre, denied a seat in the Legislative Assembly because of his previous membership in the Constituent Assembly, was able nevertheless through the Jacobin Club to rise quickly to a position of commanding influence in the affairs of France.

The capital likewise witnessed an extraordinary flourishing of the press. While the censorship of the Old Régime had been notoriously ineffective, the general atmosphere had not been conducive to the free exercise of public criticism. Now the floodgates were opened wide. The papers represented the same spectrum of opinions as was to be found in the clubs, ranging from the conservative right to the radical left. The *Moniteur,* more or less factual in content, soon became the official vehicle for news of debates, decrees and legislation. More commonly the papers were journals of opinion; some of them, indeed, resembled news-letters or pamphlets more than they resembled our present-day newspapers. Some representatives of the moderate press, such as the *Journal de Paris* or Mirabeau's *Courrier de Provence,* were quite influential, but on the whole the papers of the left grew most rapidly. Among these were Brissot's *Patriot français,* Camille Desmoulins' *Révolutions de France et de Brabant,* Dr. Marat's *Ami du peuple* and Hébert's *Père Duchesne.* These in time had an extraordinary success in arousing mob violence.

Although political parties as such hardly existed in the Assembly, they soon began to appear in rudimentary form. To the right of the presiding officer were found the conservative deputies, largely noble and clerical, who represented the forces of conservatism and privilege. In the center were the deputies of less extreme but still strongly royalist views. One would have had to look to the left to find those deputies whose influence was steadily to grow and who were to provide the leaders of the future republic. Historians have distinguished three groups among these leftist deputies: the Constitutionalists, including Sieyès, Talleyrand, Barère, Grégoire and Lafayette, whose work largely created the Constitution of 1791; a group led by "the Triumvirate" (Barnave, Duport and Lameth); and on the extreme left a number of men of whom Robespierre, at first obscure, soon emerged as the unquestioned leader. Robespierre and his group actually had very little power until the summer of 1791. The great name of Mirabeau can hardly be allotted to any party. He sought some form of limited monarchy and more than any other his voice swayed the Assembly. His work, however, was to some extent a work of improvisation. "We can never understand Mirabeau's career in the National Assembly if we conceive of him as of English statesmen, who by a regular course of promotion rise to the command of a disciplined party, and rule the state by the will of the people in the name of the sovereign. Mirabeau was only an adventurer of genius in a dissolving society." [4]

Even though the progress of the French Revolution tempts the student to focus his attention upon Paris, the developments there produced important consequences in the provinces, where local societies and newspapers were established in emulation of those in the capital. A decree of the Assembly in December, 1789, had authorized a new pattern of municipal government, each commune electing its officers and organizing a local militia. The phenomenon of "Federation" quickly followed, as the new local associations of patriots began to exchange pledges of fraternity. On July 14, 1790, the first anniversary of the fall of the Bastille, a great Festival of Federation was held in Paris. Delegations of the local National Guards assembled from all over France; Talleyrand, assisted by four hundred priests, officiated at a huge open-air Mass; and Lafayette as president of the Constituent Assembly administered a patriotic oath. Louis XVI was present and, while the crowd swore allegiance to him, above this pledge rose the new sentiment of allegiance to the country, the law and the Revolution. The fervor of Paris itself had been conveyed in some degree to the representatives of all France.

Still another phenomenon deserves attention. As soon as it became clear that Louis intended to give his assent to important measures of the Assembly, some clergy and nobles began to leave France, at first in small numbers and then in larger. Various Italian courts and a number of Rhineland cities, notably Coblenz, became centers where organized French opposition to the developments at home took shape. In the Rhineland it was possible to appeal to the local Hapsburg authorities and obtain assurances of sympathy and even some promises of eventual armed support. As the *émigrés*, looking forward to the day when they could win back their lost privileges, undertook to arm themselves, they began to constitute a force hostile and menacing to the Revolution. In consequence, the leaders of the Constituent Assembly were themselves obliged to contemplate more drastic action.

■ THE ADMINISTRATIVE PATTERN OF A NEW FRANCE

For more than two years the Constituent Assembly kept at work hammering out a new administrative machinery for France. Vote after vote, decree after decree, produced in the end an impressive body of legislation. In the process some inconsistencies developed: the Declaration of the Rights of Man, for example, proclaimed equal rights for all, whereas the voting provisions which were finally set up limited voting to certain financially privileged groups. Despite such contradictions and despite the occasional intru-

4. *The Cambridge Modern History*, VIII, p. 175.

sion of violence, the Assembly wrought well. It would be hard, indeed, to find a precedent in French history for an era of orderly change which so greatly transformed the political, economic and social fabric of the country. By 1791 a new France had come into existence.

Sweeping changes were made in the general political organization of France. The old provinces (which for administrative purposes had come to be known as "generalities" or "intendancies") disappeared. A decree of December 22, 1789, established an elaborately co-ordinated system of departments, districts, cantons and communes. The departments (more precisely defined in February, 1790) were to be 83 in number; they were to be about equal in size and were to be of such extent that the chief town was not to be more than a day's travel from any part. Some departments corresponded closely to former provinces; some were created by splitting up the larger provinces; others were made by combining small provinces. The departments were divided into districts, there being from three to nine districts in a department. The districts were divided into cantons, which were about three square leagues in extent; they turned out in the end to have very little significance save as electoral units. At the base of the pyramid were the 44,000 communes or municipalities. The importance of these was enormous, for they provided the essential democratic basis for the new France.

Each department was administered by an elected departmental council of 36 members and by other appointed officials. Their duties, which were elaborately defined, concerned such matters as assessing and collecting taxes and supervising expenditures, poor relief, public works, education, religious worship, the militia and prisons. On a lower level the districts had a roughly similar machinery and performed somewhat similar duties. The cantons served chiefly as the units for organizing the primary electoral assemblies. Elaborate rules were drawn up concerning the government of the communes. Here the elected mayors and councils became living symbols of the new revolutionary spirit, attending to the affairs of the community and having under their control the local National Guard.

A tremendous amount of administrative work was thrust into the hands of these new local officers, whose responsibility was intended to run much more to the people who elected them than to the central government in Paris. As a matter of practice, however, local authorities continued to seek instructions from the capital, as they had done under the Old Régime. The leaders of the National Assembly thus wielded the whip hand, though they would seem to have done so despite the new constitution and not because of it. In summary, then, the work of the Constituent Assembly in reorganizing the entire system of provincial and local government was far-reaching and profound, for it created the essential administrative pattern which France still retains. It established the democratic, communal structures at what might be called the grass-roots level of public life. It attempted a great work of administrative decentralization as a reaction against the inefficient centralization, as De Tocqueville called it, of the old order. It is worth observing that the new, ostensibly democratic framework could be turned to other purposes. Within a very few years Napoleon injected into the system a powerful new set of *appointed* officers (notably his prefects, sub-prefects and councillors). These were strictly tied to the central despotism at Paris. Napoleon thus kept the outward forms of democracy while at the same time perfecting the administrative machinery of his new imperial regime, a considerable part of which was also bequeathed as a legacy to the nineteenth century.

In the field of justice, where the old courts and legal procedures were hopelessly antiquated and confused, a sweeping reorganization was effected. A great decree of August 16, 1790, supplemented by much further legislation, provided the basic elements of reorganization. Hereditary and noble titles were abolished. It was announced that punishment in every case was to be proportionate to the crime and was to be stipulated precisely in the laws, leaving little to the discretion of the judges. Most of the very harsh old penalties, such as torture, the pillory, public confession and branding with hot irons, were abolished.

In place of the old courts, which had been filled by privileged officials holding their posts either by inheritance or by purchase, an entirely new court system was set up. All judgeships became elective for defined terms of years. Justices of the peace were to be elected for two years in every canton and in every town of more than 2,000 inhabitants. These would handle local and minor cases. In each district there was to be a district tribunal of five judges elected for six years. Special departmental tribunals made up of seven judges drawn from the district courts were to try criminal cases. As an innovation they were to have the assistance of grand and petty juries to determine the facts. A special Court of Cassation (from the French *casser,* to break) served the country as a whole. This court was a panel made up of judges, drawn from every department, which could reverse the judgment of lower courts for faults in procedure. Apart from this there was no system of appeals. A special High Court sat at Paris to try cases of treason and other offenses charged against important officials. Commercial tribunals of five judges were also established to deal with suits involving commerce on land or sea.

These legal reforms constituted some of the best work of the Assembly. The insistence upon elected judges and the absence of a regular system of appeal courts would seem to imply the belief that justice could safely be left to those whom the voters had directly chosen. "Justice," Mathiez wrote, "was always administered in the king's name, but it had in fact become the concern of the nation." [5] In spite of all the dangers and in spite of the excesses at the height of the revolutionary fury, the new judicial arrangements on the whole worked well.

No aspect of reorganization had a larger importance than that dealing with finances and taxation. The injustices in this field had long aroused such bitter protest that, with the new doctrine proclaimed by the Declaration of Rights, the clamor quickly grew for an end of the era of economic privilege. In a much less exalted sense it was painfully clear, too, that France must take drastic action to save itself from bankruptcy. On June 17, three days before the Tennis Court Oath, the Third Estate had adopted a declaration asserting that all existing taxes were illegal, since they were not sanctioned by the consent of the people. Such taxes were, therefore, to be regarded as only provisionally in effect. The sequel to the dramatic renunciation of feudal rights on the night of August 4 had been a decree which drastically restricted the power of the manorial lord in matters of taxation. This, however, was of no immediate assistance to the central government, which still needed the assurance of definite sources of revenue.

The Assembly moved quickly to abolish the old taxes which comprised such indirect levies as the salt tax and internal customs dues as well as the historic direct taxes, principally the *taille, capitation* and *vingtième*. Necker, however, found it extraordinarily difficult to improvise new sources of revenue quickly. The old Discount Bank (*Caisse d'Escompte*) established by Turgot in 1776 was unable to provide further advances. Bonds which Necker sought to issue in August with interest at $4\frac{1}{2}$ or 5 per cent were not taken up by the public. Appeals for "patriotic contributions" brought some funds (the king sent some of the royal silver to the mint) but the results were on the whole trivial. The national debt, estimated at over three billion francs early in 1789, reached the total of four billion francs within a year. Major remedies, it is clear, were necessary.

The enormous wealth of the Roman Catholic Church in France was estimated at something between two and four billion francs—in other words, about the equivalent of the national debt. Talleyrand, Bishop of Autun, seems to have been the first to propose (October, 1789) that all church lands be placed "at the disposal of the Nation." The epoch-marking decree of November 2, 1789, was careful to stipulate that ecclesiastical property should be transferred to the nation only on condition that the government undertook to provide for the expenses of worship, the salaries of the clergy and

5. MATHIEZ, *The French Revolution,* p. 92.

the relief of the poor. The nation, therefore, in taking over the financial assets of the church automatically assumed many of its duties.

The new wealth thus acquired was handled in a complicated and highly ingenious fashion. A vote of December, 1789, authorized the use of church lands as security for the national debt. A new kind of financial device, the *assignats,* appeared. The *assignats* were, in effect, bonds bearing interest at five per cent which could be used only for certain purposes. Holders of government bonds which normally would have been redeemed some day in cash were authorized to exchange these bonds for interest-bearing *assignats.* There was but one way to redeem *assignats:* the holders would have to purchase church lands from the state. The government would then proceed to destroy the *assignats* it received in payment for the church lands, which, of course, had been taken by the government at no cost. Everyone, presumably, would be happy—everyone except the original holders of the church lands—and even here it will be remembered that the government had undertaken to assume all the costs of public worship. Little wonder that this transaction has been described as "one of the shrewdest financial manipulations ever devised—at least on paper." [6]

Shortly after the first issue of *assignats* (400 million francs) had been authorized in December, 1789, it became clear that the public would not take readily to the new scheme unless the *assignats* were made as easily negotiable as currency. A decree of April, 1790, made the *assignats* legal tender; in May they were made legally exchangeable for metallic currency. Unavoidable as these moves seemed, they had unfortunate effects, for citizens were now in a position to compare the worth of paper money with that of their regular currency. By the end of 1791 the *assignats* as a circulating medium had lost nearly 25 per cent of their face value and by the spring of 1792 they had lost almost 40 per cent. They were to decline even further and ultimately in 1797 were to be completely repudiated. Even so, one must not forget their practical value in making possible the orderly transfer of property from the hands of the church to the hands of a substantial number of French citizens.

The search for financial stability resulted in other measures. In place of the old complicated tax system a general land tax (*contribution foncière*), a personal property tax (*contribution mobilière*) and a tax on business revenues (*patente*) were introduced early in 1791. These three continued as the basic taxes of the entire revolutionary period and, indeed, provided the essential framework for the tax system of the nineteenth century. It could not be claimed, however, that these new measures at first worked well. A

6. JOHN HALL STEWART, *A Documentary Survey of the French Revolution* (1951), p. 159.

large part of the taxes remaining unpaid, the government was forced to turn to various expedients such as ever larger issues of *assignats* in order to avoid bankruptcy.

What classes benefited by these complex economic changes? The sufferers could clearly be seen: the vested interests of nobles and clergy had been dealt a severe blow. The beneficiaries, however, are not so easy to determine. Although the peasants had been freed from many humiliating dues and services, the poorer among them did not find it easy to acquire land. The church lands which came upon the market were generally bought by the wealthier peasants or by those substantially endowed members of the urban middle class who were looking for a profitable and safe investment. What we would call the rural proletariat benefited little, if at all.

The urban workers do not seem to have been much favored. According to medieval custom they frequently had banded together in associations or *compagnonnages* sometimes for social or charitable purposes and sometimes with the direct purpose of bettering their economic conditions. Strikes had not been unknown. The Chapelier Law of June, 1791, put an end to all such associations of workmen—in deference, it would seem, to the supposed principle of "freedom." Workmen of any trade were not permitted to assemble, to organize themselves or to go on strike in defense of their common interests. Such a move is a clear indication of the middle-class orientation of the Assembly, which was unwilling to associate itself too closely with the cause of the proletariat.

A decree of October, 1790, abolished all internal tariffs and tolls on goods moving throughout France and set up a general tariff for the country as a whole to regulate goods coming in from abroad. Here the creed of the Physiocrats found practical expression. This measure, covering both import and export duties, was the basis for similar legislation during the later periods of Convention and the Directory. What is true of tariff policy is true also of most financial measures adopted in these early days of the Revolution: they established a general pattern which leaders during the immediately succeeding years were content to follow.

■ THE REORGANIZATION OF THE CHURCH

The great work of reform could hardly ignore questions of religion. France was an overwhelmingly Catholic country. Of the twenty-five million French, perhaps one million were Protestants who, ever since Louis XIV's reckless revocation of the Edict of Nantes in 1685, had been under very severe legal disabilities. In the course of time many of these disabilities had come to be ignored; even so, there could be no question of the privileged position held by the Roman Catholic Church in France on the eve of the Revolution.

The French church could properly be regarded as Gallican in that it had a considerable degree of freedom from papal control. Although it sent regular contributions to Rome in the form of annates, it was largely in charge of its own revenues. It voted periodical "free gifts" to the king. Clerical appointments lay very largely in royal hands or with the French church itself. During the course of the eighteenth century the *philosophes* had conducted a bitter attack against ecclesiastic abuses in France, with the consequence that much of this critical spirit carried over into the Constituent Assembly. The reforming zeal of this body almost of necessity, therefore, turned to church matters, all the more so because the most urgent problems of 1789 were financial and the wealth of the church was enormous.

Many steps were quickly taken in church matters. The Declaration of the Rights of Man had stipulated (Article X) that no one should be molested for his religious opinions, "provided their manifestation does not disturb the public order established by law." The famous decrees of August 4, 1789, had stipulated that tithes paid to religious bodies should end. Holding more than one religious office (plurality of benefices) was forbidden. A provisional decree in October, 1789, permitted monks to leave their cloisters; this was followed in February, 1790, by decrees abolishing all purely contemplative orders and declaring that perpetual vows henceforth were illegal in France. Another decree (December, 1789) provided that non-Catholics should be eligible for election to all public offices and for appointment to civil and military positions. All these measures breathed the new spirit of reform.

The larger issues of ecclesiastical reorganization were precipitated by the momentous decision in November, 1789, to place all church lands at the disposal of the state. The impetus for this move had clearly been financial.[7] But the government, in exchange for the advantages, assumed liabilities. Church land was to be taken over "upon condition of providing in a suitable manner for the expenses of worship, the maintenance of ministers and the relief of the poor." The Assembly clearly recognized one of its obligations when it decreed in the following April that all clerical salaries would be guaranteed by the state. In various other moves the Assembly proceeded to remake the ecclesiastical structure of France. Between May and July, 1790, it combined its work into one general document known as the Civil Constitution of the Clergy. As the word, "Civil," in the title indicated, the principal concern was with organization, not with ritual or dogma. Voted on July 12, this document finally received the reluctant approval of the king on August 24, 1790.

7. See pp. 584–585.

The essential purpose of the Civil Constitution of the Clergy was to adapt the structure of the church to the conditions of a new age. The kingdom was to be divided into ten metropolitan districts. The 139 archbishoprics and bishoprics of the old France were reduced to 83, that is, one for each department. Parishes were also reorganized, the larger in some cases being subdivided and the smaller in some cases combined. All salaries, pensions and residences for the clergy were to be provided by the state.

The most striking provision of the Civil Constitution was that all clerical appointments were to be made by the process of popular election. Bishops were to be chosen in the electoral assemblies of the departments and priests in the electoral assemblies of the districts. Certain safeguards were stipulated. To be eligible for a bishopric a candidate must have held priestly office for fifteen years in the diocese; on election he was to be examined in matters of doctrine and morals by the metropolitan or senior bishop. Similarly, in order to be eligible for election as a parish priest a candidate must have served for at least five years in orders and had to be examined and approved by his bishop. Even with these safeguards the new electoral process can well be described as revolutionary, especially as there was nothing to prevent Protestants who were members of the electoral assemblies from participating in the choice. Moreover, papal confirmation of episcopal elections was explicitly forbidden. After election the incumbent was to take an oath "to be faithful to the nation, to the law, and to the King, and to maintain with all his power the Constitution decreed by the National Assembly and accepted by the King." No cleric was to absent himself for more than fifteen days a year from his post without serious reason.

Although Louis XVI had many misgivings about the Civil Constitution of the Clergy, he nevertheless gave his approval to it in August, 1790, as he assented in the following December to the special decree requiring all clergy to take the oath to maintain the Constitution. The clergy were sharply divided, only seven of the existing bishops being prepared to take the oath and only about one-half of the parish priests. The larger proportion of the lower clergy who were amenable to the new arrangements can be explained by the fact that these men tended to come from the middle and lower classes and on the whole were disposed to accept the work of the Revolution.

The outcome was a cleavage between those clergy who were willing to take the oath (the "Jurors") and those who were not (the "Non-Jurors"). Despite the Decree of May, 1791, which permitted the "Non-Jurors" to hold public services if they so desired (even though they could take no part in the "constitutional" regime of the church), discontent increased and was made all the sharper by the attitude of the papacy. Pius VI soon began to address letters of remonstrance to the French clergy. In April, 1791, he issued the bull, *Charitas,* affirming that all who took the civic oath would be suspended from their tenure of office. The offending seven bishops were specifically named and denounced. All elections held under the Civil Constitution were declared to be "void, illegitimate, sacrilegious and absolutely non-effective." Those who refused to heed the warnings now given would be cut off from communion with the church. The pope ended with an appeal to all Frenchmen in which he gave his opinion of the influence of eighteenth-century thought upon the course of events: "Be steadily on your guard lest you lend ear to the insidious voices of the philosophy of this century which lead to death. . . ."

The Assembly's reply to this action was to decree (June, 1791) that no papal documents of any kind could be published in France unless they had been presented to the legislature and authorized by it. Clergy ignoring this provision would be severely penalized. The lines of disagreement were now so sharply drawn that Frenchmen were soon compelled to define their allegiance. Although the majority seem to have gone along with the Assembly, there remained considerable numbers, especially in some of the outlying parts of France, whose allegiance to the old order and to the non-juring clergy was very strong. The consequence was occasional riots and local disturbances, not at first serious in extent but capable under the stimulus of royalist and ultra-conservative leadership of developing into a dangerous counter-revolutionary movement.

■ THE CONSTITUTION COMPLETED

The machinery of central administration, intended to bind together and give unity to all French political life, was carefully specified in a written document. This Constitution of 1791, the first of its kind in French history and a landmark in the history of modern Europe, was declared complete on September 3, 1791. Its provisions demonstrate how far the reforming theories of the eighteenth century had expressed themselves in actuality.

A Preamble formally abolished all titles of nobility and other hereditary distinctions. Purchase of office was forbidden and exceptions to the law were declared no longer to exist. Workmen's gilds and professional associations were not to be recognized. Religious vows were no longer to be binding. Following the Preamble came a series of Fundamental Provisions echoing in general terms those of the Declaration of Rights in 1789 and adding certain great basic stipulations such as the provision of public relief for the needy, public instruction for all children, a system of national festivals and a common code of civil law for the entire kingdom. All citizens were declared to be admissible to public offices and employments despite the restrictions upon voting and office-holding which were listed later in the Constitution. The division or separation of powers was also put forth as a basic principle. Legislative power was put into the hands of a freely elected National Assembly, the executive power in the hands of a hereditary monarch and the judicial power in the hands of popularly elected judges.

The Legislative Assembly was to consist of one chamber of 745 members elected for two years and eligible only once for immediate re-election. No member of the Constituent Assembly could be a candidate. This body was to meet in regular session every May.[8] Members were chosen by a complex indirect voting system which started with the division of the population into "active" and "passive" citizens. A passive citizen, presumably, was anyone who enjoyed the general rights stipulated under the Constitution. An active citizen had to be born or naturalized as a Frenchman, to be twenty-five years old, to be domiciled for a year in his canton, not to be working as a domestic servant, and to be paying an annual direct tax equal to the local value of three days' labor. Even with these restrictive provisions it has been calculated that about 60 per cent of the adult males could vote, as compared with about 5 per cent in England. Perhaps some 4,300,000 Frenchmen were granted the suffrage and some 3,000,000 were denied it.

In order to choose deputies to the National Assembly the active citizens were to meet in primary assemblies held in each city or canton. There they would choose from their number a group of electors, on the basis of one for each hundred citizens. To be an elector, as distinguished from an ordinary voter, one had to pay a direct tax equal to ten days' labor. Electoral assemblies then met in the chief town of each department and chose the slate of deputies to be sent to Paris. The requirement for being a deputy was fixed in the so-called "silver mark" clause. This provided that deputies must own real estate and pay a substantial annual tax.[9] Thus only about 50,000 Frenchmen could serve as electors and only a fraction of these as deputies. The primary and the departmental assemblies were also the bodies which elected the officials of the districts and the departments.

The legislature, although restricted in its composition because of the complicated electoral system, was intended to be a powerful body. It was to meet every May without the need of a royal summons, could not be prorogued by the king and was to be renewed *in toto* every two years. The

8. The 745 seats were allotted on a threefold basis (1) Each of the 83 departments had three seats automatically (with the exception of Paris which had only one), giving a total of 247. (2) Another one-third of the seats were distributed to the departments on the basis of relative population, giving a total of 249. (3) Another third of the seats were allotted on the basis of direct taxes paid, giving a total of 249.

9. Voted in January, 1791, this was the actual provision under which the election of September 1791 was held. At the last minute the article was redrawn to provide that *all* active citizens could be eligible for election. but this provision was too late to be effective.

deputies had full parliamentary immunity. They initiated and voted all laws. They fixed taxes, controlled expenditures and had the full power of the purse unhampered by a royal veto. They controlled the armed forces, made declarations of war and ratified peace treaties. The legislature could arraign ministers before a special High Court.

Supreme executive power was delegated by the nation to the monarch whose hereditary title was fixed by primogeniture in the male line of the reigning family. The king was to take an oath to be faithful to the nation and the law. At the beginning of each reign he was to be voted a civil list (a sum for his own expenditures) by the legislature. In the case of high treason or leaving the realm without consent he could be deposed. He was to choose his own ministers (but not from the Assembly) and could dismiss them. He had the power to propose declarations of war, to conduct foreign affairs, to appoint ambassadors and certain high army and civil officials and to promulgate the laws. All his executive acts had to be countersigned by his ministers; he, in turn, had to sign all enactments of the legislature in order to make them into law. In this respect he had what was known as a "suspensive veto"; he could withhold his signature during two consecutive legislatures and thus delay action for at least two years. But if the Assembly persisted, it would finally prevail. Moreover, this provision did not apply to constitutional matters or taxation. In essence, therefore, Louis was to be a constitutional monarch *à l'anglaise*. One should note how essential his genuine co-operation was to the working of the new regime.

The ministers, who were appointed by the monarch, were obliged in addition to directing their departments and countersigning all royal orders to submit regular reports to the Assembly. Even though they could not be members of the Assembly, they were to have a designated place in it and in certain circumstances could demand a hearing. As actually organized, the ministries were six in number: War, Foreign Affairs, Finance, Interior, Marine and Justice.

The judiciary, representing the third branch of the division of powers, has already been described. In addition to the simplified and systematic re-arrangements of courts and the use of popular election for all judges, juries were provided for in criminal cases. Speedy trials were guaranteed. In general a system of privilege and vested interest was replaced by a system seeking equal justice for all.

By any fair estimate this Constitution of 1791 must be deemed a remarkable achievement. "Worse constitutions," it has been truthfully said, "have met with longer life." [10] It had the misfortune to go into effect at a time when war clouds were gathering abroad, when dissensions were increasing

10. LOUIS GOTTSCHALK, *The Era of the French Revolution* (1929), p. 176.

at home and when the king was to prove tragically unequal to the responsibilities which he was asked to assume. The life of this new constitution, so
laboriously and so hopefully drafted, was one year.

■ "THE REVOLUTION IS OVER": THE FLIGHT OF THE KING

When the work of constitution-making was completed in the summer of
1791, this long-hoped-for achievement was accompanied paradoxically by a
growing uneasiness and dissatisfaction. Mirabeau, who while counselling the
king to moderation had always wished to see him exercise a genuine authority, died in April, 1791.[11] Henceforth Louis was increasingly subjected to
dangerous influences. Through his wife he had a close connection with the
Austrian court, where hostility to the Revolution was on the increase. His
two *émigré* brothers, the Count of Artois and the Count of Provence, were associated with counter-revolutionary forces abroad. In France the discontent
of royalists, clericals and conservatives in general was on the increase. The
poorer classes were affected by inflation, rising prices and unemployment.
Louis saw that his powers had been diminished; more than this, perhaps,
he was gravely concerned at the sweeping changes in the religious life of
France, made inevitable by the Civil Constitution of the Clergy. This was
the part of the reform program which he accepted with the greatest repug-
nance and by which he hardly felt himself to be bound.

On June 21, 1791, Paris awoke to find itself without a king. During the
previous night, after careful preparations which had been secretly furthered
by the Swedish ambassador, the royal family had left the Tuileries in dis-
guise. Traveling for nearly twenty-four hours in a huge, specially built
coach, they were finally discovered and detained by the local militia at
Varennes, some twenty-five miles from the Luxemburg frontier. Evidence
shows that Louis had long maintained correspondence with the *émigré*
forces abroad and had looked sympathetically at the prospect of a military
demonstration by troops gathered at the frontier. His feelings had been intensified at the time of the sanctioning of the Civil Constitution of the
Clergy in August, 1790. As early as the following December he seems to
have contemplated flight, rumors of which had soon begun to circulate in the
capital. The actual attempt at escape thus was not altogether unexpected. It
came, however, as a profound shock to the Assembly. Word was sent to
Varennes that the royal family was to be brought back under guard.

For a second time Louis made a strangely unroyal entrance into his
capital. After the march of the women to Versailles in October, 1789, he
and his family had been escorted back to the Tuileries with something less

11. It is true, but in the light of the times no great criticism of Mirabeau, that he was
granted secret subsidies by the court.

than royal dignity. Now, on the morrow of his disastrous flight, a funeral-like procession brought him back to Paris: first a horseman bearing a large placard commanding complete silence, then the royal coach surrounded by a company of grenadiers, then Drouet, the innkeeper who had recognized Louis from his portrait on one of the new *assignats,* conspicuous in a separate carriage, enjoying his triumph.

At the Tuileries the royal family were to all intents under arrest. What was now to be the status of the monarchy and of the new Constitution? The Assembly, on the first news of the flight, had authorized the seizure of the royal family on the very dubious grounds that they had been abducted. Louis had left behind a statement that he had sought to recover his freedom and place his family in safety because there remained to him only "a vain semblance of liberty." His cause was not aided by a later statement that he had never really intended to leave the kingdom. On June 24 the Assembly voted that the Minister of Justice could put the seal of state on its decrees without sanction or acceptance by the king. In effect, therefore, the monarchy was suspended.

Without much question the royal flight gravely and in the end fatally injured the position of the monarchy. Early in July placards and petitions began to appear urging a republic. The entire work of the Constituent Assembly, however, was predicated upon the existence and genuine functioning of royal power. Moreover, although some hotheads might not have cared, the moderates in the Assembly had no desire to precipitate the foreign intervention that almost certainly would follow if the republicans had their way.

A compromise, therefore, was reached. A decree of July 16 stipulated that the king should remain suspended until he had accepted the new Constitution. Radical opposition was immediately aroused; crowds collected on the Champ-de-Mars to submit a petition in protest against the Assembly's action and to demand that Louis' abdication be accepted and a new government created. National Guards, summoned to maintain order, fired into the mob, with the result that nearly twenty were fatally injured. The republican cause now had its "martyrs," and thus the quickly named "Massacre of the Champ-de-Mars" dramatized the unbridgeable gap between the moderates who were still prepared to accept the Constitution of 1791 and the extremists who were now thinking in terms of a republic.

The Assembly having solemnly declared the Constitution to be complete, Louis gave his assent on September 14. Two weeks later he proclaimed, "The Revolution is over." As the elections already had taken place, the last session of the Constituent Assembly was held on September 30. On the following day the new Legislative Assembly, no members of which had sat in the previous assembly, held its first meeting. Untried and inexperienced except as a result of what they had learned in the heady atmosphere of the clubs and local political gatherings, these new men soon were to see their country swept into dangerous and terrifying waters. "Nothing turned out according to plan. It was the fate of the expiring Assembly, which believed in Liberty, Fraternity, and Equality, and had worked for a democratic state safeguarded by a universal and democratic peace, to level the path for a military tyranny and to sow the seeds of general war." [12]

12. FISHER, *History of Europe*, p. 829.

A DEPUTY ON MISSION TO THE ARMIES OF THE CONVENTION. This extraordinary painting attributed to the artist David dramatizes the spirit of the new era. Plumes and tricolor on the hat, gloves, belt, sash and sword of office all signalize the authority of a representative of the people. Courtesy, Caisse Nationale des Monuments Historiques, Paris.

Chapter 23

The Revolutionary Fever,
1792–1795

■ THE FAILURE OF LIMITED MONARCHY
   AND THE COMING OF WAR, 1791–1792

THE LEGISLATIVE ASSEMBLY, elected under the terms of the new constitution, met on October 1, 1791. Supposedly it was to inaugurate a stable era of limited monarchy and peaceful progress. Actually, France within a year was to abolish its monarchy, become a republic and find itself committed to a dangerous war with foreign enemies. In September of 1792, therefore, the legislature had little choice but to disband, having first taken steps to summon a convention that would undertake the work of constitution-making for a second time—this time under pressures far more intense than those of 1789.

The 745 members of the Legislative Assembly which met in 1791 were preponderantly the spokesmen of the middle classes. Because of the twofold system of primary and secondary elections it could truthfully be said that the new members were chosen in the last resort by the 50,000 leading property owners in France. They were relatively inexperienced, for a self-denying ordinance had forbidden members of the Constituent Assembly to stand for re-election. The training of these members came at most from their activities in local government and from their membership in the clubs and other political associations now rapidly growing up throughout France.

Although parties in the modern sense were not clearly defined, the distinctions between "right" and "left" were already marked. Seeing that all members were pledged to the Constitution of 1791 with its provisions for a limited monarchy, no place remained for those conservative royalists who were committed outright to the defense of the old order. On the right of the presiding officer sat the Feuillants—the representatives of a group that had seceded from the Jacobin Club in July, 1791, in protest against its growing radicalism. This seceding group had established its own headquarters in the former convent of a religious order known as the Feuillants. Numbering about 264, the Feuillants were moderate in outlook, hoping to maintain the monarchy and strengthen the executive. Part of the group accepted the leadership of Lafayette; another part was led by a "Triumvirate" of less prominent figures. From the Feuillants the king selected his first ministry.

On the left of the presiding officer sat a smaller group of about 130, for the most part members either of the Jacobin Club or the Cordeliers. The majority of the left gathered around Brissot de Warville, a deputy from Bordeaux, and consequently were know either as the "Brissotins," the "Bordeaux Group," or the "Girondins." Vergniaud was their great orator and Condorcet their philosopher. Others on the left—the Jacobins—accepted the leadership of Maximilien Robespierre, a provincial lawyer from Arras and a former member of the Constituent Assembly. Debarred from membership in the Legislative Assembly because of the self-denying ordinance, Robespierre was rapidly becoming the dominant figure in the powerful Jacobin Club, where he found an opportunity for public leadership almost equal to that provided by the Assembly. In time the Girondins and Jacobins were to part company; at this period they were united in a growing suspicion of the monarchy.

The Feuillants and the Bordeaux Group, it will be seen, were each a minority. In the center sat those cautious moderates—"the Prudent Ones"—

numbering about 345, who had no precise creed and who were prepared to support either right or left according as the tide turned. Many of these survived to serve under Napoleon and even under the restored Bourbon monarchy of 1814. At this moment they had no great role to play, for the tide was now running strongly to the left.

Urgent problems confronted the Legislative Assembly. The *assignats* continued to decline in value, as did French currency abroad, making trade difficult. A rise in the price of sugar, coffee and grain caused hardship and widespread protests. During the winter of 1791–1792 mobs broke into food warehouses in Paris and other towns; on occasion the canal barges and wagon-trains moving grain from one part of France to another were attacked. Many peasants deeply resented the continued exaction of a number of the old feudal services, exemption from which, according to the legislation of August, 1789, could be won only by a money payment.

This general situation had its effects on the Assembly, where a cleavage appeared between the conservative members of the Feuillant group and those who, supporting the Bordeaux Group, were willing to align themselves more closely with the masses. In times of trouble the obvious temptation was to look for scapegoats. The Assembly quickly undertook in October and November, 1791, to issue a series of decrees against those at home and abroad whom it suspected of disloyalty. The first decree ordered the king's emigrant brother, the Count of Provence, to return within two months. The second ordered all *émigrés* to return to France by January, 1792, under pain of death. A third required the "non-juring" clergy to take a new civic oath to the Constitution of 1791, under penalty of being classed as suspects and deprived of their state pensions. A fourth decree required the king to request the elector of Trèves and other Rhineland rulers to disperse the *émigrés* gathering in their territories. In December Louis accepted the first and fourth of these decrees but used his constitutional power to veto the second and third. His true attitude may be observed in a secret letter which he sent to Frederick William II of Prussia on December 3, 1791:

> I have just addressed myself to the Emperor, to the Empress of Russia [and] to the Kings of Spain and Sweden, and have presented to them the idea of a congress of the principal powers of Europe, supported by an armed force, as the best means of checking the factions here, or providing means of establishing a more desirable state of affairs. . . .

The queen had earlier been even more outspoken. "Armed force alone can make everything good," she had written in September, 1791, to her brother, Leopold, now Austrian emperor.

The dangers coming from France were not immediately apparent to the European powers. In 1789 liberal opinion throughout Europe had in general welcomed the news of the great events in Paris. Conservative opinion was not at first greatly aroused, for the public policy of France's European neighbors was directed toward other areas. In 1787 Russia and Austria had begun a war for the partition of Turkey, and in 1788 Russia was also at war with Sweden. A revolt in the Austrian Netherlands against the innovations of Joseph II began in December, 1789. The reform program of the Polish patriots was arousing the concern of Poland's two neighbors, Russia and Prussia. The European powers, in short, were concerned with their own selfish interests to which they did not at first consider that France brought any threat. Hence they saw no need to intervene. This was true despite the fact that Marie Antoinette was the sister of the Austrian emperor, and that the "Family Compact" of 1761, still operative, bound France and Spain in supposedly close alliance. Europe, in the words of the French historian, Sorel, failed to intervene at first "for the sole reason that there was no Europe." Statesmen could console themselves with the reflection that France, torn by internal conflict, counted for little in the international struggle for power. They could note that in May, 1790, the Constituent Assembly had voted to renounce all wars of conquest. Only gradually did concern for the fate of their brother-monarch in Paris and fears of what France might do abroad arouse the crowned heads of Europe to a policy of action.

Various developments contributed to a changed outlook. Trouble arose in Alsace where, ever since the Peace of Westphalia, some German princes had been guaranteed by France the exercise of their feudal rights. In abolishing such rights throughout France the Constituent Assembly had offered the German princes a cash indemnity which they refused, appealing to the Austrian emperor for backing. In December, 1791, he sent the French government a sharp note of protest, but with no success.

Other matters began to arouse European concern. One was the fate of the territory of Avignon in the south of France, which since the fourteenth century had been owned by the papacy. Following a popular rebellion in June, 1790, that led Avignon to demand annexation to France, the Constituent Assembly had finally voted to incorporate this territory in France and proceeded to do so despite papal protests. In another area France forfeited the friendship of Spain in 1790, as a result of a dispute between Spain and England over their respective rights to Nootka Sound on the northwest coast of America. When William Pitt prepared his "Spanish Armament"—a naval force to reinforce England's claims—Spain appealed to France for support. This the Assembly refused to give (August, 1790) with the result that Spain backed down and France lost its closest ally of the eighteenth century.

The Belgian revolt against Austria likewise made trouble, since its leaders made overtures to the new French government, some of which were cordially received. A further source of tension was the steadily increasing emigration from France. Particularly in the Rhineland the *émigrés* began to organize for the purpose of armed intervention, and to this end they actually began sending secret agents into France.

In England the mistrust of French developments steadily grew. When Edmund Burke, who earlier had defended in Parliament the cause of the rebellious American colonists, published his *Reflections on the Revolution in France* (November, 1790), this eloquent denunciation of what he called "the cannibal philosophers" of France undoubtedly strengthened English hostility. Burke's argument was that the French revolutionary leaders were ignoring the great historical truth that a country's roots lie deep in the past and that change should come about by an orderly, gradual and evolutionary process. To undertake a radical transformation on the basis of pure reason, according to Burke, can only lead to disaster. Soon translated into French and German, the *Reflections* had a powerful influence on conservative thought abroad.

The attempted flight of the royal family in June, 1791, intensified foreign concern. In July the Emperor Leopold issued a secret circular from Padua to his brother monarchs, proposing a joint declaration to the French government threatening to avenge "any future outrages" against the royal family. Not receiving much response, Leopold persuaded Frederick William II of Prussia to sign with him the Declaration of Pillnitz (August, 1791), urging European rulers to recognize that the fate of the French king was matter of common concern to them all and therefore that, if the other powers would cooperate, then Austria and Prussia "are resolved to act promptly, in mutual accord with the forces necessary to attain the proposed common objective." This Pillnitz declaration was deeply resented in France.

As the year 1792 began, the prospects of war increased. Most of the Girondins were in favor of war, thinking that it would unmask the king whom they now mistrusted and strengthen the position of their party. Louis XVI favored war, but for precisely opposite reasons. He expected that foreign intervention would succeed and that his opponents would be overthrown. Only Robespierre and a small group of Jacobins spoke out in favor of peace. Distrusting both the Girondins and the king, they felt that the country was unready for combat and that a military disaster might lead to a dictatorship.

War came in the spring. In March, 1792, Louis dismissed his Feuillant ministers, who had been publicly denounced in the Assembly, and chose a

Girondin ministry with General Dumouriez as Minister of Foreign Affairs and Roland head of the Department of the Interior. The Girondins, who were strong for war, dominated the legislature. Having first issued a statement that it would never undertake a war of conquest or injure the liberties of other peoples, the Legislative Assembly by an almost unanimous vote on April 20 declared war on Austria. On May 1 Prussia allied itself with Austria.

The first campaign went badly for the French. A great many regular army officers had resigned their commissions and the general quality of new leadership was not high. Some regiments went over to the enemy; others fled at the first encounter. Dumouriez's invasion of the Austrian Netherlands consequently proved an ignominious failure. Meanwhile the crisis grew at home. A decree of the Assembly that non-juring priests must be deported (May 27) and another authorizing a new army to be made up of 20,000 *Fédérés* (National Guard units from the various departments) were vetoed by Louis. When Roland protested, the king dismissed him and two of his colleagues. The new ministry selected from the Feuillant group therefore represented a temporary swing to the right.

These developments led to the "Day of June 20." A demonstration, originally planned for this date to celebrate the anniversary of the Tennis Court Oath, quickly assumed a menacing aspect. A mob appeared before the Assembly and submitted a petition protesting against Louis' dismissal of the Girondin ministers. Another mob broke into the palace of the Tuileries, found Louis and held him in humiliating conversation for several hours. Louis showed courage. He donned a revolutionary cap, drank a toast to the nation but refused to take back his veto of the decrees. Eventually the mayor of Paris arrived and rescued him from the mob.

There could be little doubt that republicanism was now a growing force. July and August, 1792, were months of crisis for the monarchy and for France. Some bourgeois opinion professed outrage at the treatment of the king. On the other hand radicalism, inspired by the Jacobins, also increased. Armed groups of *Fédérés* began to arrive in Paris, among them a group from Marseilles singing a marching-song composed by Rouget de Lisle at Strasbourg and soon to win immortality as the *Marseillaise*. On July 10 the Feuillant ministry was once again replaced by the Girondins, who immediately obtained a vote from the Assembly that the country was in danger and undertook various emergency measures to meet it.

Meanwhile an Austro-Prussian army led by the Duke of Brunswick prepared to invade France. On July 25 he issued a Manifesto to the French people which was published in the *Moniteur* at Paris on August 3. The Manifesto professed "no other aim than the welfare of France." All Frenchmen were urged to submit to the invading armies. Brunswick threatened to treat as rebels all National Guards who took up arms and to deliver Paris "to military punishment and total destruction" if the least harm was done to the royal family. The Manifesto, deplored by Louis XVI, spelled his doom.

On the night of August 9–10, organized risings through Paris overthrew the existing city government and set up a "Revolutionary Commune." The mayor, Pétion, was seized and the commander of the National Guard was shot. The Commune was the nearest thing to "direct democracy" that France had yet seen.[1] A huge mob, far uglier in temper than that of June 20, stormed the Tuileries, where the loyal Swiss guards put up a devoted resistance. The king and the royal family, with the noise of firing in their ears, hastened across the courtyard and flung themselves upon the mercy of the Legislative Assembly in session nearby in the royal riding-school. Under these conditions of violence, and menaced by the threats of the revolutionary Commune of Paris, the Assembly voted on August 10 to suspend the monarchy. On the same day it issued a decree for the summoning of a National Convention to assemble in Paris on September 20. Meanwhile, a provisional Executive Council of six ministers was authorized to act in place of Louis XVI. In essence, therefore, this step was the most revolutionary that the government of France so far had taken.

From the suspension of the monarchy on August 10 to the meeting of the Convention on September 20, power was divided between three bodies: the somewhat discredited Legislative Assembly, the revolutionary Commune of Paris and the new Executive Council. This latter body soon came to be dominated by Georges Jacques Danton (1759–1794), the new Minister of Justice. Danton was a typical product of the revolutionary age. A lawyer of modest origin from the provincial town of Arcis-sur-Aube, Danton had secured a minor governmental position in Paris before 1789. He soon identified himself with the revolutionary life of the capital, was elected president of his district and became one of the best-known men in Paris. Danton had been president of the radical Cordeliers Club. His powerful figure and magnificent eloquence also made him a dominant character at the Jacobins. Failing to be elected to the Legislative Assembly, he neverthe-less grew steadily in reputation and influence. The appearance of the revolutionary Commune in Paris after August 10 gave him still further prestige. He so dominated the Executive Council that the critical last month of the Legislative Assembly was in some sense a Danton dictatorship.

The critical problems were both domestic and foreign. By a series of

1. This Paris Commune, in the sense of being an example of popular revolutionary violence, is the source of one meaning of the modern word, "Communist."

decrees the Assembly authorized a special court to try conspirators, confiscated the property of all religious houses without exception, introduced even stricter measures against the non-juring clergy, authorized the confiscation and sale of *émigré* lands and abolished all remaining feudal dues without compensation unless the proprietor could produce his original title. Meanwhile Lafayette, despairing of the future of the monarchy, deserted to the Austrians, who put him in confinement. On August 19 the Prussians under the Duke of Brunswick entered France. On September 2 the news reached Paris that the great fortress of Verdun, the chief obstacle on the road to the capital, was about to fall. This news was the precipitant of the September Massacres—one of the bloodiest episodes in the entire history of the Revolution. The Paris mobs once again roamed the streets, inspired by provocative posters, by inflammatory speeches and by nameless rumors. It was claimed that the prisons harbored traitors who were prepared to break out in organized revolt as soon as the assembled volunteers left Paris for the front. The special criminal court authorized by the Assembly had not begun to function. Hence the mobs took justice into their own hands. Prison after prison was visited; the inmates were briefly questioned and then, in most cases, summarily executed. Piles of mutilated bodies lay at the prison gates. The total of these ghastly executions which included many non-juring clergy reached about 1,100. Equally savage massacres occurred in a number of provincial towns. Danton, as Minister of Justice, certainly condoned if he did not actually initiate these acts of violence. Editors such as Jean Paul Marat recklessly published incitements to mob violence. In a larger sense, though it is no justification of them, the massacres were the unanticipated outcome of an embittered and seemingly ominous revolutionary situation.

On September 20, 1792, the very day on which the Legislative Assembly was due to turn over its powers to the newly-elected Convention, the invading army of the Duke of Brunswick met the French near the little town of Valmy, less than a hundred miles from Paris. Obscured in the early morning mists, the defenders stood firm against the Prussian cannonade and replied with vigor. To the astonishment of all Europe the Prussian army turned in retreat. Whatever the explanation—dysentery, bad weather, muddy roads or poor morale—the Prussian retreat made the "cannonade of Valmy" one of the decisive battles of history. The direction of the entire campaign was reversed so that the Revolution, hitherto on the defensive, soon took on an aggressive, crusading character.[2]

These dramatic events should not obscure other measures undertaken by the Legislative Assembly during the one year of its existence. It authorized

2. Brunswick's decision at Valmy is one of the great understatements of history: *Hier schlagen wir nicht* ("We won't fight here").

the issuance of further *assignats* to the value of 900,000,000 francs. It issued instructions and rules for the operation of the new tax-system which the Constituent Assembly had created. It attempted on various occasions to reduce the still surviving feudal dues and to sell *émigré* lands in small parcels to peasants. As one of its last acts it legalized divorce and made the recording of births, marriages and deaths a civil rather than a church function. It conferred honorary citizenship on a number of distinguished foreigners including Tom Paine, Bentham, Wilberforce, Pestalozzi, Washington, Hamilton, Madison and the Polish patriot, Kosciuszko. On April 20, 1792, the very day on which it had declared war, the Legislative Assembly received from a committee headed by Condorcet a report on education, properly described as a landmark in French educational history.[3] This report declared education to be the birthright of all children and therefore a public responsibility. Adopting the principle of coeducation, the state should provide a network of schools which would train all according to their abilities. The study of the sciences, citizenship, the arts, literature and hygiene should be included. The goals were declared to be the welfare of the individual, of *la patrie* and of mankind as a whole.

In this mingled atmosphere of idealism, of bloody domestic strife and of foreign war the Legislative Assembly came to an end. Intended to be the established government of a new France, it had disbanded in less than a year, giving place to a new and constitutionally unauthorized body, the Convention.

■ GIRONDIN ASCENDANCE IN THE CONVENTION, 1792–1793

With the meeting of the Convention in September, 1792, the French Revolution entered another phase. In a narrow sense this body had been authorized by the Legislative Assembly in order to make the constitutional changes necessitated by the suspension of the king. In point of fact constitution-making turned out to be one of the least important duties of the new body, which came into existence just as the revolutionary storm within France rose to its climax and as the war assumed European proportions. Not until the autumn of 1795, when the fires of violent revolution had died down, was the Convention able to achieve its original purpose, to agree upon a constitution and disband.

The Legislative Assembly had taken upon itself to ignore the voting provisions stipulated in the Constitution of 1791. The distinction between "active" and "passive" citizens was now to be dropped, though the voting, as previously, was to take place in two stages. Not more than one-tenth of

---

3. Talleyrand is entitled to the credit of having first submitted a comprehensive plan for public primary and secondary education to the Constituent Assembly, in September, 1791.

the estimated seven million eligible voters went to the polls. As the balloting began on the very day of the great prison massacres of September, it is understandable that the results showed a sharp swing to the left.

Not a single royalist deputy was elected. The Girondin group, which had formerly sat on the left of the presiding officer, now sat on the right, a compact body of 165. The great majority of the deputies, some 500 in number, sat on low seats in the center of the hall, an area nicknamed "the Plain" or more contemptuously "the Marsh." Here were men such as Sieyès and Grégoire, formerly prominent in the Constituent Assembly but no longer playing a dominant role. The deputies of the Plain were clearly disposed to follow but not to lead. On the high benches at the left, from which they won the nickname of "the Mountain," sat the 90 or so Jacobin deputies. These were the extremists, schooled in the atmosphere of the clubs and the Paris *sections.* Not yet able to win control, they were nevertheless to be of steadily increasing influence. Out of the 750 deputies only two could properly be classed as artisans.

The Girondins, whose principal figures were Brissot, Vergniaud, Condorcet, Pétion and Roland, were the direct heirs of the *philosophes,* even as the Jacobins could be said to inherit something of the more radical tradition of Rousseau. The Girondins were republicans of necessity, democrats in theory, yet in fact woefully out of touch with the raw democracy of the Paris streets. They were men of property, middle-class intellectuals and cultivated theorists who were fond of meeting at the *salon* of that "republican soul," Madame Roland, in order to air their views. Their most striking difference from the Jacobins lay in their suspicion of the leadership of Paris, for which reason they were accused by the Jacobins of attempting to weaken France by creating a loosely federal state. One of their number, Pétion, was elected president of the Convention and another, Condorcet, vice-president. Others held key secretarial posts, so that the group as a whole, though not truly a party in the English sense, provided the driving force in public affairs from September, 1792, until the end of May, 1793.

The first urgent problem was to determine the nature of the new French constitution. On September 21, 1792, with notable lack of fervor the Convention unanimously declared the monarchy abolished. On the following day it was voted that all public documents should be dated from "the Year I of the French Republic." Three days later Danton's motion, that "the French Republic is one and indivisible," was accepted. By such indirect means rather than by any explicit declaration the French Republic was introduced into history. Gradually the departmental governments and the army groups sent in their loyal adherence to the new republican regime.

The fate of the monarch was still undecided. Louis was no longer king, but the debate as to whether he should be punished was dragged on for three months. The Jacobins had no hesitation in proposing extreme measures. "The king must die," Robespierre declared, "so that the country may live." His colleague, St. Just, was equally blunt: "A king deserves death, not for what he does, but for what he is." After a large number of incriminating letters proving Louis' traitorous correspondence abroad were discovered in the Tuileries, "Louis Capet" was brought to trial in December, 1792, before the full Convention on an indictment of treason. On January 14 the Convention voted unanimously that he was guilty. Subsequently the death penalty was determined by a vote of 387 to 334. On January 21, 1793, attended by a non-juring priest, Louis was escorted from his prison to the Place de la Révolution (now the Place de la Concorde) and publicly executed amid cries of "Vive la Nation." A weak man throughout his life, he had endured prison with resignation and he died bravely. The victory, if such it may be called, was that of the Jacobins, who now were in a position to appeal for still more terror in order to gain their ends.

Up to this point the war had gone well. By November, 1792, not only had the invading armies been driven from French soil, but in addition three republican armies had crossed the frontier. In the north, Dumouriez invaded the Austrian Netherlands, won the Battle of Jemappes (November 6), and seized Brussels, Antwerp and Liège. To the east, General Custine advanced into the Rhineland, winning Speyer, Worms, Frankfurt and Mainz. A third army under Montesquiou and Anselme marched southward into Savoy and Nice. The "natural frontiers" of France for which Louis XIV had fought in vain were quickly won by the new armies of the infant republic. Under these intoxicating circumstances the Convention voted two "propaganda decrees." On November 19 it promised "fraternity and aid to all peoples who wish to recover their liberty" and on December 15 it announced that it would bring "peace, aid, fraternity, liberty and equality" and suppress all feudal rights and privileges in the lands occupied by the French armies. After local plebiscites, Nice and Savoy were annexed to France, while in the Netherlands and the Rhineland, town after town likewise voted for annexation. By March, 1793, the Convention ratified these votes and declared the territories a part of the French Republic.

In consequence, the scope of the war quickly broadened. England, shocked by Louis' execution and by the threat to the Low Countries, broke off diplomatic relations with France, which in reply declared war on England and Holland on February 1, 1793. Spain, Portugal, Sardinia, Tuscany, Naples and (in 1794) the entire Holy Roman Empire likewise declared war. Among the major European powers, therefore, only Russia, busy in Poland and Turkey, failed to take up arms against France.

At this critical moment in the spring of 1793 the French government faced civil war at home. Economic conditions were bad, for the *assignats* depreciated still further, food became scarce and costly, and unemployment increased. The war demanded more troops, even though over 200,000 men were already in the field—as many as Louis XIV ever had been able to maintain at one time. To meet its military needs the Convention decreed in February, 1793, a levy of 300,000 men to be drawn from all those between the ages of eighteen and forty—a preliminary to the later development of a full-fledged system of national conscription. Under all these stresses the districts in the west of France known as the Vendée, where the influence of the non-juring priests was strongest, broke out in rebellion. At the same time General Dumouriez, whose plans to invade Holland had gone astray, was recalled. Instead of obeying, he first planned to march on Paris and restore the monarchy, and then deserted, like Lafayette, to the Austrians.

The Convention adopted drastic measures to deal with a desperate situation. Between March and May a whole series of emergency measures were decreed. A special tax was imposed on the rich, *assignats* were made legal tender, and by the first Law of the Maximum (May, 1793) local authorities were empowered to fix maximum prices for grain. The old decrees against *émigrés* were consolidated and made harsher. Various new means were devised to enforce authority. A new criminal court, later known as the Revolutionary Tribunal, was set up. Citizens were empowered to organize local "Watch Committees" to root out suspects. "Representatives on Mission" were to be sent to the armies and the provinces for the same purpose. A Committee of Public Safety, later to become the supreme agency of revolutionary power, was authorized in April to coordinate executive and legislative power.[4] By all these means the leaders of the Convention struggled to avoid disaster.

In the late spring of 1793 the general discontent with the Girondin leaders became acute. The draft of a new constitution which, despite all other urgent matters, Condorcet and his colleagues had managed to complete had been brushed aside in February as too moderate. One of the principal Jacobin leaders, Dr. Marat, who had accused the Girondins of treachery, triumphantly averted their attempt to convict him before the Revolutionary Tribunal. The Girondins, for their part, vainly attempted to stir up the departments against the capital.

At the end of May huge mobs, organized by the *sections* (or precincts) of the Paris Commune, surrounded the Convention and demanded the arrest of the Girondin leaders. Rebuffed once, the mobs returned on June 2 and

4. A Committee of General Defense had been authorized in January and reorganized in March, 1793, but was soon supplanted by the Committee of Public Safety.

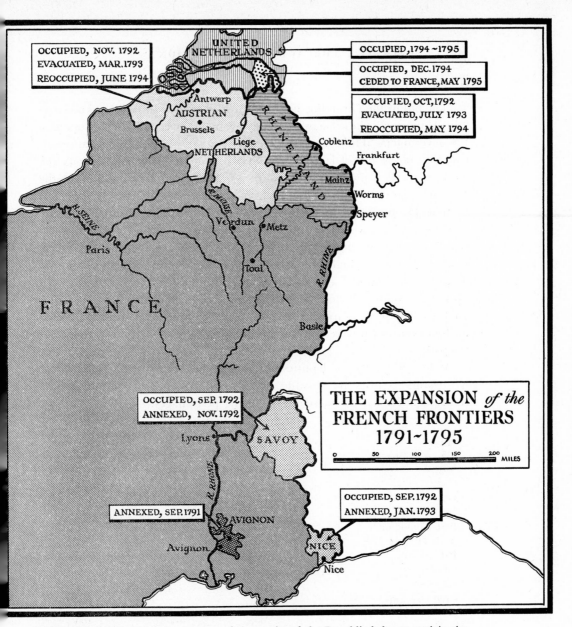

This striking evidence of the successes of the armies of the Republic helps to explain the revolutionary fervor which overtook France and the deep concern aroused in Europe.

this time so intimidated the Convention that it decreed the arrest of twenty-nine leading Girondins, among them Brissot, Vergniaud and Madame Roland (whose husband contrived to escape). Some went into hiding; others were seized later. Ultimately about 140 Girondin deputies were either arrested or dispersed, their fate lying in the hands of the Jacobins, who now assumed power. From moderate republicanism France was passing to the more extreme phase known as Jacobinism.

■ THE JACOBINS

The fall of the Girondins in June, 1793, left the radical group known as "the Mountain"—in other words, the Jacobins—in a position to dominate the government. These were the men who in the eyes of their European contemporaries and of later generations came most especially to typify the Revolution. It is important, therefore, to have some understanding of the Jacobin organization, its membership, its creed and its leaders.

The Jacobin Club in Paris, it will be recalled, had begun innocently enough in 1789 as a group of like-minded deputies, "Friends of the Constitution," meeting conveniently in a former Jacobin convent in the Rue Saint-Honoré. It had gradually become an important center of political power. Throughout 1790 and 1791 local societies, similarly organized, had grown up so that eventually there were an estimated 6,800 Jacobin clubs in France, all linked with the parent society in Paris. In 1793–1794 perhaps half a million Frenchmen were enrolled members, with an equal number in close sympathy.

Who, apart from the deputies in the Assembly, joined the Jacobin clubs? No overall statistics are possible, but a sampling of several groups where records survive has produced the following percentages:

CLASSES	GROUP I	GROUP II	GROUP III
Lawyers	6%	9%	8%
Clergy	5	4	2
Other Liberal Professions	8	11	8
Merchants	9	15	9
Petty Tradesmen	16	16	20
Artisans	22	22	31
Peasants	10	8	11
Officers	6	4	2
Soldiers	6	4	1
Civil Servants	12	7	8
	100%	100%	100%

It will be seen that the clubs included a wide range of occupations. They were dominated by no one type although there was a marked concentration of the petty bourgeois. "The Jacobin was neither noble nor beggar—though most clubs had a sprinkling of both of these—but almost anything in between." [5]

5. CRANE BRINTON, *The Jacobins* (1930), p. 70. This important study is the basis for most of what is said here about the Jacobins.

Various purposes were served by the Jacobin clubs. The parent body in Paris became a powerful pressure-group, a center where political reputations could be made and where debates and resolutions had an almost official force. Much of the work was that of propaganda—issuing statements, submitting petitions and denouncing unpopular acts. A good deal of ritual developed, some of it similar to the ritual of the Masonic lodges. The Jacobins became adept at various symbolic manifestations of patriotism such as erecting altars to *la patrie* and planting trees of liberty. Through active correspondence the parent society could exhort the Jacobin clubs in the departments and alert them to new developments. Even more important, after the fall of the monarchy and the development of various improvised, emergency techniques of administration, the local societies became a semi-official part of the government, acting as agents of surveillance and denouncing suspected traitors.

The basic creed of the Jacobins was, of course, republican. Unlike the Girondins, they accepted a centralized leadership at Paris. They were good nationalists. They believed in a secular state in which the religion of *la patrie* took precedence over that of the organized churches. They disliked privilege and professed a belief in equality. But it is hard to see the Jacobins, as some have done, as incipient socialists. They were, on the contrary, believers in private property and advocates of laissez-faire. The products of a revolutionary age, they were willing to countenance the use of ruthless force to secure ends that they believed good, and it may well be that they were at times pushed further in the direction of radicalism than in theory they would have desired. In sum, the Jacobins can be regarded as the most remarkable example before our own day of the way in which an organized and indoctrinated minority can effectively impose itself upon a country at a time of crisis.

Marat, Saint-Just and Robespierre best typify Jacobin leadership in this year of their supremacy. Danton, once active in the Jacobin Club and easily the leading figure in France when he became Minister of Justice in August, 1792, resigned from the Committee of Public Safety in July, 1793, and never again was able to dominate the public scene. Jean Paul Marat (1743–1793) was a strange figure, a medical doctor evidently of some ability who had lived in England before the Revolution and had published monographs on scientific and political subjects. In 1789 he founded a newspaper, *L'Ami du Peuple,* a bloodthirsty, vituperative and intensely popular journal, always ready to advocate violence as a means to the desired end. Marat, who dressed like a pirate and represented one of the poorest sections of Paris in the Convention, was elected president of the Jacobin Club in April, 1793. His biographers have stressed the persistent element of humanitarian sympathy which lay beneath his violent and repulsive exterior. In July he was assassinated by a country girl, Charlotte Corday, who sincerely thought she had rid the country of a tyrant. In death Marat became the greatest of the revolutionary martyrs.

Louis Antoine de Saint-Just (1767–1794) when elected a deputy to the Convention was only twenty-four. He had absorbed like a sponge the radical ideas around him in Paris and had become an ardent admirer and follower of Robespierre. A certain youthful fanaticism and tireless energy soon brought him to the front rank of Jacobin leadership. "One does not make revolutions by halves," he declared. Saint-Just was notable for his passionate oratory and for the relentless zeal with which he undertook the work of representative on mission. He has rightly been called the Apostle of the Terror for, like Marat, he was prepared always to use violence in order to win his desired goal. The violence which he employed was eventually to destroy him. At the age of twenty-six he died, with Robespierre, on the guillotine.

Maximilien Robespierre (1758–1794) was a lawyer from Arras, hardly noticed at first in the Constituent Assembly but soon rising through the Jacobins to an outstanding position. His old-fashioned dress and prim manner belied the terrifying fanaticism that inspired him. Robespierre had been a reader of Rousseau and seems to have believed that he had a mission to bring about that reign of virtue of which Rousseau dreamed. In theory he doubtless accepted the principle of the general will and popular sovereignty. In practice he took the view that virtue was usually in a minority and consequently that the burden of leadership would fall upon a few chosen spirits. Robespierre's contemporary nickname was "The Incorruptible." At the height of his power he lived modestly near the Convention in the quiet circle of a carpenter's family. No evidence has ever been found that he accumulated wealth, as did so many of his colleagues. For himself he sought nothing save power, which he never scrupled to use against any who were rash enough or, as he felt, wicked enough to oppose him.

The constitutional question was still urgent, for the Girondin draft of a republican machinery of government had been rejected. Hence a revised, Jacobin draft was hastily prepared and presented to the Convention on June 10. Its history was brief. Accepted by the Convention on June 24, it was ratified overwhelmingly by a plebiscite on August 20 and promptly shelved by the Convention on October 10. Had this Constitution of 1793 ever gone into effect, France would have found itself with universal manhood suffrage and a general system of democratic control going far beyond anything it had hitherto known. The legislature was to be elected by direct vote, was to be completely renewed every year, and was to choose an executive council from lists established by popular vote in the departments. A system of referendum and recall was provided. In the declaration of rights were statements concerning public education, public relief and the workers' rights to subsistence. Insurrection against an unjust government was declared to be "the most sacred of rights and the most indispensable of duties." In general, however, the constitution still emphasized the rights of property.

The immediate domestic problem was the "Federalist Revolt" which had flared up in some sixty departments, partly because of appeals made by the exiled Girondin leaders. By the end of July this revolt had been mastered, save for a few cities such as Lyons which held out in rebellion until October and Toulon which resisted until December. Continuing unrest in the Vendée together with the seriousness of the military situation in the summer of 1793 made it seem imperative to the Jacobins that they continue to govern by revolutionary means. On October 10 any prospect of putting into operation the new constitution was ended by a decree, voted by the Convention, to the effect that "the provisional government of France is revolutionary until the peace."

■ REVOLUTIONARY GOVERNMENT

The structure and operation of this "Revolutionary Government" now brought into operation by the Jacobins deserve careful analysis. In practice the system dated from the suspension of the king in August, 1792, when it became necessary to improvise a new means of government. As one crisis followed another, additional steps were taken until in the end an elaborate machinery of dictatorial government—the first of its kind in modern times—had come into being. This technique of government illustrates the way in which a determined group can maintain itself in power by concentrating authority in a series of self-perpetuating committees only nominally subject to the national legislative body. By means of terror and various propaganda devices public opinion can be kept under control. In this sense the revolutionary regime in the France of 1793 has some affinities with the Fascist, National Socialist and Communist regimes of the twentieth century.

The first political steps had been taken in the closing days of the Legislative Assembly where, after the suspension of the king, a Provisional Executive Council, first dominated by Danton, was set up. This Council declined in authority after the first danger of invasion waned and the newly-elected Convention began to assert itself.

Most of the revolutionary machinery which the Jacobins were to use so effectively was created during the Girondin regime in the early months of 1793. A Committee of General Security, first set up in October, 1792, to supervise police activities, was enlarged in the spring of 1793. It had twelve members supposedly replaced each month. Later overshadowed by the Committee of Public Safety, it nevertheless remained one of the two great committees by which the revolutionary machinery was directed. The Committee of Public Safety was created by decree of the Convention in April, 1793. It was an emergency executive committee of twelve (originally nine) members of the Convention, deliberating in secret and having broad executive powers. Its members were to be chosen only for a term of one month and were to make weekly reports to the Convention. Supposedly the agent of the Convention, from April to July, 1793, it was really a Danton ministry. Thenceforth the Committee of Public Safety became a self-perpetuating Jacobin instrument, dominated by Robespierre. Its powers extended to all major aspects of domestic and foreign affairs.

In March, 1793, the Convention had also created the Revolutionary Tribunal. Its purpose was to combat all counter-revolutionary activities and threats to the security of the state. Five judges were to be appointed by the Convention, as well as a public prosecutor, and twelve jurors who were to make known their decisions individually and publicly. The Tribunal, at first hesitant in its duties, soon grew in authority and confidence. Between March, 1793, and July, 1794, it sentenced to death some 2,600 French men and women, among them the principal Girondin leaders and also Marie Antoinette. Similar tribunals were established in the chief provincial cities.

Other means were simultaneously employed to guarantee the authority of the central government. In March and April, 1793, the Convention authorized representatives on mission to be sent to each department and to the armies of the Republic. Some did good work, others outrageously abused their powers and were strongly disliked by the departmental governments. Another device was to set up permanent, appointive local agents or watch committees in the departments to draw up lists of suspects and in general to see that the laws were enforced. Still another device was to make use of the local Jacobin clubs, which thus became a semi-official branch of the government.

Several economic measures were likewise undertaken. These too had their origins in the period of Girondin rule. *Assignats* had been made legal tender in April, 1793, while an attempt to fix a maximum price for grain had been made in May. In June it was provided that peasants could buy *émigré* land worth up to 500 francs by making payments over a period of twenty years without interest. The Jacobins pushed these economic measures still further. In July, 1793, the last remaining feudal dues owed by the peasants were declared abolished without compensation. Hoarding and profiteering were made capital crimes. In September a compulsory loan was exacted from wealthier citizens in proportion to their income. A "Law of the Maximum" was passed in September going much further than the measure of the preceding May. Uniform prices throughout France were fixed for grain, flour, salt, soap and tobacco. For other staples the maximum was to be fixed in each district at one-third more than the prevailing prices of 1790. Maximum wages in each commune were to be those of 1790 plus one-half. This measure was a reaction to emergency conditions rather than an expression of any radical economic philosophy. Although in the long run a failure, it had temporarily a stabilizing effect upon the price structure. In October a Commission of Supplies was established with the right to seize supplies and with power over the production, transportation, importing and exporting of agricultural and industrial products.

The most dramatic effort to mobilize France was the *Levée en Masse* proclaimed in August, 1793. This, the first attempt at full national mobilization in modern history, declared all French citizens to be in permanent requisition for army service:

> The young men will go to battle; married men will forge arms and transport foodstuffs; women will make tents and will serve in hospitals; children will tear rags into lint; old men will get themselves carried to public places, there to stir up the courage of the warriors, hatred of kings and unity in the republic.

More concretely, unmarried men from eighteen to twenty-five were called to arms, representatives on mission were sent to all departments to requisition supplies and supervise recruiting, arrears in taxes were to be collected forthwith and scientists along with experts of various kinds were pressed into industrial service.

Ruthless means were invoked to suppress opposition. The "First Terror," which ran through the closing half of 1793, brought the guillotine into action. In September the Convention declared, "Terror is the order of the day." In the same month the Law of Suspects authorized the immediate arrest of those who "by their conduct, associations, talk, or writings have shown themselves partisans of tyranny." Local watch committees were empowered to draw up lists of suspects. On October 10, as already noted, the centralized, dictatorial system of emergency government was declared to be in operation until peace. Finally, on December 4, 1793, a document known as the "Constitution of the Terror" was voted by the Convention. This brought together in one comprehensive decree the various earlier emergency measures. Although lip service was paid to the authority of the Convention, actually the Committee of Public Safety and to a lesser degree the Committee of General Security were now the central organs of government.

Some twenty thousand people throughout France lost their lives in this First Terror. Taking France as a whole and including the later Terror, the number of victims (counting those who died in prison or who were denied trial) has been reliably estimated at between 35,000 and 40,000. Less than 17,000 were actually condemned by the courts. These figures are shocking enough, even though they pale beside the mass executions of our own day. That the guillotine was used to destroy one class, the aristocracy, is a thesis not borne out by the evidence. Careful tabulation and analysis of all available figures show that the Terror was "socially indiscriminate but politically perspicacious"—it was used, in other words, not as an agent of class war but to destroy people of any class whatever who were opposed to the Revolution, to the Republic and, in the end, to the Jacobin party.[6]

Under the Jacobins the course of the war, which in the first half of 1793 had gone badly, causing the French to abandon their conquests, altered for the better. By August an army of 650,000 men was in the field under the command of new revolutionary generals: Davout, aged 24, Hoche, aged 25, Jourdan, aged 31, and Moreau, aged 32. This was by far the largest army ever yet assembled by a European power. The *Levée en Masse,* decreed in August, released trained soldiers from garrison duty. As Minister of War, Lazare Carnot, "the Organizer of Victory," worked wonders. "Demi-brigades" were formed by combining two battalions of volunteers with one battalion of the line. New officers, new tactics and new discipline were employed. Siege warfare was abandoned. Troops went into battle not in the elaborate, parade-ground, line formation of tradition, but in easily maneuverable columns with their officers at the head. Government laboratories sought improvements in weapons and powder. An observation balloon was used for the first time at the Battle of Fleurus and an "optical telegraph," or system of semaphores, made it possible to relay messages from Paris to the northeast frontier in a few hours.

By October, 1793, the menace of a second invasion of France was removed, and by the end of the year the threat of internal revolt was also stayed. The French armies once again resumed the offensive, so that Jourdan's great victory at Fleurus in June, 1794, opened the way for a second overrunning of the Austrian Netherlands. Such was the military legacy which the Jacobins were able to hand on to their successors.

■ THE REPUBLIC OF VIRTUE

In this great sweep of revolutionary change, what has been perhaps ironically called "The Republic of Virtue" came into existence. Attempts were made to create an entire new outlook for Frenchmen. Many of these attempts we might classify as political psychology and propaganda. A decree

6. See the important statistical study by DONALD GREER, *The Incidence of the Terror* (1935).

of October, 1793, created a new calendar. "The French Era" was declared to begin on September 22, 1792, the day following the abolition of monarchy and by happy coincidence the autumnal equinox. "The equality of the days and the nights," declared a committee, "was marked in the heavens at the same moment when civil and moral equality was proclaimed." This "Year I of Liberty" was divided into twelve months of thirty days each: the months were divided into three "decades" of ten days, and at the close of the year there would be five (or, in leap years, six) days of holiday, dedicated somewhat mysteriously to Virtue, Genius, Labor, Opinion and Rewards.[7] It will be observed that this revolutionary calendar, in effect until 1806, blandly ignored the practices of the rest of the world and gave no recognition to the Sabbath, the saints' days and the festivals of the Christian calendar. The government's action can thus be seen as a part of the continuing development in the direction of "civic religion" and possibly dechristianization to which many of the Jacobin leaders were committed.

The period of the Terror saw a continuing attack on religion. Little pretense was made to keep in operation the Civil Constitution of the Clergy. "Civic religion" in its various patriotic manifestations was considered by many an adequate substitute for the old faith. Examples of fanaticism were numerous. One representative on mission (Fouché) took it upon himself to proclaim at Nevers that "death is an eternal slumber." A deputy at Paris demanded that all church towers and spires be pulled down as "contrary to the principle of equality." On November 10, 1792, the Cathedral of Notre Dame in Paris became a "Temple of Reason" and in a decorous ceremony (none the less shocking to conventional opinion) an actress of the *Comédie-Française* impersonated the Goddess of Reason. Some bishops, Gobel and Talleyrand among them, renounced their orders. Local action frequently outran that of the central government. In Paris, for example, all churches were closed by a decree of the Commune in November, 1793.

The growth of the new revolutionary spirit found expression in the countless "little things" of the republican age: the use of the term, *citoyen*, instead of *monsieur*, or of the familiar *tu* in address, instead of the more formal *vous*. In dress the *sansculottes* or trousers replaced the aristocratic knee-breeches. Wigs quickly went out of fashion. The typical Paris Jacobin of 1794 wore trousers, an open necked shirt, a short jacket, a red "Phrygian"

---

7. The new names of months had a markedly poetic flavor. Beginning on September 22, the three autumn months were *Vendémiaire, Brumaire* and *Frimaire.* The winter months were *Nivôse, Pluviôse* and *Ventôse.* The spring months were *Germinal, Floréal* and *Prairial,* and the summer months *Messidor, Thermidor* and *Fructidor.* Each day of the year was given some natural, if less poetic, designation: the day of the cedar, of the cauliflower, of the pickaxe, of the plow, of manure, of the goat, etc. Revolutionaries seldom seem to have a sense of humor.

cap of liberty and in many cases wooden shoes in order to conserve leather for the army. All kinds of revolutionary symbols were in evidence—tricolor cockades, framed copies of the Rights of Man, busts of Rousseau or Marat, altars to *la patrie* and trees of liberty. Names of Roman republican heroes such as "Brutus" or "Gracchus" became common. Not only individuals but even towns changed their names so as to remove any suggestion of royalism. It became customary to organize parades, public festivals and ceremonies testifying to the new republican faith, so that the entire life of France was colored by a vivid republican symbolism. In December, 1793, the Convention, amid so many other concerns, asserted the principle of free compulsory education for all.

By the autumn of 1793 Robespierre and his group dominated the Convention as earlier they had dominated the Jacobin Club. The Girondins, victims of the Terror along with the queen and many others, were gone. The fortunes of the war once again were prospering. Such troubles as now arose in France came from those who, while accepting the Revolution, opposed the immediate policies of Robespierre or resented the enormous concentration of power in the hands of the twelve members of the Committee of Public Safety.

The *Hébertistes* were an extreme group or faction wishing to see the Revolution proceed even further to the left. Hébert was a local official of the Paris Commune who had won notoriety as editor of *Père Duchesne*, one of the most violent and scurrilous of the revolutionary newspapers. Although he had no intelligible program, he was able to gather around him a small group having strong anti-religious and proletarian sympathies. Among them was the eccentric Baron Cloots, a Prussian calling himself "Ambassador of the Human Race" who had won French citizenship and a seat in the Convention. When the *Hébertistes* made use of a food shortage in Paris to urge a new insurrection, Robespierre struck, and in March, 1794, their leaders were sent to the guillotine.

Another type of opposition to Robespierre came from the moderates, or "Indulgents," of whom Danton was the leader. Danton's great services to the Revolution during the first invasion crisis in August and September, 1792, had been sullied by subsequent revelations of his financial speculations and misdealings. For a time a member of the Committee of Public Safety, he was in retirement on his substantial country properties between October and December, 1793. He had become the principal leader of those who resented the Terror and wished to see France return to an orderly, constitutional regime. It was his misfortune that his associates were political adventurers and speculators whose corruption it was easy to expose. In April, 1794, Danton, Camille Desmoulins and others were brought before the Revolutionary Tribunal and after a caricature of a trial were guillotined. Robespierre now seemed in a position to govern France unchallenged.

The last four months of Robespierre's rule have been called the Republic of Virtue. Without much doubt he would have chosen so to regard them. Robespierre appears to the student today as a fanatic, a reader steeped in the egalitarian ideas of Rousseau and at the same time highly suspicious of his fellow-men, an idealist utterly convinced of the rightness of his own ideas. Robespierre was a prim bachelor wearing the knee-breeches, buckled shoes, blue coat and powdered hair of the Old Régime. He seemed to have little in common with the mobs of the Paris streets. The great blot upon his name is the fanatical ruthlessness with which he sought to destroy all those who in any way opposed him.

On April 1 the Committee of Public Safety decreed that the body of ministers making up the Provisional Executive Council should be replaced by twelve commissions, all subordinate to itself. Robespierre's political power now could hardly be challenged, for the Committee of Public Safety lay completely in his hands. He likewise undertook economic changes. The Ventôse Decrees (so called for the month of March, 1794, in which they were issued) declared that the property of all enemies of the Republic should be confiscated and used to indemnify needy patriots, lists of whose names were to be drawn up by the local communes. Some have seen the Ventôse Decrees as an evidence of Robespierre's socialist leanings. Actually they seem rather to have been designed as an emergency measure and in practice were not very effective.

In May Robespierre sought to consolidate the Reign of Virtue by a decree establishing the worship of the Supreme Being. Frenchmen were called upon to recognize the two dogmas of their faith, the existence of the Supreme Being and the Immortality of the Soul. The government for its part undertook to organize festivals and public instruction to assure acceptance of these beliefs. To dramatize immediate public recognition Robespierre presided on June 8 over the great Festival of the Supreme Being, the outstanding example of revolutionary symbolism. Preparations for the great event had gone on for weeks. Choirs had been trained in the various Paris *sections*. Across the Seine in the *Champ de Mars* a huge artificial mountain, symbolic of the Jacobins, had been constructed, complete with a tree of liberty, an altar, a Roman column, an antique temple, some Etruscan tombs and a grotto. Stands had been erected in the gardens of the Tuileries for the deputies. In front of them was a cloth and plaster statue of Atheism, designed to be consumed by flames while a hidden statue of Wisdom rose triumphantly to replace it. On the morning of the celebration the crowds marched from their various *sections* to the central point, the women and children in white, the men garlanded with oak leaves, and all chanting the hymns that Gossec had composed for the occasion. Robespierre, the high priest, as it were, of the festival, was resplendent with a violet coat, white breeches, lace ruffs, a red, white and blue silk sash, plumed hat and a bouquet of cornflowers, poppies and stalks of grain. It was he who at the appropriate instant set the torch to the Statue of Atheism causing Wisdom to rise somewhat unsteadily through the smoke and flames. This was Robespierre's supreme moment.

By a last irony, within two days of the Festival of the Supreme Being, the Law of Prairial (June 10, 1794) sought to speed up the work of the Revolutionary Tribunal which was now divided into four groups sitting simultaneously for greater speed. Suspects could be brought before the Tribunal on the slightest pretext; they were not to have counsel and were denied the right of rebuttal "if material or moral proof exists." The only permissible sentence was death. It is not surprising, therefore, that in the seven weeks during which this terrifying law operated, the number of daily guillotinings increased tenfold. In 49 days there were 1,376 executions. The "Second Terror" of June and July was an even bloodier repetition of the First.

The Second Terror led to the fall of Robespierre. Secret opposition to him existed in the very Committee of Public Safety which he had long dominated and among those representatives on mission who were now beginning to fear reprisals for their acts of violence. As much as anyone can be said to have organized the revolt, it was that born intriguer, Fouché. The newly elected president of the Jacobin Club, it was he who, as representative on mission at Lyons, had been responsible for the execution of more than 1,600 prisoners. Some plotters had personal grievances against Robespierre; others were concerned at the general trend of the times. On July 26 Robespierre made a long, vague speech to the Convention, hinting at conspiracy and demanding further "purification." On July 27 (the ninth Thermidor) the conspirators finally found courage to denounce Robespierre and to order him arrested along with his close associates. That night the Paris Commune rose in sympathy with the Robespierrists. These were freed from prison, whereupon they attempted to organize a last desperate revolt at the Hôtel de Ville. The people of the Paris *sections* did not rally, however, as they had in the past, so that troops sent by the Convention to the Hôtel de Ville were able to seize the leaders. Robespierre, his jaw broken by a pistol bullet, was carried back on a shutter to the Convention where through the night he lay in agony on a table outside the doors of the Committee of Public Safety while his fate was decided. Next day he, Saint-Just and twenty other associates were led to the guillotine, to add their blood to the blood of thousands before them.

■ THE THERMIDOREAN REACTION, 1794–1795

The men who overthrew Robespierre in the hot July month of Thermidor have come to be known as the Thermidoreans and the subsequent year of their rule has come to be known as the period of the Thermidorean Reaction. They would not have regarded themselves as reactionaries. They had participated in the work of the Terror. But now they were anxious somehow to save themselves from the upsurge of resentment against it. Thus they were responsive to the swing of sentiment away from the policy of revolutionary excesses. The period of their rule was marked by a general let-down of republican ardor, by a growing cynicism and by the kind of weariness to be expected after an age of violence. The new leaders were careerists such as Tallien, Fréron, Barras and Fouché. These were opportunistic, cynical, selfish and essentially petty men who swam with the tide of the times. In Paris especially, the abandonment of the era of "republican virtue" was most notable. Groups of young men known as the *Jeunesse dorée* (Gilded Youth), wearing extravagant costumes and affecting reckless manners, roamed the streets, entering cafés and theaters in order to quarrel and brawl with former Jacobins. Dancing became a mania, one especially popular entertainment being the *Bal des Victimes,* to which only relatives of those who had been guillotined were invited. Fantastically exaggerated costumes were the mark of those men who called themselves the *incroyables* and of the women known as the *merveilleuses*. A new style of hairdressing left the nape of the neck bare as if in readiness for the guillotine. In this and other ways Parisian society flaunted its differences from the preceding age.

The powerful structure of revolutionary government was soon weakened. The authority of the Committee of Public Safety was limited to the conduct of war and diplomacy, its other powers being divided among sixteen committees dependent on the Convention. The Revolutionary Tribunal was first reorganized, then sharply reduced in authority and finally, in May, 1795, abolished. The revolutionary Paris Commune, which had been proscribed on 9 Thermidor because it had backed Robespierre, was suppressed and its members outlawed. The most radical measures of the Jacobins were repealed—the Law of Prairial and the Ventôse Decrees in August, the Law of Suspects and the Law of the Maximum in December, 1794. The activities of the representatives on mission were restricted to the army and the work of the local watch committees was abolished. The great Jacobin Club at Paris, the heart of so much revolutionary activity, was closed in November. Meanwhile thousands of suspects were released from prison and the surviving members of the Gironde allowed to resume their seats in the Convention. In response to some public feeling a number of the most violent of the remaining terrorists were brought to trial. Carrier, for example, who had conducted his own savage reign of terror at Nantes, was guillotined, as was Fouquier-Tinville, the notorious public prosecutor of the Revolutionary Tribunal.

The field of religion saw some interesting developments. The policy of the new leaders was to maintain the practice of "civic religion" as the Jacobins had sought to establish it. Clerical pensions, which had been guaranteed under the Civil Constitution of the Clergy, were abolished and formal religious teaching forbidden in the schools. Such measures could not prevent a considerable revival of religion. Those clergy who had accepted the Revolution and those who had refused to take an oath to it began alike to attract large congregations. In February, 1795, therefore, the Convention rather grudgingly issued a decree recognizing religious liberty, following this in September with a formal guaranty of free worship and a complete separation of church and state.

One of the last works of the Convention was to issue the decree of October 25, 1795, on public education. It provided that there should be one or more elementary schools in each canton to teach reading, writing, arithmetic and "the elements of republican morality." Every department should have at least one secondary or central school. Various special schools were also to be founded. At Paris there was to be a National Institute of Arts and Sciences, intended to encourage all worthy developments in physical and mathematical sciences, moral and political sciences, and literature and the fine arts. Various earlier decrees had established a Conservatory of Arts and Crafts, normal schools, a Conservatory of Music, a Polytechnic School, and schools of Artillery, Military Engineering, Roads and Bridges, Mines, Geography, Naval Engineering, Law, Natural History, Medicine and Oriental Studies. In theory, at least, the new France was now provided with an impressive educational structure ranging from the lowest to the highest grades.

The work of the Thermidoreans was undertaken amid great economic hardships, for food was scarce, prices high and the winter of 1794–1795 exceptionally severe. These considerations are at least a partial explanation of the "Jacobin revolts" of 1795. In April a mob largely composed of women and children invaded the Convention demanding bread, liberty and the Constitution of 1793. It was soon dispersed. A more serious disturbance in May required the use of troops before it could be suppressed.

Another type of discontent arose from a certain resurgence of royalism. A number of returning *émigrés* associated themselves in the provinces with those who had suffered under Jacobin rule and inaugurated a "White Terror," which had considerable success in the west and south. England tried to aid the royalists by giving naval assistance to an *émigré* force which landed at Quiberon Bay in Brittany in June, 1795. The landing, though a

disastrous failure, was nevertheless symptomatic of the general unrest of this
difficult year.

The Thermidoreans had their greatest success in the field of foreign
affairs, for the First Coalition, thanks to the great French victories of 1794,
was falling apart. Following the Battle of Fleurus (June, 1794), the Austrian
Netherlands were overrun. By the end of the year the Rhine frontier was
won for a second time. During the winter Pichegru successfully invaded
Holland. Far to the south another army cleared the Pyrenees of Spanish
troops. Thus, by the spring of 1795 the French, having won their "natural
frontiers," were still on the offensive. Prussia undertook secret negotiations
in 1794, the outcome of which was the Peace of Basel (April, 1795) by which
the French were conceded the Prussian territories on the left bank of the
Rhine. Holland left the war by the Peace of The Hague (May, 1795), likewise
ceding to the French the Rhenish areas of Dutch Flanders, Maestricht and
Venloo. In July, 1795, Spain signed a peace at Basel, ceding to the French its
half of the island of Santo Domingo. About this time Tuscany, Hanover,
Hesse-Cassel and Saxony left the Coalition, so that only England and Austria
remained at war with France. Whatever the weaknesses of the Thermidoreans,
it is indisputable that they had won great prestige in the field of foreign
affairs.

Now that the foreign danger had been averted and the emergency measures of revolutionary government largely abandoned, it became all the more
important for the Convention to return to its original task, that of drafting
a constitution for republican France. It could hardly be expected to rein-
troduce, or even simply to amend, the ultra-democratic constitution of 1793.
The members chose instead to draft a new document known under the
chronology of the revolutionary calendar as the Constitution of the Year III.
This product of caution and disillusionment was in operation in France
from 1795 to 1799. More practical and less theoretical than its predecessors,
it was not unsuccessful in establishing a compromise between the royalist
and democratic viewpoints.

France's third written constitution began with a cautious Declaration of
Rights, reaffirming the sanctity of property and adding to the list of rights
a list also of duties. Property qualifications were required for voters, who
were to choose deputies by a two-stage process of indirect election. For the
first time the legislature was to consist of two chambers. Members of the
Council of Five Hundred had to own real property and be at least thirty years
old. The duties of this body were to initiate and discuss legislation. The
Council of Ancients had 250 members, likewise property owners and at least
forty years old. By a provision possibly unique in legislative history, members had to be either married or widowers. Their main duty was to accept or

reject the proposals of the Council of Five Hundred. Each house was to have one-third of its membership renewed annually so that there might be no sudden transformation of membership or policy.

The executive power was to rest in the hands of a Directory of five men, chosen by the Ancients from a list prepared by the Five Hundred. To be eligible, a member had to be forty and had to have served previously as a minister or deputy. One member was to retire annually, and the presidency was to be held in rotation for terms of three months. It is clear, then, that the constitution was intended to guarantee order by an elaborate system of checks and balances. This it did. It also retained in general the system of local government and the judicial arrangements established in 1791. The principal weakness of the constitution was not so much its caution as it was the failure to provide a method of procedure in case of a deadlock between the legislative and executive power. Lacking such a provision, the constitution made an eventual *coup d'état* all the more likely.

To provide continuity in government the Convention voted a supplementary decree to the effect that two-thirds of the membership in the new legislative bodies, that is, five hundred deputies, should be drawn from the members of the Convention. Although this stipulation proved highly unpopular with the country as a whole, the constitution was ratified in September, 1795.[8] A week before the elections were held, a rising occurred in Paris to protest against the self-perpetuating action of the Convention. It was put down by artillery under the command of a young captain named Napoleon Bonaparte. Thus the three dramatic years of the Convention came to an end and a new and supposedly permanent constitutional era was launched.

8. The constitution was ratified by a vote of about 1,000,000 to 50,000. The 2/3 provision was accepted by a vote of about 200,000 to 100,000 and only because of solidly affirmative votes from the army and navy.

THE IMPERIAL CORONATION. In this splendid scene Napoleon distinctly outshadows Pope Pius VII. From the painting in the Louvre by David, photograph by Alinari.

Chapter 24

From Republic to Empire
in France, 1795–1804

■ THE DOMESTIC ACHIEVEMENTS OF THE DIRECTORY, 1795–1799

THE RULE of the Directory in France lasted almost exactly four years. In domestic matters this was the period during which the country steadied down after the fevered excesses of the Jacobin era. Externally, France took the

623

offensive against the forces of the First Coalition, contriving to make peace on highly advantageous terms with all members save England. Such an achievement would in itself give distinction to this age. Yet the peace turned out to be only a truce, and the ensuing war was fought on an even larger scale than that of its predecessor. In the eyes of history the most fateful aspect of these years was the spectacular rise of a revolutionary officer, Napoleon Bonaparte, whose seizure of power in 1799 meant the end of the Directory, and whose career for two decades was to be almost identical with the history of Europe.

The older interpretation of the four years of the Directory as a period of political incompetence and social decadence owes much to those Napoleonic historians who have wished to see their hero as the savior of a France unable to save itself. It is an explanation which corresponds only in part with the evidence. The first five Directors were hardly as bad as they have been painted. Barras, to be sure, would doubtless qualify for as damning a verdict as any historian would care to make about him. He was an old royalist officer who had sided with the Revolution, voted for the execution of Louis XVI, supported Robespierre and then helped to destroy him. Barras accumulated a large fortune under the Directory and lived a life of ostentatious scandal. The other four original members, however, were reasonably respectable, capable men, one of whom, Carnot, had worked magnificently to organize the military forces of the Republic. The legislative branch was about as good as could be expected given the nature of the preceding years. In the army a new crop of young revolutionary generals was displaying a remarkable capacity for leadership, commanding troops that were now truly veterans. The real damage to the reputation of the Directory, it would seem, was done by those who set its social tone—the corrupt minority of cynically reckless adventurers under the leadership of hostesses such as Madame Tallien who dominated the period.

The major internal problems facing France in 1795 were twofold: the defense of the Republic against political threats to undermine it, and the creation of an orderly economic life. Political changes brought about by violence had been so much a part of the immediate past, and economic unrest had been so commonly the prelude to violence, that the efforts to reach stability were obviously a matter of the utmost urgency. It is to the credit of the Directory that it was able to make substantial progress in both fields.

The first important challenge to the authority of the government came in the "Conspiracy of the Equals." Its leader, Gracchus Babeuf, was a product of the revolutionary age and yet too extreme to be typical of it. Trained as a surveyor, he had ample opportunity to observe the vast inequalities in the landed wealth of France. He had steeped himself in the most radical writings of the *philosophes* and had become the champion of a new type of communally organized society which would exist without private property and would guarantee a living for all. Babeuf, in short, went beyond the prevalent bourgeois creed of the revolution to advocate a radical, proletarian ideal. Having been in and out of prison, he organized a conspiratorial group in 1796 which issued a number of inflammatory pamphlets and planned an insurrection in behalf of the democratic Constitution of 1793. Babeuf was betrayed to the authorities, brought to trial and in May, 1797, guillotined. The episode has only a minor importance in the history of the Revolution, yet has been singled out by later generations of socialists as one of those first acts out of which the militantly revolutionary variety of modern socialism has developed.

Other threats to the authority of the Directory were of a different type. As the destruction of Jacobin survivals continued, the advocates of royalism began to assert themselves. The conservative royalists won some support from the moderates in the government and succeeded in electing one of their adherents, Barthélemy, to the Directory as well as making General Pichegru president of the Council of Five Hundred. Another Director, Carnot, stood midway between the royalist conspirators and those in authority. In September, 1797, the government announced the discovery of a plot (the "Coup of Fructidor") intended to put the royalists in control. It forced Barthélemy and Carnot into exile, canceled the election of nearly two hundred deputies whom it mistrusted and thus, with the aid of the army, reasserted its authority. This "appeal to the soldier" was an ominous precedent for what was soon to follow.

A year later, in May, 1798, the Directors annulled by the "Coup of Floréal" the results of 106 elections which would have brought a large number of republican extremists into the legislature. These were replaced by "safe" men. Still another crisis came in June, 1799, when new elections turned the majority of the deputies against the conservative Directory. The "Coup of Prairial" was the reverse of the situation in 1798. Then the Directors had purged the legislature. Now the radical legislature was strong enough to force the resignation or dismissal of three unpopular Directors. They were replaced by three who were more in sympathy with the popular branch.

This struggle for political power, destined in November, 1799, to bring the Directory crashing to the ground, should not obscure the positive work that it was able to accomplish. From its predecessors, the Thermidoreans, it inherited an economic situation which seemed to be approaching disaster. Some measures of state regulation, therefore, seemed unavoidable. Food was requisitioned for the armies and bread-lines organized where necessary for the civil population of the larger cities. Government control was exercised over foreign exchange and the stock-market. A most urgent problem was that of the *assignats* of which billions were still in circulation at about one per cent of their face value. In 1796 an attempt was made to stabilize them at roughly one-thirtieth of their value by a process which involved exchanging them for a new type of paper money, the *mandats térritoriaux*. Since these likewise deteriorated, the government took the drastic step in February, 1797, of repudiating forty billion francs' worth of the new paper money and returning to a strictly metallic currency. In this way the long and not un-worthy history of the *assignats* came to an inglorious end.

A related problem was that of the very heavy national debt which various attempts at economy had failed to reduce. In September, 1797, by the "Law of the Consolidated Third" one-third of this debt was consolidated and two-thirds paid off in new bonds. As these bonds rapidly declined in value the practical effect was a repudiation of two-thirds of the government's indebted-ness at the expense of the new bondholders.

Other measures more or less economic in nature sought to protect French industry by a high general tariff, to provide subsidies for manufacturers, to encourage inventors and to strengthen the various technical schools of France. Plans were devised to increase the amount of poor-relief and to provide work through new road-building projects. The tax-structure was also revised. Forced loans were attempted. Some direct taxes were lowered, indirect taxes were increased and in 1798 a more efficient system of collection introduced. To carry out all these reforms a considerable revision of the general administrative machine was necessary. A large body of new officials was brought into existence. In this way the work of the Directory anticipated one of the most characteristic of Napoleon's later reforms. "The whole Napoleonic bureaucracy exists as a nucleus under the Directory. . . . It had begun to put France in order." [1]

Another field where the Directory consolidated earlier legislation with permanently important results was that connected with the metric system of weights and measures. As early as May, 1790, the Constituent Assembly had recommended the standardization of the cumbrous old French system and for this purpose had set up a special committee which included such distinguished scientists as Monge, the mathematician, Laplace, the astrono-mer, and Lavoisier, the chemist. In August, 1793, the Convention had decreed the gradual introduction of the new metric system with the meter and the gram as its basic units. This had been reaffirmed by the Thermidoreans. Thus the Directory completed work long since begun. In December, 1799, amid the confusions attending Bonaparte's seizure of power, the meter was officially

1. CRANE BRINTON, *A Decade of Revolution, 1789–1799* (1934), pp. 220–221.

defined as being one ten-millionth of the distance along the meridian from the equator to the pole; the gram was defined as being the weight of one cubic centimeter of pure water at the temperature of melting ice. In October of the same year the franc, roughly the equivalent of the old *livre,* replaced it as the official unit of currency.

Important steps were also taken in another vitally important field, that of military conscription. In September, 1798, the system of compulsory military service for all Frenchmen between the ages of 20 and 25 was decreed, it being stipulated that men from these five classes, beginning with the youngest, should be called up annually to meet the deficiencies in voluntary enlistments. The general principle of universal, compulsory, military service had been first asserted with the *Levée en Masse* at the time of the great crisis in August, 1793. The Constitution of 1795 had restored the method of voluntary enlistment, save in national emergencies. The inadequacy of this system now led to the conscription measure of 1798. Its significance was incalculable, for what France now established as a permanent system was gradually adopted by one after another of its European opponents.

The domestic measures of the Directory amount in total to a most respectable accomplishment. Many of them represent the fulfilment of policies hopefully undertaken in the earlier days of the Revolution but never brought to fruition. Regarded differently, these same measures can be said to form the solid foundation for the reforms of the more spectacular Napoleonic era.

THE DESTRUCTION OF THE FIRST COALITION AND THE RISE OF BONAPARTE

The period of the Directory was vitally important in matters of foreign policy, for the full impact of the French Revolution upon Europe was now felt. The early protestations of French leaders that France held no aggressive designs had been replaced by new slogans which took into account France's desire to keep possession of its "natural frontiers." Considerable progress in this respect had been made, notably in the Treaty of Basel of 1795 wherein Prussia accepted the fact of a French advance to the Rhine. One of the closing acts of the Convention, moreover, had been to decree on October 1, 1795, the annexation of all Belgium and with it "all other territories on this side of the Rhine which before the war were under the dominion of Austria."

When the Directory took control of French affairs at the end of October, 1795, France had made a peace with all its opponents save England, Austria and Savoy. In March it had made its first alliance with an outside state, the newly-created Batavian Republic which succeeded the old government of the Netherlands. French armies stood along the Rhine, in the French Alps and in the Pyrenees. General public sentiment in France seems to have been strongly on the side of peace. Yet England was as yet unprepared to meet such a possibility, for Pitt and Grenville strongly mistrusted the leaders of the Directory. Official sentiment in Austria was equally hostile, for it was rashly believed that France could be knocked out of the war by one great final blow.

The Directory's policy was to attack the only foe with which it could directly grapple, namely, Austria. Three campaigns were planned for 1796. Two French armies were to move across the Rhine. Jourdan was to lead the army of the Sambre-and-Meuse into Germany, while Moreau was to join him on the Danube with the army of the Rhine-and-Moselle. A third and larger military operation was to be launched in Italy under the command of a rising young officer, the twenty-seven-year-old Napoleon Bonaparte. To attack and ultimately invade Austria through northern Italy was no new strategy—it had been attempted several times in the eighteenth century— the novelty in 1796 and 1797 was the speed and effectiveness with which the plan ultimately was executed.

The character of the new commander of the Army of Italy is best revealed in the record of his accomplishments. Napoleon Bonaparte was born on the island of Corsica in 1769, a few weeks after its annexation by France. To the end of his life he spoke French with the Italian accent of his early environment. His father, a member of the minor Corsican nobility, obtained scholarships for him in French military schools, beginning at the age of nine. Commissioned as an officer at the age of sixteen, Bonaparte can truly be said to have lived almost from infancy the life of a soldier. He won experience in the service of the Revolution, gave his support to the Jacobins and became general-of-brigade at the age of twenty-four.[2] He made a fortunate marriage to Josephine Beauharnais, a widow of Creole descent from the island of Martinique whose husband had been guillotined during the Jacobin era. Josephine had played some part in the fashionable life of the Directory and was on terms of special friendship with Barras. In part because of his own evident abilities and in part because of Josephine's influence, Bonaparte was recommended by Carnot to carry out the bold strategy planned against the Austrians in Italy.

The Italian campaign demonstrated Bonaparte's uncanny skill as a military leader. Having served in the topographical branch of the army he knew the Italian terrain thoroughly. He planned boldly and, with all the details at his finger-tips, reached his decisions on tactical points very rapidly. He made brilliant use of artillery and cavalry. "The art of war," he later

2. This would not in itself be a unique distinction. Ten of Napoleon's marshals—Soult, Lannes, Ney, Davout, Victor, Macdonald, Oudinot, Marmont, Suchet and Grouchy—became generals in their twenties.

explained, "consists, with inferior forces, in always having larger numbers than the enemy at the point of attack or defence." He was also a superb showman, able to dramatize his own presence and to issue manifestoes and proclamations to his troops that over and over again won their unfaltering support.

The first move of the Italian campaign was to separate the Sardinians from the Austrians and quickly force the former to accept the Armistice of Cherasco (April, 1796). Using the River Po to screen his left flank, Bonaparte then rapidly advanced, crossed at Piacenza and won the battle of Lodi, where his passage over the River Adda gave him a European reputation.[3] By May 15 he had entered Milan, then moved rapidly eastward again to threaten Austria's key fortress position at Mantua. In June the French were able to force the Kingdom of Naples out of the war. With equal speed Bonaparte then turned southward against the Papal States and Tuscany. These were compelled to submit. Ultimately, by the Treaty of Tolentino (February, 1797), the papacy agreed to pay an indemnity of money and art treasures to France, accepted the loss of Avignon and agreed to a reorganization of the states of central Italy. Modena, Bologna and Ferrara were combined into a new Cispadane Republic (proclaimed in the previous October) south of the River Po. This, the first of many subsequent French reorganizations of Italian territory, deserves emphasis because it illustrates the technique by which French control was to be exercised over an area which ostensibly had been reorganized in answer to the demand of its own people.

Boldly renewing the campaign despite cautious instructions sent him by the Directors at Paris, Bonaparte pushed further eastward across the Lombard plain. Staving off a new Austrian thrust he won the series of victories— Castiglione (August, 1796), Arcola (November, 1796) and Rivoli (January, 1797)—which finally led to the fall of Mantua in February, 1797. The French were now able to seize Venice and move into the passes of the Julian Alps, threatening an advance on Vienna. By April, 1797, Bonaparte was at Leoben, less than a hundred miles from the Austrian capital.

While these brilliant victories were being won in Italy, the twin campaigns in Germany had not gone well for France. Moreau and Jourdan were both driven back to the Rhine by the Austrian commander, the Archduke Charles. Nevertheless, large Austrian forces were kept busy and the French were able to establish a secret understanding with Prussia. During this period of Napoleonic victories in Italy the war-weary Directory even undertook negotiations with an equally war-weary England. At Paris in October, 1796, and again at Lille in July, 1797, Lord Malmesbury went so far as to offer to recognize France's seizure of the "natural frontiers." But

---

3. Bonaparte did nothing to discourage the publication of prints showing him (inaccurately) seizing an enemy standard and leading his troops across the bridge at Lodi.

for a variety of reasons, among them the French insistence on large colonial conquests, these negotiations were broken off in September.

Meanwhile Bonaparte had brought his Italian campaign to a triumphant conclusion. The Austrians accepted the armistice of Leoben in April, 1797. Six months later, in disregard again of instructions sent by the Directory, the terms of the armistice were embodied in the formal Treaty of Campo Formio (October 17, 1797). Austria recognized France's seizure of Belgium, the Rhine frontier and (in a significant new development) the Ionian Islands. These islands, which lay off the western coast of Greece and of which Corfu was the chief, had been in the possession of Venice. Bonaparte's seizure of them can be taken as an indication of his deeply-rooted oriental ambitions, for they gave France an important naval base on the way to Constantinople. In compensation for its losses Austria was secretly promised the Archbishopric of Salzburg, in the Tyrol, and also the territory of the Venetian Republic now doomed to extinction. The Venetian territories included the Adriatic provinces of Istria and Dalmatia. It was also provided that the German princes who lost territory to France on the left bank of the Rhine were to find compensation in ecclesiastical territories on the right bank. To arrange all this a conference was to be held at Rastatt in which France would participate—a clear indication of Bonaparte's intention that France should intervene actively in German affairs. Austria, finally, was to recognize the enlargement of the Cispadane Republic into a new Cisalpine Republic.

Although the Treaty of Campo Formio was a truce rather than a permanent settlement, it dramatically illustrated the techniques and aims of Bonaparte. It was based on military victories in the field. It dealt with areas some of which were far removed from the scene of actual conflict. It confirmed France in possession of its new Rhineland gains. It undertook to reorganize large parts of Italy. It indicated Bonaparte's eagerness to meddle in German affairs and his lurking ambitions for adventure in the Near East. In the late spring of 1797 Bonaparte took up his residence at the Chateau of Mombello near Milan where he maintained almost regal state. A visitor has given a striking picture of the new conqueror of Italy:

> I was received by Bonaparte . . . in the midst of a brilliant court rather than the headquarters of an army. Strict etiquette already reigned around him; his aides-de-camp and his officers were no longer received at his table, and he had become fastidious in the choice of the guests whom he admitted to it. An invitation was an honour eagerly sought, and obtained with great difficulty. He dined, so to speak, in public; the inhabitants of the country were admitted to the room in which he was eating, and allowed to gaze at him with a keen curiosity. . . . His reception-rooms and an immense tent pitched in front of the palace were constantly full of a crowd of generals, administrators and great

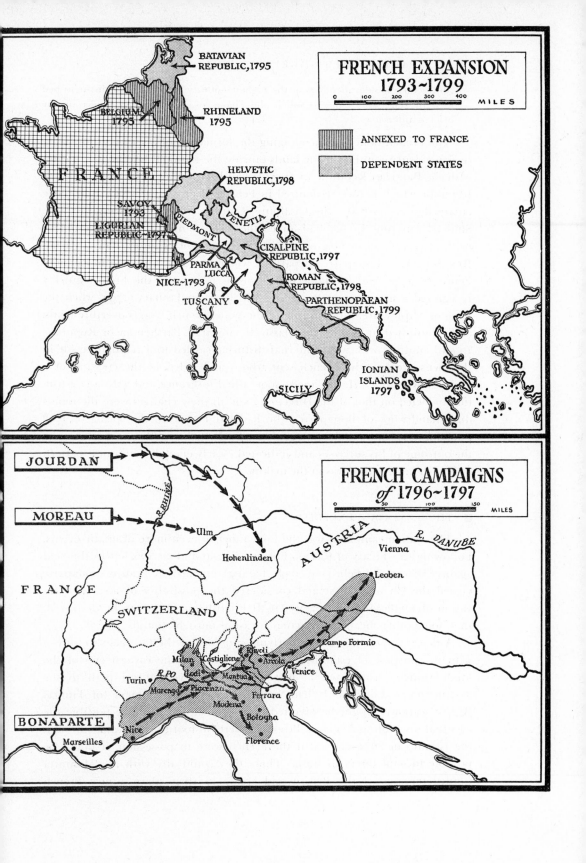

FRENCH EXPANSION
1793~1799

0   100   200   300   400   MILES

▦ ANNEXED TO FRANCE

▤ DEPENDENT STATES

BATAVIAN
REPUBLIC, 1795

BELGIUM
1795

RHINELAND
1795

FRANCE

HELVETIC
REPUBLIC, 1798

SAVOY
1793

LIGURIAN
REPUBLIC~1797

PIEDMONT

VENETIA

SAVOY
1793

NICE~1793

PARMA
LUCCA

TUSCANY

CISALPINE
REPUBLIC, 1797

ROMAN
REPUBLIC, 1798

PARTHENOPAEAN
REPUBLIC, 1799

IONIAN
ISLANDS
1797

SICILY

FRENCH CAMPAIGNS
of 1796~1797

0   50   100   150   MILES

JOURDAN

MOREAU

BONAPARTE

R. RHINE

Ulm

Hohenlinden

AUSTRIA

R. DANUBE

Vienna

Leoben

FRANCE

SWITZERLAND

Milan

Castiglione

Rivoli

Arcola

Campo Formio

Turin

R. PO

Lodi

Mantua

Venice

Marengo

Piacenza

Ferrara

Modena

Bologna

Florence

Nice

Marseilles

contractors; besides members of the highest nobility, and the most distinguished men in Italy who came to solicit the favour of a momentary glance or the briefest interview.

The French policy of encouraging the formation of a series of associated or dependent republics in the lands outside the national borders had begun with the Batavian Republic in 1795. It had been followed by the Cispadane Republic which France recognized in February, 1797, and which Bonaparte enlarged so as to make the Cisalpine Republic in the following October. Similarly, in June France had forced the dissolution of the old government of the Republic of Genoa, organizing these territories into a new Ligurian Republic. After Bonaparte's departure, when disorders broke out in Rome in February, 1798, and the pope fled from his territories, the French quickly recognized a new Roman Republic. Still later, in January, 1799, when the King of Naples attempted to restore the pope, French troops overthrew him and established at Naples the classically inspired Parthenopean Republic. In still another area, when internal disturbances led to a popular revolt in the Swiss cantons, the French sent troops and aided in the creation of a Helvetic Republic (March, 1798), soon allied to France and with a constitution modeled on that of the Directory. Not all these changes were the immediate handiwork of Bonaparte, who had left France in the spring of 1798 pursuing even more ambitious goals in the Near East. They were, however, the outcome of his successes and indicated clearly enough that a new pattern of French imperialism was in the making.

■ THE EGYPTIAN EXPEDITION

The Italian campaign was the forerunner of even more dramatic events. Following the Treaty of Campo Formio, England alone was left in the field against France. In February, 1798, having returned to France, Bonaparte visited the Channel coast and considered the possibility of an actual invasion of England, only to reject it. If English power was to be destroyed, then some other means than actual invasion must be found.

A descent upon Egypt—an outlying province of the Ottoman Empire—with the purpose of establishing French power at the eastern end of the Mediterranean would not at first sight seem a very direct path to the destruction of England. It had, nevertheless, real advantages for France. British seapower might be diverted in such a way as to make possible the eventual invasion of England. Proposals were on foot to cut a canal through the Isthmus of Suez whence, if the French were in possession, it might be possible to send forces to India. There they could ally with the Mahratta Confederacy, expel the British and create in their place a new French empire. Such plans fitted in with the long tradition of French interests in the Near East going back as far as the time of the Crusades. In 1767 the French foreign minister, Choiseul, had suggested a policy involving the annexation of Egypt, and in 1783 Vergennes had taken up this proposal again. Talleyrand, who became foreign minister of the Directory in 1797, had read a paper to the Institute pointing out the advantages France would gain from colonial establishments in the Levant. To make a splendid career for himself in the East long seems to have been a dream of Bonaparte—a dream doubtless rekindled during his Italian campaigns. His insistence upon taking the Ionian Islands for France by the Treaty of Campo Formio can best be understood as the first step to the practical realization of this oriental dream. A final consideration was that such a campaign, if successful, would heap further honors and distinction upon an ambitious soldier for whom at the moment Paris had nothing to offer but petty intrigue.

The Directory readily fell in with Bonaparte's proposals and authorized an expedition to take possession of Egypt, drive the English from their trading posts in the Near East and attempt the construction of a canal so as to control the Red Sea. He was also to seek the maintenance of good relations with the Sultan—under the circumstances hardly an easy task. A convoy of 400 transports carrying an army of 38,000 troops left Toulon in May, 1798. There also went mathematicians, geologists, antiquarians and naturalists to investigate and report upon the wonders of these ancient lands. Bonaparte undertook the study of the Koran, the better to fit him for consultation with the learned Moslem scholars of Cairo. En route to Egypt the French seized the island of Malta, small in size but of the utmost strategic importance. Little resistance was offered by its owners, the Knights of St. John, now the weak and ineffective representatives of a once famous crusading order.

Luckily avoiding the English fleet commanded by Admiral Nelson, the expedition arrived off Alexandria in July. Bonaparte put his troops ashore, marched through the Delta and won the Battle of the Pyramids against the Egyptians on July 24. Two events altered the complexion of the campaign. Nelson's fleet at last found the French ships anchored off the mouth of the Nile in Aboukir Bay, and on August 1 blew them out of the water. Turkey, with whom Bonaparte over-optimistically had hoped to remain on terms of friendship while defeating the Egyptians and the English, declared war on France in September and prepared an army to invade Egypt. This gave Bonaparte his opportunity to adopt the strategy which he always favored— the offensive. Undertaking a northward advance into Syria, he captured Jaffa in March, 1799, then pushed on to the siege of Acre, where the Turkish defenders were strongly aided by English naval reinforcements. This, however, was the end of the road. Plague affected the French troops, ammunition was running short and news came of the formation of a Second Coalition against France, of defeats in Italy and of political intrigues at Paris.[4]

Nothing was more characteristic of Bonaparte than his ability to make new decisions and then act vigorously in accordance with them. In twenty-six days he led his troops back over the 300 miles of desert to Alexandria. Here, after defeating an army the Turks put ashore at Aboukir, he resolved to return secretly to France with two ships, leaving the army to fare as best it could under General Kléber. Luck again was with him. Bonaparte sailed on August 21, 1799, avoided the English patrols and landed at Fréjus in the south of France on October 9. His unfortunate army remained for two years in Egypt until August, 1801, when the threat of a joint Turkish-British attack led its decimated remnants to surrender.

The fruits of the Egyptian expedition were largely political, for Bonaparte returned invested with a glamor of romance that brought the great majority of Frenchmen to his side. By emphasizing France's interest in Egypt, India and in the colonial problem generally—a very tender spot for the British—Bonaparte dramatized the nature of the conflict between England and France. In another sense, the ill-fated expedition was likewise important, for it inaugurated the scientific study of Egyptian antiquities. The ten folio volumes of the *Description of Egypt* and the ten further volumes of maps were the outcome of work begun by French experts during the invasion and still stand as a monumental achievement of French scholarship. At the little village of Rosetta, in the Nile Delta, a French officer uncovered the famous Rosetta stone—a trilingual inscription which unlocked the secret of Egyptian hieroglyphs. Turned over to the British at the capitulation of Alexandria in 1801, the Rosetta stone remains to this day one of the great treasures of the British Museum.

■ WAR AND POLITICS: THE SECOND COALITION
   AND THE COUP OF BRUMAIRE

Bonaparte's seizure of power by a political coup in the "foggy month" of Brumaire (November, 1799) was the outcome of a deteriorating domestic and foreign situation. At the same time it was the act of an able, successful and ruthlessly ambitious young general for whom the world seemed to offer almost limitless prizes. It has been said that the army was "full of Bonapartes." This may well have been, for the Revolution had made possible a distinguished career for many a young republican soldier. Alone among them, however, Bonaparte was able to push his advantage to the utmost and reach the position where he could play a role unique in European history.

4. Much of this bad news was obligingly provided by the British Admiral, Sir Sidney Smith, cruising off Alexandria, who sent Bonaparte a packet of French newspapers.

The First Coalition had been shattered in October, 1797, by the Treaty of Campo Formio. It was soon to be replaced by another. The renewal of the struggle owed much to the determination of England's prime minister, William Pitt, who more than any of his countrymen saw the deep significance of the struggle against France. His concern was heightened by the constant meddling of the French in Italy, the Swiss Confederation and the Netherlands. A further source of resentment, felt not only by England, was Bonaparte's seizure of Malta and his evident threats to the integrity of the Ottoman Empire. These matters particularly aroused the Tsar Paul, ruler of Russia since 1796, who had recently been made protector of the Knights of St. John. Still another irritant was the Congress at Rastatt which was held by the French and the imperialists to determine the fate of the dispossessed German princes on the left bank of the Rhine and which Bonaparte attended for a time in person. The negotiations dragged on throughout 1798 without success and with increasing bitterness.

Under these circumstances Pitt undertook to bring together a new coalition against France. In November, 1798, he outlined to the Russians his views as to an acceptable peace settlement. France should go back to her old borders, surrendering Belgium, the Rhineland and Savoy. Piedmont and Savoy should be united under the King of Sardinia. Austria was to stand guard in northern Italy. Switzerland and Holland should have their independence guaranteed, with Belgium probably united to the latter. Prussia should obtain gains in North Germany. The whole settlement should be guaranteed by England, Russia, Austria and Prussia. These general terms were restated by Pitt in 1805 and were employed by the British foreign secretary, Lord Castlereagh, as a basis for negotiations in 1814. Their importance, therefore, was greater in the future than in the immediate present. Prussia proved to be unwilling to join any coalition. By December, however, Britain, Russia, Austria, Turkey and Naples had made a series of agreements to form a loose coalition. By March, 1799, Austria was once again actively at war, fighting in the old battle-grounds of northern Italy, where for the first time in history Russian troops soon came into action.

The campaigns of 1799—a war of major scale—were fought against a France whose greatest general was far off in the deserts of Egypt and Syria. A French invasion of South Germany was forced back to the Rhine. Other French troops were driven from Naples while farther north, at Novi, they were overwhelmingly defeated by an Austro-Russian army under the command of the distinguished Russian general, Suvarov (August, 1799). The Cisalpine, Roman and Parthenopean Republics quickly collapsed. The Russians then made a spectacular march across the St. Gothard Pass into Switzerland, only to be defeated by Masséna in the Battle of Zürich (September). An Anglo-Russian expedition which invaded Holland by sea had momentary success, but by October, 1799, was compelled to evacuate the Netherlands. Such was the confused state of foreign affairs when Bonaparte returned from Egypt in that same month of October.

By this time the government of France, however creditable its general record may have been, seemed to have fallen into the hands of a Directory of mediocrities and a legislature of uncertain purpose. Barras alone remained of the original five Directors. The most recent member, chosen in May, 1799, was Emmanuel Joseph Sieyès, the former *abbé* who had distinguished himself in the Estates General, lived through the tumultuous years of the Convention, shown some skill as a constitutional draftsman, acted on various diplomatic missions and now was looking for some able leader under whom to serve.[5] The other Directors—Gohier, Ducos and Moulin—were nonentities. Sieyès and Ducos alone could be counted upon to support Bonaparte. The majority of the Council of Ancients seemed well-disposed toward him, while the majority of the Council of Five Hundred seemed distrustful. Bonaparte had one useful advantage: in October his brother, Lucien, was chosen president of the Council of Five Hundred.

It seems clear that Sieyès was looking for a military leader to take the initiative in a coup d'état. His first choice was the young general, Joubert, unfortunately killed at the Battle of Novi. He then inclined toward Bonaparte whose return resulted in an immediate intensification of speculation and intrigue. Bonaparte could count upon Sieyès, upon Lucien, upon Talleyrand, recently dismissed from the Ministry of Foreign Affairs, and upon the ex-Jacobin and arch-intriguer, Joseph Fouché, now most conveniently Minister of Police. Too young to become a Director (Bonaparte had barely reached the age of thirty), he had to contrive somehow to get the Directors to resign and have the two Councils entrust the provisional government to the architects of the conspiracy. These could then revise the constitution in the manner they desired.

The Coup of Brumaire was a classic example of cold-blooded intrigue. Bonaparte skilfully dramatized his return from Egypt. He appeared before the Directors wearing a Turkish fez, a green overcoat and a scimitar. He read a paper to the Institute on Egyptian archaeology. He appeared in the company of scientists. Meanwhile he widened his circle of acquaintances, subscribed to every newspaper in Paris, secretly prepared pamphlets and posters and completed his plans. Sieyès, aware of what was expected of a successful conspirator, took private riding-lessons in preparation for the inevitable cavalcade through the streets of Paris.

5. Sieyès is responsible for one of the most famous *mots* of the Revolution. Asked what he did during the Terror, he replied, "I survived."

On November 9, by prearrangement, those members of the Council of Ancients who were considered trustworthy were summoned to an early morning meeting at which they decreed the transfer of the entire Legislative Body to Saint-Cloud, in the environs of Paris, on the pretext of an imminent Jacobin plot. At the same time the Council appointed General Bonaparte commander of the troops of the capital. Sieyès and Ducos obligingly resigned from the Directory and somehow Talleyrand persuaded Barras to do likewise. The other two Directors were held under guard at the Luxemburg Palace.

On the following day, when the two Chambers met at Saint-Cloud, Bonaparte prepared to address them. The troops who had gathered around the chateau—so he explained to the Ancients—were necessary to forestall a Jacobin plot. On appearing before the hostile and suspicious Council of Five Hundred he provoked an uproar and was so violently denounced that he was overcome and had to be dragged, half-fainting from the hall. Lucien saved the day by rallying the grenadiers, who entered with muskets and bayonets. At this a panic ensued. The members escaped through the French windows, flinging their scarlet togas of office upon the rose bushes of Saint-Cloud as they scattered into the gathering dusk. Later in the night a small committee of both houses decreed the appointment of three provisory Consuls, Bonaparte, Sieyès and Ducos, to govern during the crisis. A few members of the scattered Council of Five Hundred were reassembled along with the members of the Council of Ancients and with this faint shadow of legality it was agreed to end the Directory, to exclude 61 specified members of the Legislative Body (which was now adjourned for six weeks) and to set up a commission of fifty to aid the Consuls in revising the constitution. In this way, by a vote of the minority of the Council of Ancients and of less than thirty of the Council of Five Hundred, Bonaparte's intrigues and threats of force were given a kind of public sanction. He had made himself the true master of France.

■ STABILIZATION AT HOME AND ABROAD

The most urgent work required of the three provisory Consuls, Bonaparte, Sieyès and Ducos, was to give France another (its fourth) written constitution. Sieyès, the inveterate phrase-maker, took the initiative, producing in six weeks a draft which doubtless reflected his varied experiences since 1789 and which sought to embody the motto: "Confidence from below, power from above." Bonaparte most characteristically condemned this draft as inefficient: "Sieyès," he said, "puts shadows everywhere." At the last moment Bonaparte rewrote the document so as to express his own ideas.

The outcome was "the Constitution of the Year VIII," announced to the French people on December 13, 1799.

The Constitution had no bill of rights. All Frenchmen 21 years old, not indentured servants and having been domiciled for a year, could vote. Yet this guarantee of universal manhood suffrage was almost meaningless. Citizens in each locality were to draw up a "communal list" of one-tenth of their number from which local officials were to be selected by the administration. Members of the "communal lists" chose one-tenth of their number to make up the "departmental lists" and these in turn chose one-tenth of their number to make up the "national lists" or "Notables of France." Legislative work was divided among four bodies. There was to be a Council of State appointed by the First Consul to draft and initiate legislation. A Conservative Senate of 80 life members with an original membership largely chosen by the Consuls was to fill its own subsequent vacancies by cooptation. The Senate's main duty was to select the names from the national lists so as to fill the other legislative bodies and high administrative posts. A Tribunate of 100 members, chosen by the Senate for five-year terms, had the right to discuss but not to vote the laws. A Legislative Body of 300, similarly chosen, had the right to vote but not to discuss.

Administrative power lay mainly in the hands of the three Consuls, eventually to be chosen by the Senate for ten-year terms, but now specifically named in the Constitution. Bonaparte altered the original plan so as to put enormous powers in the hands of the First Consul. It was he who appointed and dismissed all members of the Council of State and thus controlled the introduction of all legislation. He appointed the heads of the seven ministries, the ambassadors, high military officers, the prefects and upper magistrates. His powers were clearly superior to those of the other Consuls who in general had a consultative voice. They could sign a register to indicate their presence and they could record their opinion if they so desired; "after which," ran Article 42, "the decision of the First Consul shall suffice."

This system of supposed checks and balances in which the democratic process of election and legislation in practice disappeared, was ratified in February, 1800, by the phenomenal vote of 3,011,007 to 1,562. This vote may appear less phenomenal when it is noted that in some districts the schoolchildren were set to work copying voters' names into "registers of acceptance." Not waiting for the formal plebiscite, the provisional government had declared the Constitution to be officially in effect in the previous December. Bonaparte had devised an effective technique whereby his autocracy could function behind a façade of supposed constitutionalism. The *Gazette de France* made everything clear to its readers. "What does the Constitution contain?" it asked. "It contains Bonaparte."

The urgent cry of the French people in 1799, now that the "natural frontiers" were won, was for peace. It may well be one of the great ironies of this period that in searching for peace they should have so overwhelmingly entrusted their fortunes to one who was essentially a soldier and a conqueror of overpowering ambition and self-confidence. Bonaparte was quick to realize, however, that his immediate prestige depended upon his success in bringing the war to an end. As early as Christmas Day, 1799, he wrote therefore to the king of England and the Austrian emperor proposing that peace negotiations be considered. Under the circumstances of France's military position in Italy and Germany, to say nothing of the troops left in Egypt, Bonaparte's prospects did not look bright. His offer can hardly have been seriously received; at all events the replies were unsatisfactory.

The military defeat of Austria seemed once more the necessary prerequisite to securing peace. Hence in the spring of 1800 Bonaparte launched a lightning campaign in Italy. Masséna was ordered to engage an Austrian army in the neighborhood of Genoa. Leaving his base at Dijon, in Burgundy, Bonaparte took his troops into Switzerland and by a surprise move crossed the Alps through the Great St. Bernard Pass in seven days. The difficulties which he mastered were enormous, for even in May some fifteen miles of the route were impassable to wheeled vehicles. Bonaparte entered Milan as a conqueror and on June 14 won the dramatic victory of Marengo. This forced the Austrians to retire as far east as the Mincio River, leaving the greater part of the now reestablished Cisalpine Republic once more in French hands. General Moreau, meanwhile, who had invaded South Germany and driven the Austrians back to Ulm, on the upper Danube, won the Battle of Hohenlinden in December, 1800. He was within fifty miles of Vienna and Austrian military power for a second time had been broken.

The negotiations for peace with Austria resulted in the Treaty of Lunéville, signed on February 9, 1801. In a general sense a repetition of the Treaty of Campo Formio, the terms were now more dictatorial and more severe. France was confirmed in possession of the Belgian provinces and the entire Rhineland area. Austria was to continue in possession of Istria and Dalmatia and was to hold Venetia only as far as the Adige River. France thus was able to reassert its influence over Piedmont, the Ligurian Republic and the Cisalpine Republic which Austria was required now to recognize along with the Batavian and the Helvetic Republics. In the preceding month Bonaparte had been elected president of the Cisalpine Republic. It was once more stipulated that the German princes losing territory on the left bank of the Rhine should be compensated on the right bank, where the emperor agreed to find them land at the expense of the old ecclesiastical states. Without question, Lunéville was a shattering defeat for Austria.

Russia meanwhile had made its departure from the Second Coalition. Paul I had joined the war in pursuit of Russian interest and had contributed substantial forces to the common cause. He was resentful at what he regarded as poor support from Austria and was furious when the British seized Malta from the French in September, 1800. Paul had sent a Russian fleet through the Straits into the Mediterranean in order to set up a Republic of the Ionian Islands under Russian protection. British seapower, therefore, seemed sure to interfere with his larger Mediterranean ambitions. Hence he persuaded Sweden, Denmark and Prussia to join with him in reviving the old League of Armed Neutrality in order to resist Britain's interference with neutral shipping. Paul listened, too, with sympathy to Bonaparte's proposals for a joint partition of the Near East. The Tsar, who had shown clear signs of madness, was assassinated as the result of a palace plot in March, 1801, to be succeeded by his son, Alexander I. In the following October Russia made a formal peace with France.

During the same year the other members of the Second Coalition withdrew from the war. By the Treaty of Aranjuez Spain ceded Louisiana to France, being promised in return that Tuscany would be set up as a kingdom for the Duke of Parma, the husband of the Spanish infanta. Naples left the war in March, Portugal in June and Turkey in October. England alone remained at war with France.

Napoleon's original hope that he could use Russia as the nucleus of a great coalition against England had ended with the assassination of the Tsar Paul. Almost at the same time Lord Abercrombie won a decisive victory over the French troops in Egypt, while Nelson broke up the League of Armed Neutrality by his successful attack in April, 1801, upon the Danish fleet at Copenhagen. It seemed, therefore, that the method of negotiation would have to be undertaken. Feeling in England moved in the same direction, for trade had suffered through the closing of the continental markets and in addition the shipping losses through privateering on the high seas were substantial. After eighteen years in office, William Pitt resigned the prime ministership in February, 1801, because of George III's opposition to Pitt's proposals for Catholic emancipation in Ireland. His successor was Addington, a mediocrity who did not hesitate to seek an agreement with France that Pitt knew could only be temporary.[6]

By October, 1801, a preliminary agreement had been reached at London. This was followed by further discussions at Amiens with Lord Cornwallis as

6. A popular contemporary jingle ran as follows:

> Pitt is to Addington
> As London is to Paddington.

Paddington was then an obscure suburb of the capital.

the chief British spokesman and Talleyrand and Joseph Bonaparte representing France. The Treaty of Amiens (March, 1802) provided that England was to recognize the French Republic. England gave up most of its colonial conquests, returning the Cape of Good Hope to the Dutch, Malta to the Knights of St. John and Egypt to the Ottoman Empire. It kept only Ceylon and Trinidad. In return France was to evacuate Naples and the Papal States and to recognize the Republic of the Ionian Islands. The advantages were clearly on the side of France, while for England the peace could be little more than a breathing spell which left unsolved the great problem of French control in the Low Countries, the Rhineland and Italy. For the English it had at least this virtue, that England remained in control of the seas. In 1802 England had 202 ships of the line and 277 frigates. France had only 39 of the former and 35 of the latter. "It is a peace," Sheridan declared in the House of Commons, "of which all men are glad but of which no man can be proud." But peace it was, and for a brief interlude the guns were silent.

■ THE BIRTH OF IMPERIAL FRANCE

During the period of the Consulate (1800–1804) the general pattern of Napoleonic reconstruction in France became clear. In these years a confused, revolutionary society was turned into an orderly imperial state. Bonaparte, a child of the Revolution, preserved many of its greatest achievements. He was also a powerful tyrant who imposed his own will upon a people that at least for a time seemed happy to accept it. It is this combination of republican ideals and dictatorial authority which gives a unique character to the France of the Napoleonic age.

The Constitution of the Year VIII was so cleverly devised that its autocratic quality was not at first apparent. The attitude of the First Consul seemed to be one of moderation. As members of his Council of State he included all types ranging from former Jacobins to royalists. When Sieyès and Ducos vacated their provisional consulships by being "kicked upstairs" to the Senate, Bonaparte took as colleagues Cambacérès, a distinguished lawyer, and Lebrun, formerly a moderate royalist and something of a literary figure, the translator of Tasso and Homer. Many former deputies from the period of the Directory were nominated to the new legislative bodies. The laws against *émigrés* were relaxed and a general easing of tension displayed on all sides.

The most obvious internal threat at the outset of the Consulate came from a new royalist rising which had flared up in the Vendée. This too was counteracted, partly by police and military measures, and also by Bonaparte's rapid action in revoking the severe law of hostages of July, 1799, which made kinsmen responsible for crimes committed by their *émigré* relatives. He also restored citizenship to relatives of *émigrés* and promised full religious liberty to all Frenchmen. By February, 1800, organized resistance in the Vendée was at an end.

The time was ripe for Bonaparte's remarkable gifts as an organizer to be put into action. A decree of February, 1800, brought about a drastic change in the system of French departmental and local administration. Henceforth the prefects of the departments, the sub-prefects and the mayors of the communes were to be nominated, along with their various councils, by the First Consul. The structural pattern of revolutionary France remained, but popular election and true local self-administration were at an end. In their place arose the efficient centralization of the new Napoleonic régime—a centralization that has remained as a permanent legacy to our own day. Similarly, a decree of March, 1800, which reorganized the judicial system took as its starting point the legal reforms of the Constituent Assembly, but knit the courts into a tighter scheme comprising civil courts, criminal courts and courts of appeal, and placed the appointment of nearly all judges in the hands of the First Consul. Another indication of the trend of the times was the introduction of an efficient censorship for the press and theater and the reduction of the number of Paris newspapers in two months from 73 to 13.

Urgent steps were necessary in the field of finances and taxation, for despite the various steps taken by the Directory the economy of France was still precarious. Although nearly two-thirds of the national debt had been wiped out, finances were very shaky and government bonds had dropped to a very low value. New efforts were made to consolidate the public debt, to centralize and systematize the machinery of tax-collecting and to bring the budget into balance. A Bank of France was created in February, 1800, and its capital enlarged in 1803. The French coinage was standardized on a decimal basis. For the fiscal year 1801–1802 the budget seemed to have been brought into balance, though this balance was due in part to the tribute and exactions which were obtained from conquered lands. Some of the financial devices were more artificial than genuine, and Bonaparte's efforts to stimulate French industrial and commercial life were amateurish and unproductive. Even so, the general picture, certainly in its externals, seemed one of substantial progress.

In the field of legal reform Bonaparte's talents were ably employed. His lucid and powerful mind was admirably adapted to take up the work of legal codification which the Constituent Assembly had begun nearly ten years earlier. A committee set up by Bonaparte completed the draft of a Civil Code by December, 1800. It was then submitted to the First Consul who in a series of thirty-five meetings with the Council of State gave it vigorous revision. The outcome was the famous Civil Code which after various delays was proclaimed in March, 1804. The Code recognized some of the basic ideas which the Revolution had asserted: equality before the law, freedom of conscience and of occupation, the supremacy of the civil power. Its careful regulations concerning inheritance, landed property and mortgages, its stipulation that a testator could dispose freely of only one-half of his estate and must divide the rest among his heirs, its recognition of divorce, its careful defining of the powers of the head of a family—all these points were important in contributing to the growth of a middle-class state in which the rights of property were greatly respected. The Code had very little interest in the particular problems of the wage-earner. A Code of Civil Procedure, a Code of Criminal Procedure and Penal Law and a Commercial Code came at later dates. The Codes were one of Napoleon's greatest contributions to modern France:

> They recognized and embodied, in principle at least, the leading demands of the revolutionary program, the profound aspiration for order, for a unified national system of secular legislation, for civil equality, religious liberty, and a soil freed from feudal encumbrances. They recognized no privileges of birth, opened all careers to men of industry and talent, promoted the distribution of property and discouraged the accumulation of large landed estates. In this sense they were a summary of the Revolution. . . .[7]

One of the problems crying most urgently for solution was that of the Church. The Revolution had dealt serious blows to the former privileges of the Roman Catholic establishment and had witnessed the appearance of a variety of more or less eccentric cults. The Roman Catholic clergy had been split into two groups: the "constitutionals" who accepted the Revolution, and the "non-juring" clergy who in spite of many hardships did not. When freedom of worship was announced, it soon became evident that there was an impressive return to the churches and that the "non-juring" clergy were actually more numerous than those who had accepted the Revolution. Under these circumstances and in the interest of public order, a settlement obviously was required. Though Bonaparte's own brand of Catholicism was of the most nominal sort, he quite clearly recognized the need for active governmental measures. Hence he undertook as early as the summer of 1800 to see whether or not an accommodation could be reached with the papacy.

Following protracted negotiations the terms of a Concordat were finally accepted by both sides in July, 1801. Roman Catholicism was declared to be the religion of the majority of Frenchmen, "and especially of the three Consuls." The Roman Catholic faith was to be freely exercised in France, subject to the police power (a significant qualification). The pope was confirmed in possession of his Italian territories save for those areas (the "Legations") which had been made a part of the Cisalpine Republic. The French clergy were to accept the Republic by oath. Church lands were to remain in

7. G. BRUUN, *Europe and the French Imperium* (1938), p. 28.

the possession of their purchasers or of the French government. Clerical salaries, consequently, were to be paid by the state. Bishops were to be nominated by the First Consul and consecrated by the pope. The lower clergy were to be chosen by the bishops. These were the basic terms of a settlement so acceptable to the majority of Frenchmen that it endured until 1905. The Concordat was ratified in December, 1801.

This general atmosphere of good will was soon sharply challenged by the "Organic Articles," a series of police regulations issued by Bonaparte without any consultation with the papacy in April, 1802. These provided that no papal bulls or decrees of general church councils would have effect in France without the consent of the government, and that no papal legates would be permitted to assert their authority. The state declared its right to supervise and control the operation of Catholic schools and seminaries. One liturgy and one catechism were to be used in France. The Organic Articles, a reassertion of the old Gallican attitude of the French government, seriously embittered what otherwise must be regarded as an unusually promising relationship between church and state. The Organic Articles also dealt with the Protestants who likewise were subject to governmental supervision and who were granted certain funds for the maintenance of their faith.

In various other respects Bonaparte sought to bring order to a country that had suffered much from the fever of revolution. A decree of May, 1802, sought to consolidate the earlier program of educational reform. Elementary schools were declared to be the responsibility of the local communes, while secondary education was to be mainly in the hands of the *lycées* over which the government was to exercise a considerable degree of control. Military discipline and even military dress were standard features of the classroom. A heavy stress was put upon scientific studies, and to this end the Institute of France, first established in 1795, was reorganized in 1803 into four classes. These carried on the work of the French Academy, the Academy of Science, the Academy of Inscriptions and those academies devoted to painting, sculpture and architecture.

In other respects Bonaparte sought to dramatize the dignity of his position and the grandeur of France. Work which was now started for the beautification of Paris was carried on during his entire reign, so that many of the most notable features of the present-day city are Napoleonic in origin: the new wing of the Louvre, the Carrousel Arch and the Arch of Triumph, the Vendôme Column, the Church of the Madeleine, the Bourse and several of the Seine bridges. As a reward for ability and loyal service the Legion of Honor was established in 1802—an arrangement which provided pensions in addition to the customary outward signs of distinction.[8]

8. The Revolution, in addition to abolishing all titles of nobility, had done away with medals and decorations.

In place of the rough republican informality of the previous era Bonaparte sought to insist upon a high standard of decorum for public life. Special uniforms were designed for the consuls and other high public officials. The etiquette and ceremonial surrounding the First Consul soon became regal in spirit if not in actual fact.

The first move away from the tradition of republicanism had been taken in 1799 when Bonaparte set up the Consulate with himself as unquestioned leader. In August, 1802, a proposal was submitted to the French people that Bonaparte should become Consul for life. It was approved by an overwhelming vote (3,500,000 to a little more than 8,000). The changes which were embodied in the "Constitution of the Year X" (December, 1802) provided that Bonaparte could amend the Constitution and had exclusive power to choose the Senate, the principal initiator of legislative proposals. The Tribunate was reduced from one hundred to fifty. The trend to despotism could hardly have been more explicit.

The uncovering of a royalist plot early in 1804 played directly into Bonaparte's hands. Its leaders, including two generals—Jean Moreau and Pichegru—were seized. Evidence seemed to implicate a young member of the celebrated Condé family, the Duke of Enghien, who was living not far from France in the German territory of Baden. French hussars were sent across the border in an outrageous disregard of the rights of nations. They seized the young duke and quickly brought him back to the Château of Vincennes, near Paris, for trial on a charge of treason. As Enghien crossed the courtyard for his "trial" he passed an open grave dug in anticipation of the verdict. He was quickly found guilty and shot, to the general horror of Europe. Pichegru was found strangled in his cell. Moreau was banished. Such ruthless measures, unwise in the light of their impact upon European opinion, were indicative of Bonaparte's overpowering confidence in his own destiny.

The Empire was voted by the legislature in April, 1804, and confirmed overwhelmingly by plebiscite. In May, 1804, the Senate adopted the "Constitution of the Year XII," creating an emperorship in the lineage and family of Napoleon Bonaparte. His power was autocratic and unquestioned, yet by keeping the external pattern of the Constitution of 1799—Senate, Council of State, Tribunate and Legislative Body—Napoleon was able to preserve some sense of the republican tradition and assert his connection with those earlier momentous years.[9] The basic gains of the Revolution were not abandoned, but a new Caesarism, far different from the monarchy of the Bourbons, had imposed itself upon France.

---

9. Students of constitutional history may puzzle over the terminology of Article I of the new Constitution: "The government of the Republic is vested in an Emperor who will assume the title of Emperor of the French."

Napoleonic Europe,

1803–1810

AN IMAGINATIVE PROPOSAL FOR INVADING ENGLAND BY
TUNNEL, SEA AND AIR. The scene in this fantastic engraving of 1804 may be compared with the 1944 cross-
Channel invasion of France. The artist provides a
tunnel for artillery, while infantry, protected by Mont-
golfier balloons, are ferried across. Courtesy, Biblio-
thèque Nationale, Paris.

Chapter 25

■ THE RENEWAL OF WAR, 1803–1805

THE FRENCH EMPIRE which Napoleon had created made a profound impact
upon the life of Europe. From 1804 to 1810 the emperor steadily enlarged
his authority, making change after change affecting the pattern of European
states and even the structure of European society. By 1810 forces had arisen
which challenged his power, brought him into renewed battle and were in
the end to destroy him. The *finale* came at the Congress of Vienna where,

out of the ruins of Napoleonic Europe, statesmen were able to create a new structure providing the basis for the history of the nineteenth century.

The Empire had been decreed by the Senate in May, 1804. The full transition was achieved in the following December when in a splendid ceremony at Notre Dame Napoleon and Josephine were crowned. The sword and insignia of Charlemagne were brought to Paris from the ancient tomb at Aachen; the painter, David, recorded the occasion in one of his most famous works; and the sixty-four-year-old pontiff, Pius VII, was summoned from Rome to consecrate, though not actually to crown, the imperial couple. At the climactic moments of the ceremony Napoleon placed the crown of France upon his own head and upon Josephine's. He sought, clearly, to be the architect of his own destiny.

Before the transition from Consulate to Empire was completed France found itself again at war. In view of the clear evidence which Napoleon had time and again given of the vast sweep of his ambitions, such an outcome could not be surprising. Yet it would be an oversimplification of history to explain the new course of events merely in terms of the ambitions of one man. His actions canalized, as it were, tendencies arising from the earlier revolutionary period: among them were the widespread desire to maintain the natural frontiers, the crusading zeal of statesmen and soldiers alike, the French distrust of the old European dynasties, and the new involvements in the dependent republics along France's borders. In the light of these forces, the peace won by 1802 was really only a truce.

One important clue to the ambitions of Napoleon lay in his attitude toward the problem of colonies. His early interest in the Ionian Islands and his ambitious dreams concerning Egypt indicate his conviction that, despite England's naval superiority, France could win glory in the Levant and in distant Asia. In America, too, it will be recalled that Louisiana had been secured from Spain by the secret treaty of 1800. Its future as a French colony was tied with the further problem of the island of Santo Domingo, of which France had acquired full possession from Spain in 1795. Here a talented Negro leader, Toussaint L'Ouverture, had risen as a champion of his fellow-Negroes, now supposedly freed from slavery and eager for even further rights. By 1801 Toussaint had established what was practically a Negro republic. Hence Napoleon sent his brother-in-law, General Leclerc, to the island in February, 1802, with an army of 33,000 men—ostensibly as military governor but actually with instructions to overthrow Toussaint's rule. This he effected, and Toussaint died in 1803 in a French prison. But the victory was hollow, for the yellow fever destroyed three-quarters of the French expedition, including Leclerc himself. And two years later, in 1804, the island declared its independence under another Negro leader, Dessalines.

This fiasco led Napoleon to alter his views about Lousiana, of which France had taken actual possession in March, 1801. Under the threat of English seapower and with the difficulties in Santo Domingo, France soon accepted the offer of the American statesmen sent to Paris by President Jefferson. The Louisiana Territory, so fateful in future American history, was transferred to the United States in August, 1803, for a payment of $15,000,000.

French commercial and maritime interests persisted in other areas. In September, 1800, a scientific expedition was sent to Australia where until 1803 it remained engaged in mapping and surveying the coasts. Although no annexations were made or attempted, the publication at Paris in 1807 of an elaborate account of the expedition including a map showing half of the Australian continent under the name of "Terre Napoléon" indicates the trend of the emperor's ambitions.

Active interest was also shown in India where, since 1791, native unrest against the English had been stimulated by the Sultan of Mysore, "Tippo Sahib," a leader of the Mahratta Confederacy. At the time of the Egyptian expedition it had been the hope of Napoleon to send aid from Suez to "Citizen Tippo," as the French republicans had delighted to call him. This did not materialize, and in 1799 Tippo was killed in the siege of Mysore. Napoleon's interest nevertheless remained. In 1802 he sent General Sebastiani on a secret trade mission to Egypt, and in January, 1803, he startled Europe by publishing in the *Moniteur* Sebastiani's report to the effect that with an army of 6,000 the French could recapture Egypt. In March General Decaen sailed from Brest with nearly 2,000 troops to reinforce the French garrisons in India. Although his mission was officially one of observation, his instructions spoke of the possible "great glory" that he might win. Napoleon's oriental dreams quite clearly were still alive.

Napoleon's meddling in Europe was even more insistent than overseas, for his various treaty arrangements seemed less a "settlement" than a prelude to still further advances. In Germany, for example, the Treaty of Lunéville (1801), which conceded to France the Rhine frontier, had indicated that the compensation to be found within the Empire for the dispossessed German princes from the left bank of the Rhine should come from the ecclesiastical states on the right bank. When in 1801 the Imperial Diet appointed a deputation of eight to consider this, the real work was undertaken at Paris, where Talleyrand at the Ministry of Foreign Affairs held the strings in his hands.[1] The general principle which inspired Napoleon's reorganization of

1. Huge bribes were poured out by the German spokesmen at Paris. The representative of Baden, for example, gave Talleyrand a valuable snuffbox and 100,000 francs in banknotes. A similar sum had been reserved for Joseph Bonaparte, but on second thought it was added to Talleyrand's *douceur*.

Germany was efficiency. The ecclesiastical states, which clearly belonged to an outworn age, and even the smaller secular states must be destroyed in order to strengthen the larger and more forward-looking states. This meant that of 74 ecclesiastical states only one, the archbishopric of Mainz, could be allowed to remain. The number of free imperial cities was reduced from 51 to 6. In the end, the states principally benefiting were Prussia, Bavaria, Baden, Württemberg, Hanover and Hesse-Cassel. As an example, Prussia lost 2,750 square kilometers on the left bank of the Rhine and gained 12,000 square kilometers in Westphalia. It lost population numbering 125,000 and gained 500,000. The others made corresponding gains. Two of the three ecclesiastical members of the old electoral college lost their seats; five new states were added, so that the college ultimately had six Protestant and four Catholic members. One-sixth of the population of the Empire—in other words, about four million people—was transferred from ecclesiastical to secular hands. When all the changes were completed in Paris, they were referred to the Imperial Diet, which by the resounding decree of February, 1803—the famous *Reichsdeputationshauptschluss*—gave them its sanction. "The Germany of the Middle Ages, with its ecclesiastical states, its orders of knighthood, and the preponderance of the Hapsburgs, vanished, never to return. . . . Another stage on the road toward a united Germany was accomplished; and, for this reason, the Imperial Recess of 1803 was in its way a revolution as radical as was the French Revolution of 1789." [2]

Napoleon's other meddlings in these years may be more briefly summarized. The Grand Duchy of Tuscany was converted in June, 1801, into the Kingdom of Etruria and granted to the son-in-law of the King of Spain. The Batavian Republic was required to accept a new constitution in October, despite the fact of its rejection by a Dutch plebiscite. In the following January Napoleon accepted the presidency of the Cisalpine Republic, now renamed the Italian Republic. Piedmont, long in French hands, was formally annexed in September, 1802. The most active French intervention, however, came in Switzerland. In order to guarantee control of the vitally important Great St. Bernard and Simplon passes, Napoleon had separated the canton of Valais from the other cantons and established it as an independent republic. When civil war broke out between aristocratic and democratic Swiss factions, French troops under General Ney marched into the Helvetic Republic with the orders, "crush all opposition." Ten Swiss commissioners were invited to Paris to discuss a new constitution that Napoleon had drafted for them and there in February, 1803, they signed the Act of Mediation, accepting a federal structure of nineteen cantons, linked together by a federal diet. As distinguished from the "unitary" constitution which preceded it,

2. *The Cambridge Modern History,* IX, pp. 94–95.

the Act gave Switzerland the basic political structure which it has to this
day. In the following September Switzerland was forced into a military
alliance which gave France the sole right of recruiting troops in the Confederation.

Such moves made it difficult for France's former opponents to be convinced of Napoleon's peaceful intentions. England in particular was concerned over a pattern of intervention extending all the way from the
Netherlands to India. Although it had agreed in the Treaty of Amiens
to restore Malta to the Knights of St. John, the English government privately
instructed its representative in no circumstances to do so. Meanwhile it
sent protest after protest to Paris concerning French behavior in Holland,
Switzerland, Italy and Egypt. By the spring of 1803 it was clear that conflict
was imminent. England's final offer was to evacuate Malta in ten years' time
if France would evacuate Holland and Switzerland at once and confirm the
independence of the Italian and Ligurian republics. This offer Napoleon
would not accept; by May the two countries were again at war.

It was not at first easy for England and France to come to grips. French
troops quickly occupied Holland, Naples and Hanover and the government
declared the continental ports from the Elbe to southern Italy closed to all
British shipping. In reply, English naval squadrons blockaded Brest, Roche-
fort and Toulon. Napoleon proceeded to raise troops and funds from the
various dependent republics. His most dramatic move, however, was to make
preparations at Boulogne for the cross-Channel invasion of England. Despite
the skepticism of some historians, who regard it as a feint, this invasion seems
to have been seriously meant. Over 2,000 flat-bottomed invasion barges were
assembled, an army of nearly 170,000 was encamped at Boulogne, the harbor
was enlarged, the roads through Picardy were improved and the troops were
rigorously drilled for over a year. The close personal interest taken by the
emperor during his visits to the coast is further indication of the reality of
the project.

Meanwhile England brought pressure on the European states to oppose
Napoleon. Sweden was easily induced to take action. Tsar Alexander I
of Russia, who had ordered court mourning for the death of the Duke of
Enghien, was shocked at the French occupation of Hanover, Switzerland and
the Italian ports. In September, 1804, he broke off diplomatic relations with
France. William Pitt, once again prime minister, sent Russia his proposals
for a general European peace settlement in January, 1805, which were
strongly reminiscent of those he had drafted in 1798.[3] By July, 1805, Russia
was formally allied with England. Austria, too, showing its concern over
Napoleon's continued interference in Italy, had made a secret agreement

3. See p. 635.

with Russia as early as November, 1804, to attack Napoleon if his aggressions continued. Thus, when he declared his intention of converting the Italian Republic into a kingdom, and even more when he was crowned at Milan in May, 1805, with the historic iron crown of Lombardy, Austria felt its interests to have been seriously affected. In August it gave secret adherence to the Russo-British alliance, accepting Pitt's general proposals for a European settlement. In September Austria openly declared war on France, bringing with it the Kingdom of Naples. Prussia alone of the major powers refused at this time to commit itself to the struggle.

■ THE DEFEAT OF THE THIRD COALITION, 1805–1807

The War of the Third Coalition enabled Napoleon to win some of his greatest victories. His first problem, the invasion of England, depended upon his ability to concentrate French naval forces in the Channel. This in turn depended upon the dispersal of British seapower. With Nelson on watch at Toulouse and Cornwallis at Brest a French move was not easy. Among other feints, Villeneuve, the French admiral, was ordered to the West Indies in order to draw off Nelson's fleet and then to return. Although the maneuver was in part successful, Nelson was clever enough to follow Villeneuve back. The end result was that the French fleet, instead of dominating the Channel, found itself bottled up at Cadiz. Even before the despairing Villeneuve issued forth to meet Nelson at Trafalgar, Napoleon had made up his mind, in August, 1805, that England could not be invaded and that his most urgent need was to destroy the Austrian armies now massing along the Danube. The great English naval victory at Trafalgar (October, 1805) ended the danger of any French challenge on the high seas and thus in the long run proved one of the determinants in the epic struggle between England and France. Nelson, shot through the spine by a French sharpshooter, died on his flagship, the *Victory*. Villeneuve survived, to brood over his defeat and, within a few months, to commit suicide.

Napoleon's campaign against Austria and Russia was conducted with phenomenal speed. He met the Austrian commander, Mack, on the Danube in October, 1805, and by brilliant maneuvering forced him to surrender at Ulm with more than 20,000 men. Pushing on quickly to seize Vienna, he then advanced northward into Bohemia where, on December 2, "the sun of Austerlitz" shone on one of the greatest Napoleonic victories which he won over the combined forces of Austria and Russia.

For the third time Austria had been defeated by Napoleon, and for the third time it was compelled to accept peace on his terms. The Treaty of Pressburg (December, 1805) broke the Third Coalition by requiring Austria to cede Venetia, Istria and Dalmatia to the newly-founded Kingdom of Italy. The Tyrol was to be given to Bavaria, and other Austrian possessions went to Württemberg and Baden. In all, Austria lost some three million inhabitants. The rulers of Bavaria and Württemberg were now to be recognized as kings. Thus the prestige of Austria within the Holy Roman Empire had been seriously weakened, its position in Italy completely destroyed, and its hold in the Adriatic limited to little more than the port of Trieste. The only sop tossed to Austria was that it obtained the territory of Salzburg.

Russia and England were still at war with France, but Prussia remained an uncertain quantity. The weak Frederick William III, who had succeeded his father, Frederick William II, in 1797, showed little disposition to become involved in conflict. He had been apathetic at the French occupation of Hanover in 1803 and was aroused only when French troops, marching across Germany, violated Prussian territory at Ansbach in October, 1805. But Frederick William's tentative alignment with Austria and Russia was soon altered by the brute facts of war. Two weeks after Austerlitz Prussia accepted the Treaty of Schönbrunn with France, being promised Hanover in return for an offensive and defensive alliance. "Prussian policy," declared Charles James Fox in the Commons with feeling, "combines everything that is contemptible in servility with everything that is odious in rapacity." Despite such British outrage, in the spring of 1806, following the death of Pitt, negotiations were again undertaken between England and France. During these negotiations France proposed that Hanover be restored to England if only Napoleon's brother, Joseph, could be made ruler of Sicily. Even though the offer was refused, it served to infuriate the Prussians, who were also concerned at the drastic changes being made by Napoleon within Germany. When in August, 1806, the French shot an obscure Nuremberg bookseller, Palm, for selling a pamphlet protesting against the "deep humiliation" of Germany, Prussian emotions were quickly aroused. In September, 1806, Prussia declared war on France.

Prussia's intervention was even more poorly timed than had been Austria's. Within a month the Prussian armies were overwhelmed at Jena, the French paraded along *Unter den Linden* in Berlin, and Frederick William was required to take refuge far to the east at Memel. Advancing in pursuit, Napoleon met the Russians at Eylau, in East Prussia, where after bloody losses he claimed a victory in February, 1807. In June the decisive battle of Friedland drove Russia out of the war. The Fourth Coalition against Napoleon was at an end.

Before considering the treaties of Tilsit, by which France now made peace with Prussia and Russia, it will be advisable to note the significant political changes in Europe which Napoleon effected concurrently with his military campaigns. Nothing, indeed, is more impressive than the incredible energy with which the emperor of the French could turn first to the demands of war, then to the domestic affairs of France, to the reorganization of Germany, or to the reconstruction of Italy.

Important further changes were made in Italy and elsewhere. In March, 1805, the Italian Republic was converted into the Kingdom of Italy. Napoleon was solemnly crowned at Milan and his stepson, Eugène Beauharnais, installed as viceroy. Genoa was annexed in the same year, and the small duchies of Piombino and Lucca bestowed as "imperial fiefs" upon his sisters, Elisa and Pauline. In December, 1805, Napoleon declared that the Bourbon rulers of Naples were deposed, and in the following March his brother, Joseph, was declared King of Naples and Sicily, subject to the imperial authority of France. In June, 1806, the government of the Batavian Republic was overthrown and another brother, Louis Bonaparte, became King of Holland.

Changes of even greater significance were undertaken in Germany. The Confederation of the Rhine that came into existence in 1806 climaxed a long series of French interventions in German affairs which, beginning with the Peace of Basel and including Campo Formio, Lunéville and the secularizations of 1803, had ultimately suppressed over 120 small states. Napoleon's further changes seem to have been intended in part as a means of securing a new and commanding position in central Europe with respect to Austria and Prussia, his potential or actual enemies. The changes of 1806 can be attributed also to Napoleon's "disinterested passion for practical improvement"—to the workings of a mind that could never rest in the presence of outworn institutions or persistent inefficiencies. The fantastically outmoded Imperial Diet, which Napoleon once described as "a miserable monkeyhouse," had no place in his schemes for a new Europe, nor had the petty states which he now so ruthlessly destroyed. "No longer did the Count of Limburg-Styrum parade his army of one colonel, six officers, and two privates in the valley of the Roehr." [4] Under the direction of Talleyrand and the emperor a draft of the plans for Germany was prepared at Paris. The fifteen separate treaties made with the states involved were combined into one text and proclaimed in July, 1806.

The Confederation of the Rhine in its original form consisted of fifteen states, of which Baden, Württemberg, Bavaria, Hesse-Darmstadt, Nassau, Frankfort and the newly created Grand Duchy of Berg were the chief. Prussia and Austria, of course, remained outside, as did for a time Saxony, Hanover, Mecklenburg and Hesse-Cassel. Nearly all the free cities and petty principalities were now absorbed in the larger states. These were

4. J. HOLLAND ROSE, *The Life of Napoleon I* (1924), II, p. 78.

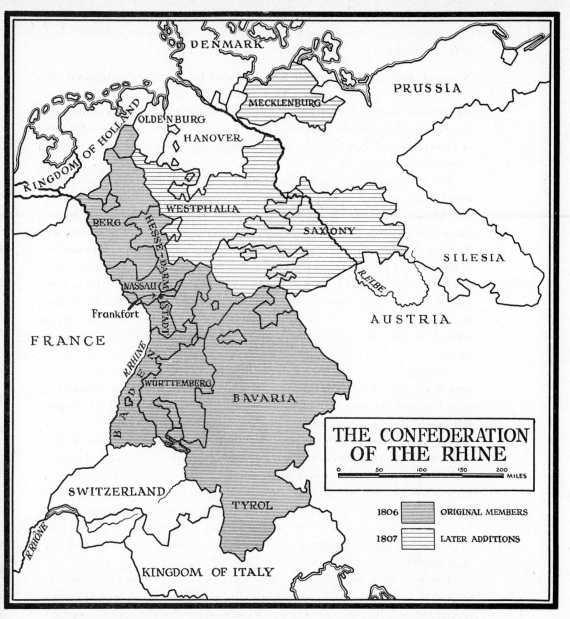

DENMARK

PRUSSIA

MECKLENBURG

KINGDOM OF HOLLAND

OLDENBURG

HANOVER

WESTPHALIA

BERG

SAXONY

HESSE-DARMSTADT

SILESIA

NASSAU

Frankfort

FRANCE

R. ELBE

AUSTRIA

R. RHINE

B A D E N

WÜRTTEMBERG

BAVARIA

THE CONFEDERATION
OF THE RHINE

0   50   100   150   200
                              MILES

SWITZERLAND

TYROL

1806 [ORIGINAL MEMBERS]

1807 [LATER ADDITIONS]

R. RHÔNE

KINGDOM OF ITALY

Compare this map with the growth of French influence in Italy (pages 631 and 665). The
number of German states is reduced, Prussia is east of the Elbe and the *Bund* touches the
Baltic.

organized in a diet with its grandiloquently named College of Kings and its
College of Princes (neither of which ever met). The emperor of the French
was protector of the Confederation, which was permanently allied with
France and obliged to furnish it with 63,000 troops.

With the proclamation of this new Confederation, the thousand-year-old
Empire lost what little meaning it still possessed. Hence, in August, 1806,

Napoleon informed the Diet at Ratisbon that he no longer recognized the existence of the Empire. Francis II renounced his ancient imperial dignities and became Francis I, Hereditary Emperor of Austria. Austria's leadership in German affairs had long represented the shadow rather than the substance of power, so that Napoleon's ruthless action was little more than a frank recognition of realities.

Still further changes in German affairs came with the treaties of Tilsit, which in the summer of 1807 brought to an end the French war with Prussia and Russia. After the victory of Friedland in June, 1807, Napoleon found himself in the little town of Tilsit on the banks of the Niemen at the Russo-Prussian frontier. Here he received Alexander I of Russia and Frederick William III of Prussia to consider the terms of peace. Alexander was warmly greeted by the French emperor, the two carrying on their first discussions privately on a raft moored in the river while Frederick William III wrung his hands unavailingly on the bank. The beautiful Queen Louise of Prussia arrived to add her appeals to those of her husband, with equally little success.

Savage terms were imposed upon Prussia. Every inch of Prussian soil west of the Elbe River was taken away so as to create with some other German territory the new Kingdom of Westphalia, to be allotted to Jerome Bonaparte and to be included as a further member of the Confederation of the Rhine. East of the Elbe most of the land taken by Prussia in the Second and Third Partitions of Poland was to be reconstituted as the Grand Duchy of Warsaw—the eastern counterpart of the Confederation of the Rhine. French troops were to garrison the remaining Prussian fortresses until an indemnity of unspecified amount was paid. Prussia was to recognize Napoleon's changes in Europe, close its harbors to English shipping and join France in war against England if by December an honorable peace had not been reached.

The Russian terms were much less onerous. Actually, the two emperors seemed to be looking forward to mutually advantageous arrangements. In return for an alliance with France, Russia recognized Napoleon's various European changes and agreed to the dismemberment of Prussia and to an eventual war with England if Russian attempts at mediation should fail. In somewhat ambiguous terms it was implied that Russia might some day share in a partition of the Ottoman Empire.

With these terms agreed upon, Napoleon was now able to proceed to enlarge the Confederation of the Rhine. By the inclusion of the kingdoms of Westphalia and Saxony and of north German territory such as Oldenburg and Mecklenburg, the Confederation was expanded so as to include ulti-

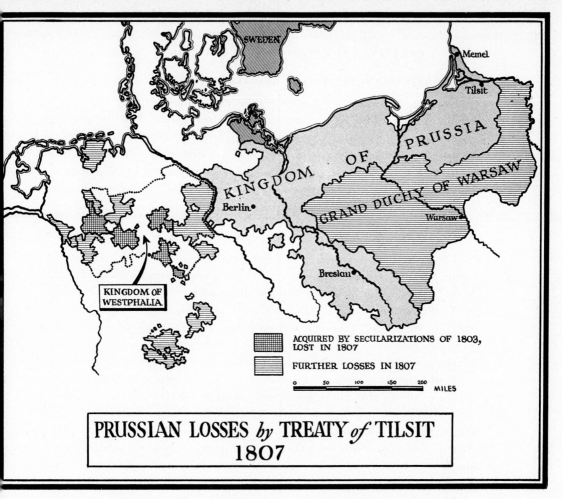

Note how Prussia's western losses contribute to the new Kingdom of Westphalia, while Posen, earlier taken from Poland, is an important part of the Grand Duchy of Warsaw.

mately thirty-two states. Subjected to close French supervision and control, it provided Napoleon with a substantial financial contribution and large numbers of troops. In a larger sense it will be noted how effectively Napoleon's policies minimized the danger from across the Rhine. The reorganizations of 1806 and 1807 had the effect of creating a threefold division—"the German Triad." A much weakened Prussia remained in the north; a much weakened Austria stood in the south and east; a Confederation of the Rhine, very clearly under the French thumb, had been constructed in the west. For the time at least Napoleon had banished the specter of a powerfully united Germany. Far more effectively than had Richelieu or Mazarin before him, he had contrived to make the division of Germany a means to ensure French preponderance upon the Continent.

■ THE CONTINENTAL SYSTEM AND ITS CONSEQUENCES

Between 1804 and 1807 Napoleon's power on the Continent had grown steadily greater, while at the same time England's control of the seas remained intact. Under such circumstances the conflict between the two great opponents was marked by vigorous efforts to destroy each other's economic strength. The expression, "Continental System," was given by Napoleon to the various economic measures which, in default of positive military action, he felt sure would bring England to its knees. If this was his immediate purpose, it may also be true that he hoped these moves would bring Europe nearer to the goal of a genuine confederation under French control.

The techniques of economic warfare developed at this time were by no means the creation of Napoleon. Several measures employed by France before 1799 had been intended to injure Britain by excluding its goods from the Continent; Britain had retaliated by blockading French ports and attempting to shut off French trade with the colonies. In these contests the advantage had been so strongly on the side of Britain that by 1799 the French merchant marine had been completely driven from the high seas.[5]

By the time of Trafalgar (October, 1805) it was clear that France could not hope to establish direct naval and maritime supremacy over England. "The sea," as the emperor put it, "will have to be subdued by land." Napoleon regarded as unsound the economic prosperity of what he scornfully chose to call a nation of shopkeepers. Seeing that England's wealth rested upon trade, he believed that a successful attack upon this trade would bring the island kingdom to disaster. Hence, by measures such as the high French tariff of April, 1803, and the announcement that continental ports would be closed to British shipping, Napoleon strove to achieve his purpose. When Prussia was brought into a French alliance at the beginning of 1806 by the promise of Hanover, one of the stipulations was that it, too, must agree to close its ports to British shipping. Similarly, one of the demands made upon the members of the Confederation of the Rhine was that they exclude all British goods from their territories. The same demands were made of the newly conquered Kingdom of Naples. Meanwhile the English kept up a blockade of the European coast from Brest to Hamburg.

After his victories of 1806 Napoleon issued his Berlin Decree in November from the Prussian capital. The British Isles were declared to be in a state of blockade; no one was to trade with them or to accept British merchandise: and all British subjects found in any country occupied by the French were to be made prisoners. All British goods found on the Continent were liable to seizure; no ship coming from a British port could have access

---

5. "Before 1789 over 2,000 French ships had been engaged in European and colonial trade; ten years later there was not a merchant ship on the high seas flying the French flag." BRUUN, *Europe and the French Imperium*, p. 86.

to any port on the Continent. "The essential underlying idea," as Admiral Mahan has written in his classic treatise on this period, "was to crush the commerce of Great Britain by closing the Continent to her products of every kind." [6] By such means Napoleon hoped to bring about the collapse of England.

The British responded with the Order in Council of January, 1807. Any ship trading between ports from which English ships were excluded would be liable to capture as a lawful prize. This Order was followed by another in November, 1807, stipulating that all ports from which the British flag was excluded were to be considered in a state of blockade. These decrees meant that England was challenging the rights of neutrals to engage in the European coastal trade or to carry goods from the French colonies to Europe. Such severe prohibitions, however, were given certain qualifications. In an attempt to placate the neutrals, Britain permitted them to run their ships from British ports to the enemy colonies. It also permitted neutral ships to carry certain goods to the blockaded ports on the Continent provided that they first call at a British port and pay heavy duty on the cargo. In December, 1807, Napoleon issued his Milan Decree declaring that all ships submitting to these British rules would be regarded as lawful prizes of war.

The general significance of these economic measures must be stressed. Lacking effective sea power, Napoleon could not impose (and indeed could not have intended to impose) an effective blockade on the British Isles. Although some damage, to be sure, could be done to British commerce by French privateers, the prime Napoleonic purpose was to ruin, rather than to starve, England; the method employed was one designed to prevent British shipping from carrying goods into the Continent. Naples, the Kingdom of Italy, Holland, the Confederation of the Rhine, the Grand Duchy of Warsaw and later Denmark, Prussia, Austria, Russia and Spain—all were forced to accept what in essence was intended to be a blockade of continental Europe by itself. England likewise was not primarily attempting to starve France or its allies. It wished to preserve its own dominant position in shipping and trade. It was prepared, therefore, to force goods upon the Continent, whether manufactured in England or coming from overseas, provided they came via a British port. Each side took steps that were clearly inconsistent with the general purposes of a blockade. From time to time the English issued special licenses for the shipment of cargoes through blockaded European ports. Customs officers were bribed; smuggling was encouraged; and devious overland trade routes, sometimes as far afield as the Balkans, were employed to force colonial wares into central Europe. The French, too, issued special import licenses, so that French troops on occasion

6. A. T. MAHAN, *The Influence of Sea Power upon the French Revolution and Empire* (London, n.d.), II, p. 272.

were equipped with greatcoats and boots made in England. One unexpected and most significant long-term result was that British merchants looked for new markets elsewhere. A rapidly growing trade with the Spanish colonies in America saved many English merchants from bankruptcy and gave England a favored economic position in the New World which it was able to maintain throughout the nineteenth century.[7]

The Continental System clearly played havoc with neutral rights. To make it effective, Napoleon was compelled to extend his European authority by ever wider annexations and to impose irksome restrictions upon the peoples subordinate to him. Such burdens stimulated a steadily growing unrest, so that the Continental System in the end proved to be one of the factors responsible for turning large parts of Europe against the Napoleonic hegemony. For the United States the persistent infringement of neutral rights by both belligerents was a source of growing indignation. Congress passed the Embargo Act late in 1807, closing American ports to foreign commerce and forbidding American ships to sail to any foreign port. When this proved unenforceable, it was replaced early in 1809 by the Non-Intercourse Act, which limited the embargo to Great Britain and France. This act was likewise unsatisfactory, as were the various measures taken after its repeal in 1810. Napoleon gave President Madison the dubious promise that the Berlin and Milan Decrees would not be invoked against the United States. This left Great Britain as the principal culprit in American eyes, all the more resented since the British invoked the right of search, stopping American ships to see if British-born seamen were on board. In 1812 the two countries went to war—a barren struggle without advantage to either.

The Continental System, though it caused England considerable hardship, clearly failed to do what Napoleon wished it to do. Its operation, moreover, involved him in further European adventures. Nothing, indeed, is more striking than the way in which he was compelled to undertake, step by step, an ever larger degree of European control. In this extension of French power the Spanish kingdom assumed a spectacular importance.

The Iberian Peninsula created urgent problems for Napoleon in 1807. Spain, which in the early days of the Revolution had abandoned the Family Compact in order to join the First Coalition against France, had left the war in 1795. Since then it had followed a policy either of benevolent neutrality or of actual alliance with France, which had reached a climax in 1805 when Napoleon forced Spain to take naval measures against Britain and to share with the French in the disaster at Trafalgar. Although Spain had

7. Napoleon developed the sugar-beet industry in France and turned French chemists to work so as to provide domestic substitutes for commodities formerly imported from abroad. To prevent Denmark from joining the Continental System, a British fleet without warning bombarded Copenhagen in 1807 and seized what was left of the Danish navy.

accepted the burden of the Continental System, Portugal, England's ancient ally, refused to do so. Hence, in October, 1807, Napoleon concluded a secret treaty with Spain for the partition of Portugal. French troops were sent through Spain and seized Lisbon, forcing the royal family of Portugal to escape under British protection to Brazil. Meanwhile, resentment grew in Spain against the French alliance which the monarchy had accepted. The unfortunate country was cursed with a dim-witted king, Charles IV, a vicious and dissolute queen, Maria Luisa, a principal minister, Godoy, who was openly the queen's lover, and an heir-apparent, Prince Ferdinand, of consuming ambition and despicable character. A conspiracy of March, 1808, overthrew both Godoy and Charles IV and gave Ferdinand the throne. Spain was now overrun by French troops. Napoleon, claiming to intervene in the interests of order, summoned the two royal contestants to Bayonne, in the south of France. Ferdinand was required to restore the crown to his father, and Charles (by the Treaty of Bayonne) then agreed to transfer it to Napoleon. The emperor was thus able to proclaim in June, 1808, that his brother, Joseph Bonaparte, had become King of Spain.

The course of Spanish events proved to be strikingly different from that in other countries occupied by Napoleon. Since French troops were now in occupation of both Spain and Portugal, he seemed to have scored a great victory. Two circumstances, however, cast their ominous shadows. Even before Joseph arrived at Madrid, the Spanish rose in revolt against the French occupancy, with such success that a French army of 20,000 was compelled to capitulate at Baylen in July. In the second place, a small British expeditionary force began in August to land in Portugal. British progress in the Peninsula turned out at first to be disappointingly slow. This intervention, nevertheless, together with the active support of the Spanish guerillas, proved in the end to be a force beyond the power of Napoleon to control. Resistance was not organized initially on a national scale, for there was no government to lead it. The fighting was directed by local committees (*juntas*) which eventually organized a supreme central committee. By 1810, when the Spanish *Cortes* was convoked at Cadiz, something in the nature of a national opposition to Napoleon had finally appeared.[8]

The Spanish crisis seemed to make it all the more necessary for Napoleon to maintain his strength elsewhere. In September, 1808, he invited the Tsar Alexander to meet him at Erfurt, in central Germany, so that they could renew their alliance and consider their common problems. In the previous spring Alexander had seized the province of Finland from Sweden as Napoleon had suggested at Tilsit. The meetings were amicable enough, and

8. Still later, in 1812, a relatively liberal constitution modeled on the French Constitution of 1791 was adopted.

in all the externals of his position the French emperor was able to dazzle the Russian ruler. The princes and kings of the Confederation of the Rhine were invited to Erfurt, as were many of the leading intellectuals of Germany, Goethe among them. The actors of the *Comédie Française* were brought from Paris to perform. Napoleon could point to the phenomenal prestige of his European position. His brothers were kings in Spain, Westphalia and Holland; his brother-in-law, Murat, formerly Grand Duke of Berg, was now King of Naples; his stepson, Eugène Beauharnais, Viceroy of Italy. Napoleon dominated Switzerland, the Confederation of the Rhine and the Grand Duchy of Warsaw. He had imposed punitive treaties upon Prussia and Austria. In Italy he had made further changes. Tuscany was annexed to France in May, 1808. At the same time the papacy, which had refused to abandon its neutrality on Napoleon's orders, lost all its temporal possessions. The greater part of the Papal States, including Rome, was annexed to France; some outlying portions (Ancona and the Legations) were added to the Kingdom of Italy. By this tripartite division of Italian soil, everything save the islands of Sicily and Sardinia came under the control of France.

The picture of Napoleonic splendor had its flaws. Troubles loomed ominously in Spain. The Continental System never worked well, so that the minor irritations that were evident from the first grew eventually to major proportions. Resentment was bitter in Prussia, as it was in some parts of Austria. The tsar, while outwardly all cordiality, was hurt at France's failure to undertake an active policy against the Ottoman Empire. England was very much in the war against France and held control of the seas. In France itself undercurrents of resentment existed. The pressure of conscription was beginning to tell, and disloyalty existed in high places. Talleyrand had resigned from his post as minister of foreign relations in August, 1807, though retaining his rank as imperial councillor. He accompanied Napoleon to Erfurt, but there he seems to have become convinced that his master was embarking upon reckless policies that would bring him to disaster. Talleyrand dropped hints to the tsar that he would be "available" in any efforts on the part of Russia and Austria to counter Napoleon's European designs. Fouché, the Napoleonic minister of police, seems likewise to have been associated with Talleyrand's intrigues. Both men were too clever to engage in the kind of outright conspiracy with which Napoleon would have been prepared to deal ruthlessly. The most that the emperor could do was to denounce Talleyrand publicly in January, 1809, in language of unparalleled violence and vulgarity, and dismiss him from office.

The spectacular development of the year 1809 was Austria's re-entry into the war—a surprising action for a country that had met defeat three times in little more than a decade. Napoleon's increasingly arrogant moves had evidently aroused bitter resentment. In the Tyrol and various other German-speaking parts of the Hapsburg lands a growing sense of Austrian national-ism was in evidence. The Peace of Pressburg (1805) had been felt as a deep humiliation, in consequence of which a new group of younger leaders arose, determined to avenge the losses that Austria had then undergone. War spirit was whipped up by a deliberately inspired press campaign—one of the first modern examples of its kind. England aided Austria to a decision by diplomatic pressure and the promise of subsidies. Believing that Napoleon was deeply involved in Spanish affairs, and hoping above all to win back the Tyrol which it had been compelled to cede to Bavaria, the Austrian government declared war on France in March, 1809.

Napoleon responded as usual with masterly speed. Failing to win a promise of armed support from Russia, he hastily assembled an army of 200,000 men in Germany and occupied Vienna in May. Both sides had heavy casualties in the Battle of Aspern, which was really a French defeat. In July, however, the Austrians were in turn defeated at Wagram, on the banks of the Danube. Britain's efforts to help the cause by landing troops on the island of Walcheren, off the Dutch coast, turned into an unmitigated disaster. A rising in the Tyrol led by a local innkeeper of remarkable abilities, Andreas Hofer, was put down and its leader shot. Thus, by October, 1809, Austria was prepared to sign the Peace of Schönbrunn. The Duchy of Salzburg and other neighboring lands were ceded to Bavaria. The port of Trieste and the provinces of Carniola and Carinthia were added to France's Illyrian Prov-inces, thereby cutting Austria off completely from the Adriatic. Austria also surrendered the territory of Galicia, north of the Carpathians, to the Grand Duchy of Warsaw. Austria had to pay war indemnities, reduce its armies, join the Continental System and accept the Napoleonic reorganiza-tion of Spain, Portugal and Italy. That the Hapsburg state should so readily have submitted to a treaty involving the loss of three and a half million subjects may be explained at least in part by the growing conviction of some of its leaders that the French Empire could not last.

■ THE PINNACLE OF EMPIRE: NAPOLEONIC FRANCE

The extraordinary transformation effected in Europe by Napoleon can perhaps best be seen in the year 1810. Then his power had reached its zenith. The bitter revolt which raged in Spain was not as yet out of hand. When Sweden had made its peace with France in January, England alone of the European states continued in armed opposition to the Napoleonic empire.

A succession of further annexations during this climactic year carried the frontiers of imperial France far beyond the famous "natural limits" of the Rhine, the Alps and the Pyrenees, which the Revolution had won. A decree of February, 1810, declared the Spanish territory between the Pyrenees and the Ebro annexed to France. In the same month Rome was declared to be the second city of the French Empire. In July Holland was annexed. In December the north German coast was also absorbed, so that the old Hanseatic towns of Hamburg, Bremen and even Lübeck, on the Baltic, had become French provincial cities. To round out the picture, the Swiss canton of Valais, formerly established as an "independent" republic, was now annexed to France. The consolidation of all these territories meant a phenomenal increase in the area directly subject to the control of the French government. The 83 departments recognized in the Constitution of 1791 had now increased to 131. By 1812 the population of this larger France was estimated at 42.7 millions, of which something short of 29 millions were found within the pre-revolutionary boundaries of the French kingdom.

A threefold area—by far the greater part of continental Europe—now lay under Napoleon's control. In central position was the greatly enlarged France just described, extending from the Pyrenees to the Baltic, from the English Channel to Rome, and including even the outlying Illyrian Provinces as a part of what was known as "The Empire of the French." Beyond this lay a second area, "The Grand Empire," made up of those puppet states which were closely under Napoleon's control and some of which were ruled by members of his family. These comprised Spain, the Confederation of the Rhine, Switzerland, the Kingdom of Italy, the Kingdom of Naples, the Principalities of Lucca and Piombino and the Grand Duchy of Warsaw. In a third category were those states allied with France and in some measure subject to it: Prussia, Austria and the joint Kingdom of Denmark and Norway. Not even Charlemagne had controlled so vast an empire.

The imperial control was not only wide but tight. There could be little question about the powerful despotism that Napoleon had imposed upon his French subjects. Gradually he minimized the representative element in the imperial constitution of France. The Tribunate was abolished in 1807. The Legislative Body was rarely summoned. Laws were issued by the Senate in the form of *Senatus-Consulta* or took the shape of imperial decrees. At the same time the activities and powers of the Ministry of Police steadily increased. A more rigorous censorship was introduced. A decree of 1810, for example, declared that there should be only one newspaper for each department and that Paris should have a total of four.

Under this despotism the splendid externals of the Empire continued to develop. The elaborate imperial hierarchy began with the emperor and extended downward through the imperial princes and princesses of the Bonaparte family, the six grand imperial dignitaries, the grand officers of the Empire and those rulers outside France whose realms fell within the French

FRENCH FRONTIER OF 1789 ---- DEPENDENT STATES

FRENCH EMPIRE FRENCH ALLIES

NAPOLEONIC EUROPE *in* 1810

0 100 200 300 400 500 600 MILES

RUSSIAN

EMPIRE

SWEDEN

DENMARK & NORWAY

PRUSSIA

GRAND DUCHY OF WARSAW

CONFEDERATION OF THE RHINE

AUSTRIAN

EMPIRE

Paris

FRENCH

EMPIRE

SWITZ.

KINGDOM OF ITALY

ILLYRIAN PROVINCES

R.DANUBE

LUCCA →
PIOMBINO

OTTOMAN

EMPIRE

PORTUGAL

SPAIN

CORSICA

SARDINIA

KINGDOM OF NAPLES

CORFU

IONIAN ISLANDS

SICILY

RUSSIAN

Borodino, Sept. 7

Moscow
Sept. 14-Oct. 19

R. DÜNA

Vitebsk.

Kovno
June 24 + Dec. 16

Vilna

Borisov

Smolensk, Aug. 17

R. NIEMEN

R. Beresina
Oct. 29

R. BERESINA

R. DNIEPER

EMPIRE

Königsberg

PRUSSIA

ELBE

ODER

GRAND DUCHY
OF WARSAW

VISTULA

Berlin

Warsaw

THE CAMPAIGN *of* 1812

0 100 200 300 MILES

orbit. Napoleon's chief servants were granted lesser principalities, or dukedoms, usually in Italy. Talleyrand, for example, became Prince of Benevento,
Fouché became Duke of Otranto, Marshal Soult became Duke of Dalmatia.
In this way a new Napoleonic nobility was created in place of the old French
aristocracy which the Revolution had abolished. Each level of public service
had its appropriate title of nobility: the grand imperial dignitaries, for
example, were princes; members of the Senate had the rank of count;
bishops, judges and certain mayors had the rank of baron. It has been estimated that Napoleon created at least 10 princes, 31 dukes, 388 counts, 1,090
barons and 1,500 chevaliers. These were given estates and large fortunes. A
new imperial ceremonial was introduced, splendid in many of its externals
and yet to those who remembered the graceful court life of the *ancien régime*
always somewhat uncouth, awkward and touched with vulgarity. Napoleon,
in truth, had little regard for such matters, or skill in them, and accepted the
routines of the court only as a necessary part of the imperial order.[9]

The imagination returns again and again to the extraordinary figure at
the center of this vast fabric of empire. As a dynamic young commander of
the Army of Italy Napoleon had first shown his great gifts as a soldier.
Assuming power as First Consul he revealed a capacity for administration
that seldom, if ever, has been equaled. He would preside for five or six hours
at a stretch over the meetings of bodies such as the Council of State, bringing a powerful and logically organized mind to bear on the problems at
issue. His working day frequently lasted for sixteen or eighteen hours. One
of his secretaries, Baron Fain, has given a striking account of the Napoleonic
routine. Often he would arise at two, work in his dressing-gown until five,
bathe and then sleep until seven. After breakfast he would sign his correspondence, look over new material, inspect the secret reports, read the
French newspapers and have the English papers read to him. The morning
would be completed by dictation, a *levée* and a survey of the military situation. After lunch (which rarely took more than fifteen or twenty minutes) the
emperor received officials and presided over the regular meetings of the
Council of State and other bodies. The daily routine was ended by six in
the afternoon. Napoleon cared little for social life; he would doze through
the *soirées* and *musicales* of the Empress Josephine, sometimes he would
play cards, checkers or billiards, and usually he would retire about ten
o'clock. On his travels an equally insistent routine was maintained. Despatches followed him wherever he went; secretaries were always in attendance; and distance never kept Napoleon from disposing of all kinds of
business. The dismissal of Stein, for example, the principal adviser to
Frederick William III of Prussia, was ordered by Napoleon from Madrid. A

9. The Duke of Wellington, celebrated for his concise judgments on men and affairs, much
later passed verdict on Napoleon: "Wasn't a gentleman."

decree reorganizing the national theater of France Napoleon issued in 1812 at Moscow.

Napoleon's unique gifts have been admirably summarized by the historian who long studied the great work of imperial administration:

> Napoleon brought to the task of government exactly that assemblage of qualities which the situation required, an unsurpassed capacity for acquiring technical information in every branch of government, a wealth of administrative inventiveness which has never been equalled, a rare power of driving and draining the energies of men, a beautiful clearness of intellect which enabled him to seize the salient features of any subject, however tough, technical, and remote, a soldierly impatience of verbiage in others combined with a serviceable gift of melodramatic eloquence in himself; above all, immense capacity for relevant labor. He could work eighteen hours at a stretch, could turn his mind at once from one subject to another entirely remote from it, and a few minutes were enough to put him in possession of the material facts.[10]

Napoleon undertook his tremendous burdens at a heavy cost to himself. By 1809, at the age of forty, he had become cynical, jealous, irritable, given to violent outbursts of temper and no longer sure in his judgments. By 1812 he was at odds in one way or another with nearly every member of his family. His last campaigns were, with some exceptions, notably inferior to his earlier.

The paradox, and in a sense the greatness, of the Napoleonic despotism is that it preserved much of the great work of the Revolution. The struggle for equality that the Revolution had inaugurated was not lost—the principle was secured by maintaining the ideal of equality before the law and by the "career open to talents"—in the Napoleonic phrase, "the field-marshal's baton in every soldier's knapsack." In a way that never formerly would have been possible, men could rise from humble beginnings to great eminence. Napoleon gave France the efficiently centralized administration which had long been sought but never before achieved. He gave it the discipline of the great legal Codes. He maintained a general policy of religious freedom and toleration. Above all, he maintained intact the great transfer of land from aristocratic and ecclesiastical hands to the middle-class and peasant owners who were to be so characteristic of nineteenth-century France. He caused to shine even more brightly the fires of French nationalism which the soldiers of the Revolution had kindled. And more perhaps than any of his predecessors he invested France and its armies with a prestige and a glamor the impact of which was felt all through the nineteenth century.

In this period of imperial magnificence Napoleon undertook the task of divorce and remarriage. It had become clear that he could expect no heir from Josephine. A marriage into one of the great royal houses of Europe

10. H. A. L. FISHER, *Bonapartism* (1914), pp. 41–42.

might be expected both to provide him with a son and to consolidate the position of his dynasty. Inquiries were made at St. Petersburg and Vienna. In a deeply emotional scene Napoleon informed Josephine in November 1809, that for reasons of state he had decided to end their marriage. Shortly afterwards the decree of divorce was obtained in the archiepiscopal court at Paris, the pope later refusing his sanction. Proposals for a new marriage were discussed in the Council of State, where four votes were given for Austria, four for Saxony and three for Russia. Napoleon ended the discussion by deciding firmly for an Austrian marriage, already secretly endorsed by Metternich. A contract was hastily drawn up and sent to Vienna, and in 1810 the eighteen-year-old archduchess Marie-Louise, daughter of Francis I, was married to Napoleon. An heir, the King of Rome, was born in March, 1811.

Despite all the strains of war and blockade, the economic life of imperial France displayed substantial vigor. In internal matters Napoleon was accustomed to exercise to the full his unique talents for close supervision. Through constant scrutiny of ministerial reports he made it possible to effect many savings and to end many abuses. Even so, the burdens borne by the average Frenchman were heavy. The direct taxes earlier established by the Revolution were lowered, but in their place the import duties and the excise taxes on liquor, salt and tobacco were increased. A special fund, the "Extraordinary Domain," handled the very substantial contributions which were demanded from the vassal states. Other funds were secured by banking transactions so complex as to make the correct determination of the overall financial situation almost impossible. The opinion has been ventured, however, that despite all contributions coming in from abroad, Frenchmen found the government of Napoleon more expensive to support than that of Louis XVI.[11]

The economy of France was fundamentally healthy. Agriculture, with the exception of some areas, was quite generally prosperous. New crops such as the sugar beet and the increased use of the mulberry for silk were developments of permanent importance. French industry, too, saw some growth behind the general tariff wall. Textile production was increased in various ways. The new Jacquard loom made possible elaborately woven silk fabrics, while between 1806 and 1810 improved cotton spinning machinery quadrupled the output of French mills. Only the metallurgical industry showed a serious lag, especially when compared with the rapid progress of its counterpart in England. To the industries manufacturing cannon, muskets and gunpowder, government subsidies and controls were applied. Workmen as a class did not fare well. They were still subject to the regulations imposed during the

11. BRUUN, *Europe and the French Imperium,* p. 75.

Revolution; their hours were long, and they were required to carry a *livret,* or passbook, to be endorsed by their employer before they could move from one post to another.

In order to further commerce, Napoleon continued the progressive road-building program of the Old Regime. Some 30,000 kilometers of imperial roads radiating from Paris were built, as well as over 18,000 kilometers of departmental highways. Carriage roads were cut through the Simplon and Mont Cenis passes in the Alps. Various rivers, notably the Rhine and the Rhône, the Somme and the Scheldt, were linked by canals. In contrast to agriculture and industry, however, French commerce suffered heavily under Napoleon. Economic life in the seaports was paralyzed by the blockade. The alternative to overseas commerce was a more vigorous trade with continental Europe, but notwithstanding official efforts in this direction success was not great. Foreign trade under the Empire was actually less than it had been in the closing days of the Old Regime.

The army, according to Napoleon, reached its maximum efficiency during the War of the Third Coalition, when veterans and recruits were combined in a military machine of superb quality. In the subsequent years the progressive inclusion of foreign levies changed the nature of the Napoleonic armies until in the campaign of 1812 the emperor commanded one of the most diverse forces that Europe had ever seen. Under the conscription law originally passed in 1798 the demands upon French manpower proved to be substantial but not overwhelming. The following table indicates the levies taken in France during the successive years of Napoleon's power:

YEAR	CONSCRIPTS	YEAR	CONSCRIPTS
1800	30,000	1807	80,000
1801	60,000	1808	240,000
1802	60,000	1809	76,000
1803	60,000	1810	160,000
1804	60,000	1811	120,000
1805	210,000	1812	237,000
1806	80,000	1813	1,140,000
		Total	2,613,000

These figures refer only to the men raised by conscription; they indicate the annual drafts, not the number of men actually under arms. They show the relatively small demands made until 1805, when the Third Coalition offered its great challenge. They show also how Napoleon, in order to meet the terrible pressure of the final military crisis, was obliged to raise in 1813 alone almost as many men as in the thirteen preceding years. Further numbers of troops were provided by volunteers, by foreign regiments serving in France, and by the contingents demanded from allied and subject states.

In 1814 a special *levée en masse* was invoked to meet the crisis caused by the invasion of France. Although the burden imposed by Napoleon upon France was heavy, it had not nearly so crushing an impact as that caused by the wars of the twentieth century. One estimate of the number of Frenchmen recruited within the ancient boundaries of France who were killed or died of wounds between 1800 and 1815 puts the figure at 400,000. For the much shorter period from 1914 to 1918 the figure would be at least 1,300,000.

In the field of education Napoleon exercised a rigorous control over France. "The essential thing," he declared in 1805, "is a teaching body like that of the Jesuits of old." The basic educational structure was capped in 1808 by the so-called "Imperial University," superimposed upon the foundations laid by the earlier reforms of 1802. This was not a university in the accepted sense but was rather the culminating point of all the teaching agencies in France, providing the means whereby every branch of instruction would be knit together in a pyramidical structure controlled and disciplined in the service of France.

Similarly, Napoleon continued the religious arrangements provided under the Concordat, for it was clearly to his advantage to have a church working in support of the Empire. For religion in any deep sense he seems to have had little use. The Organic Articles of 1802 had provided that there should be only one liturgy and one catechism for the Catholic churches of France. The *Catechism of the Empire,* drawn up in consequence under Napoleon's directions in 1806 and intended for use in all churches, contained some striking phrases: "Christians owe to the princes who govern them, and we owe in particular to our Emperor Napoleon I, love, respect, obedience, fidelity, military service and the taxes levied for the preservation and defense of the empire and his throne." [12]

Napoleon's further dreams for enhancing the splendor of his Empire included the assembling of a vast collection of art treasures at Paris—a work notably forwarded by every campaign from 1796 onward. In addition to these treasures there were also to be assembled at Paris documents from the Vatican archives, from the great Spanish collections at Simancas and from the archives of the Holy Roman Empire, as part of a great plan to make the imperial archives the principal repository for all Europe. The palaces surrounding Paris—Saint-Cloud, Fontainebleau, Versailles, Compiègne, Trianon and Rambouillet—were restored and enlarged.

Napoleon's policies were hardly favorable to the healthy and free growth of the arts and literature. "They tell me," he is reported to have said on one occasion, "that we have no literature in France. It is the fault of the minister of the interior." Under the Consulate and Empire a neo-classical style devel-

12. Translated in R. STEARNS, *Pageant of Europe* (1947), p. 424.

oped, usually known as the Empire Style, which spread rapidly from France throughout Europe. Its popularity was aided by Napoleon, who was pleased to demonstrate France's kinship with imperial Rome. The style produced some massive architectural monuments and a good deal of ornate, rectangular furniture decorated with motifs inspired by the new archaeological discoveries in Pompeii and Herculaneum and in Egypt. Bronze medallions, heavily embroidered tapestries, and the use of brown and yellow colors were all characteristic marks of the style. The paintings of David, who became the "official" artist of the Napoleonic era as he had been under the Republic, express something of this same impressive if ponderous imperial spirit.

The age saw no rich growth of imaginative literature. In 1794 the guillotine had taken one of France's purest spirits, the poet André Chénier. The greatest literary figure of the Napoleonic age, François de Chateaubriand (1768–1848), published his *Genius of Christianity* in 1802, a work of the utmost importance not only in preaching a return to Catholicism but also in opening the door to the new romantic age in French literature. "He introduced men to a new climate of magnificent or mysterious landscapes, to the surge of passions, to romantic melancholy and to a style of rich images and orchestration." [13] Chateaubriand served for a time in minor diplomatic posts but resigned in protest against the execution of the Duke of Enghien. In 1814 his pen welcomed back the Bourbons from their exile.

The only other French figure comparable to Chateaubriand was Madame de Staël (1766–1817), the daughter of the famous Genevan banker and statesman, Necker. Her novels, *Delphine* and *Corinne,* are important in the transition from the classical to the romantic age. Her most important work, *On Germany* (1810), first opened the eyes of the French to the new stirrings of romanticism in Germany and to the important literary, artistic and philosophical developments to be found across the Rhine. She, too, met the displeasure of Napoleon and carried on a long duel with him. When she protested vehemently against the rules of censorship which were applied to her book, *On Germany,* his answer was to confiscate all the 10,000 copies that had been printed and to exile her from France. In such an atmosphere of repression literature could hardly flourish.

Amid all the imperial magnificence of the Napoleonic age unrest and dissatisfaction existed and grew, for the costs of war were heavy and the prospects of peace ever more uncertain. Nevertheless, such discontent as there was remained largely beneath the surface. With censorship and other controls the opportunities for open criticism were very few. The shocks which in the end were to overthrow Napoleon had to come from abroad.

13. DANIEL MORNET, in *The European Inheritance* (1954), II, p. 342.

■ THE PINNACLE OF EMPIRE: NAPOLEONIC EUROPE

Large measures of reform were undertaken in the various non-French parts of the "Grand Empire." Here something of the same pattern of administrative improvement was undertaken as in France itself, with consequences that were to extend far beyond the immediate period of Napoleon's domination. In Italy, in Germany and to a lesser degree in Holland and the Grand Duchy of Warsaw, substantial changes were made.

In Italy, where Napoleon had first exercised his administrative talents, changes were pushed faster and further than elsewhere. Before 1789 Italy had been a complex network of kingdoms, duchies and principalities. By 1810 these divisions had been reduced to three: a Kingdom of Italy, a Kingdom of Naples and a substantial area, running from the old French frontier as far as Rome, which had been annexed to France. This great political simplification, although ended in 1815, was in itself an important anticipation of the nineteenth-century movement of national unification, the Risorgimento.

While the detailed nature of French control necessarily varied somewhat from one part of Italy to another, in general a broadly consistent pattern can be observed. Much church land was secularized. Serfdom and other feudal survivals were abolished. Measures were taken for the suppression of brigandage. A new administrative machinery, directed by Napoleonic officers and employing the French Civil and Commercial Codes, was introduced. Material improvements such as new roads, bridges and schools were introduced. Poor relief and public charity were reorganized. Currency was standardized. Cities such as Turin were given street lighting, paved roads and public gardens. In such measures one observes the characteristic efforts of Napoleon to achieve material and practical improvements.

Against these positive accomplishments must be set the negative aspects of the Napoleonic regime in Italy. Although Eugène was liked and respected as viceroy of Italy, the same cannot be said of Joseph Bonaparte and his successor, Joachim Murat, on the throne of Naples. The administration of the peninsula was usually carried out with a heavy hand. Taxes, though efficiently collected, were onerous, and only a minor fraction was used for the betterment of the Italians. Large contributions had to be sent regularly to the French treasury.[14] The Continental System, moreover, required Italy

14. The budget of 1812 for the Kingdom of Italy showed the following allotment of expenditures:

For military defense	46 million francs	
For debt charges	22 " "
For contributions to France	30 " "
For internal affairs	46 " "
Total	144 " "

not only to close its ports to British goods but also as far as possible to limit its foreign trade exclusively to France. Conscription was also a painful necessity. While statistics are uncertain, one estimate is that between 1805 and 1814 Italy contributed 120,000 conscripts to the imperial armies, of whom 60,000 perished. The papacy, resentful of Napoleon's moves and ultimately the author of a bull of excommunication against him, was in constant opposition. In 1810 Pius VII was held virtually a prisoner at Savona in northern Italy; in 1812 he was taken as an officially honored but certainly unwilling guest to Fontainebleau where he remained until 1814. It is not therefore surprising that revolts against the French occupation should have broken out in Milan in 1814, that Murat should have attempted to lead the Kingdom of Naples over to the Allies in 1814, or that in the years immediately following the downfall of the French Empire Italian patriots should have sought to blot out the memories of the French era. These were the expected reactions and should not obscure the permanent importance of the dynamic element which Napoleon injected into Italian life.

A roughly similar pattern of Napoleonic control was imposed upon Germany, specifically upon the various states making up the Confederation of the Rhine and upon those parts of the north German coast annexed in 1810. The degree of transformation, of course, varied. The Kingdom of Westphalia, ruled by Napoleon's brother, Jerome, and the Grand Duchy of Berg, ruled at first by his brother-in-law, Murat, were very closely regulated. Other states, such as Württemberg or Saxony, where the native monarchs had no enthusiasm for a reform program, were left pretty much alone. On the whole, however, the general changes were impressive. They included the abolition of serfdom, the introduction of the French legal codes, the control of the church, improvements in education, the organization of poor-relief, public health measures and a large program of public works. The burdens which were imposed were equally real. A type of administration in which the principal officers were French, an economic order which was distorted by the burden of the Continental System, a heavy load of taxes and tribute, a policy of conscription which sent German troops into the French campaigns of 1809 and 1812—these were the marks of the imperial despotism. Cowed and bullied into submission, the states of the Confederation of the Rhine at last rose against Napoleon in the autumn of 1813 when his star went into a decline, and as they did so the structure which he had created fell apart. Nothing, however, could possibly restore the old order. Napoleon had destroyed the outworn Holy Roman Empire; he had ended the era of the petty ecclesiastical states; and he had effected a permanent and impressive reduction in the number of the secular states. The legal, economic and political reforms which he introduced in the Confederation of the Rhine

left their imprint on the German peasant: west of the Elbe River his condition grew to be far better than that of the feudal-agrarian population
lying east of the Elbe.

In Holland the pattern of reforms was not so marked. Nor were the
changes made in the Grand Duchy of Warsaw substantial. A new and liberal
constitution was drafted for the duchy, now supposedly in the hands of the
king of Saxony. Actually, it remained closely under French direction, a
member of the Continental System and subject to heavy financial and military exactions. The very existence of the Grand Duchy of Warsaw was a
constant irritant to the tsar of Russia and one of the important reasons for
his turning against Napoleon.

The Napoleonic imperium in Europe remains one of the impressive
phenomena of modern times, a striking illustration of the ability of a single
man to impose his will upon millions. London, Stockholm and Constantinople were the only European capitals which Napoleon did not at some
time bring under his power. Throughout the area of his conquests one
characteristic of Napoleon's activity was always present—the search for
efficiency in the place of inefficiency, the persistent desire to create a smoothly
running, powerfully centralized machinery of government. It has been
questioned whether the vast territories which he dominated were truly an
empire; certainly, if he had any vision of a genuine federation of Europe
he took few practical steps to achieve it. Napoleon's actual control of the
new Europe at its greatest extent was based on the sword and was of surprisingly brief duration. Spain was afire with revolt before he had reached
the limits of expansion in Germany and Italy. A large element of imperma-
nence and improvisation was never absent from what he did; the political
divisions in Germany and Italy were subject to repeated changes and still
remained in process of readjustment as late as 1810. It is obvious also that
the element of exploitation was large; the administrative efficiency which
Napoleon introduced was accompanied by heavy financial and military
demands upon the subject peoples. Napoleon looked with a tolerant eye
upon the personal extravagances of Jerome and Murat in their courts at
Westphalia and Berg, and it was a cardinal element in his policy that the
subjects of the Grand Empire should carry heavier burdens than were imposed on the people of France.

In the broadest sense, despite Napoleon's exactions, his great contribution
to the larger European world was to substitute the spirit of a new age for
the spirit of the past. As the French armies carried the imperial eagles across
Europe, they brought to many peoples some element of the great social, legal
and economic reforms that were the product of the revolutionary age in
France.

"THE THIRD OF MAY." This powerful painting by the great Spanish artist, Goya, shows Spanish guerillas being executed by the French on orders of Marshal Murat, an episode of the uprising of 1808. Rarely have the brutality and terror of war been more poignantly suggested. Photograph by the Prado, Madrid.

Chapter **26**

The Close
of the Napoleonic Era
1810–1815

■ THE BEGINNING OF THE END: SPAIN, PRUSSIA AND RUSSIA

THE DECLINE AND COLLAPSE of the elaborately organized Napoleonic Empire can be attributed to a variety of causes, political, economic, military and psychological. Among these one of the most important and yet one most difficult precisely to evaluate was the growing sentiment of nationalism.

675

Ironically enough, it was revolutionary France that had produced the first great demonstrations of this powerful force. Inspired by an ardent devotion to *la patrie,* the ragged armies of the early Republic had driven the invader from their soil and carried the tricolor into foreign lands. The soldiers of Napoleon had never failed to embody something of this same spirit. There can be little doubt, on the other hand, that England's opposition to Napoleon was inspired by a strong national feeling. An upsurge of Austrian nationalism, especially in the Tyrol, was at least a partial explanation for the disastrous Austrian campaign of 1809. In the fateful years between 1810 and 1814 a growing opposition to the Napoleonic regime developed in widely separated parts of Europe—in Spain, in Prussia and in Russia. Ultimately this scattered opposition was able to combine in the form of a coalition strong enough to destroy the French hegemony. Spain, Prussia and Russia, then, constitute as it were successive chapters in the dramatic story of Napoleon's downfall.

The Spanish contribution to Napoleon's overthrow can be briefly told. Joseph's coronation as king of Spain in July, 1808, occurred amid a popular, nationwide revolt of which the British government was quick to take advantage. In a memorable speech in June, 1808, the foreign secretary, George Canning, had defined the British position:

> Whenever any nation in Europe starts up with a determination to oppose a power which . . . is alike the common enemy of all other people, that nation, whatever its former relation may be, becomes, *ipso facto,* the ally of Great Britain. . . . No interest can be so purely British as Spanish success; no conquest so advantageous to England as conquering from France the complete integrity of Spanish dominions in every quarter of the globe.

A British expeditionary force commanded by Sir Arthur Wellesley, the future Duke of Wellington, landed in Portugal in August. After the French capitulation of Baylen, Napoleon hastened to Spain, reoccupied Madrid and reorganized the French armies, putting them in the hands of his best generals, Ney and Soult. By January, 1809, the British were forced to withdraw.

A new stage in the Peninsular War came when the Duke of Wellington returned in the spring of 1809 with larger forces. Napoleon was under no illusions as to the gravity of the situation created by what he called "the Spanish ulcer." After the conclusion of the Austrian campaign of 1809 he once more turned his attention to the south, and by 1810 had 370,000 men in Spain. To maintain his position in Portugal, Wellington built up a fifty-mile-long entrenched position running to the sea—the celebrated "lines of Torres Vedras." In the first great modern demonstration of trench-warfare

Wellington defended these lines through the winter. By the spring of 1811 he was at last able to break out, with the result that by the end of the year Portugal was cleared of French troops.

The rest of the story of the Peninsular War is one of bitter fighting and of the steady advance of the combined English, Spanish and Portuguese forces to the French border. Wellington's successes at Ciudad Rodrigo, Badajos and Salamanca led to the fall of Madrid in August, 1812. The victories of Vittoria, Pamplona and San Sebastian in the summer of 1813 brought the allied armies to the Pyrenees and opened the way for an invasion of France from the south. This invasion came at a time when a vastly greater coalition had taken shape in central Europe and was forcing Napoleon to withdraw to the Rhine and ultimately across Champagne to the gates of Paris. The Peninsular War, though not in itself decisive, was "an essential sideshow." It tied down huge numbers of French troops, it revealed weaknesses in the imperial fabric, it exemplified the new force of nationalism and it permitted the British armies, as they never had been able before, to come to grips with the French.

The regeneration of Prussia in the years between 1807 and 1812 was a parallel phenomenon to the rise of national sentiment in Spain. Although Prussia had taken an active part in the First Coalition (1792–1795) and again in the unfortunate campaigns of 1806–1807 its general conduct during the revolutionary years had been undistinguished. The reign of Frederick William II (1786–1797) had stood in almost every respect as a depressing contrast to that of his predecessor, Frederick the Great, nor was Frederick William III (1797–1840), however well-intentioned, able to give Prussia strong leadership. The terms of the Treaty of Tilsit in 1807 which took away from Prussia one-third of its territory marked an acute humiliation. By subsequent arrangements the size of the Prussian army was fixed at 42,000 men, the total amount of the indemnity was put at the then huge sum of 140 million francs and Prussia was required to furnish military contingents for Napoleon's armies as well as join the Continental System. Little, if anything, of the greatness of the Frederician age remained.

The transformation occurring after Tilsit was in large part the work of an able and devoted group of Prussian civil servants. Among these Baron von Stein (1757–1831) was easily the most distinguished. This capable, well-trained administrator who had been in the Prussian civil service since 1780 was dismissed by Frederick William III as the result of personal disagreements and recalled soon after Tilsit because of the obvious need for his high abilities. Stein remained in office for only fourteen months, for Napoleon soon discovered how dangerous his work was for the French cause and in

November, 1808, ordered his dismissal. Stein escaped arrest by fleeing to Austria and to Russia, where he played an important part in mobilizing opinion against France.

Supporting Stein and carrying out his intended reforms was a remarkable group of administrators: Hardenberg, Gneisenau, Scharnhorst, Humboldt, Fichte, Niebuhr and Schön. It is a curious fact, perhaps indicative of the wider German interests beginning to crystallize against France, that of these names only two, Stein and Schön, were genuinely Prussian. The work which these men did was in one sense administrative and technical within the single state of Prussia; in another sense it was inspired by deep feelings of responsibility to a wider German fatherland. The aim of these reformers was in essence to eliminate old abuses and to mobilize every class of the population in the service of the state. Stein's statement of the great undertaking was as follows: "We started from the fundamental idea of rousing a moral, religious, patriotic spirit in the nation, of inspiring it anew with courage, self-confidence, readiness for every sacrifice in the cause of independence of the foreigner and national honor."

A series of administrative reforms were designed to remove some obvious weaknesses in the administration of the kingdom. Heavy taxes were imposed to meet the burdens of the occupation. Stein persuaded his royal master to gather the various ministers together in a royal council or cabinet that would provide more efficiency than did the antiquated General Directory of 1723. He was able to initiate useful administrative changes, carried further by his successors, in the operation of the civil service. He was responsible, too, for the Municipal Ordinance of November, 1807, which introduced the principle of elective town councils, subject to some state supervision, throughout the kingdom.

Another group of reforms dealt with social and economic matters. The most dramatic of these was the great Emancipating Edict of October, 1807, concerning serfdom. Here Stein was able to bring to completion proposals made before he took office. The decree of 1807 gave *personal* freedom to all Prussian serfs who henceforth were no longer bound to the soil, were released from menial services and could marry freely. They were not, however, made the owners of the land which they occupied, and frequently found that this land was encumbered with a variety of obligations only a little less irksome than serfdom itself. It remained for Hardenberg to sponsor in 1811 the great Agrarian Law which usually bears his name and which provided that the tenant, in return for surrendering one-third or one-half of his holding to the landlord, became the full owner of the rest without any of the previous encumbrances. Other provisions of the original Edict of 1807 were almost equally significant. Free trade in land was established, thereby ending the ancient system by which some land could be held only by noblemen and be sold only to others of the same class. Another important move was to declare (as had not been the case in the past) all occupations open to anyone. Thus noblemen could now legitimately engage in trade, and the bourgeois and peasant were free to enter previously restricted occupations. While the caste system still continued in Prussia as a powerful social force, a new element of flexibility and mobility had been introduced.

The military reforms were the outcome of the work of a special commission in which Scharnhorst and Gneisenau were the principal members. The problem first tackled, and with considerable success, was to bring about improvements in weapons, equipment, organization, tactics and morale. The next problem was to reorganize the method of recruitment. Napoleon's decree of 1808 had restricted the Prussian army to 42,000 men. By the ingenious device of the *Krümpersystem* (literally, "shrinkage system") recruits were trained very briefly and then secretly passed on to the reserve. In this way, although Prussia restricted its active army to 42,000, it was able in 1813 to put 230,000 men in the field. The final consolidation of these measures came in the great Military Law of September, 1814, the basis of all subsequent conscription in Prussia in the nineteenth century. All men from 21 to 25 were to serve three years with the colors and two in reserve (save for certain exceptional groups whose active service was limited to one year). Men from 26 to 40 were in the first reserve, or *Landwehr,* having posts in regular regiments and liable to be called up in case of war. A second reserve, the *Landsturm,* comprised all from 17 to 50 who were to be mobilized if need arose to repel an actual invasion. Here then, was an elaborately planned system of universal military service going far beyond the conscription measures devised and applied in France.

These various measures were accompanied by a remarkable invigoration of Prussian, and in a sense all German, cultural life. The eighteenth century had in general been marked by a strong current of cosmopolitanism. "It is the privilege and duty of the philosopher and of the poet," Goethe had written, "to belong to no nation and to no time, but rather to be a contemporary of all times." This viewpoint, it can hardly be doubted, did little to help the growth of a genuine German national spirit. Such a German spirit, nevertheless, was in the making, and scattered writers could be found in the late eighteenth century who were sensitive to its claims.

Johann Gottfried Herder (1744–1803) ranks as one of the first great exponents of nationalism. His interest in folklore, popular songs, legends and peasant culture had led him to see nationalism as a healthy cultural force, giving separate identity to the different European peoples but permitting them to be regarded as branches of one common tree of humanity. The great German philosopher, Immanuel Kant (1724–1804) of Königsberg, who had hailed the coming of the French Revolution, can hardly be given an important place in the history of German nationalism. Yet in seeking to rebuild philosophy anew on the basis of idealism he had enunciated his famous "categorical imperative"—that true freedom lies in obeying the moral law and that our knowledge of the moral order comes from within, from our intuitive ethical sense. A true community is one of men held together by "a stern law of duty." Kant's disciple, Johann Gottlieb Fichte (1762–1814), carried the argument further by insisting that the individual life has no real existence and that the individual can realize himself only in that group which is the nation. In his course of lectures delivered at Berlin in 1807 and 1808, the famous *Addresses to the German Nation,* Fichte appealed for a completely unselfish dedication of all Germans to the service of their country.

Imaginative literature caught something of this same spirit. Johann Friedrich Schiller's play, *William Tell* (1804), with its dramatizing of a heroic episode in the Swiss struggle for freedom had an obvious moral for Germany. On the eve of the War of Liberation a group of German poets, most notably Kleist, Arndt, Körner and Rückert employed their verse as a veritable call to arms. At Königsberg in 1808 was organized the *Tugendbund,* or League of Virtue, a small group attempting to associate liberal ideas with the further concept of devotion to the service of the fatherland.

The gospel of nationalism received stimulus in other ways. The scholarly interests which sent historians, philologists and legal students to the German past helped to emphasize the seeming uniqueness of German culture. Wilhelm Tieck's collection of folk-songs and legends (1797) was the beginning of a movement culminating in the great work of the brothers Jacob and Wilhelm Grimm. Jacob's scholarly investigations into the growth of the Teutonic languages entitle him to be called the founder of scientific philology. For most people, however, the famous collection of "Grimms' Fairy Tales" published between 1812 and 1815 will be regarded as a source of childhood delight. These volumes likewise mark the founding of the modern science of folklore and in still another sense are an important contribution to the awakening of German national sentiment. The pioneer approach of Friedrich Karl von Savigny (1779–1861) to the study of law, rejecting the rationalism of the eighteenth century and stressing instead the evolution of law in a historical manner out of ancient customs and traditions was likewise a contribution to the growing sense of national identity.

In 1809 a charter was issued for the founding of the University of Berlin. This new university was the product of the national crisis, for it was intended as a replacement for the University of Halle, lost by the territorial cessions of the Treaty of Tilsit. The names of some of its first faculty indicate the distinction which the University of Berlin possessed from the time of its foundation—Wilhelm von Humboldt as professor of science, Fichte in philosophy, Niebuhr in history, Schleiermacher in theology and Savigny in law. The university was a cradle of national sentiment, a focal point for those intellectual forces which in the year 1813 helped to galvanize the Prussian people into action against Napoleon.

A third area of growing opposition to Napoleon was Russia. While French power was being undermined in Spain and while Prussian resentment was steadily rising, the relations between Napoleon and Alexander approached the point of open hostility. The alliance first broached on the raft at Tilsit had been at best unstable. Too many incompatible interests were involved. Alexander was a strange character—a compound of liberalism and authoritarianism, of shrewd worldliness and exalted mysticism. Under the spell of some of his religious advisers he had steadily developed an extraordinary sense of his "mission" to which in many respects Napoleon seemed opposed. Alexander was intensely suspicious of the creation and the enlargement of the Grand Duchy of Warsaw. He was resentful at Napoleon's constant postponement of the partition of the Ottoman Empire. He disliked the Continental System, all the more so when in order to control the north German coast Napoleon had annexed Oldenburg, a duchy in the possession of a relative of the tsar. The Russian emperor had been offended at Napoleon's marriage to Marie-Louise of Austria which came tactlessly on the heels of inquiries concerning the suitability of Alexander's own sister. In December, 1810, Alexander issued a decree which in effect meant the abandonment of the Continental System. By 1811 it was clear that a breach between the two countries was not long distant. Throughout the year both sides began their preparations. In February, 1812, Napoleon imposed a military alliance upon Prussia, exacting the promise of 20,000 men for a prospective campaign against Russia. In March he obtained a similar promise of 30,000 men from Austria. Russia cleared the decks by a treaty of alliance with Sweden in April (the Treaty of Abo) and by ending its war with Turkey in May.

Long before these moves were undertaken, Napoleon had begun his preparations for what he meant to be the decisive stroke against Russia. An army of 600,000 men—by far the largest Europe had ever seen—was assembled. It included contingents from all those states annexed by France or subject to its authority: Prussians, Westphalians, Suabians, Dutchmen, Swiss, Austrians, Poles, Lithuanians, Croats, Spaniards, Portuguese and a minority (actually about 200,000) of Frenchmen. This monstrous force was assembled with all its supplies in East Prussia and the Grand Duchy of Warsaw. Without bothering to declare war or even to inform the French people, Napoleon crossed the River Niemen in June.

The French plan of campaign was to drive a wedge between the assembling Russian armies, destroy them separately, and winter at Smolensk, about four hundred miles from the frontier-crossing. The vast Lithuanian territories would then be annexed to the Grand Duchy of Warsaw. If Alexander I refused such terms, a second campaign in 1813 would be directed to the capture of Moscow. The Russian plan, on the other hand, was to avoid pitched battles, to withdraw, harassing the French armies, and in the modern phrase trade space for time. Alexander declared himself ready, if need be, to retreat all the way to Kamchatka. It is a telling commentary upon Napoleon's failing powers as a great commander (due in part to the ill-health of which he now showed clear signs) that he permitted himself to fight the campaign on the Russian terms.

Almost from the outset the 400,000 troops who actually invaded Russia in 1812 suffered heavy losses through illness, desertion and the harassing tactics of the Russians during the hot summer advance. Unable to bring the enemy to a pitched battle, Napoleon reached Smolensk in mid-August and there unwisely altered his plans, deciding to press on to Moscow. On September 7 the French and Russians fought the bloody and indescribably savage battle of Borodino in which there were 70,000 casualties in one day. A week later Napoleon entered Moscow, with the Russian armies still eluding him. The burning of the vast wooden city (probably on the orders of its governor) made it impossible for Napoleon to winter there. Hence on October 18 the great retreat began, with only 100,000 of Napoleon's troops remaining. By the time the French regained Smolensk, half these forces were gone and the bitter winter had set in. The French continued their retreat amid almost unendurable hardships. At the Beresina River, where French engineers hastily put two wooden bridges across the ice-choked waters, Napoleon had only 40,000 men. He completed the crossing and reached the Niemen, the point of his original departure, with but 20,000. When all the survivors, garrison troops and guard units were assembled, perhaps 100,000 remained of the 600,000 troops originally under Napoleon's command. The most brilliant commander in modern times had lost half a million men in a disastrous Russian campaign which lasted just six months.

Napoleon left the broken remnants of his armies and travelled post-haste, incognito, across Europe to Paris, for he had heard news of serious disaffection in the capital. He was preceded by despatches giving some hint of the Russian disaster, and ending with the phrase, "the health of the Emperor has never been better."

■ THE OVERTHROW OF THE NAPOLEONIC EMPIRE

The collapse of the Napoleonic Empire followed quickly on the heels of the disastrous campaign of 1812. Russia alone had dealt France this staggering military blow, and while England, of course, was still in the war and while Sweden for its own purposes had allied itself with Russia by the Treaty of Abo, no genuine coalition as yet existed. The urgent problem, therefore, was to establish the kind of coalition that would mobilize Europe's military strength to the full and that would at the same time reach some agreement as to the general terms on which peace could be concluded with France.[1]

Prussia was the first to move. In December, 1812, the East Prussian commander, General Yorck, on his own initiative signed an armistice with the Russians against whom he was supposedly allied with the French. This provoked such an outburst of patriotic fervor that in February, 1813, Prussia formed a secret alliance with Russia (the Treaty of Kalisch) and almost immediately joined the war against France. The general pledge given Prussia was that it should be restored to as strong a position as it had held before the losses incurred at Tilsit and that Germany should be free. In the ensuing months England associated itself more closely with Sweden, Russia and Prussia.

Concurrently with these first diplomatic maneuvers important military steps were taken. The Tsar Alexander of Russia had come to regard himself as the destined leader of the forces intended to overthrow the French hegemony. He was the "White Angel" from the north who would overthrow the "Black Angel," Napoleon. His military leaders, dominated by less nebulous considerations, were led to agree that their policy should be not merely to expel the French from Russian soil, but to follow the Napoleonic armies to their destruction. Napoleon's policy on returning to France was to reassure the country as to its future prospects and to obtain authorization for further large levies of troops. From all sources he counted upon 600,000 men for the spring of 1813.[2] Actually, at the opening of the spring campaign in Saxony he was able to assemble about 250,000 troops. Unable, however, to push some preliminary victories to a decisive conclusion, he agreed early in June to accept a two-months' armistice.

The armistice gave Austria its chance. After the disasters of 1809 the Emperor Francis took as foreign minister Prince Metternich (1773–1859), an able, well-trained diplomat who as ambassador at Paris had come to form

1. It may be recalled that the Fifth Coalition, now in process of formation, had been preceded by four others: the First, in 1792–1793; the Second in 1798; the Third, in 1804–1805; and the Fourth, in 1806.
2. This involved calling up immediately the conscripts for both 1813 and 1814, recalling 100,000 men formerly exempted and using the National Guard for foreign service.

a shrewd estimate of Napoleon. Metternich was determined not to make the mistakes of his predecessors by plunging Austria rashly into a war which it could not expect to win. In 1813 his policy was that of "armed mediation," designed to build up Austria's military strength while offering his services to both sides. Late in June Austria came to a secret agreement with Russia and Prussia as to the general terms it was willing to offer Napoleon: the dissolution of the Grand Duchy of Warsaw and the Confederation of the Rhine, the reconstitution of Prussia and the restoration of the Illyrian Provinces to Austria. Metternich had a nine-hour interview with Napoleon at Dresden, vividly described in his memoirs. He found the emperor adamant against the terms that Austria was ready to support with the result that, after further abortive negotiations with the French, Metternich made the great decision. In August the signal fires were lighted from Vienna to the Bohemian frontier indicating that Austria had entered the coalition against France. For the fifth time the Hapsburgs were to seek a decision against France in battle.

The military campaign of the fall of 1813 was disastrous for France. Napoleon won a great battle near Dresden, but, failing to follow it up, was unable to stem the huge tide of troops—Russian, Prussian, Austrian and Swedish—now converging upon him. Near Leipzig, between October 16 and 19, was fought the great Battle of the Nations. It was a disaster for Napoleon who fought it badly and at the end had only 40,000 men left of the 250,000 he had brought with him into Germany. Napoleon's only choice now was to retreat across Germany to France, witnessing the crumbling of the Confederation of the Rhine as he marched. By New Year's Day, 1814, he was at Basel, ready to continue the war on the soil of France. Holland had risen, Wellington was over the Pyrenees and in Italy Murat was about to seek an understanding with Austria. Napoleon's Empire, in any realistic sense, was gone.

Meanwhile the diplomatic negotiations continued. Upon what general terms were the allies prepared to treat? Some of these terms had emerged in the various treaties of alliance whipped together in 1813; they included the dissolution of the Grand Duchy of Warsaw and the Confederation of the Rhine, the reconstitution of Prussia, the re-establishment of the Netherlands and the promise of Austrian gains in Italy. No stipulation, however, had yet been made that Napoleon need be overthrown, nor had the question of France's boundaries been determined. When the great allied coalition reached Frankfort in November, the "Frankfort offer" was made to Napoleon: peace would be made with him if he would accept the "natural limits" of Belgium, the Rhine and the Alps, foregoing all further conquests. How genuine this offer was historians cannot say. At all events Napoleon refused a clear answer, so that his chance, such as it was, to make peace on terms that would have left France greater than it ever had been under its kings, was lost.

The confusions at the allied headquarters (where the tsar and the king of Prussia were present) became less when Castlereagh, the British foreign minister, arrived from England. In February and March, 1814, new proposals were submitted to Napoleon which in rough summary would have forced France back to the "ancient limits" (those of 1792) as opposed to the earlier offer of the "natural limits." Misled, however, by the victories that he was able to win on the soil of France in the first months of 1814, Napoleon refused these terms, as he had refused the even better terms from Frankfort three months before.

The allies therefore on March 9 signed among themselves the Treaty of Chaumont.[3] This treaty, largely the result of the steady pressure which Castlereagh brought to bear, was the general basis upon which the peace settlement eventually was erected. It provided that England, Austria, Russia and Prussia would pursue the war vigorously, make no peace save in common, each keep 60,000 men available in case France should violate the peace and continue their alliance for twenty years. The secret articles stipulated that France should go back to the frontiers of 1792. They also included the broad terms for the disposition of lands surrendered by France which a few weeks later were to be incorporated in the First Treaty of Paris. These secret terms were that there should be a confederated Germany, an independent Switzerland, an Italy made up of independent states, an enlarged Holland and a free Spain under its Bourbon dynasty. The Treaty of Chaumont, which in general embodied most of the proposals made by Pitt in 1805, was Castlereagh's great contribution to the forming of the alliance.[4]

The actual overthrow of Napoleon was the product of military circumstances. Despite the superb skill with which Napoleon handled his ever-dwindling forces, the armies of the Coalition, too great to be held back, moved forward relentlessly. It is an interesting commentary on the state of public morale that the French people, unlike the Spaniards, remained apathetic in the face of the invading armies. Napoleon had entrusted the defense of the capital to his brother, Joseph. Ignoring his instructions, Joseph surrendered Paris on the night of March 30, 1814, and on the following day the allied forces, with the Tsar Alexander at their head, made their triumphal entry into the city.

For Napoleon it was all over. After unavailing attempts at compromise he accepted on April 11 the Treaty of Fontainebleau by which he abdicated for himself and his family, all the members of which were to receive sub-

3. It was antedated March 1st.
4. See p. 651.

stantial financial settlements. Napoleon was to be sent to the Island of Elba which he would rule in full sovereignty with the title of emperor. The empress, Marie-Louise, and her son were granted the Italian duchies of Parma, Piacenza and Guastalla. Thither she went, never to see Napoleon again, and to console herself with the charms of the one-eyed Austrian Count Neipperg. Josephine, living in dignified seclusion at Malmaison, died in May, 1814.

The return of the Bourbons was not the automatic sequel to the overthrow of Napoleon. The Count of Provence (Louis XVI's brother and the future Louis XVIII) had long lived in England. The British government favored in a general sense his return and worked quietly for it, but did not wish to act in advance of French opinion. This had been mobilized by royalist groups in France, not without secret assistance from Talleyrand who was preparing himself for a new era. It was not clear at first, however, whether Austria would prefer a regency under Marie-Louise on behalf of her son. Nor was it clear whether the unpredictable Alexander I would support Bernadotte, the Crown Prince of Sweden, as a candidate for the throne of France or even whether he would recommend that the French people be allowed freely to choose for themselves. In the end, however, Bourbon sentiment made itself known in France. Talleyrand, professing to act in its behalf, made secret contact with the allied leaders even before Paris surrendered. The Senate, guided by Talleyrand, declared that "the French people freely call to the throne Louis-Stanislas-Xavier de France, brother of the late king." The Count of Provence consequently crossed over from England and issued the Declaration of Saint-Ouen "in the nineteenth year of our reign," promising to grant a constitution that would preserve the major gains of the Revolution.

While Napoleon was being escorted through the south of France en route to Elba, Louis XVIII made his entry into Paris. A provisional government, authorized by the Senate, took shape with Talleyrand as its principal figure and quickly drafted the Constitutional Charter of 1814. With surprisingly little difficulty, therefore, the political transition from the Bonapartes to the Bourbons had been accomplished.

The return of Napoleon from Elba in March, 1815, followed by the dramatic events of the "Hundred Days" was at best an episode. His enthusiastic welcome by the army and by a considerable segment of the French may be explained in terms of the continuing glamor of his name and the disillusionment aroused by the uninspired domestic program of the Bourbons, who fled at once into a humiliating exile at Brussels. Napoleon's bid for popularity now was to prepare the "Additional Act to the Constitution of the Empire," largely the work of the writer and liberal publicist, Benjamin

Constant. Its declared purpose was to give France truly liberal institutions which would include a responsible ministry, freedom of the press, a popularly elected legislature and a system of jury trials. The Additional Act was luke-warmly accepted by a majority of the million and a half French voters who went to the polls.

The allies, however, quickly asserted their unalterable determination to resist any further Bonapartist rule in France. They had at their disposal combined armies amounting at least to 800,000 men together with limitless reserves, in contrast to the 200,000 troops which Napoleon was able to muster and of which little more than half actually followed him into the field. The Battle of Waterloo, therefore, on June 18, 1815, was not a decisive battle in the sense that if it had turned out otherwise the fate of Europe would have been drastically different. Whatever the immediate outcome, Napoleon's ultimate defeat would surely have followed. Waterloo was decisive in the specific sense that it set a final end to Napoleon's military and political career. Surrendering to the British and asking to be allowed to live in seclusion in Scotland, he was instead sent to the remote island of St. Helena in the South Atlantic where, after nearly six years of bitter exile, in May, 1821, he died.

■ THE RECONSTRUCTION OF EUROPE, 1814–1815

The great problems of reconstruction which demanded solution after the downfall of Napoleon were threefold: they involved, first, the question of what to do with a defeated France; secondly, what to do with those large border areas which France had directly annexed; and, thirdly, how to deal with the more distant parts of Europe where the ambitions of Russia, Prussia, Austria and the lesser states were principally centered. This re-construction was to be the work of conservative statesmen who had fought the Revolution and Napoleon, who were acutely conscious of the claims of legitimacy and who, for the most part, were anxious in Castlereagh's phrase "to get the world back to peaceful habits."

The problem of France proved to be surprisingly easy to regulate. The restored Bourbons could do what Napoleon, the child of the Revolution, never could do, namely, accept the frontiers of the Old Régime. The allies were disposed to deal leniently with Louis XVIII, who had been in constant opposition to Napoleon and who symbolized in his person the principle of legitimacy. His foreign minister, Talleyrand, the successive participant in every French government since the days of the Estates General, professed general sympathy with the viewpoint of the allies. Discussions therefore went forward with such speed that on May 30, 1814, the signatures were attached to the First Treaty of Paris.[5] The open terms gave France the old limits of 1792 and in addition certain areas (part of Savoy and a number of fortified border towns in the northeast) that were intended to ensure a defensible frontier. France was required to yield Mauritius, Tobago and St. Lucia to England and to recognize England's possession of Malta. France kept the art treasures seized by Napoleon and was not required to pay an indemnity or maintain an army of occupation. Considering the troubles that France had made for Europe the terms were a model of leniency.

The Treaty of Paris also looked forward to the plans for a larger European settlement. Within two months a general congress was to meet at Vienna. In a series of secret articles it was stipulated that the territories now surrendered by France should be disposed of in the following manner: Holland was to be independent and enlarged; the left bank of the Rhine was to go to Prussia and other German states; Switzerland was to have its independence guaranteed; Piedmont was to be restored and enlarged; Austria was to be given a commanding position in northern Italy. The importance of these secret articles was twofold: the map will show that they were intended to create a zone of security or area of buffer states along the French borders; furthermore, these were provisions privately agreed upon in advance by the major powers which presumably the meetings at Vienna would merely ratify.

The Congress of Vienna assembled in September, 1814, and a vast medley of discussions, official and unofficial, continued until the Final Act was accepted on June 9, 1815. In a sense it is correct to say with Friedrich Gentz, the Austrian publicist and secretary of the gathering, that "the Congress, as such, never convened." Over two hundred delegations arrived, including representatives of special interests such as the English Quakers, the German book-publishers and the Frankfort Jews. Scores of dispossessed German princes reappeared from obscurity, as the historian, Treitschke, wrote, "like worms after the rain." The Emperor Francis I of Austria proved to be a lavish host, so that the Congress danced even more than it labored, but the efforts to create an orderly working structure and a systematic method of procedure met insuperable obstacles. A number of special commissions were established (for example, a statistical commission and a commission on the German Confederation) and did useful work. For the most part, however, the great powers, coming together as a Committee of Five, contrived to keep the principal decisions in their own hands. Much of the real work, as is probably the case in most congresses, was done in the unofficial gatherings of diplomats at dinners, balls, receptions, excursions and boudoirs.

5. The Treaty was actually signed by the "Big Five": Russia, Prussia, Austria, England and France. Three other powers, Spain, Portugal and Sweden, gave their adherence.

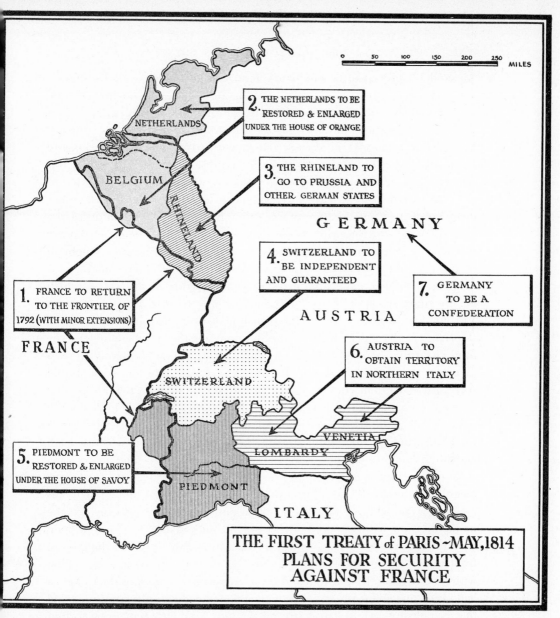

2. THE NETHERLANDS TO BE RESTORED & ENLARGED UNDER THE HOUSE OF ORANGE

3. THE RHINELAND TO GO TO PRUSSIA AND OTHER GERMAN STATES

4. SWITZERLAND TO BE INDEPENDENT AND GUARANTEED

7. GERMANY TO BE A CONFEDERATION

1. FRANCE TO RETURN TO THE FRONTIER OF 1792 (WITH MINOR EXTENSIONS)

6. AUSTRIA TO OBTAIN TERRITORY IN NORTHERN ITALY

5. PIEDMONT TO BE RESTORED & ENLARGED UNDER THE HOUSE OF SAVOY

NETHERLANDS

BELGIUM

RHINELAND

GERMANY

FRANCE

AUSTRIA

SWITZERLAND

VENETIA

LOMBARDY

PIEDMONT

ITALY

THE FIRST TREATY of PARIS ~ MAY, 1814
PLANS FOR SECURITY
AGAINST FRANCE

These tentative arrangements were made definite at the Congress of Vienna. France is actually larger than in 1792, though French Savoy, now acquired, is lost in 1815.

It was not easy to harmonize conflicting national policies. Lord Castlereagh was concerned, first, to safeguard Great Britain's maritime and colonial interests and, secondly, to build up an effective balance of power whereby neither France at one extreme of Europe nor Russia at the other could become dangerous. The Austrian chancellor, Metternich, was equally concerned about the European balance, to safeguard which he felt that Austria should maintain its power in central Europe and establish itself strongly in Italy.

Alexander I proved to be one of the most difficult figures at the Congress, with his alternating moods of romantic liberalism and sabre-rattling realism. Already in possession of Finland and Bessarabia, he now directed his main territorial aspirations toward Poland which he coveted in its entirety. Frederick William III of Prussia joined with his ministers in seeking to reconstitute their kingdom on as large a territorial basis as in 1805. For this objective the neighboring kingdom of Saxony which, unfortunately for itself, had remained in alliance with Napoleon for some time after the other members of the Confederation of the Rhine had seen the wisdom of leaving him, appeared a logical prize. These were the ambitions of the major powers, in addition to which every dispossessed German princeling now sought to be restored and every petty state sought some degree of enlargement.

In his memoirs Talleyrand gives a striking picture of the way in which he, the spokesman of a defeated country, was treated as an outcast at Vienna until by insisting upon the principle of legitimacy and championing the rights of the lesser states he was able to enter the inner councils of the four victorious powers and play a leading role in the Congress. It is a picture only partly in agreement with the evidence. He had some initial success, it is true, in converting the "Big Four" into the "Big Five." The policies of Russia and Prussia soon led them to disagree with England and Austria. When the two former joined in an attempt to secure all Poland for Russia and all Saxony for Prussia it was only natural that Castlereagh and Metternich should have sought the support of Talleyrand in resisting such overreaching claims. This, however, was as much a "victory" for Castlereagh and Metternich, who knew precisely what they were doing, as it was for Talleyrand who was not slow to claim most of the credit. In the end the major decision with respect both to Poland and Saxony was one of compromise. The return of Napoleon from Elba in March, 1815, cut the ground from under Talleyrand, for he at once became the spokesman of a king without a country. By this time, however, the principal work of the Congress had been done and it was easy for the members to adopt a declaration saying that Napoleon's actions had destroyed the only legal title remaining to him and that he was to be considered "an object of public vengeance."

The work of the Congress of Vienna was embodied in the 121 articles of the Final Act of June 9, 1815—"a general instrument . . . which served as a basis for the international life of Europe for nearly fifty years." [6] The complex provisions can be briefly summarized. Russia was permitted to keep Finland, which it had won from Sweden in 1808, and Bessarabia, ceded by the Ottoman Empire in 1812. It received about three-fifths of Poland which was to be set up as a kingdom or separate entity ("Congress Poland") within

6. Sir C. K. WEBSTER, *The Congress of Vienna, 1814–1815* (new ed., 1937), p. 81.

PRINCIPAL EUROPEAN TERRITORIAL CHANGES IN 1815

0   100   200   300   400   500   MILES

Legend:
- TO RUSSIA
- TO PRUSSIA
- TO AUSTRIA
- TO PIEDMONT
- TO NETHERLANDS
- --- GERMAN CONFEDERATION

FINLAND

NORWAY from DENMARK to SWEDEN

SWEDEN

RUSSIAN EMPIRE

WON IN 1793 AND 1795

DENMARK

SWEDISH POMERANIA

POSEN

KINGDOM OF POLAND

PRUSSIA

SAXONY

GALICIA

LUXEMBURG

SAAR

BESSARABIA

AUSTRIAN

EMPIRE

SALZBURG

FRANCE

SWITZ.D

TYROL

VENETIA

LOMBARDY

ISTRIA

PIEDMONT

DALMATIA

OTTOMAN

EMPIRE

TUSCANY

PAPAL

ELBA

STATES

CORSICA

NAPLES

SARDINIA

SICILY

IONIAN ISLANDS

MALTA (TO BRITAIN)

the Russian Empire and with its own constitution. The old Polish royal capital of Cracow was established as a "free city." Prussia, which obtained about two-fifths of Saxony, as well as Swedish Pomerania, the former Polish province of Posen, the Napoleonic Kingdom of Westphalia and much of the Rhineland, now known as Rhenish Prussia, was substantially larger than in 1805. The decision to advance Prussia's power in the Rhineland, giving it the Ruhr and Saar basins and bringing it into direct proximity to France, has been called one of the most fateful decisions of the Congress. Austria won back the Tyrol and Salzburg from Bavaria. It likewise retained those Galician territories north of the Carpathians which it had secured in the First Partition of Poland. Austria's chief gains, as it had desired, were to the south: Lombardy and Venetia in Italy; and nearby Dalmatia. England's gains were maritime: she held Malta, Ceylon, the Cape Colony, Mauritius and a few islands in the West Indies—Trinidad, St. Lucia and Tobago.

Among the lesser states, Sweden was permitted to keep Norway (which it had taken from Denmark in 1814) recognizing, however, its separate identity as a kingdom. The House of Orange was restored in the Kingdom of the Netherlands, now enlarged by the addition of Belgium. Switzerland was re-established as an independent confederation of twenty-two cantons. The Bourbon dynasty continued to rule in Spain and the House of Braganza in Portugal. The Neapolitan Bourbons, kinsmen of the Hapsburgs, were re-stored in the Kingdom of Naples.[7] The pope was restored to his territories, as were the legitimate Hapsburg rulers in Modena and Tuscany. Marie-Louise remained in possession of Parma, Piacenza and Guastalla. The Kingdom of Sardinia, an important bastion against any French attack upon Italy, was confirmed in possession of the former Republic of Genoa.

Great difficulties were encountered in reorganizing the German states once members of the Holy Roman Empire or the Confederation of the Rhine. The desire of German patriots to create a truly national state ran counter to the policies of Austria, Prussia and indeed of the other major powers. In the end a very loose confederation of thirty-eight states under the perpetual presidency of Austria was established. Those Napoleonic changes which had turned Bavaria, Saxony and Württemberg into kingdoms and in general had taken land from the smaller states in order to add to the larger were allowed to remain. In a sense, therefore, the Congress recognized Napoleon's repeated "simplifications" of the Germanies, and it may well be questioned whether without his work the three-hundred-odd states of 1789

7. Joachim Murat, who had made secret arrangements with Austria in 1814 in the hope of retaining the Neapolitan throne, proved an embarrassment to the allies. He determined his own fate by reversing his stand and attempting to side with Napoleon during the Hundred Days. On landing in Calabria he was seized by the Austrians, court-martialled and shot.

could have been reduced to the thirty-eight of 1815. This new Confederation, lacking a federal army, a federal citizenship or any genuinely parliamentary institutions satisfied the desires of Metternich, but was a poor substitute for the greater Germany that the patriots and liberals had envisaged.

The Congress can doubtless be criticized for its disregard of the principle of nationality, for its ruthless bartering of populations and its complete ignoring of popular will. In these matters it was the creature of its own age. It sought essentially to organize the balance of power in such a way that the threat from an overmighty state such as Napoleonic France could not again arise. Whatever the long-term consequences of ignoring the principles of nationality and self-determination, the Congress at least succeeded in giving Europe a long respite from the feverish excitements of the revolutionary era.

It has often been said that the Congress of Vienna was guided by the principle of "legitimacy." This at best is only partly true. Talleyrand, naturally enough, made much of this point, seeing that he wished to secure full recognition for himself as the spokesman of the legitimate Bourbon dynasty of France. A number of former rulers, dispossessed by Napoleon— Ferdinand I of Naples, Victor Emmanuel I of Sardinia and Ferdinand VII of Spain, for example—were recognized once more by the Congress. Yet there were many cases, particularly in the German states, where legitimate rulers, ousted as a result of the great Napoleonic changes, failed to win back their thrones. Expediency, rather than principle, was the rule.

The rallying of France to Napoleon on his return from Elba meant that the allies could no longer regard the generous terms of the First Treaty of Paris as satisfactory. After Waterloo and the second restoration of the Bourbons, therefore, further negotiations were undertaken during which the Prussians and the representatives of some of the lesser German states demanded that extremely harsh terms be imposed upon France. Both Alexander I and the Duke of Wellington made a stand in behalf of moderation. Ultimately a settlement was reached in the form of the Second Treaty of Paris of November 20, 1815. By its terms France, although still retaining substantially the frontier of 1792, was required to surrender those additional areas given it in 1814. An indemnity of 700 million francs was imposed, an army of occupation was to be stationed in France for five years and the most important works of art seized by Napoleon (among them the Venus de' Medici and the bronze horses taken from Venice) were later restored to their rightful owners. In the light of all the burdens France had imposed upon Europe these terms, although less generous than those of 1814, must still be regarded as moderate.

The end of the year 1815 marked the close of an era. Two further measures intended to ensure the stability of the European settlement, Alexander I's mystically inspired Treaty of Holy Alliance of September and Castle-reagh's much more realistic Quadruple Alliance signed in November, are properly a part of the post-Napoleonic period. The real conclusion of the great revolutionary era came with the final dispositions with respect to France made in the Second Treaty of Paris. These settlements ushered in what French historians have chosen to call the Age of the Restoration. How-ever conservative the intention of statesmen may have been, events were to show that they had not succeeded in restoring the old order. It will be the purpose of the concluding chapter to look back over the four preceding centuries in order to epitomize their major developments. With these devel-opments in mind it will then be possible finally to evaluate the more specific legacy left by the great Age of Revolution to the nineteenth century, the progenitor of our own troubled times.

EPILOGUE

"Napoleon is the first and only man

who could have given Europe the real equilibrium

for which she has been searching in vain for several centuries

and from which today she is farther off than ever. . . .

A real equilibrium would have rendered war well-nigh impossible.

A suitable organization would have carried

to every household the highest degree of civilization

which could possibly be attained.

Napoleon was able to do all this, and he did not do it. . . .

Posterity will say of him,

'That man was endowed with a very great intellectual force,

but . . . he was not able to enjoy prosperity with moderation,

nor to bear misfortune with dignity,

and it is because he lacked moral force

that he caused the ruin of Europe and of himself.' "

TALLEYRAND

Epilogue

AT THE CONCLUSION of a survey covering nearly four hundred years of European history certain large questions present themselves. What, in the broadest sense, seem to have been the outstanding developments of this entire period with respect to man's evolution as a member of European society? More specifically, what was the immediate legacy which the era of the French Revolution and Napoleon bestowed upon the succeeding century?

To answer such questions is not easy, for the vast historical panorama extending from the close of the Middle Ages to the opening of the nineteenth century makes up one of the most complex periods in the history of civilized man. During these years, as the patterns of European life assumed first one shape and then another, rapid movement alternated with relative stability. In the seventeenth century it was fashionable to believe that a magnificent level of achievement had been reached which it would be difficult ever to surpass. In the eighteenth century observers of the Enlightenment were convinced of the reality of continuing progress that would affect every aspect of the contemporary scene. The age of the French Revolution produced even more spectacular hopes.

At the risk of over-simplification, a summary of the major achievements in European life must be attempted. The conclusions suggested here are, of course, a distillation of the larger body of material already presented and will be fully intelligible only if related to it. The reader should be reminded, too, that while man may be regarded primarily as a member of a political society he is also deeply involved in many other activities—economic, religious, esthetic and scientific, for example—all of which demand some measure of evaluation.

The major political phenomenon at the opening of the modern era was the rise of nation-states more powerful and far more tightly organized than had been their medieval predecessors. The profound effects of this development are still with us. In a negative sense, the appearance of such nation-states meant the decline of that concept of European unity which to some extent had existed during the Middle Ages and which had found outward expression in the medieval Church and (in theory at least) in the medieval Empire. Both these institutions were subject to attack. The Protestant Reformation effectively challenged the universal authority of the Roman Catholic Church, while in a political sense the Holy Roman Empire fell into an increasing decrepitude which ended in 1806 when Napoleon finally insisted upon its abolition. Long before this, however, the divisive elements in European political life had deeply impressed themselves upon the times.

The distinctive marks of states such as France, Spain, England and Sweden during this evolution of our modern world were numerous. They clearly were beginning to be *national,* though hardly with that militantly self-conscious nationalism so characteristic of the nineteenth and twentieth centuries. They were *dynastic,* being organized in such a way as to give scope to the ambitions of powerful families such as the Tudors in England, the Bourbons in France, the Hapsburgs in Austria and the Hohenzollerns in Brandenburg-Prussia. To a large degree they were *patrimonial,* that is to say, each dynasty looked upon its realm as a patrimony or personal estate from which it drew large benefits and which it was to protect and, wherever possible, enlarge. Almost inevitably such European states were *expansionist* and aggressive in their attitude toward other states. In economic matters their general policies were for the most part *mercantilist.* A consequence of the age of exploration was that some of these states likewise became *imperialistic,* taking advantage of the outward surge of European life to establish trading posts, forts and settlements, to build navies and merchant-marines and to win vast overseas territories.

Within these states a further characteristic was the struggle to determine which hands were effectively to exercise power, for as European life became more complex the responsibilities of the central government obviously became greater. The struggle for political control had various outcomes. In late seventeenth-century England the Stuart dynasty was compelled to subordinate its authority to that of a Parliament dominated by an elected House of Commons. The United Netherlands worked out a system of federal rule for its seven provinces which, although it gave some recognition to popular will, was in reality much more oligarchical than it was democratic. Something the same could be said of the Swiss Confederation. The prevailing trend on the Continent was clearly in the direction of strong royal power. Rulers such as Louis XIV of France, Frederick William, the Great Elector of Brandenburg, and Peter the Great of Russia exercised a ruthless authority unchecked by any elected parliamentary bodies. The enlightened despots of the eighteenth century were not subject to the control of parliaments or estates, but professed instead to acknowledge the sovereignty of that Reason or Law which the *philosophes* had proclaimed. To the time of the French Revolution, then, the strengthening and consolidation of royal authority, enlightened or otherwise, seemed a far more common phenomenon than did the limiting of royal power on the English model.

The demand for political and social reform arising during the eighteenth century was dramatically answered during the French Revolution, first by the various attempts to formulate the "rights of man" and then by the several constitutions which one after another sought to put these rights into effect. During all the turmoil of this era the essential concept of some kind of written definition of powers was never lost, although such constitutional definitions seemed meaningless when Napoleon rode roughshod over the supposed rights of his subjects. The restored Bourbons, for all that they repudiated the work of the Revolution, found it necessary to issue the celebrated Charter of 1814, guaranteeing some political rights to their subjects. It may be said, therefore, that the struggle to impose constitutional limitations upon royal power was first successful in England. A century later the same struggle found dramatic expression in revolutionary France, whence in various ways its influence spread throughout the Continent.

Equally as important as this search for constitutional sanctions, and far more widely operative, was the steady growth of centralized, bureaucratic, professionally expert administrative machinery. The old bodies of noble advisers—privileged, self-seeking and often incompetent—surviving from feudal times slowly gave place to the new network of specialized functionaries drawn increasingly from the middle class. Ministers were appointed whose business it was to administer particular branches or departments of government; royal agents were sent to the provinces to supervise the work and sometimes to override the authority of privileged local bodies. Efforts were made to find men trained in the problems of finance, to appoint judges competent to administer the new codes of law which the enlightened despots were pleased to introduce and in general to create an efficient machinery of administration. Making all allowances for the continuation of a large degree of privilege, wastefulness and incompetence, it is clear that the new bureaucracies were a valuable component of the modern European states system.

One highly significant aspect of the growth of the states was found in the field of external relations. The outstanding fact would seem to be the unhesitating employment of the ruthless techniques of power politics, so that, despite the protests of some intellectuals and humanitarians, war continued to be accepted as a legitimate means to further national interests. Even in an atmosphere of recurrent war, however, it was considered impor-

tant to define the rules of conduct between states, and so the theorists expended much ink and effort in seeking to clarify and elaborate the "law of
nations." Ineffective as this "law" may have been, it nevertheless helped to
regularize diplomatic procedure and to build up a body of customs which
nations for their own advantage were disposed to accept. Steady progress
was also made in standardizing the technical and professional aspects of
diplomacy. Permanent embassies came to be maintained abroad by all the
major powers. Books were written upon the rights of ambassadors and upon
diplomatic practice in general, with useful results for the holding of conferences, the drafting of treaties and the general conduct of negotiations. Even
so, one must properly stress the large element of opportunism, cynicism and
ruthlessness which continued to show itself in a European world where the
balance of power was the controlling principle of diplomacy and where each
state maneuvered so as to avoid a position of weakness or isolation amid the
generally competitive struggle.

Only the most extreme type of wishful thinking could ignore the great
importance of war in the general history of modern Europe. Its conduct
became increasingly elaborate and specialized. In place of the old feudal
levies and crude mercenary contingents appeared standing armies with
better equipment, better tactics and better leadership. These armies (and
navies) steadily increased in size, and commanded a steadily larger share of
the national budget. From the crude system of conscription first employed
grew the great national mobilizations of French troops during the Revolution. This was followed shortly afterward by the fully articulated system of
compulsory military service which made Prussia the first modern example of
the nation in arms. No state could afford to ignore the lesson to be drawn
from such powerful examples. Wars, too, increased in scale and destructive-
ness, so that by the time of the French Revolution their impact upon national
life far exceeded what it had been in earlier centuries.

This historian will note how certain geographic areas in Europe appeared
time and again as the classic fields of military conflict. Northern Italy, for
example, was fought over by France and Austria for more than three centuries.[1] The southern shores of the Baltic became an area of rivalry between
the ambitions of Russia and Sweden, with Russia the eventual victor. In
central Europe the areas of Saxony, Bohemia and Silesia were long the stage
of Austro-Prussian conflicts. On the northern shores of the Black Sea the
Russians and the Turks were to fight intermittently for at least two centuries.
Perhaps more important than any of these was the vital territory of Flanders

1. The Emperor Louis Napoleon of France won his victories of Solferino and Magenta in
1859 over the Austrians within a radius of less than a hundred miles of Pavia, where in
1525 Francis I of France met defeat and capture at Hapsburg hands.

and the Rhineland—an age-old arena of bitter conflict. Again and again these lands suffered from the campaigns between France and her rivals across the Rhine. To England, also, Flanders and the Low Countries were of such economic and strategic importance that a threat to them coming from any major power—Spain, France or Germany—was always taken as a threat to England's own vital interests, in defense of which it never hesitated to take military action.

Some significant changes in the relative power status of various countries may finally be noted. Throughout the entire period under consideration, France and Austria could properly be called great powers, while England, quickly rising to a similar rank during the sixteenth century, successfully maintained it. Russia and Prussia are examples of states whose rise came later and more slowly. Spain, Poland and the Ottoman Empire represent major powers sinking to a minor rank; in Poland's case, indeed, the tragic outcome was to be complete political extinction. Bohemia and Hungary, once proud medieval kingdoms, were unable to preserve their independence, and managed only to retain a kind of local identity within the larger framework of the Hapsburg Empire. Despite a considerable degree of geographic, ethnic, linguistic and cultural unity, neither the German nor the Italian peoples were able to organize themselves as an effective political unit. Two European states, Sweden and the United Netherlands, contrived during the seventeenth century to rise to a level of international importance which a certain lack of fundamental strength made it impossible for them permanently to maintain.

By the opening of the nineteenth century the relative status of the great powers differed in important respects from what it had been in the sixteenth. To some extent the center of political power had moved eastward. At the Congress of Vienna in 1815 the "Big Four" who sought to keep the direction of European affairs largely in their hands were England, Austria, Russia and Prussia. Three of these states lay east of the Rhine, and two of them were relatively new arrivals as major powers—a point which strikingly illustrates the thesis of Lavisse that the capital fact of the three centuries under consideration has been the organization and growth of eastern Europe in such a way as to modify the older workings of the balance of power.[2]

The main economic changes of this period were closely connected with the growth of the modern states system. In general, the transition from medieval to modern economic life meant the decline of the old local method of regulating industry and commerce, whether by the craft gild or by the

2. ERNEST LAVISSE, *Vue générale de l'histoire politique de l'Europe* (16th ed., Paris, 1924), p. 181.

town authorities, in favor of a new type of control exercised by the central government on a nation-wide scale. This system of national regulation, or mercantilism, most strikingly illustrated in the France of Louis XIV and Colbert, had its beginnings in Tudor England, in the France of Henry IV and Sully and in the Brandenburg of the Great Elector. In a ruthlessly competitive world where all states were striving for power, it was only to be expected that rulers would mobilize their economic as well as their military resources in order to prevail over their opponents. Tariffs, industrial subsidies, navigation acts, strict rules concerning manufacture and various other methods of control were all a means to strengthen the state in what was held to be an unavoidable struggle.

Viewed from another angle, all economic life—agricultural, commercial and industrial—was profoundly affected by technological improvements. The changes which resulted were so elaborate as to defy simple summary. In agriculture the outstanding trend was the progressive weakening of the old medieval forms of village organization and the development of better methods of farming. The outcomes in various countries showed wide differences. In England, the decline of the medieval village system, the progress of enclosures and the vogue of scientific agriculture in the eighteenth century favored the accumulation of very large estates, either held and cultivated by their noble proprietors or leased out to tenant farmers. In France, the tendency to peasant ownership existing even before the Revolution was markedly accentuated by the reforms of the revolutionary period, so that France became, more than any of its contemporaries, a country of peasant proprietors. Technological improvements were made in continental agriculture, to a considerable extent as a result of the influence of England's example. East of the Elbe River serfdom remained, and in the case of eighteenth-century Russia actually underwent a substantial increase. While one effect of the Napoleonic era was Stein's great emancipation edict in Prussia, in general the abolition of serfdom in eastern Europe came later; in Poland, Russia, Austria and Hungary emancipation was to be one of the great achievements of the nineteenth century.

The world of commerce saw impressive changes. As trade grew to worldwide proportions and the wealth of Europe notably increased, the first consequences were such as to constitute what has come to be known as the Commercial Revolution. This was one of the great dynamic forces of modern times. "Colonial wares" such as spices, tea, coffee, cocoa, sugar, tobacco, calicoes and silks substantially affected the daily habits of the European population, and also brought wealth and power to the merchants who dealt in them. Such changes made possible a new economic and political status for the rising middle class, the bourgeoisie. By the end of the period this class had gone far to replace the aristocracy as the truly dynamic element in the society of Western Europe. The linking of Europe with a wider overseas world had other consequences: colonies were founded, trade grew, missionary enterprise developed, population became more mobile and intellectual horizons were widened.

Historians are now disposed to stress the evolutionary as much as the revolutionary aspects of the great changes in European industrial life. Improvements in technology, never absent from the European scene, came at an accelerated pace during the eighteenth century. Spinning, weaving, coal mining, iron manufacture, pottery making and a great many other specialized industries felt the spur. The old sources of power—the energy of man and beast, the forces of wind and water—were in process of being transformed by the incalculable new power of steam. The application of steam to industry in the closing decades of the eighteenth century and its further application to transportation during the nineteenth century meant the full development of the Industrial Revolution. The tremendous increase in the output of goods, the larger demand for labor and the cheapening of agricultural products contributed to the increased material well-being and also to the spectacular growth of the European population. The estimated European population of 200 millions at the opening of the nineteenth century was about four times what it had been in the sixteenth century.

These great political and economic changes meant important modifications in the fabric of European society. The medieval social structure had been relatively stable; one class was superimposed upon another, with each group on the whole accepting and understanding its place in the general scheme of things. The possibility of movement from one status to another doubtless existed—a prosperous merchant could become a noble, for example, or a promising peasant boy become a priest—but for the most part individuals accepted the rank to which, as it was felt, God had called them. Even during the Middle Ages, however, this regime of "status" felt the pressure of change, in part because of the gradual transformation of European economic life, and in part because of more specific causes such as the Crusades and the destructive impact of the great fourteenth-century plague known as the Black Death. In Western Europe serfdom went into a decline. The urban classes in time were likewise transformed by the great sweep of new economic and political forces. The English Revolution of 1688 made it possible for the middle class to assert itself politically as it had not previously been able to do. A century later the French Revolution, while making grand affirmations about the general "rights of man and of the citizen," was in actual practice clearing the path for a more specifically bourgeois advance.

With reason, therefore, the French refer to the period before 1789 as the *ancien régime,* an age characterized by the existence of a privileged order of society which received its death blow during the great revolutionary era.

The eighteenth century experienced an impressive growth in humanitarian sentiment leading to a larger exercise of social responsibility. Civilized man, to be sure, has hardly ever been without some feeling of responsibility toward his fellows. Those duties of charity and mercy which in medieval times had been the particular province of the Church came to be assumed by various secular bodies, sometimes by public-spirited individuals, sometimes by civic organizations, by local government or even by the larger machinery of the national state. Schools, as well as hospitals, orphanages, poorhouses, asylums and other charitable institutions became increasingly the concern of public officials. It would be unrealistic to make too much of the actual achievement, for the new spirit of humanitarianism often outran the actual performance, yet the eighteenth century gave widespread evidence of the desire to improve the lot of the suffering and the needy. "Happiness," the Jacobin leader, St. Just, declared, "is a new idea in Europe." In the spirit of this new idea, many dedicated leaders who would have been shocked to be regarded as revolutionaries sought to widen the area within which happiness could be achieved here and now upon earth.

> Without question the European poor of the eighteenth century fared badly, and their health, wealth, and happiness were sacrificed in the progress that brought prosperity and comfort to the few. Yet not only the warmest hearts but the coolest brains clearly recognized society's obligation to minister to the wants of the needy. Measured in terms of absolute social justice the humanitarian effort was calamitously inadequate; judged as an index of a new spirit, as a token of a humanity greater than that which Europe had ever experienced, it represented a memorable advance. . . . Never before in Europe's history had so many people at one time felt so generously and sought to act in accordance with their feelings.[3]

Changes in intellectual outlook and intellectual standards have been a fundamental aspect of the evolution of the modern world. The great political and economic transformations of the sixteenth, seventeenth and eighteenth centuries almost automatically provoked critical discussion as to their meaning and value. Thus, the literature of political theory which was produced during this age dealt boldly with questions concerning the nature of the state, man's obligations toward it and his rights as an individual and a citizen. So, too, the great economic changes produced conflicts of opinion as to which economic policies were best. From such discussions eventually emerged a larger understanding of the actual forces at work in society and

3. LEO GERSHOY, *From Despotism to Revolution,* p. 295.

consequently the beginning of the modern science of economics. The "Classical Economists" who wrote at the end of this period made substantial contributions to the study of man's social behavior.

The great religious conflicts of the era of the Reformation profoundly affected man's general outlook. The historian must see these developments as far more than simply a disagreement over questions of dogma. Dogmatic questions, to be sure, were at the heart of the controversy, yet in the general life of Europe the effects were felt in numerous other ways. Of permanent significance was the emergence of the Protestant faith so as to form a third major group along with the Roman Catholic and the Eastern Orthodox churches. National churches arose, closely allied in most cases with the new monarchies and giving substantial support to them. Religious reform and social progress were by no means always synonymous. Wars were fought, persecution raged and for a time intolerance actually seemed to grow. In some cases there seemed actual retrogression, as when Louis XIV revoked the Edict of Nantes issued by his more tolerant predecessor, Henry IV, or when the Clarendon Code of Restoration England imposed such harsh measures upon Roman Catholics and Dissenters. Gradually, however, the atmosphere of toleration developed, if at first on no better basis than that of "live and let live." The Roman Catholic, required to justify himself in the face of attacks and criticism, undertook a process of housecleaning and self-discipline which gave his ancient Church new vigor. The Protestant took pride in asserting the right of individual judgment and in participating more democratically in the exercise of his religion.

The active religious enthusiasms generated in the heat of the first great Reformation controversies could hardly be expected to continue at their original level. During the seventeenth century a good deal of conventionality, formalism and emptiness began to mark ecclesiastical life. By the eighteenth century a powerful body of thought assailed conventional religion; some of the critics seemed merely indifferent; some were skeptical, deistic, agnostic or even militantly atheistic. Against such forces a substantial counter-attack was carried out by German Pietism and English Methodism, with significant and impressive results. In France during the revolutionary era the prevalent tendency was one of governmental suspicion and hostility toward the organized churches. But this was not sufficient to destroy the faith or transform the customary religious behavior of the average man. Napoleon, the great realist, understood this, and made his accommodation with the Roman Catholic Church. The opening of the nineteenth century witnessed a very substantial "return to religion," a marked literary interest in the religious revival and a close association between these developments and the Romantic movement in literature and the arts. This trend, however, should not obscure the importance of other developments quite different in their general character.

The acceptance of a new "secular" point of view, in accordance with which many of the other-worldly values of the medieval period were rejected, has been a key aspect of the evolution of the modern world. To be sure, the new outlook came about slowly, and in its beginnings affected relatively small groups of people. Increased attention was given to the phenomena of the physical world and to the search for purely rational explanations in all fields. The rise of modern science, in both its theoretical and its practical aspects, gave superb luster to the seventeenth century, so much so that the historian can describe the highway which extends from Copernicus to Newton as one of the most magnificent prospects in all human achievement. As more data became available, and as the language of mathematics was employed to furnish explanations or "laws," the universe could be seen to operate under regular, ascertainable law, comprehensible to human reason. Almost every aspect of human thought was, as we have seen, colored by this new outlook. It led to what has been described as the faith of the eighteenth century—the conviction that the employment of the method of reason would lead man to one victory after another in his forward advance and to a future of almost unimaginable happiness and well-being.

Changes in standards of taste and in the modes of esthetic expression provide another illuminating chapter in man's history. Time and again one will observe how the artistic creations of a given age echo something of the spirit of its political institutions or its economic life. A Gothic cathedral represented the mobilization of the skills and ideals of medieval artists and craftsmen just as surely as a skyscraper represents a mobilization of the skills and ideals of the businessman, the city planner and the engineer. It is not always easy, however, to find the motivations or forces actually responsible for the "cultural climate" of a given age, or to do more than make a superficial correlation between the artistic standards of an epoch and the social and intellectual values to which it adheres.

The great standard terms such as "Renaissance," "Classical," "Baroque," "Rococo," "Neo-Classical" and "Romantic" all have a fairly explicit meaning to the student of the arts. At the beginning of the modern era the revival of classical forms produced a Renaissance art breaking away from the conventions of its medieval precursor. The Renaissance patterns then underwent those successive changes—Mannerist, Baroque, Rococo, Neo-Classical—which had as their outcome the rise of the Romantic era at the close of the eighteenth century. The student can not only trace such chronological sequences; he can take his stand in a given age and find those common characteristics enabling him to speak of the contemporary similarities in Baroque art, Baroque literature and Baroque music. He may be able to see how in certain climactic periods such as the Italian Renaissance or the France of Louis XIV the various aspects of human achievement—political, artistic, literary, philosophical and social—seemed to come together in one harmonious pattern. Similarly, he may be able to detect the complex ways in which the many-sided culture of one era gives place to that of another, as in the transition from the Classical to the Romantic age. The rich mass of material presented by literature, music and the arts during these centuries offers a perpetual challenge to the historian who seeks to use and interpret it. In the simplest terms this material may be regarded as one of the most impressive manifestations of the versatile, creative genius of western man.

A distinguished historian of modern culture has listed five characteristics which in his view have marked off the modern period from earlier periods of history. The first has been the growth of world unity as a result of the great explorations and the vast improvement in the means of communication. The second has been the enormous increase of population and wealth. The third he has taken to be the equalization of classes through the spread of the institutions of democracy. The fourth is listed as the growth of the secular aspects in modern society to an extent not previously known. A fifth note of modernity, closely associated with the preceding point, he has found in the growth of modern science. Together, these have characterized the new age. "The modern spirit . . . is, as distinguished from the spirit of earlier ages, rational, free, forward-looking, and self-conscious. To trust reason rather than tradition or authority, to assert the liberty of the individual, to look to the future rather than to the past, to regard the truth as relative and subjective rather than as absolute and objective, are the marks of the modern spirit." [4] Such new tendencies have vigorously asserted themselves in a world where traditional values and conventionally organized religion have continued, nevertheless, to play an important part in the life of mankind.

What has just been written is a suggestion of some major trends in the evolution of modern Europe as they can be determined from the vantage point of today. The observer of 1815, standing at the close of one political epoch and the opening of another, could hardly have possessed such a perspective. For obvious reasons he would be more aware of his immediate past than of the long centuries out of which his world had grown. Particularly in France, the observer might well have seen this immediate past in the cold light of disillusionment, for only with the passing of time would the memo-

4. PRESERVED SMITH, *A History of Modern Culture*, I, p. 7.

ries stirred up by the harsh realities of Napoleon's rule be transformed and mellowed into the romantic substance of the "Napoleonic Legend."

The man of 1815 would probably have been less aware of the constructive achievements of the Revolutionary era than of its disruptive violence. He and his fellows, consequently, would be disposed to welcome the new era of peace as an "age of restoration," when order could be established in the place of disorder, when authority could take the place of anarchy, when society could be maintained in its traditional ranks and stability appear in the place of feverish change. The Age of Revolution was in actual fact succeeded by an Age of Reaction. In country after country legitimate dynasties were restored, the marks of revolution were obliterated and subjects came docilely under the rule of authoritarian masters. In such circumstances it is not surprising that the nature of those larger forces contributing to the making of the modern world should have remained obscure and misunderstood.

In two immediate respects the revolutionary tradition was cast aside. The republican ideal, first proclaimed in the France of 1792, had few continuing adherents. The attempts to reassert it in the subsequent revolutionary movements of 1830 and 1848 were to have at best a temporary success. Not until 1871 did republicanism again take serious hold upon France. Nor had the ideal of constitutional democracy a much better fate. The constitutional guarantees which existed in the England, the Netherlands, the France, the Switzerland and the Sweden of 1815 were far from being truly democratic. Other states (but not, it will be noted, Prussia, Russia or Austria) were soon to provide themselves with constitutions and charters of a sort. Yet the efforts to extend the franchise, which won their first victories in the English Reform Bill of 1832, moved at a slow pace; this struggle was to occupy the greater part of the nineteenth century and did not achieve full success until the twentieth.

In other respects the changed climate of the new age was undeniable. A world of preponderantly bourgeois interests had come into existence. During the late eighteenth century England had shown the first impressive evidences of a new industrial society. This society, with all its virtues and with all its unhappy stresses and strains, flourished during the nineteenth century. Other countries, notably Belgium, France and western Germany followed at some distance and with some modifications along the economic and social path first opened by England. With surprising speed the impact of these changes was to be felt throughout the entire world.

After 1815 the fires of nationalism kindled by the French Revolution burned fitfully throughout Europe, despite the efforts of men such as Metternich to extinguish them. During the period from 1789 to 1815, when

France had contrived to establish the structure of a militantly self-conscious, centralized state, patriotic reactions were provoked abroad. The ardent nationalism which in France had given rise to the cult of *la patrie* found its echo in other lands: in England, in Prussia, in Spain, in Austria, in Russia and in the Balkans. This nationalism was in time to become one of the most potent forces of the nineteenth century.

Among the many changes that were in evidence at the conclusion of our period we may reemphasize the importance of the growth of a European secular society, taking its lead from the scientist and the rationalist and finding its values in the present world rather than in the world to come. These various aspects of the secular state to which the French Revolution made so notable a contribution became more clearly defined as the nineteenth century progressed:

> The march of the secular spirit is attested by the relaxation of compulsory tithes, compulsory church attendance and compulsory baptism; the reduction of clerical influence especially in education; the restriction on ecclesiastical endowments; the declining percentage of books published on religious topics, and the transference of control over matters of public decency and morals largely to lay hands. Corresponding to these changes, but of a positive nature, may be noted the extension of compulsory lay schooling and compulsory vaccination; the introduction of civil marriage and divorce; the multiplication of popular works and lectures on scientific subjects; the legalization, in the face of clerical protests, of such practices as cremation and contraception. In many countries today the only indissoluble oath recognized by law is that of allegiance to the state, the only inescapable obligation the liability to military service.[5]

Significant as the preceding generalizations must appear, the concluding words of this book should not dwell solely upon them. Organized religion has continued to be a powerful force in human affairs, influencing the feelings and actions of the masses of men. Nor should the historian insist too much upon the catalog of man's "achievements" if that concept conveys any sense of completion or finality. Surely one of the most vivid impressions derived from reading the story of the past is that of the tireless energies of man, of the ceaseless activity that leads him to accept both victory and failure as the point of departure for still further adventure. Some historians have come to the belief that the creative centuries of European genius are nearing an end. Even if this belief should prove to be true, it would hardly diminish the greatness of the period with which this book is concerned. As new centers of political power develop in areas of the world far removed from Europe, it is inconceivable that they could ever completely divorce themselves from the tremendous legacy bequeathed to mankind in these four centuries of European achievement.

5. G. BRUUN, *Europe and the French Imperium,* p. 240.

BIBLIOGRAPHY

Chronological Tables

List of Rulers

Genealogies

How to Write a History Paper

General Index

Bibliography

Suggestions for Further Reading

THE student wishing to enlarge his knowledge of modern European history will quickly discover the enormous mass of available material. The following bibliography, comprising mainly but not exclusively works in English, is intended simply as an introduction to the field. The emphasis is upon books that are readable, that are recent in date and are likely to be found in good American libraries.

A list of bibliographies, encyclopedias and other guides must begin with the indispensable *Guide to Historical Literature* (1931, reprinted 1949) edited by Dutcher, G. M., and others. This can be brought up to date by the successive volumes of the *International Bibliography of the Historical Sciences* (1930 ff.) listing books published since 1926, and by the reviews in *The American Historical Review* and *The Journal of Modern History*. Coulter, E. M., and Gerstenfeld, M., *Historical Bibliographies* (1935) will put the student on the track of further historical guides.

Accurate factual information is contained in Langer, W. L. (ed.), *An Encyclopedia of World History* (revised ed., 1956). Shepherd, W. R., *Historical Atlas* (7th ed., 1929, reprinted, 1955) is most useful, as are Sellman, R. R., *A Student's Atlas of Modern History* (1952), and *Atlas of European History* (1957) edited by E. W. Fox and H. S. Deighton. An *Atlas of World History*, edited by R. R. Palmer, is announced for forthcoming publication. The student should likewise be familiar with the type of material found in the *Encyclopedia of the Social Sciences* (15 vols., 1930–1935), the *Encyclopedia of Religion and Ethics* (13 vols., 1908–1927), the *Catholic Encyclopedia* (16 vols., 1907–1914), the *Jewish Encyclopedia* (12 vols., 1901–1906) and the *Encyclopedia Britannica* (14th ed., 24 vols., 1929).

A number of comprehensive general histories are available. *The Cambridge Modern History* (14 vols., 1902–1912), edited by Ward, Sir A. W., Prothero, Sir G. W., and Leathes, Sir Stanley, has also been published in a cheaper edition (1934) without the atlas volume or bibliographies. Heavily weighted in the direction of political and diplomatic history, it has nevertheless invaluable material on diverse aspects of modern history. For the average student *The Rise of Modern Europe* series under the editorship of W. L. Langer is more serviceable and up-to-date. Ten volumes have appeared on the period from 1250 to 1815, with a gap still remaining from 1517 to 1610. In the French series, *Peuples et civilisations* (20 vols., 1928–1951), edited by Halphen, L., and Sagnac, P., volumes VI to XIV deal with the era from the Middle Ages to 1815. There is also the *Histoire générale des civilisa-*

711

tions under the direction of M. Crouzet of which volume IV (1954) by R. Mousnier runs from 1492 to 1715, and volume V (1954) by R. Mousnier and E. LaBrousse from 1715 to 1815. The *Propyläen Weltgeschichte* (10 vols., 1929–1933), edited by W. Goetz, should be noted because of its splendid illustrations. *European Civilization, Its Origin and Development* (7 vols., 1934–1939), edited by Eyre, E., is published under Catholic auspices. *The European Inheritance* (3 vols., 1954), edited by Barker, Sir E., Clark, Sir G., and Vaucher, P., is a work of international collaboration and presents many stimulating viewpoints.

General source materials are most conveniently accessible in the following: Stearns, R. P. (ed.), *Pageant of Europe: Sources and Selections from the Renaissance to the Present Day* (1947); Baumer, F. le Van (ed.), *Main Currents of Western Thought* (1952); *Introduction to Contemporary Civilization in the West: A Source Book* (2 vols., 1946), prepared by the Contemporary Civilization staff of Columbia College, Columbia University.

On geographic matters see: Febvre, L. P. V., *A Geographic Introduction to History* (1925); Thompson, J. M., *Historical Geography of Europe 800–1789* (1929); Whittlesey, D. S., *Environmental Foundations of European History* (1949); Wright, John K., *The Geographical Basis of European History* (1928).

For economic history see: Clough, S. B., *The Rise and Fall of Civilization* (1951); Clough, S. B., and Cole, C. W., *Economic History of Europe* (1946); Eyre, E. (ed.), *Economic History of Europe* (Vol. V of *European Civilization* listed above); Gras, N. S. B., *History of Agriculture in Europe and America* (1925); Heaton, Herbert, *Economic History of Europe* (rev. ed., 1948); Irvine, Helen D., *The Making of Rural Europe* (1923); Ogg, F. A., and Sharp, W. R., *Economic Development of Europe* (rev. ed., 1949); Weber, Max, *General Economic History* (1950).

For general intellectual and cultural history see: Brinton, C., *Ideas and Men, The Story of Western Thought* (1950); Friedell, E., *A Cultural History of the Modern Age* (3 vols., 1930–1932); Randall, J. H., *Making of the Modern Mind* (rev. ed., 1940); Smith, Preserved, *A History of Modern Culture* (2 vols., 1930–1934). This runs from 1543 to 1776.

The following can be recommended as general histories of art, literature and music: Gardner, Helen, *Art through the Ages* (3rd ed., 1948); Hauser, A., *The Social History of Art* (2 vols., 1951); Robb, D. M., and Garrison, J. J., *Art in the Western World* (3rd ed., 1953); Fletcher, Sir B., *A History of Architecture on the Comparative Method* (latest ed., 1948); Goetz, W. (ed.), *Propyläen Kunstgeschichte* (18 vols., 1923–1932); Magnus, L., *A History of European Literature* (1934); Lang, P. H., *Music in Western Civilization* (1941); Leichentritt, H., *Music, History and Ideas* (1938); Nef, K., *An Outline of the History of Music* (1935); Westrup, J. A., *An Introduction to Musical History* (1955).

On religious history: Latourette, K. S., *History of the Expansion of Christianity* (4 vols., 1937–1941); Hughes, P., *A Popular History of the Catholic Church* (1949); Von Pastor, L., *History of the Popes from the Close of the Middle Ages* (Engl. transl., 38 vols., 1891–1951); Bainton, R. H., *The Church of Our Fathers* (1941); Baron, S. W., *A Social and Religious History of the Jews* (3 vols., 1937).

On military history see: Vagts, A., *A History of Militarism* (1937); Montrose, L., *War Through the Ages* (rev. ed., 1946); Fuller, J. C. F., *A Military History of the Western World* (2 vols., 1955); Stevens, W. O., and Westcott, A. F., *A History of Sea Power* (1942); Earle, E. M. (ed.), *Makers of Modern Strategy* (1943).

Miscellaneous general topics: Coon, C. S., *The Races of Europe* (1939); Huntington, E., *Civilization and Climate* (rev. ed., 1924); Forbes, R. J., *Man the Maker: A History of Technology and Engineering* (1952); Giedion, S., *Mechanization Takes Command: A Contribution to Anonymous History* (1948); Mumford, L., *Technics and Civilization* (1934); Beard, Miriam, *History of the Business Man* (1938); Oppenheim, L. F. L., *International Law* (5th ed., 1937); LIFE, *Picture History of Western Man* (1951).

Some of the most useful national histories may be listed. For England *The Oxford History of England* (1934 ff.) now has eleven of the projected fourteen volumes in print. Among the shorter histories Trevelyan, G. M., *History of England* (rev. and enl., 1937) is a classic. There is also his *English Social History* (1942) likewise published in four volumes as *Illustrated English Social History*. Other excellent single volumes are: Lunt, W. E., *History of England* (3rd ed., 1945); Smith, Goldwin, *A History of England* (1957); Eckles, R. B., and Hale, R. W., *Britain, Her Peoples and the Commonwealth* (1954); Walker, Eric A., *The British Empire, 1497–1953* (2nd ed., 1954).

For France the great history edited by E. Lavisse, *Histoire de France* and *Histoire de France contemporaine, 1789–1919* (19 vols., 1900–1922) is basic. Useful briefer works are: Grant, A. J., *The French Monarchy, 1483–1789* (4th ed., 2 vols., 1925); Guérard, A. L., *France* (1946); Guignebert, C., *A Short History of the French People* (2 vols., 1930); Maurois, A., *A History of France* (1949); Seignobos, C., *The Evolution of the French People* (1932).

For Germany, in addition to the still useful but heavily political Henderson, E. F., *A Short History of Germany* (2 vols. in one, 1928), there are: Reinhardt, K. F., *Germany, 2000 Years* (1950); Shuster, G. N., and Bergstraesser, A., *Germany, A Short History* (1944); Steinberg, S. H., *A Short History of Germany* (1945); Valentin, V., *The German People, Their History and Civilization* (1946).

For Russia, see Pares, Sir B., *History of Russia* (new ed., 1953); Miliukov, P., *Outlines of Russian Culture* (ed. M. Karpovich, 3 vols., 1942); Florinsky, M. T., *Russia: A History and Interpretation* (2 vols., 1953); Mazour, A. G., *Russia, Past and Present* (1951); Tompkins, S., *Russia Through the Ages* (1940); Vernadsky, G., *A History of Russia* (new rev. ed., 1944).

For Italy: Salvatorelli, L., *A Concise History of Italy* (1940); Trevelyan, J. P., *A Short History of the Italian People* (1920).

For Spain and Portugal: Bertrand, L., and Petrie, Sir C., *The History of Spain* (rev. ed., 1952); Castro, A., *The Structure of Spanish History* (1954); Altamira y Crevea, R., *A History of Spain* (1949), and *A History of Spanish Civilization* (1930); Livermore, H. V., *History of Portugal* (1947); Nowell, C. E., *History of Portugal* (1953).

For the Netherlands and Belgium: Blok, P. J., *History of the People of the Netherlands* (5 vols., 1898–1912); Vlekke, B. H. M., *Evolution of the Dutch Nation* (1945); Edmundsen, G., *A History of Holland* (1922); Renier, G. J., *The Dutch Nation* (1944); Van der Linden, H., *Belgium: The Making of a Nation* (1920).

For Switzerland: Martin, William, *History of Switzerland* (1931); Herold, J. C., *The Swiss Without Halos* (1948); Oechsli, W., *History of Switzerland, 1499–1914* (1922).

For Scandinavia: Toyne, S. M., *The Scandinavians in History* (1948); Bain, R. N., *Scandinavia, A Political History* (1905); Larsen, K., *A History of Norway* (1948); Hallendorff, C. and Schück, A., *A History of Sweden* (1929); Birch, J. H. S., *Denmark in History* (1938).

For other countries: Thomson, S. H., *Czechoslovakia in European History* (1943); Reddaway, W. F., and others (eds.), *The Cambridge History of Poland* (2 vols., 1941–1950); Halecky, O., *A History of Poland* (1943); Schevill, F., and Gewehr, W. M., *A History of the Balkan Peninsula* (1933); Miller, William, *The Balkans* (1908); Eversley, George, Baron, *The Turkish Empire From 1288 to 1914* (1923); Hubbard, G. E., *The Day of the Crescent* (1920); Halecky, O., *Borderlands of Western Civilization* (1952), a survey of East Central Europe.

CHAPTERS 1 and 2   Medieval Foundations of Modern Times

GENERAL HISTORIES OF THE MIDDLE AGES

Previté-Orton, C. W. (ed.), *The Shorter Cambridge Medieval History* (2 vols., 1952), a valuable abridgment of the original 8-volume work; Durant, Will, *The Age of Faith* (1950); Painter, S., *A History of the Middle Ages* (1953); Southern, R. W., *The Making of the Middle Ages* (1953); Strayer, J. R., *Western Europe in the Middle Ages: A Short History* (1955); Strayer, J. R., and Munro, D. C., *The Middle Ages, 395–1500* (1942); Thompson, J. W., and Johnson, E. N., *An Introduction to Medieval Europe* (1937); Pirenne, H., *Economic and Social History of Medieval Europe* (1936); Thompson, J. W., *Economic and Social History of Europe in the Later Middle Ages* (1931).

RURAL LIFE

Clapham, Sir J. H., and Power, E. (eds.), *The Agrarian Life of the Middle Ages* (1941), Vol. I of *The Cambridge Economic History of Europe;* Coulton, G. G., *The Medieval Village* (1931); Bennett, Henry S., *Life on the English Manor. A Study of Peasant Conditions, 1150–1400* (1937); Davis, William S., *Life on a Medieval Barony* (1923); Ernle, Lord, *English Farming Past and Present* (1927); Homans, G. C., *English Villagers of the Thirteenth Century* (1941); Neilson, Nellie, *Medieval Agrarian Economy* (1936); Cook, T. A., *Manor Life Through Four Centuries* (1938).

URBAN AND COMMERCIAL LIFE

Postan, M. M., and Rich, E. (eds.), *Trade and Industry in the Middle Ages* (1952), Vol. II of *The Cambridge Economic History of Europe;* Baldwin, Summerfield, *Business in the Middle Ages* (1937); Boissonnade, P., *Life and Work in Medieval Europe* (1927); Jusserand, J. J., *English Wayfaring Life in the Middle Ages* (new ed., 1912); Kerr, A. B., *Jacques Coeur, Merchant Prince of the Middle Ages* (1927); Nash, E. G., *The Hanse, Its History and Romance* (1929); Pirenne, H., *Medieval Cities. Their Origins and the Revival of Trade* (1925); Power, E. E., *Medieval People* (1924, reprinted 1955); Salzmann, L. F., *English Industries in the Middle Ages* (1923); Thrupp, S., *The Merchant Class of Medieval London, 1300–1500* (1948); Cram, R. A., *Walled Towns* (1949).

THE EXPANSION OF EUROPE

Useful studies are Baker, J. N. L., *History of Geographical Discovery* (rev. ed., 1937); Beazley, C. R., *The Dawn of Modern Geography* (3 vols., 1897–1906); Kimble, G. H. T., *Geography in the Middle Ages* (1938). For contacts with Asia see Olschki, L., *Marco Polo's Predecessors* (1943); Sykes, P. M., *The Quest for Cathay* (1936); Hart, H. H., *Venetian Adventurer* [Marco Polo] (3rd ed., 1947); Yule, Sir H., *The Book of Ser Marco Polo, the Venetian* (3rd rev. ed., 2 vols., 1903); Moule, A. C., *Christians in China Before the Year 1553* (1930). On the crusades there is the brief account by Newhall, R. A., *The Crusades* (1927), and the definitive work by Runciman, S., *A History of the Crusades* (3 vols., 1951–1954). For other questions see: Newton, A. P. (ed.), *Travel and Travellers of the Middle Ages* (1926); Tyler, J. E., *The Alpine Passes in the Middle Ages* (1930); and Prawdin, M. P., *The Mongol Empire, Its Rise and Legacy* (1940).

GOVERNMENT AND POLITICS

Lord Bryce's *Holy Roman Empire,* first published in 1864 and frequently enlarged and reissued (latest ed., 1950), is a classic. Various aspects of political life and thought are presented in the following: Bloch, Marc, *Feudal Society* (1956); Clark, M. V., *The Medieval City State. An Essay on Tyranny and Federation in the Later Middle Ages* (1926); Ganshof, F. L., *Feudalism* (1952); Gierke, O. F. von, *Political*

Theories of the Middle Ages (new ed., 1938); Hearnshaw, F. C. J. (ed.), *The Social and Political Ideas of Some Great Medieval Thinkers* (1923); Kern, F., *Kingship and Law in the Middle Ages* (1939); Lewis, Ewart, *Medieval Political Ideas* (2 vols., 1954), texts and commentaries; McIlwain, C. H., *The Growth of Political Thought in the West* (1932); Painter, S., *The Rise of Feudal Monarchies* (1951); Stephenson, Carl, *Medieval Feudalism* (1942); Vinogradoff, P., *Roman Law in Medieval Europe* (1929); Painter, S., *Medieval Society* (1951).

RELIGION

Adams, Henry, *Mont-Saint-Michel and Chartres* (latest ed., 1936); Baldwin, Marshall W., *The Medieval Church* (1953); Baldwin, Summerfield, *The Organization of Medieval Christianity* (1929); Boase, T. S. R., *St. Francis* (1936); Dawson, Christopher, *Medieval Religion* (1934); Evans, Joan, *Monastic Life at Cluny* (1931); Thompson, A. Hamilton, *Innocent III and the Medieval Papacy* (1950); Lunt, W. E., *Papal Revenues in the Middle Ages* (2 vols., 1934); McFarlane, K. B., *John Wycliffe and the Beginnings of English Non-conformity* (1953); Packard, S. R., *Europe and the Church Under Innocent III* (1927); Petry, R. C., *St. Francis of Assisi* (1941); Sabatier, P., *Life of St. Francis of Assisi* (1894); Tellenbach, G., *Church, State and Christian Society at the Time of the Investiture Contest* (1940); Turberville, A. S., *Medieval Heresy and the Inquisition* (1932); Williams, W., *St. Bernard* (1944).

CHAPTER 3   The Cultural Transition

GENERAL SURVEYS OF MEDIEVAL CULTURE

Artz, F. B., *The Mind of the Middle Ages* (2nd ed., 1954), a splendid work of synthesis with outstanding bibliographies; Adams, George B., *Civilization During the Middle Ages Especially in Relation to Modern Civilization* (rev. ed., 1922); Coulton, G. G., *Studies in Medieval Thought* (1940); Crump, C. G., and Jacob, E. F. (eds.), *The Legacy of the Middle Ages* (1926); Hearnshaw, F. C. J. (ed.), *Medieval Contributions to Modern Civilization* (1949); Taylor, H. O., *The Medieval Mind* (2 vols., rev. ed., 1930); Harrison, F., *Medieval Man and his Notions* (1947).

THE ROOTS OF MEDIEVAL CULTURE

Arragon, R. F., *The Transition from the Ancient to the Medieval World* (1936); Bolgar, R. R., *The Classical Heritage and Its Beneficiaries* (1954); De Burgh, W. G., *The Legacy of the Ancient World* (2 vols., 1954); Dopsch, A., *The Economic and Social Foundations of European Civilization* (2nd ed., 1937); Highet, Gilbert, *The Classical Tradition* (1949); Sandys, J., *A History of Classical Scholarship* (3 vols., 2nd ed., 1921); Snell, B., *The Discovery of the Mind, Greek Origins of European Thought* (1953). Much valuable information is given in the various "Legacy" volumes published by the Oxford Press: Livingstone, Sir R. W. (ed.), *The Legacy of Greece* (1921); Bailey, C. (ed.), *The Legacy of Rome* (1923); Bevan, E. R., and Singer, C. (eds.), *The Legacy of Israel* (2nd ed., 1928); Arnold, T., and Guillaume, A. (eds.), *The Legacy of Islam* (1931); Baynes, N. H., and Moss, H. (eds.), *Byzantium* (1948). With these may be included Faris, N. A. (ed.), *The Arab Heritage* (1944). See also Gibb, H. A. R., *Mohammedanism* (1955).

MEDIEVAL SCHOLARSHIP

Abelson, P., *The Seven Liberal Arts* (1906); Copleston, F., *Medieval Philosophy, Augustine to Scotus* (1952); Gilson, E., *Spirit of Medieval Philosophy* (1936); Haskins, C. H., *The Renaissance of the Twelfth Century* (1927), *The Rise of the Uni-*

versities (1923); Hawkins, D. J. B., *A Sketch of Medieval Philosophy* (1947); Loomis, Louise R., *Medieval Hellenism* (1906); Powicke, F. M., *Ways of Medieval Life and Thought* (1950); Rashdall, H., *The Universities of Europe in the Middle Ages* (3 vols., 2nd ed., 1936); Waddell, H., *Peter Abelard* (1933), *The Wandering Scholars* (7th ed., 1934); Walsh, Gerald G., *Medieval Humanism* (1942). For some of the scientific aspects of medieval learning consult: Crombie, A. C., *Augustine to Galileo, A. D. 400–1650* (1952), *Robert Grosseteste and the Origins of Experimental Science* (1953); Easton, S. C., *Roger Bacon and His Search for a Universal Science* (1952); Haskins, C. H., *Studies in the History of Medieval Science* (2nd ed., 1927); Mason, S. F., *A History of the Sciences* (1953); Thorndike, L., *History of Magic and Experimental Science* (6 vols., 1923–1941); Woodruff, F. W., *Roger Bacon. A Biography* (1938).

LITERATURE AND THE ARTS

On literature see: Brittain, F., *The Medieval Latin and Romance Lyric (to 1300 A. D.)* (2nd ed., 1951), an anthology; Jones, Charles W., *Medieval Literature in Translation* (1950); Smythe, B. (tr.), *Troubadour Poets* (1911); Waddell, H. (tr.), *Medieval Latin Lyrics* (4th ed., 1933); Chaytor, H. J., *The Provençal Chanson de Geste* (1946); Coghill, N., *The Poet Chaucer* (1949); Ker, W. P., *The Dark Ages* (1955); Taylor, A. B., *An Introduction to Medieval Romance* (1930); Tilley, A., *Medieval France: A Companion to French Studies* (1922); Vossler, K., *Medieval Culture: An Introduction to Dante and His Times* (2 vols., 1929); Wright, F. A., and Sinclair, T. O., *A History of Later Latin Literature* (1931). On medieval music see: Bukofzer, M. F., *Studies in Medieval and Renaissance Music* (1950); Hughes, Anselm (ed.), *Early Medieval Music up to 1300* (1954). This is Vol. II of *The New Oxford History of Music*. Reese, G., *Music in the Middle Ages* (1940). For the arts consult the following general works: Lethaby, W. R., *Medieval Art* (3rd ed., 1950); Morey, C. R., *Medieval Art* (1942). In addition see: Adams, Henry, *Mont-Saint-Michel and Chartres* (1936); Braun, H., *The English Castle* (1936); Evans, Joan, *Art in Medieval France* (1948), *English Art, 1307–1461* (1949); Harvey, J. H., *The Gothic World, 1100–1600* (1950), deals with architecture; Sitwell, Sacheverell, *The Gothick North* (1929).

MISCELLANEOUS ASPECTS OF MEDIEVAL CULTURE

Coulton, G. G., *The Medieval Scene* (1930), *Medieval Panorama, The English Scene from Conquest to Reformation* (1939); Holmes, Urban T., Jr., *Daily Living in the Twelfth Century* (1952); Kelly, Amy, *Eleanor of Aquitaine and the Four Kings* (1950); Painter, S., *French Chivalry* (1940), *Medieval Society* (1951); Powicke, Sir M., *Medieval England, 1066–1485* (1932); Prestage, E. (ed.), *Chivalry* (1928); Temko, Allan, *Notre Dame of Paris* (1955); Thompson, J. W., *The Medieval Library* (1939); Walsh, James J., *The Thirteenth, the Greatest of Centuries* (1907). The following are useful works on Byzantine civilization: Baynes, Norman H., *The Byzantine Empire* (1952); Baynes, N. H., and Moss, H., *Byzantium: An Introduction to East Roman Civilization* (1948); Diehl, C., *History of the Byzantine Empire* (1925); Hussey, Joan M., *The Byzantine World* (1948); Runciman, S., *Byzantine Civilization* (1933); Ostrogorsky, G., *The History of the Byzantine State* (1956).

ITALY AND THE REVIVAL OF LEARNING

Some useful general works on the Renaissance as a whole are: Durant, Will, *The Renaissance* (1953); Ferguson, Wallace R., *The Renaissance* (1940); Lucas, Henry S., *The Renaissance and the Reformation* (1934); Green, V. H. H., *Renaissance and Reformation* (1952); Sellery, George C., *The Renaissance: Its Nature and Origins* (1950); Sichel, Edith, *The Renaissance* (1922). The following deal specifically with

Italy: Burckhardt, J. C., *The Civilization of the Renaissance in Italy* (illustrated ed., 1937); Symonds, J. A., *The Renaissance in Italy* (7 vols., 1875–1886 and later eds.). For the political and economic setting consult: Cheyney, E. P., *The Dawn of a New Era, 1250–1453* (1936) and Schevill, F., *History of Florence* (1936). For various aspects of the Revival of Learning see: Symonds, J. A., *The Age of the Despots* (new ed., 1900) and *The Revival of Learning* (new ed., 1900), Vols. I and II of the general work listed above; Schevill, F. (ed.), *The First Century of Italian Humanism* (1928), documents; Robinson, J. H., and Rolfe, H. W., *Petrarch the First Modern Scholar and Man of Letters* (2nd ed., 1914); Whitfield, J. H., *Petrarch and the Renaissance* (1943); Hutton, E., *Some Aspects of the Genius of Boccaccio* (1922); Colman, C. B., *The Treatise of Lorenzo Valla on the Donation of Constantine* (1922). On the Medici see: Armstrong, Edward, *Lorenzo de' Medici* (1896); Gutkind, Curt W., *Cosimo de' Medici, Pater Patriae* (1939); Loth, David, *Lorenzo the Magnificent* (1929); Schevill, F., *The Medici* (1949); Young, G. F., *The Medici* (2 vols., 1909). The following are useful on the beginning of printing: Butler, P., *The Origin of Printing in Europe* (1940); Goldschmidt, E. P., *The Printed Book of the Renaissance* (1950); McMurtrie, Douglas C., *The Book. The Story of Printing and Book-making* (3rd rev. ed., 1943). See also Hutton, F., *Sigismondo Pandolfo Malatesta. Lord of Rimini* (1906); Woodward, W. H., *Vittorino da Feltre and Other Humanist Educators* (1905); Highet, G., *The Classical Tradition* (1949); Cassirer, E., and others (eds.), *The Renaissance Philosophy of Man* (reprint 1956); Kibre, Pearl, "Intellectual Interests as Reflected in the Libraries of the Fourteenth and Fifteenth Centuries," *Journal of the History of Ideas,* VII (1946).

THE TRANSFORMATION OF THE ARTS IN ITALY

Wölfflin, H., *Classic Art: An Introduction to the Italian Renaissance* (1952), a retranslation of a fundamental work first published in 1903; Symonds, J. A., *The Renaissance in Italy: The Fine Arts* (1877 and later eds.), Vol. III of the general work listed above; Berenson, Bernhard, *The Italian Painters of the Renaissance* (new ed., 1938), an authoritative study; Krey, A. C., *A City That Art Built* [Florence] (1936); Venturi, L., *Italian Painting: The Creators of the Renaissance* (1950); Vasari, Giorgio, *Lives of Seventy of the Most Eminent Painters, Sculptors, and Architects* (1896); Metropolitan Museum of Art, *The Renaissance: A Symposium* (1952); Antal, F., *Florentine Painting and Its Social Background* (1948); Cartwright, J., *The Painters of Florence from the Thirteenth to the Sixteenth Century* (1916); Wittkower, R., *Architectural Principles in the Art of Humanism* (1950); Bode, W., *Florentine Sculptors of the Renaissance* (new ed., 1928).

CHAPTER 4   The New World of Politics

GENERAL SURVEYS

The Cambridge Modern History, Vol. I; Grant, A. J., *A History of Europe, 1494–1610* (5th ed., 1952); Cheyney, E. P., *The Dawn of a New Era, 1250–1453* (4th ed., 1936); Gilmore, M. P., *The World of Humanism, 1453–1517* (1952); Johnson, A. H., *Europe in the Sixteenth Century, 1494–1598* (7th ed., 1949); Mattingly, Garrett, *Renaissance Diplomacy* (1955); Petrie, Sir Charles, *Earlier Diplomatic History, 1492–1713* (1949).

SPAIN, ENGLAND AND FRANCE

See the general histories of the various countries listed above. For Spain see also: Merriman, R. B., *Rise of the Spanish Empire in the Old World and in the New* (4 vols., 1918–1934); Salmon, E. D., *Imperial Spain* (1931); Trevor-Davies, R., *The*

Golden Century of Spain, 1501–1621 (1937). For England see also: Fisher, H. A. L., *History of England from the Accession of Henry VII to the Death of Henry VIII* (1906); Mackie, J. D., *The Early Tudors, 1485–1558* (1952); Pickthorn, K., *Early Tudor Government, Henry VII* (1949), *Early Tudor Government, Henry VIII* (1951). For France see also: Batiffol, L., *The Century of the Renaissance* (1916); Bridge, J. S. C., *History of France from the Death of Louis XI, 1483–1515* (5 vols., 1921–1936).

SPECIAL TOPICS

Further light on the politics and diplomacy of this age may be secured from the following: Acton, Lord, *Lectures on Modern History* (1921); Armstrong, E., *The Emperor Charles V* (2 vols., 1902); Brandi, Karl, *The Emperor Charles V: The Growth and Destiny of a Man and of a World Empire* (1939); Lybyer, A. H., *The Government of the Ottoman Empire in the Time of Suleiman the Magnificent* (1913); McElwee, W. L., *The Reign of Charles V* (1936); Mathew, A. H., *The Life and Times of Rodrigo Borgia* (1912); Merriman, R. B., *Suleiman the Magnificent* (1944); Vaughan, D., *Europe and the Turk: A Pattern of Alliances, 1350–1700* (1954); Oman, C. W. C., *A History of the Art of War in the Sixteenth Century* (1937); Taylor, F. L., *The Art of War in Italy, 1494–1529* (1921); Pollard, A. F., *Factors in Modern History* (1926); Portigliotti, G., *The Borgias: Alexander VI, Caesar, Lucrezia* (1928); Beuf, Carlo, *Cesare Borgia* (1942); Lucas-Dubreton, J., *The Borgias* (1955); Woodward, W. H., *Cesare Borgia: A Biography* (1913); Villari, P., *Life and Times of Girolamo Savonarola* (2 vols., 1888); Roeder, R., *Savonarola, a Study in Conscience* (1930); Putnam, R., *Charles the Bold* (1908); Wyndham Lewis, D. B., *King Spider* [Louis XI] (1929). For Machiavelli and Sir Thomas More see the references in Chapter VII.

CHAPTER 5   Overseas Expansion and Economic Change

THE GREAT VOYAGES

For general accounts of exploration and expansion see, in addition to Baker and Beazley cited in Chapter II, the following: Abbott, W. C., *The Expansion of Europe* (new ed., 2 vols. in 1, 1929); Dickinson, R. E., and Howarth, O. J. R., *The Making of Geography* (1933); Gillespie, J. E., *A History of Geographical Discovery* (1933); Herrmann, Paul, *Conquest by Man* (1954); Lamb, Harold, *New Found World* (1955), popular; Newton, A. P. (ed.), *The Great Age of Discovery* (1932); Nowell, Charles E., *The Great Discoveries and the First Colonial Empires* (1954); Parry, J. H., *Europe and a Wider World, 1415–1715* (1949); Penrose, Boies, *Travel and Discovery in the Renaissance, 1420–1620* (1952); Sykes, Sir Percy, *A History of Exploration from the Earliest Times to the Present Day* (1934).

THE FIRST EMPIRES

For Portugal see: Beazley, C. R., *Prince Henry the Navigator* (1895); Danvers, F. C., *The Portuguese in India* (2 vols., 1894); Hart, Henry R., *Sea Road to the Indies* (1950); Morison, S. E., *Portuguese Voyages to America in the Fifteenth Century* (1940); Morse Stephens, H., *Albuquerque* (1892); Prestage, Edgar, *The Portuguese Pioneers* (1933); Sanceau, Elaine, *The Land of Prester John* (1944).

For Spain see, in addition to the works of Merriman and Salmon cited in Chapter IV, the following: Benson, E. F., *Ferdinand Magellan* (1930); Chudoba, Bohdan, *Spain and the Empire* (1952); Collis, Maurice, *Cortes and Montezuma* (1955); Hanke, Lewis, *The First Social Experiments in America* (1935), *The Spanish Struggle for Justice in the Conquest of America* (1949); Haring, C. H., *The Spanish Empire in America* (1947), *Trade and Navigation Between Spain and the Indies in the*

Time of the Hapsburgs (1918); Kirkpatrick, F. A., *The Spanish Conquistadores* (1934); Madariaga, S. de, *Hernan Cortez: Conqueror of Mexico* (1941); Morison, S. E., *Admiral of the Ocean Sea* [Columbus] (1942); Parry, J. H., *The Spanish Theory of Empire in the Sixteenth Century* (1940); Simpson, Lesley B., *The Encomienda in New Spain: Forced Labor in the Spanish Colonies, 1492–1550* (1929); Zweig, Stefan, *Conqueror of the Seas* [Magellan] (1938).

For England see: Chatterton, E. K., *English Seamen and the Colonization of America* (1930); Innes, A. D., *The Maritime and Colonial Expansion of England* (1931); McCann, F. T., *The English Discovery of America to 1585* (1952); Parks, George B., *Richard Hakluyt and the English Voyages* (1928); Quinn, D. B., *Raleigh and the British Empire* (1949); Rowse, A. L., *The Expansion of Elizabethan England* (1955); Williamson, J. A., *The Age of Drake* (1938), *John and Sebastian Cabot* (1920), *Maritime Enterprise, 1485–1558* (1913), *Sir Francis Drake* (1951), *Sir John Hawkins* (1950).

For France see: Priestley, H. I., *France Overseas Through the Old Regime* (1939); Wrong, G. M., *The Rise and Fall of New France* (2 vols., 1928); Grant, W. L., *The Voyages of Champlain* (1907); Parkman, Francis, *Pioneers of France in the New World* (1865 and numerous later eds.); Windsor, Justin, *Cartier to Frontenac* (1894). Miscellaneous: Brown, L. A., *The Story of Maps* (1949); Nordenskiold, A. H., *Facsimile Atlas* (1889), for early maps; Taylor, E. G. R., *Tudor Geography 1485–1583* (1930); Tooley, R. V., *Maps and Map Makers* (2nd ed., 1952); Chatterton, E. K., *Sailing Ships* (1923).

THE NEW EUROPEAN ECONOMY

Useful material will be found in Heaton's *Economic History of Europe* and in Cheyney's *Dawn of a New Era* cited above. For the Commercial Revolution see: Packard, L. B., *The Commercial Revolution* (1927); Heckscher, E. F., *Mercantilism* (2 vols., 1935); Nussbaum, F. L., *A History of the Economic Institutions of Modern Europe: An Introduction to Der Moderne Kapitalismus of Werner Sombart* (1933); Schmoller, G. F. von, *The Mercantile System and Its Historical Significance* (1910); Sée, Henri, *Modern Capitalism: Its Origin and Evolution* (1931); Tawney, R. H., *Religion and the Rise of Capitalism* (new ed., 1937). For English commerce see: Burwash, D., *English Merchant Shipping, 1460–1540* (1948); Hannay, D., *The Great Chartered Companies* (1926); Lingelbach, W. E., *The Merchant Adventurers of England* (1902). For Spain see: Hamilton, Earl, *American Treasure and the Price Revolution in Spain, 1501–1660* (1934); Klein, J., *The Mesta. A Study in Spanish Economic History, 1273–1836* (1920); Smith, Robert S., *The Spanish Guild Merchant. A History of the Consulado, 1250–1700* (1955). For Germany see: Ehrenberg, R., *Capital and Finance in the Age of the Renaissance: A Study of the Fuggers* (1928); Klarwill, V., *The Fugger News-letters* (2nd series, 1924); Strieder, J., *Jacob Fugger the Rich* (1931). For Italy see: Lane, F. C., *Venetian Ships and Shipping of the Renaissance* (1934); Lane, F. C., *Andrea Barbarigo, Merchant of Venice, 1418–1449* (1944); Richards, G. R. B., *Florentine Merchants in the Age of the Medici* (1932); Roover, R. de, *The Medici Bank, Its Organization, Management, Operations, and Decline* (1948). For agrarian changes: Bradley, H., *The Enclosures in England* (1918); Gay, E. F., "Enclosures in England in the Sixteenth Century," *Quarterly Journal of Economics*, XVII (Aug., 1903); Gras, N. S. B., *A History of Agriculture in Europe and America* (2nd ed., 1940); Tawney, R. H., *The Agrarian Problem in the Sixteenth Century* (1912).

PATTERNS OF SOCIAL CHANGE

Harvey, J. H., *Gothic England: A Survey of National Culture, 1300–1550* (1947); Hexter, J. H., "Education of the Aristocracy in the Renaissance," *Journal of Mod-*

ern History, XXII (1950); Palm, F. C., *The Middle Classes Then and Now* (1936); Renard, G., and Weulersse, G., *Life and Work in Modern Europe (Fifteenth to Eighteenth Centuries)* (1926); Rowse, A. L., *The England of Elizabeth. The Structure of Society* (1951); Trevelyan, G. M., *English Social History* (Vol. II, 1942); Wright, Louis B., *Middle Class Culture in Elizabethan England* (1935).

CHAPTER 6   The Culmination of the Renaissance (1)

ART AND LETTERS IN ITALY

Many of the works on Italy already cited in Chapter III are useful. See also: Vaughan, Herbert M., *Studies in the Italian Renaissance* (1930); Symonds, J. A., *The Renaissance in Italy: The Fine Arts* (1877 and numerous later eds.) is Vol. III of the work cited above. Wölfflin's *The Art of the Italian Renaissance* and Berenson's *Italian Painters*, cited above, are basic. For various aspects of Italian painting see: Mather, F. J., *Western European Painting of the Renaissance* (1940); Venturi, R. S., *Italian Painting: The Renaissance* (1951); Clark, Sir K., *Leonardo da Vinci* (new ed., 1952); Lucas, E. V., *Michelangelo* (1925); Saponaro, M., *Michelangelo* (1951); Tolnay, Charles de, *Michelangelo* (4 vols., 1943–1954); Lavery, F., *Raphael* (1922); McCurdy, E., *Raphael Santi* (1917); Powers, H. H., *Venice and Its Art* (1930); Rea, H., *Titian* (1906); Stearns, F. P., *Four Great Venetians: An Account of the Lives of Giorgione, Titian, Tintoretto, and Il Veronese* (1901). For sculpture see: Valentiner, W. R., *Studies of Italian Renaissance Sculpture* (1950); Maclagen, E. R. D., *Italian Sculpture of the Renaissance* (1935). For architecture see: Anderson, W. J., and Stratton, A., *The Architecture of the Renaissance in Italy* (1927); Gromort, G., *Italian Renaissance Architecture* (1922); Scott, Geoffrey, *The Architecture of Humanism* (reprinted 1954). For music see: Bukofzer, M. F., *Studies in Medieval and Renaissance Music* (1950); Dent, E. J., *Music of the Renaissance in Italy* (1934).

    For literature see: Symonds, J. A., *The Renaissance in Italy: Italian Literature* (2 vols., 1881 and numerous later eds.), comprising Vols. IV and V of the work cited above; Fletcher, J. B., *Literature of the Italian Renaissance* (2 vols., 1934); Taylor, H. O., *Thought and Expression in the Sixteenth Century* (2 vols., 1920); Ady, J. M., *The Perfect Courtier, Baldassare Castiglione. His Life and Letters, 1478–1529* (2 vols., 1927); Cartwright, Julia, *Baldassare Castiglione* (2 vols., 1908); Castiglione, B., *The Book of the Courtier* (1901 and numerous eds.); Cust, R. H. H., *The Life of Benvenuto Cellini* (1910); Cellini, B., *Memoirs* (1907 and numerous eds.); Hutton, E., *Pietro Aretino, the Scourge of Princes* (1922); Roeder, R., *The Man of the Renaissance* (1933). For Machiavelli see the references below under Political Thought. See also Ross, J. B., and McLaughlin, M. M. (eds.), *Portable Renaissance Reader* (1953).

HUMANISM AND THE ARTS IN GERMANY AND THE NETHERLANDS

Taylor's *Thought and Expression in the Sixteenth Century*, Vol. I, cited above, is very useful for German humanism. See also: Allen, P. S., *The Age of Erasmus* (1914); *The Cambridge Modern History*, Vol. I. On Erasmus see: Allen, P. S., *Erasmus: Lectures and Wayfaring Sketches* (1934); Huizinga, J., *Erasmus* (new rev. ed., 1924); Hyma, A., *The Youth of Erasmus* (1930); Mangan, J. J., *The Life, Character, and Influence of Erasmus of Rotterdam* (2 vols., 1927); Phillips, Margaret M., *Erasmus and the Northern Renaissance* (1949); Smith, Preserved, *Erasmus. A Study of His Life, Ideals and Place in History* (1923). Extracts from Erasmus' letters and *Colloquies* are given in Hyma, A., *Erasmus and the Humanists* (1930). *The Praise of Folly* has been translated by Hudson, H. H. (1941), and also by Dean, Leonard F. (1946). *The Education of a Christian Prince* has been translated by Born, L. K. (1936). The *Colloquies* have been translated by Bailey, N. (1877). For other northern humanists see: Hildebrandt, F., *Melanchthon* (1946); Holborn, H., *Ulrich Von Hutten* (1937); Hyma, A., *The Brethren of the Common Life* (1950), *The Christian Renaissance: A History of the "Devotio Moderna"* (1924); Stokes, F. G. (ed. and transl.) *Epistolae Obscurorum Virorum* (1925); Zeydel, E. H. (ed.), *Brant's Ship of Fools* (1944).

For artistic aspects see: Benesch, O., *The Art of the Renaissance in Northern Europe* (1947); Dreusch, W. R., *German Painting of the Sixteenth Century* (1936); Mather, F. J., *Western European Painting of the Renaissance* (1939); Dickinson, Helen A., *German Masters of Art* (1914); Panofsky, E., *Albrecht Dürer* (2 vols., 1943); Reinhardt, H., *Holbein* (1938); Burkhard, Arthur, *Matthias Grünewald: Personality and Accomplishment* (1936); Fry, Roger, *Flemish Art* (1927); Rooses, M., *Art in Flanders* (1914); Valentiner, W. R., *The Art of the Low Countries* (1914); Van der Elst, Baron Joseph, *The Last Flowering of the Middle Ages* (1944); Baldass, L., *Jan Van Eyck* (1952).

THE FRENCH RENAISSANCE

Works useful for the general setting are: Grant, Arthur J., *The French Monarchy, 1483–1789* (4th ed., 2 vols., 1925); Batiffol, Louis, *The Century of the Renaissance* (1916); Huizinga, J., *Waning of the Middle Ages* (1924); Guérard, A., *The Life and Death of an Ideal: France in the Classical Age* (1928); Tilley, A., *The Dawn of the French Renaissance* (1918); Hackett, F., *Francis I* (1937); Putnam, S., *Marguerite of Navarre: The First Modern Woman* (1935); Neale, J. E., *The Age of Catherine de' Medici* (1956); Roeder, Ralph, *Catherine de' Medici and the Lost Revolution* (1939); Van Dyke, Paul, *Catherine de' Medicis* (2 vols., 1922); Sichel, E., *Women and Men of the French Renaissance* (1901); Fedden, Mrs. K. W., *Manor Life in Old France* (1933).

For the arts see: Blunt, Anthony, *Art and Architecture in France, 1500 to 1700* (1954); Hourticq, L., *Art in France* (1911); Ward, W. H., *The Architecture of the Renaissance in France* (2nd ed., 1926); Jackson, T. G., *The Renaissance of Roman Architecture: Part III, France* (1923); Museum of Fine Arts, Boston, *The French Renaissance* (1942), a portfolio. For literature and learning see: Taylor, H. O., *Thought and Expression in the Sixteenth Century*, Vol. I, cited previously; Tilley, A., *The Literature of the French Renaissance* (2 vols., 1904), *Studies in the French Renaissance* (1921); Wyndham Lewis, D. B., *François Villon. A Documented Survey* (1928). Rabelais' *Gargantua and Pantagruel* has been edited by Nock, A. J., and Wilson, C. R. (2 vols., 1931). There are lives of Rabelais by Tilley, A. (1907), Plattard, J. (1931) and Putnam, S. (1929). The Florio translation of Montaigne's *Essays* is conveniently accessible in a modern edition (1933). See also Gide, A., *The Living Thoughts of Montaigne* (1939).

CHAPTER 7   The Culmination of the Renaissance (2)

THE RENAISSANCE IN ENGLAND

For general accounts of the Tudor period see: Bindoff, S. T., *Tudor England* (Pelican History of England, Vol. V, 1952); Read, Conyers, *The Tudors. Personalities and Practical Politics in Sixteenth Century England* (1936); Fisher, H. A. L., *History of England from the Accession of Henry VII to the Death of Henry VIII, 1485–1547* (1906); Mackie, J. D., *The Earlier Tudors, 1485–1558* (1952); Pollard,

A. F., *History of England from the Accession of Edward VI to the Death of Elizabeth, 1547–1603* (1910); Black, J. B., *The Reign of Elizabeth* (1936).

For biographies see: Garvin, Katharine (ed.), *The Great Tudors* (1935); Innes, A. D., *Ten Tudor Statesmen* (1934); Lee, Sidney, *Great Englishmen of the Sixteenth Century* (1904); Pollard, A. F., *The Reign of Henry VII* (1914), *Henry VIII* (1905); Mattingly, Garrett, *Catherine of Aragon* (1941); Prescott, H. F. M., *Mary Tudor* (1953); Read, Conyers, *Mr. Secretary Walsingham* (3 vols., 1925), *Mr. Secretary Cecil* (1955). The best biography of Queen Elizabeth is Neale, J. E., *Queen Elizabeth* (1934). See also: Creighton, M., *Queen Elizabeth* (1909); Waldman, Milton, *Queen Elizabeth I* (1952); Elton, G. R., *The Tudor Revolution in Government* (1953); Williams, C. H., *Making of the Tudor Despotism* (1935); Zeeveld, W. Gordon, *Foundations of Tudor Policy* (1948).

On English humanism see: Bush, Douglas, *The Renaissance and English Humanism* (1939); Campbell, W. E., *Erasmus, Tyndale and More* (1949); Caspari, F., *Humanism and the Social Order in Tudor England* (1954); Einstein, Lewis, *The Italian Renaissance in England: Studies* (1913), *Tudor Ideals* (1921); Elliot-Binns, L. E., *England and the New Learning* (1937); Tillyard, E. M., *The Elizabethan World Picture* (1944); Weiss, Roberto, *Humanism in England During the Fifteenth Century* (1941). For literary aspects see also: Ward, A. W., and Waller, A. R. (eds.), *The Cambridge History of English Literature* (15 vols., rev. ed., 1933), Vols. III–VI; Bennett, H. S., *English Books and Readers, 1475–1557* (1952); Wilson, F. P., *Elizabethan and Jacobean* (1945); Reese, M. M., *Shakespeare: His World and His Work* (1953); Boas, F. S., *Christopher Marlowe* (1940); Chambers, R. W., *Thomas More* (1935); Hexter, J. H., *More's Utopia: The Biography of an Idea* (1952); More, Sir Thomas, *The Utopia*, translated by Ralph Robynson (1935).

For the arts see: Summerson, John, *Architecture in Britain, 1530–1830* (1954); Garner, T., and Stratton, A., *Domestic Architecture of England During the Tudor Period* (2 vols., 1929); Walker, E., *A History of Music in England* (3rd ed., 1952); Boyd, M. C., *Elizabethan Music and Musical Criticism* (1940); Fellowes, E. H., *William Byrd* (1936), *English Madrigal Composers* (1921); Woodfill, W. C., *Musicians in English Society from Elizabeth to Charles I* (1953). For miscellaneous aspects see: Byrne, M. St. C., *Elizabethan Life in Town and Country* (new ed., 1947); Camden, Carroll, *Elizabethan Woman* (1952); Chew, S. C., *The Crescent and the Rose: Islam and England During the Renaissance* (1937); Davis, W. S., *Life in Elizabethan Days* (1930); Winchester, Barbara, *Tudor Family Portrait* (1955).

SPANISH CULTURE IN THE SIXTEENTH CENTURY

For general histories see, in addition to Merriman, Salmon and Trevor-Davies cited in Chapter IV, the following: Altamira y Crevea, R., *History of Spanish Civilization* (1930); Hume, Martin, *Spain, 1479–1788* (3rd rev. ed., 1913). On literature and scholarship see: Kelly, J. F., *A New History of Spanish Literature* (1926); Trend, J. B., *The Civilization of Spain* (1944); Lyell, J., *Cardinal Ximenes* (1917); Lynn, Caro, *A College Professor of the Renaissance: Lucio Marineo Siculo* (1937); Bell, A. F. G., *Luis de León: A Study of the Spanish Renaissance* (1925); Sanceau, Elaine, *Knight of the Renaissance: A Biography of D. João de Castro* (1949); Bell, A. F. G., *Cervantes* (1947); Entwistle, W. J., *Cervantes* (1940); Schevill, R., *The Dramatic Art of Lope de Vega* (1918). On the arts in Spain see: Bevan, B., *History of Spanish Architecture* (1938); Byne, A., and Stapley, M., *Spanish Architecture of the Sixteenth Century* (1917); Whittlesey, A., *The Renaissance Architecture of Central and Northern Spain* (1920); Harris, E., *Spanish Painting* (1938); Goldscheider, L., *El Greco* (1938); Legendre, M., *El Greco* (1947); Riggs, A. S., *Velasquez* (1947).

POLITICAL THOUGHT IN THE SIXTEENTH CENTURY

In general see: Sabine, G. H., *A History of Political Theory* (1937); Allen, J. W., *A History of Political Thought in the Sixteenth Century* (1947). For special aspects see: Baumer, F. LeVan, *The Early Tudor Theory of Kingship* (1940); Cassirer, E., *The Myth of the State* (1946); Church, W. F., *Constitutional Thought in Sixteenth Century France* (1941); Figgis, J. N., *Studies of Political Thought from Gerson to Grotius* (2nd ed., 1923); Hearnshaw, F. J. C. (ed.), *Social and Political Ideas of Some Great Thinkers of the Renaissance and Reformation* (1925); McNeill, J. T., *John Calvin on God and Political Duty* (1950); Reynolds, Beatrice, *Proponents of Limited Monarchy in 16th Century France: Francis Hotman and Jean Bodin* (1931); Waring, L. H., *The Political Theories of Martin Luther* (1910); Weber, M., *The Protestant Ethic and the Spirit of Capitalism* (1930). On Machiavelli see: Machiavelli, N., *The Prince* (numerous eds.); Butterfield, H., *The Statecraft of Machiavelli* (1940); Gilbert, Allan H., *Machiavelli's "Prince" and Its Forerunners* (1938); Morley, J., *Machiavelli* (1897); Sforza, Carlo, *The Living Thoughts of Machiavelli* (1940); Whitfield, J. H., *Machiavelli* (1947).

THE BEGINNINGS OF THE SCIENTIFIC REVOLUTION

The best and most recent treatment is Hall, A. R., *The Scientific Revolution, 1500–1800* (1954). Useful general histories of science are: Butterfield, H., *The Origins of Modern Science, 1300–1800* (1951); Dampier, Sir William Cecil, *A Shorter History of Science* (3rd rev. ed., 1942); Harvey-Gibson, R., *Two Thousand Years of Science* (1931); Jeans, Sir James, *The Growth of Physical Science* (2nd ed., 1951); Mason, S. F., *Main Currents of Scientific Thought* (1953); Mees, C. E. K., *The Path of Science* (1946); Pledge, H. T., *Science Since 1500* (1939); Sarton, G., *Guide to the History of Science* (1952); Shepherd, W. B., *New Survey of Science* (1950); Taylor, F. S., *A Short History of Science and Scientific Thought* (1949); Wightman, W., *The Growth of Scientific Ideas* (1950). See also Smith's *History of Modern Culture*, Volume I, and Randall's *Making of the Modern Mind* previously cited.

Special studies of Renaissance science include: Johnson, F. R., *Astronomical Thought in Renaissance England* (1937); Sarton, G., *The Appreciation of Ancient and Medieval Science During the Renaissance, 1450–1600* (1955); Stimson, Dorothy, *The Gradual Acceptance of the Copernican Theory of the Universe* (1917); Taylor, F. S., *The Alchemists: Founders of Modern Chemistry* (1949); Thorndike, L., *Science and Thought in the Fifteenth Century* (1929); Wolf, A., *A History of Science, Technology and Philosophy in the 16th and 17th Centuries* (1935). Topical studies include: Bell, E. T., *The Development of Mathematics* (1940); Burtt, Edwin A., *The Metaphysical Foundations of Modern Philosophical Science* (new ed., 1952); Conant, James B., *On Understanding Science: An Historical Approach* (1947); Nicolson, M. H., *Voyages to the Moon* (1948); Pachter, Henry M., *Paracelsus: Magic Into Science* (1951); Parsons, William B., *Engineers and Engineering in the Renaissance* (1939); Shryock, R. H., *The Development of Modern Medicine* (1947); Singer, Charles, *The Evolution of Anatomy* (1925), *The Story of Living Things: A Short Account of the Evolution of the Biological Sciences* (1931); Usher, A. P., *A History of Mechanical Inventions* (1929).

Good biographical studies are: McCurdy, E. (ed.), *The Notebooks of Leonardo da Vinci* (2 vols., 1938); McCurdy, E., *The Mind of Leonardo da Vinci* (1932); Heydenreich, L. H., *Leonardo da Vinci* (2 vols., 1955); Saunders, J. B. de C., and O'Malley, Charles D., *The Illustrations from the Works of Andreas Vesalius of Brussels* (1950); Armitage, A., *Sun, Stand Thou Still: The Life and Work of Copernicus* (1947); Kesten, H., *Copernicus and His World* (1945); Mizwa, S. P., *Nicholas Coper-*

nicus (1943); Bacon, Francis, *The New Atlantis* (1909); Farrington, B., *Francis Bacon, Philosopher of Industrial Science* (1949); Gade, J. A., *The Life and Times of Tycho Brahe* (1947); Baumgardt, Carola, *Johannes Kepler: Life and Letters* (1951); Namer, E., *Galileo, Searcher of the Heavens* (1931); Santillana, G. de, *The Crime of Galileo* (1955); Taylor, F. S., *Galileo and Freedom of Thought* (1938); Galileo Galilei, *Dialogue on the Great World Systems,* revised and edited by G. de Santillana (1953). See also Sarton, G., *Six Wings: Men of Science in the Renaissance* (1957).

CHAPTER 8   The Age of the Reformation, 1517–1598 (1)

BACKGROUNDS

The most useful general works on the Reformation era are: Grimm, H. J., *The Reformation Era* (1954); Smith, Preserved, *The Age of the Reformation* (1920, reissued 1951); Bainton, Roland H., *The Reformation of the Sixteenth Century* (1952); Lindsay, T. M., *History of the Reformation* (2 vols., 1928); Mosse, George L., *The Reformation* (1953); Walker, W., *The Reformation* (1900); *The Cambridge Modern History*, Vol. II, "The Reformation," Vol. III, "The Wars of Religion"; Lucas, H. S., *The Renaissance and the Reformation* (1934); Green, V. H. H., *Renaissance and Reformation* (1952). For documents see: Bettenson, H., *Documents of the Christian Church* (1905); Kidd, B. J., *Documents Illustrative of the Continental Reformation* (1911), largely in Latin.

LUTHERANISM IN GERMANY AND SCANDINAVIA

Among the many Protestant lives of Martin Luther are: Bainton, Roland H., *Here I Stand. A Life of Martin Luther* (1950); Mackinnon, James, *Luther and the Reformation* (4 vols., 1925–1930); McGiffert, A. C., *Martin Luther* (1917); Schwiebert, E. G., *Luther and His Times* (1950); Smith, Preserved, *Life and Letters of Martin Luther* (1914). Studies by Catholics include: Febvre, L., *Martin Luther: A Destiny* (1929); Grisar, H., *Martin Luther: His Life and Work* (1935); Maritain, J., *Three Reformers* (1947). For Luther's writings see: Woolf, B. L. (ed.), *The Reformation Writings of Martin Luther* Vol. I (1953); Luther, Martin, *Three Treatises* (1943) giving the three pamphlets of 1520; Wace, H., and Buchheim, C. A., *Luther's Primary Works* (1896). There is much of interest in Smith, Preserved, and Gallinger, H. P. (eds.), *Conversations With Luther* (1915). Special studies include: Bax, E. Belfort, *The Peasants' War in Germany: Rise and Fall of the Anabaptists* (1903); Bruce, G. M., *Luther as an Educator* (1928); Eells, H., *Martin Bucer*, 1931; Hildebrandt, F., *Melanchthon: Alien or Ally?* (1946); Holborn, Hajo, *Ulrich von Hutten and the German Reformation* (1937); Hyma, A., *Luther's Theological Development from Erfurt to Augsburg* (1928); Pascal, Roy, *The Social Basis of the German Reformation* (1933); Reu, Michael, *The Augsburg Confession* (1930); Richardson, J. W., *Philip Melanchthon* (1907); Schapiro, J. S., *Social Reform and the Reformation* (1909); Smith, Preserved, *Erasmus. A Study of His Life, Ideals, and Place in History* (1923). For the spread of Lutheranism see: Dunckley, E. H., *The Reformation in Denmark* (1948); Waddams, H. M., *The Swedish Church* (1946); Willson, T. B., *History of Church and State in Norway* (1903); Fox, Paul, *The Reformation in Poland* (1924); Toth, W., "Highlights of the Hungarian Reformation," *Church History,* IX (1940).

THE REFORMATION IN SWITZERLAND AND FRANCE

See the general works of Grimm, Bainton and Smith cited above. Two good studies of Calvin are: Hunt, R. N. C., *Calvin* (1933); and Walker, W., *John Calvin* (1906).

Others are: Breen, Q., *John Calvin: A Study in French Humanism* (1931); Harkness, G., *John Calvin. The Man and His Ethics* (1931); Mackinnon, James, *Calvin and the Reformation* (1936); McNeill, J. T., *John Calvin on God and Political Duty* (1950). The translation of Calvin's *Institutes* by J. Allen has been revised by B. B. Warfield (2 vols., 1936). See also Kerr, H. (ed.), *A Compend of the Institutes of the Christian Religion* (1939). For Zwingli see: Farner, O., *Zwingli the Reformer* (1952); Jackson, S. M., *Huldreich Zwingli: The Reformer of German Switzerland* (1900). For various aspects of the Reformation in France see: Armstrong, E., *The French Wars of Religion* (2nd ed., 1904); Baird, Henry M., *History of the Rise of the Huguenots of France* (2 vols., 1900) and *The Huguenots and Henry of Navarre* (2 vols., 1909); Grant, A. J., *The Huguenots* (1934); Kelly, C. G., *French Protestantism, 1559–1562* (1918); Palm, F. C., *Calvinism and the Religious Wars* (1932) and *Politics and Religion in Sixteenth Century France* (1927); Thompson, J. W., *Wars of Religion in France, 1559–1576: The Huguenots, Catherine de' Medici, and Philip II* (2nd ed., 1914); Dodge, Guy, *The Political Theory of the Huguenots of the Dispersion* (1947). There are biographies of Henry of Navarre by Sedgwick, H. D. (1930); Slocombe, G. (1931); and Willert, P. F. (1893). See also Van Dyke, P., *Catherine de' Medicis* (2 vols., 1922).

CHAPTER 9 The Age of the Reformation, 1517–1598 (2)

THE ENGLISH REFORMATION

See the general histories of the Tudor period cited in Chapter VII, and the general histories of the Reformation cited in Chapter VIII. Two Protestant accounts are: Parker, Thomas M., *The English Reformation to 1558* (1950); and Powicke, F. M., *The Reformation in England* (1941). Two Catholic accounts are: Constant, G., *The Reformation in England* (2 vols., 1935, 1942); Hughes, Philip, *The Reformation in England* (Vols. I and II, 1950, 1954). For special aspects see: Mackinnon, J., *The Origins of the Reformation* (1939); Gasquet, F. A., Cardinal, *Eve of the Reformation* (3rd ed., 1905); Marti, O. A., *Economic Causes of the Reformation in England* (1929); Baskerville, G., *English Monks and the Suppression of the Monasteries* (1940); Birt, H. N., *Elizabethan Religious Settlement* (1907); Bishop, E., *Edward VI and the Book of Common Prayer* (1891); Cremeans, C. D., *The Reception of Calvinistic Thought in England* (1949); Deanesly, M., *The Lollard Bible* (1920); Foxe, John, *Acts and Monuments* (8 vols., 3rd. ed., London, 1870); Garrett, C. H., *The Marian Exiles* (1938); Gasquet, P. A., *Henry VIII and the English Monasteries* (6th ed., 1895); Jordan, W. K., *Development of Religious Toleration in England* (4 vols., 1932–1940), Vol. I; Read, Conyers, *Social and Political Forces in the English Reformation* (1953); Rupp, E. G., *Studies in the Making of the English Protestant Tradition* (1949). In addition to the various biographies listed in Chapter VII see: Gray, C. M., *Hugh Latimer* (1949); Hutchinson, F. E., *Cranmer and the English Reformation* (1951); Merriman, R. B., *The Life and Letters of Thomas Cromwell* (2 vols., 1902); Pollard, A. F., *Thomas Cranmer* (1904); Pollard, A. F., *Wolsey* (1929); Prescott, H. F. M., *Mary Tudor* (rev. ed., 1953); Schenk, W., *Reginald Pole, Cardinal of England* (1950).

THE REFORMATION IN SCOTLAND

Knox, John, *History of the Reformation in Scotland* (ed. W. C. Dickinson, 2 vols., 1950); Mitchell, A. F., *The Scottish Reformation* (1900); Lang, A., *John Knox and the Reformation* (1905); Lang, Andrew, *The Mystery of Mary Stuart* (1904); Linklater, E., *Mary Queen of Scots* (1952); Mahon, R. H., *Mary Queen of Scots* (1924); Muir, Edwin, *John Knox: Portrait of a Calvinist* (1929).

THE RADICAL SECTS

See the following: Bainton, Roland H., *The Travail of Religious Liberty* (1951); Dale, R. W. and A. W., *History of English Congregationalism* (1907); Evans, A. P., *An Episode in the Struggle for Religious Freedom: The Sectaries of Nuremberg, 1524–1528* (1924); Haller, William, *The Rise of Puritanism* (1939); Jones, Rufus M., *Spiritual Reformers in the Sixteenth and Seventeenth Centuries* (1914); Jones, Rufus M., *Studies in Mystical Religion* (1909); Kirby, E., *William Prynne. A Study in Puritanism* (1931); Knappen, M. M., *Tudor Puritanism* (1939); Schneider, H. W., *The Puritan Mind* (1930); Smithson, R., *The Anabaptists* (1935); Wilbur, E. M., *A History of Unitarianism* (1945).

THE REFORMATION IN THE CATHOLIC CHURCH

For general accounts see: Janelle, P., *The Catholic Reformation* (1949); Jourdan, G. H., *Movement Towards Catholic Reform in the Early Sixteenth Century* (1914); Kidd, B. J., *Counter Reformation, 1550–1600* (1933). For the Jesuit Order see: Boehmer, H., *The Jesuits* (1928); Brodrick, J., *The Origins of the Jesuits* (1940), *The Progress of the Jesuits, 1556–1579* (1947), *St. Peter Canisius* (1935); Campbell, T. J., *The Jesuits, 1534–1921* (2 vols., 1921); Harney, M. P., *The Jesuits in History: The Society of Jesus Through Four Centuries* (1941). For St. Ignatius see: Dudon, P., *St. Ignatius of Loyola* (1950); Fitzpatrick, Edward A., *St. Ignatius and the Ratio Studiorum* (1933); Sedgwick, H. D., *Ignatius Loyola* (1923); Van Dyke, P., *Ignatius Loyola. The Founder of the Jesuits* (1927); O'Connor, J. F. X. (ed.), *The Autobiography of Saint Ignatius* (1900); Rickaby, J. (tr.), *The Spiritual Exercises of St. Ignatius* (2nd ed., 1923). See also: Jedin, Hubert, *A History of the Council of Trent* (2 vols., 1956); Littledale, R. F., *A Short History of the Council of Trent* (1888); Evennett, H. O., *The Cardinal of Lorraine and the Council of Trent: A Study in the Counter Reformation* (1931); Lea, H. C., *History of the Inquisition in Spain* (4 vols., 1907); Roth, C., *The Spanish Inquisition* (1938); Vacandard, E., *The Inquisition* (1908); Turberville, A. S., *The Spanish Inquisition* (1932); Betten, F. S., *The Roman Index of Forbidden Books* (1935); Burke, R., *What Is the Index?* (1952); Waugh, Evelyn, *Edmund Campion* (1946); Murray, R. H., *The Political Consequences of the Reformation* (1926); Pauck, Wilhelm, *The Heritage of the Reformation* (1950).

CHAPTER 10   The Age of Philip II

GENERAL

The following works already listed in Chapters IV, V and VII are useful: Chudoba, *Spain and the Empire;* Trevor-Davies, *The Golden Century of Spain;* Hamilton, *American Treasure and the Price Revolution in Spain;* Hume, *Spain, Its Greatness and Decay;* Klein, *The Mesta;* Salmon, *Imperial Spain;* Merriman, *Rise of the Spanish Empire,* Vol. IV.

PHILIP II

See the following: Hume, M. A. S., *Philip II* (new ed., 1911); Loth, D. G., *Philip II of Spain* (1932); Maass, E., *The Dream of Philip II* (1944); Mariejol, J. H., *Philip II, the First Modern King* (1934); Prescott, W. H., *History of the Reign of Philip the Second* (3 vols., 1855–1858 and later eds.), covers only half the reign.

THE REVOLT OF THE NETHERLANDS

See Barnouw, A. J., *Pageant of Netherlands History* (1952); Blok, J. P., *History of the People of the Netherlands* (5 vols., 1898–1912), Vol. III; Geyl, P., *The Revolt of the Netherlands, 1559–1609* (1932), *The Netherlands Divided, 1609–1648* (1936);

Merriman, R. B., *Six Contemporaneous Revolutions* (1938); Motley, J. L., *Rise of the Dutch Republic* (3 vols., 1856 and later eds.); Vlekke, B. H. M., *Evolution of the Dutch Nation* (1945); De Iongh, Jane, *Margaret of Austria, Regent of the Netherlands* (1953). See also the biographies of William the Silent by Harrison, F. (1907), Putnam, R. (2 vols., 1911), and Wedgwood, C. V. (1944).

MISCELLANEOUS

Adams, N. B., *The Heritage of Spain* (1943); Anderson, R. C., *Naval Wars in the Levant, 1559–1853* (1952); Corbett, Sir Julian, *Drake and the Tudor Navy* (2 vols., 1898); Hale, J. R., *The Great Armada* (1913); Hume, M. A. S., *Two English Queens and Philip* (1908); Parry, J. H., *The Spanish Theory of Empire in the Sixteenth Century* (1940); Slocombe, G., *Don Juan of Austria* (1935). See also the references on Spanish culture in Chapter VII.

CHAPTER 11   The Age of the Thirty Years' War

GENERAL WORKS USEFUL FOR THIS PERIOD

Clark, G. N., *The Seventeenth Century* (2nd ed., 1947); Green, V. H. H., *Renaissance and Reformation* (1952); Friedrich, C. J. H., *The Age of the Baroque, 1610–1660* (1952); Mowat, R. B., *A History of European Diplomacy 1451–1789* (1928); Ogg, David, *Europe in the Seventeenth Century* (6th ed., 1952); Rayner, R. M., *European History, 1648–1789* (1952); Reddaway, W. F., *A History of Europe, 1610–1715* (1948); Wakeman, H. O., *The Ascendancy of France, 1598–1715* (4th ed., 1921); *The Cambridge Modern History*, Vol. IV, "The Thirty Years' War."

FRANCE: HENRY IV, RICHELIEU AND MAZARIN

For general histories see: Boulenger, J., *The Seventeenth Century* (1930); Grant, A. J., *The French Monarchy, 1483–1789* (4th ed., 2 vols., 1925), Vol. I; Kitchin, G. W., *A History of France* (3 vols., 1896–1903), Vols. II–III. See also: Guérard, A., *The Life and Death of an Ideal: France in the Classical Age* (1928); Lodge, Eleanor, *Sully, Colbert, Turgot: A Chapter in French Economic History* (1931); Ogg, David (ed.), *The Grand Design of Henry IV* (1921); Palm, F. C., *The Establishment of French Absolutism, 1574–1610* (1928). For biographies of Henry IV see Chapter VIII.

On Richelieu and Mazarin see: Bailly, A., *The Cardinal Dictator. A Portrait of Richelieu* (1936); Belloc, H., *Richelieu* (1929); Burckhardt, Carl J., *Richelieu: His Rise to Power* (1940); Federn, K., *Richelieu* (1928); Lodge, Sir Richard, *Richelieu* (1920); Perkins, J. B., *Richelieu and the Growth of French Power* (1900); Wedgwood, C. V., *Richelieu and the French Monarchy* (1950); Palm, F. C., *The Economic Policies of Richelieu* (1922); Huxley, Aldous, *Grey Eminence: A Study of Religion and Politics* (1941), deals with Richelieu's confidant, Father Joseph; Hassall, A., *Mazarin* (1903, reprinted 1934); Perkins, James B., *France Under Mazarin* (2 vols., 1886); Batiffol, Louis, *Marie de' Medicis and the French Court in the XVIIth Century* (1908); Bridges, J. H., *France Under Richelieu and Colbert* (1866); Doolin, P. R., *The Fronde* (1935); Steegmuller, Francis, *La Grande Mademoiselle* (1956), sister of Louis XIII.

THE THIRTY YEARS' WAR

Gardiner, S. R., *The Thirty Years' War, 1618–1648* (1897); Gindeley, Anton, *History of the Thirty Years' War* (1884); Wedgwood, C. V., *The Thirty Years' War* (1939); Ahnlund, N., *Gustav Adolf the Great* (1940); Beller, E. A., *Propaganda in Germany During the Thirty Years' War* (1940); Fletcher, C. R. L., *Gustavus Adol-*

phus and the Struggle of Protestantism for Existence (1903); Frischauer, P., *The Imperial Crown* (1939), deals with Austria; Gade, J. A., *Christian IV* (1928); Goldsmith, M., *Queen Christina of Sweden* (1933); McMunn, Sir George, *Gustavus Adolphus, the Northern Hurricane* (1930); Schwarz, Henry F., *The Imperial Privy Council in the Seventeenth Century* (1943); Watson, F., *Wallenstein: Soldier Under Saturn* (1938); Hume, M. A. S., *The Court of Philip IV. Spain in Decadence* (1907); Trevor-Davies, R., *Spain in Decline, 1621–1700* (1955).

THE AGE OF THE BAROQUE

Friedrich's *Age of the Baroque, 1610–1660*, previously cited ties its whole discussion to the concept of the Baroque. Gilbert Highet's *The Classical Tradition* (1949) is admirable on literature. For the arts see: Webb, G. F., *Baroque Art* (1949); Fokker, T. H., *Roman Baroque Art* (1938); Sitwell, Sacheverell, *German Baroque Art* (1927), *Southern Baroque Art* (3rd ed., 1931), *Spanish Baroque Art* (1931); Weisbach, W., *Spanish Baroque Art* (1941); Wittkower, R., *Gian Lorenzo Bernini: The Sculptor of the Roman Baroque* (1955); Briggs, M. S., *Baroque Architecture* (1914); Kaufmann, E., *Architecture in the Age of Reason: Baroque and Post-Baroque in England, Italy and France* (1955); McComb, A., *The Baroque Painters of Italy* (1934); Riggs, A. S., *Velasquez* (1947); Calvert, A. F., *Murillo* (1907); Von Bode, Wilhelm, *Great Masters of Dutch and Flemish Painting* (1909); Burckhardt, J., *Rubens* (1950); Cammaerts, W., *Rubens, Painter and Diplomat* (1932); Trivas, N. S., *The Paintings of Franz Hals* (1941); Valentiner, W. R., *Franz Hals* (1923); Lucas, E. V., *Vermeer the Magical* (1929); Cust, Lionel, *Anthony Van Dyck* (1911); Rosenberg, Jakob, *Rembrandt* (2 vols., 1948); Hind, Arthur M., *Rembrandt* (1932); Bredius, A. (ed.), *The Paintings of Rembrandt* (1942); Bukofzer, M. F., *Music in the Baroque Era* (1947); Parry, C. H. H., *The Music of the Seventeenth Century* (1902); Streatfield, R. A., *The Opera* (5th ed., 1925); Triggs, H. Inigo, *Garden Craft in Europe* (1913). See also references in Ch. XIII on culture of Age of Louis XIV.

CHAPTER 12   The Struggle for Parliamentary Government in England

HISTORIES OF THE PERIOD 1603–1660

Trevelyan, G. M., *England Under the Stuarts* (new ed., 1933); Davies, Godfrey, *The Early Stuarts, 1603–1660* (1937); Gardiner, S. R., *History of England . . . 1603–1642* (10 vols., 1863–1882), *History of the Great Civil War, 1642–1649* (4 vols., 1886), *History of the Commonwealth and Protectorate, 1649–1656* (3 vols., 1894–1903); Firth, C. H., *The Last Years of the Protectorate, 1656–1658* (2 vols., 1909), a continuation of Gardiner; Davies, Godfrey, *The Restoration of Charles II, 1658–1660* (1955); Wedgwood, C. V., *The King's Peace, 1637–1641* (1955), the first volume of a new history of the Civil War.

POLITICAL AND CONSTITUTIONAL PROBLEMS OF THE PURITAN REVOLUTION

Allen, J. W., *English Political Thought, 1603–1660* (1938); Brown, L. F., *The Political Activities of the Baptists and Fifth-Monarchy Men in England During the Interregnum* (1913); Figgis, J. N., *The Theory of the Divine Right of Kings* (new ed., 1922); Gardiner, S. R. (ed.), *The Constitutional Documents of the Puritan Revolution, 1625–1660* (1906); Judson, Margaret A., *The Crisis of the Constitution: An Essay in Constitutional and Political Thought, 1603–1645* (1949); McIlwain, C. H., *The High Court of Parliament and Its Supremacy* (1910); McIlwain, C. H. (ed.), *The Political Works of James I* (1918); Tanner, J. R., *English Constitutional*

Conflicts in the Seventeenth Century, 1603–1689 (new ed., 1939); Wormuth, F. D., *The Royal Prerogative, 1603–1649* (1939), *The Origins of Modern Constitutionalism* (1949); Young, G. M., *Charles I and Cromwell* (1935); Bowen, C. D., *The Lion and the Throne: The Life and Times of Sir Edward Coke* (1957).

RELIGIOUS ASPECTS OF THE PURITAN REVOLUTION

Berens, L. H., *The Digger Movement in the Days of the Commonwealth* (1906); Braithwaite, W. C., *The Beginnings of Quakerism* (1912); Jones, Rufus M., *Mysticism and Democracy in the English Commonwealth* (1932); Jordan, W. K., *The Development of Religious Toleration in England from the Accession of James I to the Convention of the Long Parliament, 1603–1640* (1936), *The Development of Religious Toleration in England, 1640–1660* (1938); Pease, T. C., *The Leveller Movement* (1916); Schenk, W., *The Concern for Social Justice in the Puritan Revolution* (1948); Schneider, H. W., *The Puritan Mind* (1930).

BIOGRAPHIES

On Oliver Cromwell, in addition to *The Writings and Speeches,* edited by Abbott, W. C. (4 vols., 1938–1947), there are biographies by Buchan, J. (1934), Firth, C. H. (1935), Gardiner, S. R. (1901), Morley, J. (1901) and Wedgwood, C. V. (1939). See also: Barker, A. E., *Milton and the Puritan Dilemma, 1641–1660* (1942); Hexter, J. H., *The Reign of King Pym* (1941); Higham, F. M. G., *Charles I* (1932); Kirby, E., *William Prynne* (1931); Pakenham, P., *Charles I* (1936); Trevor-Roper, H. R., *Archbishop Laud, 1573–1645* (1940); Wedgwood, C. V., *Strafford, 1593–1641* (1949); Williams, C., *James I* (1953); Williamson, H. R., *John Hampden* (1933); Wolfe, Don M., *Milton in the Puritan Revolution* (1941); Wormald, H. G., *Clarendon: Politics, History and Religion, 1640–1660* (1951).

MISCELLANEOUS ASPECTS, 1603–1660

Ashley, M. P., *Financial and Commercial Policy Under the Cromwellian Protectorate* (1934); Firth, C. H., *Cromwell's Army* (1902); Gooch, G. P., *History of English Democratic Ideas in the Seventeenth Century* (rev. ed., 1927); James, Margaret, *Social Problems and Policy During the Puritan Revolution, 1640–1660* (1930); Mackie, J. D., *Cavalier and Puritan* (rev. ed., 1936); Willey, Basil, *The Seventeenth Century Background* (1934); Notestein, W., *The English People on the Eve of Colonization* (1954).

GENERAL HISTORIES, 1660–1714

Trevelyan, G. M., *England Under the Stuarts* (new ed., 1933); Clark, G. N., *The Later Stuarts, 1660–1714* (1934); Ogg, David, *England in the Reign of Charles II* (2 vols., 2nd ed., 1955), *England in the Reign of James II and William III* (1955); Trevelyan, G. M., *England Under Queen Anne* (3 vols., 1930–1934).

SPECIAL ASPECTS

Bryant, A., *The England of Charles II* (1935); Feiling, Keith, *Early History of the Tory Party, 1640–1714* (1924); Morgan, W. T., *English Political Parties and Leaders in the Reign of Queen Anne, 1702–1710* (1920); Plum, Harry G., *Restoration Puritanism: A Study in the Growth of English Liberty* (1943); Tanner, J. R., *Samuel Pepys and the Royal Navy* (1920); Trevelyan, G. M., *The English Revolution, 1688–1689* (2nd ed., 1946).

BIOGRAPHIES

For Charles II see the biographies by Airy, O. (1901) and Bryant, Arthur (1946). For James II there are biographies by Belloc, H. (1928), Higham, F. G. M. (1934) and Turner, F. C. (1949). See also: Traill, H. D., *William III* (new ed., 1926); Renier, G. J., *William of Orange* (1933); Ogg, D., *William III* (1956); Connell, N., *Anne, the Last Stuart Monarch* (1937); Bryant, A., *Samuel Pepys* (3 vols., 1933–1939); Tanner, J. R., *Mr. Pepys* (1925); Churchill, Winston S., *Marlborough: His Life and Times* (6 vols., 1933–1938); Ponsonby, A., *John Evelyn* (1934).

CHAPTER 13   The Age of Louis XIV

GENERAL SURVEYS

In addition to the works of Boulenger, Clark, Guérard, Ogg, Rayner and Wakeman cited under Chapter 11 above see: *The Cambridge Modern History*, Vol. V, "The Age of Louis XIV"; Nussbaum, F. L., *The Triumph of Science and Reason, 1660–1685* (1953); Wolf, John B., *The Emergence of the Great Powers, 1685–1715* (1951); Packard, L. B., *The Age of Louis XIV* (1929); Lewis, W. H., *The Splendid Century* (1954); Lough, J., *An Introduction to Seventeenth Century France* (1954). Two fundamental accounts in French are: Lavisse, E., *Louis XIV de 1643 à 1685* (1911) and *Louis XIV, la fin du règne, 1685–1715* (1911), comprising Volumes VII and VIII of the *Histoire de France* edited by Lavisse; and Saint-Léger, A. de, and Sagnac, P., *La Prépondérance française: Louis XIV, 1661–1715* (1935), in the *Peuples et civilisations* series.

BIOGRAPHIES OF LOUIS XIV

In the absence of a definitive biography see: Ashley, M., *Louis XIV and the Greatness of France* (1948); Bertrand, L., *Louis XIV* (1928); Forester, C. S., *Louis XIV* (1928); Hassall, A., *Louis XIV and the Zenith of the French Monarchy* (1914); Ogg, David, *Louis XIV* (1933); Petrie, Sir Charles, *Louis XIV* (1940).

POLITICS AND ADMINISTRATION

King, James E., *Science and Rationalism in the Government of Louis XIV, 1661–1683* (1949); Perkins, James B., *France Under the Regency, with a Review of the Administration of Louis XIV* (1892); Halévy, D., *Vauban, Builder of Fortresses* (1925); Dodge, Guy, *The Political Theory of the Huguenots of the Dispersion* (1947); Sée, Henri, *Les Idées politiques en France au XVIIIᵉ siècle* (1923); Weygand, M., *Turenne* (1930).

ECONOMICS

Cole, C. W., *French Mercantilist Doctrines Before Colbert* (1931), *Colbert and a Century of French Mercantilism* (2 vols., 1939), *French Mercantilism, 1683–1700* (1943); Heckscher, Eli, *Mercantilism* (2 vols., 1935); Lodge, Eleanor, *Sully, Colbert, Turgot. A Chapter in French Economic History* (1931); Roberts, H. van D., *Boisguillebert, Economist of the Reign of Louis XIV* (1935); Sargent, A. J., *The Economic Policy of Colbert* (1899).

RELIGION

Abercrombie, N., *The Origins of Jansenism* (1936); Baird, H. M., *The Huguenots and the Revocation of the Edict of Nantes* (2 vols., 1895); Clark, William, *Pascal and the Port-Royalists* (1902); Grant, A. J., *The Huguenots* (1934); Sanders, E. K., *Jacques Benigne Bossuet* (1921).

SOCIETY

Bradby, G. F., *The Great Days of Versailles* (1927); Farmer, James E., *Versailles and the Court Under Louis XIV* (1906); Hugon, Cecile, *Social France in the Seventeenth Century* (1911); Sagnac, P., *La Formation de la société française moderne* (1945); Saint-Simon, Duc de, *Memoirs*, transl. by B. St. John (3 vols., 1889); Taillandier, St. René, *The Royal Ark. Louis XIV and His Court* (1931).

LITERATURE AND THE ARTS

For literary studies see: Tilley, Arthur A. (ed.), *Modern France, A Companion to French Studies* (1922), *From Montaigne to Molière* (2nd revised ed., 1923), *The De-*

cline of the Age of Louis XIV: French Literature, 1687–1715 (1929); Wright, C. H. C., *French Classicism* (1920); Hazard, P., *The European Mind: The Critical Years (1680–1715)* (1953); Clark, A. F. B., *Boileau and the French Classical Critics in England* (1925), *Jean Racine* (1940); Duclaux, M., *Racine* (1925); Hamel, F., *Jean de la Fontaine* (1911); Matthews, Brander, *Molière—His Life and His Works* (new ed., 1926); Robinson, Howard, *Bayle the Sceptic* (1931); Tilley, A., *Madame de Sévigné* (1936); Vincent, L. H., *Corneille* (1901). See also Blomfield, Sir R. T., *A History of French Architecture From the Death of Mazarin Till the Death of Louis XV, 1661–1774* (2 vols., 1921); Blunt, A., *Art and Architecture in France, 1500 to 1700* (1954).

CHAPTER 14   Monarchy in Central Europe

GENERAL ACCOUNTS
Treatments of Central Europe in the late seventeenth century are found in Nussbaum, F. L., *The Triumph of Science and Reason, 1660–1685* (1953), Wolf, John B., *The Emergence of the Great Powers, 1685–1715* (1951) and *The Cambridge Modern History*, Vols. V and VI. See also Wakeman, Mowat and Rayner, cited in Chapter XI.

THE HAPSBURG EMPIRE
Eckhardt, F., *A Short History of the Hungarian People* (1931); Frischauer, Paul, *Prince Eugene: A Man and a Hundred Years of History* (1934), *The Imperial Crown: The Story of the Rise and Fall of the Holy Roman and Austrian Empires* (1939); Halecky, O., *Borderlands of Western Civilization* (1952); Kosary, D. G., *A History of Hungary* (1941); Léger, L., *History of Austria-Hungary* (1889); MacMunn, Sir George, *Prince Eugene: Twin Marshal with Marlborough* (1934); Marczali, H., *Hungary in the Eighteenth Century* (1910); Marriott, J. A. R., *The Eastern Question. An Historical Study in European Diplomacy* (3rd. rev. ed., 1924); Morton, J. B., *Sobieski: King of Poland* (1932); Schwarz, H. F., *The Imperial Privy Council in the Seventeenth Century* (1943); Thomson, S. Harrison, *Czechoslovakia in European History* (1943).

BRANDENBURG-PRUSSIA TO 1713
In addition to the relevant sections in Nussbaum, Wolf and *The Cambridge Modern History*, Vol. V, see: Barraclough, G., *The Origins of Modern Germany* (1946); Flenley, Ralph, *Modern German History* (1953); Shuster, G. H., and Bergstraesser, A., *Germany. A Short History* (1944). For the rise of Brandenburg-Prussia see: Carsten, F. L., *The Origins of Prussia* (1954); Fay, S. B., *The Rise of Brandenburg-Prussia to 1786* (1937); Marriott, J. A. R., and Robertson, C. G., *The Evolution of Prussia* (rev. ed., 1940). Ranke, L. von, *Memoirs of the House of Brandenburg, and History of Prussia During the 17th and 18th Centuries* (3 vols., 1849), although old is still fundamentally important. See also: Tuttle, Herbert, *History of Prussia to the Accession of Frederick the Great* (1884); Innes, A. D., *The Hohenzollern* (1915); Lavisse, E., *Etudes sur l'histoire de Prusse* (1912); Schevill, F., *The Great Elector* (1947); Fay, S. B., "The Beginnings of the Standing Army in Prussia," *American Historical Review*, XXII (1917); Carsten, F. L., "The Great Elector and the Foundation of the Hohenzollern Despotism," *English Historical Review*, LXV (1950); Richardson, O. H., "The Great Elector and Religious Toleration," *English Historical Review*, XXV (1910).

CHAPTER 15   Monarchy in Eastern Europe

RUSSIA
General histories which are useful in addition to those cited in the first section of the Bibliography are: Bain, R. N., *Slavonic Europe: A Political History of Poland*

and Russia from 1447 to 1796 (1908); Kerner, R. J., *The Urge to the Sea: The Course of Russian History* (1942); Mirsky, D. S., *Russia: A Social History* (reprint, 1942); Spector, Ivar, *An Introduction to Russian History and Culture* (1949); Sumner, B. H., *A Short History of Russia* (1943); Walsh, W. B. (ed.), *Readings in Russian History* (enl. ed., 1951).

On the period before Peter the Great see: Paszkiewicz, Henryk, *The Origin of Russia* (1956); Graham, S., *Boris Godunov* (1933), *Ivan the Terrible* (1933); Waliszewski, K., *Ivan the Terrible* (1904); Lamb, Harold, *The March of Muscovy: Ivan the Terrible and the Growth of the Russian Empire, 1400–1648* (1948); Golder, F. A., *Russian Expansion on the Pacific, 1641–1850* (1914); Lobanov-Rostovsky, A., *Russia and Asia* (1933); O'Brien, C. B., *Russia Under Two Tsars, 1682–1689: The Regency of Sophia Alekseevna* (1952).

On Peter the Great see: Graham, Stephen, *Peter the Great* (2nd ed., 1950); Lamb, H., *The City and the Tsar: Peter the Great and the Move to the West, 1648–1762* (1948); Schuyler, E., *Peter the Great* (2 vols., 1884); Sumner, B. H., *Peter the Great and the Emergence of Russia* (1950), *Peter the Great and the Ottoman Empire* (1949); Waliszewski, K., *Peter the Great* (2 vols., 1897). See also: Hamilton, George H., *The Art and Architecture of Russia* (1954); Leroy-Beaulieu, A., *The Empire of the Tsars and the Russians* (3 vols., 1893–1896); Masaryk, T. G., *The Spirit of Russia* (2 vols., rev. ed., 1955); Putnam, Peter, *Seven Britons in Imperial Russia, 1698–1812* (1952).

SCANDINAVIA AND POLAND

See, in addition to the general histories listed in the first section of the Bibliography: Bain, R. N., *Scandinavia: A Political History* (1905), *Charles XII and the Collapse of the Swedish Empire, 1682–1719* (1895); Gade, J. A., *Charles the Twelfth* (1916); Godley, E., *Charles XII of Sweden: A Study in Kingship* (1928); Reddaway, W. F., and others (eds.), *The Cambridge History of Poland*, Vol. II, *From Augustus II to Pilsudski, 1697–1935* (1941); Halecki, O., *A History of Poland* (1943).

CHAPTER 16   War and Diplomacy in Europe, 1713–1789

GENERAL SURVEYS

A good account of war and diplomacy in the eighteenth century is given in the following three volumes of *The Rise of Modern Europe* series: Roberts, Penfield, *The Quest for Security, 1715–1740* (1947); Dorn, Walter L., *Competition for Empire, 1740–1763* (1940); Gershoy, Leo, *From Despotism to Revolution, 1763–1789* (1944). See also: *The Cambridge Modern History*, Vol. VI; Buffinton, A. H., *The Second Hundred Years' War, 1689–1815* (1929); Hassall, A., *The Balance of Power, 1715–1789* (4th ed., 1921); Mowat, R. B., *A History of European Diplomacy, 1451–1789* (1928); Rayner, R. M., *European History, 1648 to 1789* (1952); Petrie, Sir Charles, *Diplomatic History, 1713–1933* (1946).

SPECIAL STUDIES

Armstrong, E., *Elizabeth Farnese* (1892); Harcourt-Smith, S., *Cardinal of Spain: The Life and Strange Career of Alberoni* (1944); Wilson, A. M., *French Foreign Policy During the Administration of Cardinal Fleury* (1936); Lodge, Sir Richard, *Studies in Eighteenth Century Diplomacy, 1740–1748* (1930), *Great Britain and Prussia in the Eighteenth Century* (1923); Conn, S., *Gibraltar in British Diplomacy in the Eighteenth Century* (1942); Malcolm-Smith, E., *British Diplomacy in the 18th Century, 1700–1789* (1937); Ward, Sir A. W., *Great Britain and Hanover* (1899); Harrison, F., *Chatham* (1922); Tunstall, W. C. B., *William Pitt, Earl of*

*Chatham (*1938); Williams, Basil, *The Life of William Pitt, Earl of Chatham* (2 vols., 1914); Atkinson, C. T., *A History of Germany, 1715–1818* (1908); Temperley, H. W. V., *Frederick the Great and Kaiser Joseph* (1915). See also the biographies of Frederick II of Prussia cited in Chapter XX. An important study is: Nef, J. U., *War and Human Progress: On the Rise of Industrial Civilization* (1950).

THE PARTITIONS OF POLAND AND THE EASTERN QUESTION

For Poland see, in addition to *The Cambridge History of Poland* cited in Chapter XV: Lord, R. H., *The Second Partition of Poland. A Study in Diplomatic History* (1915); Bain, R. N., *The Last King of Poland and His Contemporaries* (1909). For the Eastern Question see: Marriott, J. A. R., *The Eastern Question* (3rd rev. ed., 1924); Creasy, Sir Edward, *History of the Ottoman Turks* (new ed., by Coolidge, A. C., and Claflin, W. H., 1906); Sorel, A., *The Eastern Question in the Eighteenth Century* (1898).

CHAPTER 17 Overseas Expansion and Imperial Conflict, 1600–1789

BACKGROUNDS

Many of the references cited in Chapter V, especially Abbott's *Expansion of Europe,* continue to be useful.

THE DUTCH COLONIAL EMPIRE

Useful general accounts are: Hyma, A., *The Dutch in the Far East* (1942); Furnivall, J. S., *Netherlands India* (1944); Vandenbosch, A., *The Dutch East Indies* (1942); Vlekke, B. H. M., *Nusantara: A History of the East Indian Archipelago* (1943); Barbour, V., *Capitalism in Amsterdam During the 17th Century* (1950); Day, C., *Policy and Administration of the Dutch in Java* (1904); Edmundson, G., *Anglo-Dutch Rivalry During the First Half of the Seventeenth Century* (1911); Shepherd, W. R., *The Story of New Amsterdam* (1926); Van Loon, H. W., *Golden Book of the Dutch Navigators* (1916).

THE RISE OF THE BRITISH EMPIRE

For general accounts see: Carrington, C. E., *The British Overseas: Exploits of a Nation of Shopkeepers* (1950); Egerton, H. E., *Short History of British Colonial Policy, 1606–1909* (12th rev. ed., 1950); Innes, A. D., *The Maritime and Colonial Expansion of England Under the Stuarts, 1603–1714* (1931); Rose, J. H., Newton, A. P. and Benians, E. A. (eds.), *The Cambridge History of the British Empire,* Vols. I and II (1929–1940); Seeley, J. R., *The Expansion of England* (new ed., 1925); Williamson, J. A., *A Short History of British Expansion* (2 vols., 2nd ed., 1930), *Great Britain and the Empire* (2nd ed., 1953), and *Cook and the Opening of the Pacific* (1948). For the American and West Indian settlements see: Andrews, C. M., *The Colonial Period of American History* (3 vols., 1934–1937); Beer, G. L., *The Origins of the British Colonial System, 1578–1660* (1908), and *The Old Colonial System, 1660–1754* (1912); Gipson, L. H., *The British Empire Before the American Revolution* (8 vols., 1936–1954); Jernegan, M. W., *The American Colonies, 1492–1750* (1929); Wertenbaker, T. J., *The First Americans, 1607–1690* (1927); Newton, A. P., *European Nations in the West Indies, 1493–1688* (1933). For India see: Allan, J., Haig, W. T., and Dodwell, H. H. (eds.), *The Cambridge Shorter History of India* (1934); Innes, A. D., *Short History of the British in India* (5th ed., 1910); Tilby, A. W., *British India, 1600–1828* (2nd rev. ed., 1911); Furber, Holden, *John Company at Work. A Study of European Expansion in India in the Late Eighteenth Century* (1948). On the slave trade see: Dow, G. F., *Slave Ships and Slaving* (1927); and Wyndham, H. A., *The Atlantic and Slavery* (1935).

FRANCE IN AMERICA AND THE INDIES

See: Priestley, H. I., *France Overseas Through the Old Regime* (1939); Dalgliesh, W. H., *The Perpetual Company of the Indies in the Days of Dupleix* (1933); Roberts, W. A., *The French in the West Indies* (1942); Crouse, N. M., *French Pioneers in the West Indies, 1624–1664* (1940), and *The French Struggle for the West Indies, 1665–1713* (1943); Burt, A. L., *The Old Province of Quebec* (1933); Wrong, G. M., *The Rise and Fall of New France* (2 vols., 1928). Two of the volumes by Francis Parkman, *Count Frontenac and New France Under Louis XIV* (1877), and *La Salle and the Discovery of the Great West* (1869), can still be read with profit.

THE IMPERIAL DUEL BETWEEN ENGLAND AND FRANCE

Graham, G. S., *Empire of the North Atlantic: The Maritime Struggle for North America* (1950); Mahan, A. T., *The Influence of Sea Power Upon History, 1660–1783* (1897); Pares, R., *War and Trade in the West Indies, 1739–1763* (1936); Pitman, F. W., *The Development of the British West Indies, 1700–1763* (1917); Schuyler, R. L., *The Fall of the Old Colonial System: A Study in British Free Trade, 1770–1870* (1945); Waugh, W. T., *James Wolfe* (1931); Whitton, F. E., *Wolfe and North America* (1929); Wrong, G. M., *The Conquest of New France* (1918); Davies, A. M., *Clive of Plassey* (1939); Dodwell, H. H., *Dupleix and Clive* (1920); Moon, P., *Warren Hastings and British India* (1949); Sutherland, L. S., *The East India Company in Eighteenth Century Politics* (1953); Rashed, Z. E., *The Peace of Paris, 1763* (1952).

THE AMERICAN REVOLUTION

From the enormous literature on the American Revolution the following are selected: Alden, J. R., *The American Revolution* (1954); Greene, E. B., *The Revolutionary Generation, 1763–1790* (1943); Becker, Carl L., *The Eve of the Revolution* (1918); Miller, J. C., *Origins of the American Revolution* (1943); Andrews, C. M., *The Colonial Background of the American Revolution* (rev. ed., 1931); Becker, Carl L., *The Declaration of Independence* (1922); Schlesinger, A. M., *Colonial Merchants and the American Revolution* (1918); McIlwain, C. H., *The American Revolution: A Constitutional Interpretation* (1923); Coupland, Sir Reginald, *The American Revolution and the British Empire* (1930); Bemis, S. F., *The Diplomacy of the American Revolution* (1935).

CHAPTER 18   The Intellectual Revolution: The World of Nature

THE NATURE OF THE ENLIGHTENMENT

See the general works on intellectual history by Brinton, Randall, Preserved Smith and Friedell listed in the introduction to the Bibliography. For the general setting see also Clark, G. N., *The Seventeenth Century* (1929). See also the histories of science listed in Chapter VII, especially Hall, *The Scientific Revolution,* Butterfield's *Origins of Modern Science* and Wolf's *History of Science, Technology and Philosophy in the 16th and 17th Centuries.* Works of fundamental importance on the Intellectual Revolution are: Burtt, E. A., *The Metaphysical Foundations of Modern Physical Science* (rev. ed., 1955); Cassirer, E., *The Philosophy of the Enlightenment* (1951, reprinted, 1955); Whitehead, A. N., *Science and the Modern World* (1925).

DESCARTES AND CARTESIANISM

The *Discourse on Method* is available in numerous editions. See also: Balz, A. G. A., *Descartes and the Modern Mind* (1952); Ginzburg, B., *The Adventure of Science* (1930), for the relations of Cartesianism and Newtonianism; Iverach, J., *Descartes, Spinoza, and the New Philosophy* (1904); Mellone, S. H., *The Dawn of Modern*

Thought: Descartes, Spinoza, Leibniz (1930); Rogers, A. K., *A Student's History of Philosophy* (3rd ed., 1934); Roth, L., *Descartes: Discourse on Method* (1937); Scott, J. F., *The Scientific Work of René Descartes* (1952).

THE NEWTONIAN SYNTHESIS

In addition to the general histories of science listed above see: Andrade, E. N., *Isaac Newton* (1950); Brodetsky, S., *Sir Isaac Newton* (1928); Clark, G. N., *Science and Social Welfare in the Age of Newton* (1937); Jeans, Sir James, *The Growth of Physical Science* (1951); More, L. T., *Isaac Newton: A Biography* (1934); Sullivan, J. W. N., *Sir Isaac Newton* (1938); Strong, E. W., "Newton and God," *Journal of the History of Ideas*, XIII (1952).

THE PHYSICAL SCIENCES

For the inventions see: Usher, A. P., *A History of Mechanical Inventions* (1929); Bell, Louis, *The Telescope* (1922); Clay, R. S., and Court, T. H., *History of the Microscope* (1932). For specific sciences Preserved Smith's *History of Modern Culture*, Vol. II, provides a useful summary. See also: Hart, Ivor B., *Makers of Science: Mathematics, Physics, Astronomy* (1924); Macpherson, H. C., *Makers of Modern Astronomy* (1933); Crew, H., *Rise of Modern Physics* (2nd ed., 1935); Semat, H., *Physics in the Modern World* (1949); Farber, E., *The Evolution of Chemistry* (1952); More, Louis T., *The Life and Works of the Honourable Robert Boyle* (1944); Bell, A. E., *Christian Huygens and the Development of Science in the Seventeenth Century* (1947).

THE BIOLOGICAL SCIENCES AND MEDICINE

Singer, Charles, *History of Biology* (1950); Nordenskiold, E., *The History of Biology* (1928); Shryock, R. H., *The Development of Modern Medicine: An Interpretation of the Social and Scientific Factors Involved* (2nd rev. ed., 1947); Adams, F. D., *The Birth and Development of the Geological Sciences* (1938); Raven, C. E., *John Ray* (1950).

THE POPULARIZATION OF SCIENCE

See, in addition to Preserved Smith's *History of Modern Culture*, Vol. II: Brown, Harcourt, *Scientific Organizations in Seventeenth Century France, 1620–1680* (1934); Lyons, Sir H. G., *The Royal Society, 1660–1940* (1944); Ornstein, Martha, *The Role of the Scientific Societies in the Seventeenth Century* (3rd ed., 1938).

CHAPTER 19 The Intellectual Revolution: The World of Man

GENERAL

Valuable analyses are provided in Preserved Smith's *History of Modern Culture*, Vol. II, in Randall's *Making of the Modern Mind* and in Brinton's *Ideas and Men*, already cited. See also the volumes by Nussbaum, Wolf, Roberts, Dorn and Gershoy in *The Rise of Modern Europe* series. Many of the references given below in Chapter XXI are useful. See also, for general interpretation: Lovejoy, A. O., *The Great Chain of Being* (1936); and Hazard, P., *European Thought in the Eighteenth Century from Montesquieu to Lessing* (1954).

HISTORY

Good general treatments of historical writing are: Thompson, J. W., *History of Historical Writing* (2 vols., 1942); Barnes, H. E., *History of Historical Writing* (1937). See also: Black, J. B., *The Art of History: A Study of Four Great Historians of the Eighteenth Century* (1926), discussing Voltaire, Hume, Robertson and Gibbon; Low, David M., *Edward Gibbon, 1734–1794* (1937); Torrey, N., *The Spirit of Voltaire* (1938); Robinson, Howard, *Bayle the Sceptic* (1931); Cheyne, T. K., *Founders of Old Testament Criticism* (1893).

POLITICAL THOUGHT

Useful general works include: Sabine, G. H., *A History of Political Theory* (1937); Cook, Thomas I., *The History of Political Philosophy from Plato to Burke* (1936); Dunning, W. A., *History of Political Theories from Luther to Montesquieu* (1905). See also: Hearnshaw, F. J. C. (ed.), *Social and Political Ideas of Some Great Thinkers of the Sixteenth and Seventeenth Centuries* (new ed., 1945), *Social and Political Ideas of Some Great French Thinkers of the Age of Reason* (1931); Gooch, G. P., *Political Thought in England from Bacon to Halifax* (2nd ed., 1923), *History of English Democratic Ideas in the Seventeenth Century* (rev. ed., 1927); Laski, H. J., *The Rise of European Liberalism* (1936), *Political Thought in England from Locke to Bentham* (1920); Catlin, G. E. C., *Thomas Hobbes* (1922); Strauss, Leo, *The Political Philosophy of Hobbes* (1936); Aaron, R. I., *John Locke* (1937); Sorel, A., *Montesquieu* (1888); Vaughan, C. E. (ed.), *The Political Writings of Rousseau* (2 vols., 1916); Cobban, A., *Rousseau and the Modern State* (1934); Mowat, R. B., *Jean-Jacques Rousseau* (1938); Wright, E. H., *The Meaning of Rousseau* (1929); Maestro, M. T., *Voltaire and Beccaria as Reformers of Criminal Law* (1942); Phillipson, C., *Three Criminal Law Reformers: Beccaria, Bentham, Romilly* (1923); Guthrie, W. B., *Socialism Before the French Revolution, A History* (1907); Gray, Alexander, *The Socialist Tradition from Moses to Lenin* (1946); Peixotto, J., *The French Revolution and Modern French Socialism* (1901).

ECONOMIC THOUGHT

See the following general treatises: Gide, C., and Rist, C., *History of Economic Doctrines from the Time of the Physiocrats to the Present Day* (latest ed., 1948); Gray, Alexander, *The Development of Economic Doctrine* (1935); Haney, Lewis H., *History of Economic Thought* (4th ed., 1949). See also: Higgs, Henry, *The Physiocrats* (reprinted, 1952); Haldane, R. B. H., *Life of Adam Smith* (1887); Scott, William R., *Adam Smith as Student and Professor* (1937); Say, Leon, *Turgot* (1888).

EDUCATION

Boyd, William, *The History of Western Education* (3rd ed., 1932); Eby, F., *The Development of Modern Education* (1952); Spinka, M., *John Amos Comenius* (1943); Adamson, J. W. (ed.), *The Educational Writings of John Locke* (1922); Davidson, T., *Rousseau and Education According to Nature* (1907).

PHILOSOPHY

Useful approaches will be found in the works of Preserved Smith, Lovejoy, Randall and Cassirer already cited. For a general history consult Rogers, A. K., *A Student's History of Philosophy* (3rd ed., 1934). In addition to the monographs of Iverach and Mellone listed in Chapter XVIII see: Hibben, J. G., *The Philosophy of the Enlightenment* (1910); Burtt, E. A., *The English Philosophers from Bacon to Mill* (1939); Carr, H. W., *Leibniz* (1929); Browne, Lewis, *Blessed Spinoza* (1932); Hendel, C. W., Jr., *Studies in the Philosophy of David Hume* (1925).

RELIGION

For the currents of rationalism, deism and skepticism see, in addition to the work of Hazard cited in Chapter XIII, the following: Stephen, Sir Leslie, *History of English Thought in the Eighteenth Century* (2 vols., 3rd ed., 1902), old but still useful; Becker, Carl L., *The Heavenly City of the Eighteenth Century Philosophers* (1932);

McCloy, S. T., *Gibbon's Antagonism to Christianity* (1933); Palmer, R. R., *Catholics and Unbelievers in Eighteenth Century France* (1939); Stromberg, R., *Religious Liberalism in Eighteenth Century England* (1954); Torrey, N. L., *Voltaire and the English Deists* (1930).

For German Pietism and the Methodist revival in England see: Pinson, Koppel S., *Pietism as a Factor in the Rise of German Nationalism* (1934); Nagler, A. W., *Pietism and Methodism* (1918); Edwards, M. L., *John Wesley and the Eighteenth Century* (rev. ed., 1955); Warner, W. J., *The Wesleyan Movement in the Industrial Revolution* (1930); Vulliamy, C. E., *John Wesley* (1931). See also: Coupland, Sir Reginald, *Wilberforce* (1923); Sykes, N., *Church and State in England in the Eighteenth Century* (1934).

THE ARTS AND LETTERS

For eighteenth century art in general see Volumes XIII and XIV of the *Propyläen Kunstgeschichte,* cited in the introduction to this Bibliography. See also Blomfield's *History of Architecture,* cited in Chapter XIII, and the following: Kimball, S. F., *Creation of the Rococo* (1943); Earp, T. W., *French Painting: From the Seventeenth Century to Today* (1945); Wilenski, R. H., *French Painting* (rev. ed., 1950), *English Painting* (1937); Fry, Roger, *Georgian Art (1760–1820)* (1929); Waterhouse, E. K., *Reynolds* (1941); Beckett, R. B., *Hogarth* (1949); Jourdain, A. M., *English Decoration and Furniture of the Later Eighteenth Century* (1922); Brackett, O., *Thomas Chippendale* (1925); Gudiol, José, *Goya* (1941); Reichwein, A., *China and Europe. Intellectual and Artistic Contacts in the Eighteenth Century* (1925); Summerson, J., *Georgian London* (1946); Fosca, F., *The Eighteenth Century: From Watteau to Tiepolo* (1953).

For literature see: Willey, B., *The Eighteenth Century Background* (1940); Neff, Emery, *A Revolution in European Poetry* (1940); Green, F. C., *Minuet. A Critical Survey of French and English Literary Ideas in the Eighteenth Century* (1935); Stephen, Sir Leslie, *English Literature and Society in the Eighteenth Century* (1903); *The Cambridge History of English Literature,* Vols. X, XI; Quennell, P., *The Profane Virtues* (1945); Green, F. C., *French Novelists: Manners and Ideas from the Renaissance to the Revolution* (1929); Francke, Kuno, *A History of German Literature as Determined by Social Forces* (new ed., 1931); Garland, H. B., *Lessing, the Founder of Modern German Literature* (1937); Robertson, J. G., *The Life and Work of Goethe* (1932). See also the references in Chapter XX.

For music see in addition to the general works cited earlier: Davison, A. T., *Bach and Handel: The Consummation of the Baroque in Music* (1951); Williams, C. F. A., *Handel* (1935); Hughes, Rosemary, *Haydn* (1950); Blom, E., *Mozart* (1935).

CHAPTER 20   Europe on the Eve of Revolution

GENERAL

See, in addition to the volumes by Roberts, Dorn and Gershoy in *The Rise of Modern Europe series,* Sorel, A., *Europe Under the Old Regime* (tr. F. H. Herrick, 1947).

ENGLAND

For a general survey of the 18th century see J. H. Plumb, *The First Four Georges* (1957) and Maccoby, S., *Eighteenth-Century England* (1931). For the period to 1760 see Williams, Basil, *The Whig Supremacy, 1714–1760* (1939). Political aspects are covered in Morley, J., *Walpole* (new ed., 1922); Stirling Taylor, G. R., *Robert Walpole and His Age* (1931); Plumb, J. H., *Sir Robert Walpole. The Making of a Statesman* (1956); Porritt, E., *The Unreformed House of Commons* (2nd ed., 1909); Laprade, W., *Public Opinion and Politics in Eighteenth-Century England* (1936); Oliver, F. S., *The Endless Adventure* (1931), on the evolution of the prime-ministership; Quennell, P., *Caroline of England* (1940), wife of George II; Vulliamy, C. E., *Royal George: A Study of King George III* (1937); Namier, L. B., *Structure of Politics at the Accession of George III* (2 vols., 1929); Pares, R., *George III and the Politicians* (1953); Williams, Basil, *Life of William Pitt, Earl of Chatham* (2 vols., 1913); Harrison, F., *Chatham* (1905, reprinted 1922); Lascelles, E. C. P., *Life of Charles James Fox* (1936); Rose, J. H., *Short Life of William Pitt* (1925).

For economic and social change see: Ashton, T. S., *The Industrial Revolution* (1948); Mantoux, P., *The Industrial Revolution of the Eighteenth Century* (rev. ed., 1929); Hammond, J. L., and Barbara, *The Village Labourer, 1760–1832* (2nd ed., 1920), *The Skilled Labourer, 1760–1832* (1919), *The Town Labourer, 1760–1832* (new ed., 1950), and *The Rise of Modern Industry* (new ed., 1937); Allen, R. J., *Life in Eighteenth-Century England* (1942); Cole, G. D. H., and Postgate, R., *The British Common People, 1746–1938* (1939); George, Dorothy, *London Life in the XVIIIth Century* (1925); Hearnshaw, F. J. C. (ed.), *Social and Political Ideas of Some English Thinkers of the Augustan Age* (1928); Shellabarger, S., *Lord Chesterfield* (1935); Turberville, A. S. (ed.), *Johnson's England, 1709–1784* (2 vols., 1933); Turberville, A. S., *English Men and Manners in the Eighteenth Century* (1929); Trevelyan, G. M., *English Social History*, Vol. III, cited before.

GERMANY AND PRUSSIA

In addition to the general histories listed in Chapter XIV see: Bruford, W. H., *Germany in the Eighteenth Century* (1935); Priest, G. M., *Germany Since 1740* (1915); Pinson, K. S., *Modern Germany: Its History and Civilization* (1954). For the reign of Frederick William I see: Ergang, R., *Potsdam Fuehrer: Frederick William I, Father of Prussian Militarism* (1941); and Dorwart, R. A., *The Administrative Reforms of Frederick William I of Prussia* (1953). There are biographies of Frederick II by Reddaway, W. F. (new ed., 1948), Young, Norwood (1919), Goldsmith, Margaret (1930), and Gaxotte, P. (1942). Gooch, G. P., *Frederick the Great, the Ruler, the Writer, the Man* (1947), is a useful series of essays. See also Easum, C. V., *Prince Henry of Prussia, Brother of Frederick the Great* (1942); Dorn, W., "The Prussian Bureaucracy in the Eighteenth Century," *Political Science Quarterly*, XLVI (1931), XLVII (1932); Small, Albion, *The Cameralists, the Pioneers of German Social Polity* (1909); Clark, R. T., Jr., *Herder: His Life and Thought* (1955); Ergang, R., *Herder and the Foundations of German Nationalism* (1931); Willoughby, L. A., *The Classical Age of German Literature, 1784–1805* (1926).

AUSTRIA

Useful information may still be obtained from Coxe, William, *History of the House of Austria, 1218–1792* (4 vols., new ed., 1893–1895). Taylor, A. J. P., *The Hapsburg Monarchy, 1815–1918* (1942) has some valuable background material in its opening chapters. For Maria Theresa see: Bright, J. F., *Maria Theresa* (1897); Goldsmith, M., *Maria Theresa of Austria* (1936); Gooch, G. P., *Maria Theresa and Other Studies* (1951). For Joseph II see Bright, J. F., *Joseph II* (1897); Padover, S. K., *The Revolutionary Emperor. Joseph the Second, 1741–1790* (1934). See also: Goodwin, Sister Mary Clare, *The Papal Conflict with Josephinism* (1938); Link, Edith M., *The Emancipation of the Austrian Peasant, 1740–1798* (1949); Kerner, R. J., *Bohemia in the Eighteenth Century . . . With Special Reference to the Reign of the Emperor Leopold II, 1790–1792* (1932); Marczali, H., *Hungary in the Eighteenth Century* (1910).

RUSSIA

See, in addition to the histories listed in Chapter XV, the following: Thomson, G. S., *Catherine the Great and the Expansion of Russia* (1950); Waliszewski, K., *Romance of an Empress: Catherine II of Russia* (1929); Reddaway, W. F. (ed.), *Documents of Catherine the Great* (1931); Gooch, G. P., *Catherine the Great and*

Other Studies (1954); Soloveytchik, G., *Potemkin* (1947); Robinson, G. T., *Rural Russia Under the Old Regime* (1932).

THE LESSER STATES

The Cambridge Modern History, Vol. VI; Bruun, G., *The Enlightened Despots* (1929); Bain, R. N., *Scandinavia. A Political History . . . From 1513 to 1900* (1905), *Gustavus III and His Contemporaries, 1746–1792* (2 vols., 1904), and *The Last King of Poland and His Contemporaries* (1909).

CHAPTER 21 The Crisis of the French Monarchy

GOVERNMENTAL AND ADMINISTRATIVE BACKGROUND

See in general Grant's *French Monarchy*, Vol. II, cited in Chapter VI. For the reign of Louis XV see: Perkins, J. B., *France Under Louis XV* (2 vols., 1897); Carré, H., *Louis XV (1715–1774)*, this being Vol. VIII of the *Histoire de France* edited by E. Lavisse; Ford, Franklin L., *Robe and Sword: The Regrouping of the French Aristocracy After Louis XIV* (1953); Gaxotte, P., *Louis XV and his Times* (1934).

SOCIAL AND ECONOMIC CONDITIONS

Barber, E., *The Bourgeoisie in 18th Century France* (1955); Ducros, L., *French Society in the 18th Century* (1926); Faÿ, Bernard, *Revolution and Freemasonry, 1680–1800* (1935); Maxwell, C., *The English Traveller in France, 1698–1815* (1932); Sée, Henri, *Economic and Social Conditions in France During the Eighteenth Century* (1927); Young, Arthur, *Travels in France During the Years 1787, 1788, 1789* (edited by C. Maxwell, 1929).

THE CRITICISMS OF THE PHILOSOPHES

Becker, Carl L., *The Heavenly City of the Eighteenth Century Philosophers* (1932); Bury, J. B., *The Idea of Progress: An Inquiry Into Its Origin and Growth* (1932); Frankel, C., *The Faith of Reason: The Idea of Progress in the French Enlightenment* (1948); Havens, G. R., *The Age of Ideas: From Reaction to Revolution in Eighteenth-Century France* (1955); Martin, Kingsley, *French Liberal Thought in the Eighteenth Century. A Study of Political Ideas from Bayle to Condorcet* (1929); Morley, J., *Diderot and the Encyclopedists* (2 vols., 1886); Mornet, D., *French Thought in the Eighteenth Century* (1929); Rocquain, F., *Revolutionary Spirit Preceding the French Revolution* (1892); Roustan, M., *Pioneers of the French Revolution* (1926); Rowe, C., *Voltaire and the State* (1955); Torrey, N. L., *The Spirit of Voltaire* (1938); Wade, Ira O., *The Clandestine Organization and Diffusion of Philosophic Ideas in France from 1700 to 1750* (1938); Wickwar, W. H., *Baron d'Holbach: A Prelude to the French Revolution* (1935).

THE TWILIGHT OF THE MONARCHY, 1774–1789

There is no very competent account in English of the reign of Louis XVI. Funck-Brentano, F., *The Old Regime in France* (1929) is strongly royalist. Two essential accounts in French are: Sagnac, P., *La fin de l'ancien régime et la Révolution américaine (1763–1789)* (1947) in the *Peuples et civilisations* series; and Carré, H., Sagnac, P., and Lavisse, E., *Louis XVI (1774–1789)* (1911), this being Vol. IX of the *Histoire de France* edited by E. Lavisse. Taine, H. A., *The Ancient Regime* (Engl. tr., new ed., 1931) is a French classic but very hostile to the Revolution. See also: Tocqueville, A. de, *L'Ancien Régime* (latest transl. 1954); Dakin, D., *Turgot and the Ancien Régime in France* (1939); Padover, S. K., *The Life and Death of Louis XVI* (1939); Belloc, H., *Marie Antoinette* (2nd ed., 1924); Castelot, A., *Queen of France. A Biography of Marie Antoinette* (1957); Funck-Brentano, F., *The Diamond Necklace* (1901); Gottschalk, Louis, *The Place of the American Revolution in the Causal Pattern of the French Revolution* (1948); Lefebvre, G., *The Coming of the French Revolution* (1947).

CHAPTERS 22 and 23   The French Revolution to 1795

GENERAL TREATMENTS

Two useful surveys covering the entire Revolutionary and Napoleonic period are: Gershoy, Leo, *The French Revolution and Napoleon* (1933); Gottschalk, Louis R., *The Era of the French Revolution (1715–1815)* (1929). The most valuable French accounts covering the decade 1789–1799 are: Lefebvre, G., Guyot, R., and Sagnac, P., *La Révolution française* (1930) in the *Peuples et civilisations* series; and Sagnac, P., *La Révolution (1789–1792)* (1920), and Pariset, G., *La Révolution (1792–1799)* (1920), these being Vols. I and II of the *Histoire de France contemporaine* edited by E. Lavisse. Other works dealing specifically with the Revolution are: Aulard, A., *The French Revolution, A Political History* (4 vols., 1910); Brinton, C., *A Decade of Revolution, 1789–1799* (1934); Gershoy, Leo, *The French Revolution, 1789–1799* (1932); Hazen, C. D., *The French Revolution* (2 vols., 1932); Kropotkin, P., *The Great French Revolution, 1789–1793* (1909), a "proletarian" interpretation; Madelin, Louis, *The French Revolution* (1925), Bonapartist; Mathiez, Albert, *The French Revolution* (1928), goes only to 1794, strongly Robespierrist; Thompson, J. M., *The French Revolution* (1945). The most valuable collection of documents is Stewart, John H., *A Documentary Survey of the French Revolution* (1951); Anderson, F. M. (ed.), *The Constitutions and Other Select Documents Illustrative of the History of France, 1789–1901* (1908); Higgins, E. L. (ed.), *The French Revolution as Told by Contemporaries* (1938); Legg, L. G. W. (ed.), *Select Documents Illustrative of the History of the French Revolution: The Constituent Assembly* (2 vols., 1905); Thompson, J. M. (ed.), *English Witnesses of the French Revolution* (1938). For contemporary illustrations see: Henderson, E. F., *Symbol and Satire in the French Revolution* (1912).

SPECIAL ASPECTS

Acton, Lord, *Lectures on the French Revolution* (1925); Brace, Richard M., *Bordeaux and the Gironde, 1789–1794* (1947); Brinton, C., *The Jacobins, an Essay in the New History* (1930); Clough, S. B., *France, a History of National Economics, 1789–1939* (1939); Elton, Godfrey, *The Revolutionary Idea in France, 1789–1871* (1923); Garrett, M. B., *The Estates General of 1789* (1935); Godfrey, J. L., *Revolutionary Justice: A Study of the Organization, Personnel and Procedure of the Paris Tribunal, 1793–1795* (1951); Greer, Donald, *The Incidence of the Terror During the French Revolution* (1935), *The Incidence of the Emigration During the French Revolution* (1951); Harris, S. E., *The Assignats* (1930); Hayes, C. J. H., *Historical Evolution of Modern Nationalism* (1931); Hearnshaw, F. J. C. (ed.), *The Social and Political Ideas of Some Representative Thinkers of the Revolutionary Era* (1931); Herbert, S., *The Fall of Feudalism in France* (1921); Hyslop, Beatrice F., *French Nationalism in 1789 According to the General Cahiers* (1934); Kerr, W. B., *The Reign of Terror, 1793–1794* (1927); Mathiez, A., *After Robespierre. The Thermidorean Reaction* (1931), *The Fall of Robespierre and Other Essays* (1927); Morris, Gouverneur, *A Diary of the French Revolution, 1789–1793* (2 vols., 1939); Nussbaum, F. L., *Commercial Policy in the French Revolution, a Study of the Career of G. J. A. Ducher* (1923); Palmer, R. R., *Twelve Who Ruled. The Committee of Public Safety During the Terror* (1941); Parker, H. T., *The Cult of Antiquity and the French Revolutionaries* (1937); Rogers, C. B., *The Spirit of Revolution in 1789* (1949); Shepard, W. F., *Price Control and the Reign of Terror* (1953); Sirich, John B., *The Revolutionary Committees in the Departments of France, 1793–1794* (1943); Thompson, E., *Popular Sovereignty and the French Constituent Assembly, 1789–1791* (1952); Wilkinson, S., *The French Army Before Napoleon* (1915).

THE REVOLUTION AND EUROPE

The great work on foreign relations, still untranslated save in small part, is Sorel, A., *L'Europe et la Révolution française* (8 vols., 1895–1904 and later eds.). For special aspects see: Birley, R., *The English Jacobins* (1924); Brown, P. A., *The French Revolution in English History* (1924); Clapham, J. H., *The Causes of the War of 1792* (1899); Cobban, A., *The Debate on the French Revolution, 1789–1800* (1950), *Edmund Burke and the Revolt Against the Eighteenth Century* (1929); Gooch, G. P., *Germany and the French Revolution* (1920); Laprade, W. T., *England and the French Revolution, 1789–1797* (1910); Mahan, A. T., *The Influence of Sea-Power upon the French Revolution and the Empire, 1793–1812* (2 vols., 1893 and later eds.).

BIOGRAPHIES

General works include: Béraud, H., *Twelve Portraits of the French Revolution* (1928); Madelin, L., *Figures of the Revolution* (1930); Thompson, J. M., *Leaders of the French Revolution* (1929); Whitham, J. M., *A Biographical History of the French Revolution* (1931).

For individual figures consult: Brucker, G. A., *Jean-Sylvain Bailly, Revolutionary Mayor of Paris* (1950); Bradby, E. D., *Life of Barnave* (2 vols., 1915); Ellery, E., *Brissot de Warville* (1915); Magnus, Sir Philip, *Edmund Burke* (1939); Dupré, Huntley, *Lazare Carnot, Republican Patriot* (1940); Schapiro, J. S., *Condorcet and the Rise of Liberalism* (1934); Belloc, H., *Danton, A Study* (1928); Madelin, L., *Danton* (1921); Dowd, David L., *Pageant-Master of the Republic: Jacques-Louis David* (1948); Morton, J. B., *Camille Desmoulins* (1951); Zweig, S., *Joseph Fouché* (1930); Sedgwick, H. R., *La Fayette* (1928); Gottschalk, Louis R., *Jean Paul Marat* (1927); Welch, O. J. G., *Mirabeau* (1951); Willert, P. F., *Mirabeau* (1898); Rose, J. H., *A Short Life of William Pitt* (1925); Belloc, H., *Robespierre* (1927); Korngold, R., *Robespierre and the Fourth Estate* (1941); Renier, G. J., *Robespierre* (1936); Thompson, J. M., *Robespierre* (2 vols., 1936), and *Robespierre and the French Revolution* (1952); Ward, Reginald S., *Maximilien Robespierre, a Study in Deterioration* (1934); Young, C., *A Lady Who Loved Herself* (1930) [Mme. Roland]; Bruun, G., *Saint-Just, Apostle of the Terror* (1932); Curtis, E. N., *Saint-Just, Colleague of Robespierre* (1935); Clapham, J. H., *The Abbé Sieyès* (1912); Van Deusen, Glyndon, G., *Sieyès: His Life and His Nationalism* (1932); Wilson, R. McNair, *Madame de Staël: High Priestess of Love* (1931); Goldsmith, M., *Madame de Staël* (1938); Brinton, C., *The Lives of Talleyrand* (1936); Duff-Cooper, A., *Talleyrand* (1932); Bowers, C., *Pierre Vergniaud* (1951).

CHAPTERS 24—26   The Napoleonic Era, 1795–1815

GENERAL

Histories of this age and biographies of Napoleon can hardly be separated. In English the most useful general works are: Bruun, G., *Europe and the French Imperium, 1799–1815* (1938), in *The Rise of Modern Europe* series; *The Cambridge Modern History*, Vol. IX; and the strongly Bonapartist Madelin, L., *The Consulate and the Empire* (2 vols., 1934–1936). In French the most useful general works are: Pariset, G., *Le Consulat et l'Empire* (1921), being Vol. III of the *Histoire de France contemporaine*, edited by E. Lavisse; and Lefebvre, G., *Napoléon* (1935).

STUDIES OF NAPOLEON

General biographies include: Bainville, J., *Napoleon* (1932); Fisher, H. A. L., *Napoleon* (1912); Fournier, A., *Napoleon the First* (1925); Kircheisen, F. M., *Napoleon* (1932); Markham, F. M. H., *Napoleon and the Awakening of Europe* (1954); Rose, J. Holland, *The Life of Napoleon I* (2 vols., 1902 and later eds.); Thompson, J. M., *Napoleon Bonaparte. His Rise and Fall* (1952).

For the period of the Directory and Bonaparte's rise to power see: Minnigerode, M., *The Magnificent Comedy: Some Aspects of Public and Private Life in Paris From the Fall of Robespierre to the Coming of Bonaparte* (1931); Thomson, David, *The Babeuf Plot: The Making of A Republican Legend* (1947); Young, Norwood, *The Growth of Napoleon* (1910); Pratt, Fletcher, *The Road to Empire: The Life and Times of Bonaparte the General* (1939); Wilkinson, S., *The Rise of General Bonaparte* (new ed., 1952); Phipps, R. W., *The Armies of the First French Republic and the Rise of the Marshals of Napoleon* (5 vols., 1926–1939); Adlow, E., *Napoleon in Italy, 1796–1797* (1948); Elgood, P. G., *Bonaparte's Adventures in Egypt* (1931). The classic account in French is Vandal, A., *L'Avènement de Bonaparte* (2 vols., 1902–1907).

Other aspects of Napoleon are dealt with in: Andrews, George G., *Napoleon in Review* (1939); Broadley, A. M., *Napoleon in Caricature, 1795–1821* (2 vols., 1910); Geyl, P., *Napoleon—For and Against* (1949); Geer, W., *Napoleon and Josephine* (1925), *Napoleon and Marie-Louise* (1925), *Napoleon and his Family* (3 vols., 1927–1929); Guérard, A., *Reflections on the Napoleonic Legend* (1924); Herold, J. C. (ed.), *The Mind of Napoleon I: A Selection from his Written and Spoken Words* (1955); Johnston, R. M., *The Corsican* (new ed., 1930), giving extracts from Napoleon's writings; Macdonell, A. G., *Napoleon and his Marshals* (1934); Pratt, Fletcher, *The Empire and the Glory, Napoleon Bonaparte, 1800–1806* (1949); Sorel, A., *Napoleon and the French Revolution, 1799–1814* (1928), excerpts, transl. by H. L. Hutton, from Sorel's great work; Thompson, J. M., *Napoleon Self-Revealed: Three Hundred Selected Letters* (1934).

FRENCH INTERNAL AFFAIRS

Fisher, H. A. L., *Bonapartism* (1914); Cachard, H., *The French Civil Code* (1930); Walsh, H. H., *The Concordat of 1801* (1933); *The Cambridge Modern History*, Vol. IX, chs. v, vi, vii; Zweig, S., *Joseph Fouché, the Portrait of a Politician* (1930); Coffin, V., "Censorship and Literature Under Napoleon I," *The American Historical Review*, XXII (1917).

EXTERNAL AFFAIRS

For colonial questions see: Priestley, H. I., *France Overseas Through the Old Regime* (1939); Lokke, C. L., *France and the Colonial Question, 1763–1801* (1932), "French Dreams of Colonial Empire Under the Directory and the Consulate," *The Journal of Modern History*, II (1930); Lyon, E. Wilson, *Louisiana in French Diplomacy, 1759–1804* (1934), *The Man Who Sold Louisiana: The Career of François Barbé-Marbois* (1942); Scott, E., *Terre Napoleon: A History of French Exploration and Projects in Australia* (1910).

For diplomatic history see, in addition to the basic work of Sorel, previously cited: Mowat, R. B., *The Diplomacy of Napoleon* (1924); Brinton, C., *The Lives of Talleyrand* (1936); Dard, E., *Napoleon and Talleyrand* (1937); Duff-Cooper, A., *Talleyrand* (1932); Deutsch, H. C., *The Genesis of Napoleonic Imperialism* (1938); Holtman, R. B., *Napoleonic Propaganda* (1950); Butterfield, H., *The Peace Tactics of Napoleon, 1806–1808* (1929); Heckscher, E., *The Continental System* (1922); Melvin, F. E., *Napoleon's Navigation System* (1919); Puryear, V. J., *Napoleon and the Dardanelles* (1951); Shupp, P. F., *The European Powers and the Near Eastern Question, 1806–1807* (1931); Buckland, C. S., *Metternich and the British Government from 1809 to 1813* (1932); Cecil, Algernon, *Metternich* (1933); Du Coudray, H., *Metternich* (1935).

For the diplomacy at the close of the Napoleonic period see: Webster, Sir Charles K., *The Foreign Policy of Castlereagh, 1812–1815* (1931), *The Congress of Vienna, 1814–1815* (reissued, 1934); Phillips, W. A., *The Confederation of Europe* (new ed., 1920); Scott, F. D., *Bernadotte and the Fall of Napoleon* (1935); Caulaincourt, General, *No Peace with Napoleon* (1936); Lockhart, J. C., *The Peacemakers, 1814–1815* (1932); Nicolson, Harold, *The Congress of Vienna* (1946); Ferrero, G., *The Reconstruction of Europe, 1814–1815* (1941); Stearns, J. B., *The Role of Metternich in Undermining Napoleon* (1948); Straus, H. A., *The Attitude of the Congress of Vienna Toward Nationalism in Germany, Italy and Poland* (1949); Gulick, E. V., *Europe's Classic Balance of Power* (1955); Sweet, Paul R., *Friedrich von Gentz, Defender of the Old Order* (1941).

For the fall of Napoleon and after, see: Browning, O., *The Fall of Napoleon* (1907); Houssaye, H., *Napoleon and the Campaign of 1814* (1914), *1815, Waterloo* (1905), *The Return of Napoleon* (1934); Rosebery, Lord, *Napoleon, The Last Phase* (1901); Wright, W., *The Pinnacle of Glory* (1935), dealing with Napoleon at St. Helena; Knapton, E. J., "Some Aspects of the Bourbon Restoration of 1814," *The Journal of Modern History*, VI (1934).

BRITISH POLICY DURING THE NAPOLEONIC ERA

Ward, Sir A. W., and Gooch, G. P. (eds.), *The Cambridge History of British Foreign Policy, 1783–1919* (3 vols., 1922–1923), Vol. I; Bryant, Sir Arthur, *Years of Endurance, 1793–1802* (1942), *Years of Victory, 1802–1812* (1945), *The Age of Elegance, 1812–1822* (1950); Cunningham, A., *British Credit in the Last Napoleonic War* (1910); Galpin, W. F., *The Grain Supply of England During the Napoleonic Period* (1925); Guedalla, P., *Wellington* (1931); Oman, Carola, *Napoleon at the Channel* (1942), *Lord Nelson* (1946); Rose, J. Holland, *Napoleonic Studies* (1904), *William Pitt and the Great War* (1911), *Pitt and Napoleon: Essays and Letters* (1912); Fortescue, J., *Wellington* (1925).

GERMANY

Anderson, E. N., *Nationalism and the Cultural Crisis in Prussia, 1806–1815* (1939); Aris, R., *History of Political Thought in Germany from 1789 to 1815* (1936); Engelbrecht, H. C., *Johann Gottlieb Fichte* (1933); Ergang, R. R., *Herder and the Foundations of German Nationalism* (1931); Fisher, H. A. L., *Studies in Napoleonic Statesmanship: Germany* (1914); Ford, Guy S., *Hanover and Prussia, 1795–1803* (1903), *Stein and the Era of Reform in Prussia* (1922); Gooch, G. P., *Germany and the French Revolution* (1920); Grunwald, C. de, *Napoleon's Nemesis: The Life of Baron Stein* (1936); Kohn, H., "The Eve of German Nationalism, 1789–1812," *Journal of the History of Ideas*, XII (1951); Langsam, W. C., *The Napoleonic Wars and German Nationalism in Austria* (1930); Pundt, A. G., *Arndt and the National Awakening in Germany* (1936); Shanahan, W. O., *Prussian Military Reforms, 1786–1813* (1945); Springer, O., and Melvin, F. E. (eds.), *A German Conscript With Napoleon: Jacob Walter's Recollections of the Campaigns of 1806–1807, 1809, and 1812–1813* (1938); Zeydel, E. H., *Ludwig Tieck, the German Romanticist* (1935); Simon, Walter M., *The Failure of the Prussian Reform Movement: 1807–1819* (1956).

ITALY

Johnston, R. M., *The Napoleonic Empire in Southern Italy and the Rise of the Secret Societies* (2 vols., 1904); McClellan, G. B., *Venice and Bonaparte* (1931); Noether, E. P., *Seeds of Italian Nationalism, 1700–1815* (1951); Rath, R. J., *The Fall of the Napoleonic Kingdom of Italy (1814)* (1941).

RUSSIA

Lobanov-Rostovsky, A. A., *Russia and Europe, 1789–1825* (1947); Caulaincourt, General, *With Napoleon in Russia* (1934); Knapton, E. J., *The Lady of the Holy Alliance: The Life of Julie de Krüdener* (1939); Paleologue, M., *The Enigmatic Czar: The Life of Alexander I of Russia* (1938); Strakhovsky, L. I., *Alexander I of Russia* (1947); Tarle, E. V., *Napoleon's Invasion of Russia* (1942).

Comparative Chronological Tables

POLITICAL		ECONOMIC AND SOCIAL		OVERSEAS EXPANSION	
711–13	Moslems conquer Spain	8th c.	DECLINE OF URBAN LIFE		
732	Charles Martel defeats Moslems at Tours				
800–14	Charlemagne, Emperor	9th c.	EUROPEAN MIGRATIONS OF THE NORTHMEN		
827ff.	Saracens in Sicily	9th c.	DEVELOPMENT OF FEUDAL PATTERN OF SOCIETY		
843	Treaty of Verdun				
929ff.	Caliphate of Cordova	10th c.	GROWTH OF "OPEN FIELD" SYSTEM OF AGRICULTURE	10th c.	NORSEMEN IN ICELAND AND GREENLAND
962–73	Otto I, Emperor				
987ff.	Capetians in France				
10th c. ff.	FEUDAL AGE	10th c.	GROWTH OF TOWNS		
1001–38	Stephen I of Hungary	11th c.	RISE OF THE GILDS		
1061–91	Normans conquer Sicily				
1066	Normans conquer England				
1212–50	Frederick II, Emperor	c. 1240	Beginnings of the Hansa League	1245	John of Carpini in Central Asia
1215	*Magna Carta* in England	1252	Gold florins issued at Florence	1271–95	Voyages of Marco Polo through Asia
1228ff.	Teutonic Knights in East Prussia				
1240	Mongols capture Kiev	1290	Expulsion of the Jews from England		
1273	Rudolf of Hapsburg, Holy Roman Emperor				
1291	Swiss League of three "Forest Cantons"				
1295	"Model Parliament" in England				
1302	Estates General, France	1317	Venetian galleys reach Antwerp	c. 1350	Discovery of Madeira, Azores and Cape Verde Islands
1337–1453	Hundred Years' War	1348–50	Black Death in Western Europe		
1356	"Golden Bull," Emperor Charles IV	1381	Peasants' Revolt in England		
1386	Polish-Lithuanian Union	1391	Massacres of Jews in Spain	1415	Portuguese capture Ceuta
1397	Union of Kalmar				
1417ff.	Hohenzollerns in Brandenburg	1401	Bank of Barcelona	1418	First expedition of Henry the Navigator (Madeira)
1434–64	Cosimo de' Medici	1407	Bank of St. George, Genoa		
1453	Turks capture Constantinople	15th c.	Rise of banking families: the Medici, the Fuggers, Jacques Coeur	15th c.	THE GREAT VOYAGES
				1445	Portuguese reach Senegal River

The following tables summarize a mass of historical data. The columns have been arranged so that different types of material may be visualized in chronological sequence and also as parts of one contemporary scene. Small capitals have been inserted occasionally to suggest major trends. Titles of books are italicized; titles of paintings are in quotation marks. The dates given are occasionally approximate. In the case of artists and authors the name and year of an important work are given rather than the less meaningful dates of birth and death.

RELIGION		SCIENCE AND LEARNING		LITERATURE AND ARTS	
718	Mission of St. Boniface to the Germans	731	Bede, *Ecclesiastical History*	c. 700	*Beowulf*
		8th c.	CAROLINGIAN RENAISSANCE	8th c.	CAROLINGIAN RENAISSANCE
				782ff.	Alcuin of York at court of Charlemagne
863–85	Missions of St. Cyril and St. Methodius to the Slavs	9th c.	John Scotus Erigena	9th c.	Great Mosque, Cordova
				9th c.	The *Book of Kells*
910	Abbey of Cluny	930–1037	Avicenna		
989	Vladimir of Kiev becomes Christian				
				11th c.	DEVELOPMENT OF ROMANESQUE ART
1054	Separation of Western and Eastern Church			1063	St. Mark's, Venice, begun
1073–85	Gregory VII, Pope	1079–1142	Peter Abelard		
1084	Carthusian Order				
1095	First Crusade preached by Urban II				
1098	Cistercian Order				
1100	Kingdom of Jerusalem			c. 1100	*Chanson de Roland*
1122	Concordat of Worms	12th–14th c.	AGE OF SCHOLASTICISM	c. 1130	Durham Cathedral, nave
1147–49	Second Crusade				
1090–1153	St. Bernard	c. 1150	*Sentences* of Peter Lombard		
1189–92	Third Crusade	c. 1150	Cathedral School, Paris		
1198–1216	Innocent III, Pope	1115–80	John of Salisbury		
		1126–98	Averroës		THE GOTHIC AGE
1202–04	Fourth Crusade	c. 1200	Charter of University of Paris	c. 1200	Rebuilding of Chartres Cathedral
1204–61	"Latin Empire of Constantinople"	1175–1253	Robert Grosseteste	c. 1220	Amiens Cathedral, nave
1218	Dominican Order	c. 1266	Roger Bacon, *Opus Maius*	c. 1235	*Romance of the Rose*
1223	Franciscan Order			c. 1250	Salisbury Cathedral
1225–74	St. Thomas Aquinas	1206–80	Albertus Magnus	c. 1250	Sainte Chapelle, Paris
1260–1327	Meister Eckhart				
1294–1303	Boniface VIII, Pope				
		?–1308	Duns Scotus	?1300ff.	Dante, *The Divine Comedy*
1305–78	"Babylonian Captivity" of the Church	?–1347	William of Occam	1305	Giotto, Arena Chapel frescoes, Padua
1340–84	Gerard Groote	1324	Marsiglio of Padua, *Defensor Pacis*		RENAISSANCE BEGINNINGS
1347–80	St. Catherine of Siena	14th c.	REVIVAL OF LEARNING: HUMANISM	1342	Petrarch crowned laureate at Rome
1378–1417	The "Great Schism"	1305–74	Petrarch, "Father of Humanism"	1353	Boccaccio, *The Decameron*
c. 1382	Wyclif translates Bible	1397ff.	Chrysoloras lectures on Greek at Florence	c. 1390	Chaucer, *Canterbury Tales*
1382ff.	Lollardry in England				
1415	John Hus burned as a heretic			1415–32	Van Eyck, "Adoration of the Lamb"
1420–31	Hussite Wars in Bohemia	1415ff.	Poggio discovers classical manuscripts	1416	Donatello, statue of St. George
1431	Joan of Arc burned as a heretic	1400–64	Nicholas of Cusa	1419	Brunelleschi, design for cathedral dome, Florence
1438	Pragmatic Sanction of Bourges	1425	Vittorino da Feltre's classical school		

POLITICAL		ECONOMIC AND SOCIAL		OVERSEAS EXPANSION	
1461–83	Louis XI of France	1485	Antwerp *Bourse*	1460	Portuguese at Cape Sierra Leone
1462–1505	Ivan III of Muscovy	1492	Moors expelled from Granada	1470	Ptolemy's *Geography* printed
1469–92	Lorenzo de' Medici	1492	Jews banished from Spain	1472	Portuguese cross the Equator
1479–1504	Ferdinand and Isabella in Spain	1494	Pacioli's treatise on bookkeeping	1480	D'Ailly's *Imago Mundi* printed
16th c.	STRONG MONARCHIES			1487–88	Diaz at Cape of Good Hope
1485–1509	Henry VII, first Tudor			1492	Columbus in America
1494–1529	Italian Wars			1497–98	Cabot's voyages to America
				1498	Vasco da Gama reaches India
				16th c.	COMMERCIAL REVOLUTION
1509–47	Henry VIII of England	16th c.	THE COMMERCIAL REVOLUTION	1500	Cabral reaches Brazil
1515–47	Francis I of France	16th c.	Development of trading companies	1501	Portuguese trading post at Calicut
1519–56	Charles V, Emperor	16th c.	Enclosure of common fields, England	1510	Portuguese at Goa
1520–66	Suleiman II			1512	Portuguese in Spice Islands
1523–60	Gustavus I of Sweden	1524–25	Peasants' Revolt, Germany	1513	Balboa at Panama
1527	Imperial troops sack Rome	1531	Antwerp Stock Exchange	1516	Portuguese at Canton
1529	Turks besiege Vienna	1536	French Capitulations in Ottoman Empire	1519–21	Cortes in Mexico
1533–84	Ivan IV of Muscovy			1519–22	Magellan's voyage around the world
1541	Turks capture Budapest	1555	Muscovy Company	1524	Spanish Council of the Indies
1547–53	Edward VI of England	1563	Statute of Apprentices, England	1532ff.	Pizarro in Peru
1547–59	Henry II of France			1534–35	Cartier explores the St. Lawrence River
1556–98	Philip II of Spain			1539	Las Casas, *Relation of the Destruction of the Indies*
1558–1603	Elizabeth I of England			1542	Portuguese in Japan
1559	Peace of Cateau-Cambrésis			1553–54	Willoughby and Chancellor reach the White Sea
1566ff.	Netherlands Revolt			1562	Negro slaves taken to Hispaniola
1568ff.	Moriscoes expelled from Spain			1571	Spaniards found Manila
1571	Battle of Lepanto			1577–80	Drake's voyage around the world
1579	Union of Utrecht			1583	Failure of Gilbert's Newfoundland colony
1580–1640	Union of Spain and Portugal			1588ff.	Hakluyt, *Voyages*
1588	Spanish Armada			1590ff.	De Bry, *Voyages*
1589–1610	Henry IV of France			1595	Dutch in East Indies
1598	Peace of Vervins				
		17th c.	DEVELOPMENT OF THE BOURGEOISIE	17th c.	GROWTH OF COLONIAL EMPIRES
1603–25	James I of England	1600	English East India Company	1605	Dutch take Amboyna
1610–43	Louis XIII of France	1602	Dutch East India Company	1607	Jamestown settlement
1611–32	Gustavus II of Sweden	1609	Bank of Amsterdam	1608	French found Quebec
1613–45	Michael Romanov	1627	Company of One Hundred Associates, France	1609	English at Bermuda
1618–48	Thirty Years' War	1651	First English Navigation Act	1612	English at Surat in India
1624–42	Richelieu ministry			1613	Dutch on Manhattan Is.
1625–49	Charles I of England			1620	Plymouth settlement
1628	Petition of Right			1624	Dutch at Formosa
1635	Peace of Prague			1629	Massachusetts Bay Colony
				1630	French in Senegal
				1634	Dutch at Curaçao

RELIGION		SCIENCE AND LEARNING		LITERATURE AND ARTS	
1441	Thomas à Kempis, *Imitation of Christ*	1440	Valla exposes *Donation of Constantine*	c. 1428	Masaccio, "Tribute Money"
1447–55	Nicholas V, "The first humanist pope"	c. 1450	Gutenberg's printing press	1403–52	Ghiberti, doors for Baptistery, Florence
1478ff.	Inquisition in Spain	1462	Platonic Academy	1430	Fra Angelico, "Coronation of the Virgin"
1492–1503	Alexander VI (Borgia), Pope	1468	Ficino completes translation of Plato	1446–51	Alberti, Rucellai Palace
1498	Execution of Savonarola at Florence	1476	Lascaris, *Greek Grammar*	c. 1456	Uccello, "Battle Piece"
		1486	Pico, *Oration on the Dignity of Man*	1465	First Italian printing press
				1478	Botticelli, "Primavera"
		1490	Aldine Press at Venice	c. 1488	Verrocchio, statue of Condottiere Colleoni
16th c.	THE AGE OF THE REFORMATION	1496	Colet's Oxford lectures	c. 1488	Leonardo, "Last Supper"
1503–13	Julius II, Pope	1498	Erasmus at Oxford		THE HIGH RENAISSANCE
1512	Lefèvre, *Commentary on St. Paul*			c. 1503	Leonardo, "Mona Lisa"
		1510–13	Erasmus at Cambridge	1504	Michelangelo, statue of David
1512–17	Fifth Lateran Council	1513	Machiavelli's *Prince*	1506	Bramante, design for St. Peter's
1513–21	Leo X, Pope	1514	*Letters of Obscure Men*		
1516	Concordat of Bologna	1516	Erasmus, *Greek Testament*	1508–12	Michelangelo, Sistine Chapel ceiling
1517	Luther, *Ninety-Five Theses*	1522	Ximenes, *Polyglot Bible*	1509–11	Raphael, Vatican frescoes
1521	Diet at Worms			1510	Giorgione, "The Concert"
1530	Confession of Augsburg		BEGINNINGS OF THE SCIENTIFIC REVOLUTION	1511	Erasmus, *Praise of Folly*
1531	Henry VIII Supreme Head of English Church	1530	Collège de France founded	1514	Dürer, "Melancolia I"
				1516	Ariosto, *Orlando Furioso*
1534–49	Paul III, Pope			c. 1515	Grünewald, Isenheim Altar
1536–39	Dissolution of English monasteries			1516	More, *Utopia*
1536	Calvin, *Institutes*			1522	Titian, "Bacchus and Ariadne"
1539	*Great Bible* in England			1524–33	Michelangelo, Medici tombs
1540	Society of Jesus			1533ff.	Rabelais, *Gargantua and Pantagruel*
1541	Calvin's *Ecclesiastical Ordinances*	1541	Mercator, terrestrial globe	1535	Holbein, "The Ambassadors"
1542	Roman Inquisition	1542	Gessner, *Catalog of Plants*	1538	Cranach, "Crucifixion"
1542–52	Mission of St. Francis Xavier	1543	Copernicus, *Revolutions of the Celestial Orbs*	1546	Michelangelo, design for St. Peter's
1546–63	Council of Trent	1543	Vesalius, *Structure of the Human Body*	1546	Lescot, Pavilion of the Louvre
1555	Peace of Augsburg	1544	Münster, *Cosmographia*	1559	Cellini, sculpture of Perseus and Medusa
1559	Act of Uniformity in England	1545	Cardan, *Ars Magna*	1567	Palestrina, Mass of Pope Marcellus
1559	*Index of Prohibited Books*	1556	Agricola, *De Re Metallica*	1568	Bruegel, "Peasant Wedding"
1561	Scottish *Book of Discipline*	1561	Guicciardini, *History of Italy*		THE BAROQUE AGE
1562–98	French Wars of Religion	1576	Bodin, *The Republic*	1568	Vignola, Church of the Gesù
1563	Thirty-Nine Articles of Religion in England	1582	Gregorian Calendar	1572	Camoëns, *The Lusiads*
1563	Close of Council of Trent	1583	Scaliger, *De Emendatione Temporum*	1574	Tasso, *Jerusalem Delivered*
1572	Massacre of St. Bartholomew	1585	Stevin, *The Decimal*	1580	Montaigne, *Essays*
1593	Conversion of Henry IV of France			1586	El Greco, "Burial of Count Orgaz"
1598	Edict of Nantes			1590ff.	Spenser, *Faerie Queen*
1611	King James Bible	c. 1600	Jansen's microscope	1591	Shakespeare, *Romeo and Juliet*
1567–1622	St. Francis de Sales	1600	Gilbert, *On the Magnet*	1594	Tintoretto, "Last Supper"
		1603	Accademia dei Lincei, Rome	1605	Cervantes, *Don Quixote*
1576–1660	St. Vincent de Paul	1608	Lippershey's telescope	1607	Monteverdi, *Orpheus*
		1609	Galileo's telescope	1611	Shakespeare, *The Tempest*
		1609	Kepler, *Astronomia Nova*	1619	Inigo Jones, Banqueting Hall, Whitehall
		1614	Napier, *Description of Logarithms*	c. 1635	Velasquez, "Surrender at Breda"
		1625	Grotius, *On the Law of War and Peace*	1636	Poussin, "Abduction of the Sabines"

POLITICAL		ECONOMIC AND SOCIAL		OVERSEAS EXPANSION	
1640–88	Great Elector, Prussia			1639	Russians at Okhotsk
1642–49	English Civil War			1642	Dutch in Tasmania
1642–61	Mazarin ministry			1651	Dutch at Cape of Good Hope
1643–1715	Louis XIV of France			1654	Portuguese expel Dutch from Brazil
1648	Peace of Westphalia			1658	Dutch at Ceylon
1649–60	Commonwealth, England			1661	English at Bombay
1652–54	First Anglo-Dutch War			1682	La Salle reaches mouth of the Mississippi
1658–1705	Leopold I of Austria				
1659	Peace of the Pyrenees			1685	French *Code Noir*
1660–85	Charles II of England	1661–83	Colbert Superintend-ent of Finances in France	1689–97	King William's War
1660	Peace of Oliva				
1665–67	2nd Anglo-Dutch War	1664	Mun, *England's Treas-ure by Forraign Trade*		
1667–68	War of Devolution	1666	Great Fire of London		
1667	Peace of Andrusovo	1670	Hudson's Bay Company		
1672–78	Dutch War	1672	Royal African Com-pany granted slave-trade monopoly		
1679	Habeas Corpus Act				
1683	Turks besiege Vienna				
1688	"Glorious Revolution" in England	1691	Petty, *Political Arith-metic*		
1689	Bill of Rights; Act of Succession	1694	Bank of England		
1689–97	War of League of Augsburg				
1699	Peace of Carlowitz				
1689–1725	Peter I of Russia				
1697–1718	Charles XII of Sweden			18th c.	AGE OF IMPERIAL RIVALRY
1700–46	Philip V of Spain			1701–13	Queen Anne's War
1700–21	Great Northern War			1707ff.	Decline of Mogul Empire
1701	Act of Settlement				
1701–13	War of the Spanish Succession				
1702–14	Queen Anne of England	1703	Methuen Treaty, Eng-land and Portugal		
1704	England wins Gibraltar				
1707	Union of England and Scotland	1703	St. Petersburg founded		
1711–40	Charles VI of Austria	1706	Newcomen's and Pa-pin's steam engine		
1713–40	Frederick William I of Prussia	1707	Vauban, *Dime royale*		
1713	Peace of Utrecht	1720	South Sea Bubble		
1714–27	George I of England				
1715–74	Louis XV of France				
1718	Peace of Passarowitz				
1721	Peace of Nystadt				
1721–42	Walpole ministry				
1723	General Directory in Prussia				
1726–43	Fleury ministry	1733	Kay's flying shuttle	1728	Vitus Bering discovers Bering Straits
1727–60	George II of England	1755	Lisbon earthquake		
1733–38	Polish Succession War	1760ff.	Bakewell's improvements in cattlebreeding	1743–48	King George's War
1738	Peace of Vienna			1748ff.	Rivalry of Clive and Dupleix in India
1739	Peace of Belgrade	1760–90	Great period of enclos-ing common fields in England		
1740–86	Frederick II of Prussia			1755–63	French and Indian Wars
1740–80	Maria Theresa of Austria			1757	Battle of Plassey, India
1740–48	War of the Austrian Succession	1761	Duke of Bridgewater's canal, Manchester	1758	English capture Louisburg
1748	Peace of Aix-la-Chapelle	1763	Prussian School Code	1759	English capture Quebec
1750–92	Kaunitz ministry, Austria	1765	Prussian State Bank	1763	Peace of Paris
1756	"Diplomatic Revolution"	1767	*Instruction* of Cather-ine II of Russia	1765	Stamp Act
1757–63	Seven Years' War			1768–79	Captain Cook's voyages
1757–61	Elder Pitt ministry				

RELIGION	SCIENCE AND LEARNING	LITERATURE AND ARTS
1647 Beginning of George Fox's preaching	1628 Harvey, *On the Motion of the Heart*	1637 Corneille, *The Cid*
1650 Usher, *Annals of the Old and New Testament*	1632 Galileo, *Dialogue on the Two Great World Systems*	1642 Rembrandt, "The Night Watch"
1654ff. Nikon's Reforms of the Russian Church	1632 Comenius, *Great Didactic*	1644 Milton, *Areopagitica*
1656 Pascal, *Provincial Letters*	1634 French Academy founded	1648 Rembrandt, "Christ at Emmaus"
1670 Bossuet, *Exposition of Catholic Doctrine*	1637 Descartes, *Discourse on Method*	1655 Murillo, "The Immaculate Conception"
1675 Spener, *Pia Desideria*	1643 Torricelli, barometer	1656 Bernini, Colonnade of St. Peter's
1678 Simon, *Critical History of the Old Testament*	1644 Descartes, *Principles of Philosophy*	1660 Vermeer, "View of Delft"
1682 French Declaration of Gallican Liberties	1651 Hobbes, *The Leviathan*	1662 Versailles begun
1685 Revocation of the Edict of Nantes	1661 Boyle, *Sceptical Chymist*	1663 Milton, *Paradise Lost*
	1662 Royal Society, London	1665 Perrault, east front of the Louvre
1688 Bossuet, *History of the Variations of Protestantism*	1666 French Academy of Science	1667 Racine, *Andromaque*
	1670 Pascal, *Thoughts*	1668ff. La Fontaine, *Fables*
1689 Toleration Act, England	1677 Spinoza, *Ethics*	1670 Molière, *Bourgeois Gentleman*
1690 Locke, *Letter on Toleration*	1681 Bossuet, *Universal History*	
	1682 Ray, *New System of Plants*	1674 Boileau, *Poetic Art*
	1686 Fontenelle, *Plurality of Worlds*	1675 Mansart, design for Invalides
	1687 Newton, *Principia*	1675 Wren, design for St. Paul's
	1689 Locke, *Treatises on Government; On the Human Understanding*	1678 Bunyan, *Pilgrim's Progress*
		1689 Purcell, *Dido and Aeneas*
	1690 Huyghens, *Treatise on Light*	1694 *Dictionary of the French Language* completed
	1697 Bayle, *Critical Dictionary*	CLASSICISM
	18th c. THE AGE OF REASON	1702ff. Poppelmann, Zwinger Palace, Dresden
		1705 Vanbrugh, design for Blenheim Palace
	1710 Berkeley, *Principles of Human Knowledge*	1711ff. Addison, *The Spectator*
	1712 St. Pierre, *Project of Perpetual Peace*	1714 Cathedral of St. Peter and St. Paul, St. Petersburg
	1714 Leibniz, *Monadology*	
	1721 Montesquieu, *Persian Letters*	1717 Watteau, "Embarkment for Cytherea"
1713 Papal Bull, *Unigenitus*, condemns Jansenists	1724 Fahrenheit, thermometer	1717 Masonic Grand Lodge established in London
1721 Holy Synod established in Russia	1725 Vico, *Scienza Nuova*	1719 Defoe, *Robinson Crusoe*
1728 William Law, *Serious Call to a Devout and Holy Life*	1735 Linnaeus, *System of Nature*	1722 Rameau, *Treatise on Harmony*
	1737 Swammerdam, *Bible of Nature*	1722ff. Bach, *Well-Tempered Clavichord*
1736 Butler, *Analogy of Religion*	1739 Hume, *Treatise on Human Nature*	1726 Swift, *Gulliver's Travels*
1739 Beginning of Wesley's preaching mission		1733 Pope, *Essay on Man*
1747 Hume, *Essay on Miracles*		1733 Voltaire, *Letters on the English*
		1735 Hogarth, "Rake's Progress"
		1740 Chardin, "Saying Grace"
		1740 Richardson, *Pamela*
	1748 Montesquieu, *Spirit of Laws*	1741 Handel, *The Messiah*
	1748 La Mettrie, *Man a Machine*	1749 Fielding, *Tom Jones*
	1749ff. Buffon, *Natural History*	CLASSICISM AND PREROMANTICISM
	1750 Rousseau, *Discourse on the Arts and Sciences*	1750 Horace Walpole's Gothic design for "Strawberry Hill"
		1750 Gray, *Elegy in a Country Churchyard*

POLITICAL		ECONOMIC AND SOCIAL		OVERSEAS EXPANSION	
1760–1820	George III of England				
1762–96	Catherine II of Russia				
1763	Peace of Paris				
1765–90	Joseph II of Austria				
1766	France gets Lorraine				
1768–74	Russo-Turkish War	1769	Wedgwood's pottery at Etruria		
1772	First Polish Partition				
1774	Kuchuk-Kainardji, Treaty	1769	Watt's improved steam engine		
1774–92	Louis XVI of France			1774–85	Warren Hastings in India
1783	Russia annexes Crimea	1769	Arkwright's water frame		
1783–1801	Younger Pitt ministry	1770	Hargreaves' spinning jenny	1774	Quebec Act
1786–97	Frederick William II of Prussia	1774	Austrian School Ordinance	1776	American Declaration of Independence
1787–92	Russo-Turkish War	1776	Turgot's Gild Ordinance	1777	American Articles of Confederation
1787	Belgian Revolution	1781–89	Freeing of serfs in Austria	1783	Peace of Paris
1789	Estates General meet	1784ff.	Young's *Annals of Husbandry*	1795	French win all Santo Domingo
1789–91	Constituent Assembly				
1791	French Constitution	1784	Cort process for wrought iron		
1791–92	Legislative Assembly				
1792–97	First Coalition	1785	Cartwright's power loom		
1792	Battle of Valmy				
1792	First French Republic	1789	French abolition of feudal rights		
1792–95	Convention in France	1789	Declaration of Rights of Man		
1793	Second Polish Partition				
1793	New French Constitution	1789	French confiscation of Church lands		
1793–94	Jacobin rule in France				
1795	Treaty of Basel	1789	Issuing of *Assignats*		
1795	New French Constitution	1791	Chapelier Law in France		
1795–99	Directory in France				
1795	Third Polish Partition	1792	Condorcet, *Report on Education*		
1796–97	Bonaparte's Italian campaign				
1797	Treaty of Campo Formio	1793	Final abolition of feudal dues in France		
1798–99	Egyptian Expedition				
1798–1802	Second Coalition	1793	French Law of the Maximum		
1799	Coup of Brumaire	1793	French Revolutionary Calendar		
1799	New French Constitution				
1799–1804	Consulate in France	1795	Decree on Public Education in France		
1801	Peace of Lunéville				
1802	Peace of Amiens	1796	Babeuf's "Conspiracy of the Equals"		
1804–07	Third Coalition				
1804–14	Napoleonic Empire	1799	Establishment of the metric system in France	1802	Defeat of Toussaint L'-Ouverture in Santo Domingo
1805	Battles of Trafalgar and Austerlitz				
1805	Peace of Pressburg	1804	French Civil Code	1803	Louisiana Purchase
1806ff.	Continental System	1806	French Code of Civil Procedure	1806	Cape Colony taken by the British
1806	Confederation of the Rhine	1807	French Commercial Code	1807	Slave-trade abolished in British Empire
1807	Treaties of Tilsit	1807	Emancipation of serfs in Prussia	1812	War of 1812
1808ff.	Spanish Rising				
1809	Austrian Rising	1808	French Criminal Code		
1812	Russian Campaign	1810	French Penal Code		
1813–14	Fifth Coalition	1811	Agrarian Law in Prussia		
1813	Battle of the Nations	1814	Conscription system in Prussia completed		
1814	Treaty of Fontainebleau				
1814	First Treaty of Paris				
1814–15	Congress of Vienna				
1815	The Hundred Days				
1815	Battle of Waterloo				
1815	Second Treaty of Paris				

RELIGION	SCIENCE AND LEARNING	LITERATURE AND ARTS
1761 Jesuit Order suppressed in Portugal	1751 Voltaire, *Age of Louis XIV*	1755 Johnson, *English Dictionary*
1764 Jesuit Order suppressed in Spain	1751–80 Diderot, *Encyclopedia*	1759 Voltaire, *Candide*
1773 Jesuit Order suppressed in Austria	1753 British Museum	1759 Boucher, "Madame Pompadour"
Jesuit Order suppressed by the papacy	1754 Voltaire, *Essay on Manners*	1760 Rousseau, *The New Héloïse*
1780 First Sunday School organized by Robert Raikes	1754 Condillac, *Treatise on the Sensations*	1762 Gluck, *Orpheus and Eurydice*
1781 Joseph II's *Patent of Toleration*	1754 Rousseau, *Origins of Inequality*	1764 Winckelmann, *Ancient Art*
1781 Contemplative monastic orders ended in Austria	1758 Quesnay, *Tableau économique*	1764 Sterne, *Tristram Shandy*
1784 Methodist Conference organized in England	1762 Harrison, chronometer	1768 Fragonard, "The Swing"
1787 Society for Abolishing the Slave Trade	1762 Rousseau, *Emile; The Social Contract*	1770 Gainsborough, "Blue Boy"
1790 Civil Constitution of the Clergy	1764 Beccaria, *On Crimes and Punishment*	1774 Goethe, *Sorrows of Werther*
1793 "Worship of Reason" in France	1771 Holbach, *System of Nature*	1781 Houdon, statue of Voltaire
1794 "Festival of the Supreme Being" in France	1773 Helvetius, *On Man*	1781 Schiller, *The Robbers*
1795 Reopening of the churches in Paris	1776 Bentham, *Fragment on Government*	1784 Beaumarchais, *Marriage of Figaro*
	1776 Smith, *Wealth of Nations*	1784 Reynolds, "Mrs. Siddons as the Tragic Muse"
	1776–87 Gibbon, *Decline and Fall of the Roman Empire*	1787 Mozart, *Don Giovanni*
	1776 Paine, *Common Sense*	1798 Wordsworth and Coleridge, *Lyrical Ballads*
	1777 Lessing, *Education of the Human Race*	1800 Goya, "The Family of Charles IV"
	1781 Kant, *Critique of Pure Reason*	1804 Schiller, *William Tell*
	1784ff. Herder, *Philosophy of History*	1804 Beethoven, *Eroica Symphony*
	1785 Hutton, *Theory of the Earth*	1804 Church of the Madeleine, Paris
1800–23 Pius VII, Pope	1789 Lavoisier, *Elementary Treatise on Chemistry*	1805 David, "Coronation of Josephine"
1801 Concordat between France and the papacy	1789 Bentham, *Principles of Morals and Legislation*	1808 Goethe, *Faust*, Part I
	1790 Burke, *Reflections on the Revolution in France*	1810 Madame de Staël, *On Germany*
1802 The Organic Articles in France	1791 Paine, *Rights of Man*	1812 Grimm's *Fairy Tales*
1802 Chateaubriand, *Genius of Christianity*	1791 Godwin, *Political Justice*	1812 Byron, *Childe Harold*
1807 Pius VII seized by the French	1794 Condorcet, *Progress of the Human Spirit*	
1809 States of the Church annexed to France	1795 Kant, *Perpetual Peace*	
1814 Papal States restored	1798 Malthus, *Essay on Population*	
1815 Jesuit Order restored	1799–1825 Laplace, *Mécanique celeste*	
	1807 Fichte, *Addresses to the German Nation*	
	1808 Dalton, *New System of Chemical Philosophy*	
	1809 Founding of the University of Berlin	

Rulers of Principal European States: 1450–1815

AUSTRIA

See genealogical tables following

DENMARK AND NORWAY

Christian I, 1448–1481
John, 1481–1513
Christian II, 1513–1523
Frederick I, 1523–1533
Christian III, 1533–1559
Frederick II, 1559–1588
Christian IV, 1588–1648
Frederick III, 1648–1670
Christian V, 1670–1699
Frederick IV, 1699–1730
Christian VI, 1730–1746
Frederick V, 1746–1766
Christian VII, 1766–1808
Frederick VI, 1808–1839

FRANCE

See genealogical tables following

GREAT BRITAIN

See genealogical tables following

HOLY ROMAN EMPIRE

House of Hapsburg

Frederick III, 1440–1493
Maximilian I, 1493–1519
Charles V, 1519–1558
Ferdinand I, 1558–1564
Maximilian II, 1564–1576
Rudolph II, 1576–1612
Matthias, 1612–1619
Ferdinand II, 1619–1637
Ferdinand III, 1637–1657
Leopold I, 1658–1705
Joseph I, 1705–1711
Charles VI, 1711–1740

House of Bavaria

Charles VII, 1742–1745

House of Hapsburg-Lorraine

Francis I, 1745–1765
Joseph II, 1765–1790
Leopold II, 1790–1792
Francis II, 1792–1806

MILAN

Francesco Sforza, 1450–1466
Galeazzo Maria Sforza, 1466–1476
Gian Galeazzo Sforza, 1476–1479
Ludovico Sforza, 1479–1500
Massimiliano Sforza, 1512–1515
Francesco II, 1522–1535
To Spain, 1535–1714
To Austria, 1714–1797
Cisalpine Republic, 1797–1805
To France, 1805–1815

NAPLES

To Spain, 1443–1713
To Austria, 1713–1738
Charles III, 1738–1759
Ferdinand IV, 1759–1806
Joseph Bonaparte, 1806–1808
Joachim Murat, 1809–1815

OTTOMAN EMPIRE

Mohammed II, 1451–1481
Bayezid II, 1481–1512
Selim I, 1512–1520
Suleiman II, "The Magnificent," 1520–1566
Selim II, 1566–1574
Murad III, 1574–1595
Mohammed III, 1595–1603
Ahmed I, 1603–1617
Mustapha I, 1617–1618
Othman II, 1618–1623
Murad IV, 1623–1640
Ibrahim, 1640–1648
Mohammed IV, 1648–1687
Suleiman III, 1687–1691
Ahmed II, 1691–1695
Mustapha II, 1695–1703
Ahmed III, 1703–1730
Mahmud I, 1730–1754
Othman III, 1754–1757
Mustapha III, 1757–1773
Abdul Hamid I, 1773–1789
Selim III, 1789–1807
Mustapha IV, 1807–1808
Mahmud II, 1808–1839

THE PAPACY

Nicholas V, 1447–1455
Calixtus III (Borgia), 1455–1458
Pius II, 1458–1464
Paul II, 1464–1471
Sixtus IV, 1471–1484
Innocent VIII, 1484–1492
Alexander VI (Borgia), 1492–1503
Pius III, 1503
Julius II, 1503–1513
Leo X (Medici), 1513–1521
Adrian VI, 1522–1523
Clement VII (Medici), 1523–1534
Paul III, 1534–1549
Julius III, 1550–1555
Marcellus II, 1555
Paul IV, 1555–1559
Pius IV (Medici), 1559–1565
Pius V, 1566–1572
Gregory XIII, 1572–1585
Sixtus V, 1585–1590
Urban VII, 1590
Gregory XIV, 1590–1591
Innocent IX, 1591
Clement VIII, 1592–1605
Leo XI (Medici), 1605
Paul V, 1605–1621
Gregory XV, 1621–1623
Urban VIII, 1623–1644
Innocent X, 1644–1655
Alexander VII, 1655–1667
Clement IX, 1667–1669
Clement X, 1670–1676
Innocent XI, 1676–1689
Alexander VIII, 1689–1691
Innocent XII, 1691–1700
Clement XI, 1700–1721
Innocent XIII, 1721–1724
Benedict XIII, 1724–1730
Clement XII, 1730–1740
Benedict XIV, 1740–1758
Clement XIII, 1758–1769
Clement XIV, 1769–1774
Pius VI, 1775–1799
Pius VII, 1800–1823

POLAND

Casimir IV, 1447–1492
John Albert, 1492–1501
Alexander, 1501–1506
Sigismund I, 1506–1548
Sigismund II, 1548–1572
Henry of Valois, 1573–1574
Stephen Bathory, 1575–1586
Sigismund III Vasa, 1587–1632
Ladislaus VII, 1632–1648

John II Casimir, 1648–1668
Michael Wisniowiecki, 1669–1673
John III Sobieski, 1674–1696
Augustus II of Saxony, 1697–1704
Stanislas I Leszczynski, 1704–1709
Augustus II (*restored*), 1709–1733
Stanislas I Leszczynski (*restored*), 1733–1734
Augustus III of Saxony, 1734–1763
Stanislas II Poniatowski, 1764–1795
Partitioned by Russia, Prussia and Austria, 1795
Grand Duchy of Warsaw, 1807–1815

PORTUGAL

Alfonso V, 1438–1481
John II, 1481–1495
Emanuel I, 1495–1521
John III, 1521–1557
Sebastian, 1557–1578
Henry, 1578–1580
To Spain, 1580–1640
John IV, 1640–1656
Alfonso VI, 1656–1667
Pedro II, 1667–1706
John V, 1706–1750
Joseph, 1750–1777
Maria I and Pedro III, 1777–1786
Maria I, 1786–1816

PRUSSIA

Electors of Brandenburg

Frederick II, 1440–1470
Albert Achilles, 1470–1486
John Cicero, 1486–1499
Joachim I, 1499–1535
Joachim II, 1535–1571
John George, 1571–1598
Joachim Frederick, 1598–1608
John Sigismund, 1608–1619
George William, 1619–1640
Frederick William, the Great Elector, 1640–1688
Frederick III, 1688–1713 (Frederick I, King in Prussia, 1701–1713)

Kings of Prussia

Frederick I, 1701–1713
Frederick William I, 1713–1740
Frederick II, 1740–1786
Frederick William II, 1786–1797
Frederick William III, 1797–1840

RUSSIA

Basil II, 1425–1462
Ivan III, "The Great," 1462–1505
Basil IV, 1505–1533
Ivan IV, "The Terrible," 1533–1584
Theodore I, 1584–1598
Boris Godunov, 1598–1605
Michael Romanov, 1613–1645
Alexius, 1645–1676
Theodore II, 1676–1682
Ivan V and Peter I, 1682–1689
Peter I, "The Great," 1689–1725
Catherine I, 1725–1727
Peter II, 1727–1730
Anna, 1730–1740
Ivan VI, 1740–1741
Elizabeth, 1741–1762
Peter III, 1762
Catherine II, "The Great," 1762–1796
Paul, 1796–1801
Alexander I, 1801–1825

SAVOY

Dukes of Savoy

Philibert II, 1497–1504
Charles III, 1504–1533
Emmanuel Philibert, 1553–1580
Charles Emmanuel I, 1580–1630
Victor Amadeus I, 1630–1637
Charles Emmanuel II, 1638–1675
Victor Amadeus II, 1675–1730

Kings of Sardinia

Victor Amadeus II, 1720–1730
Charles Emmanuel III, 1730–1773
Victor Amadeus III, 1773–1796
Charles Emmanuel IV, 1796–1802
Victor Emmanuel I, 1802–1821

SPAIN

See genealogical tables following

SWEDEN

United with Denmark, 1397–1523
Gustavus I Vasa, 1523–1560
Eric XIV, 1560–1568
John III, 1568–1592
Sigismund, 1592–1599
Charles IX, 1599–1611
Gustavus II Adolphus, 1611–1632
Christina, 1632–1654
Charles X, 1654–1660
Charles XI, 1660–1697

Charles XII, 1697–1718
Ulrica Eleonora, 1718–1720
Frederick I, 1720–1751
Adolphus Frederick, 1751–1771
Gustavus III, 1771–1792
Gustavus IV, 1792–1809
Charles XIII, 1809–1818
Charles XIV (Bernadotte), 1818–1844

TUSCANY

Rulers of Florence

Cosimo de' Medici, 1434–1464
Piero de' Medici, 1464–1469
Lorenzo and Giuliano de' Medici, 1469–1478
Lorenzo de' Medici, 1478–1492
Piero de' Medici, 1492–1494
Giuliano de' Medici, 1512–1514
Lorenzo de' Medici, 1514–1519
Giulio de' Medici, 1519–1527

Dukes of Tuscany

Alessandro, 1530–1537
Cosimo I, Grand Duke, 1537–1574
Francis I, 1574–1587
Ferdinand I, 1587–1605
Cosimo II, 1605–1621
Ferdinand II, 1621–1670
Cosimo III, 1670–1723
John Gaston, 1723–1737
Francis, 1737–1745 (Duke of Lorraine, Holy Roman Emperor, 1745–1765)
Leopold I, 1745–1790 (Holy Roman Emperor, 1790–1792)
Ferdinand III, 1790–1801
To France, 1801–1815

UNITED NETHERLANDS

William I, "The Silent," Prince of Orange, Stadholder, 1581–1584
Maurice of Nassau, 1584–1625
Frederick Henry, 1625–1647
William II, 1647–1650
John DeWitt, Grand Pensionary, 1650–1672
William III of Nassau, Stadholder, 1672–1702
John William, Nominal Stadholder, 1702–1711
William IV, Nominal Stadholder, 1711–1748
William IV, Hereditary Stadholder, 1748–1751
William V, 1751–1795
Batavian Republic, 1795–1806
Louis Bonaparte, King, 1806–1810
To France, 1810–1813
William I of Orange, King, 1813–1840

Genealogical Tables

ENGLAND: LANCASTRIANS, YORKISTS, TUDORS, STUARTS, AND HANOVERIANS

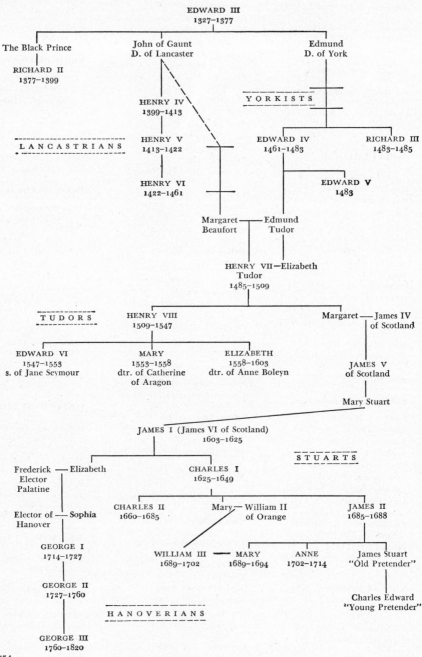

FRANCE: VALOIS AND BOURBON DYNASTIES

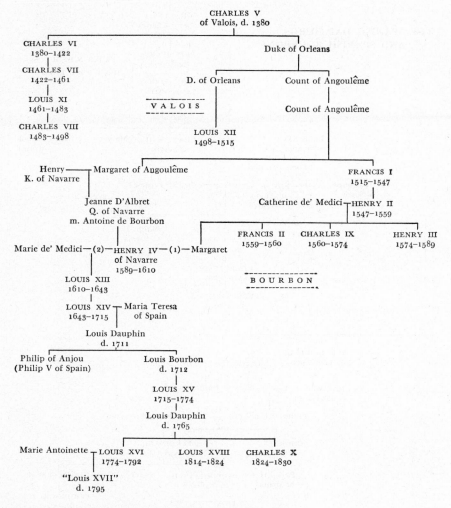

FRANCE: DYNASTY OF NAPOLEON BONAPARTE

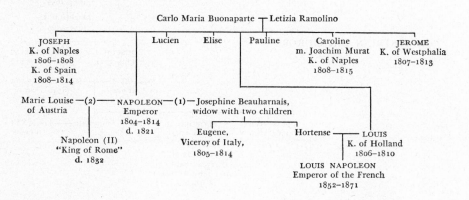

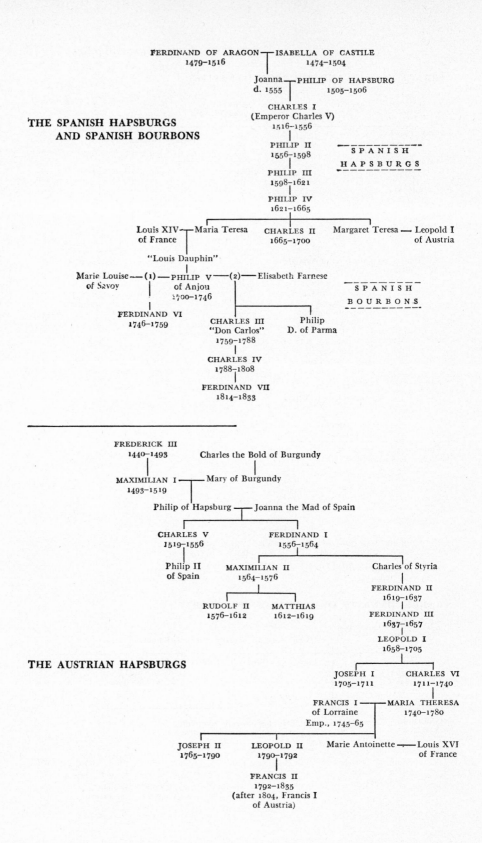

FERDINAND OF ARAGON ── ISABELLA OF CASTILE
1479–1516   1474–1504

Joanna ── PHILIP OF HAPSBURG
d. 1555   1505–1506

CHARLES I
(Emperor Charles V)
1516–1556

**THE SPANISH HAPSBURGS
AND SPANISH BOURBONS**

PHILIP II
1556–1598

⌐ ─ ─ ─ ─ ─ ─ ─ ┐
S P A N I S H
H A P S B U R G S
└ ─ ─ ─ ─ ─ ─ ─ ┘

PHILIP III
1598–1621

PHILIP IV
1621–1665

Louis XIV ── Maria Teresa   CHARLES II   Margaret Teresa ── Leopold I
of France   1665–1700   of Austria

"Louis Dauphin"

Marie Louise ── (1) ── PHILIP V ── (2) ── Elisabeth Farnese
of Savoy   of Anjou
                      1700–1746

⌐ ─ ─ ─ ─ ─ ┐
S P A N I S H
B O U R B O N S
└ ─ ─ ─ ─ ─ ┘

FERDINAND VI   CHARLES III   Philip
1746–1759   "Don Carlos"   D. of Parma
                         1759–1788

CHARLES IV
1788–1808

FERDINAND VII
1814–1833

FREDERICK III
1440–1493   Charles the Bold of Burgundy

MAXIMILIAN I ── Mary of Burgundy
1493–1519

Philip of Hapsburg ── Joanna the Mad of Spain

CHARLES V   FERDINAND I
1519–1556   1556–1564

Philip II   MAXIMILIAN II   Charles of Styria
of Spain   1564–1576
                                      FERDINAND II
                                      1619–1637

          RUDOLF II   MATTHIAS   FERDINAND III
          1576–1612   1612–1619   1637–1657

                                        LEOPOLD I
                                        1658–1705

THE AUSTRIAN HAPSBURGS

JOSEPH I   CHARLES VI
1705–1711   1711–1740

FRANCIS I ── MARIA THERESA
of Lorraine   1740–1780
Emp., 1745–65

JOSEPH II   LEOPOLD II   Marie Antoinette ── Louis XVI
1765–1790   1790–1792   of France

FRANCIS II
1792–1835
(after 1804, Francis I
of Austria)

Suggestions for Writing a History Paper

WRITTEN REPORTS and essays are an important part of college history courses, and rightly so. When you prepare a paper you become, if only in an amateur way, a member of the historian's craft. You are taking those first steps leading you to qualify as an expert practitioner. You are in one sense a "maker of history," for you are grappling with a problem that once involved real and living issues, and you are trying to work out your own explanation rather than having someone else tell you the answer. The following hints—and they do not pretend to be more than hints—should help you to undertake this kind of work with efficiency and pleasure.

Selecting a Topic

If the topic is assigned, you have no problem. If you have a choice of topics, or if you must devise your own, look over some possible subjects and then ask yourself a few questions: (1) Is the subject interesting to you? (2) Does it seem reasonable and manageable in scope? (3) Are you likely to find adequate materials for this topic conveniently at hand? (4) Does the subject lend itself to differences of opinion and to reinterpretation, or is it stale and outworn? (5) Can you, in a modest way, say something new, or at least something which is individual to yourself? (6) Finally, and this is a reasonable consideration, will the paper fit in well with the course which you are taking and contribute usefully to your progress in it? When you have hit upon a tentative subject, remember that it is something more than just a title. Mull it over and "worry" it until the topic takes shape as a problem for which you are expected to find a solution.

Finding Materials

The materials for history papers come largely from books. You must, therefore, compile a bibliography, but it is surely a mistake to try to complete this list of references before settling down to the serious work of reading. Browse around for a start, looking for some simple sketch such as you are likely to find in a chapter of a textbook or in an article from an encyclopedia. Use this reading to give you the general hang of the subject and to suggest the kind of material for which you will now start to search. Having some idea of your subject, begin to collect references bearing upon it. Use the standard 3 x 5 inch filing cards, one for each reference, being careful to fill out details of the author's name, exact title of the book, the edition if there are several, the number of volumes, the place and date of publication. Carefulness at this stage saves much rechecking later.

Your list of references can be assembled from various sources: (1) the bibliographies given in textbooks and encyclopedia articles; (2) subject classifications in your library card catalog; (3) the library shelves where books on a given subject are assembled (though you must never expect to find all the useful books on one topic in one place); (4) standard guides such as the *Guide to Historical Literature;* (5) standard guides to periodical literature; (6) the more elaborate bibliographies in collaborative histories such as *The Cambridge Modern History* and *The Rise of Modern Europe* series. A further and usually most fruitful source of material will appear when you get down to reading some of the books on your list. By watching the footnote references, especially those in the more substantial and newer books, you will come across still further items which obviously have been valuable to the author whom you are consulting. Most historians would agree that this procedure, which can be pursued to the point of diminishing returns, pays very large dividends. Note also that certain manuals and standard works provide convenient short-cuts to background information. A most useful factual source is the one-volume *Encyclopedia of World History* edited by W. L. Langer. Quite different in scope but equally indispensable is the 15-volume *Encyclopedia of the Social Sciences.* Assemble your bibliographical cards alphabetically by author, wherever possible adding brief notes to indicate the particular value of each book.

Collecting Notes

If you are tempted to accumulate your notes in the usual large loose-leaf notebook, remember that for anything but a very short paper you are making trouble for yourself. Notes thus taken are hard to rearrange. They are probably put down in haphazard order so that it is difficult to use your material efficiently in organizing an intelligent plan. Important details get buried and exact page references are frequently unclear. The best practice is to use separate slips or cards, either 3 x 5 inches, 4 x 6 inches, or 5 x 8 inches in size. Every note thus taken should have three parts: (1) the note itself, either a summary of what you have read or a precise quotation (enclosed in quotation marks) from the book consulted; (2) an exact page reference with a clear indication of the title of the book used; (3) a brief heading to show what the note is about. This last is a great help to clear thinking and to the systematic arrangement of your notes.

Your notes will obviously vary in nature. To begin with, you might try to take some that will give you a running outline of your topic. If, for example, your subject is biographical, you might summarize the main outlines of a man's life. If you spread these notes systematically over a number of sheets you will at once have a kind of crude structure around which to group your further and more detailed notes. As you read you can add specific points of detail, being careful to avoid repetitious note-taking. As you accumulate material you should have a plan or "thesis" developing in your mind or, better still, roughly written out. Keep in mind the general topic and look for interpretative passages and for new evidence to strengthen or modify the preliminary views which you hold. It is certainly legitimate to look for material that confirms your hypothesis, let us say, that Cromwell was a "wicked" man; but you must also be ready to make a record of evidence to the contrary. Look particularly for material that will fill in gaps, offer new viewpoints and state a point pungently. If you wish to use direct quotations take them accurately, indicating in your notes all omissions. If you can find and quote interesting contemporary material, so much the better. As your notes accumulate, use index cards to sort them out, or clip them together in groups. It is very helpful at times to write summarizing notes of your own which will refresh your mind later and help you to pull together scattered bits of evidence. It is also a good idea to collect passages indicating conflicting viewpoints in different authors. This will give you a fine opportunity to act as the arbitrator of such differences.

Organizing Your Material

This is probably the most difficult task to do well. Some very tentative outlines for your paper will doubtless have suggested themselves to you when you did your first exploratory reading. By all means put this outline down, but remember that it must be subjected to rigid criticism and revision. A good paper must present a genuine *thesis,* and this thesis must, to some degree at least, be your own. Do not hesitate, therefore, to let your imagination play upon your subject. If history were simply the mechanical recording of "facts" no great historical works would ever have been written. Ultimately you will have to settle for one explanation or interpretation of events that seems to make more sense than another, and you will have to give your reasons.

The more simply you organize your material the better. Plan your outline, so that it will state at the beginning what the paper intends to do, and then let it proceed by the most direct route to make the demonstration. At the end sum up. A few hints on organization may be helpful. Decide whether you wish to employ a *chronological* or a *topical* method of treatment. If you are dealing, say, with Louis XIV you may wish a chronological arrangement, in which case you would discuss in sequence the problems of his youth, his maturity and his declining years. If you decide upon the topical method you would work out a few main headings covering subjects such as politics, religion, economic matters and foreign policy. Whatever the plan, it is advisable to block out your paper in a few clearly separated divisions; following this the lesser divisions can be fitted into place. In organizing your material keep in mind the problem of proportion. A common failing seems to be to have a long-winded introduction. Bear in mind the overall scheme and do not let enthusiasm for a pet point lead you to exaggerate its importance. As you revise the organization of your paper ask yourself further questions: Does the essay indicate at the beginning what you intend to do? Does it move along by logical stages, and are these likely to be intelligible to your readers? Does the paper reach a conclusion, and is the significance of this conclusion properly underscored? If you feel impatient at all this preparatory work, and burst to get on with the actual writing, remember that the more intelligently you make your plan, the less arduous will be the actual task of translating your ideas into words.

Writing

At some point the time will come when your notes and outlines must be turned into a readable essay. Rules concerning the mechanical form of your paper are given in many college manuals. Be sure to follow the form which is standard in your institution, and above all be consistent in your usages. On almost any point of detail you can consult the University of Chicago Press publication, *A Manual of Style.* Follow the accepted rules for the use of footnotes, that is to say, use them to give the source of direct quotations, unusual and little-known materials, controversial viewpoints, important statistics and in general any matter where common sense suggests that the reader would be interested in running down the authority for a statement. Follow likewise the standard rules for the bibliography which should accompany your paper, remembering that a bibliography which is inaccurate in its citations is almost worse than useless, and that a bibliography which is uncritical—in other words, which does not indicate the value of its separate items— is a poor thing indeed. Keep in mind the simple rules of planning, of paragraph structure, of topic sentences and of transitions. Allow yourself adequate time to write your paper (this is a counsel of perfection), then put it aside for a few days, come back to it and read it afresh as if it were written by someone else. Following this usually painful experience make the inevitable corrections. Almost any paper can, with advantage, be reduced in length. Verify all quotations, factual data, footnote citations and titles in your bibliography. If you are unsure of your spelling and punctuation, try to persuade someone else to read your paper for you. If it is necessary, make final corrections neatly in your typescript by pen. Avoid "fine writing." Most readers of college history papers will be grateful if the work you submit is written in simple, intelligible English, if spelling, punctuation and grammar reach minimum standards of acceptability, if your essay has a theme and a pattern and if it reaches a conclusion not unrelated to the evidence.

The following are recommended as helpful books: Allen Johnson, *The Historian and Historical Evidence* (New York, 1926); Sherman Kent, *Writing History* (New York, 1941); Louis Gottschalk, *Understanding History, A Primer of Historical Method* (New York, 1950); University of Chicago Press, *A Manual of Style* (11th ed., Chicago, 1949); Kate L. Turabian, *A Manual for the Writing of Term Papers. Theses and Dissertations* (revised ed., Chicago, 1955).

INDEX